NATIONAL IMPLEMENTATION OF UNITED NATIONS SANCTIONS

A COMPARATIVE STUDY

The Graduate Institute of International Studies

Volume 4

National Implementation of United Nations Sanctions

A Comparative Study

Edited by

Vera Gowlland-Debbas

With the assistance of Djacoba Liva Tehindrazanarivelo

MARTINUS NIJHOFF PUBLISHERS

LEIDEN / BOSTON

A C.I.P. Catalogue record for this book is available from the Library of Congress.

Printed on acid-free paper.

ISBN 90 04 14090 5

Koninklijke Brill NV incorporates the imprint Martinus Nijhoff Publishers.
http://www.brill.nl

Printed and bound in The Netherlands.

TABLE OF CONTENTS

FOREWORD

This comparative study of national implementation of Security Council sanctions resolutions which brings together the research results of 29 academics and experts, is the second publication within the framework of a project on UN Sanctions carried out under the auspices of the Graduate Institute of International Studies and directed by Professor Vera Gowlland-Debbas. This part of the project was extended following on the events of 11 September, 2001 in order to take into account implementation of Security Council resolutions on the combatting of terrorism.

The first publication, entitled *United Nations Sanctions and International Law* (Kluwer Law International, 2001), examined a broader set of issues on the basis of papers first presented at a Colloquium organised by the Graduate Institute of International Studies in Geneva from 23 to 25 June 1999.

The overall project has been made possible by funding from The Thyssen Foundation, The United Nations University, The Swiss Federal Department of Foreign Affairs, The Swiss Federal Department of Defence, Civil Protection and Sports, and the Tokyo Club in Japan.

The Graduate Institute of International Studies would like to reiterate its thanks to the sponsors for their invaluable support. Thanks also are due to Dr. Daniel Warner, Executive Director of the Programme for the Study of International Organisation(s), who was responsible for the overall administration of the project and to Ms. Lisa Krahenbuhl and Ms. Catherine Rebord for their contribution to the coordination and secretarial tasks. Dr. Djacoba Liva Tehindrazanarivelo was responsible for the final preparation of the manuscript for publication.

This book is dedicated to the memory of Mariano Garcia-Rubio.

LIST OF ABBREVIATIONS

AFDI	*Annuaire français de droit international*
AJIL	*American Journal of International Law*
ANC	African National Congress (South Africa)
ASIL	American Society of International Law
ATF	*Arrêt du Tribunal fédéral* (Case-law of the Swiss Federal Supreme Court)
AVR	*Archiv des Völkerrechts*
CFSP	Common Foreign and Security Policy
CMLR	Common Market Law Reports
CMLRev.	*Common Market Law Review*
COCOM	Coordinating Committee on Multilateral Export Controls (COCOM Arrangements)
CSCE	Conference on Security and Cooperation in Europe
CTC	Counter-terrorism Committee of the UN Security Council
EAEC	European Atomic Energy Community (EURATOM)
EBRD	European Bank for Reconstruction and Development
EC	European Community
ECHR	European Convention on Human Rights
ECJ	European Court of Justice
ECOWAS	Economic Community of West African States
ECR	European Court Reports
ECSC	European Coal and Steel Community
EEC	European Economic Community
EFTA	European Free Trade Association
EJIL	*European Journal of International Law*
EPC	European Political Co-operation
EU	European Union
FRELIMO	Frente de Libertaçâo de Moçambique
FRY	Federal Republic of Yugoslavia
GAOR	UN General Assembly Official Records
GA Res.	UN General Assembly Resolution
GATS	General Agreement on Trade in Services
GATT	General Agreement on Tariffs and Trade
IAEA	International Atomic Energy Agency
ICAO	International Civil Aviation Organisation
ICC	International Criminal Court
ICJ	International Court of Justice
ICJ Reports	Reports of Judgments, Advisory Opinions and Orders of the ICJ
ICLQ	*International and Comparative Law Quarterly*
ICRC	International Committee of the Red Cross
ICTR	International Criminal Tribunal for Rwanda
ICTY	International Criminal Tribunal for the Former Yugoslavia
IEEPA	International Emergency Economic Powers Act (US)

ILR	International Law Reports
IMF	International Monetary Fund
INTERPOL	International Criminal Police Organisation
JDI	*Journal du droit international*
JOCE	*Journal officiel des Communautés européennes*
KAC	Kuwait Airways Corporation
MPLA	Movimento Popular de Libertaçao de Angola
NATO	North Atlantic Treaty Organisation
NEPAD	New Partnership for Africa's Development
NGO	Non-Governmental Organisation
NYUL Rev.	*New York University Law Review*
OAS	Organisation of American States
OAU	Organisation for African Unity
OECD	Organisation for Economic Cooperation and Development
OIP	Office of Iraq Program
OJ	*Official Journal (of the European Communities)*
OJEC	*Official Journal of the European Communities*
OSCE	Organisation for Security and Co-operation in Europe
PCIJ	Permanent Court of International Justice
PFLP	Popular Front for the Liberation of Palestine
PLAN	People's Liberation Army of Namibia
Pol. YBIL	*Polish Yearbook of International Law*
RBDI	*Revue belge de droit international*
RCADI	*Recueil des cours de l'Académie de droit international de La Haye/ Collected Courses of the Hague Academy of International Law*
RFDA	*Revue française de droit administratif*
RGDIP	*Revue générale de droit international public*
RIDC	*Revue internationale de droit comparé*
RUF	Revolutionary United Front (Sierra Leone)
SADC	Southern African Development Community
SADCC	Southern African Development Coordinating Conference
SAMCOMM	Sanctions Assistance Missions Command
SCR	Security Council Resolution
SEA	Single European Act
SWAPO	South West African People's Organisation
SZIER	*Schweizerische Zeitschrift für internationales und europäisches Recht*
TA	Treaty of Amsterdam
TEU	Treaty on European Union ("Maastricht Treaty")
TWEA	Trading with the Enemy Act (US)
UNSCR	United Nations Security Council Resolution
UN	United Nations
UNASMIL	United Nations Mission in Sierra Leone
UNCC	United Nations Compensation Commission
UNITA	Uniao Nacional Para a Independencia Total de Angola

UNMOVIC	United Nations Monitoring, Verification and Inspection Commission
UNPROFOR	United Nations Protection Force
UNSC	United Nations Security Council
WEU	West European Union
WHO	World Health Organisation
WLR	Weekly Law Reports (UK)
WMO	World Meteorological Organisation
WTO	World Trade Organisation
ZANU	Zimbabwe African National Union Patriotic Front
ZaöRV	*Zeitschrift für ausländisches internationales Recht und Völkerrecht*
ZAPU	Zimbabwe African People's Union
ZBJV	*Zeitschrift des Bernischen Juristenvereins*
ZSR	*Zeitschrift für schweizerisches Recht*

PART I

INTRODUCTORY OVERVIEW

SANCTIONS REGIMES UNDER ARTICLE 41 OF THE UN CHARTER

*Vera Gowlland-Debbas**

I. Scope of the Study

This book focuses on the international legal implications of domestic implementation of the mandatory decisions of the Security Council imposing sanctions under Chapter VII of the United Nations Charter. It is a comparative study of select States in Europe, Eastern Europe, America, Asia, the Middle East and Africa, including a regional dimension insofar as it covers implementation of Security Council decisions by the European Union. The book also underlines the particular problems which faces a State, Switzerland, having a status of permanent neutrality and a former non-Member State of the United Nations, as well as those arising for States, including those neighbouring sanctioned entities, that are adversely affected by the implementation of sanctions and thus face special economic problems within the meaning of Article 50 of the United Nations Charter.

A comparative approach to this topic and to the complex questions which arise from the day-to-day operations of incorporation of international decisions into domestic law has not, to our knowledge, been undertaken. While the revival of the powers of the Security Council has elicited a large number of studies of Chapter VII – academic or policy-oriented, particularly within the framework of United Nations reform schemes, general or focusing on particular crises – these have centred in particular on the legality of sanctions within the Charter framework, or on their effectiveness on target States. Particular national studies have been conducted relating to domestic implementation, but in a piecemeal fashion – for example, there is one for the Netherlands on Rhodesian sanctions,[1] and a more general study of sanctions implementation in Finland.[2] Numerous books have been written on sanctions implementation by the United States, but these have mainly concerned unilateral measures. As for States' reports to the United

* Professor of Public International Law, Graduate Institute of International Studies, Geneva.

1 See P.J. Kuyper, *The Implementation of International Sanctions: the Netherlands and Rhodesia* (Alphen aan de Rijn, Sijthoff and Noordhoff, 1978).

Vera Gowlland-Debbas (ed.), National Implementation of UN Sanctions, *3-31*.

Nations on their domestic implementation, these failed in the past to give an overall picture of the process, although reporting under the resolutions on the combatting of the financing of terrorism has been more successful.

Moreover, the broader object of this present study is to enquire into the significance of such domestic implementation of Security Council mandatory decisions for the classic relationship between domestic and international law and within the framework of the evolution of contemporary public international law.

A list of issues to be addressed by the respective chapters was drawn up at the start of the project and these constitute more or less the basic outline of each chapter. However, because of the diversity of problems faced by the States concerned, it was agreed that a certain flexibility of approach within each national study was preferable to complete uniformity.

The decisions falling within the scope of the study are those adopted by the Security Council under Article 41 of the Charter, which relate to: economic, diplomatic and financial sanctions, the International Criminal Tribunals on Yugoslavia and Rwanda, and the resolutions on the combatting of terrorism.

Since 1990, the United Nations Security Council, which has primary responsibility for maintenance of international peace and security, has made increasing use of its broad powers under Chapter VII which had long remained dormant. Article 39, which is the trigger to further action under Chapter VII, states:

> "The Security Council shall determine the existence of any threat to the peace, breach of the peace, or act of aggression and shall make recommendations, or decide what measures shall be taken in accordance with Articles 41 and 42, to maintain or restore international peace and security."

To the extent that there exists no legal definition of these terms, at least as concerns a threat to or breach of the peace, such determinations are discretionary, although adopted within the limits imposed by the Charter (see in particular, Article 24(2) which refers back to the Purposes and Principles of the United Nations) and general international law.[3] Following on such a determination, the Council again has a wide discretion in its choice of responses. In accordance with Chapter VII, it could follow any of these determinations under Article 39 by a recommendation under Article 39, by calling for provisional measures under Article 40, or by resorting to mandatory non-military measures under Articles 4l, or military measures under Article 42.

2 See Martti Koskenniemi, *Kansainväliset pakotteet ja Suomi. Ulko- ja turvallisuuspolitiikan alaan kuuluvat ei-sotilaalliset sanktiot ja niiden täytäntöönpano Suomessa* (Helsinki, Lakimiesliiton Kustannus, 1994).

3 It will be noted that the Security Council, in resorting to sanctions under Chapter VII, has generally qualified these situations as a "threat to the peace", with the exception of Iraq, whose invasion and occupation of Kuwait was determined to be a breach of the peace (the determination of a breach of the peace in the cases of Palestine, Iran-Iraq war and the Falklands war was not followed by the imposition of sanctions under Article 41). The Council has never made a formal determination under Article 39 of an act of aggression.

Article 41, which is the springboard for this study, states:

> "The Security Council may decide what measures involving the use of armed force are to be employed to give effect to its decisions, and it may call upon the Members of the United Nations to apply such measures. These may include complete or partial interruption of economic relations and of rail, sea, air, postal, telegraphic, radio, and other means of communication, and the severance of diplomatic relations."

The term sanctions is used throughout in the national studies to designate the non-military measures adopted under Article 41. It is a truism to state that the term is not to be found in the Charter and that it has been used in the past to designate only the measures provided for under Articles 5 and 6 relating to suspension and expulsion of States from the Organisation, and Article 19 relating to suspension from voting in the General Assembly as a consequence of arrears in Charter contributions. The use of the term sanctions to designate enforcement measures under Chapter VII, however, is in accordance with the current practice of States and the term has, moreover, crept into the vocabulary of Council resolutions (e.g. the preamble of Resolution 665 (1990) on Iraq), as well as confirmed by the regular reference to "Sanctions Committees", and the current use of the term "tageted sanctions".

The adoption of sanctions by the Security Council has, of course, raised numerous issues, including questions relating to their legality. Many of these issues were the focus of the previous study that was initiated within this project.[4] This chapter is only concerned with outlining briefly the panoply of measures that the Security Council has been led to adopt under Chapter VII and which States have been called on to implement. These are also set out in the Annex to this Chapter.

Article 41 has evolved over time. The feasibility of interrupting postal, telegraphic and radio communications was challenged by Member States at various times, and such severance has never taken place. On the other hand, some of the measures adopted by the Security Council are not expressly stated in Article 41 and have been extrapolated from existing measures stipulated in that Article, although in some respects, the Council has clearly gone beyond these stipulations.

One example is the call for non-recognition of entities, acts or situations, which can with difficulty be included under the term "severance of diplomatic relations", although in the case of annexation of territory, non-recognition may be seen as the corollary of Article 2(4). The Security Council has characterised State conduct as not only illegal, but also invalid, these determinations serving as the basis for a duty of collective non-recognition.

Another example is the establishment of two International Criminal Tribunals for the Former Yugoslavia and Rwanda, referred to below, which has led to the prosecution of individuals under international law. In regard to the Tribunals' legal basis, the International Criminal Tribunal for the Former Yugoslavia, in the *Tadic* case, considered that Article 41 was not exhaustive and based the legality of its establishment on the first part

4 See Vera Gowlland-Debbas (ed.), *United Nations Sanctions and International Law* (The Hague/London/Boston, Kluwer Law International, 2001).

of Article 41, i.e. as a measure short of the use of force which the Council (as opposed to the Members of the United Nations) could adopt for the purpose of contributing to the restoration and maintenance of peace in the former Yugoslavia.[5]

This comparative study is therefore not only concerned with domestic implementation of economic, financial and diplomatic sanctions in the broad sense, but also includes implementation of the decisions of the Security Council relating to cooperation with the International Criminal Tribunals.[6] Moreover, the resolutions adopted by the Security Council in the wake of the September 11 attack on the World Trade Center, which are aimed at combatting terrorist acts, have been included, even though these do not strictly speaking fit into the traditional pattern of sanctions resolutions.

The study excludes military measures. Some of the sanctions regimes referred to below have been accompanied by resort to either authorised or non-authorised military force, such as those relating to Iraq, Haiti, Kosovo, Somalia, Afghanistan and the Congo. It is, of course, well known that Article 42 no longer serves as a clear legal basis for military action and that, lacking a military force at its disposal, the Council has resorted to authorisations to States and regional organisations for the use of military force either as all-out military action, as in the case of Iraq in 1991, or for limited purposes, such as to enforce economic sanctions, to protect United Nations so-called "safe areas", to facilitate the delivery of humanitarian aid, to defend United Nations peacekeeping forces, to reinstate democratically elected regimes, or to enforce peace settlements. The Council, acting under Chapter VII, has also authorised peacekeeping operations in some of these situations to resort to limited force going beyond self-defence. Any reference to military force in this study, however, is restricted to that of enforcement at sea of economic sanctions and only to the extent that this has raised problems in domestic law.

II. Survey of Sanctions Regimes Adopted Under Article 41 of the Charter

It has been considered useful to retrace the non-military sanctions regimes imposed by the Security Council in order to gauge the extent of the network of obligations which Member States have had to implement under their domestic legal system and to set in context the measures reported on in the national studies.

The most frequently adopted sanctions have covered prohibitions of export and import, prohibition of services, prohibition of movement of funds, freezing of funds and assets, prohibition of air, sea and land communications, severance or reduction of

5 International Tribunal for the Prosecution of Persons Responsible for Serious Violations of International Humanitarian Law Committed in the Territory of the Former Yugoslavia since 1991, *The Prosecutor v. Dusko Tadic a/k/a/ "Dule"*, Decision on the Defence Motion for Interlocutory Appeal on Jurisdiction, 2 October 1995.

6 The Special Court for Sierra Leone set up under a joint agreement between the Government of Sierra Leone and the United Nations in conformity with Security Council Resolution 1315 (2000) and mandated to try those who bear the greatest responsibility for serious violations of international humanitarian law and Sierra Leonean law committed in the territory of Sierra Leone since 30 November 1996, does not fall into the same category, nor raises similar problems of implementation by Member States. It will therefore not be alluded to here.

diplomatic and other official relations, and restrictions on the movement of persons. The sanctions resolutions have also contained humanitarian and other exceptions; medical equipment and foodstuffs in humanitarian circumstances being generally excepted, although the resolutions have shown great inconsistency in other types of exceptions, as the list in the Annex to this chapter shows.

Though not mandated as a law enforcement body, the Council has come to play an important role in that respect. Its resolutions under Chapter VII have in recent years linked determinations under Article 39 of a threat to or breach of the peace with determinations of breaches of fundamental norms of international law, such as the prohibition of aggression, human rights (genocide, self-determination) and humanitarian law. In this way they have come to be generally identified with community interests.

To date, the Security Council has invoked Chapter VII for the imposition of sanctions under Article 41 against 12 States (South Africa, Iraq, the Former Yugoslavia, Somalia, Libya, Liberia, Haiti, Rwanda, Sudan, Sierra Leone, Ethiopia and Eritrea) and five non-State entities or groups (the Southern Rhodesia minority regime, UNITA in Angola, the Bosnian Serbs, the Taliban in Afghanistan, and "all foreign and Congolese armed groups and militias operating in the territory of North and South Kivu and of Ituri, and groups not party to the Global and All-inclusive agreement, in the Democratic Republic of the Congo").[7] The network of sanctions spans four continents. In addition, the Security Council has adopted resolutions aimed at combatting "acts of terrorism" which are general in nature and not targeted against specific entities.

After an initial controversy in the case of Southern Rhodesia, the Security Council now assumes the competence to decide when to terminate sanctions and therefore to review conditions for compliance periodically. This means that the same consensus has to prevail within the Council on termination as did on adoption, which is not always easy to obtain, as shown in the case of Iraq. Nevertheless, the majority of sanctions were terminated through an official resolution of the Council, some having first been suspended, and, on one occasion, restored. Apart from the resolutions on the combatting of terrorism, seven sanctions regimes are still in force at the time of writing: Iraq (military measures), Somalia, Rwanda (non-governmental forces), Liberia, Sierra Leone, and militias in the Democratic Republic of the Congo.

(1) The First United Nations Sanctions Experiments

a. Southern Rhodesia

Mandatory economic sanctions under Article 41 of the Charter were adopted for the first time in the history of the United Nations in December 1966, following on the Unilateral Declaration of Independence (UDI) in November 1965 by a white minority regime in Southern Rhodesia. The Security Council, considering the UDI to be in contravention of the right of the African majority to self-determination, declared it null and void, including all subsequent acts of the illegal regime, and imposed a duty of

7 An updated list may be found on http://www.un.org/News/ossg/sanction.htm.

non-recognition (Resolutions 216 and 217 (1965); and 277 (1970)). Southern Rhodesia thus remained unrecognised as an independent State until the establishment of the State of Zimbabwe in 1980 under majority rule. After recommending economic sanctions in November 1965 (Resolutions 216 and 217 (1965)), it determined unequivocally in December 1966, that the situation in Southern Rhodesia constituted a threat to international peace and security and proceeded to impose mandatory sanctions which were initially selective, targeting certain Southern Rhodesian exports (asbestos, iron ore, chrome, pig-iron, sugar, tobacco, copper, meat and meat products and hides, skins and leather), and then, in 1968, quasi-comprehensive, including economic, financial and diplomatic, measures (Resolutions 232 and 253, respectively). These were subsequently reinforced in regard, *inter alia,* to insurance coverage for air flights and commodities and trade names and franchises (Resolutions 277 (1970); 333 (1973); and 388 (1976)). The measures were only terminated in December 1979 when the birth of the new State of Zimbabwe in 1980 became imminent.

b. South Africa

The only other measure formally adopted under Article 41 of the Charter during this Cold War period was a mandatory arms embargo in 1977 against South Africa (Resolution 418), reinforced in 1984 (Resolution 558), as part of United Nations action to dismantle the apartheid system in South Africa – the first time that sanctions were imposed against a Member of the United Nations. However, all subsequent efforts to adopt mandatory comprehensive economic sanctions, including suspension of investments, against South Africa (which had been recommended by the General Assembly) were to fail.

(2) Comprehensive Sanctions Post-1990

The reactivation of the Security Council immediately after the end of the Cold War following on a newly-found consensus was to result in a proliferation of sanctions measures. The new era was ushered in by the invasion of Kuwait by Iraq on August 2, 1990, resulting in a broad expansion both qualitatively and quantitatively of the powers of the Security Council. However, of the post-1990 measures, only three of the sanctions regimes – those relating to Iraq, Haiti and Yugoslavia – are considered to have been quasi-comprehensive, covering the gamut of economic, financial, diplomatic and other measures.

a. Iraq

The measures adopted against Iraq under Article 41, following on its invasion of Kuwait on 2 August 1990, had as their initial objective that of ensuring the immediate and unconditional withdrawal of all of its forces from Kuwait – although other objectives, including the disarmament of Iraq, were later grafted onto these. In Resolution 662 (1990), the Council: "1. *Decides* that annexation of Kuwait by Iraq under any form and whatever pretext has no legal validity, and is considered null and void" and called on all States, international organisations and specialised agencies "to refrain from any action or dealing that might be interpreted as an indirect recognition of the annexation"; the pronouncement of invalidity also extended to all subsequent acts of the Government of Iraq relating to this purported annexation (see Resolutions 664 and 670 (1990)).

As opposed to the economic and financial sanctions against Southern Rhodesia which were only progressively tightened, those adopted against Iraq imposed from the start a near comprehensive trade embargo, financial sanctions, including the freezing of assets, and ban on all means of transportation, including air traffic and aircraft and the impounding of vessels of Iraqi registry (Resolutions 661 and 670 (1990)).

After the armed action by the Coalition against Iraq in January 1991, authorised by Resolution 678 (1990), the sanctions remained in force in order to obtain Iraqi compliance with the series of demilitarisation measures called for under Resolution 687, which included the destruction and removal of nuclear, chemical and biological weapons and the facilities for their manufacture and use. Resolution 687, however, partially lifted the sanctions in regard to foodstuffs and certain supplies for essential civilian needs, subject to the approval of the Sanctions Committee (a condition lifted by Resolution 1051 (1999)).

The importation of a limited amount of petroleum from Iraq was authorised in order, *inter alia*, to fund the United Nations Compensation Fund to meet claims against Iraq, and for the purchase of humanitarian goods under the Oil-for-Food Programme established under Resolution 986 (1995) and extended on several occasions. The ceiling on petroleum was gradually raised and subsequently lifted in December 1999 (Resolution 1284). The Council then went from restricting civilian trade to a focus on the prohibition of the import of weapons and military related goods. Resolution 1051, adopted in March 1996, established the export/import monitoring system for Iraq regarding the supply of "dual-use" items to Iraq; subsequently, a revised Goods Review List of military-related goods or commodities was adopted under Resolution 1409 (2002), thus lifting the ban from any commodities not included on the list.

The disarmament and verification regime imposed on Iraq and the steps leading to the war waged against it, is beyond the scope of this study. Briefly, it will be recalled that Resolution 1137, adopted in November 1997, imposed travel restrictions on Iraqi officials and members of the Iraqi armed forces considered responsible for non-compliance with the United Nations inspection regime and that, in December 1999, the United Nations Monitoring, Verification and Inspection Commission (UNMOVIC) was established under Resolution 1284 to undertake the responsibilities of the former UNSCOM, which had been charged with monitoring the elimination of weapons of mass destruction in Iraq. Although Resolution 1441, adopted in November 2002, warned of serious consequences if Iraq did not comply with all the relevant Council resolutions relating to this regime, the Council was unable to meet for a subsequent resolution due to lack of unanimity among its Permanent Members. There followed the unauthorised and hence illegal military action against Iraq led by the United States and the United Kingdom, and the subsequent occupation of the country by the coalition forces. This resulted in ending the remaining sanctions against Iraq, with the exception of the arms embargo, first *de facto*, and then officially under Resolution 1483, adopted in the wake of the occupation on 22 May 2003, thus ushering in a new and uncertain era for Iraq.

b. Yugoslavia

Quasi-comprehensive sanctions were also resorted to in response to the crises in the Former Yugoslavia. When heavy fighting broke out in various parts of the Socialist Federal Republic of Yugoslavia as a prelude to its dismemberment, the Security Council adopted, in September 1991, Resolution 713, which imposed a mandatory arms embargo against the territory. Following on the break-up of Yugoslavia, the continuation of the fighting, and the policies of ethnic cleansing and mass exodus of the population which ensued, the Security Council was led to take a further series of wide-ranging measures, first confirming that the arms embargo applied to all areas that had been part of Yugoslavia (Resolution 727) and then, in May 1992, taking specific measures confined to the territory of the newly proclaimed Federal Republic of Yugoslavia (Serbia and Montenegro) modelled on the Rhodesian and Iraqi sanctions, which included not only a full ban on imports and exports, a flight ban, and the severance of financial relations, but also a reduction of diplomatic representation and suspension of sporting contacts, scientific and technical co-operation and cultural exchanges (Resolution 757). Sanctions were again strengthened in November 1992 (Resolution 787) and April 1993 (Resolution 820), and by then covered also communications and transport, including river traffic along the Danube, transhipment through the FRY and the impounding and detaining of all Yugoslavian vessels, freight vehicles and aircraft and the freezing of assets.

Sanctions under Article 41 of the Charter were also associated with a policy of non-recognition. This took the form of refusal of admission of the new Serbian entity, the Security Council declaring "that the State formerly known as the Socialist Federal Republic of Yugoslavia has ceased to exist" and the suspension of Yugoslavia from voting in the General Assembly and ECOSOC (Resolution 777 (1992); and 821 (1993)). In the case of Bosnia and Herzegovina the Council also endorsed "the principle that all statements or commitments made under duress, particularly those relating to land and property, are wholly null and void" (Resolution 820 (1993)).

When the "Bosnian Serb party" refused to submit to the peace plans for Bosnia, trade sanctions were also applied to that non-State entity in September 1994 as well as the non-admission into Member States territories of Bosnian Serb officials and military officers (Resolution 942).

Though sanctions against Yugoslavia were first suspended and then lifted following on the Dayton agreement (Resolution 1074), the crisis in Kosovo led to the re-imposition of an arms embargo in 1998 (Resolution 1160) and to the subsequent establishment of a fully-fledged United Nations administration of the territory (Resolution 1244). The remaining sanctions against the FRY were lifted in September 2001 (Resolution 1367).

The International Criminal Tribunal for the Former Yugoslavia (ICTY) was established by Security Council Resolution 827 of 25 May 1993 in the face of the serious violations of international humanitarian law committed in the territory of the former Yugoslavia since 1991, such as the massive and systematic detention and rape of women, and the continuance of the practice of "ethnic cleansing", which was determined to constitute a threat to international peace and security. It will be recalled that the Tribunal has subject-matter jurisdiction over grave breaches of the 1949 Geneva Conventions, violations of the laws or customs of war, genocide and crimes against humanity, and that while it has concurrent jurisdiction with national courts over these offences, it can claim primacy over such courts and may take over national investigations and proceedings at any stage if this proves to be in the interest of international justice.

c. Haiti

Sanctions against Haiti were adopted in June 1993 (Resolution 841) in response to the political crisis triggered by the ousting of President Aristide following on a military coup. They included an oil and arms embargo and the freezing of foreign assets controlled by the *de facto* authorities of the country. Suspended two months later as a result of the adoption of the Governors Island Agreement to resolve the crisis (Resolution 861), they were reimposed in October 1993 (Resolution 873) when it was clear that this was not being respected, and tightened the following year to include all commodities and products, with the exception of medical supplies and foodstuffs (Resolution 917). Sanctions were again lifted in September 1994 (Resolution 994) when the Government of Haiti was restored to President Aristide.

(3) Selective Sanctions in Africa post-1990

With the exception of Afghanistan, and the particular case of Libya, the remaining sanctions regimes have been concentrated on the African continent in response to internal military conflicts, ethnic violence leading in one case to genocide, general collapse of internal order and State authority, economic wars fought for acquisition of natural resources, and consequent generation of refugee flows and the spilling over of armed conflicts into neighbouring countries. These sanctions have generally been more restricted in scope both in respect of the targeted entity and in terms of the measures imposed.

The measures imposed against African States, as well as non-State entities, have generally covered a mandatory embargo on the delivery of weapons and military equipment to the parties either as stand-alone or combined with an assortment of financial restrictions and select embargo of commodities (essentially petroleum and diamonds), as well as travel and flight bans.

a. Somalia

An arms embargo was imposed against Somalia in January 1992 (Resolution 733) following on the intensification of the internal armed conflict, the heavy losses of life and the looming humanitarian crisis. This was last reaffirmed by Resolution 1519 (2003), the Security Council reiterating its firm support for the Somali National Reconciliation Process, as well as its serious concern over the continued flow of weapons and ammunition supplies to and through Somalia in contravention of the arms embargo.

b. Liberia

In November 1999 an arms embargo was also imposed on Liberia (Resolution 788) as a result of the non-respect of the parties for the implementation of the Yamoussoukro

IV Accord and the general deterioration of the situation. Subsequently, following on the active support provided by the Government of Liberia for the Revolutionary United Front (RUF) in Sierra Leone, the Security Council adopted Resolution 1343 in March 2001 which, on the one hand, terminated the measures under Resolution 788 and on the other imposed a more comprehensive embargo which included a new arms embargo and a ban on the direct or indirect import of all rough diamonds from Liberia. The Resolution also called on States to take measures to prevent the entry into or transit through their territories of senior members of the Government of Liberia and its armed forces, as well as their immediate family and other select individuals. These sanctions, limited over time, were extended by Resolution 1478 (2003) following on the active support provided by the Government of Liberia also to the rebels in Côte d'Ivoire.

c. UNITA

The case of the National Union for the Total Independence of Angola (UNITA) is a complex one. In order to compel it to enter into a cease-fire agreement with the Government in accordance with the "Accordos de Paz" and to accept the 1992 United Nations supervised election results in Angola which brought the MPLA to power, an embargo on arms, petroleum and petroleum products was imposed on the territory controlled by UNITA (Resolution 864 (1993)). Following on UNITA's persistent failure to comply with its obligations under the Lusaka Protocol signed on 20 November 1994, these measures were strengthened to include restrictions on the travel of senior officials of UNITA and their immediate families, the closure of all UNITA offices, the prohibition of airflights and the supply of aircraft or aircraft components, engineering and servicing (Resolution 1127 (1997)); these came into force two months later. In June 1998, the Council in reaction to UNITA's failure to implement new undertakings on the implementation of the Lusaka Protocol, imposed further sanctions. States were to freeze funds and financial resources belonging to UNITA, including senior officials and their immediate family in accordance with the list of designated individuals drawn up by the Sanctions Committee under Resolution 1127, and to sever all official contacts with it. The Resolution also prohibited the direct or indirect import from Angola of all diamonds not controlled through the Government Certificate of Origin regime and the sale or supply to those areas of Angola controlled by UNITA of aircraft and equipment used in mining or mining services as well as ground and waterborne transportation services (Resolution 1173 (1998)). Sanctions were first suspended, then terminated in December 2002 by Resolution 1448 (2002) when UNITA undertook to implement the peace agreements.

d. Rwanda

Following on the Security Council's strong condemnation of the ongoing violence and ethnic killing in Rwanda, an arms embargo was similarly imposed on that country by Resolution 918 in May 1994 and extended to neighbouring countries by Resolution 997 (1995) if such arms were destined for Rwanda. In accordance with Resolution 1011 (1995) the Security Council first suspended and then terminated this embargo in

September 1996 but only in respect of the Government of Rwanda as opposed to non-governmental forces.

The Security Council also created the International Criminal Tribunal for Rwanda (ICTR) by Resolution 955 of 8 November 1994. The Tribunal, located in Arusha, was established for the prosecution of persons responsible for genocide and other serious violations of international humanitarian law committed in the territory of Rwanda between 1 January 1994 and 31 December 1994. It also has the competence to prosecute Rwandan citizens responsible for genocide and other such violations of international law committed in the territory of neighbouring States during the same period. *Ratione materiae,* the Tribunal has jurisdiction over genocide, crimes against humanity, violations of Article 3 common to the Geneva Conventions and of Additional Protocol II.

e. Sierra Leone

Following on the overthrow by a military junta of the democratically elected President, an oil and arms embargo was imposed on Sierra Leone in October 1997 by Security Council Resolution 1132, as well as restrictions on the travel of members of the junta. These were terminated by Resolution 1156 in March 1998 and 1171 in June 1998, respectively, when the junta was ousted by the West African Intervention Force, ECOMOG. However, since the fighting continued, the arms embargo remained in respect of non-governmental forces and Resolution 1171 also imposed a travel ban on leading members of the former military junta and of the RUF, as designated by the Committee established by Resolution 1132. In July 2000, the Security Council requested the Government of Sierra Leone to ensure that an effective Certificate of Origin regime for trade in diamonds was in operation in Sierra Leone and prohibited the import of rough diamonds not controlled by the Government under this scheme (Resolution 1306). These measures were renewed successively by Resolution 1385 (December 2001) and Resolution 1446 (December 2002).

f. Ethiopia and Eritrea

In regard to the conflict between Ethiopia and Eritrea, when fighting erupted again despite efforts at international mediation in May 2000, the Security Council adopted Resolution 1298 under which it imposed an arms embargo against the two countries, as well as a ban on the provision of related technical assistance or training. The measures expired on 16 May 2001 (see Presidential Statement S/PRST/2001/14).

g. Democratic Republic of the Congo

In July 2003, the Security Council, deeply concerned by the continuation of hostilities in the eastern part of the DRC, particularly in North and South Kivu and in Ituri, despite the conclusion of a Global and All Inclusive Agreement on the Transition in the Democratic Republic of the Congo signed in Pretoria on 17 December 2002 and the establishment of a Government of National Unity and Transition, the grave violation of human rights and humantarian law and the illegal plundering of the natural resources of the

Congo, adopted Resolution 1493 (2003). It decided, *inter alia*, that all States, including the Democratic Republic of the Congo, prevent the supply of arms and related matériel, as well as military assistance, to all "foreign and Congolese armed groups and militias operating in the territory of North and South Kuvu and of Ituri, and to groups not party to the Global and All-inclusive agreement in the Democratic Republic of the Congo". This was imposed for an initial period of 12 months.

(4) Measures for the combatting of Terrorism

Apart from encouraging States to become parties to the relevant international conventions, the Security Council has also determined that international terrorism is a threat to international peace, thus opening the way to action under Chapter VII. Initially, it was concerned with the question of State responsibility for terrorist acts, as well as for the harbouring of terrorists, leading to the adoption of sanctions against the States concerned. Its most recent action, however, has been directed towards penalisation of acts of international terrorism, as well as suppression of its financing.

a. Libya

Selective sanctions against Libya, covering an air and arms embargo and the reduction of Libyan diplomatic personnel serving abroad, were adopted in 1992 (Resolution 748) in the context of the crisis generated by the Lockerbie bombing and in response to Libya's refusal to accede to what were, in effect, requests from the Governments of the United States and United Kingdom that it surrender two Libyan suspects, accept responsibility and pay compensation. Sanctions were tightened in 1993 (Resolution 883) to include, *inter alia,* the freezing of Libyan assets abroad, including the funds of "any person identified by States as acting on behalf of the Government or public authorities of Libya", and a ban on the provision to Libya of equipment for oil refining and transportation. The sanctions were indefinitely suspended on the basis of a Presidential statement (S/PRST/1999/10) in April 1999 following on the acceptance by all the parties concerned of a trial in The Hague under Scottish law of the two accused whose surrender had been requested. They were finally lifted by Resolution 1506 on 12 September 2003 in view of Libya's acceptance of its responsibility and the payment of appropriate compensation.

b. Sudan

Following on the failure of the Sudan to comply with the Security Council's demands in Resolution 1044 (1996) that it extradite the three suspects wanted in connection with the 26 June 1995 attempted assassination of President Hosni Mubarak of Egypt and that it stop supporting terrorist activities, the Council decided under Resolution 1054 adopted in May 1996, that all States were to significantly reduce Sudanese diplomatic staff and restrict the entry into or transit through their territory of members of the Government of Sudan and other officials. Further sanctions, including a flight ban, were threatened a few months later by Resolution 1070, but these were finally not imposed and in September 2001 the Council also lifted the diplomatic sanctions (Resolution 1372).

c. Afghanistan

When the Taliban administration in Afghanistan failed to comply with the demand in Resolution 1267 of 15 October 1999 to surrender for trial Usama bin Laden to the appropriate authorities, the prohibitions contained in paragraph 4 of the Resolution, i.e. a flight ban on any aircraft owned, leased or operated by or on behalf of the Taliban, as well as a freeze on funds directly or indirectly owned or controlled by the Taliban, entered into effect on 14 November 1999. One year later, on 19 December 2000, the Security Council imposed an embargo on the supply to the territory of Afghanistan under Taliban control of arms and related materiel of all types, including technical advice or military training (Resolution 1333 (2000)). States were also called on to reduce their diplomatic staff, close all Taliban and Ariana Afghan Airlines offices in their territories, and to freeze the funds and other financial assets of Usama bin Laden and the Al-Qaida network. The flight ban was also reinforced. These measures entered into force one month later.

Following on the signature of the Bonn Agreement on provisional arrangements in Afghanistan, the establishment of a United Nations authorised International Security Assistance Force, and an Afghan interim authority, the Security Council modified the sanctions regime to take into account the fact that the Taliban were no longer in *de facto* control of Afghanistan. Thus in January 2002, the Security Council lifted the measures against Ariana Afghan Airlines (Resolution 1388). At the same time, it adopted Resolution 1390 which amended the arms embargo, imposed a travel ban and kept in place the freezing of funds, targeting the measures specifically at Usama Bin Laden and Al-Qaida, including associated members of the Taliban, rather than at a *de facto* regime. Resolution 1390 recalled Resolution 1373 (2001). Thus sanctions against Afghanistan melted into the broader framework of the response to terrorism and cooperation between the Afghanistan Committee and the newly established Counter-Terrorism Committee under Resolution 1373 was reinforced.

d. Resolution 1373

This development was taken a step further by Resolution 1373 on the prevention and suppression of the financing of terrorist acts adopted on September 28, 2001 in the aftermath of the September 11th attack on the World Trade Center and following on Security Council Resolution 1368 (2001).

The Council, after reaffirming that any act of international terrorism constitutes a threat to international peace and security, decides, *inter alia*, that all States shall:

1. (a) Prevent and suppress the financing of terrorist acts;
   (b) Criminalize the willful provision or collection, by any means, directly or indirectly, of funds by their nationals or in their territories with the intention that the funds should be used, or in the knowledge that they are to be used, in order to carry out terrorist acts;
   (c) Freeze without delay funds and other financial assets or economic resources of persons who commit, or attempt to commit, terrorist acts or participate in or facilitate the commission of terrorist acts; of entities owned or controlled directly

or indirectly by such persons; and of persons and entities acting on behalf of, or at the direction of such persons and entities, including funds derived or generated from property owned or controlled directly or indirectly by such persons and associated persons and entities;

(d) Prohibit their nationals or any persons and entities within their territories from making any funds, financial assets or economic resources or financial or other related services available, directly or indirectly, for the benefit of persons who commit or attempt to commit or facilitate or participate in the commission of terrorist acts, of entities owned or controlled, directly or indirectly, by such persons and of persons and entities acting on behalf of or at the direction of such persons;

(e) Ensure that any person who participates in the financing, planning, preparation or perpetration of terrorist acts or in supporting terrorist acts is brought to justice and ensure that, in addition to any other measures against them, such terrorist acts are established as serious criminal offences in domestic laws and regulations and that the punishment duly reflects the seriousness of such terrorist acts.

Thus paragraph 1 of the Resolution obliges States to criminalise the provision or collection of funds destined to support terrorism and to freeze the funds and other financial assets or economic resources of persons or entities that commit or attempt to commit terrorist acts or facilitate their commission, and from bringing the perpetrator to justice.

The following paragraph 2 decides that States shall refrain from supporting terrorists in any way, including through recruitment, the granting of safe haven, and the use of their territory; that they shall establish terrorist acts as serious criminal offences in their domestic laws, and cooperate in inter-state criminal investigations and proceedings. The final paragraph 3 calls, *inter alia*, for inter-State assistance and exchange of information to prevent the commission of terrorist acts, for ratification of the relevant counter-terrorism conventions, including the International Convention for the Suppression of the Financing of Terrorism of 9 December 1999, and for the adoption of measures to ensure that asylum-seekers are not involved in acts of terrorism and that refugee status is not abused. It also notes the close connection between international terrorism and transnational organized crime, illicit drugs, money-laundering, illegal arms trafficking, and illegal movement of nuclear, chemical, biological and other potentially deadly materials.

The Resolution departs from traditional sanctions resolutions in a number of ways. It imposes on Member States open-ended obligations with no temporal limitation and calls on them to adopt legislation criminalising specified conduct which up to now may not have been penalised in their domestic laws. There is an undoubted shift from the application of sanctions which in principle had a traditional non-punitive character to measures having penal connotations. The target is neither a member of a governmental or political grouping nor is it designated – Usama bin Laden, Al-Qaida, etc. – it is general and impersonal and, apart from the lists drawn up by the Afghanistan Committee, leaves it to implementing States to designate the entities that are targeted in the absence of a definition of terrorist acts. The legislative nature of the Resolution is evident from the fact that States are called on to implement provisions similar to those found in conventional instruments, such as the International Convention for the Suppression of the Financing of Terrorism, outside of any conventional obligations. Furthermore, Resolution 1373 (2001) has a potentially serious impact on asylum law in linking asylum-seeking with terrorism.

e. Black-listing as a result of the move away from comprehensive to targeted sanctions

The debate on sanctions stirred up by the Iraq case which focussed on a critique of the far-reaching and in some cases irreversible effects on the economies and population of target states of comprehensive economic sanctions, notwithstanding the humanitarian exceptions and the Oil-For-Food program, resulted at the end of the 90s decade in disillusionment with such sanctions and a call for re-evaluation of this "blunt instrument."[8] The Security Council created a commission to evaluate the humanitarian situation in Iraq and held an open session on Iraq on 26 and 28 June 2001.[9] It subsequently established a working group of the Council to develop general recommendations on how to improve the effectiveness of United Nations sanctions.[10]

This led to proposals which led to a re-orientation of sanctions away from comprehensive and towards so-called "smart sanctions" or targeted sanctions directed at government leaders and elites and other specifically designated entities responsible for the policies condemned.

As was seen in the case of the sanctions in Africa, such measures involved in particular restrictions on financial and banking operations (asset freezes, blocking of financial transactions or financial services) and travel and aviation bans, including visas, or were directed against specific commodities, such as arms and diamonds, particularly important in view of economically motivated conflicts. The aim was to increase the efficiency of sanctions, while at the same time decreasing their unwanted side-effects, particularly on the populations of targeted States.[11]

---

8 In the words of Boutros Boutros-Ghali in his Agenda for peace (see A/50/60 – S/1995/1, of 3 January 1995, para.70).

9 See S/1999/356 of 30 March 1999, pursuant to Note from the President of the Security Council dated 30 January 1999 (S/1999/100).

10 See Security Council Working Group on General Issues on Sanctions established in April 2000 pursuant to a Note by the President of the Security Council (S/2000/319).

11 Three Government initiatives contributed to developing the concept of targeted financial sanctions: the Bonn-Berlin, Interlaken and Stockholm processes. The Bonn process focused on arms embargoes and travel-related sanctions, the Interlaken process concentrated on the identification of basic legal and administrative requirements for national implementation of financial sanctions, while the Stockholm process focused on how the United Nations and Member States could ensure effective monitoring of compliance and enforcement, and how best to assist Member States in implementing sanctions regimes. The findings were presented to the Security Council at various intervals, including October 2001 and February 2003. (See e.g., *Targeted Financial Sanctions – A Manual for Design and Implementation: Contributions from the Interlaken Process*, The Swiss Confederation in cooperation with the United Nations Secretariat and the Watson Institute for International Studies, Brown University (at http://www.smartsanctions.ch).

There was also a shift from the prohibition of the movement of funds and the freezing of government assets (Iraq, Libya, Yugoslavia) to blocking the accounts of designated entities and individuals. In this connection, the relevant Sanctions Committees had been requested by the Security Council to maintain updated lists of targeted individuals as early as 1994 in connection with their respective regimes. Concerning financial and travel measures, for example, lists were drawn up of members of the military junta in Haiti, the Haitian military, and immediate family members (Resolution 917 (1994)), UNITA officials (Resolution 1127 (1997)), members of the former military junta and the RUF in Sierra Leone (Resolution 1171 (1998)), and senior members of the Government of Liberia and its armed forces, including their immediate family and other designated individuals (Resolution 1343 (2001)).[12]

Nevertheless, those targeted were still members of a government or political faction. However, the resolutions on the combatting of terrorism – those on Afghanistan and Resolution 1373 (2001) – ushered in a new era as the question of how to combat the financing of terrorism became of major importance. Thus Resolution 1333 requested the Sanctions Committee on Afghanistan to establish and maintain updated lists of individuals and entities targeted by the freezing of funds and financial assets, including those referred to under Resolution 1267. Resolution 1390 directed specifically at Usama Bin Laden and associates, does likewise; finally one consolidated list was issued which is regularly updated.[13] No reasons are given for inclusion on the list and the de-listing procedure which was finally instituted, provides individuals with a political, not judicial process. No list has been established under Resolution 1373, leaving Member States to draw up their own.

An additional listing procedure has been created under paragraph 19 of Resolution 1483 (2003) which directed the Sanctions Committee on Iraq to identify individuals and entities associated with the previous Government of Iraq who own funds or other financial assets located outside Iraq which Member States are to freeze without delay and to transfer to the Iraq Development Fund.

While the move away from comprehensive sanctions and the recent tendency to bypass the Security Council in resorting to non-authorised unilateral action, may appear to have made earlier debates over the legal consequences of Security Council sanctions resolutions outdated, targeted sanctions in the form of Resolution 1373 and the listing procedures under Resolutions 1267, 1333 and 1390, have on the contrary refuelled public debate on the competence and powers of the Security Council, the problems arising in the field of human rights, particularly due process rights, and the consequent question of judicial review and other remedies for the individual.

12 See for example, SC/7062, SC/7162, and SC/7253 adopted in May, October and December, 2001, respectively.

13 The latest comprehensive list was issued as SC/7222/rev.1* and a number of addenda have since followed. An up-to-date list is available at http://www.un.org/Docs/sc/committees/AfghanPressEng.htm. See also the reports of the Committee (S/2002/101 of 5 February 2002 and S/2002/1423 of 26 December 2002).

III. The Implications of Sanctions Implementation for Member States

(1) The Obligation to Implement

The decisions and practice of the Security Council while political in origin, have served to change the legal positions of States and also, recently, of individuals, engendering far-reaching legal consequences. The measures adopted under Chapter VII have not only resulted in a temporary suspension of the subjective legal rights of the State against which they are applied (sometimes with irreversible effects), but also, as distinct from those "horizontal" reactions (countermeasures) taken by an injured State or States within a bilateral context for the purpose of enforcing subjective rights, have resulted in the creation of a vertical relationship between the Organisation and Member States. The implications for implementing States are therefore also far-reaching for, in contrast to unilateral countermeasures, States do not have a right, but a duty to take such action.

The decisions of the Security Council are mandatory in accordance with Article 25 of the Charter under which States "agree to accept and carry out the decisions of the Security Council". It is generally agreed that the term "decisions" in Article 25 is limited to those decisions by the Security Council which in accordance with the articles under which they are adopted create obligations for Members. These decisions are taken on behalf of the entire United Nations membership (Article 24(1)). The binding effect of these articles is crowned by Articles 48 and 49 of the Charter.

States may and have contested the obligatory character of particular resolutions. There has been controversy, for example, as to whether decisions adopted under Article 40 or outside of Chapter VII can have mandatory force.[14] However, there is general agreement that the resolutions which adopt sanctions measures are binding, even if some lack an express reference to Article 25, as a result of their firm basis in Chapter VII and in most cases the express reference to Article 41. This does not mean to say that the wording of certain provisions may not give rise to controversy over their legal effects, where, for instance, the Council resorts to wording such as "calls upon", which is weaker than "decides", does not expressly spell out the clear basis under Article 41, or, exceptionally, makes no express determination under Article 39 (this is the case with respect to Resolution 1160 (1999) on Kosovo, made up for in the subsequent Resolution 1199).

Sanctions resolutions are variously addressed to "all Member States", to "all States", to "all States Members of the Specialised Agencies", or to "all States members of international and regional organisations".[15] The reference to "all States" includes States not members of the United Nations; it used to be commonly understood, however, that Article 2(6) placed the obligation to ensure the effective implementation of Security Council decisions by non-Member States, on the Organisation, rather than acted as an

14 See Advisory Opinion on Namibia in which the ICJ considered that the Security Council could adopt mandatory decisions outside Chapter VII on the basis of its broad powers under Article 24 of the Charter (ICJ Reports 1971, p. 53).

15 We are not concerned here with implementation by United Nations organs or the United Nations family, so will not refer to specialised agencies, regional organisations and other international Organisations as addressees.

infringement of the *pacta tertiis* rule, as Switzerland made clear on numerous occasions. With Switzerland among the last of the States to join the Organisation, this issue is by now moot, although the history of sanctions implementation by that country makes a most interesting study, and has thus been included in this work.

Moreover, since it is important to ensure that there are no cracks in the universal application of sanctions, no State has yet been formally dispensed by the Security Council from this implementation, even though the Council does have that discretion (Article 48(1)). States too, in accordance with Article 48(2) of the Charter, must carry out the decisions of the Security Council through their actions in other international or regional organisations.

Article 103 of the Charter, referred to expressly or by implication in some resolutions,[16] ensures that the carrying out of Charter obligations by Member States prevails over any other international agreement, and this has been interpreted as including the secondary obligations contained in Security Council resolutions.

Non-mandatory resolutions which provide an authorisation to States to use all necessary means to enforce the economic embargoes decided on by the Security Council,[17] have also resulted in the temporary suspension of (non-imperative) rules of customary international law by allowing such measures as interception, forcible search and even arrest of third-party ships on the high seas. In situations of armed conflict – the Iraq-Kuwait case – the sanctions measures have also required States to go beyond the traditional duties of neutral States, which were not bound to prevent their nationals from furnishing supplies, including military supplies, to belligerents.

(2) Provisions Relating to Domestic Implementation and Reporting

a. References to specific domestic measures

Security Council resolutions have in some cases specifically spelled out the measures which States are required to take at the domestic level (measures which are examined in the following chapters). For example, the resolutions prescribe the attitude of their courts to recognition or sovereign immunity issues,[18] or call for domestic enforcement measures, including penal sanctions.[19]

16 See, for example, SCR 670 (1990) on Iraq, Note by the President of the Security Council of 10 February 1993 (S/25270) and SCR 841 (1993) on Haiti.

17 For example SCR 221 (1966) for Rhodesia, 665 (1990) for Iraq, 787 (1992) for Yugoslavia and 841 (1993) for Haiti.

18 See, e.g., SCR 277 (1970) which calls on Member States "to ensure that any act performed by officials and institutions of the illegal regime in Southern Rhodesia shall not be accorded any recognition, official or otherwise, including judicial notice, by the competent organs of their State", or, regarding Iraq, SCR 712 (1991) and 1483 (2003) in connection with immunity from legal process of petroleum exports from Iraq in all States.

19 So, for example, SCR 333 (1973) on Southern Rhodesia calls on States to enact and enforce legislation providing for the imposition of severe penalties on persons that evade or commit breaches of sanctions; Resolution 820 on Yugoslavia "Reminds States of the importance of

The sanctions resolutions have also defined the scope of domestic implementing measures which are to apply on their territory and in respect of their nationals (i.e. even outside their territory) and "notwithstanding any contract entered into or any licence granted before the date of the resolution".

Security Council Resolutions 827 (1993) and 955 (1994) establishing the two International Criminal Tribunals call on States "to cooperate fully with the International Tribunal and its organs" and to take "any measures necessary under their domestic law to implement the provisions of the present resolution and the statute". Such cooperation was spelled out, and included the provision of evidence, the detention and transfer of accused persons, the relocation of witnesses or the enforcement of sentences handed down by the Tribunal.

Resolution 1373 is the most intrusive in the internal domain of States, calling on them under Article 1(b) to: "Criminalize the wilful provision or collection, by any means, directly or indirectly, of funds by their nationals or in their territories with the intention that the funds should be used, or in the knowledge that they are to be used, in order to carry out terrorist acts".

b. Reporting

Security Council resolutions expressly refer to Member States implementation. They require States to make regular reports on such implementation to be addressed, in some cases, to the Secretary-General, in others to the Sanctions Committees which are established under each sanctions regime. Such reporting is by implication mandatory since it follows from the obligation of States to implement the decisions of the Security Council and from the need to verify the effectiveness of the action taken. In fact, Resolution 1456 (2003) which appends a declaration on the issue of combatting terrorism specifically refers to an obligation to report under that Resolution. It also follows from the tasks assigned to the Sanctions Committee, including requesting further information from States, reminders for the submission of reports, and guidance given for their submission. The manner in which such United Nations organs and United Nations Member States interface is therefore important and numerous Council resolutions have called on Member States to cooperate with the relevant Sanctions Committees.

While in the past the resolutions did not detail the manner or frequency of reporting, with the result that reporting by States was sporadic and often laconic,[20] recent resolutions have been far more specific. Reporting under Resolution 1373 has been particularly streamlined and shows the heightened interest the Security Council has taken in States'

---

strict enforcement of measures imposed under Chapter VII of the Charter, and calls upon them to bring proceedings against persons and entities violating the measures imposed (by previous resolutions) and to impose appropriate penalties". See also SCR 841 (1993) (Haiti), 864 (1993) and 1295 (1999) (UNITA), 1267 (1999) and 1333 (2000) (Taliban).

20 See, for example, analysis of reporting on implementation of Southern Rhodesian sanctions, in Vera Gowlland-Debbas, *Collective Responses to Illegal Acts in International Law. United Nations Action in the Question of Southern Rhodesia* (Martinus Nijhoff Publishers, 1990), Chapter 8, pp. 557-640.

implementing legislation, which is reflected in the tasks assigned to the Counter-terrorism Committee established under the Resolution (CTC).

Resolution 1373 (2001) "calls upon States to report to the Committee (Counter-Terrorism Committee (CTC) established under the Resolution), no later than 90 days from the date of adoption of this resolution and thereafter, according to a timetable to be proposed by the Committee, on the steps they have taken to implement this resolution". The Annex to Resolution 1377 (2001) appending a Ministerial declaration on the global effort to combat terrorism, invites the Counter-Terrorism Committee to "explore ways in which States can be assisted, and in particular to explore with international, regional and subregional Organisations:

- the promotion of best-practice in the areas covered by resolution 1373 (2001), including the preparation of model laws as appropriate,
- the availability of existing technical, financial, regulatory, legislative or other assistance programmes which might facilitate the implementation of resolution 1373 (2001),
- the promotion of possible synergies between these assistance programmes".

The CTC, following on the "Guidance for reports required of States" drawn up by the Afghanistan Sanctions Committee, has also established a comprehensive questionnaire for States, requesting them, *inter alia*, to indicate relevant legislation or executive action in place or contemplated, and other action to implement the letter and spirit of Resolution 1373. As a result, by the end of 2003, all but three Member States had filed at least one report, though 58 States were noted as failing to submit second and third reports.

(3) Monitoring of State Implementation

a. UN monitoring of implementation

A detailed analysis of the implementation by the United Nations and its agencies of Security Council resolutions, for example the establishment of first UNSCOM and then UNMOVIC to monitor the elimination of weapons of mass destruction in Iraq under Resolution 687 (1991), is outside the scope of this study.

Monitoring of sanctions implementation by United Nations Member States, however, will be briefly alluded to. Such monitoring tasks have been assigned to the Secretary-General as well as to the Sanctions Committees established under each sanctions regime and consisting of all the members of the Council. The mandates of the Sanctions Committee have consisted, *inter alia*, in following up on sanctions implementation by States, including examining State reports, considering information brought to their attention by States regarding violations of sanctions, processing requests for exemptions from the measures, and reporting periodically to the Council, including recommendations on improvement of sanctions monitoring and their humanitarian implications. In some cases, as seen above, they have been responsible for the designation of individuals and entities targeted by sanctions.

The appointment of independent expert panels and monitoring groups has also become a regular feature of sanctions implementation to tackle in particular the illegal trade in diamonds and arms smuggling. Their mandates have included investigation of violations, information gathering, assessment of progress in implementation of resolutions, the drawing up of lists of violators and the making of recommendations on improvement of the system. They are usually established for periods of around four to six months, but are renewable.

The first such panel was established by Security Council Resolution 1013 (1995) to investigate the violations of the arms embargo against the former Rwandan Government forces. This International Commission of Inquiry issued six reports from 1996 to 1998.[21] Following on the visits to Angola by the Chairman of the Sanctions Committee, Ambassador Fowler, an expert panel was also established to undertake studies to trace violations in arms trafficking, oil supplies and the diamond trade, as well as the movement of UNITA funds (Resolutions 1237 (1999)). Following on the Fowler report and its recommendations, particularly in connection with diamond trading markets, Resolution 1295 (2000) called on the Secretary General to establish a Monitoring Mechanism to investigate violations of the sanctions resolutions identified by the Panel of Experts (1295 (2000)).[22] Similar Panels of Experts and Monitoring Groups were established in relation to Sierra Leone (Resolution 1306 (2000)), Liberia (Resolution 1343 (2001)); 1408 (2002); and 1458 (2003)) and Somalia (Resolutions 1425 (2002); 1474 (2003); and 1519 (2003)).[23]

These panels adopted a "name and shame" approach: the one on Angola, for example, identifying Governments (including two African sitting Heads of State and Belgium), companies and individuals involved in violation of United Nations sanctions, while the one on Sierra Leone implicated the Government of Liberia. The role of private industry in the enforcement of the diamond embargoes against UNITA in Angola, the rebels in Sierra Leone and the Government of Liberia, was particularly highlighted.

Although the monitoring process preceded in this case the application of sanctions against the militias in the Eastern part of the DRC under Resolution 1493 (2003), mention should be made in this context of the Panel of Experts on the Illegal Exploitation of the Natural Resources and other Forms of Wealth of the Democratic Republic of the Congo which was established by the Security Council, in a statement of its President of 2 June 2000, to collect information and to analyse these economic links with the continuation of the conflict. The mandate of the Panel of Experts was renewed on a number of occasions, the latest being under Resolution 1499 (2003).[24] The Panel named individuals and companies implicated in illegal activities and against whom restrictive measures would be taken, removing the names of those parties from its list with which the Panel had reached a resolution.

21 See Final Report of the International Commission of Inquiry (S/1996/195).

22 See Final Report of the Panel of Experts established pursuant to Resolution 1237 (1999), dated 10 March 2000 (S/2000/203), and Reports of the Monitoring Mechanism on Angola Sanctions (S/2000/1026, S/2000/1225, S/2001/363 and S/2001/966).

23 See, as examples, Reports of the Panels of Experts concerning Sierra Leone (S/2000/1195) and Liberia (S/2001/1015, S/2002/1115 and S/2003/498) and first Report of the Panel on Somalia (S/2003/223).

24 See Reports of the Panel of Experts: S/2001/357, S/2001/1072 and S/2002/1146.

Monitoring schemes have also been established in connection with the combatting of terrorism. Resolution 1333 (2000) on Afghanistan called for the establishment of a Committee of Experts to make recommendations on the monitoring of the arms embargo and the closure of terrorist training camps.[25] The Security Council established a further monitoring mechanism to oversee implementation of the measures against the Taliban, as well as to offer assistance to States bordering the territory of Afghanistan under Taliban control (Resolution 1363 (2001)).[26] Further experts were reappointed by Resolution 1455 (2003).

b. The Kimberley Process

The link identified between the diamond trade and the fueling of brutal conflicts in Africa, particularly through the funding of rebel groups such as UNITA and the RUF, has led to an international initiative to set internationally agreed minimum standards for national certification schemes which is designed to prevent the sale of "conflict diamonds". This has taken the form of a series of multilateral negotiations known as the Kimberley Process which was launched in May 2000 in South Africa and culminated in the adoption of the Kimberley Process Certification Scheme (KPCS) at a Ministerial Meeting in Interlaken, in November 2002. Fifty-one States and the European Community, are currently participating in this Scheme. It also includes the active participation of representatives from the diamond industry, as well as United Nations bodies, such as the United Nations Sanctions Committees for Angola, Sierra Leone and Liberia, the Monitoring Mechanism on the situation in Angola as well as the Expert Panel on the Illegal Exploitation of Natural Resources and other forms of Wealth in the Democratic Republic of the Congo.

The Scheme was endorsed from the beginning by the United Nations General Assembly (see Resolution 55/56 on the role of "conflict" diamonds) and more recently by the Security Council which in Resolution 1459 (2003), "Noting with deep concern the linkage between the illicit trade in rough diamonds from certain regions of the world and the fuelling of armed conflicts that affect international peace and security" and recalling its past resolutions to control the illicit trade in rough diamonds, welcomed the adoption of the Kimberley Process Certification Scheme for Rough Diamonds in Interlaken and expessed its strong support for it as well as the ongoing process to refine and implement it, including the voluntary system of industry self-regulation.[27]

c. Enforcement by Member States of the economic embargo at sea

In the cases of Southern Rhodesia, Iraq, Haiti, the Federal Republic of Yugoslavia and Sierra Leone, the Security Council has called on all States to enforce the economic embargo at sea, including interception and inspection of third-Stateships on the high

25 See Report of the Committee: S/2001/511.

26 See Report of the monitoring group: S/2002/65.

27 For further information on this process, see www.kimberleyprocess.com/documents.asp.

seas in order to prohibit any traffic from entering the targeted entity's territorial seas carrying prohibited goods. Thus Resolution 787 (1992) on Yugoslavia, calls upon all States, acting nationally or through regional agencies or arrangements, to "use such measures commensurate with the specific circumstances as may be necessary under the authority of the Council to halt all inward and outward maritime shipping in order to inspect and verify their cargoes and destinations" in implementation of economic sanctions. Acting under Chapter VIII of the Charter, it has called on regional organisations to enlist in this process. Regional organisations such as the EU, NATO and WEU (in the case of Yugoslavia sanctions), as well as ECOWAS (in respect of Sierra Leone), have thus all participated in such enforcement.[28] These resolutions are not mandatory. Nevertheless, they go far in authorising States to intercept and forcibly search third-party ships on the high seas, which is normally contrary to the international law obligations of States, for such resolutions imply or explicitly refer (in the case of the "Beira" Resolution 221) to the use of a limited amount of force.

28 See SCR 221 (1966) on Southern Rhodesia, SCR 875 (1993) and 917 (1994) on Haiti, SCR 665 (1990) on Iraq, SCR 787 (1992) on Bosnia, and SCR 1132 (1997) on Sierra Leone.

Annex: Table of Sanctions Measures Adopted by the Security Council

Below is a summary of the measures adopted by the Security Council for implementation by States. The list does not purport to be exhaustive.

(1) Non-recognition

- *Non-recognition of consequences of illegal acts.* **Southern Rhodesia**: non-recognition of the illegal racist minority régime (SCR 216, 217, 277, 288, 328), non-recognition of internal settlement concluded under auspices of illegal régime and non-recognition of results of any elections held under it (SCR 423, 445 and 448), refusal of passports issued by the illegal regime (SCR 253); **Iraq**: no actions or dealings that might be interpreted as an indirect recognition of the annexation of Kuwait (SCR 662, 664 and 670), non-recognition of any regime in Kuwait set up by the occupying power (SCR 661).
- *Non-cognisance of the laws or acts of the sanctioned entity in municipal courts.* **Southern Rhodesia** : non-recognition under domestic law of acts of illegal regime, including judicial notice (SCR 277).
- *Non-admission to, or suspension from international organisation.* **Southern Rhodesia** (SCR 277); the **Federal Republic of Yugoslavia (Serbia and Montenegro):** suspended from participation in the General Assembly and ECOSOC (SCR 777 and 821).
- *Symbolic acts.* **Southern Rhodesia**: exclusion from participation in sporting events (interpretation of SCR 253 by the Sanctions Committee, Note dated July 17, 1976); **Federal Republic of Yugoslavia**: exclusion from scientific and technical cooperation and cultural exchanges (SCR 757).

(2) Measures Flowing from Article 41

a. Severance of Diplomatic and other Relations

- *Severance or reduction of diplomatic, consular and trade relations.* **Southern Rhodesia** (SCR 217, 253, 277); **Libya** (SCR 748); **Federal Republic of Yugoslavia** (SCR 757); **Sudan** (SCR 1054); **UNITA**: official contacts with the UNITA leadership in areas of Angola to which State administration had not been extended (SCR 1173); **Taliban** (SCR 1333).
- *Closure of offices, including information and tourist offices, abroad.* **Southern Rhodesia**: tourist offices (SCR 277); **Libya**: Libyan Arab Airlines (SCR 883), **UNITA**: UNITA offices (SCR 1127); **Taliban**: Ariana Afghan Airlines and Taliban offices (SCR 1333).

b. Movement of persons

- *Restriction of entry or transit through member States' territories of persons.* **Sudan, Iraq, Liberia**: senior members of Government and armed forces, including family mem-

bers (SCR 1054, 1137, 1343, respectively); **UNITA, Bosnian Serbs, Sierra Leone, Taliban**: senior officials of *de facto* entity and members of military junta, or persons found to have violated sanctions imposed against the targeted entity (SCR 1127, 942, 1132 and 1171, 1333, respectively); Usama bin Laden, members of the Al-Qaida organisation and associates (SCR 1390).
- *Refusal of entry to residents who are acting for or on behalf of the sanctioned entity.* **Southern Rhodesia** (SCR 253), **Bosnian Serb forces** (SCR 942), **individuals connected to terrorism** (SCR 1373).

c. Economic and financial measures

1 Prohibited imports from the sanctioned State
- *Comprehensive restrictions on commodities and products.* **Southern Rhodesia** (SCR 253); **Iraq-Kuwait** (SCR 661); **Federal Republic of Yugoslavia** (SCR 757); **Bosnian Serbs** (SCR 942); **Haiti** (SCR 917).
- *Restrictions on selective imports of commodities and products.* **Southern Rhodesia**: asbestos, iron ore, chrome, pig-iron, sugar, tobacco, copper, meat products, hides, skins and leather (SCR 232); **UNITA, Sierra Leone and Liberia**: diamonds (SCR 1295, 1306 and 1385, 1343, respectively); **Taliban controlled areas**: chemical acetic anhydride (SCR 1333); Liberia: all round logs and timber products (SCR 1478).
- *Activities related to prohibited commodities or products:* prohibition of their promotion or dealings in their exports, including transfer of funds for such purposes; of their shipment in vessels or aircraft or carriage by land transport facilities, or their transshipment.

2 Prohibited exports to the sanctioned State
- *Comprehensive embargo.* **Southern Rhodesia, Iraq, Federal Republic of Yugoslavia, Bosnian Serbs, Haiti**: prohibition on sale or supply of any commodities or products whether or not originating in member States territories (SCR 253, 661, 757, 917, 942, respectively).
- *Selective embargo*
  - *Petroleum.* **Haiti, UNITA, Sierra Leone** (SCR 841, 864, 1132, respectively);
  - *Equipment for oil refining and transportation.* **Libya** (SCR 883);
  - *Arms and related matériel, including military assistance.* **South Africa** (SCR 418), **Former Yugoslavia** (SCR 713), **Somalia** (SCR 733), **Libya** (SCR 748), **Liberia** (SCR 788), **Haiti** (SCR 841), **Rwanda**, including States neighboring Rwanda if purpose is within Rwanda and Rwandan camps within neighboring State territories (SCR 918), **UNITA** (SCR 864), **Sierra Leone** (SCR 1132), **Federal Republic of Yugoslavia – Kosovo** (SCR 1160), **Afghanistan under Taliban control** (SCR 1333), **Democratic Republic of the Congo** (foreign and Congolese armed groups and militias operating in the territory of North and South Kivu and of Ituri) (SCR 1493);
  - *Aircraft and/or motor vehicles.* **Southern Rhodesia** (SCR 232), **Libya** (SCR 748), **Federal Republic of Yugoslavia** (SCR 757), **UNITA** (SCR 1129).

– *Activities related to prohibited commodities or products.* Prohibition of their promotion or dealings; prohibition of their shipment in vessels or aircraft or carriage by land transport facilities.

3 Restrictions on movements of funds
– *Freezing of funds, financial assets and economic resources.* **Federal Republic of Yugoslavia** (SCR 820), **Haiti** (SCR 841), **Libya** (SCR 883), **Bosnian Serbs** (SCR 942), **UNITA** (SCR 1173), **Taliban** (SCR 1267), **Usama bin Laden** and individual and associated entities (SCR 1333, 1390), **persons or entities involved in the commission or facilitation of terrorist acts** (SCR 1373).
– *Prohibition of funds for investment for government or commercial or other undertakings.*
– *Remission of funds to private persons in targeted State.* **Southern Rhodesia** (SCR 232), **Federal Republic of Yugoslavia** (SCR 757).
– *Collection of funds for the purpose of contravening Security Council resolutions.* **Federal Republic of Yugoslavia -Kosovo** (SCR 1160), **counter-terrorism** (SCR 1373).

4 Severance of means of communications
– *Severance of means of communication on land, sea or river*
– *Denial of permission to aircraft destined to or from the target State.* **Iraq** (SCR 665), **Libya** (SCR 748), **Federal Republic of Yugoslavia** (SCR 757), **UNITA** (SCR 1127).
– *Denial of permission to aircraft registered, owned or controlled by targeted State.* **Sudan** (SCR 1070), **Afghanistan** (SCR 1267).
– *Seizure of modes of transport registered, owned or controlled by persons in targeted State and vessels in violation of sanctions.* **Federal Republic of Yugoslavia** (SCR 820).
– *Measures in the area of telecommunications.* **UNITA** (SCR 1221).

5 Prohibited services
– *Insurance coverage of air flights and individuals, or air cargo.* **Southern Rhodesia** (SCR 333), **UNITA** (SCR 1127).
– *Insurance of commodities or products destined for the targeted entity.*
– *Granting of trade names and franchise.* **Southern Rhodesia** (SCR 388).
– *Engineering and servicing of aircraft.*

6 Penal measures
– *International Criminal Tribunals.* **Former Yugoslavia and Rwanda** (SCR 808 and 827, 955, respectively).
– *Penal sanctions under domestic law for persons who evade sanctions.* **Southern Rhodesia** (SCR 333); **Federal Republic of Yugoslavia** (SCR 820); **Haiti** (SCR 841); **UNITA** (SCR 864 and 1295); **Taliban** (SCR 1267 and 1333).
– *Criminalisation of financing, planning, preparation or perpetration of terrorist acts.* Counter-terrorism (SCR 1373).

d. Targeted entities

- *The Government of the sanctioned State,* de facto *authorities, or "all parties" to a particular conflict.*
- *Commercial, industrial or public utility undertakings in the territory of the sanctioned State.*
- *Any person or body for the purpose of any business carried on or operated from the territory.*
- *Entities abroad owned or controlled by persons in the territory.*
- *Select list of persons and entities targeted by financial sanctions.* **Haiti**: members of the military junta in Haiti, the Haitian military, and immediate family members (SCR 917); **UNITA:** officials (SCR 1127); **Sierra Leone**: members of the former military junta and the RUF (SCR 1171); **Liberia**: senior members of the Government and its armed forces, including immediate family and other designated individuals (SCR 1343); **Afghanistan**: individuals and entities targeted by the freezing of funds and financial assets (SCR 1333), **Usama Bin Laden and associates** (SCR 1390); **Iraq**: individuals and entities associated with the previous Government of Iraq who own funds or other financial assets located outside Iraq with the purpose of transferring such funds to the Iraq Development Fund (SCR 1483).

e. Humanitarian and other exceptions

- *Supplies intended strictly for medical purposes.*
- *Foodstuffs in special humanitarian circumstances.*
- *Educational and information materials.* **Southern Rhodesia** (SCR 253), **Iraq** (as of SCR 1284).
- *Payments exclusively for pensions.* **Southern Rhodesia** (SCR 253).
- *Payments intended towards excepted products.*
- *Materials and supplies for essential civilian needs.* **Iraq,** including in relation to the Oil-for-Food programme (SCR 687 and 986).
- *Petroleum or petroleum products.* **Haiti**: propane gas for cooking, for verified essential humanitarian needs (SCR 841); **Sierra Leone**: on a case-by-case basis for Government, ECOMOG or UN agencies for verified humanitarian purposes (SCR 1132).
- *Flights for medical emergencies.* **Libya:** Special arrangements for emergency medical evacuations by air from Libya (adopted by the Council on 14 October 1992 and Sanctions Committee on 17 July 1995); **UNITA**, **Taliban**: aircraft carrying food, medicine, supplies for essential humanitarian needs (SCR 1127, 1267, respectively).
- *Air flights for Hajj pilgrimage or other religious obligation.* **Iraq,** including expenses to be met by funds in the Iraqi escrow account (SCR 1210, 1284); Taliban (SCR 1267); Libya (Sanctions Committee (S/1996/2 and S/1999/1299)); Liberia (SCR 1343).
- *Nationals of implementing States in cases where such persons may be targeted by restrictions on entry or transit through their territories.* **Sierra Leone** (SCR 1171); **Bosnian Serbs** (SCR 942); **Liberia** (SCR 1343); **Al-Qaida and associates** (SCR 1390).
- *Telecommunications, postal services, legal services or services for humanitarian purposes.* **Former Yugoslavia,** express exception (SCR 820).

- *Explosives intended exclusively for demining programmes.* **Rwanda** (SCR 1005).
- *Non-lethal military equipment, protective clothing, including flak jackets and military helmets, arms.* **Kosovo, Eritrea/Ethiopia, Afghanistan, Liberia, Democratic Republic of the Congo** (SCR 1203, 1298, 1333, 1343, respectively): for use by United Nations personnel, representatives of the media, humanitarian and development workers.
- *Navigation on the Danube for riparian states.* **Federal Republic of Yugoslavia** (SCR 992).
- *Participation of government officials in peace negotiations or for purposes of judicial proceedings.* **Liberia** (SCR 1343 and 1478); **UNITA** (S/PRST/2002/7); **Taliban and Al-Qaida** (SCR 1390).

(3) Termination of Sanctions

- **Southern Rhodesia** (SCR 460, 21 December 1979).
- **South Africa** (SCR 919, 25 May 1994).
- **Haiti**: suspension of sanctions (SCR 861, 27 August 1993); termination of sanctions re-imposed by SCR 873 in October 1993 (SCR 944, 29 September 1994).
- **Rwanda**: suspension, then removal of arms embargo (SCR 1011, effective 1 September 1996); arms embargo for non-governmental forces remains prohibited.
- **Sierra Leone**: Removal of ban on petroleum (SCR 1156, 16 March 1998); termination of remaining ban on oil and arms (SCR 1171, 5 June 1998), but only in respect of the Government of Sierra Leone through named points of entry.
- **Liberia**: termination of comprehensive arms embargo (SCR 1343, 7 March 2001); targeted arms embargo and other sanctions imposed by SCR 1343 still in force.
- **Eritrea/Ethiopia**: termination of arms embargo by a Security Council presidential statement (S/PRST/2001, 15 May 2001).
- **Federal Republic of Yugoslavia**: suspension of certain sanctions for an initial period of 100 days (SCR 943, 23 September 1994); termination of arms embargo (SCR 1021, 18 June 1996); indefinite suspension of sanctions (SCR 1022, 22 November 1995); termination of sanctions, including against Bosnian Serbs (SCR 1074, 1 October 1996); termination of embargo on arms re-imposed by SCR 1160 concerning Kosovo (SCR 1367, 10 September, 2001).
- **Sudan** (SCR 1372, 28 September 2001).
- **Afghanistan:** termination of sanctions against Ariana Afghan Airlines (SCR 1388, 15 January 2002); travel and financial sanctions against the Taliban and their supporters remaining.
- **UNITA:** suspension of travel bans for a period of 90 days (SCR 1412, 17 May 2002); termination of sanctions (SCR 1448, 9 December 2002).
- **Iraq** : termination of all non military sanctions (SCR 1483, 22 May 2003).
- **Libyan Arab Jamahiriya**: suspension as of 5 April by Presidential statement adopted on 8 April 1999 noting that the conditions set out by SCR 1192 (1998) had been fulfilled (S/PRST/1999/10); termination (SCR 1506, 12 September 2003).

IMPLEMENTING SANCTIONS RESOLUTIONS IN DOMESTIC LAW

*Vera Gowlland-Debbas**

This comparative study of the international legal implications of domestic mechanisms for implementation of Security Council decisions[1] addresses three interrelated themes. The first, of a theoretical nature, relates to the traditional relationship between international and domestic law. The question raised is whether the implementation of decisions of international organisations, and in particular the derived obligations resulting from Security Council resolutions, poses problems which are in some way distinct from those raised by the implementation of other conventional international law obligations, thereby introducing a new conundrum. To what extent also may it be said that Security Council resolutions introduce a new dimension to implementation of international decisions in so far as they are perceived to be in fulfilment of community objectives?

The second theme concerns the effectiveness of the decisions of the Security Council. If they aim to change the behaviour of the targeted entity or achieve a return to international legality, sanctions must demonstrate a certain degree of effectiveness. This study is not concerned with the questions of either the effects of sanctions on the conduct of the targeted States or entities, or the effective implementation of these decisions by the United Nations itself.[2] Effectiveness in this context is viewed from the perspective of the compliance of implementing States which depends on the effective *mise en œuvre* of these decisions in national law. In this narrow sense, effectiveness concerns the availability and nature of domestic mechanisms, and the ability of implementing States to carry out the mandatory decisions of the Security Council in a speedy and comprehensive manner and in conformity with their obligations under the United Nations Charter. While some of

* Professor of Public International Law, Graduate Institute of International Studies, Geneva.

1 The general analytical framework used in this chapter has in part been drawn from: Vera Gowlland-Debbas, *Collective Responses to Illegal Acts in International Law. United Nations Action in the Question of Southern Rhodesia* (Dordrecht/Boston/London, Martinus Nijhoff Publishers, 1990), pp. 557-632, but the analysis is based on the national studies included in this book.

2 Some of these other aspects of effectiveness of sanctions are addressed in the first volume. See Vera Gowlland-Debbas (ed), *United Nations Sanctions and International Law* (The Hague/London/Boston, Kluwer Law International, 2001).

Vera Gowlland-Debbas (ed.), National Implementation of UN Sanctions, *33-78.*

the measures required are to be taken at the official level, such as the severance of diplomatic relations and policies of non-recognition, and in theory do not pose problems of implementation in domestic law, the majority require being made operative against individuals within States, and this, in turn, is dependent on the effective implementation, application and enforcement of the decisions of the Security Council within the domestic order by national legislative, executive, administrative and judicial bodies in accordance with each State's constitutional and legal requirements. Hence the importance of collaboration between what has been perceived as two autonomous legal orders.

A final theme which is addressed in this study concerns the legitimacy of Security Council resolutions as seen from the viewpoint of domestic legal systems, that is the extent to which Security Council decisions encroach on constitutionally or internationally protected individual rights and the potential role played by domestic courts in reviewing the decisions of the Security Council.[3]

I. Implementation of International Obligations into Domestic Law: A Theoretical Framework

It is obvious that international legal rules cannot be applied in the abstract and that international law has to work primarily through domestic mechanisms. Hence the importance of the theoretical relationship between international and municipal law. This relationship raises two sets of problems: that of the problem of application of international law within the domestic system, and that of the resolution of conflicts which may arise between rules of international law and rules of municipal law.

Where conflicts between municipal law and international law have been dealt with on the *international* plane, such conflicts have been resolved both in State practice and by international tribunals on the basis of the primacy of international law. States, in their relations with each other, have never accepted that one of them plead the provisions of its own municipal law or deficiencies in that law, in order to justify a breach of its obligations under international law.

The principle that under international law a State cannot invoke its domestic law as exempting it from the execution of its international obligations is well consecrated in conventional international law. The 1969 Vienna Convention on the Law of Treaties establishes the primacy of treaties over municipal law, without discriminating between constitutional or ordinary law. Article 27 provides that: "A party may not invoke the provisions of its internal law as justification for its failure to perform a treaty." There is also ample judicial and arbitral authority for this rule, beginning with the 1872 *Alabama Claims* Arbitration.[4] As the Permanent Court of International Justice put it in its Advisory Opinion in the *Greco-Bulgarian Communities Case:* "It is a generally accepted principle of international law that in the relations between Powers who are contracting Parties to a treaty, the provisions of municipal law cannot prevail over those of the treaty."[5] And

3 Issues relating to legitimacy/legality in terms of the constitutionality of the decisions of the Security Council under the Charter and general international law are also dealt with in *ibid.*

4 MOORE, 1 *International Arbitrations* 656.

5 (1930), PCIJ, Ser. B., 1930, No. 17, p. 32.

again, in the question of the *Treatment of Polish Nationals in Danzig*, the Court stated: "...a State cannot adduce as against another State its own Constitution with a view to evading obligations incumbent upon it under international law or treaties in force."[6] The Court reiterated this principle in its Advisory Opinion of April 26, 1988, relating to the impending closure by the United States of the PLO Mission to the United Nations in New York.[7] The Court has also pronounced on the conformity of internal law with international law, though it has not been concerned with its validity under domestic law.

Unlike the situation prevailing under Article 103, which upholds the primacy of Charter obligations over international agreements, the Charter is silent with respect to the internal law of Member States. The fear that States would plead provisions of their domestic legislation in order to escape their obligations under the Charter had in fact been expressed at the San Francisco Conference, and Belgium had proposed, though unsuccessfully, an amendment to prevent such claims being made.[8] Nevertheless, it is clear that under international law a State could not invoke its domestic law as exempting it from the obligation to execute a decision of the Security Council. Non-implementation of the mandatory decisions of the Security Council under Article 25 of the Charter would therefore be viewed as a violation of Charter obligations giving rise to State responsibility under international law. It is interesting to note that the question of conflict between mandatory Security Council decisions and Member States' domestic laws was raised in Security Council Resolution 320 (1972) in regard to the authorisation by the United States Congress of importation of chrome ore from Rhodesia in contravention of its obligations under Article 25 of the Charter. In this resolution, the Security Council expressed its deep concern at such a decision and urged the United States "to co-operate fully with the United Nations in the effective implementation of sanctions."

From a domestic law perspective, however, one obtains a very different picture. As opposed to the obligation to fulfil in good faith obligations flowing from treaties and the consequent incurring of State responsibility for failure to do so, which is clearly a matter for international law, the mechanisms by which States incorporate international law into their domestic system are largely left by international law to be regulated by municipal law. The domestic system, however, is structurally complex and there is a multiplicity of organs charged with the application of international legal rules. Moreover, conflicts between domestic and international law will be dealt with in accordance with the law of the forum; domestic courts bound by their own rules may not always uphold the primacy of international law and the consequences will depend on the place attributed to international law in the national system.

In theory, the relationship between international law and municipal law has traditionally been approached from the perspective of the relationship between two legal *orders*, that is from the aspect of their formal validity as legal systems. It is from this

6 (1932), PCIJ, Ser. A/B, No. 44, p. 24. See also *Exchange of Greek and Turkish Populations*, (1925), PCIJ, Ser. B, No. 10, p. 20 and *Free Zones of Upper Savoy and the District of Gex*, (1930), PCIJ, Ser. A, No. 24, p. 12.

7 *Applicability of the Obligation to Arbitrate under Section 21 of the United Nations Headquarters Agreement of 26 June 1947*, Advisory Opinion, ICJ Reports 1988, pp. 34-35.

8 *UNCIO Docs.*, Vol. 13, p. 759.

perspective that the monist/dualist controversy has taken place. The Kelsenian view, derived from the Kantian unitary conception of law, which propounds a monist thesis with preponderance of international law, has an obvious appeal to internationalists but tends to come up against the perceived reality of a plurality of autonomous domestic systems. The dualist position associated with such writers as Triepel and Anzilotti, has come up against the problem that there is by now no logical demarcation of subject matters between the two legal orders, nor is it tenable any longer to state that international law does not regulate relations between individuals, since international law does confer in exceptional cases both rights and duties directly on them. (This is not the same thing as endorsing Kelsen's view that "the behaviour of states is reducible to the behaviour of individuals representing the State. Thus the alleged difference in subject matter between international and national law cannot be a difference between the kinds of subjects whose behaviour they regulate."[9]) Without dismissing the monist/dualist controversy as "unreal, artificial and strictly beside the point", as does Sir Gerald Fitzmaurice,[10] we can shift the debate.

For the fact that the two legal orders continue to draw their validity from separate spheres – in other words that international law and domestic law form two distinct and autonomous legal orders in their modes of creation each with their own logic – does not, as Michel Virally points out, dispose of the question.[11] Both he and Krystyna Marek[12] have shown that the relationship between the two legal systems is dependent not only on the systemic relations between the two orders but in part also, on the degree of development of international law. Nor, as a recent interesting study on this evolution has shown,[13] does it signal the abandonment of internationalist aspirations for the supremacy of international law, for the omnipresence of international law in domestic systems and the permeability of these to international law has taken place in a manner compatible with dualism and regardless of an evolution towards monism.

The relationship between international and domestic law, it has been argued, should be reexamined from a substantive, rather than from a formal (or systems) perspective; this need has arisen from the new functions which international law has assumed in the international system in consequence of the complex interdependence of States as well

9 Hans Kelsen, *The Principles of International Law* (Rinehart, 1952), p. 73.

10 Sir Gerald Fitzmaurice, "The General Principles of International Law considered from the Standpoint of the Rule of Law", 92 *RCADI* (1957-II), at p. 71.

11 Michel Virally, "Sur un pont aux ânes: les rapports entre droit international et droits internes", in Michel Virally, *Le droit international en devenir* (Paris, Presses Universitaires de France/ Graduate Institute of Intenational Studies, 1990), pp. 103-117, at pp. 109-110.

12 Krystyna Marek, "Les rapports entre le droit international et le droit interne à la lumière de la jurisprudence de la Cour permanente de justice internationale", 66 *RGDIP* (1962) 260-298, at pp. 260-61.

13 See Rafâa Ben Achour et Slim Laghmani (dirs.), *Droit international et droits internes, développements récents* (Paris, Pedone, 1998) in particular, Slim Laghmani, "Droit international et droits internes: vers un renouveau du *jus gentium*?", pp. 23-44, at pp. 27-29, 40-41; Sadok Belaïd, "Droit international et droit constitutionnel: les développements récents", pp. 47-79, at pp.51-76; and Patrick Daillier, "Monisme et dualisme: un débat dépassé?", pp. 9-21, at pp. 9-11..

as recent moves towards globalisation: the evolution in international law from bilateral to community interests, the shaping of an international public policy in the form of the development of certain universal principles, such as human rights and fundamental freedoms, means that the implementation of international law in domestic law is inevitable – States can no longer opt out. As a result, contemporary international law has assumed the purpose not only of regulating interstate relations, but increasingly of harmonising domestic law. A parallel has thus been drawn with the *jus gentium* in the sense of the creation of a common legal language. This is reflected in recent constitutional trends: the adaptation of constitutions, which now increasingly accord primacy to international law within the domestic legal order, as well as the sharing by domestic legal systems of a common minimum set of international law rules and standards. (The Community legal order has of course provided a different model of the articulation between the two orders.)

This omnipresence of international law, combined with a democratic deficit in international procedures, has at the same time created a backlash to this expansion of international law. This can be seen in the efforts of legislatures to control the treaty-making process and that of domestic courts to shield the executive from the effects of importation of international law into domestic legal systems; this has been effectuated through interpretation, by determining treaties to be non-self-executing and by application of such doctrines as act of state or justiciability.[14]

The implementation of Security Council decisions by United Nations Member States illustrates this evolution in the manner in which international law is being imported into domestic legal systems, as the following overview shows.

II. Domestic Implementation of Non-Military Sanctions in the Practice of Member States

(1) Legal Basis of Domestic Measures

Resolutions of the Security Council leave to States the choice of means of implementation. A considerable gap may thus ensue between the adoption of a binding resolution by the Security Council and its execution by States. Firstly, notwithstanding that the effectiveness of economic sanctions is largely dependent on speed of implementation, there may be a notable time lag in making the decision effective in domestic law. The cause for this delay may be found in the initial enactment of legislation and/or in the entry into force of the measures. Secondly, the process of converting the international decision into domestically applicable law may result in a modification of the content of Security Council decisions, for example, by making them less comprehensive, by narrowing their

14 See Eyal Benvenisti, "Judicial Misgivings Regarding the Application of International Law: An Analysis of Attitudes of National Courts", 4 *EJIL* (1993) 159-183. See also Walter Kälin, "Implementing Treaties in Domestic Law: from 'Pacta Sunt Servanda' to 'Anything Goes'", in Vera Gowlland-Debbas (ed.), *Multilateral Treaty-Making* (The Hague/Boston/London, Martinus Nijhoff Publishers, 2000), pp. 111-128.

temporal, territorial and personal scope, and by introducing new exceptions into their content and application.

The following analysis attempts to give an overall picture of the legal issues arising from domestic implementation of Security Council sanctions. References to particular States' practice generally refer back to the related chapters included in this book and to the citations included therein, unless otherwise indicated.

a. Constitutional basis

Some reference to international organisations may be found in the more recent constitutions. In Europe, such mention has been introduced mainly following on the establishment of the European Community, for the purpose of transferring competencies or imposing limitations on legislative, executive and judicial functions. This applies also to the recent constitutions of Eastern Europe in order to allow for the accession of these countries to the European Union (see, for example, the new 1997 Polish Constitution or the 2001 "Euro-amendment" to the Constitution of the Czech Republic). The European Union, of course, establishes a clearly different supra-national legal order with directly applicable provisions which individuals may invoke before a municipal court. In the Constitution of Argentina, likewise, reference in the Constitution to the "secondary law" enacted by supra-national organisations concerns only integration treaties. Such constitutional mention, therefore, does not confer on decisions of other international organisations a force superior to that of ordinary law nor do they form a special category.[15]

Nevertheless, references, such as those in the preamble to the French Constitution, to such limitations upon State sovereignty as may be necessary for the organisation and preservation of peace, or, as in Belgium, to the transfer of the exercise of specific powers to international organisations by treaty, have been or may be interpreted as applicable also to the enforcement of Security Council resolutions, including cooperation with the International Criminal Tribunals.

Mandatory decisions of international organisations are assimilated to treaty obligations. There is little controversy today over the fact that such obligations also cover the mandatory decisions of the Security Council, seen as secondary obligations under the Charter.

It is not easy in practice to divide States into neat monist/dualist categories and Governments are themselves not always clear about what the position is within their domestic system.[16] This is often difficult to determine from a simple analysis of State constitutional provisions for constitutional practice may change over the years (see for example the controversy relating to Sweden which appears to have changed over the years from a monist to a confirmed dualist country, while the Czech Republic has

15 Lambertus Erades (ed. by M. Fitzmaurice and C. Flinterman), *Interactions between International and Municipal Law – a comparative case law study* (The Hague, TMC Asser Instituut, 1993), p. 846.

16 See Jean Dhommeaux, "Monismes et dualismes en droit international des droits de l'homme", *AFDI* (1995) 447-469, at pp. 446-47.

recently shifted from a predominantly dualist to a predominantly monist system). The United Kingdom offers one of the clearest example of a dualist State in which treaties must be transformed into UK law to be applicable within the domestic system; the United Nations Charter itself, and in consequence resolutions of the Security Council, are themselves not part of United Kingdom law and are not enforceable as such in United Kingdom courts.

However, with the possible exception of Namibia, even in the countries included here which are considered monist, such as Argentina, Belgium, France, Japan, The Netherlands, Poland, Switzerland, or the United States, where international law is declared "the law of the land", hence where no transformation of duly ratified treaties is required and promulgation is usually the condition for internal effect, the result may not be the direct applicability of Security Council resolutions. In such countries, a distinction is usually made between self-executing treaties which are sufficiently precise and complete and intended to become immediately operative against individuals on the domestic level and those which are non-self-executing and therefore require the enactment of implementing legislation to be enforceable by municipal courts.[17]

---

17 In the words of United States Chief Justice Marshall: A treaty is "to be regarded in courts of justice as equivalent to an act of the Legislature, whenever it operates of itself, without the aid of any legislative provision. But when the terms of the stipulation import a contract, when either of the parties engages to perform a particular act, the treaty addresses itself to the political, not the judicial department; and the Legislature must execute the contract, before it can become a rule for the Court" (*Foster v. Neilson*, (1829) 27 U.S. (2 Pet.) 253 at 314). See also Decision of the California Court of Appeal in *Sei Fujii v. State of California* (19 *ILR* (1952) 312): "In order for a treaty provision to be operative without the aid of implementing legislation and to have the force and effect of a statute, it must appear that the framers of the treaty intended to prescribe a rule that, standing alone, would be enforceable in the courts".
There is no universal definition of the term "self-executing" which comes from American administrative and judicial practice. The notions of "direct applicability" and "direct effect" have also been used, though they are not always synonymous. A "self-executing treaty" is a term used in domestic law to signify that a treaty gives rise to legal rights or obligations for individuals directly enforceable in the domestic courts without further implementing legislation. It is to be distinguished from the technique of incorporation of a treaty into the internal order. The treaty may well be the "law of the land" for other purposes (e.g. mandating the government to carry out certain action) and still be considered non-self-executing in this sense. There are no clear rules for courts in assessing the effect of specific treaties, but this is a matter of treaty interpretation for the courts who will look to the nature of the treaty and to the complete and precise nature of the rule. Therefore a treaty may well be considered self-executing for the courts of one State, but not for another. On the other hand, the concept of "direct applicability" has been seen as a question of international law, depending on whether the treaty *under international law* was intended by the parties to be directly applicable as such in their domestic legal orders. The concept of direct applicability has of course been developed particularly in the framework of supranational European Community law. (See Thomas Burgenthal, "Self-Executing and Non-Self-Executing Treaties in National and International Law", 235 *RCADI* (1992) 307-397, at pp. 317-340; Joe Verhoeven, "La notion d''applicabilité directe' du droit international", XV *RBDI* (1980) 244-264; Marco G. Marcoff, "Les règles d'application indirecte en droit international", 80 *RGDIP* (1976) 385-424. See also PCIJ,

Despite their important status on the international plane, sanctions decisions of the Security Council adopted under Article 41 have in general been assimilated to *non-self-executing* treaty obligations. In *Diggs v. Dent*, the United States District Court for the District of Columbia considered that Security Council Resolution 276 (1970) and 301 (1971) relating to Namibia were not self-executing though accepted by the Court as mandatory decisions of the Council under Article 25 of the Charter: "treaties do not generally confer upon citizens rights which they may enforce in the courts. It is only when a treaty is 'self-executing' that individuals derive enforceable rights from the treaty, without further legislative or executive action. The provisions of the Charter of the United Nations are not self-executing and do not vest any of the plaintiffs with any individual legal rights which they may assert in this court." The Court contrasted this with the earlier case of *Diggs v. Shultz*, relating to Rhodesian sanctions which "had been made effective in this country by Executive Orders which imposed penalties upon persons who violated their directives."[18]

More recently, in a judgement of 21 April 1995, the German Federal Court of Justice stated that economic measures adopted by the Security Council under Chapter VII of the United Nations Charter do not have direct effect for the individuals in Member States, but are binding only on the States themselves.

This position however has not been uncontested and courts have on occasion taken into account the fact that provisions of a Security Council resolution may affect the legal situation of individuals in their direct consequences on contractual obligations, even in the absence of domestic implementing legislation. Thus in Belgium, courts have on occasion indicated that some decisions of the Security Council have self-executing character, while French courts have upheld the lawfulness of individual conduct in refusing to respect certain contracts on the grounds of the existence of a Security Council resolution, though they have done this on the basis of "*force majeure*" rather than on the self-executing character of the Council resolutions.[19] It has also been suggested that courts in Argentina could well apply Security Council resolutions as self-executing provisions by analogy with their decisions in human rights cases. Interestingly, Security Council

Jurisdiction of the Courts of Danzig (1928), Ser. B, No.15, at 17-18, in which the Court considered that the "*Beamtenabkommen*", the agreement between Poland and Danzig regulating the status of certain railroad officials, was directly applicable by the national courts).

18 United States, Decision of the District Court for the District of Columbia in *Diggs v. Dent*, May 1975 (14 *ILM* (1975) 797-805 at 803-804); United States, Decision of the Court of Appeals for the District of Columbia in *Diggs v. Shultz*, October 31, 1972 (11 *ILM* (1972) 1252-58). There have been other decisions in which US courts have considered the Charter as a whole, or its provisions on human rights, or non-self-governing territories, to be non-self-executing, whereas provisions of the Charter relating to privileges and immunities or Trusteeship Agreements, have been considered self-executing (see in particular Thomas A. Schweitzer, "The United Nations as a Source of Domestic Law: Can Security Council Resolutions be Enforced in American Courts", 4 *Yale Studies in World Public Order* (1977) 162-273, at 224-230).

19 See also Gilbert Guillaume, "L'introduction et l'exécution dans les ordres juridiques des Etats des résolutions du Conseil de sécurité des Nations Unies prises en vertu du Chapitre VII de la Charte", 50 *Revue internationale de droit comparé* (1998) 539-549, at 546.

Resolution 692 (1991) establishing the United Nations Compensation Commission appears to have been given direct effect within the Polish legal order. Finally, it is suggested that in Namibia, a monist State, Security Council decisions may well be enforced by Namibian courts without the necessity of implementing laws. However, while it has been suggested that the Orders handed down by the two International Criminal Tribunals have direct effect in Member States,[20] the general practice of Member States in considering necessary the adoption of further implementing measures, has not upheld this view.

b. Prior enabling legislation

Since the self-executing character of Security Council resolutions has not been generally established, these have required the adoption of domestic implementing measures via the mechanisms generally provided for in constitutions (although these may not always be explicitly spelled out).

The existence of a general law adopted as framework legislation expressly enabling the executive branch to implement by decree the decisions of the United Nations Security Council under Article 25 of the United Nations Charter, would appear, at first glance, to be essential in order to ensure the automatic and speedy compliance so essential to the effectiveness of sanctions, whatever the position – monist or dualist – of the State concerned. The Southern Rhodesian experience showed that where a United Nations Participation Act was in existence, the time lag between adoption of the resolution by the Security Council and domestic implementation was two to three months, whereas passage of new legislation was a time-consuming process – sometimes taking as much as two to three years.

Moreover, the fact that economic and financial measures endorsed by the Security Council inevitably affect the status of individuals by encroaching on constitutionally-protected property rights and contractual obligations, means that proper enabling laws should be provided in order to ensure transparency and avoid challenges in domestic courts.

Nevertheless, few States have followed the route of adopting enabling legislation. Though Resolution 19 of the 1921 series of resolutions adopted by the League Assembly in relation to Article 16 of the Covenant[21] had reminded members of the need to adopt prior general legislation in order to avoid delay, only two States – France and Czechoslovakia – had followed up on this proposal, and finally neither of their legislation was relied upon when it came to adopting sanctions against Italy in 1935-36 following on its aggression against Abyssinia. Again, on October 16, 1935, the Committee set up by the League to coordinate sanctions against Italy, while recognising that this was a matter falling within the exclusive competence of each State, reminded members of their duty

20 Shuichi Furuya, "Legal Effect of Rules of the International Criminal Tribunals and Court upon Individuals", XLVII *Netherlands International Law Review* (2000/2) 111-145.

21 Resolutions concerning the Economic Weapon adopted by the Assembly on October 4, 1921.

to adopt necessary measures. As a result, ten States enacted permanent general legislation for the application of Article 16 of the League Covenant, while seven States passed specific legislation for the application of sanctions against Italy.[22]

There was little improvement on this situation following the establishment of the United Nations. Only a handful of States adopted permanent enabling legislation expressly authorising the executive branch to implement future mandatory decisions of the Security Council under Article 41 of the Charter by decree; these included the United States (United Nations Participation Act 1945) and the United Kingdom (United Nations Act 1946). The majority of States did not consider such legislation to constitute automatic accompaniment to membership in the United Nations, not even those who acceded much later, such as Finland and Jordan, both of which joined in 1955.

The case of Southern Rhodesia, the very first instance of mandatory economic sanctions taken under Chapter VII, was a milestone in domestic implementation. In the absence of comprehensive sanctions legislation, States initially relied on *ad hoc* implementation. However, the adoption of first selective and then comprehensive mandatory sanctions was particularly formative in the development of new enabling acts in the period 1965-1971. Finland adopted in 1967 the Act on the Implementation of Certain Obligations of Finland as a Member of the United Nations, followed by Sweden in May 1971. Denmark, Norway and Canada followed suit, while the Netherlands adopted a Sanctions Act in 1977 which went beyond Security Council sanctions. The Swedish, Finnish and Dutch acts were particularly extensive in covering also *recommendations* of the Security Council. Since Security Council resolutions were considered to affect private rights, the procedure for constitutional amendment had to be followed in some cases, as for example in Finland.

In the 1990s a number of developments placed novel demands on domestic implementing mechanisms which led to the amendment of existing enabling acts or the adoption of new ones. First, the reactivation of the Security Council led to an exponential increase in Chapter VII sanctions. Second, the expanded or new participation of European States in the regional integration process and the enlargement of European Union competence following on the Maastricht Treaty required increasing coordination of national implementing measures with actions taken within the framework of the European Union. Third, such enabling laws were necessary in order to respond to innovatory measures adopted by the Security Council, such as the International Criminal Tribunals (the case of France, Belgium, Sweden), or to cover areas not falling under European Union competence, such as penal sanctions and control of the arms trade. Finally, in some regions, political or constitutional developments necessitated a new approach to sanctions implementation: in Eastern Europe, the shift from a State monopoly on foreign trade to a market economy, as well as the adoption of democratic constitutions, and in Namibia and South Africa, independence and the ending of apartheid, respectively, with resultant adoption of new constitutions.

Such changes included Sweden's amendment in 1999 of its recently adopted 1996 Law on Certain International Sanctions, Finland's amendment of its 1967 enabling Act

22 A.E. Highley, *The First Sanctions Experiment. A Study of League Procedures* (Geneva, 1938), pp. 33-34.

following on its accession to the European Union in 1995 so as to reflect its European Union obligations, the introduction of comprehensive legislation in France in 1993 on the basis of Community law, the introduction in Belgium in 1995 of a new Federal Law on the Implementation of United Nations Security Council Decisions and the adoption by the Czech Republic, in 2000, of a General Law on implementation of international sanctions for the maintenance of international peace and security, to cover also its accession to the European Union.

However, the Legislative Council in Poland, in evaluating draft framework legislation allowing for detailed implementation of Security Council resolutions, concluded that *ad hoc* measures, including specific fast track legislation, were in fact adequate for sanctions implementation. Similarly, in South Africa, framework legislation for the Application of Resolutions of the Security Council of the United Nations never entered into force.

In the absence of enabling laws, the majority of States have been able to respond to Security Council decisions, and continue to do so, through reliance on pre-existing legislation not related to United Nations Security Council resolutions, or on the basis of *ad hoc* legislation adopted ex post facto after the adoption of a mandatory decision of the Security Council.

c. Pre-existing legislation not designed for sanctions legislation

The legal basis of State responses has been diverse. States have relied on existing laws or statutes not directly related to decisions of international organisations for the implementation of Security Council sanctions of a traditional type, such as trade sanctions, arms embargoes, restrictions on transfer of capital (the freezing of funds has been more problematic, being seen as seizure of private property), ban on air traffic and restriction of movement of persons. The legislation relied on has included trade and emergency laws, laws regulating exportation of war materials, including control of problematic dual-use goods, licensing systems requiring authorisations to trade on a case-by-case basis, customs or exchange control and banking regulations, aviation laws and immigration control.

Sweden, Germany, France and Japan, amongst others, executed measures on the basis of the Government's powers to regulate international trade relations in particular circumstances. In Argentina, Security Council resolutions have been incorporated through individual presidential decrees based on the competence of the President to conduct foreign relations, while Jordan has relied on a very simplified procedure, in which Council resolutions have been imported verbatim by means of a decision of the Council of Ministers. In South Africa, a pending Conventional Arms Control Bill of 2000 will subject arms to a licensing system, the objective being to ensure, *inter alia*, that conventional arms sales are not used in contravention of that country's international obligations, including the purposes and principles of the United Nations. South Africa has also relied on money-laundering legislation, which is important in the context of targeted sanctions, while in Namibia, the contravention of sanctions on arms and diamonds was covered by criminal law dealing with smuggling of prohibited goods.

In Poland, recent laws have contained provisions directly relating to Security Council sanctions which allow the Council of Ministers to introduce limitations on international commerce, including arms and financial relations, if it is necessary in order to meet the obligations of Poland deriving from the United Nations Charter in the field of international peace and security, in accordance with the WTO.

Even where enabling acts exist and even where, as in the UK, they provide a broad scope for the adoption of measures by the Executive, this does not entirely obviate the need to resort to other legislation. For example, the UK has resorted to other Acts of Parliament relating to defence and emergency powers, including the recent Immigration and Asylum Act 1999 which catered expressly to Security Council travel bans, while Finland has gone outside its enabling act in respect of dual use items, cultural or sports contacts.

The position of the United States in respect of sanctions is difficult to assess because of the blurring in that country of any distinction between unilateral and United Nations collective measures. Under the United Nations Enabling Act, Security Council resolutions require being made effective by Executive Orders.[23] However, it appears that only the sanctions against Rhodesia were clearly implemented on the basis of the United Nations Participation Act. In other cases, the US has additionally relied on the authority granted by domestic statutes, such as the International Emergency Economic Powers Act (IEEPA).

Federal States, such as Belgium, may face certain problems of implementation, where the federated entities retain a limited competence in respect of certain areas, such as sports and cultural relations.

d. *Ad hoc* legislation in response to specific sanctions resolutions or situations

Some States have resorted to the parliamentary process for the adoption, on a case-by-case basis, of particular sanctions laws, as, for example, Finland, where a specific law for the implementation of sanctions against Southern Rhodesia, and France, which adopted legislation implementing paragraph 29 of Resolution 687 barring Iraqi claims relating to non-fulfilment of contracts and provisions relating to cooperation with the International Criminal Tribunal. This process, required in some countries when Security Council resolutions affect property, contractual obligations, or human rights, can be a very slow one. The time lag between the adoption of the Security Council resolution and the domestic implementing act may take as long as six months to two years. In the Czech Republic, Haitian sanctions were ended by the Security Council before the special draft law which was being considered could even be adopted, while measures to implement Libyan sanctions came into force five years after the initial Security Council resolution in 1992. In The Netherlands, because of delays in implementing legislation, the Sierra Leone petroleum embargo was enforceable in that country for only two months of its five months duration.

Special sanctions legislation also raises the problem of sanctions termination, since the domestic measures can be justified only during the period of validity of the United

23 See the case of *Diggs. V. Shultz*, *supra*, note 18.

Nations measures. Domestic measures may remain in place months after the lifting of the measures by the Security Council.

While the resort to *ad hoc* pre-existing legislation not directly related to sanctions as a legal basis for implementation has not generally stopped States from formally complying with sanctions resolutions, it does have the consequence of fragmenting the legal basis of such implementation, with consequent gaps in respect of certain types of sanctions, for example those relating to financial and currency transactions or air traffic. In some cases, the targeting of non-state entities has also raised difficulties, as the case of Poland has shown in respect of the Taliban. On the other hand, the adoption of specially tailored sanctions legislation on a case-by-case basis, though having the advantage of fostering transparency of implementing measures and guaranteeing more comprehensive implementation, is a far slower process.

e. Implementation through the European Union

Although as regional organisations, both the Southern African Development Community [SADC] and the League of Arab States have participated in sanctions decision-making, feeding into the debate on sanctions at the United Nations, urging their members on the basis of their laws, to adhere to and enforce sanctions, and, in the case of SADC, participating in their monitoring and control, neither organisation has played the role that the European Union has assumed. As a supranational organisation, the European Union is the only regional body whose decisions are directly applicable within Member States legal order, hence the importance of its role in interposing itself between the Security Council and Member States implementation of sanctions.

The implementation of Security Council sanctions by the European Union has evolved dramatically over the years since the adoption by the Security Council of its first sanctions measures against Southern Rhodesia. The increasing transfers of competence from Member States to the European Union through the Maastricht Treaty and the Treaty of Amsterdam has meant the almost exclusive competence of the Community in the field of economic sanctions. This competence arises at present under the EC Treaty, based on Article 60 relating to restrictions on the movement of capital and payments (including the freezing of funds) to third countries and Article 301 providing for the interruption or reduction of economic relations with one or more third countries, providing this is required by a Common Position or Joint Action adopted in the framework of the Common and Foreign Security Provisions (CFSP) of the Treaty on European Union, which outline as one of the objectives, the preservation of peace and security in accordance with the United Nations Charter. EC regulations adopted under these provisions, even where not expressly linked to decisions of the Security Council, have nevertheless become largely sufficient as a legal basis for implementation by European Union Member States of sanctions adopted by the Security Council. These have the advantage of being directly applicable within European Union Member States, following on their promulgation. The ability of States to act independently in implementing Security Council sanctions has thus become increasingly limited as even the competence they continue to retain in foreign policy and the field of security, must be exercised in a manner consistent with Community law, as the ECJ has stated in the case of *Centro-Com*.

Security Council resolutions may however continue to address issues still in the national competence of the European Union members or not properly dealt with by the EC or CFSP, e.g. sports, diplomatic or cultural sanctions, arms trade, and penalization of individual conduct in violation of EC regulations. Moreover, European Union Member States have continued to consider that they are independently bound to carry out their obligations under the Charter. The fact that these prevail over their obligations under the EC treaty is not only confirmed by Article 103 of the Charter but also by Article 307 of the EC Treaty, even though that article has been interpreted restrictively by the ECJ. Moreover, States continue to report independently and directly to the United Nations, the totality of their implementation measures.

From the perspective of *European Union law*, implementation on the basis of EC regulations has in the past raised a host of issues, such as the legal basis for the exercise of European Union competence, the limits to such exercise, and the interplay between European Community and domestic legislation in sanctions implementation.

From the perspective of *United Nations law*, the issues which have arisen concern the extent to which the interposition of the Community between the United Nations and European Union Member States distorts, transforms or in any way impacts on the content and implementation of Security Council sanctions. The content of EC regulations are not necessarily coincidental with those of Council resolutions, in some cases going beyond their scope, or providing for a more detailed elaboration of their content. Such regulations have provided their own interpretation of terms found in Council resolutions, such as the meaning of funds, freezing of funds and financial services, as well as the definition of terrorist acts. Moreover, in certain cases the European Union will itself adopt autonomous measures, pre-empting Council decisions, or adopt additional or more restrictive measures *vis-à-vis* the same targeted entity, as it did in the case of Yugoslavia in 1998, or, on the contrary, the measures decreed may fall below the requirements of Security Council resolutions. Problems may arise from the relationship between European Union legislation, domestic measures and United Nations sanctions, where Member States apply simultaneously EC regulations and United Nations sanctions which are not coincidental against the same targeted entity (see cases in UK domestic courts).

The fact that the European Union is not a member of the United Nations, although it plays an increasingly important role in coordinating Member States actions within the United Nations, means that the separate obligations of United Nations Member States under Article 25 to carry out the decisions of the Security Council remain. The European Union is not mentioned specifically in Council resolutions; it will be recalled, however, that Article 48 (2) states that: "Such decisions shall be carried out by the Members of the United Nations directly and through their action in the appropriate international agencies of which they are members," which provides the European Union with justification to act.

(2) Content and Scope of Domestic Measures

Speed of implementation is not always synonymous with effectiveness; this is illustrated in States which have incorporated sanctions resolutions verbatim into the internal order, seemingly the most satisfactory procedure, but where this has not automatically ensured their effectiveness, since more detailed measures are required to make them applicable to individuals.

However, where Security Council decisions have required being made operative as against individuals, domestic implementing measures have not coincided in all respects with their requirements, which is inevitable. International and internal measures will differ in their material scope, territorial and personal scope, or *ratione temporis* in respect of their entry into force; they will also have differing effects on existing contracts, or vary in respect of the humanitarian exceptions or in provision of penal sanctions.

a. Material scope of the prohibitions

Measures which require being taken at an official level have generally been followed by Member States. For example, these have, with few exceptions, abstained from the recognition of entities, acts or situations declared illegal and invalid by the Security Council. This was the case in respect of the unilaterally declared State of Rhodesia, which remained unrecognized by all States, even dissident Portugal and South Africa, until the advent of Zimbabwe under majority rule. This has also been the case in respect of non-recognition of Iraq's annexation of Kuwait and Yugoslavia's status in the United Nations. On the other hand, it will be seen from the national studies that in implementing sanctions in domestic law, States have either gone well beyond, or fallen far short of what is required of them. Disparities will result in the coverage of prohibited items – whether these include trade in goods, transfer of funds, freezing of assets, trade in services, air traffic, or transit of vessels. In the case of Southern Rhodesia, for example, some States going well beyond the Security Council resolutions, adopted measures, such as a ban on telecommunication and postal links, which had been expressly rejected by the Security Council.

b. Territorial scope

Security Council resolutions invite Member States to apply the measures *in their territories* – this covers the activities of all individuals, including therefore those of non-nationals residing in the territory.

The resolutions on Southern Rhodesia contained specific provisions on territorial coverage. Thus a French decree of August 23, 1968 prohibiting trading "throughout the customs territory" *(territoire douanier français)* may have constituted a derogation from Security Council Resolution 253 prohibiting import of all commodities and products from Southern Rhodesia "whether or not they are imported in bond and whether or not any special legal status with respect to the import of goods is enjoyed by the port or other place where they are imported or stored." Resolution 232 also expressly extended the measures to territories under the administration of Member States.

Member States with overseas territories, like France, the UK and the Netherlands, have generally extended the scope of their measures to them; such territories, however, have their separate legal systems, which means that the legal basis and entry into force of sanctions may be different from those of the metropolis. United States legislation defines the term "United States" as meaning all territory subject to the jurisdiction of the United States.

c. Scope *ratione personae*

Security Council resolutions extend also to the activities of nationals residing outside the territory. States are to prohibit, *inter alia*, any activities that promote or are calculated to promote the sale or supply of prohibited items "by their nationals or from their territories"; and the shipment in vessels or aircraft of their registration or under charter to their nationals. Such Council resolutions do not extend beyond what is authorised by the rules relating to the exercise of State personal jurisdiction, since it refers only to the activities of "nationals". However, Member States are also called on to extend their legislation to aircraft "operated by an operator having his principal place of business or permanent residence" in their territory (Resolution 670 on Iraq).

The exercise of jurisdiction outside territory in order to give effect to multilateral treaty obligations entails what is a relatively novel element in international law: that of the introduction of a duty – and not only, as traditionally was the case, a right – to exercise State control over private activities abroad. In seeking in particular to enforce sanctions against evasions by multinationals operating worldwide, Security Council resolutions require States to adopt legislation with extraterritorial reach. In view of the fact that all Member States are bound to carry out the decisions of the Security Council, such exercise of competence can no longer be seen as in the past as an intervention in the domestic jurisdiction of other States. It may however raise practical and technical problems today in view of the non-territorial nature of many financial and other transactions.

States have also been called on to extend sanctions to the ships of the sanctioned entity, including, in the case of the Federal Republic of Yugoslavia, "any vessel in which a majority or controlling interest is held by a person or undertaking in or operating from the Federal Republic of Yugoslavia regardless of the flag under which the vessel sails" (Resolution 757), that is, based on the criteria of effective control.

States have in some cases made illegal activities conducted outside their territory which are carried out by their nationals or their corporations – this is the case, for example, of the UK, Sweden, the United States and The Netherlands, although this does not always mean that nationals could be tried and convicted for such acts. United States Executive Orders, for example, apply to persons subject to the jurisdiction of the United States, persons being defined as "individuals, partnerships, associations or other unincorporated body of individuals, or corporations."

On the other hand, some States have deliberately restricted the extraterritorial effects of their legislation. In connection with Rhodesian sanctions, Switzerland had initially claimed that it could not proceed in law against Swiss registered companies in respect of transactions outside Swiss territory. It stated further: "under international public law, each State is entitled to apply legal norms only in its own territory, and the Swiss authorities therefore cannot take any measures that would contravene international positive law." This position, however, was subsequently challenged in a memorandum by the United Nations Legal Counsel, supported by references, *inter alia,* to the *Lotus* case, and to State practice such as the UK Trading with the Enemy Act of 1939:[24]

24 S/11178/Rev.l dated May 8, 1973.

> "If those companies are organised under the law of the State concerned, have its nationality and are registered under its law, it would appear to be open to the competent authorities to decide whether or not to allow the companies to maintain whatever status they enjoy under local law. It would, for example, seem that the authorities may be in a position to require that the companies concerned desist from engaging in the transactions in question as a condition for the continuance of their registration under local law ... it would be at variance (moreover) with both law and precedent, to assert that public international law precludes a State from enacting laws having extraterritorial effect and providing for enforcement within the territory of the legislating State."

Switzerland, with some exceptions, continues not to extend its sanctions legislation extraterritorially, although it has applied such legislation to vessels and aircraft under the Swiss flag.

Despite EC regulations to the contrary, the provisions of which apply also to nationals of European Union Member States outside their territories, countries such as Germany continue in their sanctions legislation to address only transactions on the territory (with certain exceptions, for example the personal scope of German restrictions on trade with arms is much broader). Though Belgium introduced a personal jurisdiction clause in 1995, no such measures have been implemented, and even where implemented at the EC level, such activities outside territory have not been criminalized. The scope of extraterritorial application of Finnish sanctions legislation is restricted by the general provisions of the Penal Code.

The exercise of personal jurisdiction has thus raised constitutional and other problems for implementing States, obliging them in certain cases to enact special legislation or amend existing laws to provide for the general extraterritorial reach of sanctions or to introduce restrictions on shipping abroad.

Security Council resolutions do not explicitly require the exercise of extraterritorial jurisdiction over subsidiaries abroad. Nevertheless, this question had first been raised in connection with the sanctions against Southern Rhodesia. While such exercise has been claimed (and challenged) on numerous occasions by some States, in particular the United States, when in pursuit of domestic aims and policies,[25] these have generally been reluctant to do so when implementing United Nations sanctions. Thus the United States, Sweden, and France have refused to restrict the activities of subsidiaries abroad owned by their nationals as contrary to international law rules on jurisdiction. In France, this refusal to exercise such extended jurisdiction has even applied to the activities of branches of French corporations situated abroad, which is normally considered to be within personal jurisdiction.

Two examples of extension of jurisdiction over third parties should be noted however. The first is a claim by the United States to *enforce* Security Council resolutions unilater-

25 As, in the past, the "Siberian pipelines" case had shown (Export Administration Regulations as amended (47 Fed.Reg.5 January, 1982, pp. 141-145)), relating to exports to the USSR of oil and gas equipment, which extends to juridical bodies wherever organized or doing business that are owned or controlled by citizens or residents of the US, or persons actually within the US.

ally (i.e. without specific authorisation from the Security Council and on the basis of domestic not United Nations enabling legislation) and extraterritorially, against private third parties. This is to be found in the United States Kennedy-d'Amato Act of 1996 imposing economic sanctions on foreign companies engaging in specified transactions with Iran and Libya, one of the purposes of which is expressly stated to be that of pressuring Libya through further isolation into compliance with United Nations Security Council resolutions.

At the level of the EC, one should also note Regulation No. 990/93 concerning detention by European Union Member States of vessels suspected of having breached the sanctions against the FRY, even if the ships were flying the flag of a non-member country, belonged to non-Community nationals or companies, and the alleged breach of sanctions occurred outside Community territory. This was confirmed by the European Court of Justice, despite contrary views held by Member States.[26] This Regulation, however, was in line with the authorisation granted by the United Nations Security Council relating to enforcement of the economic embargo at sea. One would have assumed that problems would arise in domestic law from such implementation not based on a mandatory resolution, but flowing from an authorisation by the Security Council and moreover which implied overriding existing international law obligations, as well as a limited use of force. The national studies, however, have not revealed any controversy over these provisions.

d. Application of measures *ratione temporis*

In some cases, action by countries preceded a Security Council decision, or was solely based on a Security Council recommendation, hence taken on the basis of autonomous legislation. This was the case for Sweden and Finland in respect of sanctions against South Africa and Southern Rhodesia and of the UK, where supplementary legislation – and not the United Nations enabling act – conferred powers to impose measures against Iraq before 6 August 1990, the date of the Security Council resolution. In France, sanctions relating to the freezing of the assets of Iraq preceded Resolution 661 and therefore had to be based on national enabling legislation.

Even when national measures follow on Security Council decisions, it is difficult to make them coincide *ratione temporis* and there will always be a time lag. In some cases, the national measure may be adopted long after the Security Council decision.

Moreover, the entry into force of Security Council resolutions raises complex temporal issues of implementation. Some resolutions call for immediate effect, others make no mention at all of the date of their application, while some give advance warning of two to several weeks, dependent on the compliance of the targeted State, or leave it to the Sanctions Committee to determine the entry into force of sanctions against particular individuals or entities, by designating the persons, funds and aircraft.

In some cases, different provisions come into operation at different times. For example, past resolutions which prohibited exports from the sanctioned State after the date of the Security Council resolution were neither retroactive, nor did they entirely have immediate effect, for they appeared to authorise the importation of targeted products

26 See case of *Ebony Maritime, infra*, note 35.

into implementing States *after* the date of the resolution, providing these had been exported from the sanctioned territory *before* the date of the resolution. The same would have been the case for exports to the sanctioned entity which left the implementing State before the date of the Security Council resolution.[27] On the other hand, provisions relating not to import or export of commodities and products but for example to transfer of funds, means of transportation, such as severance of airlinks, or insurance, call for immediate application.

A review of state legislation shows, however, that with few exceptions (see e.g. US Executive Order 1967), most acts or decrees have immediate and not retroactive effect to the date of Security Council resolutions, even though sometimes adopted months after the relevant Security Council resolution, or, again, their entry into force may be the date of their official publication. Retroactivity would of course pose problems in criminal law. States therefore are faced with a dilemma – either their implementing measures violate the principle of retroactivity or their acts are not in strict conformity with their obligations under the Charter. As for States members of the European Union, the time factor is further complicated, since EC regulations may call for retroactive application of the Security Council measures, although, again, this may not be followed under domestic implementation of such regulations.

The time factor intervenes as well in respect of sanctions termination, domestic sanctions being lifted in some cases several months after the lifting of Security Council measures.

e. Interpretation of terms and humanitarian exceptions

The scope of prohibited items is also determined by interpretation within the domestic sphere of the terms of Security Council resolutions. Such resolutions contain a large number of open-ended and undefined terms: "goods", "food 'in humanitarian circumstances'", "military equipment", "arms and related matériel", which leave a large margin of appreciation to implementing authorities and detract from uniform implementation. The provisions relating to financial measures such as freezing of funds, have proved particularly ambiguous.

Initially, in the case of Southern Rhodesian, interpretation had been largely left up to individual States. The controversy over interpretation gathered force in the Sanctions Committee on Iraq, with respect to the exception on "foodstuffs in humanitarian circumstances". Cuba and Yemen, for instance, wished to see a general exemption for foodstuffs, stating that they could never accept any definition which would allow the supply of foodstuffs only to avert famine, since this would be in direct violation of the international human right to food.[28] However, interpretation of the terms found in Security Council resolutions is considered to fall within the competence of the Security

27 See Paul Tavernier, *Recherches sur l'application dans le temps des actes et des règles en droit international public. Problèmes de droit intertemporel ou de droit transitoire* (Paris, LGDJ, 1970).

28 See Proceedings of the Sanctions Committee, reproduced in D. Bethlehem (ed.), *The Kuwait Crisis: Sanctions and their Economic Consequences*, (Cambridge, 1991), Part II, pp. 778 and 793.

Council. The Council has sometimes clarified its terms in Presidential statements or in subsequent resolutions. Generally, however, this has been left up to the individual Sanctions Committees established for each sanctions regime; although not given a general mandate to interpret (apart, possibly, from the specific one in Resolution 666), these have been led to assume this task on a case-by-case basis (and under a no-objections procedure) in response to requests for States for processing specific items under the humanitarian exceptions, or in respect of dual-use items.[29] Generally speaking, States have regarded the interpretations of the Sanctions Committees as authoritative (but see pronouncements of the Irish High Court in the case of *Bosphorus* below).

Without clarification of certain terms, such as "essential humanitarian need", "controlling or majority interest" in the targeting of vessels, and "funds and other financial resources" which are to be frozen by States, uniform practice by States is impossible. The Sanctions Committee has, for example, interpreted the term "funds and other financial resources" to be frozen by States, drawing on a private initiative – the Interlaken process – which has included the development of building blocks of language for future use by the Security Council.[30] Nevertheless, there is still considerable leeway for interpretation in European Union law, as has been seen, and in domestic law.

Particular problems have arisen in regard to what the humanitarian exceptions cover. It has been seen that the items subject to humanitarian exceptions are not the same from one sanctions regime to another; for example, pensions, news materials and educational supplies have been exempt in one case, but not in another. But there have also been discrepancies in the humanitarian exceptions granted between Council resolutions and domestic implementing measures. States have exempted goods not included in the exceptions prescribed by the Security Council, on the grounds, for example, that they were conforming to international law; they have thus excepted commodities destined for the operation of diplomatic missions, including those of the sanctioned State, and allowed financial transactions for such purposes as pensions, study abroad and medical assistance. States have also left it to the discretion of their competent ministers to interpret the humanitarian exceptions.

f. The effects on private rights

The measures prescribed by the Security Council require restricting private rights to fulfil objectives which may appear for individuals to be far removed from their concerns. Sanctions resolutions state that the prohibitions on commodities or products and related financial transactions shall apply "notwithstanding any contract entered into or any licence granted before the date of the resolution". The consequent effects on private

29 See Michael P. Scharf and Joshua L. Dorosin, "Interpreting UN sanctions: the Rulings and Role of the Yugoslavia Sanctions Committee", XIX *Brooklyn Journal of International Law* (1993) 771-827.

30 See *Targeted Financial Sanctions – A Manual for Design and Implementation: Contributions from the Interlaken Process*, The Swiss Confederation in cooperation with the United Nations Secretariat and the Watson Institute for International Studies, Brown University (at http://www.smartsanctions.ch).

contractual rights may in some States be at variance with the constitutional or general legal order of the member State, including the law of contracts.

Difficulties arise in determining the scope of such clauses, which may include a variety of commercial transactions, such as contracts relating to sales, services, such as insurance, leasing, franchising, promotional and sub-contracting activities.[31] These provisions raise also the question of non-retroactivity, as well as their legal effects: nullity or only temporary suspension of the contract?[32] States have adopted a variety of approaches; they have also included many exceptions to such provisions, for example, transport contracts the execution of which had already begun before the date in which the decree went into effect, or where payment of goods had been made prior to the date in question. The United States has applied a "hardship provision" in some cases, the rationale being that it would only profit the sanctioned entity to keep both the funds and the goods. On the other hand, the Swiss Federal Council has turned down appeals by companies claiming that they should benefit from such a hardship clause, arguing that this would only be applicable if substantial Swiss interests were at stake, not in order to alleviate the impact of sanctions on individual claimants.

Compensation is not generally available for such unfulfilled contracts. It was clear from the decision of the Governing Council of the UNCC excluding losses suffered as a result of the trade embargo from the liability of Iraq, that compensation could not be sought at the international level. Nor is such compensation generally provided for under domestic law, which has led to some public debate. In some countries, however, such as in Finland, the constitutional protection of property rights includes compensation. Claims for compensation could be made, also, on the grounds of general principles of law.

At the same time, measures were adopted in the cases of Iraq (Resolution 687), Yugoslavia (Resolution 757), Libya (Resolution 883) and Haiti (Resolution 917), to shield individuals and companies, including banks, from the consequences of non-execution of contracts as a result of economic sanctions. States were thus called on to ensure that the targeted States were expressly excluded from making claims for such non-performance. This has raised problems where bank guaranties are concerned, as the national study on Switzerland points out.

g. Provision of penalties

In a number of cases, the Security Council has called expressly for States to adopt domestic enforcement measures, including appropriate penalties for violations of sanctions.[33]

---

31 See B. Grelon and C.-E. Gudin, "Contrats et crise du Golfe", 118 *Journal du droit international* (1991) 633-677.

32 SCR 418 (1970) imposing a mandatory arms embargo against South Africa "calls upon all States to review ... all existing contractual arrangements with and licences granted to South Africa relating to the manufacture and maintenance of arms, ammunition of all types and military equipment and vehicles **with a view to terminating them**" (emphasis added).

33 So, for example, in the case of Yugoslavia, Resolution 820 (1993) "Reminds States of the importance of strict enforcement of measures imposed under Chapter VII of the Charter, and calls upon them to bring proceedings against persons and entities violating the measures

State legislation, as the examples of Sweden, France, Belgium and Germany show, has not been uniform in this respect. Since general sanctions legislation does not always include penalties, a legal basis for the imposition of such penalties has been sought in general penal codes, in specially tailored penal measures for violations of arms embargoes and in customs codes, with consequent varying degrees of severity. Penalties have thus ranged from confiscation and fines which can be quite sizeable for serious offences such as trade in arms, to imprisonment of between two and six years for offences committed with intent. While in some cases, penalties have been extended to citizens committing such crimes abroad, in practice criminal pursuits have not always been initiated.[34]

Such penalties have also been applied for breaches of community regulations implementing Security Council sanctions. In the case of *Ebony Maritime* the ECJ addressed the question of whether confiscation of cargo carried by a tanker flying the Maltese flag, on its way to Yugoslavia in violation of Security Council resolutions, was compatible with community law; it ruled that though the choice of penalties remained within the discretion of EC Member States, such penalties against an infringement of community law should be "effective, proportionate and dissuasive."[35]

(3) Domestic Procedures for Implementation and Enforcement

The numerous technical issues arising from sanctions application and enforcement in domestic law are generally outside the scope of this study and have not been systematically studied, but some of these have been raised in the various national studies. They cover a vast range of disparate problems.

There is first the question of coordination of action between various government, administrative and financial bodies, but also the interface between central government, regions and communities. There is also the highly complex problem of implementation of sanctions in the field of banking, particularly in view of the extraterritorial nature of banking operations and the difficulties entailed by their regulation and control. The move from comprehensive sanctions to targeted sanctions, in particular the freezing of funds and the consequent technique of listing in the framework of counter-terrorism, has given banks an even more central role in implementing decisions of the Security Council, but has also challenged them in calling for new solutions very different from those for money-laundering. The feasibility of targeted financial sanctions and their efficiency has thus been the subject of much debate.

In regard to the traditional sanctions affecting exported or imported items, technical questions arise such as detection of false documents regarding the origin or destination

---

imposed (by previous resolutions) and to impose appropriate penalties". See also SCR 841 (1993) (Haiti), 864 (1993) and 1295 (1999) (UNITA), 1267 (1999) and 1333 (2000) (Taliban).

34 For cases of prosecution before domestic courts of individuals and corporations evading the sanctions against Southern Rhodesia, see *Collective Responses to Illegal Acts*, *op. cit.*, note 1, chapter 8.

35 See Case C-177/95, *Ebony Maritime SA and Loten Navigation Co.Ltd. v. Prefetto della Provincia di Brindisi and Others*, 27 February 1997, [1997] ECR I-1114, at para. 35.

of goods, particularly topical today in view of the problems arising from the trade in "conflict" diamonds, the criteria for dual use items, the problem of end-user clauses in contracts, or procedures for disclosure of information.

Finally, the problem of sanctions enforcement arises. This covers prosecution of individuals, seizure and confiscation of ships (which has proved difficult in some States, as the example of Japan shows), and sanctions busting by nationals with consequences at the international level which involve Member States' responsibility and United Nations follow-up. The participation of military forces in United Nations sanctions enforcement at sea does not seem to have raised constitutional problems in Member States.

III. Security Council Decisions before National and Regional Courts

Courts have had the opportunity to pronounce on Security Council resolutions in applying them to particular cases and there are a certain number of areas in which they can or have played a role. Courts may be called on to resolve conflicts arising between domestic law and Security Council decisions; they are then faced with problems of hierarchy. They may also be enlisted in sanctions implementation, where particular measures such as non-recognition of governmental acts or the grant of immunities before national courts, involves them directly. They may have a role in the review of the validity of national implementing measures, thus incidentally touching on the validity of Council resolutions and their interpretation. Finally, courts can play a role in the protection of human rights and fundamental freedoms where these are affected by sanctions implementation.

(1) The Resolution of Conflicts between Security Council Resolutions and Domestic Law Before National Courts

The implementation of Security Council resolutions poses the problem of compatibility between domestic and international law; such conflicts may come before domestic courts. Their resolution will depend of course on the law of the forum. Domestic courts bound by their own rules may not always uphold the primacy of international law and the consequences will depend on the place attributed to international law in the national system.

The problem of hierarchy is posed only in respect of monist States where treaties and statutes are placed on an equal footing. While some constitutions are silent as to hierarchy (e.g. Constitution of Japan), and some consecrate the *lex posterior* rule, or the primacy of the later in time (United States), a number of constitutions uphold the primacy of a self-executing treaty over municipal law, which means that a treaty will prevail over subsequent as well as earlier legislation (see, for example, the cases of Argentina, Belgium, France, Germany, Jordan, Namibia, The Netherlands and Poland).

But from that does not necessarily flow the primacy of international law over the constitution. Implementing Security Council resolutions in domestic law may therefore raise important constitutional problems. The most likely problem to arise in relation to conflicts between Security Council resolutions and constitutional provisions is that of incompatibility with fundamental rights and freedoms, including constitutionally protected property rights.

In the Southern Rhodesian crisis, certain Member States, including the United States, considered that they were barred from implementing proposals relating to severance of postal, telegraphic, radio and other means of communication, or to the prohibition of insurance on the lives of passengers, by constitutional provisions relating to fundamental freedoms, including freedom of information and freedom of movement. Where such proposals were nonetheless incorporated into the resolutions (e.g. Resolution 253 which would have entailed the barring of entry into States' territories of their own nationals residing in Southern Rhodesia), the refusal by some States to carry out these provisions on the basis that this was contrary to general principles of international law (the case, for example, of Sweden) meant that these States were not in full compliance with their obligations under the Charter. Moreover, the surrender of persons to the International Criminal Tribunals has posed problems of conflict with constitutional provisions, as the case of Germany has shown.

In *United States v. Steinberg*, a decision concerning a potential conflict between Resolution 277 (1970) relating to non-recognition and the Constitution of the United States, the Court stated:

> "This country has a continuing obligation to observe with entire good faith and scrupulous care all of its undertakings under [the United Nations Charter], including support of the resolutions adopted by the Security Council. Of course, a treaty ... cannot run counter to the provisions of the Constitution of this country. Therefore, the government ... could not choose between respecting the constitutional rights of a citizen and adhering to the provisions of a treaty."[36]

The Court found, however, that in this case the Government did not make such a choice. In the internal order, therefore, the Constitution usually prevails over decisions of the Security Council. But Security Council resolutions could also be outranked in domestic law by other treaties, Article 103 notwithstanding (see, for example, the case of Argentina). This does not only refer to treaties which are later in time, but also to those protecting fundamental human rights (such as the ECHR or the ICCPR) which may have become constitutionally entrenched and thus given the same ranking as constitutional norms.

Moreover, while in federal States such as Switzerland or the United States, where treaties are placed at the same level as federal statutes, a self-executing treaty automatically supersedes prior domestic laws which are inconsistent with it, the converse is that a new federal law will prevail over an earlier treaty in conflict with it, which leads to the State being unable to respect its international obligations. The case of *Diggs v. Shultz* arising from resumption by the United States of importation of chrome from Rhodesia under the umbrella of the Byrd amendment is a good illustration of the problems posed by the resolution of conflicts between Security Council decisions and domestic law in

36 *United States v. Steinberg*, United States District Court for the Northern District of Illinois, 478 F. Supp.29 (3 Oct. 1979). See M. Lloyd Nash (ed.), United States Department of State, *Digest of United States Practice in International Law* (Washington Publisher, 1979), pp. 436-437.

domestic courts. When legal action was initiated in 1972 to halt import of Rhodesian chrome despite the existence of a prohibition under a Security Council resolution, the United States Court of Appeals, although finding that the law authorising such imports showed "blatant disregard, of our treaty undertakings" nevertheless referred to the "constitutional power of Congress to set treaty obligations at naught" and concluded that "under our constitutional scheme, Congress can denounce treaties if it sees fit to do so, and there is nothing the other branches of government can do about it." It also rejected the contentions of the appellants that commitments to the United Nations have more force than an ordinary treaty.[37] While Courts in the United States have relied on a presumption that the legislator did not intend to violate the treaty, thus avoiding conflicts between international and municipal law,[38] it is not always possible to interpret the conflicting rules to that effect.

(2) *The Role of Domestic Courts in Implementation of Security Council Provisions on Non-Recognition and Grant of Immunities*

The Security Council has called on States not to grant certain benefits which are normally regulated by their municipal law; this has concerned non-cognisance by domestic courts of acts of unrecognised States or Governments. It has also called for the grant of immunity from judicial proceedings. Such provisions which involve domestic courts directly in sanctions implementation, may prove difficult to implement in a State in which there is separation of powers between executive and judicial bodies. In matters of recognition, for example, courts may act in complete independence from the executive branch of the Government, and tend to give at least limited effect to foreign legislation acting on the premise that a foreign State or Government exists even though it may not have been recognised by the executive, providing its effectivity is ensured and the particular act or legislation is in conformity with ordre public. In some countries, like the United Kingdom, however, the opinion of the government in matters of cognisance and interpretation is binding.

Resolution 277 which called on Member States "to take appropriate measures, at the national level, to ensure that any act performed by officials and institutions of the illegal régime in Southern Rhodesia shall not be accorded any recognition, official or otherwise, including judicial notice, by the competent organs of their States", thus prohibiting Member States from giving effect to the laws or acts of the illegal régime in their municipal law, was considered at the time controversial.

Interpreting the Resolution as including non-cognizance by domestic courts (this depended on the meaning to be ascribed to "judicial notice"), led the United States to

---

37 *Supra*, note 18, at p. 1255.

38 See the case of the threatened closure of the PLO Observer Mission to the United Nations in New York, in which Judge Palmieri applied to a Congressional act (the "Ant-Terrorism Act of 1987") a principle of interpretation which led to the finding that Congress did not "express a manifest intent" to override United States obligations under the UN Headquarters Agreement (United States District Court for the Southern District of New York. *United States v. Palestine Liberation Organisation et al.*, Decision of June 29, 1988 (27 *ILM* (1988) 1055-1088, at pp. 1079-1086).

object to the provision on the basis of the independence of the United States courts in the matter. France, on the other hand, understanding the term "judicial notice" as referring to the Rhodesian judicial decisions, hence to the types of acts to be denied effects, reserved its position on the basis that "the measures enacted would not refer to civil actions or relations governing private law, but would affect only acts under public law of these acts of judicial notice".[39]

Security Council Resolution 277 appeared to make no distinction in the matter of judicial notice between official acts under public law and those governing private law relations. Yet even in countries where the judiciary has followed the executive in non-recognition questions, courts have made that distinction in respect to rights of private persons (everyday transactions such as birth certificates, marriages and deaths) at least where the effects of non-recognition would lead to absurd or inhumane results. The importance of such a distinction has been upheld by the International Court of Justice in the *Namibia* Opinion in setting limits to Security Council non-recognition policies.[40]

This raises an important question concerning independence of domestic courts. The 1993 resolution of the *Institut de droit international* adopted in Milano states in Article 1: "National courts should be empowered by their domestic legal order to interpret and apply international law with full independence."[41] To what extent do Security Council resolutions require States to run counter to this by calling on them to ensure that their courts behave in a certain manner?

The Security Council has also decided questions of immunity from legal proceedings. This was the case for Resolutions 712 (1991) and 1483 (2003) in regard to immunity from legal process in all States of petroleum exports from Iraq. Having declared, under Resolution 1483, that all proceeds from the sale of Iraqi petroleum and natural gas shall be deposited into the Development Fund for Iraq until the emergence of an internationally recognized and representative Government, the Council decided, under paragraph 22 that:

> "until December 31, 2007, unless the Council decides otherwise, petroleum, petroleum products, and natural gas originating in Iraq shall be immune, until title passes to the initial purchaser from legal proceedings against them and not be subject to any form of attachment, garnishment, or execution, and that all States shall take any steps that may be necessary under their respective domestic legal systems to assure this protection, and that proceeds and obligations arising from sales thereof, as well as the Development Fund for Iraq, shall enjoy privileges and immunities equivalent to those enjoyed by the United Nations except that the above-mentioned privileges and immunities will not apply with respect to any legal proceeding in which recourse to such proceeds or obligations is necessary to satisfy liability for damages assessed in connection with an ecological accident, including an oil spill, that occurs after the date of adoption of this resolution."

39 SCOR, 25th yr., 1535th mtg., paras. 37 and 95, respectively.

40 ICJ Reports 1971, p. 56.

41 See 65-II *AIDI* (1994) 321.

Controversy is bound to arise over this in national courts, particularly where domestic implementation extends the immunity further than the intention of Resolution 1483. This is the case with US Executive Order 13303 implementing Resolution 1483, which, after declaring a national emergency, states in Section 1 that "any attachment, judgment, decree, lien, execution, garnishment, or other judicial process is prohibited, and shall be deemed null and void, with respect to the following: (a) the Development Fund for Iraq, and (b) all Iraqi petroleum and petroleum products, and interests therein, and proceeds, obligations, or any financial instruments of any nature whatsoever arising from or related to the sale or marketing thereof, and interests therein, in which any foreign country or a national thereof has any interest, that are in the United States, that hereafter come within the United States, or that are or hereafter come within the possession or control of United States persons." It does not contain the exception to the immunity granted under paragraph 22 of Resolution 1483 for environmental liability. Nor does it contain the temporal limitation of Resolution 1483, extending the immunity as long as the oil is marketed. It has been stated that the deviations from Resolution 1483 may lead a court to reject the implementing executive order as overbroad, and that it may also be considered illegal under the IEEPA because it dismisses claims of U.S. citizens without providing an alternate forum.[42]

(3) *Judicial Review by National Courts*

a. Judicial competence to review national implementing measures

In turning to the question of judicial review by domestic courts, reference must also be made to the role of two regional courts – the European Court of Justice and the European Court of Human Rights. EC regulations have direct effect in the domestic orders of States and in this sense, the ECJ constitutes the apex of the national judicial system. The ECtHR, for its part, is the guardian of a Convention that, as has been mentioned, has been given quasi-constitutional ranking in many of the States of the Council of Europe.

Domestic courts could only claim to control the legality of Security Council decisions in terms of their national constitutions and for domestic application purposes, since they cannot review such legality in terms of the UN Charter itself. Such judicial review can therefore only be incidental. The Federal Court of Justice of Germany has expressly held that in reviewing German implementing legislation it could only make reference to measures the Security Council had actually taken, not those it could lawfully take.

This raises the general question of the justiciability of the implementing acts of national Governments in domestic courts. As the national studies point out, however, courts do not always have the competence to review national implementation measures; moreover, where they have exercised some measure of scrutiny, they have tended to uphold the measures concerned, particularly where such legislation is tied to questions of national security, and on the basis that they draw their legitimacy from the Security Council resolutions.

42 See http://www.earthrights.org/news/eo13303memo.shtml.

In France, for example, the *Conseil d'Etat* has refused to control the legality under French law of domestic implementing measures since these could not be detached from the Security Council resolution itself which, in the eyes of the French court, constituted "*un acte de gouvernment*" (an act of State). The courts of other countries too, have refused to exercise powers of judicial review on the grounds of "act of State". In the United Kingdom, it appears from the national study that such challenges have met with little success, although the entry into force of the Human Rights Act in 1998 may be altering the picture. In the United States, the use of the International Emergency Economic Powers Act (IEEPA) as a domestic legal basis, ties sanctions to national security, which has meant that there has been so far few challenges by the courts to implementing legislation.

Refusal to control the legality of national measures has also been justified on the basis of the primacy of the United Nations Charter. In a decision of the District Court of the Hague of 31 August 2001 in the case of *Milosevic*, relating to a request that Milosevic be released unconditionally on the grounds that the Netherlands was acting unlawfully in cooperating with the ICTY,[43] it was ruled that under the Headquarters Agreement the Netherlands had lawfully transferred its jurisdiction over the ICTY's indictees to that Tribunal, that the Statute of the ICTY gave it primacy over national courts and that United Nations Charter obligations prevailed over the obligations of Member States. The Dutch Court thus argued that it had no competence to consider the request.[44]

Remedies may also not be available at the regional level. In the subsequent case of *Milosevic v. the Netherlands*,[45] the ECtHR declared inadmissible the complaint brought by Milosevic under several provisions of the ECHR, precisely for failure to exhaust local remedies ... even though it was plain that there were none that were adequate and effective.

For European Union Member States, the ECJ can and has controlled domestic implementing measures, although solely in the light of the law of the EC. However, as is evidenced in the cases cited below, the ECJ has so far not provided much satisfaction to individuals and entities affected or targeted by sanctions, although this may be a question of time.

b. Interpretation of Security Council resolutions

Faced with an individual complaint that the national implementing measure exceeds the measures required by the Security Council resolution (see for example, cases brought before UK and German Courts in this respect), domestic courts will be faced with the problem of interpreting the relevant Security Council resolution. Sanctions implemen-

43 *Slobodan Milosevic v. The State of the Netherlands* (Judgment in interlocutory injunction), 31 August 2001, President of the Hague District Court, Kort Geding 2001/258, p. 688.

44 The Dutch Court also relied on *Nalitelic v. Croatia* (Application No. 51891/99 (Decision as to Admissibility), ECtHR, 4 May 2000) to argue that the ICTY offered sufficient procedural guarantees. In consequence, it rejected as manifestly unfounded the argument that the surrender of an accused person to the ICTY would violate the right to a fair trial under Article 6(1) of the ECHR.

45 See Application No. 77631/01, *Slobodan Milosevic v. the Netherlands* (Judgment), ECtHR, 19 Mar. 2002.

tation therefore may result in a multiplicity of interpretations in the different courts of Member States and hence faces the danger of a further fragmentation of the sanctions regime. The question also arises as to the extent to which such bodies can indeed interpret Security Council resolutions.

Domestic courts have turned to the relevant Security Council resolutions as an aid to interpretation of national implementing measures or EC legislation giving effect to the sanctions, but they will normally proceed according to the methods of interpretation followed for domestic law (see examples cited in the national studies in relation to the German Federal Court of Justice and the UK House of Lords). The case of *Kuwait Airways Corporation* v. *Iraqi Airways Co.* is an illustration of the fact that even when not implemented by legislation, Security Council resolutions can serve as aids to interpretation, as well as in defining *ordre public*. Thus Security Council Resolution 662 (1990) relating to the nullity and non-recognition of the Iraqi annexation of Kuwait and the measures taken to implement it was considered relevant in determining UK public policy.[46] The sanction of nullity applied by the Security Council in Resolution 662 was thus given effect in the United Kingdom courts notwithstanding the lack of implementing measures.

The decision of the Irish High Court in the case of *Bosphorus Hava*[47] which considered that the impounding by the Irish authorities of the Turkish registered aircraft which had been leased from Yugoslav Airlines did not fall within the terms of Resolution 820 (1993), is of interest in this context. It will be recalled that this Resolution, which was implemented into the Community Legal Order by Regulation No. 990/93 of 26 April 1993, refers to the impounding of vessels "in which a majority or controlling interest is held by a person or undertaking in or operating from the Federal Republic of Yugoslavia ...".[48] The Court held that while United Nations resolutions did not form part of Irish domestic law, Resolution 820 provided the genesis for the relevant provisions of the EEC Council regulation and that therefore the Court should take into account any judicial or academic commentary on its terms to assist it in its interpretation. Nevertheless, it declared that in the absence of such commentary, the unexplained conclusion of the United Nations Sanctions Committee that the aircraft fell within the terms of Resolution 820 (1993) was of no value to the Court.

The European Court of Justice has been called on also to interpret Security Council

46 The case of *The Campaign for Nuclear Disarmament and the Prime Minister of the United Kingdom et al.* (The High Court of Justice, Queen's Bench Division (Divisional Court), [2002] England and Wales High Court Decisions 2759 QB), in which the Court refused to interpret Security Council Resolution 1441, poses different issues. The applicant had sought an advisory declaration as to whether Resolution 1441 authorised States to take military action in the event of Iraqi non-compliance. The Court considered the request non-justiciable, *inter alia* on the ground that this would involve the interpretation of Resolution 1441, itself a specific international treaty, which was not part of UK domestic law, since English courts could not presume to give an authoritative ruling on its meaning binding on other States.

47 See *infra*, note 56.

48 The Sanctions Committee has on a number of occasions (see e.g. case of *MV Crna Gora* in the Netherlands study) reaffirmed that the test as to whether sanctions should apply to particular vessels was that of effective control, not the flag under which the vessel was flying. See also SCR 787 (1992), para. 10.

resolutions in reviewing the legality of domestic implementation of EC Regulations. Faced with the same case of *Bosphorus Hava*,[49] the ECJ applied its own principles of interpretation[50] to the Community Regulation's reference to "majority or controlling interest" in finding that the wording of Article 8 did not suggest a distinction between ownership and day-to-day operation and control. It therefore concluded that the Regulation did apply to the particular case. The Advocate General has also stated: "There is no doubt in my view that the Regulation has to be interpreted in the light of the Security Council Resolutions ... It follows that the Regulation has to be interpreted in such a way as to make the sanctions fully effective."[51]

(4) Domestic and Regional Courts in the Protection of Human Rights and Fundamental Freedoms

Increasingly, courts are having to address the tensions which have arisen between the public policy nature of Security Council resolutions and individual rights. At the core lies a question of fundamental importance: the balance to be struck between the effective fulfilment of obligations to implement sanctions under the United Nations Charter and the protection of fundamental legal principles safeguarding individual rights.

Although prohibition on foreign trade has not usually been taken to encroach on fundamental freedoms, other human rights issues arising from the implementation of United Nations sanctions which have come up before domestic and regional courts have included property rights, including the question of compensation, and rights of due process which have arisen in particular in connection with surrender to the ICTY and with the listing procedures under Security Council resolutions relating to terrorism.

In regard to the freezing of funds (which has been seen as both property confiscation and penal sanction[52]), the two European regional courts have reiterated that property rights are not absolute and that their exercise may be subject to restrictions justified by objectives of general interests. These arguments were summarized by the ECJ in the *Invest Import und Export* case,[53] which concerned an EC regulation on the freezing of

---

49 See *infra*, note 55.

50 Both a literal interpretation and a teleological one. See Iris Canor, "Can Two Walk Together, Except they be Agreed? – The Relationship between International Law and European Law: The Incorporation of United Nations Sanctions against Yugoslavia into European Community Law through the Perspective of the European Court of Justice", 35 *Common Market Law Review* (1998) 137-187, at pp. 144-46.

51 See Opinion of the Advocate General, in the case of *Ebony Maritime*, *supra* note 35, p. I-1122, para. 21.

52 See *R. (on the application of Othman) v. Secretary of State for Work and Pensions*, [2001] EWHC Admin 1022 (QB2001) relating to the freezing of assets undertaken in response to alleged involvement of the individual in international terrorism.

53 See Case C-317/00 P(R), *"Invest" Import und Export GmbH and Invest Commerce SARL v. Commission*, 13 November 2000, [2000] ECR I-9541 (Order of the President of the Court on the Appeal against the Order of the President of the Second Chamber of the Ct. of First Instance of the EC of 2 August 2000).

funds and a ban on investment in pursuance of Security Council resolutions relating to the Federal Republic of Yugoslavia. The applicants had sought a suspension of the operation of the Regulation in so far as it included them in an annexed "black list." The Court reiterated its *Bosphorus* judgment[54] in arguing that "any measure imposing sanctions has, by definition, consequences which affect the right to property and the freedom to pursue a trade or business, thereby causing harm to persons who are in no way responsible for the situation which led to the adoption of the sanctions."

In assessing the proportionality of the measures taken, the ECJ has considered that the importance of the general interests of the international community embodied in Security Council resolutions – the maintenance of international peace and the protection of human rights – justified their negative consequences, even of a substantial nature.[55] Accordingly, those consequences could not be regarded as manifestly disproportionate in relation to the aims pursued.

The conclusions of the ECJ, however, reflected a very different balancing act of public and private interests from that reached by the Irish High Court in the above-mentioned *Bosphorus* case. The Irish Court, which had challenged the impounding by the Irish Government of an aircraft registered in Turkey and leased by a wholly-owned Turkish company from Yugoslav Airlines, had declared: "it is clear that the [EC regulations implementing Security Council sanctions against Yugoslavia] are not intended to punish or penalize peoples or countries who have not in any way caused or contributed to these tragic events."[56]

The *Bosphorus* verdict of the ECJ has now been challenged in the EctHR.[57] The applicant has complained under Article 1 of Protocol No. 1 ECHR that the impounding of the leased aircraft in Ireland was a disproportionate interference with the peaceful enjoyment of his possessions, arguing that Ireland's responsibility under the Convention arose from the manner in which it chose to implement the relevant EC regulation and ruling by the ECJ in that case. The Government has argued, however, that the aim of the interference with the applicant's property rights was undeniably a fundamentally important public interest, which included prevention of the breach of the right to life and freedom from genocide and torture. Given that public interest, the test was therefore whether the interference was preferable or advisable, as opposed to whether it was necessary in a democratic society. It also submitted that the State was accorded a broad margin of appreciation. It concluded that the balance struck between the conflicting interests was therefore consistent with the requirements of Article 1 of Protocol No. 1.

54 See Case C-84/95, *Bosphorus Hava Yollari Turizm ve Ticaret AS v. Minister for Transport, Energy and Communications, Ireland and others*, 30 July 1996, [1996] ECR I-3953.

55 See Opinion of Advocate General F.V. Jacobs, delivered on 30 April 1996, in the case of *Bosphorus Hava*, *ibid.*, paras. 64-69. See also *Ebony Maritime*, *supra*, note 35, paras. 33 and 44.

56 *Bosphorus Hava Yollari Turizm ve Ticaret AS v. Minister for Transport, Energy and Communications, Ireland and the Attorney General*, Irish High Court, No. 352JR, 2 *ILRM* (1994) at 551 (21 June 1994).

57 See *Bosphorus Hava Yollari Turizm ve Ticaret AS v. Ireland (Decision as to Admissibility)*, ECtHR (Fourth Section), Application No. 45036/98 (13 Sep. 2001).

It is interesting to note, in the light of the *Milosevic* judgment, that in the Court's ruling on admissibility in relation to exhaustion of local remedies, the Court found that since the detention of the aircraft was immune from challenge on constitutional grounds, being an act done in pursuance of an EC obligation entrenched in the Irish Constitution, domestic remedies offered no real prospects of success. In consequence, the Court concluded that the complaint, having raised complex and serious issues under article 1 of Protocol No. 1 requiring determination on the merits, could not be dismissed as manifestly ill-founded.

In matters of compensation, however, the buck has been passed to the Security Council, where of course no such remedy is available. In the case of *Dorsch Consult*,[58] the European Court of First Instance found that the alleged damage suffered due to non-payment by Iraq for the construction of an expressway in retaliation to the imposition of economic sanctions, could not, in the final analysis, be attributed to the EC regulation implementing the United Nations sanctions but to Security Council Resolution 661 (1990) imposing sanctions on Iraq. This ruling effectively leaves individuals without a remedy, since few national laws envisage such compensation, nor is this contemplated at the international level (as has been seen, the United Nations Compensation Commission has excluded the liability of Iraq for damage incurred as a result of the economic embargo).

Of course, the cases referred to above involved individuals affected by sanctions as third parties, not the targeted entities themselves. In the case of targeted individuals, two types of cases have arisen. The first has to do with individuals surrendered to the ICTY or ICTR, which has raised the question of conflict between international obligations and the due process afforded by domestic criminal law. This is seen below. The second has to do with the targeting of individuals suspected of terrorist activities and placed on the Security Council Sanctions Committee's lists. Undoubtedly, the conflict between fundamental rights and arbitrary targeting of sanctions following on measures such as the freezing of assets undertaken in response to alleged involvement of the individual in international terrorism will continue to raise questions in European Union and other United Nations Member States. But the fact that the removal of the name of an individual alleged to be involved in terrorism from a list results from a political process with the ultimate decision being made by the Security Council, means that judicial challenges are unlikely to be successful.

In the case of *Aden and others v. Council and Commission* before the European Court of First Instance,[59] the three Swedish nationals whose assets had been frozen in application of Resolution 1333 and subsequent EC Regulations, argued, *inter alia*, that their right to a fair hearing had been violated, since they had no possibility of domestic judicial review and hence of verification of the evidence, and that the penal sanction imposed was not the legal consequence of a precise charge filed against them. In its decision of 7 May 2002, however, the Court of First Instance refused to grant the requested provisional

58 Case T-184/95, *Dorsch Consult Ingenieurgesellschaft mbH v. Council of the European Union and Commission of the European Communities*, 28 April 1998, [1998] ECR II-667.

59 Case T-306/01 R, *Abdirisak Aden and others v. Council of the European Union and Commission of the European Communities,* Order of the President of the Court of First Instance, 7 May 2002, [2002] ECR II-239.

measures, i.e. the suspension of the European Union Regulations implementing the Security Council's resolution, on the grounds that there was no risk of grave and irreparable damages since the claimants had a minimum subsistence; the Court's reference, *inter alia*, to Articles 25 and 103 of the Charter, makes it improbable that an eventual decision on the merits would challenge the decisions of the Sanctions Committee.[60]

An action against the Council of the European Union and the Commission of the European Community has also been brought before the Court of First Instance on 6 February 2003 by Jose Maria Sison.[61] The applicant, who has been granted asylum in the Netherlands, seeks the annulment of Council Regulations and Decisions pursuant to which he has been black-listed, as a past member of the Philippini communist party. His complaint relates, *inter alia*, to a violation of the obligation to state reasons, of the principle of sound administration, of the principle of proportionality and the freedom of circulation of capital. The applicant also invokes the violation of several general principles of Community Law, such as the principles enshrined in Articles 6, 7, 10 and 11 of the European Convention on Human Rights and Article 1 of the First Protocol thereto. Finally, the illegality of Regulation 2580/2001 is invoked on the basis that Articles 60, 301 and 308 of the EC Treaty do not provide a sufficient legal basis, nor explicitly authorise the Council to issue such a Regulation.

IV. Domestic Implementation of the Provisions Relating to Cooperation with the International Criminal Tribunals

The establishment of the two International Criminal Tribunals has, understandably, raised constitutional problems in domestic law, affecting as they do, individual liberties and the organisation of justice. The International Criminal Tribunals for the Former Yugoslavia and Rwanda have jurisdiction directly over individuals who commit crimes falling within their competence; in this sense, the Statutes do not require domestic law in order to apply directly to such persons. As the Trial Chamber of the ICTR put it: "By establishing the two International Criminal Tribunals for the former Yugoslavia and Rwanda ... the Security Council explicitly extended international legal obligations and criminal responsibilities directly to individuals for violations of international humanitarian law ... ."[62] This has been justified in view, notably, of the "seriousness, the magnitude and the gravity of the crimes committed during the conflict." The rules of the Tribunals also apply directly to individuals other than the accused – for example, the rules relating to the summoning of witnesses or the production of evidence.[63]

60 See Erika de Wet and André Nollkaemper, "Review of Security Council Decisions by National Courts", 45 *GYBIL* (2002) 166-202, at pp. 169 and 177-68.

61 See Case T-47/03 R, *Jose Maria Sison v. Council of the European Union and Commission of the European Community,* Interlocutory Proceedings, Order of the President of the Court of First Instance, 15 May 2003, at http://www.curia.eu.int/en/content/aide/index.htm

62 ICTR, *Prosecutor v. Joseph Kanyabashi*, Decision on the motion challenging the jurisdiction of the Tribunal, Case No. ICTR-96-15-T, 18 June 1997, para. 35.

63 See ICTY, *The Prosecutor v. Tihomir Blaskic*, Case no. IT-95-14-AR 108bis, Appeals Chamber, Judgement of 29 October 1997 on the Request of the Republic of Croatia for Review of the

At the same time, however, United Nations Security Council Resolutions 827 and 955 establishing the two Tribunals impose specific obligations on Member States in the field of cooperation and judicial assistance. States have the obligation to take any measures necessary under their domestic law to comply with requests for assistance or orders issued by the Trial Chambers,[64] such as identification and location of persons, the taking of testimony, the production of evidence, the arrest or detention of persons and their surrender or transfer to the International Tribunals, but also the recognition of judgements passed by the Tribunals, and if necessary cooperation, in their execution. As with other Security Council decisions, these obligations have been considered non-self-executing, requiring implementing legislation for their execution by domestic organs. Some questions have arisen as to the direct effect of the Tribunals' orders within the domestic legal orders, since they are directly applicable to individuals under international law (see the case of Germany). But the Order that was issued by the Tribunal on 24 May 1999, calling for the freezing of the assets of Milosevic and associated persons, was implemented in European Union States by means of an EC Regulation.

Since they affect the rights of individuals under criminal law, the implementation of obligations relating to the Tribunal have also required a different domestic legal basis to that for the implementation of economic sanctions.[65] However, the International Criminal Tribunals being innovatory, pre-existing provisions on cooperation with such bodies was non-existent, prior legislation on judicial cooperation being conceived of as regulating relations between States.

Falling within the prerogatives of the legislature, and considered to require full Parliamentary debate, the relevant provisions in Security Council resolutions and the Statute of the Tribunals have therefore been implemented on the basis of *ad hoc* laws on recognition of the binding force of the decisions of the Tribunal and on judicial cooperation, adopted in many cases in accordance with the procedure laid down for the adoption of urgent legislative acts (see for example, the *ad hoc* laws adopted by France, Belgium, Germany and Switzerland). The United Kingdom has, exceptionally, relied on the United Nations Act for implementation of its obligations of cooperation with the Tribunals (as well as, in the Lockerbie case, for the provision for a Scottish court to sit in the Netherlands in accordance with Resolution 1198 (1998)), but this has not gone without challenge; it has been argued that this Act was intended to act as a legal basis for the implementation of economic sanctions, not extradition to an innovatory international criminal tribunal (see UK national study).

Decision of Trial Chamber II of 18 July 1997, in which the Appeals Chamber concluded: "The spirit and purpose of the Statute, as well as the aforementioned provisions, confer on the International Tribunal an incidental or ancillary jurisdiction over individuals other than those whom the International Tribunal may prosecute and try. These are individuals who may be of assistance in the task of dispensing criminal justice entrusted to the International Tribunal" (para. 48).

64 See SCR 827 (1993), Article 4, and 955 (1994), Article 2 and Articles 29 and 28 of the Statutes of the ICTY and ICTR, respectively.

65 See S. Furuya, *supra*, note 20, pp. 111-145.

Quite apart from the question of the domestic legal basis of cooperation by States with the Tribunals, numerous other issues arise from the interface between International Tribunals and domestic judicial authorities.

Domestic authorities must establish procedures for dealing with requests emanating from either of the Tribunals and render executory their arrest warrants. Domestic implementing legislation establish a general duty on the judiciary to cooperate with the International Criminal Tribunals and both the decision and procedure for handing over the accused has been considered a matter for the judicial authorities. Despite the primacy of the International Tribunals in respect of national jurisdictions as provided for in the Statutes, where it comes to the surrender of individuals, domestic courts have in some cases asserted their primacy in such matters as the qualification of the facts, including the determination of whether the alleged crimes fall into the jurisdiction of the International Tribunals, or the evaluation of the evidence, or have relied on domestic definitions of the crimes falling within the competence of the Tribunals. This could not however affect the Tribunals' inherent powers to determine their own jurisdiction.

Cooperation with the Tribunals has also raised questions of conflict between international law and domestic criminal law and extradition practice. The prohibition of extradition of nationals found in some national constitutions has come up against the rules of procedure of the two Tribunals which require States to deliver their nationals. States have avoided constitutional amendments by making a distinction between extradition – a matter for inter-State relations – and surrender to international organs, or did not consider that they would be faced with such a problem, given the localised jurisdiction of the Tribunals. In Germany, it is only following on ratification of the Statute of the International Criminal Court that a constitutional amendment in this respect has been envisaged. In Poland, the 1997 Criminal Procedure Code was amended in order to introduce such a distinction, although this has not obviated controversy over the issue. In Finland, legislation covering the extradition of Finnish citizens has had to resort to the procedure for constitutional amendments. A conflict has also arisen in Switzerland between the provisions of the Statutes of the International Criminal Tribunals and the Federal Constitution which prohibits the extradition of Swiss nationals against their will.

In the United States, controversy arose over whether extradition could proceed in the absence of a treaty in the case of Rwandan Elizaphan Ntakirutimana, the first person in that country to be surrendered to the ICTR, where he had been indicted on several counts, including genocide. The constitutionality of congressional legislation enacted in February 1996 which implemented two executive agreements concluded with the ICTY and ICTR for the purpose of arresting and surrendering to these Tribunals indicted fugitives found in the US,[66] was questioned. A Federal District Court in Texas had ruled on December 17, 1997,[67] that this Congressional legislation was unconstitutional as

66 In particular, National Defense Authorization Act, Public Law No. 104-106, Section 1342, 110 Stat. 486 (1996), implementing the United States' obligations under Security Council Resolution 955. See Robert Kushen and Kenneth J. Harris, "Surrender of Fugitives by the United States to the War Crimes Tribunals for Yugoslavia and Rwanda", 90 *AJIL* (1996) 510-518.

67 *In the Matter of Surrender of Elizaphan Ntakirutimana*, US District Court, Southern District of Texas, No. L-96-5 (Dec. 17, 1997).

extradition from the US could only be accomplished under the terms of a valid treaty of extradition, ignoring the fact that this agreement had been made pursuant to a Security Council decision, that is pursuant to a treaty obligation. On January 24, 2000, however, the United States Supreme Court refused a request to review a subsequent United States Circuit Court's ruling that ordered the surrender.

Constitutional issues have also arisen over the rights of the defence, fair trial and habeas corpus. The question is whether domestic courts can review the compatibility of the Tribunals with the international human rights conventions to ensure due process for surrendered individuals. Where challenges have been brought before domestic courts, these have presumed the conformity of the procedures of the respective Tribunal with minimum human rights standards. In Switzerland, for example, this question was raised in a decision concerning the surrender of a Rwandan national to the International Tribunal in Arusha, but the Supreme Court considered that conformity of procedures of the Tribunal with the minimum standards of the ECHR and the ICCPR could not be examined and had to be presumed. Such decisions have been facilitated by the decision of the ECtHR in *Nalitelic v. Croatia*, in which it rejected as manifestly unfounded an argument that the surrender of an accused person to the International Criminal Tribunal for the Former Yugoslavia would violate the right to a fair trial under Article 6(1) of the European Convention.

Nevertheless, States have requested certain assurances from the Tribunals before surrendering individuals. Switzerland will thus only surrender a Swiss national if it is guaranteed that he/she will be sent back to Switzerland at the end of the procedure. The 1996 Belgium Law on judicial cooperation with the International Tribunals has been interpreted as obligating the Belgium government to seek assurances from the Tribunals that persons transferred by the Belgian Government would not, if convicted, serve imprisonment in a country which is not a party to the European Convention on Human Rights.

Finally, there is the matter of enforcement of the judgements pronounced by the Tribunals and the victim's right to claim for reparation. To give the example of Switzerland, this State will only accept imprisonment on its territory of convicted persons who are either nationals or residents of Switzerland and the international sentence can only be enforced to the extent admitted by Swiss law.

V. Special Problems

(1) Implementation of Resolutions on combatting the Financing of Terrorism

The measures laid down by Security Council Resolution 1373 (2001) may be seen as preventive measures, and are treated as administrative measures in some countries, but they also have penal connotations, since they impose not only a duty to freeze all funds and other financial assets of persons who commit or attempt to commit terrorists acts or support such activities, as well as prohibit funds from being made available for the benefit of such persons, but also provide for the criminalisation of certain acts in the domestic laws of States. At the same time, Resolution 1373 does not provide a definition of terrorist acts and leaves it to implementing States to designate the entities that are targeted by the sanctions.

Although implementation of Resolution 1373 has been included in the scope of this study, and the national studies do make reference to their domestic legislation relating to counter-terrorism, it is premature to offer firm conclusions. Moreover, the national studies reveal the difficulties of disentangling the various strands of the measures to combat terrorism adopted in their domestic legal systems: those in implementation of Resolution 1373 (2001), measures taken more specifically against Al-Qaida and the Taliban under Resolutions 1267(1999), 1333 (2000), and 1390 (2002), obligations undertaken under treaties within the framework of a United Nations international strategy against terrorism, or of regional organisations, such as the web of European Union Common Positions and EC Regulations on the combatting of terrorism, the 1999 OAU Convention on the Prevention and combatting of Terrorism, or the Declaration on combatting Terrorism and Action Plan adopted at the November 2001 regional meeting of Heads of States of Central, Eastern and South-Eastern Europe. States have also adopted measures independently, either in the immediate aftermath of the terrorist attacks of September 11, 2001 or to combat particular domestic forms of terrorism.

Not all countries have found it necessary to adopt new legislation, basing themselves on pre-existing anti-terrorist provisions in their criminal code considered to cover many of the penal sanctions called for by the Security Council. Even where *ad hoc* legislation has been adopted after the passage of Security Council Resolution 1373, the range of measures relate more to the general international fight against terrorism and the links with transnational organized crime, reflecting the broad terms of paragraph 4 of the Resolution. They cover a wide range of legislative measures, including in the fields of information, money-laundering, drug-trafficking, illegal migration, and nuclear and chemical/biological proliferation.

For European Union Member States, implementation has been the result of co-ordination over a range of measures. Security Council Resolution 1373 was implemented within the European Union on the basis of a Council Common Position 2001/931/CFSP of 27 December 2001 on the application of specific measures to combat terrorism and EC Regulation 2580 (2001) on specific restrictive measures directed against certain persons and entities with a view to combatting terrorism, adopted on the same day. Both of these have been subsequently updated or amended. The European Union has adopted its own definition of the term "terrorist act" (thus filling the vacuum left by Resolution 1373 (2001)), drawn up its own lists of "persons, groups and entities involved in terrorist acts" targeted by its measures, which may include lists of names designated by the Security Council and Sanctions Committee, and provided its own measures calling for the freezing of funds and economic resources belonging to such persons, groups and entities. The lists of targeted persons, groups and entities to be communicated to the banks and financial authorities concerned have been regularly updated. The measures relating to the freezing of funds in Security Council Resolution 1390 (2002) to be taken with respect to Usama bin Laden, the Al-Qaida network and the Taliban and the updated list referred to created pursuant to Resolutions 1267 (1999) and 1333 (2000) was implemented by EC Regulation 2002/881/EC based on Common Position 2002/402/CFSP, both adopted on 27 May 2002.

Controversy has also arisen over the competence of the European Union in relation to targeted sanctions directed against named individuals, rather than measures directed against third States and hence over whether Articles 301 and 60 of the EC Treaty are a sufficient legal basis in that respect (the earlier EC Regulation concerning Milosevic and associated persons had been considered less questionable because of its clear connection with the Federal Republic of Yugoslavia). As a result, Article 308 of the EC Treaty has been used as an additional legal basis for the Community's competence; this establishes an exceptional basis for action by the Council acting on a proposal from the Commission in order to attain the objectives of the Community. This has meant that some European Union Member States have had to adapt their national legislation to include the new legal basis for EC Regulations on the combatting of terrorism.

As has been seen, the measures adopted within the Community in implementation of Security Council resolutions combatting terrorism have been challenged in the Court of First Instance in the case of *Aden* and *Jose Maria Sison.*[68] Under pressure from public opinion, Governments such as Sweden and Finland have also sought to ensure that sufficient safeguards for individual legal rights are provided for at the European Union level.

The national studies underline some of the problems and controversies which have arisen relating, for example, to the far-reaching extension of powers of intelligence agencies and police in data gathering which threaten the right to privacy, and many of the due process rights. For example, the South African 2002 Anti-Terrorism Bill which makes provision for the seizure and forfeiture of terrorist property even in the absence of criminal proceedings against an accused has been considered highly controversial. In Sweden a first initiative for expedient implementation of the Council provisions on terrorism was turned down by the Drafts Legislation Advisory Committee as unsatisfactory from a constitutional point of view.

The United States is again a case apart, since the measures it has adopted in combatting terrorism have not been the direct result of implementation of Security Council resolutions, but were adopted well before. Thus the Executive Orders directed against the Taliban, Usama Bin Laden and Al-Quaida have been issued under the IEEPA declaring a national emergency, though mention is made on occasion of Security Council resolutions. One could say in regard to Security Council action against terrorism, that the situation has not been one of domestic implementation of Security Council sanctions, but of Security Council implementation of the domestic sanctions of one of its Permanent Members.

A detailed picture of the way in which Member States have implemented Resolution 1373 may be found in their reports to the Counter-Terrorism Committee (CTC).[69] Their reports have not been included in this study, with the exception of that of Japan which serves as an illustration of the extent of the web of measures – executive, legislative, judicial – in which individuals may now find themselves entrapped with no possibility of recourse.

68 See *supra,* notes 59 and 61.

69 See http://www.un.org/Docs/sc/committees/1373/submitted_reports.html

(2) *The Case of Neutral and Non-Member States*

The chapter on Switzerland addresses important issues that had originated as far back as the League of Nations concerning the compatibility between a status of permanent neutrality and membership in universal organisations, particularly in situations in which non-military sanctions are nevertheless applied against the background of an armed conflict, as well as the effects on third States of Charter obligations. These issues may now appear moot in the light of Switzerland's admission into the United Nations on 10 September 2002 as the 190th Member State. Nevertheless, Switzerland's one-time implementation of sanctions as a *non-Member State* and its future implementation as a *permanently neutral* Member State alongside Austria, remains of great relevance; moreover, the text of Switzerland's application to join the United Nations includes a declaration of neutrality.

It will be recalled that a policy of "differential" or "qualified neutrality" was attempted by Switzerland in an effort to reconcile its obligations as a permanently neutral State with its membership in the League of Nations. The London Declaration of the League Council of February 1920 had dispensed it from participation in military sanctions whilst maintaining its obligation to participate in economic and financial sanctions under Article 16(1) of the Covenant, on the basis that a neutral's duty of impartiality applied only to military matters. This policy however foundered on the rocks of the Italo-Ethiopian conflict. While Switzerland complied with certain proposals of the League by imposing, *inter alia*, a prohibition on the export of materials to Italy, it declared itself unable to apply the prohibition on Italian imports and confined itself to limiting trade to the "courant normal", the level reached in 1934. As for the embargo on weapons, ammunition and war supplies, it relied exclusively on its status of permanent neutrality by extending the embargo to both parties to the conflict. The failure of the policy of "differential" neutrality, explains the Swiss position *vis-à-vis* the United Nations in the period before 1990.

In its practice, the Security Council did not hesitate in the past to call on non-Member States in sanctions implementation (relying on Article 2(6) of the Charter). Such one-time non-Member States as Germany and Switzerland had taken the position that they had no obligations as third parties. Both nevertheless did adopt a certain number of measures to restrict trade in pursuance of Security Council resolutions. This was the case for the Federal Republic of Germany in the case of Southern Rhodesia. As will be seen, this has also been the case for Switzerland after 1990, in the cases of Iraq, Yugoslavia and Haiti.

Although Switzerland would have been on firm ground in basing its position solely on its status as a non-Member, the official Swiss statement in the case of Southern Rhodesia stressed the position of Switzerland as a permanently neutral State. It will be noted that Austria, as a United Nations member and permanently neutral State, had, while reserving its position of principle, agreed to implement Security Council resolutions in that affair. Switzerland however had decided that for reasons likewise of principle it could not submit to the mandatory sanctions although it would see to it that Rhodesian trade would remain at the level of the courant normal.[70]

70 See for the position of neutral States in regard to Southern Rhodesia, *Collective Responses to Illegal Acts*, *supra*, note 1, pp. 514-526.

Switzerland, however, reconceptualised its status of permanent neutrality after the end of the cold war, considering that this was compatible with participation in sanctions adopted under Chapter VII of the Charter. This confirmed the view that while the United Nations could not purport to bind non-Member States, a permanently neutral non-Member State could no longer adopt a position of absolute impartiality by ignoring *authorised* collective action when taken in the interests of international peace and security or the enforcement of universal human rights. The Federal Supreme Court of Switzerland in a case concerning the sales of weapons to Croatia in violation of the United Nations embargo but not of Swiss law, held that even though the Council's resolutions were not binding on Switzerland, violation of these resolutions would be in opposition with universal *ordre public*; the contract was therefore considered null and void.

Thus, with some exceptions, the sanctions adopted by Switzerland against, for example, Iraq, Haiti or the Former Yugoslavia, were generally faithful to the provisions in Security Council resolutions, although they were adopted on an autonomous and domestic legal basis. Domestic implementation measures were taken immediately or shortly after the imposition of international sanctions.

Initially, Switzerland relied on pre-existing legislation for application of an arms embargo on a case-by-case basis, such as the Federal law on military materiél, or for the control of dual use goods, or a federal law granting a general authorisation clause to the Federal Council "if essential economic interests of Switzerland" were at stake and providing for a form of licensing. Where therefore sanctions went beyond an embargo on weapons, the Federal Council enacted specific executive orders; this power to enact sanctions without passing through lengthy parliamentary procedure is now explicitly recognised in the new constitution of Switzerland which entered into force in January 2000. It is interesting to note that even when it was a non-Member State, Switzerland co-operated with the respective Sanctions Committees in procedures set down for the handling of humanitarian goods.

For various reasons, including the fact that certain provisions in Federal executive orders regarding the imposition of penal sanctions did not meet constitutional requirements relating to individual rights, general enabling legislation on the implementation of international sanctions was passed by the Swiss Parliament on 22 March 2002 even before Switzerland became a Member of the United Nations. It is intended to serve as a legal basis for implementation of non-military sanctions measures adopted internationally.

Swedish neutrality is, of course, a very different case, since it constitutes a political choice. Sweden's neutrality included a peacetime policy element of international activism. It was not therefore in issue in the Rhodesian crisis where United Nations action against Southern Rhodesia fell in line with Sweden's foreign policy orientation towards decolonisation in Africa. Moreover, Sweden went beyond Council resolutions in adopting sanctions against South Africa, since this was also in line with the linkage between human rights and maintenance of international peace and security which has been a basic tenet of Swedish foreign security policy. In more recent cases, however, there has not been a marked national Swedish policy interest and implementation has become more of a technical matter, following closely the conditions laid down in the relevant Security Council resolutions.

(3) *States Requiring Assistance under Article 50 of the Charter*

States which suffer economic hardship as a result of sanctions implementation may either be exempt from such implementation by a discretionary decision of the Council under Article 48(1) of the Charter (never officially resorted to) or have a right to consult the Council under Article 50 of the Charter, although there is no guarantee of the actual provision of financial or technical assistance (Article 49, however, does refer to the mutual assistance that members shall afford each other in carrying out the measures adopted by the Council).

Zambia, Malawi, Botswana and Lesotho, who either bordered on or were neighbours of Southern Rhodesia or enclaves of South Africa, had invoked Article 50, raising the special economic problems they had had to face (for a detailed study see the South African study).[71] Twenty-three countries invoked Article 50 after the Security Council adopted resolution 661 imposing sanctions against Iraq and Kuwait. Similar problems arose in the case of the sanctions against Yugoslavia where seven riparian States of the Danube[72] and Uganda invoked Article 50.

The national study on Jordan, a country placed in a very difficult situation because of total dependence on oil from Iraq, in addition to loss of trade, delays and redirection of its ships arising from their interception at sea, evokes this problem and underlines the unsatisfactory nature of the solutions proposed and the need to define the scope of Article 50.

71 Also, *ibid.*, pp. 497-500.

72 Albania, Bulgaria, Hungary, Macedonia (former Yugoslav Republic), Romania, Slovakia and Ukraine.

Select Bibliography

I. Case-Law

(1) International Courts

PCIJ, *Exchange of Greek and Turkish Populations* (1925), Ser. B, No. 10.

PCIJ, *Jurisdiction of the Courts of Danzig* (1928), Ser. B, No.15.

PCIJ, *Free Zones of Upper Savoy and the District of Gex* (1930), Ser. A, No. 24.

PCIJ, *Greco-Bulgarian Communities Case* (1930), Ser. B., No. 17.

PCIJ, *Treatment of Polish Nationals and other Persons of Polish Origins or Speech in the Territory of Danzig* (1932), Ser. A/B, No. 44.

ICJ, *Legal Consequences for States of the Continued Presence of South Africa in Namibia (South West Africa) Notwithstanding Security Council Resolution 276 (1970),* Advisory Opinion of 21 June 1971, ICJ Reports 1971.

ICJ, *Applicability of the Obligation to Arbitrate under Section 21 of the United Nations Headquarters Agreement of 26 June 1947*, Advisory Opinion of 26 April 1988, ICJ Reports 1988.

ICTY, *The* Prosecutor *v. Tihomir Blaskic*, Case no. IT-95-14-AR 108bis, Appeals Chamber, Judgment of 29 October 1997 on the Request of the Republic of Croatia for Review of the Decision of Trial Chamber II of 18 July 1997.

ICTY, *The Prosecutor v. Dusko Tadic a/k/a/ "Dule",* Case No. IT-94-1, Appeals Chamber, Decision of 2 October 1995 on the Defence Motion for Interlocutory Appeal on Jurisdiction.

ICTR, *The Prosecutor v. Joseph Kanyabashi*, Case No. ICTR-96-15-T, Decision of 18 June 1997 on the motion challenging the jurisdiction of the Tribunal.

(2) European Courts

ECtHR, *Bosphorus Hava Yollari Turizm ve Ticaret AS v. Ireland (Decision as to Admissibility), ECtHR (Fourth Section), Application No. 45036/98, 13 Sep. 2001.*

ECtHR, *Nalitelic v. Croatia,* Application No. 51891/99 (Decision as to Admissibility), 4 May 2000.

EctHR, *Slobodan Milosevic v. the Netherlands,* Application No. 77631/01 (Judgment), 19 Mar. 2002.

ECJ, Case C-177/95, *Ebony Maritime SA and Loten Navigation Co. Ltd. v. Prefetto della Provincia di Brindisi and Others,* 27 February 1997, [1997] ECR I-1114.

ECJ, Case C-317/00 P(R) *"Invest" Import und Export GmbH and Invest Commerce SARL v. Commission*, 13 November 2000, [2000] ECR I-9541.

ECJ, Case C-84/95, *Bosphorus Hava Yollari Turizm ve Ticaret AS v. Minister for Transport, Energy and Communications, Ireland and others,* 30 July 1996, [1996] ECR I-3953.

ECJ, Case T-184/95 R, Dorsch Consult Ingenieurgesellschaft mbH v. Council of the European Union and Commission of the European Communities, 28 April 1998, [1998] ECR II-667.

ECJ, Case T-306/01 R, *Abdirisak Aden and others v. Council of the European Union and Commission of the European Communities,* Order of thc President of the Court of First Instance, 7 May 2002, [2002] ECR II-239.

ECJ, Case T-47/03 R, *Jose Maria Sison v. Council of the European Union and Commission of the European Community,* Interlocutory Proceedings, Order of the President of the Court of First Instance, 15 May 2003 (at http://www.curia.eu.int/en/content/aide/index.htm).

(3) National Courts

Dutch Court, *Slobodan Milosevic v. The State of The Netherlands* (Judgment in interlocutory injunction), 31 August 2001, President of the Hague Distr. Ct, Kort Geding 2001/258.

Irish High Court, No. 352JR, *Bosphorus Hava Yollari Turizm ve Ticaret AS v. Minister for Transport, Energy and Communications, Ireland and the Attorney General,* 21 June 1994, 2 *ILRM* (1994) 551.

UK High Court of Justice, Queen's Bench Division (Divisional Court), *The Campaign for Nuclear Disarmament and the Prime Minister of the United Kingdom et al.*, [2002] *England and Wales High Court Decisions* 2759 QB.

US Supreme Court, *Foster v. Neilson*, (1829) 27 U.S. (2 Pet.) 253 at 314).

US, California Court of Appeal, *Sei Fujii v. State of California,* 19 *ILR* (1952) 312.

US Court of Appeals for the District of Columbia, *Diggs v. Shultz*, 31 October 1972, 11 *ILM* (1972) 1252-58.

US District Court for the District of Columbia, *Diggs v. Dent*, May 1975, 14 *ILM* (1975) 797ff.

US District Court for the Northern District of Illinois, 478 F. Supp. 29, *United States v. Steinberg, 3 Oct. 1979, in M. Lloyd Nash (ed.), United States Department of State, Digest of United States Practice in International Law* (Washington Publisher, 1979), pp. 436-437.

US District Court for the Southern District of New York, *United States v. Palestine Liberation Organisation et al,* Decision of 29 June 1988, 27 *ILM* (1988) 1055-1088.

US District Court for the Southern District of Texas, No. L-96-5, *In the Matter of Surrender of Elizaphan Ntakirutimana*, Decision of 17 December 1997.

II. Books and Contributions to Collective Works

Ben Achour, Rafâa et Laghmani, Slim (dirs.), *Droit international et droits internes, développements récents* (Paris, Pedone, 1998).

Bethlehem, Daniel (ed.), *The Kuwait Crisis: Sanctions and their Economic Consequences*, Cambridge International Documents Series, Part II (Cambridge, Grotius Publications, 1991).

Bothe, Michael and Vinuesa, Raul E. (eds), *International Law and Municipal Law*, German-Argentinian Constitutional Law Colloquium (Berlin, Duncker & Humblot, 1982).

Cortright, David and López, George A., *The Sanctions Decade. Assessing UN Strategies in the 1990's* (International Peace Academy, 2000).

Eisemann, Pierre-Michel (ed.), *L'intégration du droit international et communautaire dans l'ordre juridique national. Etude de la pratique en Europe* (The Hague/London/Boston, Kluwer, 1996).

Erades, Lambertus (ed. by M. Fitzmaurice and C. Flinterman), *Interactions between International and Municipal Law - a comparative case law study* (The Hague, TMC Asser Instituut, 1993).

Gowlland-Debbas, Vera, *Collective Responses to Illegal Acts in International Law. United Nations Action in the Question of Southern Rhodesia* (Dordrecht/Boston/London, Martinus Nijhoff Publishers, 1990).

Gowlland-Debbas, Vera (ed), *United Nations Sanctions and International Law* (The Hague/London/Boston, Kluwer Law International, 2001).

Haguenau, Catherine, *L'application effective du droit communautaire en droit interne. Analyse comparative des problèmes rencontrés en droit français, anglais et allemand* (Bruxelles, Bruylant, 1995).

Highley, A. E., *The First Sanctions Experiment. A Study of League Procedures* (Geneva, Geneva Research Centre, 1938).

Kuyper, Peter J., *The Implementation of International Sanctions: the Netherlands and Rhodesia* (Alphen aan de Rijn, Sijthoff and Noordhoff, 1978).

Lardy, Pierre, *La force obligatoire du droit international en droit interne* (Paris, LGDJ, 1966).

Lauterpacht, Elihu and Collier, John G. (eds), *Individual Rights and the State in Foreign Affairs. An International Compendium* (New York, Praeger Publishers, 1977).

Lauterpacht, Elihu, "Implementation of Decisions of International Organisations through National Courts", in S. Scwhebel (ed), *The Effectiveness of International Decisions: Papers of A Conference of the American Society of International Law and the Proceedings of the Conference* (Leyden, Sijthoff; Dobbs Ferry, NY, Oceana Publications, 1971).

Leary, Virginia, *International Labour Conventions and National Law* (The Hague, Martinus Nijhoff, 1982).

Moussé, Jean, *Le contentieux des organisations internationales et de l'Union européenne* (Bruxelles, Bruylant, 1997).

Schreuer, Christoph, *Decisions of International Institutions Before Domestic Courts* (London, Oceana Publications, 1981).

Targeted Financial Sanctions – A Manual for Design and Implementation: Contributions from the Interlaken Process, The Swiss Confederation in cooperation with the United Nations Secretariat and the Watson Institute for International Studies, Brown University (at http://www.smartsanctions.ch).

Tavernier, Paul, *Recherches sur l'application dans le temps des actes et des règles en droit international public. Problèmes de droit intertemporel ou de droit transitoire* (Paris, LGDJ, 1970).

Tehindrazanarivelo, Djacoba Liva, *Les Effets secondaires des sanctions non militaires des Nations Unies. Aspects juridiques et influence sur le nouveau concept de sanction de l'ONU* (Doctoral Thesis, nº 662, The Graduate Institute of International Studies, Geneva, 2003)

Virally, Michel, "Sur un pont aux ânes: les rapports entre droit international et droits internes", in Michel Virally, *Le droit international en devenir* (Paris, Presses Universitaires de France/Graduate Institute of International Studies, 1990), pp. 103-117.

III. Articles

Angelet, Nicolas, "La mise en œuvre des mesures économiques des Nations Unies dans la Communauté européenne", XXVI *RBDI* (1993) 500-533.

Benvenisti, Eyal, "Judicial Misgivings Regarding the Application of International Law: An Analysis of Attitudes of National Courts", 4 *EJIL* (1993) 159-183.

Bohr, Sebastian, "Sanctions by the United Nations Security Council and the European Community", 4 *EJIL* (1993) 256-268.

Burgenthal, Thomas, "Self-Executing and Non-Self-Executing Treaties in National and International Law", 235 *RCADI* (1992-IV) 307-397.

Canor, Iris, "Can Two Walk Together, Except they be Agreed? – The Relationship between International Law and European Law: The Incorporation of United Nations Sanctions against Yugoslavia into European Community Law through the Perspective of the European Court of Justice", 35 *Common Market Law Review* (1998) 137-187.

Burci, Gian Luca, "The Indirect Effects of United Nations Sanctions on Third States: the Role of Article 50 of the UN Charter", 2 *AfYIL* (1994) 157-171.

Conlon, Paul, "Lessons from Iraq: The Functions of the Iraq Sanctions Committee as a Source of Sanctions Implementation Authority and Practice", 35 *VJIL* (1995) 633-668.

De Wet, Erika and Strydom, Hennie, "Implementing International Humanitarian Law: Developments in South Africa and other Jurisdictions with special reference to International War Crimes Tribunals", 25 *SAYIL* (2000) 42-68.

De Wet, Erika and Nollkaemper, André, "Review of Security Council Decisions by National Courts", 45 *GYBIL* (2002) 166-202.

Dhommeaux, Jean, "Monismes et dualismes en droit international des droits de l'homme", *AFDI* (1995) 447-469.

Falk, Richard, "Implementing International Law - the Role of Domestic Courts: Some Reflections on the United States Experience", 3 *Leiden Journal of International Law* (1990) (Special Issue) 67-76.

Fitzmaurice, Gerald, "The General Principles of International Law, Considered from the Standpoint of the Rule of Law", 92 *RCADI* (1957-II) 1-223.

Furuya, Shuichi, "Legal Effect of Rules of the International Criminal Tribunals and Courts upon Individuals", XLVII *Netherlands International Law Review* (2000/2) 111-145.

Gowlland-Debbas, Vera, "The Domestic Implementation of UN Sanctions", in Erika de Wet and André (eds), *Review of the Security Council by Member States* (Antwerp, Intersentia, 2003), pp. 63-76.

Grelon, B. and Gudin, C.-E., "Contrats et crise du Golfe", 118 *Journal du droit international* (1991) 633-677.

Guillaume, Gilbert, "L'introduction et l'exécution dans les ordres juridiques des Etats des résolutions du Conseil de sécurité des Nations Unies prises en vertu du Chapitre VII de la Charte", 50 *Revue internationale de droit comparé* (1998) 539-549.

Iwasawa, Yuji, "The Doctrine of Self-Executing Treaties in the United States: A Critical Analysis", 26 *Virginia Journal of International Law* (1986) 627-692.

Kälin, Walter, "Implementing Treaties in Domestic Law: from "Pacta Sunt Servanda" to "Anything Goes", in Vera Gowlland-Debbas (ed.), *Multilateral Treaty-Making* (The Hague/Boston/London, Martinus Nijhoff Publishers, 2000), pp. 111-128.

Kelsen, Hans, "Les rapports de système entre le droit interne et le droit international public", 14 *RCADI* (1926-IV) 231-329.

Koskenniemi, Martti, "Le Comité des sanctions créé par la Résolution 661 (1990) du Conseil de sécurité", *AFDI* (1991) 119-137.

Kushen, Robert and Harris, Kenneth J., "Surrender of Fugitives by the United States to the War Crimes Tribunals for Yugoslavia and Rwanda", 90 *AJIL* (1996) 510-518.

Marcoff, Marco G., "Les règles d'application indirecte en droit international", 80 *RGDIP* (1976) 385-424.

Marek, Krystyna, "Les rapports entre le droit international et le droit interne à la lumière de la jurisprudence de la Cour permanente de justice internationale", 66 *RGDIP* (1962) 260-298.

Matringe, Jean, "Problèmes et techniques de mise en œuvre des sanctions économiques de l'organisation des Nations Unies en droit interne", in *Hague Academy of International Law, Economic Sanctions in International Law*, ed. by Laura Picchio Forlati and Linos-Alexandre Sicilianos (Leiden / Boston, Martinus Nijhoff Publishers, 2004), pp. 637-681)

Paust, J., "Self-Executing Treaties", 82 *American Journal of International Law* (1988) 760-764.

Schreuer, Christoph, "The Relevance of United Nations Decisions in Domestic Litigation", 27 *ICLQ* (1978) 1-17.

Scharf, Michael P. and Dorosin, Joshua L., "Interpreting UN sanctions: the Rulings and Role of the Yugoslavia Sanctions Committee", XIX *Brooklyn Journal of International Law* (1993) 771-827.

Schweitzer, Thomas A., "The United Nations as a Source of Domestic Law: Can Security Council Resolutions be Enforced in American Courts", 4 *Yale Studies in World Public Order* (1977) 162-273.

Skubiszewski, Krzysztof, "Resolutions of International Organisations and Municipal Law", 2 *Pol. YBIL* (1968/69) 80-108.

Verhoeven, Joe, "La notion d"applicabilité directe' du droit international", XV *RBDI* (1980) 244-264.

Warner, J.P., "The Relationship between European Community Law and the National Laws of Member States", 93 *Law Quarterly Review* (1977) 349-366.

PART II

NATIONAL STUDIES

3

ARGENTINA

*Emilio J. Cárdenas and Mariano Garcia-Rubio**

I. Introduction

UN Security Council resolutions are binding upon all UN Member States and carry the full force of law. Their effects, however, cannot be appreciated without noting that actual implementation of such measures must take place at the national level. It is precisely at this level that enforcement and decisions of compliance become critical considerations.[1] Each national government has developed its own set of individual means of implementing the UN Security Council resolutions containing economic and other sanctions.

The Constitution of Argentina, first adopted in 1853/60, was understandably silent regarding the domestic legal status of decisions adopted by international organisations. Since there is no specific legislation dealing with the instrumentalities of Argentina's participation in the United Nations and the constitutional amendment of 1994 did not include any provision in this regard, the domestic implementation of UN Security Council resolutions must therefore be studied from the broader perspective of the relationship between international law and Argentine domestic law.[2]

To the current knowledge of the authors, Argentine domestic courts have not yet been confronted with cases dealing with legal issues related to the implementation of

---

* Emilio J. Cárdenas is Executive Director, HSBC Argentina Holdings S.A. in Buenos Aires, and former Permanent Representative of Argentina to the United Nations. The late Mariano Garcia Rubio was Legal Counsel, International Centre for Settlement of Investment Disputes (ICSID), The World Bank Group. The authors wish to thank Silvia Fernández and Holger Martinsen, from the Argentine Ministry of Foreign Affairs, and Alejandro Adaglio, from the Argentine Supreme Court of Justice, for their co-operation with the authors at the research stage of this paper.

1 C. Joyner; "Sanctions and International Law", in D. Cortright and G.A. López, (eds.), *Economic Sanctions. Panacea or Peacebuilding in a Post-Cold War World?* (Boulder: CO, Westview Press, 1995), p. 77.

2 Articles 610 and 631 of the Argentine Customs Code allow the President to impose restrictions on imports or exports for "international policy" reasons, but it is doubtful whether this provision can be considered as specifically enabling domestic legislation for the implementation of UN Security Council resolutions.

Vera Gowlland-Debbas (ed.), National Implementation of UN Sanctions, *81-101.*

non-military UN Security Council resolutions.[3] However, the new provisions of the 1994 constitutional amendment relating to the status of treaties in domestic law, as well as the decisions of the Argentine Supreme Court of Justice (which has been particularly active in this field) allow us to analyse four main issues which appear to be relevant for the purposes of this study: the foremost issue deals with whether the UN Security Council resolutions need to be "adopted" by or "incorporated" into domestic law, a point which is also largely dependent upon the legal nature of such decisions in international law. The second question is whether such UN Security Council resolutions, once they have become part of the Argentine legal order, are – or are not – of a "self-executing" nature, i.e. directly applicable by national courts. The third issue is directly linked to the previous point, and revolves around the situation in domestic law when the local authorities simply fail to implement a UN Security Council resolution. Lastly, the fourth point of interest is to analyse how a potential conflict between a UN Security Council resolution and the Argentine Constitution could be reconciled.

II. Security Council Resolutions as the "Law of the Land"

(1) Security Council Resolutions as Sources of International and Domestic Law

The silence of Article 38 of the Statute of the International Court of Justice with regard to the legal status of decisions taken by international organisations in general, including UN Security Council resolutions in particular, is known. However, as binding decisions taken by international organisations are not considered to be "original" sources of international law,[4] they are generally assimilated, by analogy, to the status of the legal instrument from which their respective binding power derives.[5]

Article 25 of the UN Charter grants binding power to the UN Security Council resolutions, counter balanced by Article 103 of the Charter which, on the other hand, ensures that the provisions of the Charter do prevail over any other conventional obligation binding upon the UN Member States. The application of Article 103 also extends to UN Security Council resolutions, as far as they are enacted as a consequence of the Charter itself.[6] To this effect, UN Security Council resolutions can be regarded, from an

3 For the purposes of this study, we will use the expression "UN Security Council resolutions" as meaning binding decisions adopted by the UN Security Council under Chapter VII of the UN Charter.

4 M. Pinto, "Les résolutions des organisations internationales. A propos des rapports entre le droit interne et le droit international", in M. Bothe and R. Vinuesa (eds.), *International Law and Municipal Law, German-Argentinean Constitutional Law Colloquiuim* (Berlin, Duncker & Humboldt, 1982), pp. 173-178, at p. 175.

5 M. Diaz de Velasco, *Instituciones de derecho internacional público* (8th Edition, Madrid, Tecnos) p. 118 and ff.

6 The ICJ so resolved in its Order on Provisional Measures in the *Questions of Interpretation and Application of the 1971 Montreal Convention Arising from the Aerial Incident at Lockerbie Case*, between the United States and the United Kingdom against Libya. See, ICJ Reports 1992, p. 16, para. 39: "Whereas both Libya and the United States, as Members of the United Nations,

international law perspective, as "UN secondary law", thus having a "derived" conventional character flowing from their primary source, i.e., the UN Charter.

The Argentine Constitution also allows for the possibility of drawing a similar conclusion. Argentina is an original member of the United Nations, having ratified the Charter on 24 September 1945.[7] Since then, the Charter, as per Article 31 of the Argentine Constitution, is considered to be "the supreme law of the Nation", together with the Constitution itself and the Laws enacted by the Congress.

The Constitutional amendment of 1994 specifically grants priority to all international treaties over domestic legislation.[8] It also confers such priority to the regulations or "secondary law" enacted by supranational organisations to which Argentina may have delegated competencies or jurisdictional powers. Although the provision of Article 75, paragraph 24, of the Argentine Constitution, refers only to integration treaties, its underlying assumption seems to be that the status of "secondary law" created by international organisations in domestic law is dependent upon (i) the status that the instrument granting competence to create them may itself have in international law, and (ii) the specific provisions of that instrument.[9] Consequently, it could be argued by analogy that the same principle applies with regard to UN Security Council resolutions under the collective security framework of Chapter VII of the Charter, which contains a clear delegation of competencies by all UN Member States in favour of the UN Security Council.[10]

It appears, therefore, that for the purpose of analysing their relationship with and status under Argentine domestic law, UN Security Council resolutions should in principle be treated as akin to international treaties.[11]

(2) The Status of International Treaties in Argentine Domestic Law

Article 31 of the Argentine Constitution provides that: "[T]his Constitution, the laws of the Nation that may, as a result thereof, be enacted by Congress, and the treaties entered

---

are obliged to accept and carry out the decisions of the Security Council in accordance with Article 25 of the Charter; whereas the Court, which is at the stage of proceedings on provisional measures, considers that prima facie this obligation extends to the decision contained in resolution 748 (1992); and whereas, in accordance with Article 103 of the Charter, the obligations of the Parties in that respect prevail over their obligations under any other international agreement, including the Montreal Convention..."

7 Law number 12.838.

8 Article 75, paragraph 22, of the Argentine Constitution.

9 This means that when "secondary law" is enacted as a consequence of a treaty, its binding character will also depend upon the specific terms of the treaty itself.

10 As De Visscher explains, an analogy *"...est essentiellement l'expression d'une tendance assimilatrice qui pousse la pensée à raprocher, malgré des dissemblances exterieures, de situations qu'unit entre elles 'l'identité de raison juridique'"*. See Charles De Visscher, *Problèmes d'interprétation judiciaire en droit international public* (Paris, Pedone, 1963), p. 38.

11 In agreement: H. Martinsen, "*El Ordenamiento Jurídico Argentino y la aplicación de las decisiones del Consejo de Seguridad de la ONU*" (an unpublished thesis presented to the Argentine Ministry of Foreign Affairs on March, 2000), note 1, at 4.1.1.

into with foreign powers, are the supreme law of the Nation, and the authorities of every Province are bound to conform to it, notwithstanding any provision to the contrary which the provincial laws or constitutions may contain..."[12]

The main purpose of this "supremacy clause" is to assure the primacy of federal law over legislation enacted by the various federated Provinces. According to the treaty-making provisions laid down by the Argentine Constitution, treaties must be approved by Congress[13] and subsequently ratified by the President, who both concludes and executes them.[14] Under these conditions, treaties become part of the "supreme law of the Nation" according to the above-mentioned terms of Article 31 of the Constitution, at the time of its entry into effect at the international level, without any further need of an explicit individual act of "incorporation".

(3) UN Security Council Resolutions: The Need for Incorporation?

A different pattern, however, has been applied to UN Security Council resolutions. The practice of Argentina regarding the incorporation of such resolutions into domestic law differs from the aforementioned regime applicable to international treaties.

Since the imposition of sanctions against Southern Rhodesia in 1972, most UN Security Council resolutions have been incorporated into Argentine domestic law through individual Presidential decrees, on the basis that the President conducts the foreign relations of the country.[15]

Those decrees generally contain two provisions. By the first one, the President "approves" the Security Council Resolution at issue. By the second, he calls on all organs of the State (at both the national and provincial levels) to take all necessary steps (within their respective jurisdictions) to comply with the provisions of the UN Security Council Resolution.[16]

In the case of trade embargoes, for example, it is the Central Bank, in the exercise of its police power over all banks and financial institutions, that communicates to such enti-

12 The content of this provision is analogous to Article VI, section 2, of the US Constitution: "This Constitution, and the Laws of the United States which shall be made in Pursuance thereof; and all Treaties made, or which shall be made, under the Authority of the United States, shall be the supreme Law of the Land..."

13 Article 75, paragraph 22, of the Constitution.

14 Article 99, paragraph 11, of the Constitution.

15 *Ibid.*

16 This formula was used for the first time for the implementation of UN SCR 253/68 on South Rhodesia by Law number 19.846 of 21 September 1972. It has also been used for the implementation of UN SCR 660/90 on Iraq (Decree 1560, 13 August 1990); UN SCR 670/90 on Iraq (Decree 2067, 5 October 1990); UN SCR 748/92 on Libya (Decree 651, 4 June 1992); UN SCR 841/93 on Haiti (Decree 1470, 19 July 1993); UN SCR 787/93 on Bosnia-Herzegovina (Decree 2798, 30 December 1993); UN SCR 917/94 on Haiti (Decree 784, 27 May 1994); UN SCR 883/94 on Libya (Decree 1076, 7 July 1994); UN SCR 986/96 on Iraq (Decree 582, 11 June 1996); and UN SCR 1132/97 and 1156/98 (Decree 71, 10 February 1999).

ties the prohibition of carrying out financial transactions related to exports to or imports from the country at issue. The Central Bank also enacts the same kind of directive for the purpose of the practical implementation of Security Council resolutions imposing the freezing of financial assets.[17]

The only exception to the above-mentioned formula occurs when the UN sanctions are suspended. In these particular cases, the Presidential decree also provides for the derogation of the previous decree through which the UN Security Council resolution imposing the sanctions was – in due course – implemented.[18]

These acts of "incorporation" of United Nations Security Council resolutions into domestic law could be justified only if, as some authors suggest, the legal nature of such resolutions is that of "unilateral acts of international organisations" rather than "secondary" treaty law.[19] However, as explained above, we do not share this position. A binding decision taken by the United Nations Security Council could not possibly bind UN Member States if it had been just a "unilateral" act. Such decisions derive their binding power from a treaty and therefore their legal nature is of a conventional nature rather than of a unilateral one.

Therefore, we see no need for any specific or *ad hoc* presidential "approval" or act of incorporation of United Nations Security Council resolutions into domestic law. These acts of incorporation are not required by the Constitution, according to the monist approach it adopts regarding international treaties.[20] Like treaties, United Nations Security Council resolutions become part of the law of the land from the moment they come into existence at the international level, i.e. from their adoption by the United Nations Security Council.

A different view, i.e. that an act of incorporation would be considered to be a prerequisite for Security Council resolutions to become a part of the Argentine legal system, would imply the acceptance of a "dualistic" approach to the relationship between international and domestic law, which is certainly contrary to the letter and spirit of the Argentine Constitution.

---

17 See, for instance, Central Bank communication number 5778, on the implementation of sanctions imposed on Kuwait and Iraq. After the terrorist events of September 11, 2001, the US Embassy in Buenos Aires has – twice – requested the Argentine Banking Association (ABA) to distribute among its member entities the full list of individuals and entities whose assets have been blocked or frozen by the US Government by Executive Order 13,224. Such distribution was made for information purposes.

18 Suspension of sanctions against Haiti by UN SCR 873/93 (Decree 2410, 25 November 1993); suspension of sanctions against Yugoslavia, by UN SCR 1021 and 1022/95 (Decree 753, 16 July 1996).

19 See, for instance, J. Barberis, *Formación del derecho internacional* (Buenos Aires, Ed. Abaco, de R. Depalma, 1994), pp. 159 and ff. Also C. Economides, "*Les actes institutionnels internationaux et les sources de droit international*", *Annuaire français de droit international* (1988), 161.

20 G. Bidart Campos, *Manual de la Constitución Reformada* (Buenos Aires, Ediar, 1996) v. 1, p. 287.

(4) *Publication in the Official Bulletin*

A further and somewhat controversial point related to the implementation of United Nations Security Council resolutions into Argentine domestic law is whether their publication in the Official Bulletin constitutes a *conditio sine qua non* for their effectiveness at the domestic level.

This last view has been taken in Spain by Professor Gonzalez Campos[21] when interpreting Article 96. 1 of the Spanish Constitution, which expressly requires the publication of treaties as a condition precedent for their becoming a part of the Spanish internal legal order.[22] The Spanish Council of State, for its part, accepted this interpretation in a 1993 *dictum* related to United Nations Security Council Resolution 827 (1993), on the establishment of the International Criminal Tribunal for the Prosecution of Persons Responsible for Serious Violations of International Humanitarian Law Committed in the Territory of the Former Yugoslavia. The Council of State took the view that "U.N Security Council Resolutions adopted under Chapter VII of the United Nations Charter become part of the Spanish legal system simply by their publication in the Spanish Official Bulletin".[23]

However, this principle is not transposable to the Argentine legal system, as its structure is slightly different: publication is not a specific constitutional condition for considering treaties as part of the internal legal order.

According to Article 99, paragraph 3, of the Argentine Constitution, the President participates in the enactment of all laws, "promulgates them, and has them published". Publication is – thus – a constitutional requirement for laws, and a legal requirement for treaties. Law number 24.080/92 imposes upon the State the obligation to publish a series of acts related to international treaties[24] in the Official Bulletin, such as the text of the treaties and conventions to which Argentina is a party, as well as their respective instruments of ratification, reservations, interpretative declarations, etc.

However, it must be noted that this law imposes upon the State the obligation to publish all international treaties, but it does not subject the status of treaties as part of the domestic legal system to such publication, since a law could not modify the "monist" approach taken by the Constitution, according to which international obligations become part of domestic law from their very inception at the international level without any further requirement. Therefore, publication of a ratified treaty in the Official Bulletin is a formality required by domestic legislation, but is not a *conditio sine qua non* for

21 J.D. González Campos, *Curso de Derecho Internacional Público* (Universidad Complutense, Madrid, 4th Edition, 1990) v. I, pp. 231-233.

22 Article 96, paragraph 1, of the Spanish Constitution reads as follow: "Validly concluded international treaties once officially published in Spain shall constitute part of the internal (legal) order. Their provisions may only be abolished, modified or suspended in the manner provided for in the treaties themselves or in accord with general norms of international Law."

23 M. Martin Martinez, *National Sovereignty and International Organizations*, (The Hague, Kluwer Law International, 1996), pp. 226-227.

24 Law number 24.080/1992, Official Bulletin, 18 June 1992.

considering the obligations contained in that type of legal instruments as part of the "supreme law of the Nation".

Similarly, Security Council resolutions must be considered part of the Argentine legal system from their adoption and, as in the case of international treaties, its publication in the Official Bulletin should rather be seen as a formal, though not substantial requirement, as there would be no ground to make a distinction between treaties and the United Nations Security Council Reolutions in this particular regard.

In addition, this view is consistent with the obligations imposed upon Argentina by international law. According to the customary rule now embodied in Article 27 of the Vienna Convention on the Law of Treaties, no State would be entitled to claim (at the international level) the lack of publication of a treaty as valid ground to justify its failure to comply with the international obligations imposed by such an instrument. Failure to publish a treaty would not amount to a violation of a norm of fundamental character regarding the competence to enter into treaties, and this would also exclude the potential application of Article 46 of the Vienna Convention on the Law of Treaties. This is so simply because the Argentine Constitution itself does not determine that publication has the character of a substantial condition for international obligations becoming a part of Argentina's domestic law. The same principles apply, *mutatis mutandi,* to Security Council resolutions, since the rule of Article 27 of the Vienna Convention on the Law of Treaties is a codification of the customary principle that grants supremacy to international law in general, and not only to treaties, over domestic law.[25]

At the internal level, the Supreme Court of Justice of Argentina takes the same view by stating that the impossibility to resort to domestic law to justify the failure to comply with an international obligation "is a part of the Argentine legal order". The Court adds: "The Vienna Convention on the Law of Treaties is an international treaty, constitutionally valid, that grants priority to international treaties over domestic legislation. That is certainly a recognition of the supremacy of international law vouched by Argentina's domestic law itself".[26]

Consequently, by virtue of both (i) the Argentine Constitutional provisions dealing with the status of treaties in domestic law and (ii) the customary principle laid down in Article 27 of the Vienna Convention, failure to publish a United Nations Security Council resolution in the Official Bulletin should not alter its character of "supreme law of the Nation". Again, an opposing view would imply the acceptance of a "dualist" conception, as publication in the Official Bulletin could be equated to an act of "incorporation" or "reception" into domestic law, distorting the "monist" position clearly adopted by the Argentine Constitution.

Nevertheless, a distinction could certainly be made between the obligations imposed upon the State by a United Nations Security Council resolution, on the one hand, and the obligations imposed by it upon individuals, on the other.

---

25 See, in general, M. Kohen, "*La codification du droit des traités: quelques éléments pour un bilan global*", *Revue générale de droit international public* (2000) 577-613.

26 *Ekmekdjian c. Sofovich case,* Fallos 315:1492, para. 18. Also: Raúl H. Guerrero, "*La relación entre la norma internacional correccional y la Constitución Nacional, luego de su reforma*", in *Doctrina Judicial*, La Ley, XVI, n. 3, p. 133 (December 15, 1999).

If an unpublished United Nations Security Council resolution establishes an obligation upon the State itself with which it fails to comply, an individual vested with a subjective right or a legitimate interest on the matter could go to court to have his or her right or interest, as the case may be, duly recognized and protected.

The failure of an individual or a corporation to comply with an export contract entered into with a foreign State, on the basis of an embargo imposed on that State by a United Nations Security Council resolution, is therefore legal under Argentine domestic law, even though the United Nations Security Council resolution in question might not have been published.[27] The same seems to be true for the opposite situation, i.e.: the execution of a private contract with a third State, or performance under it, after the sanctions imposed upon it have been suspended or lifted by the United Nations Security Council is licit under domestic law, irrespective of the eventual lack of publication of the pertinent United Nations Security Council resolution (or the lack of derogation of any domestic legislation implementing such resolution). It must be noted that this has been the case, for example, with United Nations Security Council Resolution 1192 (1998), suspending sanctions imposed against Libya, which has not been published in the Argentine Official Bulletin.

An entirely different situation may arise when an individual or a corporation is about to be sanctioned for violating an obligation imposed by a non-published United Nations Security Council resolution. Article 19 of the Argentine Constitution states that: "No inhabitant of the Nation shall be compelled to do what the law does not order, or be deprived of what it does not forbid." It appears that when an obligation is imposed upon individuals by international law, publication could then be considered as a condition for the law to be known and, thereafter, directly applicable to individuals.

This is the underlying principle arising from Article 3, of Law number 24.080/92,[28] which provides that treaties and conventions imposing obligations on physical and legal persons other than the State itself are applicable and binding **only** after their publication in Argentina's Official Bulletin.

Therefore, publication in the Official Bulletin is not to be considered as a *conditio sine qua non* for United Nations Security Council resolutions to become part of the Argentine legal system, but it becomes a substantial condition for their direct applicability when they impose duties and obligations on individuals.

The lack of publication would not prevent, *au contraire*, either individual claims before the courts for the protection of rights or legitimate interests that may be affected by United Nations Security Council resolutions, or the possibility for the State to elude

27 This would be the case, for instance, with respect to the obligation provided for in paragraph 29, of UN SCR 687 (1991): "*Decides* that all States, including Iraq, shall take the necessary measures to ensure that no claim shall lie at the instance of the Government of Iraq, or of any person or body in Iraq, or of any person claiming through or for the benefit of any such person or body, in connection with any contract or other transaction where its performance was affected by reason of the measures taken by the Council in resolution 661 (1990) and related resolutions."

28 In accordance with Article 2 of the Argentine Civil Code.

its international obligations either at the domestic or at the international level, as far as those international obligations could be considered as "self-executing".

III. "Self-executing" Character of United Nations Security Council Resolutions

Issues of incorporation of norms into domestic legal systems are to be distinguished from their potential "self-executing" character when applied at the domestic level.

The conditions under which international regulations become part of domestic legal systems depend on constitutional provisions, whereas their "self-executing" character depends mainly on the content and wording of such norms themselves, i.e. on international law.[29]

Our previous conclusion, namely that publication of United Nations Security Council resolutions in the Official Bulletin is not a substantial condition for considering such resolutions as part of the Argentine legal order, opens the floor to the question as to whether United Nations Security Council resolutions (or, at least, some of their provisions) may have a "self-executing" character in Argentine domestic law.

Although there is still controversy around the notion of "self-executing norms",[30] it is clear that the question arises only in "monist" countries.[31] Being basically a matter of interpretation, the final say of whether a specific regulation issued under international law is "self-executing", or not, is to be decided by the domestic judges, on a case-by-case basis.[32]

(1) The Need for Complementary Legislation as a Test of the "Self-executing" Character of a Norm

One criterion for determining the "self-executing" character of a norm is whether it can be applied at the internal level without the need for complementary domestic legislation.[33] In this regard, the language of United Nations Security Council resolutions suggest that they impose direct obligations upon the Member States, and that their

29 P. De Visscher, "Les tendances internationales des Constitutions modernes", *RCADI* (1952-I) 562. In this regard, it must be noted that Justices Boffi Boggero and Aberastury all said, in due course, in relation to the Washington Labor Convention: "The Washington Convention of 1919 has been incorporated into our legal system with the scope of (supreme law of the land) from the moment of its approval...without need for a specific law of adoption... The text of rule XIX of the Washington Convention demonstrates that no subsequent legislation is needed for it to come into force." (Fallos 256:156).

30 J. Paust; "Self-Executing Treaties", 82 *American Journal of International Law* (1988) 760-764.

31 R. Müllerson, *Ordering Anarchy- International Law in International Society* (The Hague, Martinus Nijhoff Publishers, 2000), pp. 194-195.

32 Th. Burgenthal, "Self-Executing and Non-Self-Executing Treaties in National and International Law", 235 RCADI (1992-IV) p. 395.

33 Y. Iwasawa, "The Doctrine of Self-Executing Treaties in the United States: A Critical Analysis", 26 *Virginia Journal of International Law* (1986) 627.

effective implementation depends upon the cooperation and support of individual governments.[34]

However, the fact that States do have to adopt internal measures to comply with United Nations Security Council resolutions does not necessarily imply that the obligations contained in such resolutions are not "self-executing".

A clear example is found in United Nations Security Council Resolution 1373, recently adopted in direct response to the terrorist events of 11 September 2001, in the United States. The United Nations Security Council decided, among other things, that all Member States shall:

> "(b) Criminalize the willful provision or collection, by any means, directly or indirectly, of funds by their nationals or in their territory with the intention that the funds should be used, or in the knowledge that they are to be used, in order to carry out terrorist acts;
>
> (c) Freeze without delay funds and other financial assets or economic resources of persons who commit, or attempt to commit, terrorist acts or participate in or facilitate the commission of terrorist acts; of entities owned or controlled directly or indirectly by such persons; and of persons and entities, including funds derived or generated from property owned or controlled directly or indirectly by such persons and associated persons and entities;..."

It would seem that the obligation to criminalise the supply of funds with the intention that they be used to support terrorist acts is an "obligation of means", since the respective resolution imposes the obligation upon States to enact internal criminal legislation to that effect. This is, therefore, not an "immediate" obligation. The provision of paragraph (b) could not -in fact- be implemented without further or complementary domestic legislation, for that could otherwise be understood as a violation of the principle *nullum crime sine lege*, recognized by virtually all Constitutions of the world.[35]

The obligation to "freeze" financial assets, on the contrary, is an obligation "of result" and, consequently, an "immediate" obligation is imposed upon all Member States. Nevertheless, the modalities of implementation may also require some complementary domestic legislation.

The difference between a "non self-executing" and a "self-executing" obligation (both requiring complementary domestic legislation) is that the lack of implementing legislation does not bar either the "self-executing" character of the latter, or the possibility that it may be directly invoked by individuals before national courts.

This is, in fact, the view already held by the Supreme Court of Justice of Argentina when confronted with the determination of the status in domestic law of the "right to reply" embodied in the Inter-American Convention of Human Rights.[36] It found that the Convention was of a "self-executing" nature and that the failure of the Argentine Congress to enact specific implementing legislation could not prevent the effective

34 D. Cortright and G.A. López, *The Sanctions Decade. Assessing UN Strategies in the 1990's* (International Peace Academy, 2000), p. 99.

35 Constitution of Argentina, Article 18.

36 Article 14, paragraph 1, of the Inter American Convention on Human Rights reads as follows:

protection of the right at stake, since that would otherwise amount to a breach of the Inter-American Convention.

The Court stressed that judicial decisions range among the measures to be adopted in domestic law for the effective implementation of an international obligation.[37] For this reason, the Court declared that it is its obligation to prevent the international responsibility of the State from arising, inasmuch as that is constitutionally done.[38] Consequently, the Court applied the individual right to reply in the concrete case at issue, despite the absence of supplementary domestic legislation.[39]

Therefore, the requirement of issuing some form of complementary domestic legislation seems not to be a conclusive test for the determination of the "self-executing" character or not of an international obligation.

(2) The Addressee of the Obligation as a Test of the "Self-executing" Character of a Norm

The Argentine Supreme Court has followed a different criterion for establishing the "self-executing" character of a given clause: if it directly confers rights or imposes obligations upon private parties, then it is considered to be "self-executing". If, on the contrary, the obligation is imposed upon the State, the clause at issue is meant to be a "non self-executing" one.

This is a somehow more appropriate test for determining the "self-executing" nature of an international obligation. It must be noted that, thus far, the Argentine Supreme Court has taken this particular view only in connection with private parties' subjective rights granted by international human rights treaties.

However, taking into account the Court's concern, referred to above, to try to prevent the international responsibility that may arise from its decisions, it is not unthinkable that the Argentine Supreme Court would apply the same principles regarding United Nations Security Council resolutions, even though they (i) are not human rights instruments and (ii) do not generally confer direct rights to individuals.

This finding is based on the view that a given clause does not necessarily have to establish *direct* rights or obligations in order to be considered as "self-executing". Private parties may also have a *legitimate interest* on the effective compliance by the State of an international obligation that may otherwise have an adverse impact on its legal situation under domestic law.[40]

"1. Anyone injured by inaccurate or offensive statements or ideas disseminated to the public in general by a legally regulated medium of communication has the right to reply or to make a correction using the same communications outlet, under such conditions as the law may establish."

37 *Ekmekdjian c. Sofovich Case,* Fallos 315:1492, para. 22.

38 *Ibid.* para. 19.

39 *Ibid.*, para. 19

40 Evelina Teubal de Alhadeff, "Comment on Self Executing Treaties", in M. Bothe and R. Vinuesa (eds), *International Law and Municipal Law, German-Argentinian Constitutional Law Colloquiuim (*Berlin, Duncker & Humboldt, 1982), pp. 161-172, at p. 169. A similar position seems to have been taken by the French *Cour de Cassation*, as described by Geneviève Burdeau and Brigitte Stern in their Chapter on France (see part V, "Role of National Courts").

Similar to the example referred to above,[41] a United Nations Security Council resolution imposing an embargo against State A could certainly affect the legal situation of private companies that may have concluded (though not yet performed) supply contracts with such State A. If the company decides thereafter to breach the contract on the grounds of the said embargo imposed by the United Nations Security Council, and State A sues the company before the courts of State B, the legal situation of the company in domestic law could clearly be affected by the resolution at issue, for its otherwise illicit conduct would be rendered legal by that resolution. Consequently, the norm imposing the embargo could be considered as a "self-executing" one. Otherwise, following the above-mentioned reasoning of the Supreme Court, the tribunals of State B would engage the international responsibility of the State by recognizing that the company had acted wrongfully, in disregard of the export embargo imposed by the Security Council upon State A.

By the same token, the conduct of a bank that freezes financial assets of physical or legal persons involved in the commitment or the assistance to the commitment of terrorist acts on the basis of Security Council Resolution 1373 is rendered legal under Argentine law, despite the lack of complementary legislation. If the affected physical or legal person sues the bank before a national tribunal, this tribunal should recognize the "self-executing" character of such a provision, although no subjective rights are granted at all. In this case, the mere "legal interest" of the financial institution is enough to consider the obligation imposed by the Security Council resolution as directly applicable. If the tribunal reaches a different conclusion, it would engage – as in the previous example – the international responsibility of Argentina, something that courts and tribunals are called on to avoid, according to the case law of the Supreme Court of Justice.

Therefore, it seems that international obligations likely to affect the legal situation of private parties under domestic law should enjoy a presumption in favor of their "self-executing" character. This is so because of the impact of such norms on the legal position of private parties, and also because of the international responsibility arising out of the non-recognition of this character by national courts or administrative organs.

In conclusion, it can be said that, notwithstanding the fact that different techniques can be found in comparative law, the Argentine Supreme Court of Justice has relied, at least up to now, on the following criterion to determine the "self-executing" nature of an international obligation: if the obligation is one of result and imposes upon the State an immediate obligation likely to affect the legal situation of private parties under domestic law or directly conferring rights to individuals, then that obligation could be considered as having a "self-executing" nature, provided there is no constitutional conflict. On the contrary, obligations of means requiring from the State a specific course of action seeking the achievement of a certain goal or objective in the future would not have such a character and, consequently, could not be invoked by individuals before domestic courts.

41 See above, p. 90.

IV. Failure to Implement a Security Council Resolution

This finding gains importance in connection with the third point of our discussion, namely, what would be the legal situation in domestic law when the competent authorities of the State fail to enact the implementing measures necessary to comply with a United Nations Security Council resolution?

As mentioned above, the United Nations Security Council Resolution lifting the sanctions that were imposed on Libya has never been published in the Argentine Official Bulletin. In our view, that specific resolution is nonetheless part of the supreme law of the land from the time of its adoption by the United Nations Security Council. Private parties could thus invoke its provisions before Argentine Courts, insofar as they can prove that they have a legitimate interest connected with the implementation of this resolution.

Similarly, Argentina has not taken any domestic measures in order to comply with Security Council Resolution 827 (1993), which imposed upon UN Member States the obligation to cooperate with the International Criminal Tribunals for the former Yugoslavia and Rwanda, in the following terms:

> "4. Decides that all States shall cooperate fully with the international Tribunal and its organs in accordance with the present resolution and the Statute of the International Tribunal and that consequently States shall take any measures necessary under their domestic law to implement the provisions of the present resolution and the Statute, including the obligation of States to comply with requests for assistance or orders issued by a Trial Chamber under Article 29 of the Statute."[42]

Although there have been no concrete cases in which the above-mentioned Tribunal requested the cooperation of Argentina, it is important to analyse what could be the legal situation should this Tribunal request the surrender of an individual resident in Argentina.

As mentioned before, the failure by Argentina to adopt domestic measures necessary to implement the provisions of Resolution 823 (1993) and the Statute of the International Criminal Tribunal for the former Yugoslavia would not constitute, either in international or in domestic law, a valid ground for not giving effect to the request which could eventually be made by the Tribunal.

The above-mentioned Resolution imposes an immediate obligation upon Argentina, and this obligation is part of the domestic legal system from the time of its adoption by the United Nations Security Council. On the basis of the Supreme Court decision that judicial resolutions range among the measures to be adopted in domestic law for the implementation of international obligations, it is a reasonable presumption that the failure by Argentina in adopting internal complementary legislation would not neces-

42 Some countries, such as Venezuela, have already informed the International Criminal Tribunal for the FormerYugoslavia that no complementary legislation is needed at their domestic levels in order to ensure the cooperation due to such an organ. See Doc. A/54/187-S/1998/846.

sarily prevent a domestic court from cooperating with the International Tribunal. This is so particularly because of the already mentioned concern of the Argentine Supreme Court regarding the international responsibility that may otherwise arise in the event of non-cooperation, and the concern that the process of surrendering suspected individuals to the Tribunal does not prejudge their the culpability and, consequently, does not violate the principle of legality embodied in Article 18 of the Argentine Constitution.[43]

V. UN Security Council Resolutions and the Argentine Constitution

Unlike our previous example, there may be cases where the provisions of a Security Council resolution could conflict with the Argentine Constitution, or even with other international treaties or conventions to which Argentina is a party.

In this regard, it must be noted that one of the main questions that the 1853/60 Constitution left open to judicial interpretation was the relationship between international treaties and federal legislation, with the exception of the Constitution itself.

For a long time, the Supreme Court of Justice of Argentina followed the "last in time doctrine" that the Supreme Court of the United States had already adopted in 1880 in the *Whitney v. Robertson*[44] case. The Supreme Court of Argentina, since 1963, has consistently found that "neither article 31 nor article 100 of the Constitution give priority or primacy to Treaties concluded with foreign powers with respect to Laws validly enacted by the Congress. Both, Laws and Treaties, are equally qualified to be the "supreme law of the land" and there is no normative reason to give priority to one over the other".[45]

However, in 1992, the Argentinean Supreme Court drastically changed this view, and in an *obiter dictum* on the relationship between international and municipal law, in the *Ekmekdjian* case, found that "...according with the requirements of international cooperation, harmonization and integration recognized by Argentina...the proposition that there is no legal grounds to give priority to a treaty over a law is no longer correct".[46]

43 It must be noted that the Inter-Ministerial Commission created to draft the necessary legislation establishing the modalities of co-operation with the International Criminal Court is currently considering the possibility of including a provisional clause according to which such legislation would apply, *mutatis mutandi*, to co-operation with the various International Tribunals which were created by the UN Security Council.

44 In this particular case, the US Supreme Court declared that: "By the Constitution, a treaty is placed on the same footing, and made of like obligation, with an act of legislation. Both are declared by that instrument to be the supreme law of the land, and no superior efficacy is given to either over the other. When the two relate to the same subject, the courts will always endeavour to construe them as to give effect to both, if that can be done without violating the language of either; but, if the two are inconsistent, the one last in date will control the other: provided, always, the stipulation of the treaty on the subject is self-executing..." (Supreme Court of the United States, 124 U.S. 190, 8 S Ct. 456, 31 L.Ed. 386). Also: R. Guerrero, "*Los Tratados en la Constitución de 1994*" (Buenos Aires, Ciudad Argentina, 2001) pp. 21 ff.

45 *Martin y Cia. Ltda. c/ Administración General de Puertos,* Fallos 257:99. Also Fallos 271:7.

46 *Ekmekdjian, Miguel Angel c/ Sofovich, Gerardo y otros.* Fallos 315:1492: "*...acorde con las exigencias de cooperación, armonización e integración que la República Argentina reconoce,... ya no es*

A few months after the *Ekmekdjian* case, the Court dealt again with this issue in the case of *Fibraca Constructora S.C.A. c/ Comisión Técnica Mixta Salto Grande.* Although it kept its view regarding the supremacy of treaties, it added that treaties would prevail over domestic legislation "provided due respect was paid to the principles of public law set up in the Constitution".[47] This is in line with the provision of Article 27 of the Argentine Constitution that requires international treaties to be in conformity with the "principles of public law laid down by this Constitution".[48]

This fundamental change in the Argentinean Supreme Court's case law regarding the relationship between international and domestic law was definitively taken into account in the 1994 constitutional amendment, following the trend that had already been set by other Latin-American constitutions.[49]

Articles 27 and 31 of the Constitution remained untouched by the 1994 reform.[50] In addition, the 1994 amendments provide, as a matter of principle that all international treaties prevail over domestic legislation with the exception of the Constitution itself.

Article 75, paragraph 22, of the Argentine Constitution establishes *in limine*, that international treaties and concordats concluded with the Holy See prevail over domestic

---

válida la proposición jurídica según la cual no existe fundamento normativo para acordar prioridad al tratado frente a la ley."

In the Court's view, there are two reasons by which international treaties are to be considered hierarchically superior to laws.

The first one lies on constitutional law grounds. As international treaties are concluded and signed by the President, approved by federal law of the Parliament, and subsequently ratified by the President, they are considered as being "complex or organic federal acts". In the Court's reasoning, if a federal law could derogate from an international treaty, then the distribution of competencies imposed by the Constitution itself would be violated, because an act of one branch of the Government – the Parliament – would supersede an act, the conclusion of which involves two branches of the Government. In addition, this would also be contrary to the Constitution, since under it, it is the President who conducts the foreign relations of the country.

International law, as mentioned above, is the second ground on which the Argentine Supreme Court relied to grant priority to international treaties over laws enacted by Congress. In 1980, Argentina ratified the Vienna Convention on the Law of Treaties. The Court found that Article 27 of that Convention, by stating that States cannot rely on its municipal law in order to justify its failure to comply with an international obligation contained in a treaty, "imposes the obligation to grant priority to a treaty in case of a conflict between the treaty and *any* other incompatible domestic norm on Argentina" (emphasis added). The Court concluded that the priority of treaties over domestic legislation set up in Article 27 of the Vienna Convention "is a part of the Argentine legal order. The Convention is an international treaty, constitutionally valid, that grants priority to international treaties over domestic legislation in domestic law. That is a recognition of the primacy of international law made by domestic law itself."

47 Fallos 316:1394.

48 Article 27 reads as follow: "The Federal Government is bound to strengthen its relations of peace and commerce with foreign powers by means of treaties that are in conformity with the principles of public law laid down by this Constitution".

49 Constitution of Colombia, Article 93; Constitution of Honduras, Article 18; Constitution of El Salvador, Article 144; Constitution of Costa Rica, Article 7.

50 Law Declaring the Need of the Constitutional Reform, number 24.309.

laws. In addition, paragraphs 22 and 24 of Article 75 introduce a distinction between the various kinds of treaties, placing them in a hierarchy, according to (i) their object and (ii) the special majority requirements necessary for their parliamentary approval. Such a distinction could arguably operate as a conflict resolution clause, in cases of contradictory conventional obligations. The main differentiation that can be found in the 1994 Constitution is between treaties enjoying "constitutional hierarchy" and those without such a character.

Human rights instruments which are expressly mentioned in Article 75, paragraph 22 of the Constitution,[51] and those approved by Congress after 1994 with the affirmative vote of two-thirds of both the House of Representatives and the Senate, enjoy "constitutional hierarchy".[52]

Treaties enjoying "constitutional hierarchy", in turn, do not derogate from any provision of the first part of this Constitution (the dogmatic part including the "bill of rights") and must be considered complementary to the rights and guarantees granted therein. The Supreme Court referred to this specific issue in the following terms: "Constitutional provisions and those of treaties with constitutional hierarchy have the same hierarchy, they are complementary and, therefore, they cannot cancel each other".[53]

As just mentioned, there are only two ways in Argentine domestic law by which a treaty can obtain constitutional rank: (i) either by express reference to it in the case by case listing contained in Article 75, paragraph 22, of the Constitution; or (ii) by a parliamentary decision approved by the affirmative vote of the two-thirds of the total number of members of both the House of Representatives and the Senate.

It must be noted that the United Nations Charter, surprisingly, does not rank amongst treaties listed as having constitutional status. It is neither expressly mentioned in Article 75, paragraph 22 of the Constitution, nor has it, yet, been given constitutional hierarchy following the procedure described in that article.

This means that United Nations Security Council resolutions must be in conformity not only with the principles of public law laid down in the Constitution itself (according to Article 27 of the Constitution) but also with the specific human rights instruments that, according to Article 75, paragraph 22 of the Constitution, do have constitutional standing. This is a key issue because the incompatibility of the implementation of a

51 Article 75, paragraph 22, makes reference to the following Human Rights instruments: the American Declaration of the Rights and Duties of the Man; the Universal Declaration of Human Rights; the American Convention on Human Rights; the International Covenant on Economic, Social and Cultural Rights; the International Covenant on Civil and Political Rights and its Optional Protocol; the International Convention on the Prevention and Punishment of Genocide; the International Convention on the Elimination of all Forms of Racial Discrimination; the Convention on the Elimination of all Forms of Discrimination Against Women; the Convention Against Torture and other Cruel, Inhumane or Degrading Treatment or Punishment; and the Convention on the Rights of the Child. It is interesting to note that the Argentine Constitution grants constitutional status to instruments considered as "soft law" at the international law level, i. e. the Universal Declaration of Human Rights.

52 This procedure has been used by Congress to elevate the Inter-American Convention on Forced Disappearance of Persons to constitutional standing. Law number 24.556.

53 Fallos 319: 3148.

United Nations Security Council resolution with a specific Constitutional provision is an enhanced possibility.

It must be clarified that "conformity with the principles of public law laid down in the Constitution" does not mean that treaties must conform to every single norm of the Constitution, but only to its "principles of public law".[54] It seems apparent that this provision assures, as a matter of domestic law, the supremacy of the Constitution over international treaties and, consequently, over United Nations Security Council resolutions.[55]

A somewhat less apparent point is whether the human rights instruments enjoying constitutional standing have become part of those "principles of public law" to which all other international treaties, and United Nations Security Council resolutions, must conform. The answer seems to be a positive one, for it is difficult to see what would be the practical effect of such constitutional standing, should the answer be negative.

It appears, therefore, that "regular" treaties and United Nations Security Council resolutions must respect the principles of public law laid down in the Constitution, as well as those in human rights instruments having constitutional standing.

In the view of the Argentine Supreme Court any conflict between a treaty and domestic legislation cannot be resolved in a way that frustrates the objectives of the treaty.[56] By analogy, this implies that any conflict between a "regular" treaty and a treaty with "constitutional standing" cannot be resolved in a manner that frustrates the objectives of the latter.

It would follow that, as United Nations Security Council resolutions are assimilated to "regular" treaties, they must conform to the principles of the human rights instruments having constitutional standing, and that any potential conflict among them should be resolved, avoiding the frustration of the objectives of those instruments.

This would imply the need to exercise some sort of control of legality by the Supreme Court, eventually giving priority to the norms of international law of the "constitutionalized" human rights instruments, over United Nations Security Council resolutions, should the conformity of the latter with the former come into question.[57]

This could result in a variety of rather awkward situations. While the potential conflict between the obligations imposed by a United Nations Security Council resolution

54 Justice Boggiano had briefly touched upon this point in his opinion in the case *Servini de Cubria s/ amparo*, by saying that, according to Article 27 of the Constitution, treaties must conform to the "principles" of public law set up in the Constitution, and not to its concrete norms. See S. 289, XXIV RHE, paragraph 12.

55 Rafael Bielsa, "*Observaciones sumarias sobre algunos puntos de derecho público concernientes al carácter jurídico de ciertas leyes*", *La Ley*, v. 120, 1965, p. 1079.

56 Fallos 323: 3160. "*En tanto el tratado internacional tiene, en las condiciones de su vigencia, jerarquía superior a las leyes, debe descartarse el amparo del ordenamiento hacia toda solución que comporte una frustración de los objetivos del tratado o que comprometa el futuro de los objetivos del tratado o que comprometa el futuro cumplimiento de las obligaciones que de él resultan*".

57 For instance, a pharmaceutical products exporter having concluded, though not performed yet, a supply contract with a State upon which sanctions have been imposed, could challenge the conformity of the pertinent Security Council resolution with the right to health recognized in several of the human rights instruments with constitutional standing under Argentine law.

and human rights law of a conventional nature is solved at the international law level in favor of the former, by virtue of Article 103 of the Charter; this priority seems to have been reversed in Argentine law by the Constitution.[58]

The effect of a declaration of unconstitutionality of a United Nations Security Council resolution on the basis of an alleged violation by its specific provisions of some human rights instrument with constitutional standing in Argentine law, could imply the non-application of that resolution by an Argentine judge and, consequently, a violation of Articles 25 and 103 of the United Nations Charter that would – in turn – engage the international responsibility of Argentina.[59]

It seems rather unreasonable to consider that by granting certain human rights instruments constitutional standing, the drafters of the 1994 Constitution had the intention to potentially put Argentina in violation of the United Nations Charter.

The delegation of competencies in favor of the United Nations Security Council in connection with measures necessary to preserve or restore international peace and security is, since 1945, part of the Argentine legal order. And its constitutionality has never – ever – been challenged.

In addition, the human rights instruments mentioned in Article 75, paragraph 22, of the Argentine Constitution do not, *per se,* bind the Security Council. The Security Council is bound by human rights law insofar as it becomes general international law and, therefore, it seems absurd for an individual State to claim it can exercise "control" over the legality of a United Nations Security Council decision on the basis of instruments that are not even binding for such an organ.

Such control of constitutionality, permissible under international law if made on customary law grounds, becomes illicit at the international level when made on a conventional law basis by domestic courts. First, because the United Nations Security Council is not bound by conventional law other than by the United Nations Charter itself. Second, because Articles 25 and 103 of the United Nations Charter establishes the precedence of obligations flowing from Security Council resolutions adopted under Chapter VII, in particular, and the United Nations Charter, in general, over any other conventional obligations.

Consequently, it would appear that the maximum respect for international human rights law at the domestic level intended by the drafters of the Argentine Constitution when granting constitutional standing to certain human rights instruments cannot be construed in a manner incompatible with the international obligations flowing from the Charter of the United Nations that provides the constitutional framework within which most of these human rights instruments have – in fact – been concluded.

---

58 It must be noted here that such a "control of legality" of a UN Security Council resolution should be made, according to the Constitution, against conventional international law and not against customary law. The Constitution gives constitutional status to the above-mentioned human rights treaties and other instruments as such, and not as instruments potentially reflecting the customary status of their norms.

59 Under Articles 25 and 103 of the UN Charter, binding SC resolutions issued under Chapter VII of the Charter, supersede any other international obligations of the Member States. See *supra*, footnote 6.

In our view, the simplest way of overcoming these complex legal issues would be to obtain an *ad hoc* declaration from the Congress under the terms of Article 75, paragraph 22, *in fine*, of the Argentine Constitution, specifically granting constitutional status to the Charter of the United Nations. What was overlooked in 1994 could thus be corrected.

It is difficult to predict what the attitude of the Argentine Supreme Court would be if and when confronted with this type of dilemma. But given the deep commitment of the Court during the last few years to respect for legality at the international level and its declared objective of trying to prevent any international responsibility which may arise from its decisions, it is possible that an interpretation of the Constitution like the one suggested above would be retained.

VI. Final Remarks

Our analysis of the practice and legal framework under which non-military United Nations Security Council sanctions are implemented in Argentina, lead us to the following general conclusions:

– United Nations Security Council resolutions become part of the Argentine legal system under the same terms and in the same manner as international treaties do, i.e. from their inception at the international level, and without need of any further act of incorporation.
– The current practice of "approving" United Nations Security Council resolutions through issuing specific presidential decrees seems to be contrary to the "monist" approach taken by the Argentine Constitution on the relationship between treaties and domestic law.
– Similarly, publication of United Nations Security Council resolutions in the Official Bulletin cannot be considered as a substantial *sine qua non* condition for such resolutions to become part of Argentinean law, for the same reasons explained above. Publication, however, does become a condition when the resolution at issue imposes obligations upon individuals.
– The obligations "of result" imposed upon Argentina by a United Nations Security Council resolution are to be considered "self-executing", and therefore, applicable by Argentinean national courts when invoked by individuals vested with a subjective right or a legitimate interest. On the contrary, obligations "of means" are considered to be "non self-executing", and not directly applicable by Argentine national courts.
– The failure of the legislative or administrative organs of Argentina to enact complementary legislation does not alter the "self-executing" character of obligations "of result" imposed upon it by a United Nations Security Council resolution.
– The constitutional standing granted by the Constitution to certain human rights instruments cannot reasonably be construed as meaning that Argentine national courts may be entitled to exercise control over the legality of United Nations Security Council resolutions, for three main reasons:
    1. because the United Nations Security Council is not bound by those instruments, *per se;*

2. because Articles 25 and 103 of the United Nations Charter establish, beyond doubt, the supremacy of obligations flowing from the United Nations Charter over any other conventional international obligations;
3. because it cannot be reasonably assumed that the drafters of the Argentine Constitution had – at all – the intention to enable Argentine national tribunals to exercise a "control of legality" over Security Council resolutions contrary to international law which may, in turn, engage the international responsibility of Argentina.

Select Bibliography

I. Books

Barberis, J., *Formación del derecho internacional* (Buenos Aires, Ed. Abaco, de R. Depalma, 1994).

Bidart Campos, G., *Manual de la Constitución Reformada* (Buenos Aires, Ediar, 1996).

Cortright, D. and López, G.A., *The Sanctions Decade. Assessing UN Strategies in the 1990's* (International Peace Academy, 2000).

De Visscher, Charles, *Problèmes d'interprétation judiciaire en droit international public* (Paris, Pedone, 1963).

Diaz de Velasco, M., *Instituciones de derecho internacional público* (8th Edition, Tecnos, Madrid).

González Campos, J.D., *Curso de Derecho Internacional Público* (4th Edition, Universidad Complutense, Madrid, 1990).

Martin Martinez, M., *National Sovereignty and International Organizations* (The Hague, Kluwer Law International, 1996).

Müllerson, R., *Ordering Anarchy: International Law in International Society* (The Hague, Martinus Nijhoff Publishers, 2000).

II. Articles and Contributions to Collective Works

Bielsa, R., "Observaciones sumarias sobre algunos puntos de derecho público concernientes al carácter jurídico de ciertas leyes", 120 *La Ley* (1965).

Burgenthal, Th., "Self-Executing and Non-Self-Executing Treaties in National and International Law", 235 *RCADI* (1992-IV) 303-400.

De Visscher, P, "Les tendances internationales des Constitutions modernes", 80 *RCADI* (1952-I) 511-578.

Economides, C., "Les actes institutionnels internationaux et les sources de droit international", XXXIV *Annuaire français de droit international* (1988)131-145.

Guerrero, R., "La relación entre la norma internacional correccional y la Constitución Nacional, luego de su reforma", in *Doctrina Judicial*, La Ley, XVI (1999), nr. 3.

Iwasawa, Y., "The Doctrine of Self-Executing Treaties in the United States: A Critical Analysis", 26 *Virginia Journal of International Law* (1986) 627-692.

Kohen, M., "La codification du droit des traités: quelques éléments pour un bilan global", *Revue Générale de Droit International Public* (2000-3) 577-613.

Martinsen, H., "El Ordenamiento Jurídico Argentino y la aplicación de las decisiones del Consejo de Seguridad de la ONU", an unpublished thesis presented to the Argentine Ministry of Foreign Affairs on March, 2000.

Paust, J., "Self-Executing Treaties", 82 *American Journal of International Law* (1988) 760-764.

Pinto, M., "Les résolutions des organisations internationales. A propos des rapports entre le droit interne et le droit international", *in* M. Bothe and R. Vinuesa (eds), *International Law and Municipal Law, German-Argentinean Constitutional Law Colloquiuim* (Berlin, Duncker & Humboldt, 1982), pp. 173-178.

Teubal de Alhadeff, E., "Comment on Self Executing Treaties", in M. Bothe and R. Vinuesa (eds.), *International Law and Municipal Law, German-Argentinian Constitutional Law Colloquium* (Berlin, Duncker & Humboldt, 1982), pp. 161-172.

4

BELGIUM

*Eric Suy and Nicolas Angelet**

I. Legal Basis of Domestic Measures Implementing Economic Sanctions

(1) The Relationship between Domestic and International Law in General

Article 167, paragraphs 2 and 3 of the Belgian Constitution provide that treaties shall have no effect unless they have been approved by the federal legislative Chambers, or by the Council of the federated entity competent to enter into the treaty concerned, depending on its subject matter.

Yet the Belgian constitutional order rests on a monist foundation to the extent that treaties are part of Belgian law *qualitate qua*, as treaties under international law, to the extent and only to the extent that they have been ratified by the competent Belgian authority and have entered into force at the international level. A self-executing treaty has priority over any provision of domestic, including constitutional law which is incompatible with it.[1] The self-executing character depends on the complete and precise character of the international rule, rather than on the intention of the authors of the treaty;[2]

---

* Erik Suy is Honorary Professor of Law, Université de Louvain. Nicolas Angelet is chargé de cours, Université libre de Bruxelles and Avocat, Liedekerke Wolters Waelbroeck Kirkpatrick , Belgium.

1 See in particular Cass., 27 May 1971 (N.V. Fromagerie Franco-Suisse Le Ski), *Journal des Tribunaux*, 1971, 460, conclusions Ganshof van der Meersch; and also Cass., 16 January 1968 and 12 March 1968, *Pasicrisie*, 1968, I, p. 625 and 874; Cass., 27 May 1971, *Pasicrisie*, 1971, I, p. 886; Cass. 26 September 1978, *Pasicrisie*, 1979, I, p. 126; Cass., 4 April 1984, *Pasicrisie*, 1984, I, p. 920; Cass., 16 April 1984, *Pasicrisie*, 1984, I, p. 1032; Cass., 10 May 1989, *Pasicrisie*, 1989, I, p. 953. See further the comments by J. Salmon, "Le conflit entre le traité international et la loi interne en Belgique à la suite de l'arrêt rendu le 27 mai 1971 par la Cour de cassation", *Journal des Tribunaux* (1971) p. 535; M. Waelbroeck, "Portée et critères de l'applicabilité directe des traités internationaux", *Revue critique de jurisprudence belge* (1985) 41-42; J. Verhoeven, "Chronique de jurisprudence belge relative au droit international public", XIX *Revue belge de droit international* (No. 2, 1986) 342; J. Verhoeven, "Belgique", in: P.M. Eisemann (ed.), *The Integration of International and European Community Law into the National Legal Order – A Study of the Practice in Europe* (The Hague, Kluwer, 1996), 115 ff.

2 See, in particular, Cass., 10 May 1985, *Pasicrisie*, 1985, I, p. 1123 and Cass., 6 March 1986,

Vera Gowlland-Debbas (ed.), National Implementation of UN Sanctions, *103-122*.

in other words, the international rule is self-executing to the extent that the Belgian State and its organs have no margin of appreciation.

While this monist approach has been mitigated to some extent following the creation of the Belgian Court of Arbitration (the constitutional court), which has ruled that its power of review encompasses not only the laws approving international treaties, but also the provisions contained in such treaties,[3] it remains of major importance by reason of the Court of Arbitration's competence *ratione materiae*, which is limited to reviewing whether the division of competences within the Belgian federal structure and a number of fundamental rights and freedoms have been respected.[4]

In respect of secondary legislation emanating from international organisations, Article 34 (formerly 25 bis) of the Belgian Constitution provides that the exercise of specific powers may be transferred to international organisations by treaty or by law. Although this provision was introduced into the Constitution in order to reflect the realities of the transfer of sovereign rights to the European Community, it may also apply to the transfer of responsibility to the United Nations Security Council for the maintenance of international peace and security in accordance with Articles 24 and 25 of the Charter of the United Nations. Article 34 of the Constitution has been invoked *inter alia* as a basis for Belgium's cooperation with the International Criminal Tribunals.[5]

(2) *Prior Enabling Legislation*

Prior to 1995, no specific legislation existed on the implementation of United Nations Security Council Decisions. Many Security Council decisions have thus been implemented on the basis of the Law of 11 September 1961 on the import, export and transit of goods,[6] the Law of 5 August 1991 on the import, export and transit of arms, ammunition and material specially designed for military use and technology in these fields,[7] as well as on the basis of the Decree-Law (*Décret-Loi*) of 6 October 1944 concerning foreign exchange transactions.[8] However, although it has been used for that purpose, the Decree-Law of 1944 did not provide for an adequate basis for the implementation of decisions on the freezing of assets.

This appears to be one of the main reasons why, on 11 May 1995, Belgium adopted a Federal Law on the implementation of United Nations Security Council Decisions.[9]

Pasicrisie, 1986, I, p. 853. Comp. J. Verhoeven, "Applicabilité directe des traités et 'intention des parties contractantes'", in: *Liber Amicorum E. Krings* (Brussels, Story-Scientia, 1991), p. 895 ff.

3 See *i.a.* Court of Arbitration, No. 26/91, 16 October 1991, and No. 12/94, 3 February 1994; see also the comments by Y. Lejeune and Ph. Brouwers, "La Cour d'arbitrage face au contrôle de la constitutionnalité des traités", *Journal des Tribunaux* (1992) 670.

4 Article 1 of the special Law of 6 January 1989 on the Court of Arbitration, *Moniteur belge*, 7 January 1989.

5 See also below.

6 *Moniteur belge*, 27 October 1962.

7 *Moniteur belge*, 10 September 1991.

8 *Moniteur belge*, 7 October 1944.

9 *Moniteur belge*, 29 July 1995. See P. d'Argent, "La loi du 11 mai 1995 relative à la mise en

Article 1 of the Law provides that the "King may, by Royal Decree deliberated on in the Council of Ministers, take the measures necessary for the implementation of compulsory decisions taken by the Security Council pursuant to the United Nations Charter. These measures may include complete or partial interruption of economic relations and of rail, sea, air, postal, telegraphic, radio, and other means of communication, as well as the seizure of movable and immovable goods and the freezing of financial assets". According to Article 2, the Law of 1995 does not affect the King's powers pursuant to the Law of 1961 on foreign trade, the Law of 1991 on arms trade and the Law-Decree of 1944 on foreign exchange transactions. Pursuant to Article 3, Parliament shall immediately be informed of the Decrees adopted by the King pursuant to the present Law. The King immediately notifies the Communities and Regions [*i.e.* the federated entities] of the compulsory decisions taken by the Security Council pursuant to the United Nations Charter. Article 4 provides that the violation of the measures enumerated in the Royal Decrees adopted pursuant to the Law of 1995 shall be punished with imprisonment and fines as specified in that Law. This does not affect the applicability of more severe sanctions provided for in other laws. Article 5 enables the agents appointed by the competent Minister to investigate and determine violations of the measures taken pursuant to the Law.

When the Draft Law on the implementation of United Nations Security Council Decisions was submitted to it for advice, the Legislative Section of the Belgian Council of State objected that the delegation of powers provided for in the Draft was unconstitutional, for reasons which will be fully set out below. The Government slightly amended the Draft Law in view of this advice, but maintained the main provisions criticized by the Council of State. Nor did Parliament take account of the Council of State's advice.

Although the Belgian federated entities (Regions and Communities) have a limited competence with respect to the implementation of UN sanctions, in relation to some economic matters, but also with respect to cultural and sports relations, the Regions and Communities have not, as yet, enacted a special enabling legislation similar to the Law of 11 May 1995.

(3) Ex Post Facto *Legislation, Executive Orders and Decrees*

In view of the above-mentioned legislative framework, ex post facto implementation measures are generally limited to the adoption of Royal and Ministerial Decrees. Indeed, the above-mentioned Laws of 1944, 1961, 1991 and 1995 all require the enactment of Royal Decrees. The Royal Decrees relating to financial measures are further implemented by means of Ministerial Decrees which exempt categories of transactions or provide for the possibility of obtaining individual exemptions.[10]

One exception exists with respect to the implementation measures relating to the International Criminal Tribunal for the former Yugoslavia and the International Criminal Tribunal for Rwanda. These implementation measures were not taken on the basis of the Law of 11 May 1995, but were made the object of an *ad hoc* law enacted by Parlia-

oeuvre des décisions du Conseil de sécurité de l'Organisation des Nations Unies", *Journal des Tribunaux* (1996) 357-361.

10 See below.

ment.[11] This is probably due to the fact that the implementation measures relating to these Tribunals did not meet the urgency requirement justifying the application of the Law of 1995.

It may further be noted that, following the invasion of Kuwait by Iraq, the Minister of Finance issued 'recommendations' to all Belgian financial institutions requesting them to freeze Iraqi and Kuwaiti assets located in Belgium. These recommendations had no clear legal basis, and on 7 August 1990, the President of the Brussels Commercial Court ordered a bank to release funds which had been frozen on the basis of these recommendations.[12]

II. Legal Basis of Domestic Measures Based on the Decisions of the European Union

(1) Legal Basis in Belgian Law of European Union Decisions

Article 34 of the Belgian Constitution provides that the exercise of specific powers may be transferred to international organisations by treaty or by law. As stated above, this provision was inserted in the Constitution for the purpose of European integration; as a matter of fact, most Security Council economic sanctions are presently implemented in European Community Regulations. Apart from procedural measures and criminal law aspects, the implementation measures taken at the Belgian national level since 1990 have been limited to arms trade and sanctions in the financial field. The Treaty of Maastricht of 1992 further extended European Community competence in the field, as Article 73 G of the EC Treaty now empowers the Council to take the necessary urgent measures on the movement of capital and on payments as regards the third countries concerned.[13] No particular limits apply in respect of the applicability of European Community Regulations in the Belgian domestic order.

(2) Interplay between European Union and Domestic Legislation in Sanctions Implementation

Notwithstanding some exceptions, Security Council decisions on economic sanctions are implemented through EC Regulations which have direct effect in the domestic legal order of the Member States. Therefore, the need for the Member States to adopt further implementing measures is almost non-existent. EC Regulations implementing Security Council decisions may, however, require the EC Member States to criminalise

11 Law of 22 March 1996 on the recognition of the International Criminal Tribunal for the Former Yugoslavia and the International Criminal Tribunal for Rwanda and on judicial cooperation with these Tribunals, *Moniteur belge*, 24 April 1996.

12 This unpublished Order is mentioned by Ch.-G. Winandy, "Il était une fois ... L'embargo contre l'Irak et le Koweit, ou le conte du non-droit", in: *L'embargo – actes de la journée d'études du 1er décembre 1995 organisée par l'Association Européenne pour le Droit Bancaire et Financier – Belgium* (Brussels, Bruylant, 1996), p. 233 ff., at p. 236.

13 See the contribution by Daniel Bethlehem in the present study, *infra*, pp. 123-165.

the violation of these Regulations. In Belgium, many, but not all of these violations are criminalised by the 1961 Foreign Trade Law. In that respect, the Law of 11 May 1995 suffered from a major default in that it did not criminalise the violation of measures implemented at the *European Community* level. This lacuna has now been filled by the Law of 13 April 2003 which criminalizes the violation of measures implemented at the European Community level (*Moniteur belge,* 13 June 2003).

III. The Content of Domestic Measures of Implementation

(1) Content of Prohibitions

a. Content ratione materiae

A comparison between Security Council resolutions and the implementation measures taken at the Belgian domestic level reveals two kinds of discrepancies. The first one relates to the application of economic sanctions to the sanctioned State's diplomatic missions, the second one has a more general scope.

As to the first kind of discrepancies, the implementing measures taken in Belgium since the invasion of Kuwait by Iraq contain general exemptions in respect of the functioning of diplomatic missions. The Ministerial Decree of 22 September 1990 relating to Iraq and Kuwait thus provides for an exemption of the transfer of funds for the purpose of the functioning of the Belgian diplomatic missions.[14] Case-to-case exemptions have been granted for expenses related to the functioning of the Iraqi embassy in Brussels.[15] The Ministerial Decree of 29 July 1992 concerning Yugoslavia and the Ministerial Decree of 20 June 1994 concerning Libya also contain general exemptions in respect of the expenses related to the functioning of the Yugoslav and Libyan embassies in Brussels.[16] The Royal Decree of 25 February 1994, implementing United Nations sanctions against Haiti, did not provide for such general exemptions.[17] The Belgian Government considered that the United Nations sanctions were inapplicable to the embassy of Haiti in Brussels because the ambassador had been accredited by President Aristide.[18]

While the above-mentioned specific exemptions may be linked to the status of diplomatic missions under international law, other general exemptions mitigate the measures in the light of their purpose, and may be considered based on the general principle of reasonableness. The Ministerial Decree of 22 September 1990 on Iraq thus contains general exemptions concerning the following financial transactions:

- payments made by Iraqi or Kuwaiti nationals to Belgian residents, through Belgian accounts and for the following purposes: salaries, pensions and other allowances pursuant to employment contracts entered into before 7 August 1990; taxes etc.; insur-

14 *Moniteur belge*, 4 October 1990.

15 G. Brouhns, "Les embargos financiers", in: *Mélanges Jean Pardon - Etudes en droit bancaire et financier* (Brussels, Bruylant, 1996) p. 21 ff., at p. 44-45.

16 *Moniteur belge*, 1 August 1992 and 29 June 1994, respectively.

17 *Moniteur belge*, 9 March 1994.

18 G. Brouhns, *op. cit.*, p. 66.

ance fees; studies or medical assistance; interests due to Belgian banks for credits prior to 7 August 1990, etc.; other payments to Belgian residents up to one million Belgian francs per month, as well as cash withdrawals up to one million Belgian francs per month and per account;
- investments etc., provided that the funds be held by the same person in a financial institution on Belgium;
- transfers by Belgian residents to Belgian nationals living in Iraq or Kuwait, up to 100.000 Belgian francs per month.[19]

With respect to the implementation of Security Council Resolution 757 (1992) on Yugoslavia (Serbia and Montenegro), the reasoning underlying the definition of general exemptions was that no financial resources should be made available to the Yugoslav Central Bank[20] (which is a restrictive, if not erroneous interpretation of the relevant resolutions). The Ministerial Decree of 29 July 1992 contains the same general exemptions as in the Iraqi case and adds a few more:
- financial transfers by Yugoslav nationals living in Belgium to persons living outside the territory of Yugoslavia;
- financial transfers by Belgian residents to Belgian nationals living in Yugoslavia, with a maximum of 25.000 Belgian francs a month and per person;
- payments in respect of imports from Yugoslavia prior to 6 June 1992, provided that the sum be paid on a blocked account;
- payments in respect of exports to Yugoslavia for which an export license has been obtained pursuant to EC Regulations, as well as the payment of exports to Yugoslavia prior to 6 June 1992.[21]

The Ministerial Decree of 20 June 1994 concerning Libya equally provides for certain exemptions, related to the particular nature of the financial measures taken by the Security Council.[22] Unlike the Decrees adopted in the other, above-mentioned cases, the Royal Decree of 17 March 1994 requires the relevant financial institutions to provide the Ministry of Finance with a monthly survey of the special accounts mentioned in paragraph 4 of Resolution 883 (1993).[23]

b. Humanitarian exceptions

The general exemptions in the Ministerial Decrees do not expressly refer to humanitarian circumstances. While the competent Minister's power to grant case-to-case exemptions might give rise to humanitarian exceptions, there is no information available in this respect.

19 *Moniteur belge*, 4 October 1990.

20 G. Brouhns, *op. cit.*, p. 54.

21 *Moniteur belge*, 1 August 1992.

22 *Moniteur belge*, 29 June 1994.

23 *Moniteur belge*, 31 March 1994.

c. Provisions relating to contracts

The above-mentioned financial exemptions allow for a limited performance of existing contracts, to the extent that such performance is compatible with the purpose of the United Nations measures. The financial measures thus provide for general exemptions concerning the payment of salaries etc. related to employment contracts entered into before the United Nations measures, the payment of insurance fees, and the payment of interests due to Belgian banks for grants prior to the United Nations measures. The measures against Yugoslavia also exempt payments in respect of imports from Yugoslavia prior to 6 June 1992, provided that the sum be paid on a blocked account, and the payment of exports to Yugoslavia prior to 6 June 1992.[24] To the extent that the Ministerial Decree does not expressly require that the payment for exports to Yugoslavia (or some of them) be made on a blocked account, the Decree seems to neglect the fact that such exports may require payments to companies in Yugoslavia.

d. Provisions relating to penal sanctions

The mechanism for criminalising violations of EC and national implementing measures of Security Council sanctions has already been described above. It may be noted that the sanctions provided for in the Decree-Law of 1944 and the Law of 1961 are less severe than those of the Law of 1991 on the arms trade, of the Law of 1995 and of the Law of 13 April 2003 (imprisonment up to 5 years and fines up to 1.000.000 Belgian francs). As the Law of 1995 only applies if the Security Council decisions cannot be implemented on the basis of the other above-mentioned Laws,[25] the overall criminalisation scheme does not sufficiently reflect the gravity of some violations of United Nations economic sanctions.[26]

(2) Ratione Personae *and* Ratione Loci

Security Council decisions requiring Member States to prevent activities on a *personal* jurisdiction basis have not always been adequately implemented in Belgian law. In Resolution 661 (1990), for example, the Council decided *i.a.* that "all States ... shall prevent their nationals ... from removing from their territories or otherwise making available to that Government [of Iraq] ... any ... funds or financial resources ...". This obligation to prevent said activities on a personal (extra-territorial) jurisdiction basis was not implemented in Belgian law. The Royal Decree of 8 August 1990 merely required a prior authorisation for the transfer of funds etc. "between Belgium and foreign countries", as well as for operations relating to Kuwaiti or Iraqi investments in Belgium.[27]

---

24 Ministerial Decree of 26 July 1993, *Moniteur belge*, 6 August 1993.

25 Article 2 of the Law and the Government's Report, *Pasinomie*, 1995, at p. 2375 and p. 2378, respectively.

26 For further details, see N. Angelet, "Criminal Liability for the Violation of United Nations Economic Sanctions", *European Journal of Crime, Criminal Law and Criminal Justice* (1999) 89 ff.

27 *Moniteur belge*, 9 August 1990.

While personal jurisdiction clauses may now be implemented on the basis of the Law of 11 May 1995, no such measures have been taken so far. Thus, Resolution 1160 (1998), according to which States shall prevent the arms trade with Yugoslavia on a personal jurisdiction basis, has not been implemented in Belgian law. Even when the personal jurisdiction clauses are implemented at the European Community level (which is the case for foreign trade and for financial transactions which promote prohibited sales), a problem remains because the Belgian legislation does not criminalise the violation of EC Regulations in this respect. In most cases, personal jurisdiction may, however, be exercised through a combination of pre-existing Belgian laws, such as the 1961 foreign trade law, and general provisions of criminal jurisdiction as contained *i.a.* in the Preliminary Title of the Code of Criminal Procedure.

(3) Entry Into Force (Scope Ratione Temporis*)*

Belgian implementation measures do not, as a rule, claim any retroactive effect. They enter into force on the date of their publication in the Belgian official journal. The Royal Decrees are generally published within a few days following the adoption of the Security Council resolutions they purport to implement.[28] Yet, Resolution 883 (1993) of 11 November 1993, which provided for sanctions against Libya entering into force on 1 December 1993, was only implemented by Royal Decree of 17 March 1994. In the Haitian case, Resolution 841 (1993) of 16 June 1993 and Resolution 873 (1993) of 13 October 1993 were implemented by Royal Decree of 25 February 1994, published in the Belgian official gazette of 9 March 1994 and entering into force without retroactive effect.

The suspension and lifting of measures at the national level mostly coincide with the corresponding measure taken by the Security Council. However, Resolution 944 of 29 September 1994, providing for the lifting of sanctions the day after President Aristide's arrival in Haiti, on 16 October 1994, was only implemented by Royal Decree of 1 December 1994, published in the Belgian official gazette of 24 December 1994 and, again, entering into force without retroactive effect.

More recently, however, the Belgian practice to publish lists of targeted persons or entities with respect to which implementing measures have been taken by the European Union, has led to the adoption of retroactive measures. Thus, when the United Nations decided in January 2002 to restrict the list of entities associated with the Taliban of Afghanistan, an implementing measure was adopted at EC level on 18 January 2002, and entered into force on the day of publication in the Official Journal, on 19 January 2002.[29] At the Belgian level, a Ministerial Decree was enacted on 25 March 2002. The Decree was published in the official gazette of 30 March 2002 and took effect on 19 January 2002.[30] Such retroactivity, however, is merely formal in kind, as the Royal Decree is nothing but an unnecessary duplication of the self-executing EC Regulation.

28 For example, Resolution 661 (1990) of 6 August 1990 was implemented by Royal Decree of 8 August 1990, published on 9 August 1990; Resolution 757 (1992) of 30 May 1992 was implemented by Royal Decree of 5 June 1992, published on 6 June 1992.

29 Commission Regulation (EC) No. 105/2002, *O.J.*, L 17/52 of 19 January 2002.

30 *Moniteur belge*, 30 March 2002.

As the Law of 11 May 1995 is limited to implementing Security Council decisions, national implementation measures taken on that basis could not be kept in force as countermeasures or retorting measures under general international law after they have been suspended or lifted by the Security Council. More generally, it may be noted that in Belgian practice, the lifting of restrictive measures following a Security Council decision to that effect is considered as much an international obligation as the imposition of such measures: the UN decision is interpreted, not as the termination of an international obligation to take restrictive measures, but as the enactment of an international obligation to lift measures previously taken. The above-mentioned Royal Decree of 25 March 2002 thus refers to the decision taken by the Security Council Sanctions Committee restricting the list of targeted entities, before indicating that "such measures must be taken without delay so as to comply with Belgium's international obligations in this respect".[31]

IV. Constitutional and Humanitarian Issues Raised by Sanctions Implementation

Implementing Security Council decisions on non-forcible measures has raised two important constitutional issues. The first one relates to the Law of 11 May 1995 on the Implementation of United Nations Security Council Decisions, and the second to the Law of 22 March 1996 concerning the recognition of the International Tribunal for the former Yugoslavia and the International Tribunal for Rwanda and judicial cooperation with these Tribunals.

When the Draft Law on the implementation of United Nations Security Council Decisions was submitted for advice to the Legislative Section of the Belgian Council of State, the Council objected that the delegation of powers provided for in the Draft was unconstitutional. Such delegation would only be admissible if (1) the Security Council Decisions to be implemented, or at least, the conflict in relation to which such decisions had or could be taken, were specified beforehand; (2) delegated powers may only be used for a limited period of time, and (3) measures taken were approved by Parliament. The Government contested the soundness of this advice, arguing that the delegation only related to compulsory decisions of the Security Council in accordance with the United Nations Charter, that the measures to be taken were specified *expressis verbis* in the resolutions and that they were limited in time. Furthermore, the Government argued that the national measures would not remain in force after relevant Security Council decisions had become inapplicable. The Government nevertheless agreed to complement the Draft with a provision stating that Parliament shall be informed of the measures taken. The consistency of implementing measures with the relevant Security Council decisions, the Government argued, could thus be reviewed on the basis of generally applicable constitutional procedures. It also gave the assurance that Security Council decisions would only be implemented on the basis of the Law when urgency so requested.[32]

31 *Ibid.* For an analysis of a number of legal issues involved, see N. Angelet, "L'embargo et l'ONU", in: *L'embargo - actes de la journée d'études du 1er décembre 1995 organisée par l'Association Européenne pour le Droit Bancaire et Financier - Belgium* (Brussels, Bruylant, 1996), pp. 45 ff., at 64 ff.

32 *Pasinomie*, 1995, pp. 2377-2379.

The second constitutional issue raised by sanctions implementation relates to Article 13 of the Law of 22 March 1996 on judicial cooperation with the International Tribunal for the former Yugoslavia and the International Tribunal for Rwanda, which provides that the Government shall transfer the arrested persons pursuant to the Rules of Procedure of the Tribunal and in accordance with the European Convention on Human Rights. In this respect, it was argued in the Belgian Senate that the European Convention on Human Rights prevails over Security Council resolutions.[33] The Report made on behalf of the Justice Commission of the Senate indicates, however, that the primary aim of Article 13 was to oblige the Belgian Government to seek assurance from the Tribunals that persons transferred by the Belgian Government would not, if convicted, serve imprisonment in a country which is not a party to the European Convention on Human Rights.[34]

It may also be noted that Belgian law does not provide for any compensation scheme with respect to contracts which may not be performed as a consequence of United Nations measures. While such compensation might arguably be claimed on the basis of general principles of Belgian public law,[35] no such cases have been dealt with by Belgian Courts so far.

V. Domestic Procedures for Implementation and Enforcement

(1) Coordination between Different Ministerial Activities

Generally, the Ministry of Foreign Affairs primarily acts as a letterbox. Pursuant to the Law of 11 May 1995, the federal government is under an obligation immediately to notify the Communities and Regions of the decisions taken by the Security Council.[36] As Security Council decisions must be interpreted in accordance with the Charter and with general international law, and considering that the competent ministries often provide for exemptions based on such interpretation,[37] the low-profile attitude of the Ministry of Foreign Affairs seems unjustified.

A different approach was taken in 1999, when it was alleged in a report of the Panel of Experts on violations of Security Council sanctions against UNITA that an important part of the diamonds exported from Angola in violation of Security Council sanctions against UNITA were being imported in Antwerp.[38] A "Diamond Task Force"

33 See *Parliamentary Documents*, Senate, 1-247/3, 1995--1996, Report by Mr. Erdman on behalf of the Commission of Justice of the Senate, 27 February 1996, p. 89. See also D. Vandermeersch, "La loi du 22 mars 1996 relative à la reconnaissance du TPIY et du TPIR et à la coopération avec ces tribunaux", *Revue de droit pénal* (1996) 883, note 134.

34 *Parliamentary Documents, Senate*, 1-247/3, 1995-1996. Report by Mr. Erdman on behalf of the Commission of Justice of the Senate, 27 February 1996, p. 89.

35 See R. Ergec, "L'embargo et les droits nationaux", in: *L'embargo, op. cit.*, pp. 123 ff. at p. 143 ff.

36 *Op. cit.*, Article 3, paragraph 2.

37 See above.

38 S/2000/203 of 10 March 2000. See further the Final Report, S/2000/1225 of 21 December 2000.

composed of representatives of various ministries – justice, foreign affairs, foreign trade and development, finance, economic affairs, security services – as well as of the office of the public prosecutor in Antwerp and of a national magistrate, was entrusted with the task of studying the problem and proposing measures for combating diamonds trafficking.[39]

(2) *Role of Banks*

Pursuant to the relevant Royal or Ministerial Decrees, requests for individual exemptions in the financial field must be addressed to the Governor of the National Bank of Belgium. The National Bank investigates the matter and advises the Minister of Finance.[40] However, prior to the Royal Decree of 17 March 1994 implementing sanctions against Libya, no Belgian implementation Decree required the financial institutions concerned to provide the Ministry of Finance with a periodic survey of their activities in this field.[41]

(3) *The Role of the Private Sector: The Antwerp Diamonds Market*

In 1999, allegations by the United Nations Panel of Experts that diamonds exported from Angola in violation of Security Council sanctions against UNITA were being imported in Antwerp, gave birth to a quite unprecedented initiative in sanctions implementation, when the private diamonds sector took several initiatives so as to contribute to the implementation of sanctions directed against "conflict diamonds".

The private sector's initiatives started with a public awareness action from the Diamonds High Council (HRD), the non-governmental professional organisation for the diamond sector, inviting Belgian diamond traders to sign a petition endorsing Security Council action against "conflict diamonds". This was followed by a resolution of the Belgian diamond bourses, and further by a statement of the Belgian diamond banks that diamond traders found to be trading in conflict diamonds would have all banking facilities withdrawn, and still further by an amendment of the bylaws of the Belgian Association of Rough Diamond Traders stating that any member found to be trading in conflict diamonds would be expelled from the Association and reported to the World Federation of Diamond Bourses and exposed to the competent authorities, and urging members to print a clause on their sales invoices and consignment memoranda, declaring that all appropriate measures had been taken to determine that none of the diamonds had, to the trader's best knowledge, originated in a country subject to United Nations sanctions.[42]

The Diamond High Council also intensively cooperated with the United Nations so as to work out practical solutions for preventing the trade in diamonds from conflict

39 SC/6825 of 15 March 2000.

40 See G. Brouhns, *op. cit., passim.*

41 *Moniteur belge*, 31 March 1994.

42 For further details, see the Internet site of the Diamonds High Council: www.hrd.be and more specifically www.conflictdiamonds.com.

zones. The HRD launched a mission to Luanda, Angola, and started bilateral talks with the Luanda government regarding certification, which eventually led to an agreement of structural cooperation being signed on 29 March 2000. A similar initiative was taken with respect to Sierra Leone. The HRD also participated in the "Kimberley Process" initiated by the South African Government.[43] These initiatives were welcomed and encouraged in various Security Council resolutions.[44]

(4) Parliamentary Procedures of Inquiry

When in 2000, the UN Panel of Experts on the Illegal Exploitation of Natural Resources and Other Forms of Wealth of the Democratic Republic of Congo reported that a number of Belgian companies were involved in the exploitation and import of coltan originating in DRC territory occupied by foreign troops,[45] a Parliamentary Commission of Inquiry was created so as to investigate the exploitation, both legal and illegal, of natural resources in the region of the Great Lakes as well as the role of Belgium as a center for the commercialization of such resources. The "Commission of Inquiry on the Great Lakes", delivered its report on 20 February 2003. The Commission notably put forward a number of critiques with respect to the Panel of Experts' report. Whereas the Panel of Experts had formulated complaints towards some diamond companies because of their non-respect of OECD Guidelines for Multinational Enterprises, the Commission noted that, apart from being non-binding, these Guidelines were not addressed to diamond traders who were not multi-national enterprises. Also, the Commission considered that sanctions, if any, should be applied to company directors rather than to a Belgian employee as the Panel of Experts suggested. The Commission further regretted that some of the persons and companies mentioned in the UN Report had not been heard by the UN Panel, which jeopardized the principle of due process. The Commission also concluded that, on the basis of information available to them and without prejudice to the results of further investigations, the individuals and companies which had been made the object of the Commission's inquiry had not been found to be in breach of any legal obligation.[46]

VI. Role of National Courts

The Belgian monist approach and the case law concerning the self-executing character of international treaties, which has been described above, might arguably allow for the application of (some) Security Council decisions in the domestic legal order, provided

43 For further details, see *ibid.*

44 SCR 1295 (2000) of 18 April 2000, paragraph 17; SCR 1306 (2000) of 5 July 2000, paragraph 10.

45 S/2001/357 of 12 April 2001 and S/2001/1072 of 13 November 2001.

46 Senate, Session of 2002-2003, Doc. 2-942/1 of 20 February 2003, notably pp. 196, 204-205, 216 and 226.

they be published in the Belgian official gazette.[47] It may also be argued that no such publication is required for the purpose of an individual's invoking self-executing international norms against the Belgian authorities.[48]

In *Dumez v. Iraq*, relating to the seizure of Iraqi assets located in Belgium, the French corporation Dumez argued that Iraq had lost its sovereign immunity following the adoption of Security Council Resolution 687, in particular its paragraph 16 according to which "Iraq, without prejudice to its debts and obligations arising prior to 2 August 1990, which will be addressed through the normal mechanisms, is liable under international law for any direct loss (..) as a result of its unlawful invasion and occupation of Kuwait", as well as its paragraph 17 stating that "Iraqi statements made since 2 August 1990 repudiating its foreign debt are null and void". The Brussels *Juge des Saisies* (judge of attachments) decided that there was, in principle, no objection to conferring a self-executing character to Security Council decisions, but that the relevant provisions of Resolution 687 only limited Iraq's immunity with respect to claims arising after August 2, 1990, whereas Dumez's claim arose prior to that date.[49] More recently, the Brussels Court of Appeal adopted an analogous viewpoint in *Leica v. Iraq.* Without dwelling on the issue of whether Security Council resolutions may have a self-executing character, the Court judged that Resolution 687 did not deprive Iraq of its diplomatic immunity with respect to the assets seized by Leica in relation to a debt arising prior to August 2nd, 1990.[50]

The importance of the Juge des Saisies's *obiter dictum* should, however, not be overestimated. Many Security Council decisions cannot, notwithstanding their precision, be applied as such in the Belgian domestic order in the absence of any implementation measure. For example, in *Ndayambaje, Kanyabashi and Higabino* concerning a request for transfer of these persons to the International Criminal Tribunal for Rwanda, the Minister of Justice indicated that the request for deferral could only be dealt with (by the Belgian Court of Cassation) after the entry into force of what became the Law of 22 March 1996 on judicial cooperation with the International Criminal Tribunal for the former Yugoslavia and the International Criminal Tribunal for Rwanda. In her conclusions presented to the Court of Cassation pursuant to that Law, the Advocate-General referred to this statement by the Minister of Justice, adding that the Law had entered into force by then, without making any reservation in this respect. The Court of Cassation itself did not address the issue.[51] Article 34 of the Constitution notwithstanding, and even though the Statutes of the Tribunals have been published in the Belgian official

---

47. See J. Verhoeven, "Guerre et droit international - Sur certaines questions soulevées par le conflit Iraq-Koweit", *Journal des Tribunaux* (1991) p. 141; P. d'Argent, "Le juge des saisies, le Conseil de sécurité et l'immunité d'exécution restreinte des Etats étrangers", *Journal des Tribunaux* (1995) 565 ff. at p. 570; see also N. Angelet, "L'embargo et l'ONU", in: *L'embargo, op. cit.*, pp.45 ff., in particular at pp. 55 ff.

48 See J. Verhoeven, note under Cass., 19 March 1981, *Journal des Tribunaux* (1982) 565.

49 Civ. Bruxelles (sais.), 27 February 1995, *Journal des Tribunaux* (1995) 565 ff.

50 Brussels Court of Appeal, 15 February 2000, *Journal des Tribunaux* (2001) 6 ff. with a note by M. Romero, "L'immunité d'exécution des missions diplomatiques".

51 Cass., 15 May 1996, *Pasicrisie*, 1996, I, pp. 491 ff.

gazette,[52] it appears that the request for deferral could hardly have been dealt with failing the specific procedure provided for in the Law of 22 March 1996.

Another, more delicate issue is whether domestic courts may set aside decisions taken by subsidiary organs of the Security Council which are deemed incompatible with relevant Security Council decisions or other international law standards. This is of particular importance with respect to the freezing of individuals' assets on the basis of United Nations decisions, notably as concerns the financing of terrorism. Such measures are a cause of concern to the extent that, although they are administrative rather than criminal in nature, they may affect the presumption of innocence and do not provide for any means of redress for the individuals concerned to defend their rights.

VII. Implementation of Security Council Decisions Relating to the International Criminal Tribunals for the Former Yugoslavia and Rwanda

As already stated, the Security Council resolutions on the International Criminal Tribunals have not been implemented on the basis of the Law of 11 May 1995, but through an *ad hoc* Law of 22 March 1996 on the recognition of the International Tribunal for the former Yugoslavia and the International Tribunal for Rwanda and on judicial cooperation with these Tribunals.

The obligation to cooperate with the International Tribunals is provided for in Articles 2 and 4 of the Law. Pursuant to Article 5 of the Law, the Minister of Justice is competent to receive requests to cooperate emanating from any of the Tribunals. Chapter II of the Law deals with requests by an International Tribunal to a Belgian court to defer to its competence. Article 6 provides that if an International Tribunal requests the national courts to defer to its competence in relation to facts which are within its competence, the Court of Cassation decides, on the request of the Prosecutor-General, after having heard the person concerned and having determined that there is no error in respect of his or her identity. The words "in relation to facts which are within its competence" suggest that the Belgian judge's qualification of the facts would prevail over the International Tribunal's characterization. In her above-mentioned conclusions for the Court of Cassation on requests for deferral, the Advocate-General declared that the relevant facts fell within the International Criminal Tribunal's competence *ratione materiae*, *ratione personae*, *ratione loci* and *ratione temporis*, without however presenting any further argument in this respect. The Court limited itself to referring to the decision taken by the Tribunal for Rwanda without reviewing the qualification of the facts.[54]

Article 7 of the Law further provides that the Belgian court's deferring to the International Tribunal's competence does not affect the victim's right to claim for reparation. However, the exercise of this right is suspended as long as the case is pending before the

52 See *Moniteur belge*, 27 April 1996 and *Parliamentary Documents*, Senate, 1-247/3, 1995-1996, p. 9, 22.

53 Brussels Labour Court, 21 April 1993, *Journal des Tribunaux du Travail*, (1993) 363-364.

54 See Cass., 15 May 1996, *Pasicrisie*, 1996, I, p. 491 ff.; Cass., 9 July 1996, *Pasicrisie*, 1996, I, pp. 729 ff.; Cass., 9 October 1996, *Bulletin des arrêts de la Cour de cassation* (1996) 962 ff..

Tribunal. Article 8 relates to the hypothesis that, following a Belgian court's deferral, the Tribunal's Prosecutor decides not to indict the person concerned, or the Tribunal does not confirm the indictment or finds that it has no competence to decide the case. In this hypothesis, the Court of Cassation shall determine the procedure and order that the case be referred to the competent Belgian court, tribunal or investigating judge. This Article was applied in a judgement of 13 August 1996 *re Higaniro*, where the International Criminal Tribunal for Rwanda, acting pursuant to Articles 17 and 18 of its Statute, had decided that no charges could be withheld against the accused and had refused to confirm the indictment.[55]

Chapter III of the Law deals with judicial cooperation. Pursuant to Article 9, requests made by the Tribunals or the Prosecutor relating to the conduct of the proceedings, such as the identification of persons and the gathering of evidence, shall be dealt with by the competent Belgian authorities as if the demand were made by Belgian judicial authorities. Article 10 authorises the Prosecutor or Judge of the International Tribunal by whom the request was made to attend the proceedings in Belgium. Article 11 further provides that the Minister of Justice shall be informed of any procedure pending before a Belgian court pursuant to the Law of 16 June 1993 on the repression of serious violations of the 1949 Geneva Conventions and their 1st and 2nd additional Protocols, in relation to facts which could fall within the competence of one of the International Tribunals.

Chapter IV of the Law relates to the arrest and transfer of persons. Article 12 *i.a.* provides that arrest warrants issued by a Tribunal with respect to a person located on Belgian territory are rendered executory by the *Chambre du conseil* of the place where the person concerned has his/her domicile or where he/she has been found. Again, the Belgian court is under the obligation to verify, *i.a.*, whether the facts mentioned in the warrant are within the Tribunal's competence. As stated above, Article 13 of the Law of 22 March 1996 further provides that the Government shall transfer the arrested persons pursuant to the Rules of Procedure of the Tribunal and in accordance with the European Convention on Human Rights.

Finally, Chapter V of the Law relates to the enforcement of sentences. Article 14 *i.a.* provides that to the extent that Belgium is mentioned on the list of States which have indicated to the Security Council their willingness to accept convicted persons, the sentence is directly and immediately enforceable in Belgium.

VIII. Interface between Domestic and International Implementation

Communication between national governments and competent United Nations bodies has proven of crucial importance with respect to Security Council sanctions against UNITA and, more specifically, conflict diamonds. Following the adoption by the Panel of Experts of a first report, stating that Belgium had failed to adequately implement United Nations sanctions with respect to diamonds,[56] the Belgian Permanent Representative to the United Nations stated before the Security Council that he regretted the omission

55 Cass., 13 August 1996, *Bulletin des arrêts de la Cour de cassation* (1996) 740 ff..

56 S/2000/203 of 10 March 2000, paragraphs 89-90.

of important information, as well as the inclusion of some unfounded information. He indicated that the creation of the Diamond Task Force had remained unmentioned, as well as measures taken by the Diamond High Council.[57] Security Council Resolution 1295 (2000), which was adopted subsequently,

> "welcomes the steps announced by the Government of Belgium on 3 March 2000 in support of the more effective implementation of the measures contained in Resolution 1173 (1998), welcomes also the establishment by the Government of Belgium of an inter-ministerial task force to curb sanctions violations, further welcomes the measures taken by the Diamond High Council, in conjunction with the Government of Angola, to render sanctions more effective, invites the Government of Belgium and the Diamond High Council to continue to cooperate with the Committee to devise practical measures to limit access by UNITA to the legitimate diamond market and welcomes their public affirmations in this regard."[58]

The Security Council thus appeared to acknowledge that at least some information provided by the Belgian authorities had not been duly taken into account by the Panel of Experts. The Panel of Experts, which counted only one French-speaking person among its members, may in fact have been unable to take account of information provided to it in French, while translation facilities in the United Nations are being reduced for budgetary reasons.[59] If so, it is to be feared that information provided to the United Nations in Member States' reports will not always be accorded the attention it deserves. This may have dramatic consequences for the reporting State, as well as for justice and for the United Nations' integrity, when that State is being accused of violating the United Nations sanctions regime. Apart from this hypothesis, it is also to be feared that the Sanctions Committees may be deprived of crucial information on the inadequacy of the implementation measures taken by some Member States.

IX. Conclusions and Recommendations

The great majority of Security Council sanctions under Chapter VII of the Charter are presently implemented at the level of the European Community. Belgian practice, however, reveals a number of problems which are of general interest. The implementing measures taken at the Belgian national level provide for a substantial number of general or case-to-case exemptions which are not enunciated in the relevant Security Council decisions. This confirms that Security Council resolutions may, and should be interpreted and applied in accordance with the Charter and with general international law. In particular, the measures enunciated in the Council's decisions may be mitigated in the light of their object and purpose on the basis of the principle of reasonableness. However, this possibility may engender constitutional problems. The Belgian Government's thesis that

57 SC/6825 of 15 March 2000.

58 SCR 1295 (2000) of 18 April 2000, paragraph 17.

59 See GA/AB/3289 of 22 March 1999.

the special powers which the Law of 11 May 1995 confers upon the Government are justified because the measures to be taken are enunciated *expressis verbis* in the relevant Security Council decisions, is unconvincing. While this does not necessarily deprive the Law of 1995 of its legitimacy, it may require a more stringent parliamentary control. It further requires a more intensive collaboration between the Ministry of Foreign Affairs and the 'technical' Ministries implementing the United Nations decisions in various fields.

In the second place, it is striking that the fear has been expressed that the implementation of United Nations sanctions might affect human rights, and in particular the human rights standards applicable at the European regional level. The fact that the Security Council and its subsidiary organs are extending their grip on individual behaviour is likely to create substantial problems in this field. In this respect, the main recommendation to be made is for the Security Council and its subsidiary bodies to take due account of human rights law when drafting decisions on economic sanctions.

* * *

Select Bibliography

I. United Nations Documents

- S/2000/203 of 10 March 2000, *Letter dated 10 March 2000 from the Chairman of the Security Council Committee established pursuant to Resolution 864 (1993) concerning the situation in Angola addressed to the President of the Security Council, Annex I, Letter dated 28 February 2000 from the Chairman of the Panel of Experts established by the Security Council pursuant to Resolution 1237 (1999) addressed to the Chairman of the Security Council Committee established pursuant to Resolution 864 (1993) concerning the situation in Angola, Enclosure, Report of the Panel of Experts on violations of Security Council Sanctions Against UNITA.*
- SC/6825 of 15 March 2000.
- SCR 1295 (2000) of 18 April 2000.

II. Belgian Legislation and Parliamentary Documents

(1) Legislation

- Decree-Law of 6 October 1944 concerning foreign exchange transactions, *Moniteur belge*, 7 October 1944.
- Law of 11 September 1961 on the import, export and transit of goods, *Moniteur belge*, 27 October 1962.

- Special Law of 6 January 1989 on the Court of Arbitration, *Moniteur belge*, 7 January 1989.
- Law of 5 August 1991 on the import, export and transit of arms, ammunition and material specially designed for military use and technology in these fields, *Moniteur belge*, 10 September 1991.
- Law of 11 May 1995 on the implementation of United Nations Security Council Decisions, *Moniteur belge*, 29 July 1995.
- Law of 22 March 1996 on the recognition of the International Criminal Tribunal for the Former Yugoslavia and the International Criminal Tribunal for Rwanda and on judicial cooperation with these Tribunals, *Moniteur belge*, 24 April 1996.
- Law of 13 April 2003 on the implementation of restrictive measures adopted by the Council of the European Union against States, certain persons and entities, *Moniteur belge*, 13 June 2003.
- Royal Decree of 8 August 1990 concerning the financial relations with certain countries, *Moniteur belge*, 9 August 1990.
- Royal Decree of 5 June 1992 concerning the financial relations with the Federal Republic of Yugoslavia (Serbia and Montenegro), *Moniteur belge*, 6 June 1992.
- Royal Decree of 25 February 1994 concerning the financial relations with Haiti, *Moniteur belge*, 9 March 1994.
- Royal Decree of 17 March 1994 concerning the financial relations with Libya, *Moniteur belge*, 31 March 1994.
- Royal Decree of 20 June 1994 amending the royal decree of 17 March 1994 concerning financial relations with Libya, *Moniteur belge*, 29 June 1994.
- Ministerial Decree of 8 August 1990 submitting the import, export and transit of goods to the obtention of a licence, *Moniteur belge*, 9 August 1990.
- Ministerial Decree of 22 September 1990 concerning the financial relations with certain countries, *Moniteur belge*, 4 October 1990.
- Ministerial Decree of 26 July 1993 amending the ministerial decree of 29 July 1992 implementing the royal decree of 5 June 1992 on the financial relations with the Federal Republic of Yugoslavia (Serbia and Montenegro), *Moniteur belge*, 6 August 1993.
- Ministerial Decree of 29 July 1992 implementing the royal decree of 5 June 1992 concerning the financial relations with the Federal Republic of Yugoslavia (Serbia and Montenegro), *Moniteur belge*, 1 August 1992.
- Ministerial Decree of 20 June 1994 implementing the royal decree of 17 March 1994 concerning the financial relations with Libya, *Moniteur belge*, 29 June 1994.

(2) Parliamentary Documents

- *Parliamentary Documents*, Senate, 1993-1994, n. 1173/1.
- *Parliamentary Documents*, Senate, 1995-1996, 1-247/3.

– Report of the Senate Commission of Inquiry on the Great Lakes, Doc. 2-942/1 of 20 February 2003.

III. Jurisprudence

(1) General

– Court of Arbitration, No. 26/91, 16 October 1991.
– Court of Arbitration, No. 12/94, 3 February 1994.
– Cass., 16 January 1968, *Pasicrisie*, 1968, I, p. 625.
– Cass., 12 March 1968, *Pasicrisie*, 1968, I, p. 874.
– Cass., 27 May 1971, *Pasicrisie*, 1971, I, p. 886.
– Cass. 26 September 1978, *Pasicrisie*, 1979, I, p. 126.
– Cass., 4 April 1984, *Pasicrisie*, 1984, I, p. 920.
– Cass., 16 April 1984, *Pasicrisie*, 1984, I, p. 1032.
– Cass., 10 May 1985, *Pasicrisie*, 1985, I, p. 1123.
– Cass., 6 March 1986, *Pasicrisie*, 1986, I, p. 853.
– Cass., 10 May 1989, *Pasicrisie*, 1989, I, p. 953.

(2) On United Nations Sanctions

– Cass., 15 May 1996, *Pasicrisie*, 1996, I, p. 491 ff.;
– Cass., 9 July 1996, *Pasicrisie*, 1996, I, p. 729 ff.;
– Cass., 13 August 1996, *Bulletin des arrêts de la Cour de cassation*, 1996, p. 740 ff.
– Cass., 9 October 1996, *Bulletin des arrêts de la Cour de cassation*, 1996, p. 962 ff.
– Brussels Labour Court, 21 April 1993, *Journal des Tribunaux du Travail*, 1993, p. 363-364.
– Brussels Court of Appeal, 15 February 2000, A.R. No. 1999/AR/892, unpublished.
– Civ. Bruxelles (sais.), 27 February 1995, *Journal des Tribunaux*, 1995, p. 565 ff.

IV. Books and Articles

(1) General

– Y. Lejeune and Ph. Brouwers, "La Cour d'arbitrage face au contrôle de la constitutionnalité des traités", *Journal des Tribunaux* (1992) 670.
– J. Salmon, "Le conflit entre le traité international et la loi interne en Belgique à la suite de l'arrêt rendu le 27 mai 1971 par la Cour de cassation", *Journal des Tribunaux* (1971) 535.
– J. Verhoeven, "Chronique de jurisprudence belge relative au droit international public", XIX *Revue belge de droit international*, No. 2 (1986) 342.
– J. Verhoeven, note under Cass., 19 March 1981, *Journal des Tribunaux* (1982) 565.
– J. Verhoeven, "Applicabilité directe des traités et 'intention des parties contractantes'", in: *Liber Amicorum E. Krings* (Brussels, Story-Scientia, 1991) 895 ff.

- M. Waelbroeck, "Portée et critères de l'applicabilité directe des traités internationaux", *Revue critique de jurisprudence belge* (1985) 41-42.

(2) On United Nations Sanctions

- N. Angelet, "L'embargo et l'ONU", in: *L'embargo – actes de la journée d'études du 1er décembre 1995 organisée par l'Association Européenne pour le Droit Bancaire et Financier – Belgium* (Brussels, Bruylant, 1996), pp. 45-85.
- N. Angelet, "Criminal Liability for the Violation of United Nations Economic Sanctions", 7 *European Journal of Crime, Criminal Law and Criminal Justice*, No. 2 (1999) 89-102.
- G. Brouhns, "Les embargos financiers", in: *Mélanges Jean Pardon – Etudes en droit bancaire et financier* (Brussels, Bruylant, 1996), pp. 21-83.
- P. d'Argent, "Le juge des saisies, le Conseil de sécurité et l'immunité d'exécution restreinte des Etats étrangers", *Journal des Tribunaux* (1995) 568-572.
- P. d'Argent, "La loi du 11 mai 1995 relative à la mise en oeuvre des décisions du Conseil de sécurité de l'Organisation des Nations Unies", *Journal des Tribunaux* (1996) pp. 357-361.
- D. Vandermeersch, "La loi du 22 mars 1996 relative à la reconnaissance du TPIY et du TPIR et à la coopération avec ces tribunaux", *Revue de droit pénal* (1996) 855-888.
- J. Verhoeven, "Guerre et droit international – Sur certaines questions soulevées par le conflit Iraq-Koweit", *Journal des Tribunaux* (1991) 139-142.
- Ph. Willaert, "Les sanctions économiques contre la Rhodésie (1965-1979)", XVIII *Revue belge de droit international*, No. 2 (1984-1985) 216-245.
- *L'embargo - Actes de la journée d'études du 1er décembre 1995 organisée par l'Association Européenne pour le Droit Bancaire et Financier - Belgium* (Brussels, Bruylant, 1996), p. 268.

5

THE EUROPEAN UNION

*Daniel Bethlehem**

Prefatory Note

The present chapter addresses the issue of the implementation of decisions of the UN Security Council (UNSC) imposing economic and other non-military sanctions by the European Union (EU) and its related manifestations, notably the European Community (EC).[1] It does not address the imposition of sanctions by the EU[2] independently of

* Queen's Counsel; Director, Lauterpacht Research Centre for International Law and Fellow of Clare Hall, University of Cambridge. The author would like to thank Rodney Neufeld and Penelope Nevill of the Lauterpacht Research Centre for their assistance in respect of this chapter.

1 The description "European Community" refers to the arrangements first established by the *Treaty of Rome Establishing the European Economic Community* (EEC) of 1957, as amended by various acts of accession and treaties of amendment including, most recently, Title II of the *Maastricht Treaty on European Union* (TEU) and the *Treaty of Amsterdam* (TA). The description "European Communities" refers to the three communities: the European Community, the European Coal and Steel Community (ECSC) and the European Atomic Energy Community (EAEC). The description "European Union" refers to the arrangements established by the *TEU*, as amended by the *Treaty of Amsterdam*. By Article 1 of the *TEU*, the European Union "shall be founded on the European Communities, supplemented by the policies and forms of cooperation established by this Treaty". The "policies and forms of cooperation" referred to include, in particular, those relating to the common foreign and security policy (Title V) and police and judicial cooperation in criminal matters (Title VI). In contrast to the EC, the EU does not have legal personality. The form of cooperation that characterises the Union is therefore largely inter-governmental. While a formal distinction must be made between acts of the EU and acts of the EC, it is increasingly the case, particularly in the area of the implementation of international economic sanctions, that these acts are inextricably intertwined. This matter is discussed further in the body of the present chapter. For further consideration, see Kapteyn and Verloren van Themaat, *Introduction to the Law of the European Communities* (3rd ed., 1998; Gormley, ed.), at pp. 45-76.

2 Unless a different appreciation is evident from the text, the reference herein to the "EU" is used generically to refer to both the EU and the EC (also referred to simply as "the Community").

Vera Gowlland-Debbas (ed.), National Implementation of UN Sanctions, *123-165.*

action by the UNSC, so-called "unilateral sanctions".[3] While there are good reasons for distinguishing between these two areas of action by the EU – notably because the original provenance of the measures may tell us something about their wider international legitimacy – the procedural framework and machinery of EU sanctions implementation is likely to be the same in both cases. Procedural and administrative developments that have emerged in one area of EU action are thus likely to be reflected in EU practice in the other. In particular, for present purposes, EU practice in respect of the imposition of unilateral sanctions is likely to be reflected in EU practice implementing decisions of the UNSC.

The importance of this appreciation lies in the fact that the EU sanctions implementation regime has evolved significantly over recent years and continues to develop. Thus, the *Treaty on European Union*, which entered into force on 1 November 1993, both significantly enlarged the competence of the EC in the field of sanctions and, in its establishment of the EU, created a mechanism for the articulation of policy in this area through the provisions on a Common Foreign and Security Policy (CFSP). The CFSP provisions were further amended by the *Treaty of Amsterdam*, which entered into force on 1 May 1999 (which also had the incidental effect of renumbering the articles of both the TEU and the EC Treaty).

The practice of the EU in the field of sanctions on the basis of these provisions has also evolved. Of particular importance was the approach adopted by the EU in respect of the imposition of sanctions against the Federal Republic of Yugoslavia (FRY) over

3 Examples of such measures include: an arms embargo imposed on Indonesia (Common Position 1999/624/CFSP of 16 September 1999 (OJ No L 245, 17.9.1999, p. 53) and Council Regulation (EC) No 2158/1999 of 11 October 1999 (OJ No L 265, 13.10.99, p. 1); measures against Burma/Myanmar (see, *inter alia*, Council Regulation (EC) No 1081/2000 of 22 May 2000 (OJ No L 122, 24.5.2000, p. 29), amended by Commission Regulation (EC) No 1883/2002 of 22 October 2002 (OJ No L 285, 23.10.2002, p. 17) and Commission Regulation (EC No 744/2003 of 28 April 2003 (OJ No L 106, 29.4.2003, p. 20)); an arms embargo against the Democratic Republic of the Congo (see Common Position 2002/829/CFSP of 21 October 2002 (OJ No L 285, 23.10.2002, p. 1) amending an arms embargo of 7 April 1993); sanctions against Nigeria (see Common Position 95/515/CFSP of 20 November 1995 (OJ No L 298, 11.12.1995, p. 1) as amended by Common Position 98/614/CFSP of 30 October 1998 (OJ No L 293/77, 31.10.98, p. 77) which was repealed by Council Decision 1999/347/CFSP of 17 May 1999 (OJ No L 133, 28.5.1999, p. 5)); and, most recently, restrictive measures against Zimbabwe (see Common Position 2002/145/CFSP of 18 February 2002 (OJ No L 50, 21.2.2002, p. 1), amended by Common Position 2002/600/CFSP of 22 July 2002 (OJ No L 195, 24.7.2002, p. 1), Council Decision 2002/754/CFSP of 13 September 2002 (OJ No L 247, 14.9.2002, p. 56) and Council Regulation (EC) No 310/2002 of 18 February 2002 (OJ No L 50, 21.2.2000, p. 4), amended by Commission Regulation (EC) No L 1224/2002 of 8 July 2002 (OJ No L 179, 9.7.2002, p. 10), amended for a second time by Commission Regulation (EC) No 1345/2002 of 24 July 2002 (OJ No L 196, 25.7.2002, p. 28) and for a third time by Commission Regulation (EC) No 1643/2002 of 13 September 2002 (OJ No L 247, 14.9.2002, p. 22). Common Position 2003/115/CFSP of 18 February 2003 (OJ No L 46, 20.2.2003, p. 30) extended and amended Common Position 2002/145/CFSP. See also Council Decision 2003/112/EC and Council Regulation (EC) No 313/2003, both of 18 February 2003 (OJ No L 46, 20.2.2003, pp. 25 and 6)).

events in Kosovo where measures were taken independently and in the absence of any action by the UNSC.[4] Notably, by Regulation 1294/1999 extending the freeze of funds and the ban on investment in relation to the FRY imposed by the EU in earlier measures, the EU for the first time established a licensing regime which allowed the European Commission (Commission) to authorise, by way of exception, transactions or activities that would otherwise have been prohibited by the Regulation or the lawfulness of which may have been uncertain.[5] This constituted a major, and long-overdue innovation in the EU sanctions regime, mirroring arrangements that had long been a feature of the sanctions regimes of many EU Member States, designed both to improve the effectiveness of sanctions and to reduce the unintended costs of compliance with such measures by persons affected thereby. The flexibility introduced by such procedures is becoming a common feature of EU sanctions regimes – including those implementing decisions of the UNSC – with the consequence that the sometimes cumbersome arrangements of past EU sanctions measures are being replaced by increasingly sophisticated and adaptable measures. As with other areas of EU law, the growth of administrative decision-making and secondary legislation by the Commission on the basis of primary legislation by the EU – invariably affecting the conduct of persons within the Union or having the nationality of an EU Member State in a quite significant manner – may also be expected

4 See in this regard the following: Common Position 98/240/CFSP of 19 March 1998 (OJ No L 95, 27.3.1998, p. 1) amended by Common Position 2001/719/CFSP of 8 October 2001 (OJ No L 268, 9.10.2001, p. 49); Common Position 98/326/CFSP of 7 May 1998 (OJ No L 143, 14.5.1998, p. 1); Common Position 98/374/CFSP of 8 June 1998 (OJ No L 165, 10.6.1998, p. 1); Council Regulation (EC) No 1295/98 of 22 June 1998 (OJ No L 178, 23.6.1998, p. 33); Council Regulation (EC) No 1607/98 of 24 July 1998 (OJ No L 209, 25.7.1998, p. 16). Regulations 1295/98 and 1607/98 were repealed and replaced by Council Regulation (EC) No 1294/1999 of 15 June 1999 (OJ No L 153, 19.6.1999, p. 63). On this see Common Position 1999/318/CFSP of 10 May 1999 (OJ No L 123, 13.5.1999, p. 1). Regulation 1294/1999 has been amended by the following: Commission Regulation (EC) No 1970/1999 of 15 September 1999 (OJ No L 244, 16.9.1999, p. 39); Commission Regulation (EC) No 2756/1999 of 22 December 1999 (OJ No L 331, 23.12.1999, p. 43); Council Regulation (EC) No 607/2000 of 20 March 2000 (OJ No L 73, 23.3.2000, p. 4); Council Regulation (EC) No 2488/2000 of 10 November 2000 (OJ No L 287, 14.11.2000, p. 19); Council Regulation (EC) No 723/2000 of 6 April 2000 (OJ No L 86, 7.4.2000, p. 1); Commission Regulation (EC) No 826/2000 of 25 April 2000 (OJ No L 101, 26.4.2000, p. 3); Council Regulation (EC) No 1059/2000 of 18 May 2000 (OJ No L 119, 20.5.2000, p. 1); Commission Regulation (EC) No 1094/2000 of 24 May 2000 (OJ No 124, 25.5.2000, p. 42); Commission Regulation (EC) No 1147/2000 of 29 May 2000 (OJ No L 129, 30.5.2000, p. 15); and Commission Regulation (EC) No 1440/2000 of 30 June 2000 (OJ No L 161, 1.7.2000, p. 68).

5 See Article 8 of Regulation 1294/1999, as amended by Regulation 723/2000, *op.cit.* note 2. As a precursor to this development, Article 9 of Council Regulation (EC) No 1705/98 of 28 July 1998 in respect of sanctions against Angola (OJ No L 215, 1.8.98, p. 1) empowered the Commission to supplement and/or amend the annexes to that Regulation. The Commission exercised this power in Commission Regulation (EC) No 753/1999 of 12 April 1999 (OJ No L 98, 13.4.99, p. 3).

to give rise to an increasing incidence of challenge and the consequential development of a body of jurisprudence relating to the interpretation and application of sanctions.[6]

While these developments are likely to be a feature of both EU implementation of UNSC decisions and measures adopted by the EU unilaterally, the potential ramifications of such developments may resonate differently in each area. Thus, in the case of measures adopted by the EU in the absence of UNSC decisions, it may be expected that a common ground of challenge – in respect of both the measures themselves and administrative decisions and secondary measures adopted thereunder – would be the alleged incompatibility of the EU measure with some rule of international law, invariably contained in a treaty to which both the EU and the target state are a party. Such proceedings may arise both in Community courts, notably the European Court of Justice (ECJ), as well as in international tribunals such as panels and the Appellate Body of the World Trade Organisation (WTO). Indeed, this was the essence of the challenge raised by "Yugoslavia" in December 1991 within the framework of the *General Agreement on Tariffs and Trade* (GATT 1947) against certain trade measures taken by the Community prior to the imposition of sanctions by the UNSC, a complaint that, in the end, did not proceed following the decision of the GATT Council that the FRY "could not continue automatically the contracting party status of the former Socialist Federal Republic of Yugoslavia in the GATT and that it shall not participate in the work of the Council and its subsidiary bodies".[7]

In contrast, in circumstances in which the EU has acted in implementation of a decision of the UNSC, the issue more likely to arise in legal proceedings may be the compatibility of the EU measure with the UNSC decision it purports to implement. More significant, perhaps, is that legal proceedings in such circumstances, in whatever forum, could conceivably also be used to challenge the *vires* of the UNSC decision, whether by reference to the UN *Charter* or general international law.

As this suggests, although the focus of this chapter is EU implementation of UNSC decisions imposing sanctions, a full appreciation of the evolving competence and practice of the EU in this field would also require an examination of the relevant law and practice relating to the imposition of sanctions by the EU independently and in the absence of action by the UNSC.

* * *

6 See on this issue Canor, I., "'Can Two Walk Together, Except They Be Agreed?' The Relationship Between International Law and European Law: The Incorporation of United Nations Sanctions Against Yugoslavia into European Community Law Through the Perspective of the European Court of Justice", 35 *CMLRev* (1998) 137.

7 GATT Doc. C/M/264, 14 July 1993, at p. 3. See further on this matter the *Analytical Index: Guide to GATT Law and Practice* (1995), at pp. 604-605, 644, 673, 877-878, 1014 and 1094.

I. Introduction

The EU is not a Member of the United Nations. Subject to any discussion of the obligations of non-Members of the UN to comply with decisions of the UNSC under general international law, the EU does not, therefore, have a direct obligation under the UN *Charter* to give effect to decisions of the UNSC imposing economic sanctions. If the EU has an obligation to act at all in relation to such measures, it is a derivative *obligation* based on the obligation of individual EU Member States under the *Charter* in respect of UNSC decisions and the transfer of competence in respect of such matters from the Member States to the Community.

The formality of this assessment belies, however, the fact that the stated objectives of the EU's CFSP include the preservation of peace and the strengthening of international security "in accordance with the principles of the United Nations Charter".[8] Under Article 302 of the *EC Treaty*, the Commission also has responsibility "to ensure the maintenance of all appropriate relations with the organs of the United Nations and of its specialised agencies". Article 19 of the *TEU* further provides that EU Member States shall coordinate their action in international organisations and shall uphold EU common positions in such fora.[9] As the CFSP provisions of the *TEU* require the EU Council to implement common strategies in areas where the Member States have important interests in common *inter alia* by the adoption of common positions, the EU is not therefore simply a semi-detached participant in the economic sanctions arena centred on the UNSC. While it may not speak with its own voice in the UNSC, and may not be directly bound by decisions of the UNSC, the reality is that the EU plays an increasingly important role in the formulation and coordination of policy with regard to matters addressed by the UNSC and considers itself bound, on behalf of its Member States, to take such action as is necessary to give effect to decisions of the UNSC in areas which come within its competence.

The Community's competence to act in implementation of UNSC decisions imposing sanctions has not, however, always been so evident. As already noted, the Community sanctions implementation regime has evolved significantly over recent years, a matter illustrated by the contrasting approaches adopted to the implementation of UNSC sanctions against Rhodesia in the late 1960s and 1970s and against Yugoslavia in the 1990s. Thus, in response to various Resolutions of the UNSC imposing a comprehensive regime of sanctions against Rhodesia in the period 1965 to 1979,[10] the Community not only

8 As per Article 11(1), third indent, TEU.

9 As per Article 19(1), TEU. The second paragraph of this article further provides *inter alia* that: "Member States which are also members of the United Nations Security Council will concert and keep other Member States fully informed. Member States which are permanent members of the Security Council will, in the execution of their functions, ensure the defence of the positions and the interests of the Union, without prejudice to their responsibilities under the provisions of the United Nations Charter."

10 See, in particular, Security Council Resolutions 217 (1965) of 20 November 1965, 221 (1966) of 9 April 1966, 232 (1966) of 16 December 1966, 253 (1968) of 29 May 1968, 277 (1970) of 18 March 1970, 314 (1972) of 28 February 1972, 333 (1973) of 22 May 1973, 388 (1976) of 6 April 1976 and 409 (1977) of 27 May 1977.

initially failed to take any action to implement the relevant Security Council Resolutions ("SCRs") imposing sanctions but actually included Rhodesia on the list of countries with which trade was *liberalised*.[11] It was only in 1970, with the adoption of a new regime for the importation of goods into the Community, that Rhodesia was removed from this list of countries.[12]

The Commission's attitude to the division of competence between the Community and its Member States in respect of UNSC sanctions against Rhodesia is equally revealing. Thus, in response to a Written Parliamentary Question on 23 March 1973 which, in respect of alleged infringements by certain Member States of the UNSC sanctions against Rhodesia, asked *inter alia* whether the Commission did "not feel that it should check compliance with international obligations to which Member States of the Community have, like others, subscribed",[13] the Commission responded:

> "... the Commission does not consider that it is one of its functions to check compliance with international undertakings entered into by the Member States where these do not affect the application of the Treaties of which it is the guardian."[14]

The Commission's determination not to become drawn in to questions relating to Member State implementation of UNSC sanctions against Rhodesia was reiterated subsequently.[15]

In contrast, the Community's response to the UNSC sanctions against Yugoslavia paints a very different picture. Thus, following the adoption of SCR 713 (1991) – in which the UNSC expressed concern that the continuation of the situation in Yugoslavia constituted a threat to international peace and security and imposed "a general and complete embargo on all deliveries of weapons and military equipment to Yugoslavia"[16] – the Community moved quickly to adopt a series of measures of its own against Yugoslavia which had an extensive economic effect.[17] While these measures did not purport to be in

11 See Council Regulation (EEC) No 2041/68 of 10 December 1968 (OJ No L 303, 18.12.68, p. 1). See also Council Regulation (EEC) No 2603/69 of 20 December 1969 (OJ No L 324, 27.12.69, p. 25). For a discussion of these measures, see P.J. Kuyper, "Sanctions Against Rhodesia: The EEC and the Implementation of General International Legal Rules", 12 *CMLRev* (1975) 231, at pp. 233-235.

12 Council Regulation (EEC) No 1025/70 of 25 May 1970 (OJ No L 124, 8.6.70, p. 6). See also Kuyper, *ibid.*.

13 Written Question No 5/73 by Mr Vredeling, 23 March 1973 (OJ No C 57, 17.7.73, p. 27).

14 Answer of the Commission, 4 June 1973 (OJ No C 57, 17.7.73, p. 28).

15 Written Question No 249/73 by Mr Johnston, 18 July 1973, and answer by the Commission of 6 November 1973 (OJ No C 102, 24.11.73, p. 13).

16 SCR 713 (1991) of 25 September 1991, at preambular paragraph 4 and operative paragraph 6.

17 See, for example, Council Regulation (EEC) No 3300/91 of 11 November 1991 (OJ No L 315, 15.11.91, p. 1); Council Regulation (EEC) No 3302/91 of 11 November 1991 (OJ No L 315, 15.11.91, p. 46); Decision 91/586/ECSC, EEC of 11 November 1991 (OJ No L 315, 15.11.91, p. 47); Decision 91/587/ECSC of 11 November 1991 (OJ No L 315, 15.11.91, p. 48); Deci-

implementation of SCR 713 (1991), a number of the measures referred explicitly to the Resolution and to the UNSC's expression of concern that the continuation of the situation in Yugoslavia constituted a threat to international peace and security.

Subsequent to SCR 713 (1991), the UNSC went on to adopt a series of Resolutions imposing a comprehensive regime of sanctions against the "Federal Republic of Yugoslavia (Serbia and Montenegro)". The principal measures included SCR 757 (1992) of 30 May 1992, SCR 760 (1992) of 18 June 1992, SCR 787 (1992) of 16 November 1992, SCR 820 (1992) of 17 April 1992, SCR 942 (1994) of 23 September 1994, SCR 943 (1994) of 23 September 1994,[18] SCR 992 (1995) of 11 May 1995, SCR 1021 (1995) of 22 November 1995, SCR 1022 (1995) of 22 November 1995, SCR 1074 (1996) of 1 October 1996 and SCR 1160 (1998) of 31 March 1998. These Resolutions were implemented by the Community by an almost bewildering array of often interacting measures.[19] While EU Member States also passed domestic legislation or took other action

sion 91/588/ECSC of 11 November 1991 (OJ No L 315, 15.11.91, p. 49); Decision 91/589/ECSC of 11 November 1991 (OJ No L 315, 15.11.91, p. 50); Council Decision 91/602/EEC of 25 November 1991 (OJ No L 325, 27.11.91, p. 23). See also Council Regulation (EEC) No 3567/91 of 2 December 1991 (OJ No L 342, 12.12.91, p. 1); Council Regulation (EEC) No 3587/91 of 3 December 1991 (OJ No L 341, 12.12.91, p. 1); Council Regulation (EEC) No 545/92 of 3 February 1992 (OJ No L 63, 7.3.92, p. 1); Council Regulation (EEC) No 546/92 of 3 February 1992 (OJ No L 63, 7.3.92, p. 39); Council Regulation (EEC) No 547/92 of 3 February 1992 (OJ No L 63, 7.3.92, p. 41); Council Regulation (EEC) No 548/92 3 February 1992 (OJ No L 63, 7.3.92, p. 49); Council Regulation (EEC) No 1433/92 of 1 June 1992 (OJ No L 151, 3.6.92, p. 7); and Council Regulation (EEC) No 3105/92 of 26 October 1992 (OJ No L 312, 29.10.92, p. 1).

18 As extended by SCR 970 (1995) of 12 January 1995, SCR 988 (1995) of 21 April 1995, SCR 1003 (1995) of 5 July 1995, and SCR 1015 (1995) of 15 September 1995.

19 See *inter alia* Council Regulation (EEC) No 1432/92 of 1 June 1992 (OJ No L 151, 3.6.92, p. 4), as amended or supplemented by Council Regulation (EEC) No 2015/92 of 20 July 1992 (OJ No L 205, 22.7.92, p. 2), Council Regulation (EEC) No 3534/92 of 7 December 1992 (OJ No L 358, 8.12.92, p. 16), Council Regulation (EEC) No 2656/92 of 8 September 1992 (OJ No L 266, 12.9.92, p. 27), Council Regulation (EEC) No 40/93 of 8 January 1993 (OJ No L 7, 13.1.93, p. 1); also Council Regulation (EEC) No 2655/92 of 8 September 1992 (OJ No L 266, 12.9.92, p. 26); Decision 92/285/ECSC of 1 June 1992 (OJ No L 151, 3.6.92, p. 20), as amended or supplemented by Decision 92/314/ECSC of 15 June 1992 (OJ No L 166, 20.6.92, p. 35), Decision 92/388/ECSC of 20 June 1992 (OJ No L 205, 22.7.92, p. 5), Decision 92/470/ECSC of 8 September 1992 (OJ No L 266, 12.9.92, p. 29), Decision 92/555/ECSC of 7 December 1992 (OJ No L 358, 8.12.92, p. 18), Decision 93/8/ECSC of 8 January 1993 (OJ No L 7, 13.1.93, p. 11); also Commission Regulation (EEC, ECSC) No 2725/92 of 18 September 1992 (OJ No L 276, 19.9.92, p. 18), as amended and repealed by Commission Regulation (EEC, ECSC) No 3031/92 of 21 October 1992 (OJ No L 306, 22.10.92, p. 39), Commission Regulation (ECSC, EEC) No 2068/93 of 28 July 1993 (OJ No L 187, 29.7.93, p. 37); also Council Regulation (EEC) No 990/93 of 26 April 1993 (OJ No L 102, 28.4.93, p. 14), as amended, supplemented, suspended and repealed by Council Decision 94/673/CFSP of 10 October 1994 (OJ No L 266, 15.10.94, p. 11), Council Regulation (EC) No 2472/94 of 10 October 1994 (OJ No L 266, 15.10.94, p. 8), Council Decision 95/11/CFSP of 23 January 1995 (OJ No L 20, 27.1.95, p. 2), Council Regulation (EC) No 109/95 of 23 January 1995 (OJ No L 20, 27.1.95, p. 1), Common Position 95/150/CFSP of 28 April 1995 (OJ No L 99,

to implement UNSC decisions – in many cases, for purposes of setting down penalties for the infringement of the EU measures – the sanctions regimes in EU Member States were largely characterised by EU measures.

29.4.95, p. 2), Council Regulation (EC) No 984/95 of 28 April 1995 (OJ No L 99, 29.4.95, p. 1), Common Position 95/213/CFSP of 12 June 1995 (OJ No L 138, 21.6.95, p. 2), Council Regulation (EC) No 1380/95 of 12 June 1995 (OJ No L 138, 21.6.95, p. 1), Common Position 95/254/CFSP of 7 July 1995 (OJ No L 160, 11.7.95, p. 2), Council Regulation (EC) No 1673/95 of 7 July 1995 (OJ No L 160, 11.7.95, p. 1), Common Position 95/378/CFSP of 19 September 1995 (OJ No L 227, 22.9.95, p. 2), Council Regulation (EC) No 2229/95 of 19 September 1995 (OJ No L 227, 22.9.95, p. 1), Common Position 95/511/CFSP of 4 December 1995 (OJ No L 297, 9.12.95, p. 4), Council Regulation (EC) No 2815/95 of 4 December 1995 (OJ No L 297, 9.12.95, p. 1), Council Regulation (EC) No 462/96 of 11 March 1996 (OJ No L 65, 15.3.96, p. 2), Common Position 96/708/CFSP of 9 December 1996 (OJ No L 328, 18.12.96, p. 5), Council Regulation (EC) No 2382/96 of 9 December 1996 (OJ No L 328, 18.12.96, p. 1); also Decision 93/235/ECSC of 26 April 1993 (OJ No L 102, 28.4.93, p. 17), as suspended and repealed by Decision 95/510/ECSC of 4 December 1995 (OJ No L 297, 9.12.95, p. 3), Decision 96/201/ECSC of 11 March 1996 (OJ No L 65, 15.3.96, p. 38), Decision 96/707/ECSC of 9 December 1996 (OJ No L 328, 18.12.96, p. 3); also Council Decision 94/366/CFSP of 13 June 1994 (OJ No L 165, 1.7.94, p. 1) and Council Regulation (EC) No 1733/94 of 11 July 1994 (OJ No L 182, 16.7.94, p. 1); also Council Decision 94/672/CFSP of 10 October 1994 (OJ No L 266, 15.10.94, p. 10) and Council Regulation (EC) No 2471/94 of 10 October 1994 (OJ No L 266, 15.10.94, p. 10, as repealed by Council Regulation 467/95 *supra*, and Council Regulation (EC) No 2382/96 *supra*; Common Position 96/184 of 26 February 1996 (OJ No L 85, 7.3.1996, p. 1); Common Position 98/240/CFSP of 19 March 1998 (OJ No L 95, 27.3.98, p. 1), extended by Common Position 98/326/CFSP of 7 May 1998 (OJ No L 143, 14.5.1998, p. 1) and Council Regulation (EC) No 1295/98 of 22 June 1998 (OJ No L 178, 23.6.1998, p. 33); Common Position 98/374/CFSP of 8 June 1998 (OJ No L 165, 10.6.1998, p. 1) further extending Common Position 98/326/CFSP; Council Regulation (EC) No 1607/98 of 24 July 1998 (OJ No L 209, 25.7.1998, p. 16), Common Position 98/426 of 29 June 1998 (OJ No L 190, 4.7.1998, p. 3) and Council Regulation (EC) No 1901/98 of 7 September 1998 (OJ No L 248, 8.9.1998, p. 1) as amended by Council Regulation (EC) No 214/1999 of 25 January 1999 (OJ No L 23, 30.1.1999, p. 6); Council Regulation (EC) No 926/98 of 27 April 1998 (OJ No L 130, 1.5.1998, p. 1); Common Position 1999/273/CFSP of 23 April 1999 (OJ No L 108, 27.4.1999, p. 1) and Council Regulation (EC) No 900/1999 of 29 April 1999 (OJ No L 114, 1.5.1999, p. 7) and Commission Regulation (EC) No 1084/1999 of 26 May 1999 (OJ No L 131, 27.5.1999, p. 29); Common Position 1999/318/CFSP of 10 May 1999 (OJ No L 123, 13.5.1999, p. 1), Council Regulation (EC) No 1064/1999 of 21 May 1999 (OJ No L 129, 22.5.1999, p. 27) and Council Decision 1999/319/CFSP of 10 May 1999 (OJ No L 123, 13.5.1999, p. 3), amended variously by Council Decisions 1999/357/CFSP of 1 June 1999 (OJ No L 140, 3.6.1999, p. 1), 1999/424/CFSP of 28 June 1999 (OJ No L 163, 29.6.1999, p. 86), 1999/604/CFSP of 3 September 1999 (OJ No L 236, 7.9.1999, p. 1), 1999/612/CFSP of 13 September 1999 (OJ No L 242, 14.9.1999, p. 32), 1999/812/CFSP of 6 December 1999 (OJ No L 314, 8.12.1999, p. 36), 2000/177/CFSP of 28 February 2000 (OJ No L 56, 1.3.2000, p. 2), 2000/348/CFSP of 22 May 2000 (OJ No L 122, 24.5.2000, p. 7), 2000/495/CFSP of 3 August 2000 (OJ No L 200, 8.8.2000, p. 1); Council Regulation (EC) No 1294/1999 of 15 June 1999 (OJ No L 153, 19.6.1999, p. 63); Commission Regulation (EC) 1520/1999 of 12 July 1999 amending Council Regulation 1064/1999 (OJ No L 177, 13.7.1999, p. 10); Council Regulation (EC) No 2111/1999 of 4 October 1999 (OJ No L 258,

As these two contrasting cases of UNSC sanctions implementation by the Community illustrate, there has been a quite dramatic evolution in the Community's role in this area over the period in question. As has already been commented upon, much of this has to do with the significant broadening of the Community's competence in this field as a result of the *TEU*. Further impetus to Community action also no doubt emerged as a response to the sheer volume of activity in this area by the UNSC in the period from August 1990. In this respect, SCR 661 (1990) of 6 August 1990 impos-

5.10.1999, p. 12) as amended by Council Regulation (EC) No 2421/1999 of 15 November 1999 (OJ No L 294, 16.11.1999, p. 7); Council Regulation (EC) No 2151/1999 of 11 October 1999 repealing Regulation 1064/1999 (OJ No L 264, 12.10.1999, p. 3), in turn suspended by Council Regulation (EC) No 607/2000 of 20 March 2000 (OJ No L 73, 22.3.2000, p. 4 - which also amended Regulations (EC) No 1294/1999 and (EC) No 2111/1999) and Council Regulation (EC) No 1746/2000 of 3 August 2000 (OJ No L 200, 8.8.2000, p. 24); Common Position 2000/56/CFSP of 24 January 2000 (OJ No L 21, 26.1.2000, p. 4) amending and supplementing Common Position 1999/318/CFSP; Common Position 2000/176/CFSP of 28 February 2000 (OJ No L 56, 1.3.2000, p. 1) suspending article 4 of Common Position 1999/318/CFSP; Council Regulation (EC) No 723/2000 of 6 April 2000 (OJ No L 86, 7.4.2000, p. 1) and Commission Regulation (EC) No 826/2000 of 25 April 2000 (OJ No L 101, 26.4.2000, p. 3) amending Regulation (EC) No 1294/1999; Commission Regulation (EC) No 1094/2000 (OJ No L 124, 25.5.2000, p. 42) amending Regulation (EC) No 1294/1999 and in turn amended by Commission Regulation (EC) No 1147/2000 of 29 May 2000 (OJ No L 129, 30.5.2000, p. 15); Council Regulation (EC) 1059/2000 of 18 May 2000 (OJ No L 119, 20.5.2000, p. 1) amending Regulation (EC) 723/2000; Commission Regulation (EC) No 1440/2000 of 30 June 2000 (OJ No L 161, 1.7.2000, p. 68) amending Regulation (EC) No 1294/1999; Common Position 2000/454/CFSP of 20 July 2000 (OJ No L 183, 22.7.2000, p. 1) suspending article 4 of Common Position 1999/318/CFSP; Commission Regulation (EC) No 1894/2000 of 26 July 2000 (OJ No L 228, 8.9.2000, p. 3) amending Annex V to Council Regulation (EC) No 2111/1999; Council Regulation (EC) No 2111/1999 was repealed by Council Regulation (EC) No 2228/2000 of 9 October 2000 (OJ No L 261, 14.10.2000, p. 4) adopted in support of the democratic FRY; Council Regulation (EC) No 2151/1999 was repealed by Council Regulation (EC) No 2227/2000 of 9 October 2000 (OJ No L 261, 14.10.2000, p. 3), also in support of a democratic FRY; Common Position 2000/599/CFSP of 9 October 2000 (OJ No L 261, 14.10.2000, p. 1) repealed Common Position 1999/273/CFSP (*supra*); Council Regulation (EC) No 2156/2001 of 5 November 2001 (OJ No L 289, 6.11.2001, p. 5) repealed Regulation (EC) No 926/98. While a number of Common Positions and Regulations were repealed over this period, more specific Common Positions and Regulations were imposed in respect of Mr Milosevic and persons associated with him. See: Common Position 2000/696/CFSP of 10 November 2000 (OJ No L 287, 14.11.2000, p. 1) which was amended by Common Position 2001/155/CFSP of 26 February 2001 (OJ No L 57, 27.2.2001, p. 3); Council Decision 2000/697/CFSP of 10 November 2000 (OJ No L 287, 14.11.2000, p. 2); Council Regulation (EC) No 2488/2000 of 10 November 2000 (OJ No L 287, 14.11.2000, p. 19) maintaining a freeze of funds in respect of Mr Milosevic and associated persons. This was amended by Commission Regulation (EC) No 1205/2001 of 19 June 2001 (OJ No L 163, 20.6.2001, p. 14). The UNSC lifted the sanctions in 2001 (by SCR 1367 (2001), 10 September 2001). The Council amended its Common Position in 96/184/CFSP (as amended by Decisions 98/498/CFSP, 1999/481/CFSP and 2000/722/CFSP) accordingly – see Common Position 2001/719/CFSP of 8 October 2001 (*ibid.* at note 4).

ing sanctions against Iraq, the first significant imposition of economic sanctions by the UNSC for more than a decade, set the trend for a series of subsequent measures by the UNSC imposing sanctions against the SFRY/FRY, Libya, Somalia, Liberia, Haiti, Angola (UNITA forces), Rwanda, Sudan, Sierra Leone, Ethiopia/Eritrea and Afghanistan. Effective implementation of these measures increasingly necessitated coordination across EU Member States.

As well as these spurs to EU action, momentum in favour of greater EU involvement in implementation of UNSC sanctions has also come more subtly from the growing trend of European integration. Thus, the ECJ in Case C-124/95, *Centro-Com* held that, while Member States retained their competence in the field of foreign and security policy, this has to be exercised in a manner consistent with Community law and must respect Community rules adopted under the common commercial policy.[20] The Court further stated, on the question of the application of Article 301 of the *EC Treaty* which provides for Member State compliance with treaty obligations which predate those in the *EC Treaty*,[21] that where such an agreement "allows, but does not require, a Member State to adopt a measure which appears to be contrary to Community law, the Member State must refrain from adopting such a measure".[22] In the light of this decision, the competence of Member States to act independently of the Community in implementation of decisions of the UNSC imposing sanctions is likely to become increasingly limited.

Against this background, this chapter proceeds to address EU implementation of UNSC decisions imposing sanctions under the following headings:

- the constitutional basis, competence and practice of the Community in the field of sanctions implementation;
- observations on the relationship between EU implementation and Member State implementation of UNSC sanctions;
- the scope and interpretation of EU sanctions; and
- concluding remarks.

II. The Constitutional Basis, Competence and Practice of the Community in the Field of Sanctions Implementation[23]

(1) The EEC Treaty and the Early Years of Sanctions Implementation

The *Treaty of Rome* of 1957 establishing the European Economic Community made no special provision for the imposition of economic sanctions or for the implementation of

20 Case C-124/95, *R v. HM Treasury and Bank of England*, ex parte *Centro-Com SrL* [1997] 1 CMLR 555, at paragraphs 24-30.

21 See further below.

22 *Op.cit.* note 20, at paragraph 60.

23 The following discussion is limited to the evolving competence of the Community to take measures in implementation of UNSC sanctions decisions pursuant to the *EEC* – subsequently the *EC – Treaty* and the *TEU*. To the extent that measures have been required by the Community to restrict trade in the field of coal and steel products – covered by the *ECSC Treaty* – these have been taken by a *Decision of the Representatives of the Governments of the*

decisions of the UNSC. Matters threatening the maintenance of international peace and security or that, in the language of Chapter VII of the UN *Charter*, amounted to a threat to the peace, breach of the peace or act of aggression, were however addressed in Article 224 of the *EEC Treaty* in the following terms:[24]

> "Member States shall consult each other with a view to taking together the steps needed to prevent the functioning of the common market being affected by measures which a Member State may be called upon to take in the event of serious internal disturbances affecting the maintenance of law and order, in the event of war, serious international tension constituting a threat of war, or in order to carry out obligations it has accepted for the purpose of maintaining peace and international security."

While this provision established a procedure, within the framework of the *EEC Treaty*, for addressing UNSC decisions imposing sanctions, the significant feature of these arrangements is that the matter was left essentially to the Member States. Pursuant to this provision, the implementation of decisions of the UNSC imposing sanctions was not therefore a matter for the Community.

The writ of the Community in the area of sanctions was further limited by the terms of Article 223 of the *EEC Treaty* which provided *inter alia* as follows:[25]

> "1. The provisions of this Treaty shall not preclude the application of the following rules:
> (a) No Member State shall be obliged to supply information the disclosure of which it considers contrary to the essential interests of its security;
> (b) Any Member State may take such measures as it considers necessary for the protection of the essential interests of its security which are connected with the production of or trade in arms, munitions and war material; such measures shall not adversely affect the conditions of competition in the common market regarding products which are not intended for specifically military purposes."

Member States of the European Coal and Steel Community, Meeting within the Council. See, for example, Decision 90/414/ECSC of 8 August 1990 preventing trade as regards Iraq and Kuwait (OJ No L 213, 9.8.90, p. 3). Although the provision is not referred to in such Decisions, of importance in this regard is Article 95, *ECSC* which provides *inter alia*: "In all cases not provided for in this Treaty where it becomes apparent that a decision or recommendation of the [Commission] is necessary to attain, within the common market in coal and steel and in accordance with Article 5, one of the objectives of the Community set out in Articles 2, 3 and 4, the decision may be taken or the recommendation made with the unanimous assent of the Council and after the Consultative Committee has been consulted." To the extent that Community measures have been required to restrict trade in nuclear products coming within the ambit of the *EAEC Treaty*, these have been included within the measures adopted under the *EEC Treaty*. See further on this point, MacLeod, Hendry and Hyett, *The External Relations of the European Communities* (1996), at p. 353, note 1.

24 Renumbered as Article 297 of the *EC Treaty*.

25 Renumbered, as amended, as Article 296 of the *EC Treaty*.

Pursuant to paragraph 1(b) of this article, any action required in implementation of a UNSC decision imposing an embargo on the sale or supply of arms and related *materiél* would be a matter for each Member State individually, not for the Community. This limitation on Community action was highlighted in connection with the debate over the sale of arms to southern Africa in the mid-1970s where, in response to a Written Parliamentary Question of 21 October 1976 enquiring of the Commission *inter alia* whether the Community had taken any steps to prohibit the sale or supply of arms from a Member State to any southern African country, the Commission responded that it was

> "not within the competence of the Commission to deal with the matters to which the Honourable Member refers, which are the responsibility of individual Member States."[26]

While Articles 223 and 224 of the *EEC Treaty* effectively reserved to Member States the competence to act in areas likely to be addressed by UNSC sanctions decisions, Article 225 of the Treaty did attempt to claw back some role for the Community.[27] Pursuant to this provision,

> "[i]f measures taken in the circumstances referred to in Articles 223 and 224 have the effect of distorting the conditions of competition in the common market, the Commission shall, together with the State concerned, examine how these measures can be adjusted to the rules laid down in this Treaty.
>
> By way of derogation from the procedure laid down in Articles 169 and 170 [relating to access to the ECJ], the Commission or any Member State may bring the matter directly before the Court of Justice if it considers that another Member State is making improper use of the powers provided for in Articles 223 and 224. The Court of Justice shall give its ruling in camera."

No proceedings have been brought under the second paragraph of this provision.

Also of significance to the question of the competence of the Community versus that of the Member States on the issue of the implementation of UNSC decisions was Article 234 of the *EEC Treaty* which provided as follows:[28]

> "The rights and obligations arising from agreements concluded before the entry into force of this Treaty between one or more Member States on the one hand, and one or more third countries on the other, shall not be affected by the provisions of this Treaty.
>
> To the extent that such agreements are not compatible with this Treaty, the Member State or States concerned shall take all appropriate steps to eliminate the incompatibilities

26 Written Question No 563/76 by Mr Glinne of 21 October 1976 and Answer by the Commission of 27 October 1976 (OJ No C 294, 13.12.76, p. 57).

27 Renumbered as Article 298 of the *EC Treaty*.

28 Renumbered, as amended, as Article 307 of the *EC Treaty*.

> established. Member States shall, where necessary, assist each other to this end and shall, where appropriate, adopt a common attitude.
>
> In applying the agreements referred to in the first paragraph, Member States shall take into account the fact that the advantages accorded under this Treaty by each Member State form an integral part of the establishment of the Community and are thereby inseparably linked with the creation of common institutions, the conferring of powers upon them and the granting of the same advantages by all the other Member States."

The significance of this provision arose from the fact that, for fourteen of the fifteen EU Member States, the UN *Charter* created rights and obligations that predated their rights and obligations under the *EEC Treaty*. Only for Germany, which became a Member of the UN in 1973, did the rights and obligations created by the *EEC Treaty* predate those of the *Charter*.[29] The implicit effect of Article 234 in the field of the implementation of UNSC decisions was therefore to reinforce the perception that such matters came within the reserve domain of Member States and, notwithstanding the second and third paragraphs of this Article, were not a matter of Community competence. This perception was further bolstered by the terms of Article 103 of the UN *Charter*, binding upon all EEC Member States, which provided:

> "In the event of a conflict between the obligations of the Members of the United Nations under the present Charter and their obligations under any other international agreement, their obligations under the present Charter shall prevail."

The deference afforded to obligations under pre-existing treaties within the Community legal regime under Article 234 of the *EEC Treaty* was thus complemented by a trumping provision in the UN *Charter* which reaffirmed the primacy of obligations under the *Charter* for UN Members.

While, pursuant to these provisions, the balance appeared to favour Member State competence, as opposed to that of the Community, in the field of sanctions implementation, the matter was not, however, as clear cut as appeared at first sight. Thus, in favour of Community competence in this field was the fact that, pursuant to Article 113 of the *EEC Treaty*,[30] it was the Community that was competent in the field of the common commercial policy rather than Member States. As described in paragraph 1 of this Article,

> "the common commercial policy shall be based on uniform principles, particularly in regard to changes in tariff rates, the conclusion of tariff and trade agreements, the achievement of

29 The dates of UN and EC membership respectively in the case of the EU Member States are as follows: Austria – 1955, 1995; Belgium – 1945, 1958; Denmark – 1945, 1973; Finland – 1955, 1995; France – 1945, 1958; Germany – 1973, 1958; Greece – 1945, 1981; Ireland – 1945, 1973; Italy – 1955, 1958; Luxembourg – 1945, 1958; Netherlands – 1945, 1958; Portugal – 1955, 1986; Spain – 1955, 1986; Sweden – 1946, 1995; United Kingdom – 1945, 1958.

30 Renumbered, as amended, as Article 133 of the *EC Treaty*.

> uniformity in measures of liberalisation, export policy and measures to protect trade such as those to be taken in case of dumping or subsidies."[31]

Pursuant to paragraph 2 of the Article, the Commission is required to submit proposals to the Council for implementing the common commercial policy. The Council is required to act on these proposals by a qualified majority.

As economic sanctions measures taken by the UNSC invariably require the suspension of trading relations between the Community and the target state, the implementation of such measures will usually fall within the common commercial policy and will therefore be a matter of Community competence.

In addition to Article 113 of the *EEC Treaty*, Community competence to take measures in implementation of other, non-trading elements of UNSC sanctions decisions might also be based on other general provisions of the *EEC Treaty*. Thus, for example, pursuant to Article 75 of the *EEC Treaty*, the adoption of "common rules applicable to international transport to or from the territory of a Member State or passing across the territory of one or more Member States" was a matter of Community competence (in the period after 1966), with the Council being required to act, by qualified majority, on a proposal from the Commission.

Finally, in Article 235, the *EEC Treaty* also established an exceptional basis for action to attain the objectives of the Community as follows:[32]

> "If action by the Community should prove necessary to attain, in the course of the operation of the common market, one of the objectives of the Community and this Treaty has not provided the necessary powers, the Council shall, acting unanimously on a proposal from the Commission and after consulting the European Parliament, take the appropriate measures."

The objectives of the Community as described *inter alia* in Article 3 of the *EEC Treaty* included:

> "(b) the establishment of a common customs tariff and of a common commercial policy towards third countries;
>
> ...
>
> (h) the approximation of the laws of Member States to the extent required for the proper functioning of the common market; ..."

It was against the background of these various provisions that the question of the competence of the Community, versus that of the Member States, to take measures in implementation of UNSC decisions imposing sanctions was addressed in the period prior to the entry into force of the *TEU* on 1 November 1993.

31 See also Article 111 of the *EEC Treaty*.

32 Renumbered as Article 308 of the *EC Treaty*.

a. Rhodesia

The first occasion on which the issue of Community versus Member State competence to implement UNSC sanctions decisions arose was in respect of Rhodesia. In this case,[33] the Member States – which, with the exception of Germany (until 1973), were all Members of the UN and therefore bound by the UNSC decisions – acted independently of the Community to implement sanctions. As has already been described, the irony of this situation is that, in December 1968 (ie, after sanctions had already been imposed by the UNSC), the Community included Rhodesia on a list of countries with which trade was to be liberalised[34] with the consequence that Member State measures implementing the UNSC decision appeared to be contrary to Community law and, in view of the primacy of Community law over national law, potentially illegal.[35] This situation was only rectified in May 1970 with the removal of Rhodesia from the list of countries with which trade was to be liberalised.[36]

As has already been noted, the practice of the Community in respect of sanctions against Rhodesia was fundamentally shaped by the perception that compliance with obligations laid down in UNSC decisions was a matter for the Member States, not the Community.[37] Within the panoply of *EEC Treaty* provisions identified above, the dominant appreciation was that the implementation of UNSC sanctions decisions fell within the ambit of Articles 223, 224 and 234.

While, however, practice in respect of sanctions against Rhodesia favoured Member State competence, it also bore the seeds of developing Community competence. Thus, the Regulations liberalising Community trade with Rhodesia and subsequently removing Rhodesia from this regime were made under the common commercial policy provisions of the *EEC Treaty*. The ambiguity of this practice notwithstanding, the foundations for subsequent action by the Community in implementation of UNSC sanctions under Article 113 of the *EEC Treaty* were thus laid at this point.

b. South Africa

The next case of mandatory UNSC sanctions was South Africa. As is well known, these measures were limited to the imposition of an embargo, imposed by SCR 418 (1977) of 4 November 1977, on the

> "provision to South Africa of arms and related *matériel* of all types, including the sale or transfer of weapons and ammunition, military vehicles and equipment, para-military police equipment, and spare parts for the aforementioned, and … of all types of equipment

---

33 See Kuyper, *op.cit.* note 11.

34 See Regulation 2041/68, *op.cit.* note 11.

35 This analysis does not, however, take account of Article 234 of the *EEC Treaty* which would no doubt have been relied upon to preserve the competence of the Member States in this matter.

36 See note 12 *supra*.

37 See the discussion at notes 13-15 *supra*.

and supplies and grants of licensing arrangements for the manufacture or maintenance of the aforementioned."[38]

In keeping with the appreciation that measures concerning the production of or trade in arms, munitions and war material fell within the exclusive competence of Member States pursuant to Article 223 of the *EEC Treaty*,[39] the Community did not take any action in implementation of SCR 418 (1977).[40]

Although, in the absence of any mandatory UNSC decisions imposing sanctions in the period 1977 – 1990, questions relating directly to the competence of the Community to take measures in implementation of such decisions did not arise, the debate about Community competence in the field of economic sanctions more generally continued through the 1980s. Against the background of the principle stated by the ECJ in Case 22/70, *AETR* to the effect that, once competence is exercised by the Community, it is no longer open to Member States to act,[41] the focus of the debate was whether politically inspired trade sanctions came within the *réserve de souveraineté* of Member States pursuant to Article 224 of the *EEC Treaty* or whether they fell properly within the common commercial policy competence of the Community under Article 113 of the Treaty.[42] Addressing developments during the 1980s, one commentator summed up the debate on this matter in the following terms:

38 As per paragraph 2.

39 See further the text at note 25 *supra*.

40 Various measures sanctions measures were, however, subsequently taken by the Community against South Africa independently of any action by the UNSC. See *inter alia* the following: Decision 86/459/ECSC of 16 September 1986 (OJ No L 268, 19.9.86, p. 1); Decision 86/517/EEC of 27 October 1986 (OJ No L 305, 31.10.86, p. 45); Council Regulation (EEC) No 3302/86 of 27 October 1986 (OJ No L 305, 31.10.86, p. 11); Decision 88/280/ECSC of 25 April 1988 (OJ No L 120, 7.5.88, p. 1); Decision 91/114/EEC of 25 February 1991 (OJ No L 59, 6.3.91, p. 18); Council Regulation (EEC) No 219/92 of 27 January 1992 (OJ No L 24, 1.2.92, p. 6). See also the *Resolution of the European Parliament on the implementation by the Member States of the Community of economic sanctions against the Republic of South Africa*, Doc.A2-151/87, 30 October 1987 (OJ No C 318, 30.11.87, p. 151). The constitutional basis of the various measures taken by the Community was not explicitly stated save in the case of Regulation 219/92, which repealed Regulation 3302/86 suspending imports of Krugerrands and other gold coins from South Africa, which referred to Article 113, EEC.

41 Case 22/70, *Commission v. Council* [1971] ECR 263. The case concerned the competence of the Commission in respect of road transport in the light of action by the Member States under the auspices of the United Nations Economic Commission for Europe concerning the revision of the European Road Transport Agreement. In upholding the Community's competence, as opposed to that of the Member States, in this matter, the Court stated *inter alia* as follows: "... each time the Community, with a view to implementing a common policy envisaged in the Treaty, adopts provisions laying down common rules, whatever form these may take, the Member States no longer have the right, acting individually or even collectively, to undertake obligations with third countries which affect those rules" (at paragraph 17).

42 See further P.J. Kuijper, "European Economic Community", in K.M. Meessen (ed.), *International Law of Export Control* (1992), at 57 *et seq*.

> "... past practice on politically inspired trade sanctions indicates that the Council is very reluctant to use the sole Article 113 as a basis for such measures [sic]; that there is a willingness to have recourse to framework decisions in order to make ECSC sanctions complementary to sanctions on EEC products; that the Council is willing to rely on Article 224, either alone in order to permit a minimum of consultation between Member States with the help of the Commission, or in combination with Article 113 in order to decide upon a true Regulation; and finally that within the Council some Member States at least regard Article 224 not as a normal exception to the EEC Treaty, but as provision concerning retained sovereign rights."[43]

(2) European Political Cooperation and the Single European Act[44]

In part as a result of the limitations of Community cooperation under the *EEC Treaty* in the field of political affairs, a report was adopted by the (then) six Governments of the Member States at the Luxembourg Summit in October 1970 which laid the basis for what became known as European Political Cooperation ("EPC"). This envisaged six-monthly meetings of Foreign Ministers to discuss matters of foreign policy, a practice that was significantly expanded in subsequent years to encompass discussions, at an intergovernmental level, of all important foreign policy questions of concern to Member States.

Although EPC was formally distinct from action by the Community under the *EEC Treaty*, the reality was that the two forms of cooperation were closely linked whenever the question in issue was one of foreign policy. This link was expressly recognised in December 1974 with the establishment of the European Council, distinct from the Council of the European Communities, to formalise regular meetings of Heads of Government and Foreign Ministers of Community Member States, at which matters of political cooperation would be considered.

This loose EPC framework was formalised with the entry into force of the *Single European Act* (SEA) on 1 July 1987. This treaty, which also had the effect of amending the various treaties establishing the European Communities, both formalised the existence and role of the European Council and laid down detailed provisions governing "European Cooperation in the sphere of foreign policy".[45] Thus, pursuant to Article 30 of the *SEA*, the Parties *inter alia* undertook to inform and consult each other on foreign policy matters of general interest and to "give due consideration to the desirability of adopting and implementing common European positions".

While the formalisation of EPC under the *SEA* was not focused on the implementation of UNSC sanctions, it both established a mechanism within which action by the Member States in implementation of sanctions could be brought within a cooperative framework and created an expectation that Member States would proceed in a coordi-

43 Kuijper, *ibid.*, at p. 62.

44 See generally on this issue Kapteyn and Verloren van Themaat, *op.cit.* note 1, at pp. 27-35.

45 See Article 30.

nated manner on such matters. Coupled with the wider development and acceptance of Community competence in the field of external trade under the common commercial policy – including in the field of export controls and trade sanctions taken outside the framework of action by the UNSC[46] – the formalisation of EPC resulted in a growing appreciation that the implementation of economic sanctions was properly to be addressed by the Community within the framework of the common commercial policy under Article 113 of the *EEC Treaty*. Thus, by the point at which the UNSC adopted SCR 661 (1990) imposing sanctions against Iraq, the contention that the Community was not competent to act in implementation of such measures had all but disappeared.

a. Iraq/Kuwait

The UNSC adopted a number of Resolutions imposing sanctions against Iraq in the period following its invasion of Kuwait including SCR 661 (1990) of 6 August 1990, SCR 666 (1990) of 13 September 1990, SCR 670 (1990) of 25 September 1990 and SCR 687 (1991) of 3 April 1991. Additional Resolutions were subsequently adopted to implement and operate the oil for food programme as an exception to the general prohibition on trade with Iraq.[47]

With seemingly little debate about its competence to do so, the Community acted quickly to give effect to the various UNSC restrictions.[48] Of particular interest in respect of these measures were the following features:

46 See Kuijper, *op.cit.*, note 42, at pp. 57 *et seq.*

47 See *inter alia* SCR 986 (1995) of 14 April 1995, SCR 1111 (1997) of 4 June 1997, SCR 1129 (1997) of 12 September 1997, SCR 1143 (1997) of 4 December 1997, SCR 1153 (1998) of 20 February 1998, SCR 1158 (1998) of 25 March 1998, SCR 1175 (1998) of 19 June 1998, SCR 1210 (1998) of 24 November 1998, SCR 1242 (1999) of 21 May 1999, SCR 1266 (1999) of 4 October 1999, SCR 1275 (1999) of 19 November 1999, SCR 1280 (1999) of 3 December 1999, SCR 1281 (1999) of 10 December 1999, SCR 1284 (1999) of 17 December 1999, SCR 1293 (2000) of 31 March 2000, SCR 1302 (2000) of 8 June 2000, SCR 1330 (2000) of 5 December 2000, SCR 1352 (2001) of 1 January 2001, SCR 1360 (2001) of 3 July 2001, SCR 1382 (2001) of 29 November 2001, SCR 1409 (2002) of 14 May 2002, SCR 1443 (2002) of 25 November 2002, SCR 1447 (2002) of 4 December 2002, SCR 1454 (2002) of 30 December 2002 and SCR 1472 (2003) of 28 March 2003. See also SCR 1483 (2003) of 22 May 2003.

48 See Council Regulation (EEC) No 2340/90 of 8 August 1990 (OJ No L 213, 9.8.90, at p. 1), as amended by Council Regulation (EEC) No 3155/90 of 29 October 1990 (OJ No L 304, 1.11.90, p. 1), Council Regulation (EEC) No 542/91 of 4 March 1991 (OJ No L 60, 7.3.91, p. 5), Council Regulation (EEC) No 811/91 of 27 March 1991 (OJ No L 82, 28.3.91, p. 50), Council Regulation (EEC) No 1194/91 of 7 May 1991 (OJ No L 115, 8.5.91, p. 37); also Decision 90/414/ECSC of 8 August 1990 (OJ No L 213, 9.8.90, p. 3), as amended by Decision 91/125/ECSC of 4 March 1991 (OJ No L 60, 7.3.91, p. 15), Decision 91/265/ECSC of 21 May 1991 (OJ No L 127, 23.5.91, p. 27), Decision 96/740/ECSC of 17 December 1996 (OJ No L 337, 27.12.96, p. 4); also Council Regulation (EEC) No 3541/92 of 7 December 1992 (OJ No L 361, 10.12.92, p. 1); also Common Position 96/741/CFSP of 17 December 1996 (OJ No L 337, 27.12.96, p. 5) supplemented by Common Position 2002/599/CFSP of 22 July 2002 (OJ No L 194, 23.7.2002, p. 47) and Council Regulation (EC) No 2465/96

(a) the Community measures invariably referred to a preceding declaration or other statement by the Community and its Member States adopted within the framework of political cooperation;

(b) the Community measures invariably referred expressly to the decision(s) of the UNSC to which they were in response. In so doing, while not stating explicitly that the Community measures were adopted in *implementation* of the relevant SCR, the language of the measure left no room for doubt that this was what was intended. Thus, for example, Regulation 2340/90 referred expressly to SCR 661 (1990) and went on to provide:

> "Whereas the Community and its Member States have agreed to have recourse to a Community instrument in order to ensure uniform implementation, throughout the Community, of the measures concerning trade with Iraq and Kuwait decided upon by the United Nations Security Council;"[49]

(c) in some cases, the Community measures made express references to a relevant UNSC Resolution for purposes of incorporating into the Community measure some provision of or practice relating to the UNSC resolution;[50] and

(d) in the case of measures taken under the *EEC Treaty*, the constitutional basis for the Community action was usually declared to be Article 113 of that Treaty. The notable exception to this was Regulation 3541/92 which was adopted in implementation of paragraph 29 of SCR 687 (1991) to prohibit the satisfying of Iraqi claims with regard to contracts and transactions. As this measure did not address issues of trade that could be said to fall within the common commercial policy, the basis for the Community's action in this case was Article 235 of the *EEC Treaty*.[51]

A number of observations arising from this practice can be made. First, as already intimated, action by the Community in implementation of the UNSC's decisions imposing sanctions against Iraq seemed effectively to resolve the debate about Community competence in such matters. From this point, Community competence to act in implementation of UNSC decisions under Article 113 and, where appropriate, Article 235 of the *EEC Treaty* was uncontested.

Second, Community competence was not, however, unrestricted. In particular, as the principal basis of its competence in respect of these matters was Article 113 of the *EEC Treaty*, action by the Community was limited both by the scope of the common commercial policy as well as by other exceptions to Community action under the Treaty.

---

of 17 December 1996 (OJ No L 337, 27.12.96, p. 1). Council Regulation (EC) No 2465/96 was amended by Council Regulations (EC) No 1346/2002 of 25 July 2002 (OJ No L 197, 26.7.2002, p. 1) and (EC) No 208/2003 of 3 February 2003 (OJ No L 28, 4.2.2003, p. 26).

49 Fourth recital.

50 See, for example, Regulation 2340/90 as amended by Regulation 1194/91, at Article 3(2)(b), *op.cit.* note 48.

51 See the text at note 32 *supra*.

Thus, in the light of Article 223 of the *EEC Treaty*, the Community was not competent to take measures restricting the sale or supply of arms and related *matériel*. Of greater importance was the Community's lack of competence under Article 113 in respect of financial matters, including financial services, and the provision of services involving the movement of persons. Significantly, however, the scope of Article 113 did extend to the supply services more generally, a matter subsequently confirmed by the ECJ in Opinion 1/94, *Re the Uruguay Round Treaties*.[52]

Third, notwithstanding action by the Community, in the light of the limitations on Community competence in this area, most Member States considered themselves to be under an independent obligation to act in implementation of the UNSC decisions and did so.[53] While the competence of Member States, as a matter of Community law, to act notwithstanding action by the Community was invariably left unaddressed, later practice relating to sanctions against Yugoslavia[54] suggests that the preferred basis for such action would have been Article 234, rather than Article 224, of the *EEC Treaty*. So, for example, in the case of *R v. Searle and Others*,[55] the English Court of Appeal was faced with the argument that, in the light of Community Regulations imposing sanctions against Yugoslavia, a United Kingdom Order applying in parallel was to be considered invalid. Concluding that the UK Order and the Community Regulations were not incompatible, the Court went on to hold that the Crown's reliance on Article 234 of the *EEC Treaty* as justification for the national measure was well-founded as

> "the U.K. had a duty to act directly to implement the United Nations Resolution. What was necessary to be done was a matter for the national authorities to decide. There is no question of the Order being incompatible with the Regulations or seeking to disapply them. Article 234 operates to prevent the Community from impeding the United Kingdom's performance of its obligations under the Charter."[56]

While it is undoubtedly the case that Article 234 provides for Community deference to obligations required of Member States under pre-existing treaties – a relationship

52 Opinion 1/94, *Re the Uruguay Round Treaties* [1995] 1 CMLR 205, at paragraphs 41-53.

53 Action by individual Member States in implementation of UNSC decisions goes beyond the scope of this chapter. An extensive collection of legislative material by such States is, however, available in D.L. Bethlehem (ed.), *The Kuwait Crisis: Sanctions and Their Economic Consequences* (2 vols; 1991).

54 Addressed further below.

55 *R v. Searle and Others*, Judgment of the English Court of Appeal of 24 February 1995 [1995] 3 CMLR 196. *R v. Searle* was followed by the High Court (QBD) in *Shanning International Limited (In Liquidation) and Anor v. Rasheed Bank and Anor* [2000] 3 CMLR 450. Langley J. rejected the applicants contention that Regulation 3541/92 which implemented SCR 687 was invalid. The decision was upheld on appeal by the Court of Appeal. Although the case did not turn on parallel UK legislation, the Court of Appeal noted that Member States would have been obliged to implement SCR 687 in respect of Iraq irrespective of Community action, and that one of the purposes of the Regulation was to ensure uniformity which was a legitimate Community objective under Article 235 (at paras. 31 and 31).

56 At paragraph 59 of the Judgment.

reinforced, in the case of the *Charter*, by Article 103 of that instrument – subsequent ECJ jurisprudence on the interpretation and application of Article 234 suggests that the latitude allowed to Member States under this provision is likely to be narrower than was suggested by the Court of Appeal in *Searle*. This matter is addressed further below.

Fourth, overlapping measures at national and Community level was a potential source of uncertainty, a matter of some importance given the prospect of criminal prosecutions in the case of allegations of violation of the measures.

b. Other cases involving Community measures adopted pursuant to Article 113 of the EEC Treaty

As already noted, the *TEU* entered into force on 1 November 1993. As has also been observed (and is addressed further below), this brought about a fundamental change in the Community sanctions implementation regime. Prior to this point, the Community continued to act, often in parallel with action by the Member States, in implementation of UNSC decisions under Article 113 of the *EEC Treaty*. This was notably the case in respect of key UNSC decisions imposing sanctions against Libya,[57] the FRY,[58] Haiti[59] and Angola.[60]

(3) The TEU *and the Current Regime of EU Sanctions Implementation*

The scope of the sanctions imposed by the UNSC against Iraq highlighted the shortcomings of Community competence in this area under Article 113 of the *EEC Treaty*. In parallel with other developments aimed at bringing about closer cooperation between the Member States in the field of foreign and security policy – notably the establishment of the EU and the adoption of provisions on a CFSP – the *TEU* introduced amendments to the *EEC Treaty* by adding Articles 73g and 228a. Now numbered Articles 60 and 301 of the *EC Treaty*, these provide:

57 By SCR 731 (1992) of 21 January 1992 and SCR 748 (1992) of 31 March 1992. See in this regard Council Regulation (EEC) No 945/92 of 14 April 1992 (OJ No L 101, 15.4.92, p. 53).

58 Notably by SCR 757 (1992) of 30 May 1992, SCR 760 (1992) of 18 June 1992, SCR 787 (1992) of 16 November 1992 and SCR 820 (1993) of 17 April 1993. See in this regard the measures cited in note 19 above having adoption dates prior to 1 November 1993.

59 Notably by SCR 841 (1993) of 16 June 1993, SCR 861 (1993) of 27 August 1993 and SCR 873 (1993) of 13 October 1993. See in this regard Council Regulation (EEC) No 1608/93 of 24 June 1993 (OJ No L 155, 26.6.93, p. 2), Council Regulation (EEC) No 2520/93 of 13 September 1993 (OJ No L 232, 15.9.93, p. 3) and Council Regulation (EEC) No 3028/93 of 28 October 1993 (OJ No L 270, 30.10.93, p. 73).

60 By SCR 864 (1993) of 15 September 1993. See in this regard Council Regulation (EEC) No 2967/93 of 25 October 1993 (OJ No L 268, 29.10.93, p. 1).

"Article 60

1. If, in the cases envisaged in Article 301, action by the Community is deemed necessary, the Council may, in accordance with the procedure provided for in Article 301, take the necessary urgent measures on the movement of capital and on payments as regards the third countries concerned.

2. Without prejudice to Article 297 and as long as the Council has not taken measures pursuant to paragraph 1, a Member State may, for serious political reasons and on grounds of urgency, take unilateral measures against a third country with regard to capital movements and payments. The Commission and the other Member States shall be informed of such measures by the date of their entry into force at the latest.

The Council may, acting by a qualified majority on a proposal from the Commission, decide that the Member State concerned shall amend or abolish such measures. The President of the Council shall inform the European Parliament of any such decision taken by the Council."

"Article 301

Where it is provided, in a common position or in a joint action adopted according to the provisions of the Treaty on European Union relating to the common foreign and security policy, for an action by the Community to interrupt or to reduce, in part or completely, economic relations with one or more third countries, the Council shall take the necessary urgent measures. The Council shall act by a qualified majority on a proposal from the Commission."

Article 60 addresses the shortcoming in Community competence under Article 113 of the *EEC Treaty* in respect of sanctions relating to capital movements and payments. Article 301 establishes a more general Community competence in respect of economic sanctions where this is required in a common position or in a joint action adopted in accordance with the CFSP provisions of the *TEU*.[61]

As noted, this overhaul of Community competence in respect of sanctions under the (now renamed) *EC Treaty* went hand-in-hand with the establishment of the European Union and the detailed elaboration of provisions on a Common Foreign and Security Policy. Thus, Article 2, second indent, of the *TEU* provides that one of the objectives of the Union shall be *inter alia* "to assert its identity on the international scene, in particular through the implementation of a common foreign and security policy".

In implementation of this objective, Article 11 of the *TEU* requires the Union to define and implement a common foreign and security policy the objectives of which include the preservation of peace and strengthening of international security in accor-

61 For further discussion of these matters see MacLeod, Hendry and Hyett, *The External Relations of the European Communities: A Manual of Law and Practice* (1996), at Chapter 19.

dance with the principles of the UN *Charter*.[62] Articles 12-15[63] go on to address the manner in which these objectives are to be pursued *inter alia* as follows:

"Article 12

The Union shall pursue the objectives set out in Article 11 by:

- defining the principles of and general guidelines for the common foreign and security policy;
- deciding on common strategies;
- adopting joint actions;
- adopting common positions;
- strengthening systematic cooperation between Member States in the conduct of policy.

Article 13

1. The European Council shall define the principles of and general guidelines for the common foreign and security policy, including for matters with defence implications.

2. The European Council shall decide on common strategies to be implemented by the Union in areas where the Member States have important interests in common.

Common strategies shall set out their objectives, duration and the means to be made available by the Union and the Member States.

3. The Council shall take the decisions necessary for defining and implementing the common foreign and security policy on the basis of the general guidelines defined by the European Council.

The Council shall recommend common strategies to the European Council and shall implement them, in particular by adopting joint actions and common positions.

The Council shall ensure the unity, consistency and effectiveness of action by the Union.

Article 14

1. The Council shall adopt joint actions. Joint actions shall address specific situations where operational action by the Union is deemed to be required. They shall lay down their objectives, scope, the means to be made available to the Union, if necessary their duration, and the conditions for their implementation.

62 Article 11(1), third indent, *TEU*.

63 Formerly Articles J.2 – J.5.

…

3. Joint action shall commit the Member States in the positions they adopt and in the conduct of their activity.

…

Article 15

The Council shall adopt common positions. Common positions shall define the approach of the Union to a particular matter of a geographic or thematic nature. Member States shall ensure that their national policies conform to the common positions."

Pursuant to Article 23 of the *TEU*, decisions by the Council in respect of the CFSP are to be taken unanimously save when adopting joint actions, common positions or taking any other decision on the basis of a common strategy or when adopting any decision implementing a joint action or a common position. In such cases, the Council shall act by qualified majority.

As the text of Article 301 of the *EC Treaty* (set out above) makes plain, action by the Community in the field of sanctions is fundamentally linked to action by the EU under the CSFP provisions of the *TEU*. In particular, Community legislative competence in this field is now dependent on the prior adoption of a common position or joint action providing for the Community to act "to interrupt or to reduce, in part or completely, economic relations with one or more third countries".

Three aspects of the new arrangements warrant comment. First, on the basis of these measures, the Community now has a virtually all-embracing competence in the field of economic sanctions.[64] Second, as has just been observed, the Community's competence in this area is now tied fundamentally to the CFSP framework established by the *TEU*. Third, one consequence of this linkage is to shift the initiative in respect of sanctions, albeit within certain constraints, back to the Member States. This follows from the fact that CFSP arrangements are essentially inter-governmental in nature with the power of initiative being vested, depending on the action envisaged, in either the European Council or the Council. The locus of competence in respect of sanctions implementation, at least in respect of the initiation of measures, has thus reverted to the Member States acting within the Council.

Given the changes brought about by the *TEU*, and the exclusive reliance on the CFSP provisions by the Council in the case of sanctions implementation since 1 November 1993, it is interesting to speculate whether any residual competence to act in respect of sanctions remains under the common commercial policy provisions of the *EC Treaty*. More particularly, are there any circumstances in which the Commission will

64 Given that Article 301 refers to "economic relations", it has been argued that it could not be relied upon to impose an arms embargo or to sever amateur sporting or cultural ties. See MacLeod, Hendry and Hyett, *The External Relations of the European Communities* (1996), at p. 356.

retain an independent competence to initiate sanctions under Article 133 of the *EC Treaty*, or some similar provision, notwithstanding Articles 60 and 301 of the *EC Treaty* and the CFSP provisions of the *TEU*?

Subsequent to the entry into force of the *TEU*, the EU has acted to implement UNSC decisions on sanctions against Libya,[65] Haiti,[66] Afghanistan,[67]

65 See SCR 883 (1993) of 11 November 1993 and SCR 1192 (1998) of 27 August 1998; also Council Decision 93/614/CFSP of 22 November 1993 (OJ No L 295, 30.11.93, p. 7), Council Regulation (EC) No 3274/93 of 29 November 1993 (OJ No L 295, 30.11.93, p. 1), Council Regulation (EC) No 3275/93 of 29 November 1993 (OJ No L 295, 30.11.93, p. 4), Common Position 1999/261/CFSP of 16 April 1999 (OJ No L 103, 20.4.99, p. 1), Council Regulation (EC) No 836/1999 of 20 April 1999 (OJ No L 106, 23.4.99, p. 1) and Common Position 1999/611/CFSP of 13 September 1999 (OJ No L 242, 14.9.99, p. 31).

66 See SCR 917 (1994) of 6 May 1994, SCR 940 (1994) of 31 July 1994, SCR 944 (1994) of 29 September 1994 and SCR 948 (1994) of 15 October 1994; also Council Decision 94/315/CFSP of 30 May 1994 (OJ No L 139, 2.6.94, p. 10), Council Recommendation 94/313/EC of 30 May 1994 (OJ No L 139, 2.6.94, p. 7), Decision 94/314/ECSC of 30 May 1994 (OJ No L 139, 2.6.94, p. 8), Council Regulation (EC) No 1263/94 of 30 May 1994 (OJ No L 139, 2.6.94, p. 1), Council Regulation (EC) No 1264/94 of 30 May 1994 (OJ No L 139, 2.6.94, p. 4), Council Decision 94/681/CFSP of 14 October 1994 (OJ No L 271, 21.10.94, p. 3), Council Regulation (EC) No 2543/94 of 19 October 1994 (OJ No L 271, 21.10.94, p. 1), and Decision 94/680/ECSC of 19 October 1994 (OJ No L 271, 21.10.94, p. 2).

67 See SCR 1076 (1996) of 22 October 1996 and SCR 1267 (1999) of 15 October 1999; also Common Position 96/746/CFSP of 17 December 1996 (OJ No L 342, 31.12.96, p. 1), Council Common Position 1999/727/CFSP of 15 November 1999 (OJ No L 294, 16.11.99, p. 1), Council Common Position 2000/55/CFSP of 24 January 2000 (OJ No L 21, 26.1.2000, p. 1), Council Regulation (EC) No 337/2000 of 14 February 2000 (OJ No L 43, 16.2.2000, p. 1). See also Common Position 1998/108/CFSP of 26 January 1998 (OJ No L 32, 6.2.98, p. 14) and Common Position 1999/73/CFSP of 25 January 1999 (OJ No L 23, 30.1.99, p. 1), repealed by Common Position 2000/55/CFSP of 24 January 2000 (OJ No L 21, 26.1.2000, p. 1). Common Position 1999/727/CFSP of 15 November 1999 (OJ No L 294, 16.11.1999, p. 1) and Council Regulation (EC) No 337/2000 of 14 February 2000 (OJ No L 43, 16.2.2000, p. 1) implemented SCR 1267 (1999) of 15 October 1999. Commission Regulation (EC) 1272/2000 of 16 June 2000 (OJ No L 144, 17.6.2000, p. 16) amended Council Regulation (EC) No 337/2000/CFSP. Following SCR 1333 (2000) of 19 December 2000, the EU adopted Common Position 2001/56/CFSP of 22 January 2001 (OJ No L 21, 23.1.2001, p. 1) - which also repealed Common Position 2000/55/CFSP of 24 January 2000 – and Council Regulation (EC) No 467/2001 of 6 March 2001 (OJ No L 67, 9.3.2001, p. 1), amended by Commission Regulation (EC) No 1354/2001 of 4 July 2001 (OJ No L 182, 5.7.2001, p. 15), amended for a second time by Commission Regulation (EC) No 1996/2001 of 11 October 2001 (OJ No L 271, 12.10.2001, p. 21) which also repealed Regulation (EC) No 337/2000, amended for a third time by Commission Regulation (EC) No 2062/2001 of 19 October 2001 (OJ No L 277, 20.10.2001, p. 25), amended for a fourth time by Commission Regulation (EC) No 2199/2001 of 12 November 2001 (OJ No L 295, 13.11.2001, p. 16), for a fifth time by Commission Regulation (EC) No 2373/2001 of 4 December 2001 (OJ No L 320, 5.12.2001, p. 11), for a sixth time by Commission Regulation (EC) No 2604/2001 of 28 December 2001 (OJ No L 345, 29.12.2001, p. 54), for a seventh time by Regulation (EC) No 65/2002 of 14 January 2002 (OJ No L 11, 15.1.2001, p. 3), for a eighth time by Regulation (EC) No 105/2002 of 18 January 2002 (OJ No L 17, 19.1.2002, p. 52).

Angola (UNITA forces),[68] Sierra Leone,[69] Somalia,[70] Iraq,[71] Eritrea/Ethiopia[72] and

Common Position 2001/771/CFSP of 5 November 2001 (OJ No L 289, 6.11.2001, p. 36) amended earlier Common Positions in response to SCR 1076 (2001) on Afghanistan and SCR 1333 (2001) on the Taliban. Common Position 2002/42/CFSP of 21 January 2002 (OJ No L 20, 23.1.2002, p. 1) repealed Common Position 2001/56/CFSP. Measures against Afghanistan and the Taliban were subsequently rolled into measures targeting Osama Bin Laden and Al-Qaida in Common Position 2002/402/CFSP of 27 May 2002 (OJ No L 139, 29.5.2002, p. 4) which repealed Common Positions 96/746/CFSP, 1999/727/CFSP, 2001/154/CFSP and 2001/771/CFSP. For further measures against Osama Bin Laden and the Taliban see note 76 below.

68 See SCR 1127 (1997) of 28 August 1997, SCR 1130 (1997) of 29 September 1997, SCR 1173 (1998) of 12 June 1998, SCR 1221 (1999) of 12 January 1999; also Common Position 97/759/CFSP of 30 October 1997 (OJ No L 309, 12.11.97, p. 8), Council Regulation (EC) No 2229/97 of 30 October 1997 (OJ No L 309, 12.11.97, p. 1), Common Position 98/425/CFSP of 3 July 1998 (OJ No 190, 4.7.98, p. 1), Council Regulation (EC) No 1705/98 of 28 July 1998 (OJ No L 215, 1.8.98, p. 1) and Commission Regulation (EC) No 753/1999 of 12 April 1999 (OJ No L 98, 13.4.99, p. 3). Following SCR 1295 (2000) of 18 April 2000, the EU adopted Common Position 2000/391/CFSP of 19 June 2000 (OJ No L 146, 21.6.2000, p. 1). See also Commission Regulation (EC) No 2231/2001 of 16 November 2001 (OJ No L 301, 17.11.2001, p. 17) amending Regulation (EC) No 1705/98 and repealing Regulation (EC) No 2229/97; Regulation (EC) No 1705/98 was further amended by Commission Regulation (EC) No 2536/2001 of 21 December 2001 (OJ No L 341, 22.12.2001, p. 70), Commission Regulation (EC) No 271/2002 of 14 February 2002 (OJ No L 45, 15.2.2002, p. 16) and Commission Regulation (EC) No 689/2002 of 22 April 2002 (OJ No L 106, 23.4.2002, p. 8). See also Common Position 2002/495/CFSP of 25 June 2002 (OJ No L 167, 26.6.2002, p. 9) repealing Common Position 2000/391/CFSP. Sanctions were lifted by SCR 1448 (2002) of 9 December 2002. EU action followed in Common Position 2002/991/CFSP of 19 December 2002 (OJ No L 348, 21.12.2002, p. 1) and Council Regulation (EC) No 146/2003 of 27 January 2003 (OJ No L 24, 29.1.2003, p. 1).

69 See SCR 1132 (1997) of 8 October 1997, SCR 1156 (1998) of 16 March 1998 and SCR 1171 (1998) of 5 June 1998; also Common Position 97/826/CFSP of 8 December 1997 (OJ No L 344, 15.12.97, p. 6), Council Regulation (EC) No 2465/97 of 8 December 1997 (OJ No L 344, 15.12.97, p. 1), Common Position 98/300/CFSP of 27 April 1998 (OJ No L 136, 8.5.98, p. 2), Council Regulation (EC) No 941/98 of 27 April 1998 (OJ No L 136, 8.5.98, p. 1), and Common Position 98/409/CFSP of 29 June 1998 (OJ No L 187, 1.7.98, p. 1). Following SCR 1306 (2000) of 5 July 2000 calling on Member States to take measures in respect of the illegal trade in diamonds and to implement the 1998 arms embargo, the EU adopted Common Position 2000/455/CFSP of 20 July 2000 (OJ No L 183, 22.7.2000, p. 2) and Council Regulation (EC) No 1745/2000 of 3 August 2000 (OJ No L 200, 8.8.2000, p. 21). SCR 1306 (2000) was followed by SCR 1385 (2001) of 19 December 2001 and Common Position 2002/22/CFSP of 11 January 2002 (OJ No L 10, 12.1.2002, p. 81) and Council Regulation (EC) No 303/2002 of 18 February 2002 (OJ No L 47, 19.2.2002, p. 8). SCR 1446 (2002) of 4 December 2002 was followed by Common Position 2002/992/CFSP of 19 December 2002 (OJ No L 348, 21.12.2002, p. 2) and Council Regulation (EC) No 2290/2002 of 19 December 2002 (OJ No L 348, 21.12.2002, p. 56).

70 See Common Position 2002/960/CFSP of 10 December 2002 (OJ No L 334, 11.12.2002, p. 1) implementing measures in light of SCR 733 (1992) of 23 January 1992, SCR 1356 (2001) of 19 June 2001 and SCR 1425 (2002) of 22 July 2002 and Council Regulation (EC) No 147/2003 of 27 January 2003 (OJ No L 24, 29.1.2003, p. 2).

Liberia.[73] Other examples of EU implementation of UNSC decisions include the Kimberley Process for Trade in Rough Diamonds introduced to complement state-specific diamond and arms sanctions against Angola, Sierra Leone and the Democratic Republic of the Congo,[74] general measures combating terrorism,[75] and, more specifically, measures against Al-Qaida and Osama Bin Laden.[76]

---

71 See the measures referred to in notes 47 and 48 *supra* having an adoption date after 1 November 1993.

72 See Common Position 1999/206/CFSP of 15 March 1999 (OJ No L 72, 18.3.1999, p. 1) implementing SCR 1227 (1999) of 10 February 1999, and extended by Common Positions 1999/650/CFSP of 30 September 1999 (OJ No L 257, 2.10.1999, p. 1), 2000/230/CFSP of 20 March 2000 (OJ No L 73, 22.3.2000, p. 1). Common Position 2000/584/CFSP of 29 September 2000 (OJ No L 246, 30.9.2000, p. 69) amended and extended the embargo in light of SCRs 1298 (2000), 1312 (2000) and 1320 (2000). Common Position 2001/215/CFSP of 19 March 2001 (OJ No L 80, 20.3.2001, p. 21) further extended the embargo.

73 See Common Position 2001/357/CFSP of 7 May 2001 (OJ No L 126, 8.5.2001, p. 1) implementing certain measures in light of SCR 1343 (2001) of 7 March 2001 and Council Regulation (EC) No 1146/2001 of 11 June 2001 (OJ No L 156, 13.6.2001, p. 1). The UNSC extended SCR 1343 by SCR 1408 (2002) dated 6 May 2002. The EU then adopted Common Position 2002/457/CFSP of 13 June 2002 (OJ No L 155, 14.6.2002, p. 62) which amended and extended Common Position 2001/357/CFSP. See also Council Regulation (EC) No 1318/2002 of 22 July 2002 (OJ No L 194, 23.7.2002, p. 1) and Common Position 2003/365/CFSP of 19 May 2003 (OJ No L 124, 20.5.2003, p. 49) amending Common Position 2001/357/2001.

74 See Common Position 2001/758/CFSP of 29 October 2001 (OJ No L 286, 30.10.2001, p. 2); Council Regulation (EC) No 2368/2002 of 20 December 2002 (OJ No L 358, 31.12.2002, p. 28) referring in the preambular paragraphs of Annex I to SCR 1173 (1998), 1295 (2000), 1306 (2000) and 1343 (2001), amended by Council Regulation (EC) No 254/2003 of 11 February 2003 (OJ No L 36, 12.2.2003, p. 7), and Commission Regulations (EC) No 257/2003 of 11 February 2003 (OJ No L 36, 12.2.2003, p. 11) and (EC) No 418/2003 of 6 March 2003 (OJ No L 64, 7.3.2003, p. 13).

75 See Common Positions 2001/930/CFSP and 2001/931/CFSP, both of 27 December 2001 (OJ No L 344, 28.12.2001, pp. 90 and 93) and Council Regulation (EC) No 2580/2001 of 27 December 2001 (OJ No L 344, 28.12.2001, p. 70) implementing SCR 1373 (2001) of 28 September 2001. Council Decisions 2002/334/EC of 2 May 2002 (OJ No L 116, 3.5.2002, p. 33), 2002/460/EC of 17 June 2002 (OJ No L 160, 18.6.2002, p. 26), 2002/848/EC of 28 October 2002 (OJ No L 295, 30.10.2002, p. 12) and 2002/974/EC of 12 December 2002 (OJ No L 337, 13.12.2002, p. 85) implementing article 2(3) of Regulation (EC) No 2580/2001 and repealing earlier Decisions. Common Positions 2002/340/CFSP of 2 May 2002 (OJ No L 116, 3.5.2002, p. 75), 2002/462/2002 of 17 June 2002 (OJ No L 160, 18.6.2002, p. 32), 2002/847/CFSP of 28 October 2002 (OJ No L 295, 30.10.2002, p. 1), and 2002/976/CFSP of 12 December 2002 (OJ No L 337, 13.12.2002, p. 93) updating Common Position 2001/931/CFSP. Most recently, Commission Regulation (EC) No 745/2003 of 28 April 2003 (OJ No L 106, 29.4.2003, p. 22) amended Regulation (EC) No 2580/2001.

76 See Common Position 2002/402/CFSP of 27 May 2002 (OJ No L 139, 29.5.2002, p. 4), Council Regulation (EC) No 881/2002 of 27 May 2002 (OJ No L 139, 29.5.2002, p. 9), amended by Commission Regulation (EC) No 951/2002 of 3 June 2002 (OJ No L 145, 4.6.2002, p. 14), Commission Regulation (EC) No 1644/2002 of 13 September 2002 (OJ

III. Observations on the Relationship between the Implementation of UNSC Sanctions by the EU and its Member States

The principal means by which the Community has acted to give effect to decisions of the UNSC imposing sanctions has been through the adoption of Regulations. In the period following the entry into force of the *TEU*, this approach has been supplemented, as required by Article 301 of the *EC Treaty*, by the prior adoption of a common position by the Council defining in broad terms the approach to be adopted by the Community when enacting sanctions.

Regulations are binding in their entirety and directly applicable in the Member States.[77] They are accordingly a direct source of rights and obligations for those persons subject to them independently of any measure of national law. Indeed, in accordance with the well-established case law of the ECJ, "Member States are under a duty not to obstruct the direct applicability inherent in Regulations" and, in particular,

> "are under an obligation not to introduce any measure which might affect the jurisdiction of the Court to pronounce on any question involving the interpretation of Community law or the validity of an act of the institutions of the Community, which means that no procedure is permissible whereby the Community nature of a legal rule is concealed from those subject to it."[78]

As a general rule, therefore, save where a Regulation requires some national measure of implementation – as, for example, in the case of penalties for infringement of the Regulation – Member States may not adopt measures either giving effect to the Regulation or otherwise masking or affecting the application of the Regulation. Given this principle, the question that arises is whether EU Member States are entitled, as a matter of Com-

---

No L 247, 14.9.2002, p. 25), Commission Regulation (EC) No 1754/2002 of 1 October 2002 (OJ No L 264, 2.10.2002, p. 23), Commission Regulation (EC) No 1823/2002 of 11 October 2002 (OJ No L 276, 12.10.2002, p. 26), Commission Regulation (EC) No 1893/2002 of 23 October 2002 (OJ No L 286, 24.10.2002, p. 19), Commission Regulation (EC) No 1935/2002 of 29 October 2002 (OJ No L 295, 30.10.2002, p. 11), Commission Regulation (EC) No 2083/2002 of 22 November 2002 (OJ No L 319, 23.11.2002, p. 22), Commission Regulation (EC) No 145/2003 of 27 January 2003 (OJ No L 23, 28.1.2003, p. 22), Commission Regulation (EC) No 215/2003 of 3 February 2003 (OJ No L 28, 4.2.2003, p. 41), Commission Regulation (EC) No 244/2003 of 7 February 2003 (OJ No L 33, 8.2.2003, p. 28), Commission Regulation (EC) No 342/2003 of 21 February 2003 (OJ No L 49, 22.2.2003, p. 13), Commission Regulation (EC) No 350/2003 of 25 February 2003 (OJ No L 51, 26.2.2003, p. 19), Commission Regulation (EC) No 370/2003 of 27 February 2003 (OJ No L 53, 28.2.2003, p. 33), Commission Regulation (EC) No 414/2003 of 5 March 2003 (OJ No L 62, 6.3.2003, p. 24). Common Position 2003/140/CFSP of 27 February 2003 (OJ No L 53, 28.2.3003, p. 62) and Council Regulation (EC) No 561/2003 of 27 March 2003 (OJ No L 82, 29.3.2003, p. 1) implemented SCR 1452 (2002) of 20 December 2002.

77 See Article 249, second paragraph, of the *EC Treaty* (formerly Article 189 of the *EEC Treaty*).

78 Case 34/73, *Variola* [1973] ECR 981, at paragraphs 10-11.

munity law, to take measures in implementation of UNSC decisions in circumstances in which the Community has already acted by the adoption of a Regulation.

A number of observations on this matter are warranted. First, as a matter of established practice, the Member States have acted to implement UNSC decisions on sanctions notwithstanding the adoption of an EC Regulation. Although, in the period prior to the imposition of sanctions against Iraq, such action by the Member States was frequently justified by reference to Article 224 of the *EEC Treaty*, this provision has not been relied upon in recent years. Whatever the legal basis of such action, it ought probably to be taken as an implicit indication that, in the view of the Member States, they are entitled, or perhaps bound, to act independently in fulfilment of their obligations under the UN *Charter* pursuant to Articles 25 and 48 of that instrument.[79]

Second, as a matter of international law, the primacy of obligations under the *Charter* is established by Article 103 of the *Charter* which provides that "[i]n the event of a conflict between the obligations of the Members of the United Nations under the present Charter and their obligations under any other international agreement, the obligations under the present Charter shall prevail." Addressing the scope of Articles 25 and 103 of the *Charter* in its Provisional Measures Order in the *Lockerbie* cases, the International Court of Justice stated as follows:

> "Whereas both Libya and the [United Kingdom/United States], as Members of the United Nations, are obliged to accept and carry out the decisions of the Security Council in accordance with Article 25 of the Charter; whereas the Court, which is at the stage of proceedings on provisional measures, considers that prima facie this obligation extends to the decision contained in resolution 748 (1992); and whereas, in accordance with Article 103 of the Charter, the obligations of the Parties in that respect prevail over the obligations under any other international agreement, including the Montreal Convention".[80]

While, in view of the provisional nature of these proceedings, the application of Article 103 of the *Charter* to decisions of the UNSC imposing sanctions remains to be addressed definitively, it seems likely that, pursuant to Articles 25 and 103 of the *Charter*, obligations upon Members of the United Nations to act in implementation of decisions of the UNSC will, as a matter of general international law, prevail over obligations under other treaties. As a matter of general international law, the obligation of EU Member States to

---

79 Article 25 of the *Charter* provides: "The Members of the United Nations agree to accept and carry out the decisions of the Security Council in accordance with the present Charter." Article 48 provides: "1. The action required to carry out the decisions of the Security Council for the maintenance of international peace and security shall be taken by all the Members of the United Nations or by some of them, as the Security Council may determine. 2. Such decisions shall be carried out by the Members of the United Nations directly and through their action in the appropriate international agencies of which they are members."

80 *Case Concerning Questions of Interpretation and Application of the 1971 Montreal Convention arising from the Aerial Incident at Lockerbie (Libyan Arab Jamahiriya v. United Kingdom) (Libyan Arab Jamahiriya v. United States of America), Provisional Measures, Orders of 14 April 1992, I.C.J. Reports 1992*, pp. 3 and 114 respectively, at paragraphs 39 and 42 respectively.

take action to give effect to UNSC decisions imposing sanctions would thus prevail over any obligations to the contrary under the *EC Treaty* and the *TEU*.

Third, the primacy of EU Member State obligations under the *Charter* over those in the *EC Treaty* is confirmed as a matter of Community law by Article 307 of the *EC Treaty*[81] (although subject to the formal complication in the case of Germany that its membership of the UN succeeded its membership of the Community). At first sight, therefore, Article 307 seems to preserve, as a matter of Community law, the latitude of Member States to act in implementation of UNSC decisions notwithstanding parallel action by the Community.

Fourth, the quite significant limitations on Community competence in the field of sanctions implementation in the past – as a result, notably, of the scope of the common commercial policy – suggest that there were good reasons for accepting that Member State competence and Community competence could exist side-by-side. The greater flexibility of most Member State implementation arrangements – incorporating, for example, a licensing procedure – reinforced this appreciation.

Fifth, these considerations notwithstanding, developments in the Community regime relating to sanctions implementation, as well as recent ECJ jurisprudence on the scope of Article 307 of the *EC Treaty*, suggest that, at least as a matter of Community law, independent action by Member States is likely to become increasingly difficult to justify. Considerations having a bearing on this issue include the extensive competence of the Community to act under Article 301 of the *EC Treaty*, the move towards greater flexibility in the Community sanctions regime, notably by the incorporation of a licensing regime vested in the Commission, and the restrictive interpretation given to Article 234 of the *EEC Treaty* (now renumbered as Article 307 of the *EC Treaty*) by the ECJ in Case C-124/95, *R. v. HM Treasury and Bank of England*, ex parte *Centro-Com Srl*.[82] In this case, involving a reference to the ECJ from the English Court of Appeal on a question concerning the interpretation of Regulation 1432/92, as amended, imposing sanctions against Serbia and Montenegro, the Court concluded *inter alia* that:

(a) although EC Member States retained their competence in matters of foreign and security policy, this had to be exercised in a manner consistent with Community law. In particular, Member States could not treat national measures imposing sanctions as falling outside the scope of the common commercial policy on the ground that they had foreign and security objectives;[83]
(b) where Community rules implement the necessary measures of sanction, national measures covering the same ground could not be justified;[84] and
(c) the purpose of Article of 234 was to ensure that application of the Treaty did not affect the commitment of a Member State to respect the rights of non-Member States under an earlier agreement and to comply with its corresponding obligations.

81 Previously Article 234 of the *EEC Treaty*.

82 [1997] 1 CMLR 555.

83 At paragraphs 24-30. This aspect of the Court's judgment must be read in the light of the CFSP provisions of the *TEU*.

84 At paragraphs 44-49.

> Where a prior agreement allowed, but did not require, the Member State to adopt a measure which appeared to be contrary to Community law, the Member State had to refrain from doing so.[85]

While, in the light of this Judgment, there may well be circumstances in which Member States are *required* to act in fulfilment of their obligations under UNSC sanctions decisions – with such action being permissible as a matter of Community law – it seems increasingly likely that action by the Community will effectively occupy the field.

A number of caveats to this broad assessment are, however, warranted. First, there remain areas which appear to fall outside the ambit of Article 301 of the *EC Treaty* – even if not outside the ambit of the CFSP provisions of the *TEU*. These include non-economic sanctions, such as sports, diplomatic and cultural restrictions, as well as restrictions in respect of the trade in arms and related *matériel*. Second, practice to date indicates that the enactment of penalties for the infringement of a Community Regulation imposing sanctions will be a matter for each Member State.[86] Third, notwithstanding the increasing flexibility of Community implementation of sanctions, differences in the underlying national regulatory environment may dictate that, if they are to be effective, measures of implementation should be tailored specifically to the circumstances of particular Member States. This may be the case especially in circumstances in which a Member State is specially affected by the circumstances giving rise to the sanctions or where its underlying environment has special features.

By way of example, the scale and nature of Kuwaiti financial assets in the United Kingdom and other Community Member States dictated the need for legislative measures to "ring fence" legitimate Kuwaiti transactions from the effect of the more general restrictions imposed against Iraq and Iraqi-occupied Kuwait.[87] While, given its new-found competence and flexibility, it is not beyond contemplation that such measures

85 At paragraphs 56-60.

86 In this regard, Article 10 of the *EC Treaty* provides: "Member States shall take all appropriate measures, whether general or particular, to ensure fulfilment of the obligations arising out of this Treaty or resulting from action taken by the institutions of the Community. They shall facilitate the achievement of the Community's tasks. They shall abstain from any measure which could jeopardise the attainment of the objectives of this Treaty." In Case C-177/95, *Ebony Maritime SA v. Prefetto Della Provincia di Brindisi* [1997] 2 CMLR 24, the ECJ stated as follows: "… the Court has consistently held that where a Community regulation does not specifically provide any penalty for an infringement or refers for that purpose to national laws, regulations and administrative provisions, Article 5 E.C. [now Article 10] requires the Member States to take all measures necessary to guarantee the application and effectiveness of Community law. For that purpose, while the choice of penalties remains within their discretion, they must ensure in particular that infringements of Community law are penalised under conditions, both procedural and substantive, which are analogous to those applicable to infringements of national law of a similar nature and importance and which, in any event, make the penalty effective, proportionate and dissuasive …" (at paragraph 35).

87 See D.L. Bethlehem (ed.), *The Kuwait Crisis: Sanctions and Their Economic Consequences* (2 vols, 1991), at pp. xxxix-xli.

could in the future be taken by the Community,[88] the special circumstances of particular Member States may dictate that they act independently in respect of the matter in issue, whether pursuant to Article 307 of the *EC Treaty* or by reference to some more general principle of Community law, such as, for example, subsidiarity.[89]

In the light of these considerations, while it may be expected that Community competence in respect of the implementation of UNSC sanctions decisions will increasingly occupy the field to the exclusion of the competence of Member States, it would seem to be unwise to rule out both the possibility and desirability of a parallel exercise of competence by one or more Member States when this is necessary to ensure the effective implementation of the UNSC decision. In such circumstances, Article 307 of the *EC Treaty* would be the appropriate constitutional basis, as a matter of Community law, for Member State action.

For completeness, it ought also to be observed that Member State competence to act largely outside the framework of the *EC Treaty* – ie, subject only to the requirement of consultation – "in the event of war, serious international tension constituting a threat of war, or in order to carry out obligations it has accepted for the purpose of maintaining peace and international security" remains under Article 297 of the *EC Treaty*. In the light of the CFSP provisions of the *TEU*, competence to act pursuant to this Article would seem, however, to be subject to the requirements of the CFSP.[90]

IV. The Scope and Interpretation of EU Sanctions

(1) The Relationship between the Community Measure and the Underlying UNSC Decision

In contrast to the legal bases for the implementation of UNSC decisions in a number of the Member States which refer expressly to action by the UNSC,[91] neither the provisions

88 See, in this regard, Article 2 of Regulation 3155/90, *op.cit.* note 48.

89 In this regard, Article 5 of the *EC Treaty* may be relevant, viz: "The Community shall act within the limits of the powers conferred upon it by this Treaty and of the objectives assigned to it therein. In areas which do not fall within its exclusive competence, the Community shall take action, in accordance with the principle of subsidiarity, only if and insofar as the objectives of the proposed action cannot be sufficiently achieved by the Member States and can therefore, by reason of the scale or effects of the proposed action, be better achieved by the Community. Any action by the Community shall not go beyond what is necessary to achieve the objectives of this Treaty."

90 See, however, in this regard Article 14(6), *TEU* which provides: "In cases of imperative need arising from changes in the situation and failing a Council decision, Member States may take the necessary measures as a matter of urgency having regard to the general objectives of the joint action. The Member State concerned shall inform the Council immediately of any such measures."

91 See, for example, section 1(1) of the *UK United Nations Act 1946* which provides: "If, under Article forty-one of the Charter of the United Nations ... the Security Council of the United Nations call upon His Majesty's Government in the United Kingdom to apply any measures to give effect to any decision of that Council, His Majesty may by Order in Council make such

of the CFSP nor Article 301 of the *EC Treaty* establish any express linkage between an underlying decision of the UNSC and the measures taken pursuant to these provisions by the Community. While the absence of such a linkage is not altogether surprising – as the CFSP provisions and Article 301 operate as self-standing bases for the adoption of sanctions within the Community – the consequence of this is that Community measures adopted pursuant to these provisions need not necessarily take their scope from the UNSC decisions they purport to apply. While it may purport to give effect to a UNSC decision, a Community measure may therefore, intentionally, be either wider or narrower in scope than the UNSC decision.

By way of example (although drawn from the pre-*TEU* period), the Community initially imposed sanctions against Iraq *inter alia* by Regulations 2340/90 and 3155/90.[92] By reference to the preambular paragraphs of these measures, their object was to ensure the uniform implementation throughout the Community of SCR 661 (1990), imposing a general embargo on the import, sale or supply of commodities or products in respect of Iraq, of SCR 666 (1990), addressing the issue of humanitarian supplies and supplies intended strictly for medical purposes, and of SCR 670 (1990), which imposed a ban on flights to Iraq. The scope of these measures notwithstanding, Regulation 3155/90 imposed restrictions which appeared to go beyond the scope of the underlying UNSC Resolutions. It prohibited, in Article 1(1), the provision of non-financial services with the object or effect of promoting the economy of Iraq or Kuwait. Similar discordance of varying degrees between the underlying UNSC decisions and the Community measures adopted in purported implementation thereof is also evident in other cases.[93]

One consequence of the absence of an express linkage in the *TEU* or the *EC Treaty* between the underlying UNSC decision and the Community measure designed to give effect thereto is that there may be less scope to challenge the Community measure as an excessive exercise of power than there would be, for example, in the case of a UK Order made under the *United Nations Act 1946*. In practice, however, this shortcoming may be less significant than appears at first sight as the Common Positions adopted by the Council under the CFSP which form the basis of subsequent legislative action by the Community invariably tie the Community measure directly to the relevant UNSC decision. So, for example, Council Decision 93/614/CFSP of 22 November 1993[94] which formed the basis of EU implementation of SCR 883(1993) imposing sanctions against Libya provided *inter alia* as follows:

> "THE COUNCIL OF THE EUROPEAN UNION,
> Having regard to the Treaty on European Union, and in particular Article J.2 thereof,

provision as appears to Him necessary or expedient for enabling those measures to be effectively applied, including (without prejudice to the generality of the preceding words) provision for the apprehension, trial and punishment of persons offending against the Order."

92 *Op.cit.* note 48.

93 See, for example, the differences in formulation of SCR 883 (1993) in respect of Libya and Regulation 3274/93 adopted by the Community to give effect thereto.

94 *Op.cit.* note 65.

> Having regard to Resolution 883(93) adopted by the United Nations Security Council on 11 November 1993,
>
> HAS DECIDED AS FOLLOWS:
>
> Economic relations with Libya shall be reduced in accordance with the relevant provisions of Resolution 883(93) adopted by the Security Council on 11 November 1993.
>
> ..."

Pursuant to this Common Position, the Community went on to adopt Regulation 3274/93 imposing substantive restrictions in respect of trade with Libya and, in the course thereof, referred expressly both to the Common Position and to SCR 883 (1993).

Questions relating to the *vires* of Community measures imposing sanctions have arisen in proceedings before both national courts[95] and the European Court of Justice.[96]

The scope of the relevant Community measures by comparison to the UNSC decision to which they purport to relate may also be of practical importance in circumstances in which the compatibility of a Community measure with some other provision of international law is called into question in a forum other than a Community court. Apart from the perhaps unlikely circumstance of this being in issue in proceedings before the International Court of Justice (ICJ), such questions may arise in, for example, WTO proceedings. Indeed, as has already been noted, but for the determination of the GATT Council at its meeting in May 1992 that the FRY could not be regarded as the successor to the former Socialist Federal Republic of Yugoslavia, the entity that had been a Contracting Party of GATT 1947, it seems likely that issues relating to the compatibility *vis-à-vis* the GATT of Community measures imposing sanctions against Yugoslavia would have been raised in proceedings before a GATT Panel. Given both the broader membership and substantive remit of the WTO, it is not inconceivable that issues relating to the compatibility of Community (and other) measures imposing sanctions with WTO rules may be raised in due course in proceedings before WTO panels and the Appellate Body.

While, pursuant to the CFSP and Article 301 of the *EC Treaty*, there is no necessary linkage between Community measures imposing sanctions and the underlying UNSC decision to which they purport to give effect, in practice the scope of the Community measures will generally follow that of the UNSC Resolution to which they relate, although, for reason of legislative precision, the detail of the Community measures will invariably go beyond the often general terms of the underlying UNSC Resolution.

(2) Interpreting Community Measures

Before turning to address more closely the scope of the Community measures *ratione personae, ratione materiae and ratione temporis*, two brief observations concerning the interpretation of these measures should be made.[97] First, it is clear that both national and

95 See, for example, *R v. Searle* [1995] 3 CMLR 196.

96 See, for example, Case C-162/96, *A. Racke GmbH & Co. v. Hauptzollamt Mainz* [1998] 3 CMLR 219.

97 See on this the discussion in Canor, *op.cit.* note 6.

Community courts, when called upon to interpret Community measures giving effect to UNSC decisions will have close regard to the terms of the underlying UNSC Resolution. So, for example, in Case C-84/95, *Bosphorus*, involving the interpretation of Regulation 990/93 imposing sanctions against the FRY, the Court noted as follows:

> "As to context and aims, it should be noted that by Regulation 990/93 the Council gave effect to the decision of the Community and its Member States, meeting within the framework of political cooperation, to have recourse to a Community instrument to implement in the Community certain aspects of the sanctions taken against the Federal Republic of Yugoslavia by the Security Council of the United Nations, which, on the basis of Chapter VII of the Charter of the United Nations, adopted Resolutions 713 (1991), 752 (1992) and 787 (1992) and strengthened those sanctions by Resolution 820 (1993).
>
> To determine the scope of the first paragraph of Article 8 of Regulation 990/93, account must therefore also be taken of the text and aim of those resolutions, in particular paragraph 24 of Resolution 820 (1993) ..."[98]

The same approach is evident from other cases.[99]

Second, in having regard to the underlying UNSC decision and, notably, its object and purpose, it is apparent that the ECJ will construe the restrictions imposed by Community measures expansively. Thus, for example, in Case C-84/95, *Bosphorus*, the question in issue was whether Article 8 of Regulation 990/93 – which provided *inter alia* that all "aircraft in which a majority or controlling interest is held by a person or undertaking in or operating from the Federal Republic of Yugoslavia (Serbia and Montenegro) shall be impounded" – was to be interpreted as requiring the seizure of an aircraft owned by the Yugoslav national airline, JAT, but operated on the basis of a "dry lease" by (ie, subject to the complete control of) a Turkish charter and travel company, Bosphorus. Against the background of a Judgment by the Irish High Court[100] in judicial review proceedings granting an order for the release of the impounded aircraft on the grounds that the purpose of the Regulation was to deprive JAT of the use of the aircraft (ie, that the "interest"

98 Case C-84/95, *Bosphorus Hava Yollari Turizm Ve Ticaret AS v. Minister for Transport, Energy and Communications, Ireland* [1996] 3 CMLR 257, at paragraphs 13-14.

99 See, for example, Case C-124/95, *R v. HM Treasury and Bank of England*, ex parte *Centro-Com Srl* [1997] 1 CMLR 555, at paragraphs 3-5 and 47, 53; Case C-177/95, *Ebony Maritime SA v. Prefetto Della Provincia di Brindisi* [1997] 2 CMLR 24, at paragraphs 3, 20 and 24.

100 *Bosphorus Hava Yollari Turizm Ve Ticaret AS v. Minister for Transport, Energy and Communications* [1994] 3 CMLR 464. See also Case C-317/00 P(R), *Invest and Import GmbH and Invest Commerce v. The Commission*, 13 November 2000, [2000] ECR I-9541. The Court rejected the applicants appeal against a decision of the Second Chamber of the Court of First Instance rejecting an application for interim measures suspending Regulation (EC) No 1147/2000. Citing *Bosphorus*, the Court said: "the importance of the aims pursued by the regulation at issue is such as, *prima facie*, to justify negative consequences, even of a substantial nature for some operators. ... Accordingly, those consequences cannot be regarded as manifestly disproportionate in relation to the aims pursued" (at para.60).

referred to in Article 8 of the Regulation was essentially an interest in possession or the right to enjoy, control or regulate the use of the aircraft), the ECJ held as follows:

> "Any measure imposing sanctions has, by definition, consequences which affect the right to property and the freedom to pursue a trade or business, thereby causing harm to persons who are in no way responsible for the situation which led to the adoption of the sanctions.
>
> Moreover, the importance of the aims pursued by the regulation at issue is such as to justify negative consequences, even of a substantial nature, for some operators.
>
> The provisions of Regulation 990/93 contribute in particular to the implementation at Community level of the sanctions against the Federal Republic of Yugoslavia adopted, and later strengthened, by several resolutions of the Security Council of the United Nations. The third recital in the preamble to Regulation 990/93 states that 'the prolonged direct and indirect activities of the Federal Republic of Yugoslavia (Serbia and Montenegro) in, and with regard to, the Republic of Bosnia-Hezegovina are the main cause for the dramatic developments in the Republic of Bosnia-Herzegovina'; the fourth recital states that 'a continuation of these activities will lead to a further breach of international peace and security in the region'; and the seventh recital states that 'the Bosnian Serb party has hitherto not accepted, in full, the peace plan of the International Conference on the Former Yugoslavia in spite of appeals thereto by the Security Council'.
>
> It is in the light of those circumstances that the aim pursued by the sanctions assumes especial importance, which is, in particular, in terms of Regulation 990/93 and more especially the eighth recital in the preamble thereto, to dissuade the Federal Republic of Yugoslavia from 'further violating the integrity and security of the Republic of Bosnia-Herzegovina and to induce the Bosnian Serb party to cooperate in the restoration of peace in this Republic'.
>
> As compared with an objective of general interest so fundamental for the international community, which consists in putting an end to the state of war in the region and to the massive violations of human rights and humanitarian international law in the Republic of Bosnia-Herzegovina, the impounding of the aircraft in question, which is owned by an undertaking based in or operating from the Federal Republic of Yugoslavia, cannot be regarded as inappropriate or disproportionate.
>
> The answer to the [Irish] Supreme Court's question must therefore be that Article 8 of Regulation 990/93 applies to an aircraft which is owned by an undertaking based in or operating from the Federal Republic of Yugoslavia (Serbia and Montenegro), even though the owner has leased it for four years to another undertaking, neither based in nor operating from that Republic and in which no person or undertaking based in or operating from that Republic has a majority or controlling interest."[101]

101 Case C-84/95, *Bosphorus Hava Yollari Turizm Ve Ticaret AS v. Minister for Transport, Energy and Communications, Ireland* [1996] 3 CMLR 257, at paragraphs 22-27.

A similar rationale was articulated in Case C-177/95, *Ebony Maritime*.[102]

(3) *The Scope of the Community Measures* "Ratione Personae"

The scope of the Community measures *ratione personae* can be dealt with relatively briefly. As a matter of general proposition, Community Regulations apply directly throughout the territory of the Community. They will therefore apply to all persons within the territory of the Community. In the light of this proposition, in the case of sanctions against Iraq, the personal scope of the principal Regulations was not addressed further.

The issue was, however, addressed in more detail in the case of sanctions against the FRY. Thus, Article 5 of Regulation 1432/92[103] provided as follows:

> "This Regulation shall apply within the territory of the Community, including its air space and in any aircraft or vessel under the jurisdiction of a Member State, and to any person elsewhere who is a national of a Member State and any body elsewhere which is incorporated or constituted under the law of a Member State."

With minor variations, this formula has been adopted in all key subsequent Regulations.[104] In general, therefore, Community measures implementing sanctions will apply on the basis of both territoriality and nationality.

The limits of this principle were tested, and extended, in Case C-177/95, *Ebony Maritime* in which a preliminary issue concerned the application of Regulation 990/93 to a Maltese flagged vessel, carrying a cargo owned by a Liberian company, intercepted on the high seas heading for the FRY by a NATO/Western European Union ("WEU") force, and towed to the Italian port of Brindisi.[105] The issue arose *inter alia* as Article 1(1)(c) of the Regulation prohibited the entry into the territorial sea of the FRY by all commercial traffic.

---

102 Case C-177/95, *Ebony Maritime v. Prefetto Della Provincia di Brindisi* [1997] 2 CMLR 24. Advocate-General Jacobs addressed the matter as follows: "There is no doubt in my view that the Regulation has to be interpreted in the light of the Security Council resolutions, and in particular Resolution 820 (1993). It follows that the Regulation has to be interpreted in such a way as to make the sanctions fully effective. ... If the view were taken that Member States could not apply the Regulation in cases such as the present, there is a serious risk that they would be unable to enforce the United Nations sanctions. ... It does not seem to me that that can be regarded as the intended effect of the Regulation." (At paragraphs 21 and 25)

103 *Op.cit.* note 19.

104 See, for example, Regulation 337/2000 of 14 February 2000 in respect of Afghanistan, *op.cit.* note 67; Regulation 1705/98 of 28 July 1998 in respect of Angola, *op.cit.* note 68; Regulation 3274/93 of 29 November 1993 in respect of Libya, *op.cit.* note 65; Regulation (EC) No 303/2002 of 18 February 2002 in respect of Sierra Leone, *op cit.* note 69; Regulations (EC) No 1146/2001 of 11 June 2001 and (EC) No 1318/2002 of 22 July 2002 in respect of Liberia, *op.cit.* note 73; Regulation (EC) No 881/2002 of 27 May 2002 in respect of Al-Qaida and the Taliban, *op.cit.* note 76; Regulation (EC) No 2368/2002 of 20 December 2002 in respect of the Kimberley Process, *op.cit.* note 74.

105 Case C-177/95, *Ebony Maritime v. Prefetto Della Provincia di Brindisi* [1997] 2 CMLR 24.

Contending before the ECJ that the Regulation did not apply, the United Kingdom, France and Italy referred to Article 11 of the Regulation (cast in identical terms to Article 5 of Regulation 1432/92 set out above) and argued that the Regulation applied only in the following cases: (i) within the territorial waters of the Member States; (ii) to ships under the jurisdiction of a Member State; (iii) to individuals who are nationals of a Member State; and (iv) to companies incorporated or constituted under the law of a Member State.

Noting the observations of the Commission that the case involved a continuous chain of events, some of which did take place within Community territory, Advocate-General Jacobs addressed the scope of the Regulation in the following terms:

> "In my view it is clear that the Regulation applies merely by virtue of the fact that the Lido II [the vessel] was towed to Brindisi after having been seized by the NATO/WEU forces. The Regulation was adopted so as to give effect to Resolution 820 (1993) of the Security Council. It plainly follows from the objectives and the provisions of that Resolution that it was intended to be applied as broadly as possible. ...
>
> Article 11 provides that the Regulation shall apply 'within the territory of the Community'. In the present case that is precisely how the Regulation is being applied: it is being applied by the Italian authorities within their territory. And again in accordance with Article 11, the Regulation is being applied to a ship 'under the jurisdiction of a Member State', and there is no suggestion that the ship was improperly brought within the Member State's jurisdiction. The effect of Article 11 is not, therefore, to limit the field of application of the Regulation; it makes the field of application coterminous with the jurisdiction of Member States under international law.
>
> The prohibition, on the other hand, whose alleged breach gives rise to the application of the Regulation, applies also outside the territory of the Community, and does so of necessity, since Article 1(1)(c) of the Regulation prohibits entry into the Yugoslav territorial sea, which will normally take place from outside the territory of the Community. That prohibition, moreover, applies to 'all commercial traffic'; it is not limited to ships flying the flag of a Member State."[106]

Although rather more elliptically, the Court reached the same conclusion.[107]

However desirable the result in this particular case, it may be questioned whether it is adequately sustained by the terms of Regulation 990/93. There is a aura of artificiality in the conclusion that Article 11 is confined to the adjudicatory (and enforcement) jurisdiction of a Member State while the Regulation more generally applies extra-territorially to all persons, aircraft, vessels and other bodies wherever they may be situated regardless of their connection with the Community. While the extended application in this way of a

106 Case C-177/95, *Ebony Maritime v. Prefetto Della Provincia di Brindisi* [1997] 2 CMLR 24, at paragraphs 20, 22-23 of the Advocate-General's Opinion.

107 *Ibid.*, at paragraph 19 of the Judgment.

Community measure adopted in implementation of a UNSC decision may ultimately be consistent with international law, the Community's intention to legislate extra-territorially in this way would seem to be insufficiently clear to have warranted such a conclusion in the case of Regulation 990/93. The outcome raises doubt more generally about the application of Community – and perhaps other national – measures giving effect to UNSC sanctions decisions. This hesitation notwithstanding, it is evident from this case that the scope *ratione personae* of Community measures giving effect to UNSC decisions may be considerably broader than the jurisdictional remit declared on the face of the instrument.

(4) The Scope of Community Measures "Ratione Materiae"

The scope *ratione materiae* of Community measures giving effect to UNSC decisions has already been addressed in the context of the relationship between the Community measure and the underlying UNSC decision. As was there observed, in general, Community measures will take their scope from the terms of the UNSC Resolution to which they give effect. In this regard, the mandate of the Community measure will invariably be set by the Common Position adopted by the Council under the CFSP which will usually indicate simply that economic relations with the state in question will be reduced in accordance with a specified UNSC resolution.

An examination of the instances over the past decade in which the Community has purported to give effect to UNSC decisions shows that, in general, the Community measures shadow the substantive scope, if not always the precise language, of the underlying UNSC decision relatively closely. Thus, for example, Regulation 337/2000 of 14 February 2000 concerning a flight ban and a freeze of funds and other financial resources in respect of the Taliban of Afghanistan[108] follows the terms of SCR 1267 (1999) and the designations of the UN Sanctions Committee established by that Resolution and referred to in its operative provisions.

Where Community measures tend to go beyond the terms, though arguably not the scope, of the underlying UNSC Resolution is in cases in which the effective implementation of the Resolution requires a more detailed elaboration of the restrictions. Thus, for example, the Community gave effect to the prohibition on the sale or supply *inter alia* of "petroleum and petroleum products" to UNITA set out in SCR 864 (1993) of 15 September 1993 by Regulation 2967/93.[109] In contrast, however, to the bald prohibition in the SCR, the Community gave effect to the prohibition through a detailed 24 category description, in an annex to the Regulation, of petroleum and petroleum products by reference to the appropriate CN (combined nomenclature) code used at the time for customs classification purposes. While there was nothing in the UNSC Resolution to suggest such an approach, it is difficult to argue that a detailed elaboration of the restriction set out in general terms in the SCR was either excessive or inappropriate.

Equally acceptable would seem to be the common Community practice of prohibiting, along with the activity expressly referred to in the relevant UNSC Resolution, "any

108 *Op.cit.* note 67.

109 *Op.cit.* note 60.

activity the object or effect of which is, directly or indirectly, to promote the transaction referred to". By way of example of such a practice, this was the approach adopted by the Community in the case of Regulation 2967/93 just referred to giving effect to the explicit prohibition in SCR 864 (1993) on the sale or supply of petroleum and petroleum products. The elaboration of the general prohibition to explicitly include activity having the object or effect, directly or indirectly, of promoting the prohibited transaction would seem to be a wholly acceptable way of ensuring legal certainty, particularly in circumstances in which a breach of the prohibition would attract criminal penalties.

Potentially more problematic, however, are the few instances in which the Community measure appears to go beyond the *substantive* scope of the underlying UNSC Resolution or in which the language employed by the Community measure is potentially at variance with that used in the Resolution. The example of the prohibition on the provision of non-financial services by Regulation 2340/90, as amended by Regulation 3155/90, is given above. This practice was repeated in the case of sanctions against the FRY in which Regulation 1432/92 prohibited the provision of non-financial services notwithstanding that the matter was not addressed in SCR 757 (1992) to which it was designed to give effect.

While, in the case of Regulation 1432/92 and SCR 757 (1992), it could be argued that the prohibition on non-financial services was merely a specific elaboration of the general prohibition on any activities "which would promote or are calculated to promote" the export of commodities or products originating in the FRY in SCR 757 (1992), it seems clear that the Regulation goes beyond the Resolution in important respects. The question in such circumstances is whether the *vires* of the Regulation could be impugned in proceedings before the ECJ or the compatibility of the Regulation with some other binding rule of law could be challenged in some other tribunal.

While it may be expected that any tribunal faced with a question of either the *vires* of a Community measure implementing a UNSC sanctions decision or the compatibility of such a measure with some other rule of law, would allow the Community a considerable margin of appreciation[110] – particularly in circumstances in which the Community measure was consistent with the object and purpose of the underlying UNSC Resolution – it is clear that the validity of a Community measure may, as a matter of *Community law*, be impugned on the ground of inconsistency with a rule of international law.[111] While the fact that a Community measure purporting to implement a UNSC decision went beyond the terms of the UNSC Resolution would probably not of itself be sufficient to sustain an argument of inconsistency with a rule of international law, it seems likely that, in such circumstances, the Community measure would not be able to avail itself of the shield of Article 103 of the *Charter* to the extent of any excess in circumstances in which the *vires* of the measure was impugned by reference to some other rule of international law. The same is

110 Cf. Case C-162/96, *A. Racke GmbH & Co. v. Hauptzollamt Mainz* [1998] 3 CMLR 219.

111 See, for example, Joined Cases 21 to 24/72, *International Fruit Company v. Produktschap voor Groeten en Fruit* ("Third International Fruit Case") [1972] ECR 1219, at paragraphs 6-7 of the Judgment. See also H.G. Schermers and D. Waelbroeck, *Judicial Protection in the European Communities* (5th ed., 1992), at pp. 217-8; and K.M. Meessen "The Application of Rules of Public International Law within Community Law", (1976) 13 CMLRev 485.

also likely to be true of an allegation of the incompatibility of a Community measure with some other binding rule of international law raised before a non-Community tribunal.

(5) The Scope of Community Measures "Ratione Temporis"

The scope of Community measures *ratione temporis* is largely only of significance in the context of the suspension or termination of sanctions. To the extent that the Community acts prior to any action by the UNSC, such action will amount to the unilateral imposition of sanctions by the Community. While there are some instances in which UNSC Resolutions include a start or trigger date for the imposition of sanctions, this practice has by-and-large either been incorporated into the relevant Community measure or the Community measure giving effect thereto has only been enacted or entered into force after the date in question.[112]

In the case of the suspension or termination of sanctions, Community practice has developed with the development in UNSC practice. Thus, SCR 661 (1990) of 6 August 1990, imposing sanctions against Iraq, made no provision for the termination of sanctions other than to imply that the sanctions would be lifted at the point of Iraqi compliance with the substantive demands made in the Resolution. Similarly, no provision was made in Regulation 1432/90 giving effect to SCR 661 (1990) for the termination of the Community measures.

Experience in the case of sanctions against both Iraq and Yugoslavia identified the absence of any predetermined mechanism for the suspension or termination of sanctions at the level of the UNSC as a problem. In some cases, notably Haiti, the situation on the ground caused the UNSC to impose sanctions, suspend the sanctions, re-impose the sanctions and finally terminate the sanctions. In each case, this necessitated a new Resolution by the UNSC.

In the light of this experience, it has become relatively common for UNSC Resolutions to make specific provision for the temporal application, suspension and termination of sanctions. In such circumstances, the Community has invariably followed the approach adopted by the UNSC. Thus, in the case of Haiti, the roller coaster of delayed implementation, suspension, termination of the suspension, expansion, and conditional termination at UNSC level[113] was followed closely at Community level.[114]

---

112 See, for example, Regulation 1608/93 of 24 June 1993, *op.cit.* note 59, giving effect to SCR 841 (1993) of 16 June 1993 in respect of Haiti. In this case, the SCR provided that sanctions "shall come into force at 00:01 EST on 23 June 1993" unless certain conditions were satisfied. The Regulation, which was adopted on 24 June 1993, and entered into force two days later on 26 June 1993, provided in Article 1 that "[a]s from 00.01 EST (New York time) on 23 June 1993, the following shall be prohibited".

113 See SCR 841 (1993) of 16 June 1993, SCR 861 (1993) of 27 August 1993, SCR 873 (1993) of 13 October 1993, SCR 917 (1994) of 6 May 1994, SCR 940 (1994) of 31 July 1994, SCR 944 (1994) of 29 September 1994 and SCR 948 (1994) of 15 October 1994.

114 See the following principal Community measures, *op.cit.* notes 59 and 66: Regulation 1608/93 of 24 June 1993, Regulation 2520/93 of 13 September 1993, Regulation 3028/93 of 28 October 1993, Regulation 1263/94 of 30 May 1994 and Regulation 2543/94 of 19 October 1994.

V. Concluding Remarks

By way of conclusion, one additional issue of importance warrants comment. The implementation of sanctions by the Community inevitably has economic consequences for persons affected by the measures within the Community. Typically, the performance of contracts already concluded may be prohibited. The target state may also react by adopting measures of its own freezing foreign assets within its jurisdiction. Debts due may not be paid.

While the Community has acted in the case of each of the principal cases of UNSC sanctions since 1990 to give effect to UNSC decisions prohibiting the satisfying of claims with regard to contracts and transactions the performance of which was affected by the relevant UNSC Resolution/s,[115] the question nevertheless arises as to whether either the Member States or the Community are responsible for losses caused in consequence of the sanctions imposed by the Community.

This issue has come before the courts in a number of cases. *In Re Trade with Iraq*, a case before the Landgericht Bonn,[116] the question was whether the German Government was responsible for the losses of a German trader that arose in consequence of a German decree giving effect to, and imposing penalties in respect of the breach of, Community Regulation 2340/90 imposing sanctions against Iraq. Holding that the action was unfounded, the Court stated that any injury that the plaintiff might have suffered was caused not by the decree of the German Government but by the European Community. The Court further held that, as regards the Community's export prohibition, the plaintiff had to rely on any claims for compensation it may have against the Community under Article 215, second paragraph, of the *EEC Treaty* (now Article 288 of the *EC Treaty*) and noted that the ECJ has in principle recognised that the Community is liable for injury caused by its legislative acts.

In virtually mirror image proceedings some years later in Case T-184/95, *Dorsch Consult Ingenieurgesellschaft mbH v. EU Council and EC Commission*,[117] the applicant, a German company, sought compensation from the Community for the losses suffered as a result of Iraqi legislation adopted in response to sanctions taken against it by the international community. In the applicant's contention, the Iraqi legislation had been adopted in response to Community Regulation 2340/90 imposing sanctions against Iraq and that the Community was accordingly liable either for the loss caused by its lawful act (the adoption of the Regulation) or the loss caused by its unlawful act (the failure to compensate persons who had been adversely affected by the Regulation).

The Court of First Instance of the European Community dismissed the application. In so doing, the Court held *inter alia* that (a) to the extent that the applicant's losses had become irrecoverable through the adoption of the Iraqi legislation as a foreseeable and direct counter measure to the Regulation 2340/90, the damage alleged would be attributable to the Community; (b) however, the applicant had failed to prove that the Iraqi

115 See, for example, Regulation 3541/92 of 7 December 1992 in respect of Iraq, *op.cit.* note 48.

116 Case 1 0 446/90, *Re Trade with Iraq* [1993] 1 CMLR 66.

117 [1998] 2 CMLR 758.

legislation constituted an objectively foreseeable consequence of the adoption of the Community measure; (c) in any event, even if the Iraqi legislation had been a foreseeable consequence of the Community embargo, the alleged damage could not be attributed to the Community Regulation but rather to the UNSC Resolution which had originally imposed the embargo. This finding was upheld on appeal.[118]

While the conclusion that the Community cannot be held liable for losses suffered as a result of action taken by the state targeted by UNSC and Community sanctions measures is probably to be welcomed, the two cases cited, taken together, raise difficult questions about where the locus of responsibility lies in respect of damage caused to private persons as a result of the implementation of sanctions. Just as the UN and the international community have been urged to address special economic problems encountered by states in the implementation of sanctions pursuant to Article 50 of the *Charter*, so too ought the Community and the Member States act to address special economic problems encountered by private persons subject to Community or national measures implementing sanctions.

* * *

Select Bibliography

1. Bethlehem, D.L. (ed.), *The Kuwait Crisis: Sanctions and Their Economic Consequences* (2 vols; 1991).
2. Canor, I., "'Can Two Walk Together, Except They Be Agreed?' The Relationship Between International Law and European Law: The Incorporation of United Nations Sanctions Against Yugoslavia into European Community Law Through the Perspective of the European Court of Justice", (1998) 35 CMLRev 137.
3. Kuyper, P.J., "Sanctions Against Rhodesia: The EEC and the Implementation of General International Legal Rules", (1975) 12 CMLRev 231.
4. Kuijper, P.J., "European Economic Community", in Meessen, K.M. (ed.), *International Law of Export Control* (1992), at pp. 57.
5. MacLeod, Hendry and Hyett, *The External Relations of the European Communities: A Manual of Law and Practice* (1996).

118 Case 237/98 P *Dorsch Consult v. Council and Commission* [2000] ECR I-4549. See also *Elliniki Viomichania Oplon AE (EVO) v. Council of the EU and Commission of the EU*, 24 April 2002, [2002] 2 CMLR 32, Judgment of the Court of First Instance (Fourth Chamber).

6

FINLAND

*Martti Koskenniemi, Päivi Kaukoranta and Martin Björklund**

I. Introduction

One aspect of the political transformations in the 1990's has been an increasing recourse to economic – and occasionally military – sanctions by international organisations, particularly the United Nations. The emergence of an apparent political consensus between the Great Powers has facilitated the adoption of economic measures under Article 41 of the UN Charter – often irrespective of the rather meagre historical evidence for the effectiveness of sanctions, at least if measured in terms of attaining a rapid transformation in the target State's policy.[1] Ian Smith's racist government could withstand 14 years (1965-1979) of an almost complete economic boycott declared by the Security Council on South Rhodesia. Iraq's economic isolation entered its second decade – while its government yielded only to military pressure. But although declaring an economic embargo is obviously designed to contribute to a change of heart on the targeted State's part, it may serve other purposes as well. Clearly, in some cases economic sanctions have been resorted to in the absence of alternative policy tools and without great confidence in their bringing about the desired political result. A sanctions decision may have been taken in order to manifest the determination of the "international community" or the unity of the Security Council members, for instance. Or it may have been made in order to forestall pressure towards taking military measures. Economic sanctions may thus possess an important symbolic value and contribute to the diversification of foreign policy means, lifting political pressure from taking more drastic measures. Although economic mea-

---

* Martti Koskenniemi is a Professor at the University of Helsinki, Director of the Erik Castrén Institute, and a Member of the International Law Commission; Päivi Kaukoranta is the Director of the Treaty Unit at the Finnish Ministry for Foreign Affairs; Martin Björklund is a Researcher at the Erik Castrén Institute, University of Helsinki.

1 Standard studies are Gary C. Hufbauer – Jeffrey J. Schott, *Economic Sanctions in Support of Foreign Policy Goals* (1983) and id., *Economic Sanctions Reconsidered. History and Current Policy* (1985). Assessments of effectiveness are also included in James Barber, "Economic Sanctions as a Policy Instrument", 55 *International Affairs* (1979) 373-9; Robin Renwick, *Economic Sanctions* (1981), pp. 76-81 and David Baldwin, *Economic Statecraft* (1985), pp. 55-8. Cf. also Kimberly Ann Elliott, "Remarks", *ASIL Proceedings* (1991), pp. 171-3.

Vera Gowlland-Debbas (ed.), National Implementation of UN Sanctions, *167-194.*

sures have also been much criticised – particularly because of the suffering they cause to civilian populations – it is hard to see how they could be done away with altogether. The question is not so much whether economic measures are or are not acceptable or effective in themselves, but whether they can be managed by the UN or Member States in such a fashion as to maximise their potential effectiveness as a means to influence the policies of particular States and to minimise their negative effects on the populations of those States or on the general international situation.

II. Policy or Law?

From the perspective of diplomats, economic sanctions appear as a foreign policy tool among others, situated in a scale of increasing severity somewhere between a critical communiqué and military attack. How comprehensive sanctions are, whom they are targeted against, which exceptions are allowed, and how efficiently they are managed are affairs of diplomacy, too, and decisions about them reflect complex contextual assessments of effectiveness and legitimacy. Often, however, sanctions – particularly sanctions under Chapter VII of the Charter – are seen as a means of enforcement of international law. The question of whether economic measures can properly be understood as analogous to sanctions in domestic criminal law has, of course, been a classical topic of legal commentary. During the cold war, it was not difficult to conclude that the analogy was false.[2] Unlike the domestic judge, the Security Council was completely free in determining not only how to act in case there was a "threat to the peace, breach of the peace or an act of aggression" foreseen in Article 39 but whether to act in the first place.

In the relative euphoria following the Gulf War, and increasingly in legal analysis of Chapter VII – including debates of the legal position of the Security Council vis-à-vis the International Court of Justice – the Council's activity started to appear as enforcement jurisdiction for breaches of international law. In such an atmosphere, measures under Articles 39-42 of the Charter started to appear as legally circumscribed forms of punishment, or at least as police measures, intended to bring about the vindication of the norms violated. This made it seem important to define and delimit the Council's sanctions jurisdiction more carefully and to imagine its deliberations as a form of – however rudimentary – enforcement of a new world order.

Very little of later experience in the 1990's supports such an understanding. Which countries have been targeted, how sanctions were formulated and whether openly advertised breaches were taken seriously, seemed to depend again on questions of political propriety, the complex play of alliance and adversity between Council members. Lawyers may debate whether the arms embargo decreed in Resolution 713 (1991) over the whole territory of the former Yugoslavia was in breach of the right of self-defence of Bosnia-Herzegovina under Article 51 of the Charter. This had no effect on the Council, however, which was simply determined to look elsewhere when Arab States provided arms and assistance to Bosnia – or when they received Libyan Air Lines aircraft in their territories

2 Cf. Hans Kelsen, *The Law of the United Nations* (1951), pp. 732-7.

in defiance of the sanctions set against Libya in 1992, widely held to have been problematic in their legal justification.[3]

None of this made the position of Member States any easier. The more "political" sanctions appear, the more pressure there is for individual members to think for themselves whether and to what extent to put them into effect. In principle, members are, of course, bound under Articles 25 and 48 faithfully to carry out decisions of the Council, whatever their political merit. That everyone is automatically expected to execute such measures is a key aspect of collective security and the *conditio sine qua non* of the deterrent value of the provisions. One cannot, however, fail to feel sympathy towards countries such as Jordan for which the choice to apply the embargo against Iraq would have been frankly suicidal. Again, the Council decided to look elsewhere as petroleum and other products continued to cross the Iraqi-Jordanian boundary after 1991. This situation is not unique. Countries are not in an identical position to implement and enforce particular sanctions. Neighbours act always in a key role and the decision to execute a particular boycott may sometimes be frustrated by a neighbouring State's policy just as certainly as its decision not to implement sanctions may be for it the only policy of prudence. Something of the experience of the frontline States in connection with the South Rhodesian and South African experiments is a sobering reminder of such problems. That much should not be expected in terms of the solidarity between UN members is well illustrated by the frustrating efforts by a number of small or vulnerable States to make a reality of the promises of assistance in article 50 of the Charter during the interminable discussions waged within the Charter Committee of the UN General Assembly through the 90's.

In other words, recourse to economic sanctions by the Security Council is a decision of policy of which there is no guarantee that it will respect a Member State's preferences. This does not mean that the Council's jurisdiction to order sanctions has no legal limit – though there is little hope of a centralised enforcement of any such limit. Nor does it mean that members would not be bound to implement and enforce sanctions even if they disagreed about their well-foundedness. But inasmuch as member States are the final arbiters of the lawfulness of the Council's actions, having the "right of last resort",[4] it cannot automatically be excluded that they exercise this power by a less than full implementation of the controversial measure.

Nonetheless, many Member States accept the binding force of Security Council decisions as a matter of principle and of legal culture. One of such States is Finland which has traditionally looked towards the United Nations and the system of collective security under Chapter VII as important parts of the world order and in whose functioning Finland itself had a stake.

3 SCR 748 (1992) of 30 March 1992.

4 Dan Ciobanu, *Preliminary Objections. Related to the Jurisdiction of the United Nations Political Organs* (1975), pp. 173-179.

III. Legal Basis of Finnish Implementation Legislation

The legal basis of Finnish sanctions implementation legislation has developed gradually, in connection with particular situations. Therefore, in the following it will be discussed chronologically.

(1) Membership in the United Nations

The proposal concerning Finland's membership in the United Nations was submitted to the Parliament on 12 June 1947. The proposal contained no mention of the binding force of United Nations Security Council decisions. Nor was any room devoted in the bill for a discussion of Finland's possible obligations under Article 41 of the Charter. No attention was directed to the matter by the Parliament, either. Finnish membership in the UN was accepted as a matter of course. Disappointment about the inability of the League of Nations to take effective action at the outset of the Winter War in 1939 was still fresh in mind and there must have been doubt about the functionality of Chapter VII. Nonetheless, UN membership was seen as a guarantee of Finland's independence and international position and there was no interest to express reservations or doubts about the Charter – they would anyway have been pointless. Because of the well-known difficulties in having new members accepted to the organisation, it was only in the Fall of 1955 that Finland finally became a member. The Charter was incorporated by a decree of 13 January 1956. No other implementation legislation was passed at the time.

(2) Constitutional Position of Sanctions

Most foreign policy measures – including participation in measures decided by the Security Council – pose no constitutional problem in Finland. Thus, decisions on participation in non-economic sanctions (diplomatic protests, non-recognition policies, limitation of diplomatic personnel etc.) may be taken by the President of the Republic, in co-operation with the Council of State, under his general competence as leader of Foreign Policy under Section 93 of the 2000 Constitution of Finland and the equivalent prior legislation.[5] No special implementation legislation is needed in such situations. For example, the Council has required States not to recognise the independence of South Rhodesia (1965) or of the Northern Turkish Republic of Cyprus (1983). It has called upon States not to recognise changes in the position of Jerusalem, and certain other territorial gains by Israel (1969, 1980), South Africa's presence in Namibia (1969, 1970) or its Bantustan-homelands (1969), as well as Iraq's annexation of Kuwait (1990) and annexations by force in the Yugoslavian succession wars (1991).

Such decisions have been binding on Member States. Nonetheless, no specific implementation legislation has been deemed necessary in respect of any. Finland has, however, respected them. In connection with parliamentary debates concerning tourism in Northern Cyprus, the Foreign Minister has reaffirmed Finland's obligation to refrain from such action that would constitute *de facto* recognition.

5 Act 731/1999 and Act 94/1919.

By contrast, economic sanctions that limit the right to trade of private individuals have been understood to contradict Section 6 of the old Constitution Act (1919) that lays down the principle of the protection of private property. This principle has now been transferred to Section 15 of the new Constitution of Finland (2000) and reads as follows:

> The property of everyone is protected. Provisions on the expropriation of property, for public needs and against full compensation, are laid down by an Act.

According to established practice, however, it has been deemed possible to limit the right of ownership by an Act of Parliament if such limit does not encroach upon the owner's right in an abnormal or unreasonable manner. More extensive interference is possible only through the legislative procedure designed for amending the Constitution. That is to say, such law must be passed in two successive Parliamentary sessions, first by a majority of the votes cast and then without any material alterations by at least two thirds majority, or by a two-thirds majority in a single session if first declared urgent by a five-sixths majority.[6] By contrast, international treaties that involve constitutional issues may be adopted in a single session with a two-thirds majority.[7]

As stated above, the UN Charter was incorporated into Finnish law by a decree. Even if the question of Finnish implementation of UN Security Council economic sanctions had been debated at the time (which it was not), this would not have provided a sufficient basis for a deviation from the provision on protection of private property in the Constitution Act. Hence, until the matter arose in practice, there were no provisions in force in Finland that would have enabled participation in foreign economic boycotts.

IV. The Rhodesia Sanctions Implementation Legislation (1967)

The implementation of UN Security Council resolutions under Article 41 of the Charter came up in practice in connection with the Rhodesian crisis in 1965. The first Security Council sanction decision after the Unilateral Declaration of Independence – Security Council Resolution 217 (1965) of 20 November 1965 – was formulated in non-mandatory terms. Nonetheless, it was decided in Finland that some action should be taken. According to a law on the export of war equipment,[8] such export required permission by the Council of State. Five days after the passing of Security Council Resolution 217 (1965), the Council of State decided that no export licences would be given for arms trade with Rhodesia as long as the present situation would continue. No action was taken to implement the trade embargo recommended in the said Resolution, apart from removing Rhodesia from the list of countries with whom free trade was conducted under

6 Constitution Act, Section 73.

7 Constitution Act, Section 95.

8 Act 318/1938 and Decree 319/1938.

the decree on the security of foreign trade.[9] This meant in practice that export licensing was re-established for Rhodesia.[10]

A year later, on 16 December 1966, the Security Council passed a resolution on binding, but partial economic sanctions (Security Council Resolution 232 (1966)). In this connection, Finland enacted a specific law on Rhodesian sanctions that entered into force as of 10 March 1967.[11] This act was adopted following the procedure for constitutional amendments.[12] It was an enabling act, authorising the Government to enact by decree the implementation of Security Council Resolution 232 (1966). It contained five sections:

Act
on the Implementation of Obligations under Security Council Resolution on South Rhodesia

Issued on 10 March 1967

According to the decision of Parliament, which is taken in conformity with the provisions of Section 67 of Parliament Act, the following shall be enacted:

Section 1. As the United Nations Security Council has in its decision of 16 December 1966 obliged the Member States of the United Nations in accordance with Articles 25 and 48 of the Charter to take measures of economic nature and concerning traffic, necessary measures for the implementation of those obligations for the part of Finland shall be prescribed by a decree in accordance what is provided in this Act.

Section 2. The Speaker of the Parliament shall be notified of decrees issued by virtue of this Act without delay, and he or she shall inform the Parliament immediately, or if the Parliament is not in session, as soon as they are convened, and those decrees shall be cancelled if the Parliament so decides.

Section 3. Contract or commitment entered into contrary to the purposes of this Act or which means circumvention thereof, shall be null and void.

If a contract or commitment, entered into prior to the entry into force of regulations issued by virtue of this Act, is contrary to the provisions of such regulations, enforcement of such commitment shall be interrupted immediately.

Section 4. Penalty and other sanctions for violation of directives issued by virtue of this Act or based thereupon shall be adjudged in accordance with Act on the Punishment of Acts against Certain Enabling Acts of 28 June 1958 (305/1958).

The provisions of the Act mentioned above shall also otherwise be applied in issues falling under the scope of this Act.

9 Decree 438/1965.

10 Decree 637/1965.

11 Act 187/1967.

12 Procedure for Constitutional amendments was at the time included in Section 67 of the Parliament Act.

Section 5. This Act shall be in force until the end of the year 1967 and the directives issued by virtue thereof shall also cease to be in force at that time. It may be prescribed by a decree, however, that the application of this Act or directives issued by virtue thereof shall cease already earlier.

The Act was intended to be in force only until the end of 1967. In connection with passing the Act, however, the Parliament expressed its view that there should be general legislation on the matter. It decided that a new enabling act, covering the implementation of Security Council resolutions generally should be submitted to Parliament by the expiry of the Act on South Rhodesia.

The implementation decree that incorporated those provisions of Security Council Resolution 232 (1966) that belonged to the sphere of legislation was given on 22 March 1967.[13]

V. General Enabling Act (1967)

In accordance with the wishes of Parliament, expressed in connection with the passing of the Rhodesian sanctions Act in early 1967, the government prepared a bill for a general Enabling Act on UN economic sanctions. This Act was passed at the end of 1967 following the procedure for constitutional amendments because it was considered to deviate from the principle of the protection of private property and, being an enabling act, also from Section 2 of the Constitution Act providing that the powers of the State in Finland are vested in the people, who are represented by the Parliament. The general Enabling Act entered into force as of 1.1.1968.[14]

Act
on the Implementation of Certain Obligations of Finland as a Member of the United Nations

Issued on 29 December 1967

According to the decision of Parliament, which is taken in conformity with the provisions of Section 67 of Parliament Act, the following shall be enacted:

Section 1. In order to implement the obligations of Finland as a Member of the United Nations arising from the binding resolutions adopted by the Security Council, necessary measures of economic nature or concerning communications or other traffic may be prescribed by a decree.

Section 2. The Speaker of the Parliament shall be notified of decrees issued by virtue of this Act without delay, and he or she shall inform the Parliament immediately, or if the Parliament is not in session, as soon as they are convened, and those decrees shall be cancelled if the Parliament so decides.

---

13 Decree 188/1967.

14 Act 659/1967.

> Section 3. Contract or commitment entered into contrary to this Act or directives issued by virtue thereof or in order to evade those provisions, shall not be enforced.
>
> If a contract or other commitment, entered into prior to the date of entry into force of a decree issued by virtue of this act, is contrary to the provisions of such a decree or of regulations issued by virtue thereof, enforcement of such commitment shall be interrupted immediately.
>
> Section 4. Penalty and other sanctions for violation of regulations issued by virtue of this Act or based thereupon shall be adjudged in accordance with Act on the Punishment of Acts against Certain Enabling Acts of 28 June 1958 (305/1958).
>
> The provisions of the Act mentioned above shall also otherwise be applied in issues falling under the scope of this Act.
>
> Section 5. More detailed provisions on the application of this Act shall be issued by a decree, if necessary.
>
> Section 6. This Act will enter into force on 1 January 1968.

Section 4 of the Act was amended in 1990 as follows:[15]

> Section 4. Penalty for violation or attempted violation of regulatory measures issued by authorities by virtue of this act is prescribed in Chapter 46, articles 1 – 3, of the Penal Code. Forfeitures are prescribed in articles 8 – 13 of the same Chapter.

This Act is still in force.[16] Four aspects of it are worthy of note:
1) It authorises only the implementation of *binding* Security Council Resolutions;
2) Implementation decrees have to be notified to Parliament that may, if necessary, abrogate them – even if Parliament has never used this power;
3) A contract in conflict with the implementation decree may not be implemented even if it had been concluded before the entry into force of the law;
4) As for penal sanctions, reference was made to a 1958 law concerning the punishment of acts against certain enabling acts. In 1990 reference was made to the equivalent provisions in the Penal Code.

Since 1967, this Act has provided the basis for the Finnish implementation of all binding sanctions resolutions passed by the UN Security Council. During 1967-1999, altogether 42 implementation decrees have been enacted, dealing with Resolutions on Rhodesia (1966-1979), South Africa (1977-1994), Iraq (1990-2003), Former Yugoslavia (1991-1996), Somalia (1992-2002), Liberia (1992-1999), Serbia-Montenegro and certain areas in Croatia and Bosnia Herzegovina (1992-1996), Libya (1992-), Haiti (1993-1994), Angola (UNITA) (1993-2002), Rwanda (1994-) and Sierra Leone (1998-2002).[17]

---

15 Act 824/1990.

16 For subsequent amendments see in section "Legal basis of domestic measures based on decisions of the European Union" and in section "Measures as a result of the terrorist attacks on 11 September 2001".

17 For a review of the measures until 1994, cf. Martti Koskenniemi, *Kansainvälisen pakotteet ja Suomi. Ulko-ja turvallisuuspolitiikan alaan kuuluvat ei-sotilaalliset sanktiot ja niiden täytän-*

VI. Other Relevant Legislation

Apart from the Enabling Law of 1967, other pieces of legislation have been used or have been available for the implementation of UN economic sanctions. A 1974 Law on the Protection of Foreign Trade[18] offered the possibility to limit trade in order to 1) guarantee balance of payments; 2) in severe disturbances of economic action in some fields; 3) to deal with competition restrictions. But the Law did not allow restrictions of export or import on the basis of foreign policy reasons. In 1992, a provision on the Co-ordinating Committee for Multilateral Export Control (CoCom) was added to this law. It now became possible to limit export of items that had been imported with a specific re-exportation reservation. After Finland's entry into the European Union in 1995, external trade became a matter of exclusive Union competence. Consequently, this Act has been substituted by the Act on administration of foreign trade and on control and safeguard measures in certain cases[19] and by the Act on control of exports of dual use goods.[20]

The Law on National Preparedness of 1991 becomes effective in case of an armed attack on Finland or war or a situation after the war.[21] The law becomes applicable, however, only if the crisis has an effect on Finland (it cannot thus be invoked to set up sanctions if the situation does not concern Finland).

VII. South Africa: Implementation of Non-Mandatory Sanctions

Already in the 1960's the UN General Assembly and Security Council recommended that Member States limit or terminate their arms trade with Portugal, Mozambique, South Rhodesia and South Africa. These recommendations were implemented in Finland by decisions by the Council of State in accordance with a 1933 Decree on Firearms[22] and a 1938 Law on War Equipment[23] not to export prohibited goods to the relevant territories.[24]

The implementation of binding sanctions against South Africa arose for the first time in connection with the setting up of an arms embargo by Security Council Resolution 418 (1977) on 4 November 1977. This was a binding decision, made under Chapter VII. It was implemented by a decree based on the enabling Act of 1967. It was considered that a decree was needed because merely refraining from providing licenses under the arms trade Act would not cover all the products referred to in Security Council Resolution 418 (1977). The decree entered into force on 1.1.1978.

---

töönpano Suomessa (1994), p. s. 362-3. For the implementation of binding SC resolutions as a member of the European Union, see also section 11.

18 Act 154/1974, *Ulkomaankaupan turvaamisesta annettu laki.*

19 Act 1521/1994.

20 Act 108/1997.

21 Act 1080/1991, *Valmiuslaki.*

22 Act 33/1933 and Decree 34/1933.

23 Act 318/1938.

24 Cf. Koskenniemi (1994), pp. 283-290.

Decree on the Implementation of Obligations under United Nations Security Council Resolution on South Africa

Issued in Helsinki on 23 December 1977

Upon presentation by the Minister for Foreign Affairs, the following is enacted by virtue of sections 1 and 5 of the Act (659/1967) of 29 December 1967 on the Implementation of Certain Obligations of Finland as a Member of the United Nations:

Section 1. In order to implement the obligations of Finland arising from the United Nations Security Council Resolution adopted on 4 November 1977 concerning South Africa, supply of arms and all kinds of *materiel* related thereto to the Republic of South Africa, including sale and transfer of weapons and ammunition, military vehicles and equipment and paramilitary police equipment and supply of spare parts thereto, shall be prohibited. It shall be also prohibited to supply any kind of device and equipment or to grant licences to South Africa for the purpose of production or maintenance of such equipment.

Section 2. As regards penalties and other sanctions resulting from violations of this Decree or regulations issued by virtue thereof, section 4 of the Act on the Implementation of Certain Obligations of Finland as a Member of the United Nations (659/1967) shall apply.

Section 3. The Council of State shall, if necessary, provide more detailed regulations on the application of this Decree.

In 1984 the Security Council recommended a ban also on the import of arms from South Africa. Because this was not a binding decision, it could not be implemented by recourse to the 1967 enabling Act. It was put into effect by a decision by the Council of State in August 1985 not to import arms from South Africa.

In 1985 and 1986, the Security Council recommended that Member States take a number of economic measures against South Africa ((Security Council Resolution 566 (1985), 19 June 1985, Security Council Resolution 569 (1985), 26 July 1985, and Security Council Resolution 591 (1986), 28 November 1986). Again, because the 1967 enabling Act dealt only with binding Council decisions, it could not be used as legislative basis for implementation of the 1985 and 1986 measures. Since 1963, Finland had co-ordinated its policy towards South Africa with other Nordic Countries. Within this co-ordination, it was decided that measures should be taken to implement the measures. For this purpose, special legislation was needed.

A first measure was the implementation of the recommendation in Security Council Resolution 569 (1985) against new investments in South Africa. The Finnish act on an investment ban against South Africa entered into force on 1.1.1986.[25] Because it implied limitations for the enjoyment of property rights, it was enacted under the procedure for constitutional amendments. The same procedure was used to enact a full trade boycott

25 Act 1104/1985.

against South Africa in 1987.[26] In this connection there was discussion on the possible conflict between the law and Finland's obligations under the General Agreement on Trade and Tariffs (GATT). Although no definite decision was made on the permissible justification, the Government bills did make a reference to the national security exception in Article XXI of the GATT. The 1987 Act also contained some substantive limitations: it did not cover services; the implementation of contracts made before the Act was allowed during 3 months of the entry into force of the Act; the Council of State was mandated to give both general and special exceptions to the embargo. In a Decision of the Council of State at the time three materials were left beyond its scope: 1) publications and information materials; 2) medicine and goods for humanitarian purposes; 3) travel goods by private individuals. No special permission for such exports was needed.[27]

With the transition from *apartheid* to democracy, all sanctions apart from the arms embargo of 1977 and the recommendation of 1984 not to import arms from South-Africa were abolished in 1993.[28] These measures were finally lifted in accordance with Security Council Resolution 919 (1994) on 3 June 1994.[29]

VIII. Sanctions with No Specific Implementation Legislation

As pointed out above, most types of non-economic sanctions (diplomatic protests, limitation of cultural or other contacts etc.) have not been deemed to require implementation legislation inasmuch as they have come under the foreign policy powers of the President or, with the new Constitution Act of 2000, of the President acting in co-operation with the Council of State. The same applies to measures that fall under the existing powers of other authorities. The typical example is a limitation of arms trade (either imports or exports) when such limitation can be achieved by not granting (import or export) licences. Such an "auto-limitation" has not, however, been deemed sufficient to implement a binding arms embargo decision by the Security Council. Nor have specific implementation measures been enacted to enforce a travel ban of certain persons to Finland. Implementation of such sanctions is carried out by the competent national autorities, nowadays in coordination with the other Schengen States. Also the limitation of cultural or sports contacts has been left to the discretion of the relevant ministry. The Foreign Ministry has notified such decisions and seeks to survey that they are properly followed.

In addition, no specific implementation action has been taken in regard to decisions that do not appear to concern Finland because of their geographical scope of application or other fact. As such can be mentioned a provision that prohibits the conduct of railway traffic with the target State when no connecting railway exists (Security Council Resolution 277 (1970)). Nor have implementation measures been taken against a company that has never functioned in Finland (Security Council Resolution 748 (1992) concerning the closing of the offices of the Libyan Air Lines).

26 Act 599/1987.

27 Decision of the Council of State 600/1987.

28 Act 415/1993.

29 Decree 427/1994.

No implementation measures have been taken in regard to provisions included in certain resolutions in the Yugoslavian situation concerning the transfer of the target State's property or funds to UN accounts when it has seemed reasonable to assume that no such funds or property existed in Finland (Security Council Resolution 778 (1992) and Security Council Resolution 820 (1993)). This decision may be criticised: it cannot be excluded that such property or funds will enter Finland later on – for instance for the purpose of circumventing sanctions. Accordingly, the obligation to transfer to the Development Fund for Iraq funds and other financial assets or economic resources of persons and entities identified by the Sanctions Committee under Security Council Resolution 1483 (2003) was implemented in Finland by a national Decree 757/2003 under the 1967 Enabling Act as this was considered a measure that did not fall under the competence of the European Union.

IX. Arms Embargoes

In many cases, UN sanctions policies have targeted specific items – typically weapons and military goods – rather than the whole foreign trade of the relevant country. Such measures may be defended particularly as they deal with a matter in the Government's (or the military leadership's) direct interest and avoid causing excessive hardship for the civilian population. However, domestic production and sanctions-breaking may often offset the effects of such "smart sanctions". Nonetheless, they have a great symbolic significance as may be defended as a natural countermeasure against a State involved in illegitimate military or oppressive actions.

Already as a member of the League of Nations, and then after joining the UN, Finland put into effect arms embargoes by deciding to refrain from arms trade with a particular country under the 1933 Firearms Decree and the 1938 Decree on War Equipment. These were replaced in 1990 by the Law on Defence Equipment.[30] Section 3 of the law lays down two criteria for not giving permission to export:

a) if it endangered Finland's security
b) if it conflicted with Finland's foreign policy.

In the Government Bill, it is stated that this means, among other things, that export would be prohibited to States that are targeted by the UN Security Council. Guidelines on the transfers of defence equipment[31] have been issued on the basis of this Act. According to them, when granting export permissions, the Government will observe "relevant international treaties" (listed in the Annex) as well as economic sanctions and arms embargoes set up in formally binding resolutions by the UN Security Council (sanctions, bans and recommendations in force are mentioned in the Annex). The act also covers arms embargoes decided by the European Union (also listed in the Annex) as well as restrictions decided by the OSCE or other security organisations or by international, multilaterally binding export control regimes. The Annexes are constantly updated by

30 Act 242/1990, *Puolustustarvikelaki.*

31 Decision of the Council of State 474/1995.

decisions of the Ministry for Foreign Affairs,[32] and provide thus exact references to arms embargoes and other sanctions having a bearing on the trade on defence equipment.

Furthermore, the Act on Firearms[33] requires a permission for example for import to Finland, transfer, export and transit for commercial purposes of firearms and spare parts thereto, cartridges and dangerous ammunition. The licensing authority shall establish as appropriate with the Ministry for Foreign Affairs that there are no foreign or security policy obstacles for the permission.

Irrespective of the legislative basis provided in these Acts, implementation of Security Council arms embargoes continued to take place by decrees under the 1967 Enabling Act until the year 1998.[34]

X. Types of Implemented Sanctions

Sanctions that need to be incorporated into Finnish law are those that "belong to the sphere of legislation" – in other words, that would involve the legislative powers of the Parliament by analogy with the system of the implementation of international agreements in Finland under Sections 93 – 95 of the Constitution Act of 2000. In practice, this has meant either the use of the 1967 enabling act (in the case of binding Security Council resolutions) or special legislation (South Africa). As a summary, it may be observed that the enabling Act was used between 1967 and 1993 to enforce the following measures from the Security Council resolutions:

1) Prohibition on export or import of goods and services (including arms and goods for police) to the target State. This prohibition may also have dealt with provision of insurance, patents, copyright or trademark;
2) Prohibitions of export or import of services. This group includes banking and insurance services, deliveries to the target State as well as deliveries by Finnish vessels or aircraft wherever they may be. In addition, technical services, training, servicing and other services have been covered;
3) Prohibition of the *promotion* of export or import to of from the target State. This would cover activities intended to promote trade as well as activities actually promoting it. In connection with the sanctions against Iraq, the provision has been interpreted to involve a denial of commercial services. In connection with sanctions against Serbia-Montenegro, services have been listed separately;
4) The limitation or rupture of financial transfers to or from the target State, prohibition of transfer of funds and the freezing of assets located in Finland;

32 See for example decision of the Ministry for Foreign Affairs 1002/1998.

33 Act 1/1998.

34 Iraq: SCR 661 (1990)-Decree 680/1990; Yugoslavia: SCRs 713 (1991), 1021 (1995)-Decrees 1723/1991, 152/1996, 493/1996; Somalia: SCR 733 (1992)-Decree 89/1992; Liberia: SCR 788 (1992)-Decree 1193/1993; Libya: SCR 748-Decrees 336/92, 501/1999; Haiti: SCR 841 (1993)-Decrees 658/1993, 926/1994; Angola: SCRs 864 (1993), 1127 (1997)-Decrees 848/1993, 1127/1997; Rwanda: SCRs 918 (1994), 1005 (1995), 1011 (1995)-Decrees 420/1994, 1093/1995, 679/1996; Sierra Leone: SCRs 1132 (1997), 1171 (1998)-Decrees 5/1998 and 545/1998. For a comparison of the material coverage of these measures, cf. the table in Koskenniemi (1994), p. 301.

5) Prohibition of air traffic to and from the target State as well as prohibition of transit by the vessels of the target State. They may also have included the prohibition of the transit of any vessel in Finnish territory (including territorial sea) that may be suspected of breaching the sanctions;
6) Prohibition to recognise travel documents of the target State or for instance tickets provided by an air operator of the target State.

Enforcement has invariably taken place by substantive incorporation legislation. The measures have been listed in the body of the implementation decree. The relevant Security Council Resolution has not been annexed, published or even officially translated.[35] Implementation decrees have usually been so formulated that they incorporate those measures from the Security Council Resolution that would in Finland "belong to the domain of legislation" as understood under Section 95 of the Constitution Act.

Implementation decrees have always included a provision referring to the penal sanctions in Section 4 of the 1967 Act. They have also included a provision enabling the Council of State to adopt more detailed directives on the application of the implementation decrees. In practice, the Council of State has not resorted to this possibility.

Humanitarian exceptions allowed by Security Council resolutions have been transferred to the implementation decrees by listing the supplies which are permitted – as the case may be – subject to case-by-case approval by the sanctions committee. Such supplies shall be notified to the Ministry for Foreign Affairs which forwards the notification to the sanctions committee.[36]

XI. Special Questions

(1) Co-ordination Between Different Ministries

The main responsibility of the implementation of sanctions lies with the Ministry for Foreign Affairs (MFA). It is, therefore, for the MFA to prepare and present to the President of the Republic implementation decrees – or more often nowadays – notifications related to EC sanctions regulations and keeping up to date annexes of the guidelines on the transfers of defence equipment. This work is carried out in close co-operation with the Ministry of Finance (financial sanctions), Ministry of Trade and Industry and the Customs Board (trade sanctions), Ministry of Defence and Ministry of Interior (arms embargoes), Ministry of Transport and Telecommunications and Nations Board of Aviation (flight bans, communications).

35 An exception to this rule was the SC Resolution 986 (1995) on food for oil which was published in the Finnish Treaty Series because it was considered to include detailed and useful information on the legal purposes for the use of funds from the sale of oil and on the functioning of the food for oil system as a whole. Not all this information could be included in the national legislation or in the EC regulation.

36 See for example Decree 1356/1996. Translation into English in P. Kaukoranta, "Nordic and International Practice 1996: Finland", 66 *Nordic Journal of International Law* (1997) 334.

The Ministry for Foreign Affairs is also responsible for informing other authorities and relevant quarters of current sanctions. In addition, the Ministry for Foreign Affairs, formerly the Ministry of Trade and Industry, publishes a handbook on export control which is designed to provide permanent instructions and tools for all authorities and actors in industry and commerce. In addition to proper export control arrangements[37] this handbook also covers UN and EU economic sanctions and arms embargoes. While co-ordinating the implementation of sanctions, the MFA also reports to the UN on measures taken to implement UN sanctions when required under UN Security Council resolutions. Before its entry into the European Union, Finland submitted to the UN translations of the national implementation decrees. Thereafter, reports by Finland normally merely referred to the EU measures and the related penal sanctions. After 11 September 2001 also the natonal reporting on terrorism-related sanctions to the relevant UN sanctions Committees has considerably expanded.

(2) Role of Courts

A few cases of alleged violations (counterfeit certificates of origin) were examined by customs authorities and prosecuted during the period of the enforcement of the Rhodesian sanctions. There were no convictions, however.[38] Since then, Finnish courts have never had to deal with actual or suspected violations of the sanctions decrees. In 2003 a criminal investigation was initiated with respect to a suspected violation of the export ban to Iraq, but at the time of writing this article, the matter has not yet been referred to any Court. Therefore, there has been no authoritative response to the many interpretation problems that have arisen.

(3) Effect on Contracts

Sanctions decisions as well as the implementation legislation have been regularly construed with a retroactive effect. That is to say, they have prohibited the implementation of private contracts even when such contracts were made before the sanctions decisions or even the events leading to them took place. In Finland, the legislative basis of such retroactivity is contained in an express provision of the 1967 Enabling Act.[39] Often a provision on retroactivity is also included in the domestic sanctions decree itself. Many recent sanctions resolutions prohibit the recognition of claims by the target State's authorities or other persons that are based on the non-fulfilment of its obligations by a private contractor in compliance with sanctions. This provision was not originally included in Finnish implementation decrees. Recently, however, it has been included in them. No cases of claims have arisen, but it would probably have been possible to refrain from recognising them anyway on the basis of *force majeure*. Though there has been some uncertainty about

37 See for example Decree 1356/1996. Translation into English in P. Kaukoranta "Nordic and International Practice 1996: Finland", 66 *Nordic Journal of International Law* (1997) 334.

38 Cf. Koskenniemi (1994), p. 92-97.

39 Section 3(2).

this matter, the general policy of Finnish Banks has been not to pay any claims to States targeted by sanctions.

(4) Damages

In many cases, the Finnish party may suffer loss from scrupulous compliance with sanctions. The Committee that prepared the 1967 Bill held that, in the absence of specific legislation on the matter, the Finnish party would not be able to recover damages from the Finnish State. The legislative situation has not changed. It cannot be excluded, however, that it might sometimes be reasonable or equitable to provide compensation for a private Finnish party in case his loss would be a direct result of participation in sanctions.

The issue was raised once again in connection with the sanctions concerning Iraq and Kuwait. In the opinion of the Ministry of Justice decrees given by authorities by virtue of existing legislation (which has been issued following the procedure for constitutional amendments) and within the limits of competencies provided by law cannot cause a liability to pay compensation. The opinion leaves open the possibility of voluntary compensation.

(5) Extraterritoriality

Most UN sanctions have been formulated in such a manner that they concern export into and import from the target State. In Finland, the relevant implementation decrees have also been formulated accordingly which means that they are applicable beyond Finland's territory to persons and companies under Finnish jurisdiction on the basis of the personality principle.

Scope of extraterritorial application of Finnish sanctions legislation is restricted by general provisions of the Penal Code. In accordance with Chapter 1 of the Penal Code on the territorial scope of application criminal law of Finland shall be applied to an offence committed outside of Finland for which the law of Finland provides a punishment exceeding six months of imprisonment and if the State, in the territory of which the offence was committed, has requested prosecution before a Finnish Court or has requested extradition of the offender but the request has been rejected.[40] In addition, the requirement of double punishability applies to offences committed in the territory of foreign States.[41]

(6) Implementation of War Crimes Resolutions

In 1993 the Council set up the International Criminal Tribunal for the Former Yugoslavia (ICTY) and called upon States to take necessary measures to implement its decisions.[42] The resolution was directly binding and required legislative measures in Finland as there were no pre-existing provisions on criminal assistance to an international crimi-

40 Penal Code 626/1996, Section 8.

41 Penal Code, Section 11.

42 SCR 827 (1993) of 25 May 1993.

nal tribunal. A committee set up by the Ministry of Justice prepared a bill concerning such assistance. The resulting law contains provision on the recognition of the jurisdiction of the ICTY and on the binding force of its decisions in Finland. The provisions of the law are formulated in a categorical manner. It provides for the unexceptional implementation of extradition requests by the Tribunal, for instance. It was adopted in the procedure for constitutional amendments for the reason, *inter alia*, that no exception was made for the extradition of Finnish citizens.[43]

XII. Legal Basis of Domestic Measures Based on Decisions of the European Union

(1) Legal Basis for Exercise of European Union Competence

Finland entered the European Union on 1 January 1995 together with Austria and Sweden. Provisions of the accession treaty[44] falling within the scope of legislation were incorporated by means of a *blanco* Act which Parliament enacted following the procedure of adopting international treaties which concern the Constitution.[45] Thus also provisions concerning adoption of sanctions – Articles J.2 and J.3[46] of the Treaty on European Union and Articles 73 g and 228 a (new Articles 60 and 301) of the Treaty Establishing the European Community – were incorporated in the legislation of Finland. This legislation provides the general legal basis for Finland's participation in the implementation of economic sanctions agreed by the European Union.

(2) Harmonisation of National Sanctions Legislation with European Union Sanctions

At the time of Finland entering the European Union all existing economic sanctions imposed under the common foreign and security policy were based on binding resolutions of the Security Council which had been implemented in Finland through national decrees by virtue of the 1967 Act. According to the Finnish Government EU sanctions in force at that time did not include provisions which would have required instant legislative amendments in Finland. It was also considered *in abstracto* that pure implementation of binding Security Council resolutions on economic sanctions by the EU would not necessarily require amendments to the Finnish legislation. The Government stated that it was, however, necessary to enact provisions on appropriate penalties to be imposed where provisions of European Union Council regulations were violated and on the administration of those sanctions in situations where the EU has decided on such measures independently, without a prior binding resolution of the Security Council.

---

43 Government Bill 278/1993 and Law 12/1994.

44 Treaty concerning the accession of [the Kingdom of Norway,] the Republic of Austria, the Republic of Finland and the Kingdom of Sweden to the European Union, *Official Journal NO. C 241, 29/08/1994*, p. 9.

45 Act 1540/1994.

46 In the Treaty of Amsterdam provisions of Articles J.2 and J.3 were moved to several Articles. Common positions concerning sanctions are now adopted on the basis of Article 15 of the Treaty on European Union.

At the time of accession Finnish legislation included provisions on sanctions that were similar or parallel to those of European Union Council regulations – albeit in some cases less detailed. The only real differences seemed to concern the prohibition to recognise claims in respect of contracts or other commercial transactions affected by sanctions on Iraq and Serbia and Montenegro as well as seizure and confiscation of vessels, aircraft, freight vehicles or cargoes having violated sanctions against Serbia and Montenegro. Later on, the Finnish decrees were, however, streamlined to include also those provisions.[47]

(3) *Specific Legal Basis: Amendments to the 1967 Act*

The harmonisation of national sanctions legislation with European Union sanctions legislation was an immediate remedy. A more permanent solution was found from amendments introduced to the 1967 Act in 1997.[48] While expanding the scope of the 1967 Act they also entailed modification of the title of the Act, which now reads: *Act on the Enforcement of Certain Obligations of Finland as a Member of the United Nations and the European Union.* The amended parts of the Act – contrary to the original parts – are not true enabling provisions by nature, but merely provide for the Council of State (Government) the power to issue more detailed provisions on EU sanctions as well as refer to the penalties to be applied when EU Council regulations are infringed. The decision to choose a legislative technique mixing provisions of a slightly different nature and relating to two different organisations was based, among other reasons, on the fact that most EU sanctions are implementing decisions for binding Security Council resolutions, and it seemed therefore advisable to administer them under the same Act. These amendments did not require the use of legislative procedure for constitutional amendments because Finland had already in its Treaty of Accession to the EU become bound by sanctions regulations of the EC. Furthermore, the amended parts did not provide the Government with any new enabling powers.

> Section 2a: More detailed provisions on the implementation of regulations to the common foreign and security policy of the European Union and concerning movement of capital or payment or other interruption or reduction of economic relations, adopted under Article 73g or 228a of the Treaty Establishing the European Community shall be issued by a decision of the Council of State.
>
> Information on the entry into force of regulations mentioned in paragraph 1 above and on penal provisions applicable thereto shall be published through notifications by the Ministry for Foreign Affairs in accordance with what is provided for the publication of laws in Constitution Act, Section [20, paragraph 2].[49]

47 Decree 131/1995 and 132/1995.

48 Act 705/1997. Government Bill No 262/1996. For more details, see P. Kaukoranta, "The National Implementation of EC Economic Sanctions, The case of Finland", in Marti Koskenniemi (ed.), *International Law Aspects of the European Union* (1998), pp. 99-109.

49 Now in the Constitution Act, Section 79. For subsequent amendments of the 1967 Act see in section XIII, "Measures Taken as a Result of the Terrorist Attacks on 11 September 2001".

> Section 4. Penalty for violation or attempted violation of regulatory measures issued by authorities by virtue of this act or regulations relating to the common foreign and security policy of the European Union and concerning movement of capital or payments or other interruption or reduction of economic sanctions, adopted under Article 73g or 228a of the Treaty Establishing the European Community, is prescribed in Chapter 46, Sections 1 to 3 of the Penal Code. Forfeitures are prescribed in Sections 8 to 13 of the same Chapter.

Amendments to the sanctions legislation required that provisions of the Penal Code were amended accordingly:[50]

> A person who violates or tries to violate regulatory measures issued in 1) in the Act on the Enforcement of Certain Obligations of Finland as a Member of the United Nations and the European Union;... 11) in regulations relating to the common foreign and security policy of the European Union and concerning movement of capital or payments or other interruption or reduction of economic relations, adopted under Article 73g or 228a of the Treaty Establishing the European Community or regulatory measures issued by virtue thereof shall be sentenced to pay a fine or to imprisonment of up to two years.

A new section 4 of the Sanctions Act and the subsequent amendment of the Penal Code are to a certain extent problematic in relation to the principle of legality as they extend punishability to all sanctions regulations – also to future regulations – adopted under current Articles 60 and 301 of the EC Treaty. The principle of legality which can be derived from international human rights treaties is spelled in the Constitution of Finland as follows:

> No one shall be found guilty of a criminal offence or be sentenced to a punishment on the basis of a deed, which has not been determined punishable by an Act at the time of its commission. The penalty for an offence shall not be more severe than that provided by an Act at the time of commission of the offence.

The Constitutional Law Committee of the Parliament considered these aspects extensively. Recognizing the problematic nature of the proposed provisions it came to the conclusion that they did not, however, contravene the principle of legality.[51]

The requirement that the Government publish information on the entry into force of EC regulations and penal provisions applicable thereto was to serve exactly those general principles of criminal law. Notifications by the Ministry for Foreign Affairs merely refer to those regulations and to the relevant penal provisions. Those notifications do not, thus, have any constitutive effects but are of an informative nature.[52]

50 Act 706/1997.

51 Opinion of the Constitutional Law Committee 4/1997.

52 Examples of such notifications, see for example P. Kaukoranta, "Elements of Nordic Practice 1998: Finland", 68 *Nordic Journal of International Law* (1999) 171-192.

Recent trends in the field of economic sanctions show a tendency for more detailed provisions which are updated frequently. The obligation to implement such sanctions becomes rather burdensome unless national legislation provides a certain amount of automaticity. While seeking to bear in mind the basic principles of criminal law the Finnish sanctions legislation seems to fulfil the requirement of determining swiftly penal sanctions to be imposed where provisions of EC regulations are infringed.[53]

(4) *Limits to the Exercise of European Union Competence*

The Amendments to the 1967 Act provided a necessary means to implement EU sanctions imposed in the form of Council regulations. Use of other forms of instruments available for the Council of the EU[54] could create a need for *ad hoc* legislation or for amendments to the existing legislation.

An example of another kind of legal instrument is the Council Decision 1999/319/CFSP implementing Common Position 1999/318/CFSP concerning additional restrictive measures against the Federal Republic of Yugoslavia. The authorities responsible for issuing of visas in Finland apply the Council decision directly. As the decision does not fall within the scope of the 1967 Act as amended in 1997 there are no specific provisions penalising the infringement of this decision. Unlike Council regulations this Council decision does not even set a clear obligation for a Member State of the EU to provide such provisions. This is in line with what is explained in section "Constitutional position" about participation in non-economic sanctions.

In the practice of the EU, arms embargoes have not been considered to fall within the competence of the European Community. The EU thus only adopts a common position under Article 12 of the Treaty on European Union. The implementation of such arms embargoes is carried out under the Law on Defence Equipment as explained above.

(5) *The 1997 Legislation in Practice and Interplay Between the European Union and Domestic Legislation*

Finland did not repeal national decrees enacted by virtue of the 1967 Act before its accession to the European Union but has continued to keep existing decrees up to date. One of the reasons was that economic operators accustomed to national sanctions decrees

53 Due to lengthy delays by member states of the European Union the Council has recently added in sanction regulations provisions of a following nature: "Pending the adoption, where necessary, of any legislation to this end, the sanctions to be imposed where the provisions of this Regulation are infringed, shall be those determined by member states in accordance with certain earlier regulations". See for example Article 12(2) of Council Regulation (EC) No 1294/19999 of 15 June 1999 concerning freeze of funds and a ban on investment in relation to the Former Republic of Yugoslavia (FRY) and repealing Regulations (EC) No 1295/98 and (EC) No 1607/98, OJL 153, 19/06/1999, pp. 63-82. As in the case of Finland no new legislation is needed as these kind of provisions do not apply to Finland.

54 Directives, decisions, recommendations or opinions as provided in Article 249 of the Treaty Establishing the European Community.

could have misinterpreted the repeal of such sanctions to mean that those sanctions ceased to be in force if they failed to observe that similar provisions remained in the EC legislation. Many of the national decrees based at the time on binding resolutions of the Security Council were repealed in 2002 and 2003. No new national decrees will be given in situations where the Security Council resolutions are implemented through European Union Council regulations. Thus, for example, Security Council Resolution 1267 (1999) concerning the Afghan faction known as the Taliban is implemented in Finland through Council Regulation (EC) No 337/2000 only.

It is noteworthy that while amending the 1967 Act Finland retained the possibility to implement binding Security Council resolutions should the European Union fail to implement them. In principle, this could be the case, if the Union could not agree on the issue because of political disagreements or disagreements concerning the proper ways and means of implementing a Security Council resolution. In practice, cases have occurred where the European Union has been considered to lack the competence to regulate on certain issues, namely on arms embargoes. In these cases the EU only adopted a common position on sanctions policy while the implementing measures were taken at the national level. Another example of such a case is the implementation of Security Council Resolution 1483 (2003) where the obligation to transfer certain funds to the Development Fund of Iraq was not considered to fall within the competence of the EU. Some Member States of the EU have also taken national measures while the implementation of certain binding Security Council resolutions in the EU has taken some time.

As stated above, under the 1967 Enabling Act the Government is required to notify the national implementation decrees to Parliament that may, if necessary, abrogate them. In the case of EC regulations the role of Parliament is maintained under Section 97 of the Constitution Act, which provides that the Foreign Affairs Committee of the Parliament shall receive, upon request and otherwise, a report by the Council of State on issues concerning the common foreign and security policy of the European Union. The Ministry for Foreign Affairs submits to the Foreign Affairs Committee by virtue of this provision proposals for common positions and sanctions regulations prior to the deliberations of such proposals before the Permanent Representatives Committee of the EU.

XIII. Measures Taken as a Result of the Terrorist Attacks on 11 September 2001

(1) Major International Conventions and EC Measures

The Government of Finland has co-ordinated, together with other members of the EU, a range of measures after the terrorist attacks of 11 September.[55] The most important of these are included in the EU Council Framework Decision of 13 June 2002 on combatting terrorism (2002/475/JHA).[56] The Government Bill to implement the decision was debated in the Parliament in the course of the autumn of 2002. As the controversial ini-

55 Information on the measures taken is available in Terrorism and Finland : the report submitted to the Government of Finland (updated July 10, 2002) available at the MFA website http://www.formin.fi/english/ under the heading 'Policies' last visited 6 April 2003.

56 OJ L 22.6.2002 164, pp. 3-7.

tial Commission proposal for a Framework Decision[57] was significantly modified in the course of negotiations among Member States, and as the renewed text paid due regard to the principles of criminal law followed in most Member States, as well as included provisions for safeguards on human rights and fundamental freedoms, the Bill passed without fundamental amendment.

Action against terrorism that had already been on the agenda within international co-operation for a considerable time, was given renewed attention. Twelve conventions to combat terrorism have been negotiated within the framework of the United Nations. Finland has signed and ratified all twelve UN Conventions suppressing terrorism.[58] Discussions on a further comprehensive convention against international terrorism, were discussed by an *ad hoc* committee of the UN General Assembly. Finland supported the draft convention for the suppression of acts of nuclear terrorism[59] based on the Russian initiative.

(2) Measures in Relation to Resolutions Targeting the Taliban Pre-dating 11 September

Resolutions 1267 and 1333 against the Taliban had been implemented in Finland through EC regulations and the regulation in force at the time of the terrorist attack was 467/2001. As a regulation is directly applicable law in any EU Member State there is no need for any legislative measures at the national level. Nonetheless, a notification of the Ministry for Foreign affairs is published in the Statute Book of Finland. The notification includes a mention that a specific sanctions regulation has entered into force as well as a mention that any breach of such a regulation is punishable in accordance with Sections 1-3 of Chapter 46 of the Penal Code.[60] The list of persons and entities targeted by financial sanctions was renewed by the Commission a month after the attack on 12 October 2001. The list issued by the Commission followed the Sanctions Committee Decision SC/7166 of the 8th of October which in turn corresponded with the publication of a

57 OJ C 332 E, 27.11.2001, p. 300.

58 Finland ratified the International Convention for the Suppression of the Financing of Terrorism on 28 June 2002. The Convention and the national implementing legislation, including the amendment of Chapter 34 of the Penal Code establishing the financing of terrorism as a criminal act, entered into force on 28 July 2002. The new provisions prohibiting the financing of terrorism was later, in the context of the national implementation of the EU Framework Decision on combating terrorism, inserted as such in a new Chapter of the Penal Code on terrorist offences. The Ministry of the Interior is preparing a bill for the amendment of the Act on the Provision of Assistance by the Defence Forces to the Police. It is proposed that terrorism be provided for in the amended provisions in accordance with the Government Bill (43/2002) concerning, *inter alia*, the amendment of Chapter 34 of the Penal Code. According to the draft bill, the police would be entitled to accept military support from the defence forces in situations involving terrorism.

59 Terrorism and Finland : the report submitted to the Government of Finland (updated July 10, 2002) available at the MFA website http://www.formin.fi/english/ under the heading 'policies' last visited 6 August 2002.

60 Regulation 467/2001 was adopted on 6 March and was notified on 14 March 2002 through notification 274/2001 (Ulkoasiainministeriön ilmoitus).

much publicized US Executive Order 13224 of 23 September.[61] The renewal of the list of targets would also later be repeated according to the same pattern, with some days passing from the publication of the US list to the same targets appearing on the UN list and after a brief delay on the EU list.[62] No separate notification is made for these new lists as long as they are based on the same regulation. The Ministry for Foreign Affairs merely communicates the lists to the financial supervision authority (Rahoitustarkastus) which informs banks and other financial actors. As official lists were not provided in electronic form by the UN or the EU, delays were unfortunately common.

(3) Measures Taken in Relation to SCR 1373

UN Security Council Resolution 1373, adopted under Chapter VII of the UN Charter, includes binding provisions. All Member States shall report to the Counter-terrorism Committee of the Security Council (CTC) on the steps they have taken to implement the Resolution. Finland's first report has been considered by the CTC,[63] and the second report, based on the Committee's additional questions, was submitted in July 2002.

The obligation imposed by Security Council Resolution 1373 on States to criminalise the provision or collection of funds to be used in order to carry out terrorist acts, has been implemented through the enactment of new legislative provisions upon the ratification of the International Convention for the Suppression of the Financing of Terrorism.

The other obligations set out in the Resolution, pertaining to the freezing of funds, have been implemented at the EU level. The Common Position (2001/930/CFSP) on combating terrorism and the Common Position (2001/931/CFSP) on the application of specific measures to combat terrorism, as well as the Council Regulation (2001/2580/EC) on specific restrictive measures directed against certain persons and entities with a view to combating terrorism, were adopted on 27 December 2001. The Council Decision (2002/460/EC) implementing Article 2(3) of the Regulation, containing a list of persons, groups and entities whose funds and other financial assets must be frozen, is updated on a regular basis. The first amendments to the list were made on 2 May 2002.

In Finland, the implementation of the Regulation required an amendment of the Act on the Enforcement of Certain Obligations of Finland as a Member of the United Nations and of the European Union and of Chapter 46 of the Penal Code. Until then, the relevant Finnish legislation had only provided for the penalisation of actions against EU sanctions that were based on Articles 301 and 60 of the EC treaty.[64] As the aforementioned implementing measures were no longer taken in accordance with the word-

---

61 Bush: "We will starve the terrorists", www.cnn.com/2001/US/09/24/ret.bush.transcript/index.html.

62 The connection between US measures and UN sanctions committee lists on targets has been pointed out by Per Cramér in the chapter on Sweden in this publication (at note 181) and the list of successive Commission measures may also be found in that chapter at note 187.

63 Available at the MFA website http://www.formin.fi/english/ under the heading 'policies' (last visited 6 August 2002).

64 As amended by the act 882/2001 by which the reference to Articles 73 g and 228 a EC were brought in line with the current numbering of the EC treaty .

ing of these articles, i.e. in relation to any third State, but were directed at individuals, the legal base was deemed insufficient and a reference to Article 308 of the EC treaty was included. Consequently, an amendment including reference to sanctions based on Article 308 also had to be included in the Finnish legislation.[65] From January to May a hypothetical breach of Regulation 2580 could not have been prosecuted under Finnish law. This explains why the routine notification of the Ministry for Foreign Affairs concerning Regulation 2580/2001 published on the 9th of January 2001[66] does not include any reference to the Penal Code. The amendments to the national legislation entered into force in May 2002 and a new notification was published including reference to penalties.[67]

(4) *The Connection to Third States and the Legal Base of Articles 301 and 60 EC*

The inclusion of Article 308 as a legal base for sanctions regulations has pointed to the issue of EC competence concerning the use of individually targeted sanctions. The wording of the EC Treaty Articles 301 and 60 leads to a problem with regulations, which were only based on these articles and were directed against named individuals without mentioning any connection to a targeted third State. The Finnish government proposal for the aforementioned amendment to national implementation legislation mentions one earlier EC Regulation targeting named individuals without specific mention of any third State but concludes that this Regulation 2488/2000 concerning Milosevic and persons close to him, had such a clear connection with the Federal Republic of Yugoslavia and earlier sanctions directed against that country that the legal base of Articles 301 and 60 was sufficient. The same clear connection with a third State may be seen to exist in the case of regulations which seek to affect the leaders of a third State such as in the case of sanctions against certain government officials of Burma / Myanmar (1081/2001). Nonetheless, the lists of targeted entities published by the commission in relation to regulation 467/2001 during the fall of 2001 have only a very remote connection to the third State mentioned in the regulation and these have still been based only on Article 301. The question of whether such a measure is valid has been brought to the Court of First Instance in Case T-306/01-02 by the Swedish citizens targeted by EC Regulation 467/2001.

(5) *Measures Taken in Relation to Resolution 1390*

UN Security Council Resolution 1390 concerning measures to be taken with respect to Usama bin Laden, the Al-Qaida network and the Taliban was adopted on 16 January 2002. The updated list created pursuant to earlier resolutions concerning Afghanistan, of individuals, groups, undertakings and entities whose funds and other financial assets and economic resources must be frozen by UN Member States, is attached to the Resolu-

65 Government proposal for an amendment to the Act on the Enforcement of Certain Obligations of Finland as a Member of the United Nations and of the European Union (Sanctions Act) (659/1967) and of Chapter 46 of the Penal Code, p. 6.

66 Ulkoasianministeriön ilmoitus 21/2002.

67 Ulkoasianministeriön ilmoitus 451/2002.

tion. The Council of the EU adopted, on 27 May 2002, a Regulation (2002/881/EC) implementing the Security Council resolution. The regulation was notified through the routine procedure related above.[68] So far, no funds, other financial assets or economic resources to be frozen have been found in Finland. The names of some bank clients have been found to have similarities with those indicated on the UN and EU lists, but not to the extent of justifying the freezing of funds.

(6) Fundamental Rights Issues in Relation to Measures taken within the EU

During the elaboration of the EC measures to implement Security Council Resolution 1373 Finland, among other States, demanded the inclusion of measures to guarantee at least a minimum level of respect of fundamental rights.[69] Amendments to the lists are reviewed in an ad hoc "clearing house" consisting of representatives of the Member States and the Commission. Proposals concerning new names of the persons, groups and entities that the clearing house recommends to be added to the list are submitted, after Coreper preparation, to the Council for decision-making. A unanimity decision by the Council is required for the amendment of the list. According to the relevant CFSP Act (Decision 931/2001) the target lists have to be based on reliable and accurate information or on decisions made by competent authorities. Persons included on the list by the EC Member States may challenge the decision at the European Court of First Instance. Nonetheless persons may be added regardless of these criteria based on Security Council resolutions decisions by the UN sanctions committee.

The tone in sanctions cases[70] gives the impression that the ECJ still clings firmly to the formulations of its Bosphorus[71] verdict. The EC legal framework has hitherto been unable to provide efficient legal recourse for entities targeted by sanctions. Any complaints concerning legal safeguards are simply referred to the state which has placed the targeted entity on the list.[72] Unfortunately it is often well nigh impossible to find out which State has done so in order to challenge the decision. And even if such a challenge were successful unanimity is still needed in the Council for any amendments to be made to the list. The Bosphorus verdict has now been challenged at the European Court of Human Rights[73] and increasingly the conflict between fundamental rights and apparently arbitrary targeting of sanctions raises questions in EU Member States.[74]

68 Ulkoasianministeriön ilmoitus 469/2002, published 31 May 2002.

69 Memorandum of the Foreign Affairs Committee (Ulkoasiainvaliokunnan Mietintö 15/2002 vp), p. 2.

70 *Invest Import und Export GmbH and Invest Commerce SARL v. Commission,* T-189/00 R ECR [2000] II 2993-3010 and C-317/00 ECR [2000] I 9541.

71 *Bosphorus Hava Yollari ve Ticaret AS v. Ministry for Transport, Energy and Communications,* Ireland and the Attorney General, C-84/95 ECR [1996] I-3953.

72 T-189/00 R, ECR [2000] II 3008 at paragraphs 39-41.

73 13.9.2001, Press release issued by the Registrar of the European Court of Human Rights ("Bosphorus Airways") v. Ireland.

74 Luxembourg, apparently acting unilaterally, released the funds of several targets of financial sanctions for lack of evidence to continue with the freezing. See i.a. Peter Finn, "Terrorism-

XIV. Conclusion

Active support for international organisations and particularly the United Nations has been a consistent aspect of Finland's post-war foreign policy. This is based on the assumption that a small State has much more to gain than to lose from effective international co-operation in representative multilateral organisations. It would, however, be too much to say that Finland also expects the collective security system written into Chapter VII of the Charter to provide efficient protection for its own sovereignty or its national interests. The experience of the League of Nations, of the Cold War, and internal problems with the functionality of the UN sanctions system do not permit reliance on the solidarity of UN members. But despite "realist" doubts in this respect, Finland has proved itself a reliable partner in the sanctions policies decided by the UN.

As we saw, little attention was given to economic sanctions as Finland joined the organisation in 1955. The political situation at the time must have made the collective security aspirations of the organisation seem rather remote from reality. However, as the first sanctions were decreed against South Rhodesia, Finland immediately enacted the necessary legislation to put them into effect. Finland's seriousness in implementing the Rhodesia provisions is visible in its conscientious reporting on its various measures to the sanctions committee established in New York. The legislative basis created at the time (i.e. the Enabling Act of 1967) is still in place. Co-ordinating its policy towards the racist regime in South Africa with other Nordic countries, Finland stood in the forefront of the international action against *apartheid* e.g. by legislating into effect the Council's non-mandatory sanctions in 1985 and 1986. As Iraq occupied Kuwait in 1990, Finland was itself a Member of the Security Council and supported all the sanctions that were decided against Iraq in 1990. Finland's UN representative was even elected as Chairperson of the Council's relevant sanctions committee. In the 1990's practically all UN sanctions were put into effect by in Finland by transcribing the relevant prohibitions into Finnish implementation decrees, enacted on the basis of the 1967 Act. The fact that the 1993 law on the provision of assistance to the International Criminal Tribunal on Former Yugoslavia made no exception for the extradition of Finnish citizens – in principle, it requires even the extradition of the President of Finland if the Tribunal so wished – is a remarkable symbol of the Finnish sense of obligation.

In a sense, however, Finland has been able to buy its reputation as a conscientious and perhaps even "legalistic" UN member by acting in situations in which not much has been at stake for it. Sanctions have so far concerned remote countries whose political or trade relations with Finland have been insignificant. Only the implementation of the South African measures – which were from the UN's perspective anyway only non-mandatory – gave rise to any significant discussion. And in the end they, too, were thoroughly implemented. The small gaps that might have existed in regard to non-recognition of certain claims and the non-implementation of measures against activities that nobody had ever

financing investigation falters in Luxembourg", *Washington Post*, 3 June 2002 or *Helsingin Sanomat,* 7 June 2002 "Terrorismista epäiltyjen varoja vapautettu Luxemburgissa" (Funds of terrorist suspects released in Luxemburg).

undertaken in Finland concerned technical details and can in no way be interpreted as political obstruction. This is not to say that had more been at stake, Finland would not have been so conscientious. But it leaves open the answer to a crucial question about the effectiveness of Chapter VII, or indeed any system of collective security: how far is a Member State (such as Finland) prepared to sacrifice its short-term interest in advantageous political or trade relations in furtherance of its long-term interest in a collectively ruled world order. To the extent that there is no guarantee that the Great Powers themselves, when acting as members of the Security Council, are constrained by such altruistic objectives, it would perhaps be too much to ask that other States made such an automatic commitment.

In connection with the "smart sanctions" against specific individuals especially in the aftermath of 11 September 2001, new and serious concerns have arisen with regard to the protection of individual rights of persons targeted by collective measures. The move in the later part of the 1990's from comprehensive trade sanctions to "smart" sanctions targeted at individuals named by the Security Council or subsidiary organs has passed virtually unnoticed and unchallenged until now. The move to targeting specific individuals constitutes a fundamental change in the workings of an institution formerly concerned only with States. When a Security Council Resolution targets a named individual it purports to pierce through the justice system of all Member States, setting aside any form of protection of individual rights afforded to him by the constitution or international obligations of the implementing State. The lack of review of the decisions which include or exclude individuals from the lists, and the fierce resistance by certain permanent members of the Security Council to all plans of such review as well as to any critique of the present system has brought the sanctions system into a conflict with many of the values and principles the United Nations has traditionally championed – fundamental rights, rule of law and due process. If left unaddressed, this cannot but cause grave harm to the legitimacy of Security Council acts even in the countries traditionally most in favour of them. If individually targeted sanctions are to be used in the future, issues of legitimacy and respect of fundamental rights have to be addressed as an integral part of the effectiveness of this potentially powerful tool.

* * *

Select Bibliography

I. National Legislation with Translations into English

(Available through http://www.finlex.fi/english/laws/index.php)

1. Act on the Enforcement of Certain Obligations of Finland as a Member of the United Nations and of the European Union [659/1967].
2. Act on the Export and Transit of Defence Materiel [242/1990].

3. Emergency Powers Act [1080/1991].
4. Amendment to the Penal Code [626/1996].
5. Decree on the export and transit of defence materiel [108/1997].
6. The Constitution of Finland [731/1999].

II. Government Reports

Terrorism and Finland: The report submitted to the Government of Finland available at the MFA site http://www.formin.fi/english/ under the heading 'Policies' last visited 7 April 2003.

Memorandum of the Parliament Select Committee for Foreign Affairs (*Ulkoasiainvaliokunnan Mietintö* 15/2002 vp), Helsinki: Painatuskeskus 2002.

III. Articles & Monographs

1. Baldwin, David, *Economic Statecraft* (Princeton, NJ: Princeton University Press, 1985).
2. Barber, James, "Economic Sanctions as a Policy Instrument", 55 *International Affairs* (1979) 373-379.
3. Ciobanu, Dan, *Preliminary Objections. Related to the Jurisdiction of the United Nations Political Organs* (The Hague, Nijhoff, 1975), pp. 173-179.
4. Elliott, Kimberley Ann "Remarks", *ASIL Proceedings* (1991), pp. 170-175.
5. Hufbauer, Gary C., Schott, Jeffrey J., *Economic Sanctions in Support of Foreign Policy Goals* (Washington DC, 1983).
6. Hufbauer, Gary C., Schott, Jeffrey J., *Economic Sanctions Reconsidered. History and Current Policy* (Washington DC, Institute for International Economics, 1985).
7. Kaukoranta, Päivi, "The National Implementation of EC Economic Sanctions, The case of Finland" in Koskenniemi, Martti (ed.) *International Law Aspects of the European Union* (The Hague, Kluwer Law International, 1997).
8. Kaukoranta, Päivi, "Elements of Nordic Practice 1998: Finland", 68 *Nordic Journal of International Law* (1999) 171–192.
9. Kelsen, Hans, *The Law of the United Nations. A Critical Analysis of its Fundamental Problems, with supplement* (London, Steven & Sons, 1951).
10. Koskenniemi, Martti, *Kansainväliset pakotteet ja Suomi. Ulko-ja turvallisuuspolitiikan alaan kuuluvat ei-sotilaalliset sanktiot ja niiden täytäntöönpano Suomessa* (Helsinki, Lakimiesliiton kustannus, 1994).
11. Renwick, Robin, *Economic Sanctions* (Cambridge, Mass., Harvard University, 1981).

IV. Case-Law

Bosphorus Hava Yollari ve Ticaret AS v. Ministry for Transport, Energy and Communications, Ireland and the Attorney General, Case C-84/95, [1996] ECR I-3953.

Invest Import und Export GmbH and Invest Commerce SARL v. Commission, Cases T-189/00 R, [2000] ECR II-2993-3010 and C-317/00, [2000] ECR I-9541.

7

FRANCE

*Geneviève Burdeau and Brigitte Stern**

I. Introduction

We shall first explore briefly the way in which France has, throughout the years, approached the sanctions decided by the United Nations. Then, before addressing the subject of domestic implementation of Security Council decisions in France, we shall consider the specific character of the decisions at stake and the notion of implementation.

(1) A Quick Glance at History

Concerning the attitude of France towards sanctions decided by the Security Council, a distinction must be drawn between the French doctrine relating to the use of sanctions by the Security Council on the one hand and the question of the implementation of sanctions on the other.

In view of the experience drawn from the numerous experiences since the Iraqi crisis of 1990/1991, of the serious doubts arising about the political efficiency of large economic sanctions and of the burden for the populations concerned and for third countries with economic links with the targeted State, the French doctrine about the recourse to sanctions has been reconsidered. This doctrine relies on four principles: (i) sanctions should be reserved for exceptional circumstances, (ii) sanctions should be properly targeted and proportionate, (iii) sanctions should be limited in time and open a perspective for suspension or increase, (iv) sanctions should be adaptable according to the evolution of the political situation and to the improvements which occur.[1]

---

* Professors at the University Panthéon Sorbonne (Paris I).

1 These views have been drawn from different declarations and articles by Mr Hubert Vedrine, the French Minister of Foreign Affairs from 1997 to 2002 and presented by Mr Jacques Villemain, from the French Ministry of Foreign Affairs at a conference organised jointly by the International Peace Academy, the Center for International Studies and Research and the Royal Institute of International Affairs in Paris in November 2001. Apparently these principles still reflect the current official doctrine.

Vera Gowlland-Debbas (ed.), National Implementation of UN Sanctions, *195-231.*

As regards the second aspect, France has not always been as eager as it is today to implement the sanctions decided by the United Nations. This is, at least, the view of P.M. Eisemann: "*Ainsi, certains ont-ils pu, dans le passé s'interroger sur la volonté politique du gouvernement français de se plier aux mesures internationales d'embargo contre certains Etats ou certaines entités.*"[2] And he cites as an example, which could explain the doubts expressed, the very visible presence of the French companies Total or Peugeot in Southern Africa, at the time of the economic sanctions against Rhodesia and South Africa.[3]

The situation has nevertherless apparently changed today: "*Il ne semble cependant pas que l'on puisse émettre les mêmes doutes au regard des crises de la dernière décennie. Bien au contraire, le gouvernement français aurait plutôt succombé, à New York comme à Bruxelles, à un 'enthousiasme sanctionnateur', tant cette forme de réaction lui semblait en adéquation avec les besoins des situations conflictuelles rencontrées.*"[4]

This is not the place to discuss whether this difference merely reflects divergent political preferences or illustrates a basic and systemic change of approach towards international sanctions.

(2) What Do "Non-Military Sanctions" Mean?

Given the nature of this research, a short exploration of the character and purpose of the *measures under consideration* would seem to be called for. It must be recalled first that the term "sanctions" appears nowhere in Chapter VII of the United Nations Charter and that two categories of measures are envisaged according to Articles 39, 40 and 41.

On the one hand, Article 40 provides for the possibility for the Security Council to "call upon the parties concerned to comply with such provisional measures, as it deems necessary or desirable". This first category of measures, including measures like truces, cease-fires, cessation of hostilities, withdrawal of troops, is supposed to put an end to a dangerous situation. Such measures are directly intended to restore peace and security and normally only address the parties involved in the conflict and not all Member States. On the other hand, a second category of measures, decided along with Article 41, is only indirectly linked with the objective of restoring peace. By themselves these measures do not reduce insecurity or the threat to peace: the Security Council may decide that they "are to be employed to give effect to its decisions". These measures will appear essentially as a means of pressure on the States directly concerned by the crisis and their subject matter may be highly diversified: the indicative list contained in Article 41 has been supplemented by new types of measures, such as the freezing of assets, prohibition on the delivery of visas and so on.

These two categories of measures differ not only with respect to the way they operate legally and their addressees, but also, if one refers to the wording of the relevant articles, with respect to their legal strength. Concerning the first category, Article 40 states that

2 Pierre-Michel Eisemann, "La contribution des Etats à la mise en œuvre des sanctions: le cas de la France", in *Les Nations Unies et les sanctions*, Actes du colloque d'Aix en Provence (Paris, Pedone, 2000), p. 67.

3 An action is now pending against these companies in the United States.

4 Pierre-Michel Eisemann, *op. cit.*, note 2, *ibidem.*

"the Security Council shall duly take account of failure to comply with such provisional measures". This reveals the compulsory legal force of these measures and the right for the Security Council to adopt second range measures to reinforce the binding force of the measures already taken.

On the other hand, Article 41 only states that the Security Council "may call upon (*inviter*) the Members of the United Nations to apply such measures". The formula seems to show a weaker legal force, a kind of mere invitation, without a faculty for the Security Council to control domestic implementation by Member States.

In practice, however, the measures taken by the Security Council according to Article 41 were drafted in a mandatory style (the Security Council decides...) and have generally been considered as binding by the Member States. The creation of sanctions committees has also played an important role in that respect. Moreover, non-compliance with a resolution deciding upon such measures would be considered a violation of Article 25 of the Charter, as the Security Council made clear in the Rhodesian case by Resolution 232 (1966) of 16 December 1966. Several recent resolutions express the preoccupation of the Security Council with non-compliance by Member States with measures taken under Article 41.

However, despite this apparent confusion between the two categories regarding their legal regime, it appears that measures addressed to third States still retain some specificity and that, after having been decided in a single resolution without any clear distinction (Resolution 232/1966) in the Rhodesian case, they appear more distinctly in the Security Council practice of these last years (since 1990), most of the time in separate resolutions or in distinct parts of one single resolution (see, for example, Resolution 687 (1991) of 3 April 1991).

Only the second category of measures seems to be at stake here. As for their main features, it can first be noted that they are intended to impede normal relations with the target State; not only official relations between the States will be affected, but mainly private intercourse. Private persons will thus be involved in sanctions decided between subjects of public international law. Their rights will be restricted in consideration of objectives which may seem to them rather remote.[5] This must be stressed since, conversely, a State is not generally considered as responsible for acts committed by its nationals.

Since the sanctions envisaged here serve only as a means of pressure[6] and have to be considered as a temporary disruption of normal international relations, it follows that domestic measures of implementation have to be quickly introduced and quickly raised, and that the parliamentary process which could seem necessary in view of the nature of the rights restricted, does not seem to meet this requirement of rapidity. Moreover, inasmuch as these measures may go against customary or conventional obligations of the States (for instance, a derogation to specific trade treaty provisions or to the obligation of States not to undermine property rights of aliens), the domestic measures are justified

5 See, for example, the Judgement of the Court of Justice of the European Communities delivered on 30 July 1996 in Case C-84/95, *Bosphorus Hava Yollari Turizm v. Ticaret anonim Sirketi*.

6 Some of them, like an obligation not to recognize a situation, can be permanent.

only during the period of validity of the United Nations measures and should be abrogated immediately after the latter are lifted.

A new category of measures appeared in the practice of the Security Council with Resolution 1373 (2001) of September 28, 2001 on threats to international peace and security caused by terrorist acts. This Resolution indeed does not contain proper sanctions against a definite State in the classical way, but rather calls for permanent measures to be taken by the United Nations Member States in order to prevent and suppress the financing of terrorist acts, to prevent and criminalize the commission of terrorist acts. This Resolution accords States a wide margin of appreciation with respect to the acts as well as to the persons concerned.

(3) What Do Implementation and Enforcement Mean?

The notion of "*implementation and enforcement*" includes several operations on the part of the United Nations Member States which must not only introduce definite norms into their municipal law, but must also ensure effective application of such domestic norms.

With respect to the first aspect, in the case of France, as in that of other EC Members, the incidence of increasing transfers of competence through the Maastricht and Amsterdam treaties was of paramount importance for the question of domestic implementation of economic sanctions.

Until 1990, the experience of the French authorities in implementing United Nations sanctions was rather limited. The inadequacy of the French legal framework began to appear in the 1990s, but could be compensated thanks to Community procedures which had already been experienced during the Falkland dispute, although their consistency with public international law as well as with the European treaties could be seriously challenged.[7] The provisions of Articles 228A and 73G of the Maastricht Treaty[8] were intended to answer these critics and also to provide the European Community with a serious legal basis to act in a united way in implementing Security Council decisions. It must be noted that this transfer of competence occurred precisely at a moment when the recourse to Article 41 of the Charter became more frequent on the part of the Security Council. Some difficult competence issues under French law, which had appeared during the Gulf crisis, could thus find a new solid solution along with European law.

The provisions of the Maastricht Treaty concerning economic sanctions, which entered into force in November 1993 and which were taken over by the Amsterdam Treaty, can eventually leave some place to national competence in the case of unilateral measures decided by one EC Member State alone, as was evidenced in the case of the Greek embargo against Macedonia. Conversely, in the case of economic sanctions decided by the Security Council, there seems to exist no possibility – and no need in

7 Annelies Sam-Simenot, "Les conflits de compétence entre la Communauté européenne et les Etats membres dans le domaine des sanctions économiques édictées par le Conseil de sécurité de l'ONU", D. 1998, p. 83; Jean-Louis Dewost, "La Communauté, les Dix et les sanctions économiques: de la crise iranienne à la crise des Malouines", *AFDI* (1982) 215-232; Joe Verhoeven, "Communautés européennes et sanctions internationales", *RBDI* (1984-85) 96-112.

8 Now Articles 297 and 60 of the Amsterdam Treaty.

general – in the future for the adoption of national norms of implementation. Given that all European Union members are under a duty to comply with Security Council resolutions, the adoption of a Common Position along with Article 297 of the Amsterdam Treaty (ex-228A) is not only an option, but an obligation for them; it is difficult to imagine situations in which they would set aside Article 297 and choose to act individually since the Common Position will serve as the legal basis for an EC Regulation which will provide all details so that a national norm would not normally be necessary.

It may happen that certain Security Council resolutions address issues still in the national competence of the European Union Member States needing national norms of implementation. This is the case for resolutions which require for their implementation permanent measures of criminal law, such as the resolutions creating the International Criminal Tribunals or for Resolution 1373 against terrorism. Conversely, when the Security Council decides "classical" economic sanctions against a State, in most cases the European measures will suffice and domestic implementation will consist essentially in applying EC Regulations. It follows that, if the legal framework of the French legislation still exists, it does not seem to have been of any use since 1st November 1993 and this will most probably remain the case in the future except on very rare issues, especially when, as in 1990, the French authorities want to take action immediately, without waiting for a Common Position from the European Union and a subsequent EC Regulation. This occurred again in September 2001, in order to freeze the assets belonging to individuals and organisations linked with terrorism.[9] A French freezing decree was enacted on the 25th of September 2001, about eight months before the EC Council issued Regulation Nr. 881/2202.[10] But it must be noted that an EC Regulation concerning the freezing of assets of the Taliban of Afghanistan had already been passed in March 2001.

II. Legal Basis of Domestic Measures Implementing Economic Sanctions

(1) General System of Implementing International Law in France

a. Hierarchy of norms

France is usually considered as a monist country but only for treaties. As far as the application of international law in France is concerned, reference must be made to the French Constitution.

9 Decree nr. 2001_875 of 25 September 2001 (*réglementant les relations financières avec certaines personnes ou certaines entités)*, *JORF* 25 September 2001, p. 15190; Decree nr. 2001-934 of 12 October 2001 (*complétant le décret n°2001-875)*, *JORF* 13 October 2001, p. 16089; Decree of 9 November 2001 (*complétant le décret du 25 septembre 2001)*, *JORF* 10 November 2001, p. 17881.

10 Council Regulation (EC) No 881/2002 imposing certain specific restrictive measures directed against certain persons and entities associated with Usama bin Laden, the Al-Qaida network and the Taliban and repealing Council Regulation (EC) Nr. 467/2001, 9 March 2001, prohibiting the export of certain goods and services to Afghanistan, strengthening the flight ban and extending the freeze of funds and other financial resources in respect of the Taliban of Afghanistan. This regulation has been amended 15 times since then until March 2003 (OJEC No L 062 of 6/03/2003, pp. 24-25).

First, the Preamble of the Constitution of 1946, which is embodied by reference into the Preamble of the present Constitution of 1958, states (§14) that: "The French Republic, faithful to its traditions, shall conform to the rules of international public law... ."

This is in general considered as a reference to customary international law, but does not give any clear indication on the place of customary rules in the internal hierarchy of norms. It seems rather a position of principle, stating that France is respectful of general international law. However, the French *Conseil d'Etat* considered that neither this provision nor Article 55 of the Constitution allow French judges to confer a customary rule or a general principle of international law pre-eminence over acts voted by Parliament.[11]

> "*Considérant qu'aux termes de l'article 55 de la Constitution française (...) ni cet article ni aucune autre disposition de valeur constitutionnelle ne prescrit ni n'implique que le juge administratif fasse prévaloir la coutume internationale ou même un principe général de droit international sur la loi en cas de conflit entre d'une part ces normes internationales et d'autre part la norme législative interne.*"

In the same Preamble (§15), it is also stated that:

> "Subject to reciprocity, France shall consent to the limitations upon its sovereignty necessary to the organisation and preservation of peace."

This general formula is usually interpreted as relating to the organisation of the international community of States and especially as permitting the enforcement of the decisions of the United Nations, and among those the decisions of the Security Council related to international peace and security.

Finally, the often quoted Article 55 concerns international treaties and conventions:

> "From the moment of their publication, treaties or agreements duly ratified or approved shall prevail over Acts of Parliament subject, for each agreement or treaty, to reciprocal application by the other party."

b. Publication

It is of course well known that a text can only be applied when it is known by the persons subject to its requirements: in other words, in France as everywhere, an international decision – like a national one – has to be published before one even can think about its application in the internal legal order.

Different methods of publication can be envisioned. Of course, in general an uncon-

11 C.E. Ass. 6 June 1977, Aquarone, D. 1997, IR.157; *RFDA* 1997, 1081, concl. Gilles Bachelier; C.E. 28 July 2000, Paulin, D. 2001.387, note Tixier. See also Gerard Teboul, "L'alinéa 14: droit public international", in *Le préambule de la Constitution de 1946: histoire, analyse et commentaires* (Paris, Dalloz, 2001), pp. 327-356.

tested method is publication in the *Journal Officiel de la République Française (Lois et décrets)*. Texts incorporating a United Nations resolution into French law, or adapting French law to its provisions, are usually published in such a way. Another possibility would be the direct publication of a resolution in the French *Journal Officiel*, but this has never been the case.

However, Decree nr. 53-192 of 14 March 1953 on the publication of treaties[12] also mentions the possibility to publish the resolutions of an international organisation in the official journal of the international organisation concerned. Article 3 of the Decree mentions that an international regulation can be published in such a way:

> "*les règlements émanant d'une organisation internationale lorsque ces règlements sont intégralement publiés dans le Bulletin officiel de cette organisation, offert au public, et lorsque cette publication suffit, en vertu des dispositions expresses d'une convention engageant la France, à rendre ces règlements opposables aux particuliers.*"

It is quite obvious that Security Council resolutions are published as United Nations documents, in annual reports and even on the Internet. However, no-one has ever suggested that this could amount to publication in the French legal system, rendering these resolutions directly applicable.

The issue is different indeed with European Union Common Positions, which are published in the Official Journal of the European Communities (OJEC).

(2) Constitutional Basis

No specific provision in the French Constitution of 1958 addresses the implementation of Security Council decisions and no direct effect until recently was recognised to the latter by French law.[13] The doctrinal debate has, however, been vigorous.

Some – and probably the majority of international lawyers – think that United Nations Security Council decisions only apply to States and never directly to the individuals inside those States. For example, the President of the ICJ, Judge Gilbert Guillaume, declares that "it is doubtful that they could be self-executing."[14] This view has been confirmed by an award delivered by an arbitral tribunal composed of Mr Keba Mbaye, Mr Guillaume and Mr Bennouna.[15]

---

12 Brochure nr. 1620-I, *Ministère des affaires étrangères. Attributions – organisation*, Paris, Direction des Journaux officiels, 1994, pp. 17-19.

13 Marie-Pierre Lanfranchi, "La valeur juridique en France des résolutions du Conseil de sécurité", *AFDI* (1997) 31-57. According to her, "*la place que son ordre juridique national réserve aux résolutions n'est pas clairement établie par les textes*", *idem*, p. 33.

14 Gilbert Guillaume, "L'introduction et l'exécution dans les ordres juridiques internes des Etats des résolutions du Conseil de sécurité des Nations Unies prises en vertu du chapitre VII de la Charte", *RIDC* (1998), at p. 546, our translation.

15 Affaire *Libyan Arab Airlines c/Air France*, sentence partielle nr. 2 of 11 March 2000, nr. 64 which states: the arbitral tribunal "*ne doute pas que les résolutions du Conseil de sécurité ne sont pas d'application directe*".

Others are of the opposite view, and consider that Security Council resolutions impose obligations directly on the individuals inside the States concerned: this is, for example, the position of Jean-François Lachaume, according to whom:

> "*(o)n doit admettre que les résolutions du Conseil de sécurité prises dans le cadre du chapitre VII, s'imposent, bien évidemment, aux Etats membres de l'O.N.U. mais aussi, et c'est l'un des aspects de leur effectivité, aux organes politiques, administratifs, juridictionnels de ces Etats. Les obligations auxquelles les Etats membres consentent, en vertu de la Charte, imposent une telle solution ainsi, d'ailleurs, que la volonté clairement affirmée de la République française (voir le préambule de la Constitution du 27 octobre 1946 repris par celui de la Constitution du 4 octobre 1958) de se conformer aux règles du droit public international. Il n'y a pas, non plus, de raisons décisives de ne pas faire bénéficier les résolutions en cause de la supériorité hiérarchique des règles internationales affirmées par l'article 55 de la Constitution.*"[16]

The case law, as P.M. Eisemann rightly pointed out in 2000,[17] seems confused and divided. The *Conseil d'Etat* thus considered that norms adopted by the ICAO were not directly applicable in France and were mere recommandations which needed measures of implementation,[18] but it did not have the occasion to take a position on the applicability in France of Security Council resolutions.

The *Cour d'Appel de Paris* recently decided that United Nations Security Council resolutions were to be considered by judges in France as binding :

> "*Considérant que dès que le Conseil agit pour le maintien de la paix ou son rétablissement dans le cadre du chapitre VII de la Charte des Nations Unies, ses résolutions, qui ont à la fois une fonction normative et coercitive, s'imposent aux juges des Etats membres, dont la France, comme possédant une autorité dérivée du Traité constitutif des Nations Unies.*"

This decision seems most questionable since it relies on a misunderstanding about the United Nations Charter and an erroneous parallel with the European treaties. The Court thus considers that a direct effect of Security Council resolutions in domestic law derives from the Charter.[19] There is no need to stress that no provision of the Charter grants such legal force to these resolutions. Article 25 of the United Nations Charter only states:

> "The Members of the United Nations agree to accept and carry out the decisions of the Security Council in accordance with the present Charter."

16 Jean-François Lachaume, "Jurisprudence française relative au droit international (année 1990)", *AFDI* (1991) 895.

17 *Op.cit.*

18 C.E. Section 23 November 2001, *Compagnie nationale Air France*, *RFDA* (2002), p. 188 and obs. D. Ruzié, *RFDA* (2002), p. 767.

19 C.A. Paris 1ère chambre section G, 20 February 2002, *Etat d'Irak c. Société Dumez G.T.M. et société Vinci*, *Gaz. Pal.*, 2002. p. 987 and note G. de La Pradelle, p. 1169.

Moreover, the decision of the *Cour d'Appel* leads to the application of a text even though it has never been published in the *Journal Officiel*, which is contrary to the constant position of the *Cour de Cassation*.

Even if no constitutional provision directly deals with Security Council resolutions, nevertheless some constitutional provisions may be of some importance inasmuch as they define the respective normative competences of Parliament and of the Government. More precisely, since many economic measures decided by the Security Council have effects on property rights and on contractual obligations, implementation measures should in principle be adopted pursuant to Article 34 of the Constitution which provides for the necessity of a law adopted by the Parliament, on such issues. This lengthy procedure does not seem particularly well adapted to the necessity of immediate implementation of Security Council resolutions and this explains the resort to prior enabling legislation. So, we will see that, on rare occasions, Security Council resolutions are implemented directly by a specific law, while most of the time the executive power implements them, relying on prior enabling general legislation.

(3) Enacting Legislation

Sometimes a law is necessary to implement the sanctions decided by the United Nations as far as a matter falling within the exclusive competence of the Parliament is concerned. As emphasised by different authors,[20] the implementation of Article 29 of Resolution 687 of 3 April 1991 on the protection of private economic actors from the consequences of the inexecution of their contractual obligations towards Iraq was realised by adding a "*cavalier*" to Law nr. 91-716 of 26 July 1991 "*portant diverses dispositions d'ordre économique et financier*" that provides:

> "*Il ne peut être fait droit à aucune réclamation ou demande se rapportant à un contrat ou à une garantie financière indépendante, dont l'exécution a été affectée par les mesures décidées en vertu de la résolution n° 661 et des résolutions connexes du Conseil de sécurité des Nations Unies ou des règlements communautaires n° 2340/90 du 8 août 1990 et 3155/90 du 29 octobre 1990 ou en vertu de toutes autres dispositions françaises ou étrangères adoptées en conformité avec ces mesures, si elle est présentée par l'Etat irakien, une collectivité publique irakienne, une personne physique résidant en Irak, une personne morale ayant son siège ou son centre d'activités en Irak, une personne morale dont le capital ou les droits de vote sont contrôlés directement ou indirectement par une ou plusieurs personnes ainsi définies. Il en est de même pour les réclamations ou demandes présentées par une personne physique ou morale se prévalant d'une cession de droits d'une ou plusieurs des personnes ci-dessus énumérées ou d'une personne agissant au nom ou pour le compte d'une ou plusieurs personnes mentionnées ci-dessus. Les mêmes dispositions du présent article s'appliquent, dans les mêmes conditions, à toutes les stipulations annexes au contrat ... .*"[21]

20 Geneviève Burdeau, "Les conséquences de la crise du Golfe sur les relations économiques privées", in *Les aspects juridiques de la crise et de la guerre du Golfe*, CEDIN (Paris, Montchestien 1991), p. 460 and Eisemann, *op.cit.*

21 Article 45 of Law nr. 91-716 of 26 July 1991, *JORF* 27 July 1991, p. 9955 (especially at p. 9964).

(4) *Prior Enabling Legislation*

a. General legislation

No post-war general piece of legislation exists in France specifically concerning the implementation of United Nations sanctions.

A Decree of 30 November 1944 provides for the import requirements of foreign goods into France and the French overseas territories, as well as the requirements for exportation or for re-exportation of goods out of France or out of the French overseas territories to foreign countries.[22] This text has never been abrogated, although it does not seem to have been any more used since the Rhodesian case.[23]

Just after the entry into force of the 1958 Constitution, a general text was passed, namely Ordinance nr. 59-147 of 7 January 1959 relating to the General Defence Organisation. It is drafted in a very comprehensive manner and enables the Government to take decrees in order to ensure compliance with "alliances and international treaties and agreements", a very general formula which visibly encompasses France's obligations under the United Nations Charter.[24] This text, however, has never been resorted to for

22 *JORF*, 1 December 1944, p. 1585.

23 Decree nr 68-759 of 23 August 1968 prohibiting import and export of goods originating or coming from Southern Rhodesia or exported to that country (*prohibant l'importation et l'exportation des marchandises originaires ou en provenance de la Rhodésie du Sud ou à destination de ce pays*) (*JORF*, 27 August 1968, p. 8215) and Decree nr. 79-1116 of 22 December 1979 removing the prohibition to import and export goods originating or coming from Southern Rhodesia or exported to that country (*supprimant l'interdiction d'importation et d'exportation des marchandises originaires ou en provenance de Rhodésie-Zimbabwe ou à destination de ce territoire)* (*JORF*, 23 December 1979, p. 3256).

24 According to Article 1 of Ordinance nr. 59-147 of 7 January 1959 relating to the General Defence Organisation (*portant organisation générale de la défense*): "*la défense a pour objet d'assurer en tout temps, en toutes circonstances et contre toutes les formes d'agression, la sécurité et l'intégrité du territoire, ainsi que la vie de la population. Elle pourvoit de même au respect des alliances, traités et accords internationaux*" (The defence is intended to ensure in all circumstances and against all forms of aggression, the security and integrity of the territories as well as the life of the population. It provides also for the respect of alliances, treaties and international agreements). Moreover, the Law of 11 July 1938 on the organisation of the nation during wartime (still in force), which Article 5 of the Ordinance of 1959 refers to, states that the measures provided for can be ordered and executed "*dans les cas prévus par le Pacte de la Société des Nations, soit en période de tension extérieure lorsque les circonstances l'exigent. Dans le même temps, la Société des Nations est saisie du litige*" (in the cases provided for by the Covenant of the League of Nations or in time of external emergency, whenever required by the circumstances). Although it has not been reformulated after fifty years of UN existence, that provision could be considered as applicable in the UN context. The 1959 Ordinance enables the Government, under the conditions and subject to the penalties provided for by the Law of 1938, "*de soumettre à contrôle et à répartition, les ressources en énergie, matières premières, produits industriels et produits nécessaires au ravitaillement et, à cet effet, d'imposer aux personnes physiques ou morales en leurs biens, les sujétions indispensables*" (to submit to control and repartition energy, raw materials, industrial products resources and supply commodities and to prescribe to individuals and corporate bodies the necessary obligations).

the purpose of implementing United Nations resolutions even in the Rhodesian case[25] and consequently the related penalties are not applicable.

So it appears that general enabling legislation for the implementation of Security Council legislation for some obscure reason is not considered as existing or is considered as obsolete. Therefore French authorities must either refer to specific legislation concerning limited domains, like trade or exchange control, enabling the Government to take the appropriate regulations, or ask Parliament to adopt an act.[26]

b. Enabling legislation for exceptional circumstances

The legal basis for the *arrêté* dated 24 December 1965 prohibiting exports of oil products to Rhodesia and for the Decree dated 23 August 1968 establishing an embargo on all sorts of products[27] was found in the Customs Code (*Code des Douanes*) and especially in Article 21. Article 21 deals with the powers granted to the Government in exceptional circumstances, such as war and similar situations,[28] to prohibit imports and/or exports.

As a consequence of the transfer of competence to the EC Council that provision does not seem to have any practical usefulness for the implementation of Security Council decisions. However, the *Cour de Cassation* (*Chambre criminelle*) decided that the penalties provided for by the *Code des Douanes* could not be imposed unless a decree under Article 21 had been previously adopted:[29] "*le règlement communautaire prohibant toute relation commerciale avec l'Iraq, faute de dispositions de droit interne prises conformément à l'article 21 du Code des douanes, ne pouvait servir de base aux poursuites.*" This means that, according to the position of the *Cour de Cassation*, a violation of an EC Regulation implementing a United Nations resolution could not be punished by the imposition of

25 Decree nr. 68-759 of 23 August 1968 (*relatif à la prohibition de l'importation et l'exportation des marchandises originaires ou en provenance de la Rhodésie du Sud ou à destination de ce pays).*

26 See above, for example, Article 45 of Law nr. 91-716 of 26 July 1991, implementing Article 29 of Resolution 687 of 3 April 1991.

27 *Arrêté* of 24 December 1965, *JORF*, 25 December 1965, p. 11763: Decree nr. 68-759 of 23 August 1968 prohibiting import and export of goods originating or coming from Southern Rhodesia or exported to that country (*prohibant l'importation et l'exportation de marchandises originaires ou en provenance de la Rhodésie du Sud ou à destination de ce pays*), *JORF*, 27 August 1968, p. 8215.

28 Article 21: "*En cas de mobilisation, en cas d'agression manifeste mettant le pays dans la nécessité de pourvoir à sa défense, en période de tension extérieure lorsque les circonstances l'exigent, le Gouvernement peut réglementer ou suspendre l'importation et l'exportation de certaines marchandises, par décrets pris en conseil des ministres. Ces décrets sont pris sur la proposition du ministre chargé de l'organisation de la Nation en temps de guerre.*" (In case of mobilisation, in case of evident aggression imposing the necessity on the country to provide for its own defence, in time of external emergency requiring this, the Government may regulate or suspend the import or export of certain goods by decree adopted by the Council of Ministers. Such decrees are taken on a proposal from the Minister in charge of the organisation of the Nation during wartime).

29 Cass. Crim., 30 January 1995, *Juris Classeur,* éd. entr., 27 July 1995, nr. 480 note J.Cl. Berr: Cass. Crim. 18 May 1998.

one of the sanctions provided for by the Customs Code unless a special provision under French law has been previously adopted.

This position leads to a most illogical situation: as a consequence of the transfer of competence in favour of the EC, Article 21 of the *Code des Douanes* is no longer used by the French Government to implement Security Council decisions and the *Cour de Cassation* infers therefrom that in case of infringement of an EC Regulation providing for commercial sanctions (multilateral as well as unilateral) no action can be taken, although it usually accepts the imposition of penalties on offenders for breaches of EC regulations concerning customs issues in general.[30]

So the French domestic legal situation concerning implementation appears as if a general enabling legislation does not exist or is for most obscure reasons considered as obsolete or forgotten. Nevertheless, several specific enabling laws concerning definite domains, such as external trade or exchange control, have been used in the past. To the extent that sanctions decided by the Security Council fall within these fields, these specific enabling laws can be resorted to. However, for sanctions concerning other matters it is necessary in principle to resort to Parliament. This has sometimes been done for non-urgent matters.[31] Conversely, in emergency situations, like the necessity to freeze assets of the target State, the French authorities preferred to rely on a questionable legal basis rather than to ask Parliament to adopt a new act. No general reflection has apparently been led in France in official circles on the opportunity to adopt an appropriate legislation related to such issues. The entry into force of the Maastricht Treaty contributed to this question being set aside.

c. Enabling legislation for specific domains

Apart from the *Code des Douanes*, another enabling text has been effectively used, namely Law nr. 66-1008 of 28 December 1966[32] on exchange control (*Loi relative aux relations financières avec l'étranger*) which has been codified by the ordinance of 14 December 2000 in the *Code Monétaire et Financier*[33] without any change. This law is based on the principle of freedom of financial relations with foreigners and foreign countries in accordance with France international commitments, but also grants the Government the right to exercise its control if the national interest requires it to do so. Article L.151-2 states that:

> *"Le gouvernement peut, pour assurer la défense des intérêts nationaux et par décret pris sur le rapport du ministre de l'économie et des finances:*
> *1° Soumettre à déclaration, autorisation préalable ou contrôle:*
> *a) Les opérations de change, les mouvements de capitaux et les règlements de toute nature entre la France et l'étranger;*

30 Claude Berr, Chronique de droit douanier, *Juris Classeur*, éd. Entreprises 1995, p. 480.

31 See above the example of Law nr. 91-716 of 26 July 1991.

32 *JORF*, 29 December 1966, p. 11621.

33 Les relations financières avec l'étranger, art. L.151-1 to L.165-1 of the *Code Monétaire et Financier*.

> *b) La constitution, le changement de consistance et la liquidation des avoirs français à l'étranger;*
> *c) La constitution et la liquidation des investissements étrangers en France;*
> *d) L'importation et l'exportation de l'or ainsi que tous autres mouvements matériels de valeurs entre la France et l'étranger;*
> *2° Prescrire le rapatriement des créances sur l'étranger nées de l'exportation de marchandises, de la rémunération de services et, d'une manière générale, de tous revenus ou produits à l'étranger ... ."*

This text served as the legal basis for the Decree of 2 August 1990 on financial relations with Iraq and Kuwait which established control over the constitution and liquidation of Iraqi and Kuwaiti investments. No complementary measure was considered to be necessary after Resolution 661 of 6 August 1991 demanding the freeze of Iraqi and Kuwaiti assets, although the two measures – control over foreign investments and freeze of assets – are not strictly identical.[34] The freeze of assets implied restrictions on the free disposition of private property and on contractual relations between the banks and their clients which presumably required a new law pursuant to Article 34 of the Constitution. Hence the constitutionality of the resort to the law on exchange control as the exclusive legal basis for a freezing measure is highly questionable.

This Law of 1966 was completed by Law 96-109 of 14 February 1996[35] and by Decree nr. 89-938 of 29 December 1989,[36] modified by Decree nr. 96-117 of 14 February 1996.[37] These texts, which now all together constitute *Titre V* of the *Code Monétaire et Financier,* confirm the suppression of all kinds of authorisation for movements of capital except in three series of cases, especially when the foreign investment or the movement of capital threatens the public order.[38] Every individual exporting or importing funds over 7600 euros without the intermediary of a bank has to make a special declaration.

These texts were used in the case of Libya, Haïti, and Yugoslavia.[39]

34 On that discussion, see Geneviève Burdeau, "Le gel d'avoirs étrangers", 1 *JDI* (1995) 5-57.

35 *JORF* 15 February 1996, p. 2385.

36 *JORF*, 30 December 1989, p. 16411.

37 *JORF*, 16 January 1990, p. 650.

38 Article 151-3 of the Code: *"Le ministre chargé de l'économie, s'il constate qu'un investissement étranger est de nature à mettre en cause l'ordre public, la santé publique ou la sécurité publique (...) peut enjoindre à l'investisseur de ne pas donner suite à l'opération, de la modifier ou de faire rétablir à ses frais la situation antérieure."*

39 Decree nr. 93-1264 of 29 November 1993 on financial relations with Libya (*réglementant les relations financières avec la Libye*) (*JORF*, 30 November 1993, p. 16535) suspended by Decree nr. 99-407 of 25 May 1999 (*JORF*, 26 May 1999, p. 7756). Decree nr. 91-1079 of 18 October 1991 on financial relations with the Republic of Haïti (*réglementant les relations financières avec la République d'Haïti*) (*JORF*, 19 October 1991, p. 13722), supplemented by Decree nr. 94-636 of 25 July 1994 (*JORF*, 26 July 1994, p. 10 779) [extension of Decree nr. 91-1079 to the *de facto* authorities in Haïti] and abrogated by Decree nr. 94-897 of 18 October 1994 on financial relations with the Republic of Haïti (*réglementant les relations financières avec la République*

However, since the entry into force of Article 73 G of the Maastricht Treaty, now Article 60 of the Amsterdam Treaty, most measures for freezing foreign assets decided pursuant to United Nations resolutions have been introduced through European regulations, except for the Decree of 25 September 2001 concerning the financial relations with persons linked with Al-Qaida,[40] so that the French constitutional debate on that issue has become largely theoretical. The reason why this last decree appeared to be necessary seems to be that EC Regulation nr. 467/2001 of 6 March 2001 seemed to impose a general freezing of funds of all persons identified as terrorists or belonging to a terrorist organisation.[41]

A special mention must be made of texts concerning the control of the arms trade, since this question remains in the national competence, pursuant to Article 30 (ex-36) of the EC Treaty, except for the export of dual purpose goods which are now regulated by an EC Regulation.[42] The legal basis for the control of the arms trade lies in the *décret-loi* dated 18 April 1939,[43] which prohibits arms export without special authorisation, and its uncountable texts of application.[44] The consecutive licence regime was established by an

d'Haïti) (*JORF*, 19 October 1994, p. 14 831). Decree nr. 92-487 of 4 June 1992 on financial relations with the Federal Republic of Yugoslavia (*réglementant les relations financières avec la République fédérale de Yougoslavie* (*Serbie et Monténégro*) (*JORF*, 5 June 1992, p. 7480) [authorisation required for certain operations], abrogated by Decree nr. 95-1255 of 1st December 1995 (*JORF*, 2 December 1995, p. 17604). The *arrêté* of 2 July 1992 (*JORF*, 5 July 1992, p. 8963) also refers to the Law nr. 84-46 of 24 January 1984 relating to the activities and control of credit instituions (*relative à l'activité et au contrôle des établissements de crédit*) (*JORF*, 25 January 1984, p. 390).

40 Decree nr 2001-875 of 25 September 2001 (*réglementant les relations financières avec certaines personnes ou entités)*, *JORF*, 26 September 2001.

41 On that basis the French authorities froze about 4.420.000 euros. Security Council, Letter dated 24 December addressed to the President of the Committee created along with Resolution 1373(2001) by the French permanent representative to the UN. S/2001/1274.

42 EC Regulation nr. 3381/94 of 19 December 1994 (*instituant un régime communutaire de contrôle des exportations de biens à double usage (JOCE*, L 367 du 31 décembre 1994) *et modificatif*); EC Regulation nr. 837/95 of 10 April 1995, *JOCE*, L 90 of 21 April 1995)

43 *Matériels de guerre et munitions. Textes législatifs et réglementaires*, Brochure nr. 1074, Paris, Direction des Journaux officiels, p. 1.

44 Decree nr. 73-364 of 12 March 1973 for the application of the *Décret-loi* of 1939 (*JORF*, 30 March 1973, p. 3516) and Decree nr. 83-1040 of 25 November 1983 concerning trade, conservation, expedition and transport of certain arms (*JORF*, 7 December 1983, p. 3531), replaced by Decree nr. 95-589 of 6 May 1995 relating to the application of the Decree of 18 April 1939 providing for the regime of war material, arms and ammunitions (*JORF*, May 1995, p. 7458), modified by Decree nr. 98-1148 of 16 December 1998 (*JORF*, 17 December 1998, p. 19048)]: *arrêté* of 2 April 1971 listing the war material, and assimilated to be submitted to a special procedure for their exportation (*JORF*, 4 April 1971, p. 3212), partially abrogated and replaced by the *arrêté* of 20 November 1991 listing the war material, and assimilated goods to be submitted to a special procedure for their exportation (*JORF*, 22 November 1991, p. 15235), also modified by the *arrêté* of 9 May 1997 (*JORF*, 16 May 1997, p. 7382)] ; *arrêté* of 12 March 1973 relating to the procedure of importation and exportation of war material, arms and ammunitions war material, arms and ammunitions and assimilated goods (*JORF*, 30 March

arrêté of 2 October 1992.[45] The issue of a licence is subject to a control of final destination and can in any case be refused by the administration. Moreover, special *arrêtés* prohibiting arms export can be taken to comply with Security Council prohibitions.

The sanctions which can be decided in case of infringement of the rules adopted along with Article 151-2 of the *Code Monétaire et Financier* are those provided by Article 459 of the *Code des Douanes.*[46] If the prohibitive measures rely on an EC regulation, it can be feared that the *Cour de Cassation* will take the same position as in the above-mentioned case of infringement of regulations prohibiting exports.

(5) Ex-Post Facto *Legislation, Executive Orders or Decrees*

Implementation measures taken by French authorities have almost completely disappeared since November 1993 except in two fields: arms export prohibition and implementation measures concerning International Criminal Tribunals.[47]

III. Legal Basis of Domestic Measures Based on European Union Decisions

(1) Legal Basis Under National Law for the Transfer of Competence to the European Union

As a founder Member of the EC, France has been bound by the successive provisions of the EC and of the European Union treaties. As a matter of fact, France had to modify its Constitution several times, in order to be able to enter into the different treaties through which more and more aspects of national sovereignty were transferred to the Brussels authorities.

When the Maastricht Treaty was to be ratified and incorporated into the French legal order, its text was submitted to the French Constitutional Council, for a control of its conformity with the Constitution. The decision of the Constitutional Council of 31 December 1992 declares:

> "... respect for national sovereignty does not preclude France, acting in accordance with the Preamble to the Constitution of 1946, from concluding international agreements for participation in the establishment or development of a permanent international organisation enjoying legal personality and decision-making powers on the basis of transfers of powers decided on by the Member States, subject to reciprocity.
> However, should an international agreement entered into to this end involve a clause conflicting with the Constitution or jeopardising the essential conditions for the exercise

1973, p. 3525), abrogated and replaced by the *arrêté* of 2 October 1992 (*JORF*, 6 October 1992, p. 13858).

45 *JORF*, 6 October 1992, p. 13858.

46 Article 165-1 of the *Code Monétaire et Financier.*

47 See below, Section VII pp. 224ff.

> of national sovereignty, authorization to ratify would require prior amendment of the Constitution.
> The Constitutional Council should undertake its review of the Treaty on European Union in the light of these principles."[48]

Considering that France had transferred part of its sovereignty, a modification of the Constitution was required.

The same reasoning was held for the ratification of the Amsterdam Treaty, which was controlled by the Constitutional Council in its decision of 31 December 1997, which was followed by another modification of the French Constitution.

(2) Member States' Limits to Such Exercise

European competences in regard to the implementation of United Nations sanctions raised some discussions before the Maastricht Treaty, but France, like other State Members, accepted in 1990 that European regulations would be taken instead of national measures, although Article 224 of the Rome Treaty clearly preserved national competence.

The entry into force of the Maastricht Treaty could have raised the question of the legal basis of the French existing legislation, particularly the Decree of 2 August 1990 concerning the freezing of Iraqi assets. In fact, this Decree remained in force even after the entry into force of European Regulation nr. 2465/96 of 17 December 1996 which modifies the Regulation of 6 August 1990 in the new legal context of the Oil for Food Resolution on the one hand and of the provisions of the Maastricht Treaty on the other hand.

(3) Interplay Between European Union and Domestic Legislation in Sanctions Implementation

Pursuant to Article 55 of the French Constitution, treaties to which France is a party enjoy a legal authority superior to that of the law. All French tribunals have now given European regulations priority over domestic law (except constitutional provisions) in any case.[49]

As far as economic sanctions are concerned, European regulations constitute the usual means of establishing norms applicable in the French legal order and normally they do not need other domestic texts since they are directly applicable. It may happen, however, that the administration in charge of the control of the implementation, most of the time the Ministry of Finance, finds it necessary to give some explanations to economic operators through a "*circulaire*"[50] or an "*avis aux exportateurs ou aux importa-*

48 CC, *Rec.* 1992, p. 57.

49 For the judiciary tribunals, see Cass. Ch. mixte, 24 May 1975, *Ste des Cafés Jacques Vabre*, Bull. p. 6; C.E. Ass. 20 October 1989, *Nicolo*, *Rec.* p. 748.

50 For example, the "*circulaire*" of the Ministry of National Education of 24 September 1990, asking the universities to suspend all scientific and technical cooperation with Iraq and to

teurs",[51] or a "*note*".[52] Such texts have no legal value on their own and are just intended to clarify the manner according to which the European regulation has to be applied, especially the licence procedure which is regulated by the Decree of 30 November 1944 and the *arrêté* of 30 January 1967.[53]

As for sanctions as a consequence of a breach of European regulations, full national competence still remains. As a matter of fact, no special text providing for criminal sanctions has been adopted and the usual sanctions in customs and exchange control matters are supposed to apply. This was the position expressed by the French Government in its reply to the questionnaire addressed by the Sanction Committee in 1990.[54] The effective application of such a solution supposes that French courts consider breaches of European regulations implementing United Nations resolutions as usual offences punished by domestic customs law. As has already been mentioned, the Criminal Chamber of the *Cour de Cassation* for some obscure reason did not adopt that position.

IV. Formal Comparison of Security Council Resolutions and Domestic Measures

As we know, the present study is an attempt to answer the question of how effectively States really apply United Nations sanctions in their national orders. In other words, an attempt is made to assess whether the situation today is any better than it was for example at the time of the Rhodesian sanctions: if one reads the Report of the Secretary-General on the application of Resolution 232 of 16 December 1966, the impression is

---

refrain from registering students having the Iraqi nationality for the academic year 1990-1991. See Conseil d'Etat, 23 September 1992, *GISTI*, *Recueil*, p. 346.

51 See, for instance, *Avis aux importateurs et aux exportateurs de certaines marchandises en provenance et à destination de l'Irak* , *JORF*, 5 February 1998, p. 1888, or *Avis aux exportateurs de certaines marchandises à destination de la Lybie*, *JORF*, 25 November 1998, p. 17828.

52 As an example, can be cited the "*note*" of 30 July 1992 on the "*application des mesures de réglementation des relations financières avec la Yougoslavie (Serbie et Monténégro)*", *B.O. de l'Administration centrale de l'économie, des finances et du budget*, nr. 3, 1992.

53 Decree of 30 November 1944 on the import and export requirements into and out of France and the French overseas territories (*fixant les conditions d'importation en France et dans les territoires français d'outre-mer des marchandises étrangères ainsi que les conditions d'exportation et de réexportation des marchandises hors de France et des territoires d'outre-mer à destination de l'étranger et établissant certaines formalités au point de vue des échanges entre la France et les territoires d'outre-mer*) and *arrêté* of 30 January 1967 relating to imports and exports into or from foreign countries (*relatif aux importations et aux exportations en provenance ou à destination de l'étranger)*.

54 Committee of the Security Council created by Resolution 661 (1990) concerning the situation between Iraq and Kuwait. *Note verbale* of 6 December 1990, addressed to the Secretary-General by the French permanent mission to the UN. S/AC.25/1990/69. According to that note the French penalties are those provided for in the *Code des Douanes* which include fines, seizures and confiscation of the goods or means of transportation concerned, and by the Law of 18 December 1966 on foreign financial relations, Article 5 of which provides for imprisonment from 1 to 3 months, confiscation of assets and fines from half to double of the sum involved.

that, according to Jean Combacau "*il est à peu près impossible de savoir si les Etats appliquent ou non les sanctions, dans quelle mesure et depuis quand... .*"[55]

It seems that different discrepancies can be traced between the United Nations sanctions and the manner in which these sanctions are enforced in the national legal orders.

(1) Scope of Prohibitions: A Divergence Can Exist as Far as the Content is Concerned

The national measures of implementation are not always strictly modelled on the United Nations sanction. The national sanction is sometimes broader and sometimes narrower than the United Nations sanction, although according to Article 25 of the Charter it should not in principle be narrower.

The examples developed hereafter on the two International Criminal Tribunals for the Former Yugoslavia and Rwanda perfectly illustrate this point.[56]

(2) Territorial and Personal Scope: A Divergence Can Exist as Far as the Scope (champ d'application) *is Concerned*

When the Security Council decides economic sanctions under Article 41 to be applied by the Member States, it takes into account the extent of the State's jurisdiction according to international law: in other words, the Security Council does not impose on a State to take sanctions that go beyond its powers and would for example imply an extraterritorial application of its national law, not supported by the international rules. What are very briefly these international rules?

a. The international rules on jurisdiction

Since the *Lotus* case,[57] the international rules[58] governing the State's jurisdiction are clearly established, and can be summarised as follows: jurisdiction to enforce is strictly territorial and can therefore never be extraterritorial. It means that enforcement by one State's authorities on the territory of another State is forbidden in all circumstances in international law. Jurisdiction to prescribe – and jurisdiction to adjudicate – can be

55 Jean Combacau, *Le pouvoir de sanction de l'ONU. Etude théorique de la coercition non militaire* (Paris, Pedone, 1974), p. 316. Underlined by Jean Combacau.

56 See below.

57 *S.S. Lotus* Case, 7 September 1927, PCIJ, Series A, nr. 10, pp. 18-19.

58 For a general discussion on international law and extraterritoriality, see, for a comparative approach, Brigitte Stern (ed.), *L'application extraterritoriale du droit économique,* Cahiers du CEDIN, nr. 3 (Paris, Monchrestien, 1987); for a very general theoretical approach on the topic of extraterritoriality, Brigitte Stern, "Quelques observations sur les règles internationales relatives à l'application extraterritoriale du droit", *AFDI* (1986) 7-52 and "L'extraterritorialité revisitée. Où il est question des affaires Alvarez-Machain, Pâte de bois et de quelques autres...", *AFDI* (1992) 239-312, as well as "Droit international et sanctions unilatérales", in *Sanctions unilatérales, mondialisation du commerce et ordre juridique international,* Cahiers du CEDIN, nr. 14 (Paris, Monchrestien, 1998), pp. 185-218.

extraterritorial, as long as they respect the limitations placed by international law on such exercises of jurisdiction. The adoption of an extraterritorial rule or decision is not always contrary to international law. It is only contrary to international law, when it does not have a reasonable link with the State enacting such a rule or taking such a decision. The links recognised by international law to allow a State to set rules of law are the territorial principle, the nationality principle, the protective principle and the universality principle.

The principle of territoriality means that a State has jurisdiction according to international law to establish rules or take decisions applying to persons or property on its territory or events taking place on its territory. In order to grant jurisdiction on an act to a State, it is admitted that it is enough that one constitutive element of the act has been consummated on the territory of that State. One speaks about "objective territoriality" when an act has been initiated abroad, but is consummated in the territory, and about "subjective territoriality", when an act has been initiated on the territory, but is consummated abroad. The United States extend this territorial principle by the so-called effect doctrine, according to which they can assert jurisdiction towards an act as soon as it has a substantial effect on American territory.

The principle of nationality means that a State is entitled to exercise its jurisdiction over its nationals, which can become extraterritorial when a national is outside its territory. However, this does not allow it to regulate all activities of its nationals, all over the world.

The protective principle recognises a State's extraterritorial jurisdiction over acts designed to injure its vital interests.

The universality principle gives a State jurisdiction over certain acts that qualify as international crimes, wherever committed and by whomsoever they have been committed.

b. These rules apply for the implementation of United Nations sanctions

States have to act in the framework of these recognised bases for jurisdiction. Usually States, when they adopt measures of implementation, act in the framework of their internationally recognised jurisdiction, that means that they are entitled to use their territorial and personal jurisdictions to enforce United Nations sanctions, the two other bases for jurisdiction being irrelevant here. Sometimes States do not use the full range of their powers, when they are under an obligation to do so, in order to enforce Security Council decisions correctly: this can be analysed as a partial non-enforcement of United Nations resolutions. On the other hand some resolutions go beyond the generally accepted rules concerning the territorial jurisdiction of States and require adaptation.[59]

59 In the case of the Gulf crisis, this view is shared by Judge Guillaume who underlines that Resolutions 661 and 670 resulted in extending the States jurisdiction beyond the usual limits admitted in international law and that many UN Member States did not effectively adapt their domestic legislation in that respect. Gilbert Guillaume, "La crise du Golfe et son développement jusqu'au 15 janvier 1991: sanctions économiques et blocus", in *Les aspects juridiques de la crise et de la guerre du Golfe*, sous la direction de B. Stern, Cahiers du CEDIN, (Paris, Montchrestien, 1991), pp. 287-302.

For example, in France, a "*note*" dated 21 September 1991 from the Ministry of Economy taken for the application of the Decree of 2 August 1990 on the financial relations of France with Iraq clearly states the territorial application of the Decree: "*Les dispositions du décret et de l'arrêté susvisés doivent être appliquées par les succursales et filiales françaises des établissements de crédit ou autres étrangers. En revanche les succursales ou filiales des établissements de crédit ou autres français, situées à l'étranger n'y sont pas soumises*". It is interesting to see that branches and subsidiaries are treated in the same way, which means that if France has fully used its territorial jurisdiction to impose sanctions, it has not completely used its personal jurisdiction which could have permitted France to impose the United Nations sanctions on French subsidiaries abroad.

Jean Combacau, in his thesis, has underscored the fact that States, when implementing United Nations sanctions, often use their territorial jurisdiction quite properly, but do not bother to use their personal jurisdiction: "*on peut ainsi considérer que beaucoup d'Etats, même s'ils usent correctement de leur compétence territoriale pour exécuter leurs obligations, font de leur compétence dite personnelle un usage insuffisant et non conforme aux résolutions de l'ONU: peu nombreux sont en effet ceux qui précisent que les interdictions qu'ils posent s'étendent à leur nationaux séjournant en dehors de leur territoire.*"[60]

Another example, although not French, but quite illuminating, can be given here in order to underline the possible difference in the scope of United Nations and national sanctions. This refers to Resolution 748 (1992), adopted on 31 March 1992, in which sanctions were decided against Libya. In this text, the Security Council, as usual, is very cautious and only requires from the Member States acts that they may perform: in other words they are required to forbid a certain number of actions "to their nationals or from their territories."

> "The Security Council…
> 4. Decides also that all States shall
> (a) Deny permission to any aircraft to take off from, land in or overfly *their territory* if it is destined to land in or has taken off from the territory of Libya…
> (b) Forbid, by *their nationals or from their territory*, the supply of any aircraft or aircraft components to Libya …
> 5. Decides further that all States shall:
> (c) Prohibit any provision to Libya by *their nationals or from their territory* of arms and related material of all types …
> (d) Prohibit any provision to Libya by *their nationals or from their territory* of technical advice, assistance or training related to the provision, manufacture, maintenance, or use of the items in subparagraph (a) above … ."[61]

In other words, the States could use their personal as well as their territorial jurisdiction to enforce the measures. But no other extraterritorial jurisdiction was granted to the States by this Resolution. Therefore, the United States could not, as they tried to do,

60 Jean Combacau, *Le pouvoir de sanction de l'ONU. Etude théorique de la coercition non militaire* (Paris, Pedone, 1974), p. 322.

61 Emphasis added.

justify the extraterritorial application of sanctions against Libya in the d'Amato Act to any person in the world who did not comply with the interdictions set forth in that law by relying on Resolution 748 (1992).

c. National precision on the scope of the sanctions

The extent of personal jurisdiction is often quite clearly expressed in the national or European measures of implementation: they aim at the individuals having the nationality of the State, the legal persons registered or incorporated under the law of the State, the planes and boats under the flag of the State.

The territorial jurisdiction is also often precisely defined: for example, a reference is sometimes made to the air space over the territory.

An example of these details can be given by Article 1 of the EC Regulation of 29 October 1990 for the enforcement of Resolutions 660, 661 and 666 of 1990 against Iraq:

> "*... dès l'entrée en vigueur du présent règlement est interdite dans la Communauté, y compris son espace aérien ou à partir de son territoire ou par l'intermédiaire d'aéronefs et de navires battant le pavillon d'un Etat membre ainsi qu'à tout ressortissant communautaire, la prestation de services non financiers... .*"

Sometimes, the territorial scope is geographically defined so that there is no ambiguity on the territory to which the sanction applies. A good example of this is the *arrêté* of 12 September 1990, complementing a former one on "Financial relations with some foreign countries", as a matter of fact with Iraq: according to this text, "France" means "*(l)a France métropolitaine, les départements d'outre-mer, les territoires d'outre-mer et les collectivités territoriales à statut particulier de Mayotte et de Saint Pierre et Miquelon. La principauté de Monaco est assimilée à la France.*"

(3) Entry into Force: A Divergence Can Exist in Time

a. A national sanction can be adopted *before* the United Nations sanction

Sometimes a national sanction is adopted before a United Nations sanction. Whatever its basis in the national legal order, it is difficult to see in such a national sanction the implementation of a United Nations decision to carry out sanctions.

A clear example of such a situation is given by the Iraqi sanctions in France: the French Decree nr. 90. 881 was adopted on 2 August 1990, while the decision to freeze Iraqi and Kuwaiti assets was only taken by the United Nations by means of Resolution 661 (1990) of 6 August 1990. The question whether the French sanction can be considered as an application of the United Nations sanction after the 6th of August is open to discussion.

Formally, it is certainly not, as no reference, of course, is made in the French text to the United Nations Resolution: thus, the French sanction cannot be considered as a *de jure* application of the United Nations sanction. The French Decree is, on the contrary, based on national enabling legislation: Law nr. 66-1008 of 28 December 1966 on financial relations with foreign countries, Decree nr. 89-938 of 29 December 1989 regulating financial relations with foreign countries, and their decrees of application.

Materially, it must be examined whether or not the content is the same: if it is not, the French text cannot even be considered as a *de facto* application of the United Nations Resolution; if it is, it could be considered that the French text is a *de facto* application of the United Nations text, but, in our opinion, the existence of the two sanctions should be analysed more as a situation where there are *parallel sanctions* than as a situation in which the national sanction is an enforcement of the United Nations sanction.

In fact, as early as 8 August 1990, the European Community adopted Regulation Nr. 2340/90, enforcing the sanctions decided by Resolution 661, providing in its Article 4 that it would enter into force on the day of its publication in the *Official Journal of the Communities* – which occurred on 9 August 1990 – and that it would have a direct effect in all Member States. So, as far as France is concerned, this text constitutes a measure of implementation of the United Nations Resolution. The French Decree not having been abrogated (on the contrary, it has been amended), a question could apparently arise concerning a possible discrepancy between the text of the French Decree and EC Regulation nr. 2465/96 of 17 December 1996 which modifies the above-mentioned EC Regulation of 1990 after the Oil for Food resolution and the entry into force of Article 73 of the Maastricht Treaty, which has a direct effect in France. However, in this specific case, things must be analysed closely, as the subject matter of the French Decree is only financial relations with foreign countries. So the 1990 EC Regulation only concerned imports and exports, while the French Decree regulated movements of capital, which were still under the jurisdiction of States (Article 67 and following). The 1996 Regulation is rather ambiguous in prohibiting the supply of all kinds of financial services to Iraqi nationals or undertakings, but it is not clearly contradictory with the French Decree.

b. The national sanction can be adopted *long after* the United Nations sanction

Here we find all the cases in which States, for different reasons, do not enforce United Nations sanctions quickly. Sometimes this can be for political reasons, a reluctance to apply the sanction; sometimes it can be for legal reasons, based on general constitutional restraints, that require a law for certain acts: a good example can be provided here by the Law of 2 January 1995, adopted to implement Resolution 827 (1993) of 25 May 1993, which means that almost two years elapsed between the two texts. Of course, the creation of an International Tribunal is a very special sanction, imagined for the first time in 1993, and it needed important changes in national legislation, which can explain the delay. Another example, although the delay is much shorter, is the case already mentioned of Article 45 of Law nr. 91-716 of 26 July 1991 adopted to implement Article 29 of Resolution 687 of 3 April 1991.

c. The question is in fact: does the national sanction ever coincide with the United Nations sanction?

There is always a time gap, be it short, between the adoption of a sanction through a resolution by the Security Council and its incorporation in the national legal order. The question of the respect or the violation of the principle of retroactivity is then raised and should receive some more thought. As a matter of fact, the State is faced with a dilemma: either apply the United Nations sanction from the date it has been adopted and then violate the principle of non-retroactivity, or apply the sanctions immediately, that is from the date of the national text, but then act in contradiction with its obligations under the Charter between the moment of the resolution and the moment of the enforcement of national sanctions.

Usually, States do not apply the sanctions retroactively. In order to know when the State that does not apply the resolution is acting in violation of the Charter, it could be considered that the obligation to apply United Nations sanctions means *an obligation to apply them in a reasonable time*, but this formula is never included in the United Nations resolutions.

It sometimes happens that the United Nations resolution gives a certain time to States to enact domestic measures. For example, Resolution 748 (1992) adopted on 31 March 1992, and providing for sanctions against Libya, gives States two weeks to adapt their conduct to the Resolution:

> "The Security Council,
>
> ...
>
> Convinced that the suppression of acts of international terrorism, including those in which States are directly or indirectly involved, is essential for the maintenance of international peace and security,
>
> ...
>
> Acting under Chapter VII of the Charter,
>
> ...
>
> 3. Decides that, on 15 April 1992, all States shall adopt the measures set out below, which shall apply until the Security Council decides that the Libyan Government has complied with paragraphs 1 and 2 above."

It has also sometimes happened that an EC Regulation adopted on day t, and published on day t+1, has been made retroactive to day t-1. For example, EC Regulation of 8 August 1990 against Iraq was adopted on the 8th of August, entered into force on the 9th of August 1990 when it was published in the *OJEC*, and provided in its Article 1 that importation and exportation were forbidden "from 7 August 1990". This can have far-reaching consequences when one looks at the interference of sanctions with existing contractual relations.

(4) A Divergence Can Exist as far as the Strength of the Sanction Is Concerned

If one looks, for example at the financial sanctions adopted at the beginning of the Iraqi crisis, it appears quite clearly that the two decisions adopted by France and the United Nations do not coincide, as far as the automaticity, and therefore the strength of the sanction is concerned.

The French text, adopted on August 2, 1990, reads:

> "*Art. 1er. Sont soumis à autorisation préalable du ministre chargé de l'économie les opérations de change, les mouvements de capitaux et les règlements de toute nature entre la France et l'étranger effectués pour le compte de personnes physiques ou morales résidentes au Koweit et en Irak ou de nationalité koweitienne ou irakienne.*
> *Sont également soumises à autorisation préalable du ministre chargé de l'économie, la constitution ou la liquidation d'investissements d'origine koweitienne ou irakienne en France.*"

The text of the posterior Resolution 661 (1990), dated August 6, 1990, reads (on financial questions only, as it is broader):

> "Decides that all States shall not make available to the Government of Iraq, or to any commercial, industrial, or public utility undertaking in Iraq or Kuwait, any funds or any other financial or economic resources and shall prevent their nationals and any persons within their territory from removing from their territory or otherwise making available to that Government or to any such undertaking any such funds or resources and from remitting any other funds to persons or bodies within Iraq or Kuwait, except payments exclusively for strictly medical or humanitarian purposes and, in humanitarian circumstances, foodstuffs."

There is no coincidence between the measures adopted in municipal law and the Resolution, as far as their content is concerned: freezing of assets and exchange control are different. The United Nations Resolution not only prohibits the exportation of funds, but also the possibility to leave the funds available within the territory of a United Nations Member State for Iraqi authorities or nationals. But, moreover, the United Nations Resolution implies *an obligation* to transfer no funds to Iraq, while the French text just gives *a possibility* to the Minister to forbid transfer of funds to Iraq. This leaves the door open for full compliance of the French authorities with the United Nations Resolution, if they refuse all transfer of funds, except the ones necessary for humanitarian needs, but also to partial or total non-compliance, depending on the manner in which the Minister exercises his right of authorisation.

A difficulty also appeared due to a difference of interpretation in French of a term employed in Resolution 883. Along with the English text of the Resolution, the Security Council:

> "Decides that all States, including Libya, shall take the necessary measures to ensure that no claim shall lie at the instance of the Government of Libya... or of any person or body in Libya... ."

This formula was first introduced by Resolution 687 against Iraq and was since reproduced in the same wording in several resolutions.[62] The translation in French of Article 29 of Resolution 687 was:

62 Resolution 687 (1991) on Iraq; Resolution 757 (1992) of 30 May 1992 on Yugoslavia (Article 9); Resolution 917 (1994) of 6 May 1994 on Haïti (Article 11).

> *"Décide que tous les Etats, y compris l'Iraq, prendront les mesures nécessaires pour qu'il ne puisse être fait droit à aucune réclamation présentée, etc.... ."*

The same translation was used in all similar cases except for Resolution 883. For some obscure reason, the French version of that Resolution reads:

> *"...que les gouvernements de tous les Etats, y compris le Gouvernement libyen, prendront les mesures nécessaires pour s'assurer qu'aucune réclamation ne sera instruite à l'initiative du Gouvernement libyen ou des administrations publiques libyennes, ou de tout national libyen, ou de toute entreprise libyenne (...) en liaison avec tout contrat ou toute opération commerciale dont la réalisation a été affectée en raison des mesures imposées par la présente résolution ou par suite de son application ou de l'application de résolutions connexes."*

This Resolution was implemented by a Common Position of 22 November 1993 followed by two EC Regulations 3274/93 and 3275/93 of 29 November 1993. The French version of the EC Regulation uses the same wording as the French version of the previous Security Council Resolutions: "*Il est interdit de faire droit*".

A dispute arose between Air France and the Libyan Arab Airlines about the interpretation of paragraph 8 of Resolution 883. Air France held that the expression "*Aucune réclamation ne sera instruite*" prevented any arbitrator to even consider as receivable a claim concerning a contract affected by an embargo decided by the Security Council, if the claim concerned the period during which the sanction applied to the contract.[63] The arbitral tribunal presided over by Mr Kéba Mbaye and the *Cour d'Appel de Montreal* both considered that Resolution 883 was not to be interpreted as creating a non-arbitrability case.

V. Domestic Procedures for Implementation and Enforcement

(1) Co-ordination Between Different Ministerial Activities

Regarding economic sanctions the role of the Ministry of Finance has always been a key one and especially that of the Direction of Customs and the Direction of Treasury, which is in charge of exchange control issues.

For the practical application of the trade and financial restrictions established by the Security Council, a special service has been created in the *Direction Générale des Douanes et des Droits indirects*, the so-called "*Cellule embargo*" which is the intermediary between

63 This case concerned the contractual relations between the two companies about a contract concluded before the embargo. The claim by LAA concerned the contractual relations between the parties to the contract for the period of time preceding Resolution 883. See *Cour Supérieure du Québec*, 15 February 2000 (Bull. ASA 2000, p. 116) and *Cour d'Appel de Montréal*, 31 March 2003, *Compagnie Nationale Air France c/Libyan Arab Airlines*. The *Cour d'Appel de Montréal* considered that the Arbitral Tribunal was right in not refusing to examine if the claim concerned the execution of the contract before the entry into force of the UN embargo.

the exporters and the Permanent Mission of France in New York which submits the export applications to the Sanction Committee. The *Banque de France* has apparently no role to play in implementation.

(2) *Procedures Relating to Sanctions Violations*

No specific provisions have been provided for in case of violation of implementation measures. Consequently, the usual procedures provided for in case of violation of the Customs Code or of the *Code Monétaire et Financier* are theoretically to be employed.

Concerning commercial embargoes and boycotts, controls on exports and imports will be carried out by the customs administration which has large powers of investigation and of seizure of prohibited goods, but under judiciary control. In case of infringement, the usual fiscal penalties provided for by the Customs Code can apply. They include fines and confiscation of goods. The freeze of assets having been considered as an extension of exchange control, the penalties provided for by Article 5 of the 1966 Law on external relations, now *Code Monétaire et Financier*, including imprisonment from one to three months, confiscation and fines from half to treble the amount of the sum at issue may possibly apply. The applicable procedure is that of Title XII (Article 459) of the *Code des Douanes*. In addition to these fiscal sanctions, criminal sanctions can also be incurred if the infringement can also be qualified as a criminal offence.

However, as has been already mentioned, the jurisprudence of the *Cour de Cassation* sheds doubt on the very possibility of criminal pursuits, since the *Chambre Criminelle* refuses to consider that a European regulation could serve as a basis for punishment.[64]

It must be underscored that in the case of sanctions against Iraq, the freeze of assets was introduced into French law through a Decree taken on 2 August 1990 which was drafted like an ordinary exchange control decree, providing not directly for the freeze of Iraqi assets in French banks, but for the obligation for Iraqi nationals to obtain an authorisation from the Ministry of Finance in case of exchange operations, movements of funds or of payments abroad. The control was carried out through French banks and it has been reported that first steps for pursuits were made when the Ministry of Finance was informed that, due to compensation between credits and debts, the amount of certain Iraqi accounts had changed. Finally, no criminal pursuit was initiated.[65]

VI. The Role of National Courts

(1) *The Role of Courts in Sanctioning Violations*

The first point to discuss is that of direct applicability of United Nations resolutions before French courts. Until recently, French courts did not have the opportunity to take a clear position on the constitutional basis of the legal effects of United Nations resolutions on sanctions. We must wait to see if the above-mentioned position of the *Cour*

64 See cases mentioned *supra*, note 29.

65 See Geneviève Burdeau, *op. cit.*, *supra*, note 20.

d'Appel de Paris will be confirmed or not by the *Cour de Cassation*.[66] The traditional position of French courts on United Nations resolutions in general seemed to be that they only address Member States and have no direct effect in French law.

But here apparently a distinction has to be made along with an interesting remark by Michel Cosnard in his commentary on the decision of the *Cour de Cassation* of 15 June 1999.[67] As he rightly points out, resolutions of the Security Council deciding economic sanctions are indeed double-sided. On the one hand, they have a normative aspect and in this respect their prescriptions must in principle be transposed into domestic legislation, unless some general provision, for instance in the Constitution, grants all resolutions of the Security Council a direct effect in municipal law, which is not the case in France as has already been mentioned.

But, on the other hand, provisions of a Security Council resolution may also create a situation which can be taken into account in itself by national courts and can be considered as having certain legal consequences, for instance on contractual links between private parties, irrespective of the existence or of the absence of domestic implementing measures. This last position has apparently been taken by the *Cour de Cassation* in three significant cases.

In the first case, the link with a Security Council resolution was only indirect and did not concern economic measures properly but rather the first above-mentioned category of measures under Chapter VII.[68] The plaintiff sued a tour operator for having cancelled a journey, as a consequence of the air traffic perturbations connected with the launching of Operation Desert Storm in 1991, decided pursuant to Security Council Resolution 678. The tour operator was only condemned to repay the price of the journey but not to pay damages, and the complaint was dismissed on the ground of *force majeure*. The Tribunal considered that the decision to start hostilities and to interrupt civil flights to the Middle East was a political decision imposed on the air companies.[69] It is clear that this is not a case of direct application of a Security Council resolution, but only a case in which the *situation* created by the implementation of a resolution is taken into consideration.

In the second case, an employment contract between Yugoslav Air Transport (JAT) and an employee in Paris had been suspended as a consequence of the decision of the French Government to prohibit all overfly of French territory by Yugoslav aircraft, pursuant to Resolution 757 of 30 May 1992. The employee sued JAT before the French courts. The *Cour d'Appel* condemned JAT for unfair dismissal, considering that the com-

66 See *supra*, Section II (2), pp. 201ff and notes 16 and 17.

67 *Cass. civ. 1*, 15 July 1999, *Dumez c/Etat irakien et a. JDI* (2000), p. 45, note M. Cosnard

68 See above on page 202.

69 *Tribunal d'instance du 1er arrondissement de Paris*, Judgement of 15 March 1993, *Epoux Souriau c/ Société Mondoclub, Mondial Tours et Air France, Revue française de droit aérien et spatial* (1993), p. 351. "*Attendu que le déclenchement d'une guerre n'est pas réellement prévisible, même si elle a été précédée d'ultimatums et d'embargos: qu'il s'agissait en l'espèce d'une décision relevant des seules autorités politiques, et que les compagnies aériennes ne pouvaient que s'y soumettre lorsqu'elle a été prise: qu'elle constitue donc à leur égard un véritable cas de force majeure*".

pany still retained a reduced activity of sale of air tickets for other companies. The *Cour de Cassation* approved that position and suggested *a contrario* that the total interruption of JAT's commercial activities in France could have been considered as *force majeure* justifying the dismissal of the plaintiff.[70]

This case also seems very clear: the subject matter of the United Nations Resolution is the prohibition of air transport with Yugoslavia and the implementing measures are intended to give effect to that prohibition. The Resolution is not intended to suspend employment contracts and the effect of the Resolution on the employment contract is only indirect. It is only taken into consideration as creating a situation which can prevent the air company from continuing its activities and it can therefore be qualified as a "*fait du Prince*", exonerating JAT from its responsibility to suspend the employment contract. The position of the *Cour de Cassation*, admitting that the prohibition, as applied by the French authorities, could possibly create a situation affecting labour relations within JAT, although no domestic implementation measure of the Security Council on that topic had been taken, is not contradictory with the traditional position according to which a United Nations resolution is not directly applicable in French law. Here also a distinction appears between the proper implementation in French law, which requires European or domestic implementation measures and the taking into consideration of a factual situation created by the application by Members States of a United Nations resolution.[71] The same reasoning can be found in a decision concerning the *Banque franco-yougoslave*, whose activities had been considerably reduced in consequence of the sanctions against Yugoslavia and of the freeze of assets.[72]

The third case, illustrating that distinction between implementation and taking into consideration, concerned a contract passed by a private company, Dumez, with the Iraqi Ministry of Defence before the Gulf crisis. The French company, having executed its obligations under the contract without getting payment, obtained from the *Tribunal de Grande Instance de Nanterre* a decision to the effect that the Iraqi Ministry had to pay the price. Dumez then tried to obtain the enforcement of the judgement, but its claim was rejected by the Court of Appeal because of the immunity of the defendant. The *Cour de Cassation*, on rather strange grounds criticised the *Cour d'Appel* for not having taken into account the fact that, due to United Nations sanctions under Resolution 687, the sovereignty of Iraq was no longer complete. Although this last assertion, which is in total contradiction with the clear wording of the same Resolution, cannot be accepted, the idea that a situation created as a consequence of a resolution on sanctions may affect legal relations can be approved.[73]

70 Cass. Soc., 4 June 1996, *JAT c/ Dupond*, *RGDIP* (1998), p. 495, note Michel Sastre. See also Cass. Soc., 21 January 1998, nr. 260, *JAT c/ Veselko Grebenar*, nr. 260.

71 We cannot therefore agree with the commentator M. Sastre who affirms that an *a contrario* reading of the decision shows that the Court recognizes the direct applicability of the provisions of a Security Council resolution.

72 Cass. Soc., 29 October 1997, nr. 3913, *Banque franco-yougoslave c/ Vukica Milovanovic*.

73 See above, p. 203.

The same approach, but with negative conclusions, can be observed in some decisions of the *Conseil d'Etat* relating to expulsion of aliens. The *Conseil d'Etat* considered indeed that the situation created by Resolution 678 of 29 November 1990 did not by itself justify the expulsion of aliens if no precise threat against the public order was alleged.[74]

Thus a distinction has to be drawn between the cases which really raise a question of implementation of a Security Council resolution imposing sanctions and the taking into account by the judge of factual situations which derive from the application of a resolution by the French State. If one looks very carefully at the case law, it appears that as far as actual implementation of a resolution is concerned, an enacting rule of domestic law is required to give effect to the United Nations resolution in French law. In most cases, however, the resolution does note need to be directly applied as such, but only considered as a *fait du Prince* or as an element of *force majeure.* Then no domestic implementation measure is required and the situation created by a governmental attitude or by the attitude of third States can be considered as *fait du Prince* or *force majeure.*[75]

(2) The Role of Courts in the Interpretation of Security Council Resolutions

Another issue is that of interpretation: is the national judge competent to interpret United Nations resolutions? Can the judge rely on the interpretation of the resolution if its wording is different from that of the European regulation?

The above-mentioned distinction between proper implementation and taking into consideration of the resolution imposing sanctions has a direct impact on interpretation issues.

In the case of implementation of normative provisions of a Security Council resolution by domestic measures, the issue could be raised of the interpretation of the United Nations resolution by domestic courts in view of a possible control of legality of domestic measures. Two examples can be given. In the first case, a French company, *Société Héli-Union,* complained about a Decree dated 15 April 1992 implementing Resolution 748 of 31 March 1992, which decided an air embargo against Libya. That Decree was adopted by the French Government one day before the EC Regulation was published in the Official Journal, so that the only legal basis for the French decree was the Resolution which is not directly applicable. The *Conseil d'Etat,* however, dismissed the complaint, considering that the decree was not an "*acte détachable*" from foreign relations of the French State. Thus the *Conseil d'Etat* refused to control the legality under French law of domestic implementation measures, considering that they could not be distinguished (detached) from the Resolution itself which constitutes an "*acte de gouvernement*" (political act)

74 C.E., 24 March 1993, *Ministre de l'Intérieur c/ M. Chiker*, req. nr. 134.601: 23 October 1993, *Ministre de l'Intérieur c/ M. Boudih*, req. nr. 138.239: 12 January 1994, M. Boutbila, req. nr. 136.260.

75 On that distinction between implementation and taking into consideration, which is familiar to private international lawyers, see for instance, Patrick Kinsch, *Le fait du Prince étranger* (Paris, LGDJ, 1994).

which, due to the separation of powers, escapes any form of control from judges.[76]

Interpretation and control of legality issues were also raised in relation to EC Regulations before the European Court of Justice. In the Court Judgement of 14 January 1997 in the *Centro-Com Case*, the Court stated that even when adopted in the exercise of national jurisdiction relating to foreign policy and security for the application of Resolution 757 (1992), domestic implementation measures had to comply with EC rules relating to the common commercial policy. Interpretation by national authorities of EC Member States of what is required for an efficient implementation of a Security Council Resolution can consequently be controlled by the European Court of Justice in the light of European law rules.

So it appears that the interpretation and the control of legality of a national measure implementing a Security Council resolution cannot be done by French national courts although it can be done by the European Court of Justice. This position is confirmed by the Judgement of 27 February 1997 in the *Ebony Maritime Case* in which the European Court of Justice refers to a Security Council resolution to declare how national authorities should act to comply with the resolution.

VII. Implementation of Security Council Decisions Relating to the International Criminal Tribunals for the Former Yugoslavia and Rwanda

(1) *The Necessity of a Law to Enforce the Resolutions on the Creation of the International Criminal Tribunals*

In general, it can be said that United Nations sanctions may require action from different entities:

- Action can be required from the *political organs* of the State. An example, of course, is the severance of diplomatic relations, which is decided by the Ministry of Foreign Affairs.
- Action is also very often required from *the executive branch and the administration*. This is the case when the State has to adopt commercial interdictions, in case the executive is authorised by the legal system, for example through an enabling legislation, to act.
- Action has also been considered necessary from the *judicial organs* of the States, following the two recent resolutions on the creation of International Criminal Tribunals.

In France, the organisation of the judiciary is a prerogative of the Parliament, according to Article 34 of the French Constitution of 1958:

> "Article 34
> Legislation shall be passed by Parliament.

76 C.E., 29 December 1997, *Société Héli-Union, RFDA*, 1998, p. 208. That position leads to the absurd consequence that even if the domestic measure has not been taken by a competent authority, no control is possible. See also, C.E., 12 March 1999, *Société Héli-Union*, req. nr. 162.131, *Recueil*, Tables.

The rules concerning the following matters shall be enacted by Parliament:

...

- civic rights and the fundamental guarantees accorded citizens for the exercise of their civil liberties; the obligations imposed upon citizens with respect to their person or property by the needs of National Defence;

...

- the definition of crimes and criminal offences and of the punishment prescribed therefore; criminal procedure; amnesty; changes in the court structure or the organisation of the judiciary."

Resolution 827 (1993), adopted on 25 May 1993, decided the creation of an International Tribunal for the Former Yugoslavia:

"The Security Council,

...

Expressing once again its grave alarm at continuing reports of widespread and flagrant violations of international humanitarian law occurring within the territory of the former Yugoslavia, and especially in the Republic of Bosnia and Herzegovina, including reports of mass killings, massive, organized and systematic detention and rape of women and the continuance of the practice of 'ethnic cleansing', including for the acquisition and holding of territory,

Determining that this situation continues to constitute a threat to international peace and security;

Determined to put an end to such crimes and to take effective measures to bring to justice the persons who are responsible for them,

Convinced that in the particular circumstances of the former Yugoslavia the establishment as an ad hoc measure by the Council of an international tribunal and the prosecution of the persons responsible for serious violations of international humanitarian law would enable this aim to be achieved and would contribute to the restoration and maintenance of peace,

...

Acting under Chapter VII of the Charter of the United Nations,

...

Decides hereby to establish an international tribunal for the sole purpose of prosecuting persons responsible for serious violations of humanitarian law committed in the territory of the former Yugoslavia between 1 January 1991 and a date to be determined by the Security Council upon the restoration of peace and to this end to adopt the statute of the International Tribunal annexed to the report of the Secretary-General."

The fact that the organisation of the judiciary power is a prerogative of the Parliament in France explains why a law had to be adopted in order to enforce the United Nations Resolution in France. This has been stated in the "*Exposé des motifs*" of the law adopted for the enforcement of Resolution 827:

> *"La résolution 827 du Conseil de sécurité des Nations Unies faisant obligation aux Etats d'apporter 'leur pleine coopération au tribunal international en vue du jugement des personnes présumées responsables de violations graves du droit humanitaire commises sur le territoire de l'ex-Yougoslavie', le présent projet de loi prévoit les mesures d'adaptation nécessaires à son application, en précisant les conditions dans lesquelles la France participe à la répression de ces infractions et coopère avec le tribunal international."*

The intervention of a law was necessary because individual liberties and the organisation of justice were at stake.

For example, the procedure by which the accused were to be handed over to the International Tribunal, was determined by the law, and this was necessary as underscored in the "*Exposé des motifs*" of the Law on the ICTY:

> *"Tout d'abord, la décision de remise des individus est prise exclusivement par l'autorité judiciaire française, sans aucune intervention du pouvoir exécutif, contrairement à ce qui est de règle en matière d'extradition. L'accord de l'autorité judiciaire est indispensable puisqu'en vertu de la constitution celle-ci est gardienne de la liberté individuelle."*

(2) Scope of the provisions

The adaptation of French law to the requirements of Resolution 827 (1993) of 25 May 1993 creating the International Criminal Tribunal for the Former Yugoslavia, and Resolution 995 (1994) of 8 November 1994 creating the International Criminal Tribunal for Rwanda, illustrates the possibility of divergent dispositions between the international texts on sanctions and the national texts on sanctions.

In the *draft law* on the International Criminal Tribunal for the Former Yugoslavia, the scope of the tribunal's jurisdiction as understood in French law was exactly the same as in the Security Council resolution, as it was defined by a mere reference to it:

> *"Article premier:*
> *Pour l'application de la résolution 827 du Conseil de sécurité des Nations Unies du 25 mai 1993 instituant un tribunal international en vue de juger les personnes présumées responsables de violations graves du droit international humanitaire commises sur le territoire de l'ex-Yougoslavie depuis le 1er janvier 1991, la France participe à la répression des infractions et coopère avec cette juridiction dans les conditions fixées par la loi.*
> *Les dispositions qui suivent sont applicables à toute personne poursuivie des chefs ou délits qui constituent,* au sens des articles 2 à 5 du statut du tribunal international, *des infractions graves aux conventions de Genève du 12 août 1949, des violations des lois et coutumes de la guerre, un génocide ou des crimes contre l'humanité."*[77]

It appears that in the draft law, the offences were defined in exactly the same way as they were in the text of the United Nations Resolution. However, from the "*Exposé des*

77 Emphasis added.

motifs", it must be implied that this formulation has to be understood as signifying that the crimes were only the crimes defined by the Statute of the Tribunal which were also crimes in France:

> "*Le champ d'application de la présente loi est fixé par un article premier qui rappelle que sont visés les infractions graves aux conventions de Genève de 1949, les violations des lois et coutumes de la guerre, le génocide ou les crimes contre l'humanité qui constituent des crimes et délits en droit français.*"[78]

This gave rise to a controversy before the Assembly.[79] The Rapporteur wanted the adjunction of the Senate to be deleted, but it finally remained. Therefore the text of the law, as adopted,[80] reads:

> "*Les dispositions qui suivent sont applicables à toute personne poursuivie des chefs de crimes ou délits définis par la loi française, qui constituent, au sens des articles 2 à 5 du statut du tribunal international, des infractions graves aux conventions de Genève du 12 août 1949, des violations des lois et coutumes de la guerre, un génocide ou des crimes contre l'humanité.*"[81]

Such a reference to the French definition of crimes rather than to the international definition is not without consequences.

France has a definition of genocide that is different from the international definition, narrower on some points, broader on some other points. The international definition of genocide, which is to be found in Article 2 of the Genocide Convention as well as in Article 4 of the Statutes of the International Criminal Tribunals for the Former Yugoslavia and Rwanda, reads:

> "In the present Convention, genocide means any of the following acts, committed with intent to destroy, in whole or in part, a national, ethnical, racial or religious group, as such:
> a) Killing members of the group;
> b) Causing serious bodily or mental harm to members of the group;
> c) Deliberately inflicting on the group conditions of life calculated to bring about its physical destruction in whole or in part;
> d) Imposing measures intended to prevent birth within the group;
> e) Forcibly transferring children of the group to another group."

---

78 Emphasis added.

79 See Assemblée nationale, *JO des débats, 2ième séance,* 20 December 1994, p. 9444.

80 Law nr. 95-1 of 2 January 1995 adapting the French legislation to the provisions of Security Council Resolution 827 (*portant adaptation de la législation française aux dispositions de la résolution 827 du Conseil de sécurité des Nations Unies instituant un tribunal international en vue de juger les personnes présumées responsables de violations graves du droit international humanitaire commises sur le territoire de l'ex-Yougoslavie depuis 1991*), *JORF,* 3 January 1995, p. 71.

81 Emphasis added.

The French definition given in Article 211-1 of the new *Code Pénal* is the following:

> "*Constitue un génocide le fait,* en exécution d'un plan concerté *tendant à la destruction totale ou partielle d'un groupe national, ethnique, racial ou religieux,* ou d'un groupe déterminé à partir de tout autre critère arbitraire, *de commettre ou de faire commettre, à l'encontre de membres de ce groupe l'un des actes suivants:*
> - *atteinte volontaire à la vie ;*
> - *atteinte grave à l'intégrité physique ou psychique ;*
> - *soumission à des conditions d'existence de nature à entraîner la destruction totale ou partielle du groupe ;*
> - *mesures visant à entraver les naissances;*
> - *transfert forcé d'enfants.*"[82]

This definition is much more restrictive on some points than the international definition and has been therefore criticised: it is narrower, as there must be a "concerted plan" in French law, while in international law, the intention is sufficient. But in other respects the French definition is more encompassing: for example, any group persecuted to the point of disappearance is considered as submitted to genocide; also, the national definition refers to the "destruction" of the group and not, as does the international definition, to the "physical destruction".

The same analysis is possible for crimes against humanity. In Article 5 of the Statute of the ICTY, it is stated that the crimes against humanity are:

> "The following crimes, when committed during an armed conflict, whether international or national, and committed against a civilian population:
> a) Assassination
> b) Extermination
> c) Enslavement
> d) Deportation
> e) Torture
> f) Rape
> g) Persecutions for political, racial or religious reasons."

In the French text, more precisely in Article 212-1 of the new *Code Pénal*, it is stated that:

> "*La déportation, la réduction en esclavage ou la pratique massive et systématique d'exécutions sommaires, d'enlèvements de personnes suivis de leur disparition, de la torture ou d'actes inhumains, inspirées par des motifs politiques,* philosophiques, *raciaux ou religieux et organisées* en exécution d'un plan concerté *à l'encontre d'un groupe de population civile sont punies de la réclusion criminelle à perpétuité.*"[83]

82 Some of the differences are underscored.

83 Same remark.

Considering the difficulties that such discrepancies could raise in the process of the implementation of the repression of the international crimes committed in the Former Yugoslavia, France has adopted another approach to the law implementing the Statute of the International Tribunal for Rwanda. In the Law enacting Resolution 995 (1994) of 8 November 1994, France has adopted a position more respectful of the international decision, as this Law refers simply to the international definitions, without any mention of the French definitions:[84] so, no discrepancy can appear here.

VIII. Interface Between Domestic and International Implementation

(1) *The Description of a French Exportation Under the Iraqi Embargo*

The process of exporting goods from France under the Oil for Food resolutions entails going back and forth from the national authorities to the international authorities. It is interesting to follow the countless steps that are necessary throughout this process to complete such an operation.

First, a French exporter, who wants to export under the present situation, that is under the Oil for Food resolutions, has to sign a contract with a public entity of an Iraqi Ministry: the Ministry of Trade for foodstuffs, the Ministry of Health for medical goods, the Ministry of the Interior for water and so on.

Then a request for authorisation to complete this exportation has to be presented to the "*Cellule Embargo*" of the French Ministry of Economy and Finances, which carries out a first formal check.

After this first screening, the request for authorisation is sent to the French Representation in New York, which forwards it to the Secretariat of Sanctions Committee 661.

Then, the request is dealt with on a first come first examined basis, unless Iraq asks for a priority examination. The Secretariat again checks that the purported contract meets the specifications of the authorised exportations, and transmits the request to the Sanctions Committee.

The Sanctions Committee first examines the request without any consideration for available funds to pay for the operation: at that stage it gives a *theoretical consent*, which has to be given unanimously. This aspect must be emphasised, as it means that any one of the 15 Members, which make up the Sanctions Committee, has a kind of "veto power" to stop any export operation to Iraq.

If such unanimous consent is given, then the next step is the *final approval*, when funds are available. This takes the form of a *letter of approval* signed by the President of the Sanctions Committee, and sent both to the French Mission in New York and to the Central Bank of Iraq.

---

84 Law nr. 96-432 of 22 May 1996 "*portant adaptation de la législation française aux dispositions de la résolution 955 du Conseil de sécurité des Nations Unies instituant un tribunal international en vue de juger les personnes présumées responsables d'actes de génocide ou d'autres violations graves du droit international humanitaire commis en 1994 sur le territoire du Rwanda et, s'agissant des citoyens rwandais, sur le territoire d'Etats voisins*", *JORF*, 23 May 1996, p. 7695.

The letter of approval follows the reverse road than the request for authorisation; in other words, it goes from the French Mission at the United Nations to the "*Cellule Embargo*" at the Ministry of Economy and Finances, and then to the French company.

At the same time, the process of payment starts at the other end of the transaction chain: in other words, the Central Bank of Iraq informs the BNP New York, where the Iraqi funds are deposited, to open a letter of credit. To do this, the approval of the Secretary-General of the United Nations is required.

Then the concrete implementation of the contract starts. The export company sends the goods to Iraq. At the border, experts from a supervision company working for the United Nations – at the moment, this is a Swiss company – checks that everything is in conformity with the authorisation granted by the Sanctions Committee.

When the Secretary-General is advised by the Swiss company controlling the Iraqi borders that everything is correct, it authentificates the arrival of the goods in Iraq, allowing the Secretary-General to then forward this authentification to the BNP New York, which can then proceed to the payment of the exporting company.

(2) Implementation of Resolution 1373 (2001) on the Fight Against Terrorism

As was explained in a letter addressed on 24 December 2001 by the Permanent Representative of France to the President of the Security Council, the implementation of Resolution 1373 only needed an adaptation of the French legislation against terrorism which had been seriously reinforced since 1986 with the Law of 9 September 1986 on terrorist acts and that of 12 July 1990 concerning the fight against money laundering. A new Law was enacted on 15 November 2001 introducing into the French *Code Pénal* a new specific notion of financing of acts of terrorism with new sanctions. This Law introduced new provisions to facilitate the seizure of assets before the tribunal imposes confiscation as a criminal sanction. However, most of the measures analysed in that letter already existed in the French legislation prior to Resolution 1373.

IX. Conclusion

The attitude of French tribunals, as P.M. Eisemann rightly pointed out, seems very empirical, with a preoccupation to find a fair solution in every case rather than to adopt a rigid legal reasoning, and to protect "innocent" private persons who have nothing to do with the sanctioned state.[85] Such attitude appears especially in some cases concerning independent guarantees: notwithstanding their traditional position relying on the independent and abstract character of the guarantees, French tribunals adopted rather flexible solutions, refusing to the Iraqi bank Rafidain to call the guarantee for contracts

85 For such an empirical approach, see also Tribunal de commerce de Nanterre, 31 October 1990, *S.A. Lesieur International c/ Sté Norasia, A.F.D.I.* (1991), p. 895 and *Les Petites Affiches* nr. 156, 28 December 1990, p. 21, note p. M. Martin in nr. 15, 4 February 1994. Due to the embargo against Iraq and Kuwait decided by Resolution 661, the delivery of oil boxes to Kuwait became impossible. The parties to the contract having decided to cancel the sale, the Tribunal decided to nullify the bill of lading and to authorise the seller to take back the goods.

the execution of which had been prevented by the economic sanctions decided by the Security Council.[86]

Select Bibliography

I. Books

Combacau, J., *Le pouvoir de sanction de l'ONU. Etude théorique de la coercition non militaire* (Paris, Pedone, 1974), 394 p.

Eisemann, P.-M., Coussirat-Coustere, V., *L'intégration du droit international et communautaire dans l'ordre juridique national* (The Hague, Kluwer, 1996), 587 p.

Mehdi, R., *Les Nations Unies et les sanctions*, Rencontres internationales de l'Institut d'Études Politiques d'Aix-en-Provence - Aix-en-Provence 1999 (Paris, Pedone, 2000), 246 p.

Les aspects juridiques de la crise et de la guerre du Golfe, sous la direction de B. Stern, Cahiers du CEDIN (Paris, Montchrestien, 1991), 502 p.

II. Articles

Cosnard, M., note in *JDI* (2000) 47-55

Eisemann, P.-M., "La contribution des Etats à la mise en oeuvre des sanctions: le cas de la France", in *Les Nations Unies et les sanctions*, Rencontres internationales de l'Institut d'Études Politiques d'Aix-en-Provence - Aix-en-Provence 1999 (Paris, Pedone, 2000), pp. 67-85.

Idot, L., note in *JDI* (1997) 1011-1015.

Jacquemont, A., note in *JDI* (1997) 448-451.

Lanfranchi, M.-P., "La valeur juridique en France des résolutions du Conseil de sécurité", *AFDI* (1997) 31-57.

86 These cases do not raise proper issues of implementation of Security Council resolutions. *Cour d'Appel de Paris*, 1ère Ch. Section B, 23 June 1995, *S.A. Butec c/ Union des banques arabes et françaises (UBAF) et a. JCP*, ed. Entreprises, 1995, nr. 735, note B.G. Affaki, *J.D.I.* (1997), nr. 441, note A. Jacquemont: Cass. Civ. 1ère, 24 February 1998, nr. 357, *Sté Rafidain Bank et Société State Establishment for pipelines (SEP) c/Butec et UBAF, J.D.I.* (1998), p. 963, note A. Jacquemont: Cass. Soc. 16 May 1995, nr. 1014, Beyton Ltd c/ Société Générale, *RGDIP* (1996), p. 1094, obs. M. Sastre.

8

GERMANY*

*Jochen Abr. Frowein and Nico Krisch***

I. Introduction

Germany has been a member of the United Nations since 1973,[1] but it already implemented United Nations sanctions in 1966 against Rhodesia. While these measures were still taken solely through domestic acts, the role of the European Communities in sanctions implementation grew steadily from the 1980s onwards. In the South African case, the EEC acted rather cautiously, but in the 1990s, most of the necessary measures were taken within the framework of the Community. This development was reinforced by the Maastricht Treaty, which gave the EC broader power to enact economic sanctions against third States, and provided for a stronger mechanism for intergovernmental cooperation in this field. Therefore, except for administrative execution, domestic implementation measures are now rather limited in Germany. However, they perform important functions in filling the gaps left by EC measures and in penalising sanctions violations.[2]

---

* This chapter builds, in part, upon J.A. Frowein, "Implementation of Security Council Resolutions taken under Chapter VII in Germany", in *United Nations Sanctions and International Law* (V. Gowlland-Debbas (ed.), 2001), pp. 253-65. The authors are grateful to Tono Eitel for valuable comments on an earlier draft and to Christian Schaller for his research assistance. The text was finalised in February 2002.

** Jochen Abr. Frowein is Professor Emeritus of International Law, University of Heidelberg and Director Emeritus, Max Planck Institute for Comparative Public Law and International Law, Heidelberg, Germany. Nico Krisch is Hauser Research Fellow, Institute for International Law and Justice, New York University School of Law, United States.

1 Both German States became members in 1973.

2 On the German implementation practice see Hans-Konrad Ress, *Das Handelsembargo* (2000), pp. 248 *et seq.*; Henning C. Schneider, *Wirtschaftssanktionen* (1999), pp. 55 *et seq.*

Vera Gowlland-Debbas (ed.), National Implementation of UN Sanctions, *233-264.*

II. The Legal Basis of Domestic Implementation Measures

(1) The Constitutional Basis

a. The relationship between domestic and international law

The German constitutional order rests, in principle, on a moderate dualist foundation. According to Article 32 of the German Basic Law, most treaties are concluded by the Federation. They become part of domestic law – with the status of a federal law – only by the adoption of the law of ratification under Article 59 paragraph 2 of the Basic Law,[3] as has been the case for the United Nations Charter. But it then still depends on the wording and the context of the specific provisions of the treaty if certain obligations can be considered to have direct effect in the national legal order or if they are binding only on the Member States. In the latter case, further acts are needed to implement them.

The same holds true for decisions of international bodies. Before they can be relied upon in national proceedings, they have to enter the internal legal order by way of national laws, regulations, decisions etc.

An exception to this rule exists for "general rules of international law" – customary international law and general principles of law – which are, according to Article 25, part of Federal Law without further implementation.[4] Their effect in the domestic legal order depends, as in the case of treaties, on their clarity and the need for measures concretising their content. Since sanctions resolutions and treaty law do not fall within the scope of these "general rules", the special status of these rules is of little importance in our context.

b. Direct effect of international norms in the German legal order

The most important exception to this general dualist approach is Article 24 paragraph 1 of the German Constitution, which reads:

> "The Federation may by legislation transfer sovereign powers to international organizations."

This provision has existed since 1949 and it was of great importance for the integration of Europe. The European Communities were always seen as the main examples for international organisations to which specific sovereign rights have been transferred, and Article 24 paragraph 1 provided the constitutional basis for the direct applicability of regulations

3 Article 59 para. 2 reads: "Treaties which regulate the political relations of the Federation or relate to matters of federal legislation shall require the approval or participation of the appropriate legislative body in the form of a federal law."

4 Article 25 reads: "The general rules of international law shall be an integral part of federal law. They shall override laws and directly establish rights and obligations for the inhabitants of the federal territory."

and decisions by the European Communities in the German legal order.[5] With respect to European integration, Article 24 was replaced by the new Article 23 in 1992.[6]

The "transfer of sovereign rights" under Article 24 paragraph 1 has always been interpreted as referring to the exercise of jurisdiction with direct effect within German territory. A transfer of sovereign rights does not take place where international organisations may only take measures which are binding on the Federal Republic as such. Therefore, it is so far almost generally agreed that Article 24 is not applicable to the United Nations and that, although decisions taken under Chapter VII are binding for the Federal Republic as a State, they do not have direct effect on German territory or for persons under German jurisdiction.

It should be noted, however, that this view has recently been challenged, at least with respect to "orders" which emanate from the International Criminal Tribunal for the Former Yugoslavia.[7] It is true that the Federal Government has taken the position that the decisions of the Security Council establishing the two International Criminal Tribunals for the former Yugoslavia and Rwanda and some of the activities of these Tribunals "create immediately binding obligations at least for the Member States without further implementing measures by the national legislators" and that these acts constitute an exercise of sovereign powers in the sense of Article 24 paragraph 1. Nevertheless, the Government has introduced legislation "to bring German law in accordance with the obligations for the state which derive from the resolutions and the Statute (of the Tribunal) and transfers of sovereignty and to enable a smooth fulfilment of these obligations".[8]

These ambiguous sentences, however, do not necessarily mean that "orders" or other acts by the International Tribunals have direct effect in Germany without implementing legislation. Such a position is still very much an exception in legal doctrine and it is subject to serious objections deriving from the requirement of an informed parliamentary consent. In addition, several decisions by German courts have confirmed that Security Council decisions under Chapter VII have no automatic effect. The Federal Court of Justice, e.g., decided in 1995 that decisions of the Security Council under Chapter VII have no immediate legal effects for the citizens of member states. They are only binding on the Member States as such and need specific implementation.[9]

---

5 Albrecht Randelzhofer, in: Theodor Maunz, Günter Dürig *et al.* (eds.), *Grundgesetz: Kommentar*, Article 24, MN 45.

6 Article 23 para. 1 reads: "With a view to establishing a united Europe the Federal Republic of Germany shall participate in the development of the European Union, which is committed to democratic, rule-of-law, social and federal principles as well as the principle of subsidiarity, and ensures protection of basic rights comparable in substance to that afforded by this Basic Law. To this end the Federation may transfer sovereign powers by law with the consent of the Bundesrat ..."

7 Christian Tomuschat, 'Sanktionen durch internationale Strafgerichtshöfe', in *Verhandlungen des Sechzigsten Deutschen Juristentages Münster 1994*, Bd. II/2, München 1994, p. Q 66 *et seq.*

8 *Bundestags-Drucksache* 13/57, p. 6 *et seq.* (Yugoslavia) and *Bundestags-Drucksache* 13/7953, p. 6 (Rwanda).

9 Federal Court of Justice, Judgment of 21 April 1995, *Entscheidungen des Bundesgerichtshofes in Strafsachen*, vol. 41, p. 127, 129 *et seq.*; see also Judgment of 28 September 1995, *Neue Juristische Wochenschrift* 1996, p. 602.

One decision by the Federal Constitutional Court, however, might create some doubts as to this position. According to the Court, the North Atlantic Treaty Organisation (NATO) is an international organisation to which sovereign powers in the sense of Article 24 paragraph 1 have been transferred.[10] But this decision has to be seen in its specific context. Although NATO is an organisation which in principle does not exercise jurisdiction with direct effect on the territory of its Member States, the Federal Constitutional Court applied Article 24 paragraph 1 because of the enormous impact of specific decisions on the use of certain weapons, in particular the use of nuclear weapons, on the Federal Republic of Germany. The Court held that the President of the United States, when giving permission to use nuclear weapons stationed on German territory, would exercise jurisdiction transferred to NATO under Article 24 paragraph 1 of the Federal Constitution.[11] This decision, however, can certainly not be interpreted to include the United Nations. Even a decision which is directly binding for the Federal Republic of Germany under Chapter VII of the United Nations Charter would not have a comparable direct effect without implementation by German decisions.

Therefore, it is widely agreed that under German constitutional law decisions by the United Nations Security Council, even binding decisions under Chapter VII of the Charter, do not enjoy direct effect within the municipal legal order.

(2) Prior Enabling Legislation

In the German legal order, there is no general rule on the implementation of Security Council measures, but several provisions authorise the Federal Government to take implementation measures very quickly without having recourse to Parliament.[12]

The primary basis for the implementation of Security Council sanctions resolutions in municipal law is the Law on Foreign Trade (*Außenwirtschaftsgesetz*). Its Section 2 paragraph 1 reads:

> "As far as restrictions of foreign trade are permitted by this law, a regulation may provide that transactions or acts are, generally or under certain circumstances, (1) subject to prior authorization, or (2) are prohibited."

The restriction referred to in this section that is of greatest relevance to United Nations sanctions is provided for in Section 5:

> "In order to perform international obligations, which have been approved by the legislating bodies through a federal law, transactions and acts of foreign trade may be restricted and existing restrictions may be lifted."

10 Federal Constitutional Court, Judgment of 18 December 1984, *Entscheidungen des Bundesverfassungsgerichts*, vol. 68, p. 1.

11 See *supra* note 10, at 92.

12 Cf., in general, Ress, *supra* note 2, p. 223 *et seq.*

Another possible basis for the implementation of Security Council measures is Section 7 paragraph 1:

> "Transactions and acts of foreign trade may be restricted in order (1) to ensure the security of the Federal Republic of Germany, (2) to prevent a disturbance of the peaceful coexistence of the peoples of the world, or (3) to prevent that the foreign relations of the Federal Republic of Germany are severely affected."

According to these provisions, restrictions must take the form of a governmental regulation. Another mode of implementation is indicated by Article 2 paragraph 2 of the Law on Foreign Trade which authorises the Federal Minister of Economics to order provisional restrictions of foreign trade for a period of six months. The Minister of Foreign Affairs and the Minister of Finance must consent to those orders.

Apart from these general possibilities to restrict trade in specific cases, several laws require authorisations for foreign trade in every single case. Such laws exist e.g. for arms which are usually used in armed conflicts (*Kriegswaffenkontrollgesetz*), but, with slight differences, also for other products which can be used as weapons or for the production of weapons.[13] Export prohibitions on these goods can therefore be implemented by the simple refusal of an authorisation. In practice, this is the most common way; only in some cases, a general prohibition has been inserted in the Regulation on Foreign Trade.[14] The same procedure applies with respect to travel restrictions for specific persons. Usually, visa requirements exist,[15] so no specific regulation would be adopted in the case of sanctions but the competent authorities would deny a visa to the persons concerned.

While these measures are all within the competence of the executive branch, the German Parliament (*Bundestag*) is not precluded from consideration of issues related to sanctions. Regulations by the government are, in practice, reported to the parliamentary committees and, in particular, the parliamentary subcommittee for United Nations affairs often debates the scope and impact of United Nations sanctions. Moreover, issues such as sanctions against Iraq and Yugoslavia have been brought to the plenary. However, the Parliament enjoys more limited rights with respect to United Nations sanctions than with respect to unilateral measures: in the latter case, regulations must be reported to the Parliament and have to be revoked if it so demands. This does not apply to regulations implementing obligations arising from treaties which have initially been ratified by the legislative bodies.[16] In these cases, prior participation of parliament is deemed sufficient.

However, doubts have arisen whether this limitation of parliamentary influence is in conformity with the German Constitution. The *Grundgesetz* demands that laws conferring regulatory power to the Government define precisely the aims and scope of this power; Parliament itself must decide the most important issues.[17] The Law on Foreign

13 Section 5 para. 1 of the Regulation on Foreign Trade.

14 E.g., in the case of Sierra Leone, see Section 69g of the Regulation on Foreign Trade.

15 Cf. Section 3 of the Law on Foreigners.

16 Cf. Section 27 para. 2 of the Law on Foreign Trade.

17 Cf. Article 80 para. 1 of the Basic Law.

Trade, though, does not contain any specific definition; it allows for the implementation of any treaty obligation initially approved by Parliament. If the relevant treaty itself uses precise terms, this does not pose a problem. But if, as in the case of the powers of the Security Council under the United Nations Charter, the treaty is worded very broadly, the initial parliamentary decision ratifying the treaty has not defined the obligations to be implemented in any precise manner. It is therefore doubtful whether in this case the requirements of the Basic Law are met.[18] This might present even more difficulties if, as has been described above, the Parliament does not even possess the power to review the regulations in question. The Federal Constitutional Court, however, held with respect to one of the relevant Sections of the Law on Foreign Trade that its broad wording did not violate the *Grundgesetz*.[19]

(3) Ad Hoc *Legislation, Executive Orders and Decrees*

On the basis of the Law on Foreign Trade, the Federal Government enacts, where necessary, *ad hoc* regulations to prohibit trade as required by the Security Council. Usually, this would result in a modification of the Regulation on Foreign Trade (*Außenwirtschaftsverordnung*) which contains most restrictions and prohibitions. This method of implementation has now been replaced more and more by EC legislation which is directly effective in the municipal legal order and, therefore, renders national implementation superfluous. In several cases, however, the Federal Government has inserted the EC regulation into the Regulation on Foreign Trade, e.g. in the case of Libya.[20] Most commonly, though, EC regulations are now merely published in the Federal Gazette.[21]

Where quick action by the German authorities is necessary – which is the case in areas where the EC has no power to implement or when it has not yet implemented sanctions – the Minister of Economics often makes use of the power to enact provisional executive orders as described above. Usually, they are restricted to the freezing of funds.[22]

Real *ad hoc legislation* has occurred for the cooperation with the International Criminal Tribunals for the Former Yugoslavia and for Rwanda where laws were enacted to allow for the transfer of persons to the tribunals which otherwise would not have been possible.[23]

18 For criticism see, in particular, Volker Epping, *Die Außenwirtschaftsfreiheit* (1998), p. 316 *et seq.*; cf. also Ress, *supra* note 2, p. 229 *et seq.*

19 Decision of 11 October 1994, *Entscheidungen des Bundesverfassungsgerichts*, vol. 91, p. 148, 162 *et seq.*; see, in the same vein, Federal Administrative Court, Decision of 17 October 1991, *Entscheidungen des Bundesverwaltungsgerichts*, vol. 89, p. 121, 130 *et seq.*

20 Cf. Sections 69l, 69m, 69n of the Regulation on Foreign Trade.

21 See *infra*, p. 244.

22 Cf. the Order of 2 June 1992 in the case of Yugoslavia, *Bundesanzeiger* of 4 June 1992, p. 4493. For similar recent measures against terrorists, see the German *Report to the Security Council Committee established pursuant to Resolution 1373 (2001) concerning Counter-Terrorism*, available at http://www.auswaertiges-amt.de/www/de/infoservice/download/pdf/vn/ctc_bericht.pdf (25 January 2002).

23 Cf., with respect to the ICTY, the Law of 10 April 1995, *Bundesgesetzblatt* 1995 I, p. 485; with respect to Rwanda, the Law of 4 May 1998, *Bundesgesetzblatt* 1998 I, p. 843.

Moreover, *ad hoc* legislation was enacted in the framework of efforts to cope with terrorism.[24] This very broad legislation, however, though occurring after Security Council Resolution 1373 (2001), responded rather to the general international "fight against terrorism" than to the resolution. Thus it contains a far broader range of measures than required by the Security Council, and much of its content can be regarded as independent from the Council's Chapter VII action.

(4) Other Provisions

Specific provisions exist for penal sanctions against sanctions violators. While usually violators of the Law on Foreign Trade and the Regulation on Foreign Trade only have to face administrative fines, penal sanctions exist for illegal trade with arms and related products and for other acts which endanger the security of Germany, the peaceful coexistence of peoples or the foreign relations of the Federal Republic. A much more severe penalty is, however, provided for in cases where acts violate regulations which serve to implement Security Council sanctions under Chapter VII of the United Nations Charter. In these cases, sanctions violators face imprisonment for at least two years.[25] Of course, a range of other provisions criminalise behaviour in violation of Security Council measures: e.g., in the case of Security Council Resolution 1373 (2001), the pre-existing anti-terrorist provisions of the German Criminal Code cover many of the penal sanctions called for by the Security Council.[26]

III. The Legal Basis of Domestic Measures Based on EU Decisions

(1) The Legal Basis of the Competence of the European Union

The legal basis for the implementation of sanctions by the EU and the EC is explained in detail in the report of Daniel Bethlehem. Here, it shall simply be noted that the EC now enjoys a virtually comprehensive competence to order sanctions in virtue of Article 301, but also 133 (trade) and 60 (capital movements).

(2) Limits to the competence of the European Union

Until recently, the EC had no or did not exercise its competence in three areas: the trade in arms and related materiel, entry prohibitions for foreign nationals, and capital movements. The Maastricht Treaty has removed the latter restriction, and the EC now also regulates the freezing of funds and other aspects of capital movements.[27] Arms embar-

---

24 See, in particular, the Prevention of Terrorism Act of 9 January 2002, *Bundesgesetzblatt* 2002 I, p. 361. See also the *Report*, *supra* note 22.

25 Article 34 para. 4 of the Law on Foreign Trade; for the text see *infra* p. 242.

26 See especially Article 129a of the Criminal Code and the explanations in the *Report*, *supra* note 22.

27 Cf. Article 2 of EC Regulation 1705/98 of 28 July 1998, *O.J.* 1998 L 215 of 1 August 1998, concerning Angola (UNITA); Article 3 of Regulation 337/2000 of 14 February 2000, *O.J.* 2000 L 43/1, concerning Afghanistan.

goes and entry prohibitions are, however, subject only to EU common positions, but not to EC regulations.[28] For arms embargoes, this is due to Article 296 which is interpreted as giving at least concurring jurisdiction to Member States. Therefore, in that respect only national measures are being adopted.[29] The same holds true for entry prohibitions. For instance, in the case of the arms embargo on Sierra Leone, the Federal Government inserted a new Section 69g into the Regulation on Foreign Trade which reads:

> "The following activities ... are prohibited: The sale and supply of armaments and related goods of all kinds and spare parts, including the sale and supply of weapons, munitions, military vehicles and their equipment and paramilitary equipment. ...".

However, the primacy of EC measures over national law faces limits in the German legal order. Already in 1974, the Federal Constitutional Court reserved to itself the right to evaluate the conformity of EC acts with fundamental rights as enshrined in the *Grundgesetz*, as long as the EC itself did not provide for an equally effective protection of these rights.[30] In 1986, the Court found that the required degree of protection had been achieved, but indicated that it would reclaim its right to an own evaluation in case of a change.[31] The latter reservation has been reaffirmed in the 1993 decision on the Maastricht Treaty.[32] In 2000, however, the Court clarified that it would exercise its power of review only if standards of fundamental rights protection in the EU were in general too low. In contrast, a divergence of EU standards from German constitutional standards in a single case would not suffice to draw into doubt the prevalence of the community legal order.[33] Thus, it is unlikely that EC measures will be disregarded by German courts for violation of constitutional rights. As for measures implementing United Nations sanctions, such a case could practically occur only with respect to the right to property. Up to

28 Cf. the Common Position 98/409/CFSP of 29 June 1998, *O.J.* 1998 L 187 of 1 July 1998, concerning Sierra Leone; and the Common Position 2001/154/CFSP of 26 February 2001, *O.J.* 2001 L 057/1, concerning Afghanistan (Taliban), in contrast to EC Regulation 467/2001 of 6 March 2001, *O.J.* 2001 L 067/1.

29 See *Völkerrechtliche Praxis der Bundesrepublik Deutschland*; 29 *ZaöRV* (1969) 135 *et seq.* (Southern Rhodesia); 39 *ZaöRV* (1979) 597 and 52 (1992) 946, 1041 (South Africa); 52 *ZaöRV* (1992) 944 *et seq.*, 982 *et seq.* (Iraq and Kuweit); 53 *ZaöRV* (1993) 1041, 1083 *et seq.*; 54 *ZaöRV* (1994) 962 *et seq.*; 55 *ZaöRV* (1995) 1197 *et seq.*, 1230 *et seq.*; 57 *ZaöRV* (1997) 1090 (Former Yugoslavia); 54 *ZaöRV* (1994) 962; 55 *ZaöRV* (1995) 1198; 56 *ZaöRV* (1996) 1135 (Libya); 56 *ZaöRV* (1996) 1135 (Haiti).

30 Federal Constitutional Court, Judgment of 29 May 1974, Solange I, *Entscheidungen des Bundesverfassungsgerichts*, vol. 37, p. 271, 280 *et seq.*

31 Federal Constitutional Court, Judgment of 22 October 1986, Solange II, *Entscheidungen des Bundesverfassungsgerichts*, vol. 73, p. 339, 375 *et seq.*

32 Federal Constitutional Court, Judgment of 12 October 1993, Maastricht, *Entscheidungen des Bundesverfassungsgerichts*, vol. 89, p. 155, 174 *et seq.*; on the problems of this decision, see Jochen Abr. Frowein, 'Das Maastricht-Urteil und die Grenzen der Verfassungsgerichtsbarkeit'; 54 *ZaöRV* (1994) *et seq.*

33 Federal Constitutional Court, Judgment of 7 June 2000, Bananenmarktordnung, *Entscheidungen des Bundesverfassungsgerichts*, vol. 102, p. 147 *et seq.*

now, the courts have not had to decide the issue,[34] but, as will be shown below, it seems rather improbable that they would find a violation of the core of the German constitutional guarantee of property.[35]

(3) *The Interplay Between European Union and Domestic Legislation in Sanctions Implementation*

Usually, the first step in the implementation of United Nations sanctions is the adoption of a common position in the EU which often simply refers to the Security Council resolution. Then, the EC adopts a regulation in its fields of competence, and the Member State takes measures in the areas not covered by the EC regulation.[36]

a. The example of the Libyan case

The implementation of Security Council Resolution 883 (1993) concerning Libya might serve as an example for this interplay of EU and German legislation. By this resolution, the Security Council expanded sanctions against Libya. It ordered the freezing of Libyan funds, prohibited the supply of materiel for the oil industry and for aircraft, and introduced restrictions on the activities of the Libyan airline. Thereupon, the Council of the European Union, in the framework of the intergovernmental Common Foreign and Security Policy, took the following, very general decision:

> "Economic relations with Libya shall be reduced in accordance with the relevant provisions of Resolution 883 (93) adopted by the Security Council on 11 November 1993."[37]

In order to implement this decision, the Council of the European Union took further action under the EC treaty seven days later. It adopted two regulations, one preventing the supply of certain goods and services to Libya,[38] the other prohibiting the satisfying of claims with regard to contracts affected by the sanctions.[39]

Two weeks later, the German Minister of Economics amended the German Regulation on Foreign Trade.[40] The new Section 69m was entitled:

---

34 See, e.g., Federal Court of Justice, Judgment of 27 January 1994, *Juristenzeitung* 1994, p. 725.

35 See *infra* p. 256.

36 See, e.g., in the case of Angola (UNITA), following SC Resolution 1173 (1998) and 1176 (1998), the Common Position 98/425/CFSP of 3 July 1998, *O.J.* 1998 L 190 of 4 July 1998; the EC Regulation 1705/98 of 28 July 1998, *O.J.* 1998 L 215 of 1 August 1998; and the German Runderlaß Außenwirtschaft of 10 September 1998, in *Bundesanzeiger* of 17 September 1998.

37 Decision 93/614/CFSP of 22 November 1993, *O.J.* 1993 L 295/7.

38 Regulation 3274/93 of 29 November 1993, *O.J.* 1993 L 295/1 *et seq.*

39 Regulation 3275/93 of 29 November 1993, *O.J.* 1993 L 295/4 *et seq.*

40 Thirty-first regulation amending the Regulation on Foreign Trade of 14 December 1993, *Bundesanzeiger* of 21 December 1993, p. 10937 *et seq.*

> "Provisions in order to ensure the punishment in case of a violation of restrictions by the European Communities on the basis of Security Council resolutions 748 (1992) and 883 (1993) (Chapter VII of the Charter)".

While this section repeated – in the form of German law – the provisions of the first EC regulation, punishment for violations of the second regulation was achieved in another way: it was simply published – as such – in the Federal Gazette.[41] In addition, the new Section 69n of the German Regulation on Foreign Trade contained restrictions required by the Security Council which had not been implemented by the European Community. Its main part read:

> "The disposition over [Libyan] accounts at banks based on German territory, and over [Libyan] claims, shall be prohibited."

As the example shows, until recently, the main field of national implementation was the regulation of capital movements. Now, as has been said above, domestic law need regulate only arms trade restrictions and entry prohibitions.

Although EC regulations are directly applicable in the German legal system it is nevertheless necessary that the German legislator create a separate legal basis for criminal or administrative punishment in case of violation of the prohibitions since, under German law, criminal or administrative punishment is only possible if expressly authorised by a specific legal provision. The EC has not yet gained jurisdiction to lay down such rules; therefore, it only calls in a more general way for the adoption by Member States of "effective, proportionate, and dissuasive" sanctions.[42]

As will be shown in greater detail below, German law provides for different ways to attach penal sanctions to the original EC measures. Initially, the Federal Government most often chose an option which did not seem to correspond entirely to the Community legal order since it neglected the independent importance of the EC measures. More recent practice, however, shows due respect for the primacy and direct effect of EC law.

b. The initial way of penalising sanctions violations

As has been mentioned above, the primary basis for punishment under German law is laid down in Section 34 paragraph 4 of the Law on Foreign Trade[43] which reads:

> "By imprisonment of no less than two years shall be punished a person who violates a provision of this law or of a regulation based on this law or of an EC measure to restrict foreign trade published in the Collection of Federal Statutes or in the Federal Gazette,

---

41 *Bundesanzeiger* of 21 December 1993, p. 10938 *et seq.*

42 See, e.g., Article 9 of Regulation 2580/2001 of 27 December 2001, *O.J.* 2001 L 344/70 *et seq.*

43 See also the judgments of the Federal Court of Justice in *Entscheidungen des Bundesgerichtshofes in Strafsachen*, vol. 41, p. 127; *Neue Zeitschrift für Strafrecht* 1995, p. 550; *Neue Juristische Wochenschrift* 1996, p. 602.

> which serves to implement an economic sanction measure taken by the United Nations Security Council under Chapter VII of the Charter of the United Nations..."

According to that provision, a person may be punished who violates a national or EC regulation designed to implement United Nations sanctions only if it has been published in the German Collection of Federal Statutes (*Bundesgesetzblatt*) or in the Federal Gazette (*Bundesanzeiger*). Until recently, the Federal Government achieved this most often by inserting the text of the EC regulation into the German Regulation on Foreign Trade. Such provisions were usually worded in the following manner:

> "With a view to ensuring the punishment in case of a violation of the respective provisions by the European Communities, shall be prohibited: 1. The import of all products originating in or coming from ..."

This repetition of EC rules in national law was designed to ensure that persons under German jurisdiction may inform themselves about the respective prohibitions by following carefully the German statute books on regulations concerning foreign trade.

The relationship between such national implementation acts and the respective EC measures has also been subject to decisions of the Federal Court of Justice.[44] The Court held that although the separate German legislative acts were constitutive in some respects, in particular as a basis for punishment, they were only declaratory insofar as they proclaimed EC prohibitions with direct effect in Germany. It also raised the question whether the German legislative acts should be regarded as constitutive in their entirety if the EC Regulations were illegal or even void under EC law. Even if that were the case, however, the Court reasoned, the intention of the German legislator to merely enact declaratory prohibitions precluded an interpretation of them as being constitutive.[45]

As a consequence of that system, in German practice the EC regulation was often of little importance. Usually, only the Regulation on Foreign Trade was taken note of, and the independent value and direct effect of the EC measure was denied.[46] This practice seemed also to run counter to the jurisprudence of the European Court of Justice according to which national measures may not disguise the origin of norms in community law.[47] In the case of sanctions implementation, one might have argued that repetition was necessary for penal sanctions,[48] but still the tension remained.

---

44 Federal Court of Justice, Judgment of 27 January 1994, *Juristenzeitung* 1994, p. 725.

45 See Jochen Abr. Frowein, 'Regionale Sicherheitssysteme und nationales Recht', in *Verhandlungen des Sechzigsten Deutschen Juristentages Münster 1994*, Bd. II/2, München 1994, p. Q 31.

46 For striking examples, see Federal Court of Justice, Judgment of 12 April 1995, *Neue Zeitschrift für Strafrecht* 1995, p. 550 *et seq.*; Judgment of 21 April 1995, *Entscheidungen des Bundesgerichtshofs in Strafsachen*, vol. 41, p. 127, 131 *et seq.*

47 Cf. European Court of Justice, Judgment of 10 October 1973, Variola, *Reports* 1973, p. 981, 990; for the same criticism, see in particular Schneider, *supra* note 2, p. 183 *et seq.*

48 For this view, see State Court of Braunschweig, Judgment of 18 November 1996, 36 KLs 402 Js 49043/93.

c. Recent trends

Recent practice, however, shifted from this dubious way of implementation to methods more in conformity with EC law. The first of them is the publication of the EC regulation as such in the Federal Gazette.[49] This fulfils the criteria of Section 34 paragraph 4 of the Law on Foreign Trade, but also highlights the origin of the prohibition in EC law. While already used in 1993, this way of implementation has become most common since 1996,[50] and it has also been adopted in the context of the anti-terrorism measures in 2001.[51]

In some cases, a different option has been chosen. For example, in the case of Sierra Leone, the Federal Government has simply added a reference to some conduct in violation of an EC regulation to the German Regulation on Foreign Trade.[52] Usually, this leads to the possibility of an administrative fine,[53] but if such conduct threatens "the peaceful coexistence of the peoples of the world" it is equally subject to penal sanctions under Section 34 paragraph 2 of the Law on Foreign Trade. This legal means had to be chosen especially in cases where the EC measure exceeded what was required by the Security Council resolution, since in this case Section 34 paragraph 4 of the Law on Foreign Trade was not available as a basis for punishment.[54] In some cases, however, this led to a confusing multitude of implementation measures. E.g., in order to implement the sanctions against Sierra Leone, the German Federal Government inserted Section 69g into the Regulation on Foreign Trade (regulating the trade with arms), it published the EC regulation in the Federal Gazette (with respect to trade with petroleum), and it inserted a reference to that EC measure in Section 70 of the Regulation on Foreign Trade (with respect to those forms of conduct not covered by the Security Council resolution). In the case of Angola, on the other hand, the Federal Government only added the reference to the respective EC regulation to Section 70 of the German Regulation on Foreign Trade without reproducing the text. This seems the most simple and most promising way for future instances.

49 See e.g. *Bundesanzeiger* 1993, 10938 (Council Regulation (EC) 3275/93 of 29 November 1993, *O.J.* L 295/4 (Libya)).

50 Cf. the publication of EC Regulation 2465/96 on Iraq in *Bundesanzeiger* of 28 January 1997; of EC Regulation 2465/97 on Sierra Leone in *Bundesanzeiger* of 13 January 1998; of EC Regulation 1745/2000 on Sierra Leone, in *Bundesanzeiger* of 20 September 2000; of EC Regulation 1354/2001 on Afghanistan in *Bundesanzeiger* of 17 March and 24 April 2001; and of EC Regulation 1146/2001 in *Bundesanzeiger* of 22 June 2001.

51 Cf. the publication of EC regulations in *Bundesanzeiger* of 7 November 2001, of 16 November 2001, of 21 November 2001, of 12 December 2001, and of 15 January 2002.

52 Cf. Section 70 para. 5c, 5d, and 5g (on Yugoslavia) and para. 5f (on Angola) of the Regulation on Foreign Trade. A similar provision was adopted in the case of Sierra Leone, cf. Runderlaß Außenwirtschaft Nr. 2/98 of 20 January 1998, in *Bundesanzeiger* of 29 January 1998.

53 Section 33 para. 4 of the Law on Foreign Trade.

54 Cf. Runderlaß Außenwirtschaft Nr. 2/98 of 20 January 1998 on Sierra Leone, in *Bundesanzeiger* of 29 January 1998.

IV. The Content of Domestic Implementation Measures

In principle, the Federal Republic has sought to implement Security Council sanctions resolutions to their full extent. In some cases, however, domestic implementation measures as well as their interplay with EC regulations have led to minor gaps. Some of them, e.g. those relating to the scope of the prohibitions, are likely to disappear since the EC is now competent to regulate them entirely. Others, in particular those with respect to the entry into force and to existing contracts, point to more fundamental problems.

(1) The Scope of Prohibitions

a. The prohibition on satisfying claims

Problems concerning the scope of prohibitions exist only in two areas. First, the prohibition of satisfying claims of the authorities or nationals of the target State has often been implemented with delay. The competence to regulate this area was assumed by the EC even before the entry into force of the provisions on capital movements in the Maastricht Treaty. Thus, already in December 1992, the Council enacted a regulation on this matter with respect to Iraq.[55] This regulation, however, was evidence of the main problem in the implementation of this sort of obligations: while the Security Council had adopted Resolution 687 (1991) on 3 April, the EC implemented the prohibition only twenty months later. In the meantime, no national measures were taken either: already in August 1990, after Resolution 661 (1990), Germany had frozen Iraqi funds,[56] but in April 1991, it took no steps to implement the new obligations arising from Resolution 687 (1991).

A similar gap in the implementation was to be observed in the case of the Federal Republic of Yugoslavia where the prohibition of satisfying claims in Resolution 757 (1992) of 30 May 1992 was implemented by an EC regulation only in July 1994.[57] This was not countenanced by national measures either. The Federal Republic had, as in the case of Iraq, carried out its obligations with respect to the freezing of funds immediately after the adoption of Resolution 757 (1992),[58] but no action was taken with respect to the prohibition on satisfying claims until August 1994, when Germany published the EC regulation in its Federal Gazette.[59]

Of course, an important part of the prohibition on satisfying claims is already covered by the freezing of funds: if no funds may be made available to the authorities in the FRY, no payment to them is allowed and therefore, usually, claims of such authorities cannot be satisfied any more. But the purposes of both prohibitions differ significantly: while the

55 EC Regulation 3541/92 of 7 December 1992, *O.J.* 1992 L 361.

56 Sections 69a to 69e on Iraq were inserted into the Regulation on Foreign Trade on 9 August 1990, cf. *Bundesanzeiger* of 11 August 1990, p. 4065.

57 EC Regulation 1264/94 of 30 May 1994, *O.J.* 1994 L 139, 4.

58 Executive Order of 2 June 1992, *Bundesanzeiger* of 4 June 1992, p. 4493; Regulation of 11 June 1992, *Bundesanzeiger* of 13 June 1992, p. 4705.

59 *Bundesanzeiger* of 4 August 1994, p. 8025.

freezing of funds usually serves to prevent gains of the authorities or the economy of the target state, the prohibition on satisfying claims means to ensure that transaction partners in the target State cannot claim compensation for the violation of contracts necessitated by the sanctions regime. Moreover, usually gaps exist between both prohibitions: for example, in the case of Yugoslavia the obligation to freeze funds under No. 5 of Resolution 757 (1992) encompassed only funds of the authorities and of commercial, industrial or public utility undertakings in the FRY, whereas the prohibition on satisfying claims under No. 9 of the Resolution applied to any person or body in Yugoslavia. Thus, the personal scope differed, and the German regulation of June 1992 did not cover all the cases of the prohibition under No. 9 of the Resolution. According to the official explanation of the Federal Government, it was not meant to cover those other cases either: the national regulation only served to implement No. 5 of Resolution 757 (1992).[60]

b. The freezing of funds

The other problem concerns the freezing of funds itself. Until the EC gained new powers in this area in 1994, only national authorities could effect the implementation. Germany usually took measures in this regard, but often did not exactly implement the obligations contained in Security Council resolutions.

Thus, in the case of Iraq, the Security Council had decided in Resolution 661 (1990) that States should not make available any funds to any person or body within Iraq or Kuwait. The German executive order of 7 August, however, was restricted to funds of Iraqi authorities.[61] This was remedied in part by the regulation enacted by the Federal Government three days later which covered payments to the Iraqi authorities as well as to individual persons.[62] But this regulation suffered from the fact that, contrary to the Security Council resolution, it prohibited only payments of persons within their territory, but not also of German nationals elsewhere. This latter point will be dealt with later in greater detail.

In the case of Haiti, Germany fully implemented the initial prohibition to make funds available to the Haitian authorities,[63] but failed to implement the extension of these measures effected by the Security Council in Resolution 917 (1994). In this Resolution, the Security Council had broadened the scope of the prohibition to funds of officers of the Haitian military and police, participants in the coup d'état and their families. The German Government, however, did not act upon this resolution.

A particular problem arises with respect to funds of foreign embassies which enjoy special protection under the law of diplomatic and consular relations. In Germany, embassy accounts are not generally excluded from the freezing of funds, also for the

60 Cf. *Bundesanzeiger* of 13 June 1992, p. 4706.

61 Executive Order of 7 August 1990, *Bundesanzeiger* of 8 August 1990, p. 4013.

62 Regulation of 9 August 1990, *Bundesanzeiger* of 11 August 1990, p. 4065.

63 See Executive Order of 15 July 1993, *Bundesanzeiger* of 27 July 1993, p. 6798; Executive Order of 19 October 1993, *Bundesanzeiger* of 29 October 1993, p. 9777; Regulation of 25 March 1994, *Bundesanzeiger* of 30 March 1994, p. 3593.

reason that, otherwise, they might be abused. As far as funds are necessary for the maintenance of core diplomatic and consular functions, however, the German Government authorises their use on a case-by-case basis.

(2) Personal and Extraterritorial Scope

Unlike many Security Council resolutions and the corresponding EC regulations, German measures usually address only transactions on German territory. Most often, they do not cover transactions of German nationals elsewhere, although Section 7 paragraph 3 of the Law on Foreign Trade expressly provides for this possibility.

Thus the obligation of States not to make available funds to persons in Iraq and Kuwait, created by Resolution 661 (1990), was implemented in Germany only in part. The German regulation of 9 August 1990 prohibited payments and other financial transactions only to people and bodies *within* German territory.[64] This is all the more surprising since, in the same regulation, the German Federal Government repeated EC provisions applying also to nationals of Member States outside their territories. Moreover, the Government prohibited any services of German nationals in Iraq or Kuwait connected with the trade embargo. But it did not choose to apply the same for the obligation not to make available funds. The same held true for the implementation of Security Council Resolution 757 (1992) on the Former Yugoslavia,[65] and of Security Council Resolution 883 (1993) on Libya.[66]

On the other hand, the personal scope of German restrictions on trade with arms is much broader. It includes the sale of arms or services connected with arms by German nationals outside German territory.[67]

(3) Entry into Force

While the EC often provides for retroactive application of its regulations implementing Security Council resolutions,[68] the German Federal Government never did so. Therefore, implementation measures become effective only on the day after their publication which is usually several days after the Security Council resolution. Thus, the new prohibitions on financial services decided on by the Security Council in Resolution 820 of 17 April 1993 on Yugoslavia came into force in Germany only on 29 April.[69] Likewise, the measures against Haiti required by Security Council Resolution 841 of 16 June 1993 became

---

64 Regulation of 9 August 1990, *Bundesanzeiger* of 11 August 1990, p. 4065.

65 Cf. Executive Order of 2 June 1992, *Bundesanzeiger* of 4 June 1992, p. 4493; Section 69k of the Regulation on Foreign Trade on 11 June 1992, *Bundesanzeiger* of 13 June 1992.

66 Cf. Section 69n of the Regulation on Foreign Trade, *Bundesanzeiger* of 21 December 1993, p. 10938.

67 Sections 40, 45b of the Law on Foreign Trade; and, e.g., Section 69l para. 2 of the Regulation on Foreign Trade, *Bundesanzeiger* of 21 December 1993, p. 10937, on Libya.

68 See, e.g., EC regulation 1432/92 of 1 June 1992, *O.J.* 1992 L 151, 4 of 3 June 1992 on Yugoslavia. According to Article 1, the prohibitions came into force on 31 May 1992.

69 Cf. para. 1 of the Executive Order of 26 April 1993, *Bundesanzeiger* of 28 April 1993.

effective in Germany only on 28 July, i.e. six weeks later.[70] The EC regulations in this case, however, provided for retroactive application from 23 June, the date the Security Council had fixed for the start of sanctions.[71]

Another problem with respect to timely implementation stems from the lack of clarity of Security Council resolutions. Thus, in the case of Afghanistan, the Resolution left open which were the persons, funds, and aircraft to which it applied, and left it to the sanctions committee to designate them, as had been the case in other situations.[72] Before that designation, however, implementation by the Member States and in particular the EC proved difficult, and the adoption of an EC regulation was considerably delayed.[73]

(4) *Provisions Relating to Existing Contracts*

German implementation measures, unlike most EC regulations,[74] usually do not contain specific provisions on existing contracts.[75] While it is disputed whether, in this case, they are subject to the prohibition or not, better arguments militate in favour of an interpretation which takes account of the Security Council resolution to be implemented.[76] This would, in particular, correspond with the jurisprudence of the Federal Constitutional Court according to which domestic legislation should be deemed to conform to international obligations unless there is evidence of legislative intention to the contrary.[77]

In some cases, transactions in connection with existing contracts are specifically exempted from the general prohibition, but need prior authorisation which is granted only if the purposes of the Security Council resolution are not prejudiced.[78] This particular treatment of existing contracts is rendered necessary by Section 2 paragraph 3 of the German Law on Foreign Trade which reads:

> "Restrictions must not affect existing contracts unless this severely endangers the achievement of their purpose."

70 Cf. para. 1 of the Executive Order of 15 July 1993, *Bundesanzeiger* of 27 July 1993.

71 Cf. Article 1 of EC Regulation 1608/93 of 24 June 1993, *O.J.* 1993 L 155, 2 of 26 June 1993.

72 E.g., the case of Sierra Leone. Cf. SC Resolution 1171 (1998) of 5 June 1998 and the list of persons designated by the Committee in SC/6472 of 28 January 1998.

73 Cf. EC Regulation 337/2000, which was adopted on 14 February 2000, i.e. four months after the adoption of SC resolution 1267 (1999). On the lack of clarity of the obligations deriving from the SC Resolution, see in particular para. 4 of the preamble of the EC Regulation.

74 See, e.g., Article 4 of EC regulation 1608/93 of 24 June 1993, *O.J.* 1993 L 155, 2 of 26 June 1993, on Haiti.

75 See, e.g., Section 69e of the Regulation on Foreign Trade, inserted by Regulation of 9 August 1990, *Bundesanzeiger* of 11 August 1990, p. 4066.

76 See Ernst Hocke et al. (eds.), *Außenwirtschaftsrecht*, vol. 1, commentary on Section 2 of the Law on Foreign Trade, para. 5. But see also Epping, *supra* note 18, 493 et seq., who rejects any abstract approach and regards the administrative authorities as the suitable organs to weigh the different interests and rights in cause.

77 Decision of 26 March 1987, *Entscheidungen des Bundesverfassungsgerichts*, vol. 74, p. 358, 370.

78 Cf., e.g., the Executive Order of 26 April 1993 and the regulation of 9 June 1993 implementing SC Resolution 820 (1993) on Yugoslavia, *Bundesanzeiger*, 28 April 1993, 15 June 1993.

This provision reflects the particular constitutional status of existing contracts. Since they are covered by the protection of property under Article 14 of the German Basic Law, any interference must be justified and proportional to the aim pursued. Moreover, compensation is due if the restriction amounts to an expropriation. Both the German Parliament and the German courts, however, hold the view that embargo measures affecting existing contracts do not constitute expropriations because foreign trade is generally less stable than internal trade, and suddenly changing restrictions are therefore foreseeable.[79] The question of compensation will be dealt with in greater detail below.[80]

The private law consequences of an interference with existing contracts are still unclear since courts have not yet dealt with the question. Doctrine, however, holds that an embargo can amount to a durable impossibility to perform the obligations under a contract. In this case, both parties to the contract would be freed of their obligations, but would not have to compensate one another for the losses incurred. In contrast, if a contract were entered into after the enactment of an embargo, it would be considered contrary to the law and therefore null and void.[81]

(5) Provisions for Humanitarian Exceptions

Both in material and procedural regard, the German provisions on humanitarian exceptions do not seem to deviate from those in Security Council resolutions.

(6) Provisions for Penal Sanctions

The penal sanctions system has already been outlined above.[82] It suffices to recall that Section 34 paragraph 4 of the German Law on Foreign Trade provides for specific penalties in case of violation of Security Council sanctions which are implemented in EC law or national law. While persons violating export prohibitions in general can be sentenced to up to 5 years' imprisonment, violators of United Nations sanctions face imprisonment from 2 to 15 years. This means especially that no release on probation is admitted and that preparatory acts are also punished. In addition, according to recent changes in legislation, gains deriving from prohibited transactions are subject to confiscation.[83]

Penal sanctions apply also for violations by German nationals outside German territory if the measure violated provides for such extraterritorial application.[84]

---

79 See Hocke et al., *supra* note 76, commentary on Section 2 of the Law on Foreign Trade, no. 6; but see also Ress, *supra* note 2, p. 272, 287 *et seq.*; Epping, *supra* note 18, p. 495 *et seq.*

80 See *infra* p. 252 *et seq.*

81 Cf. Ress, *supra* note 2, p. 245 *et seq.*; Stefan Oeter, 'Das UN-Embargo gegen Serbien', 16 *Praxis des Internationalen Privat- und Verfahrensrechts* (1996), p. 76 *et seq.*; Claudia Bittner, 'Die Auswirkungen des Irak-Embargos für Warenlieferungsverträge: Zivilrechtliche Folgen von Handelsbeschränkungen', *Recht der Internationalen Wirtschaft* 1994, p. 458 *et seq.*

82 See *supra* p. 242, 244.

83 See, e.g., State Court of Stuttgart, Judgment of 5 September 1997, 10 Kls 144 Js 27241/97; and Federal Court of Justice, Judgment of 18 December 1997, 1 StR 722/97.

84 Section 35 of the Law on Foreign Trade.

V. Domestic Procedures for Implementation and Enforcement

(1) Coordination between Different Ministerial Activities

Regulations for the implementation of Security Council resolutions are adopted by the Federal Government as a whole, thus with the participation of all ministers.[85] Such regulations which are designed to ensure compliance with international obligations, could also be adopted by the Federal Minister for Economics with the consent of the Foreign Minister and the Minister of Finance;[86] but for the implementation of Security Council sanctions, this way has not yet been chosen. Until now, the Federal Minister of Economics has only made use of his power to issue executive orders for a provisional phase of six months which were later replaced by an ordinary regulation. For these orders, consent of the Foreign Minister and the Minister of Finance is also required.[87]

At a later stage, and where no such regulation is needed, the implementation of sanctions is effected, in general, by the administrative authorities of the federal states (*Länder*). But in many fields, this competence has been transferred to federal institutions. The most far-reaching competence in this regard is exercised by the Federal Office of Economics and Export Control (*Bundesamt für Wirtschaft und Ausfuhrkontrolle*) which decides on all authorisations concerning trade and services. The Federal Office for Agriculture and Foodstuffs is competent for all matters concerning agricultural products, i.e. also for the supply of food for humanitarian purposes. The Federal Border Guards decide on the entry of persons. Several other specific institutions exercise competences in this field.[88] While sanctions are therefore executed mainly by Federal authorities, no real concentration of this task has occurred.

(2) The Role of Central Banks

The Federal Central Bank (*Bundesbank*) is competent for all authorisations pertaining to capital movements and financial transactions. In addition, the Federal Government must consult it before adopting any regulation or executive order in these fields.[89]

(3) Procedures Relating to Sanctions Violations

Since no specific procedures for the detection of violations and the prosecution of sanctions violators exist, the general rules apply, and, in case of suspicion, the public prosecutor would direct the prosecution and would make use of the police and the customs authorities for this purpose. The prosecution enjoys wider powers than for ordinary

85 Section 27 para. 1 of the Law on Foreign Trade.

86 Section 27 para. 1 of the Law on Foreign Trade.

87 Section 2 para. 2 of the Law on Foreign Trade.

88 Cf. Section 28 of the Law on Foreign Trade; and Hocke et al., *supra* note 76, commentary on Section 28 of the Law on Foreign Trade, no. 6.

89 Section 2 para. 2, 27 para. 1, 28 para. 2 of the Law on Foreign Trade.

crimes: it may, e.g., intercept telephone calls and listen in private rooms if necessary and authorised by a judge, in cases of danger even by the public prosecutor.[90] Similarly broad powers are granted to the authorities for preventive action.[91]

Sanctions violators have been prosecuted in a number of cases some of which have been taken to higher courts. In at least six cases, the Federal Court of Justice had to decide on appeals of persons convicted for violations of the embargo against the Federal Republic of Yugoslavia.[92] In two of these cases the accused had operated bus services from Germany to towns in Serbia. One of the accused in these cases was acquitted because the mere transport of person to and within Serbia did not yet constitute a violation of the Security Council measures.[93] The other accused, however, was convicted because he had not only run the bus service but also had for this purpose paid sub-operators in Serbia. This transfer of funds contravened the embargo.[94] In yet another case, the accused had imported goods, especially fruit, but it was unclear whether these had been actually produced or only stored in Serbia and Montenegro, and what was required by the wording "originating in" as provided for by the Security Council Resolution. After a thorough interpretation of the Resolution, the Federal Court of Justice concluded that the broader meaning had to be accepted and therefore largely confirmed the conviction of the accused by the lower courts.[95] In another case, the Federal Court of Justice had to deal with the assertion by the accused that he had not been aware of the fact that the transport of a vehicle to and its sale in Serbia contravened the embargo. According to the Court, this constituted an avoidable error in law which did not remove the guilt of the accused but could lead to less severe punishment.[96]

Violations of the embargo against the Federal Republic of Yugoslavia also formed the main part of cases before lower courts. Thus, the Supreme Court of the State of Bavaria confirmed the conviction of a person who had travelled to Serbia and had there allowed another person to use his car. Although, according to the Court, the travel by car did not yet constitute an "exportation" of the car, the fact that he made the car available to a third person did.[97] Other courts had to deal with cases relating to the import of

---

90 Cf. Sections 100a, 100c of the Code of Criminal Procedure.

91 Section 39 of the Law on Foreign Trade.

92 Cf. Judgments of 12 April 1995, *Neue Zeitschrift für Strafrecht* 1995, p. 551 *et seq.*; Judgment of 21 April 1995, *Entscheidungen des Bundesgerichtshofes in Strafsachen*, vol. 41, p. 127 *et seq.*; Judgment of 21 April 1995, 1 StR 699/94; Judgment of 11 September 1995, 1 StR 242/95; Judgment of 28 September 1995, *Neue Juristische Wochenschrift* 1996, p. 602; Judgment of 14 July 1998, *Rechtsprechung des Bundesgerichtshofs (BGHR)* AWG para. 34 UN-Embargo 4.

93 Federal Court of Justice, Judgment of 21 April 1995, 1 StR 699/94.

94 Judgment of 21 April 1995, *Entscheidungen des Bundesgerichtshofes in Strafsachen*, vol. 41, p. 127 *et seq.*

95 Federal Court of Justice, Judgment of 28 September 1995, *Neue Juristische Wochenschrift* 1996, p. 602.

96 Federal Court of Justice, Judgment of 11 September 1995, 1 StR 242/95.

97 Supreme Court of the State of Bavaria, Judgment of 10 November 1997, *Die öffentliche Verwaltung* 1998, p. 296 *et seq.*

clothes[98] and of industry equipment.[99]

Violations of sanctions against other countries came before German courts to a lesser degree. The State Court of Stuttgart, e.g., had to deal with the export of equipment for the purpose of establishing a chemical weapons factory in Libya. The case found considerable public attention, and the court convicted the accused to a sentence of four years and three months of prison.[100] Two cases with respect to Iraq concerned preparatory acts. In one of them, the Court of Appeals of Oldenburg held that the mere offer to deliver goods did not constitute the illicit promotion of sales to Iraq if it stressed that the delivery itself would require prior authorisation.[101] In the other case, the Court of Appeals of Stuttgart found that talks with a view to exporting goods to Iraq did not classify as promotion of sales, but rather as an attempt to promote.[102]

(4) Questions of Compensation

German law does not specifically provide for compensation, and it has already been mentioned with respect to existing contracts that the authorities have consistently rejected such claims. The Federal Courts did not yet have to decide on the matter, since, in all cases brought before them, EC measures were in dispute which had only been repeated by national acts. According to the Federal Court of Justice, these measures may have given rise to the responsibility of the EC. The German implementation acts, on the contrary, had only a declaratory character and did not themselves constitute an interference with the rights of the claimants. Already for this reason, Germany was not liable to pay compensation.[103]

The further question whether, in the absence of a community measure, compensation by the Federal Republic was due, was left open. Whether the total exclusion of compensation, as favoured by the practice of the authorities and lower courts, is constitutional in all circumstances, is, however, disputed in doctrine.[104] Important commentators argue that the exclusion, while justified in general, violates the right to property in extreme cases, and that the German Parliament is obliged to create a legal basis for compensation in such instances.[105]

98 State Court of Osnabrück, Judgment of 26 May 1997, 26 KLs 3 Js 17396/95 (XI 6/96).

99 State Court of Hamburg, Judgment of 6 May 1998, 620 KLs 2/96 – 150 Js 282/94.

100 State Court of Stuttgart, Judgment of 1 October 1996, *Neue Zeitschrift für Strafrecht* 1997, p. 288 *et seq.*; see also Peter Heiter, 'UN-Embargomaßnahmen gegen Libyen und die Wirkung des § 69n Außenwirtschaftsverordnung auf Verfügungen über libysches Vermögen in Deutschland', *Recht der Internationalen Wirtschaft* 1997, p. 365.

101 Court of Appeals of Oldenburg, Judgment of 6 June 1994, *Neue Juristische Wochenschrift* 1994, p. 2908.

102 Court of Appeals of Stuttgart, Judgment of 17 October 1995, *Neue Zeitschrift für Strafrecht* 1997, p. 288 *et seq.*

103 Cf., e.g., Federal Court of Justice, Judgment of 27 January 1994, *Juristenzeitung* 1994, p. 725.

104 See Hocke et al., *supra* note 76, commentary on Section 2 of the Law on Foreign Trade, no. 6.

105 Ress, *supra* note 2, p. 272 *et seq.*, 304 *et seq.*; Epping, *supra* note 18, p. 510 *et seq.*

(5) *The Problem of the Embargo at Sea*

Until recently it was highly disputed in doctrine whether German armed forces could participate in armed action other than self-defence. Such action seemed to contravene Article 87a paragraph 2 of the German Basic Law which reads:

> "Other than for defence purposes the Armed Forces may only be employed to the extent explicitly permitted by this Basic Law."

In 1994, the Federal Constitutional Court, however, decided that military action for reasons other than self-defence was allowed if taken in the framework of a system of collective security. According to the Court, the more restrictive wording of Article 87a applied only to military action in the internal sphere.[106]

This judgment reflects the openness of the German constitution towards integration in a system of collective security as evidenced in Article 24 paragraph 2. The latter provision reads:

> "With a view to maintaining peace the Federation may become a party to a system of collective security; in doing so it shall consent to such limitations upon its sovereign powers as will bring about and secure a peaceful and lasting order in Europe and among the nations of the world."

After the decision of the Court, Germany participated in the monitoring of the Adriatic Sea during the Bosnian war.

No constitutional problem therefore arises if non-defensive military action is authorised by the Security Council and remains within the system of collective security. Since the Federal Constitutional Court has regarded NATO as a system of collective security as well,[107] operations of German armed forces in a NATO context do not conflict with Articles 24 and 87a either – even without Security Council authorisation. In such a case, however, it is very doubtful whether military action is barred by Article 26 paragraph 1 of the Basic Law which provides:

> "Any activities apt or intended to disturb peaceful international relations, especially preparations for military aggression, shall be unconstitutional. They shall be made a criminal offence."

It is generally held that, for the determination if the use of force constitutes an aggression, this provision refers to the rules of international law.[108] In the case of Kosovo, the

106 Federal Constitutional Court, Judgment of 12 July 1994, *Entscheidungen des Bundesverfassungsgerichts*, vol. 90, p. 286 *et seq*. On this judgment, see Georg Nolte, 'Bundeswehreinsätze in kollektiven Sicherheitssystemen'; 54 *ZaöRV* (1994) 652 *et seq*.; Doris König, 'Putting an End to an Endless Constitutional Debate?', 38 *German Yearbook of International Law* (1995) 103 *et seq*.

107 See *supra* note 106.

108 Cf. Rudolf Streinz, in: Michael Sachs (ed.), *Grundgesetz* (2nd ed., 1999), Article 26, MN 18.

Federal prosecutor did not pursue allegations of a violation of that provision arguing that the NATO action served peaceful ends.

VI. The Implementation of Measures against Terrorism

In Resolution 1373 (2001), the Security Council has adopted the broadest set of sanctions in its history, particularly because the measures are neither confined to a specific situation nor limited in time but constitute true legislative action for the whole of the international community. This is all the more evident since many of the resolution's provisions merely mirror those in conventional instruments, such as the United Nations Convention on the Financing of Terrorism. Through the use of Chapter VII of the Charter, they have become binding even for states not party to the respective treaties.

The obligations under the Security Council Resolution are very far-reaching, but not always precisely defined. In Germany, many of them did not require specific measures of implementation since they were already part of the law, as, e.g., the criminalisation of financial and other support for terrorist action; in this respect, only slight adjustments are contemplated.[109] Other obligations fell within the competence of the European Community: thus, financial measures like the freezing of funds were mainly implemented through Community law, and Germany only took provisional administrative action before the entry into force of the EC regulations.[110] As a result, Germany took important implementing measures mainly in three areas.[111] First, the German Government proposed draft legislation to improve on the laws concerning money-laundering with a view to bringing bank supervision to the most advanced international standards.[112] Second, Germany adopted far-reaching measures for the prevention of future terrorist acts. These include an extension of the powers of intelligence services, the facilitation of information exchange between different authorities, more extensive transmission of data about foreigners, and broader competences for the Federal Criminal Police Office. Moreover, initiatives have been taken to establish similar mechanisms on the European level. Third, new legislation has sought to enhance the quality of identity papers, especially those of foreigners, and measures have been taken to further tighten border controls, to identify possible suspects before entering German territory, and to facilitate their deportation.[113]

Despite the breadth of the measures required under Security Council Resolution 1373 (2001) and the scope of the German (and European) action implementing it, it is not yet possible to draw far-reaching conclusions on future changes in the implementation of Security Council sanctions in general. This is, on the one hand, due to the extraordinary political circumstances that accompanied the Security Council Resolution – after the ter-

109 See *supra* note 26.

110 See *supra* note 22.

111 See, in general, the *Report*, *supra* note 22.

112 Cf. the draft Fourth Financial Market Promotion Act, *Bundestagsdrucksache* 14/8017 of 18 January 2002, and the *Report*, *supra* note 22.

113 See, in particular, the Prevention of Terrorism Act, *supra* note 24.

rorist attacks on the United States on September 11, 2001, Western States were in any case ready to take decisive steps against terrorism. Thus the measures described above might have been adopted even in the absence of Security Council action. On the other hand, the Security Council Resolution itself is so broad and partly so open-textured that Member States were unable to apply a standard mechanism of implementation, but had to rely on carefully crafted measures to deal with this single case. Unlike usual economic sanctions, measures of this scope require specific action by Parliament rather than mere governmental regulation; and neither is this likely to change in the near future, nor would such change be desirable in the light of the domestic separation of powers. Only if the Security Council develops new standardized and more clearly defined patterns of action will Member States be able to develop more standardized implementation mechanisms themselves.

VII. The Role of National Courts

(1) The Resolution of Conflicts between Domestic and International Obligations

As has been explained at the outset, United Nations Security Council decisions – as international obligations in general, the main exception being the EC – do not enjoy direct effect in the German legal order. Before national courts, therefore, the individual can rely only on such provisions which have become part of German (or European Community) law. This view has been confirmed by the Federal Court of Justice which reasoned that:

> "An economic sanction measure adopted by the UN Security Council under Chapter VII of the Charter does not have direct effect for the individuals in the member states, but is binding only on the member states themselves."[114]

Domestic law therefore prevails over international law, unless it is specifically modified. This holds particularly true for constitutional law if the implementation of a Security Council measure violates provisions of the German Basic Law.

The German Courts have, however, relied on Security Council resolutions for the interpretation of national implementation acts,[115] as has the European Court of Justice for measures of the European Community.[116]

(2) Interpretation of Security Council Resolutions

The Federal Court of Justice has in several cases had recourse to the interpretation of Security Council resolutions in order to clarify the content of national implementation measures.

114 Judgment of 12 April 1995, *Neue Zeitschrift für Strafrecht* 1995, p. 551; also Judgment of 21 April 1995, *Entscheidungen des Bundesgerichtshofs in Strafsachen*, vol. 41, p. 129.

115 Federal Court of Justice, Judgment of 28 September 1995, *Neue Juristische Wochenschrift* 1996, p. 603 *et seq.*

116 E.g., ECJ, *Bosphorus*, *Reports* 1996 I-3953 (3983); *Ebony Maritime*, *Reports* 1997 I-1111 (1139).

For example, in 1995, it had to decide a case that made it necessary to determine whether the Security Council sanctions extended also to goods that had been imported from Yugoslavia, but had not been produced there. This case was covered by the German implementation measure, but the formula used by the Security Council ("originating in") gave rise to doubts. The Court then proceeded to an interpretation according to the methods usually used for the interpretation of domestic law. It examined the literal meaning, the context and the object and purpose of the Council resolution and placed specific emphasis on the fact that the Council itself had, in a later resolution, indicated a broader meaning.[117] These efforts of the Court to interpret the Security Council resolution are quite unusual given the restricted role of international law in the German legal order. In this case, however, they were necessary since the severe punishment provided for by Article 34 paragraph 4 of the Law on Foreign Trade applies only if the accused has violated *UN sanctions*. If the German implementation measure exceeds the measures required by the Security Council, the penalty is less grave.

In other cases of the same year, the Federal Court of Justice had to decide whether the mere transport of persons to and within Yugoslavia violated the German provisions implementing Security Council resolutions. For this purpose, the Court turned to the interpretation of these resolutions and found that Resolution 757 (1992) did not contain a general prohibition on services but only prohibitions with respect to the transport of goods. In addition, Resolution 820 (1993) which expanded the sanctions, had left untouched the area of the transport of persons over land.[118] In one of these decisions, moreover, the Federal Court of Justice discussed whether it could review the validity of the Security Council resolutions to be implemented since the lower court had raised doubts as to the limits of Article 41 of the Charter. The Federal Court of Justice, however, held that German implementation legislation referred only to measures the Security Council had actually taken and not those it could lawfully take.[119]

Lower courts equally interpreted Security Council resolutions. In a case already mentioned, the Supreme Court of the State of Bavaria confirmed the conviction of a person who had travelled to Serbia and had there allowed another person to use his car. Although, according to the Court, the mere travel did not yet constitute an "exportation" of the car, the fact that he made it available to a third person did. In this context, the Court had explicit recourse to Security Council Resolution 757 (1992) which prohibited the "sale and supply" of any products. It found that "supply" was broader than sale and included acts by which products were made available to persons within the designated territory.[120]

In 1996, the Court of Appeals of Stuttgart was faced with the question whether there was an exception from penal sanctions for acts of minor importance. The Court found

117 Federal Court of Justice, Judgment of 28 September 1995, *Neue Juristische Wochenschrift* 1996, p. 603.

118 Federal Court of Justice, Judgment of 21 April 1995, *Entscheidungen des Bundesgerichtshofs in Strafsachen*, vol. 41, p. 134 *et seq.*; Judgment of 21 April 1995, 1 StR 699/94.

119 Federal Court of Justice, Judgment of 21 April 1995, 1 StR 699/94.

120 Supreme Court of the State of Bavaria, Judgment of 10 November 1997, *Die öffentliche Verwaltung* 1998, p. 296 *et seq.*

that neither the German government nor the Security Council had provided for such an exception, but had intended to create a comprehensive sanctions regime.[121]

Apart from criminal procedures, however, courts do not pay similar attention to Security Council resolutions as such. For instance, in 1998, the Administrative Court of Appeals of Hesse had to decide whether the export of certain goods to Libya fell within the scope of the export prohibition under German law, although it was considered to lie outside the scope of Security Council Resolution 748 (1992). Since the German regulation was, according to the explanations given by the Federal Government, meant to implement the Security Council Resolution, the lower administrative court had interpreted German law in the same way as the resolution. The Court of Appeals, however, while acknowledging the legislative intention, found that the text of the German regulation was slightly broader than that of the Security Council Resolution and that, therefore, it lent itself to a different interpretation.[122] Such an approach is likely to create a great variety of implementation measures in the different Member States and therefore endangers the unity of the Security Council sanctions regime even though the national legislator did not intend this. It is therefore to be hoped that the Federal Administrative Court will overturn this judgment.

VIII. Constitutional Issues Raised by Sanctions Implementation

The main constitutional issues arising within Germany are those related to property. German higher courts have not yet had to decide upon these issues. Only the European Court of Justice has dealt with an interference with the right to property by the seizure of a plane which it saw, however, justified by the overarching public interest evidenced in the Security Council Resolution.[123]

Prohibitions on foreign trade would usually not lead to violations of fundamental rights as enshrined in the German Basic Law. As far as trade as such and the restriction of prospective gains is concerned, only the right to exercise a profession under Article 12 of the Basic Law is at stake. Restrictions of this right are subject to less strict conditions than those of the right to property under Article 14 of the Basic Law which often require compensation. But even where property in the form of existing contracts is concerned, the interference without compensation would rather constitute a (admissible) definition of the content, not a violation of the right.[124] Only in extreme cases where the restriction has severe effects on the bearer of the right and was not foreseeable, compensation might be necessary in order to render the interference lawful.[125]

Further constitutional concerns are raised by anti-terrorism measures adopted in pursuance of Security Council Resolution 1373 (2001), especially with respect to the

121 Court of Appeals of Stuttgart, Judgment of 6 December 1996, 1 Ss 589/96.

122 Judgment of 9 October 1998, *Entscheidungssammlung des Verwaltungsgerichtshofs*, vol. 49, p. 60 *et seq.*

123 ECJ, *Bosphorus*, *Reports* 1996 I-3953 (3985 *et seq.*).

124 See *supra*, IV 5; and Ress, *supra* note 2, p. 304 *et seq.*

125 Ress, *supra* note 2, p. 327 *et seq.*; Epping, *supra* note 18, p. 510 *et seq.*

right to privacy in its specifically German form of a right to "informational self-determination". The far-reaching extension of powers of intelligence agencies and the police to gather and exchange data interferes with these rights, but it is unlikely to be eventually held unconstitutional. In any event, though, these restrictions of fundamental rights were not as such required by the Security Council which only demanded that "the necessary steps" be taken "to prevent the commission of terrorist acts". Member States enjoyed a significant latitude in implementing this demand, and they were thus not bound to interfere with fundamental rights in the way the German Government has thought fit.

Human rights issues under German constitutional law can also arise with respect to the effects of sanctions on the population in the target State. The fundamental rights guaranteed by the Basic Law protect individuals not only within German territory, but also elsewhere if they are subject to measures by German authorities.[126] Thus, if the responsibility of Germany can be established for specific effects of sanctions abroad, this may give rise to justified complaints before German courts.

The same may hold true with respect to the European Convention on Human Rights. According to the European Court of Human Rights, the responsibility of the member states can be involved because of acts of their authorities producing effects outside their own territory.[127]

IX. Cooperation with the International Criminal Tribunals Created by the Security Council

(1) Domestic Provisions Relating to the Cooperation with International Criminal Tribunals

The establishment by the Security Council of the International Criminal Tribunals for the Former Yugoslavia and Rwanda required special implementing legislation by the Member States. In Germany, the Federal Parliament has passed two virtually identical "laws on cooperation" to that effect.[128] These laws establish a general duty of the German judiciary to cooperate with the International Criminal Tribunals, in particular to discontinue and transfer proceedings to those tribunals at their request. They require further that persons be arrested and transferred at the request of the tribunals and that members of the tribunals, on the basis of a special request, even be permitted to independently

126 Cf. Federal Constitutional Court, Decision of 21 March 1957, *Entscheidungen des Bundesverfassungsgerichts*, vol. 6, p. 290, 295; see also Michael Sachs, in: Sachs, *supra* note 108, Preface to Article 1, MN 19; Rainer Hofmann, *Grundrechte und grenzüberschreitende Sachverhalte*, 1994, p. 10 *et seq.*, also on possible modifications of the extent of the applicability of the rights in question.

127 European Court of Human Rights, Judgment of 26 June 1992, *Drozd and Janousek*, *Series A*, vol. 240, p. 29, para. 91; see also Jochen Abr. Frowein and Wolfgang Peukert, *Europäische Menschenrechtskonvention*, 2nd ed., 1996, p. 19.

128 Cf., with respect to the ICTY, the Law of 10 April 1995, *Bundesgesetzblatt* 1995 I, p. 485; with respect to Rwanda, the Law of 4 May 1998, *Bundesgesetzblatt* 1998 I, p. 843.

collect evidence. The cooperation laws do, however, reserve to the German authorities the right to order and execute compulsory processes; these are subject to the applicable German law. German courts must also determine independently whether the criminal proceedings or the person which the International Tribunal seeks to be transferred relate to crimes within that tribunal's jurisdiction. It is questionable, however, whether these reservations can limit the power of the Tribunals to issue orders and their inherent power to determine the scope of their jurisdiction.[129]

(2) Procedures Relating to the Surrender of Persons to International Criminal Tribunals

According to the laws on cooperation with the international criminal tribunals for Rwanda and the Former Yugoslavia, the procedure relating to the surrender of persons largely equals an extradition procedure.[130] The decision to surrender a person is taken by the Court of Appeals (*Oberlandesgericht*) which, contrary to the case of an extradition, need not ascertain that a sufficient degree of suspicion against the person exists.[131] The Court (or the public prosecutor if the case is not yet before a court) that transfers the procedure must, however, determine whether the alleged crimes fall into the jurisdiction of the international tribunal.[132] While arrest for the sake of extradition usually is restricted to two months, no such restriction exists for the arrest prior to surrender to the International Tribunals. German authorities have already surrendered persons, e.g. Dusko Tadic, to the ICTY.

(3) Conflicts with Constitutional Conditions for Extraditions

One general constitutional problem has arisen with regard to the surrender of persons to the international criminal tribunals. In its original version, Article 16 paragraph 2 of the German Basic Law prohibited the extradition of nationals to foreign countries:

> "No German may be extradited to a foreign country."

If the surrender of persons to the international criminal tribunals were regarded as an extradition, the case of a German national accused before one of the tribunals would, under this provision, have posed severe constitutional problems to the German authorities. Whether it could indeed be equated to an extradition was disputed in doctrine, but it was widely held that the surrender of German nationals would be unconstitutional.[133]

---

129 See Jochen Abr. Frowein, Georg Nolte, Karin Oellers-Frahm and Andreas Zimmermann, 'Investigating Powers of the International Criminal Tribunal for the Former Yugoslavia vis-à-vis States and High Government Officials', 1 *Max Planck Yearbook of United Nations Law* (1997) 349, 362 and 367.

130 Section 3 para. 1, 2 of the Law on the cooperation with the ICTY, *supra* note 23.

131 Section 3 para. 2.

132 Section 2 para. 3.

133 Juliane Kokott, in: Sachs, *supra* note 108, Article 16, MN 30; Gertrude Lübbe-Wolff, in: Horst Dreier (ed.), *Grundgesetz*, vol. 1, 1996, Art. 16, MN 74.

This result could have been avoided only by accepting that Security Council resolutions enjoy supranational character and therefore prevail even over domestic constitutional law.[134]

Despite these problems, the Federal Government refrained from seeking a constitutional amendment when the criminal tribunals for Yugoslavia and Rwanda were established. It assumed that because of the temporal and spatial restrictions of the tribunals' jurisdictions, practical difficulties were unlikely to occur. However, in order to ratify the Statute of the International Criminal Court, the problem had to be solved, and the Government introduced legislation amending the Basic Law. Both Houses of Parliament eventually adopted a somewhat modified amendment with the necessary majorities, so the second clause of Article 16 paragraph 2 now reads:

> "A different regulation to cover extradition to a Member State of the European Union or to an international court of law may be laid down by law, provided that constitutional principles are observed."

The last part was inserted during the parliamentary process, and its exact meaning and the extent of its restrictive effects are not yet clear.[135] However, the amendment, coupled with the respective cooperation laws, now allows unequivocally for the surrender of German nationals to the tribunals created by the Security Council.

X. Interface between Domestic and International Implementation

Security Council resolutions oblige Member States to inform the Sanctions Committees on their implementation measures, usually within 30 days of the adoption of the Resolution.[136] The practice of member states in this regard, however, differs considerably: while some confine themselves to stating that the implementation has been accomplished, others attach copies of their specific measures. German reports usually contain only a reference to the EU report which is more specific. However, the German report on implementation of Security Council Resolution 1373 (2001) was very comprehensive.[137]

Unless a Member State is member of the Security Council and thus also member of the Sanctions Committees, its contact with the Sanctions Committees is very limited. Committee chairmen inform all interested Member States about the meetings, albeit with varying degrees of precision. On the other hand, member states address the Committee only by way of the United Nations Secretariat and only in cases where sanctions violations are to be reported or where authorisations for exceptions from the sanctions regime are requested.

134 See *supra,* p. 234 *et seq.*

135 On the history and content of the new provision, see Andreas Zimmermann, 'Die Auslieferung Deutscher an Staaten der Europäischen Union und internationale Strafgerichtshöfe', *Juristenzeitung* 56 (2001) 233-238.

136 Cf., e.g., para. 10 of SC Resolution 1267 (1999) of 15 October 1999 on Afghanistan.

137 See the reference, *supra* note 22.

Requests relating to humanitarian exceptions are addressed to the Sanctions Committees by way of the UN Secretariat. There are no reports of major problems, but it seems that the unanimity rule in the committees renders obtaining an authorisation more difficult than necessary.

In principle, such requests originate from the Member State concerned. The European Commission, however, aims at concentrating these procedures in order to avoid multiple requests with respect to very similar facts.[138] It is therefore to be expected that, in the future, the European Community rather than the individual Member States will address such requests to the Sanction Committees.

XI. Conclusions and Recommendations

In Germany, the implementation of Security Council sanctions resolutions generally did not give rise to major problems. Since the German Parliament has delegated its power to enact rules concerning the restriction of foreign trade, the Federal Government was, in most cases, able to take the necessary measures without delay. In practice, therefore, the German legal order proves to be very open to sanctions measures. However, Security Council resolutions need to be specifically implemented and do not enjoy direct effects in domestic law.

Some difficulties did, however, arise, mainly caused by the interplay of EC measures and national acts. Since the EC now enjoys very far-reaching powers with regard to sanctions implementation, future national measures will be limited to the regulation of arms trade and to penal sanctions. With respect to the latter, improvements might be advisable since the current legal regime creates some confusion.

Other problems relate to gaps in the implementation. They were mainly due to the fact that the German authorities do not merely copy the Security Council measures, but adapt them to the specific instruments governing the respective areas in domestic law. While this approach might seem advantageous in a systematic perspective, copying the Security Council provisions has the merit of greater clarity and might lead to greater unity of sanctions implementation in different countries.

If transforming Security Council measures into domestic law largely in the language of the resolution seems therefore advisable, it presupposes a sufficient degree of clarity and precision on the part of the Security Council, especially if sanctions violators are to face criminal punishment. This can only be achieved on the international level and requires the development of a coherent scheme of measures by the Council. The Council must use terms whose meaning is clarified in advance, e.g. by a general definition in a framework resolution. In addition, those terms which depend on the particular case must be further specified either by the Council or the Sanctions Committees. Such additional measures have to be taken expeditiously since otherwise uniform implementation by the member states is impossible.

On the domestic level, German law as well as European Community law provide the tools for implementing Security Council measures by way of merely copying them.

138 Cf. EC Document COM (1999) 662 of 7 December 1999 on the implementation of the sanctions against Afghanistan.

For the European Community, this power derives from Article 301 of the EC Treaty. In Germany, the power to enact regulations is largely concentrated in the Federal Government, and it would therefore suffice for it to adopt such an approach in practice. In this regard, Sections 5 and 7 of the German Law on Foreign Trade fulfil the functions of a Model Law as proposed in the Interlaken process. While such a Model Law would therefore not be strictly necessary in Germany, its development and adoption by a great number of Member States might nevertheless create a more uniform and transparent framework for sanctions implementation.

* * *

Select Bibliography

I. Legislation

Basic Law: Grundgesetz für die Bundesrepublik Deutschland, of 23 May 1949, *Bundesgesetzblatt* I, 1949, p. 1, last amended on 19 December 2000, *Bundesgesetzblatt* I, 2000, p. 1755 (reproduced in Sartorius I, *Verfassungs- und Verwaltungsgesetze*, No. 1);

Criminal Code: Strafgesetzbuch, as published on 13 November 1998, *Bundesgesetzblatt* I, 1998, p. 3322, last amended on 19 June 2001, *Bundesgesetzblatt* I, 2001, p. 1142 (reproduced in Schönfelder, *Deutsche Gesetze*, No. 85)

Law on Foreign Trade: Außenwirtschaftsgesetz, of 28 April 1961, *Bundesgesetzblatt* I, 1961, p. 481, last amended on 22 December 1999, *Bundesgesetzblatt* I, 1999, p. 2822 (reproduced in Ernst Hocke et al. (eds.), *Außenwirtschaftsrecht*, Hauptteil I)

Law on Foreigners: Gesetz über die Einreise und den Aufenthalt von Ausländern im Bundesgebiet, of 9 July 1990, in: *Bundesgesetzblatt* I, 1990 p. 1354 *et seq.*, last amended on 2 August 2000, *Bundesgesetzblatt* I, 2000, p. 1253 (reproduced in Sartorius I, *Verfassungs- und Verwaltungsgesetze*, No. 565)

Law on the Cooperation with the ICTY: Gesetz über die Zusammenarbeit mit dem Internationalen Strafgerichtshof für das ehemalige Jugoslawien, of 10 April 1995, in: *Bundesgesetzblatt* I 1995, 485 *et seq.*

Law on the Cooperation with the ICTR: Gesetz über die Zusammenarbeit mit dem Internationalen Strafgerichtshof für Ruanda, of 4 May 1998, in: *Bundesgesetzblatt* I 1998, p. 843 *et seq.*

Prevention of Terrorism Act: Terrorismusbekämpfungsgesetz of 9 January 2002, in: *Bundesgesetzblatt* I, 2002, pp. 361 *et seq.*

Regulation on Foreign Trade: Verordnung zur Durchführung des Außenwirtschaftsgesetzes, of 22 November 1993, *Bundesgesetzblatt* I, 1993, 1934, last amended on 15 December 2000, *Bundesanzeiger* of 20 December 2000 (reproduced in Ernst Hocke *et al.* (eds.), *Außenwirtschaftsrecht*, Hauptteil II)

II. Doctrine

(1) Implementation of sanctions

a. Monographs

Ress, Hans-Konrad, *Das Handelsembargo: Völker-, europa- und außenwirtschaftliche Rahmenbedingungen, Praxis und Entschädigung* (2000).

Schneider, Henning C., *Wirtschaftssanktionen: Die VN, EG und Bundesrepublik Deutschland als konkurrierende Normgeber beim Erlaß paralleler Wirtschaftssanktionen* (1999).

b. Articles

Bittner, Claudia, "Die Auswirkungen des Irak-Embargos für Warenlieferungsverträge: Zivilrechtliche Folgen von Handelsbeschränkungen", *Recht der Internationalen Wirtschaft* 1994, p. 458 *et seq.*

Frowein, Jochen Abr. / Nolte, Georg / Oellers-Frahm, Karin / Zimmermann, Andreas, "Investigating Powers of the International Criminal Tribunal for the Former Yugoslavia vis-à-vis States and High Government Officials", 1 *Max Planck Yearbook of United Nations Law* (1997) 349 *et seq.*

Frowein, Jochen Abr., "Regionale Sicherheitssysteme und nationales Recht", in *Verhandlungen des Sechzigsten Deutschen Juristentages Münster 1994*, Bd. II/2, München 1994, p. Q 31 *et seq.*

Heiter, Peter, "UN-Embargomaßnahmen gegen Libyen und die Wirkung des § 69n Außenwirtschaftsverordnung auf Verfügungen über libysches Vermögen in Deutschland", *Recht der Internationalen Wirtschaft* 1997, p. 365 *et seq.*

König, Doris, "Putting an End to an Endless Constitutional Debate?", 38 *German Yearbook of International Law* (1995) 103 *et seq.*

Nolte, Georg, "Bundeswehreinsätze in kollektiven Sicherheitssystemen", 54 *ZaöRV* (1994), p. 652 *et seq.*

Oeter, Stefan, "Das UN-Embargo gegen Serbien", 16 *Praxis des Internationalen Privat- und Verfahrensrechts* (1996) 76 *et seq.*

Tomuschat, Christian, "Sanktionen durch internationale Strafgerichtshöfe", in *Verhandlungen des Sechzigsten Deutschen Juristentages Münster 1994*, Bd. II/2, München 1994, p. Q 66 *et seq.*

Zimmermann, Andreas, "Die Auslieferung Deutscher an Staaten der Europäischen Union und internationale Strafgerichtshöfe", 56 *Juristenzeitung* (2001) 233 *et seq.*

(2) Foreign Trade Law

Epping, Volker: *Die Außenwirtschaftsfreiheit* (1998).

Hocke, Ernst *et al.* (eds.), *Außenwirtschaftsrecht*, 3 vols., looseleaf (1999).

(3) Other issues

Frowein, Jochen Abr. / Peukert, Wolfgang, *Europäische Menschenrechtskonvention* (2nd ed., 1996).
Hofmann, Rainer, *Grundrechte und grenzüberschreitende Sachverhalte* (1994).
Maunz, Theodor / Dürig, Günter *et al.* (eds.), *Grundgesetz: Kommentar* (5 vols., looseleaf, 1999).
Sachs, Michael (ed.), *Grundgesetz* (2nd ed., 1999).

9

JAPAN

Hisashi Owada[*]

I. Introduction

In the Japanese legal system, there is no legislation of a general character that purports to give legal effect in the domestic legal order of Japan to a decision of the United Nations Security Council which requires the Member States to apply sanctions against a target State. The procedure for the implementation and enforcement of United Nations Security Council sanctions in Japan is regulated on the basis of existing relevant legislation applicable in the area of the sanction concerned. If no such applicable legislation exists in the area to be covered, the issue has to be dealt with on a case by case basis through enacting new legislation or through resort to an administrative measure.

The present legal situation in Japan concerning the domestic implementation of a Security Council decision can in general terms be summarized as follows:

(a) Japan does not belong to the category of States which are endowed with an all-embracing constitutional framework of a general character that expressly provides for the legal effect *ipso jure* in the domestic legal order of all decisions of the United Nations Security Council binding upon the Member States under Article 25 of the Charter, as is the case, e.g., with the Netherlands.

(b) Japan does not belong either to the category of States which make it a practice to enact specific domestic legislation each time an international agreement is concluded, including the Charter of the United Nations, so that the obligations assumed under the agreement on the international plane are transformed and made enforceable as obligations on the domestic plane, as is the case, e.g., with the United Kingdom. The United Nations Act of 1946 of the United Kingdom confers upon the Crown (the Executive Branch) the general power to implement a decision of the Security Council taken under Article 25 of the Charter through Her Majesty's Order in Council, as the necessity arises.

(c) Within the legal framework that exists in the current legal system of Japan concerning the implementation of an international agreement into the domestic legal order,

* Judge, International Court of Justice; Former Permanent Representative of Japan to the United Nations in New York.

Vera Gowlland-Debbas (ed.), National Implementation of UN Sanctions, *265-306.*

a Security Council decision taken under Article 25 of the Charter is implemented in the following way. In each case where a decision of the Security Council is taken under Article 25 of the Charter, obligating Japan as a Member State to give legal effect to it within the domestic legal order of Japan, the Government will look to some existing legal instrument relating to the subject matter which can be invoked for the purpose of implementing the Security Council decision. This is in particular the case with economic sanctions of the traditional type which normally seek to impose economic embargos, such as restrictions on trade, prohibitions on international financial transactions and other restrictions on international economic activities in relation to the target State. In these areas, there exists a host of legislation which gives the Executive Branch power to exercise control over the economic activities of individuals and juridical persons carried out within the jurisdiction of Japan in the areas concerned. Based on these existing legal instruments, the Executive Branch can take measures to implement the decision of the Security Council, without going to the legislature to enact new legislation specifically addressed at the implementation of the decision of the Security Council concerned.

This situation, however, is clearly far from satisfactory, as there is no overall legal framework which *a priori* ensures that a decision of the Security Council will be implemented, as is the case with the States falling under category *(a)* or *(b)* of the preceding paragraphs. Thus, if a decision of the Security Council is taken which purports to apply sanctions to a target State in an area not covered by the existing legal instruments that give the Executive Branch power to take necessary action, the Government will have to enact new legislation to comply with the requirement of the Security Council. Since sanctions normally have to be applied immediately upon the adoption of a Security Council resolution, this process, which requires time, entails the danger that a legal vacuum can be created in the interval. This legal vacuum is thought to be filled in practice, if necessary, by the application of the doctrine of "primacy of international law" in the constitutional theory of Japan (see below II). According to this doctrine, an international agreement binding upon Japan on the international plane can be upheld before a Japanese court, in and of itself and without further implementing legislative action, to be binding upon a Japanese national or an individual subject to Japanese jurisdiction, either directly in a self-executing manner or indirectly through some implementing administrative measures taken by the Executive Branch without further legislative action on the basis of the decision of the Security Council.

II. The Place of the Security Council within the Constitutional Order of Japan

The relationship between international law and internal law in general within the domestic legal order of Japan is a question which is prescribed only in a general way by the Constitution. Article 98 of the Constitution provides as follows:

> "1. This Constitution shall be the supreme law of the nation and no law, ordinance, imperial rescript or other act of government, or part thereof, contrary to the provisions hereof, shall have legal force or validity.

2. The treaties concluded by Japan and established laws of nations shall be faithfully observed."

These provisions of the Constitution, however, do not specify what concrete legal status within the hierarchical legal order of Japan is to be given to an international agreement to which Japan is a party or a rule of customary international law, especially in its hierarchical relationship to the Constitution and to the laws enacted by the National Diet (an Act of Parliament).

As far as the doctrines go, there is no consensus view on this question of the hierarchical relationship between the Constitution and the laws enacted by the National Diet on the one hand, and the rules of customary international law and the treaties concluded by Japan on the other. The views of scholars are divided on this point. One extreme view held by some scholars, especially among specialists in international law, takes the position that these provisions of Article 98 of the Constitution, vague as they are, purport to prescribe the principle of primacy of international law over internal law, and that the rules of international law, including both the rules of customary international law and the rules of treaty law, are superior even to the provisions of the Constitution. This view is based not simply on the literal interpretation of the actual provisions of Article 98 of the Constitution, but more importantly on the principle of internationalism that runs through the Constitution as its guiding spirit, as exemplified in its Preamble.

This view, however, is not shared by a great majority of scholars. While they have differences among themselves, the majority view is that the rules of international law, at any rate as far as the treaties to which Japan is a part are concerned, cannot claim superior validity to the Constitution. These views of the majority of scholars can in turn be classified into three schools of thought.

One view held by a group of scholars, which is especially dominant among international law specialists, takes the position that the rules of general international law in the form of customary international law occupy a place superior both to the provisions of the Constitution and to the laws enacted by the National Diet, while the treaties that Japan has concluded will have legal validity inferior to the Constitution, but superior to the laws enacted by the National Diet. The theoretical basis of this view also is founded on the doctrine of "primacy of international law" enshrined in the Constitution, though there is no provision in the Constitution that expressly authorises this differentiation between general international law and international treaties. Thus it has been argued against this view that this doctrine of "primacy of international law" is nothing more than a constitutional doctrine and as such should be operative only within the framework of the Constitution. Since it is the Constitution that gives this doctrine its validity, it is impossible even for the Constitution based on the doctrine of "primacy of international law" to give to the rule of general international law a superior place to the Constitution itself.

On the basis of this reasoning, the second view which is strongly held especially among constitutional law specialists, takes the position that the rules of international law, including both customary law and treaty law, cannot claim a place superior to the Constitution to which they are subject, but occupy a place superior to the laws enacted by the National Diet.

The third view, held mainly by some constitutional law specialists, takes the position that, as far as treaties are concerned, the principle of *lex posterior derogat lex anterior* applies in determining the hierarchical superiority between a law enacted by the Diet and a rule of treaty law, as is the case in the United States. This view derives its rationale from the procedures prescribed by the Constitution relating to the conclusion of a treaty. According to Article 73 of the Constitution, the conclusion of a treaty belongs to the power of the Executive Branch, subject only to the approval of the Diet prior, or, if the circumstances so require, subsequent, to its conclusion. The procedure required for the approval of the Diet on the conclusion of a treaty, however, is less stringent than the procedure required for the enactment of a law by the National Diet. Article 61 of the Constitution provides that for the approval of treaties by the Diet, the procedure for the adoption of the national budget, which under Article 60 in effect requires only the decision of the House of Representatives, shall be applied *mutatis mutandis*, while Article 59 of the Constitution provides that a bill for national legislation can become a law only on passage by the two Houses of the National Diet. This means in effect that the procedure for a treaty to become part of the law of the land is placed under less stringent conditions in terms of parliamentary participation than the case of national legislation in the form of a law enacted by the National Diet. For this reason, it is argued that a treaty should not be given a legal effect which effectively overrides the legal effect of the Diet.

Another constitutional issue relating to the legal status of a treaty in the domestic legal order of Japan is the question as to whether a specific legal act to implement it into the domestic legal order is required to transform an obligation assumed by a treaty in the domain of international law into an obligation in the domain of domestic law. On this point, the doctrine seems to be unanimous in upholding that a treaty is part of the law of the land and that therefore no specific measures for its transformation are required. At least in the legal theory under the Constitution, no new legislation to transform the international obligation assumed under the treaty in question into an obligation under domestic law is required for its validity in the domain of domestic law.

Needless to say, this legal situation is without prejudice to the question of the self-executing character or otherwise of the treaty in question. If the treaty in question is one of a non-self-executing character, only imposing an obligation upon the contracting States to take measures to carry out the obligations prescribed by the treaty, then there is no question of applying the provisions of the treaty directly to individuals subject to the jurisdiction of the State at the domestic level.

It must be added, however, that while the doctrine as stated above is accepted as a consensus view both by the Government and in the academic circle of Japan, the practice followed by the Government is different. Whenever a treaty to be concluded by Japan contains a provision which creates a new obligation not yet covered by the whole body of existing legislation, it has been a consistent practice of the Government to enact a new legislation to fill the lacuna in domestic law without relying exclusively on the doctrine of primacy of international law.

On this point, the Government has made the following statement in the Diet to clarify the legal position of the Government on the question of the direct applicability of the provisions of a treaty concluded by Japan in the internal legal order of Japan:

> "Except where necessary legislation exists already, it is normally the case that some legislative measure is required for implementing an obligation under the treaty in domestic law. With respect to treaties whose provisions can in and by themselves be domestically executed, or are of a so-called self-executing nature, however, domestic legislation is not required. Nevertheless, domestic legislation is sometimes undertaken with regard to such treaties, from the consideration of the legislative techniques involved."

Finally, there is one problem which so far has not received serious attention in the academic discussion in Japan, nor has surfaced as an issue of significance in practice. It is the problem of the precise legal character, within the domestic legal order of Japan, of a decision of the Security Council adopted in the form of a resolution binding upon Member States in accordance with Article 25 of the United Nations Charter. While it is clear that such a decision will be binding upon Japan on the international plane, the question as to what exactly the legal character of the decision is to be understood in the context of the provisions of Article 98 of the Constitution has not been addressed sufficiently in depth. In essence, the question as to whether such a decision of the Security Council is in itself equivalent to "a treaty" in the language of the Constitution or something else is a point which has never come up in a serious way in an academic discussion.

Does a decision of the Security Council in and of itself have exactly the same legal status as a full-fledged treaty duly concluded with the approval of the Legislative Branch in accordance with Article 73 of the Constitution and promulgated by the Executive Branch of the Government? Or should it be regarded as something less than a full-fledged treaty in its legal status, at any rate for the purpose of the Constitution and in the domestic legal order of Japan? Could it be argued that what constitutes "a treaty" within the meaning of Article 98 of the Constitution in this case should be the Charter of the United Nations, and not the individual decisions of the Security Council which, binding as they are upon the Member States on the international plane, are nothing more than executive actions of an organ of the Organisation from the view of the domestic legal order of Japan? If the latter approach is correct, could it be further argued that a decision of the Security Council, taken under Article 25 of the Charter, being nothing more than an implementing action of an executive nature within the Organisation taken by an organ of that Organisation, does not have the legal character of "a treaty" and therefore has no binding force *ipso jure* within the domestic legal order of Japan, unless it is implemented through some concrete action of the Government – either executive or legislative – to make it legally binding in the domestic legal context?

This issue might appear only to be of academic interest. In practice, however, the issue can have a much wider implication. It raises a general problem of what is the legal status in the domestic legal order of Japan of an executive action taken within an international organisation by its competent organ in the execution of the provisions of its constitutional instrument, which is evidently a "treaty" for the purpose of Article 98 of the Constitution. We shall return to this issue later (Part IV).

III. The Domestic Legal Framework Applicable to Sanctions

As we have seen, there is no single specific legislation in Japan that provides the framework for the implementation and enforcement of economic sanctions adopted by United Nations Security Council resolutions. Domestic implementation and enforcement measures are taken normally within the framework of existing legislation relevant to the concrete measures under those resolutions.

As far as economic sanctions go, the most relevant legislation in existence to be employed in the implementation of sanctions of the traditional type is the Foreign Exchange and Foreign Trade Law (hereinafter referred to as "the FEFT Law"). Under this law, three Cabinet Orders have been promulgated with a view to delegating to the Executive Branch the power of implementation of the provisions of the law through executive action. They are *(a)* the Foreign Exchange Trade Order (hereinafter referred to as the "FE Order"); *(b)* the Export Trade Control Order (hereinafter referred to as the "ETC Order"); and *(c)* the Import Trade Control Order(hereinafter referred to as the "ITC Order"). The FEFT Law was enacted in 1949, and has up to the present been revised a number of times to cope with new situations that have arisen largely in relation to economic sanctions which in recent years have become more frequent, multifaceted and complex. The most recent revision was effected in 2004 and the present revised FEFT Law came into force on 26 February 2004.

It must be pointed out in this context that the original FEFT Law was enacted in 1949, before Japan's admission to the United Nations in 1956. The main objective of the law therefore did not lie in providing a legal framework for ensuring domestic implementation and enforcement of economic sanctions undertaken by the United Nations Security Council. Rather, the primary objective of the law lay elsewhere. As stated in Article 1, the objective of the FEFT Law was as follows:

> "The objective of this Law shall be to ensure, through necessary minimum control or adjustment over the foreign transactions on the basis of the principle of the freedom of foreign exchange, foreign trade and other foreign transactions, proper expansion of foreign transactions, and thereby to aim at the attainment of an equilibrium of balance of international payments and the stability of currency, as well as to contribute to the sound development of the national economy of Japan."[1]

Thus it is clear that the original law was enacted to provide a mechanism of control by the Government for regulating certain economic activities, primarily for the purpose of attaining an equilibrium of balance of international payments, through submitting them to a regime of prior governmental oversight. The nature and the scope of this oversight

1 There is no system of official translation of the laws of Japan available in Japan. The "*Eibun Horei Shuppan* (EHS) Law Bulletin Series (The Laws and Regulations of Japan in English Series)" is the only semi-authorised collection of the laws and regulations of Japan in English available at present, but the translation in many cases falls below the minimum level of acceptability. For this reason, the writer has taken the liberty of providing his own translation of the relevant laws and regulations throughout this article.

was to be defined in concrete terms by the relevant Cabinet Orders and further by the notification to be issued in each concrete case by the competent Minister (the Minister for Economy, Trade and Industry if the matter falls within the area of foreign trade, or the Minister for Finance, if the matter falls within the area of foreign exchange, as the case may be). The Cabinet Orders have been promulgated by the Cabinet (the Executive Branch) without the involvement of the National Diet (the Legislative Branch). The notification is issued by the competent Minister upon consultation with other relevant Ministers as specified by the FEFT Law (e.g., the Minister for Foreign Affairs), but without requiring the decision of the Cabinet as a whole, for the purpose of incorporating the sanctions adopted by the Security Council into the sphere of application of the FEFT Law. Thus, each time a person (natural or juridical) is to make a transaction in the field of foreign exchange or foreign trade which falls within the purview of the law, an application for a license has to be made to the Ministry concerned by the person involved and the application for such a transaction is subject to scrutiny by the competent Minister from the viewpoint of its relevance to the sanctions adopted by the decision of the United Nations Security Council. On the basis of this scrutiny, the Minister decides on the issuance of a license in accordance with the relevant provisions of the Order in question which reflect the substance of the decision of the Security Council. In this way, while there are no provisions in the FEFT Law or any other legislation which *a priori* prohibit certain economic activities in the field of foreign exchange or foreign trade, the Government in applying this Order can enforce the relevant economic sanctions in compliance with the decision of the Security Council through this act of notification by the competent Minister that has the effect of incorporating the substance of the decision of the Security Council on sanctions into the relevant Cabinet Order and thus into the framework of legal regulation under the FEFT Law.

The following sections deal with the relevant provisions of the FEFT Law and of the Orders relating to the procedure for the implementation of economic sanctions of the Security Council as described above.

(1) The Regulation of Capital Transactions and Overseas Payment

a. Regulation on capital transactions

When the Minister for Finance deems that a capital transaction, whether by a resident or by a non-resident, if carried out without restriction, will bring about a situation which will prevent Japan from faithfully performing its obligations under the treaties or other international agreements concluded by Japan or from contributing to international efforts for international peace and thus make an attainment of the objective of the FEFT Law difficult, or when the Cabinet deems it specifically necessary in order to maintain the peace and security of Japan and decides to take the measure, the Minister may, in accordance with what is prescribed by the Cabinet Order, impose upon the resident or non-resident concerned who intends to carry out the said capital transaction the duty to obtain a license for carrying out the capital transaction in question (FEFT Law, Article 21, paragraph 1).

When the Minister for Finance imposes upon a resident or a non-resident a duty to obtain a license to carry out a capital transaction under the provisions of Article 21, paragraph 1, of the Law, he shall do so by designating by prior notification the category or categories of capital transactions for which the license is required. However, if the Minister for Finance deems it will be difficult to attain the objective of the Law through this procedure of designation by notification in relation to a capital transaction involved, the Minister may designate such capital transaction through a public notice at the Ministry of Finance and the Bank of Japan or other appropriate means to be specified by the Ordinance of the Ministry of Finance (FE Order, Article 11, paragraph 1).

When the Minister for Economy, Trade and Industry deems that a specific capital transaction by a resident falling under the capital transactions specified in Article 20, item (2) of the FEFT Law (i.e., transactions between a resident and a non-resident relating to credits arising out of monetary loan contracts or contracts for the guarantee of debts), involving *(a)* a transaction or an act prescribed by the Cabinet Order as one which an exporter or an importer of goods carries out as the direct consequence of the export or the import of goods or *(b)* a transaction or an act prescribed by the Cabinet Order as one relating to the transfer of mining rights, industrial property rights, or other analogous rights or relating to the creation of a right to use such rights (excluding the capital transactions designated by the Cabinet Order as one for the settlement of short-term international commercial transactions), if carried out without any restriction, could lead to a situation which will prevent Japan from faithfully performing treaties and other international agreements concluded by Japan or from contributing to international efforts for international peace and thus make the attainment of the objective of the FEFT Law difficult, he may in accordance with the Cabinet Order impose upon the resident intending to carry out the specific capital transaction concerned the duty to obtain a license for carrying out the specific capital transaction concerned (FEFT Law, Article 24, paragraph 1).

When the Minister for Economy, Trade and Industry in accordance with, *inter alia*, Article 24, paragraph 1, imposes upon a resident intending to carry out a capital transaction the duty to obtain a license as provided for in Article 24, paragraph 1, of the FEFT Law, the Minister shall do so by designating by prior notification the category or categories of capital transactions requiring such license (FE Order, Article 15, paragaph 1).

b. Regulation on overseas payments

When the competent Minister deems it necessary for the faithful performance of the obligations of Japan under the treaties or other international agreements concluded by Japan, when he deems it specifically necessary in order to contribute to international efforts for the maintenance of international peace, or when the Cabinet deems it specifically necessary in order to maintain the peace and security of Japan and decides to take the measure, the Minister may, in accordance with the Cabinet Order, impose on a resident or a non-resident intending to make a payment from Japan to overseas, or a resident intending to make a payment to or receive a payment from a non-resident the duty to obtain a license for the payment in question, except for the case where the payment in question is a payment relating to a transaction or an act for which the duty to obtain a license or an approval has been imposed for the same consideration as above (FEFT Law, Article 16, paragraph 1).

When the Minister for Finance or the Minister for Economy, Trade and Industry imposes upon a resident or a non-resident intending to make a payment from Japan to a foreign country, or a resident intending to make a payment to or receive a payment from a non-resident the duty to obtain a license therefore in accordance with, *inter alia*, Article 16, paragraph 1, of the FEFT Law, the Minister shall do so by designating by prior notification the type of payment for which the license is required (FE Order, Article 6, paragraph 1).

(2) The Regulation of Service Transactions and Intermediary Trade

A resident intending to carry out a transaction of the following categories with a non-resident has to obtain a license for such a transaction from the Minister for Economy, Trade and Industry in accordance with the Cabinet Order:

(1) Transactions the object of which is to offer to specific areas technologies relating to the design, the manufacture or the use of specific categories of goods specified by the Cabinet Order as being detrimental to the maintenance of international peace and security.

(2) Transactions relating to the sale and purchase of goods involving the transfer of goods between specific foreign countries specified by the Cabinet Order as being detrimental to the maintenance of international peace and security (FEFT Law, Article 25, paragraph 1).

When the competent Minister deems that a service transaction (except for the one relating to the specific technologies specified in item (1) of paragraph 1 above and the one emanating from the conclusion of a contract for the introduction of a technology as provided for in Article 30, paragraph 1) or a transaction relating to the sale and the purchase of goods involving the transfer of goods between foreign countries and carried out between a resident and a non-resident, if carried out without any restriction, will bring about a situation which will prevent Japan from faithfully performing its obligations under treaties or other international agreements concluded by Japan or from contributing to international efforts for the maintenance of peace and thus make the attainment of the objective of the FEFT Law difficult, or when the Cabinet deems it specifically necessary in order to maintain the peace and security of Japan and decides to take the measure, the Minister may, in accordance with the provisions of the Cabinet Order, impose on the resident intending to carry out the service transaction in question the duty to obtain a license for the service transaction in question (FEFT Law, Article 25, paragraph 4).

The Minister for Finance or the Minister for Economy, Trade and Industry, when he imposes upon a resident the duty to obtain a license for carrying out a service transaction in accordance with Article 25, paragraph 4, of the FEFT Law, shall designate by prior notification the category or categories of service transactions for which the license is required (FE Order, Article 18, paragraph 3).

(3) *The Regulation of Exports and Imports*

A person intending to export a specific category of goods to a specific destination or destinations specified by the Cabinet Order as being detrimental to the maintenance of international peace and security shall in accordance with the Cabinet Order obtain a license from the Minister for Economy, Trade and Industry. The Minister for Economy, Trade and Industry, when he deems it necessary for an effective implementation of the above provision may, in accordance with the Cabinet Order, impose upon a person intending to export such a specific category of goods to a destination other than the specific areas the duty to obtain a license for such export (FEFT Law, Article 48, paragraphs 1 and 2).

However, the article of the FEFT Law (i.e., Article 48), which contains the above provisions, does not exclusively address those cases where the control of export by the Government is required for the maintenance of international peace and security. The same article also prescribes that in addition to those cases provided for above, the Minister for Economy, Trade and Industry may, in accordance with the Cabinet Order, impose upon a person intending to export a specific category or categories of goods or to a specific destination or a person intending to export goods by a specific transaction the duty to obtain the approval as prescribed by the Cabinet Order within the limits necessary for the maintenance of the equilibrium of international payments, for the sound development of foreign trade and the national economy, for the faithful performance of treaties and other international agreements concluded by Japan, for the contribution to international efforts for international peace, or for the implementation of the Cabinet decision for the maintenance of the peace and security of Japan (FEFT Law, Article 48, paragraph 3).

Thus, this provision demonstrates the fact that the FEFT Law, as has been stated earlier, has a much wider scope of application in granting the power of control over export to the Executive Branch than exclusively for the maintenance of international peace and security, inasmuch as Article 48 covers the two totally separate cases of control (the requirement of a license and that of an approval) in one article without making the distinction between the two clear.

This lack of differentiation between the case of control for the purpose of contributing to the maintenance of international peace and security (Article 48, paragraphs 1 and 2), and the case of control for the purpose of maintaining the equilibrium of international payments (Article 48, paragraph 3) becomes conspicuous when one scrutinizes the process of implementation of Article 48 as a whole. Thus the ETC Order prescribes that:

(a) export of a specific category or categories of goods destined for a specific area or areas to be specified by the Cabinet Order as provided for in Article 48, paragraph 1, of the FEFT Law shall be such export of goods as listed in Schedule No. 1 annexed to the ETC Order, and destined for such areas as listed in the same Schedule No. 1 (Article 1, paragraph 1) and a person intending to obtain a license under Article 48, paragraph 1 shall apply for such license in accordance with the procedures prescribed by the Ordinance of the Ministry of Economy, Trade and Industry (Article 1, paragraph 2); whereas

(b) a person who intends to export goods falling under any of the following items must obtain an approval of the Minister for Economy, Trade and Industry in accordance with the procedures set forth by the Ordinance of the Ministry of Economy, Trade and Industry:
   (i) export of the goods listed in Schedule No. 2 annexed to the ETC Order to the destinations listed in the same Schedule No. 2;
   (ii) [omitted] (Article 2, paragraph 1)

It should be noted in this context that Schedule No. 1 annexed to the ETC Order contains 16 categories of goods ranging over more than 270 items, whereas Schedule No. 2 annexed to the Order contains 45 categories of goods. Many of these items are listed for domestic implementation of such diverse obligations assumed by Japan as those under the Washington Treaty on Endangered Species, those under the Basel Treaty on the International Transfer of Hazardous Materials, and other obligations under various international agreements to which Japan is a party.

On the import of goods, the ITC Order provides that the Minister for International Trade and Industry shall determine the itemized list of the subject of import quota, the places of origin, or of shipment of the goods which shall be the subject of import approval and other matters required for the import of goods, and shall make them public (ITC Order, Article 3, paragraph 1).

The ITC Order further provides that a person intending to import goods falling under any of the following cases must obtain an approval of the Minister for Economy, Trade and Industry in accordance with the Ordinance of the Ministry of Economy, Trade and Industry:
(i) [Omitted]
(ii) the case where a person intends to import goods whose place of origin or of shipment has been made public under Article 3, paragraph 1 above.
(iii) [Omitted] (Article 4, paragraph 1)

IV. Concrete Measures of Implementation as Classified by Type of Sanctions

In this part, an attempt will be made to classify the measures of implementation taken in the domestic legal order of Japan, as categorized by the type of sanctions adopted by the United Nations Security Council. The sanctions most frequently applied by the United Nations Security Council can be divided into the following eight categories: (1) prohibition of export; (2) prohibition of import; (3) prohibition of services; (4) prohibition of the transfer of funds; (5) freezing of assets; (6) prohibition of traffic; (7) restriction on official relations; and (8) restriction on the movement of individuals. The following is a summary, if not the exhaustive list, of the measures taken according to the type of sanctions as classified above.

(1) Prohibition of Export

The prohibition of export of goods to the target State of a sanction can take place through two different procedures. The first is a total prohibition of exports. The second is a partial prohibition, which covers only some specific goods, such as weapons, petroleum or aircraft.

(i) A total prohibition of exports was applied in relation to Iraq at the time of the Gulf Crisis in 1990 (Security Council Resolution 661, paragraph 3 *(a)*); Yugoslavia at the time of the disintegration of the Former Yugoslavia in 1992-3 (Security Council Resolution 757, paragraph 4 *(c)* and Security Council Resolution 820, paragraph 12); and Haiti at the time of the Haitian Crisis in 1994 (Security Council Resolution 917, paragraph 6). In all these cases, its implementation in the domestic legal system of Japan was carried out on the basis of Article 48, paragraph 3 of the FEFT Law. Under this provision, the Ministry of Economy, Trade and Industry has the power to issue an ordinance to impose upon exporters the duty to obtain an approval to export in relation to some specific goods or to some specific areas prior to their exportation. The list of such specific goods or such specific areas is attached to the ETC Order and revised by the Minister for Economy, Trade and Industry as necessity arises. Thus, in all the above limited cases, in accordance with the relevant United Nations Security Council resolutions that decided on a total prohibition of exports to the specific target States, this list (Schedule No. 2 and Schedule No. 2-2) of the ETC Order was revised in each case of the adoption of the resolutions to include the target State in question in relation to all the goods to be exported to that State.

(ii) A partial prohibition of the export of some specific goods can be implemented through the same mechanism. In recent years a partial prohibition of exports covering weapons and related materials was applied in relation to Yugoslavia in 1991 (Security Council Resolution 713, paragraph 6); Libya in 1992 (Security Council Resolution 748, paragraphs 5 *(a)* and *(b)*); Somalia in 1992 (Security Council Resolution 733, paragraph 5); and Rwanda in 1994 (Security Council Resolution 918, paragraph 13). A partial prohibition of exports covering petroleum was also applied in addition to the prohibition of the export of weapons and related materials, in relation to Haiti in 1993 (Security Council Resolution 841, paragraph 5); Angola in 1993 (Security Council Resolution 864, paragraph 19); and Sierra Leone in 1997 (Security Council Resolution 1132, paragraph 6). In all these cases, the same procedure as above was followed by revising Schedule No. 2 of the ETC Order to include the target State in question in relation to the specific good in question.

It is to be noted that the Government of Japan practices the voluntary national policy described as the "Three Principles on the Export of Arms". Under this policy, the export of all the weapons and related materials to any country or area in general is restricted by Article 1, paragraph 1 of the ETC Order, and the export of petroleum is also subject to Government control by Article 2, paragraph 1, of the same Order. In these circumstances, no additional domestic measures are normally required for the implementation and enforcement of the prohibition of the export of weapons and related materials, or the export of petroleum. The Minister for Economy, Trade and Industry will simply refrain from issuing a license for such export falling under the sanctions of the United Nations Security Council resolutions involved. In addition, the control over the export of these items is doubly ensured under the system of prior approval provided for in Article 48, paragraph 3 of the FEFT Law.

Besides weapons and related materials as well as petroleum, the following are among the most prominent items that have been made the subject of sanctions by Security Council resolutions in the form of prohibition of export to the target States in recent years:

(a) aircraft and aircraft parts in relation to Libya in 1992 (Security Council Resolution 748, paragraph 4 *(b)*); and Angola in 1997 (Security Council Resolution 1127, paragraph 4 *(d) (ii)*);
(b) equipment relating to petroleum mining in relation to Libya in 1993 (Security Council Resolution 993, paragraph 5); and
(c) material for mining and vehicles in relation to Angola in 1998 (Security Council Resolution 1173, paragraph 12 *(c)*, *(d)*), among others.

The prohibition of exports of these items in the Japanese legal system has been effected under the general scheme of the FEFT Law in accordance with Article 48, paragraph 1, of the Law. In accordance with this provision, the Ministry of International Trade and Industry by an ordinance of the Ministry, can require an exporter to obtain an approval prior to the export of specific goods or the export to specific areas. Each time the United Nations Security Council took the decision to apply sanctions to a target State as mentioned above in the form of prohibition of exports of those specific goods in question to that target State, the Minister for Economy, Trade and Industry revised Attachment No. 2 and Attachment No. 2-2 of the FEFT Order by adding the name of the target State in question and the goods involved.

(2) Prohibition of Import

As distinct from the case of the prohibition of export, there is no legal differentiation in the implementation procedure for the prohibition of import from a target State of sanction between the case of a total prohibition of imports and the case of a partial prohibition of imports which covers only some specific goods.

(i) A total prohibition of imports was applied in relation to Iraq in 1990 (Security Council Resolution 661, paragraph 3 *(a)*); Yugoslavia in 1992 and 1993 (Security Council Resolution 757, paragraph 4 *(a)* and Security Council Resolution 820, paragraph 12); and Haiti in 1993 (Security Council Resolution 917, paragraph 6).
(ii) A partial prohibition of some specific goods was applied in relation to Angola in 1998 (Security Council Resolution 1173, paragraph 12 *(b)*), which decided that the import of diamonds from Angola should be prohibited.

In each of these cases, the legal basis for implementing such a prohibition was the same whether the prohibition was total or partial, i.e., Article 52 of the FEFT Law. In accordance with this article, an importer may be required to obtain a prior approval of the Minister for Economy, Trade and Industry in accordance with the relevant Cabinet Order. More specifically, this power is given to the Minister for Economy, Trade and Industry under the ITC Order in its Article 3, paragraph 1, and Article 4, paragraph 1.

Each time the United Nations Security Council takes a decision to prohibit the total import from a target State as mentioned above, or the import of specific goods as mentioned above from that State, the Minister for Economy, Trade and Industry, relying on this power given to him, publishes in the form of a notification the itemized list of the import to be subject to prior approval to include the specific goods in question and other details such as the country or the place of origin, the nationality of the carrier, and so forth.

(3) Prohibition Relating to Services

As part of economic sanctions, the United Nations Security Council sometimes takes a decision which involves the prohibition of the provision of some categories of services to a target State, especially the provision of services linked to trade with that target State.

Thus the United Nations Security Council adopted a resolution at the time of the Gulf Crisis in 1990 prescribing that all States should prevent any activities that would promote exports from Iraq or Kuwait (Security Council Resolution 661, paragraph 3 *(b)*). Furthermore, in order to make this provision effective, the Security Council adopted a series of resolutions to follow it up through further measures, including those relating to intermediary trade, so that activities promoting exports from Iraq or Kuwait would not take place (Security Council Resolution 661, paragraph 3 *(a)*, Resolution 748, paragraph 4 *(b)*, Resolution 757, paragraph 4 *(b)*, Resolution 820, paragraph 12, Resolution 841, paragraph 5, Resolution 1127, paragraph 4 *(d) (ii)*, and Resolution 1132, paragraph 6).

In relation to the prohibition of intermediary trade of this kind, the basic legal framework employed in the legal system of Japan for the implementation of such a decision of the Security Council is not different from the cases of prohibition of export and import as described above.

Apart from the case of providing services relating to trade, certain categories of services to be provided for the benefit of the target State may be restricted also as part of economic sanctions imposed under a Security Council decision. For example, the provision of certain services relating to the air service to and from the target State was prohibited in relation to Yugoslavia in 1992 (Security Council Resolution 757, paragraph 7 *(b)*) and Libya in 1992 (Security Council Resolution 748, paragraph 4 *(b)*).

In those cases, the domestic legal basis in Japan for implementing the prohibition of the provision of services can be varied depending upon the nature of the service involved. As has been stated earlier, Japan has no general legislation of an all-inclusive nature for the implementation of the Security Council decision on sanctions. As a result, each case in this area of services has to be examined in the light of the specific nature of the service to be prohibited, and the legal measures to be applied will have to be sought from among the existing legislative instruments which are available for its implementation. The most frequently employed for this purpose again is the FEFT Law. This is so for the reason that in many cases the provision of services to overseas normally takes place in the context of some commercial transactions and is normally accompanied by some financial transactions which come under the purview of this FEFT law. Under Article 25, paragraph 4, of the FEFT Law, together with its implementing Order (i.e. the FE

Order, Article 18, paragraph 3), the Minister for Finance or the Minister for Economy, Trace and Industry, as the case may be, decides in the form of a notification that a specific category of services shall be subject to licensing. Typically, the services within the purview of the Minister for Economy, Trade and Industry include: *(a)* transactions directly relating to the export or the import of goods to or from the target State; and *(b)* transactions relating to the export or the import of goods to or from a third State. Most of the transactions other than those exceptions falling within the purview of the Minister for Economy, Trade and Industry come within the purview of the Minister for Finance.

(4) Prohibition Relating to the Transfer of Funds

As an important arm of economic sanctions to be applied by the United Nations Security Council, the prohibition of the transfer of funds occupies a conspicuous place among the measures to be implemented by the Member States. Such a prohibition was applied in relation to Iraq in 1990 (Security Council Resolution 661, paragraph 4), Yugoslavia in 1992 (Security Council Resolution 757, paragraph 5), Libya in 1993 (Security Council Resolution 883, paragraph 3), Haiti in 1994 (Security Council Resolution 917, paragraph 4), and Angola in 1998 (Security Council Resolution 1173, paragraph 11).

The domestic legal basis in Japan for implementing the prohibition of the transfer of funds is found in Article 21, paragraph 1, and Article 24, paragraph 1, of the FEFT Law, which subject certain transfer of funds to a system of license. With respect to the transfer of funds within the purview of the Ministry of Finance, the FE Order in its Article 11, paragraph 1, provides for the system of notification by the Minister for Finance who is endowed with the power to make certain categories of transfer of funds subject to a prior license to be obtained from the Minister. With respect to the transfer of funds falling within the purview of the Ministry of Economy, Trade and Industry, the FE Order, in its Article 15, paragraph 1, provides for a corresponding system of notification by the Minister for Economy, Trade and Industry.

Furthermore, Article 16, paragraph 1, of the FEFT Law prescribes that certain overseas payments can be made subject to a system of license. For the implementation of this article, the FE Order, in its Article 6, paragraph 1, provides that the Minister for Finance or the Minister for Economy, Trade and Industry, as the case may be, can specify the category of payment for which a license is required. Under this scheme, when an application for a transaction is submitted that will entail a transfer of funds of a nature subject to prohibition under a United Nations Security Council decision, the competent Minister refrains from issuing the license required.

(5) Freezing of Assets

Another typical category of economic sanctions is the freezing of assets of a target State situated in other Member States. This was applied in relation to Yugoslavia in 1993 (Security Council Resolution 820, paragraph 21), Haiti in 1993 (Security Council Resolution 841, paragraph 8), Libya in 1993 (Security Council Resolution 883, paragraph 3) and Angola in 1998 (Security Council Resolution 1173, paragraph 11).

In the existing legal system of Japan, a decision of the United Nations Security Council on the freezing of assets as such cannot be implemented in a straightforward way, inasmuch as Japan lacks legislation which gives the Government the power to effect the seizure of private property situated within the country. In the absence of such legislation, what the Government can do to implement such a decision of the Security Council in this area is to go through the indirect route of restricting the transfer overseas of the capital situated within Japan, thus achieving in effect the objective of freezing the assets in question, as far as the flight of the capital involved to overseas is concerned, without, however, effecting the actual freezing or vesting of the assets in question. The legal basis for this indirect measure is again Article 16, paragraph 1 of the FEFT Law, under which any payment overseas can be made conditional upon the approval of the Minister for Finance.

(6) Prohibition of Air and Other Traffic

Very often the United Nations Security Council takes a decision to apply sanctions in the form of a prohibition of air traffic between a target State and the Member States. The Member States are often under obligation not to allow aircraft of the target State to fly within the territorial airspace of the Member States. This was the case with the sanctions applied in relation to Libya in 1992 (Security Council Resolution 748, paragraph *(a)*), Yugoslavia in 1992 (Security Council Resolution 757, paragraph 7, and Security Council Resolution 917, paragraph 2) and Angola in 1997 (Security Council Resolution 1127, paragraph 4 *(d) (i)*).

In order to implement sanctions in this area in Japan, the existing provisions of the Aviation Law are employed. Under the Aviation Law, the Minister for Land, Infrastructure and Transportation has the power to deny any aircraft permission to take off from, land in, or fly over the territory of Japan. It is this power of the Minister for Land, Infrastructure and Transportation that is utilized for implementing a Security Council decision on sanctions of this category. As a matter of fact, in each of those cases of sanctions on air traffic referred to above, no regular flight based on air traffic agreements with the target State was in service between Japan and the target State in question. As a result, no new measure, either administrative or legislative, was thought to be necessary. As a precautionary measure, however, the Government took the step of circulating the relevant information with respect to the substance of the Security Council resolution involved to the interested quarters each time the Security Council took the decision in the form of a notification of the Ministry.

With respect to sanctions in relation to the Former Yugoslavia, Security Council Resolution 820 (1993), in its paragraph 24, took further measures to tighten the control over the traffic in general from and/or to the target State. This Resolution provided for the obligation of the Member States to confiscate vessels, freight vehicles, railway rolling stocks and aircraft which came from the target area to a Member State.

In Japan, there is no domestic law which empowers the Government to effect the seizure or the confiscation of such properties. Under the circumstances, in order to implement this decision of the Security Council the Government took an exceptional measure by making use of the provisions of the Immigration Control and Refugee Recognition

Act, to ensure that no traffic under these categories could take place between Japan and the Former Yugoslavia. The purport of this action of the Government was to prevent such traffic falling under the category as specified by the Security Council decision from coming into the territory of Japan, so that the situation envisaged by the Security Council decision would not materialize.

(7) Restriction on Diplomatic Relations

There are cases where the United Nations Security Council in its resolution on sanctions has called upon the Member States to reduce the number of staff of their diplomatic and other official representations such as embassies and consulates in the territory of a target State. The examples are found in the sanctions applied to Libya in 1992 (Security Council Resolution 748, paragraph 6 *(a)*), and Yugoslavia in 1992 (Security Council Resolution 757, paragraph 8 *(a)*).

In each of these sanctions, the Government within its own power took the decision to reduce the number of resident diplomats in the target State in question drastically, on the basis of its own authority under the Law of Establishment of the Ministry of Foreign Affairs, under which the Minister for Foreign Affairs has the power to take a decision on these issues. This was done each time on an *ad hoc* basis.

(8) Restriction on the Movement of Individuals

The United Nations Security Council sometimes decides by way of sanctions on measures to restrict the exchange of people between a target State and the Member States. These measures can be divided into two categories:

(a) The first category of cases involves measures which restrict the freedom of movement of individuals intending to travel for various purposes between the target State and a Member State. With regard to this category of cases, prohibition of entry of certain categories of individuals such as government officials of the target State to the Member States was applied with regard to Haiti in 1994 (Security Council Resolution 917, paragraph 3), Angola in 1997 (Security Council Resolution 1127, paragraph 4 *(a)* and *(b)*) and Sierra Leone in 1993 (Security Council Resolution 1132, paragraph 5).

(b) The second category of cases involves measures which restrict the free flow of persons to the Member States from the target State. Thus, the interruption of official contacts, sport exchanges, scientific or technical co-operation and cultural exchanges with the target State were applied with regard to Yugoslavia in 1992 (Security Council Resolution 757, para. 8 *(b)* paragraph 8 *(b)* and *(c)*).

With regard to the first category of cases, in order to implement the sanctions decided upon by the Security Council, the Government took measures not to allow the targeted personnel who were subject to the sanctions to enter Japan, by invoking the relevant provisions of the Immigration Control and Refugees Recognition Act, which endows the Minister for Justice with full discretion to decide on the question of the admission of individual foreigners wishing to enter Japan or a case-by-case basis.

With regard to the second category of cases, the Government took measures to implement these prohibitions, as far as the official contacts between the Government of Japan and the Government of the target State in question were concerned, by suspending all the official contacts falling under the category prohibited by the Security Council decisions through an administrative decision of the Government. Concerning the contacts falling under this category, but carried out by private sector initiatives, the Government resorted to the device called the "administrative guidance (*gyosei shido*)", – the technique often employed by Governmental Agencies in Japan of informally securing the compliance of the private sector involved with the requirement of the Security Council decision through the power of administrative guidance and persuasion rather than the use of mandatory power of the Government – in the form of notifying the public of the main provisions of the Security Council resolution involved through its publication in the Official Gazette of the Government.

V. Domestic Procedures for Implementation and Enforcement

On the basis of the legal instruments available in Japan for the application of sanctions as described in Part IV, the actual process of implementation and enforcement of these sanctions takes place in accordance with certain internal procedures. In this section, an attempt is made to illustrate this domestic process of implementation through concrete steps taken within the Government from the adoption of a United Nations Security Council resolution to its enforcement in the legal order of Japan, taking as a concrete example the case of sanctions applied vis-à-vis Libya.

The United Nations Security Council, following upon the destruction of Pan Am flight 103 on 21 December 1988 and of UTA flight 772 on 19 September 1989 and determining that the failure of the Libyan Government to demonstrate by concrete actions its renunciation of terrorism and in particular its continued failure to respond fully and effectively with the United Nations Security Council in its demand as set forth in Resolution 731 (1992) constituted a threat to international peace and security, decided to take quite comprehensive wide-ranging measures of sanctions vis-à-vis Libya, with a view to securing compliance by the Libyan Government with the demand of the Security Council.

The sanctions, as applied to Libya over the crucial period of 1992-1999 went through diverse, multifaceted phases. Corresponding to these different phases, the Government of Japan took concrete steps to implement each and every aspect of the sanctions, making use of different legal instruments available to it.

(1) Implementation of United Nations Security Council Resolution 748

Security Council Resolution 748 (1992), adopted on March 31 1992, addressed to all States to take the following categories of sanction measures applicable to Libya:

(a) Denial of permission to any aircraft to take off from, land in or overfly their territory, if destined to land in or having taken off from the territory of Libya (paragraph 4 *(a)*);
(b) Prohibition, by their nationals or from their territory, of the supply of any aircraft or aircraft component to Libya, the provision of engineering and maintenance servic-

ing of Libyan aircraft or aircraft components, the certification of airworthiness for Libyan aircraft, the payment of new claims against existing insurance contracts, and the provision of new direct insurance for Libyan aircraft (paragraph 4 *(b)*);

(c) Prohibition, by their nationals or from their territory, of the provision to Libya of arms and related material of all types, ... as well as the provision of any type of equipment, supplies and grants of licensing arrangements, for the manufacture or maintenance of the aforementioned (paragraph 5 *(a)*);

(d) Prohibition, by their nationals or from their territory, of the provision to Libya of technical advice, assistance or training related to the provision, manufacture, maintenance, or use of the items in *(c)* above (paragraph 5 *(b)*);

(e) Withdrawal of any of their officials or agents present in Libya to advise the Libyan authorities on military matters (paragraph 5 *(c)*);

(f) Significant reduction in the number and the level of the staff at Libyan diplomatic missions and consular posts and restriction or control on the movement within their territory of all such staff who remain (paragraph 6 *(a)*);

(g) Prevention of the operation of all Libyan Arab Airlines offices (paragraph 6 *(b)*); and

(h) Taking all appropriate steps to deny entry to or expel Libyan nationals who have been denied entry to or expelled from other States because of their involvement in terrorist activities (paragraph 6 *(c)*).

As a result of the examination of all the provisions of the Resolution by the relevant Ministries, the following domestic measures were thought to be required:

(a) Measures under Air Traffic Law;

(b) Introduction of the requirement of approval, under the approval system on the export of aircraft and their components by amending Schedule No. 2 attached to the ETC Order (Article 48, paragraph 3 of the FEFT Law and Article 2, paragraph 1 of the ETC Order).

(c) Introduction of the requirement of permission under the licensing system on intermediary trade of aircraft and their components by issuing a notice of the then Ministry of International Trade and Industry (Article 25, paragraph 4 of the Law and Article 18, paragraph 3 of the FE Order).

(d) Introduction of the requirement of approval under the approval system on service transactions by designating through notification the provision of engineering, maintenance servicing, certification of airworthiness for Libyan aircraft, the payment of new claims against existing insurance contracts and new direct insurance for Libyan aircraft as such service transactions for which the approval is required (Article 25, paragraph 4 of the FEFT Law and Article 18, paragraph 3 of the FE Order).

(e) The Order of the Minister for Foreign Affairs in the form of an administrative decree of the Ministry to reduce the number of staff at the Libyan diplomatic mission and restricting their movements in Japan.

As for the export of arms and the provision of technical advice, assistance or training related to the provision, manufacture, maintenance or use of arms, the licensing system in relation to the whole world was already in place and thus it was thought that no new measure was necessary for this item in relation to Libya.

The measures listed in the items *(a)* to *(d)* in paragraph 2 above were introduced on April 22, 1992. On item *(e)* concerning the reduction of the number of diplomats and restriction of their movements, the Ministry of Foreign Affairs notified the Libyan Mission in Tokyo on April 15, that the Mission had to reduce the number of Libyan diplomats working there from four to three and that it had to request permission in advance when the Libyan diplomats intended to travel beyond the limits of the Tokyo Metropolitan Area and of the Narita City Area (where the New Tokyo International Airport was situated).

(2) Implementation of United Nations Security Council Resolution 883

United Nations Security Council Resolution 883 was adopted on November 11, 1993, in view of the continued failure of the Libyan Government to demonstrate by concrete actions its renunciation of terrorism and its continued failure to respond fully and effectively to the requests and decisions of previous resolutions. It addressed to all States to take the following further categories of sanction measures applicable to Libya:

(a) Freezing of funds and other financial resources owned or controlled, directly or indirectly, by the Government or public authorities of Libya or any Libyan undertaking and ensuring that neither such funds and financial resources nor any other funds and financial resources are made available, by their nationals or any persons within their territory, directly or indirectly, to or for the benefit of the Government or public authorities of Libya or any Libyan undertaking (paragraph 3);

(b) Prohibition, by their nationals or from their territory, of the provision to Libya of the items listed in the Annex to the Resolution, which comprise the following categories:

  (i) Pumps of medium or large capacity and drivers (gas turbines and electric motors) designed for use in the transportation of crude oil and natural gas

  (ii) Equipment designed for use in crude oil export terminals

  (iii) Equipment which is not specially designed for use in crude oil export terminals but which because of their large capacity can be used for this purpose

  (iv) Refinery equipment

  (v) Spare parts destined for the items in (i) to (iv) above (paragraph 5 and Annex);

(c) Immediate and complete closure of all Libyan Arab Airlines offices within their territories (paragraph 6 *(a)*);

(d) Prohibition of any commercial transactions with Libyan Arab Airlines by their nationals or from their territory (paragraph 6 *(b)*);

(e) Prohibition of the entering into, or the renewal of, arrangements by their nationals or from their territory for:

  (i) Making available, for operation within Libya, any aircraft or aircraft components, or

  (ii) the provision of engineering or maintenance servicing of any aircraft or aircraft components within Libya (paragraph 6 *(c)*);

(f) Prohibition, by their nationals and from their territory, of the supply of any materials destined for the construction, improvement or maintenance of Libyan civilian or military airfields and facilities and equipment, or of any engineering or other services or components destined for the maintenance of any Libyan civilian or military airfields or associated facilities and equipment (paragraph 6 *(d)*);
(g) Prohibition, by their nationals or from their territory, of any provision of advice, assistance, or training to Libyan pilots, flight engineers, or aircraft and ground maintenance personnel associated with the operation of aircraft and airfields within Libya (paragraph 6 *(e)*);
(h) Prohibition, by their nationals or from the territory, of any renewal of any direct insurance for Libyan aircraft (paragraph 6 *(f)*);
(i) Ensuring that no claim shall lie at the instance of the Government or public authorities of Libya, or of any Libyan national, or of any Libyan undertaking, or of any person claiming through or for the benefit of any such person or undertaking, in connection with any contract or other transaction or commercial operation where its performance is affected by reason of the measures imposed by or pursuant to this Resolution or related resolutions (paragraph 8).

At that time the relevant Ministries examined the concrete domestic measures required under this Resolution, in addition to those which had already been put into effect in 1992, and decided to take the following additional measures under the existing legislative framework:
(a) Introduction of the requirement of a permission under the licensing system on capital transactions for the purpose of control over the transfer of funds (Article 25, paragraph 4 of the EEFT Law), by issuing:
  (i) A notice of the Ministry of Finance concerning the transfer of funds controlled by the Ministry of Finance (Article 11, paragraph 1 of the FE Order); and
  (ii) A notice of the then Ministry of International Trade and Industry concerning the transfer of funds controlled by the Ministry (Article 15, paragraph 1 of the FE Order).
(b) Introduction of the requirement of a permission under the licensing system on capital transactions for the purpose of control over the payment to Libya by issuing a notice of the then Ministry of International Trade and Industry (Article 16, paragraph 1 of the FE Order).
(c) Introduction of the requirement of an approval under the approval system on export for the purpose of control over the export of petroleum-related equipment, by amending Schedule No. 2 attached to the ETC Order (Article 48, paragraph 3 of the Law and Article 2, paragraph 1 of the ETC Order).
(d) Introduction of the requirement of a permission under the licensing system on export for the purpose of control over the intermediary trade of petroleum-related equipment, by issuing a notice of the Ministry of International Trade and Industry (Article 25, paragraph 4 of the Law and Article 18, paragraph 3 of the FE Order).
(e) Introduction of the requirement of a permission under the licensing system on service transactions for the purpose of control over the provision of supplies and grants of licensing arrangements for the manufacture or maintenance of petroleum-related

equipment by issuing a notice of the then Ministry of International Trade and Industry (Article 16, paragraph 2 of the FE Order).

VI. Constitutional Issues Raised by Sanctions

Economic sanctions applied by the United Nations Security Council have increased dramatically in recent years. While their implementation and enforcement clearly constitute an obligation for all the Member States in the domain of international law, some basic questions of a constitutional nature can arise from the viewpoint of their legal validity in the domain of the internal law of a Member State when they come into conflict with the rights of individuals especially in the field of their economic activities. In Japan this question has come to surface in an acute form, especially against the background that the Government has been coping with the issue of implementation of United Nations Security Council resolutions through existing legal instruments. Most of these legal instruments employed for the purpose of implementing Security Council resolutions are either existing legislation (Acts of Parliament) enacted for different or more general purposes within the domestic legal order, or administrative measures taken at the Cabinet level (Cabinet Orders), or even at a lower level (administrative ordinances and other administrative acts of the competent Ministries).

Most of the sanctions measures, whether based on United Nations Security Council resolutions or not, must be carried out by restricting the activities of individuals in the domestic legal order. It is therefore inevitable that various legal problems may arise in a situation of dichotomy between the legal basis for such restrictions upon the freedom of individuals on the one hand, and the constitutional guarantee for such freedom as a fundamental right of individuals guaranteed by the domestic law of each Member State on the other.

While there have been no court cases in Japan so far in which the legal basis of the domestic measures taken to implement the economic sanctions based on a United Nations Security Council resolution was challenged, there has been a case in which the legality of the export control measures taken by the Government under the FEFT Law in order to implement the export control requirement under the COCOM arrangements was contested.

In 1969, a group of manufacturers called the "Japan Industrial Fair Association" (Nikko-ten) applied to the then Minister for International Trade and Industry for approval of export of 19 pieces of freight to the People's Republic of China. The application for approval was made in accordance with the FEFT Law (called at that time Order having the force of a law enacted by the National Diet) and other related legal instruments. The Nikko-ten was the organiser of an industrial fair to be held in China. The application for approval of export involved the export to the People's Republic of China of certain items of industrial goods to be sent to the exhibition. The Minister decided not to give the required approval to the application because of the export restrictions that Japan had accepted under the COCOM arrangements. Thereupon the Nikko-ten brought a case against the Government over this decision. In the proceedings before the Court, the plaintiff raised, *inter alia*, the issue of the legality of the decision made by the Minister, arguing that the decision was taken in violation of the provisions of the law, and that in any case the decision was an infringement of the fundamental rights of the individuals as guaranteed by the Constitution. In the end, the plaintiff lost the case on grounds which had nothing to do with the issue raised here, but the Court, by way of an *obiter dictum*, stated quite categorically that the decision taken by the Government was illegal.

The Judgement of the Tokyo District Court, in recognizing the illegality of the decision, stated that freedom of export was a fundamental right of individuals included in the freedom of business as guaranteed by Article 22, paragraph 1 of the Constitution.[2] The Court did further examine the issue from the viewpoint of whether such restrictions on export applied by the Government on the strength of the COCOM arrangements were justified by invoking the public policy, i.e., "the public welfare" clause contained in Article 22 of the Constitution, of the measures involved. The Court instead declared that the FEFT Law permitted the regulation of export based on economic reasons, but that in the instant case the decision taken by the Government, while based on the FEFT Law, was based on political reasons and went beyond the scope permitted to the Government by the law.

It could thus be argued under the circumstances of the case that the Court did not go into the general issue of whether such restrictions on the freedom of economic activities of individuals would or would not be compatible with the constitutional guarantee of the freedom of occupation (and business) in the context of the provisions of Article 22 of the Constitution taken as a whole, and, if so, what would be the conditions under which such restrictions were held to be justified and legal. In particular, this case did not deal with the problem of what would be the constitutional situation if these restrictions were based on an international agreement, assuming that the United Nations Security Council resolutions on economic sanctions had that character, in relation to the Charter of the United Nations and the provisions of Article 98 of the Constitution, as distinct from the case of the COCOM arrangements which had no legal basis as an international agreement.

In any case, the FEFT Law was revised in 1978 as the direct result of the judgment in the "COCOM" case. The salient point of the revision was to introduce into Article 1 of the FEFT Law, which stipulated as the objective of the law "maintaining the equilibrium and the balance of payments and the development of the national economy", an additional element of a non-economic nature to cope with the situation which had come up in the COCOM case. The revision consisted in inserting an additional criterion of "the faithful observance of international commitments". It is now believed, at any rate by the Government, that the law as revised offers an ample legal ground for the Government to take such measures as are required for the implementation of an international decision on sanctions, whether based on a UN Security Council resolution or not.

It is remarkable therefore that since the introduction of the United Nations Security Council sanctions up until now, no case has been brought before the domestic court of Japan to challenge the constitutionality or the legality of the concrete measures taken by

2 Article 22, paragraph 1 of the Constitution of Japan provides as follows: "Every person shall have freedom to choose and change his residence and to choose his occupation to the extent that it does not interfere with the public welfare."

the Government in implementation of sanctions decided upon by the Security Council of the United Nations in the form of its resolutions.

As has been noted earlier in this report, it would seem that there are two fundamental problems involved in the legal mechanism employed in the Japanese system for the purpose of domestic implementation of the sanctions as adopted and applied in the form of resolutions of the United Nations Security Council.

One is a general and somewhat doctrinal problem of what is the exact legal characterization to be attributed to a resolution of the United Nations Security Council – by itself nothing more than an executive action taken by an organ of an intergovernmental organisation – within the domestic constitutional order of the legal system of Japan.

As it was pointed out in Part I of this report, the post-war Constitution of Japan is based on the principle of internationalism, adopting the monist doctrine of supremacy of international law over the internal law of Japan. Article 98, paragraph 2, of the Constitution has generally been accepted in Japanese academic circles as well as in the officialdom of the Government as the manifestation of this doctrine.

It must be stated by way of a caveat, however, that the precise legal consequences of this doctrine in terms of the hierarchical order of different legal instruments are the subject of doctrinal controversies, in which different views have been expressed among international and constitutional scholars as has been explained earlier. The question of what precisely is the legal effect to be attached to a resolution of the Security Council in the constitutional order of Japan is the problem which falls within the scope of this caveat.

There is, of course, no question whatsoever that a decision of the Security Council, taken in the form of a Security Council resolution and having the character of a decision under Article 25 of the Charter, is binding upon the Member States in accordance with the Article. The question is how this binding obligation of a decision of the Security Council upon the Member States as States on the international plane is transformed into a binding duty upon the nationals of the Member States as individuals on the internal plane in the sphere of the domestic legal order of the Member States applicable to their own nationals. As we have seen in Part I, each Member State is obligated to take measures, in whatever way is appropriate according to its own constitutional order, to give legal effect to the decision of the Security Council in question, binding upon its own nationals, where sanctions have to be observed by the individuals involved.

If one takes a monist view of the relationship between the international legal order and the internal legal order, as is the case with the constitutional system of Japan, no implementing legislation is required, and indeed has not been taken as we have seen above, for the purpose of carrying out the obligations under the Security Council decision in such a way that they are turned into concrete duties to be imposed upon the individuals subject to the jurisdiction/competence of Japan as a member of the United Nations.

However, from the different angle of the constitutional order of Japan, a resolution of the Security Council is nothing other than an executive decision taken by an organ of an intergovernmental organisation, of which Japan is a member, taken in the performance of its executive functions in accordance with its constitutional instrument, i.e. the Charter of the United Nations. However important the Charter of the United Nations may be from a political point of view, it could be argued that it is nothing but a multilateral treaty to which Japan is a party. While Article 98, paragraph 2, of the Constitution of Japan ensures that the international treaties to which Japan is a party, of which the Charter of the United Nations is certainly one, shall be faithfully observed, can it be concluded, as its *sequitur,* that an act of an executive nature taken by one of the organs of the United Nations in the performance of its assigned functions within the constitutional structure of this organisation, has exactly the same legal status within the constitutional order of the Japanese legal system as the basic constitutional instrument, i.e., the Charter of the United Nations?

A legalistic justification for the binding force of such a resolution of the Security Council, needless to say, is that a Member State of the United Nations, by subscribing to the Charter of the United Nations, including its Article 25, has accepted, *a priori* and in the form of a blank cheque, the obligation to implement all the decisions of the Security Council, regardless of what their legal relevancies may be in relation to the rights and obligations of its own nationals within its own constitutional order. It is submitted that this may be a good enough argument for upholding the general legal validity of such decisions within the domestic constitutional order of the State concerned, but not a good enough argument to defend the proposition that such decisions of the Security Council could have a specific legal effect which supersedes, or at any rate is equal to, the legal effect of a legislation enacted by the National Diet.

Going beyond the strict scope of the existing practice on sanctions for a moment, and reflecting on the theoretical implications of this problem, let us assume that the Security Council, acting under Chapter VII of the Charter of the United Nations, decided to establish a quasi-judicial body attached to the Security Council for the purpose of overseeing and enforcing the effectiveness of the sanctions adopted by the Security Council. This body could be envisaged in the form of an international tribunal of some kind, empowered to review certain activities conducted by a person, either physical or juridical, in flagrant violation of most serious sanctions prescribed by the Security Council, thus contributing to the aggravation of the situation to such a degree that the activities in question could be regarded not only as an infraction in the domestic legal order of the State, of which he is a national, but also as amounting to an infraction that threatens peace in the international legal order. Let us further assume that the Security Council resolution in question obligated a Member State within whose jurisdiction the person suspected of the activities found himself to hand him over to the custody of the tribunal for the purpose of examination and trial.

Far-fetched as this hypothesis may seem, this is more or less the framework that has been set up by the Security Council in its Resolution 808 (1993) for trying individuals who had allegedly committed grave infractions against peace and against humanity in the Former Yugoslavia. Thus it would seem arguable that in this hypothetical case, apart from the question of constitutionality or otherwise of such an action taken by the Security Council on the ground of *ultra vires* under the Charter of the United Nations, the Member States of the United Nations are under the obligation on the international plane to hand over the person demanded to the tribunal, even without going through the normal procedure for extradition of fugitives in regular interstate relations, because this would not be the case of an extradition in the traditional sense of the term. What would happen, then, if this person to be handed over to the international tribunal were to seek for the protection of the constitutional process of his own State, within whose jurisdiction he finds himself, on the basis of *habeas corpus*?

It is submitted that this complex legal situation, which could arise in the internal legal order of any State member of the United Nations, would be made much more complex and much more difficult to solve in the context of the Japanese system where there is no overall implementing mechanism specifically addressed to the binding resolution of the Security Council on sanctions, due to the ambiguity created by the use of a legal framework designed for basically different purposes.

The other fundamental problem with the Japanese system of implementing the Security Council resolution on sanctions through the utilization of the existing laws and regulations created for essentially different purposes is that the Executive Branch which employs such existing mechanisms for control to implement sanctions is always at risk to a legal challenge by individuals, who would be in a position to question the legality of the exercise of power – largely discretionary in many cases as we have seen in Part V – granted by the law concerned to the competent authorities of the Executive Branch, as falling outside the scope of the essential objective of the law and thus being arbitrary.

The COCOM case quoted earlier in Part IV, although not directly relevant to the question of the application of sanctions adopted by the United Nations Security Council, was a case in point to illustrate the nature of the problem which is common to the case of United Nations sanctions. It is to be recalled that in this case the Court held that the invocation of the FE Order (having the status of a law enacted by the National Diet) by the Executive Branch for the purpose of restricting and/or prohibiting the export transactions with the People's Republic of China was contrary to the basic objective of the law and thus unlawful.

It is true that from a legalistic viewpoint of the legislative technique, this defect of the law was redressed by the revision of relevant articles of the law. The revision was done by the incorporation in Article 1 of the Law and other relevant articles (e.g. Article 16, paragraph 1) of the reference to the discretionary power of the competent Minister who now may control certain transactions "when he deems it necessary [to take such an action] for the faithful performance of treaties and other international agreements that Japan has concluded" or "when he deems it especially necessary [to take the action] for a contribution by Japan to the international efforts for international peace". However, the basic objective of the law as enunciated in the main part of its Article 1, as well as the basic structure of the law as it was originally envisaged in 1949, is to empower the Government to control foreign exchange and foreign trade from the viewpoint of maintaining the equilibrium of international payments of Japan and the stability of its currency and thus of contributing to a healthy development of the Japanese currency. It is self-evident, however, that the rationale for the control over and the regulation of certain economic activities of persons within the jurisdiction of Japan for the purpose of bringing about the compliance with the decision of the United Nations Security Council on sanctions has nothing to do with this stated objective of the law. The whole exercise in the implementation of the Security Council resolutions on sanctions is based on a philosophy and a policy objective which are totally different from the ones on which the FEFT Law stands.

VII. Conclusion

It is believed that the somewhat detailed description of the way in which the sanctions under the Security Council resolutions are implemented in the domestic legal order of Japan has revealed the essential characteristics of the Japanese approach to the issue of sanctions. While the present legal framework in which the issue of United Nations Security Council sanctions has been dealt with has barely enabled the Government of Japan to cope with the problem of this implementation in the domestic legal order on a case-by-case basis, it has clearly proved to be totally inadequate for squarely dealing with the issue in a consistent and systematic manner. The piecemeal approach so far adopted by the Government, based on the *ad hoc* utilization of various legislative instruments, which have been primarily enacted for wholly different purposes, in order to achieve the result of compliance with the sanctions in question rather than addressing the issue in a direct way, is proving to be growingly inadequate and unsatisfactory, because of the much more frequent and diversified use of sanctions by the international community for the purpose of securing compliance of the target State with the requirements of international public order.

Given the increasingly complicated environment in which international sanctions are expected to play an important role in securing compliance on the part of the target State, while curtailing to the minimum their adverse effect upon the welfare of the people involved on humanitarian grounds, a much more structured and comprehensive approach to the problem of sanctions is required on the part of the international community, based on a clear and persuasive rationale for restricting the freedom of commercial and other activities carried out by individuals operating in the private sector. In tandem, a much more systematic and structural approach for the implementation of sanctions in the domestic legal order of Japan, which would respond more proactively and effectively to this new development for an increasingly sophisticated approach at the international level, would seem to be in order.

Annex: Measures Adopted by Japan against International Terrorism

(1) *General Observation*

On 11 September 2001, terrorist attacks took place in New York, Washington DC and Pennsylvania in the United States, destroying the twin towers of the World Trade Centre of New York and part of the building of the Department of Defense of the United States (the Pentagon Building) , together with four civilian aircraft with passengers, and causing the death of thousands of innocent people.

The United Nations Security Council reacted to the tragic terrorist attacks of 11 September immediately and adopted Resolution 1368 (2001) of 12 September 2001 to condemn those heinous acts of international terrorism. As a follow-up to this condemnation, the Security Council adopted Resolution 1373 (2001) on 28 September 2001, in which the Council, reaffirming that such acts, like any act of international terrorism, constitute a threat to international peace and security, and reaffirming also the need to combat such threats by all means, in accordance with the Charter of the United Nations, decided, *inter alia*, that all States should take various measures to prevent and suppress the financing and support of terrorist acts, including penalising such acts in their domestic law and freezing the funds and other financial assets or economic resources of persons who commit or attempt to commit such acts. The Security Council further called upon all States to co-operate to prevent and suppress terrorist attacks and to take action against their perpetrators through bilateral and multilateral arrangements and through full implementation of relevant international conventions. It also asked States to become parties as soon as possible to the relevant international conventions and protocols relating to terrorism and to intensify inter-State collaboration, including exchange of information and co-operation on administrative and judicial matters.

In compliance with Security Council Resolution 1373 (2001), which was adopted by the Security Council acting under Chapter VII of the Charter, the Government of Japan decided to take a number of measures in response, as it reported to the Counter-Terrorism Committee pursuant to paragraph 6 of Security Council Resolution 1373 (2001), as set out in detail below.

(2) *Actions to Counter International Terrorism*

a. Legislative action

With respect to the issue of legislation against terrorist financing, the relevant Ministries and Agencies worked together intensively to identify what Japan could do within the present legal framework and what amendments and additional legal arrangements it should make. Many parts of the provisions of Security Council Resolution 1373 (2001) in fact were thought to have already been implemented through previous legislation and executive measures, including the FEFT law, and legislation regulating the control of narcotics and other drugs, arms control, and various other penal acts relating to mass murder, subversive activities and organised crime, as well as immigration and asylum laws.

In addition, the Diet passed the Anti-Terrorism Special Measures Law on October 29, 2001. The Law intends to enable Japan to contribute actively and on its own initiative to the fight against international terrorism through

(1) co-operation and support activities for the armed forces of the United States and other countries which aim to eradicate the threat of terrorist attacks,
(2) search and rescue activities for such foreign forces; and
(3) assistance to affected people.

On November 16, 2001, the Cabinet, following a meeting of the National Security Council of Japan, decided on a "Basic Plan regarding Response Measures Based on the Anti-Terrorism Special Measures Law". This was followed by implementing guidelines and included the deployment of Self-Defense Forces (SDF) vessels engaged in co-operation and support activities, such as transport activities from US bases in Japan to other areas.

b. Executive action

Japan took measures to freeze the funds and other financial assets of 398 individuals and entities (as of September 2003) including Usama bin Laden, the Taliban and those associated with them in accordance with United Nations Security Council Resolutions 1267 (1999),1333 (2000), and 1390 (2002). In addition, in accordance with United Nations Security Council Resolution 1373 (2001), Japan took steps to freeze the assets of 25 individuals and entities of non-Talibans (as of September 2003), such as Palestinian Islamic Jihad (PIJ), the military wing of Hamas and PFLP. These assets-freezing measures are taken based on the FEFT Law.

Japan is now a party to all twelve counter-terrorism conventions. Concerning the International Convention for the Suppression of Terrorist Bombings and related domestic legislative proposals, these were approved by the Diet on November 9, 2001, and the Convention took effect for Japan on December 16, 2001. On 17 May 2002, the Diet approved the International Convention for the Suppression of the Financing of Terrorism which it had signed in 2001 in preparation for the legal framework to implement the provisions related to the Convention and Security Council Resolution 1373 (2001), and on 5 June 2002, the Diet passed the necessary implementing legislation. The Convention entered into force for Japan on 11 July 2002.

(3) Concrete Measures to Implement Resolution 1373

A detailed analysis of the measures – both legislative and executive – has been given by the Government of Japan in its "Comments in Relation to the Specific Questions Posed by the Counter-Terrorism Committee", contained in its "Report to the Counter-Terrorism Committee Pursuant to Paragraph 6 of Security Council Resolution 1373 (2001) of 28 September 2001",[3] as supplemented by further reports. The following are

3 See "Japan: Report to the Counter-Terrorism Committee Pursuant to Paragraph 6 of Security Council Resolution 1373 (2001) of 28 September 2001", S/2001/1306 of 27 December 2001, S/2002/623 of 31 May 2002, S/2003/269 of 29 January 2003, S/2004/17 of 13 January 2004.

the significant points contained in those reports. The references are to paragraphs and sub-paragraphs contained in Resolution 1373 and referred to in the Counter-Terrorism Committee's questionnaire to States:

a. Paragraph 1 sub-paragraph (a)

The Government of Japan, by successive additions to the list of those who are subject to measures to freeze their assets, has designated a total of 373 organisations and individuals as being subject to such measures. Included in this list are not only those who have been designated by the Sanctions Committee of the United Nations Security Council as having affiliations with the Taliban, but also the 22 most wanted terrorists designated as being subject to measures to freeze their assets under the United States Executive Order. These organisations and individuals are listed on official gazettes, and effective measures are implemented to freeze their assets.

Financial institutions including banks, insurance companies, securities companies and other institutions subject to the Law for Customer Identification by Financial Institutions are required to report suspicious transactions to the competent authorities. When a competent authority deems that such reporting requirement has not been fulfilled, it may issue an administrative order to the financial institution concerned to fulfil the requirement, although no penalty will be imposed.

On the other hand, whether the obligation of suspicious transactions reporting (STR) should be imposed on attorneys, certified public accountants and other professions is currently under review. Imposing an obligation on an attorney to report suspicious financial transactions would cause serious problems, including an infringement of his/her right and duty to maintain confidentiality, and would damage the reliable, trustworthy relationship between the lawyer and the client. As for Japanese notaries, these do not deal with financial transactions, and thus are not specifically required to report suspicious transactions to the public authorities.

As a member of the G-20, Japan has pledged to stop abuse of informal banking networks. Under the Banking Law, banking services may be provided only by licensed banks. If a person engages in banking business without a license, it will result in a fine and/or imprisonment in accordance with the Law.

On anti money-laundering legislation, Japan has enacted the Law for Punishment of Organised Crimes, Control of Crime Proceeds and Other Matters.

Effective implementation of this paragraph 1, subparagraph 1(a), also requires the existence of legal provisions or administrative measures that ensure that funds and other economic resources collected by non-profit organisations (e.g. religious, charitable or cultural organisations) are not diverted for other than the stated purposes, particularly for financing of terrorism. On this question, under the provision of paragraph 1 of Article 41 of The Law to Promote Certain Non-profit Activities (hereinafter referred to as "the Non-profit Activities Law"), if a competent authority has an appropriate reason to suspect that a corporation that conducts certain non-profit activities has violated domestic laws and regulations, administrative orders or its articles of incorporation, the authority may ask the corporation to submit a report on its activities or finances, and it may perform an on-the-spot inspection of the offices and other facilities of the corporation and inspect the activities, properties, books, documents or other objects of the corporation.

Paragraph 2 of Article 2 of the Non-profit Activities Law stipulates that the term "corporation that conducts certain non-profit activities" refers to any organisation whose main objective is the performance of non-profit activities, which satisfies both 1 and 2 noted below, and which is incorporated in accordance with the provisions of the Non-profit Activities Law. Organisations that fulfil both of the following criteria and do not aim to make a profit are:

(a) Organisations that do not attach unjust requirements to gaining or losing membership status;
(b) Organisations in which one-third or fewer of all officers receive remuneration.

Organisations whose activities meet the following conditions:

(a) The main purpose of the activities is not the spread of religious doctrine, the performance of religious services or rituals, or preaching;
(b) The main purpose of the activities is not the promotion or support of or opposition to political principles;
(c) The purpose of the activities is not the recommendation or support of or opposition to a candidate for a certain public office (including a person who aims to be a candidate for said office), a public official, or a political party.

Paragraph 1 of Article 11 of the Non-profit Activities Law also stipulates the particulars that should be stated in the "articles of incorporation" of a "corporation that conducts certain non-profit activities", including details on the object of the corporation, its directors and the type of non-profit activities and projects, and profit activities, if any.

b. Paragraph 1, sub paragraph (b)

With respect to the activities listed in this sub-paragraph, under the Penal Code of Japan, when a principal offender commences the commission of a crime, the provision or collection of funds is punishable as aiding and abetting, or as complicity. However, if the principal did not commence the commission of a crime, the provision or collection of funds is not punishable under the Penal Code.

The Law concerning Prevention of Injury to Persons Caused by Sarin (Law No.78 of 1995) stipulates that, regardless of whether a principal offender commences the commission of a crime, the provision of funds for emission, production and importation of the prohibited substances including sarin, with the knowledge that the funds would be used for such action, is by itself punishable. Similar stipulations are provided in Narcotics and Psychotropics Control Law (Law No.14 of 1953), Law of Opium (Law No.71 of 1954), Hemp Control Law (Law No.124 of 1948), Stimulants Control Law (Law No.252 of 1951), Law Controlling Possession, etc. of Fire-Arms and Swords (Law No.6 of 1958) and other laws.

Under the legislation implementing the International Convention for the Suppression of the Financing of Terrorism it is now possible to punish the provision or collection of funds in relation to terrorism even at the stage where a principal offender has not yet initiated an overt criminal act.

c. Paragraph 1, sub-paragraph (c)

In accordance with the Foreign Exchange and Foreign Trade Law, the Minister for Finance or the Minister for Economy, Trade and Industry may apply a licensing system to block assets of non-residents or to restrict payments from Japan to foreign countries or payments between residents and non-residents. The Minister for Finance may apply a licensing system for any capital transactions such as those with respect to savings and trusts, loans and issuance or flotation of bonds. In addition, those who breach such regulations are subject to penalties.

As stated above, Japan has taken measures to freeze the funds of designated entities and individuals. For further action to be taken, the Government of Japan is working to establish an improved mechanism by which more prompt and effective freezing measures can be taken. The mechanism would make it possible for the Japanese government to block financial assets independent of the name lists maintained by the Sanctions Committee of United Nations Security Council more effectively. Indeed, since September 11, 2001, in accordance with United Nations Security Council Resolution 1373, the Government of Japan has taken measures to freeze the assets of 22 individuals and entities even when their names do not appear on lists maintained by the Sanctions Committees of the United Nations Security Council.

Concerning the basis and procedures for blocking the transfer of funds and other financial assets or economic resources between resident natural or legal persons, the Act on Punishment of Financing to Offences of Public Intimidation (hereinafter referred to as "the Act") was enacted in June 2002 as a measure to implement the International Convention for the Suppression of the Financing of Terrorism. Under this Act, financing of terrorism was criminalised and included in the list of predicate offences in the Anti-Organised Crime Law.

It became possible thereafter to regard funds collected or provided in order to carry out terrorism acts as crime proceeds, and to secure the funds for confiscation and collection of equivalent value. Financial institutions are also required by the Anti-Organised Crime Law to report to the Japanese Financial Intelligence Office (JAFIO) transactions that they suspect are related to financing of terrorism. The JAFIO classifies and analyses the information on the reported suspicious transactions, and provides law enforcement authorities with information relevant to their investigation.

In this regard, the Government of Japan can take necessary measures to secure funds related to financing of terrorism transferred between resident natural or legal persons.

On April 24, 2002, the Foreign Exchange and Foreign Trade Law was amended to facilitate information exchange among competent ministries and agencies for freezing actions. The amended Law came into force on May 7. The legal basis and procedures for sharing information related to terrorists are established by the amended Law.

Concurrently with the revision of the Foreign Exchange and Foreign Trade Law, the co-ordination mechanism among relevant authorities was formalised as "Liaison Committee for freezing assets of terrorists" within the Government.

d. Paragraph 1, sub-paragraph (d)

Generally, the financing of criminal acts, according to the Penal Code in Japan, is regarded as aiding and abetting such acts; therefore, under Japan's Penal Code the financing of an act regarded as an act of terrorism is also punishable, once the commission of the act is commenced. Furthermore, as stated in (2) above, under the current legal system in Japan, the crime of financing is stipulated with regard to the several specific criminal acts, and in the case of terrorist acts defined in the Convention on the Suppression of the Financing of Terrorism, the financing thereof is subject to punishment.

Within the financial tracking system to ensure that funds received by associations are not diverted from their stated purposes to terrorist activities, financial institutions are now required under the amended legislation to report suspicious transactions which might relate to certain serious criminal offences. This will encourage financial institutions to consider whether a transaction might be related to the financing of terrorists, and when it is so deemed, the financial institution will be obliged to report such a suspicious transaction to the Japan Financial Intelligence Office (JAFIO) of the Financial Services Agency (FSA). The JAFIO receives and analyses these reports, and disseminates the intelligence to the law enforcement authorities. Accordingly, in accordance with United Nations Security Council Resolution 1267, which noted that the Taliban benefited from illicit opium, transactions suspected of their connections with Taliban-related entities are reported to the JAFIO.

Furthermore, under the Law for Customer Identification by Financial Institutions, which has been enacted in the recent Diet session, financial institutions are required to confirm and keep records of identification of customers on the basis of documents issued by public bodies. This will strengthen the above-mentioned reporting system on terrorist financing by facilitating the collection and maintenance of customers' identification information without drawing their attention to this effort. Non-compliance with the Law will result in penalties for financial institutions as well as for customers who make fraudulent representations on their identification documents.

e. Paragraph 2, sub-paragraph (a)

(1) Measures to prohibit recruitment to terrorist groups

Concerning the measures for preventing entities and individuals from recruiting, collecting funds or soliciting other forms of support for terrorist activities to be carried out inside or outside Japan, the Subversive Activities Prevention Act and the Act Regarding the Control of Organisations Which Committed Indiscriminate Mass Murder (hereinafter "Organisation Control Act") may provide measures against the activities in question.

The purpose of these Acts is the securing of public safety in Japan, and these Acts are not directly applicable to terrorist groups and terrorists abroad. The Subversive Activities Prevention Act provides for actions to place restrictions on organisational activity (Article 5) and for the declaration of dissolution (Article 7), and the Organisation Control Act provides for surveillance action (Article 5) and action for the prevention of recommitment (Article 8).

The Act Regarding the Control of Organisations Which Committed Indiscriminate Mass Murder (Law No.147 of 1999) stipulates that a group which has committed indiscriminate mass murder as an organisational activity is to have its activities investigated and placed under observation and that necessary measures will be taken to prevent the recurrence of such an act. The Director-General may have public security investigators enter land or buildings owned or managed by the organisation. Other measures include 1) prohibition of acquisition of land or buildings; 2) prohibition of use of specific land or building owned or managed by the organisation concerned; 3) ban on a person who participated in the said indiscriminate mass murder or who was an official of the organisation concerned at the time the said indiscriminate mass murder was carried out from participating in or engaging in all or a part of the activities of the organisation concerned; 4) prohibition against forcing or soliciting entry into the organisation concerned; 5)prohibition or restriction of receipt by the organisation of donation of money, articles or other property interests. Any person who contravenes the above-mentioned measures shall be liable to imprisonment with labor for a term not exceeding two years or to a fine not exceeding one million yen.

Under the Subversive Activities Prevention Act, if there is clear and well-grounded danger of an organisation performing again in the future any terrorist subversive activities continuously or repeatedly as an intrinsic activity of the organisation, and if it is seen as not possible to effectively eliminate such danger, such an organisation may be forced to be dissolved. The purpose of the declaration of dissolution is to destroy the organisation in question. Any person who performs any act in the interest of the dissolved organisation or to evade the prohibition shall be liable to imprisonment with hard labor for a term not exceeding three years or to a fine not exceeding fifty thousand yen. It is difficult to meet these requirements. Therefore, the declaration of dissolution has never been taken (There is a case where the request for the declaration of dissolution was dismissed).

It is true that the two above mentioned Acts may not cover all terrorist groups due to the specific purpose of these Acts. Under the current legal system, the Government of Japan intends to fulfil its obligation of suppressing recruitment of members of terrorist groups and terrorists abroad by taking the following measures: (i) Not issuing visas to members of terrorist groups; (ii) Rejecting requests for landing permission from members of terrorist groups by application of provisions of the Immigration Control and Refugee Recognition Act including Article 5, which prescribes grounds for rejection of landing such as infringement of national interest and security.

(2) Measures to prohibit the supply of weapons to terrorists

Essentially it is the export control legislation of Japan that acts as a legal basis for the elimination of the export of weapons to terrorists.

The Government of Japan has been dealing with "arms" exports in accordance with the policy guideline titled Three Principles on Arms Exports (hereinafter referred to as "the Three Principles") in order to avoid any possible aggravation of international conflicts. The Three Principles have been the basic policy concerning Japan's "arms" exports since they were declared at the Diet session in 1967.[4] They concern a ban on exports to

4 "Arms" as referred to in the Three Principles are defined as goods which are used by military

Communist bloc countries, countries subject to an arms embargo under United Nations Security Council resolutions, and countries involved in or likely to be involved in international conflicts. In February 1976 the ban was extended to other areas not included in the Three Principles, the collateral policy guideline declaring that the Government of Japan shall not promote "arms" exports, regardless of the destination.

Japan's export control system is based on the FEFT Law (Law No.228 of 1948), which provides the general legal framework governing Japan's external transactions, as well as the ETC Order (Executive Order No.414 of 1949) (for goods) and the FE Order (Executive Order No.260 of 1980) (for technologies). In accordance with these regulations, the Government of Japan exercises control over exports of all items on the lists attached to the Orders by means of a licensing requirement.

Based on the FEFT Law, the Government of Japan controls exports of goods and technologies which appear as the 15 items described as "subject to control" in the ETC Order Attachment List No. 1 and the FE Order Attachment List, respectively. Goods and technologies described on these Lists correspond to the goods and technologies controlled by the four international export control regimes, namely Wassenaar Arrangement, Missile Technology Control Regime, Nuclear Suppliers Group and Australia Group.

To further strengthen export controls for the non-proliferation of weapons of mass destruction, Japan introduced the catch-all controls in December 2001. A license must be obtained from the Minister for Economy, Trade and Industry for the export of virtually all goods and technologies that are related to weapons of mass destruction.

The sale, acquisition and possession of weapons in Japan are regulated. Firearms regulations in Japan have been set up to cope with various specific types and purposes of firearms.

f. Paragraph 2, sub-paragraph (b)

The following measures have been taken to prevent the commission of terrorist acts, and in particular, to provide early warning mechanisms which allow exchange of information with other states.

Relevant terror information obtained by Japan, including warning information, is provided to foreign security agencies concerned in a timely and proper manner. Japan has enhanced this process since the September incident. Terror information involving Japan provided by foreign countries has been centralised at the post of Director of Cabinet Intelligence to enable relevant governmental agencies to co-ordinate their measures to prevent terrorist attacks.

Specifically, Japan has been gathering information that might lead to the prevention of terrorist activities by making use of existing informants etc., and has concurrently been developing a new network for information gathering. In addition, Japan has been carrying out the exchange of information which might lead to the disclosure of the activities of terrorist groups by reinforcing relations with the counterpart intelligence agencies of foreign governments concerned.

---

forces and which are directly employed in combat; specifically, 16 goods listed under Item 1 of the Annexed List 1 of the Export Trade Order (See Annex 5 to Doc. S/2001/1306).

Concerning the mechanism for inter-agency co-operation between the authorities responsible for narcotics control, financial tracking and security with particular regard to border controls preventing the movement of terrorists, in January 1997, Japan established the Headquarters for the Promotion of Measures to Prevent Drug Abuse (headed by the Prime Minister). It reviewed the drug counter-measures proposed by the relevant government bodies of Japan, and formulated the Five-Year Drug Abuse Prevention Strategy in May 1998. The Strategy is targeted at interdicting smuggling at the border; promoting international co-operation, including support for measures in illicit drug producing regions; and strengthening control not only over illicit trafficking and smuggling of ATS but also over users. Relevant government bodies of Japan are strengthening the co-operation and collaboration to implement the objectives of the Strategy.

Japan also established the Headquarters for the Promotion of Measures to Prevent International Organised Crime in July 2001. The Headquarters, headed by the Chief Secretary of the Cabinet, is comprised of 10 members from the Cabinet Secretariat and 7 relevant ministries and agencies (National Public Safety Commission (National Police Agency), Ministry of Justice, Ministry of Foreign Affairs, Ministry of Finance, Ministry of Health, Labour and Welfare, Ministry of Economy, Trade and Industry and Ministry of Land, Infrastructure and Transport). In August 2001, the Strategy to Fight against International Organised Crime, including strengthening of counter-measures against illegal entry and illegal stay, was formulated by the Headquarters, and Japan has been strengthening co-operation among relevant government agencies

The International Counter-Terrorism Co-operation Division was established in the Ministry of Foreign Affairs on 12 December 2001. The Division deals with the overall co-ordination of all activities relating to counter-terrorism policy in the Ministry, including policy planning and co-peration on counter-terrorism in the United Nations framework. The International Counter-Terrorism Co-operation Division works with other government authorities to ensure that the requirements of Security Council Resolution 1373 are appropriately implemented. Since the United Nations Policy Division is in charge of United Nations issues in the Ministry, this Division compiles and submits Japanese reports concerning the implementation of Security Council Resolution 1373. In the course of drafting these reports, the United Nations Policy Division works closely with the International Counter-Terrorism Co-operation Division.

g. Paragraph 2, sub-paragraph (c)

Concerning legislation or procedures for denying safe haven to terrorists, such as laws for excluding or expelling the types of individuals referred to in this sub-paragraph, the Government of Japan may, under Articles 5 and 24 of the Immigration Control and Refugee Recognition Act (Law No.319 of 1951), deport a foreigner from its territory (Article 24) or deny a foreigner entry into its territory (Article 5), if those persons organise, belong to, or are closely associated or affiliated with any of the following political parties or other organisations:

(a) Political parties or other organisations that encourage acts of violence or assaulting, killing, or injuring officials of the Government or local public entities for the reason of their being such officials.

(b) Political parties or other organisations that encourage illegal damage or destruction of public installations or facilities.

In addition to the above, Article 24 of the Immigration Control and Refugee Recognition Act and Article 5 of the Immigration Control and Refugee Recognition Act provide for various other conditions for deportation or denial of entry.

As for relevant actions taken, immigration inspectors at the ports of entry in Japan are able to deny entry into Japan to individuals on the alert list, including terrorists under Article 5 of the Immigration Control and Refugee Recognition Act.

h. Paragraph 2, sub-paragraph (d)

In order to prevent terrorists acting from the territory of Japan against other States or citizens, Article 4 bis. paragraph 2 of the Penal Code stipulates that the Code is applicable to those who committed an act which is punishable by Japan under international agreements to which Japan has become a party, even in a case where the act was committed outside of Japan.

Japan made punishable in its domestic laws all offences set forth in the nine relevant international conventions on counter-terrorism; the two other Conventions to which Japan is a party, namely the Convention on Offences and Certain Other Acts Committed on Board, 1963 (the "Tokyo Convention") and the Convention on the Marking of Plastic Explosives for the Purpose of Detection, 1991, do not provide specific offences to be punished.

Abduction, robbery or arson are punishable even when they are committed outside Japanese territory by Japanese nationals under Article 3 of the Penal Code.

In cases to which Article 4 bis of the Penal Code is not applicable, Japan can extradite to a requesting State in accordance with its Law of Extradition, persons, including foreigners and stateless persons, who have committed terrorist acts proscribed under the relevant anti-terrorism conventions outside Japanese territory.

On the other hand, Article 4 bis of the Penal Code embodies the principle of "*auto dedere, auto judicare*," and it enables Japan to apply its Penal Code to those, including foreigners and stateless persons, who have committed such terrorist acts outside Japanese territory, but who are currently in Japan in cases where Japan does not extradite them.

Thus, through the combination of these measures, Japan can ensure that those persons are brought to justice either by extradition or by application of its own Penal Code as requested in this Resolution.

Several international conventions related to the prevention and suppression of terrorism contemplate optional jurisdictions over the offences set forth therein when committed under certain circumstances (Article 8 (4), Convention on the Physical Protection of Nuclear Material, Article 6 (2), Convention on the Suppression of Unlawful Acts Against the Safety of Maritime Navigation, Article 3 (2), Protocol for the Suppression of Unlawful Acts against the Safety of Fixed Platforms Located on the Continental Shelf, Article 6 (2), International Convention for the Suppression of Terrorist Bombings). However, Japan has not chosen to establish its jurisdiction over those offences under these provisions.

On the question of criminalising the use of Japanese territory for terrorist acts against other States or their citizens, needed for effective implementation of paragraph 2, sub-paragraphs (d) and (e) of the Resolution, a person who finances, plans, facilitates, or commits terrorist acts inside the territory of Japan shall be punished under the jurisdiction of Japan, even if the targets of such terrorist acts are other States or their citizens, under Articles 2 and 3 of the Act on Punishment of Financing to Offences of Public Intimidation.

i. Paragraph 2, sub-paragraph (e)

Any act which constitutes an offence within the scope of and as defined in 12 treaties is punishable by imprisonment. For instance, murder, arson or detonation of an explosive is punishable by death or imprisonment, up to life; the use of biological or chemical weapons or hijacking is punishable by imprisonment, up to life; and other forms of terrorist acts are punishable by imprisonment, generally up to ten to fifteen years.

j. Paragraph 2, sub-paragraph (f)

In order to assist other States, Japan has been providing maximum possible mutual legal assistance to foreign countries in accordance with its domestic legislation. As a member of INTERPOL, Japan has also ensured its readiness to co-operate in counter-terrorism measures within the framework of the organisation.

For the implementation of paragraph 2, sub-paragraph (f) of the Resolution, Japan provides assistance referred to in sub-paragraph (f), in accordance with the Law for International Assistance in Investigation, the Law of Extradition, and the Law for Judicial Assistance to Foreign Courts.

The Law for International Assistance in Investigation prescribes the requirements and procedures under which Japan can execute requests from foreign countries for mutual legal assistance on criminal cases. The Law of Extradition prescribes the requirements and procedures of extradition of fugitives upon requests from foreign countries. The Law for Judicial Assistance to Foreign Courts prescribes the proceedings in which Japanese courts provide assistance regarding service of documents and taking evidence in connection with civil or criminal cases upon request from foreign courts.

The main institutions responsible for the implementation of sub-paragraph (f) are the Ministry of Foreign Affairs, the Ministry of Justice and the National Police Agency.

There is no legal time frame within which a request for judicial assistance in criminal investigations or criminal proceedings relating to the financing or support of terrorist acts has to be met; this depends on the circumstances of each case and the kind of assistance requested.

k. Paragraph 2, sub-paragraph (g)

On the question of border controls in Japan to prevent the movement of terrorists, the Immigration Bureau of the Ministry of Justice operates the "Document Examination Laboratory" at district offices located at both Narita Airport and Kansai International Airport. At these laboratories, the immigration inspectors examine travel documents etc. by using the latest and most sophisticated document identification devices. The Immigration Bureau provides the immigration inspectors with various training courses for improving their skill in examining documents.

As to "Refugee Travel Document", if an alien in Japan who has been recognized as a refugee seeks to depart from Japan, the Minister of Justice issues a Refugee Travel Document upon application by such alien, in accordance with the procedures provided for by the Ministry of Justice Ordinance. The Refugee Inquirer examines whether the applicant is a subject of investigation under suspicion of committing a crime provided by Article 1 F-(a) or (c) of the Convention relating to the Status of Refugees, etc. after she or he has been recognized as a refugee and determines whether to issue a Refugee Travel Document.

l. Paragraph 3, sub-paragraph (a)

In order to intensify and accelerate the exchange of operational information in the areas indicated in this sub-paragraph, and in preparation for the effective exchange of information with other countries, the relevant government agencies have reinforced the system of integrating, assessing and sharing information under the Director of Cabinet Intelligence. As mentioned above, Japan has been co-operating in the promotion and acceleration of exchange of operational information through enhancing relationships among counter-terrorism related agencies of various countries.

m. Paragraph 3, sub-paragraph (b)

In regard to co-operation to prevent the commission of terrorist acts, relevant agencies have co-operated with each other in strengthening immigration control to prevent terrorists' entry into Japan. Relevant agencies have also co-ordinated their efforts in reinforcing the checking of flight passengers to prevent aircraft hijacking. Further, relevant terror information obtained by Japan, including warning information, has been provided to foreign security agencies concerned in a timely and proper manner.

n. Paragraph 5, sub-paragraph (c)

In the areas indicated in this sub-paragraph, the Government of Japan has been taking full advantage of bilateral meetings and multilateral fora, including the United Nations and the G8, to denounce terrorism in any form regardless of motive, to strengthen the international framework for the eradication of terrorism, and to call upon other countries for the implementation of effective measures against terrorist financing. In the G8, for instance, Japan has been actively involved in drawing up an Action Plan against terrorism. In view of the importance of regional co-operation involving developing countries, in addition, Japan called for strengthening of such co-operation at the Lyon Summit, and has been taking the initiative in holding counter-terrorism meetings or criminal investigation seminars on co-operation to assist countries in Asia and other regions. Japan has been sending a specialist to the CTC to support it in providing assistance to third countries regarding the fulfilment of United Nations Security Council resolutions.

Japan has bilateral treaties on extradition with the United States concluded in 1988 and the Republic of Korea concluded in 2002. In addition, in Japan there are some laws that relate to international cooperation in criminal cases, including:

(i) Law for International Assistance in Investigation, under which Japan can execute requests from foreign countries for mutual legal assistance on criminal cases. According to that law, Japan can provide assistance in response to a request from a foreign country without a treaty if that country assures reciprocity.
(ii) Law of Extradition, under which Japan can extradite the fugitive to the requesting State on the condition of reciprocity, despite non-existence of a treaty.
(iii) Law for Judicial Assistance to Foreign Courts which prescribes the proceedings in which Japanese courts provide assistance regarding service of documents and taking evidence in connection with civil or criminal cases upon request from foreign courts under the assurance of reciprocity. This law is different from the Law for International Assistance in Investigation mainly in two ways: firstly, the court is the authority which provides assistance, and secondly, assistance can be provided not only in criminal cases, but also in civil cases (Article 1 of the law).
(iv) Anti-Drug Special Law enacted following ratification of the 1988 UN Convention which contains several provisions on mutual legal assistance in drug cases and makes provision for the granting of a request for confiscation or value-based confiscation related to drug proceeds.
(v) Anti-Organised Crime Law which expanded the scope of the international co-operation mechanism related to confiscation (including value-based confiscation) and freezing system provided in the Anti-Drug Special Law.

o. Paragraph 3, sub-paragraph (d)

Regarding signing and/or ratifying the conventions and protocols referred to in this sub-paragraph, it has already been mentioned above that Japan has ratified all counter-terrorism conventions. Approval of the Diet was required with respect to the conclusion of each of those conventions, separately from legislative action for enactment of relevant domestic laws, if any. Some of the conventions have required the enactment of new special laws, others have required the application or amendment of existing laws.

p. Paragraph 3, sub-paragraph (e)

The crimes set forth in the relevant international conventions have been included as extraditable offences in the bilateral treaties to which Japan is party, namely those with the United States and with the Republic of Korea.

q. Paragraph 3, sub-paragraph (f)

To ensure that asylum seekers have not been involved in terrorist activity before being granted refugee status, all the applicants for refugee status are investigated by the Refugee Inquirer and the Minister of Justice through interviews or reference to the public authorities.

The competence of the Refugee Inquirer to inquire about the facts is provided for in Article 61-2-3,1) of the Immigration Control and Refugee Recognition Act.[5]

5 See Annex 6 of Doc. S/2001/1306.

Should it become clear that an applicant for recognition of refugee status was involved in terrorist activities, the Minister of Justice shall deny her/his application under Article 2, (3)-2, Immigration Control and Refugee Recognition Act and Article 1 (f), Convention Relating to the Status of Refugees. Moreover, if an alien residing in Japan who has been recognized as a refugee is involved in terrorist activities, the Minister of Justice shall withdraw the recognition of refugee status under Article 61-2-2, Immigration Control and Refugee Recognition Act.

r. Paragraph 3, sub-paragraph (g)

In order to prevent the abuse of refugee status by terrorists and especially to prevent claims of political motivation being recognized as grounds for refusing requests for the extradition of alleged terrorists, terrorists will not be recognized as refugees based on paragraph F of Article 1 of the Convention relating to the Status of Refugees. They may not enjoy the non-refoulement principle in the context of Paragraph 2 Article 33 of the Convention and Paragraph 3 Article 53 of the Immigration Control and Refugee Recognition Law. As stated above, Article 61-2-2 of the Immigration Control and Refugee Recognition Law provides that the Minister of Justice shall withdraw the recognition of refugee status if the alien residing in Japan commits a crime in Article 1 F- (a) or (c) of the Convention after being recognized as a refugee.

Japanese legislation ensures that claims of political motivation are not recognized as grounds for refusing requests for the extradition of alleged terrorists through the established interpretation that offences related to terrorism as such are not deemed "political offences" provided for in Article 2, Law of Extradition, as ground for refusal.

s. Paragraph 4

In relation to the concerns expressed in paragraph 4 of the Resolution, Japan is determined to strengthen co-operation with other countries in the global campaign to combat terrorism. To examine links between international terrorism and money laundering, illegal arms-trafficking, and illegal movement of nuclear, chemical, biological and other potentially deadly materials, Japan is working closely with other countries in such international fora as the G8.

t. Other matters

After September 11, 2001, a series of inter-ministerial meetings were held under the auspices of the Cabinet Secretariat. The relevant Ministries and Agencies are in full co-operation to implement, in compliance with United Nations Security Council Resolution 1373, counter-terrorism measures including measures to enhance immigration control, strengthen efforts to obtain terrorism-related information, strengthen safety systems and security measures at airports for the prevention of hijacking and other incidents, strengthen response to NBC terrorism, reinforce the security of important facilities in Japan, and enhance and thoroughly implement customs inspections systems.

More specifically, counter-terrorism measures have been implemented on the basis of the "Seven Specific Measures" decided by a ministerial meeting concerning measures against terrorism convened on September 19, 2001, as well as on the basis of the "Emergency Response Measures" decided by a meeting of the Emergency Anti-Terrorism Headquarters convened on October 8, 2001, consisting of the Prime Minister (Chief of the Headquarters), the Chief Cabinet Secretary (Deputy-Chief of the Headquarters), and the Ministers of 16 relevant ministries.

* * *

Select Bibliography

I. Documents

Japan: Reports to the Counter-Terrorism Committee Pursuant to Paragraph 6 of Security Council Resolution 1373 (2001) of 28 September 2001:

- S/2001/1306, 27 December 2001.
- S/2002/623, 31 May 2002.
- S/2003/269, 29 January 2003.
- S/2004/17, 13 January 2004.

II. Books and Articles

Iwasawa, Yuji, "Effectuation of International Law in the Municipal Legal Order of Japan", 4 *Asian Yearbook of International Law* (1994) 143-169.

Iwasawa, Yuji, "The Relationship between International Law and National Law: Japanese Experiences", 64 *British Yearbook of International Law* (1993) 333-390.

Morikawa, Koichi, "Japan's Legal Responses to United Nations Security Council Resolutions", 45 *The Japanese Annual of International Law* (2002) 34-52.

Oda, Shigeru and Owada, Hisashi (eds.), *The Practice of Japan in International Law, 1961-1970* (Tokyo, University of Tokyo Press, 1982), 471 p.

Owada, Hisashi, "Japan, International Law and the International Community", in Nisuke Ando (ed.), *Japan and International Law: Past, Present and Future,* Proceedings of the international symposium to mark the centennial of the Japanese Association of International Law, 13-14 September 1997 (The Hague / London / Boston, Kluwer Law International, 1999), pp. 347-378.

10

JORDAN

Bisher Al-Khasawneh and Adnan Amkhan *

I. Introduction[1]

A major consequence of the end of the Cold War and demise of the bipolar world has been the reinvigoration of the United Nations Security Council and the extensive usage and action by the Council based on Chapter VII of the United Nations Charter. Until the Iraqi invasion of Kuwait on 2 August 1990, it has been correctly stated that powers of a coercive nature vested by the Charter in the Security Council were rediscovered after having seemed to be dormant for decades due to the deadlock that had overshadowed the deliberations of the Council and hindered its action during the Cold War era as a result of the extensive threat or actual use of the veto.[2] The early 1990's marked the resurrection of an active and effective Security Council. In the 45 years of the existence of the Security Council prior to the Iraqi invasion of Kuwait in 1990, the Council had passed 659 resolutions. Over a period of nine years following the invasion, the Security Council has passed over 400 resolutions. What is more significant for the purpose of this study is that the Security Council has used mandatory sanctions since then in relation to at least half a dozen countries.[3]

* Bisher H. Al-Khasawneh is a Jordanian diplomat. He is currently Director of the Information, Press and Media Department at the Jordanian Ministry of Foreign Affairs and a Legal Advisor at the Ministry. He is also a candidate for a PhD degree in law at the London School of Economics and Political Science. Adnan Amkhan is the Head of Legal Affairs, Energy Charter Secretariat; and Lecturer, Faculty of Law, University of Edinburgh.

1 All views, opinions and analysis contained in this chapter are those of the authors. They do not in any, manner, fashion or way represent the official or unofficial position, view, standpoint or interpretation of the Jordanian Government. The authors take full responsibility for all information, and any additions or omissions contained in this chapter.

2 See Akande, Dapo' "The International Court of Justice and the Security Council: Is there Room for Judicial Control of the Decisions of the Political Organs of the United Nations?" 46 *ICLQ* (1997). p. 309.

3 Prior to the Iraqi invasion of Kuwait in 1990 the Security Council had ordered mandatory sanctions only twice (comprehensive sanctions against Rhodesia and an arms embargo against South Africa). After the Iraqi invasion of Kuwait the Security Council imposed comprehensive sanctions on Iraq (SCR 661(1990)). Comprehensive sanctions were also ordered by the

Vera Gowlland-Debbas (ed.), National Implementation of UN Sanctions, *307-339.*

There is a consensus that resolutions passed by the Security Council under Chapter VII are mandatory in nature. Consequently, States are obliged to comply, respect and act in accordance with such resolutions.[4] As the Security Council was reactivated at the inception of the 1990's, and as it has been resorting to the imposition of mandatory sanctions extensively, and as States are obliged and legally bound to comply with those mandatory sanctions and carry them out, it is very significant to explore the means, avenues and ways by which various States domestically implement and put into effect these resolutions. It is of paramount importance to probe how the municipal laws of certain countries import the decisions of the United Nations into their domestic legal systems so that the dictates of such resolutions become executable within the domestic legal order of those countries. It is equally important to scrutinize the remedies available to States that are adversely affected by the enforcement and compliance with sanctions imposed by the Security Council on a particular State and which, therefore, face special economic problems as a result. This study is dedicated to the case of The Hashemite Kingdom of Jordan ("Jordan"). It aims to investigate the legal domestic framework for the implementation and enforcement of mandatory economic sanctions in Jordan that were ordered by the Security Council against Iraq as a result of the latter's occupation of Kuwait in 1990. The chapter will also, under different headings, address and examine the evolution of sanctions imposed on Iraq, including the introduction, at some stage, of the idea of "smart sanctions".[5] The reaction to this concept by Jordan and some Security Council Members will also be assessed and the fate of this concept will be examined.

Security Council on the Federal Republic of Yugoslavia (Serbia and Montenegro) (SCR757 (1992), 787(1992) and 820(1993)), Haiti (SCR 841 (1993), 861(1993), 873(1993) and 917(1994)), parts of the Republic of Bosnia and Herzegovina controlled Bosnian Serbs (SCR 820(1993) and 942(1994) and the then Areas protected by the United Nations in the Republic of Croatia (SCR 820(1993)). Partial sanctions were also imposed on Libya (SCR 748(1992) and 883(1993) and Sudan (SCR 1054(1996) and 1070 (1996)). Partial sanctions were also imposed on the territories of Angola controlled by the UNITA rebel movement (SCR 864(1993)). Arms embargoes were ordered in respect of Liberia (SCR 788(1992)), Somalia (SCR 733(1992)), Rwanda (SCR 918(1994), 1011(1995)) and the whole of the territory of the Former Yugoslavia (SCR 713(1991)).

4 There is a general debate over the nature and binding quality of resolutions passed and adopted by the Security Council outside the scope of Chapter VII. The arguments regarding such resolutions are that they are, on the one hand, non-binding as a result of not having been adopted under Chapter VII and on the other that, on the basis of Article 25 of the Charter all Security Council resolutions are binding. Article 25 stipulates that "The members of the United Nations agree to accept and carry out the decisions of the Security Council in accordance with the present Charter". According to this reading, the proponents of the view that all Council decisions carry and command the same legal force argue that Article 25 made no distinction whatsoever between decisions based on Chapter VII and other Council decisions and resolutions. Hence, they contend that all Security Council resolutions are equally binding on Member States.

5 The concept of smart sanctions was floated by the United States of America in the spring of 2001. The United States, along with the United Kingdom, attempted to pass a Security Council resolution that would significantly amend the sanctions regime that has been in place since 1990. The Council failed to pass such a resolution owing to the fact that the delegation of the

This chapter will also focus on the case of Jordan as a country which has suffered from special economic problems, owing to its implementation and enforcement of sanctions ordered by the Council against Iraq and which has resorted to Article 50 of the United Nations Charter.

II. Legal Basis of Domestic Measures Implementing Economic Sanctions

(1) Provisions of the Constitution

The Constitution of Jordan as amended was promulgated in 1952. It contains no provisions directly addressing the issue of the implementation of Security Council resolutions *per se*.[6] The Constitution does not contain any explicit provisions that address the issue of how international law is applied and absorbed into the municipal law of the Hashemite Kingdom of Jordan. This is true both in the case of treaties and customary international law. The Constitution stipulates in Article 25 that: "Legislation rests with the King and Parliament. Parliament consists of the House of Deputies and the Senate".[7] Article 26 states that: "The Executive rests with the King and he exercises it through his Ministers in accordance with the provisions of this Constitution".[8] Article 27 states that: "The Judiciary rests with the Courts. Courts issue verdicts in accordance with the law in the name of the King".

(2) Treaties in Jordanian Domestic Law

Article 33 of the Jordanian Constitution, which deals with the status of treaties and international agreements, in general, reads as follows:

> "(1) The King declares war, concludes peace and ratifies treaties and agreements.

Russian Federation threatened to use the veto if such a resolution was tabled officially at the Council. The whole concept of smart sanctions as envisaged originally by the United States and the United Kingdom never surfaced again. However, a modified regime for sanctions was introduced through Security Council Resolution 1409 that was adopted by the Council on 14 May 2002 at the Council's 4531st meeting.

6 This Constitution was enacted and adopted in 1952. It was published in the *Official Gazette of the Hashemite Kingdom of Jordan*, Vol. 1093, 8/1/1952. Hereinafter referred to as *The Jordanian Constitution*. The 1952 Constitution followed two previous Constitutions; the 1928 Basic Law and the 1947 Constitution.

7 The House of Deputies is composed of 80 deputies who are elected directly through universal suffrage every four years. Every Jordanian who is 18 years of age and above is eligible to participate in the voting for the elections of the House of Deputies. Every deputy has to be at least 30 years old. The Senate is composed of 40 dignitaries that are chosen directly by the King every four years.

8 In accordance with Article 35 of the Jordanian Constitution, The King appoints the Prime Minister, dismisses him and accepts his resignation. The King also appoints the Ministers, dismisses them and accepts their resignation upon the recommendation of the Prime Minister.

> (2) Treaties and agreements which involve financial commitments to the Treasury or affect the public or private rights of Jordanians shall not be valid unless approved by the House of Deputies. In no circumstances shall any secret terms contained in any treaty or agreement be contrary to its expressed terms."[9]

Accordingly, all other treaties and agreements that do not impose any financial obligations on the budget of the State, or do not affect the private or public rights of Jordanians, are implemented and enforced in Jordan once the King approves them and they are published in the official Gazette of the Hashemite Kingdom of Jordan. Article 33 of the Constitution is the only provision contained therein which addresses the issue of treaties and agreements and their application and enforcement in Jordan. The Constitution remains silent on the means by which customary international law is applied in the municipal legal order of Jordan. Courts, however, have established jurisprudence that customary international law has a supreme status.[10] The same is true regarding all treaties, agreements and conventions once they go through the proper domestic legislative phases or mechanisms of incorporation, reception or absorption. This means, in effect, that both treaties, once they are duly incorporated, and customary international law take precedence over all other domestic laws.[11]

(3) The United Nations Charter in Jordanian Domestic Law

The bearing that the foregoing analysis has on the issue of domestic measures implementing mandatory economic sanctions imposed by the Security Council is of paramount importance. The Charter of the United Nations is a multilateral treaty. Jordan became a member of the United Nations in 1955. The Charter, as a multilateral agreement, both confers rights and imposes obligations on the Member States. The United Nations Charter states that: "The Members of the United Nations agree to accept and carry out the decisions of the Security Council in accordance with the present Charter".[12]

9 See the Jordanian Constitution, Article 33(1).

10 Opinion given by H.E. Judge Yusuf Homud, Judge at the Court of Cassation of the Hashemite Kingdom of Jordan. The Court of Cassation is the highest Court in the Hashemite Kingdom of Jordan. It is a court of law and not a court of fact. It has developed through its jurisprudence and case review an indirect competence along with the Court of Supreme Justice to review the constitutionality of laws and statutes that are enacted in Jordan. The Court of Supreme Justice is the Administrative Court of the Hashemite Kingdom of Jordan. It is a Court of fact and its decisions and judgements are final and binding upon the executive. It is a Court of first and last instance in all administrative cases. The jurisprudence of those two Courts has developed in the field of constitutional review in Jordan, owing to the fact that there does not exist a Court or a Constitutional Council that is empowered to review the constitutional correctness of various laws, statutes, decrees and executive orders and decisions.

11 This is not to suggest in any way that the issue is as straightforward as it seems regarding treaties and agreements. They would have, in order to assume the supremacy over domestic laws, to be duly absorbed and incorporated bearing in mind the qualifications contained in Article 33 of the Constitution noted previously.

12 See Charter of the United Nations, Article 25, hereinafter referred to as *UN Charter*.

The Charter also determines that "in the event of a conflict between the obligations of the Members of the United Nations under the present Charter and their obligations under any other international agreement, their obligations under the present Charter shall prevail".[13] If one examines the provisions of Chapter VII of the United Nations Charter, the extent of obligations of Member States becomes evident. Chapter VII deals with action that is taken by the Security Council with respect to acts that constitute threats to peace, breaches of the peace and acts of aggression. It prescribes collective action by Member States and enables the Council to decide on measures that are to be taken to maintain and restore international peace and security.[14] Those measures could be of a nature that does not require the use of armed force to give effect to the decisions of the Council by the Member States. The measures may include complete or partial interruption of economic relations, services, means of communication and the severance of diplomatic relations.[15] The Security Council may also, in the event that it determines that such measures would be inadequate or that they have proven to be so, use force in order to maintain and restore international peace and security.[16] The Charter provides for members to undertake to make available for the Council, on its call and in accordance with a special agreement, armed forces, assistance and facilities, including the right of passage for the purpose of maintaining international peace and security.[17] The United Nations Charter as a treaty does impose extensive obligations on its members of a material, human, economic and financial nature. Jordan as a Member State is bound by all the obligations accruing to the members.

The problem, however, arises in the case of Jordan, at least on the theoretical level, owing to the fact that the respective Jordanian authorities never completed the legislative measures required for the Charter, as an international agreement which imposes financial obligations and may affect the private and public rights of Jordanians, to be absorbed into the domestic legal order of Jordan in accordance with Article 33(2) of the Constitution. Jordan's ratification of and accession to the Charter of the United Nations was conducted by means of a decision of the Council of Ministers that was subsequently ratified by the King in accordance with Article 33(1) of the Constitution. The constitutional basis by which the Charter was incorporated into the Jordanian domestic legal system was thus Article 33(1), which stipulates that the King makes treaties and agreements. The Council of Ministers of Jordan, back in 1955, did not seem to pay due consideration to the qualification contained in Article 33(2) of the Constitution. This part of Article 33 underscores in very clear terms the necessity of Parliament's approval of any treaty or agreement that affects the private and public rights of Jordanians or imposes on the budget of the State *any expenses*. In the event that Parliament does not approve such an agreement, by a legislative act, it does not become executable in Jordan and does not become part of the domestic law of the land, nor a superior domestic law. The Charter

13 See *ibid.*, Article 103.

14 See *ibid.*, Article 39.

15 See *ibid.*, Article 41.

16 See *ibid.*, Article 42. See also Article 2(2), (5).

17 See *ibid.*, Article 43.

of the United Nations was never presented to the Jordanian Parliament for approval, despite the fact that it does entail financial obligations and could affect private and public rights of Jordanians. This would be the case if the Security Council were to call on Jordan to make available to it, in the course of its adoption of measures that include the use of force, military personnel, equipment or airfields. The same could be said regarding the annual financial contributions that Jordan makes to the United Nations budget. Those contributions come from the budget of Jordan and clearly impose and constitute *expenses* within the meaning of Article 33(2) of the Constitution. Accordingly, the Charter should have been, in its capacity and character as an international agreement that could affect the private and public rights of Jordanians, and that impose *expenses* on the budget of Jordan, presented and approved by Parliament to meet the constitutional requirement of Article 33(2).

Nevertheless, the standing of the Charter within the scope of the domestic legal order of Jordan was never questioned, challenged or doubted. This is due to the fact that there is no set body in Jordan that is imbued with the capacity to review the constitutionality of executive decisions and acts made by the King directly or through his Ministers. Jordan does not have a Constitutional Court or Constitutional Council. Equally, the courts in Jordan do not have an explicit mandate to exercise constitutional review. They have a mandate to litigate penal and civil cases in accordance with the relevant domestic legislation of the land as enacted by Parliament or the organ empowered to make legislation by delegation.[18] Courts cannot automatically exercise constitutional interpretation or review. There is no means by which individuals are able to make claims to courts challenging the conformity of particular legislation with the Constitution, unless a party that is *directly affected* by a law that is inconsistent with the Constitution makes such a claim. In such a case, the court would not nullify such a law altogether. It would rather refuse to apply such a law in the individual case that is presented to it.[19]

18 The Jordanian Constitution gives the Council of Ministers the power to legislate in the event that Parliament is not in session or dissolved. The Constitution stipulates in Article 94(1) that: "when Parliament is not in session or dissolved, the Council of Ministers may, with the consent of the King, enact temporary laws that regulate matters requiring urgent measures that cannot be delayed or that require urgent public expenditure. Such temporary laws, which should not contravene with the provisions of the Constitution, shall have the force of Law, provided that such temporary laws are presented to Parliament in the first session that it holds. Parliament may then approve such laws or amend them. In the event that Parliament withholds approval, the Council of Ministers should, with the consent of the King declare the nullity of such temporary laws. From the date of such a declaration, the effect of such laws is nullified, provided that such a nullification does not affect contracts and rights acquired under such temporary laws". Equally, the Constitution gives the Council of Ministers the power to enact statutes concerning the administrative divisions in the Kingdom and the organisation of governmental bodies, the means of their administration, the methods of selection of public employees and their competence (Article 120 of the Constitution).

19 See the ruling of the Court of Cassation of Jordan, Case Number 107 dated 25 January 1997. In this case, the Court of Cassation was presented with an appeal by the defendant Bassam Faisal Amin Qasim. The defendant was appealing the ruling of the Court of first instance and the confirmation of the Court of appeal ruling that the conditions of extraditing the

The Jordanian Constitution envisages and establishes a High Council, which has, *inter alia,* the task of interpreting the Constitution upon a request from the Council of Ministers or one of the Houses of Parliament.[20] This Council, based on the request of the Council of Ministers, did interpret Article 33 of the Constitution.[21] The High Council in its decision interpreting Article 33 of the Constitution, stated that according to Article 33(2), all treaties and agreements are executable in Jordan without Parliament's approval *unless* such agreements are of a nature that affects the private and public rights of Jordanians or impose *any expenses* on the budget of the government. This, according to the High Council, emanates from the fact that such treaties and agreements are considered, owing to their inherent nature and subject matter, as directly impinging upon the sovereignty of the State.[22] This ruling of the High Council confirmed the competence of the Executive to enter into agreements and treaties. Such treaties and agreements become part of the Jordanian domestic law and assume supremacy, if the Executive concludes them.[23] The exception to this general competence of the Executive to make agreements and treaties remains the qualification for such agreements to be presented to Parliament for approval after they are concluded by the Executive, if they affect public or private rights of Jordanians and impose expenses on the State's budget.[24]

---

defendant to the United States of America were in conformity with the Extradition Agreement that was signed between Jordan and the United States and published in the Jordanian Official Gazette, vol. No 4055 dated 16 July 1995. The defendant claimed that the Court of First Instance and Court of Appeal were, inter alia, mistaken in giving force to the Extradition Agreement because the agreement was contrary to Article 33(2) of the Constitution and was not presented to Parliament for ratification. Hence, it was not executable in Jordan. The Court of Cassation *held* that:

> "The established Jurisprudence of this Court views Extradition Agreements as ones that affect public and private rights of Jordanians. Thus, such agreements are not in force unless they are approved by Parliament. For the provisions of executing the provisions of the Agreement in Jordan, it is not sufficient to publish the agreement in the Gazette without enacting a law putting into force its provisions and their execution."

The Court went on to say that it accepted the appeal on this ground due to the fact that the decision of the Courts of First Instance and Appeal did not address this matter and failed to provide sufficient reasoning.

20 See the Jordanian Constitution, Articles 57 and 122. Article 57 outlines the Composition of the High Council, whose primary task is to try Ministers. Article 122 states that: "The High Council mentioned in Article 57 has the right of interpreting the provisions of the Constitution, if it is so requested by a decision of the Council of Ministers or a Decision taken by a simple majority of one of the Houses of Parliament. Such an interpretation becomes valid and executable upon its publication in the official Gazette".

21 The Council of Ministers made a request to the High Council to interpret Article 33 of the Constitution in its session dated 20 February 1957. The Council of Ministers requested the High Council to highlight the treaties and agreements that require Parliament's approval.

22 See decision of the High Council. Decision no 2/ 1955. Published in The Official Gazette of the Hashemite Kingdom of Jordan, Vol. 1224, p. 369 (16 April 1955).

23 See the Jordanian Constitution, Article 33(1).

24 See *ibid.*, Article 33(2).

The Charter and its application in Jordan, as noted previously, were never contested. Issues arising from the implementation of the Charter and obligations contained therein, including the annual membership contributions, and application of Security Council imposed economic sanctions were never challenged on any grounds, including the qualifications contained in Article 33(2) of the Constitution. Jordan has been making its annual contributions to the United Nations budget since it joined the Organisation in 1955. Jordan has been participating extensively in Peacekeeping operations of the United Nations.[25] Jordan has been enforcing Security Council imposed sanctions against Iraq too.[26] All such activities conducted by the Jordanian Government were never challenged by individuals before national courts. Equally, such activities were never debated by Parliament on the grounds that they are not in conformity with Article 33(2) of the Constitution. In the case of the courts, this is attributed to the fact that they do not have the legal competence to automatically review the constitutionality of measures adopted by the Executive. Nor do courts have the ability to nullify the measures in question. They merely have the competence to declare that the measure in question is inapplicable to the individual who questioned its illegality before the court. To bring a claim before the courts in Jordan, the affected individual must be directly affected by the measure in question. In the case of enforcing economic sanctions imposed by the Security Council on Iraq, no such action was brought before the Jordanian courts by any individual who has been affected by such enforcement. Hypothetically, if a claim were to be made by an affected individual in Jordan, it would have to arise in the context of the government measures enforcing the sanctions, for example, the refusal of the Customs Department to allow a Jordanian exporter to export certain goods to Iraq. Such a refusal would con-

25 Such activities and participation could arguably be affecting the public and private rights of Jordanians too. Additionally, Article 127 of the Jordanian Constitution stipulates that: " the task of the army *is confined* to the defence of the Country and its safety". Clearly, Peacekeeping operations are not functions that fall within such a confined competence. They do entail the risks of having casualties among the members of such forces. Such a possibility does affect private and public rights too, for it does go beyond the constitutionally envisaged task of the army. However, Jordanian participation in United Nations Peacekeeping operations has been extensive during the past decade. Such participation was never challenged in terms of its legality and conformity with the Constitution.

26 See letter from Mr. Marwan Al-Qasim, the Deputy Prime Minister and Foreign Minister of the Hashemite Kingdom of Jordan, addressed to the President of the Security Council dated 20 August 1990. The letter was annexed to a letter addressed from the Permanent Representative of Jordan to the United Nations to the President of the Security Council dated 20 August 1990. See S/21620 dated 24 August 1990. Cited in D.L. Bethlehem *et al.*, *The Kuwait Crisis: Sanctions and Their Economic Consequences*, Vol. 2, Part 2, (Cambridge University Press, 1994), p. 659. Hereinafter referred to as *The Kuwait Crisis: Sanctions*. The letter reads, *inter alia*, that: "1. The Government of the Hashemite Kingdom of Jordan has taken note of the Security Council's adoption of resolution 661 on 6 August 1990. Cognisant of its obligations under the Charter, and the resolution's mandatory nature, Jordan shall comply with its provisions...". See also annex to the letter addressed from the Permanent Representative of the Hashemite Kingdom of Jordan to the Secretary-General of the United Nations dated 23 August 1990 on national measures adopted by Jordan to implement Resolution 661. Cited in D.L. Bethlehem *et al.*, *The Kuwait Crisis: Sanctions*, *ibid.*, Vol.2, pp. 207-208.

stitute an administrative decision. The individuals affected by administrative decisions have recourse and standing to bring claims before the Supreme Court of Justice to challenge decisions that affect them. Another scenario could be perceived, if a decision was made by the competent governmental authorities to bring to trial a person for allegedly breaching the sanctions by smuggling goods to Iraq. In the event that such cases emerge, it is very likely that the courts would rule that the provisions of the Charter are not executable in Jordan due to the fact that the Charter was not approved by Parliament in accordance with Article 33(2) of the Constitution. The verdict of the courts in such an event would not nullify the entire measures, but rather freeze their operation to the specific plaintiffs in the specific case/cases that were brought to the courts. This would mean that if the courts were to make such a finding, the finding would not be of a general application, but would be confined to the specific case in question. The finding would additionally and logically not apply retroactively to all other previous measures adopted by the government to enforce the sanctions.

Until now, no problem has arisen out of the application of domestic measures to enforce the Security Council sanctions against Iraq. No claims were made domestically to challenge the measures by whomsoever. The measures taken are based on decisions made by the Council of Ministers. The Council of Ministers has the responsibility to administer all the internal and external affairs of the country.[27] It is within this capacity that it adopts the domestic measures to enforce sanctions based on the obligations contained in the United Nations Charter, to which Jordan is a Member. The problems would begin to arise and would pose difficulties if certain individuals or even Parliament were to invoke the fact that the United Nations Charter, as an international agreement, which imposes financial obligations on Jordan and affects the private and public rights of its citizens, was not duly approved by Parliament in accordance with the explicit provision of Article 33(2) of the Constitution. Hence, if the implementation of sanctions against Iraq by Jordan, were based on Jordan's obligations under the Charter of the United Nations, individuals and Parliament would be in a position to question the enforceability of the measures in Jordan. Courts would most likely rule that any measure adopted on issues of enforcement or punishment for sanctions violators, which is based on Security Council resolutions and Charter imposed obligations, is not executable in Jordan. This would be ascribed to the failure to exhaust and meet the requirements of Article 33(2) of the Constitution. Whether Parliament or the courts, based on claims brought by individuals, declare that measures adopted to enforce sanctions are contrary to the constitutional requirement, this would not have, in the case of Parliament, a retroactive effect. The same is true if a court renders such a ruling and the measures would not be nullified altogether. Only the application of such measure/measures would cease in that particular case.

Therefore, it is clear that there does not exist a clear constitutional basis in Jordan for the application, adoption and enforcement of Security Council imposed sanctions.

27 See the Jordanian Constitution, Article 45(1).

(4) *Prior Enabling Legislation*

To date, there is no prior or *ex post facto* enabling legislation in Jordan which addresses the question of the implementation and enforcement of United Nations imposed economic sanctions. This does not seem to be peculiar to Jordan alone. It was established, after the adoption of Resolution 661, that few States have in place a "Sanctions Act" that is designed to provide the national basis for the implementation of Security Council imposed sanctions.[28] Neither was the imposition of sanctions at the national level in Jordan based upon "suitably amended general purpose trade and financial legislation",[29] nor an explicit provision in the Jordanian Constitution to this effect.

The domestic implementation in Jordan is transparent only inasmuch as it is based on the decisions of the Council of Ministers which is the body entrusted with the administration of all internal and external affairs of the country, in addition to the fact that the Jordanian government regards itself, irrespective of obvious deficiencies in incorporating the Charter into domestic Jordanian law, as fully bound by all resolutions of the Council.[30] Accordingly, the Council of Ministers decided that it shall adhere to and enforce Security Council resolutions imposing sanctions on Iraq and communicated this to the Security Council through the Minister of Foreign Affairs of Jordan.[31] The Council of Ministers subsequently set up a Central Committee and sub-committees for the purpose of monitoring and ensuring compliance with the resolutions of the Security Council in Jordan.[32] Accordingly, it can be said that the basis for the domestic measures in Jordan was the executive decision of the Council of Ministers in its discharge of its duties in accordance with the constitutional mandate of the Council of Ministers.[33] Additionally, it could be argued that, depending on the nature of the case, an executive decision implementing a United Nations Security Council resolution could be pegged onto existing legislation, such as the Defence Law. However, this has not happened in practice.

III. Legal Basis of Domestic Measures Based on Regional Organisation Decision

Despite the fact that Jordan is a member of the Arab League[34] and notwithstanding the potential legal effect of Article 7 of the Arab League Charter, and Article 2 of the Joint

---

28 See D.L. Bethlehem, *The Kuwait Crisis: Sanctions, op. cit.*, Volume 2, Part 1, p. xli.

29 *Ibid.*

30 See the Jordanian Constitution, Article 45(1). This Article is the constitutional provision that constitutes the basis for the actions, decisions and executive orders adopted by the Council of Ministers. This, however, ought not to be confused with other constitutional provisions that impose limitations in certain cases such as Article 33(2) mentioned earlier.

31 See D.L. Bethlehem, *op. cit.*, Volume 2, Part 2., p. 659.

32 Interview conducted by Bisher Al-Khasawneh with Omar Qasim the Head of the Iraq Affairs Division at the Customs Department at the Jordanian Ministry of Finance, on 9 April 1999. Hereinafter referred to as Interview with Qasim. The mechanism of the work of the Committee and sub committees will be discussed at length at a later stage of this study.

33 See D.L. Bethlehem, *The Kuwait Crisis: Sanctions, op. cit.*, Volume 2, Part 1, p. 15.

34 Jordan joined the Arab League on 10 May 1945.

Defence and Economic Co-operation Treaty Between the States of the Arab League, which read respectively as follows:
Article 7 of the Arab League Charter provides:

> "Unanimous decisions of the Council shall be binding upon all member-states of the League; majority decisions shall be binding only upon those states which have accepted them.
>
> In either case the decisions of the Council shall be enforced in each member-state according to its respective laws."

Article 2 of the Joint Defence and Economic Co-operation Treaty between the States of the Arab League reads as follows:

> "The Contracting States consider any (act of) armed aggression made against any one or more of them or their armed forces, to be directed against them all. Therefore, in accordance with the right of self-defence, individually and collectively, they undertake to go without delay to the aid of the State or States against which such an act of aggression is made, and immediately to take, individually and collectively, all steps available, including the use of armed force, to repel the aggression and restore security and peace. In conformity with Article 6 of the Arab League Pact and Article 51 of the United Nations Charter, the Arab League Council and U.N. Security Council shall be notified of such act of aggression and the means and procedure taken to check it."

It must be said that Jordan did not as a matter of fact vote for any resolution that the Arab League Council adopted against Iraq. When the deliberations at the Arab League took place, Jordan, along with a number of the 22 Arab League Member States, chose to abstain from voting. Hence, the resolution of the League on this matter was not binding for either Jordan or other Arab League Member States who abstained or voted against the resolution.

As to Article 2 of the Joint Defence and Economic Co-operation Treaty Between the States of the Arab League, this particular article as well as the entire treaty do not seem to be of any help in assessing the issue of compliance by Jordan on the basis of a regional organisation decision, as there was actually no invocation of this treaty nor any reference to it by States parties in the case of the Iraqi invasion of Kuwait. The reason for such absence could be ascribed to the expeditious manner by which the Security Council, which is the organ of primary responsibility and competence to preserve international peace and security, responded to the Iraqi invasion. Hence, it can be said that neither the Covenant of the Arab League nor the Joint Defence and Economic Co-operation treaty between States of the Arab League provide a legal basis for Jordan's domestic implementation and compliance with sanctions imposed by the Security Council against Iraq.

IV. Comparison of Content of Security Council Resolutions and Domestic Measures

In the absence of a separate, direct and comprehensive legislation in Jordan on the issue of domestic measures for implementing sanctions, the content of the Security Council resolutions was adopted and imported lock, stock and barrel, in terms of the scope of prohibitions and prohibited items. Imports from Iraq came to a complete stop with the exception of oil.[35] Jordan communicated to the Security Council that:

> "1. Jordan has informed Iraq that it will prevent the transport of goods imported for Iraq through the Jordanian port of Aqaba, with the exception of pharmaceutical preparations, medical products and foodstuffs for humanitarian purposes.
> 2. Jordan is imposing a ban on the exportation of all goods and products of Iraqi origin through the port of Aqaba, including petroleum and its derivatives.
> 3. Jordan is temporarily allowing foodstuffs which arrived by ship at the port of Aqaba before 6 August 1990 to cross its territory to Iraq in Jordanian and foreign trucks.
> 4[1]. Jordan will no longer issue permits for the exportation of goods and products of Jordanian origin to Iraq and Kuwait, with the exception of pharmaceutical preparations, medical products and humanitarian foodstuffs
> 5[2]. Jordan will no longer issue permits for the importation of goods and products of Iraqi origin to Jordan, with the exception of certain petroleum derivatives as set forth in paragraph 3 below.
> 6[3]. Despite the imposition of a ban on Iraqi goods and products, Jordan will continue to import certain petroleum derivatives from Iraq, particularly heavy oil, because of the lack of any immediate or foreseeable alternative and in view of Jordan's total dependence on it for the production of energy. Jordan will consider halting such imports if an alternative becomes available.
> 7[1]. The transfer of funds to Iraq and Kuwait is prohibited.

35 See Note Verbale dated 16 May 1991 from the Permanent Representative of Jordan to the United Nations to the Chairman of the Security Council Sanctions Committee established by Resolution 661 (Document S/AC.25/1991/COMM.159, dated 16 May 1991). Jordan informed the Sanctions Committee that "it has resumed on an urgent basis its importation of Oil and Oil derivatives from Iraq in limited quantities absolutely essential for Jordan's own internal needs". These imports, the letter stated, "are being funded by drawing down on Iraqi debts to Jordan". The letter went on to say that: " although the Jordanian Government has been trying to import crude oil from other available sources by sea through Aqaba port, the technical limitations for receiving, handling and discharging crude oil vessels at Aqaba port do not allow us to receive all our requirements of crude oil by sea". See also the reply of the Sanctions Committee Chairman dated 22 May 1991. The letter stated that: "… I have the honour to inform you that, given the unique position of Jordan in regard to Iraq, as the Committee has previously acknowledged, the Committee at its 41st meeting, held on 21 May 1991, took note of Jordan's resumption of the import of Iraqi oil and oil derivatives as described in your note verbale, pending any arrangements that can be made to obtain supplies from other sources, and on the understanding that such Iraqi oil exports are subject to the provision of Security Council resolution 692 (1991)".

8[2]. Jordan permits the movement of individuals and of property they are carrying; it facilitates such movement for humanitarian reasons."[36]

These measures that Jordan has communicated to the Secretary-General do echo the prohibitions contained in Resolution 661.[37] They also adhere to the allowances provided for in the resolution. The only issue that Jordan singled out was the import of oil and oil derivatives. Objective reasons and problems of serious consequence were the reason for the waiver /permission granted to Jordan to do so. Equally, Jordan had stopped operating aircraft of any sort to Iraq in accordance with Resolutions 661 and 670.[38] As to other services, they were not ones that were provided for in the Security Council resolution and were not, hence, covered by measures adopted by Jordan.

The competent Jordanian authorities began implementing the sanctions upon the adoption of the resolutions imposing them by the Security Council. Although the communication of the measures adopted did not take place until late August, effective implementation had started as early as 10 August 1990.[39]

Despite the fact that there were no reported cases of sanctions violation, the applicable law to any such violations would be the Customs Law of the Hashemite Kingdom of Jordan.[40] It would be interesting to imagine penal action taken by the Jordanian authorities against a sanctions violator in the courts. This would raise all sorts of interesting issues of a nature that was referred to earlier when addressing the constitutional basis for domestic measures. Courts would then judge on the requirements of Article 33(2) of the Constitution that was analysed earlier. If the Ministry of Finance or the public prosecution were to base the penal action on a violation that breaches an obligation accruing to Jordan by means of the Charter of the United Nations, the competent courts would then be in a position to assess the constitutional requirement of Article 33(2).

36 See Annex to letter from Permanent Representative of Jordan to the United Nations addressed to the Secretary-General (S/21614, 23 August 1990) Cited in D.L. Bethlehem, *The Kuwait Crisis: Sanctions*, *op. cit.*, pp. 207-208.

37 See Security Council Resolution 661, 6 August 1990. Cited in M. Weller et al., *Iraq and Kuwait: The Hostilities and their Aftermath* (Cambridge, 1993), pp. 2-3. Hereinafter referred to as Weller, *Iraq and Kuwait*. The resolution does make provision for continued supply of medical supplies and foodstuffs in humanitarian circumstances [para 2(c)]. It also permits the transfer of funds that are strictly and exclusively for payment of strictly medical or humanitarian purposes and, in humanitarian circumstances, foodstuffs [para 4]. The prohibitions and allowances of Resolution 661 are echoed in the measures adopted by Jordan and communicated to the Secretary-General in the letter dated 23 August 1990 (*Ibid.*)

38 Jordan resumed operating civil aircraft trips to Iraq that carry both passengers and cargo in October 2000. The procedure for such operations will be examined in ensuing parts of this chapter.

39 Interview with Qasim, *op. cit.*

40 Law No. 16, 1983 was repealed by Law No. 20, 1998.

V. Domestic Procedures for Implementation and Enforcement

The proper examination of domestic procedures adopted in Jordan for implementing and enforcing sanctions imposed by the Security Council against Iraq can only be properly understood through firstly, surveying the relevant key resolutions that deal with those sanctions, their evolution, amendment and development. Secondly, the procedure itself, within Jordan and at the United Nations, will be highlighted and explained.

(1) Survey of the Relevant Key Security Council Resolutions

The first resolution to impose mandatory sanctions on Iraq by the Security Council was Resolution 661.[41] This resolution in effect prohibits all exports to and imports from Iraq and Kuwait of all goods. However, the resolution makes provision for continued supply of medical supplies and foodstuffs in humanitarian circumstances [para 2(c)]. It also permits the transfer of funds that are strictly and exclusively for payment of strictly medical or humanitarian purposes and, in humanitarian circumstances, foodstuffs [para 4].[42] This remained the case until the Security Council adopted Resolution 687.[43] This resolution stated in paragraph 20 that the Council "Decides, effective immediately, that the prohibitions against the sale or supply to Iraq of commodities or products other than medicine and health supplies, and prohibitions against financial transactions related thereto contained in Resolution 661 (1990), shall not apply to foodstuffs notified to the Security Council Committee established by Resolution 661 (1990) concerning the situation between Iraq and Kuwait, or with the approval of that committee, under the simplified "no-objection" procedure, to materials and supplies for essential civilian needs". This paragraph expanded the scope of allowance as indicated. Accordingly, it became possible to supply Iraq with medical supplies and foodstuffs notwithstanding the qualification of humanitarian circumstances provided for in Resolution 661, as long as they are essential for civilian needs. The difference between the two concepts, is reflected in practical terms, in the fact that according to the stipulation of Resolution 661, it was not a requirement to notify or seek the consent of the Committee established by the resolution as long as the export relates to medical supplies and foodstuffs in humanitarian circumstances. It was left, it seems, to the discretion of States to determine whether such medical supplies and foodstuffs exclusively meet this qualification of humanitarian purposes and circumstances. Resolution 687 expanded the scope of allowed exports to Iraq of materials and supplies, in addition to foodstuffs that are essential for civilian needs. The determination that such materials are for essential civilian needs, however, is not left for the determination of the respective States but rather, as the language of the resolution and the ensuing practice exhibit, for the Committee established by Resolution 661. Any State, or entity therein, through the organs of the State, has to notify and seek the approval or "no objec-

41 See M. Weller et al., *Iraq and Kuwait*, *op. cit.*

42 *Ibid.*

43 See Security Council Resolution 687 (1991), adopted by the Council at its 2981st meeting on 3 April 1991.

tion" of the Committee for the export of such materials and supplies. The Committee is the sole body that decides whether the materials and supplies in question are essential for civilian needs or not.

Prior to the adoption of Resolution 687, the Security Council adopted Resolution 670 (1990).[44] In this resolution the Council, in paragraph 2 "confirms that resolution 661 (1990) applies to all means of transportation, including aircraft". The resolution also provides in paragraph 3 that the Council "decides that all States, notwithstanding the existence of any rights or obligations conferred or imposed by any international agreement or any contract entered into or any licence or permit granted before the date of the present resolution, shall deny permission to any aircraft to take off from their territory if the aircraft would carry any cargo to or from Iraq or Kuwait other than food in humanitarian circumstances, subject to authorisation by the Security Council or the Security Council Committee established by Resolution 661 (1990) concerning the situation between Iraq and Kuwait and in accordance with Resolution 666 (1990), or supplies intended strictly for medical purposes or solely for the United Nations Iran-Iraq Military Observer Group. In paragraph 4 of the resolution, the Council

> "decides also that all states shall deny permission to any aircraft destined to Iraq or Kuwait, whatever its state of registration, to overfly their territory unless:
> (a) The aircraft lands at an airfield designated by the state outside Iraq or Kuwait in order to permit inspection to ensure that there is no cargo on board in violation of resolution 661 (1990) or the present resolution, and for this purpose the aircraft may be detained for as long as necessary; or
> (b) The particular flight has been approved by the Security Council Committee; or
> (c) The flight is certified by the United Nations as solely for the purposes of the Military Observer Group."

The Council in paragraph 6 "decides moreover that all states shall notify in a timely fashion the Security Council Committee of any flight between its territory and Iraq or Kuwait to which the requirement to land in paragraph 4 above does not apply and the purpose of such flight". This entire resolution is relevant to a later part of this chapter as many States, including Jordan, resumed operating flights to Iraq as of September/October 2000. Procedures adopted by Jordan and Jordan's position will be referred to in ensuing parts of this chapter.

On 14 April 1995, the Security Council adopted Resolution 986.[45] This resolution provided for, *inter alia*, allowing States, notwithstanding other previous resolutions, to permit the import of petroleum and petroleum products originating in Iraq, including financial and other essential transactions directly relating thereto, sufficient to produce a sum not exceeding a total of one million United States dollars every 90 days for purposes set forth in the resolution that include financing the export of materials and sup-

44 See Security Council Resolution 670 (1990), adopted by the Council at its 2943rd meeting on 25 September 1990.

45 See Security Council Resolution 986 (1995), adopted by the Council at its 3519th meeting on 14 April 1995.

plies essential for human needs to Iraq, providing money for the compensation fund out of which compensation decided by the United Nations Compensation Commission (UNCC) is paid to claimants, funding the expenses of the various United Nations operations in and relating to Iraq, including those relating to disarmament, funding the purchase of equipment needed to upgrade the capacity of petroleum production facilities. The resolution also provided for the establishment of an escrow account by the Secretary General, out of which all the above mentioned payments are to be made from and it mandated the Committee established by Resolution 661 to approve such sales to ensure the transparency of each transaction and its conformity with the relevant provisions of the resolution, after submission of an application by the State concerned, endorsed by the government of Iraq, for each proposed purchase of Iraqi petroleum and petroleum products. Also the resolution provided for the full payment of the full amount of each purchase of Iraqi oil directly by the purchaser in the state concerned into the aforementioned escrow account.[46] This resolution provided for new mechanisms through the establishment of the escrow account and expanded the scope of allowable exports to Iraq to include necessary materials for enhancing the capacity of oil production in Iraq. It also, for the first time allowed the imports of Iraqi Petroleum and petroleum products by all States to meet the financing of the materials and goods that are exported to Iraq and are essential for civilian needs as provided for in Resolution 687.

The next key Security Council resolution relevant to this study is Resolution 1284 (1999).[47] In particular paragraph 17 of the resolution which states that the Council

> "directs the committee established by Resolution 661 (1990) to approve, on the basis of proposals from the Secretary General, lists of humanitarian items, including foodstuffs, pharmaceutical and medical supplies, as well as basic or standard medical and agricultural equipment and basic standard educational items, decides, notwithstanding paragraph 3 of Resolution 661 (1990) and paragraph 20 of Resolution 687 (1991), that supplies of these items will not be submitted for approval of that committee, except for items subject to the provisions of Resolution 1051 (1996),[48] and will be notified to the Secretary-General and financed in accordance with the provisions of paragraph 8 (a) and 8 (b) of Resolution 986 (1995), and requests the Secretary-General to inform the committee in a timely manner of all such notifications received and actions taken".

(2) *The Procedures within Jordan to Implement and Enforce Sanctions and the Procedure at the United Nations*

The requirements of Resolutions 661, 687, 986 and subsequently 1284 stipulate that all goods bound for Iraq are prohibited with the exceptions provided for in the resolutions.

---

46 See *ibid.*

47 See Security Council Resolution 1284 (1999) adopted by the Council at its 4084th meeting on 17 December 1999.

48 This resolution addressed "dual use" materials. Such materials can be used for both civilian and military purposes. Resolution 1051 provided an extensive list of such materials and subjected

The export to Iraq of any other goods that do not fall within the scope of the exceptions provided for in the resolutions require the explicit approval of the Sanctions Committee. Such an export request has to be filled out by the prospective exporter on a special form supplied by the authorities of the exporting State. The form contains details of the goods, including their value, origin, importing person/body in Iraq and the end uses of such goods.

In the case of Jordan, such a request is submitted to the Iraq office at the Customs Department. If the form is properly filled, it is thence sent through diplomatic mail to Jordan's Mission to the United Nations in New York. The Mission in turn sends the request to the Secretariat of the Sanctions Committee. The Committee accepts the request, rejects it or puts the request on hold pending more information and clarification.[49]

The Iraq office was established within the Customs Department by a decision in 1990 of the Council of Ministers for the purpose of ensuring compliance with the Security Council resolutions imposing sanctions on Iraq. The Council of Ministers decided further to establish a Joint Central Security Committee (JCSC) entrusted with the same task.[50] The JCSC is composed of representatives of the Customs Department, and the General Intelligence, Military Intelligence and Public Security Departments. The Committee inspects the documents and export authorisations granted by the Sanctions Committee and issues a written order for executing export approval granted by the Sanctions Committee. The JCSC's order of execution has to be signed by all its members and it has to fully conform with the original application. Sub Joint Security Committees (SJSC) were also set up at all export points in Jordan, in addition to the Karama border point, which is the border point separating Jordan and Iraq. The SJSC's are entrusted with the task of inspecting the exported goods and their conformity with the approval of the Sanctions Committee and the order of execution issued by the JCSC. The Karama SJSC is entrusted with the task of conducting a final check on the cargo to ensure that it has not been altered en route before crossing into Iraq. The membership and composition of the SJSC is similar to that of the JCSC.[51] Additionally, Lloyd's Register concluded an agreement with the Jordanian Government in 1994 whereby the former would establish and conduct a permanent onshore inspection operation at the port of Aqaba to inspect all goods and cargo that are bound to Iraq through the Aqaba port. The Jordanian government decided in early November 2000 to terminate the arrangement with Lloyds and notified the decision to the United Nations. Land-based inspections are conducted by Jordanian authorities at Aqaba and all other land boundaries.

It should be noted, however, that exporting to Iraq from Jordan takes various forms, depending on the nature of the goods, and the above-mentioned procedures vary accordingly. The first mechanism by which Jordan exports to Iraq is based on the bilateral trade

---

their export to Iraq to exceptionally strict mechanisms, assessment, approval or denial that is to be conducted by the committee established by Resolution 661 (1990).

49 Interview with Qasim, *op. cit.*

50 *Ibid.* Qasim maintained that this decision of the Council of Ministers was adopted in September 1990.

51 *Ibid.*

protocol. This is an annual barter arrangement. It provides Jordan with Iraqi petroleum and petroleum products in return for supplying Iraq with goods and materials that are essential for civilian needs and life within the meaning of Resolution 687. In this case neither Iraq nor Jordan receive cash funds. The Iraqi petroleum supplied is valuated and assessed and Jordanian individuals and entities are allowed to supply Iraq with goods and materials up to the valuated ceiling assessed for the Iraqi petroleum. The Central Bank of Jordan pays the exporting Jordanian individuals and entities for the value of the exported goods from Jordanian government funds. This arrangement is exclusive for Jordanian nationals or companies. In this case a notification to the Committee established by Security Council Resolution 661 is made identifying the goods, their end-use in Iraq and other aspects referred to above. Such notifications are subject to the simplified and accelerated "no-objection" procedure referred to in Resolution 687. At the Jordanian end, after ensuring that there is no objection by the 661 Committee, the goods are inspected at the departure point by Jordanian customs officials and again at the border point of Karama with Iraq to ensure that the goods are for essential civilian needs.

The other mechanism that exists for exporting to Iraq is the export of medical equipment and medicine and foodstuffs in humanitarian circumstances within the meaning of Resolution 661. In this case, and subject to a strict test that takes into full account the meaning given by the Security Council for medical supplies and medicine and foodstuffs in humanitarian circumstances, no communication is made to the 661 Committee. However, the exported equipment is rigorously inspected in Jordan by officials from the Ministry of Trade and Industry, Customs Department and Security Services at loading point and at the border with Iraq at Karama to ensure that the exports are fully in conformity with the allowance of Resolution 661.

The third and final means of export is outside the scope of both the bilateral trade protocol (barter arrangement) and outside the scope of medical supplies and medicine and foodstuffs in humanitarian circumstances within the scope of allowance provided for in Resolution 661. In such a case a prospective Jordanian entity or individual wishing to export goods to Iraq would have to fill out a special form supplied by the authorities at the Iraq office in the Customs Department. The form contains details of the goods including their value, origin, importing person/body in Iraq and the end uses of such goods. If the form is properly filled out, it is thence sent through diplomatic mail to Jordan's Mission to the United Nations in New York. The Mission in turn sends the request to the Secretariat of the Sanctions Committee. The Committee accepts the request, rejects it or puts the request on hold pending more information and clarification.[52] If the export is approved by the Committee, it sends its approval to the mission which in turn sends it to the Customs Department. The cargo is then rigorously inspected by the respective Jordanian authorities at loading point and at the border with Iraq in Karama and subject also to random en route inspections. In such a case the exporter receives the payment for the goods that he had supplied from the escrow account established by the Secretary-General of the United Nations in accordance with Security Council Resolution 986.

As to export permits granted to third countries and their nationals or companies, the export is conducted through the same mechanism outlined above, provided that the

52 *Ibid.*

approval of the Sanctions Committee is endorsed and authenticated by the Jordanian Embassy in that State and the third State's Embassy in Jordan.

(3) *Recent Developments Concerning Sanctions Imposed against Iraq, Including the Concept of "Smart Sanctions"*

On the 14th of May, 2002, the Security Council adopted Resolution 1409.[53] This resolution introduced and adopted a Goods Review List (GRL), in addition to revised procedures for the application of the provisions of the resolution.[54] The resolution further authorised States to permit, as of 30 May 2002, the sale or supply to Iraq of any commodities or products other than those referred to in paragraph 24 of Resolution 687 (1991) or items listed on the GRL attached to this resolution, unless such commodities or products are approved by the Committee established by Resolution 661 (1990).[55]

This resolution also revisited the procedures for trading with Iraq. The new procedures require that each application "notification or Request to Ship Goods to Iraq"[56] for the sale or supply of goods to Iraq that would be financed by the escrow account referred to in Resolution 986 and established by the Secretary-General, must be forwarded to the Office of the Iraq Program (OIP) at the United Nations Secretariat by the exporting State's Permanent or Observer Mission to the United Nations or by the United Nations' agencies or programs.[57] Such applications must contain comprehensive information about the goods and commodities in question, including technical specifications and information as to whether the goods or commodities contain any items covered by the GRL or strict military equipment covered by paragraph 24 of Resolution 687. The OIP registers and reviews the application within 10 working days and may, in case of incomplete applications, request additional information. The application is thence forwarded by the OIP to the United Nations Monitoring, Verification and Inspection Commission (UNMOVIC) and the International Atomic Energy Agency (IAEA). UNMOVIC and IAEA experts thence evaluate the applications to determine whether they contain military goods prohibited by paragraph 24 of Resolution 687 or military-related equipment covered by the GRL. UNMOVIC and/or IAEA may request additional information from the Mission or entity submitting the application and if no reply, request for information or denial of application is received from UNMOVIC and/or IAEA within 10 working days, the application will be considered approved.[58] If the application is explicitly or implicitly approved by UNMOVIC and/or IAEA, the OIP will notify the submitting Mission or entity, the Iraqi government and relevant United Nations organs. Upon verification by United Nations personnel on the ground in Iraq of the arrival of the

53 See Security Council Resolution 1409, adopted by the Security Council at its 4531st meeting on 14 May 2002, hereinafter referred to as SCR 1409.

54 See *ibid.*, operative paragraph (2).

55 See *ibid.*, operative paragraph (3).

56 The official name given at the United Nations to applications to export to Iraq.

57 See Procedures attached to SCR 1409.

58 *Ibid.*

goods or commodities, the exporter will be eligible for payment from the escrow account established in accordance with Resolution 986. If UNMOVIC and/or IAEA determine that the application in question contains military equipment within the context of paragraph 24 of Resolution 687, they will notify the submitting mission or entity, through the OIP, of the ineligibility for approval of the application in question. The OIP will forward, absent a request by the submitting Mission or entity for reconsideration within 10 working days, to the 661 Committee, applications which UNMOVIC and /or IAEA determine contain items listed on the GRL for the purposes of evaluating whether the GRL items in question can be sold to Iraq. The 661 Committee will be provided, also by OIP, UNMOVIC and IAEA, at the request of the submitting Mission or entity, an assessment of the humanitarian, economic and security implications of the approval or denial of the application in question. Upon receiving the applications, the 661 Committee will have 10 working days to determine whether the items can be sold to Iraq or not. The Committee may approve the items, deny approval, request additional information. If, however, no action is taken by the Committee within 10 working days, the application will be considered approved. The submitting Mission or entity will have 90 days to reply to additional information requested by the 661 Committee and if such additional information is not received within the 90 days period, the application will be considered supplier-inactive and if 90 further days pass without information being supplied, the application will be considered lapsed. The 661 Committee will have 20 working days to examine the application after the supply of the additional requested information and absent action within this period the application will be considered approved. The submitting Mission or entity will have 30 days to appeal to the 661 Committee for reconsideration of rejected applications and the decision of the Committee will then be final.

Delegations and missions to the United Nations have expressed more satisfaction with the efficiency and expeditious manner by which this new procedure is being conducted at the United Nations.[59]

The 661 Committee is also dealing with notifications submitted to it directly by States concerning the operation of civilian flights to Iraq. Many countries, including Jordan, have opted to resume the operation of civil commercial flights to and from Iraq. Those countries, including Jordan, seem to take the view that Resolution 670 does not in effect prohibit civil flights to Iraq as long as such flights do not carry prohibited goods and materials covered by the relevant Security Council resolution and as long as the duty to notify the 661 Committee is properly met.[60]

59 Many members at various missions to the United Nations expressed this opinion to the author but requested non-attribution of those remarks.

60 This seems to be the case, as Jordan and other countries have been operating regular flights to Iraq since late September 2000. The course of action adopted by those countries has been to notify the 661 Committee and the practice of the Committee has been thus far to accept such notifications as long as they contain adequate information regarding the nature of the cargo on board. It has been maintained by one delegation of a certain country to the United Nations that one of the representatives of one of the P5 to the 661 Committee only once placed such a request on hold and that the authorities of the notifying country in question, not convinced by the reasons for placing the application on hold, proceeded with informing that

It must be noted in the context of referring to Resolution 1409 (2002) that this resolution came as efforts were being made to introduce a new or "reformed" sanctions regime that aimed at responding more effectively to the humanitarian needs of the Iraqi people, while at the same time placing more strict controls over cash that some Security Council members were contending was finding its way, illegally as they maintained, to the Iraqi government. Those efforts began to surface in April 2001. They were subject to extensive debate both within the Security Council and beyond it. They became commonly known as the efforts to introduce "smart sanctions" intending to allow the flow of all civilian goods to Iraq in an unhindered manner while elaborating mechanisms and means to prevent any loopholes that would allow the flow into Iraq of both prohibited goods, dual use goods listed in a GRL that was to be drawn up accompanying the proposed resolution and prevent the flow of any cash to the Iraqi government outside the escrow account through illegal petroleum sales.

Efforts were exerted to put in motion this amended regime at the end of the 9th stage of the oil for food programme contained within the mechanism introduced by Resolution 986 and subsequent resolutions increasing the ceiling for Iraqi petroleum and petroleum products sales. The intention was that this new regime of smart sanctions would be in motion and operation through a Security Council Resolution by 3 July 2001. Active efforts were exerted at the Council to table resolutions that would introduce this new regime of " smart sanctions". Various drafts of the proposed resolutions raised major concerns for many Member States in the Council as well as countries neighbouring Iraq, including Jordan. The proposals contained in the initial proposed drafts of that resolution seemed to nullify any existing bilateral trade arrangement that existed between Iraq and its neighbouring countries, including Jordan, Turkey and Syria. The drafts seemed to be attempting to bring all the pre-existing bilateral barter arrangements between those countries and Iraq within the ambit of the new proposed regime. Jordan was very concerned that the proposed resolution did not seem to take into consideration its bilateral annual trade protocol with Iraq which is, as explained above, a barter arrange-

country bilaterally that it would operate that flight anyway. Accordingly that placement of the application on hold was withdrawn. The author has seen copies of such correspondence and was explicitly asked not to attribute them directly. The point of view that regards the explicit approval of the 661 Committee, and not merely notification of the Committee, as a condition and legal pre-requisite point to the fact that Security Council Resolution 1284 (1999) stated in its Operative Paragraph (26) that the Council "decides that Hajj pilgrimage flights which do not transport cargo into or out of Iraq are exempt from the provisions of paragraph 3 of resolution 661 (1990) and resolution 670 (1990), provided timely notification of each flight is made to the committee established by resolution 661 (1990)". They contend that the notification requirement only pertains to aircraft carrying hajj pilgrims that do not carry cargo and they stipulate that the fact that this type of aircraft is explicitly mentioned in the resolution means in effect that all other type of aircraft require not only notification, but also approval of the Council or Committee established by Resolution 661. The subsequent practice of the Committee and acquiescence of the Council since many States resumed flights to Iraq seems to suggest that there is an acceptance among Council members of the idea that there is only a duty to notify as long as the aircraft in question does not carry goods or materials prohibited by Resolutions 661, 687 and goods that are on the GRL.

ment subject to a special preferential petroleum price mechanism. The proposed drafts that were circulated initially by two of the permanent members of the Council failed to address this Jordanian concern and concerns of Turkey and Syria on similar bilateral arrangements. The various drafts only pointed to the fact that the Council is "determined also to consult interested stated in the region and to act in cooperation with the states neighbouring Iraq" and "requests the Secretary General to consult the States sharing land borders with Iraq on specific arrangements to be established in cooperation with those states for the import of up to 150,000 barrels per day of petroleum and petroleum products from Iraq to those states, provided that such arrangements permit payment to Iraq only in the form of commodities or products or the deposit of funds due to Iraq in escrow accounts ... and to make recommendations in this regard for the approval of the Council within 120 days of the adoption of this resolution".[61] Neighbouring countries, including Jordan, had major problems with the language of the resolution as it failed to be specific regarding existing arrangements. Jordan seems to have maintained the position that its bilateral protocol barter arrangement with Iraq would be nullified as a result of this resolution and that the language of the paragraph in effect does not exceed being general language requesting the Secretary General to make recommendations after the resolution has already been adopted and leaving options open before the Council to approve or reject such arrangements. This lack of future clarity seems to have been of serious concern for Jordan. Jordan seems to have viewed the possible nullification of its barter arrangement with Iraq, through such a resolution, as the United Nations possibly reneging on a permission it gave to Jordan in reply to Jordan's communication to the Security Council and the 661 Committee in 1991 that it faced special economic problems within the meaning of Article 50 of the United Nations Charter, and that it will continue import of Iraqi petroleum and petroleum products, and the reply it received stating that the Committee "takes note of Jordan's decision".[62] Jordan seemingly viewed such a potential resolution as further aggravating its economic problems arising directly as a result of its full implementation of the sanctions.

Neighbouring countries with land borders with Iraq also had problems with another paragraph in the draft. This paragraph provided that the Council "requests the Secretary General, to review and revise the procedures for land based monitoring of the export of commodities and products to Iraq by land and sea, to ensure the effectiveness of the arrangements at authorised border crossings, utilising United Nations personnel as appropriate and to prevent the export to Iraq at those crossings and elsewhere of commodities and products not authorised for sale or supply to Iraq".[63] The neighbouring States were uncomfortable with the insinuation in the language contained in the paragraph of the need to have border controls conducted by personnel not from their own

61 This was language contained in Operative Paragraph (6) of the draft resolution in question which the author of this chapter had the opportunity to see but as a matter of propriety is unable to attribute to a specific country and/or countries that are permanent members of the Council.

62 See *supra* note 35.

63 This was the language of proposed Operative Paragraph (17) of the proposed draft resolution. See *supra* note 61.

respective separate apparatuses and expressed in certain cases their explicit rejection of such a course of action and their intention not to permit such an arrangement, even if the draft were adopted.[64]

Additionally, during the deliberations on the possible adoption of a new resolution amending the modalities and procedures for the sanctions, Iraq had threatened that it would cut off all its oil exports if such a resolution were passed. This threat did not help some neighbouring countries who depended either fully or to a significant extent on Iraqi oil and petroleum supplies to be more receptive to elements contained in the proposed circulated drafts. Finally, certain countries felt that proposed elements contained in proposed drafts seemed to attempt to perpetuate sanctions, deviate from comprehensively addressing the issue of the relationship of Iraq and the United Nations as foreseen in Resolution 1284 and make humanitarian conditions in Iraq more difficult. Such fears were expressed by some Security Council Permanent Member States. One such Security Council Permanent Member explicitly stated in late June 2001 in a letter addressed from its foreign minister to the President of the Security Council for that month that "after we carefully considered all pros and contras we have come to the conclusion that the adoption of a Security Council resolution based on the idea of "clever sanctions" would be counterproductive. That is why we will not be able to let it pass".[65] All of these factors led to the abandonment of the smart sanctions notion and the reintroduction of only some of its elements later to be incorporated in what is now known as Resolution 1409.

(4) Role of National Courts

To date, there is no reported court case which deals with the legal status or effect of the decision taken by the Council of Ministers implementing Resolution 661. Whether the Council of Ministers' decision is open to judicial review is dependent on its legal characterisation: is it an administrative decision, or an "act of state"? If it is the former it can be challenged provided certain conditions are present.[66] If it is regarded to be an "act of

---

64 The author was able to access material containing this position of one of the neighbouring countries, but is unable to specify this country except to explicitly state that it is not Jordan.

65 The author has an unofficial translation of the letter but is unable to disclose the specific country. The letter pointed, among other important points regarding reservations, to the items contained in the proposed GRL and the unacceptability of including in such a list inventory elaborated in accordance with Resolution 1051, as well as the Wassenaar list, and the possible destabilising effect on the Middle East that such a resolution might create if Iraq did not accept it or cooperate with it and other means became necessary to enforce compliance, to the fact that "the adoption of the new sanctions scheme based only on external control will finally bury the very idea of renewal of disarmament monitoring in Iraq and hence the cancellation of the embargo." It also noted "the negative reaction from the immediate neighbours of Iraq and other regional states…as they see in the proposed novelties a threat to their socio-economic stability. This fact cannot be ignored".

66 Such as: standing, the identification of the proper defendant, exhaustion of other available remedies, time limit and the available discretion for the administrative body which issued the decision under challenge.

state", the decision will not be justiciable and thus not subject to judicial review. Generally speaking, an administrative decision is defined as "a unilateral binding decision, rendered by the administration (public authority) while exercising its legitimate power, with the effect of changing or creating a specific legal position or situation, the purpose of which is to serve public interest."[67]

It is a general principle of Arab law (including Jordan) that "acts of state" are not justiciable. This means that if a decision rendered by the government is considered to fall within this category, it will be immune from judicial control in all its forms and manifestations. "Acts of state" have been defined as "decisions/acts made by the government in its capacity as a ruling power and not as an administrative power." In addition, the government has full power to act, or to make any decision in the way it sees fit, without any judicial control over those activities. The main problem with the "acts of state" doctrine has been how to distinguish it from administrative decisions which are subject to judicial review. This has been left to the courts to decide. Various tests have been utilised in this regard. The most widely accepted test is the "judicial list" test. This entails identifying those decisions considered by courts as being "acts of state" decisions. According to this test the following decisions or acts have been considered to fall within the category of "acts of states": (a) decisions made to organise the relationship between the government and parliament;[68] (b) decisions taken in the context of international relations;[69] and (c) decisions made in connection with war and military operations.[70] It is probable that the Implementation Measure will be regarded as a *force majeure* event; its effect on private rights and contracts being: to exonerate one or both of the contracting parties from liability; and/or the suspension or termination of the contractual obligation.

(5) Interface between Domestic and International Implementation

In the case of Jordan, the issue of the interface between domestic and international implementation of Security Council sanction resolutions has arisen exclusively in the context of economic sanctions against Iraq. As mentioned above, in 1990, Jordan applied to the Security Council Sanctions Committee for an exemption from the provision which prohibited the import of oil and oil derivatives from Iraq. The way Jordan's request has been handled by Jordan on the one hand and the Committee on the other is not unproblematic and raises many interesting complex legal questions. Some of which are:

- Does the Sanctions Committee "taking-note" of Jordan's request for an exemption amount to an agreement/permission?

---

67 This general definition of an administrative decision is widely accepted in all Arab administrative law jurisdiction. In addition to this definition other criteria are also relied upon in distinguishing administrative decisions from other decisions.

68 For example, proposing bills or withdrawing them; objections made by the head of State against approved laws, calling for elections, recalling Parliament; dissolving Parliament.

69 For example, recognition of governments, severing diplomatic relations with another State; joining an international organisation.

70 For example, declaring war, decisions taken in organising military manoeuvres; imposing blockades; refusal to pay compensation for damage caused by military operations.

– Has the Committee the power or the authority to agree to Jordan's request?

While there are no explicit and unequivocal answers to such questions, it would seem that in practice, the Sanction Committee "taking note"[71] of Jordan's request and communication thereafter that it resumed importation of Iraqi oil does amount to an agreement, as this was not challenged through the course of 12 long years either by Council members or by the Committee or any other State.[72] The same seems true regarding the authority of the Committee to agree. It seems from a practical standpoint that such authority in the case of sanctions against Iraq exists, as such authority was neither questioned nor challenged in practice. However, this is not to suggest that, should the Security Council make any determination to the contrary at any point, Jordan or any other State for such a purpose can claim it has a protected acquired right. The Council can, at any time make determinations that would ultimately nullify such allowances and States would have to comply in accordance with their obligation to carry out the resolutions of the Council under Article 25 of the United Nations Charter. Additionally, if the 661 Committee does possess the authority to provide allowances, this means that it also would have the authority to nullify such allowances in the future.

VI. Special Economic Problems Facing Jordan and Remedies Provided by the Charter

Jordan was one of the countries that were profoundly affected by the imposition of economic sanctions against Iraq by the Security Council. Perhaps it would not be an exaggeration to say that the overall economic burden that Jordan has to bear as a result of the sanctions is much larger than that of any other country except Kuwait.[73] It is estimated that Jordan's exports to Iraq have declined as a result of implementing the sanctions, from $190 million in 1989 to $82 million in 1991 thence to $75 million in 1992 with a net loss of £115 million annually.[74] Transit trade has also declined considerably. Additional expenses were incurred on any imports through the port of Aqaba, owing to the inspec-

71 See *supra* note 35.

72 This is not the view taken by some. Most notably Professor Bruno Simma sees the "taking note" of Jordan's communication as acceptance as dubious.

73 See the report on a mission to Jordan undertaken by the Special Representative of the Secretary-General, Mr. Jean Ripert on 17 October 1990. Annex to letter from the Secretary-General addressed to the President of the Security Council, 22 October 1990 (S/21983, 13 November 1990). Cited in D.L. Bethlehem *et al.*, *The Kuwait Crisis: Sanctions*, *op. cit.*, pp. 730-740.

74 See Study conducted by the Amman Chamber of Commerce on *The Effects of the Gulf Crisis and the Embargo on the Gulf of Aqaba on the Jordanian Economy especially the Industrial Sector,* 16 April 1994. Hereinafter referred to as *ACC Study*. The study maintains that the decline in Jordan's exports to Iraq alone is $115 million per year. It further states that exports to Kuwait have declined from $23 million per year to zero with an aggregate loss of $23 million per year and to Saudi Arabia from $72 million in 1989 to $46 million in 1991. This decline in exports according to the ACC Study, constitutes a decline in the value of exports that reaches as high as $204 million per year.

tion and interception of ships that were bound to the port until late 1993.[75] In short, it can be said that the Jordanian economy was devastated as a result of the imposition and enforcement of sanctions against Iraq. On 20 August 1990, Jordan requested to enter into consultations with the Security Council on an urgent basis after "the competent Jordanian authorities have, after careful studies and analysis, determined that compliance with the resolution will lead to extreme economic hardships to Jordan and its population, which constitute 'special economic problems within the meaning of Article 50 of the Charters".[76] Jordan was, indeed, not the only country to embark on such a course of action. The imposition of sanctions against Iraq and Kuwait in 1990 marked a systematic and broader application of Article 50.[77] Twenty-one countries invoked Article 50 after the Security Council adopted Resolution 661 imposing sanctions against Iraq and Kuwait.[78] These applications by those affected *bona fide* third countries are entirely consistent with the objective of measures taken by the Security Council under Article 41 of Chapter VII. There is a full agreement and consensus that the measures adopted by the Security Council under Article 41 aim to restore international peace and security, and when such measures manifest themselves in the form of comprehensive economic sanctions against a particular country, it must be clearly understood that they are intended

75 See ACC Study, *ibid.* Most of the ships that were bound for Aqaba during the period stretching from the imposition of the sanctions against Iraq in August 1991 until the end of 1993 were regularly intercepted by the coalition naval ships and redirected to other ports for inspection of cargo. This measure was applied to all cargo ships that were bound to Aqaba and did not take account of the fact that the delays and redirection of the ships could and indeed have generated losses for Jordanian importers who were importing goods to the Jordanian market. The losses incurred were estimated to stand at $185 million per year. In July 1994 an agreement was signed between the Jordanian Government and Lloyd's Register Inspection Limited to replace the offshore examination and verification system that was conducted by the coalition navies with an onshore examination and verification system in the port of Aqaba in order to "continue the full implementation of UNSCR 661 and relevant subsequent resolutions and to entrust Lloyd's Register(LR) to fulfil this role". The Jordanian Government is responsible for the payment of the expense for the operation by Lloyd's. Another Umbrella Agreement was signed between Jordan, Lloyd's and the United Nations on 25 August 1994, detailing the obligations of the parties and the nature of the operation. These agreements brought the offshore inspections to an end, but only in 1994.

76 See D.L. Bethlehem, *op.cit.* Letter from the Deputy Prime Minister and Foreign Minister of Jordan addressed to the President of the Security Council dated 20 August 1990, p. 659.

77 Prior to the Gulf Crisis, Article 50 had only been applied in connection with sanctions imposed against Rhodesia exclusively as the only other instance at which sanctions were ordered was the imposition of an arms embargo against South Africa which did not involve the invocation of Article 50 by countries.

78 Bangladesh (9/10/1990), Botswana (27/9/1990), Bulgaria (12/9/1990), Czechoslovakia (13/9/1990), India (5/9/1990), Jordan (20/8/1990), Lebanon (31/8/1990), Mauritania (24/9/1990), Pakistan (14/9/1990), Palestine (16/10/1990), Philippines (5/9/1990), Poland (21/9/1990), Romania (27/8/1990), Seychelles (27/8/1990), Sri Lanka (5/9/1990), Sudan (6/11/1990), Tunisia (24/8/1990), Uruguay (13/9/1990), Vietnam (21/9/1990), Yemen (9/9/1990) and Yugoslavia (24/8/1990).

to be coercive and directed against the country that has committed a threat to peace, breach of peace or act of aggression, and they should be designed to bring about a return of legality. There could also be, arguably, a punitive element to sanctions and a protective one sometimes.[79] In all cases, though, sanctions are not designed to harm countries other than the one that has committed a threat to peace, breach of the peace or act of aggression as determined by the Security Council. However, it is clear that when countries act in accordance with Security Council resolutions adopted under Chapter VII and impose sanctions against a particular State, such countries may be affected economically and face special economic problems. Accordingly, Article 50 was designed to bring about a mechanism by which such countries would have a right to consult the Council with regard to finding a solution to these problems.

The drafters of the United Nations Charter foresaw the potential problems arising for countries due to their compliance with and enforcement of sanctions imposed by the Security Council under Chapter VII. Thus, Article 50 was included in the United Nations Charter as a safeguard and as a means of redress for countries injured through the respect, application and enforcement of sanctions. Article 50 states that " If preventive or enforcement measures against any state are taken by the Security council, any other state, whether a member of the United Nations or not, which finds itself confronted with special economic problems arising from the carrying out of those measures shall have a right to consult the Security Council with regard to the solution of those problems". It is understood that Article 50 is restricted in clear terms to measures taken by the Security Council under Chapter VII.[80] Article 50 confers a right to consult with the Security Council not only for Member States, but also for non-members of the United Nations. The logic for such an extension of the right to consult is a manifestation of the reality that non-members must not become innocent victims of United Nations measures, in addition to inducing Non-Member States to voluntarily participate in United Nations measures as did the Federal Republic of Germany in the case of sanctions imposed against Rhodesia and as did Switzerland and the Republic of Korea in the case of sanctions imposed on Iraq.[81]

79 See D.L. Bethlehem, *The Kuwait Crisis: Sanctions*, Part 1, (Cambridge University Press, 1993). p. XXXV. It is argued that sanctions are primarily designed to bring about a return to legality. Daniel Bethlehem correctly argues that in the case of Iraq, there was a punitive element to sanctions that became more evident after the termination of hostilities and the adoption of the cease-fire Resolution 687. That Resolution introduced a continuation of the sanctions imposed against Iraq until Iraq meets certain disarmament requirements that were laid out in that Resolution along with other obligations that were of a punitive nature. Bethlehem also makes the point that Resolution 661 and its imposition of sanctions against Iraq and Kuwait masked a fundamental difference in the objectives for imposing the sanctions. He correctly states that as far as Iraq was concerned, the sanctions were coercive in nature and designed to deter Iraq, while in the case of Kuwait the very same measure was protective, aiming at guaranteeing that the Iraqi Government would not be able to have access to Kuwaiti funds and assets.

80 See comments on Article 50 by Professor Brun-Otto Bryde, in B. Simma (ed.), *The Charter of The United Nations: A Commentary* (Oxford University Press, 1994), pp. 659-661.

81 *Ibid.*

A reading of Article 50 clearly suggests that countries faced with special economic problems emanating from their compliance with Security Council imposed sanctions have a right to ***consult*** the Council. This right to consult precludes, indeed, the country against which sanctions are being taken. It has been suggested that, on the basis of the reading of Article 50 and its legislative history, it could be conclusively asserted that affected States merely have a right to consult the Council without any corresponding duty on the part of the Security Council to provide a specific remedy.[82] However, it has been maintained that, in theory at least, it can be adduced that the Council has the competence under Article 50 to exempt certain states who do suffer from such serious economic problems from their duty to participate in the implementation and enforcement of sanctions. The competence of the Council to grant such an exemption, it was maintained, emanates from "Its monopoly right to lift sanctions".[83] It was suggested that another way by which the Security Council may choose to assist a country applying for consultations under Article 50 was through ordering payments to such a country/countries out of United Nations funds.[84] A third course of action for the Council would be to restrict itself to calling upon other United Nations members and specialised agencies to assist countries invoking Article 50.

The practice of the Security Council clearly suggests that the course of action adopted by the Council when certain countries invoke Article 50 has been restricted to calls of assistance made by the Council to other countries and specialised agencies. In the case of sanctions imposed against Iraq by Resolution 661, the Security Council entrusted the committee established by the resolution with the task of assessing requests of assistance made under Article 50.[85] The recommendations of this committee regarding Jordan were formulated as follows:

> "4. *Requests* the Secretary General to undertake expeditiously, in co-operation with the Government of Jordan, a full with suggestions for appropriate remedies to the problems resulting from measures it has undertaken to comply with resolution 661(1990), including especially the question of supply of petroleum and its derivatives.
>
> 5. *Appeals,* based on this assessment, to all States on an urgent basis, to provide immediate technical, financial, and material assistance to Jordan to mitigate the consequences of the difficulties faced by Jordan as a result of this crisis.
>
> 6. *Requests* the Secretary General to develop methods for the purpose of receiving information from States about the contribution which they have or are prepared to make to alleviate the longer term hardships confronting Jordan as a result of its application of economic sanctions against Iraq.

82 *Ibid.*

83 *Ibid.*, p. 660.

84 See Advisory Opinion on *Certain Expenses of the United Nations.* ICJ Reports 1962, pp. 151-196. It must be noted however that from a practical point of view it is inconceivable that the Security Council would do so. Additionally, it is common knowledge that the United Nations has not been in a financial position to enable it to follow such a course of action.

85 See SCR 669 (1990).

7. *Calls upon* the Agencies, organs, organisations and bodies of the United Nations system to intensify their programmes of assistance in response to the pressing needs of Jordan and to report to the Secretary General what they are doing or are prepared to do.
8. *Requests* the Secretary General to appoint a special representative to co-ordinate assistance being given to Jordan by agencies in the United Nations system, humanitarian organisations and States which are prepared to participate in this effort, taking into account bilateral assistance being provided by States to Jordan".

Despite these recommendations by the Sanctions Committee relating to Jordan, that were by all counts much more elaborate, sympathetic and comprehensive than other recommendations, significant assistance was not forthcoming. Thus twenty-one countries, including Jordan, dispatched a joint letter to the President of the Security Council on 25 March 1991.[86] The letter was formulated in the following terms:

"4. The problems affecting these countries persist, and in certain respects have been aggravated, while the appeals launched pursuant to the recommendations of the Security Council Committee and addressed to all concerned by the Secretary General, have not evoked response commensurate with the urgent needs of the affected countries.
5. Assistance to the affected countries in accordance with Article 50 of the Charter would reaffirm international solidarity and unity.
6. The 21 States launch a collective appeal, particularly to all donor States, to respond urgently and effectively in providing assistance to the affected countries by allocating additional financial resources both through bilateral channels and by supporting the actions of the competent organs and specialised agencies of the United Nations system.
7. The 21 States most seriously affected believe that it is essential that all member States, as well as the United Nations, the specialised agencies and other international organisations of the United Nations system, take all appropriate action to cooperate with them in the field of trade, employment, economic assistance and other areas, in order to alleviate the difficult economic problems facing them.
8. The affected Countries believe that, given the magnitude of the difficulties they face, the Security Council should give renewed attention to these problems with a view to finding quick and effective solutions."

It is evident from this letter that all twenty-one States felt that the recommendations of the Sanctions Committee fell short of their needs and expectations and failed to provide remedies that significantly mitigated their special economic problems. This remained to be the general feeling of most states that applied for consultations under Article 50. The response of the Security Council and its establishment of a Sanctions Committee by Resolution 661 and entrusting this Committee to recommend means by which countries

86 See S/22382, 25 March 1991.

that are suffering from special economic problems as a result of applying and enforcing sanctions can mitigate these problems fell short of providing a tangible remedy for such countries. It further supported the proposition that the right to consult with the Council under Article 50 does not trigger a corresponding duty by the Security Council to provide a specific remedy and consolidates the interpretation that a right to consult is not tantamount to a right to assistance. The wording of the recommendations of the Committee concerning applications made by States to consult under Article 50 does not suggest or connote any commanding or binding language for States, specialised agencies and other organisations within the United Nations system to provide assistance. The recommendations were always cast in the terms of *invites, appeals, calls upon,* etc. Furthermore, the recommendations were never part of an explicit Security Council resolution[87] and were merely recommendations of a Committee created by the Council. This further confirms the view suggesting that the Council is under no legal duty whatsoever to provide specific remedies for countries invoking Article 50. It must be mentioned at this point that Jordan was granted an exemption by the Council to continue its importation of petroleum supplies from Iraq. This grant that was given to Jordan, albeit conditionally, supports the proposition that was made earlier regarding the competence of the Security Council to exempt a State or States partially or fully from applying and enforcing sanctions against a certain country that is adduced from the monopoly of the Council to impose and lift sanctions.[88]

Another interesting yet complicated issue regarding Article 50, is the issue of the type of economic losses that are incurred by States. Would States invoking Article 50 have a right to consult regarding economic losses that emanate directly from their participation in the enforcement and application of sanctions? In other words, is the right to consult restricted to economic losses that are a direct consequence of the imposition of sanctions, such as the loss of export markets, frustration of contracts etc? Or would States invoking Article 50 be able to include losses incurred owing to the perpetration of a breach to peace, threat to peace or an act of aggression that in turn triggered the imposition of sanctions such as the increase in oil prices, loss of remittances of workers, loss of debts etc? Answering these questions requires a careful reading of Article 50. This reading would suggest that consultations must be restricted to losses emanating from "***the carrying out of preventive and enforcement measures***", which introduces a concept of causation into Article 50.[89] Yet an examination of the extensive State practice during the Kuwait crisis suggests that States invoking Article 50 tend to apply for consultations on the basis of both the losses that emanate directly from their participation in the preventive and enforcement measures, in addition to losses incurred as a result of the outbreak of hostilities. The recommendations of the Sanctions Committee seem to address both types of losses.[90] However, this debate regarding the scope of losses that

87 But see, in the sanctions against Southern Rhodesia, SC Resolutions 329 (1973) and 386 (1976).

88 See *supra* note 35 and 83.

89 See D.L. Bethlehem, *op. cit.*, p. XIIV.

90 *Ibid.* In the collection edited by Daniel Bethlehem, it is evident that States invoking Article 50 included in their application to consult under that article direct losses and indirect ones. It

are included within the ambit of Article 50 remains academic. Losses that are directly incurred by states from their participation in the enforcement of sanctions have not, so far been adequately met. States invoking Article 50 during the Kuwait crisis were practically never compensated fully or significantly for the losses incurred by them due to their participation in the application and enforcement of sanctions, needless to mention other broader losses. Additionally, the establishment by the Security Council of a Compensation Committee in the case of the Kuwait crisis would suggest that, losses incurred as a result of the invasion itself are not within the limits of Article 50 but are rather addressed through the Compensation Committee. Practice is still undeveloped and limited in this regard to the Kuwait crisis. Only future practice would determine the scope of losses to which Article 50 applies.

Jordan takes the view that its consultations with the Security Council in accordance with Article 50 have not significantly mitigated the severe economic problems it has been incurring as a result of its application, implementation and enforcement of sanctions against Iraq.[91] Furthermore, it has been maintained by some Jordanian officials that, the Sanctions Committee, instead of favouring countries like Jordan whose economy was devastated by the implementation, has systematically favoured countries with more political weight, in terms of granting permission to export to Iraq. Those Jordanian officials suggested that the practice of the Committee has been consistent in favouring Security Council Permanent Member States' requests in the field of exporting industrial goods to Iraq while denying this to Jordan, despite the fact that the applications made to the Committee by those countries and Jordan were in many instances identical.

Although Article 50 consultations were used extensively for the first time by many States during the Kuwait crisis, the response of the Security Council to these applications for consultation in this crisis did not seem to have mitigated the problems of those countries. The Council predominantly restricted itself to asking Member States, specialised agencies and other organisations within the United Nations system to support countries facing special economic problems. The Security Council did not adopt any resolution to the effect of considering the losses incurred by States applying for consultation under Article 50 as expenses that are to be covered by the United Nations as expenses of the organisation. Nor did the Security Council resort to absolving a country from applying and enforcing the sanctions with the exception of allowing Jordan to continue importing petroleum from Iraq until it found an alternative. This would militate in favour of the dominating point of view that suggests that the right to consult does not trigger a corresponding duty by the Security Council to provide an adequate remedy. Having said that, one must not lose focus of the reality that for economic sanctions to work, they have to receive the genuine support of the majority of States. Any prospects for future

is interesting to note that the recommendations of the Sanctions Committee did sometimes address economic difficulties that are not directly related to the participation of a State evoking Article 50 in the application and enforcement of the measures. The recommendations of the Committee regarding Jordan support this contention. For full text of the Committee's recommendations regarding Jordan see D.L. Bethlehem, *op. cit.*, p. 730 *et seq*).

91 Interview with Qasim, *op. cit.*

success for the imposition of sanctions is going to be influenced by the effectiveness of the solutions found for the hardships that were suffered by States during the Kuwait crisis. As the response to those problems was not all too effective, serious and detailed consideration should be given to providing adequate relief for countries facing special economic problems and invoking Article 50. Only if effective relief is devised for those countries would they willingly and fully participate in applying and enforcing Security Council sanctions in the future.

* * *

Select Bibliography

I. Sources

Court of Cassation of Jordan, Case Number 107, dated 25 January 1997.

High Council, Decision No 2 / 1955, 16 April 1955, published in the *Official Gazette of the Hashemite Kingdom of Jordan*, Vol. 1224, p. 369.

Measures adopted by the Government of Jordan in compliance with the requirement to implement Security Council Resolution 661 (1990), Annex to UN Doc. S/21614, 23 August 1990.

Letter from the Deputy Prime Minister and Foreign Minister of the Hashemite Kingdom of Jordan addressed to the President of the Security Council, 20 August 1990, Annex to UN Doc. S/21620, 24 August 1990.

Report dated 17 October 1990 on a mission to Jordan undertaken by the Special Representative of the Secretary General, Mr. Jean Ripert, Annex to UN Doc. S/21938, 13 November 1990.

Note verbale dated 16 May 1991 from the Permanent Representative of Jordan to the United Nations to the Chairman of the Security Council Sanctions Committee established by Resolution 661, UN Doc. S/AC.25/1991/COMM.159, 16 May 1991.

II. Works

Al-Khasawneh, Bisher, "Consultation under Article 50 of the United Nations Charter: the Experience of the Middle East", in V. Gowlland-Debbas (ed.), *United Nations Sanctions and International* Law (The Hague/London/Boston, Kluwer Law International, 2001), pp. 325-334.

Amman Chamber of Commerce, *The Effects of the Gulf Crisis and the Embargo on the Gulf of Aqaba on the Jordanian Economy especially the Industrial Sector*, Study of 16 April 1994.

Bethlehem, Daniel (ed.), *The Kuwait Crisis: Sanctions and Their Economic Consequences,* Cambridge International Documents Series, vol. 2 (Cambridge, Grotius Publications Ltd, 1991), Part I: pp. 207-208, Part II: pp. 659-664, 727-747 and 782.

11

THE NETHERLANDS

*Alfred H.A. Soons**

I. Introduction

It should be noted at the outset that this contribution[1] on the implementation in the Netherlands legal order of binding United Nations sanctions established under Article 41 of the United Nations Charter focuses primarily on implementation in the European part of the Kingdom of the Netherlands. The Caribbean parts of the Kingdom (the Netherlands Antilles and Aruba) have their own national legal system. However, some information on sanctions implementation in the Netherlands Antilles and Aruba will be provided in Section VIII of this chapter.

The Netherlands has a relatively long experience with collective sanctions implementation. Initially this implementation was done at a purely national level, but since the establishment of the European Economic Community for the European part of the Kingdom gradually this shifted to the Community (now European Union) level. As will be seen, this has had a significant effect on the nature and scope of national sanctions implementation measures.

Three categories of binding United Nations sanctions requiring national implementation can be distinguished: economic sanctions (including arms embargoes); co-operation with *ad hoc* international criminal tribunals; and anti-terrorism measures targeting specific groups or persons irrespective of particular territories. Each category has its own peculiarities and requires a different approach in implementation. They will therefore be given separate attention.

II. Legal Basis of Domestic Measures Implementing Sanctions

(1) *The Relationship between Domestic Law and International and European Law*

Before dealing with the Dutch national legislation specifically on sanctions implementation it is useful to outline briefly the constitutional relationship between national law and

* Professor of Public International Law, Utrecht University.

1 The author gratefully acknowledges the research assistance provided by Arie Trouwborst and Sarah Nouwen.

Vera Gowlland-Debbas (ed.), National Implementation of UN Sanctions, *341-380.*

international and European law in The Netherlands.

The Netherlands Constitution is relatively open to the international legal order. Article 90 of the Constitution explicitly charges the Government with furthering the development of the international legal order. According to Article 92 legislative, executive and judicial powers may be conferred on international organisations by treaty. If a treaty contains provisions deviating from the Constitution a qualified majority of two-thirds is required in Parliament before ratification.[2]

The Netherlands has a mitigated monist system:[3] international law constitutes part of the national legal order, and directly applicable (self-executing) treaty provisions and decisions of international organisations have priority over conflicting national legal norms, including constitutional provisions. The latter rule, however, does not apply to norms of customary international law.[4]

Already before the present constitutional provisions on the relationship between international and national law were introduced in 1953 the applicability of international law, both conventional and customary, in the Netherlands legal order without prior transformation had been confirmed in case law.[5] The two relevant current provisions of the Constitution read as follows:[6]

> *Article 93*
> Provisions of treaties and of decisions of international organisations under public international law, which may be binding on all persons by virtue of their contents shall become binding after they have been published.
>
> *Article 94*
> Statutory regulations in force within the Kingdom shall not be applicable if such application is in conflict with provisions of treaties or of decisions by international organisations under public international law which are binding on all persons.

Thus, Article 93 as such is not the basis for the immediate internal effect of treaty provisions or decisions of international organisations.[7] It must be interpreted to the effect that only treaty provisions and decisions of international organisations that (1) may be

---

2 Article 91, paragraph 3, of the Constitution.

3 On the relationship between national law and international law in The Netherlands in general, see the literature mentioned in the Bibliograpy under (I).

4 Netherlands Supreme Court, Judgment of 6 March 1959 (Nyugat II), Nederlandse Jurisprudentie (hereinafter: NJ) 1962, 2; *Netherlands International Law Review* (1963), 82-91.

5 Netherlands Supreme Court, Judgment of 3 March 1919 (Grenstractaat Aken), NJ 1919, 371.

6 The present Articles 93 and 94 date from 1983 , but their contents are the same as Articles 65-67 of the 1953 Constitution.

7 Although this is not explicitly provided in the Constitution, it is obvious that these constitutional provisions only apply to treaties which are in force for The Netherlands and decisions of international organisations of which The Netherlands is a member.

binding on all persons by virtue of their contents (are "directly applicable") and (2) have been published, can contain obligations for citizens.

Article 94 then stipulates that only directly applicable (self-executing) provisions of treaties and decisions of international organisations have priority over conflicting national legislation.

It should be noted that Article 94 refers to all statutory regulations: in case of conflict with the international norms referred to in Article 94, international law prevails over any provision of legislation, whatever its rank or nature (*posterior* or *anterior*) including rules contained in acts of Parliament and even the Constitution. Thus, whereas the Constitution in Article 120 prohibits constitutional review of acts of Parliament, all courts may review the compatibility of acts of Parliament with directly applicable provisions of treaties and decisions of international organisations.

It is the task of the judiciary to determine in concrete cases which provisions are "binding on all persons". The judge can take into account whether the legislator has expressed its view on the question. For the determination the judge takes into consideration the wording, character, purport and *travaux préparatoires* of the provision, and sometimes also the national context in which the provision is to be applied. During the parliamentary debates on the draft Articles 93 and 94 the Government expressed the view that for provisions of treaties and decisions of international organisations to be regarded as "binding on all persons", they would have to address citizens (as well), may not contain any policy instructions for the legislator and executive and should not explicitly only impose obligations on the State, something which could be apparent from the fact that the provisions need further implementation. In the present context it should be noted that so far Netherlands courts have not regarded United Nations sanctions resolutions as containing directly binding provisions. Obviously, EC sanctions regulations do contain directly binding provisions.

It is debated among constitutional lawyers in The Netherlands whether or not Articles 93 and 94 of the Constitution also provide the basis for the application and priority of European Community law in the Netherlands legal order. Some argue that that basis is rather to be found in Community law itself, as can be deduced from various judgments of the European Court of Justice (*Van Gend & Loos, Costa/ENEL, Simmenthal II* and *Factortame*). However, as pointed out by Besselink,

> "Whatever the implications of these ECJ rulings are, there can be little doubt that Articles 93 and 94 were actually intended to remove all possible doubts as to the effectiveness of Community law within the national legal order, even if the latter embodies rules conflicting with those of the Community. And to the extent that they do so, they do not form an obstacle to the effect of Community law within the national legal order, so do not need to be considered inapplicable either in terms of Community law itself or in terms of national constitutional law."[8]

---

8 L.F.M. Besselink, "An Open Constitution and European Integration: The Kingdom of the Netherlands", 44 *Sociaal-Economische Wetgeving* (1996) 205.

(2) *Prior Enabling Legislation*

a. Historical development

The Netherlands was for the first time confronted with the implementation of collective sanctions during the era of the League of Nations. Prior to this period The Netherlands had adhered to a policy of strict neutrality. In the 1930's, two instances occurred of the institution of international sanctions: the Gran Chaco War in 1934, resulting in an arms embargo against Bolivia and Paraguay, and the Abessinian campaign, resulting in economic sanctions against Italy during 1935-1936. At that time, The Netherlands did not have any prior enabling legislation and initially measures were taken on the basis of existing trade laws. Because of the inadequacy of existing legislation, special legislation was quickly drafted: the *Sanctiewet 1935* (Sanctions Act 1935) and the *Uitvoerverbodenwet 1935* (Prohibitions of Exports Act 1935).[9]

In 1962, the *In- en Uitvoerwet* (Import and Export Act) was adopted.[10] This "framework act" provides a basis for regulating import or export of goods through general rules and permits and was also intended to be used for the implementation of sanctions. However, it does not cover transit of goods. On the basis of this Act the Strategic Goods Export Decree 1963 (*Uitvoerbesluit Strategische Goederen*)[11] was promulgated which subsequently formed the basis for implementing most arms embargoes.

These three pieces of legislation were available when in 1966 the United Nations Security Council for the first time established mandatory economic sanctions, against Southern Rhodesia. They were originally also the basis for the implementation of the sanctions against South Africa. They proved to be not completely adequate for the implementation of the sanctions, especially with respect to financial sanctions. A special act had to be introduced for this purpose.[12]

On the basis of the experience gained in implementing the Southern Rhodesia sanctions a new Sanctions Act was drafted. After considerable debate in Parliament resulting in several amendments the Act (*Sanctiewet 1977*) was finally adopted and entered into force in 1980. The Sanctions Act 1935 and Prohibitions of Exports Act 1935 were revoked.

The new Sanctions Act 1977 was not only intended to enable the implementation of mandatory United Nations sanctions, but also to provide a basis for implementing non-mandatory United Nations sanctions, sanctions adopted by the European Community and even national sanctions.[13]

The main feature of the Act was a triple system for the adoption of sanction measures:

9 See P.J. Kuyper, *The Implementation of International Sanctions. The Netherlands and Rhodesia.* (Alphen aan den Rijn, 1978), p. 21.

10 Act of 5 July 1962, Staatsblad (hereinafter: Stb) 1962, 295.

11 Stb. 1963, 128; entered into force on 3 July 1963.

12 Wet betalingsverkeer Zuid-Rhodesië (Stb. 1973, 555).

13 Article 2.

- in cases of urgency, measures could be adopted immediately by a Ministerial Order (*Sanctiebeschikking*, Sanction Order), which could remain in force for a maximum period of ten months (Article 7);
- should the measures have to be maintained after such period (or if there was no urgency), they would have to be adopted by an Order in Council[14] (*Sanctiebesluit*, Sanction Decree), which could remain in force for a maximum period of three years (Articles 2 and 6, paragraph 4);
- should the measures have to be maintained after such period, they would have to be adopted by an act of Parliament (Article 6, paragraph 4).

Sanction Orders could take effect on the day after they were published in the Netherlands Government Gazette (*Staatscourant*); Sanction Decrees could take effect two months after their publication in the Bulletin of Acts and Orders (*Staatsblad*) and in principle required prior consultation with the Socio-Economic Council.

The scope of the measures that could be taken on the basis of the Act was defined in Article 3 as "(...) the movement of goods, services and capital, shipping, air transport, road traffic, post and telecommunications, in so far as they relate to the states or territories designated (...)." Article 4 extended this scope to the entry and residence of aliens.

The Act included provisions on supervision and control, exemptions and dispensations and on penalisation.

After 1992, the increasing impact of European Community sanctions regulations with their direct effect significantly diminished the role of national sanctions measures, apart from arms embargoes which were still left to the Member States. The remaining role for national legislation became limited to:

- the promulgation of urgent interim rules when necessary;
- the penalisation of offences; and
- the designation of competent national authorities for the purposes of supervision and control and the granting of exemptions and dispensations.

As a consequence of the greatly increased European Community level of implementation of United Nations sanctions the need was felt for a less cumbersome national implementation system. In combination with the demonstrated insufficiency of the defined scope of the measures which could be taken under the Sanctions Act 1977, in particular with respect to financial measures and more recently anti-terrorist measures,[15] this led to the adoption within a short period of time of several amendments to the Sanctions Act 1977.[16] The latest amendments entered into force on 7 June 2002.[17]

14 I.e., a Royal Decree with the advice of the Council of State.

15 See the Memoranda of Elucidation annexed to the Bills introducing amendments to the Sanctions Act 1977.

16 In particular the Acts amending the Sanctions Act 1977 of 13 April 2000 and of 16 May 2002 (Stb. 2000, 196 and 2002, 270).

17 Stb. 2002, 270.

b. Outline of present enabling legislation

The Sanctions Act 1977, as amended (the full text of which is annexed to this chapter) has extended the scope of the measures that can be taken as defined in Article 3 to "all that is required in order to comply with the treaties, decisions and recommendations, or the international understandings, referred to in article 2". The Act is no longer restricted to measures against States and territories, and in Article 2, which defines the purposes of the Act, explicit mention is now made of fighting terrorism.

With respect to the adoption of measures, the Act now provides for a simplified system. In case of measures relating only to the performance of obligations under binding decisions of international organisations these can be adopted by Ministerial Order (*Sanctieregeling*, Sanctions regulation) which will have effect for an indeterminate time.[18] The minister responsible for implementing the Act is the Minister of Foreign Affairs, who acts whenever necessary in concurrence with the minister whom the matter may also concern. Since all United Nations Security Council sanctions are now substantively implemented within the European Community by regulation, Sanctions Regulations are now adopted in The Netherlands only in exceptional cases for ordering substantive measures. However, in all other cases such a Sanctions Regulation is necessary for the purpose of penalisation and sometimes to designate the competent authority for the granting of exemptions.

Detailed rules have been included in the Sanctions Act on financial sanctions, in particular their supervision by financial institutions (Articles 10-10h). These will be discussed further in Section IV of this chapter.

Exemptions and dispensations can be granted by the Minister in accordance with Article 9.

The Act applies to activities within Netherlands territory and on board Netherlands ships and aircraft (under the general rules of Articles 2 and 3 of the Criminal Code), and to Dutch nationals abroad (Article 13, Sanctions Act 1977). According to a judgment of the Supreme Court of 1990, the term "nationals" also includes Netherlands legal persons.[19]

The Import and Export Act 1962 (as amended in 2001)[20] is still potentially applicable but in practice no longer used for sanctions implementation. It was for the last time used for the sanctions against Iraq. The Strategic Goods Export Decree 1963 is also still in force.

It should be noted that some of the recent United Nations sanctions measures directed specifically against groups or persons in the fight against terrorism are implemented through the Criminal Code. Further amendments to the Criminal Code, the Sanctions Act 1977 and the Civil Code are in preparation.[21]

---

18 All other sanctions measures remain to be taken by Order in Council (*Sanctiebesluit*), with a maximum period of validity of three years after which adoption of an Act of Parliament will be necessary for their prolongation (Article 6, paragraph 4, Sanctions Act 1977).

19 Judgment of 11 December 1990, NJ 1991, 466.

20 Stb. 2001, 191.

21 See the Government's Policy Paper on Terrorism and the Protection of Society submitted to Parliament on 24 June 2003.

III. Adoption and Content of Domestic Implementation Measures Relating to Economic Sanctions

The experience of The Netherlands analysed in detail for this contribution concerns mainly implementation measures relating to economic sanctions taken under the Sanctions Act as it read prior to the recent amendments. This experience led to the preparation of these amendments and therefore to a large extent no longer relates to the present legal regime. However, since this experience sheds some light on a number of the problems encountered in implementing economic sanctions and can still be of some interest, this analysis[22] is included in this chapter.[23]

(1) Entry into Force

When comparing the dates on which United Nations Security Council sanctions became effective with the dates of entry into force of corresponding Dutch legislation adopted to implement these, the main conclusion would be that it is difficult to discover any regularity in the respective time spans separating them. The latter varied from a single day to several years.[24] Calculation of an average would seem rather pointless. At the most, it could be held that usually the periods in question covered several weeks to several months.

It may be instructive to have a closer look at a number of individual sanctions regimes, ranging in time from the early 1990s to the year 2002. From this, it will become apparent that sanctions decisions taken within the framework of the European Community and European Union played an increasing role in the delays encountered. This is particularly so under more recent practice, with its extensive reliance on the adoption of sanctions regulations by European Community organs. The discussion below of concrete regimes will also illustrate that, generally, the instrument of retroactivity appears to be used only for the cancellation of sanctions orders and decrees, not for their institution. Indeed, an opposite approach would contradict the general rule withholding punishability from acts penalised *post dato* with retroactive force, as codified in the Dutch Criminal Code.[25]

---

22 This analysis was prepared by Arie Trouwborst.

23 For a detailed discussion of the Netherlands experience in implementing the Southern Rhodesia sanctions, see Kuyper, *op. cit.* note 9, pp. 77-121.

24 The South Africa Arms Transport Sanctions Order 1980 (*Sanctiebeschikking Wapenvervoer Zuidafrika 1980*) and the South Africa Licences Sanctions Order 1980 (*Sanctiebeschikking Licenties Zuidafrika 1980*) entered into force in late 1980, almost three years after the adoption of UNSC Resolution 418 (1977). See *Staatscourant* (hereafter: *Stcrt*) 1980, 228. This was due to the fact that before the entry into force of the new Sanctions Act 1977 there was no basis in law for the taking of these specific measures. Therefore, the Netherlands Government had entered into "gentlemen's agreements" with the relevant sections of industry and trade in which they agreed to abide by the UN sanctions measures. See also the subsection on South Africa below, 352.

25 Article 1, paragraph 1.

a. The Former Yugoslavia

On 25 September 1991, the United Nations Security Council called for the immediate imposition of a general prohibition on the export to Yugoslavia of weapons and military equipment.[26] Three weeks previously, the Dutch Government, in response to a similar embargo agreed upon by a meeting of the EC Ministers of Foreign Affairs on 5 July 1991, had already revoked all outstanding permits for export of military goods to Yugoslavia.[27] The elaborate set of sanctions against the Federal Republic of Yugoslavia (FRY), i.e. Serbia and Montenegro – including bans on trade, financial transactions and flights – that was adopted by the Security Council through Resolution 757 on 30 May 1992, was speedily implemented in The Netherlands by way of two separate ministerial orders, the Serbia and Montenegro Transfer of Funds and Financial Services Sanctions Order[28] and the Serbia and Montenegro Sanctions Order 1992,[29] which entered into force, respectively, 3 and 4 days afterwards.[30] Further extension of the regime was achieved by way of United Nations Security Council Resolution 787 of 16 November 1992 and found reflection in the Netherlands legal order in terms of two sanctions decrees substituting the aforementioned orders upon their simultaneous entry into force, four months and 17 days after the adoption of Resolution 787.[31] Sanctions were tightened on the FRY and the Bosnian Serbs when United Nations Security Council Resolution 820 saw the light on 26 April 1993. This decision was implemented through the Serbia and Montenegro Transfer of Funds and Financial Services Sanctions Order II, effective already the next day,[32] and an amendment of the Serbia and Montenegro Sanctions Decree 1992, which became binding nearly a year later.[33]

As a consequence of United Nations Security Council Resolution 943 (1994) the sanctions in relation to Serbia and Montenegro were partly lifted for an initial period of a hundred days, starting 5 October 1994. The Dutch order giving effect to this entered

26 Resolution 713 (1991).

27 Order of 30 August 1991, *Stcrt.* 1991, 169 (which entered into force on 4 September 1991). The permits concerned had been granted on the basis of the Strategic Goods Export Decree 1963.

28 *Sanctiebeschikking Betalingsverkeer en Financiële Dienstenverkeer Servië en Montenegro* of 1 June 1992, *Stcrt.* 1992, 104.

29 *Sanctiebeschikking Servië en Montenegro 1992* of 2 June 1992, *Stcrt.* 1992, 104.

30 An order regulating exemptions from the former entered into force on 18 June 1992: *Vrijstellingsregeling Sanctiebeschikking Betalingsverkeer en Financiële Dienstenverkeer Servië en Montenegro* of 18 June 1992, *Stcrt.* 1992, 115.

31 *Sanctiebesluit Betalingsverkeer en Financiële Dienstenverkeer Servië en Montenegro* of 28 January 1993, *Stb.* 1993, 65; *Sanctiebesluit Servië en Montenegro 1992* of 28 January 1993, *Stb.* 1993, 64 (both entered into force on 2 April 1993).

32 *Sanctiebeschikking Betalingsverkeer en Financiële Dienstenverkeer Servië en Montenegro II, Stcrt.* 1993, 80 (entered into force on 27 April 1993).

33 *Besluit tot Wijziging Sanctiebesluit Servië en Montenegro 1992* of 17 January 1994, *Stb.* 1994, 41 (entered into force on 21 April 1994).

into force one month and thirteen days afterwards.[34] On 22 November 1995 the entire sanctions regime was indefinitely suspended by United Nations Security Council Resolution 1022. A ministerial order was soon adopted suspending the Serbia and Montenegro Transfer of Funds and Financial Services Sanctions Decree with retroactive force as of 23 November 1995.[35] The Serbia and Montenegro Sanctions Decree 1992, after having been amended by a decree of 4 March 1996,[36] expired on 2 April 1996.

The measures enacted against the Bosnian Serbs by United Nations Security Council Resolution 942 of 23 September 1994 have been implemented in The Netherlands through the Bosnia-Herzegovina Sanctions Order 1994[37] and the Bosnia-Herzegovina Sanctions Decree 1995.[38] The former has been in force from 18 November 1994 until its expiry on 18 September 1995. Following a vacuum of precisely one month, the latter instrument came into effect on 18 October 1995, and remained so until, in line with EC Council Regulation 462/96,[39] it was suspended by a ministerial order with retroactive force as of 27 February 1996. This was eight months prior to the final termination of all United Nations sanctions against the FRY and the Bosnian Serbs by means of United Nations Security Council Resolution 1074 (1996).[40]

b. Libya

The embargo on arms and flights against Libya that was instituted by United Nations Security Council Resolution 748 on 31 March 1992, was implemented by the Dutch Government by means of the Libya Flights and Arms Sanctions Order 1992,[41] which entered into force sixteen days afterwards. In early 1993, the order was superseded by a similar decree.[42] On 11 November 1993, new measures, including the freezing of Libyan capital and an oil products embargo, were added to the sanctions regime by United Nations Security Council Resolution 883. They were transformed into Dutch law by two separate orders, which entered into force, respectively, 20 and 24 days after the adoption of Resolution 883.[43] In September 1994, these were replaced by two sanctions decrees of the same purport, entitled Libya Transfer of Funds and Financial Services Sanctions

34 *Sanctieregeling Buitenwerkingstelling Sanctiemaatregelen Servië en Montenegro 1994* of 31 October 1994, *Stcrt.* 1994, 221 (entered into force on 18 November 1994).

35 Order of 5 December 1995, *Stcrt.* 1995, 237 (entered into force 8 December 1995).

36 See *Stb.* 1996, 167.

37 *Sanctieregeling Bosnië-Herzegovina 1994* of 31 October 1994, *Stcrt.* 1994, 221.

38 *Sanctiebesluit Bosnië-Herzegovina 1995* of 18 September 1995, *Stb.* 1995, 485.

39 Regulation of 11 March 1996, *OJ* L 65, p. 1.

40 On 1 October 1996.

41 *Sanctiebeschikking Luchtvaart en Wapens Libië 1992* of 14 April 1992, *Stcrt.* 1992, 75.

42 *Sanctiebesluit Luchtvaart en Wapens Libië 1992* of 21 January 1993, *Stb.* 1993, 57.

43 *Sanctiebeschikking Betalingsverkeer en Financiële Dienstenverkeer Libië* of 30 March 1993, *Stcrt.* 1993, 231 (entered into force on 1 December 1993); *Sanctiebeschikking Libië 1993* of 3 December 1993, *Stcrt.* 1993, 233 (entered into force on 5 December 1993).

Decree[44] and Libya Sanctions Decree 1993.[45] As the United Nations sanctions regime for Libya endured, the effect of both instruments was prolonged in 1997.[46]

When on 5 April 1999, in accordance with Resolution 1192 (1998), the United Nations Security Council announced the immediate suspension of all economic sanctions, the decrees were similarly suspended, by ministerial orders that entered into force 17 and 45 days *post dato*, respectively, but both with retroactive effect as of 6 April 1999.[47] The Libya Transfer of Funds and Financial Services Sanctions Decree was definitively revoked on 22 February 2000.[48] Taking account also of EC Council Regulation 836/99,[49] the Libya Sanctions Decree 1993 was modified so as to prohibit only the arms trade with Libya, and came into effect again on 29 May 2000, with retroactivity as of 20 March of that year.[50] At first sight, this might appear an exception to the rule that retroactive effect is not employed in Dutch practice for the institution of sanctions orders and decrees. In the absence of such retroactive effect, however, the automatic expiry of the suspension order that would have occurred on 20 March 2000 in any case, would have entailed the revival of the decree as it was before its amendment, i.e. including the bans on petroleum products and flights that had been cancelled at the United Nations level a year before.

c. Sierra Leone

The sanctions regime against Sierra Leone, comprising mainly a petroleum (products) and arms embargo, was initiated with the adoption of United Nations Security Council Resolution 1132 on 8 October 1997. The petroleum embargo was implemented within the European Community by Council Regulation 2465/97, which became binding on 15 December 1997.[51] Yet another month later, on 14 January 1998, its breach was penalised in The Netherlands with the entry into force of the Sierra Leone Sanctions

---

44 *Sanctiebesluit Betalingsverkeer en Financiële Dienstenverkeer Libië* of 27 July 1994, *Stb.* 1994, 557 (entered into force on 29 September 1994).

45 *Sanctiebesluit Libië 1993* of 27 July 1994, *Stb.* 1994, 559 (entered into force on 29 September 1994).

46 Act of 11 September 1997, *Stb.* 1997, 392 (entered into force on 19 September 1997).

47 *Regeling Buitenwerkingstelling Sanctiebesluit Betalingsverkeer en Financiële Dienstenverkeer Libië* of 19 April 1999, *Stcrt.* 1999, 75, p. 5 (entered into force on 22 April 1999); and *Regeling Buitenwerkingstelling Sanctiebesluit Libië 1993* of 12 May 1999, *Stcrt.* 1999, 92, p. 7 (entered into force on 20 May 1999).

48 Decree of 14 December 1999, *Stb.* 2000, 4, p. 1 (entered into force on 11 March, with retroactive effect as of 22 February).

49 Regulation of 20 April 1999, *OJ* L 106.

50 Decree of 5 February 2000, *Stb.* 2000, 130. The conclusion seems warranted that between 6 April 1999 and 20 March 2000 the Libya arms embargo, affirmed at the EU level in Common Positions adopted by the Council of the European Union (Common Positions 1999/261/CFSP of 16 April 1999, *OJ* L 103 and 1999/611/CFSP of 13 September 1999, *OJ* L 242), was not regulated by Dutch sanctions legislation in force.

51 Regulation of 8 December 1997, see *OJ* L 344, p. 1.

Order 1997, which also implemented the arms embargo.[52] Whereas the latter was reinforced, in modified form, by United Nations Security Council Resolution 1171 (1998), the United Nations oil embargo and corresponding EC Regulation 2465/97 were both cancelled as of 16 March 1998.[53] Although it was not until June of the same year that the Sierra Leone Sanctions Order was revised accordingly, this was done with retroactive force from 16 March onwards.[54]

In short, it took three months and six days for the United Nations trade bans to be effectively regulated within the Dutch legal order. Consequently, of the more than five months of its formal duration, the Sierra Leone petroleum embargo was enforceable in The Netherlands for only two. In addition, it remained in place in The Netherlands for nearly three months after it had been lifted by the United Nations Security Council.

d. Afghanistan

The date set by United Nations Security Council Resolution 1267 of 15 October 1999 for the imposition in respect of the Taliban of a flight ban and the freeze of financial resources, was 14 November 1999. Nonetheless, it took the EC Council three additional months to give effect to these measures, by means of Regulation 337/2000 which entered into force on 17 February 2000.[55] Accompanying penalisation as a matter of Dutch law was provided for when the Taliban Sanctions Order 2000 came into force on 28 April – five and a half months after the date established by the Security Council.[56] After its expiry on 28 February 2001 the regulation was succeeded by the Taliban Sanctions Order 2001,[57] which came into effect on 19 April 2001, leaving a gap in the punishability of offences of some seven weeks. This new instrument, however, did not yet apply United Nations Security Council Resolution 1333 that had been adopted on 19 December 2000 to tighten sanctions, so it was replaced as of 16 May 2001 by yet another ministerial order.[58] The latter penalises violations of EC Regulation 467/2001, which implements the tightened regime and entered into force on 10 March 2001,[59] and implements the arms embargo called for by Resolution 1333. Altogether, it cost some five months to attain full effectuation of the revised sanctions regime for Afghanistan

52 *Sanctieregeling Sierra Leone 1997* of 18 December 1997, *Stcrt.* 1998, 6, p. 6.

53 See UNSC Resolution 1156 of 16 March 1998; and EC Council Regulation 941/98 of 27 April 1998, *OJ* L 136.

54 *Wijziging Sanctieregeling Sierra Leone 1997* of 4 June 1998, *Stcrt.* 1998, 105, p. 7; into force: 11 June 1998.

55 Regulation of 14 February 2000, *OJ* L 43, p. 1.

56 *Sanctieregeling Taliban 2000* of 21 April 2000, *Stcrt.* 2000, 81, p. 10.

57 *Sanctieregeling Taliban 2001* of 9 April 2001, *Stcrt.* 2001, 74, p. 8. It also incorporated the specifications that had been added to Regulation 337/2000 by another EC regulation (Commission Regulation 1272/2000 of 16 June 2000, *OJ* L 144).

58 Taliban of Afghanistan Sanctions Order 2001, *Sanctieregeling Taliban van Afghanistan 2001* of 11 May 2001, *Stcrt.* 2001, 92, p. 8.

59 Council Regulation 467/2001 of 6 March 2001, *OJ* L 67, p. 1.

in Dutch law, a delay very similar to the one accompanying the implementation of the original scheme.

(2) *Content of Substantive Provisions*

Given that under contemporary practice most Dutch sanctions instruments confine themselves to the penalisation of pertinent European Community regulations, comparison of the content or formulation of the substantive provisions of sanctions decrees and orders is nowadays largely of historic interest.[60]

What such comparison reveals is that some of these domestic instruments employ rather literal translations of relevant United Nations Security Council resolution provisions, while others contain more freely interpreted or elaborated versions. Logically, the former occur mainly where resolutions spell out sanctions in unambiguous and comprehensive terms, whereas the latter correspond to measures prescribed in a less specific fashion. By way of examples, three individual regimes will be considered in some detail below, namely those relating to South Africa, Libya and Afghanistan. These contain instances both of the further elaboration in Dutch law of Security Council sanctions drafted in general terms, as of almost literally translated provisions. In addition, they illustrate the growing influence in time of EC secondary legislation on the implementation of United Nations sanctions in The Netherlands.

a. South Africa

The arms embargo imposed against South Africa by United Nations Security Council Resolution 418 (1977)[61] was set out as follows:

> The Security Council, [..]
> 2. *Decides* that all States shall cease forthwith any provision to South Africa of arms and related *materiel* of all types, including the sale or transfer of weapons and ammunition, military vehicles and equipment, para-military police equipment, and spare parts for the aforementioned, and shall cease as well the provision of all types of equipment and supplies and grants of licensing arrangements for the manufacture or maintenance of the aforementioned; [..]
> 4. *Further decides* that all States shall refrain from any co-operation with South Africa in the manufacture and development of nuclear weapons; [..]

It was implemented in The Netherlands chiefly by means of the South Africa Arms Transport Sanctions Decree 1981[62] and the South Africa Licences Sanctions Decree

60 The question whether recently adopted Dutch sanctions instruments are in conformity with their UNSC counterparts, can only be answered by comparing relevant EC regulations to the Security Council resolutions they seek to implement.

61 4 November 1977.

62 *Sanctiebesluit Wapenvervoer Zuidafrika 1981* of 9 July 1981, *Stb.* 1981, 459 (entered into force on 22 September 1981). See the preambles to this and the next instrument. The decree was

1981,[63] supplemented by a prohibitive licensing policy under the pre-existing Strategic Goods Export Decree 1963. In approximate translation, the first mentioned instrument stipulates that "it is forbidden to transport or arrange the transport of arms or related goods with any vehicle to or destined for South Africa."[64] The decree on licences outlaws the granting to South Africa, to natural persons living or staying in South Africa, and to public and corporate bodies (or affiliations thereof) located in South Africa, of patent licences, licences of exclusive rights to drawings or models, or any related technical knowledge, for the purpose of the construction or maintenance of arms and related goods.[65] It should be borne in mind that by way of Article 3(2) of the Sanctions Act 1977, preparatory acts apparently directly aiming at the transport of weapons or the granting of licences to South Africa were also forbidden.

For a definition of "arms and related goods" both decrees refer to a substantial number of categories listed in the Annex of the Strategic Goods Export Decree 1963.[66] According to the explanatory notes attached to the two instruments by the responsible ministers, this degree of specificity was chosen, in co-operation with other European States, on account of the lack of clarity in Resolution 418 as to exactly what goods resort under the bans it institutes.[67] Likewise, the generous interpretation of the licence embargo as contained, again in conformity with the practice of other European States, in the South Africa Licences Sanctions Decree 1981 – the conveyance of technical information was included – must be viewed in light of the vague delimitation of the prohibition in the Resolution's second paragraph.[68]

Paragraph 4 of Resolution 418, banning nuclear weapons co-operation with South Africa, was not regulated separately in Dutch sanctions legislation. This was deemed superfluous, given the inclusion of military applications of nuclear energy into the definition of arms and related goods as applicable under the South Africa Arms Transport Sanctions Decree 1981,[69] and owing also to international obligations already incumbent upon The Netherlands within the framework of the 1968 Treaty on the Non-Proliferation of Nuclear Weapons.[70]

---

preceded by an order of the same purport (*Sanctiebeschikking Wapenvervoer Zuidafrika 1980*, *Stcrt.* 1980, 228).

63 *Sanctiebesluit Licenties Zuidafrika 1981* of 9 July 1981, *Stb.* 1981, 460 (entered into force on 22 September 1981). It was also preceded by an order (*Sanctiebeschikking Licenties Zuidafrika 1980*, *Stcrt.* 1980, 228).

64 Article 2 (author's translation).

65 Article 2.

66 Article 1 of both instruments.

67 See the Explanatory Note (*Nota van Toelichting*) appended to both instruments.

68 See the Explanatory Note accompanying the decree.

69 Article 1 of the South Africa Arms Transport Sanctions Decree 1981, category 0181 of the Strategic Goods Export Decree 1963.

70 See the Explanatory Notes accompanying the two 1981 decrees.

b. Libya

The Libya sanctions can serve as a good illustration again in the present context. As related above, the Libya Flights and Arms Sanctions Decree 1992 (preceded by an order of the same name) formed the implementation by The Netherlands of the flights and weapons embargo instituted by UNSC Resolution 748 (1992). In the provisions of the decree practically exact translations can be found. Clear examples are the transpositions of Resolution paragraphs 4(a), 4(b) and 6(b), on flights and related matters, into, respectively, Articles 1, 2 and 4 of the Dutch instrument. Lacking a more precise description of the military goods in respect of which export, licensing and advice to Libya was forbidden by Resolution 748, the decree provided for a number of appendices setting out more defined categories – *inter alia* by reference to the Annex of the Strategic Goods Export Decree 1963 – in a manner not unlike the South African regime just discussed.[71]

In the previously mentioned Libya Transfer of Funds and Financial Services Sanctions (Order and) Decree and the Libya Sanctions (Order and) Decree 1993, translation of United Nations Security Council Resolution 883 (1993) took place in a manner very similar to the implementation of Resolution 748 as just discussed. The annex of Resolution 883 with its enumeration of banned products represents an instance of a technical appendix transformed into national law in the form of a literal translation, *in casu* as Annex B of the Libya Sanctions Decree 1993.

c. Afghanistan

The Dutch sanctions regime imposed against the Taliban of Afghanistan is representative of recent practice, under which rules – excepting arms embargoes and some other types of measures – based on the Sanctions Act 1977 are issued only after the adoption and entry into force of relevant EC secondary legislation. Apart from Article 2 of the Taliban of Afghanistan Sanctions Order 2001, which sets out the Afghanistan arms embargo, the three domestic instruments adopted to implement United Nations Security Council Resolutions 1267 (1999) and 1333 (2000) merely prohibit actions contrary to the various European Community regulations on the topic.[72]

(3) Personal and Territorial Scope

The numerous Dutch sanctions orders and decrees themselves do not contain provisions on their respective personal and territorial ranges of application. This would lead one to assume, therefore, that the generally accepted rules of criminal jurisdiction, such as the territorial principle and the nationality principle, apply. The workings of the last mentioned principle are affirmed by Article 13 of the Sanctions Act 1977, providing for the applicability of Dutch criminal law to nationals also when committing offences outside Netherlands territory. The territorial principle has been codified in Articles 2 and 3 of the Dutch

71 Article 3 of the decree.

72 The other two instruments referred to here are the Taliban Sanctions Order 2000 and the Taliban Sanctions Order 2001.

Criminal Code, which states that Dutch criminal law is applicable to everyone acting in contravention of it within The Netherlands or on board of a Dutch vessel or aircraft.

(4) Existing Contracts

Implementation in The Netherlands legal order of United Nations Security Council resolution provisions dealing with existing contracts frequently consisted of the rather literal translation into sanctions legislation of the (often standard) formulations as found in the resolutions. On other occasions, however, this type of provision was not incorporated into pertinent domestic instruments at all. This is not to say that by failing to mention existing contracts these would be exempted from the measures in question. Quite the contrary: if exceptions are not provided for, prohibitions hold in general. A drawback of such omission is, nevertheless, that it may give rise to confusion concerning the presence or absence of transitional law.

At times, where a United Nations sanctions regime has been (partly) implemented by way of European Community regulations, the Dutch instrument(s) in question expressly declare(s) the applicability of the measures contained in the European Community instruments to existing contracts. This has been the case, for instance, with sanctions legislation relating to Angola and Sierra Leone. The brief discussion of four examples of implementation in The Netherlands of United Nations Security Council resolutions will further illustrate this diverse practice.

No instances are known of disputes between private parties to contracts the performance of which was prevented by sanctions measures having been submitted to Dutch courts.

a. Resolution 418 (1977): South Africa

In Resolution 418 the United Nations Security Council called upon States to pursue the termination of "all existing arrangements with and licences granted to South Africa relating to the manufacture and maintenance of arms, ammunition of all types and military equipment and vehicles."[73] However, no provision to this end was made in either of the two instruments adopted to implement this, formally non-legally binding, request.[74]

b. Resolution 757 (1992): The Former Yugoslavia

In Resolution 757, which complemented the arms embargo against the territory of the Former Yugoslavia with, *inter alia*, comprehensive bans on trade and flights, the Security Council determined the following:

> *Calls upon* all States, including States not members of the United Nations, and all international organizations, to act strictly in accordance with the provisions of the present resolu-

---

73 Paragraph 3.

74 See the South Africa Arms Transport Sanctions Decree 1981 and the South Africa Licences Sanctions Decree 1981.

> tion, notwithstanding the existence of any rights or obligations conferred or imposed by any international agreement or any contract entered into or any licence or permit granted prior to the date of the present resolution; [75]

The Serbia and Montenegro Sanctions Order 1992 and its successor decree represent an instance of implementation whereby the international obligation to overrule existing contracts by the sanctions concerned was not explicitly transformed into national law: neither instrument contains any provisions of this purport.

c. Resolution 841 (1993): Haiti

With the adoption in 1993 of Resolution 841,[76] the United Nations Security Council imposed a petroleum (products) and arms embargo against Haiti and also ordered the freezing of capital belonging to the Republic of Haiti. The instrument contains a clause on existing rights and duties that is similar to the provision of Resolution 757 cited above.[77] A virtually literal translation of it can be encountered in the Haiti Oil (Products) and Arms Sanctions Order 1993 II, which, as its title indicates, regulated the two embargoes.[78] In relation to the freezing of assets no such explicit statement was recorded into Dutch sanctions law; the corresponding Haiti Financial Services Sanctions Order II is silent on the matter of existing contracts.[79] It should be borne in mind, however, that, as noted *supra*, the practical outcome is equal for both instruments. Only a provision in so many words exempting existing arrangements from the binding force of the orders' prohibitive terms would actually have the effect of exonerating them from the measures set out.

d. Resolution 1132 (1997): Sierra Leone

A final instance to be considered is the eleventh paragraph of Resolution 1132 (1997), from which it follows – the well-known "notwithstanding" terminology is applied once more – that existing contracts are not to be exempted from the Sierra Leone arms and oil (products) trade bans. The Sierra Leone Sanctions Order 1997 links up nicely with this by declaring the applicability of the embargoes, as prescribed in part by EC Regulation 2465/97, "notwithstanding the existence of rights or obligations following from international agreements, contracts, licences or permits concluded or granted prior to the entry into force of the present order."[80]

75 Paragraph 11.

76 Adopted on 16 June 1993.

77 See paragraph 9.

78 *Sanctiebeschikking Aard(olie) en Wapens Haïti 1993 II* of 4 November 1993, *Stcrt.* 1993, 216 (entered into force on 12 November 1993).

79 *Sanctiebeschikking Financiële Dienstenverkeer Haïti II* of 19 October 1993, *Stcrt.* 1993, 203 (entered into force on 22 October 1993).

80 Article 4 of the Order; author's translation.

(5) *Humanitarian Exceptions*

Implementation in the Netherlands legal order of United Nations Security Council resolution provisions on derogations that may be made from sanctions measures for humanitarian purposes, has been, to say the least, quite pluriform. On certain occasions exact translations are employed; on others more broadly interpreted versions. Sometimes the national instrument specifies that exceptions are only granted on humanitarian grounds; sometimes they do not. Some instruments indicate merely that exemptions are dependent on approval by the relevant United Nations Sanctions Committee, others only specify the minister(s) to whom requests should be directed, and yet others contain statements of both kinds. What is of greater interest, however, is that regularly the content of these diverse Dutch sanctions provisions is not in conformity with the text of the United Nations Security Council resolutions they seek to implement. It also occurs that domestic arrangements provide for the possibility of exemptions where the resolution upon which it is founded does not.

The Dutch executive appears to have carried out a separate implementation policy concerning (exemptions from) sanctions of a financial nature. Examples hereof are presented by the specifically financial sanctions legislation adopted in relation to Iraq, the Former Yugoslavia, Libya and Haiti. The provisions setting out the prohibitive measures in question invariably allow for the granting – by or on behalf of the Ministers of Foreign Affairs and of Finance – of exemptions, regardless of the occurrence or not of a similar clause in corresponding resolutions.

Under current practice, exemption clauses of Security Council sanctions resolutions are habitually incorporated in the European Community Regulations implementing them. The Dutch instruments then confine themselves to the appointment of the national authority to which exemption applications should be directed. The whole range of alternative implementation methods relating to humanitarian exemptions will pass in review during the discussion of various instances following below.

a. Resolution 748 (1992): Libya

The possibility of exceptions to the Libyan flights ban instituted by Resolution 748, was offered as the Security Council phrased the obligation of all States to:

> Deny permission to any aircraft to take off from, land in or overfly their territory if it is destined to land in or has taken off from the territory of Libya, unless the particular flight has been approved on grounds of significant humanitarian need by the [Sanctions] Committee established by paragraph 9 below.[81]

In relation to the other sanctions no such possibility was created. The above provision was translated quite literally into the Libya Flights and Arms Sanctions Order 1992, and later into the decree succeeding it.[82] The instruments, however, do not indicate to

81 Paragraph 4(a) of the Resolution.

82 See the respective Articles 1 of the two instruments.

whom any private parties wanting to apply should address their petitions. In line with Resolution 748, no exemption options were introduced for Libyan sanctions other than the flights embargo.

b. Resolution 757 (1992): The Former Yugoslavia

Also the implementation of Resolution 757 is instructive once more in the present context. Its terms illustrate three different methods of allowing humanitarian exceptions. Export of supplies intended for medical purposes and food, if notified to the Yugoslavia Sanctions Committee, was kept out of the trade ban.[83] Similarly, but without the notification duty, "payments exclusively for strictly medical or humanitarian purposes and foodstuffs"[84] were excepted from the financial freeze. Furthermore, under the sanctions regime of Resolution 757 permission of any flights to and from the Federal Republic of Yugoslavia was made contingent upon prior approval, "for humanitarian or other purposes consistent with the relevant resolutions of the Council," by the Sanctions Committee.[85]

As mentioned previously, the Serbia and Montenegro Sanctions Order 1992, the Serbia and Montenegro Transfer of Funds and Financial Services Sanctions Order and their respective successor decrees arranged for the resolution's implementation in The Netherlands. The former forbids the export of goods destined for the FRY, while stating that the competent Minister can grant an exemption for goods intended for strictly medical purposes, goods destined to meet vital human needs, and foodstuffs.[86] A separate provision of the same instrument prohibits the carrying by air or water of goods to the Federal Republic, excepting any transports approved of beforehand by the Yugoslavia Sanctions Committee.[87]

Attention should be drawn to several points here. Firstly, very distinct formulations are used in the two Articles, whereas they are supposedly intended to give effect to the same clause from paragraph 4(c) of Resolution 757. A second, related curiosity is the addition, in the *export* ban exemption clause of the Serbia and Montenegro Sanctions Order 1992, of the broad category of "goods destined to meet vital human needs" to the two categories of supplies named in this respect in Resolution 757 – namely "supplies intended for medical purposes and foodstuffs." Thirdly and lastly, it is noteworthy that the *transport* prohibition just described permits exceptions only after approval by the Sanctions Committee, whereas the text of the Resolution merely mentions a notification duty. The fact that, as related above, such a condition of approval indeed exists for exceptions to the flights embargo of the Resolution's seventh paragraph, might partially account for this. It cannot do so completely, however, since the Dutch rules make humanitarian transports by sea subject to approval by the Sanctions Committee as well, whereas Resolution 757 does not.

83 See paragraph 4(c) of the Resolution.

84 Paragraph 5.

85 Paragraph 7(a).

86 Article 3.

87 Article 5.

The provision primarily intended to implement the embargo on flights is Article 7 of the Serbia and Montenegro Sanctions Order and subsequent decree. This was done in the same way as in the case of the Libyan flights ban just discussed, that is through virtually literal translation of the pertinent text of Resolution 757, including its clause on humanitarian exceptions. The transformation into Dutch law of the Resolution's sanctions relating to funds, finally, presents a typical instance of the way in which financial sanctions have mostly been effectuated, touched upon in the introduction to the present section. In the Serbia and Montenegro Transfer of Funds and Financial Services Sanctions Order and like decree, execution of the various financial acts concerned is forbidden, if carried out without a permit or exemption granted by or on behalf of the Ministers of Foreign Affairs and Finance.[88]

c. Resolution 841 (1993): Haiti

Resolution 841 can serve as an example as well. In it, a carefully delimited possibility of humanitarian exceptions to the Haiti oil and oil products ban was shaped utilizing the following words:

> [The Security Council] Decides that the [Sanctions] committee established by paragraph 10 below may authorize on an exceptional case-by-case basis under a no-objection procedure the importation, in non-commercial quantities and only in barrels or bottles, of petroleum or petroleum products, including propane gas for cooking, for verified essential human needs, subject to acceptable arrangements for effective monitoring of delivery and use.[89]

Exemptions from the arms and financial sanctions were not provided for. The corresponding Haiti Oil (Products) and Arms Sanctions Order 1993 II very concisely stipulated that "The Minister of Economic Affairs can grant exemptions from the terms of Article 1,"[90] with that provision implementing the petroleum (products) embargo. No exemption clause was created in relation to the arms embargo.

Strikingly, however, in the Haiti Financial Services Sanctions Order II – adopted to give effect to the freeze of Haitian capital as prescribed by the Resolution – the above discussed standard formulation on exemptions surfaced once again. The Order outlawed the commission of any acts in respect of assets belonging to or accessible by the Republic of Haiti or those *de facto* exercising powers in that country, "without an exemption granted by or on behalf of the Ministers of Foreign Affairs and Finance."[91] A separate provision expressly empowered the two Ministers to jointly grant such exemptions.[92] Thus, whereas the Dutch implementation regulations coincided with Resolution 841 as

88 See Articles 1 through 4 of the respective instruments.

89 Paragraph 7.

90 Article 2; author's translation.

91 Articles 1 and 2; author's translation.

92 Article 3.

far as the presence of an exemption clause in respect of the oil (products) embargo and the absence thereof in respect of the arms embargo were concerned, in the domestic instrument applying the financial sanctions an exemption possibility was offered that cannot be traced back to the Resolution.

d. Resolution 986 (1995): Iraq

Implementation on the part of The Netherlands of the denominated "oil-for-food" programme as set out in Resolution 986 (1995),[93] allowing Iraq, under certain conditions, to sell oil for the acquisition of humanitarian goods, happened through EC Regulation 2465/96[94] in combination with the Iraq Sanctions Decree 1997.[95] The various exceptions to the Iraqi sanctions as created by the Resolution were incorporated in Regulation 2465/96 and further specified in the pertinent provisions of the Dutch instrument, which latter, in approximate translation, read:

> Article 3
> The prior approval by the sanctions committee of the export by Iraq, as referred to in Article 2, first part, under *b*, of the regulation [2465/96, ed.] is obtained through the medium of the minister.
>
> Article 4
> The authority referred to in Article 2, third part, under *a*, of the regulation is the minister.
>
> Article 5
> The prior notification to the sanctions committee, as referred to in Article 2, third part, under *b*, of the regulation is given through the medium of the minister.
>
> Article 6
> The prior approval by the sanctions committee of the export to Iraq, as referred to in Article 2, third part, under *c*, *d* and *e*, of the regulation is obtained through the medium of the minister.[96]

This vividly illustrates the more recent practice in the field of humanitarian exceptions to Security Council sanctions, strongly influenced as it is by European Community law.

---

93 Adopted on 14 April 1995.

94 Regulation of 17 December 1996, *OJ* L 337.

95 *Sanctiebesluit Irak 1997* of 2 August 1997, *Stb.* 1997, 377 (entered into force on 1 October 1997).

96 Author's translation.

IV. Enforcement of Domestic Implementation Measures Relating to Economic Sanctions

The actual penalisation of infringements of Dutch sanctions law has been provided for by means of the Economic Offences Act, a piece of framework legislation for the prosecution and sentence of offenders of domestic regulations of an economic kind.[97] Violations of duties and prohibitions laid down in the Sanctions Act 1977, the Import and Export Act 1962, or orders and decrees adopted pursuant to their respective terms, are qualified as "economic offences".[98] This means, among other things, that the array of powers at the disposal of the officials charged with the prosecution of sanctions law violations, is wider than under ordinary criminal law.[99]

Violations of the Sanctions Act 1977 and of rules of the Import and Export Act and related instruments that concern trade in arms and other strategic goods are rated in the category of most serious offences.[100] When committed with guilty intent, such offences are punished by a maximum of six years of imprisonment or the imposition of a fine of, at the most, 45.000 Euro.[101] In the absence of such intent, their non-compliance is considered substantially less severe and may result in a detention sentence of one year only, or a maximum fine of 11.250 Euro.[102] Additional sentences and judicial orders that may be imposed include the disqualification to exercise a particular profession, the placing under custody or temporary closure of the convicted person's corporations related to pertinent offences or the publication of the conviction.[103]

Article 10, paragraph 1 of the Sanctions Act 1977 provides that the supervision of the compliance with the provisions of the Act and its implementing rules will be charged to the officials to be designated by the Minister. The Minister has designated as such the Customs officers and the officials of the Fiscal Intelligence and Investigation Department (FIOD) of the Ministry of Finance, the officials of the Economic Surveillance Department (ECD; Ministry of Economic Affairs), the officials of the General Inspection Department (AID; Ministry of Agriculture) and the commanders of Netherlands warships.[104]

There have been a number of criminal proceedings related to violations of sanctions regulations, in particular with respect to Southern Rhodesia[105] and Yugoslavia.[106]

---

97 See *Wet op de Economische Delicten*, *Stb.* 1950, K 258, as amended.

98 See the first and second paragraphs of Article 1 of the Economic Offences Act.

99 Articles 18 through 27.

100 Article 1(1).

101 See Article 6(1), under 1, of the Economic Offences Act and Article 23(4) of the Criminal Code.

102 Article 6(1), under 3.

103 Generally, see Articles 7 and 8. For the measures mentioned, see Articles 7(c) and 8(b).

104 Article 1 of the *Regeling toezichthoudende ambtenaren Sanctiewet 1977. Stcrt.* 1994, 221.

105 See Kuyper, *op.cit.*, note 9, pp. 99-119.

106 A.P.M. Coopmans et al., "Doorwerking en effecten van sanctiemaatregelen van de Verenigde Naties", *Sociaal-Economische Wetgeving* 1995, pp. 501-502.

Apart from these criminal law enforcement possibilities there are also significant other options, in particular through administrative supervision. The Minister has designated all financial institutions listed in Article 10, paragraph 2 of the Sanctions Act 1977 for the purpose of exercising supervision over financial transactions.[107]

Of particular interest in this context, especially in view of the importance of international co-operation in enforcing sanctions measures, is Article 10h of the Sanctions Act 1977, which reads as follows:

> Without prejudice to the relevant provisions in binding decisions of organs of the European Union or of other international organisations, and in derogation of article 10g, Our Minister of Finance is authorised to supply data or information obtained in the performance of his duties charged to him under this Act, to Netherlands or foreign government authorities or to Netherlands or foreign authorities charged by their governments with the supervision of the compliance with the treaties, decisions, recommendations and understandings as referred to in article 2, in the field of financial transactions and the rules laid down pursuant to that article or pursuant to article 7, unless:
>
> a. The purpose for which the data or information will be used is insufficiently made clear;
> b. Providing the data or information would be incompatible with Netherlands law or with public order;
> c. The confidentiality of the data or information is insufficiently guaranteed;
> d. Providing the data or information is or would reasonably be, or could become, in conflict with the interests this Act intends to protect; or
> e. It is insufficiently guaranteed that the data or information will not be used for purposes other than for which they are provided.

V. Role and Practice of Dutch Courts

(1) General

Apart from in criminal proceedings, Dutch courts may play a role in sanctions implementation issues also in administrative or civil proceedings.

The Sanctions Act 1977 provides for the possibility of appeal against decisions (on behalf) of the Minister of Economic Affairs granting or refusing exemptions from provisions of sanctions decrees and orders (Article 14). Such appeal must be lodged with the Trade and Industry Appeals Tribunal in accordance with the provisions of the Act on Administrative Jurisdiction for Public Corporations. In normal circumstances the handling of such an appeal could take several months. The latter Act therefore provides for the possibility of requesting provisional measures, in order to protect interests in urgent situations. Such requests are heard by the President of the Trade and Industry Appeals Tribunal and, if necessary, can be handled within several days. Decisions of the President

107 *Besluit van 13 juli 2002 tot uitvoering van artikel 10f van de Sanctiewet 1977 (Overdrachtsbesluit Sanctiewet 1977)*, *Stb.* 2002, 403.

are not subject to appeal. Judgments of the Trade and Industry Appeals Tribunal are also not subject to appeal. The general administrative law procedures for the review of Government acts are not applicable to sanctions measures because of the availability of the above-mentioned specific procedure under the Sanctions Act 1977.

Under the general law on civil procedure the Government can be sued before a District Court in cases of alleged unlawful behaviour (tort action). It is also possible to start interim injunction proceedings before the President of the District Court for the purpose of obtaining an injunction in urgent situations. Such interim injunction proceedings can, if necessary, be handled within several days. Decisions of the President of the District Court are subject to appeal before the Court of Appeal. Such appeal normally takes several months. When Dutch courts have to judge governmental acts performed in the exercise of governmental authority in a tort action they apply a so-called "marginal" test, viz., the acts must be found to be manifestly unreasonable or arbitrary.

(2) Excursion: the MV Crna Gora-case

It may be instructive to examine in some detail the case of the *MV Crna Gora* to appreciate the role of Dutch courts as well as the position taken by the Dutch Government in a concrete case where entities subjected to the sanctions regime took recourse to the courts. It should be noted that this case dates back to the period before the amendments to the Sanctions Act 1977.

In early September 1992 the Dutch authorities became aware that the *MV Crna Gora*,[108] flying the Maltese flag and loaded with coal taken on board in Colombia, was approaching the port of Rotterdam with the intention of berthing there. On 4 September the Economic Surveillance Department (ECD) informed the ship's agent in Rotterdam, as well as other companies potentially involved in providing services to the ship, that the *MV Crna Gora* was subject to the sanctions regime for Yugoslavia (Serbia and Montenegro). Consequently, the provision of services to the ship to berth at the port of Rotterdam would constitute violations of the sanctions. The ECD position was laid down in a Report of the same day. As a result, the ship could not enter the port of Rotterdam and anchored off the Dutch coast.

The Dutch authorities' opinion that the *MV Crna Gora* was subject to the sanctions regime, notwithstanding the fact that it was registered in Malta (and not in the FRY), was based on information indicating that ownership of the ship rested with persons or organisations residing in the FRY. Consequently, the provision of services to the ship would amount to promoting the economy of the FRY through the owners of the ship, who would benefit from the continued operation of the ship resulting in revenue. This would constitute a violation of Article 9 of the Sanctions Order Serbia and Montenegro.

Twice, interim injunction proceedings were instituted against the Government of The Netherlands before the President of the Rotterdam District Court. The first such

108 "Crna Gora" means Black Mountain in Montenegran: an obvious signal to any alert sanctions supervision official at that time.

proceedings were instituted on 5 September 1992 by BOCIMAR N.V., the charterer of the *MV Crna Gora*, and ENERCO B.V., one of the consignees of the cargo of coal on board the ship. The applicants alleged that the ECD Report was based on wrong information and a wrong interpretation of Article 9 of the Sanctions Order. They demanded that the government should not attach any consequences to the Report. However, the President of the District Court was of the opinion that the ECD Report was sufficiently motivated and justified. He took the view that the applicants could attempt to have the report withdrawn by providing information casting another light on the ownership relations of the ship. Alternatively, they could apply for an exemption for the present case. The President therefore declined the requested measures in his decision of 7 September 1992.[109] The applicants did not lodge an appeal.

The second interim injunction proceedings were instituted on 8 September 1992 by Zeta Ocean Shipping Ltd., the owner of the *MV Crna Gora*. The applicant demanded that the Government reconsider the ECD Report, or remove the obstacles resulting from the ECD Report in order to allow the vessel to enter the port, unload its cargo and depart again. The Government provided further details concerning the ownership situation of the vessel, insisting that Montenegran entities still had an economic interest in the ownership of the vessel.

The President of the Rotterdam District Court came to the conclusion that, for the time being, there was sufficient evidence that the Government's position was justified that the sanctions applied to the vessel. The President consequently declined the requested measures in his decision of 9 September 1992.[110] The applicant subsequently lodged an appeal with the Court of Appeal; this appeal was withdrawn on 18 November 1992.

ENERCO B.V. on 7 September 1992 applied for an exemption under Article 9 of the Sanctions Act. This was refused by the Director of the Central Department for Import and Export on behalf of the Minister of Economic Affairs on 9 September 1992. ENERCO then lodged an objection to this decision on 10 September 1992 with the Minister of Economic Affairs and at the same time requested a provisional measure from the President of the Trade and Industry Appeals Tribunal[111] to the effect that action would be taken with regard to the *MV Crna Gora* as if the requested exemption had been granted.

In his decision of 11 September 1992, the President denied this request on the grounds that none of the three situations used as criteria by the Minister of Economic Affairs for the purpose of applying Article 9 of the Sanctions Act were present in this case. These criteria are:

- where the provision of legal assistance would be prevented by the application of sanctions;
- where there is a situation of imminent danger to persons or goods;
- where dispensations from the United Nations Sanctions Committee have been obtained.

109 *Schip en Schade* (hereinafter: S&S) 1993, 112.

110 On file with the author.

111 *College van Beroep voor het Bedrijfsleven*, CBB.

The President also considered that the alleged extent of the damages to be suffered by the applicant could not constitute a ground for granting an exemption under the Sanctions Order and consequently also not for allowing the requested provisional measures.[112]

The Permanent Mission of The Netherlands to the United Nations, by letter of 10 September 1992 to the Yugoslavia Sanctions Committee, inquired as to the Committee's position concerning the application of the sanctions to ships owned by companies registered in the FRY but sailing under the flag of some other country. The Sanctions Committee considered the issue on 23 September 1992, and reaffirmed its previous finding (in response to a US request)[113] that the decisive question in determining whether sanctions should apply to a given vessel is who exercises effective control over the vessel, not simply what flag the vessel is flying. This finding was communicated to the Netherlands Permanent Mission on 29 September 1992.[114] The Security Council on 16 November 1992 reconfirmed this view in paragraph 10 of Resolution 787.

On the application of ZETA (dated 11 September 1992), an exemption was granted on 16 October 1992 by the Director of the Central Department for Import and Export on behalf of the Minister of Economic Affairs. Based on the existence of an "humanitarian emergency situation" on board the *MV Crna Gora* (still anchored off the Dutch coast), entailing an acute risk for the safety of navigation, the ship was allowed to berth at Rotterdam. However, the exemption did not allow the unloading of the cargo. Having regard to the limited nature of the exemption granted, the position of the Netherlands authorities apparently was that the unloading of the cargo would constitute a service to the ship, and, consequently, would violate Article 9 of the Sanctions Order.

During this period there were no further applications for an exemption to unload the cargo, and no further court proceedings. Several discussions with Netherlands government officials to seek solutions for the problems were held.

On 18 November 1992, the Netherlands Permanent Mission to the United Nations requested approval of the Yugoslavia Sanctions Committee for the unloading of the cargo, in view of the fact that the continued confinement of the cargo of coal on board could develop into a serious safety hazard. In response to this request, the United Nations Sanctions Committee decided on 2 December 1992 to authorise the unloading of the cargo because of the safety hazards involved. However, the approval for unloading the vessel was granted on the condition that the cargo remained under impoundment by the Netherlands authorities for the duration of the sanctions. The communication from the chairman of the Sanctions Committee to the Netherlands Permanent Mission notifying its decision was dated 8 December 1992.

On 15 December 1992 the Director of the Central Department for Import and Export granted two exemptions, on the grounds that on board the *MV Crna Gora* a situation had arisen entailing an acute risk for the safety of the ship, her crew, and for the other

112 KG 1992, 318. Also in AB 1993, 317.

113 M.P. Scharf and J.L. Dorosin, "Interpreting UN Sanctions: The Rulings and Role of the Yugoslavia Sanctions Committee", *Brooklyn Journal of International Law (*1993), p. 800.

114 *Id.*, p. 802.

shipping traffic in her vicinity. One exemption was to the effect that services could be rendered to the vessel for the purpose of moving her to a place for unloading, and afterwards, for moving her to a berth in the port of Rotterdam to be designated by the port authorities. The other exemption was to the effect that services could be rendered for the purpose of the unloading and storage of the cargo. The *MV Crna Gora* was then moved to the coal terminal and unloaded on 16-18 December 1992. The cargo of coal was stored, and the Netherlands Government took the position that it could not be released.

Discussions with the Dutch government officials in order to obtain release of the cargo continued. On 15 and 23 December 1992 the Permanent Mission of Colombia (where the *MV Crna Gora* had been loaded) to the United Nations addressed letters to the Yugoslavia Sanctions Committee concerning the cargo of the *MV Crna Gora*. After several discussions the Committee decided on 20 January 1993 that the unloaded cargo could be released, subject to a decision by the Dutch authorities.[115] This decision was communicated by the chairman of the Committee to the Permanent Mission of Colombia by letter dated 11 March 1993. The Netherlands Government was informed by the Embassy of Colombia in The Hague on 23 March 1993.

In the meantime, on 27 and 28 January 1993, Zeta Ocean Shipping Ltd had instituted interim injunction proceedings before the President of the Rotterdam District Court against (1) INTERCOR (the shipper of the coal); and (2) the Netherlands Government. It requested the President to (1) order the Government to release the unloaded cargo of coal, or at least not to enforce the Sanctions Order with respect to that coal; and (2) order INTERCOR to take the necessary steps to prevent or limit the damages to be suffered by it and to return to Zeta the original Bills of Lading. The Government took the position that it had to comply with the condition imposed by the United Nations Sanctions Committee that the cargo of coal should not be released. This condition was attached to the Committee's decision of 8 December 1992 that the unloading of the cargo could be allowed in a case of emergency.[116] The attorney representing the Government mentioned during the hearing on 3 February 1993 that the matter was still under discussion in the Sanctions Committee and that it would be dealt with at the next meeting of the Committee on 9 February. The President then decided to adjourn the hearing until 10 February. During the resumed hearing on that day the attorney representing the Government stated that the Sanctions Committee had not yet taken a decision.

The President, in his decision of 10 February 1993, judged that the cargo of coal should be considered separate from the vessel after it had been unloaded. The cargo was to be regarded as neutral, and therefore not subject to the sanctions regime. In his opinion, the fact that the vessel was unloaded on the basis of a case of emergency and that the unloading constitutes a provision of service to the vessel which is subject to the sanctions regime does not mean that for that reason the unloaded cargo can be lawfully retained. Consequently, the President ordered the Government to release the unloaded cargo of coal, or at least not to enforce the Sanctions Order with respect to that coal.[117]

---

115 *Id.*, p. 780.

116 *Id.*, p. 803.

117 S&S 1993, 113.

The Government, having no other choice, subsequently acted in accordance with the President's order. However, consistent with its prior views, the Government considered the judgment to be wrong and resulting in a breach of obligations of the Kingdom of The Netherlands under international law. On 26 February 1993, the Government lodged an appeal with the Court of Appeal. This appeal was later withdrawn (June 1993), in view of subsequent developments. Since the implementation of the District Court President's order was factually in accordance with the Sanctions Committee's decision (of which the Government had become aware in the meantime), it was apparently considered that there was no longer any practical need to pursue the appeal.

The most interesting feature of the *MV Crna Gora* case is that the Netherlands Government consistently viewed the Sanctions Committee's communications as providing guidance which the Government was bound to follow: these communications were regarded as authoritative interpretations of the Security Council's resolutions. Netherlands judges accepted the Government's view. Ultimately, however, a judge was prepared to overrule the Government's position as manifestly unreasonable.

Subsequently, a dispute between some of the private parties concerning the liability for financial losses incurred as a result of the Dutch Government's decisions was submitted to arbitration. In the proceedings questions were raised about the lawfulness of the Dutch governmental actions. However, the dispute was settled before an award was made.

VI. Enforcement of the Economic Embargo at Sea

In some cases of sanctions the United Nations Security Council had explicitly authorised the actual enforcement of economic embargoes at sea against non-flag vessels. This was the case with Southern Rhodesia, Iraq, Haiti, the territory of the Former Yugoslavia, Federal Republic of Yugoslavia (Serbia and Montenegro) and again the FRY over Kosovo.[118] Apart from Southern Rhodesia, where only the United Kingdom was authorised to enforce at sea, The Netherlands has participated in all cases of naval interdiction operations with naval assets (frigates, submarines and patrol aircraft). These operations all took place within multilateral frameworks (*ad hoc* coalitions for Iraq and Haiti, WEU and NATO for the other cases).

Commanders of Netherlands naval vessels are designated inspection officials for violations of the Sanctions Act 1977. However, no instances have occurred where Netherlands flag vessels had been involved in interdiction operations by Netherlands warships and a violation of the Sanctions Act was established.

The participation by Netherlands military forces in United Nations sanctions enforcement operations at sea has not raised any constitutional problems. It is the competence of the Government to decide to deploy such forces, under the ultimate control of Parliament. The practice of the Government to inform Parliament in advance of any

118 On the UN Security Council's practice with respect to the enforcement of economic embargoes at sea in general, see A.H.A. Soons, "Enforcing the economic embargo at sea", in V. Gowlland-Debbas (ed.), *United Nations Sanctions and International Law* (Dordrecht, Kluwer Law International, 2001), pp. 307-324.

decision to deploy forces in the framework of UN-authorised operations has recently been confirmed by an amendment of the Constitution. Article 100 of the Constitution now provides that the Government must notify Parliament in advance of any intention to deploy military assets for the maintenance or furtherance of the international legal order. In exceptional cases of urgency such notification may be done afterwards.

VII. Cooperation with the International Criminal Tribunals for the Former Yugoslavia and Rwanda

This contribution will not deal with the arrangements made by The Netherlands in its particular capacity of host State of the International Criminal Tribunal for the Former Yugoslavia (ICTY).

In April 1994, the Act on the International Criminal Tribunal for the Former Yugoslavia (ICTY Act) was passed.[119] It enables and sets out procedures for the deferral of proceedings, transfer of accused persons, various other forms of judicial assistance, including the acquisition and transfer of evidence, and the execution of imprisonment sentences on behalf of the Tribunals.[120] Three and a half years after its Yugoslav counterpart came into being, the Act on the International Criminal Tribunal for Rwanda (ICTR Act) was adopted, which entered into force on 30 December 1997.[121] Its terms plainly declare the applicability in relation to the Rwanda Tribunal of the substantive provisions of the 1994 ICTY Act.[122]

Thus far there have been few requests for deferral, transfer or other types of assistance by either of the Tribunals which have been tested before Dutch courts.

One case of transfer involved the Rwandese genocide suspect Simon Bikindi, who was arrested by Dutch police in the city of Leiden on 12 July 2001 after a request by the ICTR for transfer dated 9 July 2001. Bikindi objected to the transfer, pleading his innocence to any of the crimes he was charged with and claiming that he would run significant risk to being killed both in case of an acquittal and a conviction; accordingly, he requested that a transfer would only be permitted on condition that he would be retransferred to The Netherlands after the proceedings before the ICTR. The Hague District Court decided that the ICTR request must be complied with, that it was not competent to deal with any of the claims of innocence, and that the transfer was per-

119 *Wet van 21 April 1994, Houdende Bepalingen Verband Houdende met de Instelling van het Internationaal Tribunaal voor de Vervolging van Personen Aansprakelijk voor Ernstige Schendingen van het Internationale Humanitaire Recht, Begaan op het Grondgebied van het Voormalige Joegoslavië Sedert 1991* of 21 April 1994, *Stb.* 1994, 308 (entered into force on 4 May 1994).

120 Articles 2 through 17.

121 *Wet van 18 December 1997, Houdende Bepalingen Verband Houdende met de Instelling van het Internationaal Tribunaal voor de Vervolging van Personen Aansprakelijk voor Genocide en Andere Ernstige Schendingen van het Internationale Humanitaire Recht, Begaan op het Grondgebied van Rwanda en van Rwandese Burgers Aansprakelijk voor Genocide en Andere van Dergelijke Schendingen, Begaan op het Grondgebied van Buurlanden, Tussen 1 Januari 1994 en 31 December 1994* of 18 December 1997, *Stb.* 1997, 754.

122 See Article 2(2).

missible. However, it decided to recommend to the Minister of Justice, who ultimately decides on transfer requests, to conclude an agreement with the ICTR to the effect that Bikindi, should he be convicted, would be returned to The Netherlands for the execution of any imprisonment.[123]

Also noteworthy is the fact that the two acts, like the legislation of many other States, do not offer a solid basis for compliance with the order that was issued in the Milosevic (et al.) case by ICTY Judge Hunt on 24 May 1999, calling for the tracing and freezing of the assets of the accused persons.[124] Eventually, this order was implemented at EC level by Council Regulation No. 1294/1999 of 15 June 1999. This in turn resulted in a Sanctions Order based on the Sanctions Act 1977, although it could be doubted that the Sanctions Act provided an adequate basis for such an order.

Finally, mention should be made of two interim injunction proceedings that have arisen in the present context before the President of the Hague District Court although they are primarily related to the position of The Netherlands as the host State of the ICTY.

In the first case the applicant, Dragan Opacic, who had been placed at the disposal of the ICTY as a witness by Bosnia-Herzegovina, claimed that The Netherlands should not co-operate with the ICTY for the purpose of his return to Bosnia-Herzegovina over Dutch territory. He feared for serious violations of his human rights after such return, and argued that by co-operating The Netherlands would violate its own obligations under human rights conventions. The President of the District Court, however, in his decision of 30 May 1997 affirmed that the Netherlands Government is to abide by the decisions of the International Criminal Tribunals established under Chapter VII of the United Nations Charter and that, in principle, there is no room for judicial review by national courts in this respect.[125]

The second case involved a request by Slobodan Milosevic to be released unconditionally from the prison in The Hague or returned to the Federal Republic of Yugoslavia on the grounds that The Netherlands had acted unlawfully in allowing his transit over Dutch territory to the ICTY. He argued that he had been illegally abducted from the FRY, that the ICTY had no basis in law and was not an independent and impartial tribunal within the meaning of Article 6 ECHR and that he had immunity as former Head of State. The President, in his decision of 31 August 2001, rejected all these contentions. The President concluded that the ICTY had been lawfully established and that it offered sufficient procedural guarantees. In consequence he rejected the argument that surrender of an accused person to the ICTY would violate Article 6 ECHR. The President found that The Netherlands had lawfully, under the Host State Agreement, transferred its jurisdiction over the ICTY's indictees to the Tribunal. Since the Statute of the ICTY gave it primacy over national courts, and in view of Article 103 United Nations Charter, he concluded that he was not competent to consider Milosevic's request for release.[126]

123 Decision (Advice concerning transfer) of 16 October 2001. No CU 2001.RT.EX.01.

124 See *Milosevic et al.*, Case (IT-99-37). Decision of 24 May 1999, paragraph 26.

125 *Dragan Opacic v Staat der Nederlanden*, Case 97/742.

126 *Slobodan Milosevic v. Staat der Nederlanden*, Case 01/975. *Netherlands International Law Review* (2001), p. 357. *International Legal Materials* (2002), pp. 143-147. Milosevic subse-

VIII. Sanctions Implementation in the Netherlands Antilles and Aruba

(1) General

The Netherlands Antilles and Aruba are autonomous parts of the Kingdom of the Netherlands. The Charter for the Kingdom of The Netherlands (*Statuut voor het Koninkrijk der Nederlanden*) defines which matters belong to the competence of the Kingdom ("matters of the Kingdom"); all other matters are to be considered within the competence of the constituent countries: The Netherlands ("the Kingdom in Europe"), Aruba and the Netherlands Antilles. Defence, Foreign Affairs and nationality are the main "matters of the Kingdom". Legislation on such matters is done by Acts of the Kingdom. Treaties are always concluded by the Kingdom, although their application could be restricted to one or two of the countries. The Kingdom is ultimately responsible for compliance with international legal obligations. The Constitutions of the three countries must be in conformity with the Charter. The relationship between international law and national law in the Netherlands Antilles and Aruba is similar to the situation in The Netherlands as described above in subsection II.1. The two countries in the Caribbean are not part of the European Community.

The Netherlands Antilles and Aruba thus have their own legal system. They are exclusively competent to legislate on matters relating to the implementation of sanctions. The situation with respect to prior enabling legislation for the Netherlands Antilles[127] is as follows.

In 1968, the *Landsverordening In- en Uitvoer* (Act on Import and Export)[128] was enacted, also for the purpose of implementing sanctions measures. It entered into force on 28 March 1968. It is a framework act: regulations can be adopted by decree (Article 4) or, in cases of urgency, by ministerial order (Article 6, paragraph 1); such an order has a maximum period of validity of three months after which it should be replaced by a decree. Article 5 allows for the introduction in decrees and orders of permits and exemptions.

In only a few cases have actually decrees or orders been adopted for the implementation of United Nations sanctions. In 1990 a decree based on Article 4 of the Act on Import and Export was adopted to implement United Nations Security Council Resolution 661 on Iraq (including a complete ban of import of oil from Iraq and Kuwait); it entered into force on 29 September 1990.[129] Only in 2001 was this decree amended to

quently applied to the European Court of Human Rights, which declared his complaints inadmissible. European Court of Human Rights, *Slobodan Milosevic v. The Netherlands*, Judgment of 19 March 2002 (Application no. 77631/01).

127 The situation for Aruba is similar. It should be noted that until 1986 Aruba was part of the Netherlands Antilles. On 1 January 1986 Aruba became a separate country within the Kingdom. Legislation of the Netherlands Antilles in force on that date remained in force for Aruba until repealed by a new Act.

128 *Publicatieblad* 1968, 42.

129 *Publicatieblad* 1990, 79.

take into account the "oil for food" programme of the United Nations based on Security Council Resolution 986, allowing the export of certain oil shipments permitted by the competent United Nations authority under the auspices of the Iraq Sanctions Committee (and deleting the reference to Kuwait).[130] The amendment entered into force on 24 October 2001.

Mainly because of their location the Netherlands Antilles and Aruba have had little experience with economic sanctions implementation. During the period of the institution of sanctions against Haiti there apparently were a few cases of attempted sanction evasions. The frequency of sanctions measures during the 1990's made it difficult for small countries with limited resources like the Netherlands Antilles and Aruba to achieve timely implementation of the various sanctions measures. Especially when they are located at a large distance from the targeted states the urgency to act may be limited.

(2) Excursion: The Trafigura Case

In this context it is instructive to briefly mention the recent incident involving a violation of the Iraqi sanctions affecting the Netherlands Antilles and The Netherlands, and possibly other countries.[131]

On 19 October 2001 authorities of the Netherlands Antilles received information that the tanker *Essex* was on its way to Curacao with a cargo of oil originating from Iraq which was partially illegal: 270.000 barrels of crude oil had been loaded in excess of the 1.000.000 barrels allowed under the "oil for food" programme. The oil was destined for the refinery of the Venezuelan company PdVSA (*Petroleos de Venezuela SA*) on Curacao where it was to be distilled and exported to the US. Owner of the oil was the Dutch company Trafigura B.V., which had bought the shipment from Ibex Energy France (a designated company under the "oil for food" programme) and had agreed to sell it to PdVSA. The *Essex* was registered in Liberia and owned by a Greek company.

The Netherlands Antilles authorities prohibited PdVSA from accepting the oil from the *Essex* since it would be impossible to distinguish the 270.000 illegal barrels from the legal part of the cargo. The *Essex* arrived at Curacao on 24 October but was not allowed to berth and stayed at sea, circling the island. In the meantime, the Iraq Sanctions Decree had been amended on 23 October in order to make it possible that oil shipments allowed under the "oil for food" programme could be lawfully imported. Trafigura, as the owner of the oil, claimed to have been unaware of the illegal portion of the cargo and attempted to negotiate a solution with the authorities (now also involving the Ministry of Foreign Affairs in The Hague). The solution agreed to was to pay an amount in US dollars equal to the market value of the illegal portion of the cargo on an United Nations escrow account. The cargo would then be allowed to be unloaded and sold to PdVSA. However, PdVSA was only prepared to agree to this arrangement if the United Nations Iraq Sanctions Committee had explicitly accepted it. This position was apparently taken in view of the subsequent export of the refined oil to the US.

---

130 Ministerial Order, *Publicatieblad* 2001, 119.

131 This account is based on reports in the Netherlands Antillean newspaper *Amigoe*.

The Sanctions Committee requested a full report on this incident from the various Member States involved in some way in the shipment, before it wanted to take a decision. However, the investigations were taking so much time that eventually the Sanctions Committee decided to accept the arrangement as proposed and allowed the oil to be unloaded. This happened in early March 2002. For over four months the *Essex* had been waiting off the coast of Curacao.

Since Trafigura is a Dutch company the Netherlands authorities have undertaken a full investigation into the incident in order to establish if any violations of the Sanctions Act 1977 have occurred. The results of this investigation are not yet available.

IX. Concluding Remarks

The domestic implementation of United Nations sanctions within the Member States of the European Union, such as The Netherlands, has in the past decade changed considerably: from mainly national legislative measures to mainly European Union level measures with a limited role for the Member States. However, supervision and penalisation are still completely the responsibility of the Member States. Therefore, national enabling legislation remains an important part of the mechanisms to effect United Nations sanctions. The Netherlands has repeatedly amended its enabling legislation in order to take into account the growing role of EC Regulations and to improve the effectiveness of the measures. The challenges posed by ever-changing problems to be addressed by the United Nations Security Council, such as the fighting of terrorism, will undoubtedly require constant refinement of national and European Union-level legislative measures. At the same time, the safeguarding of constitutional rights leads to new questions that also need to be addressed in order to maintain the legitimacy of sanctions measures. This is certainly not unique to The Netherlands.

Relatively speaking, the domestic implementation of United Nations sanctions has been carried out in The Netherlands in an effective and efficient way. An absolutely perfect system may probably never be achieved, but lessons learnt have helped to develop the existence at present of adequate sanctions implementation mechanisms. Further developments within the European Union with respect to supervision and penalisation of sanctions measures at community level will undoubtedly over time result in yet new changes to the Netherlands sanctions implementation efforts.

Select Bibliography

I. On the relationship between international law and national law in The Netherlands

- Alkema, E.A., "Foreign Relations in the Netherlands Constitution of 1983", 31 *Netherlands International Law Review* (1984) 307-331.
- Besselink, L.F.M., "An Open Constitution and European Integration: the Kingdom of the Netherlands", 44 *Sociaal-Economische Wetgeving* (1996) 192-206.
- Brölman, C.M. and Vierdag, E.W., "Netherlands", in Eisemann, P.M. (ed.), *The Integration of International and European Community Law into the National Legal Order: A Study of the Practice of Europe* (The Hague, 1996), pp. 433-460.
- Erades, L., "International law and the Netherlands legal order", in Van Panhuys *et al.* (eds), *International Law in the Netherlands,* vol. III (Alphen aan den Rijn, 1980), pp. 375-434.
- Schermers, H.G., "Netherlands", in: Jacobs, F.G. & Roberts, S. (eds.), *The Effects of Treaties in Domestic Law* (London, 1987), pp. 109-122.

II. On sanctions implementation in The Netherlands

- Bulterman, M.K., "Sancties van de Europese Unie in de praktijk", *Nederlands Tijdschrift voor Europees recht* (1998) 169-174.
- Bulterman, M.K., "Financiële sancties. De totstandkoming en implementatie van financiële VN-sancties en hun gevolgen voor financiële instellingen", *Bankjuridische reeks* nr. 47 (2003).
- Coomans, A.P.M., Grünfeld, F., Hartogh, K.J., and Jansen, J.F.R., "Doorwerking en Effecten van Sanctiemaatregelen van de Verenigde Naties", 43 *Sociaal-Economische Wetgeving* (1995) 501-513.
- Hustinx, P.J., "Wetgeving: Sanctiewet 1977", 30 *Ars Aequi* (1981) 72-77.
- Klip, A.H., "Enforcement of Sanctions Imposed by the International Criminal Tribunals for Rwanda and the Former Yugoslavia", 5 *European Journal of Crime, Criminal Law and Criminal Justice* (1997) 144-164.
- Klip, A.H., "Nederland en de Internationale Strafgerechtshoven voor Rwanda en het Voormalige Joegoslavië", 20 *Trema* (1997) 22-29.
- Kuyper, P.J., *The Implementation of International Sanctions* (Alphen aan den Rijn, 1978).
- Kuyper, P.J., "De Nieuwe Sanctiewet", 28 *Sociaal-Economische Wetgeving* (1980) 319-342.
- Kuyper, P.J., "Trade Sanctions, Security and Human Rights", in Maresceau, M. (ed.), *The European Community's Commercial Policy after 1992: The Legal Dimension* (Dordrecht/Boston/London, 1993).
- Scharf, M.P. and Dorosin, J.L., "Interpreting UN Sanctions: The Rulings and Role of the Yugoslavia Sanctions Committee", 19 *Brooklyn Journal of International Law* (1993) 771-827.

Annex: Sanctions Act 1977, as Amended, in Force since 7 June 2002

Part 1. Definitions

Article 1

For the purpose of the application of the provisions of or pursuant to this Act:

a. Sanction order means: an Order in Council as referred to in article 2;
b. Sanction regulation means: a regulation as referred to in article 2, paragraph two, or in article 7;
c. Our Minister means: Our Minister for Foreign Affairs in concurrence with Our Minister whom it may also concern;
d. Corporate body means: a corporate body within the meaning of article 66, paragraph four, of the Industrial Organisation Act.

Part 2. Administration of international sanctions

Article 2

1. By Order in Council, rules may be adopted with regard to the subjects referred to in articles 3 and 4, in order to comply with treaties, decisions or recommendations of organs of international organisations, or with international understandings, related to the keeping or restoring of international peace and security, or to the furthering of the international legal order, or to the fighting of terrorism.
2. If the rules to be adopted relate only to the performance of obligations under treaties or binding decisions of international organisations, they may be adopted by Our Minister.

Article 3

1. The rules referred to in article 2 may apply to the movement of goods and services, financial transactions, shipping, aviation, road transport, post and telecommunication, and all that is required in order to comply with the treaties, decisions, and recommendations, or the international understandings, referred to in article 2.
2. The traffic referred to in subsection one also includes every act that apparently is directly aimed at realising such traffic.
3. The rules referred to in article 2 may also include regulations regarding the documents normally used in relation with the subjects mentioned in paragraph one.
4. This Act is without prejudice to the powers conferred under the Import and Export Act.

Article 4

The rules referred to in article 2 may also apply to the admittance and residence of aliens, insofar as where necessary, and in derogation of articles 3 and 12 of the Aliens Act 2000, the admittance and residence of aliens indicated in the rules may be refused, and that Our Minister of Justice may revoke the residence permits within the meaning of articles 14 and 20 of the Aliens Act 2000 with respect to the said aliens. Revocation under this section shall be regarded as revocation pursuant to articles 19 and 22, respectively, of the Aliens Act 2000.

Article 5
(repealed)

Part 3. Temporary regulations

Article 6

1. A sanction order, as well as a decision to amend or revoke such order, comes into effect two months after the date of publication of the Bulletin of Acts and Decrees in which it is placed.
2. Regarding sanction orders other than those that are given in order to comply with an obligation under a treaty or binding decision of an international organisation, or regarding a decision to revoke or amend such order, either of the Houses of the States General may express the wish, or such wish may be made on their behalf, or by at least one-fifth of either of these Houses, within one month after the date of publication in the Bulletin of Acts and Decrees in which the order is placed, that the relevant order shall be confirmed by an act. If such wish is expressed, We shall propose a bill to that end as quickly as possible.
3. If either of the Houses of the States General rejects a bill proposed in accordance with paragraph two, the relevant order shall be withdrawn immediately.
4. If not previously revoked, a sanction order ceases to have effect three years after it has come into effect, unless it is decreed otherwise by a further act.

Article 7
If Our Minister is considering making a recommendation for the adoption, amendment, or revocation of a sanction order and an urgent cause requires an immediate provision in his opinion, Our Minister may, by regulation, adopt rules in accordance with the order under consideration as well as render inoperative rules stipulated in an existing sanction order.

Article 8
If not previously revoked, a sanction regulation pursuant to article 7 shall remain in force until an order adopted pursuant to article 2 regarding the same subject comes into effect, but with a maximum of ten months after that regulation has come into effect.

Part 4. Exemption and dispensation

Article 9

1. Our Minister, as designated in the sanction order or in the sanction regulation, may grant exemption, and upon request may grant dispensation, from regulations in rules laid down in accordance with article 2 or with article 7 regarding the subjects referred to in article 3.
2. Exemption or dispensation may be granted subject to restrictions. Conditions may be attached to exemptions and dispensations.
3. Our Minister as referred to in subsection one may revoke a dispensation if the information submitted in order to obtain such dispensation turns out to be incorrect or incomplete to such extent, that a different decision would have been taken with regard to the request if the true circumstances were fully known when the request was considered.
4. Our Minister as referred to in subsection one may revoke the dispensations forming part of a group designated by him, if this is so required in his opinion due to urgent cause. Notice of a decision adopted in accordance with subsection one will be given by publication in the Bulletin of Acts and Decrees.

Part 5. Supervision

Article 10

1. The supervision of the compliance with the provisions of or pursuant to this Act will be charged to the officials or other persons designated by Our Minister.
2. Without prejudice to subsection one, Our Minister of Finance may designate one or more legal entities who will be charged with the supervision of the compliance with the provisions of or pursuant to this part 5 with respect to financial transactions carried out by:
   a. The credit institutions and financial institutions registered pursuant to article 52, paragraph two, under a, b, c, e, and f of the Credit Institutions Supervision Act 1992,
   b. The investment institutions registered pursuant to article 18, paragraph one, under a and c, of the Investment Institutions Supervision Act,
   c. The exchange offices registered pursuant to article 2 of the Exchange Offices Act,
   d. The securities institutions within the meaning of in article 7, paragraph two, under i, and the securities institutions who possess a permit pursuant to article 7, paragraph four, of the Securities Transactions Supervision Act 1995,
   e. The pension funds within the meaning of article 1, paragraph one, under b, c, d, and l, of the Pension and Savings Funds Guarantee Act,
   f. The insurers that are placed on a list within the meaning of article 9, paragraph one, under a and b, of the Insurance Industry Supervision Act 1993,
   g. The pension fund within the meaning of article 13, paragraph three, under d, of the Insurance Industry Supervision Act 1993, and

   h. The insurers that are placed on a list within the meaning of article 4, paragraph one, under a, of the Funeral Insurance In Kind Supervision Act.
3. The provisions of Chapter 5, part 5.2, of the General Administrative Law Act apply *mutatis mutandis* to persons who are charged by a legal entity designated in accordance with subsection two with the supervision of the compliance with the provisions of or pursuant to this part 5.
4. Notice of a designation order given in accordance with paragraph one or two shall be given by publication in the Government Gazette.

Article 10a
Our Minister of Finance may offer the legal entities designated in accordance with article 10, paragraph two, the opportunity to voice their opinions regarding the assessment of requests for dispensation within the meaning of article 9, paragraph one, as well as regarding the implementation of the rules adopted in accordance with article 2 or article 7 regarding financial transactions.

Article 10b
1. Our Minister of Finance may adopt rules for the management of the administrative organisation and the internal inspection of the institutions as referred to in article 10, paragraph two, under a to and including h.
2. Our Minister of Finance may adopt rules regarding providing information, whether or not upon request, by the institutions as referred to in article 10, paragraph two, under a to and including h.
3. Our Minister of Finance may grant exemption or dispensation from the rules laid down in accordance with paragraphs one and two.

Article 10c
1. Our Minister of Finance may impose an order, under pains of a penalty, with respect to violation of the rules laid down pursuant to article 10b. Article 5:32, paragraphs two through five, and articles 5:33 through 5:35, of the General Administrative Law Act are applicable.
2. Our Minister of Finance may adopt rules regarding the exercise of the power as referred to in the first sentence of paragraph one.

Article 10d
1. Our Minister of Finance may impose an administrative fine with respect to the violation of the rules laid down pursuant to article 10b.
2. The administrative fine will revert to the State.
3. Regarding the institutions as referred to in article 10, paragraph two, under a, articles 90e, 90f, 90g, 90h, 90i, 90k, 90l, and the classification in article 2 of the schedule as referred to in article 90d, of the Credit System Supervision Act 1992, apply mutatis mutandis.
4. Regarding the institutions as referred to in article 10, paragraph two, under b, articles 33e, 33f, 33g, 33h, 33i, 33k, 33l, and the classification in article 2 of the schedule

as referred to in article 33d, of the Investment Institutions Supervision Act, apply mutatis mutandis.

5. Regarding the institutions as referred to in article 10, paragraph two, under c, articles 23, 24,25, 26, 27, 29 and 30, and the classification in article 2 of the schedule as referred to in article 22, of the Exchange Offices Act, apply mutatis mutandis.
6. Regarding the institutions as referred to in article 10 paragraph two, under d, articles 48e, 48f, 48g, 48h, 48i, 48k, 48l, and the classification in article 2 of the schedule as referred to in article 48d, of the Securities Transactions Supervision Act 1995, apply mutatis mutandis.
7. Regarding the institutions as referred to in article 10, paragraph two, under e, articles 23d, 23e, 23f, 23g, 23h, 23j, 23k, and the classification in article 2 of the schedule as referred to in article 23c, of the Pension and Savings Funds Guarantee Act, apply mutatis mutandis.
8. Regarding the institutions as referred to in article 10, paragraph two, under f and g, articles 188e, 188f, 188g, 188h, 188i, 188k, 188l, and the classification in article 2 of the schedule as referred to in article 188d, of the Insurance Industry Supervision Act 1993, apply mutatis mutandis.
9. Regarding the institutions as referred to in article 10, paragraph two, under h, articles 93e, 93f, 93h, 93i, 93k, 93l, and the classification van article 2 of the schedule as referred to in article 93d, of the Funeral Insurance In Kind Supervision Act, apply mutatis mutandis.

Article 10e

1. The amount of the fine shall be determined in the manner as provided in paragraph two, on the understanding that the fine shall not exceed the amount of € 200,000.
2. The amount of the fine shall be determined by multiplying the amount of € 5445 with a factor that is applicable in accordance with the classification in article 2 of the schedule referred to in article 10d, paragraphs three, four, five, six, seven, eight, or nine.
3. Our Minister of Finance may impose in certain events a lower fine than the fine stipulated in paragraph one if the amount of the fine is unreasonably high due to extraordinary circumstances.

Article 10f

1. The powers of Our Minister of Finance pursuant to this part may be transferred by Order in Council to one or more legal entities designated in accordance with article 10, paragraph two. In this event, the obligations that exist towards Our Minister of Finance pursuant to this part 5 shall exist as obligations towards the relevant legal entities.
2. The transfer as referred to in paragraph one may be subjected to restrictions and regulations.

Article 10g

1. All data and information that have been provided or obtained regarding separate undertakings, institutions, or persons, in accordance with the provisions of this part 5

and all data and information received from an authority as referred to in article 10h, shall not be made public and shall remain classified.

2. Anyone who performs any duties under the application of this part 5 or pursuant to decisions adopted in this part, is prohibited from making any further or different use of data or information provided pursuant to the said articles or received from an authority as referred to in article 10h, or of data or information obtained through the examination of business data and documents, or to make such data and information public, other than is required for the performance of his duties in accordance with this part 5.
3. With respect to the person to who paragraph two is applicable, paragraphs one and two are without prejudice to the applicability of the provisions of the Code of Criminal Procedure.
4. Likewise, with respect to the person to who paragraph two is applicable, the provisions of paragraphs one and two are without prejudice to the applicability of the provisions of the Code of Civil Procedure and of article 66 of the Bankruptcy Act that relate to the making of a statement as a witness in a personal appearance of parties or as an expert in civil cases regarding the data or information that have been obtained in the performance of his duties in accordance with this part 5, insofar as it concerns data or information regarding a credit institution that is declared bankrupt or that has been dissolved pursuant to a court ruling. The provisions of the preceding sentence are not applicable to data or information that relate to undertakings or institutions involved in, or that have been involved in, an attempt to allow the relevant credit institution to continue its business.

Article 10h

Without prejudice to the relevant provisions in binding decisions of organs of the European Union or of other international organisations, and in derogation of article 10g, Our Minister of Finance is authorised to supply data or information obtained in the performance of his duties charged to him under this Act, to Netherlands or foreign government authorities or to Netherlands or foreign authorities charged by their governments with the supervision of the compliance with the treaties, decisions, recommendations and understandings as referred to in article 2, in the field of financial transactions and the rules laid down pursuant to that article or pursuant to article 7, unless:

a. The purpose for which the data or information will be used is insufficiently made clear;
b. Providing the data or information would be incompatible with Netherlands law or with public order;
c. The confidentiality of the data or information is insufficiently guaranteed;
d. Providing the data or information is or would reasonably be, or could become, in conflict with the interests this Act intends to protect; or
e. It is insufficiently guaranteed that the data or information will not be used for purposes other than for which they are provided.

Article 11

1. Our Minister may delegate powers vested in him pursuant to a sanction order or a sanction regulation, or pursuant to article 9, to the board of a corporate body or the board of a body having the status of a legal entity within the meaning of article 110 of the Industrial Organisations Act, unless the provisions of or pursuant to this Act would oppose this. Our Minister may subject a delegation in accordance with the first sentence to restrictions.
2. Decisions of a general nature, adopted in view of the exercise of a power delegated in accordance with subsection one, require the approval of Our Minister. Such approval shall only be withheld if such decision would be in conflict with the law or with the common interest.
3. Notice of a decision of Our Minister in accordance with subsection one will be given in the Government Gazette.

Section 12
(repealed)

Part 6. Other provisions

Article 13
Netherlands criminal law is applicable to any Dutch national who commits an act that is punishable under or pursuant to this Act abroad.

Article 14
Interested parties may lodge an appeal against a decision taken in accordance with article 9, paragraph three, with the Trade and Industry Appeals Tribunal.

Article 15
The Export Prohibition Act 1935 (Bulletin of Acts and Decrees 599) and the Sanctions Act 1935 (Bulletin of Acts and Decrees 621) cease to have effect with respect to the Netherlands.

Article 16

1. This Act may be cited as Sanctions Act 1977.
2. The day on which this Act is to come into effect shall be decided by Us.

12

POLAND AND THE CZECH REPUBLIC

Władysław Czapliński and Pavel Šturma[*]

I. Foreign Relations Power and the Constitutions of Poland and the Czech Republic

(1) *The Polish Constitution of 1997*

The present regulation in the Constitution of 2 April 1997 of the relationship between international law and domestic law marks an important step forward compared to former developments;[1] however, it is far from being fully satisfactory.[2]

The constitutional provisions dealing with the relationship between international law and Polish domestic law start with Article 9. This states that the Republic of Poland respects international law binding on it. The provision covers all international law notwithstanding its origin (whether conventional or customary). It is purely declaratory in nature and is situated in the chapter of the Constitution dealing with the principles of the political, social and legal system of Poland. In fact, this provision has been referred to as constituting a possible basis of validity in the municipal legal order for those norms which have not been indicated in the remaining provisions of the Constitution as sources

* Władysław Czapliński is Jean Monnet Professor of International and European Law, Institute of Law Studies, Polish Academy of Sciences, Warsaw, Poland. Pavel Šturma is Associate Professor of Law, Head Department of International Law, Faculty of Law, Charles University, Prague, Czech Republic.

1 Cf. Wl. Czapliński, 'International Law and Polish Municipal Law', in *Constitutional Reform and International Law in Central and Eastern Europe* (The Hague, Kluwer Law International, 1998), p. 15 ff.

2 Among numerous publications dealing with the issue we mention: A. Wyrozumska, "Legal Bases of the Polish External Competence", 36 *AVR* (1998), No. 4, p. 386; S. Biernat, "Constitutional Aspects of Poland's Future Membership in the European Union", *ibidem*, p. 398; A. Wasilkowski, "International Law and International Relations in the New Polish Constitution of 2 April 1997", 23 *PolYBIL* (1997-1998), p. 7; J. Barcz, "Membership of Poland in the European Union in the Light of the Constitution of 2 April 1997. Constitutional Act of Integration", *ibidem*, p. 21.

Vera Gowlland-Debbas (ed.), National Implementation of UN Sanctions, *381-401*.

of Polish domestic law: i.e. customary law,[3] non-ratified treaties and covenants, unilateral obligations, and binding norms elaborated by international organisations (if any).

Article 87 of the Constitution opens Chapter III concerning sources of law. According to this article, international agreements duly ratified constitute the source of Polish law. There are two kinds of ratified treaties. Certain treaties can be ratified by the President directly on the basis of his personal prerogatives. The other categories of agreements can be ratified exclusively after the prior approval of Parliament expressed in the form of a so-called ratification law (Article 89.1 of the Constitution). The Constitution extends the competence of Parliament to: treaties dealing with peace, alliances, political and military treaties; treaties concerning fundamental freedoms, rights and duties defined in the Constitution; membership in international organisations; treaties imposing important financial burdens upon the State budget; and international agreements reserved for regulation by the laws of Parliament. Every case of ratification of the agreement by the President must be notified to Parliament. It is interesting that although the competence of the Constitutional Court has been extended to the control of compatibility of international agreements with the Constitution, and of domestic law with international agreements duly ratified, it does not cover the legality of the ratification itself. The competence of the Court is limited to the control of conformity of legal (legislative) acts, and does not cover the legality of administrative acts (and it seems to be indisputable that the nature of the President's act of ratification is administrative and not legislative).

The position of ratified international agreements in the Polish legal order has been regulated in Article 91(1) of the Constitution. According to this provision, ratified treaties, upon their publication in the Official Journal of the Polish Republic, form part of the domestic legal order and are directly applicable unless their application is dependent upon the adoption of an Act of Parliament. The wording of this Article has been modified compared to the draft presented by the Constitutional Commission of the Parliamentary Assembly. The draft situated ratified international agreements among sources of Polish domestic law, so that it suggested a requirement of transformation of international agreements into domestic law (either by law of Parliament or by an act of ratification by the President of the Republic) and implied that the provision on direct applicability was meaningless. Furthermore, the Constitution suggests making a distinction between the position of treaties ratified after the prior approval of Parliament and other ratified treaties. The former should enjoy priority above laws (Acts of Parliament), while the latter are subordinated to them.

Such a solution does not exclude the possibility of the Government concluding international agreements which are contrary to municipal instruments already in force.

---

3 The only decision of a Polish court dealing with customary law concerned state immunity (Supreme Court, 15 May 1959, OSPiKA 1960, Item 2). Customary rules can be applied on the basis of *renvoi* by specific municipal acts (like maritime law, aerial transportation law etc.). We would like, however, to quote the regulation of the Minister of Foreign Affairs of 17 June 1998, Dz.U. 1998, No. 78, Item 512, on the rules of granting visas to diplomatic representatives according to which visas should be granted in accordance with domestic acts in force, binding international agreements, and existing international customs. The regulation therefore introduces customary law into municipal law without any specific constitutional basis.

The ratification of such a law should simply be accompanied by measures amending and modifying domestic Acts.

Summing up the above considerations, it should be emphasised that from the theoretical point of view ratified international agreements are incorporated into municipal law rather than transformed into domestic law.

The position of other international agreements in the Polish domestic legal order remains unclear. In theory, agreements of this kind should not be directly applicable and should not concern issues listed in Article 89(1); according to the Constitution, they do not constitute a source of Polish domestic law and they are not directly applicable. In practice, numerous international agreements and compacts are concluded in a simplified form, they are neither published in the Official Journal nor (sometimes) translated. An example of such a treaty is the statute of the EBRD. It might be supposed that such treaties are subordinated to laws of Parliament; such a solution, however, would be contrary to Article 9 of the Constitution. On the other hand, it is unclear on what basis agreements concluded in this simplified form should be applied in the Polish legal system. The Constitution neither incorporates them nor transforms them into domestic law. The position of these agreements should be regulated by the proposed law on the conclusion and implementation of international treaties (to be passed by Parliament in the forthcoming months) or it should be regulated by decisions of the Constitutional Court or Supreme Court. It might be suggested that agreements concluded in simplified form require implementation by a specific domestic Act. The rank of such an Act is, however, unclear as the catalogue of instruments of municipal law contained in Chapter III of the Constitution is exhaustive, and in particular governmental regulations can be passed exclusively on the basis of, and within the limits of, prior authorisation by law (Act of Parliament). In principle, these agreements should not create either rights or obligations for individuals, and they should be addressed to different State agencies responsible for their implementation. If so, they could be transformed into domestic law by resolutions of the Council of Ministers and regulations by the Council of Ministers, Prime Minister or respective Ministers under Article 93 of the Constitution. According to this provision, Acts of this kind are binding exclusively upon the state administration and they are of an internal nature. In reality, however, they often touch issues of direct concern for individuals. In such cases, the agreements concluded in simplified form should be implemented either by law or by governmental regulation according to a pattern adopted in domestic law. In the former case, a risk is present that Parliament will fail to adopt the Act required on time or change its content in relation to the agreement concluded (in violation of Article 9 of the Constitution). In the latter hypothesis, the legal basis of the regulation would be unclear, as the Constitution does not provide for regulations passed on the basis of international agreements. Finally, it is also possible to introduce a delegation by a general agreement ratified upon the prior approval of Parliament or by a specific law of Parliament for the Government to conclude an agreement in simplified form dealing with questions reserved for the competence of Parliament according to Article 89, if the need to conclude such an instrument arises urgently.[4]

4 Agreements concerning rights and (mainly jurisdictional) immunities of members of foreign armed forces stationed temporarily for the time of manoeuvres in the territory of Poland have been invoked in this context.

It is important to note that according to Article 241 of the Constitution, the provision of Article 91 concerning the position of international instruments in the Polish domestic legal order should be applied to international agreements concluded before the entry into force of the Constitution, provided that these agreements were ratified and published in the Official Journal, and that their content concerns the matters referred to in Article 89(1) of the Constitution (i.e. international agreements subject to the approval of Parliament).

The Constitution invokes international law not only in the context of sources of law, but also in relation to certain other/occurrences. Thus, for instance, Article 42.1 proclaims the rule *nullum crimen sine lege*, and states that this principle does not exclude punishing perpetrators of crimes under international law. The provision could cause important difficulties in connection with the entry into force of international instruments on crimes against peace and humanity, including the Statute of the International Criminal Court, in the event that judges are forced to decide whether specific acts constitute crimes of aggression or other acts prohibited directly under customary international law. Difficulties connected with the application of customary law within the Polish municipal legal order would be multiplied by the necessity to interpret international rules themselves (like the question whether specific activities can constitute aggression without being qualified as such by the UN Security Council).

(2) The Czech Constitution of 1992 (as Amended in 2001)

The Constitution of the Czech Republic of 1992 (which entered into force on 1 January 1993) did not contain any reference to the concept "international law" in general. This omission can be explained by the fact that the *travaux préparatoires* of the new draft constitution had to be accelerated due to the forthcoming dissolution of Czechoslovakia in Autumn 1992 and this legislative work obviously followed the model of the first Constitution of the Czechoslovak Republic of 1920. At the time of the "First Republic" (1918-1938), there were no constitutional rules on the relationship between international law and internal law. The case law of the highest judicial authorities at that time (the Supreme Court and the Supreme Administrative Court) was based on a strictly dualistic approach. This lacuna in the constitutional texts and this dualistic practice continued also after World War II and during the period of the socialist Czechoslovakia from the 1940s to the end of 1980s.

The Constitution of the Czech Republic of 1992 remains silent on the issue of international customary law, as well as on that of obligations arising from unilateral acts and binding norms adopted by international organisations. The only provision of Article 10 refers exclusively to one category of international treaties ratified and promulgated (i.e. human rights treaties). Such a situation is far from being satisfactory.

However, the amendment to the Constitution adopted in October 2001 (which became effective on 1 June 2002), the so-called "Euro-amendment"[5] brings some very important changes. First of all, it adds a new article, Article1(2), to the Constitution, which deals in general terms with the relationship between international law and inter-

5 See the Constitutional Act No. 395/2001 Coll.

nal law. It states: "The Czech Republic respects obligations binding on it which arise from international law". At first glance, this provision seems to cover all international law, notwithstanding its origin (custom, treaty or binding decision of an international organisation). On balance, it is of a purely declaratory nature. According to some commentaries, it does not bring any change to the existing legal situation, because the obligation of the Czech Republic to respect its international obligations could be deduced from the constitutional concept of the state of law (rule of law).[6]

It is true that the Chamber of Deputies of the Parliament deleted from the governmental /proposal for the text of Article 1(2) the important words "rules of international law", referring to customary international law and general principles of law, and left merely "international obligations". This concept is often linked with the content of treaty law in its broad meaning, not necessarily only the treaties subject to Articles 10, 10a and 49 (see below). However, the correct interpretation may lead to an intermediate, compromise solution. On the one hand, there is no doubt that Article 1(2) is declaratory and does not mean the direct incorporation of general international law (customs, general principles, etc.) into the Czech internal legal order. Consequently, individuals and other internal subjects will not be able to invoke directly rights arising from customary law. On the other hand, obligations arising from international law (irrespective of source) are binding on the Czech Republic, which means also its public authorities (e.g. the Government, the Parliament, the Constitutional Court). All State authorities are supposed to act in conformity with international obligations in their executive, law-making or even judicial activities, at least on the supreme level of the hierarchy of power (e.g. governmental or judicial). And last but not least, the placement of the provision on international law at the very beginning of the Constitution (its first Article) also gives interpretative guidance: all other constitutional norms are to be interpreted in the light of this basic rule.

As to international treaties, until the recent amendment, the Constitution of 1992 provided for the incorporation (direct effect) in Czech law only of treaties on human rights and fundamental freedoms. The former wording of Article 10 (valid until the end of May 2002) stated that "the ratified and promulgated international treaties on human rights and fundamental freedoms binding on the Czech Republic shall be directly applicable and have primacy over laws". However, the Constitution did not give any guidance concerning the internal status of other international treaties. The eminent position reserved only for one category of treaties because of their subject-matter was introduced for the first time into the constitutional order by the Parliament of Czechoslovakia in early 1991 (in connection with the constitutional Act introducing the Charter of Fundamental Rights and Freedoms).[7] Similar provisions can be found only in the Constitutions of the Slovak Republic (a heritage of the last Czechoslovak Constitution) and of Romania (where, however, also other treaties are covered by constitutional provisions). The originality of Article 10 of the Czech Constitution, although it constituted a step forward in comparison with the past situation (until 1990), created more and more prob-

6 Cf. J. Filip, "The Czech Parliament approved the Draft Euro-amendment to the Constitution of CR", *Pravni zpravodaj*, 2001, No. 11, p. 4. (in Czech).

7 See the Constitutional Act No. 23/1991 Coll.

lems of interpretation during the last decade. Therefore, the insufficient regulation of the "international dimension" in the Czech Constitution was rightly criticized.[8]

Consequently, the above-mentioned 2001 amendment to the Constitution provides for the new, substantially modified version of Article 10. It states that "the promulgated international treaties, which ratification was approved by the Parliament, and binding on the Czech Republic shall be part of the legal order; if an international treaty lays down otherwise than a law, the international treaty shall be applied". This is the most important constitutional change since the adoption of the Constitution of the independent Czech Republic. It means a shift from a predominantly dualistic system to a predominantly monistic system. On balance, under the new Article 10, international treaties will not have supralegal (constitutional) force, unlike treaties on human rights under the old Article 10. The hierarchical position of certain treaties only (standing above regular laws and on the level of constitutional laws) seems to be replaced by priority of application (so-called application hierarchy) of all duly ratified and promulgated international treaties if they depart from the provisions of the law. The new position of international treaties as a part of the Czech legal order applies not only to the newly ratified treaties (after 1 June 2002), but to all international treaties ever ratified by the Parliament of the Czech Republic and even its predecessors, provided that the treaty is still binding.

Only so-called presidential treaties, which means international treaties ratified by the President of the Republic after the approval of both Chambers of Parliament (i.e. the Chamber of Deputies and the Senate), will be included as part of the Czech legal order. The categories of treaties subject to this approval and ratification are specified in the slightly amended Article 49 of the Constitution. It extends the competence of the Parliament to: (a) treaties concerning rights and duties of persons, (b) treaties dealing with alliances, peace and other political matters, (c) treaties creating the membership of the Czech Republic in an international organisation, (d) economic treaties of a general nature, (e) treaties on other matters reserved for regulation by the laws. In spite of a different wording, the amended Article 49 covers basically the same range of international treaties. However, there is an important change concerning the competence of the Constitutional Court, introduced by this amendment to the Constitution and the amendment to the Law on the Constitutional Court.[9] According to Article 87(2) of the Constitution, from June 1st, 2002, the Constitutional Court has the competence to control *a priori* compatibility of international treaties with the constitutional order (i.e. the Constitution and other constitutional laws). Until the Constitutional Court has taken a decision, a treaty cannot be ratified. An application for examination of compatibility may be lodged by any Chamber of Parliament until its approval of a treaty, by a group of deputies or senators, from the approval of Parliament until the Act of Ratification of the treaty by the President, or by the President from the moment of submission of the treaty for his ratification. A decision by the Constitutional Court on non-compatibility of the treaty with the constitutional order prevents its ratification until such time that the non-compatibility has been removed.

8 Cf. J. Malenovský, *Relationship between International and Internal Law in General and in the Czech Law in Particular* (Masaryk University, Brno, 2000), p. 68-72 (in Czech).

9 Law No. 48/2002 Coll. amending the Law No. 182/1993 Coll., on the Constitutional Court.

The position of other international agreements (except of treaties subject to ratification) in the Czech domestic legal order remains unclear. They are covered by the new Article 1(2) of the Constitution, according to which the State authorities must respect international obligations, even though they are not as such part of the Czech legal order. Nevertheless, even such international agreements may have priority of application over a law if there is a specific reference to an international agreement in the law in question. Such a reference does not amount to the incorporation clause made by the Constitution, but it has been widely used in past practice and may be of a certain utility even in the future. However, the constitutionality of such laws referring to international agreements could be open to question, although neither Parliament nor the Constitutional Court will be able to exercise control over these agreements.

II. International and Supranational Organisations and Domestic Legal Orders

(1) Polish Law and International Organisations

The provision of Article 90.1 has been manifestly introduced in order to enable Poland's accession to the European Union. According to its wording, the Republic of Poland can transfer to international organisations or international agencies certain powers (legislative, executive or judiciary, according to Article 10.1 of the Constitution). The treaty transferring these powers should be either ratified by the President of the Republic upon the prior approval by a qualified 2/3 majority of the members of both Houses of Parliament or should be subject to a popular referendum. In the latter case therefore the referendum would replace approval by Act of Parliament, which is regular procedure with respect to international agreements supposed to be directly effective. We must emphasise that a referendum concerning possible accession creates potentially difficult problems, such as the question of what is to happen if participation does not exceed 50% of voters. The law enacted by the organisation should be directly applicable and directly effective if the statute of that organisation so provides, and it should enjoy priority over statutes (Article 91.3). This provision should constitute a basis for the implementation of the *acquis communautaire* within the Polish domestic legal system. It will, however, require modification and amendment in the Accession Act, as certain elements of the *acquis* are not based directly on the founding treaties (like the question of the direct effect of directives).

The view was expressed that UN Security Council resolutions should be treated in the same way as Acts of international organs within the meaning of Articles 90 and 91(3) of the Constitution. Formally, such a position is justified, as the Constitution contains transitional provisions concerning presumption as to the ratification of international agreements concluded in the period preceding the entry into force of the Constitution. No formal obstacle can be invoked in order to prevent the application of Acts passed by supranational organs. However, in our opinion, such a stance, putting UN Security Council resolutions on an equal footing with EC institutions, would be contrary to the purpose of the regulation (by a teleological interpretation of the Constitution).

It is worth presenting here a discussion which took place in Poland in connection with the ratification by Poland of the Statute of the International Criminal Court. In the opinion of a number of MPs, as well as of the Legislative Council (the board of legal advisers to the Prime Minister), the Statute had to be ratified on the basis of the procedure referred to in Article 90 of the Constitution, as the transfer of criminal jurisdiction implies a serious restriction of the sovereignty of the State. On the other hand, the Ministers of Foreign Affairs and of Justice presented the view that there was no qualitative difference between numerous international agreements providing for the transfer of private or commercial jurisdiction to different arbitral tribunals, and the transfer of criminal jurisdiction to the ICC. If so, it would be unreasonable to require the use of the Article 90 procedure in the case of the ICC, and of Article 89 in the event of other transfers of jurisdiction. Finally, the stance of the two Ministries was accepted and Poland ratified the Statute of the Rome Tribunal using the regular procedure.

The provisions of the Polish Constitution of 2 April 1997 constitute an important step forward in the regulation of the relationship between international law and Polish municipal law. They specify the position of international agreements and legal acts of international organisations (*ditto*: European Union) within domestic law, and establish a basis for implementation of international obligations by Poland. This regulation is not sufficient. Chapter III of the Constitution was drafted by experts, especially specialising in constitutional law. Because of their experience from the Communist era they tried to construct an exhaustive system of sources of law in order to avoid possible abuses. This is also the reason why the Constitution contains so many gaps which need to be filled by the legislation and jurisprudence of the courts, in particular—but not exclusively—of the Constitutional Court and the Supreme Court.

As to OECD Acts, the Statute does not provide for any requirements concerning domestic procedures of implementation; it states only (Article 6) that decisions can be binding upon Member States exclusively upon their transformation into domestic Acts. Finally, the statutes of other international organisations (WMO, WHO) introduce a system of contracting-out in respect of their recommendations. In the latter system, the issue of direct applicability of Acts of international organisations in the Polish domestic order does not arise, as the direct effect of these Acts should be provided for by the Statute itself.

(2) Czech Law and Supranational Organisations

The above-mentioned amendment to the Czech Constitution was adopted not only to regulate the relationship between international law and Czech law in general, but also—and in particular—in order to enable the accession of the Czech Republic to the European Union. This is the purpose of the new Articles 10a and 10b. According to the provision of Article 10a, certain powers of the Czech authorities can be transferred by an international treaty to an international organisation or institution. The above-mentioned treaty should be ratified by a special majority in Parliament (this means, under Article 39(4), a majority of 3/5 of all deputies and 3/5 of the senators present and voting?), unless a special constitutional law provides for consent by popular referendum. This constitutional law has not yet been passed by Parliament. The provision of Article 10a constitutes a basis for future accession to the EU and for the implementation of the *acquis communautaire* within the Czech legal order.

This provision could hardly be applicable for UN Security Council resolutions concerning sanctions. There are several reasons for this interpretation. First, the *travaux préparatoires* of the amendment to the Constitution clearly show that its purpose is accession to the European Union, without contemplating the issue of UN sanctions. Second, the provision of Article 10a deals with the transfer of powers from the Czech authorities to the international organisation, which seems to create a completely new situation where some of the sovereign powers of the State will pass to the international or rather supranational organisation. This is different from a situation in an organisation based on cooperation. Except for the use of force, the Member States of the United Nations keep all sovereign powers and do not transfer them to the Security Council. They are only obliged to cooperate with, and to implement the binding resolutions of the UN Security Council. Third, the provision of Article 10a should be read in context with Article 10b, according to which the Government shall regularly and in advance inform Parliament about issues relating to obligations arising from the membership of the Czech Republic in such an international organisation. The Chambers of the Parliament are consulted and give an opinion on preparing decisions of the international organisation. This is possible if applied to legislation of the European Union, but not practicable in the case of resolutions of the Security Council, which are often adopted in urgent situations and without consultation with other Member States not represented within the Security Council. The last reason is that the Czech Republic does not need to resort to the complicated interpretation of general provisions in the Constitution, because it has special legislation implementing UN Security Council sanctions.

However, the provision of Article 10a could be used as a legal basis for approval by the Czech Parliament of ratification of the Rome Statute of the International Criminal Court. The ratification of the Statute means a limited transfer of criminal jurisdiction to the International Criminal Court. Because of the political and constitutional obstacles, it is very likely that, unfortunately, the Czech Parliament will not take any decision on this issue before the beginning of June 2002. Since the amendment to the Constitution has become effective on 1 June 2002, Parliament is able to treat the Statute as a treaty under Article 10a or a treaty under Article 49. (In any case, another amendment to the Constitution may prove to be necessary, in particular concerning the possibility to hand over (transfer) Czech nationals to the International Criminal Court and the non-applicability of constitutional immunities of certain officials for the purpose of prosecution before the ICC.

III. Implementation of UN Security Council Sanctions in the Domestic Legal Orders: Current Practice

(1) The Situation of Poland

Anticipating future membership in the European Union, the fathers of the Constitution proposed the introduction of provisions dealing with the transfer of certain competencies of State powers to international organisations and international organs, as well as with the implementation of law enacted in the framework of international organisations in the Polish legal system. This problem has become actual under the current international obligations of Poland, in particular as far as it concerns resolutions of the UN Security Council (decisions within the meaning of Article 25 of the UN Charter which are based upon Chapter VII), decisions of the Council of the OECD and of the Council of the GATS. The latter are addressed to the Member States (decisions of the Council of the OECD are based on Article 5.2 and leave to the Member States the choice of adopting measures of municipal law to implement them (Article 6.3); the same applies to Acts adopted on the basis of GATS). As to the decisions of the Security Council, they were implemented in the following way:[10] the Government passed resolutions or enacted regulations addressed to respective competent Ministers requiring them to take necessary measures to implement the UN Security Council resolutions, and subsequently the Ministers adopted these measures taking into account the requirements of municipal law. Thus, for example, the sanctions against Libya imposed on the basis of UN Security Council Resolution 883 of 11 November 1993 were approved by the Council of Ministers (Government) on 7 March 1994 (Resolution No. 8),[11] and subsequently introduced into the Polish legal order in a universally binding Act (Regulation of 12 May 1994).[12] With the exception of this one Act dealing with Libya, the above-mentioned instruments did not invoke the UN Security Council resolutions but referred to municipal Acts (Statutes) as their bases. They were published in *Dziennik Ustaw* (Official Gazette) or in *Monitor Polski* (official gazette of a lower rank than *Dziennik Ustaw*, normally containing Acts which are not generally binding). In some respects, the solution applied was abused. We can quote the announcement by the Council of Ministers of 27 May 1994 that "it is declared that limitations upon arms commerce with Yugoslavia was introduced in implementation of the UNSC resolution", without publishing the relevant resolution nor specifying the State Agency which enacted the ban on arm exports, or the legal basis of this ban under municipal law.

A specific measure was adopted on 8 June 1994. The announcement signed by the Minister of Foreign Affairs, Mr. Andrzej Olechowski, and published in *Monitor Polski*.[13] The Minister declared that the Security Council, in specified resolutions, proclaimed a ban on delivery of arms and military material to Iraq, post-Yugoslav states, Somalia, Libya, Liberia, Haiti, Angola, and Rwanda. This announcement referred to the Resolution of the Council of Ministers No. 30 i of 27 May 1994 quoted above, but also to the Regulation by the Minister of International Economic Cooperation (Foreign Trade) of 29 June 1993 concerning the list of goods subjected to concessions in international commerce. The form of that instrument testifies to the fact that the Government of Poland, in the beginning of the process of democratization, was not experienced in dealing with the relationship between international law and domestic law, and that it tried to implement the resolutions of the Security Council in a pragmatic way, using a functional/teleological approach to law.

10 Cf. P. Daranowski, "The Resolutions of the Security Council of the United Nations Aimed at Maintenance or Restoration of International Peace and Security and the Polish Legal Order. The Practice of Implementation and Its Prospects", 21 *PolYBIL* (1994) 55 ff.

11 MP 1994, No. 17, Item 129.

12 Dz.U. 1994, No. 61, Item 255.

13 MP 1994, No. 39, Item 336.

This practice cannot be upheld under the new Constitution, in particular when the UN Security Council resolutions—even if addressed to the Member States—include provisions dealing with the status of individuals. They can contain provisions requiring the State agencies to act in a way contrary to constitutional norms. Article 55 forbids, for instance, the extradition of Polish nationals. Such a solution is fully compatible with international law. On the other hand, UN Security Council resolution 748 (1992) dealing with the *Lockerbie Case* demanded that Libya hand over her nationals to the international community and subject them to the jurisdiction of foreign courts. The same is true with respect to the Yugoslavia tribunal. The solution adopted to resolve this problem[14] was a distinction between extradition and delivery to an international judicial body, introduced in Article 615.2 of the Criminal Procedure Code of 1997. The reason given for that provision was that Poland had certain influence upon the activities of international courts, as based upon international agreements, while it has no influence on criminal procedures in third States. It is worth remembering that the Criminal Procedure Code was passed by Parliament after the establishment of the Tribunal for the Former Yugoslavia by the UN Security Council. Up to now, however, no case of delivery of a Polish national to the Yugoslavia Tribunal nor request thereto has been reported. To sum up, as long as there is no control of legality of the Acts of UN agencies (the ICJ consequently rejected such a possibility in its *Namibia* [1971] and *Lockerbie* [1992] decisions), Poland can be confronted with the problem of implementation of UN instruments as a constitutional issue. The catalogue of sources of domestic law is exhaustive, and it does not provide for the enactment of regulations in order to implement international agreements (although one could suggest that these regulations could be treated as remaining within the scope of international agreements duly ratified by Parliament, so that the constitutional requirement of defining the scope of regulations by law is fulfilled)—which is not to say that questions related to the status of individuals can, under the new Constitution, be regulated exclusively by Acts of Parliament. It seems necessary therefore either to implement UN Security Council resolutions by Parliamentary statute (which would not necessarily be effective enough but "proper" from the legislative point of view) or to pass a law allowing the Government to act in order to implement the UN Security Council decisions. Neither solution is of course adequate in the case of instruments conflicting with constitutional provisions.

It is worth noting that at least some of the recently passed laws contain provisions concerning possible sanctions imposed either by Security Council resolutions or by other international organisations. For instance, Articles 2, 6(1)(19), 22(1)(9) of the Law of 11 December 1997 on the administration of international trade of goods, technologies and services relevant to national security[15] allows the Council of Ministers to introduce limitations upon said commerce if the national interest or fundamental economic interest of the State so require, in accordance with WTO regulations, if it is necessary in order to meet the obligations of Poland deriving from the UN Charter in the field of

14 Posed again in connection with the ratification of the Statute of the International Criminal Court.

15 Dz.U. 1997, No. 157, Item 1057. Amended on 29 November 2000, Dz.U. No. 119, Item 1250.

international peace and security. The instrument which provides for the implementation of these provisions is a governmental regulation (*rozporz?dzenie*). This law was invoked as a basis for the ban on trade of arms and ammunition in the territory of Afghanistan in the context of UN Security Council Resolution 1333 (2000), although no application for the certificate necessary for the commercial transactions under that law was reported. Article 9.1 of the Customs Act of 28 December 1989[16] contains similar provisions. The same solution was adopted in Article 19 of the Law of 18 December 1998 on foreign currency.[17] The provision states that the Council of Ministers can enact regulations in order to implement resolutions of the UN Security Council imposing limitation upon payments to or financial relations with specific states. Finally, the imposition of restrictions on air traffic can be introduced on the basis of Article 15 of the Air Transportation Law of 1 May 1962,[18] according to which the provisions of this Law should be applied conform to international agreements concluded by Poland in the field of civil aviation; the implementation of these agreements was left to the Minister of Transportation by means of regulations. All these provisions are compatible with the Constitution of 1997.[19] Generally the Constitution does not allow the enactment of executive measures by the Council of Ministers to implement international obligations. It is possible to enact such measures exclusively on the basis of specific provisions of a law (Act of Parliament), in the framework specified by the law. Under these circumstances it seems necessary for Ministers to act on the basis of domestic Acts.

In some cases, the Resolutions of the Council of Ministers ordered the competent Ministers to use their right of legislative initiative in order to amend specific laws, the application of which might be necessary or useful for the implementation of the UN Security Council sanctions. Such a solution was applied, for instance, with respect to penal sanctions introduced by the UN Security Council; the Minister of Justice was requested to propose amendments to the Criminal Code concerning the criminalisation of acts punishable under the resolutions.

A specific solution was applied with respect to Resolution 986 (1995) of 14 April 1995 establishing the UN Compensation Commission. This resolution defined the principles governing claims for damages suffered by UN Member States, corporations and individuals as a result of the aggression of Iraq against Kuwait. The Polish State, companies, and individual persons brought claims against the Iraqi government amounting to USD 187 mio. The resolution was not implemented within the Polish legal system properly speaking; no information on the resolution and its consequences was published in the Official Journal (*Dziennik Ustaw* or *Monitor Polski*). All information concerning the measures applicable to the claims was disseminated exclusively by the press and electronic media. All documentation concerning claims should have been sent by the persons

16 Dz.U. 1989, No. 75, Item 445.

17 Dz.U. 1998, No. 160, Item 1063.

18 Dz.U. 1962, No. 32, Item 153.

19 In practice, the resolutions declaring the ban on commercial flights provided for in Resolutions 1267 (1999) and 1333 (2000) were implemented in such a way that no aircraft owned or controlled by the Taliban was allowed to start or land in Poland. However, no such attempts were reported.

concerned directly to the UNCC. A special agency within the Ministry of Economic Affairs was created; however, its task was exclusively to transfer the documents to Geneva without adding a single sheet of paper. In fact, therefore, Resolution 986 became directly effective within the Polish legal order.

Another interesting solution was adopted with respect to the sanctions imposed against Yugoslavia (Serbia-Montenegro). The ban on export of oil and oil-made products was introduced by a Regulation passed by the Government on 27 April 1999[20] and amended by the Regulation of 22 September 1999.[21] Both Regulations did not refer to the resolutions of the Security Council, but instead invoked two Common Positions of the European Union: 1999/273/CFSP of 23 April 1999, and 1999/604/CFSP of 3 September 1999. In those cases the Government acted relatively quickly and efficiently. This was not always the case—the lapse of time between the passing of the respective resolutions of the UN Security Council and the adoption of the implementing domestic measures was usually much longer. Thus, for instance, Resolution 820 (1993) of 18 April 1993 concerning Yugoslavia was implemented by the Government by means of Resolution No. 54 of 24 June 1994, i.e. after more than 2 months; Resolution 883 (1993) of 11 November 1993 concerning Libya was implemented by Resolution No. 8 of the Council of Ministers of 7 March 1994, and the sanctions were finally introduced on 12 May 1994, i.e. after around 6 months. By contrast, the lifting of the sanctions took place very quickly. The sanctions against the Republic of Yugoslavia were suspended by UN Security Council Resolution 1022 of 22 November 1995, and two Polish domestic legal Acts implementing this resolution were adopted on 28 November 1995 (Resolution No. 135 of the Council of Ministers) and 3 January 1996 (Governmental Regulation), respectively.[22]

(2) The UN Security Council and the Czech Domestic Legal Order

Even some years before drafting and enacting the above-mentioned amendment to the Constitution, anticipating future membership of the European Union, the Czech Republic had to react to its international obligations arising in particular from its membership of the United Nations. The implementation of Acts of international organisations is one of the most difficult issues arising from the relationship between international law and internal law. These Acts have a dual quality, they are both international legal norms (sources of obligations) and acts of application of international law by the law-making or decision-making process in the competent international organisation. The validity and legal effects of such Acts depend on the treaty (statute) establishing this international organisation. The implementation of such Acts in internal law is not therefore a simple operation, but rather a two-fold process. The first step is the binding effect of the treaty (and its possible reception), the second step is the implementation of the Act enacted by

20 Dz.U, No. 39, Item 386.

21 Dz.U, No. 78, Item 877.

22 The Resolution of the Council of Ministers No. 135 obligated the competent ministers to undertake all necessary steps to suspend the sanctions against Yugoslavia; however, the provision of para. 3 emphasised that all the effects of measures imposed by the Resolution should remain valid.

a competent organ of the organisation. While the internal status of international treaties is often governed by basic (general) incorporation norms in the Constitution, the internal implementation of the Acts of international organisations is, as a rule, subordinated to a statutory norm on reception (with the force of simple law).[23] This is the situation in the Czech Republic. We should however make a distinction between economic or other sanctions based on Chapter VII of the UN Charter and peace-keeping operations. They have a fundamentally different legal basis from the point of view of international law as well as of their implementation in the Czech legal order. We shall focus on UN Security Council sanctions first.

The Czech Constitution does not contain any specific rule concerning the internal implementation of the Acts of international organisations in general and of UN Security Council decisions in particular. The above-mentioned new provision of Article 1(2) is too general. Although it provides for the duty of the Czech Republic to respect its international obligations, which certainly includes sanction obligations arising from UN Security Council resolutions, it does not make them directly applicable as part of the internal legal order (by way of incorporation). Therefore some specific internal legal Acts have been necessary for implementation of Security Council sanctions. However, the internal mechanism of sanctions implementation in Czech law went through an interesting legislative development in the 1990s.

In the beginning, the international sanctions decided by the UN Security Council were implemented by decrees of the Ministry of Foreign Trade issued on the basis of Article 56 of Law No. 42/1980 Coll., concerning international economic relations, which authorised the Ministry to limit or to ban certain commercial activities with foreign States or the transit of certain goods on Czech (former Czechoslovak) territory. This was the practice until the dissolution of Czechoslovakia at the end of 1992. For example, Decree No. 380/1990 Coll., on the ban on trade with the Republic of Iraq and the State of Kuwait, prohibited—in implementation of the UN Security Council sanctions against Iraq after its aggression against Kuwait—import or export of goods and services from or to Iraq.[24] This solution ensured a speedy and flexible reaction to the resolutions of the Security Council concerning economic sanctions. Unfortunately, the legal basis, which derives from the period of command economy and State monopoly on foreign trade, does not fit the new conditions of the market economy and the rule of law in the present Czech Republic. It became incompatible with Article 2(4) of the Czech Constitution, which stated that "every citizen is free to do anything, that is not forbidden by law, and nobody must be forced to do anything that is not prescribed by law".

That is why the Czech authorities had to employ special legislation in order to be able to make Czech persons (natural and juridical) respect the obligations imposed by the UN Security Council resolutions. The first years of the independent Czech Republic, i.e. especially the period between 1993 and 1997, can be described as the period of hesitation and "legislative experiments". Although Parliament prevented the Government

23 Cf. J. Malenovský, *Relationship between International and Internal Law in General and in the Czech Law in Particular*, *op. cit.*, p. 42-44, 84.

24 Cf. Z. Kučera, M. Pauknerová et al., *Introduction into Studies of the Czech Law of International Trade* (West Bohemian University Press, Plzen, 1997), p. 85 (in Czech).

from using decrees, it did not show the necessary flexibility in adopting the legislative measures needed for implementation of the UN Security Council sanctions. For example, the sanctions regime established by Security Council Resolution 724 (1991) in reaction to the conflict in the Former Yugoslavia was modified about ten times during the next four years. However, the Czechoslovak and later Czech legislators were not always able to react as quickly as expected by the UN Security Council resolutions.[25] For instance, the sanctions against Yugoslavia were introduced by Decree-Law No. 366/1992 Coll. of the former Presidency of the Federal Assembly (the Czechoslovak Federal Parliament) and extended by Law No. 215/1993 Coll.

The weakness and deficiencies of this legislative practice can be demonstrated in the case of the economic sanctions (embargo) against Haiti, imposed by UN Security Council Resolution 841 (1993), amended by UN Security Council Resolution 873 (1994) and finally lifted by UN Security Council Resolution 944 (1994). The Czech Government had decided to prepare draft legislation on the implementation of sanctions against Haiti, but the special law was not adopted before the end of sanctions. Similarly, the sanctions against Libya, introduced by a UN Security Council Resolution in Spring 1992, were implemented in Czech law, but only in 1997, i.e. five years later, by Law No. 78/1997 Coll. This is one of the special laws adopted by the Czech Parliament to implement the sanctions regimes of the UN Security Council. Next, Parliament adopted Law No. 304/1999 Coll. and Law No. 48/2000 Coll., dealing with the sanctions against the Federal Republic of Yugoslavia (concerning the situation in Kosovo) and the Afghan movement Taliban, respectively. Nevertheless, this form of special, ad hoc adopted laws did not allow a prompt reaction to the introduction, suspension or lifting of international sanctions. The last special law on the sanctions against the Afghan movement Taliban, however, delegated to the Government the power to implement such measures by its regulation. Consequently, the Government has specified and extended the scope of the sanctions by Regulation No. 164/2000 Coll. and Regulation No. 327/2001. The latter has extended the sanctions also to Usama bin Laden, persons connected with him and to the organisation Al-Qaida.

The urgent needs of Czech foreign policy prompted the adoption of a general law on the implementation of international sanctions for the maintenance of international peace and security (No. 98/2000 Coll.). This legislative Act has some new and important features in comparison with previous legislation. It is a framework law which delegates to the Government the implementation of all sanction regimes within the Czech Republic by way of its regulation. It enables the Czech Government to react promptly in introducing, amending, suspending or lifting sanctions. The obligations imposed on private persons are based on the law, which defines the maximum scope of limitations *ratione materiae* applied in this framework fully or partly by Governmental regulation as appropriate for the implementation of the specific international sanctions. The law provides also for penalties in case of its violation. At the same time, Parliament keeps

25 Cf. I. Janda, "Implementation of the Security Council Decisions in the Internal Legal Order", in: *On the Relationship between Constitutional and International Law*, (Acta Universitatis Carolinae Iuridica, Charles University Press, Prague, 1/1997), p. 53 (in Czech).

general political control on sanctions, as the regulation of the Government is subject to preliminary approval in the competent committee of the Chamber of Deputies.

It is worth noting that the scope of the above-mentioned law is not limited to sanctions imposed by UN Security Council decisions only (binding on the Czech Republic under international law); it may also be applied in relation to sanctions arising from the common actions or common positions of the European Union which are not binding on the Czech Republic as a Non-Member State. Indeed, once adopted in legislative form, these sanctions too become obligatory for Czech persons within the internal legal order. In view of the forthcoming accession to the EU, the Czech Republic thus adopted a necessary legal mechanism making it possible to join Community sanctions, whenever adopted in the framework of the Common Foreign and Security Policy.

As a result of the above-mentioned changes, the implementation of international sanctions in the Czech legal order could be faster. In practice, the Ministry of Foreign Affairs only notifies other governmental bodies of sanctions imposed by UN Security Council decisions or EU common positions. The method of implementation depends on the content of the sanctions. Restrictions on travel to or from the target country may be implemented by a simple Decree of the Ministry of Interior. Similarly, for an arms embargo, a Decree of the Ministry of Industry and Trade, based on a special law on licensing, is sufficient. The regulation of the Government is needed only for financial sanctions where the cooperation between the Ministry of Finance and Ministry of Foreign Affairs is at stake. Up to now, no regulation based on the general law on international sanctions (No. 98/2000 Coll.) has been adopted, although there is a need to implement sanctions against Angola and Iraq. However, the experience from the implementation of sanctions against the Taliban shows that the delay necessary for adoption of a regulation by the Government should not exceed three months.

Of a different nature seems to be the problem of the internal implementation of peace-keeping operations. The Czech Constitution (Article 43, paragraphs 4 and 6), as amended by Constitutional Law No. 300/2000 Coll., provides that the Government is competent to adopt urgent measures in implementing the decision to participate in such operations adopted by an international organisations, of which the Czech Republic is a Member State. However, Parliament is able to cancel such a decision of the Government.

IV. Proposals for Amendments and Improvements in Poland: An Opinion of the Advisory Board by the Ministry of Foreign Affairs of the Republic of Poland as to the Position of UN Security Council Resolutions

The Opinion of 10 May 1999 (unpublished) stated in general terms that UN Security Council resolutions were not directly applicable within the Polish legal order. They had to be transformed into domestic Acts. Some laws of Parliament contain a delegation for the competent Ministers to enact legislation concerning the implementation of these resolutions (commerce of goods and services, arms, finances, limitation on air transport). The Advisory Committee emphasises that the solution mentioned above is not universal. It is necessary therefore either to enact the resolution or Ordinance by the Council of Ministers, including a respective passage of the resolution; the Act of domestic law being based directly upon Articles 24 and 25 of the UN Charter, or to pass a general law by Parliament concerning the implementation of UN Security Council resolutions. The former solution would be in fact *contra* (or at least *infra*) *legem*; it would amount to an amendment of the constitutional gap; but on the other hand it would be a logical solution allowing rapid implementation of UN Security Council decisions. Examples of modification of the Constitution by constitutional practice can be found in the Polish legal system, and it should be not excluded in the context of UN sanctions.

V. Polish Draft Legislation Concerning the Implementation of UN Security Council Sanctions

On 12 February 2001 the Ministry of Foreign Affairs proposed the adoption of a set of statutes concerning the implementation of UN Security Council resolutions and the use of countermeasures in international relations, and the implementation of the Acts of international organisations in the domestic legal system. According to the draft, immediately after the imposing of sanctions by the UN Security Council, the Government, acting at the request of the Minister of Foreign Affairs, should pass a Resolution defining the steps to be taken in order to implement the sanctions. On the basis of this Resolution competent Ministers should adopt necessary measures, passing regulations founded either on respective specific legislation or on the law on the implementation of resolutions of the UN Security Council. The regulations adopted should refer to the resolution of the UN Security Council in question and specify the scope of rights and duties of both State agencies and individuals. The draft indicates certain kinds of actions by the UN Security Council and states that sanctions can consist of the limitation of movement of persons, goods and services, the freezing of financial means, the limitation of air, sea and land traffic, as well as of postal and telecommunication services. The implementation of sanctions cannot be restricted by any international agreement prior to the imposing of sanctions, by any contract of a private legal nature, or any previous authorisation. Finally, the draft proposed a number of criminal law measures aimed at the control of the implementation and at the possible punishment of violations of the sanctions.

In accordance with the procedural regulations in force, draft legislation must be evaluated by the Legislative Council from the point of view of its conformity with the Constitution and with the legal system as a whole. The Council passed its Opinion on 28 February 2001. The position of the Council was decisively critical. First of all, it expressed important doubts as to the necessity of adopting such a statute, as in practice the sanctions imposed by the UN Security Council could be implemented on the basis of the specific substantive legislation in force. The normal procedure required the enacting by competent Ministers of regulations based on the respective statutes. The Ministers acted within their own competence, undertaking their actions automatically, and they did not need any additional authorisation in the form of a Resolution of the Council of Ministers. In the opinion of the Council, although the competence of the UN Security Council as defined in Chapter VII of the UN Charter is not regulated in an exhaustive way and the UN Security Council can order every possible kind of action against any State violating the international legal order, in practice it has never applied any sanctions not provided by the Charter. Taking into account this practice, the regulations contained in the Polish legal system are sufficient to cover all the actions ordered by the UN Security Council. The only exception was the currency law which required urgent modification. Under these circumstances the Legislative Council decided not to recommend that the draft legislation proceed further. It suggested, however, that instead of passing the special law on UN Security Council resolutions, it would have been desirable to create a "fast legislative track" (provided under Article 123 of the Constitution) to cover situations in which the UN Security Council ordered sanctions not regulated by domestic Acts. Three main disputable points were, according to the Opinion: the scope of the suggested competence of the Government to pass regulations which would be contrary to Article 92 of the Constitution; the proposal concerning the publication in the Official Journal (*Dziennik Ustaw*) of the UN Security Council resolutions accompanied by the governmental announcement on their binding force (one cannot publish a legal Act without defining its legal nature); finally, the Legislative Council criticized the penal dispositions proposed by the draft as too detailed and for transferring the burden of observance of sanctions to individuals (contrary to the basic concept that the implementation of resolutions belonged to the competence of State authorities). It was also emphasised that the procedures proposed were regulated in a very detailed manner.

The Opinion of the majority of the Legislative Council met with the opposition of some of its members.[26] It was suggested that instead of a grammatical interpretation of the Constitution the Council in this case should have adopted a teleological approach: if the Constitution grants the Government specific competences (to implement international obligations, including sanctions imposed by the UN Security Council), it should also give competence to carry these out effectively, promptly and quickly, avoiding possible discussions within Parliament and the violation of Article 9 of the Constitution (referred to above). The delegation to adopt regulations proposed in the draft legislation would also meet the requirements of Article 91.1 of the Constitution, as it was detailed and its scope was limited by the action of the Security Council. It should, however, be recalled that the competence of the UN Security Council is in fact unlimited, and actions by the Government to implement its resolutions cannot be exhaustively specified by any domestic legislation. In particular, there is an urgent necessity to amend the banking law,[27] as controversies arose in the field of application in the Afghanistan crisis (some banks asked the Ministry of Foreign Affairs the possible basis and scope of restrictions in the field of banking; the Ministry of Finance refused to apply restrictions against the Taliban regime on the basis of the currency law actually in force, as this law allows the imposition of sanctions exclusively against States, and not against *de facto* regimes)—thus Resolution 1267 (1999) has never been correctly implemented nor applied by Poland; the air transportation law is also not precise enough, and a new draft has not yet been adopted by Parliament (the previous version was vetoed by the President on 25 August 2001 as he found the security measures at the airports proposed by the legislation insufficient). Respective provisions can be found in the drafts of this legislation.[28]

26 The resolutions are adopted by consensus and no separate opinions are allowed.

27 Law of 29 August 1997, Dz.U. 1997, No. 140, Item 939.

28 E.g. draft Article 5a of the banking law allows the restricting of financial transactions and other banking activities if such restrictions are required by international obligations of Poland,

VI. The Implementation by Poland of Sanctions against Terrorism/Afghanistan

In order to implement UN Security Council Resolution 1373 (2001), at the request of the Minister of Foreign Affairs, the Council of Ministers (Government) adopted on 5 November 2001 the resolution requiring the Ministers of Finance, Economic Affairs, Interior and Justice to undertake steps necessary to implement the said resolution. The implementation of this governmental instrument was reported in a note by the Permanent Representative of Poland to the UN to the Chairman of the Counter-Terrorism Committee (S/2001/1275 of 27 December 2001). This information shows the insufficiencies of the Polish legal system in applying UN Security Council sanctions, in particular if the sanctions concern non-State actors. The Ministry of Finance rejected firmly the possibility of applying sanctions against the Taliban, as the law on foreign currency allowed exclusively the restriction of the movement of capital with foreign States and not with *de facto* regimes or other entities. Because of this stance, Resolution 1267 (1999) remained unimplemented by Poland.[29]

Notwithstanding these Government activities, certain steps were also undertaken by the President of Poland, Mr. A. Kwasniewski. In particular the Presidents of the Central and Eastern European States invited by him to Warsaw adopted on 6 November 2001 the Declaration on Combating Terrorism and Action Plan in this field. The Declaration expressed the view that combating terrorism is an act directed against barbarism and not against any culture or religion; it fully supports all the efforts and measures adopted by the UN Security Council and other organisations, in particular the NATO and the European Council at its Extraordinary Meeting on 21 September 2001, and urged all States to implement Resolutions 1333 and 1373, as well as to ratify 12 international instruments concerning terrorism. It also emphasised that the existing domestic and international legislation against terrorism and connected issues (including arms trade control) can be implemented more efficiently, and security measures can be strengthened, although without infringing the rights of individuals. The Action Plan provided for a closer cooperation enabling the exchange of information on possible sources and threats of terrorism; adoption of legislative measures in particular in the fields of money-laundering and drug-trafficking; elaboration of more effective measures for combating illegal migration, including passport and customs control; as well for establishing new international institutions to research issues connected with terrorism.

VII. Concluding Remarks

It seems that in general—according to the official position of the Government—the domestic legal system in Poland is adequate and provides sufficient possibilities to

in particular in order to implement UN Security Council resolutions adopted on the basis of Chapter VII of the Charter. The list of states and individuals covered by the restrictions should be published by governmental regulation.

29 There were no such problems with respect to sanctions against Bosnian Serbs which were introduced by the regulations based upon other domestic legal acts and concerned the limitation of movement of goods.

implement UN Security Council resolutions. The proposal to draft special legislation concerning the implementation of these Acts was therefore abandoned, partially due to the critical Opinion of the Legislative Council. However, the implementation of UN Security Council Resolution 1373 clearly shows that there still are certain important gaps both in the fields of legislation and its application which should be urgently fulfilled in order to ensure the proper implementation of Article 9 of the Constitution, but also in view of the future accession of Poland to the European Union (i.e. in order to ensure the correct and full implementation of the possible future regulations of the EC). Certain legislative initiatives have just been undertaken: for instance, the Ministry of Finance has proposed amendments to the currency legislation, and modification of the Law of 16 November 2000 on counteracting the introduction of financial transactions of property values originating from unclear or illegal sources (money-laundering) in order to allow the freezing of suspected financial assets.

Similarly, it seems that, as of today, the internal legal order of the Czech Republic is adequate and provides sufficient possibilities to respect and implement international obligations arising from various sources. First, the last amendment to enter into force on June 1st, 2002, has improved substantially the "international dimension" of the Czech Constitution in general (Article 1(2)), and introduced the wide incorporation of international treaties in particular (Article 10). As to the source of international law, one can say that the Czech Republic shifted from a "dualistic" to a "monistic" system. This conclusion, however, cannot be extended to the Acts of international organizations, in particular UN Security Council resolutions on sanctions. Therefore, similar to the situation in other countries, the Czech Republic has basically followed the dualistic model. After a period of legislative hesitation and inefficiency in implementation of UN Security Council sanctions, due to a case-by-case approach (adopting special laws for each case) in the 1990s, the Czech legal order has now been adapted to the new situation. The general law on the implementation of international sanctions for the maintenance of international peace and security (No. 98/2000 Coll.) seems to provide an adequate response not only to the obligations arising from the membership of the Czech Republic in the United Nations, but also in anticipation of its possible participation in actions decided by the European Union in its CFSP.

* * *

Select Bibliography

Filip, J., "Parlament ÈR schválil návrh euronovely Ústavy ÈR [The Czech Parliament approved the draft Euro-amendment to the Constitution of CR]", *Právní zpravodaj*, No. 11/2001.

Hofmann, M., "Status of International Treaties on Environmental Protection in the Internal Law: The Case of the Czech Republic", in P. Šturma (ed.), *Implementation and Enforcement of International Environmental Law*, sborník zkolokvia, Edièní støedisko PF UK, Praha, 2002.

Janda, I., "Implementace rozhodnutí Rady bezpeènosti v našem vnitrostátním právním øádu", in: *O vztahu ústavního a mezinárodního práva* ["Implementation of the Security Council decisions in the internal legal order", in: *On the Relationship between Constitutional and International Law*], Acta Universitatis Carolinae Iuridica, 1/1997.

Malenovský, J., "K potøebnosti poctivého výkladu obratu 'pøednost pøed zákonem' v èlánku 10 èeské Ústavy" ["On the Necessity of a Honest Interpretation of the Term 'priority over law' in Article 10 of the Czech Constitution"], in: *O vztahu ústavního a mezinárodního práva*, Acta Universitatis Carolinae Iuridica, 1/1997.

Malenovský, J., "O 'chudokrevnosti' mezinárodního rozmìru èeské ústavy a možných terapiích" ["On 'anemia' of the international dimension of the Czech Constitution and possible therapies"], *Právník,* No. 7/1997.

Malenovský, J., *Pomìr mezinárodního a vnitrostátního práva obecnì a v èeském právu zvláštì* [*Relationship between International and Internal Law in General and in the Czech Law in particular*], Doplnìk - Masaryk University Press, Brno, 2000.

Malenovský, J., "Pøípad praktické aplikace èlánku 10 Ústavy Èeské republiky: Rámcová úmluva na ochranu národnostních menšin" ["A case of Practical Application of Article 10 of the Constitution of the Czech Republic: Framework Convention for the Protection of National Minorities"], *Právník* No. 9/1995.

Malenovský, J., "K ratifikaci Rámcové úmluvy o ochranì národnostních menšin Èeskou republikou" ["On the Ratification of the Framework Convention for the Protection of National Minorities by the Czech Republic"], *Právník* No. 3/1998.

Pavlíèek, V., "Nìkteré otázky vztahu mezinárodního a vnitrostátního práva se zøetelem na èlánek 10 Ústavy" ["Some Issues of the Relationship between International Law and Constitutional Law"], in: *O vztahu ústavního a mezinárodního práva*, AUC-Iuridica 1/1997.

Týè, V., *O vnitrostátní pøímé závaznosti mezinárodních smluv* [*On Direct Effect of Intenational Treaties in Internal Law*], AUB Iuridica No. 173, Masaryk University, Brno, 1996.

Pogatschnigg, I. M., *Die Tschechische Republik und die Gemeinsame Außen- und Sicherheitspolitik der EU*, Peter Lang, Frankfurt am Main, 2003 (*this is a new book by a former Erasmus student coming to Prague; she quoted our article several times in the book*).

13

SOUTH AFRICA AND NAMIBIA

*Hennie Strydom and Tunguru Huaraka**

PART I: SOUTH AFRICA

by

Hennie Strydom

I. Introduction

The outline of themes by means of which contributions to this project are guided towards a certain minimum level of uniformity is to a great extent informed by an image of the modern State as a member of a relatively well-organised international community whose activities are increasingly subjected to scrutiny for compliance with international standards of conduct. This image is largely made up of a projection of political entities which either individually or through regional organisations have reached such a level of legal and political sophistication that sanctions enforcement against delinquent members through a complex of legal and administrative mechanisms has reached an advanced stage.

Very few, if any, of the States in Africa that will feature in this chapter could, until very recently, realistically live up to this image for several reasons. In the early stages of decolonisation, the newly independent states of Africa could barely manage the challenges of independent statehood and economic survival, let alone carry the burden of international obligations which ensued from over-eagerly acquired membership in international and regional organisations. Developments since then have compounded many of the initial problems. Firstly, the growing sophistication in United Nations sanctions measures has even further outpaced the ability of the national legal and administrative enforcement systems. Secondly, regional organisations, forced to inaction by statist concepts of governance have failed to instill confidence in the ability of such organisations to develop and enforce transnational codes of conduct. Thirdly, in many of the States responsible for the enforcement of sanctions the governing elite is either directly

* Hennie Strydom is Professor, Faculty of Law, Rand Afrikaans University, Johannesburg, South Africa. Tunguru Huaraka, LLB (Hons) Accra, LLM London, PhD Geneva, is Special Adviser to the Minister, Ministry of Justice; First Ambassador Extraordinary and Plenipotentiary/Permanent Representative of the Republic of Namibia to the United Nations (1991-1996).

Vera Gowlland-Debbas (ed.), National Implementation of UN Sanctions, *403-471.*

or indirectly involved in sanctions busting or wars of enrichment.[1] Fourthly, in several parts of the continent relentless armed conflicts and civil strife have over long periods of time crippled fledgling economies and destroyed fragile infrastructures.

It is within this context that the prospects of the enforcement of Security Council sanctions in Africa must be understood. As will become clear, the scales are rather tipped to the side of sanctions evasion as opposed to sanctions enforcement. However, some recent developments offer a glimmer of hope. After a false and dismal start, reconsidered and refocused efforts and measures in the case of Angola at least suggest improved co-operation between States in compliance with Security Council resolutions.[2] As regards future developments, changes at the regional institutional level could open up new and interesting possibilities. Here one must take note of the Constitutive Act establishing the African Union and adopted by the African Heads of State and Government on July 11, 2000 in Togo. Amongst the objectives of the Union are counted the encouragement of international co-operation, taking into account the Charter of the United Nations; and the promotion of peace, security and stability on the African continent. In this context, one is also eagerly waiting to see what results will ensue from the restructuring that is currently undertaken with regard to SADC organs. Another interesting development which is in the process of unfolding is the position of countries under newly adopted systems of constitutional democracy and human rights protection, such as South Africa and Namibia. How these countries will react when tension develops between compliance with constitutional obligations and compliance with sanctions enforcement measures is still very much a matter for speculation.

It is within this uncertain and fluid context that developments since the imposition of sanctions against Rhodesia will be documented and explained. Where appropriate, the actions required by Security Council sanctions have been dealt with in more detail than was perhaps necessary in view of the information provided in the introductory part of the project. However, this approach was considered necessary in view of the enforcement problems that usually arise when Security Council resolutions and government responses thereto are not in agreement, as the case studies dealt with below clearly demonstrate.

---

1 See, for instance, P. Collier & A. Hoeffler, "On the incidence of civil war in Africa", 16 August 2000 and "Greed and grievance in civil war", 4 January 2001, at www.worldbank.org; I. Elbadawi & N. Sambanis, "Why are there so many civil wars in Africa?" (2000) at ditto; K Tomaševski, *Responding to Human Rights Violations* (2000) 236; W. Reno "Clandestine Economies, Violence and States in Africa," 2 *Journal of International Affairs* (2000) 434, 435; A. Zack-Williams, 'Sierra Leone: the Political Economy of Civil War 1991-1998' 20 *Third World Quarterly* (1999) 143 *et seq*; R. Rotberg, "Mess, Mugabe's mayhem", 79 *Foreign Affairs* (2000) 47 *et seq*.

2 See Report of the SC Committee concerning the situation in Angola S/2000/1255 of 29 December 2000, para. 34: "In 2000 it became increasingly clear that the measures against UNITA were having an impact and were succeeding in their objective of preventing UNITA from pursuing its objectives through military means".

II. The Nature and Scope of the Security Council's Sanctions

(1) The Case of Rhodesia[3]

a. The failure of optional sanctions

Both Resolution 216 (12 November 1965) and 217 (20 November 1965) attempted to reconcile the seriousness of the situation with a set of measures that would bear a resemblance to the kind of moderate stance the supporting States in the Security Council would feel comfortable with. The need for such an approach was underscored by the rejection in the Council of a draft resolution submitted by the Ivory Coast which called for the implementation of enforcement measures under Articles 41, 42 and 43 of the Charter.[4]

The first principle the two Resolutions wanted to establish was the illegality of the UDI and likewise of the white minority Government in Rhodesia.[5] From this basis Resolution 217 moved to the determination of the situation as "extremely grave" and its continuance in time "a threat to international peace and security,"[6] thereby beckoning enforcement action in terms of Chapter VII of the Charter. However, the measures the Resolution envisaged in response to this situation, including a variety of sanctions, were optional and not mandatory. The language of the Resolution and the absence of a finding by the Security Council in terms of *Article* 39 of the Charter have nevertheless given rise to considerable speculation on whether the measures were intended to fall under Chapter VI or VII of the Charter.[7]

The measures were threefold. First, the United Kingdom – apparently still considered responsible as colonial overseer – was called upon to (a) "quell the rebellion",[8] (b) take "immediate measures" in pursuance of the inhabitants' right to self-determination,[9] and (c) "enforce urgently and with vigour" all measures it has undertaken to adopt.[10] Second, the OAU was called upon to "do all in its power to assist in the implementation of the resolution".[11] A specific reference to Chapter VIII of the Charter in this instance indi-

3 For a commendable study on the UN involvement in Rhodesia see V. Gowlland-Debbas, *Collective Responses to Illegal Acts in International Law: United Nations Action in the Question of Rhodesia* (1990). See also R. Zacklin, *The United Nations and Rhodesia: A Study in International Law* (1974); C. Lloyd Brown-John, *Multilateral Sanctions in International Law: A Comparative Analysis* (1975).

4 Cf. Zacklin, n 3 above, 48.

5 SC Resolution 216, para. 1 and 217, para. 3.

6 *Ibid.*, para. 1.

7 Cf. also Gowlland-Debbas, n 3 above, 381 *et seq.*

8 SC Resolution 217, para. 4.

9 *Ibid.*, para. 7. This was probably the most impractical of all the measures envisaged by the resolution.

10 *Ibid.*, para. 9.

11 *Ibid.*, para. 10.

cated the willingness of the Security Council to utilize regional arrangements or agencies for enforcement action. Third, all States were called upon to desist from providing the "illegal régime" with "arms, equipment and military material, and to do their utmost in order to break all economic relations with Southern Rhodesia, including an embargo on oil and petroleum products".[12]

Embargo as means of enforcement

The inadequacies and inefficiencies of optional sanctions as a coercive instrument were soon illustrated by the *Joanna V* incident. On April 4, 1966 the British frigate, *Plymouth*, intercepted the *Joanna V*, an oil tanker bound for Beira under a Greek flag in the course of intensified surveillance by the British air and naval forces to prevent oil supplies from reaching Rhodesia via the Mozambique port of Beira.[13] The vessel, owned by a Panamian company was chartered to a South African company. The contents of Resolution 217 were transmitted to the Captain of the *Joanna V* with instructions to change course, but the Captain refused, stating that his cargo was destined for Djibouti in Somaliland. When the *Joanna V* dropped anchor two miles offshore from Beira the United Kingdom requested an emergency meeting of the Security Council to consider proposals from preventing contraventions of the oil embargo. The result was somewhat unprecedented. Invoking the enforcement provisions of Chapter VII of the Charter, the Security Council in Resolution 221 of April 9, 1966 authorised, on the strength of a finding that the situation "constitutes a threat to the peace,"[14] the United Kingdom –

> to prevent, by the use of force if necessary, the arrival at Beira of vessels reasonably believed to be carrying oil destined for Southern Rhodesia [and] to arrest and detain the tanker known as the *Joanna V* upon her departure from Beira in the event her oil cargo is discharged there.[15]

The *Johanna V* did not discharge her cargo in Beira but the United Kingdom used these powers to intercept another vessel, the *Manuela*, within twenty-four hours after adoption of the resolution. Although this Resolution made no specific reference to Chapter VII of the Charter the finding that the situation constituted a "threat to the peace" was the clearest indication yet that the Rhodesian issue was gradually drawn into the ambit of Chapter VII, perhaps also for reasons of political expediency. For instance, the legal basis of an authorisation to use force for the enforcement of a non-mandatory oil-embargo is less likely to be questioned if language everybody understands suggests a shift in legal basis.

Ambiguities in formulation and legal basis aside, the factual evidence of overt and covert breaches of sanctions against Rhodesia made it increasingly clear that measures

12 *Ibid.*, para. 8.

13 On these developments see Gowlland-Debbas, n 3 above, 402 *et seq*; Zacklin, n 3 above, 48, 49.

14 SC Resolution 221, para. 1.

15 *Ibid.*, para. 5.

that fell short of mandatory sanctions were inherently flawed. No amount of forcible measures or an intensification of surveillance by British air and naval forces seemed capable of isolating the Rhodesian economy to the extent necessary for bringing the Government to a fall or to a negotiated settlement.

b. Selective mandatory sanctions

The historical event that turned the tide in favour of mandatory sanctions was the failed talks for a negotiated settlement between Prime Minister Harold Wilson and Ian Smith on *HMS Tiger* in December 1966. Recognising that the optional measures did not bring about the desired economic and political consequences, that a quick end to the rebellion was a fallacy, and that a continuation of the situation could have far-reaching consequences for international peace and security, the United Kingdom's new strategy turned to more targeted economic sanctions. The proposition put forward had in mind "those export commodities which would cause the greatest economic damage to the régime and those against which sanctions could be most effectively applied by Member States."[16]

Based on this initiative and on amendments by African states to a United Kingdom draft, the Security Council, on December 16, 1966 adopted Resolution 232. With specific reference to Articles 39 and 41 of the Charter, the Security Council determined that "the present situation in Southern Rhodesia constitute[d] a threat to international peace and security."[17] On this basis the Council *decided* that States *shall* take the action authorised by the Resolution[18] and reminded them of their obligations in terms of Article 25 of the Charter.[19]

The extraterritorial and retrospective operation of the sanctions

The first aim of the Resolution was to prevent from the date of the Resolution the importation by Member States of certain commodities which originated in Rhodesia, namely asbestos, iron ore, chrome, pig-iron, sugar, tobacco, copper, meat, meat products and hides, skins and leather.[20] Secondly, the Resolution was intended to operate extraterritorially as well. This is clear from the provision that prohibited activities in the territory of Member States *or by their nationals* which promoted or were calculated to promote the export of the above commodities from Rhodesia. Included in the prohibition was the transfer of funds for the purpose of export transactions,[21] the shipment of such commodities in vessels or aircraft registered in any of the Member States[22] and the sale or shipment to Rhodesia of "arms, ammunition of all types, military aircraft, military vehicles, and equipment and materials for the manufacture and maintenance of arms

16 Gowlland-Debbas, n 3 above, 424.

17 SC Resolution 232, para. 1.

18 *Ibid.*, para. 2.

19 *Ibid.*, paras. 3 and 6.

20 *Ibid.*, para. 2(a).

21 *Ibid.*, para. 2(b).

22 *Ibid.*, para. 2(c).

and ammunition in Rhodesia."[23] As regards the prohibition of the supply of oil or oil products to Rhodesia the Resolution not only operated extraterritorially, but also retrospectively in the sense that supply in terms of "contracts entered into or licenses granted" before the Resolution came into operation, was also prohibited.[24]

There is evidence that selective mandatory sanctions came too late. For instance, economic surveys of the time indicated that when Resolution 232 was adopted the Rhodesian economy was on the upswing. At the same time the sanctioned commodities had already diminished in importance as far as the country's immediate neighbours were concerned, a consequence of a change in patterns of commerce and enterprise the country undertook to weaken the impact of the sanctions.[25]

c. Comprehensive mandatory sanctions

In March 1968 four Africans reprieved by the Queen were executed in Rhodesia. This incident, considered as an outrage, prompted the meeting of the Security Council in May 1968, at the request of 36 African states, to consider more comprehensive mandatory sanctions. However, there was also the larger issue that selective mandatory sanctions have failed to bring an end to an increasing intolerable situation. In response the Council, acting again under Chapter VII of the Charter, adopted Resolution 253 (29 May 1968), making it clear in the preamble that it is "gravely concerned that the measures taken by the Security Council have not been complied with by all States and that some States, contrary to Resolution 232 (1966) ... and to their obligations under Article 25 of the Charter ..., have failed to prevent trade with the illegal régime in Southern Rhodesia."[26]

Consequently, the Security Council, reaffirming its determination that the situation in Southern Rhodesia constituted "a threat to international peace and security", *decided* that the following will be prohibited –

- The importation into the territories of Member States or the exportation from Rhodesia of "all commodities or products" including the sale, supply or shipment of such commodities or products;[27]
- The making available of funds or investments, or any other financial or economic resources to any commercial, industrial or public utility undertaking, including tourist enterprises in Rhodesia;[28]
- The entry into the territories of Member States of persons carrying a Rhodesian passport or who were reasonably suspected of residing in Rhodesia and who were suspected of having furthered or encouraged the unlawful actions of the authorities or the evasion of sanctions;[29] and

23 *Ibid.*, para. 2(d).

24 *Ibid.*, para. 2(f).

25 Cf. Brown-John, n 3 above, 331 *et seq.*

26 See also operative para. 12 of SC Resolution 253.

27 SC Resolution 253, para. 3.

28 *Ibid.*, para. 4.

29 *Ibid.*, para. 5.

– The operation of air services between Member States and Rhodesia and the linking up with any airline company constituted or aircraft registered in Rhodesia.[30]

Humanitarian exceptions
As in the previous Resolution, the above measures operated retrospectively in that States were obligated to give effect to the Resolution "notwithstanding any contract entered into or licence granted before the date of this Resolution."[31] Humanitarian exemptions were granted in two instances. Firstly, excluded from the prohibition on the sale or supply of commodities or products were supplies "intended strictly for medical purposes, educational equipment and material for use in schools and other educational institutions, publications, news material and, in special humanitarian circumstances, foodstuffs."[32] Secondly, restrictions on travel by certain categories of persons could be suspended "on exceptional humanitarian grounds."[33] Further, country-specific assistance was considered in the case of Zambia. Thus, Member States, the United Nations and specialized agencies were requested to provide assistance to Zambia "as a matter of priority with a view to helping it solve such special economic problems as it may be confronted with arising from the carrying out of these decisions of the Security Council."[34] This need for assistance must be understood against Zambia's vulnerable economic position in the region. Its economy, for instance, was inextricably linked to that of Rhodesia. The two countries shared a railway and a hydroelectric dam with the result that Zambian copper exports were dependent on the use of the shared railway and the operation of its mines on the use of the shared hydroelectric facility. In general Zambian trade with Rhodesia was a necessity and the use of alternative markets and routes have proved to be of little use.[35]

The role of the Sanctions Committee
Resolution 253 introduced another exceptional element in the United Nations attempt to make sanctions against Rhodesia more effective. By virtue of paragraph 20 a Sanctions Committee of the Security Council was established to –
– Examine reports on the implementation of the Resolution; and
– To seek additional information on trade with Rhodesia and on activities which could constitute an evasion of measures decided upon by the Security Council.

In Resolution 277 (18 March 1970) these functions of the Sanctions Committee were extended to include the "studying of ways and means by which Member States could carry out more effectively the decisions of the Security Council ... and making recommendations to the Council."[36] This Resolution, taking into account reports of the Com-

30 *Ibid.*, para. 6.
31 *Ibid.*, para. 7.
32 *Ibid.*, para. 3(d).
33 *Ibid.*, para. 5(a).
34 *Ibid.*, para. 15.
35 Cf. Brown-John, n 3 above, 325.
36 SC Resolution 277, para. 21(c).

mittee since its establishment, also, with reference to Article 41 of the Charter, extended the mandatory measures against Rhodesia to include the severance of all diplomatic, consular, trade, military and other relations and the interruption of any existing means of transportation to and from Rhodesia.[37] In language less mandatory, Member States and international and regional organisations were either *called upon* or *urged* to suspend the membership of the Rhodesian Government and to refuse any request for membership from it.[38]

d. National enforcement measures required by Security Council resolutions

Most of the resolutions that followed on these were merely confirming earlier decisions of the Security Council and urging States to fully comply with the resolutions and to take more effective measures.[39] Another turn towards better enforcement came with Resolution 333 (22 May 1973) which aimed at the criminalisation of sanctions evasion in the domestic legal system of Member States. Thus, States were called upon to enact and enforce legislation providing for the imposition of "severe penalties" on persons that evade or commit breaches of sanctions by –

- Importing any goods from Rhodesia;
- Exporting any goods to Rhodesia;
- Providing facilities for the transport of goods to and from Rhodesia;
- Conducting or facilitating any transaction or trade with Rhodesia, or
- Continuing to deal with clients in South Africa, Angola, Mozambique, Guinea (Bissau) and Namibia.[40]

Secondly, States were called upon to "pass legislation forbidding insurance companies under their jurisdiction from covering air flights into and out of Southern Rhodesia and individuals or air cargo carried on them."[41] Furthermore States were to undertake "appropriate legislative measures to ensure that al valid marine insurance contracts contain specific provisions that no goods of Southern Rhodesia origin or destined to Southern Rhodesia shall be covered by such contracts."[42] In Resolution 388 (6 April 1976) this measure was extended to contracts providing insurance cover for any commodity or product exported from or imported into Rhodesia.[43] By the same token States were obligated to prevent any commercial, industrial or public utility undertaking in Rhodesia from using "any trade name or from entering into any franchising agreement involving the use of any trade name, trade mark or registered design in connexion with the sale or

37 *Ibid.*, para. 9.

38 *Ibid.*, paras. 12, 13.

39 See, for instance, SC Resolutions 288 (17 November 1970); 314 (28 February 1972); 318 (28 July 1972) and 320 (29 September 1972).

40 SC Resolution 333, para. 4.

41 *Ibid.*, para. 6.

42 *Ibid.*, para. 7.

43 SC Resolution 388, para. 1.

distribution of any products, commodities or services of such an undertaking."[44] In Resolution 409 (27 May 1977) the net was cast wider with the Security Council's decision – again under Chapter VII of the Charter – that all Member States –

> "shall prohibit the use or transfer of any funds in their territories by the illegal régime in Southern Rhodesia, including any office or agent thereof, or by other persons or bodies within Southern Rhodesia, for the purposes of any office or agency of the illegal régime that is established within their territories other than an office or agency so established exclusively for pension purposes."[45]

Such were the measures that remained in force until December 1979 when the Security Council, by Resolution 460 (21 December 1979), decided to "call upon States Members of the United Nations to terminate the measures taken against Southern Rhodesia under Chapter VII of the Charter .... The signal for this step was the agreement reached at Lancaster House, signed by all parties on December 21 and which put in motion the political process that ended in the final decolonization of Rhodesia and the birth of a new State, Zimbabwe, in 1980.

Nature and scope of domestic measures taken by individual States

The issue of internal enforcement measures in the case of Rhodesia must be understood in its historical context. From the perspective of international politics two factors can not not be ignored. Firstly, the Cold War was at its apex with the result that the ideological divide between East and West was bound to cause perspectives on the interpretation of the decolonization process to differ. That this in turn could impact negatively on certain States' enthusiasm for the Security Council's sanctions programme stands to reason. Secondly, while the Rhodesian saga was unfolding, many African states were either in the process of becoming independent or had just gained independence. Their economies were fragile and in some cases they were heavily dependent on trade with Rhodesia and South Africa. In the case of economic sanctions their economies were therefore bound to suffer too. In addition, it was unrealistic in such circumstances to expect internal enforcement mechanisms in these states to have operated at a sophisticated level. In general, few states at the time had permanent legislative frameworks for the enforcement of United Nations sanctions in place with the result that ad hoc arrangements had to be adopted.

Already in December 1965, shortly after the imposition of non-mandatory sanctions by Security Council Resolution 217(1965), the Kenyan Government passed Legal Notices nos 108 and 109 of 8 December 1965 on the bases of which two orders were made. In the first, entitled *Prohibited Exports Order* 1965, the exportation "of any goods to, or any goods ultimately destined for, Rhodesia, including goods in transit, or for transshipment, or stores for any aircraft or vessel" was prohibited. By the same token the *Prohibited Imports Order* of 1965 prohibited the "direct or indirect importation into

44 *Ibid.*, para. 2.

45 SC Resolution 409, para. 1.

Kenya of any goods consigned from Rhodesia, including goods in transit, or for trans-shipment, or stores for any aircraft or vessel."[46]

In addition administrative measures were taken to –

- Refuse the recognition of Rhodesian travel documents;
- End telegraphic, telephonic and other communication with Rhodesia; and
- Terminate all Central African Airways Services with Rhodesia.[47]

Notices to banks under the title: *Exchange Control – Rhodesia* were issued on November 27, 1965. Subsequently, Rhodesia became a non-Sterling area and accounts of Rhodesian residents were designated Rhodesian accounts with the result that all credits and debits involving such accounts were subject to Treasury approval. The notices also restricted transactions by Kenyan residents in securities payable in Rhodesian pounds and suspended general permission for credits, loans and overdrafts.

It was reported that the implementation of the 1965 Orders effectively cut off trade with Rhodesia. Prior to the trade ban imports from Rhodesia amounted to £32,590 while exports were £10,072. In December these figures dropped to £2,330 and £1,102 respectively. The report also stated that "since January 1966 there ha[d] been no recorded trade whatsoever."[48]

A similar early response to developments in Rhodesia was taken by Tanzania. Acting under the *East African Customs Management Act* of 1952, Government Orders placing a comprehensive ban on the importation from and exportation to Rhodesia of "any goods" were issued. The only excluded items were goods that were the property of Tanzanian residents and exported from Rhodesia before November 11, 1965; used personal or household goods, and letters and postcards.[49]

Whether measures such as the above were also effective against the "laundering" of Rhodesian products through third States is difficult to tell. Although the legislative measures in question showed the necessary scope and intent, it is difficult to know whether a sophisticated administrative enforcement system existed that could uncover the laundering schemes usually associated with sanctions evasion. Problems of enforcement may also arise when sanctions legislation excluded certain categories of persons from its operation. An example is the *Southern Rhodesia Boycott Act* of 1966 adopted by Sudan and which intended to bring into its ambit contracts, imports, exports and carriage of goods in ships and aircraft. However, in Section 2, the Act determined that "notwithstanding anything hereinafter contained the prohibition shall not include African nationals of African origin and their interests whether resident in or outside Southern Rhodesia".[50] It stands to reason that such an exclusionary rule makes it all the more difficult to separate embargoed from unembargoed goods.

46 S/7781, Annex 2 (17 February 1967) 32.

47 *Ibid.*

48 *Ibid.*, 33.

49 *Ibid.*, 73, 74.

50 S/9853, Annex II, 48 (1 July 1970).

A characteristic of the legislative measures referred to above, is their broad and non-specific nature. By contrast, in at least two other cases Governments have adopted legislative measures that followed more closely the wording of the relevant Security Council Resolution. This happened, for instance, with the measures taken by Ghana and Togo in response to Security Council Resolution 232 (1966). In the case of Ghana the measures were contained in *The Southern Rhodesia Sanctions Decree* of 11 March 1967[51] and in the case of Togo in *Decree* No 67/36 of 14 February 1967.[52] In both instances the prohibitions followed the Resolution rather closely and used similar wording to specifically list the banned commodities, regulate extraterritorial application and identify the kind of transactions and activities that were henceforth considered illegal.

While the Ghana law also provided for penalties in case of violation, the Togo measures, like those in Kenya and Tanzania (at least on the face of it), were silent on the issue. The Ghana law also contained other interesting features. For instance, the owner of a vessel or aircraft in connection with which an offence was committed, and the master or captain or other person who had command of the vessel or aircraft at the time of the commission of the offence were considered guilty in addition to the offender (s10). This presumption of guilt shifted the onus onto the relevant person to prove that the offence was committed without his or her knowledge and that due diligence was exercised to prevent the commission of the offence. This presumption and onus also applied to the directors and officers of a body corporate and to the partners in a partnership.

e. Requests for economic and financial assistance under Article 50 of the United Nations Charter

That economic hardship could ensue from preventive or enforcement measures taken against a State has been foreseen by the United Nations Charter. Hence the right created by Article 50 of the Charter by virtue of which any State "which finds itself confronted with special economic problems arising from the carrying out of those measures" could consult with the Security Council with regard to a solution of the problem. The Article is clear in its wording and intent: economic hardship does not absolve a State from its international obligations, but creates an opportunity for a distinct burden to be raised when forced upon a victim State by extraordinary circumstances which normally follow in the wake of enforcement action against an offender State. The obligation to find a solution is at least a moral one.

Already in Resolution 253 (1968) the Security Council requested Members of the United Nations, specialised agencies and other international organisations to "extend assistance to Zambia as a matter of priority with a view to helping it solve such special economic problems as it may be confronted with arising from the carrying out of these decisions of the Security Council" (paragraph 15). The particularly critical position of Zambia – a leftover of its historical federal-political and economic entanglement with Rhodesia – was relayed to the Secretary-General the year before as a consequence of the

51 S/7781, Add. 4, Annex A (30 November 1967) 3.
52 S/7781 Add. 3 (27 July 1967) 32.

country's compliance with Resolution 232 (1966) which called for selective economic sanctions against Rhodesia. The difficulties that were identified related in particular to transportation, communications, storage of fuel and alternative supplies for some commodities. The call for a technical mission to visit Zambia and to assist the country in finding solutions to these problems was therefore granted.[53] However, in 1970, in a report on the effects of resolutions 232(1966), 253 (1968) and 277 (1970), the Zambian Government, with reference to the request for assistance in Resolution 253, expressed its "deep regret that no Member States, specialized agencies or other international organisations [had] given Zambia effective assistance as a result of these resolutions."[54] The country could nevertheless report that imports from Rhodesia had fallen from 31% in 1965 to below 2,5% in 1969 and that exports experienced a drop of nearly 96%.[55]

The Government of Malawi gave effect to the provisions of Resolution 232 by invoking its *Control of Goods (Import and Export) (Commerce) Regulations* of 1967 and by means of a subsequent Order based thereon banned the importation from Rhodesia of tobacco, asbestos, hides and skins, leather, chromium ore, iron ore, copper and pig-iron. However, in its report on the measures taken, the Government, with specific reference to Article 50 of the United Nations Charter, pointed out that, "in view of its geographical situation, Malawi is confronted with certain special economic problems" which related "specifically to the supply of sugar, meat and meat products."[56] Since Malawi was dependent on Rhodesia for the supply of these commodities it was not possible to prohibit altogether the importation of these commodities, with the result that Malawi declared itself ready "to enter into consultations in terms of Article 50 of the Charter...."[57]

The more extensive reach of Resolution 253 (1968) caused the Government of Malawi to inform the Secretary-General of the United Nations that "the country will not be able to effect significant new measures above what has already been done."[58] As regards imports it was reported that the establishment of alternative supply routes "would mean the loss of the existing extensive credit arrangements Malawi receive[d] from Rhodesian wholesalers, and would involve increased transport charges."[59] It was further pointed out that the cost of living at the time had already risen sharply as a result of devaluation, a situation that could only be exacerbated by additional restrictive measures. Moreover, since a substantial number of industrial and commercial firms in Malawi were operating from a Rhodesian base, a freeze on the transfer of funds, as required by the Resolution, would put them out of business and have a considerable impact on the banking industry.

The severance of air links with Rhodesia proved to be another problematic matter. Such a step would have resulted in a loss of £150,000 a year to Air Malawi, apart from a serious interruption of travel arrangements between southern African countries and

53 S/7720 (6 February 1967).

54 S/9853/Add. 1, Annex 1 (1 October 1970) 5 at 6.

55 *Ibid.*, 5, 6.

56 S/7781, Annex 2 (21 February 1967) 36.

57 *Ibid.*

58 S/8786, Annex II (28 August 1968) 48.

59 *Ibid.*

Malawi itself, and delays and extra expense would have resulted in the case of a switch to South Africa and Britain.[60] A ban on emigration to Rhodesia would have brought an end to the income of 10,000 migrant labourers who went to Rhodesia for work on an annual basis.[61]

Consequently, compliance with new sanctions, the Malawian Government pointed out, could take place "only at the cost of severely imperiling its own economy, if not breaking it". In view of this, the Malawian Government bemoaned the fact that Resolution 253 called for economic assistance to be given to Zambia without recognizing a similar plight in the case of Malawi.[62]

Another country that proved to be extremely vulnerable was Botswana, at the time one of the poorest countries in Africa, if not the world, with an economy that was heavily grant-aided and largely dependent on the cattle industry. In normal times approximately 23% of the country's import requirements came from Rhodesia while 17% of total exports of meat and related products had to pass through Rhodesia.[63] Strategically vital for the country's imports and exports was the railway line that ran from Rhodesia via Botswana to South Africa and which was owned and operated by Rhodesian Railways. The Botswana's Government fear at the time was that retaliatory measures by the Rhodesian Government could end or curtail the operation of the railway line in which case Botswana would have been faced by "an economic threat to the utmost gravity". Thus, the Government made it clear that while Botswana "could not survive without the railway" the railway was not vital to Rhodesia "since goods could be moved to and from South Africa by alternative routes without much difficulty, albeit at increased expenses."[64] In these circumstances the Botswana Government felt that the "application by it of additional sanctions against Southern Rhodesia under Resolution 232 (1966) would pose, in the terms of Article 50 of the Charter, special economic problems for Botswana."[65]

f. Reaction by the OAU

In such circumstances any steps taken by the OAU to ensure compliance with the Security Council resolutions had to encounter similar difficulties and could mean little beyond the symbolic. In 1965, in response to the adoption of non-mandatory sanctions against Rhodesia by the Security Council, the OAU decided that all Member States should bring into effect a complete blockade against Southern Rhodesia with a special focus on the following measures[66] –

60 *Ibid.*, 49.

61 *Ibid.*, 49, 50.

62 *Ibid.*, 50.

63 S/7781/Add.2, Annex 6 (9 March 1967).

64 *Ibid.*, 14.

65 *Ibid.*

66 ECM/Res. 13 (VI).

- A suspension of all economic relations, including trade and payment transactions with Rhodesia and a denial of sterling area facilities in respect of Commonwealth trade;
- A blocking of all Rhodesian accounts;
- The invalidation of all travel documents issued by the Rhodesian Government;
- Denial of rights to overfly and of all services to aircraft or other modes of transport;
- The severance of all modes of communication with Rhodesia.

After the imposition of mandatory sanctions by the Security Council, the OAU nevertheless reaffirmed that the situation in Rhodesia constituted a threat to international peace and security and condemned the action and domestic policies of the Rhodesian Government, and the Governments of South Africa and Portugal for their refusal to comply with Security Council resolutions.[67]

(2) *A New Generation of Sanctions: The Case of Angola*

a. Introduction

In explaining more recent experiments with United Nations sanctions in Africa one could have chosen several case studies. However, Angola is singled out for a number of reasons. Firstly, the country has been involved in a devastating civil war for more than three decades; secondly, the United Nations has had several attempts through different stages at solving the dispute with little success, and thirdly, the pattern and nature of the conflict and the international responses to it are exemplary of other experiences on the continent.

Furthermore, the UNITA problem in Angola, like others elsewhere in Africa, provides an interesting testing ground for the utility of the United Nation's new generation of targeted financial sanctions in an area of the world where corruption and criminality are pervasive and the persons or entities targeted for financial strangulation are aided by an extensive regional and international network of collaborators.[68]

b. Sanctions on arms and military equipment and their retrospective and extraterritorial nature

The refusal of UNITA to accept the results of the September 1992 Angolan election in which Jonas Savimbi lost to President Dos Santos led to the Security Council adopting Resolution 864 (1993) in terms of Chapter VII of the United Nations Charter "with a view to prohibiting all sale or supply to UNITA of arms and related matériel and military assistance, as well as petroleum and petroleum products".[69] Related matériel included "weapons and ammunition, military vehicles and equipment and spare parts".

67 CM/Res. 153 (XI).

68 Cf. also D. Cortright & G.A. Lopez, *The Sanctions Decade: Assessing UN Strategies in the 1990's* (2000), 158.

69 SC Resolution 864 (1993), para. 19.

These measures were intended to operate extraterritorially and retrospectively. As a result States were obligated to prevent the sale or supply of contraband "by their nationals or from their territories"[70] and "notwithstanding the existence of any rights or obligations conferred or imposed by any international agreement or any contract entered into or any licence or permit granted prior to the date of adoption of this resolution".[71]

c. Sanctions on the illicit trade in diamonds

Mandatory measures were also introduced by the Security Council in Resolution 1173 (1998) with a view to interrupt the stream of earnings UNITA derived from the illicit trade in diamonds. Acting under Chapter VII of the Charter, the Council decided that all States must take the necessary measures to –

- Prohibit the direct or indirect import from Angola to their territory of all diamonds not controlled through a Certificate of Origin issued by the authorities in Angola;
- Prohibit the sale or supply to persons or entities in Angola of equipment used in mining or mining services.[72]

These measures, like the arms embargo, operated extraterritorially and with retrospective effect.[73] However, whether they were suitable and of sufficient scope to address the magnitude of the illicit trade in diamonds is questionable. Recommendations made in the Fowler report, for instance, highlighted a number of concerns such as the easy access UNITA gained into legitimate diamond markets, the absence of transparency and accountability in the control of diamonds from source to trading market, and the lack of criminal law sanctions and forfeiture procedures to discourage diamond smuggling and sanctions evasion.[74]

Subsequently, the Security Council, in Resolution 1295 (2000) endorsed the proposal for devising a system of controls that will facilitate the implementation of measures already adopted by the Security Council "including arrangements that would allow for increased transparency and accountability in the control of diamonds from their point of origin to the bourses...".[75] In recognising the need for internal industry controls, the Security Council also called on States to co-operate with the diamond industry to "develop and implement more effective arrangements" to ensure that members of the industry abide by the measures adopted by the Council.[76]

The prospects for stronger action and controls are not entirely absent. Regarding the need for an effective Certificate of Origin arrangement, notice was taken by the

70 *Ibid.*

71 *Ibid.*, para. 20.

72 SC Resolution 1173 (1998), para. 12 (b) and (c).

73 *Ibid.*, paras.12 (c) and 17.

74 See Final Report of the UN Panel of Experts on Violations of Security Council Sanctions Against Unita, in S/2000/203 (10 March 2000), para. 109-114. Hereinafter Fowler Report.

75 SC Resolution 1295 (2000), para. 18.

76 *Ibid.*, para. 19.

Security Council of steps the Angolan Government were taking to introduce an effective Certificate of Origin regime. In Belgium, where the main trading market operates, the Government announced the establishment of an inter-ministerial task force to curb sanction evasion, while the Diamond High Council, in conjunction with the Angolan Government publicly affirmed their taking measures to limit UNITA's access to legitimate markets.[77]

At this point perspectives from the Sierra Leone experience are also noteworthy, especially in view of the similar way in which the illegal trade in diamonds and weapons sustains the RUF's military offensive against the Government of Sierra Leone. Like in the case of Angola a procurement and payment network is sustained through the connivance or active participation of neighbouring countries, a practice in which the role of the Taylor regime in Liberia has been singled out for special concern.[78] The Security Council's response to this problem, like in the case of Angola, concentrated on prohibiting the direct or indirect importation by countries of rough diamonds originating in Sierra Leone and on requesting the Sierra Leone Government to ensure the implementation of an effective Certificate of Origin regime.[79]

Already in 1999 the Chairman of the Security Council Committee established pursuant to Resolution 864(1993) hinted at the problems experienced with the enforcement and monitoring of sanctions as follows[80] –

> In the course of the Chairman's visit, at one point or another, a significant number of SADC members were alleged to be involved in the violation of sanctions. In the majority of cases, this was believed to be the consequence of private interests acting without the knowledge and, sometimes, despite the efforts of their Governments. Countries outside the region, including in particular several in Central and West Africa and Eastern Europe, were also widely rumoured to be implicated in the systematic violation of Council-imposed sanctions against UNITA. The situation amounted to what one minister described as "a crisis of African solidarity."

As regards the violation of sanctions against the illicit trade in diamonds one development that offers hope is the collective efforts by a number of African and other States, the organised diamond industry and NGO's to establish minimum acceptable international standards for national certification schemes relating to the import and export of rough diamonds. This process, commonly referred to as the Kimberley Process, involves a series of multi-lateral negotiations under the chairmanship of South Africa which commenced in May 2000 in Kimberley, South Africa. Through a system of certification, which must comply with mutually agreed essential standards, the participants in this process seek to control the international trade in diamonds and in creating measures

77 *Ibid.,* paras. 16, 17.

78 By Resolution 1343 of 7 March 2001 the Security Council imposed sanctions against Liberia.

79 SC Resolution 1306 (2000), paras. 1, 2. See also SC Resolution 1171 (1998) for the arms embargo. See also SC Resolution 1343 of 7 March 2001.

80 S/1999/644 of 4 June 1999, para. 7.

for the outlawing and punishment of the illegal trade in diamonds. This process is still underway and some final proposals are expected at the end of 2001.[81]

d. Sanctions on financial assets

The reorientation that has taken place since the nineties with regard to the imposition of targeted financial sanctions is also visible in the case of Angola. In 1998 the Security Council, again acting under Chapter VII of the Charter, decided to direct attention to the financial assets of UNITA and of its members. Thus, by Resolution 1173 (1998) states and all persons and entities within their territories, were charged with the obligation to freeze funds and financial resources under their control, if such assets were derived or generated from property of[82] –
- UNITA as an organisation;
- Senior officials of UNITA; or
- Adult members of their immediate families.

"Property" is not defined by the Resolution. Further regulation of such matters by national law, as is usually the case, must remain fanciful in view of the particular geopolitical setup in the region, the lack of resources and the largely unsophisticated legal systems and infrastructure in a vast number of African countries. Investigations into the funds and financial resources of UNITA or its members are further hampered by bank secrecy laws that prevail in many countries.[83] Evidence also suggests that UNITA minimizes its exposure to banks and financial institutions and channels and that increased emphasis is placed on the stockpiling of packaged rough diamonds as a medium of currency and exchange. Moreover, Savimbi's network of cronies in several African Governments – who are not targeted by the sanctions – makes it easy to conceal the origin and use of financial assets.[84]

e. Sanctions on travel

The Security Council ban under Chapter VII of the Charter on travel and on making available travel facilities is the most comprehensive of all the measures taken till date against UNITA. The measures have three broad aims in mind. Firstly, the isolation of senior officials of UNITA and of adult members of their immediate families; secondly, the denial of landing and overflight rights to UNITA aircraft, and thirdly preventing UNITA from obtaining services and other benefits relating to air transport.

Consequently, in respect of the first aim, States are required to take measures that will prevent entry into or transit through their territories of all senior officials of UNITA and of adult members of their families and to suspend or cancel all travel documents or resi-

81 For further information on this process see www.dfa.gov/events/kimberley2.htm/.

82 SC Resolution 1173 (1998), para. 11.

83 Fowler report, above n 74, para. 116.

84 Cf. *Ibid.*, paras. 120 *et seq.*

dence permits issued to such officials or family members. The immediate and complete closure of all UNITA offices is also required.[85] Secondly, States are to prevent UNITA aircraft from taking off from, land in, or overfly their territories when such aircraft has taken off from or is destined to land at certain designated places in Angola.[86] Thirdly, States or their nationals are prohibited from making available any aircraft or aircraft components, or providing engineering or maintenance services, airworthiness certification or insurance cover to certain designated aircraft registered in Angola.[87] Excluded from the operation of these measures are medical emergency flights and aircraft "carrying food, medicine, or supplies for essential humanitarian needs, as approved in advance by the Committee created pursuant to Resolution 864 (1993).[88]

f. Problems with enforcement

The enforcement of these measures is hampered by a number of factors. In the first instance the evasion of these Security Council measures is effected by a procurement and payment network involving persons in various countries in Europe, especially Eastern Europe, and Africa. The procurement network is made up of arms brokers in South Africa, Namibia and several Eastern European countries. Through (official) links with political leaders in the Democratic Republic of the Congo, Rwanda, Burkina Faso and Togo, UNITA succeeded in obtaining false end-user certificates and assistance in the transfer and storage of weapons.[89]

In the payment network smuggled diamonds have assumed a uniquely important role in sustaining UNITA's political and military economy and in remunerating Heads of State (in Zaïre (now DRC), Togo and Burkina Faso), dealers and corrupt officials for their goodwill, services and commodities. This payment scheme was found to be facilitated by Unita's control over diamond producing areas, the lax regulatory environment in which diamond dealers conducted the diamond trade in Antwerp, which accounts for nearly 80% of the world's rough diamond trade, the lack of controls in diamond producing countries and the apparent impunity with which transaction partners operated in countries such as South Africa, Namibia, Rwanda and Burkina Faso.[90]

Another obstacle is the blessing with which UNITA conducts relations in different countries. In several African states (Togo, Zaïre, Ivory Coast, Burkino Faso, Rwanda) UNITA offices operate(d) with the direct support of host country authorities, often through personal links with heads of state.[91] Through a network of personal ties, travel and access to supplies are facilitated, a practice that can only be eradicated if sanctions are refined enough to also target the responsible persons in the different host countries,

85 SC Resolution 1127 (1997), para. 4 (a)-(c).

86 *Ibid.,* para. 4 (d)(i).

87 *Ibid.,* para. 4 (d)(ii) and (iii).

88 *Ibid.,* para. 5.

89 Fowler Report, n 74 above, paras. 15 *et seq.*

90 *Ibid.,* paras. 76 *et seq.*

91 *Ibid.,* paras. 132 *et seq.*

which is currently not the case. In other countries (Belgium, Portugal, USA, France, Switzerland) UNITA offices operate(d) without the support of the host country, but their activities are either tolerated or not detected.[92] In some of these instances one must of cause reckon with legal or constitutional constraints some countries, especially in Europe, are facing when measures against travel and residence are taken, a matter that brings into play the relationship between a State's international obligations and domestic laws.[93] On the other hand it has also been pointed out that states in central and Southern Africa imperfectly understood their obligations with regard to the implementation of Security Council resolutions, hence the absence of specific implementing legislative measures in most of these countries.[94]

Namibian, Zambian and South African territories are also often used for UNITA related activities, apparently without the knowledge of the respective Governments. In the case of South Africa the Fowler report[95] makes the following observation –

> The easy access of UNITA personnel to South Africa is at least in part due to the large size and open nature of the country. However, senior UNITA officials claim to have been received by South African Government officials subsequent to the imposition of Security Council sanctions prohibiting such contacts, and South African nationals with political connections were said to have been received in Andulo in August 1999. The Government of South Africa has undertaken to work to strengthen detection mechanisms in order to be better able to restrict the movements and activities of UNITA personnel in that country.

The problem with undertakings of this nature is that they are often not made public, with the result that their enforcement and efficiency cannot be subjected to proper scrutiny. An additional problem is that the countries geographically close to Angola, including South Africa, generally lack legislative measures specifically designed for the enforcement of the kind of measures foreseen in the various Security Council resolutions. That the absence of such measures is of special concern is clear from the recommendation in the Fowler report that "states should take immediate steps to enforce, strengthen or enact legislation making it a criminal offence under domestic law for their citizens or other individuals operating on their territory to violate sanctions imposed by the Security Council against UNITA." As regards enforcement, the recommendation further requires states to communicate to the Sanctions Committee the results of all prosecutions or investigations of violations,[96] an indication that States have either not satisfactorily complied with their reporting duties in terms of the Security Council resolutions, or that there is nothing to report on.

---

92 *Ibid.*, para. 135.

93 See, for instance, S/2000/1225 of 21 December 2000, para. 71.

94 S/1999/644 of 4 June 1999.

95 Above n 74, para. 149.

96 *Ibid.*, para. 173.

Another related matter that should be of concern is the tendency of States to merely report that the "necessary measures" have been taken to implement the provisions of Security Council resolutions without spelling out the content and scope of the measures or attaching a copy thereof to their reports.[97] One would expect the United Nations sanctions committees to request full information about the measures taken by States, and to include such information in their monitoring reports, especially in view of the current proposals by the Security Council to improve the work of the sanctions committees and to secure greater transparency.[98] Since the measures taken by States in response to Security Council resolutions are of international as opposed to domestic interest, the publication of such measures in United Nations documents should be standard practice. Moreover, if Member States can be required to "provide the sanctions committees with all information available on alleged violations of sanctions regimes"[99] there is no reason why the same obligation should not also be applicable with regard to measures designed to effectively enforce sanctions and to prevent violations.

Problems with enforcement identified in the Fowler and other reports have been elaborated on in reports of the Monitoring Mechanism[100] established pursuant to Security Council Resolution 1295 (2000) to investigate violations of Security Council measures and to develop a mechanism designed to improve the implementation of sanctions. These latter reports not only confirm much of what is contained in the Fowler report, but provide additional insight into the scale of the difficulties a sanctions enforcement regime in the region is faced with.

(3) *Modern Constitutional Developments and the Enforcement of Security Council Resolutions*

a. Background: the sanctions era

Like in the case of Rhodesia, the South African issue started to feature as a regular item on the agendas of the political organs of the United Nations because of internal governmental policies. As early as 1946 the General Assembly started to take note of the racial policies in South Africa in a matter that involved an application by the Indian Government regarding the treatment of the Indian population in South Africa.[101] It was this matter which first resulted in the Assembly making reference to the policy of *apartheid*[102] which in time became such a notorious word in domestic and international debates on South Africa.

97 Cf., for instance, S/AC.31/1999/1 of 9 February; S/AC.31/1999/2 of 9 February 1999; S/AC.31/1999/3 of 10 February 1999; S/AC.31/1999/5 of 19 February 1999; S/AC.31/1999/7 of 23 February 1999; S/AC.31/1999/10 of 23 March 1999. In contrast see the report of the USA in S/AC.31/1999/6 of 23 February 1999.

98 See S/1999/92 of 29 January 1999.

99 *Ibid.*, para. 3.

100 S/2000/1225 of 21 December 2000 and S/2001/966 of 12 October 2001.

101 GA Resolution 44 (I).

102 GA Resolution 395 (V), 2 December 1950.

The mood in the General Assembly was conciliatory at first and numerous attempts were made to bring about change through negotiations and good offices,[103] but the South African Government failed to co-operate and did not heed the Assembly's appeals. Since the sixties a number of incidents occurred which caused responses by the international community to become more action oriented. In 1960 the Sharpeville massacre occurred which resulted in an international outcry. In the same year the *Declaration on the Granting of Independence to Colonial Countries and Peoples* was adopted,[104] followed in 1963 by the *Declaration on the Elimination of All Forms of Racial Discrimination*[105] and in 1965 by the *International Convention on the Elimination of All Forms of Racial Discrimination,*[106] all instruments which reflected growing international collective support for majority rule based on self-determination, and condemnation of racial segregation and discriminatory policies. These developments, coupled with the admission of newly independent African states to the United Nations, turned the international mood towards more specific measures against South Africa.

In 1961 the General Assembly called on states to consider taking collective and separate action against South Africa[107] followed the next year by a call on States to break off diplomatic relations with South Africa, close their ports to South African vessels, boycott South African goods, seize imports from and exports to South Africa and refuse landing and passage facilities to South African aircraft.[108] This latter Resolution also requested the Security Council to take appropriate measures, including sanctions, to secure South Africa's compliance with resolutions of the General Assembly and to consider the expulsion of South Africa from the United Nations in terms of Article 6 of the Charter.

These measures, although recommendatory in nature, were gradually paving the way for the isolation of the white minority Government in South Africa. Despite the reluctance of South Africa's main trade partners to effectively implement the non-mandatory measures called for by the General Assembly, many States have decided to act upon these recommendations which resulted in the severance of diplomatic, cultural, educational and sport relationships, bans on overflight and the curtailment of trade.[109] That there was significant support for stronger action against South Africa is illustrated by the positive vote of 126 Member States in 1986 for a resolution calling on the Security Council to impose mandatory economic sanctions against South Africa. However, these and other attempts[110] at economic sanctions failed through the use or the threat of a veto by the US, France and the United Kingdom. The feeling against mandatory

103 See, for instance, GA Resolutions 511 (VI); 615 (VII); 719 (VIII); 816 (IX); 919 (X).

104 GA Resolution 1514 (XV).

105 GA Resolution 1904 (XVIII).

106 GA Resolution 2106 A (XX).

107 GA Resolution 1598 (XV).

108 GA Resolution 1761 (XVII).

109 Cf. J. Dugard, "Sanctions against South Africa", in M. Orkin (ed), *Sanctions against Apartheid* (1989), 113 at 118.

110 In February 1987 the non-aligned members of the Security Council introduced a draft resolution that would have imposed mandatory economic sanctions. See S/18705 (1987).

economic sanctions was probably best summed up by the following statement by the US representative in 1987 which also illustrated the dilemmas that faced the international community at the time –

> [My] government is convinced that mandatory sanctions would fail to bring an end to apartheid in a peaceful manner and would make it difficult, if not impossible, to achieve internal reconciliation and regional economic development. ... [M]andatory sanctions imposed by the international community at this time would result in the progressive destruction of the South African economy and the heightening of repression in that country as those now in power attempt to consolidate their hold. Who doubts the capacity of the current South African government to inflict much of the cost of mandatory sanctions on its own black citizens as well as on its immediate neighbours? It is highly unrealistic to believe that aid from the industrialized democracies will be able to cover the costs which mandatory sanctions would inevitably impose upon South Africa's immediate neighbours ....[111]

b. The arms embargo

The Security Council first voted for a voluntary arms embargo against South Africa in 1963[112] and 1964,[113] based on the determination that the situation "seriously disturbed" international peace under Chapter VI of the Charter. Attempts to make it mandatory or to have it extended to economic sanctions failed through a series of vetoes in the sixties. In 1970 the Council gave indication of the need to strengthen the arms embargo called for earlier, characterised the situation in South Africa as a potential threat to international peace and security, condemned the violations of the (recommendatory) arms embargo, and called for additional measures to be taken by States in the economic and military fields.[114] In 1975/76 the Western Powers in the Security Council vetoed attempts to impose a mandatory arms embargo against South Africa on the ground that there was no threat to international peace and security in the sense of Article 39 of the Charter.

Several events in the seventies laid the foundation for attitudes in the Security Council to harden against South Africa. In 1976/77 the Soweto uprising and subsequent repressive police reaction called forth universal condemnation of the South African Government. In September 1977 a prominent black political leader, Steve Biko, was tortured and killed in police custody, and in October of that year, following wide-spread

111 S/PV 2738 (1987). For literature on the pros and cons of economic sanctions against South Africa, see, *inter alia*, J. Hanlon & R. Omond, *The Sanctions Handbook* (1987); M. Orkin (ed), *Sanctions Against Apartheid* (1989); J. Hanlon, *South Africa: The Sanctions Report: Documents and Statistics* (1990); and T. Koenderman, *Sanctions: The Threat to South Africa* (1982).

112 SC Resolutions 181 and 183 (1963).

113 SC Resolution 191 (1964).

114 SC Resolution 282 (1970).

unrest in the country, the South African Government banned a number of political dissidents, organisations and publications.

Finally, these events caused the Security Council to adopt, for the first time in its history, mandatory sanctions against a member of the United Nations, which, in this instance came in the form of a mandatory arms embargo. The motivation for this step was captured in the preamble to Resolution 418 (1977) which expressed concern about the military build-up in South Africa, the country's acts of aggression against neighbouring states and the potential threat posed by the country's nuclear capabilities. From this prelude followed the recognition that the "existing arms embargo must be strengthened and universally applied without any reservations or qualifications whatsoever...". Clearly stating that it was acting under Chapter VII of the Charter, the Security Council *determined* that "the acquisition by South Africa of arms and related matérial constitute[d] a threat to the maintenance of international peace and security."[115] Consequently it was *decided* that –

> all States shall cease forthwith any provision to South Africa of arms and related matérial of all types, including the sale or transfer of weapons and ammunition, military vehicles and equipment, paramilitary police equipment, and spare parts for the aforementioned, and shall cease as well the provision of all types of equipment and supplies, and grants for licensing arrangements, for the manufacture or maintenance of the aforementioned.

In addition States were *called* upon to review, within the objectives of the Resolution, "all existing contractual arrangements with and licences granted to South Africa relating to the manufacture and maintenance of arms, ammunition of all types and military equipment and vehicles, with a view to terminating them."[116] This was followed by a *decision* that States "shall refrain from any co-operation with South Africa in the manufacture and development of nuclear weapons."[117]

Subsequently, in Resolution 421 (9 December 1977) the Security Council established, in accordance with Rule 28 of the Council's provisional rules of procedure, a Committee, consisting of all members of the Council with the mandate to –

- examine the Secretary-General's report on the progress of the implementation of Resolution 418(1977);
- study ways and means by which the mandatory arms embargo could be made more effective;
- seek from all States information regarding the steps they have taken concerning the effective implementation of the embargo.

This was followed the next year by Resolution 473 (13 June 1980) in which the Council called on all States to strictly and scrupulously comply with Resolution 418 and to enact appropriate national legislation for that purpose (par 10). In paragraph 11 the Security

115 SC Resolution 418 (1977), para. 1.

116 *Ibid.*, para. 3.

117 *Ibid.*, para. 4.

Council Committee was requested to "redouble its efforts to secure full implementation of the arms embargo against South Africa by recommending ... measures to close all loop-holes in the arms embargo, reinforce and make it more comprehensive."

c. National enforcement measures and the reasons for their failure

Several reasons made the effective enforcement of the arms embargo problematic. From the perspective of the African countries, especially those, which, as frontline states, grouped themselves together under the umbrella of the Southern African Development Coordinating Conference (SADCC),[118] the arms embargo was of little use as an enforcement instrument. These countries neither sold arms nor oil to South Africa and did not invest there. The sanctions they did impose were limited to unilateral action involving sports and culture, trade and transport. Moreover, trade with these states was much less important to South Africa than trade with Europe, Japan and the US. If one adds to this the decisions by the OAU and the Commonwealth to exempt the countries neighbouring South Africa from the obligation to impose sanctions[119] in view of their economic vulnerability it must be clear that numerous opportunities for evasion existed.

In a report of the Security Council Committee[120] on the effectiveness of the arms embargo the existence of loopholes and difficulties with interpretation were cited as reasons undermining the effectiveness of the embargo. Means of circumvention included the delivery of embargoed equipment and components through third parties, the sub-contracting of third parties for the manufacturing of component parts of embargoed aircraft and the transshipment of small arms through neighbouring African countries. As regards national enforcement measures responses by 118 countries have showed that state action was far from uniform. While some countries have enacted new legislation, others have resorted to existing administrative and regulatory measures with the majority satisfied with the expression of an intent to comply fully with the provisions of Resolution 418. Concerns were also raised that penalties were inadequate to act as deterrent and that existing lists of embargoed goods were, for lack of appropriate criteria specific to South Africa, unsuitable.[121]

Statutory frameworks used by foreign Governments to enforce the embargo also caused problems related to interpretation or changes in government policy. In the case of the US, for instance, the embargo was enforced through the *International Security Assistance and Arms Export Control Act* of 1987 (AECA).[122] In terms of this Act the President was empowered to determine that a Government to Government arms sale was not in the national interest. The regulation of commercial sales by private companies was subject to the granting of licences by the State Department and the Department of

118 This was later transformed into the Southern African Development Community (SADC).

119 Cf. J. Hanlon "Destabilisation, the SADCC states and sanctions", in M. Orkin (ed.), *Sanctions Against Apartheid* (1989), 173 at 185-187.

120 S/14179, 19 September 1980.

121 *Ibid.*, 11.

122 22 USCA §§ 2751-94 (1976).

Defence without a prior presidential determination. Mehlman and others have shown that between 1960 and 1977 the State Department "approved more commercial exports of items on the Munition List to South Africa than to any other African country". Moreover, the Department of Commerce, which was responsible for the licensing of all other commercial exports to both governmental and civilian users under the Export Administration Act of 1969 granted the exportation to South Africa or other clients of, inter alia, dual-use equipment such as non-combat aircraft, computers and electronic equipment and US licenced manufacturing technology or US parts or material which could be used for the production of or use in military-related items.[123] With regard to changes in policy relating to the licensing system, the observation has been made that –

> "The structure of the Commerce Department's regulatory scheme for the control of commercial exports reveals relatively little about the actual implementation of restrictions on trade with South Africa. Prior to February 22, 1978, the requirements did not expressly forbid the export to South Africa of military-related equipment on the Commodity Control List, but merely called for a validated license for these exports. In practice, the implementation of this requirement varied from the Johnson administration's policy to the more lenient post-1970 practices of the Nixon administration."[124]

This regulatory scheme was amended in 1978 through the promulgation of more stringent regulations. Henceforth, not only military-related commodities, but all commodities, including technical data exported or *re-exported* to South Africa *and Namibia* were prohibited "where the exporter or reexporter [knew] or had reason to know that the commodity will be sold to or used by or for military or police entities ... or used to service equipment owned, controlled or used by or for such military or police entities".[125]

Despite the more stringent measures, enforcement problems still remained. The broad and unreviewable licensing discretion of the Commerce Department with regard to dual-use equipment remainded intact, prohibition of sales were only possible in instances where the exporter or re-exporter knew or had reason to believe that the items will end up in the wrong hands, and the regulations did not apply to the activities of foreign subsidiaries of US corporations either in South Africa or elsewhere.[126]

The US position was not exceptional. Enforcement problems resulting from defaulting legislation or other reasons were widespread. The Chairman of the Special Committee against Apartheid, for instance, has noted that "where national legislation had been reported to the Security Council, there had been a tendency to regard Security Council Resolution 418 (1977) merely as confirmation of the discredited voluntary arms embargo and to define arms in the most restricted way. Thus, these legislation

123 M.J. Mehlman, T.H. Milch & M.V. Toumanoff, "United States restrictions on exports to South Africa", 73 *AJIL* (1979), 581 at 586, 587.

124 *Ibid.*, 588, 589.

125 See *ibid.*, 589, 590.

126 *Ibid.*, 592-596.

contain[ed] many ommissions and [did] not provide for sufficiently severe penalties in cases of violation."[127]

The phraseology of Resolution 418 also facilitated evasion. The terms "arms and related matérial" in operative paragraph 2 were subjected to differing interpretations by States with the result that a uniform practice became impossible. While some States prohibited all supplies to the South African military establishment regardless of their nature other States distinguished between military and non-military equipment.[128] A more precise definition of what was covered by the phrase "arms and related matérial" or a checklist of prohibited items could have remedied the situation.

One of the main loopholes in the attempt to hurt the South African arms production industry was the question of existing agreements and licenses. Operative paragraph 3, which called on States to review existing contractual relationships with a view to terminating them, was understood to mean that termination was (a) conditional upon and subsequent in time to a review; or that (b) termination was optional subsequent to a review, and therefore that (c) a particular Government may not deem it an obligation to terminate certain types of existing contractual obligations.[129] The obligation to "refrain from any co-operation with South Africa in the manufacture and development of nuclear weapons" in operative paragraph 4 was also considered deficient. The Special Committee against Apartheid has stated –

> that the formulation of paragraph 4 of resolution 418 (1977) was totally inadequate in preventing the apartheid régime from acquiring nuclear capability since, as interpreted by South Africa's nuclear collaborators, namely, France, the Federal Republic of Germany, the United Kingdom and the United States, it allowed the transfer of technology, capital equipment and fissionable material to South Africa."[130]

In some instances States have taken special care to ensure that sold items were not passed on to or used by the military establishment. United States regulations, for instance, required the purchaser to certify that the merchandise would not be used for military or police purposes and that US Government approval would be obtained prior to a resell of the merchandise by the purchaser.[131] However, South African law existing at the time made these restrictions pointless. Section 100 of the *Defence Act*, Act 44 of 1957 authorised the State President to obtain from any person or any public or other body, and without the consent of such person or body buildings and other premises, vehicles, aircraft, vessels, machinery, equipment, materials, articles or things necessary for the mobilisation or the maintenance of the South African Defence Force or of other forces acting in co-operation therewith. The purposes for which this power could be exercised ranged from the prevention or suppression of terrorism or internal disorder to operations

127 S/14179, 15.

128 *Ibid.*, 16, 17.

129 *Ibid.*, 19.

130 *Ibid.*, 22.

131 *Ibid.*, 18.

in defence of the Republic. In 1970 Parliament passed the *National Supplies Procurement Act*, Act 89 of 1970. In terms of Section 3 of the Act, the Minister of Economic Affairs, whenever he "deemed it necessary or expedient for the security of the Republic", could order any person capable of supplying, manufacturing or producing goods or services to supply, deliver or sell such goods or services to the Minister. In case of a wilful refusal to comply with such an order Section 4 allowed for the seizure of the goods or the use of any service provision facility by the State.

Through these measures the South African Government could undo any foreign attempt to prevent the military and police from benefitting from the sale of commodities to private users. Inter-governmental transfers were further facilitated by the *Procurement Act* in that the powers and functions conferred on the Minister of Economic Affairs could be exercised or performed by any other Minister in accordance with inter-ministerial arrangements.[132]

d. The impact of the new constitutional dispensation: changes in law and policy since the nineties

Between 1990 and 1994 a remarkable bargaining process between the white minority Government and black opposition organisations, with the African National Congress (ANC) in the vanguard, succeeded in transforming the old apartheid order and laying the foundation for a peaceful transition to a new political and constitutional dispensation. One of the major catalysts that set the process in motion was the landmark speech of President FW de Klerk on the February 2, 1990 in which the unbanning of the ANC and other political organisations and the release of Nelson Mandela and other political prisoners were announced.

A few brief remarks about the internal and external forces that fashioned this historical moment is perhaps necessary for placing at least some of the developments that will be described later on, in perspective. In the eighties internal dissent and violent protest action followed by successive states of emergency and repressive and equally violent government action brought the country to the brink of anarchy. In the face of an imminent catastrophe the possibility of a negotiated settlement caused the triumph of reason over unreason. Other contributing factors were of cause the constant threat of economic sanctions and the erosion of the governing party's traditional support base. Furthermore, the demise of the cold war stand-off which coincided with the collapse of communism had profound implications for the opposing forces in South Africa. In the words of one commentator[133] –

> The government, now unable to appeal to a wider crusade against Communism, stood out starkly as merely a minority government seeking to maintain the status quo in the face of majority opinion at home and an international consensus abroad. In the long run this was clearly an untenable position both in terms of ethics and power.... The government realisitcally had no option but to turn to reform.

132 Act 89 of 1970, s 1A.

133 M. Frost "Preparing for democracy in an authoritarian state", in R.W. Johnson & L. Schlemmer (eds.), *Launching Democracy in South Africa* (1996), 16 at 20-21.

> In like manner the anti-apartheid forces had to change their rhetoric and practice. The states both in Africa and abroad which had supported the military struggle against apartheid were no longer prepared to do so. Non-violent forms of protest, spectacularly successful in bringing down communist regimes in Central and Eastern Europe, were now widely seen as models to be followed.... In its quest for international support, the ANC had to modify its language and practice from an anti-capitalist revolutionary discourse to one which stressed democratisation and which played down violence as a method of liberation."

The influence of these developments on the design of a new constitutional dispensation cannot be ignored. That both the 1993 Interim Constitution[134] and the final 1996 Constitution[135] bear the hallmarks of modern-day democratic constitutionalism is perhaps not so self-evident. A similar understanding of historical influences should inform ones observation of the country's new foreign policy of which the main characteristics will be alluded to below.

Sanctions legislation
Prior to the nineties legislation specifically designed for the enforcement of United Nations sanctions was not an issue – for obvious reasons. The coincidence of the death of apartheid rule and the birth of a new world order based on multilateralism and regionalism in the early nineties caused a significant change in policy outlook.

When the Security Council imposed sanctions against the former Yugoslavia in the early nineties the only enabling legislation available in South Africa at the time was the *Import and Export Control Act*, 45 of 1963. Section 2 of the Act empowered the Minister of Trade and Industry to restrict the importation or exportation of certain goods to and from South Africa whenever "he deem[ed] it necessary or expedient in the public interest". Goods could be classified "according to the source or origin or the intermediate or final destination of goods or according to the channels along which or manner in which goods are imported or exported or according to the purpose for which goods are intended to be used".[136] By virtue of these powers the Minister in 1993 gave notice in the *Government Gazette* that "no goods shall be imported from or exported to the Federal Republic of Yugoslavia (Serbia and Montenegro) with effect from 16 March 1993".[137] The term 'goods' in the Act includes any commodity, article, merchandise, animal, bird, currency, material or object of whatever nature.[138] The enforcement of the Act and of any notice given in terms thereof is entrusted to inspectors who enjoy wide powers of entry, search and seizure.[139] Violation of the Act or a notice is punishable by a fine not exceeding R40, 000 or imprisonment for a period not exceeding ten years or both such

134 *Constitution of the Republic of South Africa*, Act 200 of 1993.

135 *Constitution of the Republic of South Africa*, Act 108 of 1996.

136 Act 45 of 1963, s 2(2).

137 GN R451 in *Government Gazette* nr. 14658 of 16 March 1993.

138 Act 45 of 1963, s 1 "goods".

139 *Ibid.*, s 3A.

fine and imprisonment.[140] In addition a court convicting an offender may also declare the goods in question forfeited to the State.[141] Such a declaration "shall not affect any rights which any person other than the convicted person may have to the goods in question, if it is proved that he did not know that the goods were being dealt with in contravention of the said provisions...".

It is doubtful whether the nature and scope of the South African measures even remotely complied with what the Security Council had in mind. It is therefore justifiable to question whether any steps were possible or taken under authority of the laws mentioned above to deal with Security Council requests for mandatory measures with regard to the following –

- The implementation of a general and complete embargo on all deliveries of weapons and military equipment to Yugoslavia;[142]
- The extraterritorial prohibition of transactions by South African citizens in violation of Security Council resolutions;[143]
- The denial of landing and overflight rights to aircraft destined for Yugoslavia[144];
- The suspension of sport relationships and of scientific, technical and cultural exchanges;[145]
- The freezing of funds (in South Africa) derived from property belonging to Yugoslav public or private enterprises or funds directly or indirectly controlled by such enterprises;[146]
- The impounding and forfeiture of vessels, freight vehicles and aircraft controlled by persons or undertakings in Yugoslavia;[147] and
- The prevention of all economic activities carried on by any entity, wherever incorporated or constituted, which is owned or controlled by any person or entity in Yugoslavia.[148]

Shortly after the imposition of sanctions against the former Yugoslavia and less than a year before the first democratic elections in South Africa in April 1994, the then Minister of Foreign Affairs introduced new legislation in Parliament aimed at the enforcement of Security Council resolutions. In explaining the need for such legislation it was stated that

> South Africa would have to adopt policy positions on the important world issues that will dominate the international stage in the period that lies ahead. There is no way in which

140 *Ibid.*, s 4(1).

141 *Ibid.*, s 4(2).

142 SC Resolution 713 of 25 September 1991, para. 6.

143 SC Resolution 757 of 30 May 1992, paras. 4(b) and (c), 5.

144 *Ibid.*, para. 7(a).

145 *Ibid.*, para. 8(b) and (c).

146 SC Resolution 820 of 17 April 1993.

147 *Ibid.*, para. 24.

148 SC Resolution 942 of 23 September 1994, para. 7.

> South Africa can escape this challenge. Indeed, we should welcome it, since we are now equipped to face it.[149]

Against this background the inadequacy of South African legislation for the comprehensive implementation of Security Council resolutions was highlighted and the following specific problems noted[150] –

- Since the *Import and Export Control Act* of 1963 was only to the avail of the Department of Trade and Industry other state departments could not adopt enforcement measures;
- Security Council resolutions, by virtue of South African legislation and common law, were not automatically enforceable in South African law; and
- The lack of a general enabling legislative measure delayed and fragmented the implementation process.

The solution to these problems, according to the Minister, was the *Application of Resolutions of the Security Council of the United Nations Act*, Act 172 of 1993. In terms of Section 1 the State President could by proclamation in the *Government Gazette* declare that any resolution of the Security Council shall apply in the Republic to the extent specified in the proclamation. Any such proclamation was subject to parliamentary approval in terms of Section 2. A person found guilty of contravening the proclamation was liable to a fine or imprisonment for a period not exceeding fifteen years (Section 3). The Act was assented to on December 8, 1993 but its date of commencement was never proclaimed. Less than six months later the new democratic South Africa was born with a new constitutional dispensation in terms of which legislative measures by executive sleight of hand were unlikely to pass constitutional muster. The result is that the *Import and Export Control Act* of 1963 is still the most likely measure to be invoked should South Africa decide to comply with a Security Council resolution to impose sanctions against another State.

Apart from the *Import and Export Control Act* two recent legislative measures, although not sanctions-specific in nature, could fulfil a reinforcing or supplementary function. The first is the *Regulation of Foreign Military Assistance Act*, 15 of 1998. This Act outlaws mercenary activities[151] and makes the rendering of foreign military assistance subject to authorisation by the National Conventional Arms Control Committee[152] which may refuse authorisation[153] if the rendering of the service would –

- be in conflict with the Republic's international law obligations;
- result in the infringement of human rights and fundamental freedoms;
- endanger the peace by introducing destabilising military capabilities in the region where the assistance is to be rendered;

149 *Hansard*, 26 November 1993, col 14122.

150 *Ibid.*, col 14123.

151 Section 2.

152 Sections 3 and 4.

153 Section 7.

- support or encourage terrorism;
- contribute to the escalation of regional conflicts;
- prejudice the Republic's national or international interests;
- be unacceptable for any other reason.

Contraventions are punishable by a fine or imprisonment or both[154] and the Act operates extraterritorially in that the courts will assume jurisdiction over nationals irrespective of the place of the contravention.[155]

The *Financial Intelligence Centre Act* 38 of 2001 is the second legislative measure and, although in essence a money-laundering combatting instrument, it could be of special significance in the case of targeted financial sanctions. Once operational the Centre that is envisaged by the Act will play an important role in the combatting of organised crime and money-laundering activities. Its relevance for targeted financial sanctions, which are often circumvented by the type of illegal activities the Centre is supposed to expose, will derive from its function to collect, process, analyse and interpret information about suspicious financial transactions and to co-operate with investigating authorities (Section 4) including foreign institutions and foreign investigating authorities (Section 5).

Changes in foreign policy and arms control

The advent of democracy in 1994 raised domestic and international expectations regarding South Africa's role as a responsible and respected member of the international community. Included in these expectations was the hope that South Africa would be in a position to play a leading role in Africa and in the Southern African region with regard to international peace and security matters in an environment that offered greater potential for co-operative efforts in international and regional settings. Thus, in addition to the constitutional reconstruction, the country's foreign policy likewise had to be transformed from an adversarial mode to bilateral and multilateral co-operation. After all, the official business of the Department of Foreign Affairs in the apartheid years was mainly directed at warding off or busting international sanctions and at building strong relations with sympathetic Governments. Relations with the rest of Africa were largely hostile.

Thus, in 1999 it was announced that South Africa's new foreign policy would be based on six key principles[156] –

- A commitment to the promotion of human rights;
- A commitment to the promotion of democracy;
- A commitment to justice and international law in the conduct of relations between nations;
- A commitment to international peace and to internationally agreed-upon mechanisms for the resolution of conflicts;
- A commitment to the interests of Africa in world affairs;
- A commitment to economic development through regional and international co-operation in an inter-dependent world.

---

154 Section 8.

155 Section 9.

156 Department of Foreign Affairs *White Paper on South African Participation in International Peace Missions*, Notice 2216 of 1999, *Government Gazette* No 20518, 4 October 1999, 22.

A Defence *White Paper* of 1996[157] declared that "as a responsible member of the international community, South Africa will conduct its foreign policy, arms trade and external defence activities in accordance with international law and norms." In pursuance of these goals the *White Paper* developed a number of principles intended to govern South Africa's future conduct in these areas. Of specific importance for the region and sub-region are the principles on conventional arms trade. At the outset the *White Paper* intended to subject the import and export of conventional arms, and the transit of arms through South Africa to a control process and permit system under the auspices of a cabinet committee, called the National Conventional Arms Control Committee (NCACC).[158] In future, openness and transparency, core values enshrined in the new Constitution, would also apply to arms trade, and be limited "only by national security interests."[159] On this basis the *White Paper* also affirmed South Africa's commitment to a legitimate arms control system that will ensure a responsible approach to arms sales and transfers, taking into account a number of considerations, including the following[160] –

- The need to ensure that conventional arms sales and transfers are not used in violation of the purposes and principles of the United Nations Charter;
- Respect for human rights and fundamental freedoms in the recipient country;
- The security situation in the recipient country;
- The degree to which arms sales are supportive of South Africa's national and foreign interests;
- Whether arms sales and transfers will amount to a contravention of South Africa's international commitments, "in particular its obligations under arms embargoes adopted by the United Nations Security Council and other arms control agreements or responsibilities in terms of internationally accepted custom."

The intended arms control process subjects the import, transfer, marketing and export of conventional armaments and related technology through South Africa and abroad to the granting of a duly authorised permit. Export permits will not be granted in the absence of an End-User Certificate (EUC) issued by the importing Government. Such a certificate must clearly identify the issuing authority, the specifications and quantity of the armaments in question, and a commitment by the purchaser not to resell or transfer the arms without the permission of the South African Government. In case of a breach of a commitment by the importing country the transgression will be publicised internationally and all further arms sales with the transgressor State will be barred.[161]

157 *Defence in a Democracy White Paper on National Defence for the Republic of South Africa*, May 1996, Chapter 4, para. 6.5. The changes brought about by this policy document, especially in the field of arms trading had its origin in the recommendations of the Cameron Commission of Enquiry into an arms-related scandal that surfaced shortly after the ANC-led government came to power in 1994.

158 *Ibid.,* Chapter 8, para. 9.

159 *Ibid.,* para. 12.

160 *Ibid.,* paras. 14 *et seq.*

161 *Ibid.,* paras. 18-20.

Applications will be subjected to a multi-departmental review process and to scrutiny by the Secretary for Defence and the Directors-General of the Departments of Foreign Affairs and Trade and Industry who make recommendations to the NCACC,[162] which is accountable to the Cabinet.

Although South Africa has refused to sell arms to a number of Governments in terms of its new policies, there were instances of theoretical commitments and practice not squaring up. In 1999, the Commonwealth Human Rights Initiative reported that among the ten top destinations for South African arms exports, five countries (India, Colombia, Congo-Brazzaville, Algeria and Chad) experienced some form of armed conflict in the past five years. Weapons were also supplied to major participants in the war in the Democratic Republic of the Congo, a country with an abysmal human rights record. Sales to Rwanda were only suspended in 1996 but resumed a year later at a time when fighting flared up in western Rwanda and Rwandan troops were accused of involvement in a number of atrocities.[163]

Improved control over the arms trade and less scope for subverting the above policy framework will probably result once the policy framework is consummated as law. This process is underway and has already produced draft legislation, which is currently considered by Parliament in the form of the *Conventional Arms Control Bill* 2000. Once enacted into law, the Bill will provide the legal basis for the establishment of the NCACC and regulate the process for the control of the trade in conventional arms. A few matters relevant within the context of sanctions enforcement may be alluded to at this point in time.

In addition to giving a broad definition to "import" and "export", the Bill also covers "re-exportation" which, in relation to conventional arms, means "to export imported conventional arms, or to cause imported conventional arms to be exported to any place other than that from which the conventional arms were originally imported, whether or not it is carried out in exchange for currency or any other commodity" (Clause 1). If ownership in conventional arms is transferred, the NCACC must satisfy itself that the "recipient country has given an undertaking regarding its accountability in respect of the arms in question which must be in accordance with international practice." If transfer of ownership does not take place the NCACC must –

- Obtain a statement from the recipient country regarding the intended use of the arms in question; and
- Satisfy itself that the conventional arms are returned to the Republic in accordance with the statement (Clause 15).

---

162 This Committee comprises the Ministers and Deputy Ministers of Defence, Trade and Industry, Foreign Affairs and Safety and Security; the Ministers of General Services and Arts, Culture, Science and Technology; and the Deputy Minister of Intelligence Services. For further information on the NCACC and South Africa's arms trade and policy see http://www.mil.za/sandf/dro/ncacc/ncacc.htm.

163 For these and other discrepancies between policy and practice see B. Manby, "Human rights and South Africa's foreign policy: a guiding light or flickering candle?", 2 *South African Journal on Human Rights* (2000) 372 *et seq.*

To ensure that trade in conventional arms is conducted in terms of the Bill, the Minister of Defence must establish an Inspectorate (Clause 9) whose powers of entry, search and seizure are circumscribed in the Bill (Clauses 17, 18 and 20). If in the course of a search a person claims that an article or document found upon or in the premises contains privileged information and refuses inspection of the article or document, an inspector may apply to the High Court for an order granting the attachment and removal of the article or document for safe custody until a court has made a ruling on the question whether the information in question is privileged or not (Clause 19). The Bill also allows for the suppression of information if disclosure would be detrimental to the national or security interests of the Republic or to the commercial interests of the manufacturer (Clause 23).

For the sake of completeness reference must also be made to two other developments regarding the disclosure or suppression of information. Firstly, Section 32 of the 1996 Constitution guarantees everyone the right of access to information held by the State or any other person if the information is required for the exercise or protection of a right. Secondly, in compliance with a constitutional instruction, Parliament enacted the *Promotion of Access to Information Act* 2 of 2000 to give further effect to the constitutional right enshrined in Section 32 of the Constitution. The Preamble of the Act recognises that "the system of government in South Africa before 27 April 1994, amongst others, resulted in a secretive and unresponsive culture in public and private bodies which often led to an abuse of power and human rights violations". Hence, the Act proclaims as one of its objectives the promotion of "transparency, accountability and effective governance of all public and private bodies ...."[164] This Act applies to the exclusion of any provision of other legislation (except the Constitution) that prohibits or restricts the disclosure of information and that is materially inconsistent with an object or specific provision of the Act.[165] Apart from regulating the availability of public and private records and the procedures for obtaining information, the grounds on which access to records can be refused are regulated extensively in the Act. One such ground relates to defence, security and international relations of the Republic which includes records pertaining to the deployment of weapons or "anything being designed, developed, produced or considered for use as weapons or such other equipment."[166] In like manner the Act protects the trade secrets and the financial, commercial, scientific or technical information of a third party who can be either a public or private body.[167]

Two safeguards may be invoked against an abuse of power under the exclusionary provisions of the Act. The one is contained in Section 46 of the Act, which provides for mandatory disclosure if the disclosure of the record would reveal evidence of a substantial contravention of, or failure to comply with, the law. Whether "law" includes international law, is a matter of construction and will certainly depend, at least in certain instances, on the nature and scope of the law in question. For instance, legislation

164 Act 2 of 2000, s 9(e).

165 *Ibid.*, s 5.

166 *Ibid.*, s 41.

167 *Ibid.*, ss 36, 68.

incorporating international law will certainly be unproblematic. Another solution may be contained in Section 233 of the Constitution which obliges the courts to "prefer any reasonable interpretation of the legislation that is consistent with international law over any alternative interpretation that is inconsistent with international law." However, by far the most important safeguard is contained in Section 36 of the Constitution which contains the general requirements for a limitation of fundamental rights to be justifiable. Thus, a non-disclosure infringing a fundamental right (Chapter 2 of the Constitution) must derive from a law of general application and must be reasonable and justifiable in an open and democratic society based on human dignity, equality and freedom. Factors that may be taken into account in coming to a conclusion include –

- The nature of the right;
- The importance of the purpose of the limitation;
- The nature and extent of the limitation;
- The relation between the limitation and its purpose; and
- Less restrictive means to achieve the purpose.

What remains uncertain is how South African courts will approach matters involving foreign relations under the 1996 Constitution. Up until now the opportunity has not arisen for the courts to demonstrate whether or not, or to what extent, a certain 'margin of appreciation' will be tolerated in such instances.

The 1996 Constitution and sanctions enforcement: rule of law and human rights considerations

South Africa's future role in the enforcement of Security Council sanctions is set to become more prominent, especially in view of the country's understanding of and commitment to its international and, above all, regional responsibilities. However, any such involvement cannot escape an orientation that derives from the values underlying the new Constitution, i.e. if the country wants to remain true to what it considers to be the supreme law of the land.[168] Some salient features of the Constitution relevant to the subject of sanctions enforcement therefore need to be considered.

Section 1 of the Constitution declares that South Africa is a sovereign, democratic State founded on values such as the advancement of human rights and freedoms, the rule of law and a democratic system of government to ensure accountability, responsiveness and openness. In interpreting and applying values such as these under the post 1994 constitutional dispensation, the courts have assumed the obligation to progressively develop these values. Thus, in *S v Williams* 1995 7 BCLR 861 (CC) the approach courts should adopt was spelled out by the Constitutional Court in the following words –

> Courts do have a role to play in the promotion and development of a new culture 'founded on the recognition of human rights', in particular, with regard to those rights which are enshrined in the Constitution. It is a role, which demands that a court should be particu-

168 Section 2 of the Constitution reads as follows: This Constitution is the supreme law of the Republic; law or conduct inconsistent with it is invalid, and the obligations imposed by it must be fulfilled.

> larly sensitive the impact which the exercise of judicial functions may have on the rights of individuals .... One of the implications of the new order is that old rules and practices can no longer be taken for granted; they must be subjected to constant re-assessment to bring them into line with the provisions of the Constitution" (at 866).[169]

For current purposes the references to the rule of law and the advancement of human rights and fundamental freedoms must be singled out.

With regard to the rule of law, the Constitutional Court, in one of its first cases under the Interim Constitution of 1993 on the death penalty[170] stated per Ackermann J that –

> In reaction to our past, the concept and values of the constitutional state ... are deeply foundational to the creation of the 'new order' referred to in the preamble. ... We have moved from a past characterised by much which was arbitrary and unequal in the operation of the law to a present and a future in a constitutional State where State action must be such that it is capable of being analysed and justified rationally. The idea of the constitutional State presupposes a system whose operation can be rationally tested against or in terms of the law.

In more recent decisions the courts have referred to the rule of law as "a foundational value" of the new South African State which must be promoted under the duty established by Section 39(1) of the Constitution.[171] This Section determines that a court, when interpreting the Bill of Rights (Chapter 2 of the Constitution), must promote the values that underlie an open and democratic society based on human dignity, equality and freedom.

These views on the rule of law bear relevance to domestic measures on the enforcement of sanctions in two respects. Firstly, measures that operate retrospectively might be considered constitutionally inadmissible. On the issue of the arbitrary application of the law, which is often raised in the context of retrospective legislation, the Constitutional Court in *President of the Republic of South Africa v Hugo* 1997 4 SA 1 (CC) made it clear that –

> The need for accessibility, precision and general application flow from the concept of the rule of law. A person should be able to know the law, and be able to conform his or her conduct to the law (para. 102).

In *Pharmaceutical Manufacturers Association of South Africa; In re Application of the President of the RSA and Others* 2000 3 BCLR 241 (CC) the Constitutional Court cited the following remarks by the British authors De Smith, Woolf and Jowels on the rule of law with approval –

169 This case was decided under the Interim Constitution (1993). See also *Larbi-Odam v Member of the Executive Council for Education and Another,* 1996 12 BCLR 1612 at 1622-1623.

170 *S v Makwanyane* 1995 3 SA 391 (CC) at 454 C-D.

171 Cf. *De Lange v Smuts and Others* 1998 7 BCLR 779 (CC) at 799; *National Coalition for Gay and Lesbian Equality and Others v Minister of Justice and Others,* 1998 6 BCLR 726 (W) at 741.

> The rule of law is another such principle of the greatest importance. ... The scope of the rule of law is broad. It has managed to justify a great deal of the specific content of judicial review .... In addition, the rule of law embraces some internal qualities of all public law: that it should be certain, that is, ascertainable in advance so as to be predictable and not retrospective in its operation....

In all likelihood South African jurisprudence on this point will be informed by principles established in European jurisprudence, and more particularly in German constitutional law. Much of what is contained in the South African constitution on these issues find their reference in the German *Rechtsstaat* concept.

Secondly, the requirements of transparency and opennes, and their relation to the rule of law, necessitate a re-assessment of government practice hitherto followed in announcing the imposition of sanctions against another State in pursuance of Security Council resolutions. There is reason to believe that very few private entities involved in trade were aware of the fact that South Africa imposed sanctions against Yugoslavia in the early nineties.[172] Apart from undermining the efficiency of sanction enforcement, laws that are not reasonably accessible or ascertainable may lead to constitutional challenges in the future.

The issue of the dissemination of sanction information is of course linked to two other matters, namely the enactment of national legislation specifically designed for the enforcement of United Nations sanctions which is long overdue, and the constitutional obligations on co-operative government. The latter are regulated in Chapter 3 of the Constitution. This Chapter contains a long list of principles aimed at promoting co-operative governance,[173] which all spheres of government are obliged to follow.[174] Relevant for present purposes are the provisions that –

- Effective, transparent, accountable and coherent government for the whole of the Republic must be provided, and
- The different spheres of government must co-ordinate their actions and legislation with one another.[175]

Complying with these obligations is rather essential for any national sanction enforcement scheme that wants to be effective. One of the problems though is that the South African Government has as yet not established, by an Act of Parliament, the structures and institutions to facilitate and promote intergovernmental relations as is required by Section 41(2) of the Constitution. Thus, the problems associated with the delays in and fragmentation of the process of implementing United Nations sanctions highlighted in 1993 by the then Minister of Foreign Affairs, still exist.

172 As far as could be established South Africa considered but never promulgated regulations on sanctions against Iraq. Enquiries at the Department of Foreign Affairs about South Africa's response uncovered nothing but confusion.

173 This is based on the German concept of *Bundestreue*.

174 See Constitution s 40(2).

175 *Ibid.*, s 41(1)(c) and (h)(iv).

In returning to the value concerning the advancement of human rights and fundamental freedoms, it must be noted that the Constitution ensures that the fundamental rights provisions in Chapter 2 of the Constitution are interpreted in accordance with international law. Above reference was already made to Section 233 of the Constitution. The international law "openness" of the Constitution is further illustrated by Section 39(1) which determines that a court, when interpreting the Bill of Rights, (a) must consider international law and (b) may consider foreign law. In applying a similar reference to international law in Section 35(1) of the Interim Constitution, the Constitutional Court in *S v Makwanyane* (supra) ruled as follows (at 413-414) –

> In the context of Section 35(1), public international law would include non-binding as well as binding law. They may both be used under the Section as tools of interpretation. International agreements and customary international law accordingly provide a framework within which [the Bill of Rights] can be evaluated and understood, and for that purpose, decisions of tribunals dealing with comparable instruments, such as the United Nations Committee of Human Rights, the Inter-American Commission on Human Rights, the Inter-American Court of Human Rights, The European Commission on Human Rights, and the European Court of Human Rights and, in appropriate cases, reports of specialised agencies such as the International Labour Organisation, may provide guidance as to the correct interpretation of particular provisions of the [Bill of Rights].

Since the establishment of the new constitutional order South Africa has also become a participant in a number of international instruments dealing with human rights. For instance, the *International Covenant on Civil and Political Rights* (except the first protocol) was ratified in 1998 and the *International Covenant on Social, Economic and Cultural Rights* signed in 1994 but not ratified yet. These developments must eventually become part of the equation when the imposition of sanctions is considered.

A question South African lawmakers and courts will not be able to escape in the field of sanctions implementation is the one about the relationship between economic sanctions and human rights. In 1997 this matter came before the Committee on Economic, Social and Cultural Rights, established in terms of the International Covenant on Economic, Social and Cultural Rights (1996). While the Committee did not call into question the necessity for the imposition of sanctions in appropriate circumstances, it emphasised that a resort to sanctions in terms of Chapter VII of the Charter cannot exclude altogether a consideration of the human rights provisions contained in Articles 1, 55 and 56 of the Charter.[176]

The Committee's first and foremost concern was with the impact of sanctions on the rights and privileges recognised in the Covenant, which after all, is a further realisation and elaboration of the broad, non-specific Charter provisions on the need for human rights protection. The concern of the Committee relates to matters raised in the following statement[177] –

176 Committee on Economic, Social and Cultural Rights, *General Comment* No 8, *IHRR* May 1998, 302.

177 *Ibid.*, para. 3.

> [Sanctions] ... often cause significant disruption in the distribution of food, pharmaceuticals and sanitation supplies, jeopardize the quality of food and the availability of clean drinking water, severely interfere with the functioning of basic health and education systems, and undermine the right to work. In addition their unintended consequences can include reinforcement of the power of oppressive élites, the emergence, almost invariable, of a black market and the generation of huge windfall profits for the privileged élites which manage it, enhancement of the control of the governing élites over the population at large, and restriction of opportunities to seek asylum or to manifest political opposition.

Available evidence has also moved the Committee to conclude that insufficient attention is being paid to the impact of sanctions on vulnerable groups, and studies into humanitarian exemptions have not paid special attention to the consequences that ensue from sanctions for the enjoyment of social, cultural and economic rights. Thus, the point made is that a human rights dimension must be injected into deliberations on the imposition of sanctions.[178]

From the perspective of a State's accession to or ratification of the Covenant, the Committee envisages two sets of obligations.[179] In the first instance the Committee is entrusted with the task of scrutinizing the extent to which a State party has taken steps, within the scope of available resources, to provide the greatest possible protection for economic, social and cultural rights without discrimination, and "to take all possible measures, including negotiations with other States and the international community, to reduce to a minimum the negative impact upon the rights of vulnerable groups within society."

The second set of obligations relates to the States responsible for the imposition of sanctions. In this regard the Committee makes the following conclusions:

- Economic, social and cultural rights must be taken into consideration by the States concerned. Improved protection for these rights could be achieved through a mechanism for anticipating and tracking sanctions impacts, a more transparent set of agreed principles and procedures, the identification of a wider range of exempt goods and services, etc.
- Effective monitoring must be undertaken throughout the period that sanctions are imposed.
- States have an obligation to take steps, unilaterally or collectively, to counter any disproportionate suffering caused by a sanctions programme.

The importance of the Committee's involvement in these matters lies in the fact that it contributes significantly to a growing body of consensus that executive decisions cannot be taken and implemented in isolation of substantive provisions dealing with the protection of human rights. This is especially true when the source which is invoked in support of an executive decision of a political organ is the same source from which the international body of human rights law has sprung. Moreover, logic is defied when sanctions

178 *Ibid.*, para. 6.

179 *Ibid.*, paras. 10-14.

are imposed to force the target State to respect the political and civil rights of its citizens, without assuming an obligation on the part of those responsible for the implementation of the sanctions programme to duly take into account those same considerations.

A final matter that needs to be addressed is the justiciability of the executive acts of the South African Government in foreign relations. Under South African common law executive powers enjoyed considerable immunity against judicial scrutiny. The power of the courts in such instances was limited to an enquiry about the existence of the executive prerogative and whether the power fell within the scope of the prerogative. Since in terms of the 1996 Constitution the powers of the executive derive from the Constitution, full judicial review of even the manner in which the power was exercised will now be possible.[180] Although a certain "margin of appreciation" will apply, executive decisions in the realm of foreign policy are likely to suffer the same fate. Of relevance in this regard are the following –

- In terms of Section 8(1) of the Constitution the Bill of Rights applies to all law, and binds the legislature, the executive, the judiciary and all organs of State.[181]
- In terms of Section 34 of the Constitution any person has the right to have any dispute that can be resolved by the application of law decided by a court of law.
- The courts have the power to apply international treaty and customary law[182] to enquire whether an executive act complies with international law.

The Anti-Terrorism Bill

Prior to the September 11, 2001 terrorist attack in the United States,[183] South Africa's security legislation came under review with a view to consider its appropriateness in criminalising conduct and related activities associated with modern forms of terrorism. This investigation, undertaken by the South African Law Commission,[184] was *inter alia* prompted by the United Nations efforts to develop a common international strategy against terrorism and more specifically by developments that have taken place under the auspices of the OAU, such as the adoption in July 1999 of the OAU Convention on the Prevention and Combatting of Terrorism. South Africa is amongst the thirty odd countries that signed the OAU Convention which, *inter alia*, obliges States parties to review their national laws and establish criminal offences as defined in the Convention.

180 Cf. *President of the Republic of South Africa v Hugo* 1997 6 BCLR 708 (CC); G. Carpenter, "Prerogative powers in South Africa – dead and gone at last?", 22 *South African Yearbook of International Law* (1997), 104; *Mohamed v President of the Republic of South Africa* CCT 17/10, 28 May 2001.

181 Section 239 of the Constitution defines an organ of state as "any department of state or administration …or any other functionary or institution exercising a power or performing a function in terms of the Constitution…".

182 Section 232 of the Constitution makes customary international law part of the law of South Africa to the extent that it is consistent with the Constitution or an Act of Parliament. See also J. Dugard, *International Law: A South African Perspective* (2000), 68.

183 See SC Resolution 1373 of 28 September 2001.

184 South African Law Commission, *Review of Security Legislation*, Discussion Paper 92, Project 105 (2000).

The approach of the South African Law Commission was to draft new legislation addressing the issue of terrorism in all its modern complexities on a broader basis, as opposed to amending existing legislation, such as the *Internal Security Act* of 1982, which relates only to terrorism in respect of the South African Government or the South African population. This approach seems to find its orientation in the approach followed in the OAU Convention[185] which defines a "terrorist act" as –

> (a) any act which is a violation of the criminal laws of a State Party and which may endanger the life, physical integrity or freedom of or cause serious injury or death to any person, any number or group of persons or causes or may cause damage to public or private property, natural resources, environmental or cultural heritage and is calculated to:
> (i) intimidate, put in fear, force, coerce or induce any government, body, institution, the general public or any segment thereof, to do or abstain from doing any act, or to adopt or abandon a particular standpoint, or to act according to certain principles; or
> (ii) disrupt any public service, the delivery of any essential service to the public or to create a public emergency; or
> (iii) create general insurrection in a State;
> (b) any promotion, sponsoring, contribution to, command, aid, incitement, encouragement, attempt, threat, conspiracy, organizing, or procurement of any person, with the intent to commit any act referred to in paragraph (a) (i) to (iii).

The work undertaken by the South African law Commission, which also resulted in a Draft Anti-Terrorism Bill 2000, was halted and had to be reconsidered in view of the developments that have taken place subsequent to the September 11 terrorist attack in the United States. Consequently the Law Commission presented a new Anti-Terrorism Bill in 2002, which provided for a comprehensive legislative framework for the prevention and combating of terrorism, the criminalisation of terrorist acts and of their financing and facilitation.[186]

However, in 2003/4 the 2002 Bill was again replaced by another attempt under the cumbersome title of the Protection of Constitutional Democracy Against Terrorist and Related Activities Bill,[187] which will soon be enacted into law. Reinforcing the title's sentiment, the Preamble warns that terrorist and related activities are intended to achieve political and other aims in a violent or otherwise unconstitutional manner, and undermine democratic rights and constitutional values. However, South Africa's responsibility

185 Cf. *Ibid.*, Chapter 2.

186 It must be noted, however, that the Bill casts a wide net to cover also matters such as the hijacking of aircraft (Clause 5), endangering of maritime navigation (Clause 6), acts of bombing (Clause 7), the taking of hostages (Clause 8), offences relating to fixed platforms (Clause 10), offences with regard to nuclear matters or facilities (Clause 10), and the use of weapons of mass destruction (Clause 13).

187 B 12B-2003.

to give domestic effect to its international obligations[188] with regard to the combatting of terrorism is also duly recognised in the Preambule.

Broadly speaking, the offences created by the Bill fall into three categories. The first is the offence of terrorism itself which relates to certain activities outlawed by the Bill and committed in or outside the Republic[189] and which involve the systematic, repeated or arbitrary use of violence or release into the environment, or exposing the public to dangerous, hazardous or radioactive substances or any toxic chemical or biological agent or toxin and as a result of which certain consequences are brought about. These include endangering the life or physical integrity of a person, causing a serious health risk, the destruction of or substantial damage to property, serious interference with or disruption of an essential service, causing a major economic loss or creating a serious public emergency. It is immaterial whether the harm is suffered in or outside the Republic and the activity can be committed by any means or method. Criminal intent exists when the activity is directly or indirectly meant to threaten the unity and territorial integrity of any State; intimidate or cause feelings of insecurity, or induce fear or spread feelings of terror in the civilian population; unduly compel, intimidate, force or induce a person, a government, the general public, or a domestic or international organisation to do or to abstain or refrain from doing something, or to adopt or abandon a certain standpoint. It must also be shown that the activity was committed for the purpose of the advancement of an individual or collective political, religious, ideological or philosophical motive, objective, cause or undertaking. Specifically excluded from the operation of the definition of terrorist activity is any act committed during a struggle, including an armed struggle, for the exercise of furtherance of a legitimate right to national liberation, self-determination and independence against colonialism, occupation, aggression or domination by alien forces in accordance with the principles of international law and international humanitarian law.[190] This provision was included in response to criticism against an overbroad definition in an earlier draft making a distinction of this nature impossible. However, it is also

188 South Africa is party to the following international instruments: Convention on Offences and Certain Other Acts Committed on Board Aircraft (1963), Convention for the Suppression of Unlawful Seizure of Aircraft (1970), Convention for the Suppression of Unlawful Acts Against the Safety of Civil Aviation (1971), Convention for the Prevention and Punishment of Crimes Against Internationally Protected Persons including Diplomatic Agents (1973), International Convention Against the Taking of Hostages (1979), Protocol for the Suppression of Unlawful Acts of Violence at Airports Serving International Civil Aviation (1988), Convention for the Marking of Plastic Explosives for the Purpose of Detection (1991), International Convention for the Suppression of Terrorist Bombings (1997), International Convention on the Suppression of the Financing of Terrorism (1999), and the OAU Convention on the Prevention and Combating of Terrorism (1999). The government has also indicated its willingness to become party to the following instruments not yet ratified or acceeded to: Convention for the Suppresion of Unlawful Acts Against the Safety of Maritime Navigation (1988), Protocol for the Suppression of Unlawful Acts Against the Safety of Fixed Platforms on the Continental Shelf (1988), and the Convention on the Physical Protection of Nuclear Material (1979).

189 B 12B (2003) clause 2 read with clause 1 (xxiv) "terrorist activity".

190 Clause 1 (4).

naïve not to realise that the distinction between legitimate and illegitimate activities often becomes blurred and that organisations with diverging ideological objectives often engage in symbiotic relationships and derive mutual benefits from such a relationship.

The second category of offences relates to conduct which in general contributes to or facilitates the commission of a terrorist activity such as the recruitment of persons or entities, the provisions of training, weapons, documents and other objects either in the knowledge, or while the person ought reasonable to have known, that the conduct in question is connected to a terrorist activity.[191]

The third category relates to the so-called convention offences which include offences created in fulfillment of the Republic's international obligations in terms of international instruments dealing with terrorist and terrorist related activities.[192] The purpose here is to give domestic effect to international and regional conventions to which South Africa has become a party and in so doing offences associated with the financing of terrorist activities feature prominently.[193] Provision has also been made to give domestic effect to Security Council resolutions adopted in terms of Chapter VII of the UN Charter. For instance, the President is under an obligation to give notice in the *Government Gazette* that the Security Council has identified a specific entity as being involved in terrorist activities or as an entity against whom UN members must take action specified in Security Council resolutions with a view to combat or prevent terrorist and related activites.[194] Proclamations of this nature are subject to parliamentary scrutiny and Parliament is also empowered to decide on the appropriate way in which domestic effect must be given to such resolutions.[195]

The jurisdiction of the South African courts to adjudicate in criminal proceedings under the Bill is based on traditional grounds such as territoriality, nationality and domestic effect or national interest, but also on factual presumptions.[196] Hence, the courts will assume jurisdiction if the accused was arrested, or if the offence was committed in the Republic, in its territorial waters or on board a ship or aircraft registered in the Republic. If the offence was committed elsewhere jurisdiction will derive from the nationality or place of residence of the offender, or from the nationality or place of residence of the victim. Jurisdiction will also be asserted if the offence was committed against the Republic, or a governement facility abroad, or if the offence is aimed at compelling the Republic to do or to abstain from doing any act. These grounds for jurisdiction are not a closed list. The Bill specifically leaves the matter open by determining that jurisdiction may also derive from any other basis recognized by law,[197] a phrase which is broad enough to include international law.

191 Clauses 2 (2) and 3.

192 Chapter 2, Part 2 read with clause 1 (1) (ii).

193 See clause 4.

194 Clause 25.

195 Clause 26.

196 Clause 15.

197 Clause 15 (1) (c).

Factual presumptions become relevant when an offence is committed outside the Republic by a person, or against a person, who has no nationality link with the country. In such instances the courts shall be deemed to have jurisdiction if the act:

- Affects or is intended to affect a public body, any person or business in the Republic;
- The offender is found in the Republic; and
- Is not extradited or there is no application for extradition.

For the purpose of determining the jurisdiction of the court to try the offence in these circumstances the offence shall be deemed to have been committed at the place where the accused was ordinarily resident or at the accused's principal place of business.

The decision to prosecute rests with the National Director of Public Prosecutions (NDPP).[198] No guidelines are provided on the basis of which such a decision must be taken and it can be presumed that the *National Prosecuting Authority Act* 32 of 1998 will apply. This Act empowers the NDPP to determine policy with regard to the institution of prosecutions and renders the NDPP accountable to Parliament in respect to the powers and functions performed or exercised in terms of the Act, including decisions regarding the institution of prosecutions. This, at least, will provide some kind of parliamentary oversight over decisions by the NDPP to prosecute or not to prosecute in certain cases.

Lastly, the Bill makes provision for the seizure and forfeiture of terrorist property even in the absence of criminal proceedings against an accused and involving the property in question.[199] This part of the Bill is modeled on the civil recovery of property proceedings in Chapter 6 of the Prevention of Organised Crime Act 121 of 1998, a mechanism which is also used in other jurisdictions for depriving criminals of the financial fruits of their illegal activities. However, from a constitutional point of view the proceedings in question are highly controversial and a ruling on the constitutional validity of Chapter 6 is still awaited.[200]

III. Conclusion

In considering the enforcement of Security Council resolutions in the above instances a number of obstacles have emerged. In the first place economic conditions in many of the States are such that State action beyond the partial or limited implementation of import and export embargoes becomes self-destructive. Secondly, a lack of resources and skills coupled with a defaulting legal framework and infrastructure in many States, create ample opportunity for system abuse and sanctions evasion, a situation that is worsened by the absence or fragility of government by the rule of law.

198 Clause 16.

199 Clause 23.

200 Recently, the Constitutional Court has referred a matter back to the High Court for argument and a ruling on the constitutionality of Chapter 6. See *National Director of Public Prosecutions v Minister of Justice and Constitutional Development* CCT 13/02 of 12 June 2002.

Thirdly, in a region largely made up of strong, stable democratic States, sanctions enforcement is facilitated by the ability of such States to more or less uniformly act against and isolate a delinquent member. In African conflict zones the obverse is often true. A delinquent State or State-like entity targeted by United Nations sanctions often shares borders with other delinquent or failing political entities with the result that the enforcement network is replaced with an evasion network.

Fourthly, given these circumstances the efficiency of regional organisations in facilitating the enforcement of United Nations measures must be seriously compromised. At the time of writing Member States of the Southern African Development Community (SADC) were preparing a joint position on the restriction of trade in conflict diamonds. Similar initiatives are on the agenda of the OAU and the Economic Community of West African States (ECOWAS) has placed a moratorium on arms shipments to West Africa. However, when member countries are weak and their enforcement capabilities suspect, the regional super-structure must suffer from the same malaise. Moreover, the historical track record of these organisations in dealing with conflict situations is abysmal and there is a general notion that they need not be taken seriously. Whether the new initiatives referred to in the introduction will rescue the situation remains to be seen. As longer term prospects are concerned, the initiatives that will be undertaken (and hopefully implemented) in terms of the New Partnership for Africa's Development (NEPAD) offer some hope in the sense that there is recognition of the need for institutional strengthening and development in a variety of areas with a view to achieving the objectives spelled out in the NEPAD document. As regards the peace and security initiative, for instance, efforts to build Africa's capacity to manage all aspects of conflict are linked to the enhancing of African institution's capacity to prevent, manage and resolve conflicts and to a focus on the means necessary to strengthen existing regional and sub-regional institutions.[201] Perhaps even more encouraging though is the undertaking to respect the global standards of democracy and to contribute to the strengthening of the political and administrative frameworks of the Member States in line "with the principles of democracy, transparency, accountability, integrity, respect for human rights and promotion of the rule of law."[202]

201 NEPAD 2001, paras. 71-74.

202 *Ibid.*, paras. 79, 80.

PART II: NAMIBIA

by

*Tunguru Huaraka**

I. Introduction

The Southern African Development Community [SADC], established by the Treaty of Windhoek of 19 August 1992, replaced the Southern African Development Co-ordinating Conference [SADCC] which had been set-up by the Lusaka Declaration of 1 April 1980. While SADCC was an instrument in the struggle for the emancipation of the region from colonialism and apartheid, SADC is an international organisation, with legal personality, aimed at the economic development of the region.

The SADC region, then the Southern African region,[1] had the infamy of attracting the first ever Security Council decision on sanctions, as well as the second: the 1966 sanctions against the racist minority regime of Southern Rhodesian[2] and the 1977 arms embargo against the racist apartheid in South Africa, respectively. These early Security Council decisions on sanctions, taken at the height of the Cold War, dealt with situations of decolonisation and racism.

At the end of the Cold War, the Security Council was unshackled from the chilly veto of the Cold War and thus regained its authority as the supreme international organ for the maintenance of international peace and security. The Security Council has since taken an unprecedented number of decisions on sanctions dealing with conflicts in all parts of the world. Most of these decisions on sanctions dealt with conflicts in Africa, namely, UNITA (Angola), Liberia, Libya, Rwanda, Sierra Leone, Somalia and Sudan.[3]

The majority of these conflicts in Africa which attracted Security Council decisions under Chapter VII of the Charter of the United Nations are resource-based, intra-state conflicts. The exception is only the decision with regard to Libya. In resource-based, intra-state conflicts various groups, regionally or ethnically or religiously based, battle for control of the natural resources, in most cases diamonds. In most resource-based, intra-

* The views expressed in this study are solely those of the author.

1 The Southern African region, under the division of the Organisation of African Unity (now African Union), is composed of the following: Angola, Botswana, Lesotho, Malawi, Mozambique, Namibia, South Africa, Swaziland, Zambia and Zimbabwe; and to make up SADC the following are added: Democratic Republic of Congo, Mauritius, Seychelles and Tanzania.

2 For a scholarly study on the United Nations sanctions against Southern Rhodesia see Vera Gowlland-Debbas, *Collective Responses to Illegal Acts in International Law: United Nations Action in the Question of Southern Rhodesia* (Martinus Nijhoff Publishers, Dordrecht/Boston/London,1990).

3 The others are related to: Haiti, Iraq and several parts of the former Yugoslavia.

state conflicts the legitimacy of the central government is also challenged.

To some extent it could be said that resource-based, intra-state conflicts could be considered as manifestations of under-development and poverty. What is relevant to the consideration of the enforcement of Security Council resolutions on sanctions is that in intra-state conflicts, the entities concerned are non-state entities and in most cases have no discernable territory, infrastructures or, for that matter, authority.

This chapter deals largely with the experiences of only two SADC Member States, South Africa and Namibia, in implementing Security Council decisions on sanctions, although references to other countries in the region may be appropriate.

II. Namibia

(1) Historical Background

The implementation of the Security Council resolutions on sanctions against UNITA (Angola) by the countries of the SADC region, in particular Namibia, should be situated in the geographical and developmental context as well as the historical perspectives of the region.

The conflict in Angola is a spill-over from the armed struggle against Portuguese colonialism. Various nationalist movements, especially the *Movimento Popular de Libertaçâo de Angola* [MPLA] and *Uniao Nacional Para a Independencia Total de Angola* [UNITA], fought against Portuguese colonial forces for the liberation of the country. As the Portuguese colonial regime was collapsing in 1974, simmering armed conflict between MPLA and UNITA intensified, each attempting to gain total control. As a result, the country was turned into a Cold War battleground; with western countries and racist apartheid South Africa supporting UNITA, while the eastern block and Cuba sided with MPLA. The Cuban ground troops were decisive in preventing the fast-moving apartheid South African forces from entering the capital, Luanda. The South African forces were pushed back and retreated to the south of Angola; and MPLA proclaimed the independent People's Republic of Angola on 11 November 1975. But UNITA recouped its strength under the protective umbrella of apartheid South Africa and the United States, and since then continued to carry on its attacks against the Angolan army, the civilian population and infrastructure. It could be fairly asserted that the scale and longevity of the UNITA insurgency were largely due to apartheid South Africa's aggressive efforts to maintain its control in Namibia.

It should be noted that the People's Liberation Army of Namibia [PLAN], the armed wing of SWAPO, was engaged, in fact since the mid-1960s, in the armed liberation war against the racist apartheid South African regime in Namibia, often using bases in Angola. Thus, when apartheid South Africa entered into the conflict in Angola on the side of UNITA, inevitably UNITA became part of apartheid South Africa's machinery, fighting against the armed struggle of the Namibian people for liberation.[4]

---

4 For the negotiations leading to the withdrawal of apartheid South African forces from Angola, see generally, Chester A. Crocker, *High Noon in Southern Africa. Making Peace in a Rough Neighborhood* (W.W. Norton and Co., 1992).

It was only in September 1988 that the apartheid South African forces left Angola, after having suffered a major military defeat at Cuito Cuanavale, Angola, in May of the same year, at the combined hands of Cuba, Angola and SWAPO. It is important to note that the withdrawal of apartheid South African troops from Angola was a part of the agreement for the implementation of Security Council Resolution 435 of 29 September 1978 providing for independent elections in Namibia.[5]

Namibia and Angola share a long border, of more than 1200 kilometers, which is very difficult to properly control. Furthermore, the ethnic bondage, traditions and customs of the various ethnic groups which straddle the border, though legally divided by the colonial borders, have never been broken or extinguished by such borders. Movements of persons and goods, including animals, across the border are considered as normal. It is, indeed, difficult to prevent cross-border movements when uncles and aunts are separated by the border from nephews and nieces; and when cross-border marriages are normal and common.

However, it should be emphasised that these traditional cross-border movements between Angola and Namibia are not likely to violate Security Council sanctions against UNITA, for what is transported is for domestic use or for the performance of ethnic rituals.

(2) Sanctions against UNITA

As stated above, the conflict in Angola was a resource-based, intra-state conflict. Sanctions were thus imposed against a non-state entity, namely UNITA, with frequently shifting territorial control and thus not easily discernible. The enforcement of sanctions measures against UNITA was thus only applicable to individuals, either in the enforcing country or from the targeted entity.

The first decision on sanctions against UNITA was taken by the Security Council on 15 September 1993 – Resolution 864 (1993). The Security Council determined that the refusal of UNITA to comply with its obligations under the "Accord de Paz" and its rejection of the results of the United Nations supervised September 1992 election constituted a threat to international peace and security in the region and, therefore, under Chapter VII of the Charter of the United Nations adopted the said resolution.

Resolution 864 (1993) states:

> "19. *Decides further*, with a view to prohibiting all sale or supply to the National Union of arms and related *matériel* and military assistance, as well as petroleum and petroleum products, that all States shall prevent the sale or supply, by their nationals or from their territories or using their flag vessels or aircraft, of arms and related *matériel* of all types, including weapons and ammunitions, military vehicles and equipment for the aforementioned, as well as of petroleum and petroleum products, whether or not originating in their territory, to the territory of Angola other than through named points of entry on a list to be supplied by the Government of Angola to the Secretary-General ...".

---

5 See Security Council Resolution 435 (1978) of 29 September 1978.

The said Resolution further called upon all States to strictly comply with the terms of the said Resolution.

It is interesting to note that although the sanctions measures were directed against UNITA, no dialogue with UNITA was anticipated. All that was expected of UNITA was compliance. There are a number of factors that could have inhibited the United Nations from entering into negotiations with UNITA. In the first place, intra-state violent conflicts are relatively new phenomena to face the United Nations. Ordinarily, groups which take up arms to challenge the central authority are dealt with according to domestic criminal law, because such groups are nothing but rebels. Secondly, the United Nations was established on the premise that States are the primary actors on the international plane.

Yet in a situation of wide-scale and prolonged revolt against the central authority, such as was the case in Angola, the United Nations cannot do otherwise but get involved. Such intra-state violent conflicts cause massive violations of human rights of the civilian population, resulting in huge civilian casualties, total disruption of normal civilian activities, leading to a considerable internal displacement of persons and producing a massive influx of refugees into the neighbouring countries. In such situations, the magnitude of suffering of the civilian population threatens regional international peace and security, and thus necessitates the intervention of the Security Council of the United Nations. Intra-state conflicts have produced a curious phenomenon: not only could the magnitude of the violence be a threat to international peace and security, but the actor, the non-state entity, is not a player on the international plane. As stated above, although the first resolution on sanctions against UNITA did not provide for a dialogue with UNITA, it did, on the other hand, contain an in-built mechanism to trigger off an escalation of sanctions. And these sanctions were extended to include "motorised vehicles or water craft of spare parts for such vehicles or ground or water borne transportation services".[6]

With the refusal of UNITA to comply with its obligations, and its intensification of the war, the Security Council increased the sanctions measures. The second decision on sanctions against UNITA, adopted four years later, targeted the movements of the leadership of UNITA. Sanctions which target the individuals who are carrying out the conflict, sometimes referred to as "smart sanctions", are designed not to hurt ordinary innocent people. Indeed, sanctions targeting only the leadership could be the most effective measures in intra-state conflicts.

All countries were obliged not to allow leaders of UNITA to enter their territory. Since UNITA had no legal authority in Angola, it had to carry out its activities mostly outside Angola. Therefore, the restriction of the movements of the leaders of UNITA was an important tool to curb its capacity to prosecute the war and, as the territory under its control shrank, these sanctions measures became very effective.

Resolution 1127 (1997) of 28 August 1997 states:

> "4 *Decides* that all States shall take the necessary measures:
> (a) To prevent the entry into or transit through their territories of all senior officials of UNITA and of adult members of their immediate families, ... provided that noth-

6 Security Council Resolution 1173 (1998) of 12 June 1998.

ing in this paragraph shall oblige a State to refuse entry into its territory to its own nationals;
(b) To suspend or cancel all travel documents, visas or resident permits issued to senior UNITA officials and adult members of their immediate families ...;
(c) To require the immediate and complete closure of all UNITA offices in their territories;"

The neighbouring countries, in particular Namibia and Zambia, which received a great influx of refugees from Angola had problems in sorting out the genuine refugees from senior UNITA officials.

The final, and probably the highest in intensity, sanctions measures were imposed by the Council the following year, 1998. This time the Council ultimately touched on the cause of the whole conflict, that is, as stated above, control of natural resources – diamonds. Sanctions dealing with diamonds proved not only the most important, but equally the most complicated to enforce. This will be analysed in detail shortly.

Resolution 1173 (1998) of 12 June 1998, states:

"11 *Decides* that all States, except Angola, in which there are funds and financial resources, including any funds derived or generated from property of UNITA as an organisation or of senior officials of UNITA or adult members of their immediate families ... shall require all persons and entities within their own territories holding such funds and financial resources to freeze them and ensure that they are not available directly or indirectly to or for the benefit of UNITA as an organisation or of senior officials of UNITA or adult members of their immediate families ...
12 *Decides also* that all States shall take the necessary measures:
(a) To prevent all official contacts with the UNITA leadership in areas of Angola to which State administration has not been extended ...;
(b) To prohibit the direct or indirect import from Angola to their territory of all diamonds that are not controlled through the Certificate of Origin regime of the GURN;
(c) To prohibit ... the sale or supply to persons or entities in areas of Angola to which State administration has not been extended, by their nationals or from their territory, or using their flag vessels or aircraft, of equipment used in mining or mining services;"

These sanctions measures against UNITA, covering arms, fuel, travel, diplomatic representation, diamonds and finances, were aimed at curtailing the capacity of UNITA to pursue the war; indeed, these are the life-blood of rebel movements. In this respect, effective and forceful enforcement of such sanctions measures would bring internal violent conflict swiftly to an end.

(3) Enforcement of the Decisions on Sanctions of the Security Council

It should be stated at the outset that this section will be confined only to the enforcement of Security Council resolutions on sanctions against UNITA and mostly only by the countries of SADC. Furthermore, it will not consider in detail the legality[7] of Security Council sanctions measures under the law of the Charter of the United Nations as such. It will be noted in passing that since the end of the Cold War the Security Council has been accused of being hasty in taking decisions under Chapter VII of the Charter.[8]

However, it is worth noting that the International Court of Justice in 1971 in its Advisory Opinion concerning *Legal Consequences for States of the Continued Presence of South Africa in Namibia (South West Africa) notwithstanding Security Council Resolution 276 (1970)* stated:

> "Undoubtedly, the court does not possess powers of judicial review or appeal in respect of the decisions taken by the United Nations organisations concerned."[9]

On the other hand, it cannot be doubted that dubiously founded decisions of sanctions could be challenged.[10] But to consider this in depth would be an unwarranted digression at this juncture.

As members of the United Nations, all the SADC Member States are thus, in accordance with Articles 25 and 103 of the Charter of the United Nations, under the obligation to enforce resolutions of the Security Council on sanctions taken under Chapter VII.

The Charter Law, since decisions on sanctions are taken under Chapter VII, leaves the Member States of the United Nations with no option but to enforce them. As has been stated, the failure of UNITA to enter into a cease-fire agreement with the Government in accordance with "Accordos de Paz", its rejection of the 1992 election results, as well as the subsequent non-compliance with the Lusaka Protocol of 1994[11] were all factors considered to create a situation constituting a threat to international peace and security in the region. UNITA, as a non-state entity and in fact a rebel movement, had no international obligations pertaining to international peace and security except those its leadership had entered into with the Government. The legitimacy of the central Government on which it could have based its non-compliance had been confirmed. In the 30 September 1992 United Nations supervised elections, UNITA was defeated; President dos Santos won 49.6 percent of the vote to Savimbi's 40.7 percent, while MPLA won 54 percent of the vote for the legislature and UNITA got 34 percent.[12]

---

7 See generally Vera Gowlland-Debbas (ed.), *United Nations Sanctions and International Law* (The Hague, Kluwer Law International, 2001).

8 See generally, Nicolas Angelet "International Law Limits to the Security Council", in *United Nations Sanctions and International Law, op. cit.*, pp. 71-82.

9 ICJ Reports 1971, p. 45. For a detailed consideration of this and other opinions relating to Namibia see generally, Tunguru Huaraka, *Namibia by Resolutions: A Legal Analysis of International Organisations' Attempts at Decolonization* (Unpublished Doctoral Thesis, Graduate Institute of International Studies, University of Geneva), 1979.

10 See *Case Concerning the Question of Interpretation and Application of the 1971 Montreal Convention Arising from the Aerial Incident at Lockerbie (Libya v United Kingdom)*, ICJ Reports 1992, p. 3.

11 20 November 1994, S/2000/203, para. 3.

12 *Ibid.*

It could be stated in passing that diplomats accredited to the United Nations take discussion in the Security Council very seriously, particularly when Chapter VII of the Charter is invoked. In the situation like that which prevailed in Angola, which countries of the region considered as a threat to regional security, participation was often elevated to the ministerial levels, and in most cases the decisions of the Council were crafted by the regional caucus. In this respect, the Security Council decision on sanctions will not only have the legal force of being mandatory, but will equally have regional acceptance.[13]

Those are some of the realities in light of which the enforcement of sanctions against UNITA should be viewed – this could be termed the "institutional authority".

a. Domestic Law

The emphasis here will be on the domestic laws of Namibia. But it could be generally stated that SADC countries have not indicated any legal impediment to enforcing resolutions on sanctions against UNITA. In fact, the contrary could be assumed from their decisions in SADC. Furthermore, the countries of SADC, through the Protocol on Legal Affairs, are in the process of harmonizing their legal systems. The SADC Protocol on Legal Affairs has established the Legal Sector which is charged to:

- "facilitate the adoption of appropriate schemes of co-operation in criminal and civil matters;
- promote the adoption of mutual assistance agreements and arrangements in criminal and civil matters;
- develop, as far as possible, common strategies and standards dealing with the administration of justice and law enforcement."[14]

Once this Protocol becomes fully operational it will be easy for one SADC country to obtain legal assistance from or to have its judicial decisions executed in another SADC country.

Namibia, being the only monist State in the region, is in rather a unique position. International treaties which Namibia enters into are self-executing. The Constitution of the Republic of Namibia is very explicit, it has provided in Article 144 as follows:

> "Unless otherwise provided by this Constitution or Act of Parliament, *the general rules of public international law*[15] and international agreements binding upon Namibia under this Constitution shall form part of the law of Namibia."

---

13 See generally James P. Muldoon Jr., John Fagot Aviel, Reichard Reitano and Earl Sullivan (eds.), *Multilateral Diplomacy and the United Nations Today* (Boulder, Colorado, Westview Press, 1999).

14 Protocol on Legal Affairs, Article 2(d), (e) and (g), signed and opened for ratification and accession, at Windhoek on 7 August 2000.

15 Emphasis added. It will be observed that since the Namibian people were subjected under the obnoxious apartheid administration of racist South Africa to a policy which attempted to separate races on the false basis of superiority of race, the Constitution of Namibia is a

In this respect, the Constitution of the Republic of Namibia consecrates the primacy of not only international treaties, which include the Charter of the United Nations, but equally principles of international law over domestic law. In this regard, the Namibian Constitution is much more advanced than most constitutions in Africa. The above-quoted provision is buttressed by the principles of State, also found in the Constitution, which by Article 96 states:

> "The state shall endeavour to ensure that in its international relations it:
> ...
> (b) promotes international co-operation, peace and security;
> ...
> (d) fosters respect for international law and treaty obligations;"

Obviously, these are principles of State policy which have great persuasive force upon the courts of the country.

The impact of treaty obligations upon domestic law as provided for in Article 144 of the Constitution was recently considered by the Supreme Court of Namibia. In a matter not related to enforcement of sanctions against UNITA, but a matter dealing with the rights of an accused person to be provided with legal aid by the State,[16] the Supreme Court had an opportunity to interpret Article 144 of the Constitution.

The point at issue was the granting of legal aid to an indigent accused person.

Article 95 of the Constitution provides:

> "The State shall actively promote and maintain the welfare of the people by adopting, *inter alia*, policies aimed at the following:
> (h) a legal system seeking to promote justice on the basis of equal opportunity by providing free legal aid in defined cases with due regard to the resources of the State;"

The enabling legislation left the determination of the "defined cases" to the courts. If the "Court is of the opinion that there is sufficient reason why the accused should be granted legal aid, the Court may issue a legal aid certificate"[17] and the Director of Legal Aid was obliged to grant legal aid to any person to whom a legal aid certificate has been issued by the Court.[18]

An amendment of the Legal Aid Act, 1990, removed the power of courts to issue legal aid certificates and correspondingly the obligation of the Director of Legal Aid to

---

national statement that no Namibian will ever again be denied fundamental human rights and freedoms. In the entrenched provisions of "fundamental human rights and freedoms" the Constitution often uses the phrase "as is necessary in a democratic society" which means that those clauses will be broadly interpreted.

16 *The Government of the Republic of Namibia and Others v Geofrey Kupuzo Mwilima and Other 128 Respondents*, Case No: SA 29/2001, Unreported, Heard on 25-28 March 2002.

17 Legal Aid Act, 1990, Act No. 29 of 1990, Section 8 (2).

18 *Ibid.*, Section 10 (1) (a).

grant legal aid was equally expunged.[19]

The point in dispute was whether the amendments, referred to above, had diminished the right of the indigent accused persons. After quoting Article 14 (3) (d) of the International Covenant on Civil and Political Rights, 1966, which Namibia had acceded to on 28 November 1994, the Supreme Court held that the provisions of the Covenant being part of the law of Namibia must be given effect. The Supreme Court stated in this regard, "Although no law is permitted to limit the rights set out under Chapter 3 of the Constitution , except as is provided for under the Chapter itself, the interest of justice lies at the root of fair trial and the provisions of the *Covenant* is therefore clearly compatible with the tenets of a fair trial."[20] The Supreme Court then pertinently stated:

> "the State not only has an obligation to foster respect for international law and treaties as laid down by Article 96 (d) of the Constitution but it is also clear that the International Covenant on Civil and Political Rights is binding upon the State and forms part of the law of Namibia by virtue of Article 144 of the Constitution.[21]

Following this historic ruling of the Supreme Court, it is now a settled law that the courts of Namibia will apply applicable provisions from any treaty to which Namibia is a party. This undoubtedly will include the Charter of the United Nations. Consequently, decisions of the Security Council on sanctions taken under Chapter VII will be fully enforced by the Namibian courts.

Unfortunately, in a recent case which involved the detention of an Angolan national, who was said to be a UNITA official, the obligation of Namibia to enforce Security Council sanctions against UNITA was not argued. In the appeal by the Government to the Supreme Court, in *The Government of the Republic of Namibia v Ngeve Raphael Sikunda*,[22] Sikunda, an alleged senior UNITA official and with a permanent resident permit in Namibia, having lived in the country since 1986, was detained on 17 October 2000 for deportation on the grounds that his presence in Namibia was considered a security threat.

Now, any non-national found in Namibia could be removed from the country only on the recommendation of the Security Commission established by Article 114 of the Constitution and consisting of: the Chairperson of the Public Service Commission, the Chief of the Defence Force, the Inspector General of Police, the Commissioner of Prisons and two members of the National Assembly (Parliament). The Minister of Home Affairs sought the recommendation[23] of the Security Commission to detain and deport

19 Legal Aid Amendment Act, 2000, Act No. 17, 2000, Section 4 and 5.

20 *Ibid.*, p. 40.

21 *Ibid.*

22 Case No: SA/5/2001, Unreported, Judgement Delivered on 21 February 2002.

23 The Immigration Control Act of 1993, Act No. 7 of 1993, by Section 49 (1) provides: "Notwithstanding anything to the contrary in this Act or any other law, the Minister may, on the recommendation of the Security Commission established under Article 114 of the Namibian Constitution, forthwith remove or cause to be removed from Namibia by warrant issued under his or her hand any person who enters or has entered or is found in Namibia and whose

Sikunda. The reason given, *inter alia*, was security threat and the Minister also stated in his letter that "Furthermore, Namibia being a member State of the UN Security Council and committed to making sure that the UN Security Council resolutions 1127 (1997) and 1135 (1997) imposing sanctions on UNITA are observed, should not be seen to be accommodating elements who are furthering the cause of UNITA ... in violation of UN Security Council resolutions ..."[24]

The Minister of Home Affairs, speaking in the National Assembly (Parliament), stated that "Namibia is implementing Resolution 1173 of 1998 and Resolution 1127 of 1997. We are implementing that and we are obliged."[25] He further stated that 82 activists of UNITA whose names had been provided by the Panel of Experts as operating in Namibia had been arrested.

The Security Commission responded accordingly and endorsed the request of the Minister, but when the Security Commission took its decision the two members of the National Assembly had not yet been appointed and secondly Sikunda was not given an opportunity to appear before the Commission. The Supreme Court found that both administrative law, whether the Commission was properly constituted, and, on the principle of natural justice, "*audi alteram*", the recommendation of the Security Commission was flawed and therefore invalid. On these grounds the Supreme Court ordered Sikunda to be released and not to be deported.

It is very likely that even if the question of the enforcement of sanctions against UNITA was advanced as the sole grounds for the detention and deportation of Sikunda, the same defects would have proved fatal. For the enforcement of Security Council sanctions must be carried out according to the laws of the country concerned.

However, it was important to demonstrate by the Mwilima's case, discussed above, that in Namibia, as a monist state, decisions on sanctions of the Security Council will be enforced by the Namibian courts without the necessity of enacting an enabling law.

Equally, it is illustrative to note that none of the other countries of SADC have found it necessary to enact special laws to make Security Council sanctions against UNITA enforceable in their respective domestic jurisdiction.[26] It is thus reasonable to assume that the domestic courts of these countries of SADC, if called upon, would have enforced Security Council sanctions against UNITA. In any case, the evasion of the sanctions dealing with arms and related *matériel* and diamonds will fall under the crimi-

activities endanger or are calculated to endanger the security of the State, whether or not such person is a prohibited immigrant in respect of Namibia."

24 *The Government of the Republic of Namibia vs Ngeve Raphael Sikunda*, *loc. cit.*, p. 12. Further, according to the submission by the State, altogether about 80 foreign nationals were detained as soldiers of UNITA, *ibid.*, p. 14.

25 Republic of Namibia, Debates of National Assembly, 5 October 2000, p. 110. According to the local newspaper up until September 2002, these detained UNITA activists had remained in detention. *The Namibian*, Windhoek, 27 September 2002.

26 The Monitoring Mechanism on Sanctions against UNITA, for example, concluded: "Many countries had not passed national laws enacting the implementation of Security Council Resolution 1173 (1998). Several States claim that existing national laws are sufficient for this purpose". S/2001/363, para. 107(a).

nal law of smuggling prohibited goods.

The Security Council sanctions against UNITA, as the United Nations Panel of Experts on Violations of Security Council Sanctions against UNITA, as well as its successor, the Monitoring Mechanism on Sanctions against UNITA found, were made ineffective as a result of smuggling.[27] For instance, the Panel of Experts reported that "Credible and reliable reports were received of significant fuel smuggling across the Zambia border ... information has also been received on relatively small scale fuel sales across the Angola-Namibia border, but these appear to be primarily of a private nature."[28] In order to effectively enforce the sanctions against UNITA dealing with petroleum, the Panel of Experts recommended that SADC should take the lead in ensuring that proper monitory systems were put in place.[29] We will revert to this shortly.

Diamonds and arms, particularly the former, are the most smuggled commodities in the world. Namibia is a diamond producing country; in the SADC Region other diamond-producing countries are Botswana, the Democratic Republic of Congo, South Africa and of course Angola. In fact, the economy of the country depends heavily on diamond mining, and Namibia therefore has very stringent laws against diamond smuggling. Any dealings with unpolished diamonds, whether sale or disposal, receipt or purchase, export or import, are strictly prohibited.[30]

In view of the fact that the SADC Region was one of the battlegrounds of the Cold War, notably Angola and Mozambique, as well as being the only region, except Algeria, where bitter and protracted armed liberation wars were fought (in Angola, Mozambique, Namibia, South Africa and Zimbabwe), the Region is consequently saturated with all types of arms.

Namibia also has a stringent law dealing with arms, the Arms and Ammunition Act, 1996 (Act No. 7 of 1996), which stipulates, in Section 22 (1):

> "... No person shall, except on behalf of the State, import or export from Namibia any arms or ammunition, including any arms or ammunition in transit through Namibia to any place outside Namibia."

Namibia has thus sufficient laws to enforce the Security Council sanctions against UNITA. In Namibia, UNITA could only resort to criminal activities of smuggling.

In its response to the Report of the Panel of Experts on Violations of Security Council Sanctions against UNITA,[31] the Government of Namibia responded that its investigation revealed that some of those listed as UNITA officials were refugees at the Osire Refugee Camp. The Government of Namibia further reiterated its determination to fully implement the Security Council sanctions against UNITA.[32]

---

27 See S/2000/203, S/2000/1225, S/2001/363 and S/2001/966.

28 S/2000/203, para. 68.

29 *Ibid.,* para. 70.

30 Diamond Act, 1999 (Act No. 13 of 1999), Part IV.

31 S/2000/203.

32 Letter dated 27 July 2000 from the Permanent Representative of Namibia to the United

As stated above, during the liberation war of Namibia UNITA fought alongside the apartheid racist forces of South Africa against the People's Liberation Army of Namibia [PLAN], the armed wing of the SWAPO Party, now the ruling party in Namibia since independence. In this respect, it is inconceivable that the Government of the Republic of Namibia would have in any way assisted UNITA to circumvent the Security Council sanctions.

By the end of 1999, UNITA had suffered heavy military defeats at the hands of the Government forces and had lost its operational headquarters and much of the areas it had controlled,[33] and UNITA, by mid-2000, had disintegrated into small groups of bandits.[34] These bandits often crossed over into Namibia to attack villages and steal livestock and food. Obviously, the Namibian Defence Force had to pursue these bandits into Angola. The Monitoring Mechanism on Sanctions against UNITA on its visit to Namibia was informed that on one such cross-border aggressive pursuit operation, the Namibian Defence Force discovered petroleum dumps in Angola and 32 full 5,000 liter petroleum containers were unearthed.[35]

The Mechanism was also given an opportunity to view the military equipment captured by Namibian defence forces from UNITA.[36]

It is evident from the above that Namibia was determined to ensure enforcement of Security Council sanctions against UNITA. The country had the necessary laws in place to legally enforce these measures in its courts. If at all, what may have hampered effective enforcement of the sanctions against UNITA and which is not limited to Namibia alone, but applicable to the entire region, is the constraint of under-development, particularly of advanced devices to detect smuggling of prohibited items.

b. The role of the Southern African Development Community

The countries of SADC, among others, aim to evolve common political values, systems and institutions, promote and defend peace and security. Consequently, internal conflict in a Member State, as was the case in Angola, is the concern of all the Member States.

It will be noted that UNITA was a rebel movement waging war against a Member State of SADC. In that respect the Government of Angola had the institutional support of SADC. As an institution, SADC had the legal framework to urge its members to enforce Security Council resolutions on sanctions against UNITA. The founding Treaty has among its principles that of "solidarity, peace and security".[37] This general principle has been elaborated in the Protocol on Politics, Defence and Security Cooperation of 2001,[38]

Nations to the President of the Security Council, S/2000/752.

33 S/2001/966.

34 S/2000/1225, para. 15.

35 S/2001/363, para. 108.

36 *Ibid.*, para. 28.

37 Treaty of the Southern African Development Community, Article 4(b).

38 For SADC in general, see T. Huaraka, "The Southern African Development Community", in L. Boisson de Chazournes and V. Gowlland-Debbas (eds.), *The International Legal System in*

which established the Organ on Politics, Defence and Security Cooperation.

In the area of conflict prevention, management and resolution the Organ has, *inter alia*, the following obligation:"to ensure that the State Parties adhere to and enforce all sanctions and arms embargoes imposed on any party by the United Nations Security Council."[39]

In this respect, at one of its meeting held in Luanda, Angola, from 17-18 December 2001, the Member States agreed to never allow their countries to be used for activities meant to violate the sanctions imposed by the Security Council of the UN against UNITA.[40]

As early as 1998 at the SADC Summit of Heads of State or Government held at Grand Baie, Mauritius, from 13-14 September, SADC stated, *inter alia:*

> "The Summit urged Member States to ensure tight regulations and improved control of airports and airspace to ensure effective implementation of the UN sanctions against UNITA."[41]

SADC, as a regional organisation, thus supported fully the Security Council's sanctions against UNITA. For SADC, sanctions against UNITA, a rebel movement, are intended to bring peace, security and stability to one of its Member, and consequently to the Region as a whole.

The Panel of Experts recognised the important role SADC could play to ensure that sanctions against UNITA were effectively implemented. To this end, the Panel of Experts recommended that SADC should set up mechanisms to ensure that in the Region sanctions against UNITA were not evaded.[42] Subsequently, the Security Council specifically requested SADC to consider implementing the recommendations of the Panel of Experts.[43] In response, SADC, at its 2001 Summit in Blantyre, Malawi, endorsed the establishment of the following measures:

(a) the installation of a Mobile Radar System in the SADC Region to detect illegal flights across SADC national borders;
(b) the mechanism for the international certification system for trade in rough diamonds; and
(c) the creation of a task force to compile data and to formulate a strategy to stop the supply of petroleum products to UNITA.[44]

Quest of Equity and Universality, Liber Amicorum Georges Abi-Saab (The Hague, Kluwer Law International, 2001), pp. 797-806.

39 Article 11 (1) (d) of the Protocol on Politics, Defence and Security Cooperation. It could not be established whether the adoption of the Protocol was prompted by the failure of some of the countries of SADC to implement the sanctions against UNITA.

40 See *The Namibian*, Windhoek, Thursday, 20 December 2001.

41 S/1999/915.

42 S/2000/203, in particular paras. 70, 71 and 170.

43 Security Council Resolution 1295 (2000) of 18 April 2000.

44 2001 SADC Summit Final Communiqué, Blantyre, Malawi, 12-14 August 2001.

At the same time, the Summit directed the intersectoral committees of SADC, namely those of transport, energy and mining, to conduct studies and make recommendations on how Security Council Resolution 1295 (2000) could be implemented. Further, the Summit approved, in principle, the concept of establishing a SADC Upper Airspace Control Centre as an initial step in the integration of the air traffic services of Member States.

Also at the 2001 Summit the Protocol on the Control of Firearms, Ammunition and Other Related Material was signed and opened for ratification and accession. The stated objectives of the Protocol, among others, are to:

> "co-operate closely at the regional level as well as at international fora to effectively prevent, combat, and eradicate the illicit manufacturing of, excessive and destabilising use and accumulation of, trafficking in, possession and use of, firearms, ammunition and other related materials in collaboration with international partners."[45]

As stated above, this Protocol was necessitated by the commitment of the countries of SADC to rid the Region of illegal firearms, which are often used by criminals. But the provisions of this Protocol could help the implementation of the Security Council sanctions prohibiting the supply of arms and related materials to UNITA, for the Protocol urges the State Parties to establish and improve national databases and to acquire equipment for monitoring and controlling the movement of firearms across borders. This is what the Panel of Experts on Violations of Security Council Sanctions against UNITA had identified as important tools for effective implementation of sanctions against UNITA related to firearms.[46]

Although this Protocol has not yet entered into force, nevertheless the legal regime it intends to create in the SADC Region could already be adhered to.

SADC is fast evolving as a regional organisation capable of maintaining peace and security. The newly established Organ on Politics, Defence and Security has the necessary legal force to intervene in intra-state conflicts which threaten regional peace, security and stability. However, as demonstrated above, the efforts of countries of SADC to implement the Security Council sanctions against UNITA were, in some instances, hampered by the constraint of under-developed infrastructures. But even then, the measures taken by the various countries of SADC did have an impact on the capability of UNITA to prosecute the war. SADC made tremendous efforts to make sanctions against UNITA effective; it was, after all, in the interest of SADC to maintain peace and security in the Region.

(4) Sanctions Busting: UNITA

Since the end of the Cold War and the subsequent disintegration of the Soviet Union and the eastern block, resulting further in the collapse of the state export control system,

45 Article 3(c).

46 S/2000/203.

unlimited supplies of arms became easily and cheaply available practically to anyone with the means to purchase them. The Panel of Experts on Violations of Security Council Sanctions against UNITA discovered that "as a result of the end of the Cold War and the dissolution of the Warsaw Pact international arms markets were being filled with surplus weaponry, much of it of Eastern Europe origin offered at below market prices."[47] The Panel of Experts concluded that "the desire of a number of former Warsaw Pact countries to join NATO may have resulted in those countries selling off non-NATO standard equipment at a discount – with much of this equipment going to Africa."[48]

The international syndicates, in some cases criminal, such as arms dealers, drug traffickers, diamonds dealers and money launderers hover over resource-based intra-state conflict areas like vultures. As the busting of the Security Council sanctions against UNITA has shown, these syndicates are very powerful with elaborate international networks and are the ones who fuel resource-based intra-state conflicts. Most of the time these international syndicates operate just on the verge of the law. Equally, in some cases, particularly in arms sales, even the host Government, being eager to get rid of its huge surplus of arms, would turn a blind eye to irregularities.

When UNITA restarted the war in 1998 after the collapse of the Lusaka Protocol of 1994, it became evident that UNITA had used the period from 1996 of positive political development to undertake a major rearmament exercise. It was also revealed that significant UNITA combatants had been kept in hiding in preparation for a major offensive. UNITA's rearmament was facilitated by the fact that the movement was controlling big towns with reasonably well-functioning infrastructures, such as Andulo and Bailundo, and extensive territory in the highland as well as areas of diamond mines in Cuango, Kwanza, Milange and Mavinga.[49] UNITA thus had sufficient resources to finance its acquisition of arms, fuel and supplies. It is worth noting that Angola is one of the largest diamond resources in Africa[50] and at the time UNITA was controlling a significant part of the production. The international syndicates were thus eager to supply any commodity UNITA demanded.

It will be expected that these international syndicates, which most of the time operate on the fringes of domestic legality, will hardly be deterred by the decisions of the Security Council. The scene was thus set for sanctions busting!

The ineffectiveness of the Security Council sanctions against UNITA up until early 2000 was, therefore, basically due to two factors. In the first place, UNITA's control of some of the most lucrative diamond mines in Angola assured it huge sources of finance; secondly, the insatiable demand of the rich for diamonds made smuggling of diamonds, particularly across such long poorly controlled borders, inevitable.

The Security Council was faced with the problem of trying to determine how UNITA was able to evade the sanctions and rearm so massively, even with tanks and ground-to-air missiles. In this respect, the Security Council, by Resolution 1237 (1999)

47 S/2000/203, para. 39.

48 *Ibid.*

49 S/2000/1225, paras. 8-19.

50 *Ibid.*, para. 145.

of 7 May 1999, established the Panel of Experts on Violations of Security Council Sanctions against UNITA. The Panel of Experts was requested to investigate the violations of the sanctions and to inform the Security Council on

(a) how the sanctions against UNITA were being violated,
(b) who was violating them, and
(c) what could be done to make sanctions more effective.[51]

The Panel of Experts' report,[52] which was released on 10 March 2000, was anything but diplomatic, as was the expected norm of United Nations reports. It adopted a new "name and shame" approach by which it named the countries and even heads of state which were involved in violations of Security Council sanctions against UNITA. It was described as "a bombshell" that "shattered the United Nations' normal diplomatic niceties."[53] The Panel of Experts found the major suppliers of arms and related materials were mainly Ukraine and Bulgaria. The Panel further established that the Democratic Republic of Congo, then Zaire under the late President Mobutu, was the main transit point. After the change of Government in the DRC, Burkina Faso and Togo became the main transit points.[54]

The Monitoring Mechanism on Angola Sanctions established by Security Council Resolution 1295 (2000) of 18 April 2000 to replace the Panel of Experts, noted that the traditional allies of UNITA and arms suppliers had become more hesitant as a result of publicity and the "name and shame" approach. This is an indication that the use by the Security Council of independent investigators and the public exposure of the violators, bore some positive results. The Mechanism, however, confirmed the findings of the Panel of Experts to the effect that Burkina Faso and Togo had become the major transit points for arms as well as other commodities, such as fuel, after the fall of Mobutu in Zaire. It will be recalled that the countries mentioned by the Panel of Experts as having violated the Security Council sanctions against UNITA protested that these findings were not corraborated. As a result, the Security Council retained its diplomatic niceties and welcomed "the decisions of several of the States referred to in the report of the Panel of Experts to establish interdepartmental commissions and other mechanisms to investigate the allegations contained in the report."[55] However, the Mechanism on the contrary confirmed that Lome in Togo was turned into an external headquarters of UNITA; apparently senior officials of UNITA and their families found safe haven in Togo. The Mechanism also discovered that the Togolese authorities issued the UNITA representative with a genuine end-user certificate.[56] The Mechanism stated: "It is therefore reason-

51 S/200/203, para. 2.

52 S/2000/203.

53 David Cortright and George A. Lopez (eds.) with Linda Gerber, *Sanctions and the Search for Security (Challenges to UN Action)*, International Peace Academy (Boulder/London, Lynne Rienner Publishers, 2002), p. 66.

54 S/2000/203, paras. 20-43.

55 Security Council Resolution 1295 (2000), para. 7.

56 S/2000/1225, para. 56.

able to conclude that all events described concerning Togo could not have taken place without the consent or complicity of the authorities in the country".[57] This was irrefutable evidence of a Member State violating Security Council sanctions resolutions.

Furthermore, the Mechanism in their Supplement Report released on 12 October 2001, more than a year since the Panel's report which named countries, not only confirmed the findings of the Panel, but established that Burkina Faso had become the most important base for UNITA Senior Officials. It seems that those expelled from Togo went to Burkina Faso.[58]

With regard to Security Council Resolution 864 (1993) which prohibited all sale or supply of arms to UNITA, the Panel of Experts had found that the major suppliers were mainly Ukraine and Bulgaria, and that after the change of government in Zaire, now the Democratic Republic of Congo, Burkina Faso and Togo had became the main transit points.[59]

The Panel of Experts also found out that these countries supplied UNITA officials with end-user certificates.[60] However, Burkina Faso denied having ever issued end-user certificates and claimed that they were forged. But the Mechanism contacted forensic study of end-user certificates and established that "the end-user certificates featuring Burkina Faso as the country of origin were authentic."[61]

One thing the Panel and the Mechanism both discovered is that international arms dealers transactions were worldwide. In brokering of arms transactions, off-shore companies, scattered all over the globe, from Gibraltar to Panama and to the Bahamas were involved.[62]

The leaders of the countries mentioned as having violated sanctions against arms and petroleum were allegedly paid by UNITA in diamonds. The President of Burkina Faso, Blaise Compaore[63] and of Togo, Eyadema, were specifically mentioned in this regard. The latter was apparently given "a 'passport sized' packet of diamonds when Eyadema agreed to allow Savimbi's children to come to Togo and be educated there."[64]

The Mechanism in its Supplement Report, the last available report of the investigation, concluded that the sanctions dealing with diamonds continued to be violated.[65] The Mechanism stated that "given the very large size of this trade, which of necessity involves many players in as many countries, it is not possible"[66] to monitor and evaluate every sector of the trade.

57 *Ibid.*

58 S/2001/966, paras. 46-49.

59 S/2000/203, para. 39-43.

60 *Ibid.,* para. 51.

61 S/2000/1225, para. 49(d).

62 S/2001/363, para. 12.

63 S/2000/203, para. 103.

64 *Ibid.,* para. 102.

65 S/2000/966, para. 141.

66 *Ibid.,* para. 142.

The Panel of Experts had observed that the ease with which UNITA diamonds could be sold to diamond traders and polishers in Antwerp (Belgium) made sanctions against diamonds difficult to control; and remarked that "the extremely lax control and regulations governing the Antwerp market facilitate and perhaps even encourage illegal trading activity."[67]

The Panel of Experts had found that the Belgian authorities had failed to establish an effective import identification regime with respect to diamonds.[68] As soon as the content of the report became known, even before it was officially released, some countries took measures to rectify the defects reported. The Belgian Government, for instance, announced on 3 March 2000 the establishment of an inter-ministerial task force to curb sanctions violations.[69]

The Mechanism, however, observed that the United Nations sanctions against UNITA have provided the impetus for worldwide controls on diamonds – the certificate of origin scheme.[70] This is an indication that the use of independent investigators did affect the enforcement by Member States of Security Council sanctions. The Mechanism in this regard also found: "Another positive development in West Africa is the decision of the current Government of Côte d'Ivoire to cancel the passports issued to UNITA officials and family members."[71] This was a direct result of the Security Council sanctions against UNITA.

(5) Conclusion

The establishment of the Panel of Experts on Violations of Security Council Sanctions against UNITA in May 1999[72] and its successor, the Monitoring Mechanism on Angola Sanctions,[73] were novel procedures in the monitoring process of implementation of sanctions resolutions. Judging, in particular, by the ground-breaking report[74] of the Panel of Experts which was unprecedentedly very candid and direct, naming names to shame, it appears that the use of independent experts had made a substantial difference in the implementation of sanctions.

The main recommendations of the Panel of Experts were far-reaching and unconventional. The Panel recommended, among other things, that the Security Council:

(a) "apply appropriate sanctions against Governments found to have been intentionally breaking the sanctions";
(b) "formally declar(e) the offending countries to be sanctions breakers";

67 S/2000/203, para. 87.

68 *Ibid.,* paras. 89-90.

69 Security Council Resolution 1295 (2000), para. 17.

70 S/2001/363, para. 107(e).

71 S/2001/966, para. 51.

72 Security Council Resolution 1237 (1999) of 7 May 1999.

73 Security Council Resolution 1295 (2000) of 18 April 2000.

74 S/2000/203, issued on 10 March 2000.

(c) "discourag(e) Member States from supporting the candidacies of nationals from listed countries for senior positions within the United Nations system until the listed countries are declared to be complying with the sanctions";
(d) impose "a ban on the holding of United Nations conferences or meetings in the listed countries";
(e) "discouraging other international organisations from holding conferences or meetings in the listed countries, or electing the country concerned as Chairman in office of an organisations"; and
(f) "compile and distribute a 'Blacklist' or 'Watchlist' of individuals and commercial entities involved in UNITA sanctions busting."[75]

The Security Council considered the report of the Panel of Experts containing these recommendations and decided to establish another body, the Monitoring Mechanism on Angola Sanctions, "to collect additional relevant leads relating to any allegations of violations ... including any relevant leads indicated by the Panel of Experts."[76]

The Council did not in any way refer specifically to the recommendations by the Panel of Experts. The main recommendations of the Panel of Experts, listed above, as stated were far-reaching and unconventional. Some of the recommendations would probably pose legal and institutional problems for the United Nations. Of course, the Security Council under Article 41 of the Charter could employ any measures to ensure that sanctions are effectively implemented; the Panel of Experts and the Mechanism were in fact such measures. But it would be a different issue for the Security Council, as recommended by the Panel of Experts, to impose sanctions, apparently mandatory, on "sanctions breakers". The legal hurdle to be overcome is the determination that "sanctions breakers" constitute a threat to international peace and security. That appears to be indeed a tenuous link.

The other recommendations could be implemented without stretching the provisions of the Charter to breaking point. The General Assembly could recommend that the Member States do not support the candidacies of countries declared "sanctions breakers" by the Security Council. It is possible that Article 5 of the Charter could be the route to follow in this regard. But to overcome the usual horse-trading that determines the outcome of elections in the General Assembly, the decision of the Security Council declaring a country a "sanctions breaker" must have some force.

In view of the decisive role international companies and syndicates play in fuelling and sustaining resource-based intra-state conflicts the recommendation of the Panel of Experts for the Security Council to compile and distribute a "blacklist" of such companies and even individuals should be seriously considered. As the Panel of Experts has found, such companies and individuals at times operate outside the law.

In the light of the involvement of powerful non-state entities in resource-based intra-state conflicts, the Security Council should develop new strategies to deal with such new complex phenomena. The threat to international peace and security is no longer premised only on territorial integrity, but, especially in intra-state conflicts, the deterioration of the humanitarian requirements of the population is in most cases the decisive factor

75 *Ibid.*, paras. 178-179.

76 Security Council Resolution 1295 (2000), para. 3.

for the intervention of the Security Council. In this respect sanctions as instruments for maintenance of peace and security must be revisited.

It could be observed that the Charter of the United Nations is a product of the Second World War, the most brutal and devastating armed conflict of the last century. This experience placed the defence of the notion of "international peace and security", which the international community was determined to maintain, on the use of military force. But with a precaution, through the use of the veto, that there will not be a military conflict between or among the five powerful States.

On the other hand, the international community of the 21st century, of the global village and globalization, political transparency and governance, would place the maintenance of international peace and security not only on the use of military force but also on the desire for international acceptance and assistance. The policy of "name and shame" used by the Panel of Experts could thus become an effective tool for the maintenance of international peace and security. No state in the "global village" could damn the international community and go it alone.

Although the recommendations of the Panel of Experts as well as those of the Mechanism have not been implemented, the device to use independent experts to assist the sanctions committees of the Security Council has had an impact. In this regard, the Mechanism concluded that "There is no doubt that the sanctions, together with the military operations carried out by the Angolan armed forces and the vigilance of the international community, are hurting UNITA's ability to wage war."[77] It is likely, as a result of the measures used in monitoring the Security Council sanctions against UNITA, that henceforth the implementation of sanctions will follow different patterns.

The conflict in Angola, to all intents and purposes, came to an end when Jonas Savimbi, the founder and the long-time leader of UNITA, was killed in battle on 22 February 2002. Subsequently, on 4 April 2002, the Government of Angola and *União Nacional para a Independência Total de Angola* (UNITA) signed the Memorandum of Understanding Addendum to the Lusaka Protocol for Cessation of Hostilities and the Resolution of the Outstanding Military Issues under the Lusaka Protocol (S/1994/1441, Annex). At long last, peace has been restored.

Nevertheless, the Security Council retained all the sanctions measures against UNITA and suspended only those on travel restrictions for 90 days, to allow UNITA officials to consult and thus to facilitate the peace process and national reconciliation in Angola.[78] However, on 9 December 2002, the Security Council, welcoming the progress on the peace process and the reintegration of UNITA forces in the national system lifted all the other sanctions against UNITA.[79]

❊ ❊ ❊

77 S/2000/1225, para. 250.

78 Security Council Resolution 1412 (2002) of 17 May 2002, suspension renewed by Security Council Resolution 1432 (2002) of 15 August 2002.

79 Security Council Resolution 1448 (2002) of 9 December 2002.

Select Bibliography

I. Case Law

(1) *South Africa*

De Lange v. Smuts and Others, 1998 6 BCLR 726 (W).

Larbi-Odam v. Member of the Executive Council for Education and Another, 1996 12 BCLR 1612.

Mohamed v. President of the Republic of South Africa, CCT 17/10, 28 May 2001.

National Director of Public Prosecutions v. Minister of Justice and Constitutional Development, CCT 13/02 of 12 June 2002.

President of the Republic of South Africa v. Hugo, 1997 6 BCLR 708 (CC).

S v. Makwanyane, 1995 3 SA 391 (CC).

S v. Coetzee, 1997 (1) SACR 379 (CC).

Scagell v. Attorney-General of West Cape 1996 (2) SACR 579 (CC).

(2) *Namibia*

The Government of the Republic of Namibia and Others v Geofrey Kupuzo Mwilima and Other 128 Respondents, Supreme Court, Case No: SA 29/2001, Unreported, Heard on 25-28 March 2002.

The Government of the Republic of Namibia v Ngeve Raphael Sikunda, Supreme Court, Case No: SA/5/2001, Unreported, Judgement Delivered on 21 February 2002.

II. United Nations Documents (chronological)

S/7720 of 6 February 1967.

S/7781, Annex 2 (17 February 1967).

S/7781, Annex 2 (21 February 1967).

S/7781/Add.2, Annex 6 (9 March 1967).

S/7781/Add. 3 (27 July 1967).

S/7781/Add. 4, Annex A (30 November 1967).

S/8786, Annex II (28 August 1968).

S/9853, Annex II, 48 (1 July 1970).

S/9853/Add. 1, Annex 1 (1 October 1970).

S/14179, 19 September 1980.

S/18705 (1987).

S/PV 2738 (1987).

S/1999/92 of 29 January 1999.

S/AC.31/1999/1 of 9 February 1999.

S/AC.31/1999/2 of 9 February 1999.

S/AC.31/1999/3 of 10 February 1999.

S/AC.31/1999/5 of 19 February 1999.

S/AC.31/1999/6 of 23 February 1999.

S/AC.31/1999/7 of 23 February 1999.

S/AC.31/1999/10 of 23 March 1999.

S/1999/644 of 4 June 1999.

S/2000/1255 of 29 December 2000.

S/2000/203 of 10 March 2000.

S/2000/752 of 27 July 2000.

S/2000/966 of 6 October 2000.

S/2000/1225 of 21 December 2000.

S/2001/363 of 18 April 2001.

S/2001/966 of 12 October 2001.

III. Books and Articles

Carpenter, G., "Prerogative Powers in South Africa – Dead and Gone at Last?", 22 *South African Yearbook of International Law* (1997).

Collier, P. & Hoeffler, A., "On the Incidence of Civil War in Africa", at www.worldbank.org (16 August 2000).

Collier, P. & Hoeffler, A., "Greed and Grievance in Civil War", at www.worldbank.org (4 January 2001).

Cortright, D. & Lopez, G.A., *The Sanction Decade: Assessing UN Strategies in the 1990's* (2000).

Cortright, D. & Lopez, G.A. (eds.), with Linda Gerber, *Sanctions and the Search for Security. Challenges to UN Action* (Boulder/London, Lynne Rienner Publishers, 2002).

Crocker, Chester A., *High Noon in Southern Africa. Making Peace in a Rough Neighborhood* (W. W. Norton and Co., 1992).

Dugard, J. "Sanctions against South Africa", in M. Orkin (ed.), *Sanctions Against Apartheid* (1989).

Dugard, J., *International Law: A South African Perspective* (2000).

Elbadawi, I. & Sambanis, N., "Why Are There So Many Civil Wars in Africa?", at ditto (2000).

Frost, M., "Preparing for Democracy in an Authoritarian State", in R.W. Johnson & L. Schlemmer (eds.), *Launching Democracy in South Africa* (1996).

Gowlland-Debbas, V., *Collective Responses to Illegal Acts in International Law: United Nations Actions to the Question of Rhodesia* (1990).

Hanlon, J., & Omond, R., *The Sanctions Handbook* (1987).

Hanlon, J., "Destabilisation, the SADCC States and Sanctions", in M. Orkin (ed.), *Sanctions Against Apartheid* (1989).

Hanlon, J., *South Africa: The Sanctions Report: Documents and Statistics* (1990).

Huaraka, Tunguru, "The Southern African Development Community", in L. Boisson de Chazournes and V. Gowlland-Debbas (eds.), *The International Legal System in Quest of Equity and Universality. Liber Amicorum Georges Abi-Saab* (The Hague, Kluwer Law International, 2001), pp. 797-806.

Koenderman, T., *Sanctions: The Threat to South Africa* (1982).

Lloyd, Brown-John C., *Multilateral Sanctions in International Law: A Comparative Analysis* (1975).

Manby, B., "Human Rights and South Africa's Foreign Policy: A Guiding Light or Flickering Candle?", 2 *South African Journal on Human Rights* (2000).

Mehlman, M.J., Milch, T.H. & Toumanoff, M.V., "United States Restrictions on Exports to South Africa", 73 *AJIL* (1979).

Muldoon Jr., James P.; Aviel, John Fagot; Reitano, Reichard and Sullivan, Earl (eds.), *Multilateral Diplomacy and the United Nations Today* (Boulder, Colorado, Westview Press, 1999).

Orkin, M. (ed.), *Sanctions Against Apartheid* (1989).

Reno, W., "Clandestine Economies, Violence and States in Africa", 2 *Journal of International Affairs* (2000).

Rotberg, R., "Mess, Mugabe's Mayhem", 79 *Foreign Affairs* (2000).

Tomasevski, K., *Responding to Human Rights Violations* (2000).

Zacklin, R., *The United Nations and Rhodesia: A Study in International Law* (1974).

Zack-Williams, A., "Sierra Leone: the Political Economy of Civil War 1991-1998", 20 *Third World Quarterly* (1999).

14

SWEDEN

*Ove Bring, Per Cramér and Göran Lysén**

I. The Constitutional and Dualistic Setting

The former Swedish Constitution of 1809 did not contain any specific regulation on the relationship between international obligations and national law, but the Instrument of Government (*Regeringsformen,* RF) did include a provision giving the King an exclusive treaty-making power (RF 12). In fact, this provision conveyed a message similar to the American Constitution that all treaties concluded under the authority of the executive power were "the supreme Law of the Land". This monistic perception was confirmed by the fact that all treaties were published in an official legislative collection, The Swedish Code of Statutes (*Svensk Författningssamling*, SFS), where they were included in order to be readily available for easy implementation. Treaties, laws, statutes and ordinances were published here on an equal footing, and in theory they were all directly applicable *vis-à-vis* the courts and administrative authorities. From an international law point of view, Sweden seemed to be a country of "constitutional monism".

This perception changed, however, from 1912 onwards, when a different constitutional practice was introduced. Treaties were now published separately in a new publication, *Sveriges överenskommelser med främmande makter*, SÖ (edited by the Ministry for Foreign Affairs) and treaties now lost their linkage to statutes and the system of direct applicability.

When Sweden joined the United Nations in 1946, this constitutional setting had produced a presumption that the country "had gone dualist" and was now relying on the Parliament (*Riksdag)* to transform international treaty obligations into national legislation. However, not everyone shared this new perception. A few Swedish lawyers continued to argue that Sweden was part of the monist tradition.

The Swedish membership of the United Nations (prepared by Government Bill 1946: 196) brought with it the well-known obligations of the United Nations Charter. Under Article 25 Member States agree "to accept and carry out the decisions of the Security Council". Under Article 48(2) the decisions of the Security Council for the maintenance of international peace and security (Chapter VII decisions) "shall be carried out by the

* Professors of Law at the Universities of Stockholm, Göteborg and Upsala, respectively.

Vera Gowlland-Debbas (ed.), National Implementation of UN Sanctions, *473-522.*

Members of the United Nations directly and through their actions in the appropriate international agencies of which they are members". Another, more general, obligation of the Charter is included in Article 2(5), which obliges Member States to give the UN "every assistance in any action it takes" in accordance with the Charter, and requires them to "refrain from giving assistance to any state against which the United Nations is taking preventive or enforcement action".

During the first three decades of Swedish membership in the UN there was no attempt made by the *Riksdag* to incorporate or transform into Swedish law the obligations flowing from the UN Charter. Only when the Rhodesia crisis unfolded did the Swedish authorities have to grapple with the implementation of Security Council decisions, and this was done in a typically dualistic fashion. The following section tells the story of how Sweden first relied on a provisional legislation followed by Governmental Ordinances restricting Swedish shipping etc in line with Security Council resolutions. At the same time the Government saw the need to introduce a general piece of legislation enabling it to expand its regulative powers, so as to guarantee (through Governmental Ordinance) an efficient implementation of Security Council decisions on multilateral sanctions.

Although a committee had been established in the beginning of 1966 to look at the matter of an enabling law, it took until April 1970 before a proposal was on the table. Although it was controversial in the *Riksdag*, due to the fact that the Government could introduce far-reaching implementation measures without any parliamentary debate, the bill in question was adopted as law in May 1971.

The so-called UN Law (*FN-lagen om sanktioner*) was thus adopted as a framework piece of legislation, through which the Government was enabled to respond to concrete needs of implementation. The 1971 Law was not affected by the new Constitution that was adopted in 1974 and entered into force in 1975. The new Instrument of Government did not introduce any provisions on the relationship between international and national law, but judicial practice in the 1970's had confirmed that Sweden was a dualist country. Clear examples to this effect were one case before the Labour Court in 1972, one before the Supreme Court in 1973 and one before the Supreme Administrative Court in 1974.

The 1971 law was not limited to implementation of legally binding Security Council decisions, it also covered recommendations by the Council and thus gave the Government the possibility to issue ordinances to implement such recommendations on sanctions. The law did not cover General Assembly recommendations, nor did it (in the beginning) refer to organisations other than the UN. A later reference to the OSCE did not survive the revision of the law in 1996, while a reference to the European Community (introduced in 1992) was not enough to satisfy the requirements flowing from the Swedish membership of the EU as of January 1995.

At that time – and before the Law on International Sanctions was revised – another revolutionary development had taken place in Swedish legal history. During 1994 the Swedish *Riksdag* had decided to incorporate *in extenso* the European Convention on Human Rights (ECHR) into Swedish law. The ECHR had been ratified by Sweden in 1952 and had since that time been treated by the legal system in a typically dualist fashion. It was presumed that existing Swedish law was up to European human rights standards and only a few elements of the European Convention were transformed into concrete legislation. In the long run, this reliance on benevolent interpretation of existing law was not considered sufficient. As to appeal of administrative decisions, the law was changed in 1988 in order to better fit with Article 6 of the ECHR, but this kind of *ad hoc* legislation would not suffice in the long run either. As EU membership approached, incorporation of the ECHR became unavoidable. The incorporation was a fact as of January 1 1995 and the event signified a certain shift in the Swedish attitude towards dualism and monism; the former was no longer sacrosanct and the latter (it could be argued) was in effect tolerated on a parallel basis. The strengthened position of human rights in Sweden was confirmed in the Constitution. This may be relevant to the issue of sanctions in the sense that the implementation of sanctions could be challenged by an adherence to overriding human rights obligations.

Although it is clear that the European Convention on Human Rights only has the status of ordinary law in Sweden as an Act of Parliament, Chapter 2, Section 23 of the Instrument of Government provides that no subsequent law or regulation may be adopted contrary to Sweden's obligations under the ECHR. The exact meaning of this is obscure, although it seems clear that the incorporated human rights provisions enjoy some special status in Swedish law. Nevertheless, in a conflict between constitutionally protected human rights and subsequent sanctions legislation (should such a conflict materialise), the latter may well prevail. The reason for this is that the kind of human rights which may be at least partially eroded by sanctions – private property rights, the right to exercise a trade and practice a profession – seem to be offered a lower level of protection than other human rights. The practical consequences are indicated in Chapter 11, Section 14 of the Instrument of Government, which limits the effects of judicial review to clear-cut cases. It is thus clear that a sanctions provision, which is alleged to conflict with a human rights provision, may only be set aside if the incompatibility with a constitutional or otherwise superior provision is "manifest". In a clash between the protection of property or business rights on the one hand, and sanctions obligations on the other, such a manifest incompatibility will not be an easy thing to prove.

A new enabling sanctions law was introduced in 1996 (SFS 1996:95). The title of the new law is the same as before, namely "Law on certain international sanctions". It has kept the substantial content of the former law as it related to UN sanctions, but in addition it has introduced a new regime in relationship to the EU. This development is covered below in the section on Sweden and the EU from the sanctions perspective. But it all started as a consequence of Rhodesia.

II. Sweden and the UN Sanctions against South Rhodesia and the Republic of South Africa: The Development of a Comprehensive National Legal Basis for Implementation

(1) *The UN Sanctions against Southern Rhodesia 1965-1979, A New Challenge for the Swedish Lawmakers*

The UN measures against South Rhodesia 1965-1979 were the very first instance for the Security Council of the UN to impose mandatory economic sanctions under Chapter VII of the UN Charter. It thus constituted a milestone in the concrete development of the functioning of the UN system.

The sanctions against South Rhodesia essentially consisted of an extensive ban on trade in goods supplemented by restrictions on trade in intellectual property rights, a prohibition on credits and payments, and a prohibition on sea and air transportation. These sanctions were decided upon by the Security Council in a series of resolutions obligating the Member States to introduce legal measures for their implementation. The Member States were thereby challenged to develop instruments in national law for the effective implementation of their duties under the Charter.[1]

However, in order to analyse the implementation mechanism from a Swedish perspective, it is necessary to look upon the actions taken by the Security Council from a somewhat wider perspective, going beyond the binding resolutions based on Chapter VII of the UN Charter. In addition to the binding obligations the policy with regard to South Rhodesia, formulated by the Security Council, also included a number of recommendations on sanctions and appeals for support to states that were suffering hardship as a result of the sanctions. All these decisions constitute parts of the same policy and should therefore not be seen in isolation.

a. Swedish implementation of the UN sanctions against Southern Rhodesia

The Cold War Swedish foreign and security policy was based on the principle of non-alliance in peace in order to be neutral in the case of war. This principle was combined with a loyal participation in the global collective security system of the UN. The duties under the UN Charter were given supremacy to the political aim of neutrality and the UN was seen as a *natural framework for the pursuit of an active foreign policy by a neutral nation*.[2] Neutrality was thus considered as a "fallback position" in case the collective security system of the UN did not function. In cases where the Security Council was able to take a decision under Chapter VII of the Charter, neutrality was not a valid political choice for action.[3] The Minister of Foreign Affairs, Östen Undén reconfirmed this line of thinking, when Sweden took its seat at the UN in 1946:

1 The UN Charter, Articles 2(5) and 25.

2 "Government statement in the *Riksdag* debate on foreign affairs; 23rd April", DFSP 1963, pp. 7-18, p. 14.

3 Compare the Government Bill 1946:196 "*Angående medgivande att vidtaga de åtgärder som erfordras för Sveriges anslutning till Förenta Nationerna*", pp. 11-15.

> By entering the United Nations, Sweden is accepting important restrictions on her liberty of actions in cases where collective steps may be taken to prevent threats to peace. In the Swedish Riksdag there was no difference of opinion when it came to accepting these international obligations. We undertook them with full realisation of their implications.[4]

The question of neutrality was not an issue that was cited in the national political debate concerning implementation of the sanctions against South Rhodesia. The Swedish policy with respect to South Rhodesia was based on loyalty to the UN system and the Swedish Government acted with clear political intentions to comply with Security Council recommendations and requests for economic sanctions without any inhibitions caused by the policy of neutrality.

It should furthermore be noted that the peacetime policy of neutrality included an element of international activism, which at the time was focused on the process of de-colonisation in Africa.[5] Thus, the UN actions against South Rhodesia fell well in line with the Swedish foreign policy orientation. Hans Blix who was legal adviser to the Swedish Ministry for Foreign Affairs commented on the Swedish reaction to the requests for actions against the minority regime in Salisbury in the following way:

> In contrast to its reaction in the Korean case, Sweden's reaction to the United Nation's requests in the case of Rhodesia was wholehearted from the outset and throughout. The explanations are easy to find: the government warmly supported the action, no serious doubts existed as to the legality of the action and – as a matter of crucial importance – there was no great-power conflict. In these circumstances Sweden showed no inhibitions in applying sanctions fully.[6]

Despite the political support for the UN policy, the Swedish State powers were hardly equipped to enact effective implementation measures. As a consequence of the national application of the doctrine of dualism concerning the relationship between national and international law, Security Council resolutions lacked direct effect within the Swedish legal system. Reception measures on national level were therefore necessary. However, there existed no comprehensive national legislation enabling the Government to transform or incorporate decisions by the Security Council. Initially, the sanctions against

---

This Swedish position reflects the communicating character between the scope for a State's neutrality and the establishment of a regime for collective security. Hersh Lauterpacht formulated the essence of this balance in a very clear way in 1936: *In so far as words are used with due regard to their ordinary meaning, not befogged by the deliberate artificialities of diplomatic language, it is true to say that collective security and neutrality are mutually exclusive. The more there is of the one, the less there is of the other.* "Neutrality and Collective Security", *Politica* 1936, pp. 133-155, p. 149.

4 GAOR 1946, pp. 968-969.

5 Nils Andrén, "*Maktbalans och alliansfrihet*", Norstedts Stockholm 1996, pp. 226-241.

6 Hans Blix, "Neutrality, Non-alignment and Membership of International Organisation", in *Sovereignty, Aggression and Neutrality*, (Stockholm, Almquist & Wiksell, 1970), pp. 41-62, at p. 51.

South Rhodesia decided upon by the Security Council therefore had to be implemented in an *ad hoc* manner.

The South Rhodesian crisis thereby provoked the Government and *Riksdag* to reconsider these questions and the period 1965-1971 became formative for the development of the first comprehensive Swedish legislation concerning economic sanctions.

The initial phase – Sweden precedes the Security Council

11 November 1965, the same day that the South Rhodesian unilateral declaration of independence was issued by the Salisbury regime, the Swedish Government issued a communiqué that it stated that Sweden had no intention of recognising the new regime. The Swedish consulate in Salisbury was withdrawn with immediate effect and it was declared that the Government would actively consider what further steps could be taken in line with expected forthcoming resolutions from the Security Council.[7]

Resolution 217, which was passed by the Security Council 20 November 1965, recommended a trade embargo against South Rhodesia. The Swedish Government declared its affirmative support of this resolution and urged other states to follow the same line of action. The Prime Minister stated: *It is the self-evident duty of all states to defend the United Nations and the principles of the UN Charter*.[8] In order to comply with the recommendation for an economic embargo, all trade between Sweden and South Rhodesia was placed under licensing control executed by the Swedish Board of Commerce and the Swedish Board of Agriculture. Through the application of this licensing system virtually all trade in goods between Sweden and South Rhodesia was suspended by the end of November 1965.[9]

All these measures were executed through administrative decisions based on the Government's power to regulate Sweden's international trade relations. However, in the absence of a comprehensive national legislation for implementing economic sanctions the Swedish Government had to use a fragmented legal basis for its implementation measures. The measures were partly based on a 1947 Government ordinance on a general import prohibition[10], partly on a corresponding ordinance concerning a general export prohibition enacted in 1950[11] and partly on a special ordinance on the prohibition of exportation of war materials from 1949.[12]

Implementation of the first mandatory decision on sanctions – The need for an enabling law

Through the measures taken in November 1965 Sweden had well in advance fulfilled almost all its obligations under Resolution 232 which was adopted by the Security Council on 16 December 1966. In addition to the restrictions on trade in certain goods,

7 DFSP 1965, p. 120. SC/RES/216/1965 was adopted 12 November.

8 "Statement by the Prime Minister; 22nd November", DFSP 1965, pp. 128-129.

9 "Statement by the Prime Minister; 22nd November", DFSP 1965, pp. 128-129. See also SOU 1970:19, p. 27.

10 SFS 1947:82.

11 SFS 1950:324.

12 SFS 1949:614.

Resolution 232 included a duty to prevent shipment of any of the restricted products in vessels belonging to a Member State. This caused problems when the Government lacked the necessary power to enact restrictions on Swedish shipping in accordance with the Resolution. With regard to regulation of shipping the Government possessed extraordinary powers by two laws which had been introduced during the early stages of the Second World War.[13] However, these laws were only applicable in times of war and did not empower the Government to seize Swedish shipping in times of peace. Thus the Government lacked the necessary authorisation to interfere with Swedish ships believed to carry goods for final destinations in South Rhodesia. Already shortly after the incident with the tankers outside the port of Beira, and the Security Council's adoption of Resolution 221, 6 April, the Swedish Government deemed it necessary to amend the existing legislation in order to expand the scope of its regulative power. Such an amendment was completed on 13 May through the *Riksdag's* enactment of a special law,[14] which empowered the Government to introduce restrictions on shipping in order to execute obligatory sanctions or recommendations, decided upon by the Security Council. This piece of legislation was of a provisional character, being valid only until 30 June 1968. Its validity was, however, later extended up until December 1971.[15]

The provisional law made it possible for the Government to enact a ordinance restricting Swedish shipping in accordance with Resolution 232 of December 1966.[16]

The introduction of these trade restrictions was followed by a formal statement whereby the Government undertook to report all national measures to the UN Secretariat in accordance with paragraph 8 of Resolution 232.[17]

Also the implementation of the additional sanctions laid down in Resolution 253, 28 May 1968 was partly made by a Government ordinance based on Article 2 of the Shipping Restriction Law.[18] This ordinance prohibited both direct and indirect shipment of goods to and from Rhodesia.

However, due to the lacunae in its regulative competencies the Swedish Government was unable to execute the duties arising from Resolution 253 in full:[19] Sweden had not enacted any general prohibitions against the supply of goods to South Rhodesia.[20] Other insufficiently implemented obligations were the duty to restrict trade in intellectual property rights and the duty to prohibit South Rhodesian passport holders, as

13 SFS 1939:299 and SFS 1940:176.

14 SFS 1966:158.

15 SFS 1968:135 extending the validity to 30 June 1970 and SFS 1970:750 extending the validity to the end of 1971. The 1966 law was formulated in anticipation of a permanent and comprehensive national legislation on the execution of economic sanctions. This was, however, not completed until May 1971.

16 SFS 1966:766.

17 UN Doc. S/7781, Annex II 1967, pp. 57-58.

18 SFS 1968:449.

19 Compare the analysis in SOU 1970:19.

20 The licensing system established in November 1965 only covered exports *from Sweden* to destinations in South Rhodesia.

well as certain foreigners residing in South Rhodesia from entering Sweden. It should also be noted that the duty to prevent national air carriers from operating in and out of South Rhodesia was not implemented in law, but through an informal agreement with Scandinavian Airlines System (SAS). These deficiencies were not redressed before a year later, through the *Riksdag's* enactment of a specific law on sanctions against South Rhodesia.[21]

Despite the deficiencies in the implementation of the duties under Resolution 253 it seems clear that the Swedish Government did not only apply the embargo before most other Member States, its actions in November 1965 even preceded relevant Security Council decisions. It should in this context be noted that the Swedish Government already in December 1965 expressed the opinion that the situation in South Rhodesia in fact constituted a threat to peace and that the Security Council would have grounds for a mandatory decision on economic sanctions.[22] Swedish representatives to the UN repeatedly pronounced this view.[23]

The Government evidently recognised the problems of inefficiency resulting from the lack of a comprehensive enabling law on implementation of UN sanctions. A committee with the task to investigate this issue was mandated in February 1966, however its final report was not presented before April 1970.[24]

The 1969 special law on certain sanctions against Southern Rhodesia

In order to redress the kaleidoscopic and incomplete implementation of the mandatory sanctions the Swedish Government, in May 1969, presented before the *Riksdag* a proposition for a Law on certain sanctions against Rhodesia.[25] The *Riksdag* enacted the proposition as law on 27 May 1969.[26]

The 1969 law was formulated with the express aim to fully implement the extended sanctions requested in Resolution 253.[27] However, the Government emphasised the general aims of the relevant resolutions rather than the wording of specific provisions. In the proposition the Minister of Justice stated that the Government and *Riksdag* ought to:

21 SFS 1969:232.

22 Parliamentary protocol 1965:40, p. 6.

23 See as example DFSP 1965, p. 130. One of the reasons for the Swedish insistence on mandatory sanctions was the concern that non-obligatory recommendations would prove inadequate which might lead to a loss of credibility for the UN system. The experiences from the demise of the League of Nations undoubtedly influenced Swedish foreign policy-making on the issue of sanctions.

24 SOU 1970:19.

25 Government Bill 1969:78

26 SFS 1969:232.

27 Government Bill 1969:78, pp. 36-37.

> ...interpret the Resolutions in accordance with their general spirit and to formulate the national rules for their implementation in a reasonable manner in order to fulfil their fundamental aim; namely to isolate Rhodesia and thereby remove the illegal regime.[28]

It should furthermore be noted that the Government judged Resolution 253 to be so comprehensive that further decisions on sanctions by the Security Council were unlikely.[29]

The special law on sanctions against Rhodesia was applicable to Swedish subjects acting within or outside, Swedish territory, as well as foreign subjects acting within Swedish territory.[30]

The central provision, laid down in § 2 of the law, prohibited importation of goods into, and exportation of goods from, South Rhodesia with the humanitarian exceptions stated in Resolution 253.[31] The term goods was defined to include all movables, also including electricity, with the general exception of goods for personal consumption by the proprietor.[32]

Supplementary provisions outlawed activities promoting, or calculated to promote breaches of the prohibition in § 2. Most important, these provisions restricted production, maintenance, repairs, insurance, the sale or acquisition of goods or special rights relating to goods, as well as transportation of goods.[33] In addition, payments and credits related to economic activities in South Rhodesia were prohibited with the exception of pensions and payments or credits for humanitarian, educational or medical purposes.[34] The law also prohibited national airline operations to and from South Rhodesia and co-operation with South Rhodesia airline operators.[35] Finally, express provisions on judicial procedures and penalties for breach of the prohibitions were included in the law.[36]

It should be noted that the law did not prohibit the importation of South Rhodesian goods into Sweden or the exportation of goods from Sweden to South Rhodesia as prescribed by the Security Council resolutions. These central components of the sanction policy were still to be regulated by administrative decisions taken within the framework of the established licensing system.[37]

The law was originally set to expire at the end of 1970, although it was later extended for one year.[38] Simultaneous to the enactment of the special law on sanctions against

28 Government Bill 1969:78, p. 33. Translation PC.

29 *Ibid.*, p. 37.

30 *Ibid.*, pp. 37-38.

31 SFS 1969:232, § 2.

32 *Ibid.*, § 1.

33 *Ibid.*, §§ 3-4.

34 *Ibid.*, § 5.

35 *Ibid.*, § 6.

36 *Ibid.*, §§ 8-12.

37 SFS 1947:82, SFS 1949:614 and SFS 1950:324.

38 Government Bill 1970:202. SFS 1970:750.

South Rhodesia the Government repealed the 1968 ordinance on shipping restrictions, which had become superfluous.[39]

At the same time as the enactment of the special law on sanctions against Rhodesia the *Riksdag* enacted an amendment of the Alien Law, regulating the right of foreigners to enter and reside within Swedish jurisdiction. This amendment established an express power for Swedish authorities to refuse entry to foreigners in accordance with ordinances relating to resolutions from the Security Council.[40] Thus, within this specific area an express permanent competence to implement UN sanctions was established. It should in this connection be noted that, with references to general principles of international law, the Government stated Swedish citizens residing in South Rhodesia were not to be prohibited from entering Sweden.[41] It could be argued that this limitation was not in full compliance with Resolution 253, paragraph 5(b).

As a result of these legislative acts Sweden was finally able to formally comply with Resolution 253. This legislative development did not, however, resolve the basic principal problems arising from the lack of permanent Government competencies to implement sanctions by ordinance.

b. The development of a comprehensive governmental competence to implement UN sanctions

As a result of the measures taken the total volume of trade between Sweden and South Rhodesia was reduced to less than US$ 10 000 in 1969.[42] The successful implementation of the economic sanctions against South Rhodesia was an issue for pride on behalf of the Swedish policymakers. At the annual conference of the Social Democratic Party in 1969 the Minister of Commerce stated that: "*In regard to Rhodesia it can be said without exaggeration that no nation has applied [the Security Council resolutions] more strictly than Sweden*".[43]

However, from a constitutional point of view the problems in connection with the implementation of the sanctions highlighted the need to enact a comprehensive legislation permanently enabling the Government to execute decisions and recommendations decided upon by the Security Council. As early as February 1966 the Swedish Government had appointed a special committee on the issue which presented its report in April 1970.[44] The report included a proposal for such an enabling law. The dominating interest behind the proposed legislation was to increase Sweden's capability to comply with its duties under the UN Charter without delay.[45] This interest was undoubtedly boosted by

39 SFS 1969:234 repealing SFS 1968:449.

40 SFS 1969: 233.

41 Government Bill 1969:78, pp. 57-58.

42 "Official statistics of Sweden; Foreign Trade 1969", part 2, p. 331.

43 DFSP 1969, pp. 54-64, p. 57.

44 SOU 1970:19.

45 *Ibid.*, p. 66.

the experiences during the period June 1968-May 1969 when Sweden was unable to fully implement its duties under Resolution 253.[46]

The proposal was debated extensively during the spring of 1970. The main criticism concerned the influence of the opposition in the *Riksdag* that would be encroached upon since the law would eliminate the necessity for a parliamentary debate prior to governmental action.[47] With some minor alterations the Government, as a proposition to the *Riksdag*, adopted the Committee's proposal.[48] The Government's bill was enacted as law by the *Riksdag* – the UN Law of 27 May 1971.[49]

c. The 1971 enabling law on the implementation of UN sanctions

The UN Law was given the character of an enabling law investing the Government with powers to take decisions by ordinance in order to implement recommended or mandatory economic sanctions decided upon by the Security Council. Thus, action by the Government had to be preceded by a Security Council decision calling, or requesting, the Member States to apply non-military sanctions. The purpose of this limitation was to establish a clear borderline to decisions taken by the UN General Assembly: it asserted that any proposals to extend the General Assembly's authority to decree sanctions could be rejected by the *Riksdag*. The interest to emphasise this distinction between the Council and the Assembly should be seen as an outflow of the policy of neutrality. The Minister for Foreign Affairs stated in the *Riksdag:*

> Only the Security Council has competence to take decisions on compulsory measures. Strict observance of this rule is of vital importance for a neutral state's membership in the UN. We have as a UN member given up our neutrality only to the very limited extent which follows the voting regulations in the Security Council.[50]

In the case of a Security Council Resolution calling for or requesting the Member States to sever their economic relations with a specified state the law empowered the Government to temporarily extend its competencies in order to implement UN sanctions. Such an expansion of Government competence would expire if not confirmed by the *Riksdag* within one month.[51]

---

46 Compare SOU 1970:19, p. 29.

47 The proposition was opposed by the non-socialist opposition in the Parliament and was passed by 152 votes to 144. For the liberal/conservative criticism focusing on the reduced parliamentary influence see Parliamentary protocol 1971:89, pp. 110-112. Another point of criticism was the absence of any provisions for public reimbursement of economic losses resulting from the sanctions. Compare Parliamentary Protocol 1971:89, pp. 104-15, 116-117. See also the reservation by the representative of the political opposition in SOU 1970:19, pp. 108-110.

48 Government Bill 1971:77.

49 SFS 1971:176.

50 Parliamentary Protocol AK 1969:13, p. 39. Translation PC.

51 SFS 1971:176, § 1.

The extraordinary power established by the law was explicitly limited to the restriction on trade in goods, with the exception of goods for personal consumption.[52] The competencies listed included, most importantly, the power to introduce: prohibitions on importation to, and exportation from, Sweden;[53] prohibitions on the supply of goods to, and the acquisition of goods from a State under blockade;[54] restrictions on transportation, production, maintenance, storage and insurance of prohibited goods and the licensing of intellectual property rights relating to goods;[55] prohibitions to give credits and to execute payments;[56] and prohibitions on air and sea communications to and from the territory of a State under blockade.[57] Finally, the law laid down rules on penalties for breach of Government ordinances, which had been based on the powers established by the law.[58]

It should be noted that the law did not include any provisions for public reimbursement of economic losses to commercial actors resulting from the implementation of economic sanctions.[59]

After its enactment, the new law was immediately used as an instrument for implementation. On the basis of this general legislation the Government enacted an ordinance on application of the law for implementation of sanctions against South Rhodesia.[60] This ordinance was in its turn used as a basis for an ordinance on the concrete implementation of the relevant resolutions,[61] also taking into account Resolution 277, adopted on 18 March 1970.[62]

This implementation measure was intended to cover the requested restrictions on the relations with South Rhodesia, with the exception of the duty to prevent the entrance of certain persons into the Swedish territory. In this part the sanctions were still to be implemented through application of the Alien Law.[63]

From a material point of view the ordinance covered all restrictions enacted by the 1966 special law on sanctions against South Rhodesia. In addition it also prohibited the importation into Sweden of goods originating in South Rhodesia and the exportation of goods from Sweden to South Rhodesia.[64] Thereby the administrative licensing system, established in November 1965, was no longer needed as an instrument for implementa-

52 SFS 1971:176, § 2.

53 *Ibid.*, § 3.

54 *Ibid.*, § 4.

55 *Ibid.*, § 5.

56 *Ibid.*, § 7.

57 *Ibid.*, § 8.

58 *Ibid.*, §§ 11-15.

59 See Government Bill 1971:77, pp. 29-33, 62-64.

60 SFS 1971:177. The Parliament confirmed this ordinance before its publication.

61 SFS 1971:178. The ordinance entered into force on 1 July 1971.

62 Government Bill 1971:77, p. 99.

63 SFS 1954:193 as amended by SFS 1969:233.

64 SFS 1971:178, § 1.

tion. It should also be noted that, in addition to the 1966 law, the ordinance explicitly prohibited trade in intellectual property rights.[65] In December 1972 both the law and the implementation ordinance were amended to add that also Swedish citizens found to be in breach of the ordinance outside Swedish territory could be tried and convicted in a Swedish court.[66]

As a response to Security Council Resolution 388, 6 April 1976, a further amendment of the Swedish UN Law took place on 1 July 1979. Through this amendment a government competence to impose general restrictions to trade in intellectual property rights was established.[67] This new governmental competence was thereafter used in order to fully comply with the UN sanctions policy.[68]

The implementation measures were in force until the Security Council in December 1979 decided to recall Resolutions 232 (1966), 253 (1968) and related resolutions.[69]

However, the UN Law, which had been formulated in order to answer to the specific needs raised by the resolutions on sanctions against South Rhodesia, remained in force as a *general* instrument available for future application.

d. Swedish responses to the appeals for financial and material support to the front-line states

In addition to the implementation of the recommended and requested economic sanctions Sweden responded positively to the appeals for assistance to the front-line States in Southern Africa.[70] Such behaviour fell well in line with the Swedish foreign policy priorities, which had been formulated during the 1960's, establishing a clear focus on the questions of de-colonisation and development. The principles for the development policy had been laid down in the Government's proposition 1962:100 expressing four aims for Swedish international development programs: economic growth, economic and social convergence, economic and political independence and political democracy. These aims were formative for the Swedish policy with regard to Southern Africa in general and were specifically applied to the situation in South Rhodesia.

The Swedish Government proposed as early as in 1966 a special UN study on the sharing of economic burdens resulting from sanctions.[71] Sweden was also among those

---

65 SFS 1971:178, § 3(4).

66 SFS 1972:815 and SFS 1972:817.

67 SFS 1971:176, § 5a as amended by SFS 1979:515, Government Bill 1978/79:91.

68 SFS 1979:517.

69 SFS 1979:1170-1171.

70 See as examples SC/RES/403/1977 which included an appeal to the Member States to grant Botswana financial and material support. SC/RES/445/1979 with a request to the Member States to give the front-line States (Angola, Botswana, Mozambique and Zambia) substantial material support to strengthen their defence capability. SC/RES/455/1979, paragraph 6 calling on the Member States to give assistance for the reconstruction of the economic infrastructure in Zambia.

71 "Speech by the Foreign Minister at the UN General Assembly; 10th October", DFSP 1966, pp. 41-47, p.44.

states that strongly advocated that sanctions had to be supplemented by support for third States, which were adversely affected by the sanctions.[72]

The support for co-ordinated actions was, after 1968, combined with increased Swedish humanitarian aid to the independent front-line States and to liberation movements fighting colonial rule. The Minister for Foreign Affairs stated in 1970:

> We are giving humanitarian assistance to the liberation movements in accordance with the resolutions of the UN Assembly. We intend to continue furnishing aid to Southern Africa as a moral and material expression of our sense of solidarity with those who are leading the fight for material liberation, the right of self-determination, human rights and a reasonable material and cultural standard of living.[73]

These operations included humanitarian aid to the liberation movements FRELIMO in Mozambique, MPLA in Angola and ZAPU and ZANU in South Rhodesia, as well as to the Government in Zambia. After the fall of the minority regime in Salisbury and the establishment of the Republic of Zimbabwe in April 1980 Sweden maintained high levels of aid, helping to keep the economy running during the transition phase.[74]

e. Final comments

The loyal Swedish implementation of the UN policy against South Rhodesia should be seen as an outflow from the foreign policy priorities then dominant in Sweden which could be described as an active peacetime policy of non-alliance. The combination of a pronounced interest to strengthen the multilateral UN system, an active support for the process of de-colonisation and a willingness to support economic, political and cultural development in the developing world, was very well fit suited to South Rhodesian situation. In concrete terms this political willingness was transformed into active humanitarian and financial aid to the forces promoting de-colonisation and majority rule, as well as a loyal implementation of the recommendations and requests for sanctions decided upon by the Security Council. However, initially there existed an imbalance between a dominating political opinion supporting sanctions and a lack of the legal instruments needed for efficient implementation. Up until 1969 the implementation of the relevant resolutions was incomplete and made in an *ad hoc* manner, using various legal instruments. The awareness of a need for a comprehensive law enabling the Government to implement sanctions through ordinance grew slowly among political decision-makers. The development of such a law started in 1966 by the establishment of a special committee and was concluded by the enactment of the UN law in May 1971. In spite of a strong political

72 It should in this connection be noted that Sweden as a non-permanent member of the Security Council co-sponsored SC/RES/386/1976 appealing for aid to Mozambique.

73 "Speech by the Foreign Minister; 5th May", DFSP 1970, p. 181.

74 See "Statement by Foreign Minister Ullsten; 21st December", DFSP 1979, pp. 186-187. DFSP 1980, pp. 190-191. "*Zimbabwe – svenskt u-landssamarbete*", SIDA:s informationsbyrå, Stockholm, 1980, p. 8.

opinion pronouncing loyalty to the UN system in general and to the UN policy with regard to South Rhodesia in particular, this legislative endeavour took almost five years to complete. One of the main reasons for this delay was the reluctance of the parliamentary opposition to accept a loss of political influence over the issue of implementation.

The development leading to the enactment of the Swedish UN Law in May 1971 can largely be described as a responsive behaviour in order to redress the specific problems which were encountered in connection with the implementation of the UN sanctions against South Rhodesia. The law was to a large degree formulated in order to guarantee compliance with the relevant resolutions, most importantly the comprehensive Resolution 253 (1968). After the sanctions against South Rhodesia were lifted the UN Law, which had been formulated in order to answer *specific* needs, remained in force as a *general* applicable instrument enabling the Government to implement future resolutions on economic sanctions adopted by the Security Council.

In spite of its close relation to a specific set of resolutions, the law was not substantially amended until the 1990's. This time in order to answer new needs resulting from innovations by the Security Council concerning the formulation of sanctions and from Sweden's membership in the European Union.

(2) The Swedish Implementation of Economic Sanctions against South Africa 1977-1994

Parallel to the issue of the establishment of white minority rule in South Rhodesia, the UN system was faced with a similar situation of racially based repression in the neighbouring Republic of South Africa. A UN policy with regard to the situation in South Africa was successively developed from the early 1960's and onwards. The Security Council condemned the Apartheid policy for the first time in 1960.[75] The Council then recognised that the situation in the Union of South Africa had led to *international friction* which, if continued, might endanger international peace and security.[76] South Africa was accordingly called upon to initiate measures aimed at bringing about racial harmony based on equality and to abandon its policy of Apartheid and racial discrimination.[77] This initial critique of the policy conducted by the Pretoria government was gradually developed and intensified during the following years.[78] Recommendations and demands for sanctions against South Africa supported the calls for political change.

In order to restrict the Pretoria Government's capacity for repression by military force the Security Council, already in August 1963, decided upon a recommendation addressed to all states to prohibit the export of armaments to South Africa.[79] However, it was not before the late 1970's that the Security Council made use of its power to decide upon mandatory sanctions against South Africa.

75 SC/RES/134/1960.

76 *Ibid.*, para. 1.

77 *Ibid.*, para. 4.

78 See SC/RES/181/1963, 182/1963, 191/1964, 282/1970, 392/1976 and 417/1977.

79 SC/RES/181/1963, para. 3.

In November 1977, the Security Council determined that the Apartheid system, *in combination* with the importation of armaments into South Africa constituted a threat to the maintenance of international peace and security in the meaning of Article 39 of the UN Charter.[80] Acting under Chapter VII of the UN Charter, the Council decided to establish a mandatory arms embargo against South Africa. All States were thereby obliged to cease any provision to South Africa of arms and related products as well as the grants of licensing agreements for the manufacture and maintenance of such commodities.[81] In addition the Resolution included a duty for all States to refrain from any co-operation with South Africa in the manufacture and development of nuclear weapons.[82]

This Resolution was the first time the Security Council made use of its powers under Chapter VII of the UN Charter *against a UN member*. Thus it constituted a further important principal development of the application of the UN system.

The Swedish policy with regard to the South African Republic 1960-1994 was motivated by the same national foreign policy considerations as those valid for the policy with regard to South Rhodesia: the coupling between human rights and the maintenance of international peace and security constituted a basic tenet of Swedish foreign and security policy. Accordingly, the demands for introduction of majority rule in South Africa were given a high priority on the Swedish foreign policy agenda. When this question was not directly linked to the balance of power between East and West the room for action without compromising the peacetime policy of neutrality was relatively wide. One central arena for Swedish political action was the UN where Swedish representatives strongly advocated the adoption of comprehensive mandatory sanctions against South Africa. This willingness to take action was also reflected in the Swedish implementation of the decisions on sanctions adopted by the Security Council.

a. Implementation of demands and recommendations on restrictions of trade in armaments

In Sweden the exportation of armaments had been under strict state control since 1949[83] and no permissions for exportation of armaments to South Africa were granted after 1960. The Security Council recommendation adopted in August 1963[84] had thus already been implemented through administrative decisions. Accordingly, the Swedish implementation of the mandatory prohibition of the export of armaments to South Africa decided upon by the Security Council in November 1977[85] was merely seen as a formal-

80 SC/RES/418/1977. The Resolution was adopted with unanimity in the Security Council and no States abstaining.

81 *Ibid.*, para. 2.

82 *Ibid.*, para. 4.

83 SFS 1949:614.

84 SC/RES/181/1963, para. 3.

85 SC/RES/418/1977.

ity. It was made in the form of an ordinance based on the 1971 UN law, and entered into force on 1 January 1978.[86] The ordinance was addressed to all Swedish citizens and foreign nationals with regard to activities within Swedish jurisdiction.[87] It prohibited the exportation from Sweden to South Africa, as well as the importation into South Africa, of armaments, police equipment and commodities for the repair or production of such goods.[88] Finally, the licensing for production of the embargoed categories of goods in South Africa was prohibited.[89] The complementary Security Council request to prohibit the importation of armaments originating in South Africa[90] was implemented by a special Government ordinance.[91]

b. Unilateral Swedish economic sanctions against South Africa 1977-1985

In the wake of the inability of the Security Council to adopt stricter sanctions against South Africa, Sweden deliberately acted unilaterally.

On June 7, 1979, the Swedish *Riksdag* enacted a special law, banning new Swedish investments in South Africa *and* Namibia after 1 July 1979. [92] In order to establish an effective control the law obliged all Swedish subjects who already conducted business in South Africa and Namibia to declare their sources for financing new investments and report the development of their business activities.[93] As a safety valve the government was empowered to give special permissions *in casu* for reinvestments and substitution of scrapped fixed assets under condition that the business activities were not expanded.[94] This Swedish ban on investments preceded the Security Council recommendation on similar measures by six years.[95] It was motivated by national foreign and security policy considerations in support of the struggle for majority rule in South Africa and backed by wide popular domestic support.[96]

The adoption of the law constituted an instrument within the development of a unilateral Swedish policy of sanctions and, accordingly, it was given the form of a special law and not a Government ordinance based on the 1971 UN Law.

In March 1985 the *Riksdag* enacted a new law on the prohibition of investments in South Africa and Namibia.[97] This law made the prohibition more comprehensive and a

86 SFS 1977:1126 and SFS 1977:1127.

87 SFS 1977:1127, § 6.

88 *Ibid.*, §§ 1-3.

89 *Ibid.*, §§ 4-5.

90 SC/RES/558/1984.

91 SFS 1983:870.

92 SFS 1979:487. An implementing ordinance was adopted by the Government the same day, SFS 1979:488.

93 SFS 1979:487, §§ 2-3.

94 *Ibid.*, §§ 4-5.

95 SC/RES/569/1985.

96 Government Bill 1978/79:196, pp. 6-18.

97 SFS 1985:98.

number of loopholes that were found in the 1979 Law were mended.[98] Most importantly the extending of commercial credits to agents of the South African State was prohibited,[99] and a monitoring and licensing system for the transfer of intellectual property rights to South African subjects was introduced.[100] In addition, the control mechanisms for enforcement of the ban on investments were reinforced.

c. Implementation of the recommendations laid down in Security Council Resolution 569 (1985)

To a large extent, the recommendations on further economic sanctions formulated by the Security Council in July 1985[101] were already covered by Swedish measures restricting economic relations with South Africa and Namibia.; most importantly, the general prohibition on investments that had been adopted already on 7 June 1979.

To the extent that national measures covering the recommendation had not been adopted, Sweden implemented the Security Council's urging through a Government ordinance based on the 1971 UN Law with specific references to Resolution 569.[102] Thus the Government established a competence for itself to make use of the UN Law in order to decree upon specific measures for the implementation of the recommendations framed by the Resolution. This competence was in its turn used in order to adopt a special ordinance prohibiting the importation and circulation of Krugerrands.[103]

d. The introduction of further unilateral economic sanctions against South Africa and Namibia

The restrictions on the economic relations between Sweden and South Africa were further extended on 17 December 1985, when the Swedish *Riksdag* enacted a special law prohibiting the importation of agricultural goods originating in South Africa.[104] In addition regional and local Swedish authorities were legally empowered by the *Riksdag* to discriminate against South African interests in public procurement offerings in order to show solidarity with the struggle against the policy of Apartheid.[105]

These measures were not explicitly covered by the Security Council's recommendation laid down in Resolution 569. Accordingly, they fell outside of the scope of competence established by the 1971 UN Law. The adoption of these unilateral Swedish acts of sanctions against South Africa was motivated by the need for an international reaction to the increased brutality exercised in implementing the policy of Apartheid. Within

98 Government Bill 1984/85:56.
99 SFS 1985: 98, § 1 (3).
100 SFS 1985:98 §§ 9-10.
101 SC/RES/569/1985.
102 SFS 1985:792.
103 SFS 1985:793.
104 SFS 1985:1050
105 SFS 1985:1052.

the UN, Sweden had strongly, but unsuccessfully, advocated the adoption of collective economic mandatory sanctions. The unilateral measures were seen as a substitute for collective action and in a way set an example for other States to follow.[106]

Simultaneously, the system for enforcement of measures based on the UN Law was strengthened in cases of serious infringements.[107]

In early June 1987, shortly after it became clear that the Security Council would not adopt any of the proposed draft resolutions on more comprehensive economic sanctions against South Africa, Sweden extended its unilateral actions.[108] In doing this, the Swedish Government and *Riksdag* departed from the established method for introduction of unilateral economic sanctions: On the basis of a proposition from the Government, the *Riksdag* gave the Government a special authorisation, in the form of a law, to make use of the 1971 UN Law to decree on sanctions against South Africa and Namibia *without* any recommendation or mandatory decision from the Security Council.[109] On the basis of this special authorisation the Government decreed on a comprehensive trade embargo against South Africa and Namibia on 1 July 1987.[110] This trade embargo covered importation into Sweden of goods originating in South Africa or Namibia, as well as the exportation of goods out of Sweden to final destinations in South Africa or Namibia.[111] The restrictions covered all goods with the exceptions of news materials, goods for religious or humanitarian use, medical products as enumerated in a special appendix and armaments.[112] In addition, the ordinance included a prohibition of activities promoting trade in goods with South Africa and Namibia, including the rendering of transportation services.[113]

The ordinance establishing the embargo included a power for the Government to grant individual exceptions.[114] However, the Government explicitly made it clear that exceptions from the ban could only be granted if, in a specific case, a prohibition would counteract the purpose of the boycott.[115]

When the general trade embargo included Krugerrands, the ordinance implementing the Security Council recommendation on banning the import and circulation of

106 Government Bill 1985/86:52, pp. 5-13.

107 SFS 1985:1053. This amendment, which introduced a special scale of penalties in cases of serious infringements, was motivated by legal technical reasons. See Government Bill 1985/86:52, pp. 19-20.

108 Compare Government Bill 1986/87:110, pp. 12-13.

109 SFS 1987:474.

110 SFS 1987:477.

111 *Ibid.*, §§ 2-3.

112 SFS 1977:477, § 1. The existing Swedish restrictions on trade in armaments laid down by the ordinances implementing Security Council Resolutions 418/1977 and 558/1984 were not repealed or amended. SFS 1977:1127 and SFS 1983:870.

113 SFS 1987:477, § 4.

114 *Ibid.*, § 5.

115 Government Bill 1986/87:110, p. 21. Speech by the Under-Secretary of State for Foreign Affairs, Mr Pierre Schori; 5 May 1987, DFSP 1987, p. 206.

such goods was accordingly repealed.[116] In a corresponding manner the 1985 special law prohibiting imports of agricultural goods was repealed.[117]

This *in casu* expansion of the Government's competence to decree on unilateral economic sanctions on the basis of the competence given by the 1971 UN Law was primarily motivated by reasons related to expediency. It was furthermore expected that the Security Council soon would adopt a corresponding Resolution on mandatory sanctions on the trade in goods with South Africa. Thus once again Sweden saw itself as a vanguard for discriminative actions against South Africa setting an example which supposedly would be followed.[118]

e. The need to control Swedish subsidiaries abroad and the initiation of an examination of the possibility to amend the development of the UN law

It should be noted that the ban on trade with South Africa and Namibia established by the Government on 1 July 1987 implicitly included a prohibition against evasive transactions by Swedish subjects by way of third States.[119] However, the prohibition did not cover activities conducted by Swedish subsidiaries abroad. In the Government's proposition for the 1987 ordinance it was stated as a problem that the 1971 UN Law did not empower the Government to restrict activities by subsidiaries abroad owned by Swedish companies. However, at the same time the Government noted that such an extraterritorial application was contrary to general legal principles on the limits of national jurisdiction maintained by Sweden.[120] A special parliamentary Committee was therefore charged with examining to what extent trade prohibitions could be extended to include foreign subsidiaries to Swedish companies without compromising the Swedish principal position. This Committee was furthermore charged with the task to examine if the 1971 UN Law ought to be amended in order to also include the possibility to decree on restrictions on trade in services not connected with trade in goods or technological transfers.[121] The Committee delivered its report in March 1990. The report included a concrete proposal for the amendment of the UN Law in order to cover restrictions on trade in services not related to trade in goods or intellectual property rights. The Committee did, however, take a negative view on the question of extended jurisdiction in order to cover actions conducted by foreign subsidiaries to Swedish companies. Such an expansion of Swedish jurisdiction would, in the view of the Committee, be contrary to such internationally established principles of jurisdiction that Sweden had a national interest to uphold.[122]

The Committee's proposal, which was triggered by the experiences gained from the

116 SFS 1987:476.

117 SFS 1987:475

118 Government Bill 1986/87:110, pp. 17-19.

119 *Ibid.*, pp. 20, 23-24.

120 *Ibid.*, pp. XXX.

121 *Ibid.*, p. 24.

122 SOU 1990:6, pp. 77-84.

introduction of sanctions against South Africa, was not translated into legislation, however, until 1993.[123]

f. The termination of sanctions against South Africa and Namibia

The unilateral Swedish sanctions were repealed gradually as the political situation in South Africa and Namibia developed. The Swedish Foreign Service independently monitored the situation in the region and the Swedish political decision-makers were free to make a judgement from the horizon of Stockholm.

The trade embargo against Namibia and the ban on Swedish investments in Namibia were lifted when Namibia became independent on 1 April 1990.[124]

As a reaction to the successful transition process in South Africa the Swedish trade embargo against South Africa was lifted on 13 September 1993.[125] The ban on Swedish investments in South Africa was repealed by the end of November 1993.[126] This decision was motivated by the need to support the ongoing process of transition to majority rule. Great importance was, in this case, given to the statements of Nelson Mandela on the issue of repealing the sanctions.[127]

The Swedish implementation measures of the mandatory prohibition of exportation of armaments to South Africa, as well as the prohibition of importation of armaments originating in South Africa, were finally lifted on 2 June 1994, one week after the demand for sanctions had been recalled by the Security Council.[128]

g. Final comments on the Swedish implementation of sanctions against South Africa

As a result of domestic foreign policy priorities, Sweden "over-implemented" the UN decisions on sanctions against South Africa. The unilateral Swedish measures can be said to have been in concordance with the general UN condemnation of the Apartheid policy conducted by the government in Pretoria. However, they went far beyond the obligations or recommendations decided upon by the Security Council. The unilateral Swedish measures were, from a material point of view, more comprehensive than the Security Council demanded. Furthermore, from a geographical point of view it should be noted that the Swedish actions explicitly covered both South Africa and Namibia.

This unilateral Swedish policy with regard to South Africa gained strong domestic political and public support. It was furthermore closely co-ordinated with the corresponding measures taken by Norway, Denmark and Finland. In May 1987 the general

123 See below under III, p. 496.

124 SFS 1990:78 relating to the ban on investments and SFS 1990:81 relating to the trade embargo.

125 SFS 1993:1026.

126 SFS 1993:1207.

127 Government Bill 1993/94:47, pp. 7-8.

128 SFS 1994:538 and SFS 1994:539.

Swedish position was summed up by the Under-Secretary of State for Foreign Affairs in the following way:

> Sweden has condemned the policy of apartheid since the beginning of the 1960s, both bilaterally and in the United Nations and other international fora. Since 1965 we have lent our support to the view that the situation in South Africa is a threat to international peace and security and that it is therefore justifiable and necessary for the Security Council to introduce mandatory sanctions in line with Chapter VII of the UN Charter. At that time too, Sweden became the first country in Europe to provide humanitarian assistance to the liberation movements of southern Africa…Rejection of apartheid is a worldwide concern, a stand for democracy. In Sweden, the Government and various popular movements, not least the trade unions, have supported the forces of democracy in South Africa for over two decades. In the Riksdag all the parties – with the exception of the Moderates – are agreed that we should contribute to the country's liberation with all possible vigour.[129]

Nevertheless, decisions on unilateral sanctions were publicly criticised from a number of different angles.

From a national foreign policy perspective the introduction of unilateral sanctions constituted a breach from the well-established policy principle that sanctions against another State must be based on a mandate or a recommendation from the UN Security Council. The Government was quite harshly criticised for abandoning this principle which was considered to be an important element of the peacetime policy of neutrality.[130]

A second type of critique consisted of arguments based on public international law. In a general way it was argued that the Swedish unilateral measures constituted a breach against the fundamental principle of non-intervention.[131] To this general argument was added that the Swedish unilateral restrictions on trade in goods constituted a legally unjustifiable breach of Sweden's duties under the GATT.[132]

These two strains of critique were recognised and analysed by the Swedish Government in the 1987 Bill on introducing a comprehensive ban on economic relations with South Africa. As a political justification it was, however, pointed out that the situation in South Africa constituted an extreme and unique situation which motivated an *in casu* derogation from established principles.[133] In the Bill the Minister stated that:

129 "Speech by the Under-Secretary of State for Foreign Affairs, Mr Pierre Schori, in Gothenburg on Sweden's policy towards South Africa", DFSP 1987, pp. 205-211.

130 Compare Government Bill 1978/79:196, pp. 75-180.

131 Compare Government Bill 1978/79:196, pp. 102-131.

132 This view had, as late as in 1985, been maintained by the Swedish Government. Compare Government Bill 1984/85, p. 24. In addition the 1984 parliamentary Committee on the Swedish policy with regard to South Africa had ruled out the introduction of comprehensive unilateral economic sanctions, with reference to Sweden's obligations under the GATT. See SOU 1984:52 "*Svensk sydafrikapolitik*", pp. 179-181.

133 Government Bill 1986/87:110, p. 13. It should also be noted that in spite of the formal inconsistency with the GATT the unilateral Swedish measures seem to have gained acceptance within the GATT framework and there were no official protests filed.

> ...in the light of the recent events in the United Nations and the failure of the efforts to achieve mandatory sanctions against South Africa, we must weigh our principles with regard to sanctions against the need to take as extensive measures as possible against the unique system of oppression prevailing in South Africa...I have come to the conclusion that, pending an effective decision by the Security Council, the Swedish Government should present a Bill to Parliament concerning prohibition of trade...despite the fact that this would departure from Sweden's avowed policy with regard to sanctions....I am convinced that this action will expedite the process in the United Nations, so that a broader and thus more effective economic boycott of South Africa may result at a later stage.[134]

In the eyes of the Swedish Government the unilateral measures taken against South Africa were seen as an isolated case, motivated by the uniqueness of apartheid and it did *not* constitute a precedent.

It should furthermore be noted that the unilateral sanctions were politically, but not legally, justified by references to the relevant Security Council recommendations and General Assembly resolutions.[135]

As in the case of the sanctions against South Rhodesia, the Swedish measures taken to restrict economic relations with South Africa were formulated in various types of legal instruments. However, the kaleidoscopic picture of special laws and ordinances was not a result of the lack of a comprehensive competence for efficient implementation of mandatory Security Council decisions. It was rather an outcome of the desire to separate the legal basis used for implementation of UN sanctions from the one used for decisions on unilateral actions. Unfortunately, this demarcation line became blurred in 1987 when the 1971 UN Law was used as a basis for sanctions which had no explicit reference to a mandatory demand or a recommendation from the Security Council.

Nevertheless, from the perspective of legal efficiency in implementation of UN mandated sanctions the 1971 UN Law proved itself to be a sufficient instrument. The only amendment to the law resulting from the experiences gained during the period of sanctions against South Africa being a technical modification of the penal rules. However, it was noted by the Government in 1987, when proposing the unilateral prohibition on trade in goods, that it was a future need to amend the UN Law in order to also cover general restrictions on trade in services.[136]

The expedient Swedish implementation of sanctions against South Rhodesia and South Africa was motivated by the country's loyalty to its obligations under the UN Charter and dominating national policy considerations. These two forces coincided which resulted in the enactment and successive calibration of the instruments for legal implementation of Security Council decisions. The Security Council reactions to the political situation in the Southern part of the African continent thus became formative for the general Swedish enabling legislation.

---

134 Government Bill 1986/87:110, as reprinted in English in DSFP 1987, ss. 199-204.

135 Government Bill 1978/79: 196, pp. 12-15 and Government Bill 1986/87:110, pp. 7-13.

136 Government Bill 1986/87:110. See above under 2.2.5.

III. Swedish Implementation During the Period Immediately Following the End of the Cold War : 1990-1995

During the period immediately following the end of the Cold War, the increase of Security Council Resolutions on economic sanctions was reflected in Swedish implementation measures in the form of ordinances based on the 1971 UN Law. However, in none of the cases actualised by the Security Council there existed a national Swedish policy interest comparable to the interest that had been pronounced for promoting political change in Southern Africa. Thus the Swedish implementation measures became more of a technical matter and closely followed the conditions laid down in the relevant Security Council resolutions concerning sanctions against Iraq and Kuwait,[137] Libya,[138] The Federal Republic of Yugoslavia (Serbia-Montenegro),[139] Haiti,[140] Angola (UNITA)[141] and territories in Bosnia-Herzegovina controlled by Serbian forces.[142] In response to new Security Council resolutions these measures were amended successively.[143] However, as a result of the limits of Government competencies established by the 1971 UN Law, Sweden was not able to implement certain parts of the Resolutions expediently. These deficiencies in the Swedish implementation most importantly concerned the demands on the freezing of funds and the duty to prohibit the fulfilment of claims based on contracts where its performance had been affected by the sanctions pronounced by the Security Council in Resolutions 687 (1991) against Iraq and 757 (1992) and 820 (1993), against the Federal Republic of Yugoslavia.

These gaps induced the Government to propose amendments of the 1971 UN Law in order to make it possible to execute the demanded implementation measures.

The *Riksdag* enacted these proposed amendments on 1 July 1993[144] whereby the Government was given power to decree on the freezing of funds of a sanctioned state[145]

137 The UN Law was applied with regard to Iraq from 7 August 1990. SFS 1990:885. The implementation measures against Kuwait were terminated on 7 March 1991. SFS 1991:107.

138 The UN Law was applied with regard to Libya from 24 April 1992. SFS 1992:187.

139 The UN Law was applied with regard to The Federal Republic of Yugoslavia (Serbia-Montenegro) from 30 May 1992, SFS 1992:470.

140 The UN Law was applied with regard to Haiti from 1 July 1993, SFS 1993:955. The implementation measures were terminated on 16 October 1994, SFS 1994:1326.

141 The UN Law was applied with regard to Angola (UNITA) from 7 October 1993, SFS 1993: 1061.

142 The UN Law was applied with regard to Serbian controlled territories in Bosnia and Herzegovina from 3 October 1994. SFS 1994:1307.

143 Concerning Iraq see: SFS 1990:954, 1991:107, 1991:136, 1991:918, 1991:1305, 1994:1666. Concerning the Federal Republic of Yugoslavia see: SFS 1992:893, 1993:665, 1994:1668. Concerning Libya see: SFS 1992:1306. Concerning Haiti see: SFS 1993:1107. Concerning Libya see SFS 1994:69, 1994:1667.

144 SFS 1993:664, Government Bill 1992/93:229.

145 SFS 1971:176 § 7a, introduced by SFS 1993:664. This amendment was explicitly motivated by the need for an efficient implementation of the obligations laid down in SC/RES/820/1993, para. 21 (Federal Republic of Yugoslavia).

and to introduce general restrictions on trade in services.[146] The Government was furthermore empowered to prohibit the fulfilment of claims based on contracts and transactions where its performance had been affected by the sanctions imposed.[147] These new Government powers were immediately used in order to comply with the relevant resolutions[148]

It should also be noted that the end of the Cold War led to a reorientation of the Swedish policies concerning the participation in the European integration process. In January 1993, this development was reflected in an amendment to the UN Law according to which the law could also be applied in cases when Sweden's co-operation with the European Communities in order to preserve peace and security called for it and it was a Swedish interest to take immediate action. In addition a parallel reference to decisions on economic sanctions taken within the framework of the CSCE was introduced.[149]

The experiences gained during the early 1990's sparked off a more general debate on the question of a general revision of the 1971 UN Law. In December 1993 a special parliamentary Committee was entrusted with the task to examine the law with the objective to propose a general modernisation in order to make it possible for Sweden to meet the new demands that were posed by the international community.[150] These demands were emanating both from the development of the sanctions instrument by the Security Council and from the increasing Swedish ambition to participate in the European integration process, which was manifested by Sweden's accession to the European Union on 1 January 1995.[151]

The Committee presented its report in February 1995, in which it proposed the adoption of a new enabling law, including a more general enabling clause reiterating the relevant parts of the constitutional provisions on the *Riksdag's* competence to delegate power.[152] Furthermore, the report took into account the need to co-ordinate national implementation measures with actions taken within the framework of the European Union. The report constituted the foundation for the development of the Swedish legisla-

146 SFS 1971:176 § 7b, introduced by SFS 1993:664. This amendment was explicitly motivated by the need for an efficient implementation of the obligations laid down in SC/RES/820/1993, para. 27 (Federal Republic of Yugoslavia). It was furthermore in line with the proposal presented by the Parliamentary Committee on Sanctions against South Africa 1990, SOU 1990: 6. Compare above under II.2.e, 492.

147 SFS 1993:664, § 7c, introduced by SFS 1993:664. This amendment was explicitly motivated by the need for an efficient implementation of the obligations laid down in SC/RES/687/1991, para. 29 (Iraq) and SC/RES/757/1992, para. 9 (Federal Republic of Yugoslavia).

148 SFS 1993:665-666 relating to SC/RES/757/1992 and 820/1993 on sanctions against the Federal Republic of Yugoslavia. SFS 1993:667-668 relating to SC/RES/687/1991 on sanctions against Iraq.

149 SFS 1993:1257. Government Bill 1992/93:57.

150 Dir 1993:144.

151 A direct result of the Swedish entrance as a member of the European Union were those national Swedish implementation measures that were covered by corresponding EC regulations and ECSC decisions repealed on 1 January 1995. SFS 1994:1666-1670.

152 Instrument of Government (*Regeringsformen*) Ch 8, §§ 7 and 9, SOU 1995:28, pp. 63-69.

tion for implementation of international economic sanctions that took place after 1995.

IV. EU Membership and the New Law on International Sanctions

(1) *The Legal Setting in 1995*

Since Sweden became a member of the United Nations in 1946, it has legally been obliged to give effect to binding Security Council Resolutions. In addition, under Article 48(2) of the UN Charter, it is under the obligation to ensure that such Resolutions are implemented by the international organisations of which Sweden is a member. Under UN practice, the obligations are in effect limited to giving effect to non-military measures under Article 41 of the Charter, since the matter of military enforcement by the UN itself under Article 42 is depending on the agreements envisaged by Article 43, and so far no such agreements exist. The Security Council practice of authorising members to use military force is still another matter. This practice (which is not explicitly foreseen under the Charter) implies "a coalition of the willing". It is not the practice of the Council to try to force unwilling states to accept the burden of military action.[153]

The Swedish membership (since 1995) of the European Union (EU) has further focused on the obligation in Article 48 of the Charter as far as the European Communities are concerned.[154] A further level has also been added by the Common Foreign and Security Policy (CFSP) as enshrined in the Second Pillar of the Union by the Maastricht Treaty and subsequently amended by the Amsterdam and Nice Treaties.[155]

With regard to binding Security Council Resolutions, a Member State of the UN and at the same time a member of the EU may face a rather complex situation in implementing such resolutions. According to the procedure of the Treaty on European Union (TEU), a principal political decision, in the form of a Joint Position on common implementation, is taken by the Member States within the framework of the CFSP. This decision may interpret and amend the Security Council Resolution. To the extent that the legislative measures needed for implementation are covered by Community competence implementation is executed by the adoption of acts of secondary community law. To the

153 The measures that may be undertaken by the UN relative to a Member State rest, of course, *au fond*, on the contractual obligations subscribed to by all contracting States to the Charter. The legal basis for the UN to take actions directed against a non-Member State remains nebulous in many instances, although at least parts of the global system of the UN Charter constitute general international law in today´s world.

154 Whether binding UN Security Resolutions also bind the Communities may be debated. It is thought here that they do not, because the general nature of public international law is contractual in nature as expressed in Article 34 of the Vienna Convention on the Law of Treaties and the EC is not a party to the UN Charter. Nor is there a case of State succession, or the application of the GATT criteria set out by the EC Court of Justice in, for example, *International Fruit*, [1972] *ECR* 1219.

155 See for example, S. Bohr, "Sanctions by the United Nations Security Council and the European Communities", *EJIL* (1993) 256-68, and M. Vaucher, "L'évolution récente de la pratique des sanctions communautaire à l'encontre des Etats tiers", *RTDE* (1993) 39-59.

extent the duties of implementation fall outside Community competencies, or when it has not been dealt with properly by the EC, national legal, administrative and judicial decisions are needed in order to fulfil the Member State's duties under the UN Charter. These lacunae in Community competence primarily relate to restrictions on trade in armaments, the freezing of diplomatic relations, conditions for the entry of foreigners and the introduction of penalty provisions. The "superiority" of binding UN resolutions is, of course, due to the obligation of Article 103 of the UN Charter.

The co-operation within the EU on foreign and security matters does not only include what the Security Council may decide in this context. The EU may pursue its own foreign policy and it may encompass not only political pressure in general as allowed by public international law, but also more specific measures described as retorsion, reprisals or economic sanctions. These measures may require adequate national legislation in addition to the measures decided upon by the EC.

The new Swedish legislation is intended to meet all treaty obligations, including those flowing from the EU membership.

(2) *The New Swedish Legislation on Sanctions 1996*

a. The new Swedish legislation[156]

The Law on Certain International Sanctions entered into force on 1 July 1996.[157] In the governmental proposal to the *Riksdag* it was said that the new legislation was a legal-technical and linguistic review of the previous one. The Law was also a further adaptation to the requirements of the United Nations and the changes of the situation caused by the Swedish membership of the European Union.[158] However, the Law soon proved to be insufficient relative to the treaty obligations assumed by Sweden and because of that the Law has been amended quite recently.[159] The new Law was constructed as is described below (hereafter the tense of present will be used, regardless of later changes on some points).

The purpose and also the field of application of the Law is to give effect to sanctions (1) decided upon or recommended by the Security Council of the UN *or* (2) decided upon "in accordance with the provisions for a Common Foreign and Security Policy in the Treaty of the European Union and in order to restore or maintain international peace and security" (Article 1). The measures may be directed towards a State, a territory or an "organisation" or a "regime" (Article 2).

Article 3 of the Law empowers the Government, through the issuing of Ordinances, to provide for sanctions in accordance with the Law. The governmental decision to apply the Law relative to decisions or recommendations mentioned in Article 1 must be submitted to the *Riksdag* for approval; this does not mean that the regulation (Ordinance)

156 *Lag om vissa internationella sanktioner.*

157 SFS 1996:95.

158 Government Bill 1995/96:35, p. 1, based on SOU 1995:28.

159 Government Bill 1998/99:27. SFS 1998:309 and 1998:1451 and 1452 (SFS 1999:185).

containing the actual prohibition must be submitted. The decision will lapse, if it is not submitted to the *Riksdag* within one month after it was taken by the Government, or if the *Riksdag* fails to approve the decision within two months after it was submitted to the *Riksdag*. Should one of these cases occur, any regulations based on the decision would be rendered invalid *ab initio*.

According to the Instrument of Government, the *Riksdag* may delegate legislative powers to the Government within specific fields enumerated, and the matter of sanctions is covered among those fields.[160] By issuing Ordinances the Government will use the mandate of the Law in adapting Swedish legislation to international decisions on sanctions. According to Article 4, the governmental regulations may refer to any of the following subject matters:
(1) the presence of aliens in the Kingdom of Sweden;
(2) the cross-border circulation of commodities, money or other assets;
(3) production;
(4) communications;
(5) loans and various credit arrangements;
(6) activities of commercial undertakings;
(7) traffic; or
(8) education.

The powers delegated to the Government may only be used to give effect to decisions or recommendations mentioned in Article 1 of the Law.

Sanctions should not continue when they are no longer needed and Article 6 contains provisions to this effect. The decision to put the Law into operation in a certain case, or the regulations issued in pursuance thereof, shall be repealed, when and to the extent that an international decision or recommendation on sanctions has been lifted or ceased to be valid, or when changed circumstances have rendered the purpose of a CFSP decision out of date.

According to Article 7, the Government or a governmental agency may grant exemptions from the prohibitions provided for in accordance with Article 4.

Breaches of the national provisions (whether intentional or committed by gross negligence) are penalised by means of fines or imprisonment of up to four years (Article 8). The same applies to breaches of Community Regulations implementing Security Council sanctions – be it a Resolution or a Recommendation. As to Swedish citizens who have committed such a crime abroad, there is no requirement that this crime also was a crime at the place where the crime was committed. It should be noted that this exception is applicable to Swedish citizens only (Article 9). Foreigners in Sweden are liable to penalty sanctions according to the normally applicable rules as regards Swedish penal jurisdiction – crimes committed in Sweden are prosecuted there.[161] According to Article 10, prosecution may only be initiated following a decision by the Government or

160 Instrument of Government (*Regeringsformen*) Ch. 8, § 7, sec. 1.

161 Compare the ruling by the Supreme Court, *NJA* 1998:107.

by an agency, which the Government has appointed for this purpose.[162]

Articles 11-14 deal with the "forfeiting of profit from crimes", "expulsion" and "coercive measures". According to Article 15, the Government is obliged to make known in the official gazette relevant EC Regulations linked to Security Council decisions or recommendations. Breaches of prohibitions in such Regulations are penalised according to Article 8. There are also transitional provisions maintaining the validity of decisions or regulations taken under the former law on UN sanctions.

b. Some legal issues

In public international law there is no legal definition of "sanctions", but the expression must be understood to mean the exercise of pressure relative to some political entity in order to make that entity do something or abstain from doing it. This does not necessarily imply that the entity against which the measures are directed has committed any breach of legal duty under public international law. Nor does the application of Article 39 of the Charter necessarily imply that there is a breach of legal duty by the State that threatens international peace and security. Breach of legal duty may, however, occur if the situation – subsequently – is not properly redressed – at least as far as a UN member is concerned. If there is no breach of legal duty, the States exercising pressure would only be allowed to undertake measures in conformity with the law, although some may be overtly unfriendly (retorsion). The pressurising States could also commit breaches of their own legal obligations. If, on the other hand, the State which is the object of sanctions has committed a breach of legal duty, it has also exposed itself to reprisals from other States purporting to induce the breaching State to cease doing so and remedy the situation. The issue of what reprisals would be lawfully permitted is, of course, another matter. Sanctions ordered or recommended by the Security Council fall in a category of its own, because of the system created by the Charter and the Charter's "superiority".

The Swedish Law of 1996 does not define "sanctions", but contents itself to state that it deals with international sanctions, which have been decided upon or recommended by the UN Security Council. Thus it would seem that the field of application of the Law, or rather the criteria for the initiation of the application of the Law, would depend on what the UN decisions or recommendations contain with regard to "sanctions". The same applies to decisions taken within the CFSP.

It is worth noting that the Law's reference to UN sanctions includes the phrase "in accordance with the Charter of the United Nations" (Article 1), and one may wonder if these words in any way could qualify the UN decisions and recommendations. Normally one would presume that such decisions or recommendations are taken in accordance with the procedural requirements of the Charter and also that the content of the resolution in question does not exceed the powers of the UN Security Council. However, if these words are supposed to have any meaning, they should furnish a basis for the Government to omit to put the Law into operation in obvious cases of *ultra vires* decisions. Since there is no legal review of Security Council decisions, the normal rule of auto-interpretation applies. Still, the scope for auto-interpretation appears limited, as UN

162 The Chief Public Prosecutor of Sweden has been appointed for this task.

Member States have to comply *bona fide* with Articles 2(5) and 25 of the UN Charter (as with other treaty provisions).

Nevertheless, the limited/remaining scope of auto-interpretation as to Security Council resolutions will obviously affect the understanding of these resolutions in a material sense, and a national interpretation may result in implementing measures being more or less ambitious. Under the Swedish Law on International Sanctions, national interpretation will determine the nature and extent of regulative measures provided for on the basis of Article 4 of the Law.

With regard to decisions on sanctions within the CFSP, the law in a similar way presumes that these sanctions are "in accordance with" the provisions of the Union Treaty on the formation of these policies. The same considerations, which concern the Security Council decisions, are relevant here. However, with regard to the CFSP there is also the qualification that the decision must aim at maintaining or restoring international peace and security, a condition which is implied as far as Security Council Resolutions under Chapter VII of the Charter are concerned.

Considering the field of application of the Law, it is important to note that the field is limited to UN or EU efforts with a view to maintaining or restoring international peace and security. With regard to other cases of sanctions, e.g. those decided within the CFSP but devoid of the specific purpose mentioned in the Law, it could happen that the Government must turn to the *Riksdag* for additional legislation, in order to be able to implement the sanctions.

Generally, in these cases it seems that the nature of the sanctions would be crucial. For example, the severance of diplomatic relations would cause no problem. The Government, on the basis of its already existing powers under the Instrument of Government, could undertake such action. Many other actions would also fall under the same ambit of power. Only if these powers were not sufficient to implement the sanctions concerned, the Government would have to turn to the *Riksdag* with a bill for the enactment of new legislation. Such cases could concern the criminalisation of breaches of prohibitions, and the intervention in commercial and other relationships of individuals, if such provisions were not already in existence and were applicable. The foreign policy implications would, however, in many cases, cause the Government to inform or consult with the *Riksdag*.

Regardless of whether sanctions decided by the EU have the purpose of maintaining or restoring international peace and security, it would in most cases be a matter of the EC issuing implementing Regulations. Such Regulations would be directly applicable in Sweden as in the other Member States of the EU and the provisions of these Regulations would in their operative parts produce direct effect relative to individuals. To the extent that a CFSP decision could not totally be implemented by the EC, the Government would have to prescribe appropriate provisions in an Ordinance based on Article 4 of the Law or turn to the *Riksdag* for new legislation. The latter position would undoubtedly present itself, if CFSP decisions were devoid of the purpose of maintaining international peace and security.

Concerning penal measures the picture is rather complex. The situation with regard to Security Council Resolutions is clear, because breaches of prohibitions under Article 4 are penalised as well as breaches of EC Regulations (Article 8). As a consequence, the Government must for this reason make known all EC Regulations implementing Resolutions on sanctions (Article 15). To the extent that the EC has no competence or has not acted, it is thus a matter for the Government to issue Article 4 prohibitions with due regard to decisions taken on the matter by the CFSP.

A decision within the CFSP, not being based on a Security Council Resolution, but nevertheless purporting to maintain or restore international peace and security, would generally require the Government to issue prohibitions according to Article 4. However, should the EC have acted by means of a Regulation, such a Regulation has no penal support in Swedish law as far as breaches of its provisions are concerned. This situation cannot be mended without changing the Law.

All decisions on sanctions within the CFSP, which are devoid of the purpose of maintaining international peace and security, fall outside the scope of the Law. Should such a decision be implemented by an EC Regulation, criminalisation of breaches may be dependent upon a new enactment.

In conclusion, it is obvious that the field of application of the Law initially failed to give effect to all treaty obligations of Sweden and also to provide for penal sanctions in certain instances. Some of these deficiencies have been redressed by subsequent legislation.

(3) Subsequent Amendments of the Law of 1996

a. The *ad hoc* amendment

The Council of the EU took a unanimous decision about a Common Position on restrictive measures against the Federal Republic of Yugoslavia on March 19, 1998 (98/240/CFSP).[163] In order to implement certain of these measures the EC adopted Regulation 926/98 dated 27 April 1998.[164] The Swedish Government could implement the remaining parts of the Common Position basing itself on Article 4 of the enabling law. Since the measures in the Common Position were not based on any Security Council Resolution, the provisions of the EC Regulation lacked penal support, when at the time the Swedish law required that EU sanctions should be covered by UN decisions or recommendations. In fact, the Security Council issued Resolution 1160 (1998) on 31 March 1998 including *inter alia* an embargo on weapons to Yugoslavia (and also Kosovo). Nevertheless, the EC Regulation went further in certain aspects than the Security Council Resolution. Even if the EC Regulation were to be seen as retroactively covered by the UN Resolution, there would have been no penal backing of those parts going further than the Resolution.

The problem in Swedish law was that the penal provisions of Article 8 of the 1996 Law presupposed that any EC Regulations were adopted in *pursuance* of Security Council Resolutions. In the case of Yugoslavia the Government considered that the EC Regulation had not been issued on the basis of a Security Council Resolution, but on a decision made by the CFSP, although with a view to maintaining international peace and security. The situation could not be mended without a change of the Law.

---

163 O.J. L 95, 27 March 1998, p. 1.

164 O.J. L 130, 1 May 1998, p. 1.

Realising this situation the Government made the *Riksdag* aware of this fact and a committee of the *Riksdag* took the initiative to issue a temporary law, adding Article 16 to the Law, an Article which was valid from 1 July 1998 and expired on 31 December 1998.[165] Further amendments were accordingly to follow. Article 16 provided that the penal sanctions stipulated in Article 8 also were applicable to breaches of EC Regulations adopted as a result of a Common EU Position in order to maintain or restore international peace and security. For that reason such EC Regulations were to be made known to the general public as prescribed for in Article 15.

b. The 1999 amendment

In October 1998 the Government introduced to the *Riksdag*[166] a bill for amending the Law, and these amendments entered into force on 1 January 1999.[167] The field of application of the Law was extended in so far as EC Regulations on economic sanctions were included, *regardless* of the purpose of the sanctions. Sanctions decided within the CFSP, which are devoid of the purpose of maintaining or restoring international peace and security, are still outside the ambit of the Law, unless provided for in an EC Regulation.

Furthermore, the penal provisions of § 8 were changed.[168] Breaches of prohibitions in EC Regulations are penalised, on condition that such Regulations are based on Articles 60 and 301 of the EC Treaty only. The obligation of §15 of the Swedish Law, to make EC Regulations on sanctions known to the general public, now covers all such Regulations, whether they are based upon UN Resolutions or not.

(4) Specific Problems Relating to the Freezing of Funds and other Financial Resources Controlled by Specifically Designated Entities

In late 2001, a heated debate on the implementation of UN sanctions developed in Sweden. The debate, which still has not reached its bottom line, is in concrete terms related to the implementation of the obligation to freeze financial resources belonging to specifically identified persons and organisations laid down in Security Council Resolutions 1267 (1999) and 1333 (2000).

At the core, however, lies a question of fundamental importance: where should a balance be struck between the effective fulfilment of obligations to implement sanctions under the UN Charter and the protection of fundamental legal principles safeguarding individual rights?

This question has moreover become of central importance for Sweden with regard to the implementation of Security Council Resolution 1373 (2001) and has motivated the Swedish government to take initiatives for a reformation of the technique for formulating targeted sanctions.

165 SFS 1998:309.

166 Government Bill 1998/99:27.

167 SFS 1998:1451.

168 SFS 1998:1452.

a. Implementation of Security Council Resolutions 1267, 1333 and 1390.

On 15 October 1999, the Security Council adopted Resolution 1267. In paragraph 2 of the Resolution the Security Council demanded that the Taliban administration in Afghanistan turn Usama bin Laden over without delay to the appropriate authorities in a State where he would be brought to justice.[169]

Furthermore, acting under Chapter VII of the UN Charter, the Security Council decided that economic sanctions should be imposed on 14 November 1999 unless the Security Council decided that the Taliban had fully complied with its obligations according to the Resolution.[170]

These sanctions included an obligation for all States to freeze funds and other financial resources controlled directly or indirectly by the Taliban or by any undertaking owned or controlled by the Taliban. Furthermore, all States should ensure that no financial resources were made available to the subjects concerned. The designation of the individual targets for these sanctions was entrusted to the specially established Taliban Sanctions Committee.[171]

From a Swedish perspective, the obligation to freeze funds belonging to the individuals or entities designated by the Taliban Sanctions Committee was primarily implemented on the European Union level through CFSP and EC measures. On the basis of a Common position adopted on 15 November 1999,[172] the Council adopted an EC Regulation on economic sanctions, including the freezing of financial assets and the prohibition of financial transactions as set out in Resolution 1267.[173] To this Regulation was annexed the Taliban Sanctions Committee's first listing of individuals and organisations whose funds should be frozen. For reasons of expediency, the Commission was empowered to supplement and amend this annex in accordance with future decisions adopted by the Security Council or the Taliban Sanctions Committee.[174]

In Sweden, the rules of the Regulation constitute directly applicable law.[175] The substantive provisions of the Regulation were supplemented by the penalty provisions of the Swedish Law on International Sanctions.[176] In addition, the Swedish Financial Supervisory Authority (*Finansinspektionen*) was instructed by the Ministry of Foreign Affairs to

169 In the preambular text of the Resolution it was noted that Usama Bin Laden and his associates had been indicted in the USA for the 7 August 1998 bombings of the US embassies in Nairobi and Dar es Salaam and that the USA had requested the Taliban to surrender them for trial.

170 SC/RES/1267/1999, para. 3.

171 SC/RES/1267/1999, para. 4(b). The Sanctions Committee was established by SC/RES/1267/1999, para. 6.

172 Common Position 1999/727/CFSP, O.J. L 294, 16 November 1999, p. 1, Article 2.

173 Council Regulation 337/2000, O. J. L 43, 16 February 2000, p. 1. The Regulation was adopted on the basis of the EC-Treaty, Articles 60 and 301.

174 Council Regulation 337/2000, Article 7.

175 EC Treaty, Article 249.

176 SFS 1996:95, § 8. A notification referring to the sanction provisions of Council Regulation 337/2000 was publicised in the official gazette in accordance with SFS 1996:95, § 15. See SFS 2000:82.

inform the financial sector about, and to monitor the implementation of, the sanctions.[177] Finally, the actors in the financial sector were obliged to report all actions taken to freeze funds in accordance with the EC Regulation to the Supervisory Authority.

Security Council Resolution 1333, adopted on 19 December 2000, strengthened the sanctions against the Taliban regime. In addition, it laid down a duty for all States to, without delay, freeze all funds controlled by, and prohibiting that funds were made available to, Usama bin Laden as well as individuals and entities associated with him – including Al-Qaida – as designated by the Taliban Sanctions Committee established by Resolution 1267.[178] The Committee was furthermore explicitly requested to establish and maintain updated lists of such individuals and entities, based on information provided by States and regional organisations.[179] These lists have successively been updated through decisions taken by the Sanctions Committee.[180] It should be noted that the amendments closely correspond to preceding changes of the enumeration of entities designated as "Global Terrorist Entities" made by the US administration.[181] Thus, it seems that the decisions taken by the Taliban Sanctions Committee have largely been based on information provided by the US Government.

From a Swedish horizon the implementation of Resolution 1333 followed the same scheme as the implementation of Resolution 1267: On the basis of a Common Position[182] adopted within the framework of CFSP, an EC Council Regulation was adopted on March 6.[183] The Regulation included directly applicable rules on the freezing of financial assets controlled by any natural or legal person designated by the Taliban Sanctions Committee and listed in Annex I of the Regulation. Furthermore, the Regulation

177 Information about the administration of the implementation measures by the Swedish Financial Supervisory Authority is found at http://www.fi.se.

178 SC/RES/1333/2000, para. 8(c)

179 SC/RES/1333/2000, para. 16 (b).

180 Consolidated lists of entities whose funds should be frozen in accordance with Resolutions 1267 (2000) and 1333 (2001) have continuously been made available at http://www.un.org/Docs/sc/committees/Afghanistan/Afg_list_eng.htm. The latest updated version was published on 28 June 2004.

181 Executive Order 13224 of 23 September 2001 on Blocking Property and Prohibiting Transactions with Persons who Commit, Threaten to Commit, or Support Terrorism. See information provided by the U.S Department of the Treasury at http://treasury.gov/terrorism.html

Compare Sanctions Committee Decision SC/7166, adopted on 8 October 2001, corresponding to new designation of "Global Terrorist Entities" adopted on 23 September. Sanctions Committee Decision SC/7180, adopted on 19 October 2001, corresponding to new designation of "Global Terrorist Entities" adopted on 12 October. Sanctions Committee Decision SC/7206, adopted on 9 November 2001, corresponding to new designation of "Global Terrorist Entities" adopted on 7 November. Sanctions Committee Decision SC/7252, adopted on 26 December 2001, corresponding to new designation of "Global Terrorist Entities" adopted on 20 December. Sanctions Committee Decision SC/7265, adopted on 14 January 2002, corresponding to new designation of "Global Terrorist Entities" adopted on 9 January.

182 Common Position 2001/154/CFSP, O. J. L 57, 27.2.2001, p. 1, Article 4.

183 Council Regulation 467/2001, O. J. L 67, 9 March 2001, p. 1. This Regulation included measures for implementation of both SC/RES/1267/1999 and SC/RES/1333/2000.

prohibited making financial resources available for the benefit of the listed subjects.[184] It should be noted that this new Regulation laid down a consolidated system for implementation of both Resolution 1267 and Resolution 1333.[185]

In order to efficiently respond to future changes, the Commission was empowered to amend or supplement the listing in Annex I on the basis of determinations made by either the Security Council or the Taliban Sanctions Committee.[186] Such amendments, in the form of Commission Regulations, have been adopted eight times up until January 18 2002.[187]

In Sweden the prohibitive rules laid down in the EC Council Regulation were supplemented by a notification that the penalty provisions of the Law on International Sanctions would apply in cases of infringements of the Regulation.[188] As with regard to the implementation of Resolution 1267, the Swedish Financial Supervisory Authority (*Finansinspektionen*) was instructed by the Ministry of Foreign Affairs to inform the financial sector about, and to monitor the implementation of, the sanctions.

It should finally be noted that the sanctions system established by Resolutions 1267 and 1333 was somewhat modified by the Security Council in January 2002. On January 15, the sanctions relating to the operation of Ariana Afghan Airlines were terminated.[189] Subsequently, the system for freezing of funds controlled by entities designated by the Taliban Sanctions Committee, laid down in Resolutions 1267[190] and 1333,[191] was reconfirmed by the Security Council in Resolution 1390 (2002) adopted on January 16 2002.[192] Through this Resolution the sanctions were also strengthened by an additional obligation for all States to prevent the entry into, or the transit through, their territories of persons listed by the Sanctions Committee.[193]

Concerning the procedural aspects it should be noted that the Security Council, in Resolution 1390, requested the Sanctions Committee to regularly update the list on the

184 Council Regulation 467/2001, Article 2.

185 As a consequence Council Regulation 337/2000 was repealed; Council Regulation 467/2001, Article 14.

186 Council Regulation 467/2001, Article 10.

187 Commission Regulation 1354/2001, O. J. L 182, 5 July 2001, p. 15; Commission Regulation 1996/2001, O. J. L 271 12 October 2001, p. 21; Commission Regulation 2026/2001, O. J. L 277, 20 October 2001, p. 25; Commission Regulation 2199/2001, O. J. L 295, 13 November 2001, p. 16; Commission Regulation 2373/2001, O. J. L 320, 5 December 2001, p. 11; Commission Regulation 2604/2001, O. J. L 345, 29 December 2001, p. 54; Commission Regulation 65/2002, O. J. L 11, 15 January 2002, p. 3; Commission Regulation 105/2002, O. J. L 17, 19 January 2002, p. 52.

188 SFS 2001:126, 27 March 2001.

189 SC/RES/1388/2002.

190 SC/RES/1267/2000, Article 4 (b).

191 SC/RES/1333/2001, Article 8 (c). Formally the economic sanctions established by Resolution 1333 expired 19 December 2001; SC/RES/1333/2001, Article 23.

192 SC/RES/1390/2002, Article 2(a).

193 SC/RES/1390/2002, Article 2(b). This additional obligation was implemented in Sweden through the administrative application of the national Law on Aliens, SFS 1989:526, in co-operation with the other EU Member States within the Schengen group.

basis of relevant information from the UN Member States and regional organisations. In addition, the Sanctions Committee was instructed to draw up necessary guidelines and criteria for the implementation of the sanctions.[194]

At the time of writing of this chapter, no new implementation measures regarding the obligation to freeze financial funds have been adopted as a consequence of Resolution 1390.[195] However, the EC Council Regulation for the implementation of Resolutions 1267 and 1333 remains in force.

b. Concrete reactions in Sweden

Initially, neither the Security Council Resolutions on sanctions, nor the implementation measures were publicly debated. The debate in Sweden commenced on 7 November 2001 when two organisations seated in Sweden and three Swedish citizens, associated with these organisations, appeared on a list of entities designated as "Global Terrorists Entities" by the US administration.[196] On November 9 the Taliban Sanctions Committee amended the list of entities whose financial assets should be frozen in accordance with Resolutions 1267 and 1333.[197] This amendment was in concordance with the US designation of terrorist entities of November 7. The decision by the Sanctions Committee was in its turn implemented through a Commission Regulation,[198] adopted on November 12. In order to abide by their legal duties, Swedish financial institutions immediately froze all financial assets controlled by the organisations and individuals concerned.

From the perspective of the targeted persons the sanctions had a punitive character. The three individuals, as well as representatives for the organisations whose funds had been frozen argued their innocence, but found themselves without a possibility to defend themselves against the accusation of directly or indirectly supporting international terrorist movements connected to Usama bin Laden. No procedure for a judicial, or effective administrative review of a binding Security Council decision was available, neither in international, nor in national law.[199] Thus, primarily only political methods of action remained open.

The Swedish Government very soon approached the Taliban Sanctions Committee and the US administration for further information about the evidence proving that the Swedish subjects in question had connections with international terrorist activities. The documentation presented by the US administration was not made available to the accused individuals. However, it was analysed by the Swedish Security Police. On 14 December 2001 a representative of the Security Police publicly stated that the documentation pre-

194 SC/RES/1390/2002, Article 5.

195 A Council Regulation on measures for the implementation of economic sanctions in accordance with Resolution 1390 is expected to be adopted by the end of April 2002.

196 Barakaat International Foundation, Somali Network AB, Abdirisak Aden, Abdulaziz Abdi Ali and Yusaf, Ahmed Ali.

197 Sanctions Committee Decision SC/7206, 9 November 2001.

198 Commission Regulation 2199/2001 amending Annex I of Council Regulation 467/2001.

199 This does not mean that the possibility for judicial review of the legal acts for implementation is precluded. See below, p. 510.

sented, contained nothing that confirmed the accusations.[200] Furthermore, the head of the National Criminal Investigation Department of the Swedish police publicly declared that the individuals concerned were not suspected of any crime under national law.[201]

In spite of these statements, Swedish public authorities have remained loyal in implementing the sanctions in accordance with the UN Charter. The financial assets of the subjects concerned remain frozen by Swedish financial institutions.

This situation was strongly criticised in the Swedish media and in the general political debate.[202] Nor did the Swedish Government consider the situation to be satisfactory. In connection with the visit of UN Secretary-General Kofi Annan to Stockholm on 11 December the question was raised and Swedish Prime Minister Göran Persson commented:

> This is a conflict between principles that we have not previously seen. I have stated worries for this... We are learning to handle a new situation and I hope to reach greater understanding along the way[203]

When it comes to further concrete action it should be noted that the Swedish Government has handled the issue with restraint. In late November the Ministry of Foreign Affairs established a working group entrusted with the task to analyse possible methods to safeguard the legal position of individuals targeted by UN sanctions. Swedish authorities did not, however, immediately approach the Taliban Sanctions Committee with a request to reconsider the decision to designate the concerned Swedish subjects as targets for sanctions.[204] Not before 22 January 2002 did the Swedish Government file a request with the Sanctions Committee for a general review of the list of entities whose funds should be frozen.[205] This motion for a general review was motivated by the

---

200 Public statement by Margareta Linderoth, supreme commander at the Swedish Security Police, Swedish National Broadcasting, "*Dagens Eko*", 14 December 2001.

201 Statement by Leif Nylén, head of the National Criminal Investigation Department of the Swedish police, *Svenska Dagbladet,* 14 November 2001.

202 See as examples: *Svenska Dagbladet,* Editorial 24 November 2001 and *Dagens Nyheter,* Editorial 8 December 2001.

203 "*Vaga svar om terrorlistan*", *Dagens Nyheter* 011212. (Translation by P.C.) See also "*Göran Persson diskuterade sanktioner mot terrorutpekade svenskar med FN-chefen*", *Svenska Dagbladet* 13 December 2001 and statement by the Minister of Foreign Affairs Anna Lind: *We immediately raised the issue of the lack of protection for the legal rights of the individual with the UN sanctions committee. We also made our concerns known to UN Secretary-General Kofi Annan, both in New York and on his visit to Stockholm. He was well aware of the shortcomings of the system and welcomed proposals from Sweden*, Ministry for Foreign Affairs press release, 20 December 2001, http: //www.regeringen.se

204 In December 2001 the Swedish Ministry of Foreign Affairs did, however, offer to forward documentation produced by the accused individuals to the Taliban Sanctions Committe. See "*UD agerar för utpekade somaliasvenskar*", *Dagens Nyheter,* 15 December 2001.

205 "Government requests revision of UN sanctions list", Ministry of Foreign Affairs press release, 22 January 2002, http://www.regeringen.se.

instructions given to the Sanctions Committee by the Security Council in Resolution 1390, adopted on 16 January, to formulate necessary criteria for the implementation of the targeted sanctions.[206] The Government interpreted this instruction as the opening up of a possibility to argue in favour of a more transparent evaluation of evidence based on set legal criteria when designating individual targets for sanctions. The Minister of Foreign Affairs stated:

> The Swedish Government welcomes the Security Council's decision. If the sanctions are adopted with appropriate concern for the rule of law, this can only strengthen the confidence in the UN system... Now that the new resolution has been adopted, the Swedish Government will today request in its own name a review of the names on the sanctions list, including the three Swedes. In the Government's view only the names of people who fulfil the criteria previously adopted by the EU should appear on the list.[207]

Based on this request Sweden has entered into discussions with a number of the members of the Sanctions Committee.[208]

In addition the three Swedish citizens concerned filed a request to be removed from the list. On January 25, the Swedish Government forwarded this request to the Sanctions Committee. This request was, however, not successful. The Sanctions Committee undertook the review process by a silent non-objection procedure in which three of the Committee members, the United States, Russia and Great Britain, objected to remove the concerned individuals from the list of designated terrorist entities. The negative answer to the request was communicated on February 1.[209] On the same day the Swedish Government declared that, without taking a position on the issue of guilt, it would file a new request for an objective examination of the evidence supporting the accusations against the three Swedish citizens.[210] The final outcome of this official request remains to be seen.

The possibilities for a legal review of the implementation measures

From a European Community, or a national Swedish legal perspective it can be argued that a possibility exists for review of the *implementation measures* in the light of fundamental constitutional rules laid down in European as well as in national law.[211] This is

206 SC/RES/1390/2002, Article 5 (d). Compare above under IV.4a, p. 505.

207 "Government requests revision of UN sanctions list", Ministry of Foreign Affairs press release, 22 January 2002, http://www.regeringen.se.The criteria on the definition of terrorist acts referred to in the statement were adopted by the EU 27 December 2001; Common Position 2001/931/CSFP, O.J.L 344, 28 January 2001, p.93, Article 1. See below under 4.4.2b.

208 "The USA opposes removal of Swedish citizens from UN sanctions list", Ministry of Foreign Affairs press release, 1 February 2002, http://www.regeringen.se.

209 "Svenskar stryks inte från terrorlista", *Dagens Nyheter,* 1 February 2002.

210 "The USA opposes removal of Swedish citizens from UN sanctions list", Ministry of Foreign Affairs press release, 1 February 2002, http://www.regeringen.se.

211 *Compare the reasoning by the ECJ in case C-84/95 Bosphorous Hava Yollari Turizm Ve Ticaret AS v. Minister of Transport, Energy and Communications, Ireland,* ECR [1996] I-3953.

said recognising that an annulment of the implementation measures would constitute an infringement of obligations under public international law that incurs state responsibility.

It should in this connection be noted that on December 14 the three Swedish citizens targeted by the sanctions, initiated a plea at the Court of First Instance of the European Communities for annulment of the relevant implementation measures; [212] Commission Regulation 2199/2001 as well as the preceding Council Regulation.[213] The central ground for the plea is the claim that the Regulations infringe fundamental human rights that constitute an integrated part of European Community Law,[214] most importantly the right to a fair and public hearing in accordance with Article 6 of the 1950 European Convention on Human Rights.[215]

At the time of writing of this chapter, no plea challenging the implementation measures has been filed with a Swedish national court. However, this will presumably happen in the near future. It should in this connection be observed that it is a clearly expressed Swedish position that acts of Community Law which stand in conflict with fundamental human rights, safeguarded by the Swedish Constitution, should not be given legal effect within the national legal system. Such an act is considered to fall outside the legislative competence attributed by Sweden to the Community institutions.[216]

A devaluation of the general confidence in the Security Council?

From a general perspective the method to freeze financial assets belonging to specifically designated entities in the implementing State is a type of "smart" sanction that has been developed since the early 1990's and has gained general acceptance.[217] However, the concrete Swedish experience in late 2001 put the spotlight on a potentially problematic development of UN sanctions policy. When a system of rules based on an inter-state paradigm establishes sanctions against individuals, fundamental legal rights of these individuals, guaranteed in national law could be infringed. If there are no legal procedures available for safeguarding the rights of the individual, this might lead to erosion of

212 Case T-306/01, *Aden and others* v. *Council and Commission.*

213 Council Regulation 467/2001.

214 TEU, Article 6.

215 In addition the claimants argue that the Regulations fall outside the competence of the Council's legislative power under Articles 60 and 301 of the EC Treaty and that they do not fulfil the character of Regulations as stipulated in the EC Treaty, Article 249.

216 See Report by the Parliamentary Constitutional Committee 1993/94 KU21, p. 29 and Government Bill on Swedish Membership in the European Union 1994/95:19, p. 498. The Swedish position is thus analogous to the position expressed by the German Bundesvervassungsgericht in case 2BvR 2134 and 2153/92 *Manfred Brunner and others* v. *The European Union Treaty*, 89 BverfGE, p. 155, [1994] *CMLR* 57, paras 48-49.

217 This type of sanction has been used by the Security Council on a number of occasions; SC/RES/841/1993 (Freezing of funds directly or indirectly belonging to, or controlled by, the Government of Haiti): SC/RES/883/1993 (Freezing of funds directly or indirectly belong to, or controlled by, the Government or public authorities of Libya, or any Libyan undertaking controlled by the Government or public authorities); SC/RES/942/1994 (Freezing of funds directly or indirectly belonging to, or controlled by, the Bosnian-Serb administration).

the confidence in the international legal system.

In the Swedish debate the criticism of the regime of sanctions set up by Resolutions 1267 and 1333 and reconfirmed by Resolution 1390 has been focusing on two interrelated issues.

One strain of criticism concerns the mode of operation of the Taliban Sanctions Committee. It has in this connection been questioned to what extent the Sanctions Committee has conducted, and possesses the capacity to conduct, a sufficient independent evaluation of the information presented to it before adopting amendments to the list of designated entities. In addition, the lack of transparency in the deliberations of the Committee has been criticised.

The second interrelated strain of criticism focusses on the rightlessness of the individuals concerned. There exist no formal administrative or judicial procedures whereby a person or organisation that has been designated as a target for sanctions by the Security Council may challenge the decision as factually wrong. The individual is left with no legal possibilities to defend himself against the accusation. Thus principles that are fundamental to any legal order, such as the presumption of innocence and the right to be heard, are set aside.

The common interest of establishing an efficient sanctions regime, furthering international peace and security, is thus given priority to the interest of safeguarding these fundamental legal principles. Such an order of priority might be acceptable but it requires a fundamental trust in the good judgement of the Security Council. This in its turn requires that the Council, or a special Sanctions Committee, when taking decisions on designating persons or organisations as targets for sanctions, has to base this decision on a thorough transparent evaluation of information presented to it. As a final resort a possibility for judicial review of the decision by the Security Council ought to be made available for the individual directly concerned.

It seems that in Swedish general opinion trust in the Security Council has been seriously devalued as a result of recent experiences.

These experiences became important for the formulation of a Swedish position on the implementation of further sanctions to combat international terrorism, including the freezing of financial assets, laid down in Security Council Resolution 1373 (2001).

c. The implementation of Security Council Resolution 1373 (2001)

Through Resolution 1373 (2001), adopted on 28 September, the Security Council established a general scheme of economic and legal sanctions with the objective to combat international terrorism. The Resolution obliges all States to take a wide variety of measures in order to prevent and suppress terrorist acts. These measures include the criminalisation of terrorist acts and the funding of such acts, the active prevention of financing, planning and facilitation of terrorist acts, including the freezing of financial assets, the duty to afford international assistance in connection with criminal investigations relating to terrorism and the prevention of the international movement of terrorists.[218] Finally, all

218 SC/RES/1373/2001, Articles 1-2.

States were called upon to report within 90 days their implementation of the Resolution to a specially established committee, the Counter Terrorism Committee.[219]

Thus Resolution 1373 supplemented Resolutions 1287 and 1333, which were specifically targeted at the Taliban administration, Usama bin Laden and associated entities.

It should be underlined that the Resolution, in contrast to the preceding Resolutions 1267 and 1333, left it to the implementing States to designate the entities that are targeted by the sanctions. Thus the system for sanctions laid down in Resolution 1373 has been given a far more decentralised character.

In Sweden all the duties to take action under Resolution 1373, with the exception of the freezing of financial resources, were fulfilled by existing legislation.[220] This obligation, remaining to be implemented, included a duty to freeze all funds and other financial assets of persons who commit or attempt to commit terrorists acts or support such activities. In addition, measures should be taken to prohibit funds from being made available for the benefit of such persons.[221]

The formulation of adequate measures to be used for implementation was publicly debated in the light of the experiences gained from the implementation of Resolutions 1267 and 1333. A first initiative for expedient implementation of the sanctions in national law was turned down by the Drafts Legislation Advisory Committee as unsatisfactory from a constitutional point of view.[222] The Swedish Government then concentrated its efforts to participate in the elaboration of implementation measures on the European Union level. Under pressure from general opinion, the Minister of Foreign Affairs argued strongly that sufficient safeguards for the individuals legal rights must be included in the EU acts for implementation.[223]

Implementation was executed by a combination of EU and national Swedish measures. In a Common Position, adopted on 27 December, the Member States laid the foundation for a common implementation through acts of EC law.[224] This Common Position included a definition of the term "terrorist act"[225] as well as an annexed list of persons and organisations whose financial assets should be frozen and to whom no funds should made available.[226] This political decision presupposed legislative implementation measures adopted within the EC framework.[227] Based on this Common Position, the

---

219 SC/RES/1373/2001, Article 6. Concerning the deliberations of the Counter Terrorism Committeee see http://www.un.org/terrorism/sc.htm.

220 See the Swedish report pursuant to Article 6 of SC/RES/1373/2001; S/2001/1233.

221 SC/RES/1373/2001, Article 1.

222 *"Ingen snar frysning av terroristtillgångar", Svenska Dagbladet,* 9 November 2001.

223 From its own perspective the Swedish Government's efforts were crowned with success. In a press release from the Ministry of Foreign Affairs it was stated that Swedish action resulted in that the EU implementation measures included a higher degree of protection for the legal rights of the individual. Ministry for Foreign Affairs press release, 20 December 2001, http://www.regeringen.se

224 Common Position 2001/931/CFSP, O. J. L 344, 28 January 2001, p. 93.

225 Common Position 2001/931/CFSP, Article 1.

226 Common Position 2001/931/CFSP, Annex I.

227 Common Position 2001/931/CFSP, Articles 2-3.

Council the same day decided upon a Regulation[228] prescribing specific restrictive measures against those persons and entities also listed in the annex of the Common Position, with a reference to the definition of the term "terrorist act" as laid down in the Common Position.[229] These restrictive measures include the freezing of financial assets and the prohibiting of making financial assets available to persons or organisations listed in a separate Council Decision.[230] This listing was based on the enumeration of persons and organisations in Annex I to the preceding Common Position.[231]

The decentralised nature of this scheme for sanctions is underlined by the power of the Council, acting by unanimity, to amend and review the list of persons and organisations to which the Regulation applies.[232] In order to ensure that there are grounds for keeping persons or organisations on the list a review should take place at least once every six months.[233]

Furthermore, the Regulation includes a number of safeguards for protecting the legal rights of the individuals concerned. A decision to enter a person or an organisation to the list of subjects covered by the Regulation is a decision of Community Law that may be challenged at the European Court of First Instance.[234] Secondly, the Member States are given certain national discretion to handle the question of releasing frozen funds. Thus, the Member States are empowered to grant specific authorisations to use frozen funds for essential human needs of a natural person included in the list or members of his family.[235] The Member States may also grant specific authorisations to unfreeze funds after consultations with the other Member States, the Council and the Commission. Such a specific authorisation shall be "with a view to the protection of the interests of the Community, which include the interests of its citizens and residents".[236]

In Sweden, the National Police Board,[237] the Swedish Financial Supervisory Authority[238] and The National Social Insurance Board[239] have been instructed to administrate

228 Council Regulation 2580/2001, O. J. L 344, 28 November 2001, p. 70. With regard to measures directed against persons and entities linked or related to third countries the Regulation is based on Articles 60 and 301 of the EC Treaty. With regard to measures against subjects with no such international relevance the Regulation is based on Article 308 of the EC Treaty.

229 Council Regulation 2580/2001, Article 1.

230 Council Regulation 2580/2001, Article 2.

231 Council Decision 2001/927/EC, O.J. L 344, 28 December 2001, p. 83.

232 Council Regulation 2580/2001, Article 2(3) with reference to Common Position 2001/931/CFSP, Article 1 (4-6).

233 Common Position 2001/931/CFSP, Article 1 (6).

234 EC Treaty Article 230. Alternatively a judicial review could be conducted by way of a preliminary reference from a national court to the ECJ in accordance with the EC Treaty, Article 234.

235 Council Regulation 2580/2001, Article 5(2).

236 Council Regulation 2580/2001, Article 6.

237 Decisions under Article 3 of Council Regulation 2580/2001.

238 Decisions under Articles 4 and 6 of Council Regulation 2580/2001.

239 Decisions under Article 5 of Council Regulation 2580/2001.

the implementation measures. However, it should be noted that the EU measures implementing Resolution 1373 have not yet, at the end of February 2002, been supplemented by a notification that the penal provisions of the national Law on International Sanctions will apply with regard to the directly effective provisions of the Regulation. One possible reason for this hesitation is of a legal-technical nature: Council Regulation 2580/2001 is based on Articles 60, 301 and 308 of the EC Treaty, while the Swedish Law on International Sanctions only refers to EC acts based on Articles 60 and 301.[240] In the interest of public transparency in the national implementation of economic sanctions a solution of this incompatibility between the two systems has to be found.

Nevertheless, the scheme of sanctions established by Resolution 1373 and the measures adopted for its implementation have been viewed very favourably by the Swedish Government as a way to re-establish legitimacy for the use of targeted sanctions. The implementation measures are also seen as a success for Swedish negotiation positions within the European Union.[241]

Finally it should be noted that the experiences gained from the implementation of targeted economic sanctions after September 11 2001 has motivated the Swedish Government to take a more general initiative for future reform with the objective to strengthen the legal rights of individuals.

d. A Swedish initiative for improvement of the system for execution of targeted sanctions

In December 2001 the Swedish Government voiced the ambition to actively promote a reformation of the system for implementing and monitoring targeted sanctions. This initiative constitutes a response to the critique that has been raised against the execution of sanctions under Resolutions 1267 and 1333. In connection with the presentation of this initiative the Minister of Foreign Affairs, Anna Lind stated:

> "The United Nations must develop a system that better safeguards the legal rights of individuals in cases where sanctions affect individual people."[242]

In concrete terms Sweden, in association with Switzerland and other interested countries, has the ambition to draw up proposals for ways in which the UN can develop sanctions regimes that make better provision for the legal rights of the individual. In its presentation of the initiative, the Swedish Government points at the decentralised EU

---

240 SFS 1996:95, § 8.

241 See statement by the Minister of Foreign Affairs Anna Lind, *Dagens Nyheter*, December 10 2001.

242 Minister of Foreign Affairs Anna Lind: "Targeted UN sanctions should give stronger protection to legal rights", Ministry for Foreign Affairs Press release, 20 December 2001. The question of the protection of the legal rights of the individual under sanctions regimes will be part of a project which the Government approved on 13 December, the "Stockholm process". At that time, the Government earmarked SEK 6.5 million for an international project on the implementation and monitoring of targeted sanctions, http://www.regeringen.se.

implementation of Resolution 1373 as one possible model from which to draw inspiration.[243]

(5) *Some Concluding Remarks on EU Implementation of UN Sanctions in the Light of the Swedish Law on International Sanctions*

The multi-layered system of implementation by a combination of EU/EC and national measures undoubtedly gives rise to legal-technical challenges as well as problems of transparency.

EU-measures on implementation ought to be seen as instruments used by the 15 Member States to fulfil their duties as signatories of the UN Charter. However, the sphere of competence of the EU does not cover all issues that might be covered by a decision on mandatory sanctions taken by the Security Council. There is a risk of *lacunæ* and thus the complexity of implementation has increased. This fact underlines the demands on the legal expertise vested in the national ministries responsible for implementation of UN sanctions. In concrete terms there exist technical and transparency difficulties in ascertaining the content of EU and Swedish Law on International Sanctions, since changes have been numerous as a consequence of new political developments. In this connection the legitimate public demands on transparency and clarity in the communication of implementation measures to the national legal subjects has to be underlined.

From a legal/political perspective, it should be observed that the EU-membership has induced a shift of arenas for Swedish political action on the question of UN mandated economic sanctions. In principle, EU membership legally precludes an individual Member State from conducting an activist sanctions policy of the kind Sweden conducted with regard to Southern Africa.[244] From a Swedish horizon this fact could be seen as partly reflected in the shift towards a legal-technical, rather than a political activist approach to the use and implementation of UN mandated economic sanctions.

Finally, it should be pointed out that the increased use of regional EU-sanctions undoubtedly opens up a series of interesting questions relating to efficiency and the future legitimacy of the universal UN system that needs a deeper analysis. This is, however, outside the scope of the present study.

V. Implementation of Resolutions on the International War Crimes Tribunals

(1) *Implementation of Security Council Resolution 827 (1993), Establishing the Tribunal on the Former Yugoslavia*

By the way of a Resolution, based on Chapter VII of the UN Charter, the Security Council, on 25 May 1993, established the International Tribunal for the prosecution of

243 Ministry for Foreign Affairs press release, 20 December 2001, http://www.regeringen.se.

244 It should in this connection be noted that the room for derogation from the duties within the sphere of EC competence with reference to Article 297 EC does not lend itself to a wide intepretation. Compare Case C-120/94R, *Commission* v. *Hellenic Republic*, [1994] ECR, para. 47.

persons responsible for serious violations of international humanitarian law committed in the territory of the Former Yugoslavia. The Resolution included an obligation addressed to all States to take any measures necessary to comply with requests for assistance issued by the Tribunal.[245] Since there existed no prior Swedish legislation on the question of assistance to international criminal tribunals and the question was seen as falling outside the scope of the Enabling Law, implementation had to be executed by the enactment of a specific law by the *Riksdag*. A special committee was set up by the Ministry of Justice in order to prepare a bill on the implementation of the duties on assistance laid down by the Resolution. The Committee finalised its deliberations 24 February 1994 by presenting a thoroughly motivated bill to the *Riksdag*.[246] The proposed Implementation Law was enacted by the Parliament on 2 June 1994 and entered into force on 1 July.[247]

The Implementation Law recognised the competence of the Tribunal and laid down rules on the formal procedure and division of responsibility for assisting the Tribunal. In general terms this system was given the following layout: Requests for assistance from the judges or the prosecutor of the Tribunal shall be addressed to the Swedish Ministry of Justice, which is given the main responsibility for the Government's co-operation with the Tribunal.[248] Specific rules on the procedure by Swedish authorities are subsequently laid down for the rendering of assistance in the form of extradition,[249] sequestration,[250] securing evidence[251] and the transfer of detained persons for testimony before the Tribunal.[252] The Government takes the final decision on each request for assistance.

The most far-reaching, and debated form of assistance is unquestionably the execution of requests for extradition. On this issue constitutional concerns were raised and the Swedish law reserved a limited room for national discretion. This question therefore deserves a further analysis.

a. Limitations on the duty to extradite individuals to the Tribunal

Initially it should be observed that the duty to assist the Tribunal laid down by the Security Council Resolution is unconditional. Nevertheless, the Swedish Implementation Law reserves a competence for the Government to take a decision in each individual case, this in order to safeguard the rule of law from a national perspective. Potentially this concern has its most central importance with regard to a request for extradition.

The Implementation Law states that the Government shall remit a request for extradition of an individual residing in Sweden to the Chief Public Prosecutor. The opinion

245 SC/RES/827/1993.

246 Government Bill 1993/94:142.

247 SFS 1994:569.

248 SFS 1994:569, § 2 as amended by SFS 2000:573. According to the original wording an application should be addressed to the Ministry for Foreign Affairs.

249 SFS 1994:569, §§ 3-8.

250 SFS 1994:569, § 9.

251 SFS 1994:569, §§ 10-11.

252 SFS 1994:569, § 12.

subsequently delivered by the Chief Public Prosecutor constitutes the basis for the Government's decision. If it is found to be motivated, the Government may choose to turn to the National Supreme Court for an additional opinion before taking its decision.[253] Nevertheless, the law explicitly includes a presumption that a judgement, or a decision on detention, taken by the Tribunal, constitutes a necessary prerequisite for extradition *if Swedish authorities cannot conclude that the judgement, or the decision on detention, is manifestly wrong*.[254] Thus, the room for discretion by Swedish authorities seems to be extremely limited. However, it should be noted that the Preparatory Ac to the Implementation Law states that the discretion left to the Swedish Government should also be used for safeguarding interests of an *ordre public* character. As examples of such situations are mentioned the medical status of the individual in question and the case where an individual already has been convicted for the same crime by a Swedish court (*Res Judicata).*[255] In the Preparatory Act this balance between fundamental national legal principles and the abidance to the duties under the UN Charter is commented on in the following non-conclusive way:

The interest to take regard to Swedish legal principles must however be weighed against the duty under Public International Law to co-operate with the Tribunal.[256]

b. Extradition of Swedish nationals

In the Preparatory Act for the Implementation Law it was explicitly noted that the Statute of the Tribunal does not allow a State to refuse the extradition of its own citizens. *Prima facie* this fact does not create a constitutional legal problem in Sweden. This is because, in contrast to that of a number of other States, Swedish constitutional law does not prohibit extradition of Swedish citizens.[257] However, the Instrument of Government does include a prohibition against the *expatriation* of Swedish citizens.[258] According to the Preparatory Acts related to this provision, the prohibition against expatriation establishes a constitutional limit to the possibility to extradite Swedish citizens. This is the case when the extradited individual might face a conviction to imprisonment so long that he or she hardly has a possibility to return to Sweden.[259] Nevertheless, the provisions of the Implementation Law relating to extradition cover all individuals residing in Sweden, including Swedish citizens.

This potential tension between the loyal implementation of the Security Council Resolution and the constitutional prohibition against expatriation was observed in the

253 SFS 1994:569, § 4.

254 SFS 1994:569, § 3.

255 Government Bill 1993/94:142, pp. 29-30.

256 Government Bill 1993/94:142, p. 30. Translation by PC.

257 Such a prohibition is however laid down in the general Swedish legislation on extradition; SFS 1957:668, § 2. When formulating the bill for the Implementation Law the Swedish Government carefully avoided any reference to this provision. Compare Government Bill 1993/94:142, p. 30.

258 Instrument of Government (Regeringsformen), Ch 2, § 7.

259 1975/76:KU 56, p. 32.

Preparatory Act of the Implementation Law but consciously left unsolved. It was stated that a future solution could be that Swedish citizens sentenced to imprisonment by the Tribunal served their sentence in Sweden. This would, however, require an agreement with the Tribunal and amendments to the Swedish law.[260]

(2) *The Rwanda Tribunal and Amendments to the Implementation Law*

On November 8 1994 the Security Council, acting under Chapter VII of the UN Charter, adopted a Resolution on the establishment of an International Tribunal for the prosecution of persons responsible for serious violations of international humanitarian law in the territory of Rwanda. As in the Resolution on the Tribunal for the Former Yugoslavia, the Security Council obliged all States to co-operate fully with the newly established Tribunal, including compliance with a request for assistance.[261] The Swedish implementation of the duty to render assistance to the Rwanda Tribunal was executed by a brief amendment to the Implementation Law relating to the establishment of the Tribunal on the Former Yugoslavia.[262] This amendment entered into force on January 1, 1996.

Simultaneously, the potential constitutional problems relating to the extradition of Swedish citizens were solved through precautionary measures. The Implementation Law was amended by a provision stipulating that in the case of a Swedish citizen, or a foreigner with strong connections to Sweden, being sentenced to imprisonment by anyone of the two Tribunals, it shall be made possible to serve the sentence in Sweden.[263] In this connection the Swedish Government offered the Tribunal on the Former Yugoslavia prison accommodation for Swedish citizens and for other persons residing in Sweden whom the Tribunal has sentenced to imprisonment.[264] Through these measures the constitutional restraints on extraditing Swedish citizens were diffused.

Finally it should be noted that the Implementation Law was amended in October 2000 as a consequence of a comprehensive legal reform of the Swedish legislation on international co-operation regarding the enforcement of criminal law.[265] These amendments were largely of an editorial character.[266]

---

260 Government Bill 1993/94:142, p. 30.

261 SC/RES/955/1994.

262 SFS 1995:1306 amending § 1 of SFS 1994:569.

263 SFS 1995:1306 amending new § 12a to SFS 1994:569. See Government Bill 1995/96:48, pp. 15-16.

264 According to the Swedish Government this offer did implicitly also relate to the Rwanda Tribunal. Government Bill 1995/96:48, p. 16. An agreement between the Swedish Government and the Tribunal on the Former Yugoslavia was concluded on 23 February 1999.

265 SFS 2000:573, Government Bill 1999/00:61.

266 It should be noted that the responsibility for handling requests from the Tribunals was shifted from the Ministry of Foreign Affairs to the Ministry of Justice. See SFS 1994:569, § 2.

VI. Concluding Remarks

All in all, the Swedish legal measures on the implementation of UN sanctions seem to have worked well in practice over the years. The original possibilities to restrict trade, certain services, payments and traffic have been extended to cover all financial and technical services and freezing of assets. The law on implementation of international sanctions of 1996 has confirmed this legal situation through more general provisions in order to match the demands that result from the development of the sanctions instrument.

After 1 January 1995, when Sweden became a member of the EU, the national implementation measures were integrated into a multi-layered system for the implementation of UN sanctions in which acts of secondary Community Law are supplemented by national legislative and administrative decisions. This in order to secure full and effective *national* implementation.[267] It should be underlined that, from the Swedish position, the Community acts are seen as instruments within a national policy for implementation of UN sanctions.[268] This view is emphasised by the fact that Sweden independently reports the totality of implementation measures directly to the UN.

Furthermore it ought to be noted that the legislation in question has not been a dead letter. Although it has mainly filled a preventive function, there is good reason to believe that the Swedish sanctions legislation is efficient. Nevertheless, during the 1990's the application of legal implementation measures resulted in a number of cases where the Chief Public Prosecutor brought alleged violations to national courts for criminal proceedings.[269]

267 The integration of Sweden into the system of common EU implementation was reflected in amendments to the national implementation ordinances in force 31 December 1994: SFS 1994:1666 (Iraq), SFS 1994:1667 (Libya), SFS 1994:1668 (Yugoslavia), SFS 1994:1669 (Angola) and SFS 1994:1670 (Serbian controlled territories in Bosnia and Herzegovina).

In order to comply with changes in the sanction regimes a number of national implementation ordinances have been adopted after Sweden's entry as Member of the EU: SFS 1997:4, 1998: 1353 (Iraq), SFS 1998:12, 1998:1354 (Angola), SFS 1995:1272, 1996:17, 1998:280, 1998: 1015, 1998:1194, 1999:255, 1999:584, 1999:709, 1999:794, 2000:134, 2000:206, 2000:897 (Yugoslavia), SFS 1999:232 (Libya), SFS 1996:154 (Serbian controlled territories in Bosnia and Herzegovina). In addition, lists of those EC regulations on sanctions that fall under the penal provisions of the Swedish law on economic sanctions have regularly been published in the Official Gazette. The latest publication took place on December 13, 2001; SFS 2001: 1271.

268 This is in concordance with the view stated by the ECJ in case C-84/95, *Bosphorous Hava Yollari Turizm Ve Ticaret AS* v. *Minister of Transport, Energy and Communications, Ireland* [1996] 3 CMLR 257, paras 13-14.

269 The following cases have led to verdicts in Swedish Courts 1990-2000:

Göteborgs Tingsrätt, case B 2560-90, "Svenska ICI AB", violation of SFS 1987:477 on sanctions against South Africa. The defendants were sentenced to fines.

Stockholms Tingsrätt, case B-14-10176-92, "Octavian AB", violation of SFS 1992:470, 1992: 371 and 1993:665 on sanctions against the FRY, appealed to Svea Hovrätt, case B 1178-94. The defendant was sentenced to 1 1/2 years imprisonment. The Supreme Court denied review.

Nevertheless, the latest development of the sanctions instrument, especially the targeting of specific individuals, has given rise to new challenges that threatens to erode the deep-rooted Swedish trust in the UN system. In Sweden there exists a great sensitivity that the implementation of sanctions should not infringe fundamental legal principles laid down in national law safeguarding the rights of individuals. In order to maintain the necessary confidence in the UN sanctions mechanism, it has to be applied in ways that avoid such tensions. With this in mind, it is today the ambition of the Swedish Government to actively participate in a process for reformation of the UN system for targeted economic sanctions.

Select Bibliography

I. Reports of Parliamentary Committees

1. SOU 1970:19 *Svensk FN-lag.*
2. SOU 1984:52 *Svensk sydafrikapolitik.*
3. SOU 1990:6 *Förbud mot tjänstehandel med Sydafrika mm.*
4. SOU 1995:28 *Lagen om vissa internationella sanktioner.*

Växjö Tingsrätt, case B 554-94, "Importation of Rubber Boots", violation of SFS 1992:470, 1992:471 and 1993:665 on sanctions against the FRY, appealed to Göta Hovrätt, Case B 1150-96, RH1998:18. The main defendant was sentenced to 1 1/2 years imprisonment.

Göteborgs Tingsrätt, case B 865-94, "Quad Petroleum", violation of SFS 1992:470 and 1993: 665 on sanctions against the FRY. The defendant was sentenced to ten months imprisonment.

Stockholms Tingsrätt, case B-14-1631-95, "Tälje Touring AB", violation of SFS 1992:470, 1992:471, 1993:66 and 1994:1668 on sanctions against the FRY, appealed to Svea Hovrätt, case B 1790-95. The defendant was sentenced to one-year imprisonment. The Supreme Court denied review.

Malmö Tingsrätt, case B 12611-95, "Importation of fruit juices and berries", violation of SFS 1992:470, 1992:471, 1993:665 and 1994:1668 on sanctions against the FRY. The defendant was sentenced to fines.

Helsinborgs Tingsrätt, case B 409-96, violation of SFS 1992:470, 1992:471, 1993:665 and 1994:1668 on sanctions against the FRY.

Helsinborgs Tingsrätt, case B 739-96, violation of SFS 1992:470, 1992:471, 1993:665 and 1994:1668 on sanctions against the FRY.

II. Monographs

1. Andrén, Nils, *Power-balance and Non-alignment* (Stockholm, Almquist & Wiksell, 1967).
2. Andrén, Nils, *Maktbalans och alliansfrihet* (Stockholm, Norstedts Juridik, 1996).
3. Blix, Hans, *Sovereignty, Aggression and Neutrality* (Stockholm, Almquist & Wiksell, 1970).
4. Bring, Ove; Mahmoudi, Said, *Sverige och folkrätten* (Stockholm, Norstedts Juridik, 1998).
5. Lysén, Göran, *Folkrättsligt ansvar. En studie av EG/EU och dess medlemsstater*, SIFIR N° 14 (Iustus förlag, 2002).

III. Articles

1. Cameron, Iain, "Targeted Sanctions, Legal Safeguards and the European Convention on Human Rights", 72 *Nordic Journal of International Law* (2003).
2. Cramér, Per, "Recent Swedish experiences with Targeted UN Sanctions: The Erosion of Trust in the Security Council", *in* Erika De Wet, André Nollkaemper (eds.), *Review of the Security Council by the Member States* (Antwerp/Oxford/New York, Intersentia, 2003).
3. Lysén, Göran, "Targeted UN Sanctions: Application of Legal Sources and Procedural Matters", 72 *Nordic Journal of International Law* (2003).

IV. Abbreviations

DFSP Documents on Swedish Foreign Policy

NJA *Nytt juridiskt arkiv*

SFS *Svensk författningssamling*

SOU *Statens offentliga utredningar*

SÖ *Sveriges överenskommelser med främmande makter*

15

SWITZERLAND

Mathias-Charles Krafft, Daniel Thürer and Julie-Antoinette Stadelhofer *

I. Historic Review**[1]

Switzerland, being a permanently neutral State and having been until recently a non-member State of the United Nations, was long considered a special case with respect to United Nations sanctions. While this qualification may have been justified prior to 1990, it can no longer hold true post Cold War. With its full participation in the international sanctions regime against Iraq, an important change of practice occurred in Switzerland. This change of practice accompanied a re-conceptualisation of Swiss neutrality, which had long posed a problem with respect to participation in international sanctions measures. At the same time, Switzerland reconsidered its relationship with the United Nations.

* Mathias-Charles Krafft is a former Ambassador and Emeritus Professor of the University of Lausanne. Daniel Thürer, LLM Cambridge, Dr. h.c. rer. publ., is Professor at the University of Zurich, Chair of Public International Law, European Law, Public Law and Comparative Constitutional Law. Julie-Antoinette Stadelhofer was formerly Assistant to the Law Faculty, University of Geneva, and now works for the State Secretariat for Economic Affairs, Switzerland (the views expressed in this study are solely those of the author).

** The authors are grateful to Joanna Bourke-Martignoni and Malcolm MacLaren for their most valuable assistance in reviewing the English text.

1 This study, written in the years 2001 and 2002, examines the implementation of UN sanctions by Switzerland since the beginning of the 1990s. With Switzerland's admission to the UN on 10 September 2002, the starting point for analysis has fundamentally changed from that for the time period under consideration. On the one hand, the days of sovereign decision-making are numbered, since Switzerland as a Member State is in future obligated in principle to implement sanctions resolutions. On the other, UN law, including the sanctions resolutions of the Security Council, is accorded automatic effect in the Swiss legal order. Moreover, in particular circumstances, it can be directly applied. Apart from these changes, which in the text will be explained in more detail and variously referred to as well as the entry into force of the Federal Law on the Implementation of International Sanctions, the previous implementation system remains authoritative. The following presentation is therefore still of current interest.

Vera Gowlland-Debbas (ed.), National Implementation of UN Sanctions, *523-579.*

This process led to Switzerland joining the United Nations in September 2002.

As concerns Swiss neutrality, a distinction must be made from the outset between the *law of neutrality* and the *policy of neutrality*.

The scope of the law of neutrality, as it derives from the Hague Conventions of 1907 and international customary law, is limited, applying only to international armed conflicts, i.e. armed conflicts between States.[2] In such conflicts, the neutral State is essentially bound by two complementary obligations: the obligation not to take part in the hostilities and the obligation of impartiality.[3] Strictly speaking, the law of neutrality pertains only to the military relations between a neutral State and the belligerent States and not to other relations, even economic.[4] Beyond these obligations, a neutral State enjoys considerable room for manoeuvre. The extent that a State wants to exercise this leeway depends on its policy of neutrality.

The *policy of neutrality* pertains to all the measures that a permanently neutral State adopts in peacetime in order to maintain the credibility of its neutrality.

Throughout the 19th century, States interpreted the obligation of impartiality expansively, i.e. as not limited to military matters but as covering economic matters as well.

---

2 The relevant Hague Conventions are: the Convention Respecting the Rights and Duties of Neutral Powers and Persons in Case of War on Land (V. Convention) of 18 October 1907 and the Convention Concerning the Rights and Duties of Neutral Powers in Naval War (XIII. Convention) of 18 October 1907. The importance of these two conventions as sources of the law of neutrality has to be relativised. International customary law is largely considered today by state practice and legal writers as the primary source of the law of neutrality.

3 Jürg Martin Gabriel, *Schweizer Neutralität im Wandel* (Frauenfeld, 1990); Giorgio Malinverni, "L'indépendance de la suisse dans un monde interdépendant", 117 *ZSR* (1998) II, pp. 105 ff.; Alois Riklin, "Die Neutralität der Schweiz", in: A. Riklin, A. Haug, R. Probst (eds.), *Neues Handbuch der schweizerischen Aussenpolitik* (Bern/Stuttgart/Wien, 1992), pp. 191-209; Alois Riklin, "La neutralité suisse et son évolution", in: *Mélanges en l'honneur de Jacques-Michel Grossen* (Bâle/Francfort-sur-le-Main, 1992), pp. 453-468; Dietrich Schindler, "Aspects contemporains de la neutralité", 121 *RCADI* (1967-II) 225-319; Dietrich Schindler, "Kollektive Sicherheit der Vereinten Nationen und dauernde Neutralität der Schweiz," *SZIER* (1992) 437-439 and 464-466; Daniel Thürer, "Vorstellungen über die dauernde Neutralität vor dem ersten Weltkrieg, heute und für die Zukunft", XLV *Schweizerisches Jahrbuch für internationales Recht*, Jubiläumsband, (1989) 73-103; Daniel Thürer, "Sicherheitspolitik und Neutralität", R. Rhinow (ed.), *Die schweizerische Sicherheitspolitik im internationalen Umfeld* (Basel/Frankfurt am Main, 1995), pp. 121-136.

4 It is thus forbidden for a neutral State to support one party to the conflict in its military operations (e.g. by making its territory available for military purposes including granting fly-over rights, by contributing armed forces or by exporting (State to State) arms and military goods). According to Art. 7 of the V. Hague Convention, private trade in arms and military goods remains permissible: "A neutral Power is not called upon to prevent the export or transport, on behalf of one or other of the belligerents, of arms, munitions of war, or, in general, of anything which can be of use to an army or a fleet". However, if a neutral State restricts trade in such goods, the principle of impartiality has to be respected: "Every measure of restriction or prohibition taken by a neutral Power in regard to the matters referred to in Articles 7 and 8 must be impartially applied by it to both belligerents" (Art. 9 of the V. Hague Convention). See Schindler, "Kollektive Sicherheit", *op. cit.* (note 3), p. 437 f.

This concept of neutrality is known as *integral neutrality*.

With the establishment of the League of Nations, the question of the compatibility of international sanctions as provided for in the Covenant with Switzerland's status of permanent neutrality arose. Swiss neutrality then underwent an important re-conceptualisation. In order to join the League, the concept of the *differential neutrality* was adopted. This concept of neutrality enables a neutral State to take part in economic sanctions but not in military sanctions adopted by an organisation of collective security.[5]

The negative experience with the League's sanctions regime against Italy in the Abyssinian conflict motivated Switzerland to return as soon as 1938 to the concept of *integral neutrality*. From that time, it became a matter of principle for the Federal Council not to take part in international sanctions for reasons of neutrality (policy of neutrality). Switzerland's decision not to become a member of the United Nations in 1945 is to be seen in this context.

In the case of the sanctions adopted against Rhodesia, the first mandatory sanctions ever adopted by the United Nations, the Federal Council reaffirmed this principle.[6] In its response to the notification of United Nations Security Council Resolution 232, the Swiss Federal Council stated that, due to its status as a permanently neutral State, Switzerland was not in the position to take part in the sanctions. Arguments based on the policy of neutrality, which emphasised the fact that by remaining outside of the United Nations sanctions regime Switzerland could become a hub for sanction-busting operations, proved particularly persuasive. Switzerland therefore decided to introduce the practice of the *courant normal* (stabilisation of the volume of bi-national trade at an average level for a period of reference – usually three years – prior to the adoption of the sanctions) for imports from Southern Rhodesia. Switzerland officially insisted that it had adopted these measures as a logical consequence of its policy of neutrality and stressed that their adoption could not be interpreted as a recognition of a legal obligation on non-Member States to apply economic sanctions. The measures were adopted on a purely autonomous and voluntary basis.

The sanctions adopted against South Africa raised no problems from the perspective of the policy of neutrality as they were not adopted in the context of an international armed conflict. When the Security Council adopted Resolution 418 (1977) calling for an embargo on weapons exports to South Africa, Switzerland was already applying a weapons embargo in conformity with the federal law on war material, which prohibits weapons exports to regions of political tensions.[7]

In its 1981 report, issued on the occasion of a popular referendum on Swiss entry to the United Nations, the Federal Council took a restrictive approach to the compatibility

5 FF 1919 IV 592-615. Correspondingly, Switzerland was exempted by the London Declaration to take part in military sanctions.

6 See also "Das Problem der Beteiligung der Schweiz an Sanktionen der Vereinten Nationen, besonders im Falle Rhodesiens by Rudolf Bindschedler, legal advisor to the Swiss Foreign Ministry in that period", 28 *ZaöRV* (1968) 1-15.

7 See *infra*, Section II.2, p. 533. For a comprehensive study of the relationship between Switzerland and South Africa see Groupe de travail interdépartemental Suisse-Afrique du Sud, *Les relations entre la Suisse et l'Afrique du Sud*, Berne, July 1999.

of neutrality and participation in sanctions. Though unproblematic under the law of neutrality, the adoption of economic sanctions is problematic under the policy of neutrality.[8] In a 1986 popular referendum, Swiss voters rejected a proposal to join the United Nations. Their rejection may have been partly influenced by doubts about the compatibility of permanent neutrality status with participation in United Nations sanctions.

The end of the bipolar world order led the Swiss Federal Council to abandon its restrictive policy of neutrality. Full participation by Switzerland in the economic sanctions adopted against Iraq was now considered to be compatible with the policy of neutrality. The Federal Council held that non-participation in the universal sanctions measures would practically amount to partisanship in favour of Iraq. Due to their universality it is no longer participation in economic sanctions but non-participation that risks jeopardising neutrality as such and the neutral position of Switzerland.[9] Accordingly, Switzerland adopted economic sanctions against Iraq in conformity with the relevant United Nations measures. The Federal Council insisted that Switzerland participate in these sanctions not because it was legally bound to do so, but autonomously and voluntarily (*autonomer Nachvollzug*).

This change prompted a re-conceptualisation of Switzerland's policy of neutrality. In 1993, the Federal Council issued a report that is still considered the basis for the conduct of the Swiss policy of neutrality.[10] The report reaffirmed the compatibility of Switzerland's status as a permanently neutral State with her participation in sanctions adopted by the Security Council under Chapter VII, as regards both non-military and military sanctions.[11] Put otherwise, the Federal Council believes, in conformity with prevailing legal opinion, that the law of neutrality does not apply to such sanctions.[12]

8 FF 1982 I 549-557.

9 Swiss Neutrality in Practice – Current Aspects, Report of 30 August 2000 by the Interdepartmental Working Group, p. 4, available on the website of the Federal Department of Foreign Affairs: http://www.eda.admin.ch, under "Publications".

10 Rapport sur la neutralité – Annexe au Rapport sur la politique extérieure de la Suisse dans les années 90, in: FF 1994 I 201-237. An English translation of this report is available under the title "White Paper on Neutrality – Annex to the Report on Swiss Foreign Policy for the Nineties" on the website of the Federal Department of Foreign Affairs (note 9). See as well the expert opinion issued by Professor Dietrich Schindler, "Kollektive Sicherheit der Vereinten Nationen und dauernde Neutralität der Schweiz", *op. cit.* (note 3), pp. 435-479 and *La neutralité de la Suisse sous la loupe – La politique étrangère suisse face à un monde en mutation*, Rapport du groupe d'étude sur la neutralité de la Suisse, Federal Department of Foreign Affairs, Berne.

11 FF 1994 I 222-224. In 1981, the Federal Council held that the participation of a neutral State in *economic sanctions* was not problematic from the perspective of the law of neutrality, whereas participation in *military sanctions* contradicts the law of neutrality (FF 1982 I 549-557).

12 According to this view, military sanctions cannot be considered as war for the purposes of the law of neutrality, but as legal measures for the enforcement of Security Council decisions. Consequently, the Security Council and the States adopting military sanctions do not act as belligerents, but as organs of international law enforcement. For this reason, even neutral States can participate in military sanctions (FF 1994 I 222-224). See Christian Dominicé, "La neutralité Suisse au carrefour de l'Europe", 113 *La semaine judiciaire* (1991) 398-433; Gabriel Jürg Martin, "Die Stellung der Schweiz zu Wirtschaftssanktionen", in: A. Riklin, H. Haug, R.

As guidelines for the conduct of the policy of neutrality with respect to international sanctions, the Federal Council sets out the following:

– with respect to *non-military sanctions* adopted by the Security Council under Chapter VII: participation in such measures if this is in the interest of Switzerland, defined according to considerations of solidarity, and if the measures are supported by a united community of States; however, Switzerland reserves the right not to participate if important States refrain from the outset or if the unity of the community of States is broken subsequently;
– with respect to *military sanctions* adopted by the Security Council under Chapter VII: without excluding participation in such sanctions in principle, the Federal Council nevertheless imposes a certain restraint on itself. Participation has to be examined in each case with reference to all the interests and goods at stake. As a rule, Switzerland will not obstruct such measures;
– with respect to *economic sanctions adopted outside of the United Nations*: the Federal Council is in principle ready to take part in such measures as well.[13]

In keeping with these guidelines, Switzerland has consistently followed all the non-military sanctions adopted so far by the Security Council. The federal authorities always insisted that Switzerland was taking part in these measures on an autonomous and voluntary basis (*autonomer Nachvollzug*) and that there was no legal obligation arising from Charter law for the non-Member State Switzerland to participate.[14] It is precisely the implementation of these non-military sanctions measures in the Swiss legal order and the questions and problems that have thereby arisen that will be analysed in the following sections. Looking beyond the scope of the present study, it is interesting to note, as regards the evolution of Swiss neutrality and participation in military United Nations sanctions, that Switzerland has on several occasions since 1993 conceded fly-over and transit-rights to foreign troops for United Nations operations in the Former Yugoslavia.[15]

In 1998, Switzerland participated for the first time also in economic sanctions taken outside the United Nations. In reaction to the massive human rights abuses committed

Probst, (eds.), *Neues Handbuch der schweizerischen Aussenpolitik* (Bern/Stuttgart/Wien, 1992), pp. 919-928; Dietrich Schindler, "Kollektive Sicherheit", *op. cit.* (note 3), pp. 452-458 and 473-475; Daniel Thürer, "UN Enforcement Measures and Neutrality: The Case of Switzerland", 30 *Archiv des Völkerrechts* (1992) 63-85.

13 FF 1994 I 224-227.

14 Of the same opinion was Daniel Thürer, "UN Enforcement Measures and Neutrality", *op. cit.* (note 12), pp. 69 ff. Various authors defended the point of view that even as a non-member State of the UN, Switzerland is by virtue of general international law bound to implement Security Council sanctions: Schindler, "Kollektive Sicherheit", *op. cit.* (note 3), pp. 458-464; Christian Linsi, *Gegenmassnahmen in der Form des Embargos zur Durchsetzung elementarer Völkerrechtsverpflichtungen in der schweizerischen Aussenpolitik* (Basel/Frankfurt am Main, 1994), pp. 103-116; Adrian R. Schaub, *Neutralität und Kollektive Sicherheit* (Basel/Frankfurt am Main, 1995), pp. 124-125; Christian Tomuschat, "Obligations arising for States without or against their will", 241 *RCADI* (1993-IV) 256-257.

15 Swiss Neutrality in Practice, *op. cit.* (note 9), p. 4 f. In the case of the military operation against Iraq, Switzerland refused to make available its air space and territory to foreign troops (*loc. cit.*).

against the Albanian population in Kosovo, the European Union adopted without a prior corresponding United Nations resolution economic sanctions against the Federal Republic of Yugoslavia, which were in general adopted by the EFTA and associated States.[16] It has to be noted that, in this situation, the law of neutrality was not applicable, as the conflict in Kosovo cannot be qualified as an international armed conflict.[17]

In spring 1999, however, when the NATO States began their military operation against the Federal Republic of Yugoslavia, the Federal Council declared the law of neutrality to be applicable, as the NATO operation had not been authorised by the Security Council. Switzerland was thus required to respect the obligations of a neutral State per the law of neutrality.[18] Accordingly, Switzerland did not concede fly-over rights to NATO aircraft for military missions. Flights for humanitarian missions remained, however, possible.[19] This precedent demonstrates that Swiss participation in military sanctions is only possible if the corresponding measures conform to international law.[20]

The practice of Swiss neutrality in the 1990s clearly shows that the narrow, Cold-War understanding of the policy of neutrality (*integral neutrality*) has been abandoned in favour of a more flexible understanding, amounting in effect to a focus on the military essence of neutrality.[21] By permitting even participation in military sanctions, provided that they are authorised or mandated by the United Nations Security Council, this new concept of neutrality goes beyond the inter-war concept of differential neutrality, which expressly excluded participation in military measures.

The evolution of the Swiss position with respect to participation in international sanctions measures accompanied a reconsideration of Switzerland's relationship with the United Nations. With the end of the bipolar world order, the general national attitude regarding United Nations membership changed.[22] During the second half of the nineties, several parliamentary interventions were made in favour of Switzerland joining the United Nations. On 1 March 2000, the Swiss Federal Council declared United Nations entry to be the strategic objective for the 1999-2003 legislative period. In March 2000, a

16 *Ordonnance instituant des mesures à l'encontre de la République fédérale de Yougoslavie* of 23 June 1999 (RS 946.207). See also the sanctions adopted in 2000 by the EU against Myanmar in which Switzerland also participated (*Ordonnance instituant des mesures à l'encontre du Myanmar* of 2 October 2000 (RS 946.208.2)).

17 Swiss Neutrality in Practice, *op. cit.* (note 9), p. 6.

18 *Ibid.*, p. 7.

19 An in-depth analysis of the Swiss position in respect to military and non-military sanctions against the FRY in the Kosovo crisis can be found in Swiss Neutrality in Practice, *op. cit.* (note 9), pp. 5 ff.

20 *Ibid.*, p. 18.

21 *Ibid.*, p. 2.

22 As late as in 1986, Swiss voters had refused to join the UN in a popular referendum. For an evaluation of Switzerland's relationship to the UN see Daniel Thürer, "Die Schweiz und die Vereinten Nationen", in: A. Riklin, H. Haug, R. Probst (eds.), *Neues Handbuch der schweizerischen Aussenpolitik* (Bern/Stuttgart/Wien, 1992), pp. 307-337. For a commentary on the referendum see Luzius Wildhaber "Das Schweizer Nein zu einer Vollmitgliedschaft in den Vereinten Nationen", 41 *Europa-Archiv* (1986) 461-468.

popular initiative organised by a committee of Swiss citizens proposing the entry of Switzerland in the United Nations was filed. Extensive consultation in summer 2000 revealed widespread support among political parties, political actors and civil society. In December 2000, the Federal Council sent the relevant *dossier* to the Swiss Parliament, which approved the attempt in autumn 2001.[23] The last word on this matter lay, however, with the Swiss people who had to accept entry by a double majority (majority of voting citizens and majority of cantons) according to the Federal Constitution. This vote was held in March 2002. With a clear majority of the voting citizens, but with only the narrowest possible majority of the cantons, United Nations entry was approved and the Federal Council instructed to take the necessary preparatory steps.[24] Accordingly, the Federal Council requested in June 2002 that the United Nations admit Switzerland, making it in the process clear, however, that Switzerland as a Member State would maintain its neutrality.[25] With its Resolution of 24 July 2002, the Security Council recommended the admission of Switzerland to the General Assembly and through its president declared itself satisfied with Swiss readiness to fulfil the obligations of the United Nations Charter.[26] On 10 September 2002, at the commencement of the 57th Session of the General Assembly, Switzerland was admitted by acclamation to the United Nations.[27]

With Switzerland's United Nations admission, her special status as a non-Member State has come to an end. Switzerland has thereby obligated herself per Article 25 of the United Nations Charter to implement sanctions resolutions adopted by the Security Council under Chapter VII. This obligation is important first in relation to peaceful sanctions measures, since in the case of military sanctions measures it is in principal limited to a duty to negotiate with a view to the special agreements provided for in Charter Article 43. Although as mentioned the present Swiss conception of neutrality considers both types of sanctions as being compatible with neutrality, the Federal Council's admission application contains, besides a declaration of Swiss performance of Charter obligations, a declaration of neutrality. A similar declaration was also lodged on the occasion of the General Assembly admission.[28] It was thereby to be made known

23 *Message relatif à l'initiative populaire pour l'adhésion de la Suisse à l'Organisation des Nations Unies (ONU)*, of 4 December 2000 in: FF 2001 1117.

24 54.6% of citizens and 12 cantons accepted entry, while 45.4% of citizens and 11 cantons rejected it. For a commentary on the referendum and the modification of Switzerland's constitution see Daniel Thürer and Pascal Baur, Artikel 197 Ziff. 1, in: B. Ehrenzeller, P. Mastronardi, R.J. Schweizer, K. Vallender (eds.), *St. Galler Kurzkommentar zur neuen Bundesverfassung* (Zürich/Lachen, 2002).

25 See the text of the admission application in the original French version at www.eda.admin.ch/sub_uno/ f/uno/publi/press/011024.

26 See SC Res. 1426 (2002), and Presidential Statement S/PRST/2002/23, both of 24 July 2002.

27 See GA Res. 57/1 of 10 September 2002.

28 See speech of Kaspar Villiger, President of the Confederation, in the GA on the occasion of Swiss UN-admission on 10 September 2002, <www.uno.admin.ch/sub_uno/g/uno/publi/speech.Par.0029.UpFile.pdf/sp_020910_speechFC_g>. See also speech of Federal Councilor Joseph Deiss in the GA on 13 September 2002, <www.admin.ch/sub_uno/g/uno/publi/

internationally that Swiss neutrality is an "integral component" of its United Nations admission and membership.[29] A reservation to the United Nations Charter is not, however, intended; the Charter should rather in all its aspects be adopted.[30] Nonetheless, some Parliamentary and Federal Council statements give the impression that the declaration should provide the Swiss policy of neutrality with room to manoeuvre that would enable the country to avoid participating in coercive measures should the system of collective security not function correctly or should the measures be problematic for Switzerland. Such scenarios[31] are at present rather unlikely; the actual importance of the declaration of neutrality so interpreted is therefore limited. Legally, it constitutes an interpretive declaration. It is not a reservation that would restrict the obligatory nature of certain Charter provisions as such. Instead, it sets out Switzerland's understanding of her rights and duties as a Member State and her political position in the United Nations, which understanding United Nations organs and Member States must in good faith take into consideration. Despite the declaration of neutrality, an obligation on Switzerland to implement Security Council sanctions resolutions is in principle therefore to be assumed. The Swiss room to manoeuvre that hitherto at least legally existed is thereby restricted; deviations from the sanctions resolutions are in principle prohibited in future.

In view of the post-Cold-War developments, Switzerland can no longer be qualified as a "special case" in relation to the implementation of Security Council sanctions resolutions.

II. Legal Basis of Domestic Measures Implementing Economic Sanctions

The conduct of foreign policy in Switzerland has traditionally been considered as falling within the competence of the Confederation, despite the fact that the previous Federal Constitution did not explicitly deal with this matter.[32] The revision of the Federal Constitution – which entered into force on 1 January 2000 – explicitly recognises the competence of the Confederation in foreign affairs in Article 54, while Articles 55 and 56 prescribe a limited right of cantons to participate in foreign affairs. Accordingly, in

speech.Par0031.UpFile.pdf/sp_020913_SpeechFC_g>.

29 See statement of Federal Councilor Joseph Deiss in the National Council, in: Official Bulletin of the Federal Assembly: National Council 2001, p. 1036. From the Winter session 1995, the Bulletin is available on-line via the Homepage of the Federal Assembly (www.parlament.ch).

30 *Ibid.*, p. 1037.

31 Examples could be the collapse of the universality of the UN or of the unity of the sanctioning States, the non-participation of leading States in coercive measures or sanctions that are directed at neighbouring States. See Dietrich Schindler, "Kollektive Sicherheit", *op. cit.* (note 3), pp. 457 f., 464, 474.

32 According to Wildhaber, the general distribution of competence between the Federal State and the cantons as provided for in the previous constitution as well as the whole constitutional context clearly show that the foreign affairs competence is based on an implied or implicit power of the Confederation. Luzius Wildhaber, "Aussenpolitische Kompetenzausscheidung im schweizerischen Bundesstaat", in: A. Riklin, H. Haug, R. Probst (eds.), *Neues Handbuch der schweizerischen Aussenpolitik* (Bern/Stuttgart/Wien, 1992), pp. 122 f.

the Swiss Federal State, the adoption of sanctions and the implementation of sanctions adopted by international organisations fall exclusively within the Confederation's competence.

(1) Constitutional Basis

Being previously neither a Member of the United Nations nor of the European Union, there was never a real need for Switzerland to enact constitutional or legal provisions concerning the domestic implementation of decisions adopted by international organisations. Nevertheless, there are provisions in the Swiss Constitution that can be used to give effect to such decisions.

In Switzerland, the Executive has traditionally played a primary role in decision-making on foreign affairs. There has been a recent trend, however, toward granting more influence to the Parliament in this field. The new Federal Constitution describes this trend as follows:

> "*La conduite de la politique étrangère ... relève en principe de l'organe gouvernemental. Compte tenu du parallélisme et de la complémentarité de leurs compétences, l'Assemblée fédérale et le Conseil fédéral sont nécessairement appelés à collaborer, mais le droit constitutionnel attribue au Conseil fédéral la majeure partie des fonctions de direction (opérationnelle) dans le domaine de la politique étrangère.*"[33]

The Constitution thus provides in Article 184, paragraph 1:

> "The Federal Government shall conduct foreign relations safeguarding the Federal Parliament's participation rights; it shall represent Switzerland abroad".

Article 102, paragraph 8 of the previous Constitution of 1848 contained a similar provision that had to be read together with subsequent paragraphs 9 and 10. The latter conferred on the Federal Council responsibility for matters of external security, the maintenance of independence and neutrality (paragraph 9), as well as the maintenance of internal peace and order (paragraph 10). These three paragraphs of the previous Constitution, which was in force until 31 December 1999, have been interpreted as authorising the Federal Council to enact executive orders.[34] As such, executive orders are directly founded on the Federal Constitution, being characterised in Swiss constitutional theory as *ordonnances indépendantes / selbständige Verordnungen*, whereas executive orders based on a legislative act are characterised as *ordonnances dépendantes / unselbständige Verordnungen*.[35] There was, however, an important difference in the scope of the three

33 Message relatif à une nouvelle constitution fédérale, in: FF 1997 I 424.

34 Jean-François Aubert, *Bundesstaatsrecht der Schweiz*, Fassung von 1967, Neubearbeiteter Nachtrag bis 1994, vol. II, Basel/Frankfurt am Main 1995, p. 726; Kurt Eichenberger/Dietrich Schindler, Art. 102, in: *Kommentar zur Bundesverfassung der Schweizerischen Eidgenossenschaft*, vol. IV, Basel/Zürich/Bern, p. 39/4 and p. 39/6.

35 Andreas Auer/Giorgio Malinverni/Michel Hottelier, *Droit constitutionnel suisse* (Berne, 2000),

paragraphs. Paragraphs 9 and 10 of Article 102 were to be interpreted very restrictively, authorising merely the adoption of executive orders when police measures were deemed necessary. Paragraph 8, which was not limited to police measures (even if these were included within its scope), authorised the adoption of executive orders more broadly, that is to say on foreign policy grounds in general. In situations where these constitutional provisions were used for the adoption of executive orders, they could be invoked both separately and together.[36]

This regulatory scheme has been taken over in the new Federal Constitution, which entered into force on 1 January 2000, through the adoption of Articles 184 (Foreign Relations) and 185 (External and Internal Security).[37] The official comment on Article 184 explicitly states that the ability to adopt sanctions falls within the competence conferred on the Federal Council by this provision.[38] With the new Article 184, paragraph 3 and Article 185, paragraph 3 the formerly implicit right of the Federal Council to adopt executive orders has been made explicit.[39] Contrary to the previous Constitution, which was silent as to the duration of such executive orders, the new Constitution provides that the latter must be time-limited.

The advantage of these new constitutional provisions is that they give the Executive an effective instrument with which to react rapidly to a situation without having to pass through the lengthy parliamentary procedure. When adopting such executive orders, the Federal Council is bound by the Constitution and existing legislative acts.[40]

---

vol. I, p. 522; Kurt Eichenberger/Dietrich Schindler, *op. cit.* (note 34), p. 39/4.

36 Kurt Eichenberger/Dietrich Schindler, *op. cit.* (note 34), p. 39/4.

37 Article 184, corresponding to the former Article 102, para. 8, reads as follows:

> "1. The Federal Government shall conduct foreign relations safeguarding the Federal Parliament's participation rights; it shall represent Switzerland abroad. ...
>
> 3. When the safeguard of the interests of the country so require, the Federal Government may issue ordinances and orders. Ordinances must be limited in time."

Article 185, corresponding to the previous Article 102, para. 9 and para. 10, reads as follows:

> "1. The Federal Government shall take measures to secure the external security, the independence, and the neutrality of Switzerland.
>
> 2. It shall take measures to safeguard internal security.
>
> 3. It may base itself directly on the present article to issue ordinances and orders to obviate existing or imminent great disturbances of the public order, the external or internal security. Such ordinances shall be limited in time."

38 Message relatif à une nouvelle constitution fédérale, in: FF 1997 I 424.

39 *Supra*, note 35.

40 Andreas Auer/Giorgio Malinverni/Michel Hottelier, *op. cit.* (note 35), pp. 535-537; Jean-Francois Aubert, *op. cit.* (note 34), p. 726.
In 1995, the Federal Council explicitly recognised that while adopting such orders, it is bound by the Constitution and pre-existing law, but that it is at the same time entitled to adopt rules *praeter legem* (JAAC 1996, 60/III, Nr. 88, pp. 783-789). According to Kurt Eichenberger/Dietrich Schindler, (*op. cit.* (note 34), p. 39/7), a departure from both the Constitution and legislative acts is permitted in very exceptional cases.

The extent to which the Swiss Federal Council has relied on these provisions to implement sanctions measures adopted by the United Nations Security Council will be examined below in Section II.3.

(2) Prior Enabling Legislation

On 22 March 2002, the Federal Assembly passed general prior enabling legislation for the implementation of international sanctions measures in the form of the *Loi fédérale sur l'application de sanctions internationales* (*Loi sur les embargos*, LEmb). This legislation will be examined separately (Section II.4).

Several pieces of pre-existing legislation have been used in the past to implement specific sanctions measures adopted by the Security Council. These include the *Loi fédérale sur le matériel de guerre* of 13 December 1996,[41] the *Loi fédérale sur le contrôle des biens utilisables à des fins civiles et militaires* (also called *Loi sur le contrôle des biens*) of 13 December 1996[42] and finally the *Loi fédérale sur les mesures économiques extérieures* of 25 June 1982.[43]

The *Loi fédérale sur le matériel de guerre* has a clear foreign policy objective and, as such, forms part of the Swiss legislation on foreign economic relations.[44] It requires that the production, trade, commission, import, export and transit of war material, as well as the transfer of intellectual property rights including know-how related to war material be submitted for authorisation (Article 2).[45] The requirements for the granting of authorisation for transactions abroad underwent a substantial change following the revision of this legislation in 1996. Under the previous 1972 legislation,[46] authorisation for exports of war material could be refused if the material concerned was destined for use in regions in which an armed conflict was ongoing or was imminent or in which there were other forms of dangerous tensions (Article 11). With the revision of 13 December 1996, which came into force on 1 April 1998, these requirements were adapted to the foreign policy function of this legislation. Article 22 of the revised legislation provides that,

> "*la fabrication, le courtage, l'exportation et le transit de matériel de guerre pour des destinataires à l'étranger seront autorisés si ces activités ne contreviennent pas au droit international et ne sont pas contraires aux principes de la politique étrangère de la Suisse et à ses obligations internationales.*"

---

41 RS 514.51.

42 RS 946.202.

43 RS 946.201.

44 RS 514.51, Article 1; see also Hansjörg Meyer, "Kriegsmaterialgesetz", in: Th. Cottier, R. Arpagaus (eds.), *Schweizerisches Bundesverwaltungsrecht – Schweizerisches Aussenwirtschafts- und Binnenmarktrecht* (Basel/Frankfurt am Main, 1999), p. 1.

45 The definition of war material adopted in Article 5 is a very restrictive one, excluding any dual-use goods. Dual use goods are covered by the Loi Fédérale sur le Contrôle des biens (*infra*, p. 534).

46 RO 1973 108.

A new provision (Article 25) was also included in the legislation that enables the Federal Council to decide, in accordance with decisions previously taken by the international community, that no authorisation shall be given for a specified country or region. Under the previous legislation, decisions could only be taken on a case-by-case basis. In view of these shortcomings, it was felt that legislation enabling the Federal Council to declare a general embargo on weapons exports to a particular country or region was necessary.[47] Such embargo declarations can, however, only be made in conformity with decisions adopted by the international community.[48]

The *Loi sur le contrôle des biens*[49] is an instrument for the control of strategically problematic dual-use goods[50] and specific military goods,[51] which are the object either of binding international agreements or non-binding international measures of control.[52] This legislation enables the Federal Council to introduce a system for the granting of permits (*régime de permis*) and an obligation to declare as well as monitor measures for the production, storage, transfer, utilisation, import, export, transit and commission of goods covered by binding international agreements (Article 4). As far as non-binding international measures of control are concerned, the Federal Council is enabled to apply measures for the import, export, transit and commission of such goods (Article 5) identical to those applied for binding international agreements. According to Article 6, paragraph 1, authorisation shall be refused if the activity envisaged is contrary to binding international agreements or non-binding international measures of control supported by Switzerland. Article 6, paragraph 2, which contains another ground upon which permits may be refused, constitutes a clear legal basis for Switzerland's participation in sanctions measures adopted by the Security Council:

> "*Les permis concernant les biens militaires spécifiques sont en outre refusés lorsque les Nations Unies ou certains Etats qui, comme la Suisse, participent à des mesures internationales de contrôle des exportations, interdisent l'exportation de tels biens, et si les principaux partenaires commerciaux de la Suisse s'associent à ces mesures d'interdiction.*"

47 According to the Swiss Federal Council , "… *il serait parfois utile que des décisions puissent être prises aussi en l'absence de demande concrète. Tel est le cas lorsque la Suisse désire faire savoir qu'elle se joindra à un embargo décidé par la communauté internationale … Le prononcé d'un embargo a en effet une portée politique plus grande qu'une simple information selon laquelle une éventuelle demande d'autorisation d'exporter vers un tel ou tel pays se heurterait à une décision négative.*" (*Message concernant l'initiative populaire pour l'interdiction d'exporter du matériel de guerre et la révision de la loi fédérale sur le matériel de guerre*, FF 1995 II 1029).

48 *Ibid.*, p. 1039; see also Art. 25.

49 RS 946.202.

50 Dual-use goods are goods that can be used for military as well as for civilian purposes (Art. 3b).

51 Specific military goods are goods that have been conceived or modified for military purposes but that are not arms, ammunition, explosives or any other type of weapon (Art. 3c).

52 Articles 1 and 2. See also Karl Weber, "Das Güterkontrollgesetz", in: Th. Cottier, R. Arpagaus (eds.), *Schweizerisches Bundesverwaltungsrecht – Schweizerisches Aussenwirtschafts- und Binnenmarktrecht* (Basel/Frankfurt am Main, 1999), p. 1.

This provision means that a possible United Nations embargo would *de facto* imply a prohibition of export for the corresponding goods, if they were covered by the *Loi sur le contrôle des biens.*[53]

The *Loi fédérale sur les mesures économiques extérieures* has several different purposes. One is to serve as the legal basis for the adoption of protectionist measures directed against economic measures adopted by other countries or to deal with exceptional economic conditions abroad. To that end, Article 1 provides for a general enabling clause in favour of the Federal Council if essential economic interests of Switzerland are at stake. The Council is enabled to control the import, export and transit of goods and services, to submit these to a system of permits and to limit or prohibit them (Article 1, let. a). The Federal Council is also enabled to regulate financial transactions with certain countries and under certain conditions, to impose taxes on these transactions (Article 1, let. b).[54]

(3) Ex-Post Facto *Legislation, Executive Orders or Decrees*

In the Swiss legal order, international sanctions are generally implemented by *ad hoc* instruments. In situations where these international measures are limited to a weapons embargo, however, it is not necessary to enact *ad hoc* legislation, as such measures may be implemented on the basis of pre-existing legislation, such as the *Loi fédérale sur le matériel de guerre* and the *Loi fédérale sur le contrôle des biens* mentioned above. In all other situations, the adoption of an *ad hoc* instrument, which takes the form of an executive order under the Constitution, is necessary.[55] This is why in each recent case of Security Council sanctions that went beyond an embargo on weapons, the Federal Council enacted specific executive orders, namely: *Ordonnance instituant des mesures économiques envers la République d'Irak* of 7 August 1990[56] (hereafter *Ordonnance Irak*), *Ordonnance concernant des mesures à l'encontre de la Libye* of 15 April 1992[57] (hereafter *Ordonnance Libye I*), which was replaced by a new executive order of 12 January 1994[58] (hereafter *Ordonnance Libye II*), *Ordonnance instituant des mesures économiques à l'encontre de la Yougoslavie (Serbie et Monténégro)* of 3 June 1992[59] (hereafter *Ordonnance Yougoslavie I),* which was replaced by the *Ordonnance instituant des mesures économiques à l'encontre de la Yougoslavie (Serbie et Monténégro) et d'autres régions contrôlées par les Serbes* of 3 October 1994[60] (hereafter *Ordonnance Yougoslavie II*), *Ordonnance instituant des mesures économiques à l'encontre d'Haïti* of 30 June 1993[61] (here-

---

53 Karl Weber, *op. cit.* (note 52), p. 29.

54 Karl Weber, "Das Bundesgesetz über aussenwirtschaftliche Massnahmen", in: Th. Cottier, R. Arpagaus (eds.), *Schweizerisches Bundesverwaltungsrecht – Schweizerisches Aussenwirtschafts- und Binnenmarktrecht* (Basel/Frankfurt am Main, 1999), p. 1 and p. 3. See also FF 1982 I 65ff.

55 *Supra*, Section II.1, pp. 523ff.

56 RS 946.206.

57 RO 1992 958.

58 RO 1994 108.

59 RO 1992 1203.

60 RO 1994 2194.

61 RO 1993 2053.

after *Ordonnance Haïti I*), which was replaced by the executive order of 22 June 1994[62] (hereafter *Ordonnance Haïti II*), *Ordonnance instituant des mesures à l'encontre de l'UNITA* of 25 November 1998[63] (hereafter *Ordonnance UNITA*), *Ordonnance instituant des mesures à l'encontre de la Sierra Leone* of 8 December 1997[64] (hereafter *Ordonnance Sierra Leone)*, *Ordonnance instituant des mesures à l'encontre de la République fédérale de Yougoslavie* of 23 June 1999[65] (hereafter *Ordonnance Yougoslavie III*), the *Ordonnance instituant des mesures à l'encontre des Taliban (Afghanistan)* of 2 October 2000 (hereafter *Ordonnance Taliban*)[66] and lastly the *Ordonnance instituant des mesures à l'encontre du Liberia* of 27 June 2001 (hereafter *Ordonnance Liberia*).[67]

Each of these executive orders was based on the aforementioned Article 102, paragraph 8 and/or paragraph 9 of the previous Federal Constitution. The differences between the provisions of the previous Constitution and those in the new Constitution have already been examined. Whereas in the first of these executive orders (*Ordonnance Irak*) reference was made to both paragraphs 8 and 9 of Article 102, all of the subsequent executive orders relied exclusively on paragraph 8 of the 1848 Constitution. Only the two latest executive orders (*Ordonnance Taliban* and *Ordonnance Liberia*) were adopted under the new Federal Constitution.

As far as United Nations Security Council Resolutions 827 and 955 calling on all States to co-operate with the International Criminal Tribunals for the Former Yugoslavia and Rwanda are concerned, *ad hoc* legislation was also adopted: *Arrêté fédéral relatif à la coopération avec les tribunaux internationaux chargés de poursuivre les violations graves du droit international humanitaire* of 21 December 1995.[68] According to the Federal Council,

> "*une base légale est nécessaire pour que la Suisse puisse satisfaire pleinement aux exigences énoncées par les Statuts et soit à même de collaborer pleinement avec les tribunaux.*"[69]

The pre-existing *Loi fédérale sur l'entraide internationale en matière pénale* of 20 March 1981[70] could not serve as a basis for co-operation with the International Criminal Tribunals. As the Federal Council stressed, this legislation was conceived for co-operation

62 RO 1994 1453.

63 RO 1999 151.

64 RS 946.209.

65 RS 946.207. Inasmuch as this executive order refers to a trade embargo on war material, it is properly implementing UN sanctions. In respect of all the other sanctions measures laid down therein, the executive order is implementing the comprehensive sanctions measures decided within the EU. With the adoption of this executive order, Switzerland has thus participated for the first time in sanctions measures decided outside of the UN.

66 RS 946.203.

67 RS 946.208.1.

68 RS 351.20.

69 FF 1995 IV 1065.

70 RS 351.1.

between States and could therefore not apply *telle quelle* to co-operation with the Tribunals, which raises different problems. Nevertheless, it was decided that it was possible to apply the pre-existing law on judicial assistance *mutatis mutandis*. The 1981 legislation thus served as a source of inspiration for the subsequent *Arrêté fédéral*, and it continues to apply by analogy to issues where the latter is silent (Article 2 of the *Arrêté*).[71] The *Arrêté fédéral* addresses some of the specific problems raised by the co-operation with the Tribunals; it also simplifies the procedures provided for in the law on judicial assistance. The scope of the *Arrêté* is limited to co-operation with the International Criminal Tribunals for ex-Yugoslavia and Rwanda (Article 1, (a) and (b)). The Federal Council stressed that this *ad hoc* legislation should not go beyond this scope and that the aim was not to regulate co-operation with the International Criminal Court. Nevertheless, in the event that other *ad hoc* criminal tribunals are established by the Security Council, Article 1, paragraph 2 authorises the Federal Council to extend the scope of the *Arrêté fédéral* to them.[72]

It is interesting to note that this *ad hoc* legislation was not enacted by the Federal Council in the form of an executive order, but by the Swiss Parliament in accordance with the procedure laid down for the adoption of urgent legislative acts (*Arrêté fédéral urgent*).

The three sections below will mainly focus on these *ad hoc* instruments, examining first the scope of these domestic measures as compared to Security Council resolutions (Section III), second the domestic procedures established by these instruments for the implementation and enforcement of international sanctions measures (Section IV) and third the implementation of Security Council resolutions relating to the International Criminal Tribunals (Section V). Before we undertake this examination, however, the new *Loi fédérale sur l'application de sanctions internationales* (*Loi sur les embargos*, LEmb) of 22 March 2002 will be presented.

(4) Framework Legislation on the Implementation of International Sanctions

As mentioned, in order to apply sanctions measures adopted by the United Nations Security Council, the Swiss Federal Council has enacted executive orders directly based on the Federal Constitution. These executive orders provide for the comprehensive regulation of the specific sanctions cases, including the modalities for their national implementation, such as provisions on the sphere of competence of the authorities involved, provisions on the treatment of data regarding sanctions measures, provisions on co-operation between national and international authorities, as well as provisions on penal sanctions and on criminal procedure for sanctions violators. The fact that these modalities are regulated by an executive order raises some problems. Due to their impact on individual rights, the treatment of sensitive data by State authorities must be explicitly provided for by what Swiss constitutional theory calls *loi formelle / formelles Gesetz*, that is to say, by an act adopted by Parliament according to the ordinary legislative procedure and subjected

71 FF 1995 IV 1071.

72 *Ibid.*, p. 1067, p. 1072 and p. 1074.

to a popular referendum if so requested by 50,000 Swiss citizens (*référendum facultatif*).[73] The same holds true for punishment by imprisonment. Although the various executive orders did generally provide only for fines, the additional possibility of punishment by imprisonment was introduced in order to increase the deterrent effect.

In view of these problems, it was felt necessary to create a framework legislation on the implementation of international sanctions. This legislation, the *Loi fédérale sur l'application de sanctions internationales (Loi sur les embargos, LEmb)*, was passed by the Swiss Parliament on 22 March 2002.[74] As is evident from its title and its first provision, this legislation is intended to serve as a legal basis for the implementation in Switzerland of non-military sanctions measures adopted internationally.[75] To that end, the legislation makes a clear distinction between sanctions (*sanctions / Sanktionen*) and coercive measures (*mesures de coercition/Zwangsmassnahmen*). The term "sanction" is used for international measures, that is to say measures adopted by the United Nations, the OSCE or the major trading partners of Switzerland, whereas the term "coercive measure" is only used for national measures that are necessary for the implementation of international sanctions.[76] In addition to serving as a legal basis for the implementation of international sanctions measures, the draft framework legislation has three objectives. It elaborates the necessary legal basis for the treatment of sensitive data and for penalties of imprisonment in the context of coercive measures as well as allowing for the standardisation of the general conditions for the actual implementation of coercive measures.[77] As outlined above, these general conditions have previously been established separately for each sanctions regime through specific executive orders. With the current regulation already based on *ad hoc* legislation, these general conditions are submitted to a single regime, as the relevant executive orders contain largely identical provisions on these issues. With the entry into force of the *Loi sur les embargos,* these general conditions are pre-defined, thereby making it unnecessary for the Federal Council to establish modalities. The *Loi sur les embargos*, after setting out the general provisions governing the national imple-

73 According to Art. 17, para. 2, of the Federal Law on Data Protection (*Loi fédérale sur la protection des données* of 19 June 1992 (RS 235.1) data of a particularly sensitive nature (which includes data on the violation of sanctions measures) may only be treated by federal authorities if a *loi au sens formel* explicitly so provides.
According to the Federal Supreme Court, any sanction of imprisonment requires a legal basis in the form of a *loi formelle*, as it is a particularly serious restriction of personal freedom (ATF 118 Ia 305, para. 7a (p. 318f); ATF 112 Ia 107, para. 3b (p. 112f); ATF 123 IV, para. 3d (p. 38)).

74 RS 946.231; see also the official comment in: *Message concernant la loi fédérale sur l'application de sanctions internationales* of 20 December 2000 (FF 2001 1341). The legislation entered into force on 1 January 2003.

75 Art. 1, para. 1 reads as follows: "*La Confédération peut édicter des mesures de coercition pour appliquer les sanctions visant à faire respecter le droit international public, en particulier les droits de l'homme, décrétées par l'Organisation des Nations Unies, par l'Organisation pour la sécurité et la coopération en Europe, ou par les principaux partenaires commerciaux de la Suisse.*"

76 FF 2001 1363.

77 FF 2001 1344 f.

mentation of sanctions (Section 1 (Article 1 and Article 2)), specifies the verification procedure (Section 2 (Article 3 and Article 4))[78] and provides for data protection and co-operation between national and international authorities (Section 3 (Arts. 5-7)),[79] appeal procedures (Section 4 (Article 8)) and penal sanctions for sanctions violators (Section 5 (Arts. 9-14)).[80] By creating a legal framework for the national implementation of coercive measures, this legislation will standardise these measures.

The legislation as such does not, however, constitute a sufficient legal basis for the direct implementation of international sanctions. In each situation where sanctions are applied, it will be necessary to enact a legal instrument specifying the exact content of the national coercive measures to be taken. According to Article 2, the Swiss Federal Council is competent to adopt these instruments (Article 2, paragraph 1), which take the form of executive orders (Article 2, paragraph 3). In contrast to the executive orders that the Federal Council has previously adopted based on the Federal Constitution (as described in Sections II.1 and II.3), executive orders are, with the entry into force of the new legislation, based directly on the *Loi sur les embargos*. In Swiss constitutional theory, executive orders based on the Federal Constitution are called *ordonnances indépendantes / selbständige Verordnungen*, whereas executive orders based on a prior legislative act are called *ordonnances dépendantes / unselbständige Verordnungen.*[81] Accordingly, under the *Loi sur les embargos*, executive orders adopted for the purposes of implementing international sanctions will undergo a change in nature. The Swiss Federal Council will continue, however, to be authorised to adopt sanctions by virtue of its constitutional powers (Article 184 of the Federal Constitution) even if such measures have not previously been adopted internationally (unilateral measures), since such measures are in principle authorised according to public international law.[82]

In its Official Comment on the *Loi sur les embargos*, the Federal Council emphasises that the framework legislation should not be interpreted as binding it to adopt coercive measures in order to apply international sanctions. Even following the adoption of the framework legislation, it will remain within the Federal Council's discretion to decide whether and to what extent Switzerland should apply international sanctions.[83] The Federal Council further insists that the framework legislation is in no way connected to the matter of Switzerland joining the United Nations or the EU.[84] However, with Switzerland's admission to the United Nations, the Federal Council's margin of appre-

78 Art. 3 states that persons affected by coercive measures must provide any information required in order to allow for the particular case to be determined.

Art. 4 authorises authorities competent for the verification of sanctions measures to undertake investigations on the commercial premises of any legal person subject to the duty to inform under Art. 3 and to consult any document useful to that effect.

79 See *infra,* Section VII, p. 570.

80 See *infra,* Section III.6, p. 557.

81 See *supra,* Section II.1, p. 531.

82 FF 2001 1360.

83 FF 2001 1364.

84 FF 2001 1361.

ciation whether and to what extent to apply international sanctions has been considerably reduced.[85]

This legislation, which is officially called framework legislation (*loi-cadre*),[86] in reality approximates prior enabling legislation, as it was defined in the introductory section to this chapter.

III. Comparison of the Content of Security Council Resolutions with Domestic Measures

(1) *Scope of Prohibitions*

The scope of the sanctions measures adopted by the United Nations Security Council is very broad, ranging from trade embargoes to embargoes on air traffic and aircraft, financial embargoes, travel restrictions and miscellaneous embargo measures that vary depending on the context. Whereas at the beginning of the nineties – the so-called sanctions decade[87] – sanctions measures were often comprehensive, i.e. directed indiscriminately against the whole population of a State, they have become increasingly targeted at specific groups of persons. Recently, various comprehensive measures to fight terrorism have been agreed. These measures have generally been implemented by Switzerland through sovereign decisions. In most cases, the domestic implementation measures have taken the form of *ad hoc* legislation adopted by the Federal Council under its constitutional powers. In other cases, particularly in relation to embargoes on weapons and related material as well as miscellaneous sanctions measures, *ad hoc* legislation was not necessary, since the measures in question could be implemented on the basis of pre-existing legislation. In the fight against terrorism, action was taken at different levels in the Swiss legal order.

The purpose of this section is to examine to what extent the sanctions resolutions of the Security Council have been fully implemented by Switzerland, that is to say, whether the measures on the domestic level are coterminous with the measures on the international level; whether they fall short of such requirements; or whether they in fact go beyond the Security Council resolutions. To that end, a distinction will be made between the different categories of measures (trade embargoes, financial embargoes, embargoes on air traffic and aircraft, travel restrictions, other miscellaneous sanctions measures and measures to fight terrorism).

a. Trade embargoes

Trade embargoes in one form or another have been adopted in each sanctions regime. The material scope of the trade embargoes varies greatly, ranging from extremely selec-

85 See *supra*, Section I and *infra*, Section VI.1, pp. 529 and 566.

86 FF 2001 1359.

87 David Cortright/George A. Lopez, *The Sanctions Decade – Assessing UN Strategies in the 1990s* (Colorado, 2000).

tive trade embargoes limited to specific items, to comprehensive trade embargoes including all kinds of goods (Iraq sanctions regime).

In the cases where the Security Council sanctions regime was limited to an embargo on weapons and related material (Somalia (Resolutions 733 and 751), Armenia/Azerbaijan (Resolutions 822 and 853), Rwanda (Resolutions 918, 997 and 1011) and Yemen (Resolution 924)), Switzerland adopted no national implementing legislation, as these measures could be implemented on the basis of pre-existing legislation, such as the *Loi fédérale sur le matériel de guerre* and the *Loi fédérale sur le contrôle des biens utilisables à des fins civiles et militaires et des biens militaires spécifiques*, both of 1996, or their respective predecessor legislation.[88]

In the cases where the Security Council sanctions regime provided for measures going beyond an embargo on weapons and related material, *ad hoc* legislation in the form of executive orders was adopted by the Federal Council. As far as trade embargoes on weapons and related material are concerned, Switzerland has always been keen to implement these measures in the relevant executive orders, while at the same time stressing their subordination to pre-existing national legislation.[89]

If one compares the scope *ratione materiae* of the executive orders with that of the relevant provisions of the Security Council resolutions, one has to conclude that, insofar as trade embargoes are concerned, Security Council measures have been fully implemented by Switzerland. Nevertheless, the effective scope of sanctions measures even when fully implemented in domestic law may be seriously affected by certain exception clauses.[90]

With respect to trade embargoes, particular mention must be made of conflict diamonds. In its efforts to put an end to civil wars in Angola and Sierra Leone, the Security Council directed its attention to the trade in rough diamonds that funds the rebel groups UNITA in Angola and RUF in Sierra Leone. Security Council Resolutions 1173 (1998) and 1306 (2000) prohibit the direct or indirect import from Angola and Sierra Leone, respectively of all rough diamonds that are not controlled through a certificate of origin issued by the government in Luanda or Freetown. As it was suspected that Liberia was disregarding Resolution 1306 and supporting the RUF, the import of rough diamonds from Liberia was prohibited by Resolution 1343 (2001). Switzerland implemented the rough diamond embargoes against UNITA, RUF and Liberia through executive orders.[91] Nevertheless, Switzerland was criticised by the United Nations expert panels responsible, especially for procedures at the customs warehouses at Zurich and Geneva airports, where until September 2000, rough diamonds could be stored without any declaration. The United Nations and NGOs feared that these customs warehouses might serve as hubs

---

88 See *supra*, Section II.2, p. 533.

89 Art. 3, para. 5 of the *Ordonnance concernant des mesures à l'encontre de la Libye* of 15 April 1992 (RO 1992 958) reads as follows: "*Les 1er à 4e alinéas ne s'appliquent que dans la mesure où la loi fédérale du 30 juin 1972 sur le matériel de guerre, la loi fédérale du 23 décembre 1959 sur l'utilisation pacifique de l'énergie atomique et la protection contre les radiations et leurs ordonnances d'application, ainsi que l'ordonnance du 12 février 1992 sur l'exportation et le transit de marchandises et de technologies ayant trait aux armes ABC et aux missiles ne sont pas applicables.*"

90 See *infra*, Section III.5, p. 553.

91 Art. 2a *Ordonnance Sierra Leone*, Art. 5 *Ordonnance UNITA*, Art. 2 *Ordonnance Liberia.*

for the trade in conflict diamonds. In an attempt to further tighten its control system, the Swiss Government has undertaken to regulate transactions in customs warehouses more closely through two sets of measures. Since 15 March 2001, customs warehouses have been requested to produce an inventory of rough diamonds that are both stored on and cleared from their premises. Switzerland now requires declarations of history and origin not only for rough diamond imports into Switzerland but also for transits through customs warehouses in Switzerland, thus going beyond United Nations requirements. These measures have been well received by the United Nations and may have contributed to the lifting of the suspicion that Switzerland is a hub for the trade in conflict diamonds.

Switzerland is also actively taking part in the Kimberley Process, which is seeking to develop an international certification scheme for rough diamonds. In this context, Switzerland did host the November 2002 conference of the Kimberley Group, at which the international certification scheme for rough diamonds was launched.[92]

b. Financial embargoes

Financial embargoes with measures of varying intensity, ranging from the prohibition on the transfer of funds to the freezing of assets, were instituted against Iraq, Libya, Haiti, Yugoslavia, UNITA (Angola) and the Taliban (Afghanistan). As this section makes clear, financial sanctions have undergone an interesting change in nature. From being comprehensive in the case of Iraq, they have increasingly come to be targeted at specific groups of persons (mostly ruling elites or rebel groups). While comprehensive financial sanctions do not raise special problems for the financial actors who have to implement them in the field, targeted financial sanctions do. During the last few years, considerable effort has been made to analyse the feasibility of targeted financial sanctions and to increase their efficiency. The concept of targeted financial sanctions is also of major importance in the fight against terrorism in general and terrorism financing in particular.

The prohibition of Security Council Resolution 661 to transfer funds to Iraq was implemented with the adoption of the corresponding sanctions regulation on 7 August 1990.[93]

In the cases of Libya and Haiti, the Security Council required the freezing of funds and financial resources owned or controlled by the Government or public authorities of Libya/Haiti as well as by any related entity (Resolution 841, paragraph 8; Resolution 883, paragraph 3; and Resolution 917, paragraph 4). These measures were fully implemented in Switzerland in the relevant executive orders.[94] In the case of Yugoslavia, the various

92 With Resolution 55/56 of 1 December 2000, the UN General Assembly mandated the international community to adopt measures against the trade in conflict diamonds. In this context, States having a leading position in the production and trade in rough diamonds have begun to develop an international certification scheme for rough diamonds.

93 Othmar Wyss, "Wirtschaftliche Embargomassnahmen", in: Th. Cottier, R. Arpagaus (eds.), *Schweizerisches Bundesverwaltungsrecht – Schweizerisches Aussenwirtschafts – und Binnenmarktrecht* (Basel/Frankfurt am Main, 1999), p. 25.

94 Art. 7 of the *Ordonnance concernant des mesures à l'encontre de la Libye* of 12 January 1994 (RO 1994 108) and Art. 4 of the *Ordonnance instituant des mesures économiques à l'encontre de Haïti*

financial sanctions measures of the Security Council (Resolution 757, paragraph 5; Resolution 820, paragraph 21; and Resolution 942, paragraph11) were also fully implemented in the respective *ad hoc* legislation.[95] The financial sanctions measures internationally adopted against UNITA and the Taliban (Afghanistan) were similarly handled.[96]

Although the financial embargo measures were in general fully implemented by Switzerland, even a verbatim implementation does not necessarily guarantee the effectiveness of the measures adopted, due to the particular problems raised by financial embargoes. All too often, provisions calling for financial embargo measures are drafted in equivocal terms, thereby leaving a large margin of appreciation to the implementing authorities in each State and lessening the likelihood that these measures will be uniformly applied worldwide. Moreover, once adopted, the uniform implementation of the domestic measures by financial actors in the field cannot always be guaranteed. In order to ensure a more consistent application of the Federal Council's executive orders throughout Switzerland, the Swiss Bankers Association has, in co-operation with the competent governmental authority,[97] drafted a circular for its members on how to interpret and apply these *ad hoc* legislations in everyday practice.[98]

Another problem in the implementation of financial embargoes lies in the identification of the individuals and entities targeted. Such identification did not raise particular problems in the case of Iraqi or Yugoslav companies as long as the companies were located in Iraq or Yugoslavia (Serbia and Montenegro). In the case of Yugoslavia, however, the financial sanctions that were fully implemented by Switzerland also applied to entities controlled by Yugoslavia but operating abroad (Resolution 820, paragraph 21),[99] a list of which the United Nations did not possess. A further problem related to the financial embargo against Yugoslavia was that the sanctions also applied to the funds and assets of entities located in Bosnian territories under Serb control (Resolution 942, paragraph 11). The fact that the borders of these Serb-controlled territories were in constant flux during the conflict meant that the identification of the targeted entities was very

(RO 1993 2053), taken over by the *Ordonnance instituant des mesures à l'encontre de la République d'Haïti* of 22 June 1994 (RO 1994 1453).

95 Art. 4 of the *Ordonnance instituant des mesures économiques à l'encontre de la Yougoslavie (Serbie et Monténégro)* of 3 June 1992 (RO 1992 1203); Art. 4, para. 3bis, of the same legislation as introduced by the modification of 26 April 1993 (RO 1993 1500); Art. 4 of the *Ordonnance instituant des mesures économiques à l'encontre de la Yougoslavie (Serbie et Monténégro) et d'autres régions contrôlées par les Serbes* of 3 October 1994, which replaced the former.

96 *Ordonnance instituant des mesures à l'encontre de l'UNITA (Angola)* of 25 October 1998 (RO 1999 151); *Ordonnance instituant des mesures à l'encontre des Taliban (Afghanistan)* of 2 October 2000 (RS 946.203).

97 The former Federal Office for Foreign Economic Affairs and current State Secretariat for Economic Affairs, see *infra*, Section IV.1, p. 559.

98 Othmar Wyss, *op. cit.* (note 93), p. 23.

99 *Ordonnance instituant des mesures économiques à l'encontre de la Yougoslavie (Serbie et Monténégro),* Art. 4, para. 3 bis, as introduced by the modification of 26 April 1993 (RO 1993 1500): "*les personnes morales, où qu'elles aient leur siège et où qu'elles déploient leurs activités, qui sont manifestement contrôlées par des autorités ou des personnes morales au sens de...*".

difficult, especially as there were no updated maps available at the United Nations.[100]

In the case of Libya, the financial embargo also applied not only to the funds of enterprises controlled by the Libyan Government and by Libyan public authorities but also to funds of "any person identified by States as acting on behalf of the Government or public authorities of Libya" (Resolution 883, paragraph 3b, iii). As with Yugoslavia, there was no United Nations list of the targeted Libyan entities available. A list was published by the US Department of Finance, but many governments had serious misgivings about using lists not issued by the United Nations.[101] Switzerland's decision not to implement the aforementioned passage in the relevant executive order has to be seen in this context.[102]

The United Nations published an official list of individuals targeted by financial sanctions for the first time in connection with the sanctions imposed on Haiti. The list named 800 persons with financial dealings connected to Haiti. The provisions of the Security Council resolution calling for the freezing of the funds of their businesses were not, however, mandatory. Mandatory financial sanctions were adopted against named individuals and organisations for the first time in relation to UNITA (Resolution 1173, paragraph 11). These measures, including the list of UNITA officials drawn up by the Security Council Sanctions Committee, were fully implemented in Swiss domestic law by means of an executive order.[103] The financial sanctions adopted against the Taliban were similarly implemented.[104]

As the UNITA and Taliban sanctions regimes show, the concept of targeted financial sanctions has found its way into Security Council practice. Being an important financial centre with a corresponding know-how, Switzerland has taken the initiative to examine the concept of targeted financial sanctions in order to increase their efficiency and decrease unwanted side-effects, in particular on civilian populations. Switzerland hosted two seminars on this issue in 1998 and 1999 in Interlaken at the United Nations' request. This initiative, which has become known as the *Interlaken Process*, met with considerable interest in the international community.[105] At the seminars, the feasibility of

100 Othmar Wyss, *op. cit.* (note 93), p. 26.

101 What is more, this list was seriously contested by several European States for containing entities that were allegedly not Libyan controlled. *Ibid.*, p. 26.

102 Art. 7, para. 1, of the *Ordonnance concernant des mesures à l'encontre de la Libye* of 12 January 1994 (RO 1994 108).

103 Art. 6 and annex 3 of the *Ordonnance instituant des mesures à l'encontre de l'UNITA*, adopted on 25 November 1998 (RO 1999 151).

104 *Ordonnance instituant des mesures à l'encontre des Taliban (Afghanistan)* of 2 October 2000 (RS 946.203). Annex 2 of the Ordinance containing the names of individuals and entities against which the financial sanctions are targeted has been updated several times since 11 September 2001 in order to incorporate the different lists of names issued by the UN Sanctions Committee on Afghanistan. (For further details, see the chapter on the fight against terrorism and terrorism financing.).

105 The competent authorities also established a website on targeted financial sanctions, http://www.smartsanctions.ch, which presents the proceedings from the two Interlaken seminars as well as other important data and links.

targeted financial sanctions was examined, and model language for sanctions resolutions and implementation legislation was developed. The findings of the Interlaken Process were presented to the Security Council in October 2001 in the form of a manual.[106] The manual deals with the design of United Nations Security Council resolutions on targeted financial sanctions and with national implementation of targeted financial sanctions. It contains mock targeted financial sanctions resolutions and model implementing legislation.

Due to its leading role in the Interlaken Process, Switzerland was asked by the former Canadian chair of the Sanctions Committee on Angola "to convene a conference of experts to explore possibilities to strengthen the implementation of the financial measures imposed against UNITA contained in resolution 1173 (1998)" as proposed in Security Council Resolution 1295. Recommendations for the strengthening of the UNITA sanctions regime were duly presented based on the results of the Interlaken process and the experts' practical experience with targeted financial sanctions.

c. Embargoes on air traffic and aircraft

Embargo measures on air traffic and aircraft were instituted against Iraq, Libya, Haiti, Yugoslavia and the Taliban. Resolution 661 applying sanctions against Iraq did not explicitly require embargo measures on air traffic or aircraft. It was only with Resolution 670, paragraph 2 that the Security Council confirmed that Resolution 661 applied to all means of transport, including aircraft, and specified the corresponding measures for States to adopt (paragraph 3 and paragraph 4). These embargo measures were not immediately implemented by Switzerland, probably due to the fact that in line with the Security Council's opinion, Switzerland believed that such measures were already completely covered by the comprehensive trade embargo set out in Article 1 of the relevant executive order. It was not until 1998 that a provision was included in the executive order prohibiting the use of Swiss airspace by aircraft travelling to and from Iraq.[107] The embargo measures on air traffic and, where adopted, on aircraft instituted against Haiti (Resolution 917), Libya (Resolution 748 and Resolution 883), Yugoslavia (Resolution 757) and the Taliban (Resolution 1267) were all implemented at the national level through *ad hoc* legislation.[108]

---

106 *Targeted Financial Sanctions – A Manual for Design and Implementation: Contributions from the Interlaken Process*; A Cooperation of the Watson Institute for International Studies at Brown University, the United Nations Secretariat and the Swiss Confederation. Available at http://www.smartsanctions.ch.

107 Art. 1, para. 3 of the *Ordonnance instituant des mesures économiques envers la République d'Irak*, as introduced by the modification of 27 April 1998 (RO 1998 1487).

108 Art. 2 of the *Ordonnance instituant des mesures à l'encontre de la République d'Haïti* of 22 June 1994 (RO 1994 1453); Arts. 1 and 2 of the *Ordonnance concernant des mesures à l'encontre de la Libye* of 15 April 1992 (RO 1992 958), which was replaced by the *Ordonnance concernant des mesures à l'encontre de la Libye* of 12 January 1994 (Arts. 1 and 3) (RO 1994 108); Arts. 1 and 2 of the *Ordonnance instituant des mesures économiques à l'encontre de la Yougoslavie (Serbie et Monténégro)* of 3 June 1992 (RO 1992 1203), replaced by Arts. 1 and 2 of the *Ordonnance*

d. Travel restrictions

Travel restrictions were adopted in the case of Iraq, Haiti, UNITA, Sierra Leone, the Taliban and Liberia. In the cases where travel restrictions were imposed on a clearly specified group of persons (e.g. senior UNITA officials or adult members of their immediate families, leading members of the former military junta and of the RUF in Sierra Leone, the Taliban), these measures were fully implemented via the relevant *ad hoc* legislation.[109] It has to be stressed, however, that the Swiss Federal Council or the competent Federal Department can pronounce travel restrictions against individuals without a corresponding provision in the *ad hoc* legislation.[110]

e. Other measures

Other miscellaneous sanctions measures, including reduction of the number and level of the staff at Libyan and Yugoslav diplomatic missions and consular posts (Resolution 748, paragraph 6 and Resolution 757, paragraph 8a), denial of entry to or expulsion of Libyan nationals who had previously been denied entry to or expelled from other States due to their involvement in terrorist activities (Resolution 748, paragraph 6c), withdrawal of officials or agents present in Libya to advise the Libyan authorities on military matters (Resolution 748, paragraph 5c), prevention of persons or groups representing the Federal Republic of Yugoslavia from participating in sporting events (Resolution 757, paragraph 8b), suspension of scientific and technical co-operation, cultural exchanges and visits involving persons or groups officially sponsored by or representing the Federal Republic of Yugoslavia (Resolution 757, paragraph 8c)) did not require the adoption of legislative acts.

f. Fighting terrorism and its financing

Swiss efforts to fight terrorism and its financing are documented in Switzerland's report of 19 December 2001 to the Counter Terrorism Committee established by Security Council Resolution 1373.[111]

> "Following the attacks of 11 September 2001, the Attorney General of the Swiss Confederation opened a criminal inquiry to cast light on possible connections between events

---

instituant des mesures économiques à l'encontre de la Yougoslavie (Serbie et Monténégro) et d'autres régions contrôlées par les Serbes of 3 October 1994 (RO 1994 2194); Art. 2 of the *Ordonnance instituant des mesures à l'encontre des Taliban (Afghanistan)* of 2 October 2000 (RS 946.203).

109 Art. 9 and annex 3 of the *Ordonnance instituant des mesures à l'encontre de l'UNITA,* of 25 November 1998 (RO 1999 151); Art. 3 of the *Ordonnance instituant des mesures à l'encontre de la Sierra Leone* of 8 December 1997 (RO 1997 3010); in the case of Haiti, the travel restrictions instituted by Resolution 917, para. 3 were implemented in Art. 4 of the *Ordonnance instituant des mesures à l'encontre de la République d'Haïti* of 22 June 1994 (RO 1994 1453).

110 FF 2001 1354.

111 The Report is available under the title "Report on the Fight against Terrorism" at http://www.admin.ch/eda/e/home/rep/terrorism.html.

which had taken place in Switzerland and the terrorist acts perpetrated in the United States. Switzerland promptly provided information asked for by the United States in the context of a request for mutual assistance, and it has transmitted information on its own initiative. Switzerland has also addressed requests for international mutual assistance to the US authorities. In addition, the Swiss Government has banned all activities of the al-Qaeda organisation on Swiss territory. Switzerland has systematically implemented the decisions concerning Afghanistan taken by the Sanctions Committee of the UN Security Council following the 11 September attacks (including freezing the assets of natural persons or legal entities linked to terrorism). In addition, the competent Swiss authorities have transmitted to all financial intermediaries in Switzerland the list of natural persons and legal entities which was supplied by the American authorities and reminded these institutions of their obligation to exercise due diligence in particular with regard to money laundering. About 30 bank accounts involving a total sum of approximately CHF 20 million have been blocked.

Switzerland wants to protect at all costs its financial centre from abuse for criminal purposes. In this context, it stresses that banking secrecy is not an obstacle to the execution of justice since it can be lifted as soon as a request for international mutual assistance is submitted or a criminal procedure is opened. If necessary, the competent authorities have the power to freeze immediately financial assets used for pursuing such activities. Moreover, the Swiss Money Laundering Act obliges financial intermediaries to report to the competent authorities, and to block the assets of persons whom the intermediaries have grounds to suspect are linked to criminal activities. As one of the major financial centres of the world, Switzerland wants to see more ambitious international standards developed to counter flows of criminal money. Switzerland is a member of the Financial Action Task Force (FATF) and was actively involved in drafting the FATF's 40 recommendations on measures to fight money laundering. These recommendations constitute the internationally recognised standard for the measures which a country must take to fight money laundering effectively. Switzerland has integrated them entirely within its own legal order. Following the events of 11 September 2001, it has supported the adoption of the specific recommendations of the FATF on fighting terrorism and has committed itself to implementing them by June 2002 (Swiss legal provisions in this matter are already largely compatible with the FATF's recommendations).

Finally, a special unit, known as 'Task Force Terror USA', has been set up at the Swiss Federal Department of Justice and Police for the purpose of co-ordinating the criminal inquiry opened in Switzerland and to ensure co-operation with foreign authorities. Parallel to this, an interdepartmental group on terrorism, bringing together the offices concerned from the different federal departments, has been instructed to co-ordinate the measures to fight terrorism."[112]

112 Summary of the aforementioned report (see note 111), pp. 1-3, available under the same address.

g. From comprehensive sanctions toward smart sanctions

As this third part of the report shows, the sanctions decade was characterised by a shift away from comprehensive sanctions directed indiscriminately against the whole population of a State toward smart or targeted sanctions. Having a long humanitarian tradition, Switzerland is especially sensitive to the negative effects sanctions may have on civilian populations. Switzerland has therefore been very interested in the current debate on international sanctions measures and particularly in research on targeted sanctions. As has been shown, Switzerland has encouraged the development of the concept of targeted financial sanctions. Initiatives have also been taken in other areas to develop targeted sanctions measures. Germany initiated the Bonn-Berlin Process aimed at developing the concept of targeted sanctions in the field of weapons exports, flight restrictions and visas bans.[113]

(2) Personal and Extraterritorial Scope

Beginning with the resolutions adopted in the aftermath of the Iraqi invasion of Kuwait, all Security Council sanctions resolutions have extended the scope of the sanctions' application beyond the territory of the State concerned to the State's nationals, thereby providing for the extraterritorial application of Security Council resolutions and corresponding national implementing legislation.

Switzerland has traditionally had reservations about the extraterritorial exercise of its jurisdiction. It is true that in a statement made as sanctions were adopted against Southern Rhodesia, Switzerland maintained that it could not proceed in law against Swiss-registered companies in respect of their transactions outside Swiss territory. Federal authorities later revised this position, however, and adopted an executive order that was aimed at preventing triangular operations from Swiss territory.[114]

In light of the above, it is not surprising that Switzerland has never – except in two cases to be examined below – adopted sanctions measures on an extraterritorial basis. The relevant *ad hoc* legislation has remained silent as to their scope of application and the scope of application of the measures that they provide for. This means that Swiss implementing measures and legislation have only been applied on a territorial basis. As far as ships and aircraft are concerned, the measures have generally been extended to vessels and aircraft under the Swiss flag.[115]

There have only been two cases in which sanctions measures have been applied extraterritorially. The extraterritorial reach of the measures set out in Resolution 748, paragraph 4b, which provided that all States shall b) "prohibit, by their nationals or from their

113 See on this topic http://www.auswaertiges-amt.de/www/de/aussenpolitik/vn/sanktionen-html.

114 *Ordonnance sur les transactions avec la Rhodésie du Sud* of 12 December 1977 (RO 1977 2180). On the whole question, see Linsi, *op. cit.* (note 14), pp. 270-284.

115 *Ordonnance Libye I*, Art. 1, para. 2; *Ordonnance Libye II*, Art. 1, para. 2; *Ordonnance Haiti II*, Art. 2, paras. 2 and 3; *Ordonnance Yougoslavie I*, Art. 1, para. 2; *Ordonnance Yougoslavie II*, Art. 1, para. 2.

territory... the provision of engineering and maintenance servicing of Libyan aircraft or aircraft components", was partially implemented by Switzerland. The relevant executive order prohibited such activities on Swiss territory, and this prohibition was extended to all companies holding Swiss licences for maintenance of aircraft. The order did not, however, go as far as prohibiting all Swiss nationals from engaging in these activities.[116] As the measures only applied to companies holding Swiss licences, they cannot be regarded as an unequivocal departure from the principle of the non-exercise of Swiss jurisdiction on an extraterritorial basis.

A real exception to the traditional Swiss reservations about extraterritoriality can be found in the *ad hoc* legislation in the case of UNITA. In its implementation of the various Security Council resolutions on UNITA, the Swiss Federal Council provided for an extraterritorial application as far as the trade embargo and the measures on aircraft and related services were concerned:

> "*La vente, l'exportation et le transport*, par des ressortissants suisses ou depuis le territoire suisse *des marchandises suivantes... sont interdits.* [117]"

> "*La fourniture ou la livraison*, par des ressortissants suisses ou depuis le territoire suisse, *de tout aéronef ou de toute pièce d'aéronef à l'UNITA ou à destination du territoire angolais est interdite....*"[118]

Nevertheless, in the subsequent *ad hoc* legislation in the case of the Taliban, the Swiss Federal Council did not continue with the practice of emulating the extraterritorial reach of Security Council sanctions.[119]

Although this position may appear somewhat outdated today, the fact remains that, as a non-Member State of the United Nations, Switzerland was previously not legally bound by Security Council resolutions adopting sanctions and as such was under no duty to implement sanctions on an extraterritorial basis. With Switzerland's admission to the United Nations, this no longer holds true.[120]

(3) Entry into Force

As mentioned above, Switzerland, as a non-Member State of the United Nations, was not obligated to implement sanctions imposed by the Security Council. The matter of the entry into force of domestic implementation measures based on a sovereign decision was therefore somewhat different than for United Nations Member States. Nevertheless, the

116 Art. 2, para. 2 of the *Ordonnance concernant des mesures à l'encontre de la Libye* of 15 April 1992 (RO 1992 958) reads: "*L'exécution de travaux d'entretien sur des aéronefs inscrits au registre de l'aviation libyen ou appartenant à l'Etat libyen, à des ressortissants ou des entreprises libyens est interdite en Suisse ainsi qu'aux entreprises qui sont au bénéfice d'une licence suisse pour l'entretien des aéronefs.*"

117 *Ordonnance UNITA,* Art. 4. (emphasis added).

118 *Ibid.,* Art. 8 (emphasis added).

119 RS 946.203.

120 Regarding the consequences of UN admission, see *supra*, Section I and *infra*, Section VI.1.

immediate domestic implementation of sanctions by non-Member States is desirable in order to guarantee the effectiveness of the international sanctions regime. This holds particularly true for financial sanctions measures, which should be implemented overnight by both the national authorities and the financial actors in the field. It must be noted in this regard that Switzerland has generally adopted domestic implementation measures immediately or shortly after the imposition of sanctions by the Security Council.

In instances where Security Council resolutions have specified deadlines for the domestic implementation of sanctions, Switzerland has generally respected these.[121] In instances where the Security Council adopted sanctions with immediate effect, Swiss implementation in most cases took place within one or two working days[122] or within a very short period of time (some days).[123] In some cases, however, implementation only took place over a month after the adoption of the relevant resolution.[124] In the Taliban case,

121 Para. 3 of Resolution 748 of 31 March 1992 provided that on 15 April 1992 all States shall adopt the measures set out by that resolution. The executive order (*Ordonnance concernant des mesures à l'encontre de la Libye* (RO 1992 958)) was adopted on 15 April 1992 and came into force on 16 April 1992 at 12 a.m. (Art. 7).

Similarly, see Resolution 820 of 17 April 1993 providing for new measures against Yugoslavia, which specified that these measures should come into force nine days later. These new measures were implemented on 26 April 1993 (RO 1993 1500) and came into force on 28 April 1993, that is to say within the deadline fixed by the Resolution.

122 Resolution 661 of 6 August 1990 instituting sanctions against Iraq was immediately implemented through the adoption of the *Ordonnance instituant des mesures économiques envers la République d'Irak et l'Etat du Koweït* (RO 1990 1316) adopted on 7 August 1990 and coming into force on 7 August 1990 at 11 a.m. as well as by the *Ordonnance sur la protection des valeurs patrimoniales de l'Etat du Koweït en Suisse* (RO 1990 1341) adopted on 10 August 1990 and coming into force on 10 August 1990 at 12 a.m. (Art. 6).

Resolution 757 of 30 May 1992 instituting sanctions against Yugoslavia was implemented by the adoption of the *Ordonnance instituant des mesures économiques à l'encontre de la Yougoslavie (Serbie et Monténégro)* (RO 1992 1203) adopted on 3 June 1992 and coming into force on 3 June 1992 at 12 a.m.

123 Resolution 873 of 13 October 1993 terminating the suspension of the sanctions instituted by previous resolutions against Haiti by 18 October 1993 was implemented on 20 October 1993 taking effect on 21 October 1993 (RO 1993 2953).

Resolution 942 of 23 September 1994 providing for further sanctions against Yugoslavia and territories controlled by the Serbs was implemented by the adoption of the *Ordonnance instituant des mesures économiques à l'encontre de la Yougoslavie (Serbie et Monténégro) et d'autres régions contrôlées par les Serbes* (RO 1994 2195) on 3 October 1994 and coming into force on 4 October 1994.

Resolution 841, para. 3 of 16 June 1993 instituting sanctions against Haiti provides that these sanctions shall come into force on 23 June 1993. The corresponding executive order, *Ordonnance instituant des mesures économiques à l'encontre d'Haïti* (RO 1993 2053) was adopted on 30 June 1993 and came into force on 1 July 1993 (Art. 11).

124 Resolution 883 of 11 November 1993 adopted further sanctions against Libya to come into force on 1 December 1993. These measures were taken over 12 January 1994 by the adoption of a new executive order replacing the previous one (*Ordonnance concernant des mesures à l'encontre de la Libye* (RO 1994 108)) and came into force on 13 January 1994 (Art. 17),

Resolution 1267 of 15 October 1999 took almost a year to be implemented by an executive order.[125] It is interesting to note that the *ad hoc* legislation in the Taliban and Liberia cases are the only ones so far to be time-limited, which limitation is due to the fact that they are based on the new Federal Constitution.[126] Observations similar to those concerning entry into force can be made concerning suspension or termination of sanctions.[127]

No implementation measures have been thus far adopted with retroactive effect. It is unlikely that any ever will be, as this would be contrary to the principle of non-retroactivity of legislative acts.[128]

(4) Provisions Relating to Existing Contracts

Provisions relating to existing contracts were contained in the sanctions measures taken against Libya, UNITA, Haiti and Yugoslavia. These provisions can be grouped into two categories. Provisions regarding insurance contracts for aircraft comprise the first category. In the cases of Libya (Resolution 748, paragraph 4b and Resolution 832, paragraph 6f), Yugoslavia (Resolution 757, paragraph 7b) and UNITA (Resolution 1127, paragraph 4d), the payment of new claims against existing insurance contracts and the

---

that is to say two days before the deadline provided for by Resolution 883 (para. 13) for the reporting to the Secretary General by all States of the measures they have adopted to fulfil the resolution's obligations.

The sanctions instituted against Sierra Leone by Resolution 1132 of 8 October 1997 were implemented on 8 December 1997 by the adoption of the *Ordonnance instituant des mesures à l'encontre de la Sierra Leone* (RO 1997 3010) coming into force on 16 December 1997 (Art. 8). In the case of the sanctions taken against UNITA, the Security Council strengthened the measures adopted by Resolution 864 and Resolution 1127 (implemented without *ad hoc* legislation), by Resolution 1173 of 12 June 1998 specifying that these measures should come into force on 25 June 1998. The domestic measures were adopted in this case on 25 November 1998, coming into force on the following day (*Ordonnance instituant des mesures à l'encontre de l'UNITA* (RO 1999 151)).

125 *Ordonnance instituant des mesures à l'encontre des Taliban (Afghanistan)* of 2 October 2000 (RS 946.203).

126 See *supra*, Section II.1, p. 532.

127 The suspension of the sanctions against the Federal Republic of Yugoslavia provided for in Resolution 1022 of 22 November 1995 was adopted on 24 November and came into force on the following day (RO 1995 5025).

The suspension of the embargo on petroleum and petroleum products against Sierra Leone by Resolution 1156 of 16 March 1998 was adopted on 27 April 1998 (RO 1998 1490). In the case of Haiti, Resolution 861 of 27 August 1993 suspended sanctions instituted by earlier resolutions with immediate effect. This suspension was adopted on 8 September 1993 with effect from 9 September 1993.

128 The only arguable exception is the *Ordonnance du DFEP instituant des mesures économiques envers la République d'Irak* (RO 1990 1319) adopted on 8 August 1990 and coming into force retroactively on 7 August 1990 11 a.m.: "*La présente ordonnance entre en vigueur rétroactivement le 7 août 1990 à 11 heures*" (Art. 5) (RO 1319). As this act is only an *ordonnance d'exécution* referring to the corresponding executive order of 7 August 1990, however, it cannot really be considered an exception to the non-retroactivity principle.

provision of new direct insurance for aircraft or the renewal of pre-existing contracts were prohibited. In all three cases, these measures were fully implemented in the relevant *ad hoc* legislation.[129]

The second category comprises the provisions laid out in Resolution 687, paragraph 29; Resolution 757, paragraph 9 (restated in Resolution 1022, paragraph 7); Resolution 883, paragraph 8; and Resolution 917, paragraph 11 regarding claims arising out of contracts whose performance was affected by sanctions measures. For example, Resolution 883, paragraph 8 reads: "the Governments of all States, and the Government of Libya, shall take the necessary measures to ensure that no claim shall lie at the instance of the Government or public authorities of Libya, or of any Libyan national, or of any Libyan undertaking [...] or of any person claiming through or for the benefit of any such person or undertaking, in connection with any contract or other transaction or commercial operation where its performance was affected by reason of the measures imposed by or pursuant to the present resolution or related resolutions."

This measure was aimed at the long-term protection of companies against claims arising out of obligations that could not be fulfilled due to the embargo measures, especially in relation to bank guaranties.[130] In contrast to the case of Iraq, bank guaranties were not considered to be of significance in the application by Switzerland of sanctions against Libya and Yugoslavia.[131] Even in the case of Iraq, however, the corresponding provision on bank guaranties was not implemented. Since all payments in connection with operations covered by the trade embargo were already prohibited per Article 2, paragraph 1 of the relevant executive order, it was not considered necessary to implement the provision on bank guaranties set out in paragraph 29 of Resolution 687. On the one hand, this failure to implement sanctions measures concerning bank guaranties against Iraq may become problematic when the sanctions are eventually terminated. If Switzerland has not before then taken steps to prohibit the payment of these bank guaranties, Iraqi entities may claim their payment in order to cover the cost of obligations that could not be fulfilled due to the embargo measures. To avoid this risk, the European Union and many other countries have already prohibited the improper use of bank guaranties by Iraq. On the other, the banks themselves may have reservations about a general prohibition on bank guaranties. As a bank guaranty is an autonomous commitment that is not dependent on the contract between creditor and debtor, Iraqi entities could compensate these guaranties where this form of transaction is prohibited through the use of outstanding debt claims that the bank has toward Iraq or Iraqi entities. That would mean in practice that banks would have to bear the consequences of such a prohibition on the improper use of bank guaranties, despite the fact that these guaranties were initially granted to benefit exporters.[132]

129 *Ordonnance Libye I*, Art. 2, para. 3; *Ordonnance Libye II*, Art. 3, para. 3; *Ordonnance Yougoslavie I*, Art. 2, para. 2; *Ordonnance Yougoslavie II*, Art. 2, para. 2; *Ordonnance UNITA*, Art. 8, para. 2.

130 By means of a bank guaranty a bank irrevocably engages itself to fulfil a monetary obligation in the case that a third party does not fulfil its obligation. The bank is thereby obligated to pay if the stipulations are fulfilled.

131 Othmar Wyss, *op. cit.* (note 93), pp. 24 f.

132 *Ibid.*, p. 25.

The matter of the fate of existing contracts affected by the embargo measures has not so far been addressed in Swiss implementing legislation. In the absence of explicit provisions dealing with the relationship between sanctions and pre-existing contractual agreements, the general rules of the law of contracts (*Code des obligations*[133]) are applicable. The way in which Swiss tribunals have interpreted and applied these rules will be examined in Section VI.2. below.

In order to ascertain how many and which companies were affected by the embargo measures instituted against Iraq, the relevant Swiss *ad hoc* legislation provided that all companies were under an obligation to declare any outstanding operations and negotiations.[134] Similarly, the executive orders providing for financial sanctions obligate any person holding or administering funds covered by the sanctions to declare this fact without delay to the competent authority.[135]

(5) Provisions for Humanitarian Exceptions

Security Council sanctions resolutions usually contain clauses providing for humanitarian exceptions to enforcement of the regime. These clauses are not contingent on the kind of measures adopted (i.e. trade embargoes, financial embargoes, embargoes on air traffic and aircraft, travel restrictions).

a. Trade embargoes

In the case of Iraq, Swiss implementation of humanitarian exceptions to the sanctions regime closely followed the relevant Security Council resolution that exempted "supplies intended strictly for medical purposes, and, in humanitarian circumstances, foodstuffs..." and the practice of the United Nations.[136]

The Federal Office for Foreign Economic Affairs, the Swiss authority competent to grant such exceptions, refused to authorise the export of grain silos and grain silo spare parts as well as the export of empty aluminium tubes in which medicines were to be packaged once in Iraq. Basing itself on the Security Council resolution, the Federal Office decided that the silos did not fall under the exception clause for foodstuffs. In order for the Office to have granted exceptional permission for the export of the silos, the exporter concerned would have had to have attested to the existence of a recognised humanitarian need for the goods. The Federal Council upheld these two decisions upon appeal.[137]

---

133 RS 220.

134 Art. 3, *Ordonnance Irak,* (RO 1990 1316).

135 Art. 6a *Ordonnance UNITA*, Art. 6 *Ordonnance Yougoslavie III*, Art. 4 *Ordonnance Taliban.*

136 See Resolutions 661 and 670 as well as Art. 4 of the *Ordonnance instituant des mesures économiques envers la République d'Irak et l'Etat du Koweït* of 7 August 1990 (RO 1990 1316). Othmar Wyss, *op. cit.* (note 93), pp. 19 f.

137 *Loc. cit.*

Security Council Resolution 687 extended the exception clause contained in Resolution 661. At the time of the adoption of Resolution 687, the export of foodstuffs to Iraq was allowed on a general basis (i.e. no longer only in cases of demonstrated humanitarian need) on condition that such exports were notified to the United Nations Sanctions Committee. The same resolution also allowed the exportation of other civilian humanitarian goods under the "no-objection" procedure.[138]

It is interesting to note that even as a non-Member State, Switzerland co-operated fully with the United Nations procedures for the handling of humanitarian exceptions. Not only did Switzerland notify the United Nations Sanctions Committee concerning the export of foodstuffs, but demands for other humanitarian goods were also submitted for the Committee's consideration under the no-objection procedure. Such compliance was, however, required for practical reasons. If Switzerland had not complied with these international procedures, exports authorised by Switzerland could well have run the risk of being confiscated abroad. It is therefore understandable that in cases where the Committee refused to approve an export, the competent Swiss authority also refused to grant the exemption.[139] Moreover, it was often difficult for exporters to obtain the necessary financing.[140]

These measures were later extended by the Oil-for-Food Program, which came into being following the adoption of Resolution 986. Under this program, States are authorised "to permit the import of petroleum and petroleum products originating in Iraq, including financial and other essential transactions directly relating thereto, sufficient to produce a sum not exceeding a total of one billion United States dollars every 90 days…" (paragraph 1). The Swiss executive order relating to Iraqi sanctions was modified in order to allow Swiss companies to participate in this program and in the construction of the Kirkuk-Yumurtalik pipeline from Iraq to Turkey provided for in the same resolution (paragraph 6).[141]

Apart from the Oil-for-Food Program, the Swiss handling of the humanitarian exception clauses was similar in the case of Yugoslavia. The Federal Office for Foreign Economic Affairs granted the exceptions in accordance with the corresponding United Nations resolutions. Resolution 757 exempted only "supplies intended strictly for medical purposes and foodstuffs" on condition that these supplies were notified to the United Nations Sanctions Committee. In contrast to the case of Iraq, there was a duty in the case of Yugoslavia to notify the Sanctions Committee of the intended export of goods

138 The no-objection procedure means that an export is to be authorised if none of the 15 members of the Sanctions Committee objects.

139 This was the case as regards filters for cigarettes, batteries and car tires as well as spare parts for a production plant for cooking salt. Othmar Wyss, *op. cit.* (note 93), p. 20.

140 The following data from the Yugoslav case is particularly clear in this respect. From November 1993 to October 1994, the Federal Office for Foreign Economic Affairs authorised 617 requests for exports of foodstuffs to Yugoslavia (Serbia and Montenegro) for medical or humanitarian purposes in the value of 391 million Swiss Francs. In the event, actual exports were worth only 119 million Swiss Francs. On the whole question, see Othmar Wyss, *op. cit.* (note 93), p. 20.

141 Adoption of Article 4, para. 1, let. h, by the modification of 26 June 1996 (RO 1996 1995).

for medical purposes. The subsequent Resolution 820 permitted exports of other important humanitarian goods to Yugoslavia under the no-objection procedure.

As far as the Swiss implementation of trade embargoes is concerned, executive orders have provided for additional exceptions on non-humanitarian grounds: exceptions for the export and transit of commodities destined for the Swiss diplomatic and consular representations, the ICRC and Swiss companies in the State concerned as well as, in the case of Yugoslavia, to the UNPROFOR, the Conference on Yugoslavia and the Mission of Verification of the European Communities; exceptions for the import of commodities destined for the diplomatic and consular representation of the sanctioned State in Switzerland; and exceptions for the transport of baggage with individuals.[142] These exceptions did not raise any problems in terms of their compatibility with the relevant Security Council resolutions. This cannot be said of the "hardship" clause introduced into the Swiss executive order relating to the Iraqi sanctions regime, despite the fact that the corresponding Security Council resolution did not provide for such an exception.[143]

Several companies claimed that they should benefit from the hardship clause in order to be granted the exemption necessary to allow them to export, arguing either that the commodities were ready for delivery or that the payment by Iraq was dependent on the delivery. Each of the claims made on the basis of the hardship clause was refused by the competent authority. All of the appeals to the Swiss Federal Council were also rejected on the grounds that hardship would only be accepted if substantial Swiss interests were at stake. In one of the appeals, the Council noted that the hardship clause was only applicable to cases involving State interests and that it was not to be invoked in order to attenuate the impact of the sanctions on the individual claimant. The Council stressed that the embargo against Iraq has been detrimental not only to the economic interests of Switzerland, but also to those of other countries, emphasising that other States have been more severely affected by the embargo measures than Switzerland. The Council went on to say that solidarity with the international community required Switzerland to continue its uncompromising implementation of the sanctions and therefore to adhere to a restrictive interpretation of the hardship clause.[144] With this restrictive interpretation, the Swiss Federal Council prevented the dilution of the international embargo measures through a potentially very broad exception clause.

It must be noted, however, that even if an exceptional permission had been granted through the hardship clause, the export of the corresponding commodities would probably have been impossible due to the international blockade.[145]

It remains to be seen whether such additional exception clauses will still be relevant

142 See Article 4, para. 1, let. c to e, of the *Ordonnance instituant des mesures économiques envers la République d'Irak et l'Etat du Koweït* of 7 August 1990 (RO 1990 1316). Article 5, para. 1, let. e to g, of the *Ordonnance instituant des mesures économiques à l'encontre de la Yougoslavie (Serbie et Monténégro)* of 3 June 1992 (RO 1992 1203).

143 Article 4, para. 1, let. f.

144 Othmar Wyss, *op. cit.* (note 93), p. 21; VPB 55/III (1991) No. 41, 5.

145 Othmar Wyss, *op. cit.* (note 93), p. 21; the hardship clause has in the meantime been deleted (RO 1998 1487).

following Switzerland's admission to the United Nations and the thereby changed demands on it.[146]

b. Financial embargoes

Humanitarian exceptions have also been provided for in the context of financial embargoes. In the case of Iraq, Resolution 661, paragraph 4 allowed for an exception in favour of "payments exclusively for strictly medical or humanitarian purposes and, in humanitarian circumstances, foodstuffs."

While financial transactions were initially authorised by Switzerland also for the payment of imports by Iraq from countries other than Switzerland, this practice was soon reversed, and it was decided that Iraqi funds should be used exclusively to finance deliveries from Switzerland.[147]

In keeping with what has been said in the context of exception clauses to trade embargoes, financial transactions are generally authorised with respect to payments to Swiss diplomatic and consular representations, the ICRC and Swiss companies in the sanctioned State as well as, in the case of Yugoslavia, to the UNPROFOR, the Conference on Yugoslavia and the Mission of Verification of the European communities.[148] In the case of Yugoslavia, financial transactions were also allowed for the payment of social security benefits and private allocations.[149]

In the cases of Libya[150] and Haiti,[151] the relevant Security Council resolutions did not exempt payments made from frozen accounts. Nevertheless, in the respective executive orders, the Swiss Federal Council provided for such an exception based not on humanitarian grounds, but on Swiss economic interest.

The rationale for exemptions relating to financial embargoes is that a greater degree of flexibility in the handling of financial sanctions may be necessary in special cases. Indeed, some have argued that it would be contrary to the purpose of sanctions if the sanctioning State suffered greater harm than the sanctioned State. These exemptions enabled Swiss companies carrying out transactions that were not covered by the embargo measures and that required regular payments to Libya (e.g. for salaries and infrastructure) to effect these payments. If Switzerland failed to make allowance for these kinds of payments, the fulfilment of contracts unrelated to the object of the embargo would be put at risk.[152]

146 Regarding the consequences of UN admission, see *supra*, Section I and *infra*, Section VI.1.

147 Othmar Wyss, *op. cit.* (note 93), pp. 20 f.

148 Article 4, paras. d and e of the *Ordonnance instituant des mesures économiques envers la République d'Irak et l'Etat du Koweït* of 7 August 1990 (RO 1990 1318); Article 7, paras. f and g of the *Ordonnance instituant des mesures économiques à l'encontre de la Yougoslavie (Serbie et Monténégro) et d'autres régions contrôlées par les Serbes* of 3 October 1994 (RO 1994 2194).

149 *Ibid.*, Article 7, para. 1, let. c and d.

150 Art. 7, para. 4 of the *Ordonnance concernant des mesures à l'encontre de la Libye* of 12 January 1994 (RO 1994 108).

151 Article 5, para. 2 of the *Ordonnance instituant des mesures à l'encontre de la République d'Haïti* of 22 June 1994 (RO 1994 1453).

152 Othmar Wyss, *op. cit.* (note 93), pp. 23 f.

In the Taliban case, the relevant *ad hoc* legislation enables payments for projects in favour of democratisation. In the same executive order, there is also a hardship clause enabling payments from frozen accounts.[153]

Here as well it remains to be seen whether such additional exception clauses will still be relevant following Switzerland's admission to the United Nations and the thereby changed demands on it.[154]

(6) Provisions for Penal Sanctions

Security Council resolutions instituting sanctions have only rarely contained provisions requiring States to bring criminal proceedings against other States and entities violating the sanctions measures and to impose appropriate penalties.[155] Nevertheless, beginning with the sanctions instituted against Iraq, all subsequent Swiss *ad hoc* legislation for the implementation of sanctions has contained provisions for penal sanctions, even where the relevant Security Council resolution has not. The Swiss *Ordonnance instituant des mesures économiques envers la République d'Irak et l'Etat du Koweït* set out a regime of penal sanctions for sanctions violators.[156] In the case of violations against trade and financial embargoes, the maximum fine was up to ten times the internal value of the commodities concerned, this internal value being calculated in accordance with the market price of the commodity at the moment of the disclosure of the violation. In the case of other financial transactions, the maximum fine was up to ten times the sum of money concerned. The violation of the obligation to declare outstanding operations and negotiations was to be punished by fines of up to 2,000 Swiss Francs. All of the subsequent implementing legislation adopted by the Federal Council has provided for a uniform regime of penal sanctions.[157] Intentional infringements are to be punished by fines of up to 500,000 Swiss Francs and negligent infringements up to 50,000 Swiss Francs. In both cases, mere attempts to violate the sanctions regime are punishable. This uniform system of penal sanctions for sanctions violators also contains a subsidiary clause specifying that the measures apply only inasmuch as other relevant legislation is not applicable. For the rest, the relevant provisions refer to the *Loi fédérale sur le droit pénal administratif* of 22 March 1974.[158]

Unfortunately, this regime of penal sanctions has not always been entirely satisfactory. On the one hand, the provision on the limitation period for penal prosecutions

153 Art. 3, *Ordonnance Taliban.*

154 Regarding the consequences of UN admission, see *supra*, Section I and *infra*, Section VI.1.

155 For example, see Resolution 820, para. 19 instituting sanctions against Yugoslavia; Resolution 841, para. 12 instituting sanctions against Haiti; and Resolution 864, para. 21 imposing sanctions against UNITA.

156 Art. 5 (RO 1990 1316).

157 The aforementioned provision in the *Ordonnance Irak* was later adapted to this uniform regime of penal sanctions (RO 1996 1995).

158 RS 631.0.

contained in Article 11 of the *Loi fédérale sur le droit pénal administratif* (applicable by *renvoi*) sets the limitation period for prosecutions in cases of *contravention* (infringements punishable by fines or imprisonment of three months maximum)[159] at two years. The period of limitations was later extended to five years.[160] On the other, the penalties for sanctions violators are limited to fines and do not provide for the possibility of imprisonment. However, in the executive order adopted in the case of Yugoslavia (which is implementing EU and not United Nations sanctions), the Swiss Federal Council for the first time permitted imprisonment for sanctions violators.[161] This practice was continued in the case of the sanctions adopted against UNITA, Sierra Leone and the Taliban.[162] This solution raises some problems, since according to general principles of Swiss constitutional law, penalties of imprisonment have to be laid down in a *loi formelle*, that is to say an act adopted by Parliament and subjected to an optional vote by the Swiss people. For this reason, a framework legislation for the implementation of sanctions (*Loi sur les embargos*, LEmb) containing *inter alia* provisions on penal sanctions against sanctions violators was adopted by Parliament.[163]

As for embargo measures that do not require the adoption of *ad hoc* legislation but that can instead be implemented on the basis of pre-existing legislation (e.g. in the case of embargoes on weapons and related material), the provisions on penal sanctions contained in this legislation will apply and will have priority over provisions on penal sanctions contained in *ad hoc* sanctions legislation adopted by the Federal Council.[164]

Articles 33-37 of the *Loi fédérale sur le matériel de guerre* provide for a wide range of penal sanctions. The penalties vary in cases of serious breaches from a maximum penalty of 10 years' imprisonment (*réclusion*), which can be combined with a fine of up to 5,000,000 Swiss Francs in cases of intentional infringement (Articles 33, paragraph 2; 34, paragraph 1 and 35, paragraphs 1 and 2), and imprisonment for a period of 6 months (*emprisonnement*) or a fine of up to 100,000 Swiss Francs in cases of negligence (Articles 33, paragraph 3; 34, paragraph 3; and 35, paragraph 3). In cases of minor breaches, the penalties vary from imprisonment of a maximum of 3 months (*arrêts*) or a fine of up to 100,000 Swiss Francs in cases of intentional violation and a fine of up to 40,000 Swiss Francs in cases of negligence (Article 36, paragraphs 1 and 3). The legislation also provides for the punishment of breaches committed abroad (Articles 33, paragraph 4 and 34, paragraph 4).

The *Loi fédérale sur le contrôle des biens utilisables à des fins civiles et militaires et des biens militaires spécifiques* provides for analogous penalties.

Although it follows the current regime for penal sanctions as here presented, the framework legislation on the implementation of international sanctions develops it fur-

159 Code pénal suisse, Articles 39 and 101 (RS 311.0).

160 Modification of 27 April 1998 (RO 1998 1487/1489/1490).

161 Art. 7, *Ordonnance Yougoslavie III.*

162 Art. 13, *Ordonnance UNITA;* Art. 4, *Ordonnance Sierra Leone;* Art. 6, *Ordonnance Taliban.*

163 See *supra,* Section II.4, p. 538.

164 E.g. Art. 14, *Ordonnance UNITA.*

ther by providing for the possibility of punishment by imprisonment and the confiscation of assets covered by coercive measures.[165]

IV. Domestic Procedures for Implementation and Enforcement

(1) Co-ordination among Different Ministerial Activities

The overall responsibility for the implementation of sanctions adopted by the United Nations Security Council belongs to the State Secretariat for Economic Affairs (SECO; the former Federal Office for Foreign Economic Affairs).[166] This office is responsible for the implementation of the corresponding United Nations sanctions through implementing legislation and for the legislation's actual enforcement. In the exercise of its duties, SECO works closely with the Federal Department of Foreign Affairs and, depending on the issues involved, with other units within the Swiss Government.

Requests for exemptions from the different embargo measures are generally dealt with, at least as far as trade and financial embargoes are concerned, by an interdepartmental working group under SECO's direction. Representatives of the Federal Department of Foreign Affairs, the Swiss Federal Department of Finance and the customs authorities also take part in this working group. Other offices may be consulted if necessary. For example, in relation to embargoes on weapons and related material, the Federal Department of Defence, Civil Protection and Sports is consulted as well.

In general, the competence to grant exemptions to embargoes on air traffic and maritime navigation (Haiti being the only case of the latter) lies with the Federal Office for Civil Aviation or with the Swiss Maritime Navigation Office of the Federal Department of Foreign Affairs.[167] In the case of travel restrictions, the Swiss Federal Aliens Office is competent to grant the exemptions requested.[168]

In relation to sanctions concerning the export or import of commodities, customs authorities play an important role. It is these authorities that actually retain goods covered by the sanctions measures at the border. They are then required to inform SECO.

Appeals against decisions of these authorities are to be addressed to the Federal Council.[169]

165 Articles 9-14 of the framework legislation (*Loi fédérale sur l'application de sanctions internationales*), FF 2002 2595 and *supra*, Section II.4, p. 538.

166 There is a special unit in charge of the implementation and enforcement of international sanctions measures.

167 In the case of the sanctions adopted against UNITA, however, the competence to grant such exemptions lies with the State Secretariat for Economic Affairs in co-ordination with the aforementioned Federal Office for Civil Aviation (Articles 7 and 11 of the relevant executive order of 25 November 1998).

168 In the case of the sanctions adopted against UNITA, the competence to grant exemptions to travel restrictions lies with the State Secretariat for Economic Affairs (Article 11 of the relevant executive order of 25 November 1998).

169 Appeal according to Article 72ff of the *Loi fédérale sur la procédure administrative* (RS 172.021).

The procedure for prosecution of sanctions violators will be dealt with in Section IV.3 below.

(2) Role of the Central Bank

The role of central banks in the implementation of economic sanctions depends on their foreign policy role. According to the Federal Constitution, competence with respect to foreign relations belongs exclusively to the Swiss Confederation (Federal State).[170] The Swiss National Bank, as an independent institution, therefore has no responsibility at all in the field of foreign relations. Likewise, the Swiss National Bank is not directly involved in the implementation and enforcement of international sanctions, which are, as shown in the previous chapter, the responsibility of the State Secretariat for Economic Affairs. Nevertheless, international sanctions, especially financial, may have consequences for the activities of the Swiss National Bank. As soon as financial sanctions have entered into force in Switzerland, the National Bank freezes the relevant assets, just like any other bank is required to do. This may entail, especially when the frozen assets belong to another central bank, interventions by the Government or the Central Bank of the target State. It may also happen that transactions to or from these accounts have to be made, especially in cases of exemptions to the sanctions regime (e.g. for humanitarian goods, contributions for membership in international organisations). After co-ordination with the aforementioned federal authority, the Swiss National Bank decides whether or not such transactions can be completed. Moreover, the National Bank is the office for federal authorities and private entities to turn to in regard to complex questions about monetary transactions and sanctions, e.g. whether a factual situation is prohibited or whether trade with the currency of a target State is allowed abroad. The Swiss National Bank has so far assumed responsibility for no other activities with respect to international sanctions.

(3) Procedures Relating to Sanctions Violators

As outlined above, provisions on penal sanctions for sanctions violators contained in *ad hoc* legislation enacted by the Federal Council apply on the basis of subsidiarity, that is, only to the extent that pre-existing legislation is not applicable.[171]

This *ad hoc* legislation will, to the extent of its applicability, also regulate the issue of the competence to prosecute and judge sanctions violators. This issue is generally regulated in an analogous way to the competence to determine exemptions to embargo measures.[172] The general competence for both the granting of exemptions to sanctions regimes and for the commencement of proceedings in cases of sanctions violations lies with SECO, at least as far as trade and financial embargoes are concerned. The latter is also competent to order the seizure of goods being imported to or exported from Switzerland in violation of the embargo.

170 See *supra*, Section II, p. 531.

171 See *supra*, Section III.6, p. 557.

172 See *supra*, Section IV.1, p. 559.

For violations of embargoes on air traffic and maritime navigation, the competence lies with the Federal Office for Civil Aviation or with the Swiss Maritime Navigation Office, respectively, and for violations of travel restrictions, with the Swiss Federal Aliens Office.

The procedure for the prosecution and judgement of sanctions violators as well as for appeals against decisions on sanctions violations is regulated by the *Loi fédérale sur le droit pénal administrative.*[173]

Inasmuch as special pre-existing legislation applies by virtue of the priority clause, the procedure relating to sanctions violations is regulated by this legislation. According to Article 40 of the *Loi fédérale sur le matériel de guerre* and Article 18 of the *Loi fédérale sur le contrôle des biens utilisables à des fins civiles et militaires et des biens militaires spécifiques*, the competence to prosecute and judge violations of this pre-existing legislation lies with the federal penal jurisdiction (*Juridiction pénale fédérale*). According to the same provisions, the authorities charged with the application and the control of this legislation, as well as customs authorities and cantonal and municipal police, are required to report suspected violations to the Prosecutor of the Swiss Confederation. In contrast to the *ad hoc* legislation adopted by the Federal Council, prosecutions under pre-existing legislation, the procedure for the prosecution and judgement of sanctions violators as well as appellate proceedings are regulated by the *Loi fédérale sur la procédure pénale.*[174]

(4) Prosecution of Sanctions Violators

A major problem in prosecuting sanctions violators lies in the detection of the violations. National customs authorities are frequently left to work on their own and are therefore unable to proceed in a co-ordinated way.[175]

In order to remedy this problem, a special border control system was established in the case of Yugoslavia (Serbia and Montenegro). The borders of Serbia and Montenegro were kept under surveillance by SAMCOMM (Sanctions Assistance Missions Command).[176] Thanks to SAMCOMM, an important number of potential sanctions violations were discovered and reported to the competent national authorities, some of which concerned Switzerland. Once the suspected sanctions violations have been reported, it is up to the authorities to prosecute the alleged violators under domestic legislation.[177]

In this context, mention must also be made of the confiscation of assets originating in sanctions violations. Such confiscation can raise interesting legal questions. In a case currently in abeyance before the Genevan courts, the question arose as to what extent the Genevan authorities have jurisdiction to confiscate assets originating in the breach of

173 RS 313.0.

174 RS 312.0.

175 Othmar Wyss, *op. cit.* (note 93), pp. 27 f.

176 SAMCOMM is a common organ of the EU and the former CSCE in which Switzerland participated through the provision of personnel and funding. During the embargo, 26 civil servants worked at the SAMCOMM headquarters in Brussels. Seven teams of customs officers were deployed at the borders of Serbia/Montenegro in Albania, Bulgaria, Croatia, Hungary, Romania, Macedonia and Ukraine.

177 Othmar Wyss, *op. cit.* (note 93), p. 28.

sanctions. The breach consisted here of the illegal traffic of arms to Croatia and Bosnia-Herzegovina by a Syrian national resident in Spain committed on Spanish territory. The only link with Switzerland lies in the fact that the profits from the sanctions violations are deposited in a Genevan bank. Ruling on a question that the Federal Supreme Court has yet to clearly decide, the Genevan Court of Appeals held that confiscation in question is possible provided that the condition of double criminality applies.[178] Under Swiss law, the traffic of arms to the countries of the Former Yugoslavia was prohibited.[179] The question thus remains whether this activity also violates Spanish law.[180]

(5) Compensation

The question of compensation in favour of companies affected by embargo measures was examined in the context of the sanctions measures adopted against Iraq by the Swiss Federal Council. During a parliamentary debate, the question was raised whether the Swiss Federal Council could adopt an executive order to assist small businesses suffering financial hardship due to the sanctions imposed against Iraq. The Council answered that it did not have the necessary competence to adopt such an executive order.[181] The Council stressed that if companies had suffered serious losses due to the Iraq sanctions, it should be kept in mind that a one-sided orientation of the business policy always carries high risks. Finally, the Council stated that it would examine whether commodities that were ready for export but that could not be exported due to the embargo could be bought by the Swiss Confederation or public undertakings. In the event, as most of the commodities concerned were special manufactures, the Confederation and other public bodies were not in a position to buy them.[182]

(6) Problems Raised by Extraterritorial Enforcement

Switzerland has adopted sanctions measures on an extraterritorial basis only in the case of Libya and of UNITA (see Section III.2.). Those cases did not raise any particular problems.

---

178 République et canton de Genève, Pouvoir Judiciaire, Cour de cassation, Arrêt N° ACAS/61/00 of 15 September 2000 in the case N° 97/99.

179 Art. 10, *Ordonnance Yougoslavie II.*

180 The UN weapons embargo could not serve as a basis for the infringement, because the embargo had not yet been implemented by the EU when the infringement took place. The Court of Appeals also excluded UN SC Res. 713 as a legal basis, since the infringement of UN resolutions does not have immediate effect under Spanish law. The only remaining possibility is an infringement of the Spanish law on the trade in weapons. In order to examine this possibility in more detail, the case has been sent back to the Court of First Instance.

181 The Council admitted that Article 31bis of the previous Constitution enabled the adoption of rules for the protection of important branches of industry and geographic regions that are seriously threatened, but it denied that these requirements were actually fulfilled in the present case. Othmar Wyss, *op. cit.* (note 93), pp. 21 f.

182 *Loc. cit.*

(7) *Problems of Embargo at Sea*

No such problems have arisen for Switzerland.

V. Implementation of Security Council Decisions Relating to the International Criminal Tribunals for the Former Yugoslavia and Rwanda

(1) *Provisions Relating to Co-operation with the International Criminal Tribunals*

As the two *ad hoc* International Criminal Tribunals established by Resolutions 827 and 955 must co-operate closely with state authorities, these Security Council resolutions and the Statutes of the Tribunals provide for the co-operation not merely of United Nations Member States, but of all States. Apart from the very general obligation "to cooperate fully with the International Tribunal and its organs" and to take "any measures necessary under their domestic law to implement the provisions of the present resolution and the statute", States are bound by more specific obligations in the field of co-operation and judicial assistance. The Statutes of the two *ad hoc* Tribunals (Article 28, paragraph 2 or Article 29, paragraph 2, respectively) obligate States to co-operate in the identification and location of persons, in gathering testimony and in the handing over of evidence as well as in the arrest or detention of persons and the surrender or transfer of the accused to the Tribunals. Additional obligations to co-operate are provided for in the Statutes, including the obligation to allow the Prosecutor to investigate on State territory (Articles 18, paragraphs 2 and 29 or Articles 17, paragraphs 2 and 29, respectively), to recognise judgments passed by the Tribunals and, if necessary, to co-operate in the execution of measures ordered in addition to imprisonment (Article 24, paragraph 3 or Article 23, paragraph 3, respectively).

As mentioned above, in order to assure full co-operation with the International Criminal Tribunals, the Swiss Parliament adopted *ad hoc* legislation, namely the *Arrêté fédéral relatif à la coopération avec les tribunaux internationaux chargés de poursuivre les violations graves du droit international humanitaire.*[183] An overview of the legislation's means of co-operation can be found in Article 3, paragraph 1. It was enacted to respond to the specific problems raised by co-operation with the Tribunals and to simplify procedures for co-operation and judicial assistance, in particular to reduce delays. For this reason, the provisions of the Swiss legislation on co-operation with the Tribunals are partly new and partly inspired by the pre-existing legislation on international judicial assistance in criminal matters.[184]

Requests for judicial assistance are granted if the criminal act falls under the jurisdiction of the Tribunal and if it is punishable under Swiss law (Article 17, paragraph 1); no other requirements have to be met. Article 22 on criminal investigation taking place on Swiss territory implements the aforementioned obligations of the Statutes providing that the Prosecutor may conduct investigations on the territory of third States. Provided that

183 RS 351.20, see *supra*, Section II.3, p. 536.

184 RS 351.1.

the Prosecutor has an authorisation – which must be granted if the conditions for judicial assistance (Article 17, paragraph 1) are met – the latter is allowed to conduct investigations on Swiss territory. The direct notification by mail of acts of procedure and judicial decisions to persons in Switzerland is also provided for (Article 23). This possibility manifests a clear intention to accelerate and optimise the judicial assistance provided by Switzerland to the *ad hoc* Tribunals. This intention is also made plain in the procedure to be followed for the granting of judicial assistance, which is relatively simple when compared to the legislation on international judicial assistance in criminal matters.

The question of the surrender or transfer of accused persons will be examined in Section VI.2 below.

The execution of measures ordered in addition to imprisonment (especially the return to the rightful owners of any property and proceeds criminally acquired, including by duress) can be carried out under the Swiss law on international judicial assistance in criminal matters.[185]

Article 8 authorises Swiss authorities to transmit relevant information and evidence unilaterally to the International Criminal Tribunals. Article 9 on the discontinuance of national proceedings in favour of the Tribunals (*dessaisissement en faveur des tribunaux internationaux*) implements the rule of the primacy of the Tribunals in respect of national jurisdictions as set out in the Statutes (Article 8, paragraph 2 or Article 9, paragraph 2, respectively). Discontinuance of proceedings commenced in Switzerland and transfer of these to the Tribunals will occur in cases where the Tribunal's request concerns the same facts and where the criminal act alleged comes within the jurisdiction of the requesting authority (Article 9, paragraph 2).

Articles 29-33 on the enforcement of sentences provide for the practical implementation of Article 26 or Article 27, respectively, of the Statute, according to which "imprisonment shall be served in a State designated by the International Tribunal from a list of States which have indicated to the Security Council their willingness to accept convicted persons." A final sentence of the Tribunals may be enforced in Switzerland (*peut être exécutée*) if there is a corresponding request by the Tribunal; if the person convicted is usually resident in Switzerland; and if the criminal act is punishable under Swiss law (Article 29, paragraph 1). Switzerland thereby limited its offer to co-operate in the enforcement of sentences of the *ad hoc* Tribunals to convicted persons usually resident in Switzerland. Foreigners residing in Switzerland do not, however, have the right under Swiss law to serve their sentences in Switzerland; such a right only exists for Swiss nationals (Article 29, paragraph 2). In a 1997 decision concerning the surrender of a national from Rwanda to the International Tribunal in Arusha, the Federal Supreme Court explicitly stated that

> "*... en dehors des cas où le condamné est un ressortissant suisse ... il n'existe aucun droit à l'exécution en Suisse de la peine prononcée par le Tribunal international.*"[186]

185 RS 351.1; Art. 74, para. 2.

186 ATF 123 II 175, cons. 7)c).

The Court further stressed that sentences pronounced against foreign nationals can only be enforced in Switzerland at the request of the Tribunals.[187]

In order to execute a foreign judgment requiring a term of imprisonment to be served in Switzerland, a procedure of exequatur is required.[188] This procedure permits the international sentence to be adapted to correspond to penal sanctions allowed under Swiss law. If the prison sentence imposed by the Tribunals goes beyond the maximum sanction prescribed by Swiss law for the criminal act concerned, the international sentence can only be enforced to the extent admitted by Swiss law.[189]

(2) Procedures Relating to the Surrender of Persons to the International Criminal Tribunals

The surrender of persons to the International Criminal Tribunals is regulated by Articles 10-16 of the aforementioned *Arrêté fédéral relatif à la coopération avec les tribunaux internationaux chargés de poursuivre les violations graves du droit international humanitaire.* These provisions are largely based on the relevant provisions of Swiss extradition law. Nevertheless, the use of the term "*extradition*" has intentionally been avoided, as the surrender of persons to the Tribunals cannot be considered an ordinary act under the extradition law. It is for this reason that the *Arrêté fédéral* speaks exclusively of "*transfèrement de personnes poursuivies aux tribunaux internationaux*".

The conditions for the surrender are set out in Article 10, paragraph 1, according to which any person may be surrendered to the International Criminal Tribunals if (a) the criminal act comes within the jurisdiction of the latter and if (b) the criminal act is punishable under Swiss law. As the principle of double criminality is of fundamental importance in any extradition procedure, the Swiss legislation specifies that it be met before permission for the surrender of persons to the Tribunals will be granted. In order to assure full co-operation with the Tribunals, surrender cannot be submitted for any other condition or exception.

Mention must also be made of Article 10, paragraph 2 concerning the surrender of Swiss nationals. Article 45 of the previous Federal Constitution provided that no Swiss citizen could be expelled from Switzerland. According to Article 7 of the law on international judicial assistance in criminal matters, extradition of Swiss nationals to foreign authorities is prohibited. Security Council Resolutions 827 and 955 as well as the Statutes of the two International Criminal Tribunals do not, however, provide for an exception for the surrender of nationals. With the adoption of Article 10, paragraph 2 of the *Arrêté fédéral,* Switzerland has developed an innovative method for reconciling its obligations under international law with the constitution's human rights guarantees. According to Article 10, paragraph 2, a Swiss national may only be surrendered to the Tribunals if the latter guarantees that the former will be sent back to Switzerland at the

187 *Loc. cit.*

188 FF 1995 IV 1087.

189 Application by analogy of Article 94, para. 2, of the law on international judicial assistance in criminal matters (RS. 351.1); see also FF 1995 IV 1086.

end of the procedure. Correspondingly, Article 45 of the previous Federal Constitution (now Article 25) was adapted when the Constitution was revised:

> "*Les Suisses et les Suissesses ne peuvent être expulsés du pays; ils ne peuvent être remis à une autorité étrangère que s'ils y consentent.*"[190]

As for the procedure of surrender, Articles 11-15 of the *Arrêté* are inspired by the relevant provisions of the law on international judicial assistance in criminal matters, while at the same time setting up simplified and more rapid procedures than for ordinary extradition. The legality of this simplified procedure has been confirmed by the Federal Supreme Court.[191]

VI. Role of National Courts

(1) Resolution of Conflicts between Domestic and International Obligations

It has to be recalled in this context that Switzerland, as a non-Member State of the United Nations adopting sanctions measures in conformity with Security Council resolutions, was not implementing international obligations that were legally binding; it was implementing these measures voluntarily through a sovereign decision (*autonomer Nachvollzug*).[192] This fact had far-reaching consequences for litigation before Swiss courts. As the Security Council resolutions did not bind Switzerland, there could be no conflict between domestic and international obligations.

With Switzerland's admission to the United Nations, this no longer holds true. According to the monist tradition and the adoption theory of Swiss constitutional law, international law is automatically effective in the Swiss legal order, that is without any act of transformation or incorporation being necessary.[193] International legal norms – if

190 It is also for this reason that Article 29, para. 1 of the *Arrêté* concerning the enforcement of prison sentences in Switzerland explicitly states that the sentences passed on Swiss nationals are to be enforced in Switzerland if the latter so wishes.

191 ATF 123 II 175.

192 See *supra*, Section I, p. 527.

193 Since its earliest days, the Federal Supreme Court has maintained that Switzerland is a monist State (BGE 7 782). This opinion has been unanimously followed by the practice of authorities and legal writers: Gemeinsame Stellungnahme des Bundesamtes für Justiz und der Direktion für Völkerrecht vom 26. April 1989: Das Verhältnis zwischen Völkerrecht und Landesrecht im Rahmen der schweizerischen Rechtsordnung, in: VPB 53/IV (1989) No. 54, pp. 393 ff.; Yvo Hangartner, "Völkerrecht und schweizerisches Landesrecht", in: *Festschrift für Arnold Koller* (Bern/Stuttgart/Wien, 1993), pp. 651-681; Olivier Jacot-Guillarmot, "Fondements juridiques internationaux de la primauté du droit international dans l'ordre juridique suisse", 120 *ZBJV* (1984) 227-246; Mathias-Charles Krafft, "Observations sur les rapports entre le droit international et le droit suisse, à la lumière notamment de certains développements récents de la jurisprudence de la Cour européenne des droits de l'homme", in: *Mélanges Georges Perrin*, (Lausanne, 1984), pp. 187-197; Jörg Paul Müller, "Völkerrecht und schweizerische Rechtsordnung", in: A. Riklin, H. Haug, C. Binswanger (eds.), *Handbuch der schweizerischen Aussenpolitik*

endowed with a self-executing character – are also directly applicable in particular circumstances,[194] which means that they can be appealed to in a given case and are to be applied by the authorities in favour of the individual. Because United Nations law automatically becomes part of the Swiss legal order with Switzerland's admission to the United Nations, contradictions between sanctions resolutions and national law lead to novel norm conflicts within the Swiss legal order that must be resolved. How is this to come about?

In case of a conflict between international and domestic obligations, different principles have to be taken into consideration. It is unanimously accepted that international treaties prevail over cantonal law, inter-cantonal law and executive orders adopted by the Federal Council.[195] For conflicts between treaties and the Federal Constitution, a distinction has to be made. If the treaty that is jeopardised by a revision of the Constitution is not considered to be very important, Swiss practice has generally been to prohibit the international treaty from limiting the scope of the Federal Constitution. If, however, the treaty is considered to be very important, practice and writers hold that the latter cannot be jeopardised by a revision of the Constitution. Article 139, paragraph 3 and Article 194, paragraph 2 of the new Federal Constitution lay down this principle, stating that popular initiatives calling for constitutional reform may not violate *jus cogens* norms. The most common conflicts between international and domestic obligations are conflicts between treaties and federal laws adopted by Parliament after the entry into force of the treaty. Such conflicts are generally resolved by the principle of the primacy of international law over domestic law.[196] In some very exceptional cases, the Federal Supreme Court has given priority to a federal act. According to the Court, the Swiss Parliament may, with full knowledge of the facts, enact a law that is contrary to international law if important interests of Switzerland are at stake.[197] Apart from these principles, the matter of the hierarchy of norms seems largely unresolved.[198]

In keeping with the preceding, conflicts between Federal Council implementation measures and Security Council sanctions resolutions are in principle to be resolved in latter's favour.[199] At most, it could be considered in exceptional cases whether priority should not be given to the implementation measures where the collision of norms was deliberately accepted for reasons of neutrality. This approach would accord with the emphatically declared intention of Switzerland to remain neutral even as a United

(Bern/Stuttgart, 1975), pp. 223-236; Dietrich Schindler, "Die Schweiz und das Völkerrecht", in: A. Riklin, H. Haug, R. Probst (eds.), *Neues Handbuch der Schweizerischen Aussenpolitik* (Bern/Stuttgart/Wien, 1992), pp. 99-119; Daniel Thürer, "Verfassungsrecht und Völkerrecht", in: D. Thürer, J.-P. Aubert, J.P. Müller, (eds.), *Verfassungsrecht der Schweiz* (Zürich, 2001), pp. 179-206.

194 The matter of the self-executing nature of international legal norms is to be distinguished from the one of their automatic effect in Swiss legal order.

195 ATF 109 V 244.

196 ATF 125 II 417.

197 ATF 99 Ib, 39, 44; ATF 111 V 201; ATF 116 IV 262, 268; ATF 117 IV 124, 128; ATF 118 Ib 277, 281f.

198 See Daniel Thürer, *op. cit.* (note 193), pp. 188 ff.

199 It is to be noted, however, that genuine conflicts can possibly be avoided through an interpretation of the implementation measures that is in conformity with international law.

Nations Member State, as expressed in both of the Federal Council declarations of neutrality. No direct solution arises out of the aforementioned principles to resolve the conflicts between sanctions resolutions and constitutional provisions, in particular fundamental rights. The relationship between the Constitution and international law has to date been only rarely considered in Swiss practice.[200] In principle, a discriminating approach seems to be called for.[201] Article 191 of the Swiss Federal Constitution stipulates, however, that the Federal Supreme Court and the other law-applying authorities are to follow federal statutes and international law even when they are unconstitutional. Besides international treaties and customary law, the general principles of international law and the resolutions of international organisations that bind Switzerland belong to authoritative international law.[202] Accordingly, insofar as the Federal Council implementation measures are coterminous with the Security Council sanctions resolutions, they are in principle to be followed despite any unconstitutionality.[203] The conflict of norms is thereby at least practically resolved in favour of the sanctions resolutions.

(2) *Adjudication of Disputes Relating to the Execution of Contracts or the Ownership of Goods*

In a 1993 decision, the Federal Supreme Court ruled on a dispute about a contract of commission allegedly affected by the economic embargo against Iraq.[204] Two questions were put to the Court: first, whether the embargo extended to activities of commission and second, whether it retroactively extended to activities contracted and fully executed prior to the embargo's coming into force.

In answer to the first question, the Federal Supreme Court held that the economic embargo extended to legal acts facilitating or leading to the conclusion and execution of contracts contrary to the embargo. However, it is not necessary, the Court held in

200 See Ulrich Häfelin/Walter Haller, *Schweizerisches Bundesstaatsrecht* (Zürich, 2001), p. 564.

201 *Ibid.*, p. 564; Daniel Thürer, *op. cit.* (note 193), pp. 188 ff.

202 See René Rhinow, *Die Bundesverfassung 2000* (Basel/Genf/München, 2000), pp. 197 f.

203 This presumes that the *Loi sur les embargos* fully empowers the Federal Council to issue implementation measures.

204 Two Italian undertakings producing war material concluded a contract in the early 1980s with an individual to serve as a middle-man for the sale of warships and other military equipment by the Italian undertakings to the State of Iraq. Until 1987, the contracts subsequently concluded between the Italian undertakings and the State of Iraq were regularly executed. Thereafter, problems arose: first, the Iraqi authorities suspended payment and then the Security Council embargo prevented the supply of any further commodities. As the middle-man had not been fully paid for his work, he brought a case before the International Chamber of Commerce Court of Arbitration, which he won. The two Italian undertakings lodged an appeal (per Article 191 of the Federal law on private international law) against the arbitral award at the Swiss Federal Supreme Court. The plaintiffs argued that the arbitral award was contrary to international *ordre public*. According to the plaintiffs, the contract between them and the middle-man was affected by the economic embargo imposed on Iraq. The Court of Arbitration, in taking the position of the middle-man, had allegedly issued an award contrary to international *ordre public* (ATF 119 II 386).

answer to the second question, to examine whether such contracts were nullified by the application of the principle of international *ordre public*. Considerations related to the principle of international *ordre public* do not have retroactive effect and thus cannot nullify contractual relations in cases where the main obligation had already been executed before the coming into force of the embargo:

> "*ledit ordre public ne déploie aucun effet rétroactif de nature à entraîner la nullité de relations contractuelles dans le cadre desquelles la prestation principale a déjà été exécutée avant l'entrée en vigueur de l'embargo*".[205]

In the present case, the contracts in question had been concluded in 1980 and 1981 and were therefore clearly not prohibited. The activity of commission provided for in the contracts had come to an end before the embargo's entry into force. For this reason, the Federal Supreme Court concluded:

> "*exiger l'exécution d'engagements valablement contractés, à une époque où ceux-ci ne peuvent plus être stipulés de manière licite en raison de dispositions de politique économique adoptées entretemps, ne viole nullement l'ordre public*".[206]

In a recent decision, the Federal Supreme Court considered the effects of United Nations sanctions on private contracts, especially the question of the nullity of a contract for illegality or immorality (Article 20 of the Law of Contracts (*Code des obligations*[207])). The question arose out of weapons sales to Croatia in violation of the United Nations embargo against Yugoslavia. The Court held that the sales were not illegal in Swiss law on the sole basis of the United Nations embargo, as the corresponding Security Council Resolution was not binding for the non-Member State Switzerland, and could therefore not serve as a prohibition per Article 20 of the *Code des obligations*.[208] Nevertheless, the Court held that, in view of the universal importance of the United Nations weapons embargo, the violation of the United Nations Resolution was in opposition with universal *ordre public*. Accordingly, it judged the sales to be immoral under Swiss law, which entailed the nullity of the contract.[209]

(3) Interpretation of Security Council Resolutions

What has been said earlier about the legal effects of Security Council resolutions on Switzerland before it joined the United Nations had direct consequences for the inter-

---

205 *Ibid.*, cons. 2b).

206 *Loc. cit.*

207 RS 220.

208 In the present case, the sales did not fall under the provisions of the *Loi fédérale sur le materiel de guerre*.

209 The case is only available on the website of the Federal Supreme Court: http://www.bger.ch under the reference 4C.172/2000/rnd, see in particular 5a) to 5g).

pretation of Security Council resolutions by Swiss courts. It should thus come as no surprise that in judgements dealing with sanctions measures, the Federal Supreme Court has never interpreted Security Council resolutions. Very often in fact, the pertinent resolutions are not even mentioned, the Court's reasoning relying exclusively on the relevant domestic provisions. It is to be expected that this practice will undergo a change with the Swiss admission to the United Nations.[210]

VII. Constitutional Issues Raised for States by Sanction Implementation

(1) *Human Rights Issues, such as Freedom of Movement, Freedom of Information, Protection of Acquired Rights*

Human rights issues raised by sanctions measures adopted on a voluntary basis by Switzerland mostly concerned economic freedom as guaranteed by Article 27 of the new Federal Constitution. It was on the basis of the analogous provisions in the old Constitution that the Federal Supreme Court ruled in two decisions on the conformity of the executive order instituting measures against Southern Rhodesia, especially the stabilisation of the binational volume of trade at the average level of the three-year period prior to the sanctions' adoption.[211] The main interests at stake in these two cases related to the criteria upon which authorisations were granted to import meat from Southern Rhodesia.

It has to be stressed that due to the inherently political nature of executive orders instituting sanctions measures, the review of these orders by the Federal Supreme Court is usually very limited in practice.[212]

Reference has been made elsewhere to the possibility of new norm conflicts arising from Switzerland's United Nations admission between constitutional laws and Security Council resolutions or coterminous Federal Council implementation measures as well as to the resolution of such conflicts.[213]

(2) *Issues Arising from Conflicts with Domestic Criminal Law Provisions and Extradition Practice*

The conflict between the provisions of the Statutes of the International Criminal Tribunals prohibiting exceptions for the surrender of state nationals and Article 25 of the new Federal Constitution prohibiting the extradition of Swiss nationals against their will as well as the solution to that conflict have already been covered elsewhere.[214]

210 Regarding the consequences of UN admission see *supra*, Section 1 and Section VI.1.

211 *ZBl.* 75 (1974) 93; ATF 100 Ib 318. For a short commentary on the decision and a general discussion of human rights and foreign politics see Luzius Wildhaber, "Menschenrechte – Föderalismus – Demokratie und die verfassungsrechtliche Verankerung der Aussenpolitik", in: *Festschrift Werner Kägi* (Zürich, 1979), pp. 436 ff.

212 ATF 64 I 365, 369.

213 See *supra*, Section VI.1, p. 566.

214 See *supra*, Section V.2, p. 565.

Other constitutional issues that have arisen in this context before the Swiss Supreme Court concern the rights of the defence,[215] fair trial and *Habeas Corpus*.

In a decision concerning the surrender of a Rwandan national to the International Tribunal in Arusha, the Federal Supreme Court was asked to determine whether principles developed in the context of judicial assistance and extradition between States also applied to the International Criminal Tribunals. When Switzerland grants judicial assistance and extradition warrants to authorities abroad, it must verify whether the procedures for which co-operation is being sought guarantee the suspect the minimum standards of protection contained in the European Convention on Human Rights and the United Nations Covenant on Civil and Political Rights. According to a large body of case law, Switzerland would violate its international obligations by granting judicial assistance or extradition to a State in which there was a serious danger of treatment contrary to the two human rights instruments. Switzerland may therefore seek a guarantee from the requesting State that the accused will be treated in accordance with international standards. The Court has held, however, that these principles that have been developed in the context of judicial assistance and extradition between States cannot be transposed *telles quelles* to the Tribunals:

> "*En effet, en décidant d'appliquer à titre autonome les Résolutions 827 (1993) et 955 (1994), le Conseil fédéral, puis le législateur suisse, sont partis de la considération que ces tribunaux, émanations de la communauté des Etats, offraient des garanties suffisantes quant à un déroulement correct des procédures. … Le législateur a ainsi délibérement exclu l'application des règles de l'EIMP relatives à la procédure menée à l'étranger … et aux conditions dont peut être assortie la décision de transfèrement. … Il n'y a donc pas lieu d'examiner, comme le voudrait le recourant, si la procédure devant le TPR est conforme aux standards minimaux posés par la CEDH et le Pacte ONU II, cette conformité devant être présumée. … (D)ans le cadre d'une mesure d'entraide accordée sur la base de la confiance légitime* inspirée par la juridiction requérante il n'y a *pas lieu de poser des conditions au transfèrement ….*"[216]

As concerns *Habeas Corpus*, the Rwandan national remanded in custody had presented a request for release. The Court dismissed the request, noting that Parliament had explicitly foregone the possibility under the general extradition law of permitting such a release due to the seriousness of the criminal acts with which the Tribunals are faced. Consequently, no exception to custody is made for individuals to be surrendered to the Tribunals, not even where there is no danger of flight.[217]

VIII. Interface between Domestic and International Implementation

Security Council resolutions requiring States to inform the United Nations Sanctions Committees about the implementation measures that they have adopted are often not

215 See on this point: ATF 123 II 175 para. 6)a)-6)e).

216 *Ibid.*, para. 7(b).

217 *Ibid.*, para. 8.

merely addressed to Member States but to all States. In this context, reference should be made to earlier remarks as regards the question of whether Switzerland was legally bound as a non-Member State by Security Council resolutions instituting sanctions.[218]

Nevertheless, Swiss practice has also undergone an important change. In the case of sanctions adopted against Southern Rhodesia, Switzerland could, due to its domestic regulation, comply only to a limited extent with the Sanctions Committee's request for reporting and exchange of information.[219] Consequently, Switzerland was confronted with international criticism. This situation changed in the 1990s with the adoption of identical provisions on co-operation with foreign authorities and especially the United Nations[220] in the pertinent *ad hoc* legislation. These provisions provided the federal authorities with the necessary legal basis to collaborate with the Sanctions Committees that was still lacking in the Rhodesian case.

These provisions authorise the federal authorities in charge of application, control, prevention and penal prosecution in relation to sanctions to collaborate with foreign authorities and the United Nations. A further provision sets out the conditions under which information can be transmitted to foreign authorities or to the United Nations. These conditions seek in particular to protect official secrecy and assure reciprocity. On the basis of these provisions, Switzerland regularly reports through its Permanent Observer Mission in New York to the different Sanctions Committees in charge of monitoring national implementation of United Nations sanctions.[221] The framework legislation on the implementation of international sanctions (Article 7) largely follows the aforementioned provisions contained in the different *ad hoc* legislation.[222]

As far as humanitarian exceptions are concerned, it has already been shown that as a non-Member State, Switzerland collaborated very closely with the Sanctions Committees, under both its obligation to notify and the no-objection procedure.[223]

IX. Concluding Remarks

The effectiveness of Security Council sanctions depends very much on their prompt, integral and universal implementation in domestic law. This holds particularly true for financial sanctions, which should, in view of the rapidity of global financial transactions, be adopted and implemented overnight by the United Nations, national authorities and financial actors

218 See *supra*, Section I, pp. 523 ff.

219 Swiss legislation did not then provide for a possibility of reporting to foreign organisations. For a presentation of the whole problematic, see Linsi, *op. cit.* (note 14), pp. 264-266.

220 E.g. Art. 9 and 10 of *Ordonnance Yougoslavie I*; Art. 9 and 10 of *Ordonnance Haïti I*; Art. 12 and 13 of *Ordonnance Libye II*; Art. 15 and 16 of *Ordonnance UNITA*; Art. 5 and 6 of *Ordonnance Sierra Leone;* Art. 7 and 8 of *Ordonnance Taliban.*

221 The latest report is available on the website of the Federal Department of Foreign Affairs: http://www.eda.admin.ch/eda/e/home/rep/terrorism.html. Extracts from the summary of this report have been presented in chapter III.1 under the title "fighting terrorism and its financing".

222 RS 946.231.

223 See *supra*, Section III.5, p. 554.

in the field. As a non-Member State of the United Nations, Switzerland implemented all the sanctions regimes adopted since 1990 by the United Nations Security Council on the basis of autonomous decisions (*autonomer Nachvollzug*). It did this in general immediately or shortly after the imposition of sanctions by the Security Council, and it did so to the extent prescribed by the latter. The implementation and enforcement framework used for that purpose did not give rise to major problems. Minor problems arose in the context of penal sanctions for sanctions violators and data protection, which in turn led to the adoption of framework legislation for the implementation of international sanctions.

Switzerland has taken an active role in the international efforts to enhance the effectiveness of international sanctions and to develop the concept of smart or targeted sanctions. As an important financial centre, Switzerland initiated in 1998 the so-called Interlaken Process aimed at examining the feasibility of targeted financial sanctions and at working out the know-how for the drafting of Security Council resolutions and national implementing legislation for targeted financial sanctions. As an important diamond trading centre, Switzerland has also been actively involved in the Kimberley Process to adopt an international certification scheme for conflict diamonds.

With this active role in the implementation of Security Council sanctions and in the development of techniques to enhance their effectiveness, Switzerland could by the nineties no longer be considered as a special case with respect to United Nations sanctions, as it had been in the Cold War era due to its status of permanent neutrality and its non-membership in the United Nations. As this status has undergone an important re-conceptualisation according to which permanent Swiss neutrality no longer affects participation in international sanctions and as Switzerland sought to join the United Nations, these two characteristics of Swiss foreign policy could not longer be considered decisive with respect to participation in international sanctions measures. With Switzerland's admission to the United Nations in 2002, the days of being a special case are definitely over.

* * *

Select Bibliography

I. Official Documents [224]

(1) *Legislation*

Loi fédérale sur les mesures économiques extérieures du 25 juin 1982 (RS 946.201);

– Message relatif à la loi fédérale sur les mesures économiques extérieures (FF 1982 I 65).

224 Most of these official documents are available on the official website of the Swiss Confederation: http://www.admin.ch under one of the following links:

Loi fédérale sur le contrôle des biens utilisables à des fins civiles et militaires et des biens militaires spécifiques du 13 décembre 1996 (RS 946.202);

- Message concernant la loi fédérale sur le contrôle des biens utilisables à des fins civiles et militaires (FF 1995 II 1251).

Loi fédérale sur le matériel de guerre du 13 décembre 1996 (RS 514.51);

- Message concernant l'initiative populaire 'pour l'interdiction d'exporter du matériel de guerre' et la révision de la loi fédérale sur le matériel de guerre (FF 1995 II 988).

Loi fédérale sur l'application de sanctions internationales du 18 juillet 2002 (RS 946.231);

- Message concernant la loi fédérale sur l'application de sanctions internationales du 20 décembre 2000 (FF 2001 1341).

Loi fédérale d'organisation judiciaire du 16 décembre 1943 (RS 173.110).

Loi fédérale sur la procédure administrative du 20 décembre 1968 (RS 172.021).

Loi fédérale sur la procédure pénale du 15 juin 1934 (RS 312.0).

Loi fédérale sur le droit pénal administratif du 22 mars 1974 (RS 313.0).

Loi fédérale sur l'entraide internationale en matière pénale du 20 mars 1981 (RS 351.1).

Arrêté fédéral relatif à la coopération avec les tribunaux internationaux chargés de poursuivre les violations graves du droit international humanitaire du 21 décembre 1995 (RS 351.20);

- Message concernant l'arrêté fédéral relatif à la coopération avec les tribunaux internationaux chargés de poursuivre les violations graves du droit international humanitaire (FF 1995 IV 1065).

Ordonnance instituant des mesures économiques envers la République d'Irak, du 7 août 1990 (RS 946.206).

Ordonnance concernant des mesures à l'encontre de la Libye, du 15 avril 1992 (RO 1992 958) replaced by Ordonnance concernant des mesures à l'encontre de la Libye, du 12 janvier 1994 (RO 1994 108).

Ordonnance instituant des mesures économiques à l'encontre de la Yougoslavie (Serbie et Monténégro), du 3 juin 1992 (RO 1992 1203) replaced by Ordonnance instituant des mesures économiques à l'encontre de la Yougoslavie (Serbie et Monténégro) et d'autres régions contrôlées par les Serbes, du 3 octobre 1994 (RO 1994 2194).

Ordonnance instituant des mesures économiques à l'encontre d'Haïti, du 30 juin 1993 (RO 1993 2053) replaced by Ordonnance instituant des mesures à l'encontre de la République d'Haïti, du 22 juin 1994 (RO 1994 1453).

Ordonnance instituant des mesures à l'encontre de la Sierra Leone, du 8 décembre 1997 (RS 946.209).

Ordonnance instituant des mesures à l'encontre de l'UNITA, du 25 novembre 1998 (RO 1991 151).

- RS under "Recueil systématique" (systematic collection by theme of all the legislative acts in force in the Swiss legal order).
- RO under "Recueil officiel" (chronological collection of the legislative acts adopted by the different organs of the Swiss Confederation).
- FF under "Feuille Fédérale" (official publication journal of the Swiss Confederation).

Ordonnance instituant des mesures à l'encontre de la République fédérale de Yougoslavie, du 1er juillet 1998 (RO 1998 1845).

Ordonnance instituant des mesures à l'encontre de la République fédérale de Yougoslavie, du 23 juin 1999 (RS 946.207).

Ordonnance instituant des mesures à l'encontre des personnes et entités liées à Oussama ben Laden, au groupe "Al-Qaïda" ou aux Taliban, du 20 octobre 2000 (RS 946.203).

Ordonnance instituant des mesures à l'encontre du Myanmar, du 2 octobre 2000 (RS 946.208.2).

Ordonnance instituant des mesures à l'encontre du Liberia, du 27 juin 2001 (RS 946.208.1).

Ordonnance instituant des mesures à l'encontre du Zimbabwe, du 19 mars 2002 (RS 946.209.2).

(2) Official Reports[225]

The yearly "Rapport sur la politique économique extérieure", published in the FF gives a good overview on the sanctions measures in force in the Swiss legal order:

- Rapport sur la politique économique extérieure 99/1+2 (FF 2000 1291).
- Rapport sur la politique économique extérieure 2000/1+2 (FF 2001 778).

see also the website of the State Secretariat for Economic Affairs: http://www.seco.admin.ch, under "Publications et formulaires", "Etudes et rapports".

Rapport sur la neutralité – Annexe au Rapport sur la politique extérieure de la Suisse dans les années 90 (FF 1994 I 201-237). An English translation of this report is available under the title "White Paper on Neutrality – Annex to the Report on Swiss Foreign Policy for the Nineties" on the aforementioned website (note 225).

Rapport du Conseil fédéral sur les relations entre la Suisse et l'Organisation des Nations Unies (ONU) du 1er juillet 1998 (FF 1998 4606).

Groupe de travail interdépartemental Suisse – Afrique du Sud, 'Les relations entre la Suisse et l'Afrique du Sud', Berne, July 1999.

Rapport sur la politique extérieure 2000 – Présence et coopération: la sauvegarde des intérêts dans un monde en cours d'intégration (FF 2001 261). An English translation of this report is available under the title "Switzerland's Foreign Policy Report" on the aforementioned website (note 225).

Pratique Suisse de la neutralité – aspects actuels, Rapport du groupe de travail interdépartemental du 30 août 2000. An English translation of this report is available under the title "Swiss Neutrality in Practice – Current Aspects", on the aforementioned website (note 225).

Message relatif à l'initiative populaire pour l'adhésion de la Suisse à l'Organisation des Nations Unies (ONU), du 4 décembre 2000, (FF 2001 1117).

Rapport concernant la lutte antiterroriste présenté par la Suisse au Comité du Conseil de sécurité créé par la résolution 1373 (2001), du 19 décembre 2001. An English translation of this report is available under the title "Report on the Fight against Terrorism", on the aforementioned website (note 225).

225 Some of these reports are available on the website of the Federal Department of Foreign Affairs: http://www.eda.admin.ch, under "Publications".

(3) Case Law of the Federal Supreme Court[226]

ATF 64 I 365

ATF 99 Ib 39

ZBl. 75 (1974) 93

ATF 100 Ib 318

ATF 109 V 244

ATF 111 V 201

ATF 116 IV 262

ATF 117 IV 124

ATF 118 Ib 277

ATF 119 II 386

ATF 123 II 175

ATF 125 II 417

II. Literature

(1) Monographs

Aubert, Jean-François, *Bundesstaatsrecht der Schweiz*, Fassung von 1967, Neubearbeiteter Nachtrag bis 1994 (Basel/Frankfurt am Main, 1995).

Auer, Andreas/Malinverni, Giorgio/Hottelier, Michel, *Droit constitutionnel suisse* (Berne, 2000).

Cottier, Thomas/Arpagaus, Remo (eds.), *Schweizerisches Bundesverwaltungsrecht – Schweizerisches Aussenwirtschafts – und Binnenmarktrecht* (Basel/Frankfurt am Main, 1999).

Ehrenzeller, Bernhard/Mastronardi, Philippe/Schweizer, Rainer J./Vallender, Klaus Arnold (eds.), *St. Galler Kurzkommentar zur neuen Bundesverfassung* (Zürich/Lachen, 2002).

Gabriel, Jürg Martin, *Schweizer Neutralität im Wandel* (Frauenfeld, 1990).

Häfelin, Ulrich/Haller, Walter, *Schweizerisches Bundesstaatsrecht* (Zürich, 2001).

Kommentar zur Bundesverfassung der Schweizerischen Eidgenossenschaft (Basel/Zürich/Bern, 1987-1996).

Linsi, Christian, *Gegenmassnahmen in der Form des Embargos zur Durchsetzung elementarer Völkerrechtsverpflichtungen in der schweizerischen Aussenpolitik*, Schriftenreihe für internationales Recht und internationale Beziehungen, Band 67, Basel/Frankfurt am Main 1994 (Diss. Univ. Basel, 1993).

Rhinow, René, *Die Bundesverfassung 2000* (Basel/Genf/München, 2000).

Riklin, Alois/Haug, Hans/Binswanger, Hans Christoph (eds.), *Handbuch der schweizerischen Aussenpolitik* (Bern/Stuttgart, 1975).

Riklin, Alois/Haug, Hans/Probst, Raymond (eds.), *Neues Handbuch der schweizerischen Aussenpolitik – Nouveau manuel de la politique extérieure suisse* (Bern/Stuttgart/Wien, 1992).

226 All the case law of the Federal Supreme Court is available at: http://www.bger.ch.

Ross, John F.L., *Neutrality and International Sanctions – Sweden, Switzerland and Collective Security* (New York, 1989).

Schaub, Adrian R., *Neutralität und Kollektive Sicherheit – Gegenüberstellung zweier unvereinbarer Verhaltenskonzepte in bewaffneten Konflikten und These zu einem zeit- und völkerrechtsgemässen modus vivendi*, Basel/Frankfurt am Main 1995 (Diss. Univ. Basel, 1995).

2nd Interlaken Seminar on Targeting United Nations Financial Sanctions, 29-31 March 1999, Swiss Federal Office for Foreign Economic Affairs in co-operation with the United Nations Secretariat; also available on http://www.smartsanctions.ch.

Targeted Financial Sanctions – A Manual for Design and Implementation: Contributions from the Interlaken Process; A cooperation of the Watson Institute for International Studies Brown University, the United Nations Secretariat and the Swiss Confederation (Providence, Rhode Island, 2001); also available on http://www.smartsanctions.ch.

Thürer, Daniel/Aubert, Jean-François/ Müller, Jörg Paul (eds.), *Verfassungsrecht der Schweiz – Droit constitutionnel suisse* (Zürich, 2001).

(2) Articles

Bindschedler, Rudolf, "Die Neutralität im modernen Völkerrecht", 17 *ZaöRV* (1956/57) 1-37.

Bindschedler, Rudolf, "Das Problem der Beteiligung der Schweiz an Sanktionen der Vereinten Nationen, besonders im Falle Rhodesiens", 28 *ZaöRV* (1968) 1-15.

Cottier, Michael, "Resolutionen des UN-Sicherheitsrats auf der Grundlage von Kap. VII und die Schweiz", *Rapports suisses présentés au XVème Congrès international de droit comparé: Bristol, 27 juillet au 1er août 1998* (Zürich, 1998), pp. 167-197.

Eichenberger, Kurt/Schindler, Dietrich, "Art. 102", in: *Kommentar zur Bundesverfassung der Schweizerischen Eidgenossenschaft*, vol. IV (Basel/Zürich/Bern, 1987-1996).

Gabriel, Jürg Martin, "Die Stellung der Schweiz zu Wirtschaftssanktionen", in: Riklin, A./Haug, H./Probst, R. (eds.), *Neues Handbuch der schweizerischen Aussenpolitik* (Bern/Stuttgart/Wien, 1992), pp. 919-928.

Hangartner, Yvo, "Völkerrecht und schweizerisches Landesrecht", in: *Festschrift für Arnold Koller* (Bern/Stuttgart/Wien, 1993), pp. 651-681.

Jacot-Guillarmot, Olivier, "Fondements juridiques internationaux de la primauté du droit international dans l'ordre juridique suisse", 120 *ZBJV* (1984) 227-244.

Krafft, Mathias-Charles, "Observations sur les rapports entre le droit international et le droit suisse, à la lumière notamment de certains développements récents de la jurisprudence de la Cour européenne des droits de l'homme", in: *Mélanges Georges Perrin* (Lausanne, 1984), pp. 187-197.

Malinverni, Giorgio, "L'indépendance de la suisse dans un monde interdépendant" 117 *ZSR* (1998) II, pp. 1-137.

Meyer, Hansjörg, "Kriegsmaterialgesetz", in: Cottier, Th./Arpagaus, R. (eds.), *Schweizerisches Bundesverwaltungsrecht – Schweizerisches Aussenwirtschafts- und Binnenmarktrecht* (Basel/ Frankfurt am Main, 1999), pp. 1-22.

Müller, Jörg Paul, "Völkerrecht und schweizerische Rechtsordnung", in: Riklin, A./Haug, H./ Binswanger, C. (eds.), *Handbuch der schweizerischen Aussenpolitik* (Bern/Stuttgart, 1975), pp. 223-236.

Riklin, Alois, "Die Neutralität der Schweiz", in: Riklin, A./Haug, H./Probst, R. (eds.), *Neues Handbuch der schweizerischen Aussenpolitik* (Bern/Stuttgart/Wien, 1992), pp. 191-209.

Riklin, Alois, "La neutralité suisse et son évolution", in: *Mélanges en l'honneur de Jacques-Michel Grossen* (Bâle/Francfort-sur-le-Main, 1992), pp. 453-468.

Schaller, André, "Die Teilnahme der Schweiz an den gegen Irak gerichteten wirtschaftlichen Massnahmen der UNO: Wandel und Kontinuität in der schweizerischen Aussenpolitik", in: 181 *Beiträge und Berichte des Instituts für Politikwissenschaft der Hochschule St. Gallen* (1992).

Schindler, Dietrich, "Aspects contemporains de la neutralité", 121 *RCADI* (1967-II) 225-319.

Schindler, Dietrich, "Die Schweiz und das Völkerrecht", in: Riklin, A./Haug, H./Probst, R. (eds.), *Neues Handbuch der schweizerischen Aussenpolitik* (Bern/Stuttgart/Wien, 1992), pp. 99-119.

Schindler, Dietrich, "Kollektive Sicherheit der Vereinten Nationen und dauernde Neutralität der Schweiz", *SZIER* (1992), pp. 435-479.

Thürer, Daniel, "Vorstellungen über die dauernde Neutralität vor dem ersten Weltkrieg, heute und für die Zukunft" XLV *Schweizerisches Jahrbuch für internationales Recht*, Jubiläumsband (1989) 73-103.

Thürer, Daniel, "UN Enforcement Measures and Neutrality – The Case of Switzerland", 30 *Archiv des Völkerrechts* (1992) 63-85.

Thürer, Daniel, "Die Schweiz und die Vereinten Nationen", in: Riklin, A./Haug, H./Probst, R. (eds.), *Neues Handbuch der schweizerischen Aussenpolitik* (Bern/Stuttgart/Wien, 1992), pp. 307-337.

Thürer, Daniel, "Sicherheitspolitik und Neutralität", in: Rhinow, R. (ed.), *Die Schweizerische Sicherheitspolitik im internationalen Umfeld* (Basel/Frankfurt am Main, 1995), pp. 121-136.

Thürer, Daniel, "Verfassungsrecht und Völkerrecht", in: Thürer, D./Aubert, J.-F./ Müller, J.P. (eds.), *Verfassungsrecht der Schweiz* (Zürich, 2001), pp. 179-206.

Thürer, Daniel/Baur, Pascal, "Artikel 197 Ziff. 1", in: Ehrenzeller, B./Mastronardi, P./Schweizer, R. J./Vallender, K. (eds.), *St. Galler Kurzkommentar zur neuen Bundesverfassung*, (Zürich/Lachen, 2002).

Tomuschat, Christian, "Obligations Arising for States without or against Their Will", 241 *RCADI* (1993-IV) 199-374.

Weber, Karl, "Das Bundesgesetz über aussenwirtschaftliche Massnahmen", in: Cottier, Th./ Arpagaus, R. (eds.), *Schweizerisches Bundesverwaltungsrecht – Schweizerisches Aussenwirtschafts- und Binnenmarktrecht* (Basel/Frankfurt am Main, 1999), pp. 1-21.

Weber, Karl, "Das Güterkontrollgesetz", in: Cottier, Th./Arpagaus, R. (eds.), *Schweizerisches Bundesverwaltungsrecht – Schweizerisches Aussenwirtschafts- und Binnenmarktrecht* (Basel/ Frankfurt am Main, 1999), pp. 1-33.

Wildhaber, "Luzius, Menschenrechte – Föderalismus – Demokratie und die verfassungsrechtliche Verankerung der Aussenpolitik", in: *Festschrift Werner Kägi* (Zürich, 1979), pp. 423-441.

Wildhaber, Luzius, "Das Schweizer Nein zu einer Vollmitgliedschaft in den Vereinten Nationen", 41 *Europa-Archiv* (1986) 461-468.

Wildhaber, Luzius, "Aussenpolitische Kompetenzordnung im schweizerischen Bundesstaat", in: Riklin, A./Haug, H./Probst, R. (eds.), *Neues Handbuch der schweizerischen Aussenpolitik* (Bern/ Stuttgart/Wien, 1992), pp. 121-149.

Wyss, Othmar, "Wirtschaftliche Embargomassnahmen", in: Cottier, Th./Arpagaus, R. (eds.), *Schweizerisches Bundesverwaltungsrecht – Schweizerisches Aussenwirtschafts- und Binnenmarktrecht* (Basel/Frankfurt am Main, 1999), pp. 1-31.

UNITED KINGDOM

*Christopher Greenwood, CMG, QC**

Introduction

This Report will consider the implementation of Security Council sanctions regimes in United Kingdom law. The structure of the Report broadly follows that of the other Reports in the present volume in order to facilitate the comparative study of sanctions regimes. The Report is divided into six main sections:- the legal basis for the implementation of Security Council sanctions (Part 1), the legal basis for the implementation of decisions of regional organisations (Part 2), the comparison between the content of Security Council decisions and domestic measures (Part 3), an outline of domestic procedures for enforcement and implementation (Part 4), a review of the role of national courts (Part 5) and a discussion of constitutional issues (Part 6). The conclusions of the report are set out in Part 7. The United Kingdom measures implementing United Nations sanctions regimes in force are listed on the website of the Department of Trade and Industry's Export Controls Unit (http://www.dti.gov.uk/export.control).

It is, however, necessary first to make a few introductory remarks. One issue which needs to be considered at the outset is what measures are encompassed by the term "sanctions". This term is usually employed to describe economic measures, such as trade embargoes (total or partial) and assets freezes. It is important to bear in mind, however, that such measures are only some of those envisaged by Article 41 of the United Nations Charter. Article 41 provides that:

> The Security Council may decide what measures not involving the use of armed force are to be employed to give effect to its decisions, and it may call upon the Members of the United Nations to apply such measures. These may include complete or partial interruption of economic relations and of rail, sea, air, postal, telegraphic, radio, and other means of communication, and the severance of diplomatic relations.

* Professor of International Law, London School of Economic and Political Science; Barrister, Essex Court Chambers, 24 Lincoln's Inn Fields, London WC2A 3EG. The author gratefully acknowledges the research assistance of Mr Jonathan Drakeford, LLM. Except where otherwise indicated, this Report is based on the law as it stood on 1 August 2002.

Vera Gowlland-Debbas (ed.), National Implementation of UN Sanctions, *581-604.*

The structure of the article is important. The first sentence confers a broad power to decide upon measures to give effect to the decisions taken by the Security Council under Article 39 and to call upon the Members of the United Nations to apply those measures. The only limitation is that the measures in question must not involve the use of armed force. The second sentence then gives a non-exhaustive list of examples of the type of measure which the Security Council may decide upon in the exercise of the power conferred by the first sentence.

The Appeals Chamber of the International Criminal Tribunal for the Former Yugoslavia has quite rightly commented that:-

> It is evident that the measures set out in Article 41 are merely illustrative *examples* which obviously do not exclude other measures. All the Article requires is that they do not involve "the use of force". It is a negative definition.[1]

Since the Iraqi invasion of Kuwait in 1990, the Council has decided upon a broad range of measures not involving the use of armed force in order to give effect to its decisions.[2] It has imposed sanctions of an economic character in respect of Afghanistan,[3] Angola,[4] the Federal Republic of Yugoslavia,[5] Eritrea and Ethiopia,[6] Haiti,[7] Iraq,[8] Liberia,[9] Libya,[10] Rwanda,[11] Sierra Leone, [12] Somalia [13] and Sudan.[14] Following the events of

1 *Prosecutor* v. *Tadic (Jurisdiction)* (1995) 105 *International Law Reports,* 419 at 469.

2 Most of the relevant Security Council decisions, together with the implementing measures adopted in the United Kingdom can be found in Carver and Others (eds), *Economic Sanctions Reports* (2 volumes, 1999) and the *Economic Sanctions Reporter* (looseleaf, first issued in 2000).

3 SCRs 1267 (1999); 1333 (2000), 1363 (2001), 1388 (2002) and 1390 (2002).

4 First imposed by SCR 864 (1993) and tightened in several subsequent resolutions, including SCR 1237 (1999). At the time of writing, these sanctions were being eased, following the conclusion of a ceasefire in Angola; see SCR 1412 (2002).

5 There were, in effect, two distinct sets of sanctions measures: those in connection with the initial break-up of the old Socialist Federal Republic of Yugoslavia and the war in Bosnia-Herzegovina, which were imposed by Resolutions 713 (1991), 757 (1992) and 820 (1993) and then varied by numerous later resolutions, and those in connection with the situation in Kosovo, which were imposed by SCR 1160 (1998). The sanctions were lifted by SCR 1367 (2001).

6 SCR 1298 (2000).

7 SCR 841 (1993).

8 First imposed by SCR 661 (1990) and varied by numerous subsequent resolutions, particularly SCRs 670 (1990), 687 (1991) and 986 (1995).

9 SCR 788 (1992).

10 SCRs 748 (1992), 883 (1993) and 1192 (1998).

11 SCR 918 (1994).

12 SCR 1132 (1997) and subsequent resolutions.

13 SCR 733 (1992).

14 SCRs 1054 (1996) and 1070 (1996).

11 September 2001, the Council has imposed far-reaching economic measures against persons suspected of terrorism.[15] the Council has also adopted other non-military measures which are not of an economic character. For example, it has called upon States not to extend any form of recognition to Iraq's annexation of Kuwait or the Iraqi measures consequent thereon.[16] More remarkably, it has established two international criminal tribunals for the Former Yugoslavia[17] and Rwanda[18] and called upon States to take the necessary measures to co-operate with those Tribunals by, for example, surrendering suspects to the two tribunals and making available evidence requested by them. In each case, it seems clear that the legal basis on which the Security Council acted was Article 41 of the Charter but the Council's practice has been to refer only to Chapter VII and not to identify the specific article on which it relies.

While the emphasis of the present Report will be on economic sanctions, it will be necessary to refer in passing to the implementation by the United Kingdom of some of the other non-military measures adopted by the Security Council.

A second matter which calls for introductory comment concerns the attitude of the United Kingdom towards sanctions imposed by the Security Council. In contrast to the initial reluctance which existed in some other States, [19] the United Kingdom has always been a strong supporter of the sanctions regimes and has implemented them with great rigour. That reflects both the position of the United Kingdom as a permanent member of the Security Council and the fact that the first sanctions regime, against the breakaway government of Southern Rhodesia between 1966 and 1979, was imposed at the request of the United Kingdom and in response to a rebellion by the white settlers who were resisting majority rule in what was then a British colony. It also reflects the fact that, in general, legislation in the United Kingdom is quite strictly enforced and attempts to evade United Kingdom export controls have been severely penalised.[20]

The British approach to sanctions has also been influenced by the fact that, as will be seen in Part 1 of this Report, the United Kingdom has a comparatively simple means for the implementation of sanctions imposed by the Security Council. While the measures adopted by the United Kingdom are sometimes quite complex, their adoption has been a relatively simple task and has not required primary legislation or given rise to any constitutional debate.

Finally, it is necessary to bear in mind that Security Council sanctions are implemented in the United Kingdom by a mixture of United Kingdom laws and European Community legislation. In order to avoid unnecessary duplication with Mr Bethlehem's

15 SCRs 1373 (2001) and 1377 (2001).

16 SCR 662 (1990). See below for discussion of the effect of this resolution in the English courts, p. 600.

17 SCR 827 (1993).

18 SCR 955 (1994)

19 See, e.g, the comments on France in the Report by Professors Burdeau and Stern, Chapter 7 of this volume, *supra*, pp 195 ff.

20 The Legg Report (*Report of the Sierra Leone Arms Investigation*, (1998), HC Paper No. 1016) examined problems in the implementation of those controls but also demonstrated just how seriously those failures were regarded.

Report on the European Community, EC measures are not discussed in detail here, although it has been necessary to refer to some of them in passing. It follows that in order to gain a full picture of the implementation of sanctions in the United Kingdom, it will be necessary to consult Mr Bethlehem's Report as well as the present Report.

I. Legal Basis of Domestic Measures Implementing Economic Sanctions

(1) The General Legal Framework

Unlike most other European States, the United Kingdom does not have a single constitutional text, so there is no formal, constitutional basis for sanctions implementation, nor any constitutional provision under which a challenge to the legality of a sanctions regime might be brought.

It is, however, a well established rule of United Kingdom law – which might be said to have 'constitutional status' – that a treaty concluded by the United Kingdom is not part of United Kingdom law and cannot be enforced by the United Kingdom courts unless Parliament otherwise provides.[21] That does not mean that United Kingdom courts completely ignore or disregard treaties which have not been incorporated into United Kingdom law by Parliament. The courts apply a presumption that Parliament does not intend to legislate contrary to the treaty obligations of the United Kingdom and thus take account of treaty provisions when interpreting legislation[22] and when resolving ambiguities in the common law.[23] The provisions of a treaty which has not been given effect by Parliament, either in an Act of Parliament or by delegated legislation authorised by an Act of Parliament, cannot, however, create rights or obligations under United Kingdom law or be enforced by a United Kingdom court.

The United Nations Charter, to which the United Kingdom, as an original member of the United Nations, has been party since 1945, has not been incorporated into United

21 See, e.g., the decisions of the House of Lords in *British Airways Board* v. *Laker Airways Ltd.* [1985] AC 58 and *JH Rayner Ltd.* v. *Department of Trade and Industry* [1990] 2 AC 418. The effect of treaties in English law is surveyed by Judge Higgins in Jacobs and Roberts (eds), *The Effect of Treaties in Domestic Law* (1987), pp. 123-140. A number of treaties have, of course, been given effect in United Kingdom law by Parliament, noticeably the European Communities treaties which are made part of United Kingdom law by the European Communities Act 1972. Most of the substantive provisions of the European Convention on Human Rights became part of United Kingdom law on 2 October 2000 under the terms of the Human Rights Act 1998. Until that date, however, the Convention had been the unincorporated treaty most frequently cited before United Kingdom courts. The rule that treaties not incorporated by Parliament cannot be enforced by the courts results from the fact that the legal authority under United Kingdom law to conclude a treaty vests in the Crown by virtue of the royal prerogative. It has been a principle of English (and later United Kingdom) law since the early seventeenth century that the royal prerogative cannot alter English law.

22 See, e.g., *Salomon* v. *Commissioners of Customs and Excise* [1967] 2 QB 116.

23 See, e.g., *Derbyshire County Council* v. *Times Newspapers* [1992] QB 772 (Court of Appeal), affirmed on different grounds by the House of Lords, [1993] AC 534.

Kingdom law. It follows that the Charter is not itself enforceable in a United Kingdom court. Resolutions of the Security Council which are in binding form[24] impose obligations on member States by virtue of Article 25 of the Charter, which provides that "the Members of the United Nations agree to accept and carry out the decisions of the Security Council in accordance with the present Charter." Consequently, resolutions of the Security Council, as instruments adopted under a treaty which has not been made part of United Kingdom law and which derive their binding force from such a treaty, are themselves not part of United Kingdom law and are not enforceable as such in the United Kingdom courts.

That does not mean, however, that decisions of the Council are of no significance in the United Kingdom courts. It is clear, for example, that reference may be made to Security Council resolutions as an aid to construction of United Kingdom and European Community laws. In *Shanning International Ltd* v. *Lloyds TSB Bank plc*,[25] the House of Lords had regard to the Security Council resolutions imposing sanctions on Iraq and, in particular, Resolution 687 (1991), as an aid to construction of EC legislation giving effect to those sanctions.

More striking, however, was the decision in *Kuwait Airways Corporation* v. *Iraqi Airways Co. (Nos. 4 and 5)*,[26] which shows that Security Council resolutions, even when not implemented by legislation binding on the United Kingdom courts, may be of relevance in determining United Kingdom public policy. That case concerned the seizure, following the Iraqi invasion of Kuwait, of ten aircraft belonging to Kuwait Airways Corporation (KAC). The aircraft were transferred by Iraqi legislation (Revolutionary Command Council Decree No. 369 (1990)) to Iraqi Airways Co. (IAC) in September 1990. KAC brought proceedings for conversion in the English courts and IAC (after its earlier plea of sovereign immunity had failed)[27] relied upon RCC Decree 369 as a defence. KAC argued that RCC 369 was manifestly contrary to international law and to United Kingdom public policy. It relied, *inter alia* on the fact that the Security Council had decided, in Resolution 662 (1990), that the Iraqi annexation of Kuwait and the measures taken to implement it were null and void. IAC countered that the act of State doctrine precluded the English courts from sitting in judgement on the validity of acts of the Iraqi Government within Iraq and pointed to the fact that Resolution 662 (in contrast to the resolutions imposing economic sanctions on Iraq) had not been implemented by legislation in the United Kingdom. The House of Lords unanimously rejected IAC's argument on this

24 This is not the place to attempt a discussion of the question which decisions of the Security Council are legally binding under international law. Suffice it to say that the practice since at least 1990 has been that a decision is binding if it is contained in a resolution adopted under Chapter VII of the Charter and the relevant provisions are in mandatory language. Resolutions imposing sanctions are always in this form.

25 Case [2001] UKHL 31; [2001] 1 WLR 1462.

26 Case [2002] UKHL 19; [2002] 2 AC 883; see also the decision of the Court of Appeal, *ibid.* and of Mance J, 116 *International Law Reports* 534. The present author appeared as counsel for KAC in this litigation.

27 [1995] 1 WLR 1147.

point.[28] The House of Lords made extensive reference to Resolution 662 and the other resolutions on Iraq as putting beyond doubt the fact that the Iraqi invasion of Kuwait and its subsequent annexation and despoliation were flagrantly unlawful in international law and held that English courts were entitled to take account of that fact and decline to recognize RCC Resolution 369.[29] Lord Steyn described the argument that the courts had to disregard the Security Council resolutions as they had not been incorporated into United Kingdom law as "marching logic to its ultimate unreality" and approved the statement of the Court of Appeal that

> ... the very matters which are before the court, and which KAC seek to rely on for the purpose of showing that [RCC] Resolution 369 should not be recognized, have already been determined, if not by an international court, at any rate by an international forum, of which nearly all the nations of the world are members, and whose decisions are binding on all those nations, including the United Kingdom and Iraq.[30]

(2) The United Nations Act 1946 and Related Legislation

The relevant legislation is the United Nations Act 1946. This is a very short statute, section 1(1) of which provides that:

> If, under Article forty-one of the Charter of the United Nations ... (being the Article which relates to measures not involving the use of armed force) the Security Council of the United Nations call upon His Majesty's Government in the United Kingdom to apply any measures to give effect to any decision of that Council, His Majesty may by Order in Council make such provision as appears to Him necessary or expedient for enabling those measures to be effectively applied, including (without prejudice to the generality of the preceding words) provision for the apprehension, trial and punishment of persons offending against the Order.

This Act was passed principally (although not, as will be seen, exclusively) to enable the United Kingdom to implement economic sanctions imposed by the Security Council. As the Lord Chancellor explained to the House of Lords when introducing the Bill:

> Article 41 ... says that the Security Council may decide what measures, not involving the use of armed force, are to be employed to give effect to its decisions –that, of course, is its decisions under Article 39 – and it may call upon members of the United Nations to apply such measures. These may include complete or partial interruption of economic relations and of rail, sea, air, postal, telegraphic, radio and other means of communication, and the severance of diplomatic relations.

---

28 Lord Scott of Foscote dissented on another issue.

29 See the speeches of Lord Nicholls at paras. 20-23, Lord Steyn at para. 114, Lord Hope at paras. 141-149 and Lord Scott at para. 192.

30 Lord Steyn at para. 114, quoting the Court of Appeal at para. 378.

...

> ...assuming the Security Council takes such a decision ... there is an obligation on our Government to give effect to it. At present, the Government have no powers to impose upon its nationals the duty to comply with such a decision. Hence this Bill, and the main part of the Bill, Clause 1(1), provides that if under Article 41 of the Charter the Security Council call upon His Majesty's Government to take certain decisions, then His Majesty's Government may, by Order in Council, in their turn, impose upon their nationals the obligation and the duty to observe the provisions of the Order in Council.[31]

As the Divisional Court explained in *R.* v. *HM Treasury, ex parte Centro-Com srl* –

> Section 1 of the 1946 Act ... is the medium by which that international obligation [sc the obligation under Article 25 of the Charter to give effect to the decision of the Security Council] may become part of United Kingdom law. We say 'may become' because Section 1 is an enabling provision. It empowers but does not oblige, the United Kingdom Government to take measures in support of United Nations sanctions. Moreover, it is a wide enabling power, leaving much to the discretion of the Government, namely to make such provision as appears to it 'necessary or expedient for enabling those measures effectively to be applied'.[32]

The United Kingdom thus has a tailor-made basis for implementing sanctions resolutions swiftly. Moreover, the scope of the section is very broad and enables the Government to adopt delegated legislation making whatever provision appears 'necessary or expedient' to implement the relevant Security Council resolution. That could, of course, include, for example, penal provisions, interference with existing contracts, freezing or sequestrating assets in the United Kingdom and authorising action by the Royal Navy against shipping. The United Nations Act gives the United Kingdom Government a legal basis for giving effect to sanctions which is simple, flexible and in the broadest of terms.

The United Nations Act has been employed on numerous occasions during the decade since the Iraqi invasion of Kuwait. As at 1 August 2002, Orders adopted under the Act were in force in respect of Afghanistan, Al-Qa'ida and the Taleban, Angola, Iraq, Liberia, Rwanda, Sierra Leone and Somalia. Earlier regimes in respect of Eritrea, Ethiopia, the Federal Republic of Yugoslavia, Haiti, Libya and Sudan had been terminated or suspended. The fact that the resolutions which were implemented by these Orders contained no specific reference to Article 41 was not considered an obstacle to the use of the Act, since the resolutions in question were clearly based upon that Article.

While the necessity for the United Nations Act stems from the rule of United Kingdom law which precludes unincorporated treaties from being enforced in the United Kingdom courts – a rule which might seem arcane to observers from many other States where the Constitution expressly provides for the effect of treaties in domestic law – the

31 House of Lords Debates, Vol. 139, col. 375 (12 February 1946).

32 117 *International Law Reports* 444 at 460.

result is actually very efficient. The United Kingdom has precisely that legislative vehicle for giving full and swift effect to decisions of the Security Council which other Reports have called for in other States.[33]

The implementation of sanctions in the United Kingdom is, however, somewhat more complex than the simple provisions of the United Nations Act would suggest. There are several reasons.

First, the United Nations Act is not the only legal basis which can be – and has been – used for giving effect to Security Council sanctions. There are also two other Acts of Parliament which give power to pass delegated legislation in relation to economic sanctions.

The Import, Export and Customs Powers (Defence) Act 1939, which was passed immediately before the outbreak of the Second World War and which remains in force (albeit with substantial amendments), gives a broad power to the Board of Trade (effectively to the Secretary of State for Trade) to make orders prohibiting or regulating imports and exports. Section 1 provides:

> (1) The Board of Trade may by order make such provisions as the Board think expedient for prohibiting or regulating, in all cases or in specified classes of cases, and subject to such exceptions, if any, as may be made by or under the order, the importation into, or exportation from, the United Kingdom or any specified part thereof, or the carriage coastwise or the shipment as ships' stores, of all goods or goods of any specified description.

While this provision relates only to imports and exports, the interdiction of these is generally an important – though not the only – feature of United Nations sanctions. There are two important pieces of delegated legislation of a general character which have been adopted under this Act. The Import of Goods (Control) Order 1954[34] and the licences granted thereunder provide the means for regulation of certain imports into the United Kingdom. At the time this paper went to press, the Export of Goods (Control) Order 1994[35] performed the same function in respect of exports from the United Kingdom. The provisions of the 1939 Act relating to exports from the United Kingdom (and the 1994 Order) are, however, about to be superseded by the Export Control Act 2002, which received the royal assent on 24 July 2002.

In addition, the Emergency Laws (Re-enactments and Repeals) Act 1964, which re-enacted certain war legislation, gives the Treasury broad powers to freeze foreign assets in the United Kingdom. Section 2(1) of that Act provides:

> Where the Treasury are satisfied that action to the detriment of the economic position of the United Kingdom is being, or is likely to be, taken by the government of, or persons

33 See, in particular, the Report on France by Professors Burdeau and Stern, Chapter 7 of this volume, pp. 195 ff.

34 SI 1954 No. 23 (Delegated legislation in the United Kingdom usually takes the form of Statutory Instruments. These are referred to as follows: SI 1954 N. 23 refers to the 23rd Statutory Instrument for 1954. This form of reference is used throughout this Report.)

35 SI 1994 No. 1191, as amended.

> resident in, any country or territory outside the United Kingdom, the Treasury may give general or special directions prohibiting, either absolutely or to such extent as may be specified in the directions, the carrying out, except with permission granted by or on behalf of the Treasury, of any order given by or on behalf of the government of that country or territory or any person resident therein at the time when the directions were given or at any later time while the directions are in force, in so far as the order –
> (i) requires the person to whom the order is given to make any payment or to part with any gold or securities; or
> (ii) requires any change to be made in the persons to whose credit any sum is to stand or to whose order any gold or securities are to be held.

Since the freezing of assets may also be an important part of economic sanctions, this provision also provides a basis for action to implement certain sanctions.

The 1939 and 1964 Acts and the 1954 and 1994 Orders are not specifically designed for the implementation of United Nations sanctions – indeed, the regimes which they create have their origins in the pre-Charter era. Their principal importance lies in giving effect to sanctions which are not ordered by the Security Council. They have, however, on occasions been used to give effect to United Nations sanctions or in ways which are closely connected with such sanctions. In particular, they confer powers which have been used to impose sanctions in anticipation of a decision of the Security Council,[36] to give effect to a non-binding recommendation of the Security Council[37] and to apply unilateral measures or measures decided on by the European Union which sometimes exist alongside United Nations sanctions and which may be more far-reaching.[38]

Secondly, as pointed out above, the United Kingdom legislative bases for the implementation of sanctions are not the only means by which sanctions can be given effect in the United Kingdom. EC legislation must also be taken into account. As Mr Bethlehem shows in his report, the balance between EC and national measures for giving effect to sanctions has varied from one case of sanctions to another.

Thirdly, there have been a number of cases in which the United Kingdom has simultaneously applied unilateral or European sanctions and United Nations sanctions against the same State, the unilateral or European measures going beyond what was ordered by the Security Council. In such circumstances, the United Nations Act cannot provide a legal basis for all of the measures in question.

---

36 See, e.g., their use in relation to Iraq, which is discussed below.

37 For example, before the Security Council took a binding decision on sanctions against Eritrea and Ethiopia, it adopted a non-binding recommendation concerning an arms embargo (SCR 1227 (1999)). That was given effect in the United Kingdom by the Export of Goods (Control) (Amendment No. 2) Order 1999, SI 1999 No. 335, adopted under the 1939 Act as an amendment to the main 1994 Order. The United Kingdom Government could not have used the United Nations Act 1946 because that Act only applies where the Security Council has adopted a binding decision.

38 See, e.g., the Export of Goods (Federal Republic of Yugoslavia) Order 1998, SI 1998 No. 1530.

Fourthly, it is also an important feature of the 1964 Act and of much of the secondary legislation under all three United Kingdom statutes that particular government bodies (eg, under the 1964 Act the Treasury or the Bank of England) are given powers to relax certain aspects of sanctions. This power is, of course, essential if a sanctions regime is to work properly but it creates yet another layer of regulation in the form of documents, such as Bank of England notices, which have to be consulted by anyone seeking to ascertain the current state of the law.

Finally, mention should be made of a new statutory provision designed to give effect to a form of sanction which has become widely used in recent years, namely the selective travel ban. On a number of occasions, the United Nations Security Council has required or recommended that States deny entry into their territory to certain persons. For example, Resolution 1171 (1998), paragraph 5, on Sierra Leone requires States to deny entry to "leading members of the former military junta and of the revolutionary United Front" designated by the Sierra Leone Sanctions Committee. Such personalised travel bans have also been adopted by the European Union.[39]

The Immigration and Asylum Act 1999 added a new Section 8B to the Immigration Act 1971. The new Section 8B provides for the exclusion from the United Kingdom of a person named by, or falling within a description contained in, "a designated instrument". Section 8B(5) provides that:

> The Secretary of State may by order designate an instrument if it is a resolution of the Security Council of the United Nations or an instrument made by the Council of the European Union and it –
> (a) requires that a person is not to be admitted to the United Kingdom (however that requirement is expressed); or
> (b) recommends that a person should not be admitted to the United Kingdom (however that recommendation is expressed).

The Immigration (Designation of Travel Bans) Order 2000 (SI 2000 No. 2724), which entered into force on 10 October 2000, designated Security Council Resolutions 1127 (1997) on Angola and 1171 (1998) on Sierra Leone.

Section 8B goes further than the United Nations Act 1946 because it applies to travel bans adopted by the European Union as well as those adopted by the Security Council. In addition, it is not limited to binding decisions of the Security Council adopted under Article 41 of the Charter but includes recommendations made by the Council.

(3) The Implementation of Sanctions against Iraq

The complexity of the legal regime which results from the use of the different legal bases for action under United Kingdom law is particularly apparent in the case of Iraq. The United Nations measures themselves were contained in relatively few instruments.

39 See, e.g., Council Decision 2000/177/CFSP of 28 February 2000, regarding the Federal Republic of Yugoslavia.

Following the invasion of Kuwait on 2 August 1990, the Security Council imposed economic sanctions of very broad scope on 6 August 1990 (Security Council Resolution 661). These sanctions were extended by Resolution 670 in September 1990. Following the defeat of Iraq, Resolution 687 (adopted in April 1991) further altered the sanctions regime. Finally, a series of resolutions adopted under the "oil-for-food programme" relaxed sanctions by allowing Iraq to export limited quantities of oil.

The first United Kingdom measures,[40] were taken before the adoption of Resolution 661 on 6 August 1990 and by way of a unilateral response to the invasion. On the day of the invasion, the Treasury, acting under the 1964 Act, adopted the Control of Gold, Securities, Payments and Credits (Kuwait) Directions, 1990[41] freezing Kuwaiti assets in the United Kingdom in order to prevent Iraq (or Kuwaitis acting under Iraqi direction) from transferring them. Iraqi assets were frozen by a similar order two days later.[42] These were unilateral United Kingdom measures. Had they not been taken when they were, the Iraqi administration would almost certainly have attempted to move all Iraqi and Kuwaiti assets out of the United Kingdom. As it was, Iraq never secured control of Kuwaiti assets in the United Kingdom and lost control of its own assets there.

On 4 August 1990 the European Community Member States agreed, within the framework of political co-operation, that the Member States would take certain measures to restrict the import of oil from Iraq and Kuwait. That decision was implemented in the United Kingdom by a Notice to Importers.[43] This time, the legal basis for the action was more complicated. The Notice was an amendment to the Open General Import Licence 1987, which was itself adopted under the Import of Goods (Control) Order 1954. As explained above, the 1954 Order is a standing measure adopted under the 1939 Act.

Thus, when the first United Nations measures were adopted on 6 August, the United Kingdom already had in place more limited sanctions under the authority of the 1939 and 1964 Acts. The advantage of these Acts is that they enable action to be taken very quickly. The existence of the 1954 Order meant that the United Kingdom did not even have to adopt secondary legislation in order to block oil imports. That could be done by the simple process of issuing a Notice to Importers. The measures adopted under the 1964 Act, although in the form of statutory instruments, could be adopted by the relevant Treasury Minister with little formality. Moreover, the Bank of England was then able to

40 These measures are collected in D. Bethlehem (ed.), *The Kuwait Crisis: Sanctions and their Economic Consequences* (Cambridge, 1991) (hereinafter 'Bethlehem') at pp. 324-378. For commentary, see Fox and Wickremasinghe, 'British Implementation of United Nations Sanctions against Iraq', 41 *ICLQ* (1992) 920 and 'United Kingdom Implementation of United Nations Sanctions', 42 *ICLQ* (1993) 945. The United Kingdom Government adopted separate measures for the United Kingdom dependent territories, the Isle of man and the Channel Islands. These were modelled on the measures adopted for the United Kingdom itself and are not considered further in this Report.

41 Statutory Instrument 1990, No. 1591 (Bethlehem 324).

42 The Control of Gold, Securities, Payments and Credits (Iraq) Directions, 1990 (Statutory Instrument 1990, No.1616) (Bethlehem 325).

43 Notice No. 2774 (Bethlehem 326).

add flesh to the bones of these two short instruments by giving details of the payments etc which would be permitted.[44] These measures meant that the United Kingdom was already applying some of the sanctions ordered by the Council when it adopted Resolution 661 on 6 August 1990.

In so far as it had not already taken the necessary steps, the United Kingdom implemented Resolution 661 itself by three separate measures.

(a) The Secretary of State for Trade made a brief Order under the 1939 Act prohibiting exports to Iraq or Kuwait;[45]
(b) The Secretary of State for Trade also used his powers under the 1954 Order to modify or revoke various licences and thus restrict imports from Iraq or Kuwait;[46]
(c) Finally, the Queen in Council adopted the Iraq and Kuwait (United Nations Sanctions) Order 1990.[47] This Order is a more formal and detailed instrument giving effect to the sanctions imposed by Resolution 661 in their entirety.

In addition, the EC Council adopted its own measure to give effect to Resolution 661. Regulation 2340/90,[48] adopted on 9 August 1990, has direct effect in all EC Member States, including the United Kingdom.

All of these measures were the subject of various amendments which need not be catalogued here. The question is why did there have to be so many different measures to implement a single sanctions resolution? In part the answer lies in the fact that the United Kingdom took action against Iraq before the Security Council did so. The measures adopted before 6 August 1990, therefore, could not have been based upon the United Nations Act and the Government had to rely upon a different legal basis in United Kingdom law. The 1939 Act, the 1954 Order and the 1964 Act provided that basis.[49]

That does not explain, however, why several different measures were adopted immediately after the adoption of Resolution 661, rather than a single measure under the United Nations Act. One reason appears to be that, although the United Nations Act and the 1939 and 1964 Acts all provide for implementation by delegated legislation which takes the form of a statutory instrument, different degrees of formality are required. The 1939 and 1964 Acts give a minister the power to make Orders or give Directions. The United Nations Act requires an Order in Council. That necessitates a meeting of the Privy Council and can take longer. In fact, by holding the Privy Council on the Royal Yacht

44 See, e.g., Bank of England Notice of 7 August 1990 regarding the effect of Statutory Instrument 1990 No. 1591 (Bethlehem 327).

45 The Export of Goods (Control) (Iraq and Kuwait) Order 1990, Statutory Instrument 1990, No. 1640 (Bethlehem 337).

46 See documents 123.7, 123.8 and 123.9 at Bethlehem 338, 339 and 340.

47 Statutory Instrument 1990, No. 1651 (Bethlehem 341).

48 See Report by Mr Bethlehem, Chapter 5 of this volume, pp. 123 ff. The text appears at Bethlehem 112.

49 Whether these measures were lawful in international law is a different matter which will not be discussed here, although the author firmly believes that they were both lawful and necessary.

Britannia, it proved possible to adopt the main United Nations Sanctions Order on the same day as the less formal instruments under the 1939 Act and the 1954 Order.

A further complicating factor is the overlapping competence of the United Kingdom authorities and the European Community. This matter is considered more fully in Mr Bethlehem's Report. As Mr Bethlehem explains, the scope of the EC's competence to implement United Nations sanctions is clearer today than it was in 1990-1991. Nevertheless, even where a matter falls within EC competence, it remains the case that only national law can impose criminal penalties for non-compliance. In the case of the Iraq sanctions, that meant that EC Regulation 2340/90 applied alongside the various United Kingdom measures but depended upon the United Kingdom measures for criminal sanctions as a means of enforcement. It is interesting to note, however, that when it came to implementing Resolution 687 (1991), EC law was left to deal with one important matter on its own. Paragraph 29 of that Resolution required States to provide that no claim should lie at the instance of any Iraqi body in respect of a contract the performance of which was affected by sanctions. In the EC States, that provision was implemented exclusively by EC Regulation 3541/92.[50]

The confusing mixture of implementing measures in respect of the sanctions against Iraq can be explained by these factors and also by the fact that sanctions had to be imposed as an urgent reaction to the wholly unexpected invasion of Kuwait. Moreover, apart from the Rhodesian sanctions, which had terminated more than ten years earlier, and the limited arms embargo against South Africa, the Iraq sanctions were the first occasion on which the United Kingdom had had to apply a United Nations sanctions regime. The implementation of the United Nations sanctions in the United Kingdom was carried out with great efficiency and must be accounted a success in the sense that it achieved its immediate goal of ending trade with Iraq (and, during the occupation, with Kuwait) and preserved Iraqi and Kuwaiti assets in the United Kingdom.[51]

Nevertheless, the result was, to say the least, untidy. Even at 1 August 2002, nearly twelve years after the first sanctions were imposed, a reader seeking to discover the extent of implementation of the Iraq sanctions in the United Kingdom would have to consult:

(a) the Iraq and Kuwait (United Nations Sanctions) Order 1990 (SI 1990 No. 1651, as amended by SI 1990 No. 1768 and SI 1990 No. 2144), the Iraq and Kuwait (United Nations Sanctions) (No. 2) Order 1990 (SI 1990/1987), the Iraq and Kuwait (United Nations Sanctions) (Amendment) Order 1998 (SI 1998 No. 3163, the Iraq (United Nations) (Sequestration of Assets) Order 1993 (SI 1993 No. 1233) and the United Nations (Sanctions) (Amendments) Order 2000 (SI 2000 No. 1106),[52] the Iraq (United Nations Sanctions) Order 2000 (SI 2000 No. 3241) adopted under the United Nations Act 1946;

(b) the Export of Goods (Control) (Iraq and Kuwait Sanctions) Order 1990 (SI 1990 No. 1640) as amended by the Export of Goods (Control) (Iraq and Kuwait Sanc-

50 The effect of this regulation was considered by the House of Lords in the *Shanning* case, discussed above, p. 585.

51 This is not the place to consider whether the sanctions regime imposed by the Security Council can be said to have been a success.

52 The 2000 Order is a minor amending measure applying to a number of sanctions regimes.

tions) Order 1999 (SI 1999 No. 1776), adopted under the Import, Export and Customs Powers (Defence) Act 1939;

(c) EC Council Regulations 2340/90, 3541/92 and 2465/96 (as amended on 22nd July 2002); and

(d) various General Licences adopted by the Department of Trade and Industry and Bank of England Notices.[53]

Most Iraq sanctions were lifted (after this Chapter had gone to press), pursuant to Security Council Resolution 1483 (2003), by the Iraq (United Nations Sanctions) Order 2003, SI 203 No. 1519).

(4) The Implementation of Sanctions in the Sierra Leone Case

The implementation of later sanctions regimes has tended to be less complex with most measures being based upon the United Nations Act 1946. The Sierra Leone sanctions are a useful example.

Following the expulsion from Sierra Leone of the democratically elected government by a military junta in 1997, the Security Council, in Resolution 1132 (1997) imposed a ban on the supply of arms and petroleum to Sierra Leone. This decision was implemented in the United Kingdom by the Sierra Leone (United Nations Sanctions) Order 1997 (SI 1997 No. 2592), which implemented the arms embargo, and EC Council Regulation 2465/97, which implemented the oil embargo. The United Kingdom Order was adopted under the United Nations Act, although it made reference to the Export of Goods (Control) Order 1994 (which had been adopted under the Import, Export and Customs Powers (Defence) Act 1939) in order to define the types of equipment to which the prohibitions in the Order applied.

When the democratically elected government was restored in 1998, the Security Council terminated the oil embargo by Resolution 1156 (1998) and, by Resolution 1171 (1998) replaced the arms embargo with a more limited prohibition on supplies to non-government parties. That led the EC Council to repeal Regulation 2465/97.[54] The United Kingdom repealed the 1997 Order and in its place amended the United Nations Arms Embargoes (Liberia, Somalia and the Former Yugoslavia) Order 1993 (SI 1993 No. 1787, as amended) so as to incorporate the new regime on arms supplies to Sierra Leone.[55] The Immigration (Designation of Travel Bans) Order 2000 extends Section 8B of the Immigration Act 1971 to persons covered by Resolution 1171 (1998). The United Kingdom has also implemented subsequent decisions of the Security Council regarding the import of diamonds by means of amendments to the Open General Import Licence.[56]

---

53 See Department of Trade and Industry Guidance Note, *United Nations Sanctions against Iraq* (1 February 1999).

54 EC Council Regulation 941/98.

55 See the United Nations Arms Embargoes (Amendment) (Sierra Leone) Order 1998 (SI 1998 No. 1501).

56 Amendments No. 175 and 176 implementing SCR 1306 (2000).

II. Legal Basis of Domestic Measures Based on Regional Organisation Decision

The legal basis for domestic implementation of measures decided upon by regional organisations, as opposed to the Security Council, has received far less attention in the United Kingdom. Apart from unilateral measures, the only substantial body of sanctions applied by the United Kingdom which are not derived from decisions of the Security Council originate with the European Union.

Where the EC adopts legislation to give effect to United Nations sanctions, that legislation would normally be directly effective in the United Kingdom. In so far as measures by the United Kingdom were required as a matter of EC law to implement the EC measure, these could be adopted under section 2(2) of the European Communities Act 1972.

Where the EC States adopt a decision on sanctions which is not itself legally binding on the United Kingdom or which does not take effect in EC law, that decision can frequently be given effect by measures under the 1939 and 1964 Acts and the 1954 Order (as was the case with the Notice to Importers under the 1954 Order used to implement the sanctions decision of the EC States regarding the import of petroleum from Iraq and Kuwait on 5 August 1990).

The same legal basis could be employed to give effect to sanctions decisions of another regional body (eg NATO). It should, however, be noted that the 1964 Act requires that the Treasury is satisfied that 'action to the detriment of the economic position of the United Kingdom is being, or is likely to be, taken.' This Act is not, therefore, ideally suited as a legal basis for sanctions designed to meet more general concerns.

The implementation by the United Kingdom of sanctions against the Federal Republic of Yugoslavia in connection with the situation in Kosovo provides a useful example. Although some of the sanctions in question were imposed by the Security Council, the EU States decided to impose more far-reaching sanctions, including a travel ban for selected individuals, an asset freeze, a flight ban and an arms embargo which did not entirely overlap with that imposed by the Security Council. Some of the EU measures were applied by means of directly effective EC legislation. Where implementation by United Kingdom legislation was required, the measures were generally based upon section 2(2) of the European Communities Act 1972.[57] The remaining restrictions were given effect by Orders under the Import, Export and Customs Powers (Defence) Act 1939[58] and the Immigration (Designation of Travel Bans) Order 2000.

57 See, e.g., the Federal Republic of Yugoslavia (Supply and Sale of Equipment) (Penalties and Licences) Regulations 1998 (SI 1998 No. 1531) and the Yugoslavia (Prohibition of Flights) (No. 2) Order 1999 (SI 1999 No. 3166).

58 See, e.g., the Export of Goods (Federal Republic of Yugoslavia) (Control) Order 1998 (SI 1998 No. 1530).

III. Comparison of Content of Security Council Resolutions and Domestic Measures

It is not intended here to give a detailed comparison between United Kingdom measures and the Security Council resolutions to which they give effect. In general, the United Kingdom measures have tracked quite closely the requirements of the relevant Security Council resolutions and there have been no suggestions that the United Kingdom has not taken the steps required by the Security Council. On the contrary, the approach of the United Kingdom Government has generally been to impose prohibitions in language which, if anything, was more extensive than that used by the Security Council. The draconian effect of the broad prohibitions laid down by the relevant United Kingdom instruments has then been mitigated by conferring on the Department of Trade and Industry or the Bank of England a power to permit certain transactions. This has been done by a combination of general licences and Bank of England Notices and specific permissions granted in individual cases.[59]

The relationship between the Security Council resolution and the implementing Order has been the subject of one challenge before a court. That is discussed in Part 5, below. However, the most notorious case in which arguments arose regarding the relationship between the Security Council resolution and the United Kingdom implementing measures did not go before a court. Early in 1998 questions were raised about the supply of arms by a United Kingdom company, Sandline International, to the forces of the democratic government of Sierra Leone, which at that time had been ousted by a coup, and the attitude of certain Foreign Office officials to that action. The details of the controversy are unimportant for present purposes and the rapporteur makes no comment on them. Nevertheless, the incident highlights the importance of the relationship between a Security Council resolution and the national implementing measures.

Security Council Resolution 1132 (1997), adopted in the aftermath of the coup, required States to impose a number of measures. The object of these measures was to weaken the military junta which had seized power and to facilitate the reinstatement of the democratic government. Paragraph 6 of the Resolution went on to provide that all States were to prohibit 'the sale or supply *to Sierra Leone* … of arms and related matériel of all types.' There was, however, a degree of uncertainty in the United Nations (to say the least) about whether this paragraph required States to ban supplies of weapons to the democratic government as well as to the rebels.

The United Kingdom implemented Resolution 1132 principally by means of an Order under the United Nations Act.[60] That Order made it a criminal offence to supply arms to or to the order of "any person connected with Sierra Leone". Article 2 of the Order defined the expression "person connected with Sierra Leone" as including "the Government of Sierra Leone". Whatever the correct interpretation of the Resolution,

59 See, e.g., Article 2(3) of the Iraq and Kuwait (United Nations Sanctions) Order 1990 (SI 1990 No. 1651.

60 The Sierra Leone (United Nations Sanctions) Order 1997 (Statutory Instrument 1997 No. 2592).

therefore, it was difficult to read the Order as meaning that arms might lawfully be supplied to the democratic government.

In the aftermath of this controversy, the Foreign Secretary commissioned an independent investigation by Sir Thomas Legg and Sir Robin Ibbs. The Legg Report[61] stressed the importance of looking to the detailed provisions of United Kingdom implementing legislation and not focussing exclusively upon the debate over interpretation of the resolution. The House of Commons Foreign Affairs Committee went further and urged the Government to adopt a policy of not voting for any Security Council resolution which contained any element of ambiguity. It would be interesting to speculate how many of the more than 1300 resolutions adopted by the Security Council to date would meet that stringent standard.

Three other points arising under this main heading of the Framework require comment at this stage. First, the United Kingdom measures have contained severe penal sanctions for those persons and companies convicted of breaching sanctions.

Secondly, with regard to the territorial scope of United Kingdom implementing measures, these normally apply to any person in the United Kingdom, to the activities of United Kingdom companies and nationals outside the United Kingdom and to British ships anywhere in the world.

Finally, the United Nations Act has also been used to adopt Orders giving effect to the requirement to co-operate with the International Criminal Tribunals for Former Yugoslavia and Rwanda[62] and, most recently, to provide for a Scottish court to sit in the Netherlands in accordance with Resolution 1198 (1998) to try the two men accused of the destruction of a Pan Am flight over Lockerbie and the murder of 270 people in 1988.[63]

IV. Domestic Procedures for Implementation and Enforcement

United Nations sanctions involve the responsibility of several different government departments in the United Kingdom. The adoption of the sanctions resolution in the United Nations is the responsibility of the Foreign and Commonwealth Office, which is also involved in the application of those sanctions in the United Kingdom. The Treasury, Bank of England and Department of Trade and Industry will also be involved. Delegated legislation under the United Nations Act is the responsibility of the Foreign and Commonwealth Office, whereas delegated legislation under the Import, Export and Customs Powers (Defence) Act 1939 is primarily a matter for the Department of Trade and Industry. Prosecution of those accused of sanctions violations is normally a matter for Customs and Excise. The enforcement of sanctions at sea will be undertaken by the Royal Navy.

61 Report of the Sierra Leone Arms Investigation, 27 July 1998 (HC Paper 1016).

62 The United Nations (International Tribunal) (Former Yugoslavia) Order, 1996 (Statutory Instrument 1996 No. 716) and the United Nations (International Tribunal) (Rwanda) Order 1996 (Statutory Instrument, 1996 No. 1296).

63 The High Court of Justiciary (Proceedings in the Netherlands) (United Nations) Order 1998 (Statutory Instrument, 1998 No. 2251).

In order to avoid confusion, the Government established an Embargo Enforcement Unit when sanctions against Iraq were first instituted. This was organised by the Cabinet Office. Similar arrangements have been used for other sanctions regimes. The Department of Trade and Industry publishes a series of useful guidance notes explaining the scope of different sanctions regimes.[64]

Maritime embargo measures have varied from one case to another. When the sanctions regime includes a requirement that States prevent their flag vessels from engaging in trade with the target State, the United Kingdom implementation measures will reflect that requirement and will authorise Royal Navy officers to board and search British ships if they suspect that these are sanctions-breaking (see, e.g., Article 6 of the Iraq and Kuwait (United Nations Sanctions) Order 1990,[65] which also authorises such an officer to use reasonable force if necessary).

In some cases, however, the United Nations sanctions resolutions have gone further and called upon States to use their naval forces not merely to enforce sanctions against their own flag vessels but to conduct a naval embargo and prevent vessels of other States from violating the sanctions regime. That was the case with the sanctions imposed upon Iraq in 1990.[66] The Royal Navy participated, along with navies from numerous other States, in extensive visit and search in and around the Gulf and the Red Sea.[67] Whether a State or group of States may take action against shipping not flying their flags without the specific authority of the Security Council is, of course, a difficult question.

The approach which the United Kingdom tends to take towards the implementation of Security Council decisions regarding sanctions is also illustrated by its response to the measures adopted by the Council following the 11 September 2001 attacks on New York and Washington. While these measures have been rather different from sanctions in the classical sense, not least because they have involved measures targeted on specific individuals, they also display many of the features of economic sanctions. They also repay study, because the Council has taken unusually extensive steps to check on implementation by States.

The principal Security Council measures are contained in Resolution 1373 (2001) and Resolution 1390 (2002). In summary, Resolution 1373 required States:

(1) to take specific steps to combat the financing of terrorism, including freezing the assets of persons and entities who commit, attempt to commit or facilitate the commission of acts of terrorism and preventing persons within their jurisdiction from providing funds or services to those engaged in terrorism (operative paragraph 1);
(2) make support for terrorism and participation in the financing, planning, preparation or perpetration of terrorist acts a criminal offence (operative paragraph 2);

---

64 See, e.g., the DTI Guidance Note, *United Nations Sanctions against Iraq* (February 1999), *Economic Sanctions Reporter*, p. 593 and the *Notice to Exporters: Federal Republic of Yugoslavia, Sanctions Measures in Fore at 8 March 2000*, *ibid.*, p. 367.

65 Statutory Instrument 1990, No. 1651 (Bethlehem 341).

66 Resolution 665 (1990).

67 For a description of Royal Naval activities, see Lyons, 'Naval Operations in the Gulf', in P. Rowe (ed.), *The Gulf War 1990-91 in International Law and English Law* (1993), p. 155.

(3) take active steps to co-operate in the fight against terrorism.

A committee to monitor implementation, chaired by Sir Jeremy Greenstock, the United Kingdom Permanent Representative, was established by paragraph 6 of the Security Counsil Resolution, which required all States to report within ninety days on the measures they had taken to implement Resolution 1373.

The United Kingdom Report,[68] detailed the following measures:-

(1) the financial sanctions imposed by Resolution 1373 were implemented by the Terrorism (United Nations Measures) Order 2001 (SI 2001 No. 3365), delegated legislation adopted under the United Nations Act 1946.[69] This was a classical example of the use of the main legislative vehicle for the implementation of United Nations sanctions;
(2) the Bank of England then published a list of persons and organisations whose funds in the United Kingdom were frozen. That list, which has been updated on several occasions,[70] was originally based upon lists issued by the United States Government;
(3) the provisions requiring the criminalisation of certain types of conduct were already dealt with, in large part, by the Terrorism Act 2000. The Anti-terrorism, Crime and Security Act 2001, enacted after the 11 September 2001, strengthened those provisions;
(4) the supply of weapons and other sensitive items to terrorist groups was controlled under the Export of Goods (Control) Order 1994. The Export Control Act 2002 was passed in part to strengthen these controls.

Security Council Resolution 1390 (2002) introduced further measures against the Taliban and Al-Qaida. These were implemented in the United Kingdom by the Al-Qaida and Taliban (United Nations Measures) Order 2002 (SI 2002 No. 111), adopted under the United Nations Act.

While certain other measures (not directly connected to the United Nations sanctions) taken by the United Kingdom in the wake of the 11 September attacks have aroused considerable debate and, in one case, been challenged in the courts,[71] the financial sanctions have not, so far, been the subject of such a challenge. An obvious question

68 For the first such report, see United Nations Doc. S/2001/1232.

69 See the discussion of this Act above, pp. **586 ff**.

70 The list can be found at the Bank's website, http://www.bankofengland.co.uk.

71 On 30 July 2002 the Special Immigration Appeals Commission, a body chaired by a High Court judge, gave its judgment in *A and Others* v. *Secretary of State for the Home Department* (to be reported in volume 126 of the *International Law Reports*). The SIAC held that the detention without trial of certain foreign nationals suspected of terrorist activity (but whose deportation was precluded because there was no country to which they could be deported where they would not be at risk of torture or arbitrary execution) was contrary to the European Convention on Human Rights. The SIAC accepted that the United Kingdom had been entitled to derogate from the Convention on grounds of national emergency but held that a derogation which discriminated against non-nationals was unjustified. The decision was reversed by the Court of Appeal [2003] 2 WLR 564.

is whether an individual whose assets were frozen would be able to challenge the application of the sanctions to him on the ground that he was not in fact involved in terrorism. To date, the removal of names from the lists issued by the Bank of England has been the result of decisions made by the Security Council, rather than challenges brought in the United Kingdom courts.

V. Role of National Courts

One consequence of the status of treaties in United Kingdom law (which is discussed in Part 1, above) is that a United Kingdom court enforces the United Kingdom implementing measures and the relevant EC measures (if there are any), not the Security Council resolutions as such. That does not mean, however, that the Security Council resolutions are not important in proceedings in United Kingdom courts.

A United Kingdom court faced with a question about the interpretation of a United Kingdom Order implementing United Nations sanctions would look to the relevant Security Council resolution as an aid to interpretation, as was done in, for example, *R.* v. *Her Majesty's Treasury, ex parte Centro-Com srl*[72] where the Court considered Resolution 757(1992), imposing sanctions on the Federal Republic of Yugoslavia in order to interpret the relevant United Kingdom and EC legislation. The Court of Justice of the European Communities has taken the same approach.[73]

It has occasionally been argued that a United Kingdom measure implementing United Nations sanctions is invalid on the ground that it goes beyond what is required by the relevant Security Council resolution and is therefore *ultra vires* the powers granted by the United Nations Act. Such an argument was raised, for example, in *Wahda Bank* v. *Arab Bank* in 1992.[74] This argument is, however, unlikely to succeed in anything but an extreme case, because the terms of section 1(1) of the United Nations Act are so broad, giving the Queen in Council power to make such provision as appears 'necessary or expedient' to give effect to the relevant sanctions resolution. A ground of challenge which has succeeded in at least one case, however, is that the United Kingdom measures went beyond what was required by the Security Council and in doing so contravened a principle of EC law.[75]

VI. Constitutional Issues

Since the United Kingdom does not, for the most part, have a written Constitution and there is no scope for a constitutional challenge in the courts of the kind that exists in, e.g., the United States of America, it will come as no surprise that, to date, sanctions measures have not given rise to any problems which might be said to fall within this category. The entry into force on 2 October 2000 of the Human Rights Act 1998 may

72 117 *International Law Reports* 444. The case subsequently went to the Court of Justice of the European Communities and is discussed in this context in Mr Bethlehem's report.

73 See Mr Bethlehem's report, *supra*, p. 157.

74 Decision of Phillips J, 11 December 1992, unreported.

75 Case C-124/95 *R.* v. *Her Majesty's Treasury, ex parte Centro-Com srl,* 117 *International Law Reports* 444.

well lead to attempts being made to challenge individual sanctions measures on human rights grounds, although it is noticeable that no such challenge appears to have succeeded in other States party to the European Convention on Human Rights or before the European Court of Human Rights.[76]

Nevertheless, there have been a number of issues raised which might be described as "constitutional" in the broader, political sense of the word. The Sierra Leone controversy, considered in Part 3, above, could be regarded as a constitutional question in this sense. The entire apparatus of sanctions has also been heavily criticised by a House of Commons Committee,[77] although the objection was to the nature of some United Nations sanctions rather than the manner of their implementation by the United Kingdom.

The use of secondary legislation under the United Nations Act to give effect to the Security Council resolutions requiring co-operation with the Yugoslav and Rwanda Tribunals, rather than primary legislation which would have required full debate in Parliament, has been criticised by Lady Fox on what may reasonably be described as constitutional grounds.[78] Lady Fox takes issue with the use of the United Nations Act in these two cases on two grounds. First, she maintains that the Orders adopted are *ultra vires* the 1946 Act and thus open to challenge in the courts. Secondly, she criticises the use of delegated legislation, as opposed to an Act of Parliament, on the ground that it does not involve sufficient transparency and that such a major step as providing for the surrender of suspects to an international tribunal without the normal safeguards of extradition should have been fully debated in Parliament.

With regard to the challenge to the legality of the relevant Orders, Lady Fox argues that the United Nations Act was intended to provide only for the implementation of economic sanctions and not for a form of extradition to a type of criminal tribunal not hitherto seen. She contends that "the Act, as piecemeal legislation, was enacted in a hurry specifically to give national effect to economic sanctions ordered by the Security Council" and cannot be used for other purposes.[79]

The language of Section 1(1) of the 1946 Act is not, however, confined in this way. It applies to any case in which the Security Council has called upon the United Kingdom

76 The Court has rejected as manifestly unfounded an argument that the surrender of an accused person to the International Criminal Tribunal for the Former Yugoslavia would violate the right to a fair trial under Article 6(1) of the European Convention; *Naletilic* v. *Croatia*, 121 *International Law Reports* 209. There is no scope in this paper for discussing the interesting question of the relationship between the obligations of States under the Convention and obligations under the Charter to implement a decision of the Security Council. Article 103 of the Charter provides, of course, that obligations arising under the Charter prevail over obligations under any other international agreement in the event of a conflict. It is interesting to note, however, that the European Court of Human Rights has held admissible (i.e. not 'manifestly unfounded') an action by Bosphorus airlines against Ireland in respect of the application to Bosphorus of the United Nations sanctions against the FRY.

77 Second Report of the International Development Committee, 1999-2000.

78 Fox, 'Objections to the Transfer of Criminal Jurisdiction to the United Nations Tribunal', 46 *ICLQ* (1997) 434.

79 *Ibid.*, p. 440.

Government under Article 41 of the Charter to apply *any* measures to give effect to *any* decision of the Council. As has been explained in the Introduction to this Report, the powers of the Security Council under Article 41 are not limited to the imposition of sanctions, nor have they been interpreted by the Security Council as being limited in that way. Given the language of the Section and the stated purpose of the Act, if, under Article 41, the Security Council can impose upon the United Kingdom Government an obligation to apply a particular measure, then the normal interpretation of Section 1(1) of the Act is that it confers the power to make any delegated legislation which might seem necessary or expedient in order to comply with that obligation. The fact that the measure in question is not the application of economic sanctions but provision for the transfer of a suspect to an international tribunal would not take the matter outside the scope of the Act.

Nor do the debates on the 1946 Act, brief as they were, provide much support for this thesis. The very brief statements made by the ministers who proposed the legislation show that the main concern was to enable the Government to ensure that the United Kingdom could discharge its obligations under the Charter by requiring that United Kingdom nationals act in accordance with a decision of the Security Council. Such a situation was most likely to arise when the Council called upon States to apply the kind of measures listed in the second sentence of Article 41. Nevertheless, there is no suggestion that the Act could not be used in order to meet an obligation imposed by the Security Council under Article 41 for which legislative action was needed but which did not involve economic sanctions or the actions of private individuals. On the contrary, the Lord Chancellor's speech[80] and that of Mr Noel-Baker in the House of Commons[81] closely track the language of Article 41, with the emphasis upon the power conferred by the first sentence of that Article.

There is a further reason for rejecting the argument advanced by Lady Fox. That is the presumption that Parliament, when passing legislation, intends to act consistently with the obligations of the United Kingdom under public international law.[82] As has been explained, the Security Council has the power under the Charter to require States to take action outside the field of economic sanctions. If it does so, then there is a corresponding international obligation for States. To construe Section 1(1) of the 1946 Act as confined to cases of economic sanctions would be to construe it in such a way as to deprive the Government of the capacity to implement some of its obligations under the United Nations Charter. In the absence of clear wording to that effect, it would be contrary to the presumption to interpret the 1946 Act in that way.[83]

80 House of Lords Debates, vol. 139, columns 373-7 (12 February 1946).

81 House of Commons Debates, vol. 421, columns 1513-1516 (5 April 1946).

82 See Part 1, above.

83 At the time of writing, the English courts had considered only one case in which the surrender of an accused person was sought by one of the international criminal tribunals, *R* v. *Bow Street Magistrate*, ex parte *Tharcisse Muvunyi*, unreported, 12 October 2000. Although the Applicant initially indicated an intention of challenging the legality of his surrender to the Tribunal, he withdrew his application for *habeas corpus*.

Lady Fox's second argument, which is a political rather than a legal challenge, raises issues which fall outside the scope of the present Report. There was certainly a case for the proposition that, even though the United Nations Act could be used to implement the resolutions establishing the two international criminal tribunals, it would have been preferable to have used primary legislation. Against that can be set the argument that primary legislation can frequently be a very slow vehicle for giving effect to the international obligations of a State and that the provision for trial by international criminal tribunals involves no departure from the principles of a fair trial.

VII. Conclusion

The last thirteen years has seen, for the first time, the extensive use of sanctions by the Security Council. A full assessment of the value of those sanctions requires a consideration both of their efficiency – i.e. how rigorously they were applied – and their effectiveness in achieving their goals. The second element, however, falls outside the scope of a national report.

With regard to the first consideration, it is clear that the efficiency of United Nations sanctions is entirely dependent on the manner in which they are implemented by States. On the whole the United Kingdom system for the implementation of sanctions has worked well. The United Kingdom has been able to give effect to United Nations sanctions in United Kingdom law with scarcely any delay and the paucity of challenges in the courts is testimony to the care with which the implementing legislation has been drafted. The principal problem to have arisen in the courts has concerned not the sanctions themselves but the relationship between national and European Community powers.

The principal criticism that can be made is that the implementation of sanctions has all too often involved a bewildering mixture of different instruments adopted under different Acts of Parliament and accompanied by a large number of announcements, notices and licences which make it difficult to discover what the relevant law on a particular point may be. There are, however, signs that this problem is not as great as it was at the start of the period. That is a welcome development.

Select Bibliography

I. Official Documents

Department of Trade and Industry, 'Guidance Note: United Nations Sanctions against Iraq' (1999).

House of Commons, *Report of the Sierra Leone Arms Investigation* ("The Legg Report"), HC 1997-98 No. 1016.

House of Commons, *The Future of Sanctions*, Second Report of the International Development Committee, 1999-2000; HC 1999-2000 No.67.

II. Works

Bethlehem, Daniel, (ed.), *The Kuwait Crisis: Sanctions and their Economic Consequences*, 2 vols. (Cambridge, 1991).

Carver, Jeremy (ed.), *Economic Sanctions Reports*, 2 vols (London, 1999).

Carver, Jeremy (ed.), *Economic Sanctions Reporter*, looseleaf (London, 2000-).

Fox, Hazel, 'Objections to the Transfer of Criminal Jurisdiction to the United Nations Tribunal' 46 *International and Comparative Law Quarterly* (1997) 434.

Fox, Hazel and Wickremasinghe, Chanaka, 'British Implementation of United Nations Sanctions against Iraq, 41 *International and Comparative Law Quarterly* (1992) 920.

Fox, Hazel and Wickremasinghe, Chanaka, 'British Implementation of United Nations Sanctions', 42 *International and Comparative Law Quarterly* (1993) 945.

THE UNITED STATES

*Andreas F. Lowenfeld**

I. Introduction

Since World War II, no country has applied international economic sanctions to the extent that the United States has done – in some instances in implementation of United Nations resolutions; in other instances in implementation of resolutions of regional organizations, i.e., the Organization of American States; in still other contexts in collaboration with other states when the effort to secure a United Nations Resolution was frustrated by veto; and in some instances on a unilateral basis. In some instances, the effort has been to compel a particular result or action, in many others, the effort has been to demonstrate that actions that the United States views as reprehensible cannot be taken or continued without cost. When the United States sought to organize a boycott of the 1980 Summer Olympic games in Moscow, some referred to the USA as the Champion of Olympic Sanctions, others as the Olympic Champion of Sanctions. Either way the history of the period 1945 to date has demonstrated that in many situations, the United States usually looks for a middle way between "business as usual" and the use of force, and that middle way generally turns out to be economic sanctions of some sort. Of course, this pattern was not followed with respect to Iraq in 2003.

II. Legal Bases of US Economic Sanctions[1]

In contrast to other aspects of American economic regulations which are subject to detailed legislation adopted (and frequently amended) by Congress and closely supervised by the courts, the law of international economic sanctions relies on broad general delegation to the President in the name of national security, and virtually no supervision by the courts. Attempts from time to time to curb the exercise of Presidential power in connection with economic sanctions have either failed completely, or been channeled

* Herbert and Rose Rubin Professor of International Law, New York University School of Law.

1 For a general discussion by the present author of the legal basis of economic sanctions, see A. Lowenfeld, *International Economic Law* (2002), Chapters 22-23.

Vera Gowlland-Debbas (ed.), National Implementation of UN Sanctions, *605-642.*

into requirements for a Presidential declaration of national emergency, a declaration that was at one time regarded as a grave act but recently has become routine and ritualistic.

(1) *Some History*

Economic sanctions imposed by the United States go back a long way. As early as 1794, only five years after the entry into effect of the US Constitution, Congress authorized the President to lay embargoes on all ships and vessels in the ports of the United States, whenever in his opinion the public safety shall so require.[2] The embargo was seen as a way to avoid a declaration of war against England, whose warships had regularly seized US flagships and "impressed" American seamen into service of the Crown. Similar legislation was adopted in 1798, 1799, and 1800. In 1806, during the war between France and Great Britain, Congress imposed an embargo on imports of specified merchandise from Great Britain, Ireland, or any of the colonies or dependencies of Great Britain. Importation of the specified goods would lead to confiscation, a penalty of treble the value of the goods, and if the owner or master of the vessel on which the goods were shipped had knowledge of the prohibited shipment, the vessel was subject to forfeit and the owner and master were to pay treble the value of the goods.[3]

In the following years, in response to the respective embargoes imposed by France and Great Britain, an embargo was laid by the US Congress on all ships within the jurisdiction of the United States bound to any foreign port or place except vessels under the immediate direction of the President,[4] and in 1809 a more specific interdiction was adopted prohibiting all commercial intercourse between the United States and Great Britain and France and their dependencies,[5] while permitting commercial intercourse by ships owned by citizens of other countries and with countries other than Great Britain or France. Several more embargoes and interdictions were adopted by Congress in the following years, prior to the declaration of war against Great Britain in June 1812.

(2) *The Four Principal Statutes*

a. The Trading with the Enemy Act (1917-77)

The modern era of US political trade controls began with the Trading with the Enemy Act of 1917,[6] adapted from a British statute of the same name.[7] As amended in 1941, just

2 1 U.S. Statutes at Large [hereafter "Stat."] 372, 4 June 1794.

3 See An Act to Prohibit the implementation of certain goods, wares and merchandise, 2 U.S. Stat. 379 (18 April 1806).

4 An Act laying an Embargo on all ships and vessels in the ports and harbors of the United States, 2 Stat. 451 (22 December 1807).

5 2 Stat. 528, (1 March 1809), renewed and amended 2 Stat. 550 (28 June 1809); 2 Stat. 605 (1 May 1810), 2 Stat. 654 (2 March 1911); 3 Stat. 88 (17 December 1813); repealed 3 Stat. 123 (14 April 1814).

6 40 Stat. 415 (Oct. 6, 1917).

7 Trading with the Enemy Act, 1914, 4 & 5 Geo. 5, c. 87.

after the United States entered the Second World War, the Trading with the Enemy Act (TWEA) authorized the President, "during the time of war or during any other period of national emergency declared by the President" to prohibit (except under license) any kind of activity – export, imports, financial transactions remittances, travel, investment, or any other transaction – with designated countries or nationals of designated countries.[8] The prohibitions or regulations could be directed to any person, or with respect to any property, "subject to the jurisdiction of the United States." How the quoted words were interpreted is discussed in detail in Section II(3) below. For purposes of this first survey, it is necessary to point out only that the proclamation of national emergency was left to the sole discretion of the President, and successive Presidents have relied on that authority for a variety of purposes, some related to national security, others to financial regulations, such as closing of all banks by President Roosevelt as the first act of his administration in 1933,[9] and imposition of restraints on foreign investment by President Johnson for balance of payments reasons in 1968.[10]

When the armies of Communist China crossed the Yalu River in December 1950 and thereby overtly entered the Korean War, President Truman issued a Proclamation of National Emergency, which (*inter alia*) brought the authorities granted the Trading with the Enemy Act into operation.[11] The Proclamation remained in effect for more than a quarter century, and supported sanctions not only against the People's Republic of China and North Korea, but later against North Vietnam, Laos, Cambodia, and even Cuba, as well as President Nixon's suspension in 1971 of the United States' obligations under the Articles of Agreement of the International Monetary Fund.[12]

b. The United Nations Participation Act

When the United States joined the United Nations Organization in 1945, Congress adopted the United Nations Participation Act,[13] including section 5, concerning sanctions not involving the use of force. In its original version, section 5 read in pertinent part as follows:

> (a) Notwithstanding the provision of any other law, whenever the United States is called upon by the Security Council to apply measures which said Council has decided, pursuant to article 41 of said Charter, are to be employed to give effect to its decisions under said Charter, the President may, to the extent necessary to apply such measures, through any agency which he may designate, and under such orders, rules, and regulations as may be prescribed by him, investigate, regulate, or prohibit, in whole or in part, economic relations

8 Trading with the Enemy Act §5(b), 50 U.S.C. App. §5(b) as it read from 1941-1977.

9 Presidential Proclamation No. 2039 of 6 March 1933, 48 Stat. 1689; No. 2040 of 9 March 1933, 48 Stat. 1691.

10 Excecutive Order 11387 of 1 January 1968, 33 Fed. Reg. 49 (1968).

11 Pres. Procl. No. 2914 of 16 December 1950, 15 Fed. Reg. 9029, 64 Stat. A454.

12 See note 10 *supra*.

13 59 Stat. 619, 20 December 1945, presently (with some amendments) 22 U.S.C. §§287-287e.

> or rail, sea, air, postal, telegraphic, radio, and other means of communication between any foreign country or any national thereof or any person therein and the United States or any person subject to the jurisdiction thereof, or involving any property subject to the jurisdiction of the United States.

Paragraph (b) provided for fines, imprisonment and forfeit of property for violation of paragraph 5(a).

The operative provisions of section 5 of the United Nations Participation Act – "investigate, regulate, or prohibit ... economic relations between any foreign country or any national thereof or any person therein and the United States or any person subject to the jurisdiction of the United States" – closely followed the text of paragraph 5(b) of the Trading with the Enemy Act, and it was understood that if the conditions for application of the United Nations Participation Act were met, the powers of the President (or his delegate) would be the same as those granted under the Trading with the Enemy Act. In the legislative report accompanying the Bill, the Committee on Foreign Affairs of the House of Representatives wrote:

> The committee realizes that the powers proposed to be granted are very great. However, the basic decision in this regard was made when the Charter was ratified and this provision is simply a necessary corollary to our membership in this Organization. The Committee also believes that the Security Council must be placed in the most effective position possible to act under Article 41 since the prompt and effective application of economic and diplomatic sanctions by all the United Nations (or even the threat or possibility thereof) may avoid the necessity for the use of the armed forces available to the Security Council.
>
> The better prepared this country is to participate promptly in action of this kind, the more effective will be the Security Council and the more hope there will be that the United Nations may serve its major purpose, namely, the prevention of armed conflict.[14]

The key to the authority conferred by the United Nations Participation Act is in the words "...measures which [the Security] Council *has decided* pursuant to Article 41 of [the] Charter are to be employed..."[15] Thus section 5 of the United Nations Participation Act is applicable only to actions taken by the Security Council under Chapter VII, relating to threats to the peace, breaches of the peace, and acts of aggression. Resolutions of the Security Council under Chapter VI concerning Pacific Settlement of Disputes would not activate the powers under section 5. Further, the United Nations Charter provides, in Article 39, that the Security Council "shall determine the existence of any threat to the peace..." and shall make recommendations, *or* decide, what measures shall be taken in accordance with Article 41 and 42..." A *recommendation* under Article 39 does not serve

14 House Committee on Foreign Affairs, *United Nations Participation Act of 1945*, H.R. Rep. No. 1383, 12 December 1945, 1945 U.S. Code Cong. Service p. 927 at 932.

15 Note that Section 1 of the British United Nations Act 1946, 9 & 10 Geo. 6 c. 45, 10 Halsbury's Statutes 553 (4th ed. 1995) uses almost the same wording as the United States Act, and to the same effect.

to activate the powers under section 5 of the United Nations Participation Act, even when it calls for action pursuant to Article 41. This distinction is consistent with Article 25 of the United Nations Charter, which provides that the Members of the United Nations "agree to accept and carry out *the decisions* of the Security Council" in accordance with the Charter, but contains no comparable obligations with respect to recommendations.

Many proponents of action against Rhodesia after its Unilateral Declaration of Independence (UDI) in 1965 were critical of the United States government for not enforcing an embargo on oil and petroleum products, or indeed breaking all diplomatic relations with the illegal authorities in Southern Rhodesia, as called for by the Security Council.[16] Whatever the underlying attitude of the US government was at the time, the legal reason for imposing only export controls but no restraints or imports or financial transactions, was that there was general authority for export controls, as described in Section II(2)d, but no general authority for import restraints; since the Security Council had not *decided* pursuant to Article 41 that all states shall enforce an embargo, section 5 of the United Nations Participation Act, which authorizes restraints of all kinds, was not applicable at this time in respect of Rhodesia. A year later, when the Security Council adopted so-called selective *mandatory* sanctions,[17] the Act was made applicable, but only "to the extent necessary" to apply the measures specified by the Security Council.[18] It was not until the Security Council adopted comprehensive mandatory sanctions in 1968[19] that the full range of the powers granted by the United Nations Participation Act could be exercised by the President, and President Johnson did so.[20]

The suggestion was made in 1965 that the President could impose sanctions against Rhodesia under the Trading with the Enemy Act, relying on the Truman Proclamation of National Emergency of December 1950, which had not been revoked. That Proclamation, as mentioned above, had been relied on by President Kennedy in imposing an embargo against Cuba, and some proponents of sanctions against Rhodesia urged that this example be followed with respect to Rhodesia. But Cuba and North Korea/People's Republic of China had in common at least the threat of communism, as well as the perceived threat to the national security of the United States. The consensus in the Johnson Administration in the period 1965-68 was that relying on the TWEA and the 1950 Proclamation in taking action on Rhodesia would be too great a stretch, and that the events of UDI would not justify a new proclamation of national emergency.

16 Security Council Res. 217 (20 November 1965).

17 Security Council Res. 232 (16 December 1966).

18 Executive Order 11322 Relating to Trade and Other Transactions Involving Southern Rhodesia, 5 January, 1967, 32 Fed. Reg. 119 (1967).

19 Security Council Res. 253 (29 May 1968).

20 Executive Order 11419 Relating to Trade and Other Transactions Involving Southern Rhodesia, July 29, 1968, 33 Fed. Reg. 10,837 (1968). There is more to the Rhodesia story, set out in Section III(3) below, p. 619. The brief narrative here is designed only to explain the scope and limits of the power granted to the President by the UN Participation Act.

c. The International Emergency Economic Powers Act

In the mid-1970s, Congress came to believe that the Trading with the Enemy Act had been abused in a series of actions by nearly every President since Franklin Roosevelt.[21] In part this was a response to the actual invocations of the TWEA; in part it was a reaction to a more generalized perception of the abuse of Presidential power in the wake of the Watergate scandal and the Vietnam War. Consideration was given to simply repealing the TWEA, or to limiting the authorities granted in paragraph 5(b) to time of war only.[22] The Administration, however, persuaded Congress that such action would immediately force an end to various programs of economic sanctions, in particular the embargo against trade with Cuba, just as Fidel Castro was again interfering with American interests in Africa and Central America. Moreover, the Administration argued that an American President should never be without power to act in emergencies that could not now be foreseen.

The eventual compromise was to leave existing programs established under the TWEA in place, but to limit future actions under the TWEA to time of war. For use in emergencies short of war, Congress adopted a new law, the International Emergency Economic Powers Act (IEEPA), granting authorities to the President to be exercised "to deal with an unusual and extraordinary threat with respect to which a national emergency has been declared".[23] The Act went on to specify that any exercise of the authorities granted in the Act to deal with any new threat shall be based on a new declaration of national emergency "which must be with respect to such threat." The powers granted were substantially the same as those contained in paragraph 5(b) of the TWEA, except that the power to block property was not accompanied, as in the TWEA, by the power to vest property in the U.S. government.[24]

The first resort to IEEPA came when President Carter issued an Executive Order blocking Iranian assets shortly after the U.S. Embassy in Teheran was taken over by the Iranian "students" in November 1979.[25] Subsequently IEEPA provided the authority to make various additional moves during the 444 days of the Hostage Crisis, including suspending private litigation in US courts and establishing the Iran-United States Claims Tribunal.[26] IEEPA was also used as authority for prohibiting trade with Libya and blocking assets of Libya in January 1986.

---

21 See *Emergency Controls on International Economic Transactions*. Hearings before Subcomm. on Int'l Economic Policy and Trade of House Comm. on Int'l. Relations, 95th Cong. 1st Sess. (1977). The present writer's testimony, consistent with the statement in the text, appears at pp. 2-20.

22 See H.R. 1560, "A Bill to Repeal Section 5(b) of the Trading with the Enemy Act," 95th Cong., 1st Sess. (10 January 1977).

23 Pub. L. 95-223, 91 Stat. 1625 (28 December 1977), codified as 50 U.S.C. §1701 *et seq.*

24 During the Iran Hostage Crisis, serious consideration was given to seeking authority to vest some or all of the $6 billion plus of Iranian assets that had been blocked in the United States, but the Carter administration decided against such a move, out of a combination of political and constitutional concerns.

25 Executive Order 12170. 14 November, 1979, 44 Fed. Reg. 65729 (1979).

26 See, e.g., A. Lowenfeld, L. Newman, J. Walker (eds.), *Revolutionary Days: The Iran Hostage Crisis and the Hague Claims Tribunal: a Look Back* (1998), esp. pp. 40-46.

When Iraq invaded Kuwait on August 2, 1990, President Bush immediately declared a national emergency pursuant to IEEPA to deal with the threat posed by Iraq's actions, and ordered Iraqi government property and Kuwaiti government property blocked, as described in Section IV(2)a. below. Other resort to IEEPA has concerned transactions with Libya, Haiti, Yugoslavia and its former constituents, Burma, Sudan, UNITA (Angola), organizations designated as "Terrorist" that threatened to disrupt the Middle East Peace Process,[27] and the Taliban and Al-Qaida.[28]

d. The Export Control/Export Administration Act

Under the Export Control Act of 1949[29] and successor statutes, all commercial exports from the United States – of technology as well as of goods – require a license as a condition for leaving a United States port. Most exports can be made under general license regardless of destination; for some products a particular or validated license is required, which may or may not be granted depending on the country in question and the proposed end-user. In principle, validated licenses are required for products that may have strategic uses, but many products have both civilian and military uses.[30] Further, many of the products requiring a validated license for exports are readily available from other countries. Over the years, there has been a continuing controversy over which products should be subject to the requirement of a validated license, under what circumstances such licenses should be granted, and which executive departments – Defense, State, or Commerce – should have primary responsibility for making the relevant decisions.

The other element in export controls as they have developed is a classification of different countries, which are declared eligible for exports under different categories of licenses. Exports from the United States to Canada, for instance, were virtually always permitted, provided the purchaser could show that he was an end-user or would pledge not to re-export to specific countries or purchasers. Exports to Latin America (Cuba excepted) and to Western Europe were lightly controlled, and the classification of other

---

27 Exec. Order No. 12947 of 23 January 1995, (60 Fed Reg. 5079 (1995); Exec. Order 13099 of 20 August 1998, 63 Fed. Reg. 45167 (1998)).

28 Exec. Order 13129 Blocking Property and Prohibiting Transactions with the Taliban, 4 July 1999, 64 Fed. Reg. 36750 (1999); Exec. Order 13223 Blocking Property and Prohibiting Transactions with Persons Who Commit, Threaten to Commit, or Support Terrorism, 23 September 2001, 66 Fed. Reg. 49079 (2001).

29 50 U.S.C. App. §§2021-2032 (1949-69). The Export Control Act was never adopted as permanent legislation, and was replaced in 1969 by the Export Administration Act, 50 U.S.C. App. §§2401-2420. On several occasions, the Export Control Act or Export Administration Act expired, but each time the President continued the authorities and implementation of the controls by executive order, relying on the TWEA or the IEEPA. These extensions of authority, though questionable, have never been challenged. For the most recent such extension, see Presidential Notice of 7 August 2003 on Continuation of Emergency Regarding Export Control Regulations, 68 Fed. Reg. 47833, (11 August 2003).

30 Premier Khrushchev once suggested that buttons should be controlled, since they could be used to hold up soldiers' trousers.

countries for purposes of export controls have varied according to the current state of political relations with the United States. For instance, under the Export Administration Regulations applicable in 1982, the world was divided into eight country groups, from Group P – People's Republic of China, through Group T – North and South America except Canada and Cuba, to Group Y – Soviet Union and other Communist states except Romania, Hungary and Poland, to Group Z – Cuba, Kampuchea, North Korea and Vietnam.

Traditionally, the purpose of export controls was focused on concerns of national security, particularly in the context of the Cold War. The statute also gave the President authority to impose export controls "to further the foreign policy of the United States and to aid in fulfilling its international responsibilities."[31] Even before the end of the Cold War, however, export controls were used for other purposes – some stated, others not. For instance, since 1977 US export controls have been directed to counter the Arab Boycott of Israel.[32] Also, export controls have been used to enforce sanctions against apartheid in South Africa, UDI in Rhodesia, terrorism, human rights abuses, failure to sign or implement treaties on chemical and biological weapons, nuclear non-proliferation, lack of crime control, and non-cooperation in the fight against narcotic drugs, and comparable objectives that do not neatly fit into any one category.[33]

While Congress has from time to time made declarations of policy that the President is supposed to carry out by use of export controls, the basic authority (except for the anti-Arab Boycott provisions adopted in 1977) has always been stated extremely broadly. The Congress has made "declarations of policy" – fourteen as of year-end 2003[34] – and then authorized the President to "prohibit or curtail the exportation from the United States ... of any articles, materials, or supplies, including technical data" under such regulations as he may prescribe.[35]

In contrast to regulations under the TWEA and IEEPA, which have been used to enforce complete embargoes – for instance against Cuba since 1962, against the Peoples' Republic of China 1950-72, against North Korea 1950 to date – there has always been some trade with countries subject only to export controls. The principal target of US export controls from the end of World War II to the end of the Cold War was, of course, the Soviet Union, but even at the height of the Cold War the United States never imposed a complete embargo on trade with the Soviet Union. The level of permitted commerce went up and down in response to changing perceptions of political and military developments, and to some extent in response to availability of controlled items from other countries willing to trade with the Soviet Union. Since the latitude of the

31 Export Control Act of 1949 §§2(1)(b) and 3(a). Since 1979 the authority is divided into National Security Controls and Foreign Policy Controls, but the effect of the division is scarcely noticeable. See 50 U.S.C. App. §2404 (National Security Controls), §2405 (Foreign Policy Controls).

32 See, e.g., A. Lowenfeld, *Trade Controls for Political Ends* (2nd ed. 1983) ch. III.

33 For the policy declarations governing the export controls, see 15 C.F.R. Part 738 and Supplement No. 1 thereto.

34 See 50 U.S.C. App. §2402 (1)-(14).

35 See e.g., 50 U.S.C. App. §2404 (a)(1), §2405(a)(1).

President under the Export Control Act was virtually unchecked, President Johnson was able, as mentioned earlier, to impose an almost complete ban on exports to Rhodesia in the period 1965-68, while he lacked authority to impose financial controls and controls on imports beyond what was mandated by the Security Council. The Department of Commerce, which administers export controls, established a country group for Rhodesia, for which a validated license was required for virtually all items of export from the United States, and such licenses were almost never granted.

(3) The Reach of United States Sanctions

In the administration of United States economic sanctions under the Trading with the Enemy Act or the statutes modeled on that Act (i.e., the UN Participation Act and IEEPA), the focus has typically been on interpretation of the term "Person subject to the jurisdiction of the United States." When the aim has been maximum effect of the sanction, that term has been defined (with small variation in the several regulations) as including:

(1) Any person, wheresoever located, who is a citizen or resident of the United States;
(2) Any person actually within the United States;
(3) Any corporation organized under the laws of the United States or of any State, territory, possession, or district of the United States; and
(4) Any partnership, association, corporation, or other organization, wheresoever organized or doing business, which is owned or controlled by persons specified in subparagraph (1), (2), or (3) of this paragraph.[36]

The extraterritorial aspect of US sanctions has been centered on paragraph (4), directed to foreign subsidiaries of companies based in the United States. The United States has taken the position that any company, regardless of where it is established or operated, more than 50 percent of whose shares are held by a company defined in paragraph (3), fits the definition of paragraph (4), and indeed that a company less than 50 percent of whose shares are held by a US-based company may also fit the definition, if other shares are widely dispersed or if the parent company exercises *de facto* control through a management agreement, through provisions in a credit agreement, or otherwise.

In many instances, particularly with respect to subsidiaries established in Canada, but also with respect to subsidiaries established in European and Latin American countries, assertion of jurisdiction on this basis has led to major controversies. In some instances, while maintaining the assertion of jurisdiction to prescribe, the relevant regulations have contained licenses permitting specified transactions not involving US currency or par-

36 The precise text is drawn from the Foreign Assets Control Regulations, 31 C.F.R. §500.329. Several but not all of the regulations implementing U.S. sanctions programs are substantially the same, but in some instances paragraph (4) is more limited or is omitted entirely. Paragraph (4) did not appear in the Rhodesian Sanctions Regulations, because the Security Council Resolutions on which the U.S. regulations were based were addressed only to "activities by their nationals or in their territories," without the "owned or controlled" term contained in most of the emergency regulations of the United States.

ticipation by US citizens. For instance, for a time, but not as of year-end 2003, an Argentine or Mexican corporation owned or controlled by a US corporation, was permitted to engage in commerce with Cuba, although the parent was prohibited from engaging in such commerce. If no such license has been issued, the United States has taken the position that a violator may be punished, by fines, by blacklisting, or in rare cases by proceeding against the parent corporation on the basis that it, or its management, had the power to prevent the prohibited conduct.

Generally the regulations issued pursuant to the Export Control or Export Administration Act did not define "person subject to the regulation" to include the substance of paragraph (4), but concentrated rather on the US origin of a particular product or technology subject to control. Thus a corporation established, say, in France, would not be subject to US export controls even if owned or controlled by a U.S. parent corporation, so long as it did not deal in US-origin products or technology. A well known exception to this statement was the effort in 1982 by the United States, in response to imposition of martial law in Poland, to extend its export controls (i) to foreign corporations owned or controlled by US persons, and (ii) to foreign corporations utilizing technology originating in the United States under commercial licenses from US-based firms. This effort, directed to interfering with construction of the natural gas pipeline from Northern Siberia to Western Europe, led to major protests on behalf of all of the states of Western Europe, and was abandoned by the United States within some six months of its adoption.[37]

The American Law Institute *Restatement (Third) of the Foreign Relations Law of the United States* (1987) attempted to state a middle position between the assertion on behalf of the US government that jurisdiction over subsidiaries established abroad was generally permissible and the opposite assertion that a corporation owed allegiance and obedience only to the state where it was established, regardless of the actual ownership or control. The proposed rule distinguishes between jurisdiction over branches and jurisdiction over subsidiaries, but does not preclude assertion of jurisdiction over the latter even when these are established abroad in the context of economic sanctions applicable within the state exercising jurisdiction. The references in the section to other sections of the Restatement are addressed to the problem of direct conflict between assertion of jurisdiction on the basis of territoriality and assertion on the basis of nationality, or the analogy to nationality derived from "ownership or control," and in general adopt a territorial preference if both states in question have genuine interest in the subject of the regulation:

> §414. Jurisdiction with Respect to Activities of Foreign Branches and Subsidiaries
>
> (1) Subject to §403 [Limitations on Jurisdiction to prescribe] and §441 [Foreign State Compulsion], a state may exercise jurisdiction to prescribe for limited purposes with respect to activities of foreign branches of corporations organized under its laws.

37 The story of the *Pipeline Sanctions* has been reported in numerous publications. The present author's account appears in A. Lowenfeld, *Trade Controls for Political Ends*, (2nd ed. 1983), pp. 267-396, and in abridged form, in A. Lowenfeld, *The Role of Government in International Trade: Essays over Three Decades* (2000), pp. 345-360. See also, e.g., Bernard Audit, "Extraterritorialité et commerce international: l'Affaire Gazoduc sibérien," 72 *Revue Critique de Droit International Privé* (1983) 401.

(2) A state may not ordinarily regulate activities of corporations organized under the laws of a foreign state on the basis that they are owned or controlled by nationals of the regulating state. However, under §403 and subject to §441, it may not be unreasonable for a state to exercise jurisdiction for limited purposes with respect to activities of affiliated foreign entities
   (a) by direction to the parent corporation in respect of such matters as uniform accounting, disclosure to investors, or preparation of consolidated tax returns of multinational enterprises; or
   (b) by direction to either the parent or the subsidiary in exceptional cases, depending on all relevant factors, including the extent to which
      (i) the regulation is essential to implementation of a program to further a major national interest of the state exercising jurisdiction;
      (ii) the national program of which the regulation is a part can be carried out effectively only if it is applied also to foreign subsidiaries;
      (iii) the regulation conflicts or is likely to conflict with the law or policy of the state where the subsidiary is established.
   (c) In the exceptional cases referred to in paragraph (b), the burden of establishing reasonableness is heavier when the direction is issued to the foreign subsidiary than when it is issued to the parent corporation.

It is not clear that the *Restatement* formulation represents the prevailing view in the United States, and indeed the comments and notes to paragraph 414 take up twelve printed pages. It can be said that the United States government officials charged with implementing programs of sanctions are more conscious of the costs of exercise of extraterritorial jurisdiction than they were two decades ago, in particular when the policy of the United States is not shared by other states. For instance, the Libyan Sanctions Regulations[38] and the Yugoslavia Sanctions regulations[39] did not contain the controversial paragraph (4) quoted above; the Iranian Assets Control Regulations did, but the Iranian Transaction Regulations did not contain the controversial paragraph quoted at note 36 above.[40]

(4) Enforcement

In some instances, violation of the economic sanctions statutes has been prosecuted criminally. For instance, in one recent case a British subject was convicted of violation of IEEPA and the prohibitions against trade with Libya promulgated thereunder for arranging to export a variety of computer equipment to the government of Libya, listing Greece or Cyprus as the country of ultimate destination. Under Federal sentenc-

38 See 31 C.F.R. §550.308 (1986-), defining "United States person" rather than "person subject to the jurisdiction of the United States."

39 See 31 C.F.R. §585.317 (1993-) same.

40 Compare 31 C.F.R. §535.329 (1979-) with §560.314 (1987-). Nor did the Taliban (Afghanistan) Sanctions Regulations, 31 C.F.R. §545.315 (1999-).

ing guidelines, the defendant was sentenced to 51 months in prison. *United States v. McKeeve*, 131 F.3d 1 (1st Cir. 1997).

More commonly, enforcement has been by administrative action. Typically, the Department of the Treasury, Office of Foreign Assets Control, or the Department of Commerce, Bureau of Export Administration, sends a charging letter or Prepenalty Notice to the firm believed to be in violation. The firm may contest the charge, either informally or in a hearing before an administrative law judge, and may offer any evidence in mitigation. Generally, thereafter, the agency will suggest a settlement, consisting of a fine, which may range from a few thousand dollars to several million dollars, plus in rare cases, blacklisting or probation.

In June 2002, in response to a Freedom of Information proceeding brought by a private publication, the Office of Foreign Assets Control released documents concerning 115 enforcement cases for the period March 1998-March 2002.[41] The documents were heavily blacked out, but one can nevertheless see that respondents included major companies such as Boeing, Merrill Lynch, Morgan Stanley, Citigroup, and Goodyear. Several companies paid fines for shipping food or medical supplies to Iraq. Others made shipments of various kinds to Haiti while sanctions were in force with respect to that country (see Section IV(2)b below); to Sudan, Libya, Iran, Federal Republic of Yugoslavia (Serbia & Montenegro), North Korea, and Taliban-controlled areas of Afghanistan (see Section V below). One company was fined an undisclosed amount for shipping $700,000 worth of oil well rig parts to an unaffiliated company in the United Arab Emirates, for transshipment to Iraq. The largest fine appears to have been $2.2 million paid by British subsidiaries of the US-based insurance company CNA in respect of payment of claims and receipt of premiums under reinsurance contracts with a Cuban insurer.

In some instances, settlement is reached after court proceedings have been initiated by the Department of Justice. In most instances, the settlement is reached prior to commencement of litigation, but with the threat of prosecution in the background. In all cases of settlement through administrative proceedings, the accused is required to undertake not to contest the legality of the settlement at any time in the future.

III. Economic Sanctions and the US Constitution

To anyone familiar with the American penchant for subjecting laws and administrative acts to constitutional scrutiny, it will come as a surprise that there have been few challenges, and no successful ones, of any of the Acts summarized in the preceding section.

(1) Excessive Delegation and National Security

All of the authorities discussed might be thought to be vulnerable to challenge on the grounds of excessive delegation to the executive branch. But while this basis for invali-

41 For a description of the documents released, see "U.S. Companies Pay Penalties for Trade with Certain Nations," *New York Times*, 3 July 2002, p. A9. The complete set of 174 pages, heavily censored, was placed on the web site of the Department of the Treasury at http: //www.treas.gov/foia/ofac/06252002.

dating acts of Congress or exercise of authority lacking standards was successful in connection with domestic programs, particularly in the early years of the administration of Franklin Roosevelt,[42] the same challenge in connection with an authority to be exercised internationally was unsuccessful. The leading case involved an arms embargo issued by President Roosevelt during the so-called Chaco War between Bolivia and Paraguay. *United States v. Curtiss-Wright Export Corporation*, 299 US 304 (1936). Congress had authorized but not required the President to proclaim an arms embargo against the participants in the Chaco War. The joint resolution at issue was similar to the Trading with the Enemy Act and the Export Control Act, in providing

> That if the President finds that the prohibition on the sale of arms and munitions of war in the United States to those countries now engaged in the Chaco may contribute to the reestablishment of peace between countries, and if ... he makes proclamation to that effect, it shall be unlawful to sell, except under such limitations and exceptions as the President prescribes, any arms or munitions of war in any place in the United States to the countries now engaged in that armed conflict, or to any person, company or association acting in the interest of either country, until otherwise ordered by the President or by Congress.

Violation was punishable as a crime, by fine, imprisonment, or both. The law was challenged on the ground, *inter alia*, that its operation, including creation of a crime, was conditional on the uncontrolled discretion of the President, and that the law granted to the President the power to issue exceptions to the statutory prohibition "as he may see fit, guided by no rule or standard whatever."

The Supreme Court, in a famous opinion by Justice George Sutherland, wrote:

> Whether, if the Joint Resolution had related solely to internal affairs it would be open to the challenge that it constituted an unlawful delegation of legislative power to the Executive we find it unnecessary to determine. The whole aim of the resolution is to affect a situation entirely external to the United States, and falling within the category of foreign affairs...
> It is quite apparent that if, in the maintenance of our international relations, embarrassment – perhaps serious embarrassment – is to be avoided and success for our aims achieved, congressional legislation which is to be made effective through negotiations and inquiry within the international field must often accord to the President a degree of discretion and freedom from statutory restriction which would not be admissible were domestic affairs alone involved...[43]

The broad authority of the Executive to block assets and transactions affecting blocked assets under the Trading with the Enemy Act was sustained by the Supreme Court in several cases arising out of actions taken in wartime,[44] and the precedents there estab-

42 See e.g., *Panama Refining Co. v. Ryan* (the "hot oil" case), 293 U.S. 388 (1935); *Schechter Poultry Corp. v. United States*, (the "sick chicken" case) 295 U.S. 495 (1935).

43 299 U.S. at 315, 320.

44 See e.g., *Propper v. Clark*, 337 U.S. 472 (1949); *Zittman v. McGrath*, 341 U.S. 446 (1951); *Orvis. v. Brownell*, 345 U.S. 183 (1953).

lished were in turn relied on in a challenge to action taken by the President in connection with the Iranian Hostage Crisis under the International Emergency Economic Powers Act. In *Dames & Moore v. Regan*, 453 US 654 (1981), the Supreme Court sustained the action by President Carter (confirmed by President Reagan) as part of the settlement of the Hostage Crisis, suspending all litigation against Iran brought in US courts by persons whose property or contract rights had been taken by the Iranian Revolutionary Regime, and transferring the claims of American plaintiffs to the Iran-US Claims Tribunal.

(2) *Taking Property without Due Process or Just Compensation*

Efforts have been made from time to time to challenge blocking of assets or prohibition of commercial transactions on the ground that they amount to expropriation without compensation. The argument has never succeeded in cases arising out of actions based on the emergency or national security powers granted in the statutes cited in the previous section. Perhaps an extreme case, illustrating the degree of deference shown by the U.S. courts in the national security context, was *Sardino v. Federal Reserve Bank of New York*, 361 F.2d 106 (2d Cir. 1966), with opinion by Judge Henry Friendly, one of the most esteemed federal judges. Mr. Sardino was a Cuban national residing in Havana who had a savings account of some $7,000 in a New York bank, derived from the proceeds of an insurance policy on the life of his son, who had died in New York. The funds were frozen pursuant to the Cuban Assets Control Regulations issued under the Trading with the Enemy Act, and when he applied for a license to transfer the funds, the application was denied, on the ground that "transactions of this type are not consistent with the present policy of this government with respect to Cuba." Sardino brought suit, and the court agreed with his contention that the controls deprived him of property and that the Constitution applied to nonresident aliens:

> It does not follow, however [the court wrote], that in dealing with the property of an alien the United States must be blind to the acts of the country of which he is a national; the Constitution protects the alien from arbitrary action by our government, but not from reasonable response to such action by his own...[45]

A more recent case involved a constitutional challenge to measures taken by President Reagan under the International Emergency Economic Powers Act in imposing sanctions against Libya in retaliation for that country's support of terrorism.[46] The Libyan Sanctions Regulations[47] provided, *inter alia*, that

> except as authorized, no U.S. person may perform any contract in support of an industrial or other commercial or governmental project in Libya.[48]

45 361 F.2d at 111.

46 *Chang v. United States,* 859 F.2d 893 (Fed. Cir. 1988).

47 51 Fed. Reg. 1354-59 (10 January 1986), presently codified in 31 Code of Federal Regulations [C.F.R.] Part 550.

48 31 C.F.R. §550.205.

The plaintiffs, who were US persons as defined, had been employed by the Sirte Oil Company to work in Libya, but returned home in obedience to the sanction order. They then bought suit against the United States in the Claims Court, asserting that the termination of their employment contracts under order of the United States was a taking, and that they were owed "just compensation" under the Fifth Amendment to the US Constitution.

The court accepted the contention that contracts are property. But "plaintiffs' contracts were in every sense subordinate to the President's power under the IEEPA," and, quoting an old case,

> a valid governmental exercise of its constitutional power to regulate commerce with foreign nations can have the consequential effect of altering the obligations of preexisting contracts without giving rise to a taking.[49]

Other cases could be cited involving claims that one or another of the many sanctions regulations and orders issued by the United States (i) exceeded the statutory grant; or (ii) were unconstitutional in general or as applied to the particular claims. No appellate court decision, it is believed, and certainly no Supreme Court decision, has ever invalidated or given compensation in respect of an economic sanction imposed by the U.S. government.[50]

(3) Conflict between Domestic and International Obligations: The Byrd Amendment

As stated above, economic sanctions have been applied by the United States in a variety of situations, on the basis of one of four principal statutes, each of which grants wide authorities to the executive branch. International obligations in conflict with the law of the United States have arisen in the sanctions context only once, as the US Congress attempted to curb mandatory sanctions decided upon by the UN Security Council during the period of Rhodesia's Unilateral Declaration of Independence. The story of the Byrd Amendment was widely discussed in the early 1970s, and remains the example par excellence of conflict between international obligations and domestic law in the United States. As a generation has passed since the events that gave rise to the conflict, the story is worth retelling in some detail.

Selective mandatory sanctions against Rhodesia – the former Southern Rhodesia – were adopted by the UN Security Council in 1966,[51] and comprehensive mandatory sanctions were adopted in 1968.[52] In the first five years of the UN sanctions program, no country – with the possible exception of Great Britain – enforced the sanctions as effectively as the United States. Of course, the United States had the resources, and it also

49 859 F.2d at 897.

50 We speak here of economic sanctions. Some cases have invalidated restraints on travel or publication, in reliance on the personal guarantees in the First Amendment to the Constitution.

51 Security Council Res. 232, 16 December 1966.

52 Security Council Res. 253, 29 May 1968.

had the experience of enforcing the Foreign Assets Control Regulations directed since 1950 at North Korea, the People's Republic of China, and the states of Southeast Asia under communist domination, as well as the Cuban Assets Control Regulations issued in 1963. The Rhodesia Sanctions Regulations[53] followed the pattern of the cited regulations, except that the definition of "persons subject to the jurisdiction of the United States" did not include foreign subsidiaries of US companies other than those having their principal place of business in Southern Rhodesia. None of the cases of sanctions violation reported to the United Nations through 1971 seems to have involved trade to or from the United States. One New York firm was indicted by a federal grand jury for importing and conspiracy to import chrome concentrates from Southern Rhodesia, in violation of paragraph 5 of the UN Participation Act and regulations issued thereunder; the firm pleaded guilty and paid a fine of $10,000.[54]

Nevertheless, sanctions against Rhodesia had not been approved by Congress, and doubt about the wisdom, efficacy, and even legality of the program lingered in some sectors of American public opinion and in Congress.[55] Moreover, it seemed odd to some members of Congress that at a time when sanctions against communist countries were being relaxed, sanctions should be rigidly enforced against a clearly non-communist country.

Legislation to qualify adherence by the United States to UN sanctions was introduced regularly in the Congress from 1967 on, but created little attention. In 1971, the anti-sanctions (or anti-United Nations) members of Congress developed a new argument. The embargo on trade with Rhodesia, they said, was depriving the United States of an important source of chrome, and forcing American users to turn to the Soviet Union to meet their needs. Not only did the embargo enable the Soviet Union to raise its prices, the argument went, but by cutting itself off from an alternate source of supply the United States was opening itself up to potential blackmail in connection with an important strategic commodity.[56]

In February 1971, a bill was introduced in the House of Representatives to amend the UN Participation Act to prohibit "the imposition thereunder of any prohibition on the importation into the United States of any metal-bearing ore from any free world country so long as the importation of any like ore from any communist country is not prohibited by law." Subsequently the bill was modified and introduced also in the Senate, under the sponsorship of Senator Harry Byrd of Virginia.[57] As an amendment to the

---

53 31 C.F.R. Part 525.

54 *United States v. Wm. H. Muller & Co.*, 2 Crim. 227 (S.D.N.Y. 1970).

55 The legal doubt pertained to the question of whether the Security Council had legitimately acted pursuant to Chapter VII of the UN Charter, since, it was argued, UDI did not pose a threat to breach of the peace or aggression, but rather was an internal matter. The general view, supported by the precedent of the Rhodesia sanctions, is that a threat to the peace under Chapter VII of the UN Charter is whatever the Security Council, voting in accordance with Article 27, says it is, without regard to "objective" external standards.

56 The fact that substantial mining interests in Rhodesia were owned by American companies doubtless also played a role in the Congressional debates.

57 Not the same senator who became Majority Leader, Senator Robert Byrd of West Virginia.

UN Participation Act, the bill was referred to the Foreign Affairs Committees of both Houses, and both committees rejected the bill. But the bill was then offered as a rider to a Military Procurement Authorization Act. The proposed amendment of the UN Participation Act was deleted, and replaced by a provision reading

> Notwithstanding any other provision of law, ... the President may not prohibit ... the importation of any [strategic material] ... for so long as the importation into the United States [from any] Communist-dominated countries or areas is not prohibited ....

In that form the amendment was sent not to the Senate Foreign Relations Committee but to the Armed Services Committee, which unanimously approved it, and subsequently it was approved by the full Senate. The Byrd Amendment came before a Senate-House Committee of Conference just as the United Nations was admitting the People's Republic of China and expelling Nationalist China, with the press and television showing pictures of African delegates jumping for joy at the humiliation of the United States.

Arguments about America's obligations to the United Nations, about Articles 25 and 41 of the UN Charter were not well received in Congress. While the State Department opposed the Byrd Amendment, the White House, and President Nixon personally, did not participate in the debate. Since the Byrd Amendment was now part of a major military authorization bill, it was difficult for the President to veto the bill, and he did not do so. The Byrd Amendment became law in November 1971. Chrome, and particularly a processed alloy, high carbon ferrochrome, began to be imported again into the United States from Rhodesia. More than the economic gain to Rhodesia, the symbolic effect of the Byrd Amendment, both to the white rulers of Rhodesia and to its opponents at the United Nations and in the United States, was significant.

Efforts were made by the administration every year to repeal the Byrd Amendment, but did not succeed until March 1977, in the early months of the administration of President Carter. At the United Nations, meanwhile, the reaction was one of shock, especially among the African delegates. In 1972 the General Assembly, for the first time, passed a resolution expressly condemning United States policy as "in open contravention" of Security Council resolutions and "contrary to the specific obligations assumed under Article 25 of the Charter."[58] The Security Council adopted three more resolutions on Rhodesia, all essentially directed at the United States and the Byrd Amendment.[59]

In April 1972, a group of concerned individuals and organizations, led by a member of Congress from Michigan, brought an action in the federal court in Washington D.C. seeking (i) a declaration that the Byrd Amendment was in violation of law, and (ii) a decree enjoining importation of chrome and other metals from Southern Rhodesia. The district court dismissed the case for lack of standing, but on this issue the Court of

58 G.A. Res. 2946 of 7 December 1972, 27 G.A.O.R. Supp. 30, at 78. See also G.A. Res. 2765 of 17 November 1971, 26 G.A.O.R. Supp. 29 (A/8429) at 97 adopted just before President Nixon signed the bill containing the Byrd Amendment.

59 Security Council Res. 314, 28 February 1972; 318, 28 July 1972; and 320, 29 September 1972. The United States abstained on each resolution, but did not cast a veto.

Appeals reversed. *Diggs v. Shultz*, 470 F. 2d 461 (D.C. Cir. 1972). On the merits, however, the Court of Appeals concluded that (i) a mandatory resolution of the Security Council carries the same obligation as a treaty; (ii) the intent of the Byrd Amendment was to detach the United States from the UN boycott of Southern Rhodesia "in blatant disregard of our treaty undertakings;" but (iii) the court lacked the authority to overrule the Congress in these circumstances and to compel the President to do what the statute prohibited:

> Under our constitutional scheme, Congress can denounce treaties if it sees fit to do so, and there is nothing the other branches of government can do about it. We consider that this is precisely what Congress has done in this case; and therefore the District Court was correct to the extent it found the complaint to state no tenable claim in law.[60]

No other instance has arisen placing the United States in direct conflict with a mandatory resolution of the Security Council under Article 41 of the Charter. Of course if the United States were opposed at the outset to a proposal for mandatory sanctions under Article 41, it could exercise its veto under Article 27(3), and indeed it did so, alone or in concert with Great Britain and France, a number of times in connection with proposed sanctions against South Africa.[61]

IV. Implementing UN Sanctions

(1) The Range of US Sanctions – UN-Related and Other

As of year-end 2003, the United States was maintaining sanctions against North Korea, Cuba, Iran, Iraq, Sudan, Burma, Libya, the Federal Republic of Yugoslavia (Serbia and Montenegro), Taliban-controlled territories of Afghanistan, named Narcotics Trafficking Organizations, and named Terrorist Organizations. It also was maintaining the Rough Diamonds (Sierra Leone & Liberia) Sanctions Regulations,[62] intended to deprive rebel forces in Sierra Leone and Liberia of the proceeds of the sale of rough diamonds that were said to be financing their attacks and atrocities in the named countries and neighboring states. Only the sanctions against Iraq and Yugoslavia are based directly on Security Council resolutions; the sanctions concerning "conflict diamonds", as discussed in Section IV(2)c, followed resolutions of the Security Council adopted with strong support from the United States, but the implementation of those sanctions was in some instances delayed by up to six months and was based both on the Security Council

60 470 F.2d at 466-67. The Supreme Court denied review. 411 U.S. 931 (1973).

61 See Anjali V. Patil, *The UN Veto in World Affairs 1946-1990* (1992), pp. 471-486. According to this compilation, the United States exercised its veto ten times in connection with the question of South Africa or closely allied questions; most of the resolutions in question called for selective mandatory sanctions.

62 31 C.F.R. Part 591 (2001-).

resolutions (and hence under the UN Participation Act) and on a declaration of national emergency under the International Emergency Economic Powers Act (IEEPA).

When the UN Security Council, at the urging of Great Britain and the United States, adopted a mandatory resolution requiring a boycott of aviation to or from Libya as well as an arms embargo based on Libya's failure to respond to inquiries concerning the bombing of Pan Am Flight 103 over Lockerbie, Scotland,[63] President Bush issued a complementary executive order,[64] although it seems that flights between Libya and the United States were already prohibited by the Libyan Sanctions Regulations based on President Reagan's Proclamation of National Emergency in January 1986, following a terrorist incident in Berlin attributed to Libya.[65] In August of 1998, as negotiations with the Libyan government for surrender of the two men charged with carrying out the bombing of Pan Am Flight 103 seemed to be making progress, the Security Council adopted another resolution calling for the Libyan government to ensure the appearance in the Netherlands of the two accused, and *deciding* that the prior sanctions ordered by the Security Council "shall be suspended immediately" if the two accused have arrived in the Netherlands for the purpose of trial.[66] When, after months of further negotiations, the two men were delivered up to the Netherlands on 5 April 1999, most countries, including Great Britain and France, immediately permitted their airlines to resume air service to and from Libya. The United States did not.

Tracing the relation between UN-ordered sanctions and the United States implementation would take up many pages and show small variations. Some sanctions are enforced through the Office of Foreign Assets Control of the Department of the Treasury, and if a violation is found, through criminal penalties. Others, including the arms embargo to Rwanda, are enforced under the Export Administration Act by the Department of Commerce, which generally punishes violators in administrative proceedings leading to fines or suspension of "export privileges," and by the Department of State under the Arms Export Control Act, subject to either criminal or civil penalties.[67] As noted earlier, one clue to the intensity of the American enforcement effort is the definition of "person subject to the jurisdiction of the United States" or "US person": some regulations apply only to US citizens and individuals or business entities actually in the United States or organized under the laws of the United States; some add foreign branches of corporations organized in the United States; and some add corporations organized abroad but owned or controlled by persons in the United States or organized

63 Security Council Res. 748 of 31 March 1992.

64 Exec. Order 12801 of 15 April 1992, 57 Fed. Reg. 14319 (17 April 1992). Also, the Department of Transportation issued a Special Federal Aviation Regulation (SFAR) No.65-1, 6 April 1992) prohibiting flights between the United States and Libya.

65 31 C.F.R. Part 550, esp. §550.203, implementing Exec. Order 12543 of 7 January 1986, 51 Fed. Reg. 875 (9 January 1986).

66 Security Council Res. 1192 of 27 August 1998.

67 22 U.S.C. §2751 *et seq.* In addition to the countries and areas mentioned above that are subject to sanction, arms export licenses were denied as of year-end 2003 to Afghanistan, Belarus, China, Congo (Kinshasa), Liberia, Rwanda, Somalia, Sudan, Syria, and Vietnam. See 22 C.F.R. §126.1.

under the laws of the United States, i.e., foreign subsidiaries of US corporations.[68] In connection with blocking or freezing assets, the term "subject to the jurisdiction of the United States" has sometimes been used to attempt to block funds of designated nationals deposited in foreign branches or subsidiaries of US banks.[69]

(2) Three Cases

The interplay between the United States and the United Nations in connection with economic sanctions, as well as the uncertain relation between Congress and the Executive Branch with respect to the United Nations may be illustrated by three well-known cases in which both the United States, under the authorities described in Section I of this chapter, and the Security Council, under Chapter VII of the UN Charter, exercised their respective powers.

a. Iraq (1990-2003)

On August 2, 1990, the military forces of Iraq invaded Kuwait, and quickly overran the entire country. The Security Council immediately condemned the invasion, determining under Articles 39 and 40 of the UN Charter that the invasion constituted a breach of international peace and security.[70] But in that first resolution, adopted on the morning of the invasion, the Security Council did not decide on sanctions, hoping, it seems, that Iraq might be persuaded to withdraw.[71] President George Bush did not wait.

On the same day, August 2, 1990, President Bush issued two executive orders pursuant to IEEPA, blocking all properties and interests in property of Iraq and Kuwait in the United States, and prohibiting virtually all trade between the United States and Iraq and Kuwait.[72] The Security Council adopted mandatory economic sanctions under Article 41 on August 6, 1990,[73] but in a second pair of executive orders President Bush went beyond the sanctions required by the Security Council's decision, and thus both the UN Participation Act and the International Emergency Economic Powers Act were relied on as authority for these orders.[74]

---

68 See notes 38-40 *supra*.

69 For a discussion of this issue, in particular with reference to the Iranian sanctions and the Libyan sanctions, see Peter S. Smedresman and Andreas F. Lowenfeld, *Eurodollars, Multinational Banks, and National Laws*, 64 *N.Y.U. L. Rev.* (1989) 733.

70 Security Council Res. 660 of 2 August 1990.

71 See, e.g., *New York Times*, 3 August 1990, p. A-10, quoting the British Foreign Secretary as saying "it is perfectly clear" that collective measures against Iraq will be necessary if Baghdad ignores the Council's call for withdrawal, and that Iraq had "one or two days" to respond.

72 Executive Order 12722 of 2 August 1990, 55 Fed. Reg. 31803 (1990) (concerning Iraq); Executive Order 12723 of 2 August 1990, 55 Fed. Reg. 31805 (1990) (concerning Kuwait).

73 Security Council Res. 661 of 6 August 1990.

74 Executive Order 12724 of 9 August 1990, 55 Fed. Reg. 33089 (1990) (concerning Iraq); Executive Order 12725 of 9 August 1990, 55 Fed. Reg. 33091 (1990) (concerning Kuwait).

The Security Council resolutions said nothing about enforcement of the required prohibitions. The United States, for its part, moved energetically. On August 12, 1990, President Bush ordered the U.S. Navy to halt all ships involved in commerce to and from Iraq.[75] The word "blockade" was not used, as that might have seemed to require further authorization from the Security Council. But Secretary of State Baker said that the Administration was responding to a request from the exiled Emir of Kuwait, and that this would satisfy the requirements of Article 51 of the UN Charter.[76] The White House statement said, "The President stressed that these efforts will complement, not substitute, for individual and collective compliance...." and that the United States "will coordinate its efforts with the governments of other nations to whom the Kuwaiti government has made similar requests. Two weeks later, on initiative of the United States, the Security Council adopted another resolution, calling upon

> those Member States co-operating with the Government of Kuwait which are deploying maritime forces to the area to use such measures commensurate to the specific circumstances as may be necessary under the authority of the Security Council to halt all inward and outward maritime shipping in order to inspect and verify their cargoes and destinations and to ensure strict implementation of the provisions related to such shipping laid down in resolution 661.[77]

Though the Security Council did not use the words "minimum force," as the United States had urged, the US Representative to the UN said the resolution was "sufficiently broad to use armed force – indeed, minimum force – depending upon the circumstances."[78] That the authorization came thirteen days after deployment of the US Navy in the Gulf was seen as a ratification of the US initiative, not usurpation by the United States.[79]

Domestic enforcement, of course, depended on legislative authority, or to be more precise, on enforcement of orders by the President acting in accordance with statutory authorization – in this case the UN Participation Act and IEEPA.[80] Enforcement was rigorous even before the implementing regulations were in final form. For example, on August 27, 1990, a company in Newbury, Ohio, was blocked from sending to Iraq a scin-

---

In addition to prohibitions on all imports from and exports to Iraq, the US sanctions included a blocking of all Iraqi government-owned assets that "are or hereafter come within the possession or control of United States persons, including their overseas branches." See Iraqi Sanctions Regulations, 31 C.F.R. §575.301 (1990-).

75 See White House Statement, 12 August 1990, repr. in *New York Times*, 13 August, p. A-11.

76 See *New York Times*, 13 August 1990, p. A-1.

77 Security Council Res. 665 of 25 August 1990.

78 See *New York Times*, 26 August 1990, p. 1.

79 In fact, the United States for a time considered a proposal made by the Soviet Union to revive the Military Staff Committee pursuant to Articles 46 and 47 of the UN Charter, possibly with a view to joint action under Articles 42 or 43. Eventually nothing came of this proposal. See *New York Times*, 15 August 1990, p. A-19.

80 The detailed Iraqi Sanctions Regulations, 31 C.F.R. Part 575, were not issued until 18 January 1991, 56 Fed. Reg. 2112 (1991).

tillation detector that belonged to the Iraqi Atomic Energy Commission. On September 17, 1990, a machine tool distribution company in Solon, Ohio, owned by an English company, was shut down on information that the English company was ultimately owned and controlled by a trading company controlled by the government of Iraq. At the same time the US government was coordinating its enforcement efforts with the UN, the OECD, the European Community, and in respect of financial movements, with central banks through the Bank for International Settlements.[81]

The US Congress was uneasy both about the exercise of the President's emergency powers, which might well include starting a war, and about authority said to be derived from resolutions of the UN Security Council. On the other hand, Congress was reluctant, as has nearly always been true, to tie the President's hands on matters of national security. The solution, as in other instances, was not to curb the President's authority, but to confer specific authority on him by legislation, the implication – for those who wished to draw it – being that without such authority, the President could not act.

In November 1990, Congress adopted the Iraq Sanctions Act as part of a larger appropriation bill, condemning "the brutal occupation of Kuwait," supporting the "efforts of the UN Security Council to end the violation of international law and threat to international peace," and prescribing specific civil and criminal penalties for violation of the US sanctions.[82] But the statute also provided, for the first time, that the President "shall consult with the Congress with respect to current and anticipated events regarding the international crisis caused by Iraq's invasion of Kuwait, including with respect to United States actions."[83] Further, Congress provided that the President "shall continue to impose the trade embargo and other economic sanctions,"[84] and that he shall not provide any foreign assistance to any country that is not in compliance with the Security Council sanctions against Iraq, unless he determines and certifies to Congress that such assistance is in the national interest or will directly benefit the needy people of that country.[85]

As debates raged throughout the fall of 1990 in the United Nations, in the United States, and in Europe and the Middle East about whether sanctions would work and how long one could wait to see, the United States deployed several hundred thousand troops in the Gulf area, but did not order them into action. At the same time, many of the partners of the United States in the coalition supporting economic sanctions made clear that they would not support any offensive military action against Iraq unless expressly authorized by the Security Council. Almost four months after the invasion, the Security Council did so, subject to "one final opportunity" for Iraq to avoid war. The

81 Letter from the President to Congressional Leaders Reporting on the National Emergency with Respect to Iraq, 11 February 1991, 27 Weekly Comp. Pres. Docs. 158 (1991).

82 Iraq Sanctions Act of 1990, 101 Pub. L. 513, Title V, §586-586j, 104 Stat. 2047.

83 Id. §586b.

84 Id. §586c(a).

85 Id. §586d(a). Subsection (b) adds an authorization (not a requirement) to the President to prohibit importation into the United States of all products of any foreign country that has not prohibited imports of products of Iraq into its territory or exports of its products to Iraq. So far as is known, this secondary boycott authority has not been used in implementation of sanctions against Iraq or other sanctions implementing UN resolutions.

Council authorized Member States "to use all necessary means" to uphold and implement the resolutions and to restore international peace and security, unless Iraq on or before January 15, 1991 fully implemented all the prior resolutions demanding complete withdrawal from Kuwait.[86]

The US administration took the position that this was all the authority that it needed to commit military forces to the liberation of Kuwait. Some members of Congress rejected the proposition that the Security Council could confer such authority on the President without the consent of Congress, because it is Congress that has the power to declare war under the United States Constitution. A law suit seeking to enjoin the President from initiating an attack against Iraq without first obtaining authorization from Congress was unsuccessful on the grounds that it was not ripe for decision,[87] but both the suit and widespread debate throughout the United States led President George Bush to conclude that relying on the UN resolution and his inherent powers as Commander-in-Chief would not suffice – at least as a political matter.[88]

Reluctantly, the President asked the Congress to adopt a resolution stating that "Congress supports the use of all means to implement UN Security Council Resolution 678." After much debate, Congress adopted a joint resolution substantially in accord with the President's request, but by a close vote, and subject to a requirement that the President issue a determination that all appropriate diplomatic and other peaceful means had been used to obtain compliance by Iraq with the Security Council resolutions and that "those efforts have not been and would not be successful in obtaining such compliance."[89] Passage of the resolution came on January 14, 1991, one day before the deadline set by the Security Council for withdrawal by Iraqi forces from Kuwait. Two days later the United States and allied forces began an air war against Iraq, bombing Baghdad and targets in Kuwait.

The military campaign need not be described here – six weeks of bombing, followed by six days of ground offensive. The aftermath of the campaign, however, focused again on economic sanctions.

By Resolution 687, adopted by the Security Council a month after hostilities ceased (plus several follow-up resolutions), an elaborate program of sanctions was created, including limitations on Iraq's ability to produce and sell oil, requirements that Iraq contribute to a UN Gulf War Compensation Fund, and later UN supervision of the purchase and distribution of food and medicine in Iraq under an Oil for Food Program, all linked to compliance by Iraq with a variety of conditions.[90] Among the conditions, as

86 Security Council Res. 678 of 29 November, 1990. The vote was 12-2, with China abstaining, and Cuba and Yemen opposed.

87 *Dellums v. Bush*, 752 F. Supp. 1141 D.D.C. (13 December 1990).

88 Note that the Security Council had *authorized*, not *mandated* the use of force, and the United Nations Participation Act covered only economic and diplomatic action, not the use of force.

89 Pub. L. 102-1 (H.J. Res. 77), 14 January 1991. The vote was 52-47 in the Senate, 250-183 in the House of Representatives.

90 Security Council Res. 687 of 3 April 1991 was followed by Res. 689, 692, 705, 706, 707, 712 (all in 1991); 778 in 1992; 806 and 833 in 1993; 986 in 1995; 1060 in 1996; and 1115 and 1134 in 1997, all concerned in part with the implementation and to some extent modifications of sanctions, and incidents in which the government of Iraq impeded in some way the disarma-

became critical in 2002-03, were agreements by Iraq not to acquire or develop nuclear weapons, to destroy all chemical and biological weapons and related facilities, and to eliminate ballistic missiles with a range in excess of 150 kilometers.[91]

Tracing the ups and downs of Iraqi compliance or non-compliance with the sanctions and verification program over more than a decade since the cease-fire resolutions of 1991 would require a major diversion from the theme of this chapter. Suffice it to say here that the United States at all times pressed for maximum enforcement of the sanctions.[92] In particular, the US Navy regularly patrolled the Persian Gulf to enforce the embargo against oil exported in violation of the UN restrictions. When an illegal cargo was seized, it would be sold, the ship would be put up for auction, and the proceeds would be turned over to the UN compensation fund.

As the sanctions against Iraq remained in place for over a decade, critics, including at various times at least two member states of the Security Council (France and Russia), urged termination or substantial modification of the sanctions, on the ground that they had failed to bring down the government of Saddam Hussein but had caused massive damage to the civilian population in Iraq, particularly to children deprived of food and medicines. The United States, however, maintained the position that the civilian suffering was attributable to the Iraqi government, and that relaxing sanctions would be rewarding the cruel actions of that government.[93]

Eventually in May 2002 the Security Council revised the program of sanctions against Iraq to concentrate on so-called "smart sanctions," i.e., sanctions designed more explicitly to target the regime, while providing for the civilian needs of the Iraqi people.[94] While sales of oil from Iraq would remain under control of the UN, and a portion of the proceeds would continue to be placed in the Compensation Fund to pay reparations of the Gulf War, the procedure for reviewing purchases made by Iraq was simplified and the Goods Review List was reduced and focused more sharply on products with military uses.

---

ment and inspection functions of UN missions operating in Iraq pursuant to the cease-fire conditions laid down in Resolution 687.

91 "Agreement" by Iraq may be questioned. The government did, however, formally notify the Secretary General and the Security Council of its acceptance of the provisions of Resolution 687, as required by paragraph 33 of that resolution.

92 President George Bush revoked the executive orders mandating the trade embargo against Kuwait, Executive Order 12271, of 25 July 1991, 56 Fed. Reg. 35993 (1991). The executive orders and implementing regulations directed against Iraq, however, remained in place. On 23 October 1992, the President authorized the transfer of certain Iraqi government assets being held by domestic financial institutions to the U.N. Compensation Fund. Executive Order 12817 of 23 October 1992, 57 Fed. Reg. 48433 (1992).

93 See, e.g., F. Gregory Gause III, "Getting It Backward on Iraq," 78 *Foreign Affairs* No. 3, p. 54 (May/June 1999). The article quotes, *inter alia*, the U.S. Secretary of State, Madeleine K. Albright, saying in May 1998:

> ...the fact that Iraqi children are dying is not the fault of the United States, but of Saddam Hussein...[I]t is ridiculous for the United States to be blamed for the dictatorial and cruel, barbaric ways that Saddam Hussein treats his people.

94 Security Council Res. 1409 of 14 May 2002.

Resolution 1409, whatever its ultimate effects might have been, appeared to end two years of controversy between the United States and Great Britain on one side, France and Russia on the other, concerning the scope and enforcement of the sanctions. As the United States, joined by Great Britain, sought to persuade the international community in the fall of 2002 that Saddam Hussein posed an imminent threat to use weapons of mass destruction, the positions shifted. France and Russia, previously critical of the sanctions, now favored relying on continuance of the sanctions (as modified) as pressure on the Iraqi regime to admit the UN weapons inspectors who had been expelled in 1998. The United States administration, on the other hand, concluded that the effect of sanctions would be too slow in view of the "imminent threat", and that even if Saddam Hussein readmitted the UN inspectors – as he did in late November 2002 – their findings could not be relied on.

As in the fall of 1990, the United States assembled a large military force in the Persian Gulf area in the fall of 2002, even as debates about the next steps were going on in the United States Congress and the UN Security Council. In September, President George W. Bush addressed the UN General Assembly in a forceful speech, calling upon the Security Council to "meet our common challenge":

> We will work with the Security Council for the necessary resolutions. But the purposes of the United States should not be doubted. The Security Council resolutions will be enforced, and the just demands of peace and security will be met, or action will be unavoidable, and a regime that has lost its legitimacy will also lose its power.[95]

On 11 October 2002, the U.S. Congress passed a Joint Resolution authorizing the President to use the Armed Forces of the United States "as he determines to be necessary and appropriate" in order to

(1) defend the national security of the United States against the continuing threat posed by Iraq; and
(2) enforce all relevant United Nations Security Council resolutions regarding Iraq.[96]

Passage of the Joint Resolution came only after considerable debate, and Congress insisted on inserting a provision supporting the efforts by the President to:

(1) strictly enforce through the United Nations Security Council all relevant Security Council resolutions applicable to Iraq and encourag[ing] him in those efforts; and
(2) obtain prompt and decisive action by the Security Council to ensure that Iraq abandons its strategy of delay, evasion and noncompliance and promptly and strictly complies with all relevant Security Council resolutions regarding Iraq.[97]

Three weeks later, as the world knows, the Security Council unanimously adopted Resolution 1441, containing detailed instructions and authorities for the UN weapons inspectors (UNMOVIC and IAEA) and demands for compliance by Iraq with the

95 UN Doc. A/57/PV.2 (12 September 2002), p. 6 at 9.

96 Pub. L. 107-243 (16 October 2002), para. 3.

97 *Ibid.*, para. 2.

requirements of the inspection teams.[98] No further sanctions were adopted in Resolution 1441, but the Security Council confirmed that it was acting under Chapter VII of the UN Charter, and in the last operative paragraph, the Council recalled in that context

> that the Council has repeatedly warned Iraq that it will face serious consequences as a result of its continued violations of its obligations.

Whatever one thinks of the legal basis or the factual basis for the American-led invasion – both beyond the scope of this chapter – there can be no doubt that the prediction in the last paragraph of Resolution 1441 came true. Serious consequences followed: sanctions as the middle way between business as usual and war, though they had held for twelve years, in the end proved inadequate.

b. Haiti (1991-94)[99]

On 29-30 September 1991, a military coup overthrew President Jean-Bertrand Aristide, who had been inaugurated in February of the same year following an election in which he had received 67 percent of the vote. Aristide was permitted to leave the country, and first from Venezuela and later from the United States he mobilized the international community in his favor and against the military and police leaders who had taken over the government.

President George Bush almost immediately declared a national emergency under IEEPA, blocked all assets of Haiti, its national bank, and other Haitian entities within the jurisdiction of the United States, including overseas branches of US persons, and prohibited virtually all financial transactions with Haiti.[100] An *ad hoc* meeting of Foreign Ministers of the OAS sent a special mission to Haiti, and when that failed to change the situation, adopted a resolution on October 8, 1991,[101] urging member states to proceed immediately to freeze the assets of the Haitian state, as the United States had already done on its own, and to impose a trade embargo on Haiti, which the United States promptly did as well.[102] The UN General Assembly also adopted resolutions concerned

98 Security Council Res. 1441, 8 November 2002.

99 For a more comprehensive account, addressing also the underlying political institutions, see David M. Malone, *Decision-Making in the UN Security Council: The Case of Haiti* (1998).

100 Exec. Order 12775, 4 October 1991, 56 Fed. Reg. 12775 (1991). Note that under IEEPA, this action required the proclamation of a national emergency, and President Bush duly issued the required proclamation. Thus the legislative effort in the 1970s to restrain Presidential power by requiring the proclamation of a national emergency was shown – not for the first time – to have been quite ineffective, requiring simply a paragraph in an executive order and periodic reports, not a determination importing gravity and a threat to the United States. Needless to say, no one regarded the events in Haiti, however tragic for that unhappy country, to constitute a real threat to the security of the United States.

101 OAS-MRE Res. 2/91, 8 October 1991.

102 President Bush issued a second Executive Order, No. 12779 of 28 October 1991, 56 Fed. Reg. 55975 (1991) taking account of the action of the OAS, and adding a trade embargo to the sanctions previously ordered.

with Haiti, sponsoring various missions to Haiti and endorsing the sanctions imposed pursuant to OAS resolutions.[103]

The Security Council did not become actively involved in the Haiti question until June 1993, apparently on the basis that the situation fell within the purview of the OAS in accordance with Chapter VIII of the UN Charter. On 16 June 1993, the Security Council, acting under Chapter VII, adopted a resolution jointly sponsored by France, the United States, and Venezuela, ordering selective mandatory sanctions against Haiti, unless the Security General, within a week, reported that as a result of negotiations conducted by the Special Envoy of the UN and the OAS the imposition of such measures is not warranted.[104] The President of the Security Council announced that he had been asked to state that the resolution was warranted by the "unique and exceptional situation" in Haiti, and should not be regarded as a precedent. President Clinton promptly issued an Executive Order essentially restating the restrictions in the earlier executive orders and implementing regulations, but reciting §5 of the UN Participation Act and Security Council Resolution 841 as additional authorities for his action.[105]

On 3 July 1993, President Aristide and General Raoul Cedras, the leader of the *de facto* regime in Haiti, entered into the so-called Governors Island Agreement, looking to the resignation of General Cedras and the other members of the Junta, and to the return of President Aristide. The UN Secretary General recommended that the sanctions imposed pursuant to the order of the Security Council be suspended when undertakings in accordance with the Governors Island Agreement reached a certain stage. On 27 August 1993, the Security Council (as well as the OAS) called on Member States to suspend but not terminate sanctions against Haiti.[106] Accordingly, the United States prospectively suspended trade and financial sanctions against Haiti, but continued to keep specified Haitian assets blocked.[107]

On 11 October 1993, a UN Mission to Haiti consisting of 50 Canadian police and 30 American soldiers arrived in Haiti by ship, but was not permitted to land. President Clinton called for reimposition of sanctions, and on October 13, the Security Council adopted a resolution terminating the suspension ordered in Resolution 861 and reinstating the sanctions mandated in Resolution 841.[108] On October 18, President Clinton issued a new executive order, reinstating the earlier US sanctions and adding blocking of assets of persons "who have contributed to the obstruction of the implementation of the Security Council Resolutions, the Governors Island Agreement, or the activities of the UN mission in Haiti," as well as persons who have "perpetuated or contributed to the violence in Haiti."[109]

103 See e.g., G.A. Res 46/7 of 11 October 1991; 47/20A of 24 November 1992.

104 Security Council Res. 841 of 16 June 1993.

105 Exec. Order 12853 of 30 June 1993, 58 Fed. Reg. 35843 (1993).

106 Security Council Res. 861 of 27 August 1993.

107 Haitian Transaction Regulations Amendment eff. 31 August 1993, 31 C.F.R. Part 580, 58 Fed. Reg. 46540 (1993).

108 Security Council Res. 873 of 13 October 1993.

109 Executive Order 12872 of 18 October 1993, 58 Fed. Reg. 54029 (1993), implemented by

Meanwhile, following the assassination of Haiti's minister of justice, first Canada and then the United States, withdrew their personnel from the UN mission in Haiti.[110] But on American initiative, the Security Council adopted a resolution under Chapter VII and VIII

> calling upon all member states... to use such measures... as may be necessary under the authority of the Security Council to insure implementation of the [prior sanctions resolutions]... and in particular to halt inward shipping as necessary...

in other words, to impose a naval blockade.[111] Of course the main burden fell on the United States, but Argentina, Canada, France, and the Netherlands contributed to the blockade.

One more round of sanctions was effected in May 1994, after the octogenarian President of the Supreme Court of Haiti was installed by the military leaders as President of the Republic. The Security Council and the OAS condemned the action, and the Security Council now adopted Comprehensive Mandatory Sanctions,[112] followed by four more US executive orders.[113]

Eventually, in the fall of 1994 the Haitian crisis was resolved with the departure of the leaders of the coup, as a multinational force assembled by the United States was apparently ready to invade, while former President Carter was on the island negotiating with the *de facto* regime for a safe withdrawal from the island. On September 26, the United States suspended all unilateral sanctions against Haiti, and three days later, the Security Council terminated the sanctions set out in its sanctions resolutions of 1993 and 1994.[114] The United States Haitian Transaction Regulations were suspended (except for continued blocking of assets of the participants in the coup d'état) on October 6, 1994,[115] and President Clinton issued an executive order terminating the National Emergency with respect to Haiti on October 14, 1994, the day before President Aristide returned to Haiti.[116] On the following day the Security Council adopted one more resolution, welcoming the lifting of sanctions now that President Aristide had returned to his country.[117]

---

amendment to Haitian Transaction Regulations, 31 C.F.R. Part 580, 19 October 1993, 58 Fed. Reg. 54024 (1993).

110 Note that this took place just after 18 U.S. soldiers had been killed in Mogadishu, Somalia on another UN mission.

111 Security Council Res. 873 of 16 October 1993. The Resolution recited that the Council was acting under Chapter VII and Chapter VIII.

112 Security Council Res. 917 of 6 May 1994.

113 Exec. Order 12914 of 7 May 1994, 59 Fed. Reg. 24339 (1994); Exec. Order 12917 of 21 May 1994, 59 Fed. Reg. 26925 (1994); Exec. Order 12920 of 10 June 1994, 59 Fed. Reg. 30501 (1994); Exec. Order 12922 of 22 June 1994, 59 Fed. Reg. 32645 (1994).

114 Security Council Res. 944 of 29 September 1994.

115 59 Fed. Reg. 51066 (1994).

116 Exec. Order 12932 of 14 October 1994, 59 Fed. Reg. 52403 (1994).

117 Security Council Res. 948 of 15 October 1994.

Some observers have pointed to the Haiti affair as evidence of the inadequacy of economic sanctions, as contrasted with the threat or actual use of military force. For present purposes, we use this narrative only to illustrate the interaction between the United States and the UN Security Council in circumstances where the United States is the leader, but seeks support from the UN and the relevant regional organization as well.

c. Diamonds and arms in Africa

Angola (1998-)

Despite efforts by the United Nations and the Organization for African Unity (OAU) for many years, civil war between the government of the People's Republic of Angola and the National Union for the Total Independence of Angola (UNITA) went on almost continuously since the independence of Angola in 1975. On September 15, 1993, following rejection by UNITA of a UN-monitored election, the Security Council, acting under Chapter VII of the UN Charter (but not expressly under Article 41), decided that unless an effective cease-fire had been established within ten days, "all states shall prevent the sale or supply by their nationals or from their territories... of arms and related material... as well as petroleum and petroleum products," other than through named points of entry for supply to the government of Angola.[118] The Council also expressed its readiness to consider imposition of further measures against UNITA, including trade measures and restrictions on travel of UNITA personnel, unless an effective cease-fire had been established by November 1, 1993.[119]

Ten days passed without an effective cease-fire, and on the eleventh day President Clinton issued an Executive Order stating that UNITA's continued military actions including attacks on United Nations personnel seeking to provide humanitarian assistance, refusal to accept the results of the election, and failing to abide by the *Acordos de Paz* signed earlier, constituted "an unusual and extraordinary threat to the foreign policy of the United States" (tracking the text of IEEPA). Accordingly, the President declared a national emergency to deal with that threat, and ordered an immediate embargo on sale or supply of arms and of petroleum and products of petroleum as called for by the Security Council.[120]

Peace talks between the government of Angola and UNITA began in November 1993 and a disarmament and peace protocol – the Lusaka Protocol – was signed in 1994, but UNITA did not disarm and the civil war continued. Evidently, UNITA found means to finance its campaign and to purchase arms and fuel; a major source both of finance and of access to weapons was the trade in diamonds. After tightening sanctions against UNITA in 1997 by imposing prohibitions on travel,[121] the Security Council in the following year not only decided that all States (except Angola) shall freeze assets of UNITA and its senior officials in their territories, but, for the first time, decided that all states

118 Security Council Res. 864 of 15 September 1993, para. 17.

119 *Ibid.* para. 26.

120 Executive Order 12865 of 26 September 1993, 58 Fed. Reg. 51005 (1993).

121 Security Council Res. 1127 of 28 August 1997.

"shall take the necessary measures" to prohibit the direct or indirect import from Angola of all diamonds not controlled through a certificate of origin issued by the Angolan government.[122] Again, the United States complied, though with some delay. President Clinton issued another Executive Order in August 1998,[123] followed a year later by implementing regulations, retroactive to the date of the Executive Order.[124] Under the regulations, importation of diamonds from Angola directly or indirectly would require a certificate of origin satisfactory to the customs inspector issued by the recognized government of Angola. Importers were required to keep the certificate of origin on file for five years.

Sierra Leone, Liberia, and the Revolutionary United Front (RUF) (1999-)

In July 1999, after more than eight years of conflict, the government of Sierra Leone and the Revolutionary United Front, a rebel group operating in Sierra Leone and neighboring Liberia signed the so-called Lomé Peace Agreement, negotiated with the help of the United Nations and the Economic Community of West African States (ECOWAS). The Security Council had previously imposed travel restrictions and an arms and petroleum embargo against Sierra Leone while it was under control of a military junta.[125] Those sanctions had been terminated when the elected government returned to power in the spring of 1998, and had been replaced by prohibition on supply of arms and petroleum to non-government forces in Sierra Leone.[126] Following the Lomé Agreement, the Security Council established a United Nations Mission in Sierra Leone (UNSAMIL) to help oversee implementation of the Lomé Agreement.[127]

In the event, fighting continued in Sierra Leone, also involving combatants from neighboring Liberia. Each day brought reports of taking of hostages, including personnel from UNSAMIL and other UN missions, and of continuing atrocities by the RUF against civilians and prisoners. Clearly, the rebels were well armed, and it became evident, as it had been in Angola and Congo (Zaire) several years earlier, that diamonds were the means by which the rebels paid for arms and for their transport to combat areas.

On July 5, 2000, the Security Council, again acting under Chapter VII, adopted a resolution with respect to Sierra Leone similar to the resolution adopted two years earlier regarding diamonds from Angola.[128] All States were required to "take the necessary measures to prohibit the direct or indirect import of all rough diamonds from Sierra Leone to their territory," except if accompanied by a Certificate of Origin from the government. The Council also called for a Panel of Experts to advise on implementation of the prohibition, and such a committee was created, including a diamond expert from

122 Security Council Res. 1173 of 12 June 1998; Res. 1176 of 24 June 1998.

123 Executive Order 13098 of 19 August 1998, 63 Fed. Reg. 44771 (1998).

124 64 Fed. Reg. 43924, 12 August 1999, amending 31 C.F.R. Part 590, Angola (UNITA) Sanctions Regulations. See esp. 31 C.F.R. §§208, 306(c).

125 Security Council Res. 1132 of 8 October 1997.

126 Security Council Res. 1171 of 5 June 1998.

127 Security Council Res. 1276 of 22 October 1999.

128 Security Council Res. 1306 of 5 July 2000.

Canada, an arms trade expert from Belgium, a representative of Interpol, and a representative of the International Civil Aviation Organization (ICAO).[129] The Council also called for an exploratory hearing in New York to assess the role of diamonds in the Sierra Leone conflict, including not only interested governments, but representatives of the International Diamond Manufacturers Association, the World Federation of Diamond Bourses, the Diamond High Council and the De Beers organization.

As with other mandatory sanctions resolutions, the United States carried out the order of the Security Council with an Executive Order and implementing regulations, though in this instance with a delay of six months. On January 18, 2001, two days before he left office, President Clinton proclaimed yet another national emergency, and prohibited the importation, direct or indirect, of all rough diamonds from Sierra Leone, unless accompanied by a certificate of origin, issued by the government of Sierra Leone.[130]

The UN Panel of Experts reported that officials of the government of Liberia were actively supporting the Revolutionary United Front in Liberia through the illicit diamond trade. In response, the Security Council on March 7, 2001 adopted a resolution demanding that Liberia immediately cease its support for the RUF. Further, the resolution required all states to prevent the direct or indirect import of rough diamonds from Liberia, whether or not such diamonds originated in Liberia. The resolution was to take effect two months after the date of its adoption, unless the Security Council determined prior to that date that Liberia had ceased supporting the RUF.[131] The Security Council did not make such a determination, and as soon as the deadline expired, President George W. Bush expanded President Clinton's executive order to cover importation of rough diamonds from Liberia as well.[132]

Enforcement

Enforcement of embargoes against rebel-controlled diamond trade has been difficult, because even in rough form it is hard to trace the origin of diamonds, and once they are cut and polished, there appears to be no practicable way to determine their origin. The United States, with the longest experience in enforcing economic sanctions of various kinds, was not in good position to enforce the conflict diamond embargoes, because while it accounts for about 45 percent of the market for finished diamonds, it accounts for only four percent of the market for uncut stones.[133] Thus even though the UN resolutions and the American regulations spoke of imports from Angola, Sierra Leone and Liberia *directly or indirectly*, interdiction of diamonds of rebel-controlled territories in Africa was not comparable to, for instance, interdiction of cigars made in Mexico containing Cuban leaf, or interdiction (formerly) of brushes from Hong Kong containing

129 See Letter of 26 December 2000 from Chairman of the Security Council Committee concerning Sierra Leone, S/2000/1238.

130 Executive Order 13194 of 18 January 2001, 66 Fed. Reg. 7389 (2001).

131 Security Council Res. 1343 of 7 March 2001.

132 Executive Order 13213 of 22 May 2001, 66 Fed. Reg. 28829 (2001). The implementing regulations, 31 C.F.R. Part 591, were issued on 6 February 2002, 67 Fed. Reg. 5472 (2002).

133 The principal centers for cutting and polishing diamonds are in Antwerp, Tel Aviv, and London, with smaller facilities in South Africa and The Netherlands.

bristles from Mainland China.

Nevertheless the US Bureau of Customs has employed intelligence sources and informers to seek out prohibited diamonds, and has reported at least two instances in which the embargo has been enforced. On 31 December 2001, U.S. customs inspectors at Baltimore-Washington International Airport seized 37 diamonds from a passenger who had arrived on an international flight. A search of the passenger's luggage revealed documents suggesting that he might be carrying diamonds, and when he was questioned, the passenger removed a package from his pocket containing diamonds which were detained for formal customs entry. Since the diamonds contained no accompanying certificate from the government of Sierra Leone, the diamonds were seized by Customs. In another instance at the same airport a few days later, an arriving passenger declared his diamonds to Customs and tendered a certificate of origin, but US customs inspectors noticed inconsistencies in the document, leading them to believe that it was fraudulent. Accordingly, Customs seized both the stones and the accompanying documents.[134]

More significant in the long run may be what became known as the "Kimberly Process", after the city in South Africa in which an international conference on conflict diamonds was held in May 2000. The participants, including the United States, the United Kingdom, Belgium, African diamond producers, the De Beers organization, and others, reached agreement in principle on four key points: (1) the need to establish an international certification scheme for all diamonds; (2) the need for a formal code of conduct on practices in the diamond industry; (3) the need for an independent monitoring agency to oversee the certification scheme and the code of conduct; and (4) the establishment of a working group to implement the certification scheme and the code of conduct.

The Kimberly Process was endorsed in December 2000 by the UN General Assembly,[135] and six meetings, involving more than 35 governments as well as representatives of the diamond industry, took place in 2001. The system, which became effective on 1 January 2003, calls for each shipment of rough diamonds, regardless of origin, to be accompanied by a certificate at each point of exportation, validated by the country of export and checked by the country of import. Since, as noted above, the United States is only a minor importer of rough diamonds, the success of the Kimberly system in reducing trade in conflict diamonds, if it is put into effect, does not depend on the United States, but on the principal European importers, plus commitment on the part of exporting countries to avoiding all forms of smuggling in the diamond industry.[136] It is fair to add that since

134 These two incidents were reported in Testimony of Timothy Skud, Acting Deputy assistant Secretary, Regulatory, Tariff and Trade Enforcement, U.S. Department of the Treasury, before the Senate Committee on Governmental Affairs, 13 February 2001.

135 G.A. Res. 55/56 of 1 December 2000.

136 In 2001 the U.S. House of Representatives passed a bill that would authorize (but not require) the President to prohibit importation of rough diamonds from any country that does not take effective measures to stop the trade in conflict diamonds. Further, the bill would authorize the President to prohibit entry of polished diamonds and jewelry containing such diamonds upon evidence that the polished diamonds were produced with conflict diamonds. H.R. 2722, 107th Cong. 1st Sess. (2001). As of year-end 2003, the proposed legislation was pending in the Senate, but had not been adopted.

the events of September 11, 2001, and world-wide pursuance of terrorists, there has been a sharpened focus on trade in diamonds – not only from the named African countries – because diamonds can be used to transfer money when normal financial channels are closed to money launderers and terrorists. It may well be that the often indifferent response to sanctions, including sanctions mandated by the UN Security Council, will change as a result.

V. Afghanistan, the Taliban and 11 September 2001

A report concerning implementation by the United States of sanctions recommended or mandated by the UN Security Council need not, strictly speaking, address the subject of the Taliban and the response to 11 September because the United States regularly took action ahead of or beyond the requirements of the Security Council, rather than implementation of Security Council resolutions that it itself sponsored. Nevertheless, this paper would seem incomplete without at least some account of the interplay between the United States and the United Nations in response to the threat of international terrorism. It turns out that, well before 11 September 2001, there was much more activity both by the United States and by the United Nations in connection with terrorism and Al Qaida than most people were aware of.

On 7 August 1998, two almost simultaneous acts of terrorism took place at United States embassies in Nairobi, Kenya and Dar-es-Salaam, Tanzania, with large loss of life. The Security Council promptly adopted a resolution strongly condemning the attacks, and calling upon all States to adopt, "in accordance with international law and as a matter of priority, effective and practical measures for security cooperation, for the prevention of such acts of terrorism, and for the prosecution and punishment of their perpetrators."[137] However, the Resolution did not recite that the Council was acting under Chapter VII. No mention was made of sanctions, and no individual or group was mentioned as having responsibility for the terrorist acts.[138]

On 28 August 1998, the United States, which had previously indicted Usama Bin Laden for bombings of the World Trade Center in New York in 1993 as well as other terrorist acts, issued an indictment against him for the attacks against the African embassies, on the basis of the testimony of two suspects brought to New York from Kenya.[139] In the course of fall 1998 and spring 1999 the U.S. government sought the assistance of European and African nations in investigation of the Bin Laden/Al-Qaida network, with some successes, but evidently these efforts did not break up the network or capture its leaders. On 4 July 1999, President Clinton issued an Executive Order under IEEPA declaring a national emergency, blocking all property and interests of the Taliban in the United States, and prohibiting all transactions with the Taliban except for

137 Security Council Res. 1189 of 13 August 1998.

138 Two weeks later the Security Council adopted a Resolution expressing concern at the continuing presence of terrorists in Afghanistan and condemning attacks on UN personnel in Taliban-held territories of Afghanistan, but made no connection between those attacks and the attacks in Kenya and Tanzania. Security Council Res. 1193 of 28 August 1998.

139 See *New York Times*, 29 August 1998, p. A-4.

food and medicines, on the ground that Taliban had allowed territory under its control in Afghanistan to be used as a safe haven and base of operations for Usama Bin Laden and the Al-Qaida organization.[140]

Three months later the Security Council, "deploring the fact that the Taliban continues to provide safe haven to Usama bin Laden and to allow him ...to operate a network of terrorist training camps from Taliban-controlled territory...," and noting the indictment of bin Laden by the United States, adopted a mandatory sanctions resolution under Chapter VII of the Charter. All States were required to prohibit flights to or from Taliban-controlled territory unless approved in advance by a new Committee to be established, and States were required to freeze funds controlled directly or indirectly by the Taliban and to prevent financial resources from being made available by their nationals by any persons within their territory.[141] Thus essentially the Security Council made mandatory for all states what the United States had already ordered for its territory and its nationals, including branches (but not subsidiaries) of its corporations. The sanctions were to continue until the Taliban turned over bin Laden to appropriate authorities in a country where he has been indicted.[142] In a resolution adopted at year-end 2000, also pursuant to Chapter VII, the Council demanded that the Taliban comply with the 1999 resolution, and added an arms embargo to the existing sanctions.[143] Further, the Council ordered that all funds and other financial assets of Usama bin Laden and his associates and the Al-Qaida organization be frozen without delay. Again, the United States had already taken all the measures required by the Security Council. When the formal regulations implementing the President's executive order were issued in January 2001, the authority cited was IEEPA and Executive Order 13129 of July 1999, "consistent with Security Council Resolution 1267."[144]

When the World Trade Center and the Pentagon were struck on 11 September 2001, the first reaction of the Security Council was an expression of shock and condemnation, plus "readiness to take all necessary steps to respond to the terrorist attacks ... and to combat all forms of terrorism."[145] For his part, President Bush almost immediately proclaimed a new state of national emergency by reason of the terrorist attacks.[146] On 23 September 2001, he issued a new Executive Order blocking property of and prohibiting transactions with a list of foreign individuals and organizations, including Al-Qaida/Islamic Army, Usama bin Laden, and some 25 other individuals and organiza-

140 Exec. Order 13129 of 4 July 1999, 64 Fed. Reg. 36750 (1999). Note that neither the United States nor all but three member states of the UN or the UN itself had recognized the Taliban as the government of Afghanistan. Thus the sanctions were not at this time directed at Afghanistan, but at the Taliban and territory under its control.

141 Security Council Res. 1267 of 15 October 1999.

142 See also a Statement by the President of the Security Council on behalf of the Council of 22 October 1999, S/PRST/1999/29.

143 Security Council Res. 1333 of 19 December 2000.

144 Taliban (Afghanistan) Sanctions Regulations, 31 C.F.R. Part 545, issued on 11 January 2001, 66 Fed. Reg. 2726 (2001).

145 Security Council Res. 1368 of 12 September 2001.

146 Proclamation 7463 of 14 September 2001, 64 Fed. Reg. 48199 (2001).

tions determined to have committed, or to pose a significant risk of committing, acts of terrorism against the United States.[147] Three days later, on initiative of the United States, the Security Council acting under Chapter VII, unanimously adopted Resolution 1373 requiring all States to prevent and suppress the financing of terrorist acts, to criminalize the provision of funds by their nationals or in their territories for the purpose of terrorist acts, and assisting one another in investigations and prosecutions relating to terrorist acts.[148] The resolution also created yet another committee of the Security Council, to monitor implementation of the resolution.[149]

The Counter-Terrorism Committee (CTC), under the chairmanship of the British Ambassador to the UN, set out not only to monitor, but to encourage implementation of the counter-terrorism program, and to offer technical advice where needed. The Committee circulated a detailed questionnaire on implementation of the program, and 155 States responded, an unprecedented response for a UN operation.[150] The United States replied not only by quoting President Bush to the effect that:

> We will direct every resource at our command ...,

but by declaring that the United States is ready to provide technical assistance to help those states who lack the expertise and resources to achieve full implementation.[151] The American report to the CTC listed numerous and continuing additions to the list of individuals and organizations linked to terrorist activity and therefore subject to the sanctions previously announced. Also, the United States reported coordinating – and generally leading – efforts with the International Civil Aviation Organization (ICAO), the IMF, a special Financial Action Task Force under the auspices of the Group of Seven, and other formal and informal international organizations.

It could not quite be said that the United States was implementing Security Council mandates in the campaign against terrorism post September 11. But clearly the United States saw the value of collaborating through the Security Council with other states, and it has sought to build on paragraph 4 of Resolution 1373 to address international drug trafficking, money laundering, nuclear proliferation, and the threat of chemical/biological weapons – all in the context of international terrorism.

VI. Conclusions

Putting together the four major statutes discussed above, the unique episode of the Byrd Amendment, and the experience of American economic sanctions with and without the

147 Executive Order 13224 of 23 September 2001, 66 Fed. Reg. 49079 (2001).

148 Security Council Res. 1373 of 28 September 2001.

149 Subsequent Security Council Resolutions essentially restated and reaffirmed Resolution 1373. See Security Council resolutions 1377 of 12 November 2001; 1390 of 16 January 2002.

150 See Presentation by Ambassador Greenstock (U.K.), Chairman of the Counter-Terrorism Committee, Vienna, 3-4 June 2002, UN Doc./SC/Committee 1373.

151 See Report from United States to Chairman, Counter-Terrorism Committee, S/2001/1220, 21 December 2001.

United Nations, one may reach the following conclusions:

1) The United States executive branch has very broad authority to impose economic sanctions unilaterally. While Congress could in theory, curb these authorities, in practice efforts to do so have failed, either in Congress itself, or in implementation by successive administrations.[152]
2) Once "national security" is recited in a measure of economic sanction or control, the courts have shown extreme deference to actions of the executive branch. Concepts of "taking," of "due process," of separation of powers, while not completely absent, seem to have different meanings in the economic sanctions context from their meanings in domestic controversies.
3) A mandatory sanction ordered by the Security Council under Article 39 and 41 of the Charter contains both an obligation and an authority for the United States to carry it out. A recommendation of the Security Council does not bring the UN Participation Act into effect, but may or may not be implemented pursuant to other authorities. Generally, a non-mandatory call for export controls can be implemented without the need to proclaim a national emergency; implementation of a non-mandatory call for import or financial controls requires either special legislation or proclamation of a national emergency, but such a proclamation is no longer perceived as a grave act or one linked to an actual threat to the United States.
4) The prevailing rule in the United States is that a treaty (or its equivalent) and a statute stand on an equal plane; that their texts are to be construed so as to avoid a conflict between them if that is fairly possible; and that if a conflict is unavoidable, the instrument that is later in time will prevail.[153] The leading court decision (though not by the Supreme Court) has held that a binding resolution of the UN Security Council is equivalent for this purpose to a treaty, so that breach of such a resolution is a violation, but probably is not curable by a court. An attempt by Congress to resist implementation of a mandatory sanction resolution by the Security Council has occurred only once, in unusual circumstances unlikely to occur again.

152 For instance, the change in 1969 in the title of the Export Control Act to Export Administration Act was designed to loosen the controls, and to narrow the understanding of "national security". In practice, while the regulations became more detailed, administration of the regulations remained roughly the same. See, e.g., A Lowenfeld, *Trade Controls for Political Ends* (2nd ed. 1983), pp. 132-36, 223-33. The changes that were made over time – fewer items on the positive control list, easier policy on granting licenses – reflected changing policies in the administration, not legislative restrictions.

153 See American Law Institute, *Restatement (Third) of the Foreign Relations Law of the United States*, §§114, 115 and comments and Reporters' Notes thereto (1987). Of course the statement in the text leaves open the question of the breach of an international obligation. Compliance with domestic law cannot serve as a defense to breach of an international obligation, and in theory, the United States remained liable to its treaty partners under Article 25 of the Charter for violating a binding resolution of the Security Council. See, e.g., *Restatement* §115, Comment *b*, "International legal obligation continues." See also Vera Gowlland-Debbas, *Collective Responses to Illegal Acts in International Law* (1990), pp. 500-514.

5) When the United States has been the leader in seeking UN sanctions, as in the sanctions against Iraq in 1990, it has relied on the authority granted by the UN Participation Act as well as on authority granted by domestic statutes. When it has been reluctant, or content to follow other states, as in the sanctions against Rhodesia, the United States has relied only on the UN Participation Act, and accordingly has implemented sanctions only to the extent required by the pertinent Security Council resolution.
6) With the single exception of the Byrd Amendment in connection with sanctions against Rhodesia, the United States has always implemented mandatory UN sanctions, and indeed has usually taken the sanctions further than required by the resolution in question. Generally, the United States has been the driving force behind sanctions resolutions, and also the principal enforcer. On many occasions prior to the end of the Cold War, the United States was not able to secure approval from the Security Council for the sanctions it sought to impose, but imposed the sanctions anyway, sometimes jointly with its allies, at other times alone.

❄ ❄ ❄

Select Bibliography

Adler-Karlson, Gunnar, *Western Economic Warfare, 1947-67: A Case Study of Foreign Economic Policy* (Stockholm, Almquist & Wiksell, 1968).

Carter, Barry E., *International Economic Sanctions: Improving the Haphazard U.S. Legal Regime* (Cambridge/New York, Cambridge University Press, 1988).

Cortright, David and Lopez, George H., *The Sanctions Decade: Assessing UN Strategies in the 1990s* (Boulder, Colorado, Lynne Rienner, 2000).

Damrosch, Lori F. (ed.), *Enforcing Restraint: Collective Intervention in Internal Conflicts* (New York, Council on Foreign Relations, 1993).

De Mestral, A.L.C. and Gruchalla-Wesierski, T., *Extraterritorial Application of Export Control Legislation: Canada and the U.S.A.* (Dordrecht/Boston, Martinus Nijhoff, 1990).

Hufbauer, Gary Clyde and Schott, Jeffrey J., *Economic Sanctions Reconsidered: History and Current Policy* (Washington, D.C., Institute for International Economics, 1985).

Gowlland-Debbas, Vera, *Collective Responses to Illegal Acts in International Law: United Nations Action in the Question of Southern Rhodesia* (Dordrecht /Boston, Martinus Nijhoff, 1990).

Gowlland-Debbas, Vera (ed.), *United Sanctions and International Law* (The Hague/London/ Boston, Kluwer Law International, 2001).

Lowenfeld, Andreas F., *Trade Controls for Political Ends* (New York/San Francisco, Matthew Bender, 2nd ed, 1983).

Lowenfeld, Andreas F., "Trade Controls for Political Ends: Four Perspectives", 4 *Chicago Journal of International Law* (2003) 355.

Malloy, Michael P., *Economic Sanctions and U.S. Trade* (Boston, Little Brown, 1990).

Malloy, Michael P., *United States Economic Sanctions: Theory and Practice* (The Hague/London/Boston, Kluwer Law International, 2001).

Moyer, Homer E., Jr., and Mabry, Linda A., *Export Controls As Instruments of Foreign Policy: The History, Legal Issues and Policy Lesson of Three Recent Cases* (Washington, D.C., International Law Institute, 1985).

Preeg, Ernest H., *Feeling Good or Doing Good With Sanctions: Unilateral Economic Sanctions and the U.S. National Interest* (Washington, D.C., Center for Strategic and International Studies, 1999).

Rodman, Kenneth A., *Sanctions Beyond Borders: Multinational Corporations and U.S. Economic Strategies* (Lanham, Md./Oxford, Rowan & Littlefield, 2001).

18

CONCLUDING REMARKS

Vera Gowlland-Debbas

As was stated from the outset, this comparative study of the international legal implications of domestic mechanisms for implementing Security Council sanctions addressed three interrelated themes*.

The first, of a theoretical nature, related to the classic relationship between domestic and international law. It raised the question of whether implementation of Security Council resolutions poses problems which are in some way distinct from those arising from implementation of other conventional international law obligations and it underlined the contrast between the status of Security Council resolutions under international law and that accorded to them within each State's domestic legal order.

The second concerned the effectiveness of the decisions of the Security Council from the perspective of the compliance of implementing States. Effectiveness, it was pointed out, concerned here solely the effective *mise en œuvre* of the decisions of the Security Council by Member States within their national legal orders and the extent of conformity of this implementation with States' obligations under the Charter. The scope of the study did not purport to go beyond formal legal implementation. In this narrow sense, effectiveness was examined in terms of the availability and nature of the domestic mechanisms relied on and their ability to process the decisions of the Security Council in a speedy and comprehensive manner. It is evident however that in order to be complete, a comprehensive study of the effectiveness of sanctions implementation should go beyond an analysis of formal implementation, and take into account the political willingness and or/ability of States to give effect to the resolutions.

The third theme concerned the question of the legitimacy of Security Council resolutions, notably, but not exclusively, from the viewpoint of domestic legal systems. Legitimacy in this context was touched on from the perspective of the encroachment of Security Council decisions on constitutionally protected individual rights, and in relation to the role played by domestic courts in a possible review of Security Council decisions. But it is also a question of States' perceptions of the legitimacy – as opposed to the legal-

* This concluding chapter has in large part been drawn from a working-paper presented by Nicolas Angelet, and the comments and conclusions of a working group composed of Martin Bjorklund, Emilio Cárdenas, Per Cramér, Mariano Garcia-Rubio, Brigitte Stern, Alfred Soons, and Erik Suy, which met in Geneva for a brainstorming session.

Vera Gowlland-Debbas (ed.), National Implementation of UN Sanctions, *643-658.*

ity – of Security Council resolutions and of the authority of the Security Council itself within the framework of national implementation. Effectiveness and legitimacy are of course interrelated and sometimes in tension, for a perception of the lack of legitimacy of the Security Council may result in the weakening of States' resolve to implement.

This chapter offers some tentative conclusions on these three themes which have emerged in the course of this comparative study.

I. Domestic Implementation of Sanctions in Light of the Relationship between Domestic and International Law

This comparative study of national implementing mechanisms has shown that the quasi-constitutional nature of Security Council resolutions at the international level contrasts with the place and formal ranking given to these resolutions in domestic law.

Even the more recent national constitutions do not single out the decisions of the Security Council and when they refer to the decisions of international organisations this is usually for the purpose of transferring competences to supranational institutions. In most of the countries studied, Security Council mandatory resolutions are assimilated to non-self-executing conventional obligations and are therefore not treated in a manner distinct from other treaty obligations. This means that they are superseded by domestic constitutions, and even in some cases, other conventional obligations where these are accorded constitutional ranking, in particular, treaties protecting fundamental human rights. In addition, the domestic techniques that will be used to resolve conflicts between domestic law and Security Council resolutions are no different from those applied to conflicts between domestic and treaty law. This means that in certain cases the resolutions could be superseded by the domestic legislation later in time. In general, therefore, it may be said that despite the proliferation of sanctions, their widening scope, and the increasingly complex nature of their implementation, they are in general implemented no differently on the internal plane than other non self-executing treaty obligations.

This contrasts with the unique place occupied by Security Council resolutions at the international level: superior hierarchical ranking of Security Council decisions in relation to other international agreements (Article 103); and increasing perception at the international and regional levels (see, for example, decisions of the European Court of Justice) of Security Council decisions as aspects of public policy in fulfilment of community objectives.

But there is another paradox. The formal ranking in domestic law of Security Council resolutions, in turn, does not reflect the increasing intrusion of UN Security Council decisions into the domestic sphere, requiring adaptation of legislation and even of constitutions, as well as extraterritorial reach, and encroaching on constitutionally protected rights; this is particularly evident in respect of the more recent Security Council resolutions on combating the financing of terrorism.

Nor does the formal ranking of Security Council mandatory resolutions give the whole picture of their status within domestic law. Certain municipal law decisions suggest that Security Council resolutions can be applied by domestic courts in fact if not in law as self-executing in the sense that individuals in their business dealings could rely on these decisions before the courts notwithstanding the absence of implementing measures. Moreover, the perception of Security Council resolutions as part of international public policy is increasingly reflected in domestic courts. This may be seen in particular in the attitude of these courts to the two International Criminal Tribunals and this development may also be strengthening as a result of the perceived community interest in the combating of terrorism. Furthermore, in States which are members of the European Union, Security Council resolutions when implemented as EC Council Regulations will have a superior ranking as well as direct effect in domestic law.

Finally, it may be said that there has also been an evolution in the political will to implement such resolutions – from the initial dragging of feet at the time of sanctions against Southern Rhodesia, to the zeal with which some States are implementing Security Council resolutions in the framework of counter-terrorism.

While it can only be concluded that the traditional neat distinction between monist and dualist States is not of significant relevance in arriving at conclusions on the relationship between Security Council decisions and domestic law, the implementation of Security Council decisions by UN Member States illustrates an interesting evolution in the manner in which international law is being imported into domestic legal systems. As has been pointed out in an introductory chapter, recent studies have underlined that the omnipresence of international law in domestic systems and the permeability of these to international law has taken place regardless of whether there has been a general evolution towards monism. This has largely been due to the new functions assumed by international law and the move towards complex interdependence and globalisation, represented, in our case, by the extension of the powers and competences of the Security Council into hitherto undreamt of areas, with a resultant broad intrusion into the domestic sphere. In implementing decisions of the Security Council increasingly concerned with areas of shared common interest, such as the enforcement of human rights and humanitarian law, or the combating of terrorism, States while resorting to disparate measures and means, have nevertheless succeeded in adapting their domestic legal systems to include a common minimum – though by no means monolothic – set of international norms.

II. The Effectiveness of Sanctions from the Perspective of Domestic Implementation

From the perspective of UN decision-making, Security Council decisions are mandatory on all Member States under Article 25 of the Charter and since the effectiveness of sanctions also depends on universality of its implementation, the Security Council has dispensed no State from such implementation, nor has a State been allowed to rely on *force majeure* to evade its obligations. From the perspective of domestic implementation, however, the problem of effectiveness is anything but a monolithic one. On the contrary, it manifests itself in wholly different terms, depending on the countries in which implementation is taking place.

(1) Evaluating the Effectiveness of Domestic Mechanisms

It has been seen that States have a variety of means at their disposal to effectively implement Security Council decisions. These means can be roughly categorized in the following way: pre-existing legislation in the form of enabling legislation directly related to sanctions implementation; pre-existing legislation not designed for sanctions legislation; and *ad hoc* legislation in response to specific sanctions resolutions or situations. What is the most effective type of implementing mechanisms?

United Nations Enabling Acts would appear to be the most appropriate method of implementation, particularly important in dualist States, in order to give effect to Security Council resolutions. Such acts allow for speed and comprehensiveness in implementation as opposed to *ex post facto* legislation, even if these are specifically aimed at the implementation of Security Council decisions, and they provide a transparent and clear legal basis.

Enabling Acts tend however to give a blanket competence to the executive which does not play in favour of a democratic debate in regard to the procedural – though not substantive – implementation of sanctions. Moreover, they are by far not the most widely used means resorted to. Only a handful of States adopted such acts immediately after the UN Charter came into force, a small increase taking place in reaction to the Southern Rhodesian sanctions experiment and again, after the 1990s in response to new Security Council demands, as well as to the changes taking place in Eastern Europe and elsewhere. In addition, an analysis of national practice on the use that is in effect made of such existing sanctions legislation suggests that they have not always been sufficient to adequately implement the more innovative Security Council decisions. For example, they were not consistently relied upon for the purpose of implementing Security Council decisions on the creation of the International Criminal Tribunals for the former Yugoslavia and for Rwanda. Moreover, such legislation does not obviate the need for the adoption of specific administrative procedures and measures both to apply and enforce Council decisions. One example is where existing procedures for implementing into domestic law Security Council decisions prohibiting imports of diamonds from a number of African countries proved insufficient to effectively halt such imports; as a result, a brand-new certification scheme had to be devised.

Generally, the legal basis of sanctions can be found in the domestic law of States in a mix of different instruments. It has been seen that States have relied either on a wide range of measures based on pre-existing legislation not specifically designed for the purpose of implementing Security Council decisions, such as trade, customs, fiscal and emergency laws, or on *ex post facto ad hoc* legislation for particular sanctions situations, adopted for the purpose of widening the scope of sanctions or for the introduction of enforcement procedures.

While pre-existing legislation not specifically designed for sanctions has not prevented States in general from formally being able to comply with sanctions resolutions, it does have the consequence of fragmenting the legal basis for such implementation, revealing also important gaps in the implementation of certain types of sanctions.

In the absence of UN Enabling Acts, *ex post facto* legislation relating to particular sanctions regimes plays an important role. First, it may be deemed necessary to address the innovative character of many Security Council sanctions and their extension beyond the scope that could traditionally be covered by pre-existing legislation on customs and excises or financial relations. Second, implementing Security Council decisions on the basis of legislation specifically designed for that purpose fosters transparency of implementing measures; it also clearly identifies the particular Security Council decisions, and therefore the community interest as a basis for the measures taken, which may influence the attitude of courts and tribunals, as well as of national parliaments and public opinion. Such legislation while a slower method than that of pre-existing legislation which is not sanctions specific, is therefore of importance for the protection of individual rights. The preference for *ad hoc* legislative measures, important delays in implementation notwithstanding, thus addresses a legitimacy concern; this is illustrated by the case of the International Tribunals which affected both the organisation of the domestic judicial system and the constitutionally and internationally protected rights of the accused.

Such legislation tailored to particular sanctions regimes will be even more important in the light of the evolving practice of the Security Council in the field of sanctions. Comprehensive trade sanctions of the kind imposed against Iraq are not likely to be resorted to in the future. So-called "smart" sanctions or more targeted sanctions directed at government leaders, elites and other designated entities responsible for the policies in question, and which include specifically targeted measures, in particular financial restrictions, may require particularly tailored legislation directed at financial and banking operations. Moreover, the recent resolutions on the combating of terrorism impose an obligation on States to adopt specific legislation criminalising conduct which up to now may not have been penalised in domestic law.

While the implementation of Security Council sanctions by EU Member States is now based on EC Regulations, in the – increasingly shrinking – areas not covered by the Community, such as penal sanctions, States have continued to rely on national legislation, so that the legal basis of domestic sanctions regimes is to be found in a mix of both domestic and community law. Basing national implementation on EC regulations rather than directly on Security Council resolutions may blur the lines between unilateral (including regional) and collective sanctions where EC measures may have been adopted independently of Security Council resolutions or where they do not have the same scope and comprehensiveness. (A similar problem but in an entirely different context, arises in the United States where the lines between implementation of unilateral and collective sanctions may likewise be blurred.) The interposition of Community legislation between the United Nations and States members of both organisations may affect the scope, timing and interpretation of Security Council resolutions, factors which must be taken into account in evaluating their effects on sanctions implementation. On the other hand, the direct effect of Community Regulations undoubtedly contributes to enhancing the reception of Security Council resolutions in domestic law.

Effective sanctions implementation also requires legislation which reproduces the scope and comprehensiveness of the corresponding Security Council resolutions. But domestic measures will and can never totally coincide with the international measures, whether in respect of their content, timing or scope. As is clear from the national studies, implementation, in particular cases, has either gone well below or in some cases well beyond Security Council resolutions.

To avoid the retroactive effect of Security Council decisions which generally have immediate effect, national decisions have aligned the entry into force of the measures with the date of adoption of the particular national legislative provision or decree. This means that these measures are not always in conformity *ratione temporis* with the Security

Council resolutions. The same applies to termination of the measures where the dates of termination at the international and domestic levels do not coincide; this has raised the issue of the legitimacy of the continued existence of the domestic measures when their international legal basis has been ended. The problem is further exacerbated with different dates of entry into force arising from the implementation of EC Regulations.

Sanctions resolutions have required control of the activities of private parties, even extraterritorially, which may be at variance with the constitutional or general legal order of the State concerned. States have shown a reluctance to extend enforcement of their domestic legislation to the activities of their nationals abroad despite the fact that the Security Council imposes a duty on them to do so and that extension of jurisdiction to nationals outside territory is not prohibited by international law. Yet from the perspective of the effectiveness of sanctions, the theoretical possibility for a Member State to prosecute its nationals violating UN sanctions outside its territory may effectively fill the gap created by the unwillingness or inability of other States having territorial jurisdiction over such acts.

As has been seen, sanctions decisions of the Security Council have extensive effects on private contractual rights, raising the question of retroactivity, that of the nullity or temporary suspension of the execution of contracts and that of compensation. This study has shown that States have brought their own solutions to this problem, although the tendency has been to temporarily suspend the execution of contracts. Moreover, State practice indicates that, with few exceptions, individuals are not compensated for contractual losses at the domestic level. While individuals are on the one hand protected from claims raised by the targeted States in domestic courts, there are on the other hand few instances at the domestic level, and no venues at the international level, where they can bring claims for losses suffered as a result of economic embargoes. Nevertheless, the question of compensation to individuals has been raised in some countries as a problem of legitimacy.

Penalising the acts of nationals who violate sanctions legislation on which may depend the effective implementation of sanctions has so far proven problematic. Again, States have had to rely on a variety of legal bases in order to do so, including in their implementation of EU measures. There are few indications however that States have carried out prosecutions in a consistent and across the board manner.

States have also faced special problems arising from the provisions regarding surrender of individuals to the ICTY and ICTR. The fact that Security Council resolutions in establishing the Tribunals resulted in the extension of international legal obligations and criminal responsibily directly to individuals, as well as to the direct application of Tribunal Orders to individuals other than the accused – as for example, to witnesses – has not obviated the need for domestic implementing measures relating to States' cooperation with the Tribunals. This has required in some cases, adaptation of extradition law and criminal procedures, even though States have avoided constitutional problems, in particular in regard to nationals, by treating the handing over of individuals to the Tribunals as "surrender" rather than extradition.

It is particularly difficult to assess the effectiveness of implementation in regard to Security Council resolutions combating terrorism. Firstly, one lacks hindsight in this respect. Secondly, the national studies have revealed how difficult it is to disentangle national or regional measures taken autonomously, or on the basis of treaty obligations, from those adopted strictly on the basis of Security Council decisions, such as those implementing Resolution 1373 (2001), or specifically targeting Al-Qaida and the Taliban. Thirdly, in the absence of a definition of international terrorism at the international level, States and regional organisations have adopted their own definitions, thus opening the way to targeting also unwanted local opposition groups.

The implementation of financial sanctions, particularly in combating terrorism, has moreover raised sophisticated questions relating to the operation of financial centres in regard to control of the flow of funds. While the national studies have alluded to such issues, it has been difficult to provide a meaningful analysis of the problems which have ensued particularly in the context of the globalisation of financial and banking transactions. Further studies on the implementation of such sanctions should be envisaged, however. In part, this question has been examined within the framework of the so-called Interlaken process on targeted sanctions and more recently, of a Swiss government initiative on combatting the financing of terrorism within the framework of Nato's Partnership for Peace.

Problems of sanctions implementation which have arisen before domestic courts have included the resolution of conflicts between Security Council decisions and constitutional provisions of implementing States, particularly where these measures affect human rights. As has been stated, such conflicts can only be resolved in accordance with the law of the forum. Where Security Council resolutions call on States to ensure that their courts adopt a particular conduct – in matters of non-cognisance or of immunities – this may interfere in the separation of powers between executive and judiciary. Courts have also been faced with problems of interpretation, since the language of Security Council resolutions is often obscure, sometimes deliberately, for it tends to reflect what some Security Council members have euphemistically called "constructive ambiguity". Moreover, while interpretation of the scope of Security Council resolutions and the humanitarian exceptions contained therein has in practice been entrusted to the respective Sanctions Committees, such interpretation has frequently been inconsistent and lacking in transparency. This has therefore not obviated the problem for States in their domestic legislative, administrative and judicial fora. With sanctions implementation becoming more complex, the problem of multiplication of decisions and a widening of the possibility of divergent interpretations will arise. Consistency of sanctions implementation across national boundaries is therefore impossible to achieve.

(2) The Impact of Particular Problems of States on the Effectiveness of Sanctions

a. The special case of Switzerland as a permanently neutral and former non-Member State

In terms of effectiveness, it is interesting to note that this former non-Member State, after its initial reluctance in the Southern Rhodesian case to apply trade sanctions beyond the "courant normal", went a considerable way, after 1990, towards matching the requirements of Security Council sanctions, despite potential constitutional problems such as the prospect of surrender of nationals to the Tribunals. It adopted on an autonomous basis, innovative solutions and drafted framework legislation. Even before its admission into the United Nations, Switzerland also participated in the UN process of enhancing the effectiveness of sanctions and addressing humanitarian concerns by contributing to the development of the concept of "smart" or targeted sanctions. Switzerland's recent practice in this field thus illustrates how Security Council decisions are increasingly being perceived in terms of international public policy. This has meant that, while insisting that it was not formally bound, it has found it hard in the past to ignore such decisions. Switzerland has also been conscious that a position of strict neutrality could lead to its acting as a clearing-house for sanctions evasions, a position which could not easily be sustained where the international community as a whole acted against a recalcitrant State.

b. The special case of States with problems addressed by Article 50 of the UN Charter

As has been stated, in order to ensure universality in sanctions implementation, the Security Council has never dispensed particular States from the application of sanctions. The problem of States which, when complying with sanctions face major disruption of trading patterns, such as neighbouring States or significant trading partners of the sanctioned State, is in theory to be addressed within the ambit of Article 50 of the UN Charter. Nevertheless, it has been seen that a mere right to consult the Council is inadequate. Article 50 therefore raises an important question of international burden-sharing and requires an institutionalised approach to address the difficulties faced by such States, rather than the present practice of largely ignoring their concerns or addressing them through unilateral and therefore politically partisan action.

c. The inability or unwillingness of States to implement sanctions

A number of factors facilitate sanctions evasion. The length and nature of State borders and the lack of adequate resources may make it impossible for a State to effectively control imports from, and exports to, the State or entity targeted by the Security Council. This problem has been particularly marked in Africa in the context of control of trade in diamonds, where, for example, Namibia and Angola share a long border of more than 1,200 kms and where there still exists traditional cross-border movements of persons and goods. This problem is also visible in the case of the neighbouring countries bordering on Afghanistan as signalled by the reports of the Committee of Experts established by Security Council Resolution 1333 (2000). States lacking the material means to effectively control their borders or otherwise to implement sanctions may be granted assistance, including through United Nations or other international organisations monitoring missions, but this may be viewed with suspicion by these States as indication of encroachments on sovereignty.

The scarcity of economic resources, and of technical, legal and institutional means, may constitute another factor in preventing certain States from effectively implementing sanctions. This may increasingly be so due to the growing complexity of targeted financial sanctions. In this connection, there is a marked gap between States, particularly in

Africa, who face numerous difficulties of implementation and who are themselves situated in conflict zones, and the economically and technically advanced States in Europe, Asia and the Americas, which combine the advantages of highly developed regulatory systems in the economic, financial and other relevant fields, with the fact that they have, until now, seldom been directly affected by the situations Security Council sanctions seek to address. Sanctions implementation thus further underlines the disparities existing between States.

Finally, in the context of globalisation and the internet, permeability of borders, the increasingly non-territorial nature of banking and financial operations, the expanding and elusive role of non-State actors in the international arena and the growing problem of organised crime makes it increasingly difficult for States, even those which are technically advanced, to control the private activities of nationals. This is particularly evident in the framework of wars fought for economic resources such as diamonds, and in the combating of terrorism.

There are also many reasons why States may sometimes be motivated not to implement sanctions. States may be sympathetic with or allies of the targeted State. They may unilaterally terminate sanctions measures in place on the basis of their own determination that these measures have achieved their objectives or that they can be achieved through other means: for example, the case of the United States and United Kingdom in respect of Southern Rhodesia, or concerning the invasion and occupation of Iraq. Again, States may refuse to implement sanctions on the basis of their perceived illegitimacy and dire humanitarian consequences, or on grounds that their termination is being obstructed by the action of one or two Permanent members: the case of some of the States Members of the League of Arab States or of the OAU in respect of sanctions against Libya and Iraq. The nationals of some States may likewise resort to private "sanctions-busting" initiatives, not for commercial, but humanitarian reasons, such as the initative to supply Iraq with millions of pencils – embargoed for their so-called dual-use potential – by, *inter alia*, Jordanian, US and UK citizens.

This study concludes therefore that it is difficult and inopportune to attempt a distinction between "law-abiding" States and those that are unable or unwilling to implement sanctions, for this runs the risk of oversimplification if seen from the perspective of evaluating the effectiveness of sanctions implementation. States which implement these measures formally may in fact not pursue their effective application at the national level. On the other hand, the inability or unwillingness of States to effectively implement Security Council decisions may be due to complex reasons and may not necessarily affect the effectiveness of the sanctions themselves, for example the situation of States which are too remote from the target or which have no trade relations with it (although in the matter of financial sanctions these arguments may be increasingly less tenable). Moreover, there can be no categorisation of States in one camp or another consistently for each and every sanctions situation. Whether a State is enthusiastic about sanctions or not depends on the particular political situation, as the reluctance of some Western countries to apply sanctions against Southern Rhodesia and South Africa at the time clearly showed. In addition, the universal nature and scope of recent Council resolutions on terrorism now affect individuals the world over; by listing individuals who are nationals of States which have heretofore been strong supporters of sanctions implementation, such decisions may indeed lead those States to question their legitimacy and to call for a re-evaluation of the system.

(3) *State Responsibility and UN Measures of Enforcement and Control of Domestic Implementation*

Whatever the reasons invoked, including issues of legitimacy examined below, non-implementation by States of Security Council decisions is plainly contrary to their obligations under the UN Charter, for the Security Council has clearly asserted in a consistent practice its sole competence to determine the objectives of sanctions, the means to be used and the achievement of these objectives as a prelude to lifting of sanctions. From a strictly legal perspective, therefore, such non-implementation will give rise to State responsibility, and no distinction can be drawn here between States unable and those unwilling to carry out sanctions on certain grounds, for so long as there is no formal dispensation from the Security Council. The question may arise, however, as to when a breach has actually occurred: for example is the mere absence of legislation a violation of sanctions, or does one have to wait for positive conduct leading to sanctions-busting, or for a failure to show due diligence in taking measures to prevent or to punish such violations?

The question next arises as to how the Security Council is to address such sanctions evasion. Some measures in response which affect implementing States may be briefly mentioned, although these are beyond the scope of this study. One is the adoption of sanctions under Chapter VII against States that are unwilling to implement measures against the initial target; this was envisaged as early as the Southern Rhodesian crisis, and has recently been considered in respect of certain conflicts in Africa. This approach however may create a snowball effect, notably to the extent that third States who were implementing the measures adopted against the initial target may be less able, or less willing, to adopt still further sanctions against other countries in their region. Another alternative which has been developed in the past few years so as to cope with the unwillingness of States to effectively implement Security Council sanctions is that of "naming and shaming" States, their leaders and private individuals for their alleged role in the violation of sanctions; this was notably done in connection with sanctions against UNITA, the Democratic Republic of the Congo and Sierra Leone. This process has a number of drawbacks and the "naming and shaming" campaign has been criticized on grounds of lack of due process, although it must be borne in mind that the findings of the UN Panels of Experts were part of a factual not judicial process and were in no way binding on the Sanctions Committees.

At the level of more technical and concrete concerns, one can mention recommendations and guidelines on the interface between national and international implementation. Guidelines have been drawn up for improving relations between Member States and Sanctions Committees which have to some degree addressed the question of transparency via the submission of Committee reports and press releases. Loopholes to avoid individual sanctions-evasions have been addressed – this was already envisaged by the first Sanctions Committee on sanctions against Southern Rhodesia; recommendations have called, for example, for more effective procedures for determining the origin of goods, for certification, for inclusion of end-user clauses in government contracts, or for more effective domestic enforcement measures against individuals caught in sanctions evasions. In the framework of the combating of terrorism, measures have also been adopted by the Security Council and Sanctions Committees for streamlining national implementation, through for example the establishment of comprehensive questionnaires for purposes of State reports, assistance proferred to States by international organisations in the field of national implementation, and the building of model laws.

III. The Question of Legitimacy of the Decisions of the Security Council from the Perspective of Domestic Implementation

This study has been concerned with legitimacy issues only to the extent that they arise from the impact which domestic implementation of sanctions has on individuals and individual rights within the countries examined. The question of legitimacy begins at the international level. At a more general level, legitimacy issues have underlied recent debates on the evolution of the legal system. Sanctions in particular have highlighed certain contradictions in the current international system as well as in the prospects for global governance. On the one hand, they continue to be considered necessary instruments for the achievement of certain important priorities of the international community, such as the maintenance of international peace and security and the protection of human rights, to name only two. But in the proclaimed pursuit of such general interests (action possible only when the general interest coincides with the subjective interests of Security Council Members), the Security Council has adopted measures that may not always appear compatible with basic principles such as the rule of law which is presumed as underpinning both the international and domestic legal orders. For at the same time as their express objectives concern, *inter alia,* the promotion of human rights as part and parcel of international peace and security, sanctions inevitably affect the rights of populations in the sanctioned entity and call on implementing States to circumscribe constitutionally protected rights of individuals in their territories. This process is exacerbated by the creeping extension of the powers of the Security Council in fields heretofore not considered to fall within its competence. The recent resolutions on terrorism are an illustration.

We are faced then with new threats and a serious conflict of priorities each of which may appear necessary to the construction of global order. This conflict of priorities must be seen in the context of the broader tension between a State-oriented international law and one more concerned with the individual.

Enthusiasm for comprehensive sanctions so manifest at the turn of the 90s decade – and even earlier in respect of apartheid in South Africa – has evidently waned. As their serious long-term detrimental effects on populations – including women, children and future generations – and infrastructures of targeted entities, have gradually become apparent, it is now increasingly unlikely that the United Nations will resort in the future to such global trade sanctions. Here the effectiveness of sanctions in fact worked against their legitimacy, for the more water-tight the blockade, the worse their negative long-term effects on the country concerned.

But while the move towards targeted sanctions – targeting in respect of both persons and measures – has been the logical response to this humanitarian crisis engendered by sanctions, it has in turn raised further human rights problems.

It is evident that the general "war on terrorism" has placed tremendous pressures on the UN Charter regime of international protection of the individual. The adoption of Security Council 1373 on the prevention and suppression of the financing of terrorist acts which has been central to States' counter-terrorism legislation, as well as the listing procedures under Resolutions 1267, 1333 and 1390, have also resulted in refueling public debate on the competence and powers of the Security Council (for can one consider that individuals *per se,* and not States or groups of individuals, may threaten international peace and security and that this does not represent a radical change of UN sanctions mechanisms?).

These resolutions have also raised serious questions concerning the rule of law, in relation to due process and other fundamental human rights, as well as that of judicial review and other remedies for the individual. If traditional international sanctions were seen as a means to induce a change in the behaviour of the targeted entity, individually targeted measures have changed the nature of such sanctions. For the effects of such individually targeted financial or travel sanctions are indeed those of penalties. Yet at the same time, the procedure for drawing up lists of individual targets and its lack of transparency raise serious doubts over the safeguard and protection of individual rights in sanctions implementation, such as the right to a fair and public hearing for those who are listed. Moreover, there is little possibility for a person who has been listed to effectively demonstrate his or her own innocence and the delisting processes are not judicial but diplomatic and hence discretionary. Security Council Resolution 1373, moreover, which criminalises certain individual conduct without defining it, while imposing on States the obligation to criminalise such conduct in their domestic law, leaves a wide margin of appreciation to implementing authorities in individual States, including in the identification of targeted persons and entities. This introduces a decentralisation of sanctions decision-making, without requiring adequate human rights guarantees to be exercised by the implementing member States. At the same time, due to the recent anti-terrorist measures, the increase of individuals targeted has greatly increased the risk for mistakes in targeting.

The need to protect human rights in the struggle against terrorism has been highlighted by the UN Secretary-General and the UN High Commissioner for Human Rights.[1] The human rights bodies at the United Nations have also drawn attention to the dangers inherent in the indiscriminate use of the term "terrorism" and expressed alarm at the consequent threats that anti-terrorism legislation and policies poses to the enjoyment of virtually all human rights – civil, cultural, economic, political and social.[2] The Human Rights Committee, in reviewing individual State reports under the Covenant, has stressed that legislation enacted pursuant to Security Council resolution 1373

1 See UNHCHR, *Digest of Jurisprudence of the UN and Regional Organizations on the Protection of Human Rights while Countering Terrorism*, 2003, <http://www.unhchr.ch/html/menu6/2/digest.doc>.

2 See Report of the chairpersons of the human rights treaty bodies on their fifteenth meeting at Geneva, 23-27 June 2003, *Effective Implementation of International Instruments on Human Rights, including reporting obligations,* <http://www.unhchr.ch/html/menu2/finalreport15th>; Report of the Secretary-General on *Protection of Human Rights and Fundamental Freedoms while countering terrorism* (A/58/266, 8 August 2003).

must be in conformity with the International Covenant on Civil and Political Rights. Moreover, there is the possibility of conflicts between Security Council resolutions and *jus cogens* or non-derogable human rights, for example where deportation of individuals suspected of terrorist activities to countries where they may face torture may infringe the prohibitions under Article 3 of the European Convention on Human Rights or Article 3 of the UN Convention Against Torture. Where sanctions are imposed with the objective of enforcing the target State to respect the political and civil rights of its citizens, there has to be a corollary obligation on the part of those implementing these sanctions to take into account those same rights.

Yet at the same time, remedies for the individual from potential abuses in implementation of such decisions appear to be slim and there is a notable gap in judicial redress.

At the international level there appears to be little possibility of judicial or other forms of review of either Security Council resolutions in this respect, or of States' implementing legislation.[3]

At the domestic level, which has been the focus of this study, it appears that individuals are also left with little recourse for adequate and effective remedies. From a theoretical and domestic law perspective, conflicts between non self-executing Security Council obligations and constitutionally or regionally protected human rights obligations should in principle be resolved by domestic courts in favour of the latter. Yet increasingly in practice a new picture is emerging. It appears that so far there have been few individual challenges to implementing measures, while at the same time, national and regional courts have not been willing to challenge head on the legitimacy of Security Council resolutions. Of course, national courts may not always have the competence to review national implementing measures, particularly where the domestic basis of such legislation is tied to questions of national security and, in the light of Articles 25 and 103 of the UN Charter, where these measures draw their legitimacy from Security Council resolutions. Even assuming such a competence, national or regional courts could obviously only consider issues of legitimacy or legality of Security Council resolutions in terms of their own constitutions, not under the UN Charter.

Such judicial decisions as have been handed down have tended to be cautious. In regard to the freezing of funds, for example, courts have reiterated that property rights are not absolute and that their exercise may be subject to restrictions. In assessing the proportionality of the measures taken, they have argued that the importance of the general interest embodied in Security Council resolutions – the maintenance of international peace – justified their negative consequences even of a substantial nature. In matters of compensation, they have passed the buck to the Security Council, where of course no such remedy is available. Such decisions have concerned claims from individuals affected by sanctions implementation as third parties. It remains to be seen whether this situation will change in the near future to the extent that the resolutions concerning the

3 It has been pointed out that there is little opportunity under human rights mechanisms, to review Member States' efforts in implementing resolution 1373, for only three-fourths of the States reporting to the CTC on their implementation of Resolution 1373 are parties to the International Covenant of Civil and Political Rights (CCPR), and only one tenth of those members appear before the Human Rights Committee each year.

combating of terrorism may lead to increased challenges before domestic and regional courts by individuals who are directly targeted. Such challenges have already been raised on the grounds that Security Council resolutions violate due process and other rights in not allowing any possibility of domestic judicial review and hence of verification of the evidence, and that the penal sanction imposed in the form of freezing of funds is not the legal consequence of a precise charge filed against such individuals. Nevertheless, it remains doubtful that courts will satisfactorily address these charges.

Flowing from the above, however, is the question of where such legitimacy/legality problems concerning the limits to the legislative powers of the Security Council may be brought up and dealt with in the process of implementation. Is the domestic fora indeed the proper place to raise such questions in a broader and more general sense, i.e. in terms of international legality?

There is no doubt that domestic and regional courts and tribunals have their role to play. Sanctions implementation cannot obviously be fully centralised at the UN level. It is carried out in parallel through UN mechanisms – for example the Sanctions Committees – and through UN Member States within their regional or domestic orders. The fact that Security Council decisions are, in general, not considered self-executing in domestic legal systems, does not mean that domestic courts and tribunals can, or should apply domestic implementation measures in total isolation from Security Council decisions and other relevant rules of international law. Moreover, the need for domestic courts to resort to auto-interpretation of Security Council decisions is particularly important in view of the fact that in many instances, domestic implementation measures are adopted at great speed for the purpose of implementing hurriedly drafted Council decisions that cannot take into account each and every specific hypothesis.

A right balance therefore should be struck in seeking a solution to these issues between domestic and UN mechanisms of implementation in matters of interpretation, allowing room for an autonomous interpretation and application by domestic courts and tribunals. At the same time, it is important for the purposes of legitimacy within a domestic law framework, that the Security Council develop, perhaps in the form of presidential statements, general guidelines and a legal framework outside the ambit of a specific sanctions regime. This may assist in addressing another legitimacy issue, relating to the role of national parliaments. The development of general guidelines by the Security Council, also dealing with due process where individuals are concerned, and outside the emergency context of a given case, would offer the opportunity for parliaments to have an in-depth reflection on sanctions regimes and their relation to general international law, which would contribute to alleviating legitimacy concerns when sanctions are adopted in the future.

On-going interface between implementing States and Security Council is also important; this includes transparency in the work of the Sanctions Committee and in the publication of their proceedings in order to contribute to precedent-building.

At the same time, however, allowing each State and its courts to determine for itself the legality of Security Council decisions, would run the risk of reversion to a form of auto-interpretation counter to the requirements of collective action, nor could such determinations serve as authoritative interpretations of UN obligations binding on all

Member States. Such action would only succeed in eroding the efforts to condition and circumscribe unilateral responses to violations of community norms.

Yet the erosion of trust in the Security Council's authority, that of its subsidiary organs, and that of the UN system itself, could seriously undermine in the longer-term the willingness of States to continue to implement these measures effectively. It is therefore of vital importance that this debate on legality/legitimacy (the former dealing with formal legitimacy, i.e. the compatibility between UN obligations and the protection of human rights, the other with social legitimacy which is a political question), which includes reflecting on the limits of the powers of the Security Council, the desirability of future centralisation of sanctions and the very place of coercion in international law, be taken up at the international level. Security Council resolutions would otherwise consist in open-ended obligations which States have undertaken to implement in their domestic law with no limits set.

In the absence of formal judicial review mechanisms by third parties, such challenges have indeed taken place in the context of inter-State discussions both within and without the Security Council with certain notable results. For example, the questioning of the effectiveness and consequences of broad, indiscriminate sanctions whose human cost is clearly unproportional to the objectives of the sanctions did lead to a focus on targeted or "smart" sanctions. Some reflection is now taking place on how to address the human rights problems engendered by those same targeted sanctions. But, as has been stated elsewhere in this study, the increasing and diversified use of sanctions as a means of ensuring compliance with international public policy within an increasingly complex and globalised environment and the need, at the same time, of ensuring that their adverse effects on individuals and populations and their restrictions on commercial and financial freedoms are curtailed to the minimum, requires moving away from a piecemeal approach to one which is more structured and comprehensive.

More generally, reflection should take place on the place of sanctions in the UN system, on the balance to be struck between the different priorities of the UN Charter – peace maintenance and longer-term peace building – and between organs, principally concerning the role that the General Assembly could and should play in this process.

Some final remarks can be made relating to the direction which international law is taking. First, in looking to State practice in sanctions implementation, as in sanctions decision-making, this comparative study has revealed the tendency to look to First World legislatures, domestic and regional courts, in determining new developments in international law; sanctions have thus heightened regional disparities and led to regimes *à deux vitesses*.

Second, this study of sanctions implementation has led to some interesting theoretical conclusions on the extent of the growing permeability between the two legal orders, not only in terms of substance or normative content, but also, in view of the considerable impact of sanctions on private and individual rights, of legal subjects. This is increasingly the case as we go from sanctions resolutions imposing obligations of result – e.g. severance of trade and of financial transactions – to ones which impose on States an obligation of means, for example, the adoption of particular national legislation criminalising individual conduct, co-operation with international criminal tribunals, or the elaboration of model laws. It has been pointed out that the individual lives his life in both legal orders, for one must not ignore "the all-prevailing reality of the universum of human experience" and even while both may claim to be autonomous, they are nevertheless "harmonious in that in their totality the several rules aim at a basic human good".[4]

This study of domestic implementation of sanctions began with some simplistic premises concerning the articulation of domestic and international law. It has revealed, however, that traditional solutions to the interrelationship between the two legal orders, including monist and dualist theories, no longer adequately address the complexity of the issues that arise today from implementation of Security Council resolutions, nor the current framework of the international legal order that juxtaposes an objective international law, based on community interest, alongside subjective and bilateral relations between states.

4 D.P. O'Connell, *International Law*, vol.1, 2nd ed. (London, Stevens & Sons, 1970), pp. 43-44.

INDEX